DVD DELIRIUM
VOLUME 1

First edition published by FAB Press, July 2002
This second edition published by FAB Press, June 2003

FAB Press
Grange Suite
Surrey Place
Mill Lane
Godalming
GU7 1EY
England, U.K.

www.fabpress.com

edited by
Nathaniel Thompson

A CIP catalogue record for this book is available from the British Library.

ISBN 1-903254-04-3

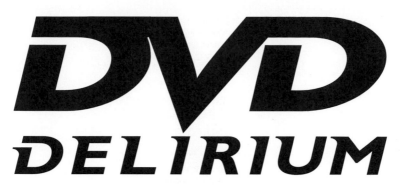

DVD DELIRIUM

The International Guide to Weird and Wonderful Films on DVD
Volume 1

edited by
Nathaniel Thompson

CREDITS

Main Text:

Nathaniel Thompson

Additional reviews were kindly contributed by:

Tim Greaves and **Stephen Thrower**

Copy Editing and Design:

Harvey Fenton

Adrian Luther-Smith came up with the *DVD Delirium* concept and provided the initial impetus.

Special Thanks also to the following individuals whose contributions were invaluable:

Francis Brewster
(picture research)

Harvey Fenton, **David Flint**, **Marc Morris**, **Brad Stevens** and **Marc Walkow**
(additional information)

DVD cover designs are copyright © the respective DVD companies,
and the covers are reproduced here in the spirit of publicity.
Picture credits:
A&E, ADV Films, AllDay, Alliance, Anchor Bay, A-Pix, Arrow, Arthaus, Artisan, Astro, Barrel
Entertainment, Beverly Wilshire, BFI, BFS, Bluelight, Bridge Pictures Classics, Buena Vista, Carlton,
Carnival, Cinema Club, Columbia, Crash Cinema, Criterion, Critical Mass, CTN, Cult Epics, Cult Video,
Culture, CVC, Dead Alive, Diamond Entertainment, Digital Entertainment, Divid 2000, Dragon,
Dreamworks, Dutch Filmworks, DVD Video International, EC Entertainment, Elite Entertainment, EMS,
Entertainment In Video (EIV), ERA, Eros International, Eurovista, Fantoma, 4 Front, Film 2000, Filmax,
FilmFour, First Run Features, Fox Video, Full Moon, GCTHV, Golden Scene, Goodtimes, HBO, Hen's
Tooth, High Fliers, Home Vision, Hong Kong Legends, Image, Indies, Indura, International Licensing,
Italian Shock, Japan Shock, Kim Stim, Kino, Koch, KultDVD, Laser Paradise, Lions Gate, Lucertola Media,
Madacy, Manga, Media Asia, Media Blasters, Medusa, Mega Star, Mei Ah, Metrodome, MGM, MIA,
Miramax, Momentum, MPI, MTI, Music Video, New Concorde, New Line, New Video, New Yorker,
Nouveaux, Ocean Shores, Odyssey, Opening Distribution, Opening Edition, Pagan, Palm, PAND,
Paramount, Parc Video, Passport, Pathé, Pioneer, Platinum, Polygram, PT Video, Redemption, Republic,
Revelation, Rhino, The Roan Group, Ruscico, Salvation, Scanbox, Second Sight, Seduction Cinema,
Shochiku, Shock-o-Rama Cinema, Sogepaq, Something Weird, Sterling, Stonevision, Strand, Synapse, Tai
Seng, Tartan, TFI, Trimark, Troma, 20th Century Fox Home Entertainment, United American, Universal,
Universe, Univideo, USA, Vanguard, VCA, VCI, Ventura, VIP, Vipco, Vision, Warner Bros, Wellspring,
Xenon, York, Zeitgeist **Any omissions will be corrected in future editions.**

INTRODUCTION

Everything happens for a reason. So goes the common refrain, but the rise of DVD offers a solid argument in its favour. These shiny silver discs arrived with a roar in the late 1990s, driven by the support of several major studios and pin sharp picture quality which quickly laid waste to its predecessor, the comparatively bulky laserdisc which had long been cherished by die hard movie fanatics. Contrary to popular belief, DVD is essentially a souped-up, pocket sized progression from laserdiscs rather than a direct improvement over videotape; laserdisc specialty companies like Criterion, Image, Elite, The Roan Group, Pioneer, and others made the leap to DVD, while new DVD companies like Anchor Bay, Synapse, Fantoma, AllDay, Ventura, and many others entered the fray. The simultaneous widespread use of the Internet promoted cheap bargains online (though we all know how that turned out), spawned several resource websites, and created a new community of fans for whom technology and film appreciation finally became inseparable.

And so we arrive at the subject of this book: films off the beaten path. Some of these titles never would have been considered for immaculate digital transfers; many were thrown onto VHS years ago in cropped, edited, or otherwise woeful transfers, now rendered obsolete. Some titles come from major studios but have become offbeat cult items or even university drinking favourites, while others are largely forgotten; even a few had been considered lost altogether until their DVD revival. These are not films to casually choose from for happy family viewing; instead, the best way to use this guide is to keep an open mind, to feel free to browse and hunt through a video shop looking for buried treasure. Be adventurous, and try to accept or even cherish qualities that mainstream sensibilities spit upon; awkward dubbing, confusing or random plotting, and outrageous visual excess can yield rich rewards to those willing to fall under the spell of a movie unafraid to break the rules. Also bear in mind that this is merely a sampling of the exotic delights available on DVD; consider this a doorway through which one can discover more international gems like Hong Kong action, Bollywood musical madness, or Russian fantasy, for example. You'll also find other rewarding genres like Italian murder mysteries, Asian martial arts and monster romps, subtitled art films, '70s erotica, spaghetti westerns, classic black and white horror, sleazy drive-in and exploitation - and the list goes on...

The tandem infiltration of DVD players and online buying has also created far more ease for discs to move over borders from one country to another, gladly falling into the hands of eager collectors. DVD players come in all variety of international standards and region codes, essentially designed to restrict the playback of certain titles from one country to another. While a "Region 0" or "Region Free" disc will play anywhere, many titles are designated from Region 1 to Region 6. Furthermore, the use of the PAL video standard in Europe and Australia is incompatible with the NTSC standard used in countries like the United States and Japan. However, many UK players can surmount these obstacles, and region free/all standard players have become more widespread in other countries as well. This book covers a wide array of regions and standards, and most titles can be purchased online. American titles (marked US) are widely available and imported through a countless number of websites, while the various international permutations of Amazon offer titles from the US (www.amazon.com), the United Kingdom (www.amazon.co.uk), France (www.amazon.fr), and Germany (www.amazon.de). Other international resources include Spain (www.dvdgo.com), Italy (www.dvd.it), Japan (www.cdjapan.co.jp), Canada (www.dvdbox-office.com), and many more; just using your favourite handy search engine can turn up a fine selection of competitive purchasing options. Code free DVD players are also widely available online in almost every major country.

Note that this guide contains a series of shorthand terms to describe a DVD's specifications. The first line indicates whether the film is "**Colour**" or "Black and White" (**B&W**), followed by the **year** of theatrical release (where applicable) and the running time in minutes (**m.**). After the major **director** and **actor** credits, you will see the name of the **studio** (or studios) who released the disc, followed by the designation of "**WS**" (widescreen) if the film is presented in a widescreen or "letterboxed" format to preserve its original visual dimensions ("aspect ratio") as seen in the theatre. Many DVDs are **16:9** enhanced, which means a higher resolution when played back on widescreen (hi-definition) television sets. You will also note a specification for the video standard (**PAL** or **NTSC**) along with the region coding ("**R**"); titles which have been released by the same studio in all major regions, formats and standards, such as the James Bond or *Alien* titles, are simply indicated by studio. Often a DVD will remain the same despite a change in the company's name and/or studio ownership; for example, several DVDs released by MGM were later repackaged with identical transfers by Warner Bros., so the most current available version will be listed. A particularly confusing example is the American company Wellspring, which was previously known as Fox Lorber, then Winstar; any of these names may be found on their packaging, but the DVDs are the same regardless. The groundbreaking UK horror-friendly company Redemption also releases titles under other banners like Salvation and Jezebel, but for our purposes their original name will be used; subsidiaries of Buena Vista like Disney, Touchstone, Miramax, and Hollywood will likewise be referred to under the banner of their parent company who released the discs. Obviously the field of DVD is always growing and evolving; readers who note any alternate versions or pertinent facts relating to these titles are encouraged to write in and let us know.

Now with these technicalities aside, brace yourself for a wild ride through the strangest, the silliest, and the most shocking celluloid offerings available for your home viewing pleasure. But be warned: once you've tasted this forbidden fruit, there's no going back.

Nathaniel Thompson

THE ABOMINABLE DR. PHIBES

Colour, 1971, 94m. / Directed by Robert Fuest / Starring Vincent Price, Joseph Cotten, Terry-Thomas / MGM (US R1 NTSC) / WS (1.85:1) (16:9)

While Vincent Price was no stranger to mixing horror and camp dating back to the days of William Castle, he found the perfect vehicle to fuse the two together within one character: the unforgettable Dr. Anton Phibes, a renowned organist turned avenging antihero. *The Abominable Dr. Phibes*, a slick art deco haunted house propelled by an outlandish presence and its magnetic star, became an unexpected hit for American International, who quickly rushed out a similar sequel from the same director, *The Avengers* helmer Robert Fuest. The tale begins when a prominent London physician passes away under the most peculiar of circumstances: death by bats. Inspector Trout (Peter Jeffrey) of Scotland Yard is perplexed by the grotesque crime, which reminds his partner of a similar recent murder involving bees. Meanwhile the facially immobile Dr. Phibes and his beautiful mute assistant, Vulnavia (Virginia North), emerge from their elaborate underground hideout to wreak vengeance on a succession of other doctors and nurses with elaborate death schemes drawn from the ten Old Testament plagues visited upon Egypt. The curses of rats, blood, frogs, and hail are just a few of the creative challenges surmounted by the fiendish Phibes, who turns each murder into a work of art designed to confound the authorities. Dr. Vesalius (Joseph Cotten) pieces together the mystery when he realizes all of the victims worked together in vain at the operating table to save Phibes' wife, Victoria (an uncredited Caroline Munro), while her husband rushed to her side and perished in a fiery car accident. As the police scramble to protect the surviving medical personnel, Phibes pushes on with his macabre mission destined to culminate in the most fearsome plague of all: darkness.

Obviously this kind of black humour isn't to everyone's taste, but Price fans have long held this film and its sequel (*Dr. Phibes Rises Again*) close to their hearts. The potentially sick and morbid subject matter is kept in check by the script's dashes of silly humour, ranging from Trout's hilarious discussions with his superiors to Phibes' bizarre methods of communicating via gramophone and consuming champagne through... well, you'll just have to see for yourself. The same formula was later perfected by Price in the similar but classier *Theatre of Blood*, but in visual terms at least, the first Phibes remains one

of Price's most striking films. The clockwork ragtime band, the luminous organ, and the vibrant decors make this a unique chunk of eye candy, while the escalating tension of the plot is aided by the viewer's guilty rooting for Phibes to finish off his adversaries as quickly as possible. The climax involving a particularly nasty surgical procedure is masterfully executed and suspenseful, with pros Cotten and Price playing off each other marvellously. *The Abominable Dr. Phibes* has gone through several different video editions over the years, from a muted full frame Vestron edition on VHS and laserdisc to a more colourful widescreen Orion/Image laserdisc that lost as much on the top and bottom as it gained on the sides. Overall, MGM's DVD outdoes them all with a beautifully crisp, colourful presentation. In fact, the level of detail is so vivid one can clearly see the string holding up the bat which charges at the maid following the first murder. As with some of MGM's other AIP transfers, the black levels are a little pale and overly bright, but players equipped with black enhancement features can remedy this problem. More difficult to assess is the 1.85:1 framing, which is about as tight as it could possibly be without destructively shearing off vital information. (It comes very close during the opening credits, however.) Less vertical information is visible compared to the laserdiscs, but the framing looks balanced and pleasing enough throughout the film. However, one can't help wondering whether a more British-friendly aspect ratio of 1.78:1 or even 1.66:1 would have been closer to what Fuest intended. Otherwise this spectacular appearance makes this the best way to become acquainted with Dr. Phibes and company, and the disc also includes the original US trailer (which only sports the shortened promotional title, *Dr. Phibes*), anamorphically enhanced and unfortunately guaranteed to spoil many of the film's highlights.

THE ABOMINABLE SNOWMAN

B&W, 1957, 91m. / Directed by Val Guest / Starring Peter Cushing, Forrest Tucker / Anchor Bay (US R1 NTSC) / WS (2.35:1) (16:9)

A solidly crafted monster movie which manipulates viewers' imaginations with the precise skill of a surgeon, *The Abominable Snowman of the Himalayas* (or just *The Abominable Snowman* to Yanks) features much of the crew present for early Hammer Films classics like the *Quatermass* sci-fi yarns. Here writer Nigel Kneale wisely relies on atmosphere and characterization to deliver palpable chills instead of a man in a shaggy suit romping through the snow. In the icy wilds of the Himalayan Mountains, botanist John Rollason (Peter Cushing) angers his wife (Maureen Connell) when he announces his intention to join an American-led expedition headed by craven adventurer Jon Friend (Forrest Tucker). These explorers ascend the mountains in search of the mysterious Yeti, or as history now calls it, the Abominable Snowman. The peaceful Lama explains that the Yeti are a race of superhuman creatures meant to be preserved in the mountains until mankind destroys itself and allows them to take over the world. The men press on anyway, with Rollason embarking in the name of scientific curiosity and Friend intending only to make a fast buck. All of the men get more than they bargained for, however, when a creature finally rears its head in the snowy darkness.

More of a meditation on man's inability to cope with strange forces than a standard campfire tale, *The Abominable Snowman* compares favourably to Howard Hawks' similarly themed *The Thing (from Another World)*, both of which make excellent use of snowy isolation as a springboard for a microcosm of universal ideas. Cushing as usual turns in an excellent performance, both sympathetic and deeply flawed, while Tucker provides shadings beyond the standard evil great white hunter. Guest once again proves his sure hand behind the camera as he guides the viewer through a creepy world most people never see first person, and the chilling sound effects are far more horrifying than anything the filmmakers could have shown onscreen. Previously issued as a widescreen laserdisc from The Roan Group, this film looks even better on DVD thanks to Anchor Bay's immaculate 16:9 transfer. The beautiful black and white scope photography has never been so effective, and Guest's effective, careful visual compositions are well preserved throughout. The usual great Hammer extras are included, such as the laser's commentary track with Kneale and Guest (largely concerned with the story's development from an early treatment by Kneale and the difficulties of recreating Himalayan snow storms on film), the American trailer, and a *World of Hammer* episode devoted to Peter Cushing. Even if you don't watch this on a dark wintry evening, this DVD will give you chills.

THE ADULT VERSION OF JEKYLL & HIDE

Colour, 1972, 91m. / Directed by Byron Mabe and Lee Raymond / Starring Jack Buddliner, Rene Bond / Image (US R0 NTSC)

Now here's a really sick one! An unapologetic wallow in the grindhouse gutter, *The Adult Version of Jekyll and Hide* pushes the sexploitation "roughie" genre to ridiculous extremes as it pulls out one perverse twist after another on the classic Robert Louis Stevenson novel. Amazingly enough, Britain's Hammer Films produced a similarly plotted variation, *Dr. Jekyll and Sister Hyde*, which left far more to the viewer's imagination... but then more isn't always less, is it? Dr. Leeder (Jack Buddliner - hmm, think that's a pseudonym?), a creepy guy who looks like Harry Reems after a really bad night, comes across the medical notebook of the legendary Dr. Jekyll (just like *Young Frankenstein*!). Naturally he feels compelled to duplicate his predecessor's formula, which has the unexpected result of turning the doc into... a voluptuous blonde woman with a heavy murderous streak! The new Miss Hide promptly seduces everyone in sight, including '70s porn kitten Rene Bond (as his secretary) and a skanky sailor who winds up losing a valuable portion of his anatomy. Whippings, canings, and other nastiness soon wash over the screen until Hide finally gets the idea of going after the Doc's innocent young fiancée, with nasty results.

Considering this film is supposed to look cheap and grimy, the DVD looks just fine and definitely crisper than the earlier Something Weird VHS version. Gritty shades of brown and grey contrast against the vivid flesh tones of the many naked bodies on display. The audio was never slickly recorded to begin with, but sounds clear enough here and delivers each moan and scream with perfect clarity. The disc also includes a running commentary by producer David Friedman, who offers some frequently humorous production anecdotes and a succinct history of the transition within the adult industry from "nudie cuties" to rougher fare like this. The theatrical trailer is astoundingly rude, closing with the film's title card emblazoned over a shot of Leeder's, er, manhood. An amusing and probably educational gallery of Friedman's exploitation ad mats is also included.

AFTER LIFE

Colour, 1998, 118m. / Directed by Hirokazu Kore-eda / Starring Erika Oda, Arata, Susumu Terajima / New Yorker (US R1 NTSC) / WS (1.66:1) / DD2.0

The question of what happens after we die has been addressed in hundreds of films, but the approach of

After Life (originally known in Japan as *Wandafuru raifu*, or *Wonderful Life*) will seem fresh and completely original to most viewers. The decidedly Eastern approach to the central issue resonates regardless of one's religious or cultural background, and what emerges is a deeply affecting, quiet little gem of a film.

After death, people's spirits find themselves at a large, remote compound where they consult with an assigned counsellor. On this particular week, twenty-two people arrive, divided among three counsellors and one trainee, Shiori (Erika Oda). The counsellors help their cases choose one moment from their lives to recreate, after which that person will spend eternity contemplating and residing within that single perfect setting. Some people cannot choose; others change their minds. A young girl wants to relive her trip to Disneyland, but Shiori convinces her to choose something more unique and personal. An older man cannot recall his ideal moment, so he endlessly scans videotapes of his life searching for a solution. And then there's the matter of another young man who, unwilling to depart into the great beyond, simply refuses to choose at all. Meanwhile the counsellors find their own perceptions changing as well, particularly Takashi (Arata), conflicted between his growing friendship with Shiori and another more abstract demand which could finally put his mind at rest.

The most striking innovation of *After Life* is its portrayal of a spiritual plane without any kind of camera filters, special effects, wispy new age music, or emotive dramatics. The camerawork is often hand held, filming in subdued and often gritty colours, while dialogue is presented as recorded on the set. The result is a feeling of startling immediacy and an almost painful intimacy with the characters, which makes the transcendent final third of the film all the more effective. The film ultimately raises more questions than it answers - just imagine some of the "perfect moment" scenarios that could not possibly ever be recreated - and the continuity between dream memories and real memories, not to mention recreation with the people themselves versus actors, is never really resolved. However, these ambiguous touches also enrich the film, which gains in mystery after the end credits have rolled. The ultimate question, of course, is then posed to the viewer: how would you choose one moment, and would that really feel like heaven to you?

New Yorker's DVD of *After Life* looks as good as could be expected from the borderline *vérité* shooting style. The image is moderately letterboxed at just under 1.66:1, revealing a bit more than was visible in US theatrical screenings, while the audio gets the job done without much fuss. The compression job appears to be competent, while extras include both the US and Japanese trailers, as well as an intriguingly designed inner booklet. Already something of a cult hit in the making, this is a film well worth visiting and recommended to anyone who enjoys a solid, thoughtful contemplation on mortality and the ultimate longing for happiness.

THE AGES OF LULU

Colour, 1990, 95m. / Directed by Bigas Luna / Starring Francesca Neri, Óscar Ladoire / Manga (Spain R0 PAL) / WS (1.85:1) / DD2.0

Never one to shy away from touchy subject matter, Bigas Luna seems determined to become to Spain what Russ Meyer is to America and Tinto Brass is to Italy. One of his most explicit works to date, *The Ages of Lulu (Les edades de Lulú)* begins like a fairly standard knockoff of *9 1/2 Weeks* but swerves into far more dangerous waters that could only be explored in Europe. Sweet little Lulu (*Live Flesh*'s Francesca Neri) discovers her sexual awakening at the hands of older, self-absorbed Pablo (Óscar Ladoire), who makes her acquaintance by shaving her nether regions ("...so you'll look prettier"). Naturally they become a couple and experiment with various kinky situations, such as a blindfolded threesome with her brother. Lulu also becomes friends with a transvestite prostitute, Ely (played by female María Barranco with an added latex appendage), who joins them in the sack as well. Soon Lulu decides she's tired of being a sex object and goes off on her own. "Men enjoy looking at lesbians, so why can't I enjoy gays?" she ponders as she saunters into a local boy bar, where she hands over some cash to one male couple (including a young Javier Bardem) and frolics with them in a back room. Things turn much, much nastier, however, with a gruelling finale that can only be described as what might happen if David Lynch directed William Friedkin's S&M shocker *Cruising*.

The Ages of Lulu is one of the many Luna films that remain difficult to see outside their native country - perhaps due to several scenes treading perilously close to hardcore and the abundant bare flesh on display. Neri's engaging, uninhibited performance really carries most of the film as she makes a convincing transformation from a naïve teenybopper to a sadder but wiser pleasure seeker.

A

The Spanish DVD from Manga offers a nice widescreen presentation of the film, taken from a mostly clean print with only a couple of minor blemishes near the beginning. Optional English subtitles are easy to read and seem to be accurate, while the stereo audio mostly comes to life during the song passages (such as one memorable encounter set to Lou Reed's "Walk on the Wild Side"). The disc also includes a trailer set entirely to the same song.

AGUIRRE, THE WRATH OF GOD

Colour, 1972, 93m. / Directed by Werner Herzog / Starring Klaus Kinski, Cecilia Rivera / Anchor Bay (US R1 NTSC) / DD5.1 / Stonevision (UK R1 PAL)

 A film whose shooting difficulties have become at least as legendary as the final product, *Aguirre, the Wrath of God* became Werner Herzog's international break-through film and established an entirely new age of German cinema. Like all of his other films, this one will certainly not appeal to every taste thanks to its slow pace and maniacal, unsympathetic lead character. However, as with all collaborations between Herzog and Klaus Kinski, *Aguirre* is crucial, unforgettable cinema, and arguably the finest collaboration ever between this volatile pair. In 1560, the depths of the jungles lining the Amazon River are infiltrated by a Spanish expedition trudging through endless miles of green wilderness. They search for the remains of the fallen Inconnu Empire, which may lead them to discover the mythical El Dorado, a city of gold. The greedy and incestuous Don Lope de Aguirre (Kinski), who has brought his own daughter (Cecilia Rivera) along on his quest, becomes the tyrannical leader of the rapidly diminishing explorers, who are being picked off by pestilence, cannibals, violent mishaps, and even murder by their own leader when they plot desertion. Still Aguirre pushes on, driven by his own lust for gold and glory regardless of the consequences to himself and his companions.

Firmly anchored by Kinski's fearless and harrowing portrayal, this film spins out one unforget-table image after another, culminating in a justifiably famous final image that will leave most viewers astounded that it was ever committed to film.

Reports of Kinski and Herzog's clashes during the filming have now become hopelessly tangled by contradictions, with both parties plotting to murder each other and Kinski's infamous tantrums draining him out so completely that his performance in front of the camera comes across as wasted and

introspective. The sublime, unsettling, and often glorious music by long-time Herzog collaborators Popol Vuh sets just the right mood, with the eerie, long opening shots of mountains dotted with struggling human forms accompanied by sounds apparently drifting in from the ether. Unlike *Fitzcarraldo*, which balanced its insane spectacle with a narrative laced with human warmth and ultimate redemption, *Aguirre* is essentially a trip straight into hell, a damned expedition whose likes would not appear on film again until the similarly lunatic venture of *Apocalypse Now* seven years later.

Anchor Bay's DVD contains an open matte presentation which offers a little more information on the top and bottom compared to the very mildly letterboxed tape from New Yorker; more importantly, the colours look much more robust and piercing, from the glittering gold and silver surfaces of the armour to those frightening, impenetrable greens within the jungle. Never has nature looked more terrifying. The 5.1 remix does what it can with the limited early '70s sound recording; the music fares best, often drifting ominously from different speakers, while the dialogue and sound effects are a bit more strident. The original mono English language track is also included but isn't worth the trouble unless you absolutely can't stand subtitles. In a priceless gesture for film history, Herzog contributes a commentary track with Norman Hill in which he offers his own linear take on the film's arduous production. Though not a true story, Herzog essentially set out to capture a time and place never seen before, one which seems to burst from western civilization's collective unconscious and mirrors the mad follies committed by inept leaders over the centuries. Of course the irony of Herzog himself often falling into this mad scheme of civilization isn't lost on him, resulting in a peculiar "hall of mirrors" effect when he discusses this film. The original German theatrical trailer is also included, along with an English language variant, neither of which probably went over too well in commercial theatres. The UK disc from Stonevision is full frame as well but features an inferior transfer with no extras.

AIRBAG

Colour, 1997, 98m. / Directed by Juanma Bajo Ulloa / Starring Karra Elejalde, Maria de Medeiros / Columbia (Spain R2 PAL) / WS (2.35:1) (16:9) / DD5.1

A wild and often tasteless attempt to beat Quentin Tarantino at his own game, *Airbag* speeds through a motley cast of eccentric characters and bizarre sequences which often play more like the skits of a particularly deranged comedy troupe; this welcome shot of adrenaline may be hit or miss but deserves to find its target audience outside of Spain.

Mild-mannered Juantxo (Karra Elejalde), a homely and not terribly bright man, celebrates the arrival of his unlikely marriage to a beautiful blonde with his eccentric and wealthy future in-laws. The bride's mother gives him a pair of valuable engagement rings, one of which he immediately puts on his finger. Later his buddies Konradín (Fernando Guillen Cuervo) and Pako (Alberto San Juan) take him out for a wild bachelor party at a country whorehouse, where virginal Juantxo discovers a few surprises about himself with the aid of a feisty hooker. Unfortunately he notices during the drive back that he lost his ring, err, inside the prostitute, so they go back to retrieve it. Juantxo learns that the ring has fallen into the hands of a sadistic pimp and gangster named Villambrosa (Francisco Rabal), and on the way home the boys accidentally flip their car over by the roadside. A passing motorist stops to help and turns out to be, sure enough, Villambrosa. When Juantxo demands his ring back, the mobster responds by dropping a lighter next to the car's leaking stream of gasoline, and only a freak of nature manages to save them. Soon the three men's attempts to hunt down the ring places them in the middle of a mob war between Villambrosa and another rival gang spearheaded by levitating, platinum blonde Fátima (an unrecognizable Maria de Medeiros).

Packed with weird incidents and memorable character bits, *Airbag* giddily skips along its merry way, delivering high amounts of gunplay, stunts, and graphic but comical sex and nudity. The plot often pauses for some weird tangents, such as cocaine-filled car airbags and a hilarious spoof of low budget Latino soap operas entitled *Obsolete Love*. Director Juanma Bajo Ulloa outdoes his previous gem *The Dead Mother (La madre muerta)* in the eccentricity department, producing a twisted film that defies any rational genre classification.

Columbia's Spanish PAL format DVD lives up the standards of their American output, with a crystal clear and colourful scope transfer, enhanced for anamorphic televisions and featuring optional English subtitles. The 5.1 audio features some amusing split surround effects, even during music and dialogue passages, and the hyperactive trailer is entirely appropriate.

ALICE, SWEET ALICE

Colour, 1976, 106m. / Directed by Alfred Sole / Starring Linda Miller, Paula E. Sheppard, Niles McMaster / Anchor Bay (US R0 NTSC) / WS (1.85:1)

Along with Pete Walker's underrated *House of Mortal Sin*, the jarring *Communion* attacks the foundations of Catholicism as swiftly and viciously as any film of its era. Most low-budget horror films offer little in the way of political substance or sustain any kind of sociological viewpoint, but *Communion* jumps in headfirst and practically dares viewers to remain passive. Later reissued under its most famous title, *Alice, Sweet Alice* (and in a sliced-up 96 minute edition called *Holy Terror*), this caustic little gem has built a reputation for itself outside the mere presence of child star Brooke Shields in a small supporting role.

Catherine Spages (Linda Miller), a devout young Catholic woman, has two daughters, Alice (*Liquid Sky*'s Paula Sheppard) and Karen (Shields). While Karen is a sweet good girl looking forward to her first communion, the older Alice becomes increasingly jealous and dislocated from her family. In fact, Alice often retreats to her apartment basement where she keeps cockroaches in a jar and causes various kinds of mayhem involving the other tenants. When Karen is brutally murdered at the church before receiving communion, suspicion immediately falls upon Alice. Catherine's estranged husband, Dom (*Bloodsucking Freaks'* Niles McMaster), arrives for the funeral and becomes entangled in the twisted murder plot as more attacks occur.

Crammed with surprises and offbeat touches, this can be a disorienting experience on first viewing but yields countless rewards along the way. Even minor characters are memorably sketched, particularly Alice's ridiculously obese neighbour, Mr. Alphonso (DeNoble, another *Bloodsucking Freaks* alumnus). The knife attacks remain genuinely shocking and frightening even now, with one agonizing and brilliantly sustained murder sequence stealing the show entirely near the end. The film's low budget actually helps, with unusual New Jersey locations lending a surreal, all too believable atmosphere of religious repression and domestic tension ready to explode. Organized religion remains at the centre as the primary corrupting force, favouring certain people at random over others and instigating malice and betrayal at every turn. The film treats people in the same manner to drive the point home, randomly knocking off characters whether they deserve it or not.

Though similar on the surface, Anchor Bay's DVD improves on the previous Roan Group laserdisc by toning down much of the oversaturated, distorted colours (especially red) which marred that transfer. The source materials are also in much better shape, freed from the distracting speckles and other damage littering the laserdisc, and the 1.85:1 framing is much more accurate than the squeezed Roan version. The laser was touted as a "director's cut" on the packaging and the print itself, which meant Sole actually tightened the film a little bit, as he felt the editing was rushed and incomplete when the film was originally released. As noted in *Video Watchdog*, the most significant cut removes a phone call from Dom's current wife, a deletion that seems to sharply divide the film's admirers. Overall the fleeting trims amount to about a minute and a half, allowing Sole to copyright this print and finally reclaim the film as his own. The DVD reinstates the footage, allowing it to be promoted as the "uncut version," and Sole's commentary has been readjusted accordingly. Sole provides some nice anecdotes about the making of the film, including a revelation of Shepherd's real age at the time and an explanation for the absence of music over the end credits (the closing music is now restored for the first time ever). Unfortunately, Sole was never again given the opportunity to shine like he does here; this was actually his second film, made after a gothic hardcore porn effort called *Deep Sleep*, and his subsequent efforts included the surreal "Vanity shags a monkey" vehicle *Tanya's Island* and the slasher parody *Pandemonium*. The DVD also replicates the extras from the Roan disc, namely the alternate *Communion* opening credits and a collection of stills from the film.

ALIEN

Colour, 1979, 117m. / Directed by Ridley Scott / Starring Sigourney Weaver, Tom Skerritt / Fox / WS (2.35:1) (16:9) / DD5.1

Though director Ridley Scott had made an art house splash with his first feature, *The Duellists*, he seemed an odd choice for a big studio project containing elements of drive-in sci-fi B movies *like It!* *The Terror from Beyond Space* and *Planet of the Vampires*. However, his immense visual gifts and cinematic storytelling skill produced a classic. The excellent ensemble cast, Dan O'Bannon's primal, terrifying narrative, and Jerry

Goldsmith's ferocious score managed to give class to what could have easily been a failure in lesser hands. Aboard the spaceship Nostromo, a seven man crew awakens from hypersleep to answer what appears to be a distress signal. The captain, Dallas (Tom Skerritt), instructs the crew to land and explore the signal from a seemingly desolate planet containing only caverns and the remains of an ancient crashed spaceship. One crew member, Kane (John Hurt), discovers vast numbers of strange egg-like formations... one of which promptly opens and discharges a face-hugging alien onto his face. Kane is brought back aboard, despite the protests of second in command Ripley (Sigourney Weaver). After scientific tests at the hands of the cold, manipulative science officer Ash (Ian Holm), the face hugger mysteriously falls off, crawls away, and dies. Kane revives, and all seems well... but not for long. After one of the screen's most memorable dinner sequences, it appears a rapidly growing alien is on board, and like the classic movie monster it is, the alien's primary intent is to wipe out the entire crew as nastily as possible. As the crew's number dwindles, the survivors try to outwit the seemingly indestructible presence and escape with their lives.

Marvellously designed by pioneering artist H.R. Giger, the alien itself is quite a beauty and still scares the bejeezus out of many viewers. Scott wisely drops most of the clichés associated with earlier science fiction films (weak secondary women, cutesy romantic subplots, etc.) in favour of a ruthless haunted house thrill ride approach that gives the film a timeless appeal. In fact, along with Scott's *Blade Runner*, this is one of the few futuristic movies that remains amazingly modern in its attitude and appearance and will likely remain so for several decades. Weaver's tough performance, her first major role, quickly established her with audiences worldwide, though Ripley would obviously reveal much deeper character traits in the sequels. By now this film has become so iconic that its youngest audiences may have difficulty believing this was actually panned by a number of critics on its original release, primarily for its gore content which, in fact, is actually quite low when you really pay attention; only the chestburster is even close to being graphic. Like *Psycho* and *The Texas Chainsaw Massacre*, this is a prime example of how to manipulate an audience into thinking they've seen far more than they really have.

Fox's laserdisc special edition of *Alien* was something of a watershed for its time, and the DVD manages to take it a step further. The anamorphically enhanced transfer from the original 35mm release materials (unlike the alternate 70mm sound mix included on the CLV laser version) benefits greatly from the enhanced shadows and chiaroscuro effects offered by DVD; also, the 5.1 remix sounds terrific considering the film's age. Few films use sound in a more manipulative fashion than this, and on a good sound system, you'll be cowering up in your sofa. The extras encompass the majority of the laser's supplements (ten deleted scenes including the notorious cocoon sequence, production art, effects demos, etc.) plus a new running commentary with Scott. The DVD also includes the isolated Goldsmith score as it appears in the film, as well as an earlier production audio track with the Goldsmith music placed as it was originally intended (plus some odd early sound effects and alternate dialogue). Less historically significant but interesting is the inclusion of the film's real theatrical trailer - it's a keeper! - along with the teaser included on the LD. Hats off to Sharpline for the striking menu design and excellent organization of the extra features. Incidentally, some Toshiba players have experienced problems with this title due to its CD-ROM compatible features.

ALIENS

Colour, 1986, 154m. / Directed by James Cameron / Starring Sigourney Weaver, Michael Biehn / Fox / WS (1.85:1) (16:9) / DD5.1

 If sequels by definition are lesser products than their originals, James Cameron's kinetic *Aliens* is a sterling exception. A relentless rollercoaster that extends the premise of the first film into startling new directions, this is that rare film that holds up after countless viewings and represents everyone involved at the peak of their craft. After her narrow escape in the first film, Ripley (Weaver) is rescued from her escape pod which has been sent floating adrift in space. Unfortunately, it's fifty-seven years later... After recovering from the shock, Ripley finds everyone unwilling to accept her explanation of the Nostromo's destruction and has her pilot's license stripped. After yuppie Burke (Paul Reiser in between his stints on *My Two Dads* and *Mad About You*) informs her that her Earth families inhabiting the alien-hosting planet as a colony have disappeared, Ripley begrudgingly agrees to accompany a group of gung-ho space marines to investigate. Among the marines are Hicks (Michael Biehn), android Bishop, smartass Hudson, and tough gal Vasquez (Lance Henrikson, Bill Paxton, and Jenette Goldstein, all re-teamed later in *Near Dark*). What they find, of course, is not pretty.

Though the film originally ran 137 minutes, Cameron expanded it with several deleted scenes for its laserdisc special edition. The extra footage, notably footage of the colonists before the alien takeover and some valuable insight into Weaver's maternal instincts, generally helps the film and doesn't slow it down at all. While purists may object at seeing the colony thriving with life instead of its original first appearance as an ominous ghost town, the scene is nevertheless fascinating and works well within the film. While a truly immaculate edition of *Aliens* may never exist, this DVD is much closer to it than the laser, which was impenetrably grainy at times. Some persistent grain still pops up here during scenes with extra footage, but a lot of clean up has obviously been done. The 16:9 transfer is more detailed than but similar to the earlier LD in terms of colour and general appearance, while the 5.1 mix gives a little more dimension to Horner's high-throttle score and the numerous bursts of firepower. The extras are the same as the LD (behind the scenes FX footage, production drawings, etc.), though this time the trailer is also included. The film itself continues to hold up well, with Weaver's remarkable Oscar-nominated performance shining as brightly as ever. Her relationship with Newt (Carrie Henn), a young colony survivor found in the abandoned corridors, gives the film a human resonance that lingers even beyond the thrilling action setpieces (and boy, are there quite a few of them). As with most Cameron films, this one continues to deliver long after other films would have called it quits. Just when you think it can't get better, it does... and when you think it's all over, you're not even close.

ALIEN 3

Colour, 1992, 117m. / Directed by David Fincher / Starring Sigourney Weaver, Charles S. Dutton / Fox / WS (2.35:1) (16:9) / DD5.1

 Easily the most controversial instalment in the series. First time director David Fincher (who cut his teeth on Madonna videos) begins with a series of merciless jabs at series fans that immediately alienated (er, sorry) much of the primary audience, and as part of the continuing saga, these bleak twists which continue all the way to the infamous downer finale obscure whatever virtues the film may contain. Looking back, it's hard to believe anyone involved, particularly the studio, expected this film to have a warm reception, and its notorious production difficulties (which involved extensive

A

cutting and reshooting up to the last minute) would have made this perhaps the most fascinating special edition out of the bunch. However, Fox has given this film (and its successor) a fairly chilly treatment on DVD. In this case, the viewer gets the film itself (at least given a sharp new 16:9 transfer, far surpassing the mediocre laserdisc), the trailer, and the HBO half-hour documentary issued on video upon the film's theatrical release. Still, its inclusion does welcome a re-evaluation of the film, and while it's not even close to a success, time has made it a somewhat more interesting viewing experience on its own terms.

After the breathless escape at the end of *Aliens*, Ripley wakes up to find her escape pod crash landed on a windy, desolate planet, Fury 161. It seems the planet, out in the space equivalent of the middle of nowhere, contains the remaining inmates of a prison colony; the prisoners have taken on fundamentalist religion as a means of psychological survival but find their beliefs tested by the presence of a woman. Ripley's companions, Hicks and Newt, died in the crash (nice, huh?), so within the first few minutes the viewer is treated to a charming autopsy on a twelve year old girl to determine whether her body bears an alien inside her chest. She's clean (no one thinks to check out Hicks' remains for some reason), but a face hugger was on board and has infested a local dog. Pretty soon it's alien stalking time all over again, and Ripley's momentary happiness in the arms of a local prison doctor (Charles Dance) offers only temporary solace as she finds herself up against the demonic force once again.

While Fincher is undoubtedly a talented director and showed remarkable artistic growth with *Fight Club* and *The Game*, here he seems to be flailing around at times to deliver both a personally satisfying product and a commercially viable instalment in a Hollywood series. As a result, his nihilist outlook is constantly at odds with the action and thrills the fans would expect. Gore splashes constantly, but it's consistently ugly and unpleasant; furthermore, the extremely slow pace and dour characters (think Ingmar Bergman in space) will test the patience of many viewers. The striking visuals manage to compensate, while Elliot Goldenthal's marvellous score (the best thing about the film, though the cues aren't always in the correct scenes) entertains the ear even when the eyes and brain have nothing to do. The rushed ending screams studio interference, though at least it gave Fincher the artistic presence to play with audience expectations later on for a similar sequence at the end of *The Game*. An enriched and expanded cut of the film would probably help its reputation, though many will never forgive it (perhaps deservedly) for the callous opening sequence, which basically destroys the entire purpose of the second film. Beyond the obvious flaws and general wrongheaded aspects of the project, however, *Alien 3* does offer some food for thought here and there, and at least the bald prison cast is a little easier to keep track of now that a few actors (namely Pete Postlethwaite and *Dr. Who*'s Paul McGann) can be recognized.

ALIEN RESURRECTION

Colour, 1997, 109m. / Directed by Jean-Pierre Jeunet / Starring Sigourney Weaver, Winona Ryder / Fox / WS (2.35:1) (16:9) / DD5.1

Hiring the director of such wild and woolly art house favourites as *Amelie* and *City of Lost Children* to helm an *Alien* movie may seem quite insane, and the results understandably split series fans down the middle. The extreme visual quirkiness and bizarre stylish flourishes which characterize director Jeunet's work are in great abundance here, and the presence of the wildly erratic Winona Ryder only serves to make the experience even more surreal. While *Alien 3* was essentially a film long on substance but woefully short on ideas outside of its vaguely defined religious symbolism, *Alien: Resurrection* is so packed with new, funky concepts from beginning to end that it really should have been much longer to reach its full potential. By far the shortest entry in the series, this one speeds by so quickly that it takes multiple viewings to absorb exactly what happened. If you haven't seen *Alien 3*, read no further as some necessary spoilers are contained below.

After Ripley's suicidal plunge to destroy the baby alien queen inside her at the end of the previous film, screenwriters resorted to one of the hoariest concepts in the book: let's clone her! (At least they didn't write off the last film as a dream, which was a rumour going around for a while.) However, the cloning concept is taken to such a marvellously surreal extreme that it actually works. See, the scientists have cloned Ripley so they can remove the alien foetus inside her; as a result, the new "Ripley" has retained some of the alien's DNA characteristics: retained memory, super strength, and acid for blood. The idiot military scientists (led by Brad Dourif with a really odd hairdo) smuggle in some human specimens via a band of space pirates including Jeunet regulars Dominique Pinon and Ron Perlman (TV's *Beauty and the Beast*). Soon aliens are popping up all over the lab and conspire a very funny method of escape. Determined to preserve herself, Ripley tags along with the freelancers for a wild ride through the ship as they manoeuvre the aliens and discover a few more nasty secrets about the DNA splicing process.

Boasting a nifty underwater chase sequence, outrageous camerawork by pro Darius Khondji, and yet another fantastic Weaver performance, *Alien: Resurrection* bends over backward to give the viewers their money's worth. The new Ripley confused fans who were used to the strong but tender leader of the other films, but it's interesting to see a familiar character turned inside out. Her relationship with the aliens obviously takes some new turns, and the bizarre final act resembles nothing seen recently in science fiction cinema. The huge doses of humour sit oddly with the grim basic material, though the bloodshed this time (and there is quite a lot) is far too cartoonish to be taken seriously. A few less one-liners would have probably been better, though some penned by *Buffy the Vampire Slayer* guru Joss Whedon hit the mark. Like *Alien 3*, Fox's DVD treatment is basically a throwaway. The transfer itself is the crispest of the bunch (this is the most recent title, after all). Strangely, this was the first entry shot in Super 35; in theatres it was exhibited at 2.35:1 and is presented as such (in 16:9) on the DVD. However, the previous laserdisc release opened the matte to 1.85:1, revealing a tremendous amount of information on the top and bottom of the screen. The scope framing really works greater for the film, lending it a sense of epic sweep missing in the postcard framing of the LD. The 5.1 mix sounds terrific, not surprisingly, though John Frizzell's serviceable score remains largely buried deep within the mix. Skimpy extras include the original trailer and a very brief studio promotion piece (too bad they couldn't include the entire made-for-cable half hour special). This disc is also available in a special box set with a fifth DVD (available by mail only in the US), containing a 66 minute documentary on the making of *Alien*. The US box contains a small packet of collector's photo cards and fold out booklets with liner notes for each film. (Unfortunately, the *Alien: Resurrection* booklet makes the regrettable goof of mixing up the cast pictures, rather hilariously - doughy faced Dominique Pinon is placed above the bio of J.E. Freeman, who isn't pictured at all, while Leland Orser's picture contains no bio at all).

ALL LADIES DO IT

Colour, 1992, 87m. / Directed by Tinto Brass / Starring Claudia Koll, Paolo Lanza / Cult Epics (US R0 NTSC), Arrow (UK R2 PAL), Dutch Filmworks (Holland R2 PAL) / WS (1.66:1), CVC (Italy R2 PAL) / WS (1.85:1) (16:9)

Deriving its title from Mozart's famous comic opera, *Cosi Fan Tutti*, the 1993 romp *All Ladies Do It (Cosi Fan Tutte)* is one of Tinto Brass' lightest and (literally) brightest films. Most likely influenced by the growing European popularity of Pedro Almodóvar, Brass spends just as much time leering on women's posteriors but also devotes more attention than usual to the intricacies of his decors and some delicious background details. This time our rump-heavy heroine is Diana (Claudia Koll), a happily married woman who nevertheless spends her time romping with a number of men. Fortunately her husband, Paul (Paolo Lanza), doesn't mind her little escapades; in fact, he rather enjoys hearing about them. Things get out of control, however, when Diana has a fling with an ass-obsessed poet named Alphonse and takes off to a wild jet-set, omnisexual outdoor party, where literally anything goes. With this film Brass teamed up for the first time with the gifted Venetian composer, Pino Donaggio, whose music adds a considerable flourish to the proceedings, working in pop motifs and lifts from Mozart with equal aplomb.

Contrary to the packaging, the film actually is widescreen (apart from open matte titles) and appears to be the same in its three English language DVD incarnations from the US, UK, and Holland. Image quality is passable if overly pale during dark scenes, with very robust colours and a relatively smooth compression job. However, the anamorphic Italian DVD (containing the original, less shrill language track) features an entirely different cut of the film, running 92 minutes, containing several brief sequences that tread into hardcore territory. Non-anamorphic extras on the Italian disc include the English language trailer and a nine minute reel of behind the scenes, deleted takes, and alternate footage, missing the final sound mix.

ALL THE COLORS OF THE DARK

Colour, 1972, 95m. / Directed by Sergio Martino / Starring Edwige Fenech, George Hilton / Astro (Germany R0 PAL) / WS (2.35:1)

While Dario Argento was busy making his "animal trilogy" of *giallo* classics during the early 1970s, the lesser known but fascinating Sergio Martino cranked out five highly accomplished horror-thrillers of his own: *The Strange Vice of Signora Ward* (a.k.a. *Next!* and *Blade of the Ripper*), *Case of the Scorpion's Tail*, *Gently Before She Dies* (a.k.a. *Excite Me*), *Torso*, and the wonderfully stylish *All the Colors of the Dark*.

This feverish cross between a murder mystery and *Rosemary's Baby* supernatural horror stars the gorgeous Edwige Fenech, who enlivened three of Martino's other *gialli* as well, and teams her up with genre regular George Hilton, who appeared in too many of these things to count. Here they play Jane and Richard, a posh London couple coping with the stress of Jane's recent miscarriage due to a car accident. Meanwhile Jane has also been having intense, recurring nightmares involving the murder of her mother and a blue-eyed, knife-wielding Ivan Rassimov, so she seeks help from her sister's psychiatrist, Dr. Burton (George Rigaud). Jane's mysterious new neighbour, Mary (Marina Malfatti), has a far more radical solution in mind; she initiates Jane into a satanic cult! Here the main devil worshipper (Julian Ugarte), a goateed creep with long gold fingernails, forces Jane to drink some fox's blood from a golden goblet and tosses her on the floor for a druggy orgy scene. As Jane's sanity begins to crumble, she wonders whether her horrific visions might actually be premonitions of a violent future; even worse, it could be connected to a sinister man who seems intent on terrorizing and stalking her no matter where she goes.

Loaded with enough twists and turns to keep the most fanatical whodunit fans busy, *All the Colors of the Dark* starts off with a bang thanks to Jane's unforgettable nightmare sequence, which would have established Martino as a powerful director to be reckoned with had anyone ever seen it outside Italy. Unfortunately this amazing curtain raiser, along with several vital dialogue scenes and the *entire climax*, was removed by Independent International when this circulated under the odd title of *They're Coming to Get You* and then on video as *Day of the Maniac*. In its original version, Martino's film is a one of the strongest of its ilk thanks to some terrific scope photography, Fenech at her finest, and a top drawer music score from Bruno Nicolai, who even returns to *Eugenie* territory during the trippy devil mass scenes. Despite some actual location shooting, the London setting doesn't really come off thanks to some peculiar dubbing and the fact that no one looks even remotely British, but it's a small quibble in an otherwise worthwhile film.

To say that this German DVD (under the title of *Die Farben der Nacht*) looks better than any other video version of this title wouldn't mean much considering its history. English language tapes have

been a botched mess, containing the heavily cut version (with awful new credits) in an unwatchable cropped transfer. The Italian language VHS was uncut but only halfway letterboxed to 1.85:1; grey market dealers circulated a version marrying what remained of the English language track to this extended transfer, but the results were still confusing and visually unsatisfying. On DVD, the audacity of the film's very wide compositions can be appreciated, and most importantly, viewers can finally enjoy the entire English soundtrack. This is especially crucial for a third act scene involving Jane's husband and sister, which has only been seen before by most viewers in Italian. The non-anamorphic transfer looks colourful and sharp enough, though blacks tend to get a little muddy or washed out depending on the scene. An odd cheese-cloth type visual pattern is barely visible in portions of some lighter scenes, but it isn't a major distraction. The dubbed German soundtrack is also offered in an extremely annoying 5.1 or 2.0 surround mix; aside from sounding phoney and wildly unbalanced, it muffles the music and seems to be taking place underwater. Luckily the English track is in the original mono. Extras include a surprisingly good makeshift trailer set to Nicolai's music, a small still gallery, and a whopping twenty trailers for other Astro/Marketing-Film releases. Though in German, these trailers offer a few odd novelties: *Randy* (apparently a re-edited job containing Sylvester Stallone footage from *A Party at Kitty and Stud's*), *The Hearse*, *Der Joker* (a barely seen 1987 thriller written by fantasy novelist Jonathan Carroll, who later disowned the final product), and best of all, a 16:9 trailer for *Der Fan,* better known to horror fans as the chilling German pop fan shocker, *Trance*.

THE ALLEY CATS

B&W, 1966, 83m. / Directed by Radley Metzger / Starring Anne Arthur, Karin Field / Image (US R0 NTSC) / WS (2.35:1)

Metzger's first erotic film with a single linear storyline, *The Alley Cats* snugly fits in with the swinging naughty foreign cinema of its day. Overripe dialogue, mildly kinky sex scenes, and a spectacular surf/lounge score combine to make this one sinfully entertaining piece of Eurokitsch, and though it's not as polished or intellectually stimulating as Metzger's later literary works, *The Alley Cats* is quite enjoyable and satisfying on its own modest terms.

Leslie (Anne Arthur), a lovely young society girl, is engaged to the seemingly straitlaced Logan (Charlie Hickman). However, Logan's carrying on an affair with a sultry blonde, Agnes (Karin Field), who's prone to comments such as "I like you because you're always... ready." A few swinging parties later, Leslie drops her inhibitions thanks to the advances of that old '60s erotica standby, the crafty lesbian. In this case the guilty party is Irena (Sabrina Koch), a slinky man-hater who passes the time by spanking guys with her garter belt. Will Leslie still honour her engagement to Logan? Will either of them learn the meaning of fidelity? How many parties can either of them endure before they pass out?

Sporting one of Metzger's most physically appealing casts, *The Alley Cats* takes expert advantage of Hans Jura's widescreen compositions and velvety black and white cinematography. Arthur is just as gorgeous and appealing as any of Metzger's future female protagonists, and the supporting cast looks appropriately well-groomed and enthusiastic. That future *Carmen, Baby*, Uta Levka, even turns up in a supporting role as one of the wanton young women.

The DVD looks comparable to the other Metzger transfers from First Run: accurate letterboxing, fine image quality, slightly worn print, and elegant menu design. Considering the rarity of this particular title (the only light "erotica" release not issued in any form before First Run's line of Metzger releases), the presentation is definitely acceptable and better than many other black and white titles released so far on DVD. As with many Euro features of the day, the trailer incorporates several photos and saucy snippets of footage rejected from the final cut of the film; in fact, this particular trailer contains far more nudity and kinkiness than the film itself.

ALTERED STATES

Colour, 1980, 109m. / Directed by Ken Russell / Starring William Hurt, Blair Brown / Warner (US R1 NTSC) / WS (1.85:1) / DD5.1

Most actors don't usually start out successful, award-winning careers by playing giant pulsating blobs of protoplasm, but that's exactly how William Hurt spent his first leading role on the big screen. Of course, considering it was in a Ken Russell film, this should really come as no surprise. Exactly how you respond to this visually relentless jackhammer of a film will depend on your tolerance for Russell's orgiastic camera pyrotechnics, which actually surpass what he achieved a few years earlier in *Tommy*. Fortunately Russell also keeps a firm grip on the narrative and characterizations (a skill with which has been credited far too rarely), keeping this from descending into a mindless sci-fi freakshow. Based on the novel by Paddy Chayefsky (who wrote the screenplay but disowned the final project before its release),

Altered States follows the unusual relationship between university research scientist Eddie Jessup (Hurt) and his wife and intellectual equal, Blair Brown (*The Days and Nights of Molly Dodd*) as he experiments with the process of de-evolution on his own body. Beginning with simple isolation tank flashbacks and descending into dangerous mixtures of mind-altering chemicals, the socially challenged Jessup finds his body and mind transforming beyond prehistoric man and into realms beyond the grasp of religion and science. Predominantly a horror film at heart (Hurt's apeman zoo chase recalls any number of 1950s monster on the loose films, and the dazzling, ear-bursting lightshow finale anticipates *Poltergeist* by a couple of years), this film managed to beat the odds (no big stars, an unbankable director, endless behind the scenes troubles) to become the most successful head trip movie since *2001*. Able support from Bob Balaban (who later directed the bizarre cult item *Parents*) and Charles Haid, as well as early appearances by Drew Darrymore (her first film) and John Larroquette, should satisfy more traditionally demanding viewers.

While decent prints of *Altered States* have circulated on cable for over a decade, its fate on video has been very messy. The first VHS and laserdisc edition was impenetrably dark and muddy-looking; the "remastered" edition some years later featured greenish skin tones and way too much grain. Luckily, the third time's the charm: both versions on the DVD look terrific, with rich colours and sharp detail. The widescreen version, enhanced for 16:9 monitors, looks a bit crisper, though the image has been matted- it gains a little on the sides and loses a bit on the bottom, but honestly the film is so centrally composed it doesn't really matter either way. The Dolby Digital 5.1 remix is nothing short of room-shaking, with John Corigliano's remarkable avant garde score and the swirling sound effects demanding this be viewed with the volume at full blast. After watching this, though, two obvious questions come to mind: why hasn't Russell directed another Hollywood film in over ten years, and when is Warner going to get around to an uncut DVD of Russell's *The Devils*?

A

AMERICAN PSYCHO

Colour, 2000, 102m. / Directed by Mary Harron / Starring Christian Bale, Willem Dafoe / Universal (US R1 NTSC), Entertainment in Video (UK R2 PAL), Intercom (Hungary R2 PAL) / WS (2.35:1) (16:9) / DD5.1

The first major American social satire posing as a slasher film since *The Stepfather* tackles the unenviable task of transferring novelist Brett Easton Ellis' notorious yuppie torture fest to the big screen. For the most part director Mary Harron (*I Shot Andy Warhol*) and co-writer Guinevere Turner have succeeded, creating an eerie and often blackly humorous antiseptic nightmare that casts a ghoulish reflection on our recent past.

Handsome, affluent Wall Street broker Patrick Bateman (Christian Bale) leads a numbing existence in which he compensates for his lack of soul or conscience by engaging in casual acts of butchery. No one is safe from his wrath, be it homeless people, prostitutes, or his fellow co-workers, whom he's willing to dispatch over something as trivial as a business card. No one around him seems to notice or even bothers to distinguish him from his fellow preening materialists. The only moral person in the film, his secretary Jean (Chloe Sevigny), views Patrick as her ideal and sets herself up for a chilly awakening, while a curious police detective (Willem Dafoe) makes repeated visits to Patrick without even scratching the surface. Or does he? Gradually Patrick's grip on sanity begins to loosen until reality and fantasy become indistinguishable, and perhaps irrelevant.

Though widely publicized thanks to its source material, the loss of leading man Leonardo DiCaprio, and a nasty scuffle with the MPAA, Lions Gate botched the American release of *American Psycho* by treating this ironic art film like a major blockbuster release, leaving many patrons shaking their heads. Seen outside its PR trappings, the film is quite satisfying as a brutal dissection of 1980s superficiality, particularly during Bale's hilarious and imminently quotable monologues on the finer points of Huey Lewis, Whitney Houston, and Phil Collins. The film slips a bit by placing itself in 1987 while including a strange barrage of songs recording long before and after that year (a similar flaw with *The Wedding Singer*), but the presentation of cutthroat yuppie self-love is dead on. All of Ellis' clinically explicit torture sequences have been removed, leaving instead a few judicious, comic book displays of bloodshed. Unfortunately this also numbs the book's analogy between the narrator's fastidious attention to detail in his personal hygiene and the fiendish care he invests into dispatching his victims. Bale still manages to make Bateman a compelling and utterly loathsome creature, all shimmering surface with muddy, poisonous waters underneath. Sevigny and Dafoe are accomplished as usual, while Leto (who seems to be making a career out of changing his hair colour) has a limited but memorable role. Only Witherspoon seems out of place; even dressed in haute couture, she looks too young and giggly to play an icy society bitch. Modernist composer John Cale contributes a marvellous, minimalist score, while the scope photography provides a succession of images worthy of a fashion magazine, albeit a highly depraved one.

Though surprisingly light on supplemental material, Universal's DVD is a worthy presentation of the film. The unrated version restores two lengthy shots to Bale's threesome frolic to "Sussudio" and longer facial blood splashing during the first axe murder. Image quality is razor sharp throughout, while the 5.1 audio is used sparingly for ambient effect during musical passages and the ironic eruption of pop tunes. Apart from the theatrical trailer, the disc includes a brief featurette in which Harron and Bale explain their reasons for wanting to do the project, as well as a chaptered on-camera interview with Bale (back in his familiar Brit accent) going more in depth into his interpretations of Bateman's character, or lack thereof. All Region 2 releases of the film are intact and contain an alternate set of extras, including some chatty deleted scenes and on the set interviews with the cast and crew.

AMERICAN PSYCHO 2

Colour, 2002, 88m. / Directed by Morgan J. Freeman / Starring Mila Kunis, William Shatner / Trimark/Lions Gate (US R1 NTSC) / WS (1.85:1) (16:9) / DD5.1

There are worse ways to kill an hour and a half in front of a television, but *American Psycho 2* is certainly one of the more expendable. Trading in all of the social commentary and gruesome wit of the Bret Easton Ellis novel and subsequent Mary Harron film with Christian Bale, this marginal sequel patches together its less than compelling narrative with far too much narration and a bizarre refusal to indulge in either full-blooded horror or outrageous comedy. The result is a peculiar and ultimately pointless exercise, skirting the edge of the teen horror, art house, and camp movie trends without ever finding any kind of voice of its own. The film begins with pretty college student Rachael (*That '70s Show*'s Mila Kunis) explaining how she became fascinated with serial killers at the tender age of twelve after killing off legendary '80s psycho Patrick Bateman and leaving the scene of the crime undetected. Now setting her sights on the FBI, freshman Rachael decides to become the teaching assistant to former agent Prof. Robert Starkman (William Shatner) - who coincidentally left the Bureau after the Bateman case collapsed. Unfortunately Rachael faces some tough competition for the coveted position with Starkman, and soon she's bumping off her rivals (and anyone else who gets in her way). Only psychiatrist Dr. Daniels (Gerant Wyn Davis) suspects that something may be dangerously awry with this all American beauty.

Though it moves along at a steady clip and tries to spike the viewer's interest with a barrage of irritating pseudo-alternative tunes, *American Psycho 2* would be thoroughly bland even if it didn't try to posit itself as a sequel to one of the more controversial tales of the past two decades. The connection to Bateman (obviously played in flashback by someone other than Christian Bale) merely serves as a reminder of how little this film has on its mind; the cutthroat college/prep school routine has already been done to death in films like *Gossip, The In Crowd, The Curve*, and so on. The few attempts to inject some pop culture irony fall dismally flat (such as one victim's dog carrying the name of Ricky Martin), and the entire script feels like an unpolished first draft that went before the cameras far too soon. At least the lead actors try their best, chewing into their roles with an almost disconcerting amount of enthusiasm. Fans of the beautiful Kunis should find plenty to ogle here, as she struts around in a wide array of low-cut leather outfits and tank tops, carrying the extremely light weight of this film on her slim, often bared shoulders. The anamorphic transfer from Lions Gate looks fine considering this film never had a real theatrical run; presumably the aspect ratio is correct. Colours are rich and stable, though the low budget results in some grain and inconsistent lighting at times (exacerbated by a few awkward shots apparently captured with a zoom lens). Surround channels remain active primarily through the music, while dialogue and ambient effects are generally centred. It's a pretty standard affair, audio and video-wise, with little to complain about. The disc also contains the trailer, English and Spanish subtitles, a handful of deleted scenes, and director's and producer's commentary.

AN AMERICAN WEREWOLF IN LONDON

Colour, 1981, 97m. / Directed by John Landis / Starring David Naughton, Jenny Agutter, Griffin Dunne / Universal (US R1 NTSC; R2, 4 PAL) / WS (1.85:1) (16:9) / DD5.1/DTS, Artisan (US R1 NTSC) / WS (1.85:1), DD5.1

Americans David Kessler (Naughton) and Jack Goodman (Dunne) are on a hiking holiday in the Yorkshire moors. Attacked by a werewolf, Jack is mauled to death and David is hospitalised. Fated to become a werewolf himself during the next full moon, David is visited by the decaying spirit of Jack who tells him he must kill himself to avoid the horrors that will otherwise ensue. Vacillating between being inordinately scary and blackly comic, there are a few dodgy moments when director Landis almost allows the rich vein of humour *in An American Werewolf in London* to degenerate into slapstick. Fortunately these are eclipsed by such inspirational sequences as the one in the back row of a Piccadilly Circus porno fleapit, where Jack introduces David to his undead victims who cheerfully trade ideas as to how their murderer might commit suicide. In contrast to such deliciously funny splashes, David's dreams are fast-paced and revolting, culminating in a double-whammy nightmare that warrants a niche in the annals of all time classic screen shocks.

The stomach-knotting minutes during which the lads hasten across the moors, stalked by something hostile just out of sight through the darkness, are so unbearable that it's almost a blessed relief when poor old Jack is torn to bits and the tension is allowed to dissipate. Naughton and Dunne share the best lines, though Agutter as David's nurse-cum-lover seems a touch uneasy with some of her dialogue. John Woodvine and a particularly surly Brian Glover provide puissant support. Rick Baker and his crew's show-stopping transformation effects when David becomes a werewolf are astounding; black hair rustles as it sprouts, sinews and muscles stretch until they scream, bone structure crunches and cracks as he shapeshifts into a snarling, ravenous beast of the night. Given that this was all achieved without the aid of computer morphing, it's all the more amazing. An unmitigated classic, and rest assured you'll never travel the labyrinthine tunnels that constitute Tottenham Court Road tube station in such a carefree manner again. The unexpectedly "final" ending didn't stop the money-men scheduling a belated sequel, but be warned *An American Werewolf in Paris* is worthless tosh.

Universal's Collectors Edition DVD by far supersedes the previous Live/Artisan Entertainment release, the only bonus on which was the atmospheric teaser trailer; curiously, a trailer of any kind is the one element absent from Universal's disc. How rewatchable is the lengthy segment in which make-up supremo Baker takes a cast of Naughton's arm? I'm not sure. However, it is but one among a number of extremely worthy extra goodies. There are fresh interviews with Baker and the sometimes irritatingly over-enthusiastic Landis, which include some previously unseen outtake footage. Then there's an additional two minutes of outtakes (sadly without sound, save for the rattle of the projector!), a section entitled "Mysterious Footage" (again without sound, this is a staged blunder, the purpose of which is unclear, with Landis and the cast of his film-within-a-film porno movie "See You Next Wednesday"), an original 1981 featurette, an entertaining commentary from Naughton and Dunne, a storyboard/scene comparison of the Piccadilly Circus mayhem, illustrated production notes, cast filmography/bios, and a rather nice slideshow of stills which plays out to snatches of Elmer Bernstein's moody score. The 20-chapter transfer of the film itself is as sharp as a werewolf's canines, with choices of English Dolby 5.1 Surround or English DTS 5.1 Surround, plus subtitling in English, Spanish and French.

- Tim Greaves

AMIN: THE RISE AND FALL

Colour, 1980, 97m. / Directed by Sharad Patel / Starring Joseph Olita, Geoffrey Keen / Parc Video (R0 PAL)

Ah, the '70s. In the wake of Vietnam, the news was filled with bizarre atrocities like the mass suicides at Jonestown and bizarre political upheaval in Africa and the Middle East. Among the most notorious "celebrities" from this period was General Idi Amin, who took control of Uganda and embarked on one of the most notorious reigns of terror in history. While the real man was chronicled with unforgettable irony and horror in Barbet Schroeder's *Idi Amin Dada* (1974), an exploitative biopic was unleashed in 1980, entitled *Amin: The Rise and Fall* in the US and *The Rise and Fall of Idi Amin* in Europe. After a quick thumbnail history lesson about Uganda, we're introduced to our villain (portrayed by lookalike Joseph Olita) as he rises to power following the previous ruler, Milton Obote. Visiting British and Israeli diplomats are openly courted by Amin, who horrifies occasional visitors with the two severed heads he keeps stashed in the refrigerator. Soon he decides to undertake a ritual of "ethnic cleansing" on the population, culminating in the show-stopping sequence in which Amin cannibalizes one of the corpses. Using Adolph Hitler as his role model, Amin captures and wipes out hordes of rebels (a body count of over 100,000), rapes his enemies' wives, and, with the help of voodoo and a gang of thug compatriots, soon becomes known as "Big Daddy." A large scale attempt to usurp the leader forms the climax after his failed invasion of Tanzania, though as history buffs will know, he continues to live in anonymity to this day in the Middle East.

At first glance, *Amin* looks like your average made-for-TV biography with a sick twist along the lines of *The Guyana Tragedy*, but grindhouse fans during its release were shocked by some truly grotesque flourishes that seem to come out of nowhere. The refrigerator bit has become the sleaze fan's equivalent of Faye Dunaway's wire hanger tirade in *Mommie Dearest*, and while the real life tragedy involved prevents this from descending into pure camp, the sheer outrageousness of the material makes it compelling and, well, just plain weird. Olita's uncanny resemblance to the ousted leader can't quite cover the fact that he's unable to deliver a genuine performance, but with a film this heavy handed and randomly structured, it hardly matters. Several slumming international actors make appearances, including a significant role for the James Bond series' Geoffrey Keen, but the film skims along through the pertinent events so quickly it's hard for anyone to make an impression. The direction by Sharad Patel (who went on to executive produce *Bachelor Party*!) is competent but rarely distinguished; at least he delivers the action scenes with some panache and never lets the viewer lose interest.

The PAL DVD release from Parc Video (which contains no indication of its country of origin) features the European title on the cover, but the print itself and three trailers (two G-rated, one R-rated) bear the US name instead. The video quality is definitely generations ahead of the fleeting US VHS prerecord edition, though anyone expecting a snazzy digital restoration will be disappointed. Image is soft but passable, and while colours are reasonably accurate, detail tends to smear and bleed, especially in long shots. The open matte framing is occasionally disrupted by the odd hard matted (1.55:1) shot, but compositions overall are fine. Be sure to watch the trailer, which offers a gruesome recap of the film's many "highlights."

THE AMITYVILLE HORROR

Colour, 1979, 118m. / Directed by Stuart Rosenberg / Starring James Brolin, Margot Kidder, Rod Steiger / MGM (US R1 NTSC) / WS (1.85:1), MGM (UK R2 PAL) / WS (1.85:1) (16:9)

A media sensation during the late '70s, the "haunted" house of Amityville became a familiar horror icon, its creepy eye-windows symbolizing the public's fascination with the unknown and the occult. Profiles and cash-ins ran all the way into the '80s, with an episode of *That's Incredible!* (remember that one?) even devoted to the craze. The frenzy first began with Jay Anson's undeniably creepy book, purportedly the true story of George and Kathy Lutz, a financially strained newlywed couple forced to move from their house after living in it for only 28 days. Naturally a movie followed soon after, and while it wanders so far afield from the original narrative that the "true story" claim was dropped from the posters, it's an undeniably entertaining ghost story in its own right.

On a dark and stormy night at 3:15 a.m., a young man takes a shotgun and kills his entire family as they sleep. After a long period on the market, the house is finally snapped up by the Lutzes, whose recent marriage brings along three of Kathy's children from a prior husband. Kathy's priest, Father Delaney (Rod Steiger), shows up to bless the house and is horrified to discover massive swarmings of flies and a demonic voice ordering him to "get out!" Strange events occur at 3:15 every night, with George becoming more withdrawn and subject to cold spells while Kathy occasionally pops up in bed, screams "She was shot in the head!," and falls back to sleep (the unintentional high point of tasteless hilarity in the film). More mishaps occur, such as a window falling on one child's hand and a wad of money disappearing before a wedding reception. Meanwhile the young daughter develops a friendship with "Jody," an invisible friend who might actually be real... and connected to the evil past of the house.

By any standards of mainstream filmmaking, *The Amityville Horror* should have been a resounding flop. The exploitative nature of the story, coupled with a bizarre hambone performance from Steiger (whose role has little relationship to the book) would have been enough to sink even the strongest film. However, love it or hate it, the film simply works on a primal level. Kidder and Brolin make a believable and sympathetic couple (despite her amusing fondness for nude leglifts), and Lalo Schifrin provides a superb, utterly creepy score which went

on to be nominated for an Oscar and, contrary to rumour, is not the same as his rejected score for *The Exorcist*. For what it's worth, MGM's DVD of *The Amityville Horror* is a tremendous improvement over any other home video version. The letterboxed image restores some much needed breathing room to the hard matted compositions (avoid the pan and scan version like the plague), while the colours that were absent on Vestron's horrendous laserdisc have now been properly restored. MGM's decision to release an anamorphic transfer in the UK but not in the US is inexplicable, but even more galling is the absence of the film's original, primitive non-Dolby stereo soundtrack. The mono sound here is fine, but it wouldn't have been difficult to punch up the original stereo tracks for DVD. Also, apart from the original trailer, the absence of extras is amazing. The disc doesn't even include some much-needed background information on the film and the events that inspired it, and the acres of existing video material on both the house itself and the making of the film could have made for one hell of a special edition. Still, while this is something of a missed opportunity, horror fans can at least finally enjoy a decent presentation of this key work of '70s horror.

AMPHIBIAN MAN

Colour, 1961, 92m. / Directed by Vladimir Chebotaryov & Gennadi Kazansky / Starring Vladimir Korenev, Anastasia Vertinskaya / Ruscico (R0 NTSC) / DD5.1

A virtually unclassifiable nautical reverie, *Amphibian Man (Chelovek-Amfibiya)* combines seafaring adventure, romance, monstrous fantasy, water choreography, and tragedy into a strange, beguiling dream of a film. A likely influence on Luc Besson's *The Big Blue*, with which it shares several nearly identical sequences and a similar story arc, this is a good place to start for newcomers to Russian cinema fantastique.

The sailors and fishermen of a remote Spanish town are sent into a panic when divers spot a glittering man, a "sea beast," lurking beneath the depths. However, his nature is more benevolent when expected when he rescues the young Guttiere (Anastasia Vertinskaya), who unfortunately becomes betrothed to the unscrupulous sea captain Don Pedro (Mikhail Kozakov). This amphibious denizen of the deep reveals himself by emerging into the town, where he turns out to be Ichthyander (Vladimir Korenev), the blond son of a local professor (Nikolai

A

Simonov) who saved his ailing son's life by transplanting to him the lungs of a shark. Ichthyander's love for Guttiere forces him to confront some of the less than receptive villagers, who make life difficult indeed for the aquatic outcast.

Rarely seen in anything resembling its intended form thanks to dubbed, muddy bootleg video and TV prints, *Amphibian Man* has largely been consigned to oddball fringe status by American viewers, though apparently its reputation flourished in Europe. The fantasy and science fiction elements are well integrated into the period setting, coupled with a haunting music score and exquisite colour photography (MGM could have easily remade this). Of course, an American studio would have most likely nixed the unexpected ending, so it's probably best that this gem remains a quiet little treasure to be discovered by adventurous viewers.

As with its other major restored films, Ruscico's DVD is a stunner. The negative has obviously undergone a great deal of loving care, while the beautiful 5.1 remix balances both the music and sound effects between each speaker to a surprisingly robust degree. The English dub track is the same one seen on TV, albeit in much cleaner form here, but the Russian version with English subtitles (or with any other optional subtitle option one might choose) is really the way to go. The disc includes the English language trailer (in much less pristine shape), a "Soundtrack" spotlight, two B&W behind-the-scenes shorts, trailers for other Ruscico titles, artwork and other elements of preliminary design, and a revealing short (11 min.) documentary, "In Search of Ichthyander," which reveals how some of the more astonishing underwater shots were achieved.

AMUCK!

Colour, 1971, 98m. / Directed by Silvio Amadio / Starring Farley Granger, Barbara Bouchet, Rosalba Neri / Eurovista (US R0 NTSC)

Italian murder mysteries don't come any sexier than *Amuck!*, originally titled *Alla ricera del piacere (In the Pursuit of Pleasure)*. Though the story may be another retread of the old *Whatever Happened to Aunt Alice?* gimmick of seemingly innocent assistants turning out to be much more than they appear, there's thankfully much more here than meets the eye.

Lovely blonde Greta (Barbara Bouchet) has just begun a new job as the secretary to prominent writer and art snob Richard Stuart (Farley Granger), who lives in an isolated Venetian country home with his perverse wife, Eleanora (Rosalba Neri). After the wife and secretary enjoy a slo-mo tumble in the sheets, it turns out Greta has actually come to investigate the disappearance of the Stuarts' last assistant, Sally, who happened to be Greta's lesbian lover. During a petting party, Richard shows off a porno version of "Little Red Riding Hood" which he shuts off abruptly when Sally appears in the frame. Then a casual hunting trip into the marshes turns nasty when Greta nearly loses her life in quicksand, and Richard's latest whodunit novel begins to bear a sinister resemblance to the deadly events occurring inside his house...

Thanks to the inspired teaming of Eurocult goddesses Bouchet and Neri, both of whom have copious nude scenes ensuring a strong fan following, *Amuck!* succeeds as a slinky thriller guaranteed to raise one's temperature a few degrees, even if the mystery angle itself is rather limited. All three leads offer enthusiastic performances, with Granger's shifty, wooden demeanour actually serving him well in contrast to some of his less memorable giallo turns in *The Slasher Is the Sex Maniac* and *What Have They Done to Your Daughters?* Meanwhile Neri takes top acting honours for her nasty bitch in heat routine, which really comes into play during the feverish drawing room climax.

For once all of the sex scenes and bare skin are genuinely integral to the story, which features a haunting flashback near the end accompanied by Teo Usuelli's catchy, repetitive theme song in which a woman repeatedly purrs, "Sexually!" This nifty piece has become a retro music staple in recent years thanks to CD compilations, gaining a familiarity to rival *Vampyros Lesbos*, but the entire score is up there with the best of its time and deserves a CD release.

While the movie itself may be an unheralded gem, the DVD presentation is unfortunately much less impressive. The transfer appears to be culled directly from a VHS master, complete with dropouts (with one particularly nasty one during the finale). Overall it looks like a very good, colourful, sharp bootleg videotape, which is obviously well below the standards for DVD. The original 2.35:1 Cromoscope compositions have been cropped to full frame, though thanks to the static camerawork, the effect is at least not as disastrous as many other similar titles. Extras include some spicy promotional photographs and two warm videotaped 2001 interviews with Bouchet and Neri, both of whom offer some nice reminiscences about making the film. Apparently the two are still next door neighbours, which makes you wonder what on earth goes on in that neighbourhood...

ANATOMY

Colour, 2000, 95m. / Directed by Stefan Ruzowitzky / Starring Franka Potente, Benno Furmann / Columbia (US R1 NTSC, UK R2 PAL) / WS (2.35:1) (16:9) / DD5.1

 Paula (Potente), an ambitious anatomy student, is accepted into the prestigious medical college where her grandfather introduced revolutionary practices still being taught. On the train journey there she saves the life of a young man with a heart condition, and is startled a few days later when his corpse turns up on the slab in her dissection class. Probing the lad's death, she uncovers information which indicates the existence of a secret society operating within the walls of the school, a society willing to go to any lengths for the advancement of medicine... even murder.

If *Anatomie* (or *Anatomy* as it was marketed in the UK and US) had been the product of Hollywood it would probably have slipped past as just another horror escapade. That it came out of Germany - and with Columbia's backing boasted the production values of a major league player - set it apart from the slew of disappointing and forgettable slasher flicks of the past few years, earning it more attention than it probably deserves. Ruzowitzky's film has a polished, slick and intelligent veneer, though after a decidedly intriguing and nasty opening in which a man wakes on an operating table to find his hand has been partially stripped of flesh to resemble an anatomical sculpture, it fails to be either particularly original or frightening. Potente, fresh out of the exceptional *Run Lola Run*, makes for a gutsy enough heroine and Benno is the convincing psycho-with-a-scalpel. Best seen in its original German language; the dubbed version is feeble in the extreme.

Columbia Tristar's 2.35:1 matted 28-chapter presentation is beautiful quality and the disc is loaded with more bonus materials than you can waggle a dermatome at. There's commentary from director Ruzowitzky, two featurettes, two theatrical trailers, a couple of deleted scenes, cast and crew interviews, some storyboard-to-scene comparisons and an excellent music video ("My Truth," performed in English by one of the film's German actresses, Anna Loos). Language choices are in English, Spanish and the preferred German, with nine subtitles options including English, Hindi and Icelandic. - TG

ANCHORESS

B&W, 1993, 106m. / Directed by Chris Newby / Starring Natalie Morse, Gene Bervoets, Toyah Wilcox / Vanguard (US R1 NTSC) / WS (1.66:1) / DD2.0

 Stark medieval dramas are usually a tough sell in the film market, and the 1993 British film *Anchoress* appears to be no exception. "Ecstasy and orthodoxy in the 14th Century!" proclaims the cover art for the film, though the ecstasy is entirely of a spiritual nature. Sort of a modern, post-feminist response to films like *The Seventh Seal*, this film may prove difficult for the average consumer but rewards patient viewers with stunning imagery and plenty of food for thought.

Christine Carpenter (Natalie Morse), a devout peasant girl, becomes enraptured with a statue of the Virgin Mary and develops a strong bond with the young local priest (Christopher Eccleston). Her parents, William (Pete Postlethwaite) and Pauline (pop star and TV staple Toyah Wilcox), are not as devoted to the church but allow their daughter to become an anchoress - a woman who is walled in to be at one with the Virgin and offer blessings to the outside people. The villagers congregate to a small window at Christine's self-imposed prison, where the priest controls how long and with whom she interacts. However, Christine's introspective existence causes her to move away from her religious faith and become focused on her more earthy dedication to the female goddess herself, Mother Earth. When her mother falls prey to the persecuting religious practices of the day, Christine comes to realize that perhaps she was not destined to remain an anchoress after all.

Featuring a very strong cast of art house regulars (including *The Vanishing*'s Gene Bervoets and a virtually unrecognizable Wilcox), *Anchoress* is first and foremost a convincing, gritty depiction of the Middle Ages, a time when religious convictions dominated every word and deed. The beautiful black and white photography perfectly captures the appearance of a delicate wood carving on film, while the surrealist eye of director Chris Newby (who directed some high profile gay shorts and features like *Madagascar Skin*) pays off during the delirious, haunting final twenty minutes. Fans of experimental British filmmakers like Derek Jarman and Peter Greenaway will be especially receptive to this film's unique, strangely resonant tone, which seems to spring out of some odd historically-tinged dream state.

Vanguard's DVD presents an accurately letterboxed transfer of the film with every bit of grain and visual grit intact. The film wasn't intended to look sleek and glossy, so the appearance here is appropriate at least. More dynamic is the Dolby Surround audio track, which bristles with life throughout the film. Ambient noises flood the surround speakers, offering a surprising amount of range that will have you often glancing over your shoulder.

AND GOD CREATED WOMAN

Colour, 1956, 95m. / Directed by Roger Vadim / Starring Brigitte Bardot, Jean-Louis Trintignant / Criterion (US R1 NTSC) / WS (2.35:1) (16:9)

A film so iconic most people don't even remember it has a plot, *And God Created Woman (Et Dieu créa la femme)* introduced the world to Brigitte Bardot, gave Roger Vadim his first break as a director, smashed down censorship barriers in the United States, and blurred the line between the arthouse and the grindhouse. So, is the film itself any good? Yes, but probably not in the way most viewers would now expect.

Rescued from a hellish life in an orphanage by a stern moralistic couple, young Juliette Hardy (Brigitte Bardot) spends her days working in a bookshop in St. Tropez and her nights partying with the locals. She spurns the advances of millionaire shipyard owner Mr. Carradine (Curd/Curt Jürgens, the villain from *The Spy Who Loved Me*), hoping instead to leave town with the handsome Antoine Tardieu (Christian Marquand, who later directed *Candy* and had sex with ice cubes in *The Other Side of Midnight*). Unfortunately Antoine regards her as nothing more than a one night stand and takes off alone. Antoine's kinder, weaker brother, Michel (Jean-Louis Trintignant), takes pity on the young beauty and, against the advice of his family and the townspeople, marries Juliette. Domestic life proves to be a problem when Mr. Carradine buys out the Tardieu shipyards, with Antoine returning home to assume duties as a chief of operations. Now saddled with three men longing to possess her, Juliette begins to crumble.

While the late Vadim earned a reputation as a womanizer and a materialist, it's interesting to note that this film remained progressive even after countless imitations. Most American directors would have probably gunned Juliette down in a hail of bullets for her transgressions (see Russ Meyer's *Lorna* for a good comparison), but Vadim is squarely on the side of his heroine. None of the men really deserve her, and the final scene leaves interpretations completely open about the characters' future happiness. Despite their wealth and prestige, businessmen like Carradine and Antoine fail to comprehend Juliette or the entire female gender for that matter; their remarks that she "destroys men" are quite ironic indeed. Of course all of these considerations take a back seat to Bardot herself, more of a force than a character.

While the film contains no actual nudity *per se*, apart from the legendary opening profile shot of Bardot's derriere and a few gauzy skin shots behind curtains, the film conveys a powerful atmosphere of sensuality from the opening frames. Bardot's hair becomes wilder and more dishevelled as the film progresses, and she provides some unforgettable iconic images along the way. Look no further than the haunting beach scene between Bardot and Marquand, in which she effectively revives him from nearly drowning with a single provocative gesture of her foot.

For such a high profile film, *And God Created Woman* has had a disastrous history on home video. The first VHS version from Vestron was the familiar English dubbed version, with sloppy panning and scanning which demolished the scope photography. Vadim's camera often sets up actors at opposing ends of the frame, and every inch is necessary to appreciate even the simplest dialogue scene. While the familiar Vadim visual flourishes only break out during the powerful Mambo finale, this is a film to be viewed in widescreen or not at all. The problem was only slightly remedied by a British VHS release, in French with English subtitles and partially letterboxed at 1.85:1.

Fortunately those versions are obsolete thanks to Criterion's amazing restoration job, which is perfectly letterboxed and boasts an astounding palette of colours. The St. Tropez waters now glow a luminous aquamarine, and Bardot's red dress is saturated a pure, noise-free crimson. The optional English subtitles restore some surprising profanity to the dialogue and fly by quickly at times, so get ready to speed read. Also included is the surprisingly dull American trailer and a restoration demonstration. (Note: Vadim remade this film less successfully in 1986 with Rebecca De Mornay, turning the female lead into a more emancipated former criminal who longs to be a pop star! Pioneer's US R1 DVD is much better than one might expect, and contrary to the packaging, it's letterboxed at 1.85:1, 16:9 enhanced, and contains the full unrated version.)

AND THE SHIP SAILS ON

Colour, 1984, 127m. / Directed by Federico Fellini / Starring Freddie Jones, Barbara Jefford / Criterion (US R1 NTSC) / WS (1.78:1)

Probably because it features few of his recognizable standard performers nor the requisite Nino Rota music score, Fellini's *E la nave va* (*And the Ship Sails On*) has never enjoyed a reputation equal to most of his earlier films. However, on both technical and artist levels, the film is easily as good some of the more famous films from his "excessive" period (*Satyricon, Casanova, City of Women*, etc.), and foreign film addicts would do well to discover this unheralded little gem.

In the summer of 1914, a luxury liner (filmed completely on the soundstages of Cinecittà!) departs from the Italian coast. The passengers on board have all congregated with one mission in mind: to pay tribute and scatter the ashes of Tetua, a revered opera diva. The events are presented for the audience through the eyes of Orlando (David Lynch favourite Freddie Jones), a gregarious reporter who spends most of his time addressing the camera. This delirious ship of exotic fools revels in lavish banquets, self indulgent soirees, and other idle dalliances of the rich. Their chic self absorption begins to crack when the captain rescues a band of Serbian refugees who have been set adrift to escape the imminent terror of World War I. As the passengers soon realize, even in the middle of the ocean, you cannot escape reality.

One of Fellini's most visually sumptuous efforts, *And the Ship Sails On* basks in its own glorious artifice. Characters often make ironic remarks while staring at the ultra-saturated backdrops ("Look at that sunset - it almost appears to be painted on!") and change costumes more often than their expressions. Like most Fellini films, this film was shot without sound and later dubbed in due to the motley international players (Jones' dubbing is especially distracting), but the Italian version is as authentic as any. The opening sequence ranks as one of the most audacious of Fellini's many cinematic feats; the film begins as a silent, sepia-toned depiction of the ship's preparations before departure, with sound effects gradually layered on as the passengers begin to arrive. One by one the actors begin to sing, with Plenizio's operatic works continuing to appear throughout the film as musical accompaniment. Upon the arrival of the ashes, the film bursts into colour - and the voyage begins. Without giving anything away, the finale is perhaps even more audacious and reminiscent of *8 1/2* in its puckish cinematic trickery. Criterion's edition of *And the Ship Sails On* clocks in at just over 127 minutes, though versions running as long as 134 minutes have been reported in Europe. Whether this discrepancy is due to Fellini's last minute trims (not an uncommon occurrence) or the vagaries of converting European video for the US is uncertain, but the film doesn't appear to be missing anything significant. The image quality is very good, especially considering the condition of most pre-1990 Italian films, though not as dazzling and clear as *Nights of Cabiria*. The easily legible English subtitles are optional and usually very accurate. No extras aside from a fold out booklet with excerpts from the book, *I, Fellini*. Amazingly, this disc is not time encoded.

AND THEN THERE WERE NONE

B&W, 1945, 97m. / Directed by René Clair / Starring Barry Fitzgerald, Walter Huston / Image, VCI (US R1 NTSC), MPIC (UK R2 PAL)

Even for those who have never seen this film or read the Agatha Christie novel on which it was based, the plot will seem very familiar. Ten strangers arrive at a large house on the mysterious Indian Island, invited by an unknown host. During dinner, a voice on a record album from their host, "Mr. Owen," accuses each of them of a murder of which they were never convicted. The house contains a sculpture and sheet music referring to a familiar nursery rhyme, "Ten Little Indians," which recounts the ghastly fates of ten Indian boys; soon the guests begin to die, one by one, through grisly and imaginative methods echoing each Indian death. The intelligent guests, including a judge and a doctor, deduce that the nefarious Mr. Owen is actually one of them, and so they must determine the killer's identity while attempting to stay alive.

One of Christie's most brilliant plot constructions, this tale began as a novel outrageously entitled *Ten Little Niggers* but was changed to *Ten Little Indians* in the US, for obvious reasons. Christie soon translated her popular novel into a stage play, using the *Ten Little Indians* title and replacing the book's nihilistic finale (in which the killer's identity is revealed through a long expository note) with a more upbeat but no less clever resolution. The 1945 film adaptation uses the book's third, least familiar title, and remains one of the finest of all cinematic mysteries. Amazingly, this was remade no less than three times by Harry Alan Towers, with each version actually worse than the last as the setting changed from Switzerland to Iran to Africa. The tale's influence over the years cannot be overestimated; aside from obvious twists like *Alien* and *Friday the 13th*, even Mario Bava made no less than two variations on the story, *Five Dolls for an August Moon* and *Bay of Blood*. Despite the passing of time, the original film remains fresh and involving, thanks to the visually imaginative direction of Rene Clair (along with *The Ghost Goes West* and *I Married a Witch*, this was one of his few English-language efforts). Clair's avant garde background serves him well here as he deftly avoids becoming stagebound with all the characters puttering around the house. Clever touches like the judge's pool table demonstration of the murderer's plan and the recurring image of a cat playing with Judith Anderson's ball of yarn (which pays off with a terrific visual punchline) provide a fascinating cinematic counterpart to Christie's witty, precise writing style (though the script includes several brilliant lines of its own). Clair also makes intelligent use of a moving camera and inventive manipulation of props (statuettes, keyholes, axes, knives). Despite the potentially morbid and creepy subject matter, the film remains balanced thanks to the pitch-perfect performances all around (Huston, Fitzgerald, and Anderson are astonishing) and a general atmosphere of jovial mystery. Not an easy task to pull off with lines like "He brought the axe down and split the cranium in half," but sure enough, it works. Long out of circulation on both television and video, *And Then There Were None* made its long-awaited legitimate video debut after the rights for the 20th Century Fox apparently expired.

The print used by VCI for its DVD is watchable, with only mild signs of wear and tear around the reel changes, but it's soft and dupey, looking more like a VHS tape. More distracting is the audio, which goes wildly out of synch through several major scenes. The Image DVD features a much crisper 35mm transfer from the BFI's preserved film element. Some damage still remains, mostly in the opening reel, but contrast and clarity are much better - and the sound matches up. This version also includes the original UK title sequence, with a title card explaining its historical context.

ANGEL HEART

Colour, 1987, 109m. / Directed by Alan Parker / Starring Mickey Rourke, Robert De Niro, Lisa Bonet / Artisan (US R1 NTSC), Momentum (UK R2 PAL) / WS (1.85:1) (16:9) / DD2.0

Director Alan Parker's bone-chilling combination of detective yarn and occult thriller (billed in the oblique trailer as *The Exorcist* meets *Chinatown*) has aged extremely well and now stands as one of the most accomplished horror efforts of the 1990s.

Mickey Rourke stars as seedy private eye Harry Angel, who investigates the disappearance of a popular crooner indebted to the mysterious Louis Cypher (Robert De Niro). Along the way he encounters an odd collection of occultists and oddballs from New York to Louisiana, leading to a nightmarish finale packed with twists and turns.

Contrary to the R rating on the American DVD's packaging, it contains the full unrated cut with those extra few moments of Mickey Rourke's bloody derriere. The shock value of seeing *Cosby* kid Lisa Bonet bare it all and frug with a sliced-up chicken has worn off by now, but each viewing of the film still manages to get under the skin. The UK DVD preserves the same cut but adds on a welcome Alan Parker commentary, along with a making-of documentary and a photo montage. The Dolby Digital soundtrack remains constantly active and generates much of the film's atmosphere of unease; image quality is crisp and attractive (though not necessarily demo piece material thanks to the film's age and Parker's penchant for hazy long shots).

ANGUISH

Colour, 1986, 89m. / Directed by Bigas Luna / Starring Zelda Rubinstein, Michael Lerner / Anchor Bay (US R1 NTSC) / WS (2.35:1) (16:9) / DD5.1

Best known to foreign film fans for his sexy, off-kilter films like *Golden Balls* and the incredible *Jamón Jamón*, director Bigas Luna first assaulted the international market with the bizarre thriller *Reborn* and the even stranger *Anguish*, a novel twist on the old film-within-a-film gimmick. The opening of the film (and even its original print ads!) warned viewers that they would be subjected to hypnotic suggestion throughout the film, but this is probably the least of the audience's problems as the overlapping narratives veer wildly between reality and illusion until the viewer is left completely disoriented. John (Michael Lerner), an unstable, nearsighted mama's boy working in an ophthalmologist's office, loses his grasp on sanity after being laid off. His creepy and domineering mother, Alice (*Poltergeist*'s Zelda Rubinstein) urges him to seek revenge and carve out the eyeballs of his victims to compensate for the wrongs the world has committed against him. Then... well, let's just say this is one film where the less said, the better. An insanely difficult film to warm up to, *Anguish* relentlessly confounds expectations by turning in on itself and turning into a series of Chinese boxes. While its central conceit has turned up in films ranging from *Targets* to *Demons*, this odd, gruesome variation interweaves its narratives so completely that the knee jerk, nonsensical shock ending almost starts to make sense in retrospect. Lerner and Rubinstein both deliver ridiculous, over the top psychotic performances which are difficult to assess, while Luna shows great visual flair in his use of hazy gold, scope photography (later duplicated in Dario Argento's *Trauma*).

Finally restored to its original, desperately needed widescreen format, *Anguish* works much better on DVD than on the previous VHS and laserdisc editions from Fox. The highly creative and manipulative stereo soundtrack, which only kicks in full force half an hour into the film, was always the strongest point of Fox's version, and Anchor Bay goes one better by presenting it in 5.1. The listener's ears can't help but be jolted by the enveloping, highly directional sound mix, one of the most creative uses of audio design imaginable. Just watch and experience it for yourself. The disc also includes a mediocre Spanish trailer with subtitles; presumably the one used in American movie houses has been lost, which is a shame. Definitely a rent before you buy it kind of movie, but its fans should be quite pleased.

ANOTHER DAY, ANOTHER MAN
B&W, 1966, 63m. / Directed by Doris Wishman / Starring Barbi Kemp, Tony Gregory
BAD GIRLS GO TO HELL
Colour, 1965, 65m. / Directed by Doris Wishman / Starring Gigi Darlene
Image (US R0 NTSC)

Oh, dear God, it's time for a double dose of Doris Wishman. For the uninitiated, Doris' films are a cataclysmic fusion of looped dialogue, maddening "plotting," and irrelevant shots of shag carpeting, furniture, and actors' feet, all punctuated with dizzying sex scenes and random acts of violence. Nobody does 'em quite like this, and Something Weird's epic drive-in DVD will show you why.

First up is *Bad Girls Go to Hell*, a black and white grindhouse roughie in which a sweet housewife is raped by her building's janitor and kills him (with an ashtray!) in self defence. Naturally she decides to flee to the anonymity of the big city, a hotbed of seedy guys just looking to put the moves on an innocent little thing like her. Apart from dealing with guys wearing the ugliest boxer shorts known to man, our heroine must preserve her sanity at all costs and winds up befriending another older woman whose son turns out to be, alas, a cop hot on her trail. What's a girl to do?

For another walk on the sordid side, take a gander at *Another Day, Another Man*, in which lady of the evening Tess tries to explain to her prudish friend Ann why being a hooker ain't so bad after all. Naturally financial disaster forces Ann to take up hooking for Tess' employer, Bert, just to make ends meet, and it all leads where such things must - disaster! Sex doesn't pay, at least in Wishman's world, but it's so darn fun on the road to ruin that few will care about the message.

Unlike the soapy dramas being churned out by Hollywood at the time, Wishman's roughie morality plays make no attempts at pandering to the masses like, say, *Peyton Place*. What we get instead is acres of sad-looking women in lingerie, trashy and all-too-catchy jazz music designed to lodge itself in your brain, and shaky camerawork that looks more accidental than cinema *vérité*. While Doris eventually turned towards candy coloured lounge nightmares like her Chesty Morgan double header, these earlier gems belong to an era unto themselves and deserve a slot, no matter how disreputable, in a history of '60s cinema in America.

The image quality is excellent for films neglected by the ravages of time; luckily Mike Vraney at Something Weird managed to grab up the original source materials for many of Doris' cracked epics, and the results will stun anyone who thinks these films should look scratchy and beaten up. Debauchery has never looked so pristine. While the films themselves are fun enough in their own down'n'dirty way, the real star of this DVD is the presentation. Decked out with tons of drive-in ephemera, this is a real treat, which perfectly shows off just what DVD can do. You get cartoon promos for drive-in etiquette, snack bar and intermission ditties, and a ton of other Wishman trailers (such as the unforgettable Indecent Desires), including one special Easter Egg trailer for Wishman's stunning anti-masterpiece, *The Amazing Transplant*. It's hours and hours of seedy fun, right at your fingertips and safely in the privacy of your own home. Get your sweaty hands on this one!

ANY NUMBER CAN WIN

Colour, 1963, 103m. / Directed by Henri Verneuil / Starring Jean Gabin, Alain Delon / Image (US R1 NTSC), Amuse (Japan R2 NTSC) / WS (2.35:1) (16:9)

Based on the novel John Trinian novel *The Big Grab*, the French thriller *Mélodie en sous-sol* (retitled *Any Number Can Win* for the US) belongs squarely in the tradition of cool crime studies like *Breathless* and *Le Samouri*, albeit with a welcome humanist edge. A typically sleek and cool French thriller in the best '60s mould, this offers a showcase for two great pros of Euro cinema, Jean Gabin (*Grand Illusion*) and Alain Delon (*Purple Noon*), at the top of their form.

Just out of prison, aging con Charles (Gabin) is torn between the demands of his wife to settle down and the urge to pull off one last heist before he retires. For his partner in crime, Charles picks the young, cocky Francis (Delon), to whom he bestows the blueprints for a lavish Cannes casino. Francis infiltrates the casino's hotel, where he mingles with the local beauties (including a visiting Palm Beach ballet troupe!) and scopes out a path to the casino vault through the air ducts. When the day of the heist arrives, both men hope their plan will be foolproof... but of course, it isn't.

More concerned with character development and fetching scenery than fast paced action or twists, *Any Number Can Win* follows in the footsteps of such leisurely Riviera caper films as Hitchcock's *To Catch a Thief*. Gabin and Delon make a good team, with the latter at the height of his poster boy career, and the catchy jazz/lounge score keeps the proceedings from ever bogging down under the sure hand of crime film specialist Henri Verneuil (*Public Enemy Number One*). Not a classic by most standards, this nifty little cocktail aspires only to entertain and does so quite efficiently, and the final ironic scene is truly marvellous.

Though the Image packaging offers no information about the film's presentation, this film has been preserved on DVD in its original Dyaliscope aspect ratio, and it's anamorphically enhanced, to boot. The quality is as impressive as possible for a black and white '60s film; the background detail remains constantly sharp and crisp, though some scenes are deliberately bright and overexposed, particularly during close ups and swimming pool scenes. Optional yellow English subtitles offer a faithful translation of the French dialogue, and the mono audio is clean and free of distortion throughout. The print sports an MGM logo before the credits. For completists a Japanese release boasts an anamorphic widescreen transfer of both the standard international 103 minute cut and a 121 minute version consisting of longer and alternate takes, both in French with optional Japanese subtitles.

THE ARABIAN NIGHTS

Colour, 1974, 131m. / Directed by Pier Paolo Pasolini / Image (US R1 NTSC), BFI (UK R2 PAL) / WS (1.85:1)

Pier Paolo Pasolini's directorial career hit a lavish high point with *The Arabian Nights*, a conclusion to his "Trilogy of Life." As with the Image and BFI releases of *The Decameron* and *The Canterbury Tales*, this DVD has been culled from the Museum of Modern Art print, which means that it's letterboxed (approximately 1:85:1, a little more severe than the 1.75:1 indicated on the package), with subtitles that cannot be removed from the picture. Considering the film's low budget and ragged history, the print looks acceptable; the colours are much punchier than any other version available on video, and the grain isn't as noticeable as it is on *The Decameron*.

The film itself is generally regarded as Pasolini's most accomplished entry in the trilogy, and it certainly is the most visually sumptuous. The framing device involves a slave girl, Pelligrini, around whom the numerous tales are spun as she rises to power and schemes to reunite with the man she loves. The graphic violence and frontal nudity may put off casual viewers, but this is one of Pasolini's more accessible films. The stunning visual settings, which were shot on location, give the proceedings a strange, hallucinatory edge, and even the most extreme moments have a touch of elegance that should prevent anyone from becoming offended enough to turn it off (as opposed to, say, the shocking *Salò*).

The notes on the back claim this is the "original uncut version," but rumours persist that an even longer, 155 minute edition existed at one point. It's hard to imagine what could have been cut, unless it was an entire story, but this will most likely remain the definitive edition unless someone in Italy uncovers the lost footage someday (if it exists). (Note: It's too bad the DVDs couldn't include the trilogy's original (and graphic) English language trailers, which are quite a riot.)

THE ARENA

Colour, 1973, 82m. / Directed by Steve Carver and Joe D'Amato / Starring Pam Grier, Margaret Markov / New Concorde (US R1 NTSC)

What's not to love about an early '70s Roger Corman drive-in movie? Fashionable feminism, gratuitous nudity, catfights, over-dramatic dialogue... yes, indeed, it's all right here in *The Arena*, a lavish spectacle (by New World standards) in which the audience is treated to *Caged Heat* in gladiator drag. Of course, most will snag this one for Pam Grier, doing by far the most explicit and unabashed nudity of her career. Luckily, it also happens to be quite a fun film. Back in the old days when the Roman Empire was at its height (and right after the Spartacus revolt, as one minor character is quick to point out), the Romans took delight in pillaging other cultures, slaughtering innocents, and taking the most beautiful women back with them as servants. Bodicia (Margaret Markhov) of Brittany is the token blonde goddess captive, while Mamawi (Grier) is a tribal woman; miraculously, both apparently know how to speak Latin. Along with two other women, Bodicia and Mamawi are subjected to such indignities as public hose-downs and handwaiting on Roman political slobs. When the girls start a catfight (the first of many OTT highlights), the nasty Romans, headed by the token gay comic character Priscium (Sid Lawrence), decide that their new acquisitions might make for more entertainment in the gladiator arena. However, after the women witness the brutal treatment of the male gladiators, who are promised their freedom and summarily executed, they decide that this isn't the most efficient system of government and plan an escape. Not surprisingly, the last third of the film is devoted to the "jailbreak," filled with plenty of sword clashing and spilled blood.

Markhov and Grier make a nice team after their previous stint on Corman's *Black Mama, White Mama*, and visually, the film looks terrific. Though credited to Steve Carver (*Big Bad Mama, Lone Wolf McQuade*), directorial chores were reportedly handled mostly by the film's cinematographer, Joe D'Amato (Aristide Massaccesi), who later found a profitable career helming horror films (*The Grim Reaper*) and a slew of highbrow Rocco Siffredi hard porn titles. And believe it or not, this was edited by Joe Dante, long before Corman gave him his big break as director of *Piranha*. The good news first: while the box indicates that this is the same chopped-up 78 minute version released on video as *Naked Warriors* back in the '80s, this is actually the complete 82 minute original release edition. Finally! Now for the bad: *The Arena* was skilfully shot in Technicope, and the opening and closing credits (as well as the great trailer) are presented letterboxed at 2.35:1... while the rest of the film is fullscreen. Aiigh! On the positive side, the transfer quality is amazingly good, with rich, vibrant colours and impeccable detail; coupled with the thoughtful recomposing of the image, you'd have a hard time guessing this was scope for a few minutes without deliberately looking for it. Still, shame on New Concorde for not presenting this film as it was meant to be seen.

A

ARIA

Colour, 1987, 88m. / Directed by Nicolas Roeg, Bruce Beresford, Charles Sturridge, Julien Temple, Ken Russell, Jean-Luc Godard, Derek Jarman, Robert Altman, Franc Roddam, Bill Bryden / Starring Theresa Russell, John Hurt, Elizabeth Hurley, Bridget Fonda / Image (US R1 NTSC) / WS (1.78:1) (16:9) / DD5.1

Usually dismissed as an attempt to meld MTV stylistics to the classical form of an operatic aria, this truly deranged film actually hearkens back to those loony continental omnibus movies of the 1960s in which some producer with too much money would tell a few notable French and Italian directors to go shoot some short films around a common theme. Here we get ten directors, and needless to say, the results are highly uneven but often surprising.

Like the literal translation of its title - "air" - *Aria* is essentially a cream puff of a film that kicks off with Theresa Russell in male drag as King Zorg, a ruler in love who becomes the subject of an assassination attempt at an opera house. Typical of Nicholas Roeg, this sequence ("Un Ballo in Maschera") makes little sense but is fun to look at, with plenty of arty shots of blood flying onto Austrian snow. Of course, this looks downright commercial compared to Jean-Luc Godard's adaptation of "Armide," in which two naked girls frolic around a gym amidst oblivious studly bodybuilders. Julien Temple takes his shot at "Rigoletto" by transplanting the look of *his Earth Girls Are Easy* into the story of a married couple (Buck Henry and Anita Morris) whose infidelities in a kitschy tourist trap are caught by a very, very long Steadicam shot that even manages to work in an opera-singing gold lame Elvis. If you're looking for celebrity skin, of course, this "superbly sensual experience" (according to the box) definitely delivers, with a young and almost unrecognizable Elizabeth Hurley doffing it all for Bruce Beresford's beautifully shot and laughably lip-synched version of Korngold's "Die Tote Stadt." So how many of these sequences are actually good? Well, the highlight is probably Franc Roddam's visually arresting "Liebestod" which presents Tristan and Isolde as a teen couple in Las Vegas living out a death pact. Making her film debut, Bridget Fonda doesn't keep clothes on for long either, enough to ensure this film's perpetual popularity on late night television, but Roddam's clip is a beautiful work in and of itself. Ken Russell also goes all out for "Nessun Dorma" by drawing a striking parallel between Egyptian goddess worship and a beautiful blonde being salvaged from a car wreck. The late Derek Jarman presents his usual skilful melange of austere theatrics and home movie footage for "Depuis le Jour," with his usual muse, Tilda Swinton, making a welcome appearance. Less impressive, unfortunately, are Robert Altman's draggy period version of "Les Boréades" and Bill Bryden's dull "Pagliacci," which attempts to tie everything together by showing John Hurt throughout preparing his clown makeup. Even at its worst, the film is never less than beautifully shot, however, and seems best designed for viewing on the small screen, particularly on DVD when the viewer can simply skip around and avoid the dull parts.

Originally unrated on its theatrical release, *Aria* was subsequently rated R without any cuts for its lacklustre video version from Academy. Long out of print, the film now looks far better on DVD, most likely derived from a hi-definition source intended for European transfer and thankfully presented as an anamorphic transfer here. The running time is about two minutes shorter, thanks to the PAL source origins, but has no discernable effect on the film. The European 1.78:1 standard framing looks accurate, and the detail and richness of colour easily blow away any other version released in the US The sound is quite good, considering, and should give any surround system a decent workout; Image has released the title in two variants, one in standard stereo surround and one with a 5.1 audio remix.

ARMY OF DARKNESS

Colour, 1993, 81 / 96m. / Directed by Sam Raimi / Starring Bruce Campbell, Embeth Davidtz / Anchor Bay (US R1 NTSC) / WS (1.66:1) (16:9) / DD5.1

Continuing the evolution of the *Evil Dead* films from pure visceral horror to dizzy genre-bending comic monsterfests, *Army of Darkness* thrusts that familiar

hapless, one-armed hero, Ash (Bruce Campbell), into the same timeslip where viewers last saw him in *Evil Dead 2*. However, the horror aspects of the series have been twisted in *Army* into a screwy homage to the likes of Ray Harryhausen, H.P. Lovecraft, Jonathan Swift, and the Three Stooges. While we may never see a fourth instalment in the series, the films at least currently stand as a satisfying trilogy with a quasi-epic final instalment.

The dim-witted Ash, armed with a shotgun and little else, finds himself in a medieval land where the horrible Deadites terrorize the countryside. After a nasty encounter in a well, Ash agrees to retrieve the notorious Necronomicon ex Mortis ("the Book of the Dead") from a desolate burial ground, in exchange for which he will be returned to his own time. Along the way, thanks in part to his own carelessness, Ash winds up fighting miniature versions of himself, splits in two (Manster-style), and even gathers an army to fight hordes of rampaging skeletons.

Held up for years due to legal wranglings with the properties of Dino De Laurentiis, *Army of Darkness* first emerged in theatres in a slimmed-down, audience-approved 81 minute edition. However, Raimi fans were still entranced by the results and rushed out to find the legendary extended cut, which soon circulated on the bootleg market. While most versions open and conclude with wraparound segments showing Ash as a contented employee at "S-Mart," the original director's cut featured a much darker, more ironic finale, available on smudgy-looking bootleg tapes and as a supplement on the longer Japanese laserdisc, *Captain Supermarket: Evil Dead III*. However, a variant expanded edition even turned up on the Sci-Fi Channel with even more alternate footage, including some unique comic bits during the long, infamous windmill sequence. (See *Video Watchdog* #46 for a full catalogue of the various cuts and reshoots.) Thankfully, Anchor Bay performed the seemingly impossible by stitching together the 96 minute director's cut with the original ending, the abbreviated US cut with added comic lines, and several expanded scenes trimmed from the final assembly. Obviously, Raimi's longer original cut is more expansive in scope and more impressive in its achievements than the more familiar edition, which was always quite a blast to begin with.

Campbell is at his best, working at the height of his cavalier *Brisco County, Jr.* persona, and Embeth Davidtz does a fine job as the damsel in distress, Sheila. Interestingly, both Campbell and Davidtz wind up playing alternate, evil versions of themselves and do quite a convincing job of it. Raimi shows his usual cinematic virtuosity, cramming bizarre camerawork and startling effects into virtually every scene to craft a slick rollercoaster ride of a film. From Joseph Lo Duca's rousing score to the goofy anachronistic humour, this also serves as a bridge between Raimi's delirious big screen joyrides and his popular TV series, *Hercules: The Legendary Journeys* and *Xena: Warrior Princess.* (However, it has nothing whatsoever to do with *For Love of the Game.*)

Anchor Bay's anamorphic, THX-approved transfers of both cuts look excellent; derived from the finest surviving material, the director's cut is obviously not quite as pristine all the way through (particularly during the windmill sequence) but, compared to what fans have been watching for the past few years, it's probably as good as it's going to get. The US cut looks astonishing and improves in every respect upon the prior Universal DVD; not surprisingly, the 5.1 sound mix is a sonic delight. The regular surround track for the director's cut is quite serviceable, too, and obviously includes some additional sound effects and music now available in stereo for the first time. The additional deleted scenes are in rough cut form, which is better than nothing. Viewers get the original opening as it was first scripted, two additional exposition scenes, and a much longer prelude to the "tiny Ashes" sequence in the windmill. The plentiful extras include the trailer, a funny half hour featurette ("The Men Behind the Army") devoted to the eclectic mixture of special effects techniques used in the film, storyboard comparisons, and a rollicking audio commentary with Campbell and Sam and Ivan Raimi (on the director's cut only). As usual, these men make for good company and provide some handy tips in making a maverick genre film, even when a big studio is involved in the production. They also helpfully provide information on most of the reinstated footage (including Ash's different retorts after shooting "Bad Ash") and even continue their commentary onto the deleted scenes, a particularly helpful gesture during the windmill intro. Bravo to everyone involved, and while *Army* may not have been the blockbuster hit Universal hoped for, it's nice to see a film with such a rapidly growing cult following get the treatment it truly deserves. The double set has become something of a collector's item, but the separate standard and director's cuts have also remained perpetually on the market in one form or another, including a brown wrap cover entitled "The Official Bootleg Edition," whatever that may mean.

ASHES OF TIME

Colour, 1994, 100m. / Directed by Wong Kar-wai / Starring Brigitte Lin, Leslie Cheung, Maggie Cheung / Mei Ah (HK R0 NTSC), World Video and Supply (US R0 NTSC) / WS (1.85:1)

That rarest of beasts, a delicate sword-swinging action film, *Ashes of Time* revolutionizes the period heroic format in much the same way director Wong Kar-wai created a new vocabulary for '90s urban action and domestic drama (*Chungking Express, Happy Together, Fallen Angels*, etc.). Most viewers will have difficulty piecing together any sort of linear narrative for at least the first half of the film, but the familiar character tropes should be enough to at least convey the basic concepts: Ou-yan Feng (Leslie Cheung, of course), a wandering, alienated swordsman; Yin and Yang (the lovely Brigitte Lin), who may or may not be the same person and the object of our hero's vengeful quest; and a blind swordsman (Tony Leung) who uses his other heightened senses to improve his physical skills.

Obvious similarities to the films of Sergio Leone abound, of course, ranging from the music to the wide open vistas and jarring close ups. However, a modern sensibility consistently infiltrates the proceedings: the jagged, often dreamlike storytelling techniques; the jaded, unsatisfied attitudes of the characters; and the lyrical sensuality of Christopher Doyle's breathtaking cinematography, which can make the simple image like a woman's leg straddling a rock over a covered stream into an aesthetic creation of exquisite beauty. The seemingly random introduction of fantastic elements, such as an elixir which brings on memory loss and causes numerous subsequent plot complications, are integrated so naturally into the film's fabric that the viewer is never even given a moment to question them. An unusually sensitive and sweeping score by Frankie Chan (thankfully available on CD) fills in the rest of the emotional holes, making this an experience that gains in significance and richness long after the end credits have rolled.

Loosely based upon Louis Cha's classic Chinese novel, *The Eagle Shooting Heroes* (given a lighter cinematic treatment under its original title one year earlier), *Ashes of Time* never received as much acclaim or recognition as its director's other films in the US, remaining largely ignored outside the festival and cult film circuits. This situation has not been helped by the most widely available US DVD edition from World Video and Supply, an overmatted nightmare that makes the film well nigh unwatchable. Fortunately, the Mei Ah DVD, available from Chinese video shops and online retailers, provides a much closer replication of the theatrical experience. (Both versions lack any extras; amazingly, the Mei Ah version doesn't even have a menu.) Some distracting print damage remains evident throughout, a sad commentary on the preservation of even the most recent films, but at least the image is framed correctly and features legible English subtitles (burned in, alas). Sound quality is not perfect but acceptable, with the dialogue, music, and sound effects delivered quite well for mono. If ever a film cried out for a 5.1 remix, this would be it; in the meantime, this bare bones option will have to do.

THE ASPHYX

Colour, 1972, 99m. / Directed by Peter Newbrook / Starring Robert Stephens, Robert Powell / AllDay (US R1 NTSC) / WS (2.35:1)

The Asphyx, also known as *Spirit of the Dead*, hinges on a concept straight out of *The Twilight Zone* or, more likely, *Night Gallery*. In turn of the century England, an up and coming scientist (Robert Stephens) discovers through a series of photographs and films the existence of an "asphyx" - an amorphous spirit hovering over people at the moment of death or in situations of mortal peril. With the assistance of Robert Powell (a fine, very intense actor best known as Franco Zeffirelli's *Jesus of Nazareth* and for his appearances in Ken Russell's *Mahler* and *Tommy*), Stephens manages to capture the asphyx of a guinea pig, thus rendering the animal unable to die. Giddy with the thought of immortality, the two men arrange to capture Stephens' asphyx as well. Naturally, the subsequent events do not go as planned, and several tragic twists ensue.

A real curio, the film boasts first-rate performances from all involved and is truly amazing to look at, with some gorgeously ornate set design and silky photography, which admirably captures the misty feeling of an era gone by. The reason for the film's lack of recognition probably lies in the fact that it can't really be classified. Though it contains elements of horror, fantasy, and period drama, *The Asphyx* exists in a sort of hazy netherworld between the three. The potentially campy subject matter receives a deadpan and brooding treatment which causes more impatient viewers to dismiss it as talky or boring. Imagine an Amicus horror film crossed with a very cerebral *Dr. Who* episode, and you'll get the idea.

Past video editions have been a pretty sorry bunch, usually from public domain video labels with scratchy, miserable pan and scan editions that destroy any sense of visual style. Fortunately, this edition perfectly letterboxes the scope image and reveals of number of imaginative camera setups and lighting schemes impossible to appreciate on past editions. For example, a full five years before *Suspiria*, note the way Stephens and Powell are often placed within the same frame but lit with completely different colours, bright red and blue respectively. In fact, the obsessive use of the colour blue adds to the chilly, uneasy atmosphere the film creates and has never been presented so strongly as it is here. The only drawback is the soundtrack, which sounds fine on a TV monitor but reveals some unfortunate deterioration and scratchiness when listened to carefully. Also includes the original US pressbook and a scene selection feature.

ASTRO-ZOMBIES

Colour, 1969, 92m. / Directed by Ted V. Mikels / Starring Wendell Corey, John Carradine, Tura Satana / Image (US R1 NTSC) / WS (1.85:1) (16:9)

Often regarded as the most deranged and ridiculous of director Ted V. Mikels' no-budget horror quickies, *Astro-Zombies* throws all pretence of coherent linear storytelling out the window in the first few minutes and never looks back. From the opening credits, which fixate endlessly on twitching toy robots to the feverish and wholly incomprehensible climax, this film is truly one of a kind. Whether that's a good thing is, of course, up to you to decide.

The bloody murder of a woman in her garage by a skull-faced zombie is apparently the latest handiwork of Dr. DeMarco (John Carradine at his hammiest), a scientist booted out by the military while he was developing a project to create remote-controlled zombies for use during space exploration. (Um... okay.) CIA head Holman (Wendell Corey) assigns two of his agents to track down DeMarco, who is in the process of developing another "astro-zombie" in his lab with the help of his leering dwarf assistant, Franchot (Mikels regular William Bagdad). Meanwhile the first zombie, which has apparently gone haywire due to its creation from a psychotic's body, sets its sights on DeMarco's ex-assistant, Janine (*Dr. Kildare*'s Joan Patrick), and a group of spies led by Tura Satana takes a keen interest in the doctor's experiments as well. All of our characters collide at the end, of course, but not before viewers are treated to an extended body-painted strip routine (complete with Mikels himself at the bongos) and one truly unbelievable incident involving solar energy drawn from a flashlight. See it if you dare...

Thanks to the cast alone, *Astro Zombies* is substantially more interesting than your standard drive-in junk. Just seeing Satana (most legendary for her leading role in Russ Meyer's *Faster, Pussycat! Kill! Kill!*) rubbing shoulders with vets like Carradine and Corey makes for an odd experience, not to mention the fact that the script was co-written by *M*A*S*H* actor Wayne Rogers(!).

Though notorious in the annals of bad movie history, the film made a bundle for Mikels and became a home video staple, where it sometimes appeared under the title of *Space Zombies*. Unfortunately most of the VHS versions were drawn from the master used by Wizard Video, which scissored out literally every single drop of blood along with the strip sequence. Even the film's trailer focused on the gory highlights, which are fairly startling (but not convincing) for a 1969 film, including severed heads and bits of torn flesh being pelted at cars, walls, and anything else the filmmakers could easily clean up. Film historians can now rejoice, however, as *Astro Zombies* has been restored to its full sexy, violent glory on DVD. The print is by far the most colourful presentation ever witnessed on the small screen, and the widescreen framing creates a sense of composition where none should really exist. Given the bizarre distribution history of the film (one of the few not controlled directly by Mikels himself), the print is in good condition overall. Only the opening pre-credit scene and the main titles are damaged to the point of distraction, with scratches and speckles littering the screen before letting up for a much cleaner, more satisfying appearance. The full juicy trailer is also included in less pristine condition. Get out your flashlights, throw back enough alcohol to numb your brain, and prepare for an entirely new kind of cinematic experience.

ASYLUM

Colour, 1972, 88m. / Directed by Roy Ward Baker / Starring Peter Cushing, Herbert Lom, Robert Powell / Image (US R0 NTSC)

During the heyday of British horror films in the '60s and '70s, a number of studios attempted to compete with Hammer Films for the international terror market. The best of these, Amicus, specialized in anthology films, with chilling stories linked together

by a clever framing device. Along with their blood-freezing 1972 version of *Tales from the Crypt*, the studio's high point remains *Asylum*, an ingenious compendium of tales by Robert Bloch (*Psycho*) boosted by an astonishing international cast.

The presumptuous young Dr. Martin (Robert Powell) arrives at a sprawling mental institution out in the British countryside to apply for a position as head of the facility. The orderly informs him that the previous director, Dr. Starr, went completely mad and now resides within the asylum walls. In order to win the job, Dr. Martin must guess which of the inmates is actually the former Dr. Starr by listening to the case histories directly from the patients themselves. In the first, a young woman named Bonnie (Barbara Parkins) relates how her married lover (Richard Todd) chopped up his wife and stored her carefully wrapped body parts in his basement freezer. Unfortunately, revenge has a nasty habit of striking from beyond the grave. Next, a kindly tailor named Bruno (Barry Morse) is hired by an eccentric customer (Peter Cushing) to design a most unusual, occult suit for his son. Then the beautiful Barbara (Charlotte Rampling) explains how her return home after a period of mental treatment was upset by the arrival of Lucy (Britt Ekland), an impish prankster who ultimately turns to murder. Finally, the gruff Byron (Herbert Lom) shows off a series of miniature, anatomically correct robot-dolls which follow the bidding of their creator's will. So does Dr. Martin guess correctly? Watch the film and find out...

Thanks to its fast pacing, clever use of classical music, and assured direction by Roy Ward Baker (*Quatermass and the Pit*), this film (which was reissued as *House of Crazies* in the US) consists of many high points, with even the most predictable moments still pulled off with admirable panache. The second tale, "The Weird Tailor," had previously been filmed as an episode of the classic horror series *Thriller*, but this remake doesn't suffer in comparison. Powell does well with a difficult role, while Lom steals every moment near the end of the film. The final twist is a delicious surprise and will not be discussed any further here.

A long-time staple of public domain video lines, *Asylum* received its best video treatment on laserdisc from Prism and Image (and oddly enough never hit video under its alternate title). The DVD duplicates the same transfer, including a freeze frame, computer generated title card to remove the old copyright information. The colour looks a little punchier on DVD, while the extra clarity also brings out some scratches and other flaws in the print. Still, this is the best the film has looked anywhere, and any self-respecting horror fan should find a welcome place in their collection for this one. Incidentally, the image (which was probably intended to be matted at 1.78:1) has been presented open matte, with plenty of extraneous headroom visible throughout the film.

AT MIDNIGHT I'LL TAKE YOUR SOUL
B&W, 1963, 81m. / Directed by José Mojica Marins / Fantoma (US R1 NTSC) / WS (1.66:1)

 Years before Freddy Krueger, another maniacal fiend with long fingernails stalked world cinemas for years in Brazil. José Mojica Marins, one of the most unforgettable director/actors ever, began his bizarre career in 1963 with *At Midnight I'll Take Your Soul*, a film shot on scraps that turned out to be a huge hit in screens across the nation. With his top hat, chiselled beard, piercing eyes, flowing black cape, and inhumanly long fingernails, Marins became a celebrity as Zé do Caixão, or "Coffin Joe," a self-centred man who becomes more of a demigod with each film.

Here the audience receives not one but two introductions delivered directly to the screen, first from Coffin Joe himself and then from a cackling gypsy woman. We then meet our antihero, Coffin Joe, the undertaker of a small village who terrorizes the citizens with his self centred, violent behaviour. Just for kicks he ties up a woman and lets spiders crawl over her, he voraciously eats meat on Good Friday, and he regularly picks fights at local bars and cuts off his competitors' fingers with a broken bottle during a game of poker. The goal of Coffin Joe's unholy search is the perfect woman who can bear his son, but even including his own less than satisfactory wife, the locals don't offer a prime candidate... or so it seems, until he meets the lovely Terezinha (Magda Mei).

Though Marins is known for his extreme, personalized filmmaking, which often puts the actors through the kind of humiliations normally, reserved for carnival freakshows, *At Midnight* is surprisingly strong in both the story and atmosphere departments. The desolate, shadowy village is photographed in a stylish manner to conceal the limited budget; in fact, some of the nocturnal graveyard sequences recall the similar feats accomplished by Mario Bava in *Black Sunday* and several of Terence Fisher's earlier Hammer films, not to mention the classic Universal horrors which crop up in numerous little homages.

All of the actors were amateurs, either friends or relatives, and Marins handled most of the technical duties himself. As far as homemade horrors go, however, this is a stunning achievement.

Bearing in mind that it was probably spliced together with Scotch tape, *At Midnight* looks terrific on DVD. Some of the process shots, such as the opening titles, still look as ragged as they ever did, but the image quality is crisp and the negative appears to have been well preserved. The previous subtitled VHS edition from Something Weird looked pretty good, but this one is even better. The Portuguese dialogue is presented with optional English subtitles, and the disc includes trailers for all three Fantoma Coffin Joe titles (identical to the ones on SW's previous compilation tape). The real treat here is a ten-minute interview with Marins in which he discusses the making of the film, pointing out various locales which had to be altered and explaining how he accomplished that memorable shimmering shot of a spectre offering Coffin Joe a light in a graveyard.

AUDITION
Colour, 1999, 116m. / Directed by Takashi Miike / Starring Ryo Ishibashi, Eihi Shiina / Tartan (UK R0 PAL) / WS (1.85:1) (16:9), Universe (HK R3 NTSC), Art Port (Japan R2 NTSC) / WS (1.85:1) / DD2.0

 Mainstream movies don't come much more disturbing than *Audition*, a crafty little sucker punch of a film that runs for its first hour like an offbeat romantic drama about a man dealing with his midlife crisis by seeking the company of a pretty young woman. However, let's just say that this film has some nasty teeth and isn't afraid to bite its viewers, so those with strong stomachs should simply seek out this astonishing film without any further description. Now here's a taste of the initial premise. After recovering from the death of his beloved wife Yoko, middle-aged Aoyama (Ryo Ishibashi) is left to raise his son all alone for several years. Aoyama discusses his loneliness with his best friend, a movie producer, who suggests an interesting new twist to avoid the complexity of dating rituals. The two men decide to hold an audition for a movie which will actually serve as a method of finding a new wife for Aoyama. The ideal woman should have some kind of artistic talent and a genial nature, qualities which appear in abundance in the form of Asami Yamazaki (Eihi Shiina), a former ballet dancer and aspiring actress.

The two tentatively begin a relationship, though her past acquaintances either tell cryptic stories or appear to have vanished completely. And that's just the beginning...

Best known as the director of kinetic, gory action fare like *Fudoh* and *Dead or Alive,* Takashi Miike restrains himself somewhat by confining the graphic horrors to the final act of this film, which laces most of its chills through the rest of the running time with quick, subtle shivers that pass by almost unnoticed. In particular, one beautifully executed scene involves Asami sitting in the foreground listening to a ringing telephone while something very sinister happens in the background. Acting, direction, and photography are all first rate, and the story expertly pulls the rug out from under the audience several times, deftly moving back and forth between reality and illusion as the narrative glides towards its grisly, inevitable resolution. Watch this one at night, and prepare to be seriously rattled.

The UK disc from Tartan boasts a fairly clean 16:9 enhanced image with nice colours and good, optional English subtitles, along with a Miike interview, film notes by Chris Campion, and the European and Japanese trailers. The stereo soundtrack is relatively inactive during the first half of the film, but the soundtrack becomes more powerful and aggressive during later scenes when chilling noises and musical stings proliferate for atmospheric effect. The Universe Region 3 disc is non-anamorphic, with rather high black levels. The subtitle translation is different and considerably more awkward. The disc also includes a Hong Kong trailer loaded with spoilers, in Japanese with Chinese subtitles. The non-anamorphic Japanese DVD features the original language track with no subtitles. A Region 1 release from the American Cinematheque is also forthcoming at the time of this writing, with several Miike-involved extras.

AUTOPSY

Colour, 1975, 100m. / Directed by Armando Crispino / Starring Mimsy Farmer, Barry Primus, Ray Lovelock / Anchor Bay (US R1 NTSC) / WS (1.85:1) (16:9)

One of the odder Italian mysteries around, *Autopsy* gained notoriety upon its original theatrical release when the US distributor encouraged rumours that real autopsies were conducted and filmed during production. Of course, this is about as believable as the final "real"

murder in *Snuff,* but the movie became a 42nd Street and drive-in favourite anyway. What viewers really got was a twisted, unconventional giallo packed with creepy set pieces and a truly novel setting.

While a stifling heat wave strikes Rome and sends many of the denizens fleeing into the countryside, a wave of suicides provoked by sunspots(!) causes more activity than usual in the local morgues. Sensitive pathologist Simona (Mimsy Farmer) is working on a thesis examining real versus staged suicides, and her work begins to get to her. Simona's disturbing hallucinations feature the fresh, mutilated corpses rising from their slabs, mugging for the camera, and even having sex on the morgue floor! Simona's piggish boyfriend, Ed (Ray Lovelock, the memorable bearded Scot from *Let Sleeping Corpses Lie*), is peeved when her visions interfere with their sex life. One day a gunshot suicide victim found on the beach is wheeled in, and Simona recognizes the victim as her father's mistress. The brother of the deceased, a slightly sinister priest (Barry Primus), believes the woman's death was actually murder, and Simona's research indicates he may be correct.

The second trip into the macabre from director Crispino (*The Etruscan Kills Again*), this film was originally released as *Macchie Solari* and, according to the apparently erroneous press materials, was listed with an inflated running time of 125 minutes! Joseph Brenner picked the film up for the US and re-edited the opening sequence to omit the opening titles, instead cutting new credits with an unforgettable funky beat into the harrowing suicide montage that kicks off the film. A few dialogue trims were made, and the entire end credits wound up on the floor as well. The result was not a substantially different film, and all of its strengths remained intact. Farmer's jittery, shrill performance was apparently intended, while one can only wonder what she sees in the shifty Primus, one of the screen's most unlikely men of the cloth. Lovelock easily takes the acting honours, as usual, with his misogynist pig getting all of the most memorable lines. The film is astoundingly graphic at times, particularly during some very revealing sex scenes and a chilling, suspenseful peek inside a crime museum that isn't easily forgotten. Some of the film rambles on a little more slowly than it should, but that's '70s Italian mysteries for ya. Ennio Morricone also contributes a lovely, haunting main theme, which was stupidly left off the soundtrack album and most memorably accompanies the film's final poetic scene.

By far the most impressive release of this film in any edition, Anchor Bay's DVD of *Autopsy* is completely uncut and looks fantastic. The weird, often subdued colour schemes don't offer many opportunities for an eye-popping video transfer, but the materials used are absolutely pristine and vividly realized. An uncut letterboxed edition was previously available on Japanese VHS, but that version was marred by optical censoring of all frontal nudity (which is a lot in this film). However, the Japanese version also contained an effective two channel stereo soundtrack, while the Anchor Bay disc is mono; the loss isn't tremendous, but it's odd they didn't include that version as an option. The disc also includes an alternate Italian language track - minus subtitles, alas - as well as the US trailer (which blows the entire ending) and a European trailer as *The Victim*.

AUTUMN SONATA

Colour, 1978, 97m. / Directed by Ingmar Bergman / Starring Ingrid Berman, Liv Ullmann / Criterion (US R1 NTSC) / WS (1.66:1)

Another excursion into the emotional torment that is the human family unit, *Autumn Sonata (Höstsonaten)* presents the expected level of angst found in Ingmar Bergman's '70s work but also offers some welcome indica-tions of redemption and grace. Eschewing the fantasy elements which characterized some of his most famous work (*Fanny and Alexander, The Seventh Seal*), Bergman instead pared down his formula to the same basic "characters in a room" method he previously mined in *Cries and Whispers*.

Seven years after their last meeting, renowned pianist Charlotte (Ingrid Bergman) decides to visit her daughter, Eva (Liv Ullmann). Now living a tender but strangely loveless marriage with the sensitive Viktor (soft porn actor Halvar Björk), Charlotte has taken on the duty of caring for her younger, mentally handicapped sister, Helena (Lena Nyman), whom Charlotte had placed in an institution years earlier. Though the women seem civil enough on the surface, Charlotte's stay eventually unearths a host of seething emotions and resentments which force both mother and daughter to confront their demons and grow as human beings.

The only collaboration between the two famous Bergmans (who weren't related), this small chamber piece meant to serve as more of an introduction to his style than a major advancement of any major themes in Ingmar Bergman's work. Ullmann once again proves her range as she deglamorizes herself and, thanks to her ponytails, takes on the appearance of a fragile and ultimately enraged little girl, saddled with a mother who also finds herself unable to cope with the demands of adulthood. Sven Nykvist's sensitive photography drenches the screen in unnaturally saturated levels of orange and gold, appropriate to the title, while he and Bergman create some of the most imaginative and psychologically penetrating compositions in his work since *Persona*.

Criterion's DVD looks extremely similar to their previous laserdisc and the VHS edition from Home Vision, though the problematic distortion of many of the colour schemes is noticeably more under control here. The marginally letterboxed image looks satisfying throughout, though some shadows have a tendency to become pale and slightly bluish (a flaw in the source print, most likely). Despite a couple of speckles, the source materials are in excellent shape, though for some reason the English opening titles have been spliced onto a mint Swedish print (thus allowing for optional English subtitles). The disc also includes an optional English-dubbed track, which is frankly ludicrous considering Bergman speaks some of her lines in English in the original film anyway. The clash between her natural voice and the English dubbing by another actress is quite surreal, to say the least. Peter Cowie contributes a truly stellar audio commentary, one of Criterion's best, in which he makes a solid case for this often dismissed film as one of Bergman's most significant achievements. His combination of amusing anecdotes, biographical detail, and critical insight make for very good listening which dramatically enriches one's enjoyment of the film. A brief and very worn theatrical trailer is also included.

AWAKENING OF THE BEAST

B&W/Colour, 1969, 91m. / Directed by José Mojica Marins / Fantoma (US R1 NTSC) / WS (1.66:1)

When is a Coffin Joe film not a Coffin Joe film? When it's *Awakening of the Beast*, a scathing portrait of drugs and decay in modern day Brazil. While the famous caped villain does make an extended appearance in the final half hour, the bulk of the film is devoted not to sadistic torture but to the lurid debauchery wrought by chemical abuse and unchecked crime in an urban environment - all the more remarkable considering it was mostly shot in one room. Banned in Brazil until 1986, this was promptly hailed as Marins' masterpiece. Though many may find it doesn't quite live up to the hype,

Awakening is both essential Marins viewing and a fascinating look at drug-fuelled hysteria.

After an extended, lurid curtain raiser in which a woman in bobby socks provokes a group of stoned men into group debauchery, the film's plot (for lack of a more refined term) begins as the renowned Dr. Sergio introduces case studies to convince the public that drugs and crime are inextricably linked. For undeniable proof, he presents four human guinea pigs who were dosed with LSD and forced to stare at a Coffin Joe poster (following a viewing of *This Night I'll Possess Your Corpse*, of course). Then, in colour and sepia tone, the viewer witnesses each subject's plunge into delusions involving Coffin Joe, whose appearances are comprised of both new footage and censored or alternate clips from his previous films.

More or less a feature length extension on the final "case study" story in Marins' most demented film, *The Strange World of Coffin Joe*, this film was most likely banned more for its political subtext than its exploitation elements. The sex is stronger and more deviant than the violence in this case, with a strong and unsettling fixation on bodily functions, but that's really nothing compared to what viewers witnessed from Mr. Marins during the 1970s. The drug material would snugly fit with any roughie exploitation title from the US during the period, making this an ideal companion piece for such fare as *Mantis in Lace* and *Alice in Acidland*, but the presence of Marins (both as Coffin Joe and himself in the memorable denouement) makes this a genuinely unique experience.

Since it was never used to strike a massive number of prints, this film's negative is in great shape. The colour sequences are a marvel to behold, and the black and white footage is crisp and features excellent contrast. Marins contributes a video interview to discuss the importance of the film, its personal message to him, and the potentially disastrous circumstances under which it was carried out. As with the other three Coffin Joe discs from Fantoma, it comes packaged with a complete reproduction of a *Coffin Joe* comic book, with translated English dialogue replaced over the original Portuguese. The comics alone are virtually worth the expense of picking up these discs, but the quality of the films and the extras should be enough to convince the sceptical.

THE AWFUL DR. ORLOFF

B&W, 1962, 90m. / Directed by Jess Franco / Starring Howard Vernon, Diana Lorys / Image (US R1 NTSC) / WS (1.66:1)

 The first major horror film by absurdly prolific Spanish director Jess Franco, *The Awful Dr. Orlof* (Spanish title: *Gritos en la noche*, or *Cries in the Night*) dragged the familiar Universal horror motifs of shambling monsters and decaying crypts into the more permissive 1960s, complete with jazz music, blood, and nudity. Though extremely tame by today's standards, this vital entry in Spanish horror history remains a compelling and stylish experiment as well as the genesis of the themes that run throughout Franco's highly personal body of work.

In a plot derived not very subtly from Georges Franju's *Eyes without a Face*, the seemingly normal Dr. Orlof (Howard Vernon) has embarked on a crusade to restore the face of his suspiciously mature-looking daughter by grafting on the facial skin tissue of beautiful women. A former prison doctor, he has recruited a robotic, deformed assistant, Morpho (Ricardo Valle), who displays an unhealthy penchant for assaulting the young women before their operations. Meanwhile the resourceful Inspector Tanner (Conrado San Martin) and a plucky dancer (Diana Lorys) set up a trap to catch the mad doctor before he strikes again...

Deliberately paced and obviously designed with a love for the horror/fantasy genre, *The Awful Dr. Orlof* (or *Orloff*, as it is more commonly known) played drive-ins and matinee houses for years on double bills in a censored version which has since turned up on several public domain video labels. This DVD from the Eurociné vaults marks the first availability in the US of the European edition (though it's still several minutes shorter than the original Spanish version), and includes such taboo images as Vernon making a gory scalpel incision on a topless woman, some scantily clad nightclub dancers, and Morpho engaging in some lecherous groping. It's rather muted material to contemporary viewers, but this was still very shocking at the time of General Franco's rule. Jess Franco later tried to top this with several sequels, and both Orlof and Morpho popped up repeatedly in tweaked incarnations in dozens of his films. This is the original, though, and time has been very kind indeed.

The DVD quality itself is stunning, with excellent contrast, accurate widescreen framing, and an amazingly clean, defect-free print. The dubbed English audio is as good an option as any, since the film was apparently subjected to post-production dubbing in every language. An alternate French language track is also included and sounds comparable. The sole extra consists of thorough, affectionate liner notes by Tim Lucas, which place both the film and Franco's entire career in their historical and artistic perspectives.

AXE
Colour, 1974, 82m. / Directed by Frederick R. Friedel / Starring Leslie Lee, Jack Canon
THE ELECTRIC CHAIR
B&W, 1972, 80m. / Directed by J.G. Patterson
Image (US R1 NTSC)

Three down-at-heel hoodlums are on the run after a bungled killing. They hide out at a remote farmhouse occupied by a withdrawn teenage girl and her catatonic grandfather. It seems an ideal hidey-hole: but as the gang discover, there's something very strange about little Lisa... Axe doesn't play by the rules. It lacks the forward motion most people expect from a story, but if you watch it at the right time of night, in the right mood, it can take you somewhere special, unlike ordinary films that take you no further than their accountant's ambition.

Directed by the intriguing Frederick Friedel, who also acts in the film as an ambivalent gangster, this is a weird little psychodrama, soaked in ambient menace. There's no real pay-off as such but it still haunts you, from the naggingly beautiful piano/synthesizer theme tune, through the nothing plot to the artistic vagueness that envelops the story. Films like this deserve to be celebrated because there's something different going on. Friedel clearly feels he has nothing to prove but his style adds up anyway: the film stays around, lingering in the mind like a dream you almost forgot but not quite. Friedel also directed *Date with a Kidnapper*, another dreamy exercise in sideways storytelling. This DVD version of *Axe* from Something Weird is as good as it's likely to get, given the moderate graininess of the original material and the limited commercial appeal of the title. There is some speckling at reel ends and occasional mild smearing of colour during longer camera pans, but the picture is generally stable. Still shots have an almost Russ Meyerish quality to their colour, with Friedel shooting faces against sharp blue skies and white wooden walls. All in all, a very watchable treatment of a weird little movie.

The "bonus" second feature here is 1977's *The Electric Chair*. When a lonely South Carolina priest and the unhappy wife of a fat lorry-driving bully have an affair, it's not long before the congregation gets to talkin'. Soon the couple are found murdered and horribly mutilated - but who was the killer? The priest's bitter, frigid wife? The lardass husband? Or one of the flock of weirdos and dimwits who inhabit the area? This Deep South issue-exploiter wastes too much time on court-room drama but is well worth seeing for its genuinely intense recreation of an execution by electric chair. Shot in what looks to be a real County Prison facility with a genuine "Old Sparky," complete with leather and iron accoutrements, the film achieves a real "charge" as it sheds light on the South's extra-special frying process. Look out for Southern director and Earl Owensby alumni Worth Keeter (*Wolfman*) as a boy who gets shot during the court-house finale. The picture is scratchy and rather worn but still adequate - no-one is ever going to lavish digital remastering on a title like this, so to have it turn up in a watchable state as an extra is the ideal compromise.

Once again, well done and thanks to Something Weird! Further extras include theatrical trailers for *Axe* and other Harry Novak productions, the educational shorts "Mental Health: Keeping Mentally Fit" and "We Still Don't Believe It" (with sword-swallower Maria Cortez), and a gallery of horror drive-in exploitation art with radio spots.
- Stephen Thrower

THE BABY
Colour, 1972, 85m. / Directed by Ted Post / Starring Ruth Roman, Anjanette Comer / Image (US R1 NTSC)

One of the sickest movies to ever receive a PG rating, *The Baby* offers more insanity per minute than our current politically correct climate would ever allow. Boosted by a surprisingly good performance by Ruth Roman (best known as the wooden leading lady of such films as *Strangers on a Train*), this gem may have limited appeal but delivers the goods for those in the right frame of mind.

Ann Gentry (Anjanette Comer), a kindly social worker, becomes intrigued by the case of Baby, a full grown young man whose suffocating mother (Ruth Roman) and sisters (Mariana Hill and Susanne Zenor) have kept him in a state of mental infancy, even forbidding him from learning to walk. Ann devotes most of her time to Baby, much to the consternation of her boss - who points out that the last social worker to take on Baby disappeared without a trace. Still grieving from her husband's debilitation in a car accident, Ann finds herself growing more attached to Baby and concerned for his welfare, while Roman and company sink deeper into insanity, indulging in such activities as whipping Baby's overly affectionate babysitter. Despite the film's obvious low budget (Baby's crying is awkwardly dubbed with the sound of a real infant) and frequent lapses in taste (Ann's visit to a class for the mentally handicapped), *The Baby* remains compelling viewing and has aged quite well. Stanley Kubrick's first composer, Gerald Fried, contributes a poignant and haunting score, while Comer makes a reasonably sympathetic central character... though her pronunciation of the word "cost" is unintentionally hilarious. Best of all, the twist ending is unforgettable and absolutely bonkers.

Not exactly a film that would seem a prime candidate for DVD, *The Baby* has been brought to the format by Image with more care than anyone could have expected. A drastic improvement over the old, long out of print VHS editions, the print exhibits some noticeable damage during the opening credits and two reel changes, but otherwise the quality is excellent. Colour saturation is rich and vivid, particularly for an early '70s title (an era widely known for its bad film stock), while the audio is clear and features no evident signs of wear. The film is presented completely open matte, with a great deal of extra unused space exposed at the top and bottom of the frame throughout. The disc also includes an extremely melodramatic Spanish language track and an alternate isolated music and sound effects track, all the better to appreciate Fried's contribution to the film. Incidentally, the original press materials indicated a running time of 102 minutes, a length which has perpetuated through such sources as Leonard Maltin. However, the true running time appears to be the 85 minutes presented here, as no material seems to be missing.

BAD MOON

Colour, 1996, 79m. / Directed by Eric Red / Starring Mariel Hemingway, Michael Paré / Warner (US R1 NTSC) / WS (2.35:1) (16:9) / DD5.1

 Competing with the theatrical cut of *Army of Darkness* as the shortest studio horror film of the '90s, *Bad Moon* must count as a missed opportunity. A loose adaptation of Wayne Smith's novel, *Thor*, which narrated events from the title dog's point of view, this shaggy werewolf tale would seem a lot more unique if Stephen King's *Cycle of the Werewolf* (and its movie adaptation, *Silver Bullet*) hadn't already beat it to the punch. What we get instead is a slickly produced and fast paced little programmer, more interesting than your average slasher flick but unlikely to appeal beyond the die hard monster crowd. In the surprisingly graphic prologue, Ted (Michael Paré) finds his Nepalese expedition screeching to a halt when his camping tent tryst with a naked local is interrupted by a marauding werewolf. After the beast tears up his conquest for the evening, Ted blows its head off with a shotgun, but not without receiving a couple of nasty scratches in the process. Flash forward to the sylvan wilds of British Columbia, where Ted's sister, Janet (Mariel Hemingway), lives in a trailer with her son, Brett (Dennis the Menace himself, Mason Gamble), and their dog, Thor. Uncle Ted arrives for a visit and behaves very suspiciously. For one thing, he vanishes into the woods every night, only to return in the morning looking very haggard indeed. Also, some mysterious deaths in the area trigger suspicions that Ted may not be entirely on the level here. And, as Thor no doubt wonders, why does Ted keep handcuffing himself to a tree at night?

Though often clumsy in execution (the whole moon thing, for example, is never remotely explained in a logical manner), *Bad Moon* has some good points. The short running time keeps things going at a fast clip, the dog ("Primo") is actually a pretty engaging screen performer, and it's always fun to see a werewolf stomping through a house and ripping people to shreds. The effects range from pretty good (mostly the initial transformations) to painfully awkward, but at least the film moves fast enough to gloss over some of the goofy animatronic wolf head shots. Director Eric Red (whose tragic subsequent history now taints his entire body of work, including *Body Parts* and *The Hitcher*) shows a keen eye for creating atmosphere out of visual basics like forests and confined rooms, while the elegant scope framing is well judged and gives the film a great visual veneer that compensates for the obvious budgetary limitations. Fortunately Warner's budget priced DVD does justice to the film's visual palette, with striking colours and excellent definition. The 5.1 audio mix is also better than anticipated, with some strong directional effects and some hefty ambient support for the score by horror regular Daniel Licht. The disc also includes a trailer for the film's extremely brief theatrical run, along with a grab bag of other trailers from Morgan Creek.

BARBARA BROADCAST

Colour, 1977, 76m. / Directed by Henry Paris (Radley Metzger) / Starring Annette Haven, C.J. Laing / VCA (US R1 NTSC)

Having established himself as a successful XXX director under the name Henry Paris, elegant erotica specialist Radley Metzger quickly followed up his ground-breaking *The Opening of Misty Beethoven* the following year *with Barbara Broadcast*, another fusion of lavish visuals and sharp wit with down and dirty sex scenes. This time any semblance of a plot is purely accidental, as the entire film revolves entirely around a goofy concept and manages to turn grindhouse filmmaking into pure surrealism.

At a posh New York restaurant, renowned sex expert Barbara Broadcast (Annette Haven) is interviewed by adventurous reporter Robert (C.J. Laing). However, people don't just eat food here, as the wait-staff delivers a variety of sexual services straight off the menu. Barbara's interview is constantly disrupted by autograph requests, sexual favours, and visits from old friends, while the clientele dallies on the tables, enjoys unorthodox salad dressing, and watches the maitre'd exact a most perverse revenge against waitresses who break the restaurant's expensive plates. Eventually Roberta decides to get in on the action by traipsing off to the kitchen, where she enjoys a steamy session with a dishwasher (Wade Nichols). That night she and Barbara meet up again at a disco, where they engage in some public displays with the libidinous Curley (Jamie Gillis) and listen to his story involving a disciplinarian approach to a Protestant American Princess (Constance Money).

The opening half hour of *Barbara Broadcast* is a delirious delight, as the elegant restaurant setting provides a perfectly Buñuelian backdrop for a variety of sexual activities. Unfortunately the film has nowhere to go from there, with the story simply tacking on one encounter after another but only barely bothering to explain them. The kitchen sequence is by far the most intense moment of the film, and all of the performers (particularly Jennifer Grey lookalike Laing) seem to be putting their all into their roles. Mildly diverting fun and unmistakably Metzger, this isn't *Misty Beethoven*, but then how could it be?

Like many '70s "Henry Paris" titles, *Barbara Broadcast* has been chopped to pieces over the years due to various censorship laws governing the home video industry; the home video from VCA (running a scant 69 minutes!) lost the entire final seven minutes of the film featuring Gillis. In fact this chilly S&M sequence was an excised scene from *Misty Beethoven*, which provoked Money into a successful lawsuit for additional payment. The DVD restores this rarely seen finale, presented by Gillis as a flashback, though a few close up shots are still missing (legally a film can't mix hardcore with physical restraints in the same scene). The kitchen scene also contains the same softened opening from the earlier VCA release; originally Laing relieved herself on camera, but most versions substitute Nichols' reaction shots instead combined with some vivid sound effects. Therefore the disc still comes up a bit short compared to the original running time, but it's still far more complete than anything before. As with the *Misty Beethoven* disc, Gillis and Leonard return for an audio commentary, though their specific recollections are rather limited due to the fact that Leonard had nothing to do with the film and Gillis merely had a glorified cameo. Instead they offer more of an overview of the whole '70s adult film scene, Metzger's filmmaking techniques, and the histories behind the various performers.

BARBARA THE FAIR WITH THE SILKEN HAIR

Colour, 1970, 81m. / Directed by Aleksandr Row / Starring Georgi Millyar, Andrei Katyshev / Ruscico (R0 NTSC) / WS (2.35:1) (16:9) / DD5.1

Though ostensibly aimed at a family audience, this enchanting Russian fairy tale contains enough glorious eye candy and bizarre touches to keep fans of filmic fantasy thoroughly engaged for its all too brief running time. Directed with a sure hand by Aleksandr Row (*Father Frost*), this follows the basic template of Jean Cocteau's *Beauty and the Beast* by deftly interweaving the mundane with the surreal, creating a cinematic banquet that easily transcends the "kiddie" label.

The powerful but jovial czar Yeremey the Bearded (Mikhail Pugovkin) lives in a sunny kingdom, though his idyllic life is turned upside down one day when he stares into a well and finds himself confronted by a magical subterranean ruler, the green, pointy-eared Chudo Yudo the Lawless (Georgi Millyar), who clutches onto the tsar's orange beard and threatens to drag him down into the fairy kingdom. Yeremey's freedom can only be granted if he agrees to provide Chudo Yudo with anything from the kingdom with which the tsar is not already familiar; finding these terms agreeable, the tsar returns home to discover that a new heir has been born. Chudo Yudo's demand for the baby results in a thwarted infant swap, leaving the false baby raised by the czar and the real heir spoiled into stunted infancy.

Both named Andrei, the men enter a wild confusion of identity when Chudo Yudo's beautiful daughter, Barbara (Tatiana Klyuyeva), decides to marry and falls in love with the good Andrei, unaware of the challenges in store for both of them.

Though definitely Russian in flavour, *Barbara* deals enough with universal fairy tale motifs (not to mention a smattering of "The Prince and the Pauper") to make it appealing to viewers of all ages. While the presence of potentially cutesy devices like talking baby bears could have made the film cloying, Row's stunning evocation of an underworld lit like a Christmas tree makes this more ideal viewing on a double bill with Mario Bava's *Hercules in the Haunted World* or even Dario Argento's *Suspiria*. You rarely see colours like this, folks. The costumes, musical numbers, and performances are all sincere and professionally executed, and the fantastic characters are imaginatively conceived and thoroughly charming.

Appropriately, the Russian Cinema Council transfer on DVD is simply stunning and rivals *Singin' in the Rain* for the most eye-popping colour transfer ever seen on a home video screen. However, for some reason the disc has been encoded to play in a squeezed format in 4:3 playback, leaving it letterboxed at 1.85:1 with everyone looking a bit squished. If you have a 16:9 compatible monitor, however, the image looks just fine and snaps back to the correct aspect ratio. (Note: this still doesn't work on DVD-Rom drives, however.) As with other Ruscico titles, the film comes in three different languages (the original Russian or well dubbed into English, Spanish, and French) with the usual array of nine optional subtitles. The 5.1 mix is extremely well done, with the music nicely spread among the speakers without sounding artificial or strained. A soundtrack sampler of three songs also kicks off the supplements, which also include clips from other upcoming fairy tale films (including more Aleksandr Ptushko titles!), a five minute featurette on the making of *Barbara*, a theatrical trailer, and a still gallery of photos, facts, and filmmaker bios.

BARBARELLA

Colour, 1968, 98m. / Directed by Roger Vadim / Starring Jane Fonda, John Phillip Law / Paramount (US R1 NTSC, UK R2 PAL) / WS (2.35:1) (16:9)

Okay, everybody sing along now: "Barbarella, psychedella..." Paramount atones for some of its DVD sins with *Barbarella*, the campy thorn in the side of Jane Fonda's curtailed film career. Before the former Mrs. Ted Turner was winning Oscars and

traipsing over enemy lines during controversial wars, she was married to director Roger Vadim (the French film equivalent of Hugh Hefner). Vadim placed Jane in a number of sexy arthouse vehicles like *Circle of Love, Spirits of the Dead*, and the memorably bizarre *The Game Is Over*. However, their relationship will always be best remembered for *Barbarella*, an adaptation of the classic S&M French comic strip in which Jane whizzes through the galaxy in various states of undress.

The "plot" is almost completely irrelevant but has something to do with Barbarella being sent by the President of Earth to find the missing scientist Durand Durand (or Duran Duran, as it's commonly spelled and where the Brit pop group got their name). Her quest leads her through numerous kinky misadventures: she's attacked by snapping dolls, makes love to blind angel Pygar (John Phillip Law in a far more plastic performance here than in *Diabolik*), and winds up in the diabolical kingdom of SoGo, led by the evil, omnisexual Black Queen (Anita Pallenberg, underused but fantastic anyway). The film sports more quotable lines than virtually any other '60s title ("Decrucify the angel or I'll melt your face!," "Here, pretty pretty," and so on) and piles on the colourfully trippy scenery with garish aplomb. This kind of joking facetiousness has turned off a number of viewers unable to get into the campy spirit, and unfortunately the fun does stop occasionally for a few draggy spots; on the whole, however, *Barbarella* survived its era far better than its counterparts and will no doubt continue to amuse and delight fans of sci-fi kitsch for decades to come.

Okay, good news first: *Barbarella* looks better on DVD than ever before on video. While the VHS and widescreen laserdisc presentations have been acceptable, its subsequent revival house screenings throughout the country in mint scope condition showed viewers just how much the small screen transfers suffered. The colours on the DVD are much richer and cleaner than the laser, and the sound quality is razor-sharp (identical to the LD). The Bob Crewe/Glitterhouse soundtrack pulses and twangs so richly you'd almost swear it was stereo (too bad the soundtrack only exists legitimately on vinyl). Now for the bad news. While watchable, the letterboxed laserdisc unfortunately sheared slivers of information off all four edges of the screen (note how Jane's full body shots when lying down in her ship across the horizontal frame are always chopped off at the forehead and ankles on the laser), while the VHS versions have been a panned and scanned mess. The

B

DVD is framed similarly to the laser... except that even more information is missing on the right side! The picture loss isn't crippling, but it's a shame the folks supervising this at Paramount couldn't have presented the complete image while they were doing the new anamorphic transfer, which looks smashing otherwise. The compositions aren't unduly harmed, and it's better to watch this in scope. And yes, the DVD is the original naughty "Rated M" version with all of Jane's naughty bits intact during the opening credits. Also includes the amusing original theatrical trailer as well as the original French language track, which finds Jane doing her own dubbing (strangely, her French is much more fluid and natural here than in the next year's *Spirits of the Dead* - maybe she just has trouble sounding mean in a foreign language).

BARON BLOOD

Colour, 1972, 97m. / Directed by Mario Bava / Starring Joseph Cotten, Elke Sommer / Image (US R0 NTSC) / WS (1.85:1)

 Following the apocalyptic black humour of his body count classic *Bay of Blood*, in 1972 Italian horror maestro Mario Bava found himself in the odd position of trying to cater to modern bloodthirsty audiences while adhering to his own need for artistic expression. Given the opportunity to shoot on a larger budget in an elaborate gothic castle, Bava agreed to tackle *Baron Blood (Gli orrori del castello di Norimberga)*, which became a drive-in favourite thanks to AIP's typically hyperbolic sales job.

In a small Austrian town, naive young Peter Kleist (Antonio Cantafora) arrives to research his family background, which involves the bloodthirsty Baron Otto von Kleist and his foreboding castle. Peter and the beautiful young Eva (Elke Sommer) decide to investigate the castle, and just for kicks, they decide to read aloud an incantation Peter has discovered on a rare parchment in America. It seems this incantation can bring the Baron back to life, and sure enough, a mysterious form starts shuffling outside the door. The parchment accidentally burns (a nice nod to Jacques Tourneur's *Curse of the Demon*), leaving Peter and Eva helpless as the Baron begins to ravage the countryside. First the Baron, who has not aged well over the centuries, seeks the aid of a doctor who winds up on the wrong end of his scalpel. Eva has a menacing encounter with the cloaked menace in the fog-shrouded streets at night, and then the local handymen begin turning up dead

and impaled at the top of the castle (great tourist idea!). Thanks to the testimony of a spooky little red-haired girl named Gretchen (*Deep Red*'s Nicoletta Elmi), our protagonists deduce that the Baron has returned to his old stomping grounds and is gradually regenerating with each passing day. Peter and Eva seek the aid of Christina Hoffman (Rada Rassimov), who invokes the spirit of the Baron's archrival, Elizabeth Holly, and reveals the only means by which he can be destroyed. Meanwhile, a new owner for the castle shows up- the wheelchair-bound Alfred Becker (Joseph Cotten). Becker seems pleasant enough at first, of course, but astute viewers shouldn't have much difficulty figuring out his true intentions. Before long, Eva and Peter get a much closer look at the Baron's infamous torture chamber than they ever expected.

Like many Bava films, *Baron Blood* runs more on visual style and psychological manipulation than linear storytelling or character development. Bava's painterly visual sense manages to wring every drop of tension out of the threadbare storyline, which simply serves as a catalyst for one macabre setpiece after another. Filled with nods to his previous films (the resurrected marauder from *Black Sunday* and the fog-shrouded village from *Kill Baby, Kill!*, for example), *Baron Blood* marks Bava's nostalgic farewell to the '60s gothic tradition. Thanks to the oft-mentioned Coke machine in the castle and the deliberately gimmicky trappings of modern Austria, Bava wittily offers a dissertation on the transforming powers of horror from one decade to the next. His subsequent film for producer Alfredo Leone, *Lisa and the Devil*, grapples with many of the same concepts, albeit in a more lyrical, eroticized context. While *Baron Blood* drags the past (represented by the Baron and Elizabeth) kicking and screaming into the present, *Lisa* reverses the tide and sombrely draws its characters from the present into the past. In *Baron*, the plush airplane of the opening scene brings the audience forward (accompanied by Stelvio Cipriani's deliberately kitschy music), while *Lisa* concludes with the exact same plane completely abandoned and transformed into a vessel of death.

While *Baron Blood* is obviously an enjoyable if slight film on its own terms, its significance becomes much more apparent in context with the rest of Bava's work. For years most viewers only saw it in the shortened AIP print, which clocked in at just over 90 minutes. Featuring a much more overtly spooky score by Les Baxter (who also rescored *Black Sunday, Black Sabbath*, and *The Evil Eye*), this version featured an alternate, bloodless take of the doctor's murder and deleted several minor dialogue and travelogue passages. The HBO/Image laserdisc (paired with *Circus of Horrors*) preserves this edition for those who want to keep the Baxter score (one of his best efforts, actually), but purists will most likely opt for Image's DVD edition, which contains the full strength version with Cipriani's original, highly diverse music.

The image quality is comparable to the earlier Elite Entertainment laserdisc and PAL VHS release from Redemption: clear, colourful, but obviously a product of its time. Like many early '70s European films, some grittiness can be spotted over a few of the darker scenes, but this is vastly superior to the US version and, thankfully, is accurately letterboxed. The muddy fleshtones that plagued the Elite version look a bit more robust here, and the sound is consistently clear and distortion-free. Though DVD and laserdisc share the same murky-looking television trailer, the DVD also contains far more extras (and much better packaging!), thanks to a diverting and revealing gallery of production and promotional photographs from this film and Bava's career in general, accessible from the amusing menu design. Italian horror buffs should chuckle with blood-sated glee.

BARRY LYNDON

Colour, 1975, 185m. / Directed by Stanley Kubrick / Starring Ryan O'Neal, Marisa Berenson / Warner / WS (1.66:1) / DD5.1

After his foray into gaudy future shock, Kubrick made the obvious choice for his next film: a subdued costume drama! Despite critical acclaim, his three hour adaptation of William Makepeace Thackeray's novel failed to connect with audiences on the same historic level as his previous films and is usually dismissed. Too bad, really, because it's an excellent film and one of Kubrick's most exquisitely crafted and tragically human efforts. Part of the blame for the film's relative obscurity may lie with the presence of Ryan O'Neal, normally a bland actor used to good effect here (probably his only good performance aside from *Paper Moon*). On a sensory level, *Barry Lyndon* is also one of Kubrick's most controlled and best-realized efforts, with his typically piecemeal classical score functioning better than usual thanks to the careful orchestrations of Leonard Rosenman (who makes particularly good use of Handel's "Sarabande"). Despite the absence of shock value or trippy visuals, this is ultimately pure Kubrick and well worth the hefty time investment.

The first half of the film, as announced by its title card, concerns the social rise of Redmond Barry (O'Neal), a ne'er-do-well determined to claw his way to the top. Finding himself tossed into the winds of history through battle, Redmond wins the approval of the powers that be in Dublin and uses his status to win the hand of the lovely Lady Lyndon (Marisa Berenson) following the death of her husband. His relationship with Lady Lyndon's son begins well, but ultimately Barry's ambitions to succeed at any cost return to haunt him in the second half as the years pass on and fate begins to take a nasty turn. One of the most visually stunning films of its day, *Barry Lyndon* in many ways represents the height of Kubrick's exacting eye for minute detail. Each costume, each shot, each note of music is precisely applied and presented for the maximum aesthetic effect; however, this austere and literary approach may not be to all tastes.

The remastered DVD (with a subtle but engaging 5.1 track) looks better than the laserdisc and first DVD versions, which were flawed by a speckled pressing and lousy compression, respectively. Like the other Kubrick titles, the technical limitations of the sound recording prevent it from really bursting forth, but the audio is more pleasing and well-rounded than most films of its era. Also includes a lengthy "the critics are raving" trailer.

BASKET CASE

Colour, 1981, 90m. / Directed by Frank Henenlotter / Starring Kevin Van Hentenryck / Image (US R1 NTSC), Tartan (UK R0 PAL)

Though best known today to trash movie addicts for his collection of "Sexy Shockers from the Vault" for Something Weird Video, New York auteur Frank Henenlotter got his start back in the early '80s with *Basket Case*, which many critics pegged as the midnight movie alternative to its closest Hollywood contemporary, *E.T.: The Extra-Terrestrial*. In this case, the boy's relationship with a short mutant takes a very unhealthy turn, as separated Siamese twins Duane (Kevin Van Hentenryck) and the misshapen Belial try to get by in a run down New York hotel. Though he spends most of the film hidden in a wicker basket, Belial does emerge occasionally to wreak gory havoc on the surgeons who separated the boys at their parents' request. Henenlotter immediately touted to the press his strong affinity to the films of goremeister Herschell Gordon Lewis, but the acting and photography are actually much stronger than anything H.G. ever had at his disposal.

The transfer for Image's first DVD was taken from the same materials used for the laserdisc release, a huge improvement over those old, muddy-looking Media videotapes. The film underwent another facelift for a Something Weird special edition, with a more colourful transfer and a bounty of extras including commentary (with Henenlotter and the gang), a retrospective tour documentary, a hilarious blooper reel, and a sampler of Beverly Bonner's public access TV work. Looking back on *Basket Case* over fifteen years later, it's a shame Henenlotter never really had the chance to dig his cinematic claws in deeper after the censorship-plagued *Brain Damage* and *Frankenhooker*, not to mention the obvious *Basket Case 2* and *3*. In fact, it's really too bad you don't see movies like this playing at the multiplex anymore; we could use more ticket takers handing out "surgical masks...to keep the blood off your face" as they did during this film's initial run. The disc issued in the UK by Tartan is uncut but is missing much of this extra material.

THE BAT WHISPERS

B&W, 1930, 82m. / Directed by Roland West / Starring Chester Morris, Chance Ward / Image (US R0 NTSC) / WS (2.00:1)

 A better than average entry in the old "dark stormy night with a mysterious animalistic killer" genre, *The Bat Whispers* marked director Roland West's second take on the popular play, a contemporary of other similar films and stage works like *The Cat and the Canary*. Well, as it turns out, West had to actually make *The Bat Whispers* twice more, at the same time - once in standard full frame, and once in 65mm. Using different takes and framing throughout, the two may be identical in terms of casting and dialogue but often play like completely different films.

An arch criminal known as "The Bat" taunts police officers by providing clues about his upcoming crimes and carrying them out undiscovered anyway. After swiping a valuable necklace and knocking over a bank for good measure, The Bat sets out for a country home where a number of occupants are spending a creepy, rainy evening. All the usual suspects are here: the no-nonsense socialite Cornelia van Gorder (Grayce Hampton), the innocent romantic couple, the dubious doctor, and so on. Is one of these seemingly innocent people really The Bat?

Though formulaic in the extreme, *The Bat Whispers* distinguishes itself entirely through a succession of astonishing, gorgeous visual sequences, which render the dialogue almost irrelevant. The camera swoops, glides, and dollies around more than the collective works of Orson Welles and Dario Argento combined, and the filmmakers use miniatures to create some astonishing effects in which the viewer is suddenly transported down hallways, out windows, and into small corners with breathtaking ease.

The full frame version has become more familiar to horror and mystery buffs, and on the whole, it seems to be a more polished cut. In the 65mm version (letterboxed at an approximation of the later Panavision aspect ratio), the camera remains more distant and sedentary, with entire scenes of dialogue running by with nary an edit. However, this also pumps up the atmosphere even more, with the set dressing and moody lighting taking complete precedence over the actors. Unfortunately, the 65mm process apparently proved too expensive for many retakes, as the actors often flub their lines and seem less confident than in the standard version. The comedy in the 65mm version suffers in particular, with several punchlines and bits of quirky character acting lost in the process. As with other horror films shot twice (a practice continued at least all the way until 1979's *Nosferatu the Vampyre*), the results are quite fascinating, and Image has done a major service by providing both variants on a single dual-layered disc for side to side comparisons. The 35mm version looks quite well preserved apart from the expected nick and scratch caused by the ravages of time; the contrast is especially impressive and appropriately dark. The 65mm version, preserved by the UCLA archives, looks noticeably more battered in spots, but it's a miracle it's managed to survive at all considering the rate of deteriorating film classics these days. Aside from the visual gimmickry and historical significance, *The Bat Whispers* contains a number of other points of interest that allow it to play like a rough draft for a William Castle film. In particular, one character emerges from a curtain after the finale to deliver a tongue-in-cheek admonishment to any audience members who might reveal The Bat's identity. Incidentally, this film was remade again far more traditionally in 1959 as *The Bat*, with Vincent Price and Agnes Moorehead.

BATMAN AND ROBIN

Colour, 1997, 125m. / Directed by Joel Schumacher / Starring George Clooney, Arnold Schwarzenegger, Uma Thurman / Warner / WS (1.85:1) (16:9) / DD5.1

Mr. Freeze (Schwarzenegger) plots to bring permanent winter to Gotham City, allying with Poison Ivy (Thurman) who believes that the world belongs to plants. Whilst grappling with this dual threat, Batman (Clooney) and Robin (Chris O'Donnell) must also contend with the impending death of faithful butler Alfred (Michael Gough) and the arrival of his tearaway niece Barbara (Alicia Silverstone).

Here the distinctly undynamic duo, Joel Schumacher and Akiva Goldsman, have a fine old time hammering nails into the coffin of Warner's Batman franchise. How strange though that the same critics who fell over each other to heap praise upon the director's *Batman Forever* should have banded together to hurl rotten tomatoes at this one. Given that *Batman and Robin* is more of the same throw-it-all-on-the-screen-whether-it-makes-sense-or-not formula, the self-contradiction is baffling; how could anyone who liked that mess not like this mess? - indeed, even Schumacher was floored by the turnabout. Actually, *Batman and Robin* is the better of the two films, though only marginally, not leastwise because it doesn't star the unbearably egotistical Val Kilmer. Regardless of what cavillers might claim, George Clooney makes for a far superior Batman. Yet his presence is one of the film's (very few) plusses. Schwarzenegger and Thurman look super-cool in their outfits, but their performances continue the backslide (started in *Forever*) towards the camp villainy of 60s TV show; if they aren't taking their dialogue seriously, how can the audience be expected to?

Much like *Batman Forever*, this one also suffers from ham-fisted overcrowding in the characters department; not only are three new villains crow-barred into the mix (along with Freeze and Ivy, there's the steroid-enhanced powerhouse Bane), but there's a new addition to the ranks of the good in the leather-clad form of Batgirl (a slightly chunky but not unappetising Alicia Silverstone). With so many origins to establish it's no surprise that everyone ends up being underwritten, shortfalls in motivation being feebly disguised with a veil of witless one-line quips. And the less said about the (intended to be funny?) bickering for Ivy's affections between Batman and Robin the better! This is the film that stopped Warner Brothers' series dead in its tracks and, despite much rumbling and mumbling, any tangible sign of a rebirth has yet to emerge. Unforgivable.

Warner Brothers' DVD release follows the trend established by the first three films and offers a choice of viewing ratios (1.85:1 theatrical or fullscreen) on a double sided disc. The quality of the film (which is sub-divided by an exceptionally generous 42 chapter stops) faithfully recreates the garish neon comic book look of the theatrical experience. Once again the opportunity to view anything remotely interesting pertaining to the film's inception is discarded in favour of a small selection of biographies and some production notes. The film can be viewed with English or French sound, and there is English, French and Spanish subtitling. - TG

BATMAN FOREVER

Colour, 1995, 121m. / Directed by Joel Schumacher / Starring Val Kilmer, Jim Carrey, Tommy Lee Jones / Warner / WS (1.85:1) (16:9) / DD5.1

The citizens of Gotham City come under threat from the disfigured and vengeance-driven Harvey Dent (Jones), aka Two-Face, and bitter under-achiever Edward Nygma (Carrey), aka The Riddler. Batman (Kilmer) battles both diabolical menaces whilst, in his true persona as Bruce Wayne, taking the orphaned Dick Grayson (Chris O'Donnell) - soon to become ally Robin - under his wing.

Calamity! When Tim Burton left the series, Michael Keaton and Danny Elfman upped sticks and went with him. These three men to all intents and purposes were the Batman films, and their contribution to the legend was going to be a tough act to follow. Thus, rather than attempting to emulate, Joel Schumacher (together with writers Lee Batchler, Janet Scott Batchler and Akiva Goldsman) did away with the sinister and shadowy Gotham and emblazoned his vision with brash comic book colours and ludicrous characters more akin to the 1960s TV show than the world of Tim Burton's finely crafted Gothic visions. If Burton's *Batman* and *Batman Returns* could be likened to luscious, mouth-watering desserts, then Schumacher's *Batman Forever* is the pint of congealed gravy poured rudely over the top. Never has there been a starker example of style over substance (except perhaps in Schumacher's own follow-up, *Batman and Robin*) - style by the bin-load, substance nada! Jim Carrey is as frenetically manic a Riddler as you'd expect but Tommy Lee Jones is superfluous and wasted as Two-Face. Chris O'Donnell's Robin is an irritating reprobate and it was a mistake to introduce him; Schumacher barely manages to restrain himself with the latent homoerotic implications. Nicole Kidman is vapid as the lust interest. The biggest crook of all,

B

however, is supercilious Val Kilmer in the title role, who brings his intolerably bland mien to the party with truly ruinous effect. With insufficient (yet still poorly constructed) narrative to sustain the running time, there are superfluous action scenes thrown in for no other reason than to brandish another ill-conceived showpiece (the Batmobile climbing a vertical wall, for example!) and the cutting is often so fast that it's hard to register what on earth is going on. The revamped Bat-hardware, particularly the new Batmobile (with tail wings which look like they'd fall off with a puff of wind) are largely a bunch of misjudged ideas that should have been rejected at treatment stage. Elliot Goldenthal's score , though a brave effort, pales in comparison to Danny Elfman's compositions. All said and done, I'm not sure how *Batman Forever* could have been worse.

No surprise that the only feature - and a negligible one at that - on Warner's DVD is a choice of viewing ratios: 1.85:1 theatrical or fullscreen. The Region 1 disc may be uncut (where the UK version has over a minute and a half cut from it), but the film is so bad, who cares? The quality of the movie itself (which is sub-divided by 39 chapter points) is nonetheless pristine. Biographies and production notes are the only supplementary features. The disc offers English or French sound, with English, French and Spanish subtitling.

- TG

BATMAN RETURNS

Colour, 1992, 126m. / Directed by Tim Burton / Starring Michael Keaton, Danny DeVito, Michelle Pfeiffer / Warner / WS (1.85:1) (16:9) / DD5.1

As Christmas descends on Gotham City, artful megalomaniac businessman Max Schreck (Christopher Walken) sets in motion a plot to plunder its power resources to his own profit. When his mousy secretary Selina Kyle (Pfeiffer) stumbles upon his plans, Schreck pushes her out of his office window. Surviving the fall, her psyche shatters unleashing an inner rage and Catwoman is born. Meanwhile, deformed outcast Oswald Cobblepot (DeVito), alias The Penguin, has retribution of his own in mind. Batman (Keaton) must deal with all three of these treacherous characters to ensure that Gotham is once again a safe place to live.

One of those all too rare occasions when a sequel betters its already outstanding predecessor. Funny, haunting, exciting, romantic, and endlessly original,

Batman Returns is the best Bat flick in Warner's quartet and also boasts the best villains. DeVito's Penguin is a repulsive conception with a gruesome Academy Award nominated Lon Chaney/*London After Midnight* make-up; whether gnawing on raw fish, biting a chunk out of a detractor's face, or teetering on the brink of death with blood dribbling from every orifice, he's a nightmarish monster of the highest calibre. Add to this Pfeiffer's PVC-clad, fetishistically tantalising Catwoman - sado-masochistically wielding a whip, popping a live canary into her mouth and grooming herself by licking her "paws" - and it's little wonder that parents were up in arms over what was ostensibly intended as entertainment for all the family. Indeed, this is a seriously twisted, tragic and pitch black fantasy from which no-one walks away unscathed, not even Batman himself.

Danny Elfman does the nigh on impossible by delivering a score that tops his original for *Batman*. Bo Welch's production design is more fantastically malevolent than Anton Furst's but not so aesthetically inspired. Unlike most of the Batman films, this one has staying power, in fact the only downside to watching it is that it makes the two subsequent films (helmed by Joel Schumacher) even more bitter pills to swallow.

Beware British cassette and DVD versions, which are devoid of several short sequences, one involving nunchukas, another in which Catwoman drops aerosol canisters into a microwave oven to explosive effect. Warner's Region 1 DVD retains all this footage, yet it's regrettably another disappointing Bat-disc where extras are concerned. It's very easy to get wound up complaining about a lack of bonus materials and forget why you wanted to make your purchase in the first place - (presumably) because the film itself is excellent! Yet the absence of even a basic trailer does seem just cause for lament, biographies and production notes once again being the only additional features. As with the other entries in the series, the double sided platter offers up a choice between 1.85:1 theatrical and fullscreen presentations. The picture quality of the 39-chapter marked film itself betters the original (slightly too dark) theatrical presentation. The movie can be viewed with either English or French sound, and there are subtitle choices in English, French and Spanish. - TG

THE BEAST (LA BÊTE)

Colour, 1975, 94m. / Directed by Walerian Borowczyk / Starring Sirpa Lane, Lisbeth Hummel / Cult Epics (US R1 NTSC) / WS (1.66:1), Nouveaux (UK R0 PAL) / WS (1.66:1) (16:9)

THE BEAST

After earning a certain degree of arthouse acclaim with *Immoral Tales*, Walerian Borowczyk immediately lost almost all of it shortly thereafter with *La Bête (The Beast)*, a randy and explicit exploration of the underlying sexual motifs running through such fairy tales as "Beauty and the Beast" and "Little Red Riding Hood." The wordless 20 minute centrepiece of the film, in which noblewoman Sirpa Lane is pursued and ravished by a hairy and anatomically gifted beast, began as an instalment of *Immoral Tales* but circulated instead as a short. Borowczyk devised a crafty, Buñuelian narrative film to surround this explosive little short, and soon he had quite a *success du scandale* on his hands. Banned or censored almost everywhere, *The Beast* has only recently resurfaced more or less intact on the English film circuit where its comical charms can be better appreciated.

The theme of the film is spelled out immediately by the sight of horses breeding in the driveway of a country estate owned by the Esperance family, a dysfunctional household of lunatics intent on maintaining a sense of normalcy. Their financial stability depends on a marriage between the brutish son, Mathurin (Pierre Benedetti), and young English rose Lucy Broadhurst (Lisbeth Hummel), due to arrive with her aunt. Meanwhile the priest arrives for the baptism along with his uncomfortably close altar boys, the younger daughter cavorts with the virile black valet instead of tending to the children, and the entire house is rife with artefacts relating to the family's most infamous ancestor, Romilda, whose torn corset now hangs encased in glass in the drawing room. Lucy is welcoming into the house, where she immediately becomes fascinated with the story of Romilda after leafing through an illustrated diary. That night she feverishly relives Romilda's beastly ordeal in the nearby woods, and most surprisingly, these events will have an immediate, surreal impact on the upcoming wedding.

Though filled with images usually suited for porn, *The Beast* still remains at heart a poisonous comedy of manners. Borowczyk's wry observation of mankind's animalistic impulses results in some odd, beautiful imagery, such as Lucy's use of a rose for sexual stimulation or the odd recurring visual of snails gliding across human hands and polished surfaces. Accompanied by a maddening harpsichord piece by Scarlatti, the beast sequence is a masterpiece of cinematic outrage, calculated to have audiences doubled over with both laughter and shock as it forges into increasingly dangerous waters. Fortunately Borowczyk manages to top even this

with his berserk finale, which foreshadows a similar denouement in his equally fascinating and thematically similar *Dr. Jekyll and His Women*. The video history of *The Beast* is long and complex, with various languages and alternate cuts floating around for over a decade. The most widely seen English language version, *Death's Ecstasy*, deleted most of the horse footage and all images of the beast's prosthetic phallus. A French language print subtitled in English reinstated all of the graphic footage and appeared in UK cinemas in 2001, with a limited run in American art theatres shortly thereafter. As Borowczyk website Mondo Erotico reported, this version was complete except for two small bits of footage which may have only appeared during the film's initial European run.

Amazingly, two different versions of *The Beast* appeared concurrently on DVD in the US and UK; the latter from Nouveaux contains the aforementioned French version with burned-in subtitles. The Cult Epics version (sporting the Argos logo at the beginning, as with Anchor Bay's *Immoral Tales*) instead has the English dubbed soundtrack. The merits of these audio options are tricky, as the film was post-synched in both languages. The English dub sounds rather canned, but Hummel was clearly speaking English throughout the film and this is the only version that matches her lip movements. However, the French track remains a more dry, elegant atmosphere and bolsters the film's effect as an intellectual comedy rather than a chunk of sleaze. Fans of the film with multiregion capability may want to just bite the bullet and get both, which are identical in terms of visual content. The Nouveaux version looks very attractive and is enhanced for 16:9 monitors, while the non-anamorphic Cult Epics transfer is a bit too bright and requires some TV adjustment to get the colours and shadows to pop out correctly. Inexplicably, the picture looked unstable and riddled with artefacts during the first few minutes on a Toshiba player but seemed fine and perfectly smooth on a Pioneer. Alas, the hysterical and intentionally grating French trailer is not included on either version, but the Nouveaux disc includes one entire segment from *Immoral Tales*, "The Tide."

BEAST FROM HAUNTED CAVE

B&W, 1959, 72m. / Directed by Monte Hellman / Starring Michael Forest, Sheila Carol, Frank Wolff / Synapse (US R1 NTSC) / WS (1.85:1) (16:9)

Best known for bucking the Hollywood system during the 1970s, director Monte Hellman developed a knack for using drive-in subject matter

B

to craft his own unique, personal statements on film, for better or worse. He turned the conventional western on its head with *The Shooting, Ride in the Whirlwind*, and *China 9, Liberty 37*, mined the untapped philosophical implications of car racing in *Two-Lane Blacktop*, and finally defied genre categories altogether with *Cockfighter* and *Iguana*. Though he wasn't considered an auteur in 1959 when he made his first film, *Beast from Haunted Cave*, Hellman already thwarted audience expectations by spending most of the running time developing his characters trapped in an elaborate heist plot, with the monster mainly confined to the sidelines before suddenly taking over during the startling, unforgettable final ten minutes.

Near a ski resort in South Dakota, a quartet of thieves set off a mine explosion to cover up for a bank robbery in which they make off with a cache of gold from the vault. After much bickering, flirting, and random exploring, all with the help of a hunky ski instructor (Michael Forest), the robbers come to realize that their little stunt has awakened a bloodthirsty beast in a nearby cave, and the locals are now paying the price with their blood.

Familiar to non-cult viewers as the executive producer and intended director of *Reservoir Dogs*, Hellman seems much more intrigued by the execution and aftermath of the robbery and its impact on the environment than the demands of creating a monster film, at least until he finally cuts loose for the nightmarish ending. The shots of helpless victims, swathed in cocoons while lashed to cave walls, screaming as their essence is drained by the vaguely defined creature, are difficult to forget and must have sent drive-in patrons into a mild hysteria at the time. The cast is fine if unremarkable, with late sleaze vet Frank Wolff (*The Lickerish Quartet, Cold Eyes of Fear*) scoring some of the best moments as one of the head schemers. The icy ski setting in the wilderness makes for a nice change of pace for a monster film, and Hellman does a good job of maintaining suspense while withholding a good view of the monster until the last possible moment.

As with many drive-in films of the period, *Beast from Haunted Cave* originally clocked in at barely over an hour, with Hellman rounding up the cast and shooting additional footage to pad it out for a TV sale in 1962. This expanded cut has been widely seen over the years, and Synapse's disc marks by far its cleanest presentation to date. The additional scenes, in which Frank Wolff (who had moved to Italy) did not participate, consist of a pre-credits sequence, a section in which in which Monte Hellman's wife Jaclyn plays Forest's sister, and a sequence shot showing Richard Sinatra talking to Forest on a small bridge (ostensibly outside Forest's cabin). A few hairline scratches aside, the source material is in very satisfying condition, with a surprising lack of dirt. The film is presented in both full frame and anamorphically enhanced widescreen transfers; the latter adds as much to the sides as it loses from the top and bottom, but benefits greatly from the added lines of resolution. The disc includes a theatrical trailer (with some alternate takes), which has certainly seen better days. A budget bin public domain DVD is also available and best avoided.

THE BEAST MUST DIE

Colour, 1974, 93m. / Directed by Paul Annett / Starring Peter Cushing, Marlene Clark, Anton Diffring / Image (US R0 NTSC) / WS (1.66:1) /

Amicus Studios became sort of the anthology horror alternative to Hammer Films during the 1960s and '70s with such favourites as *Dr. Terror's House of Horrors* and *Asylum*, but they occasionally ventured into full single narrative films as well. Some were more successful than others, and *The Beast Must Die*, sort of a shaggy werewolf cross between *Ten Little Indians* and *The Most Dangerous Game*, ranks as one of their more interesting attempts despite its shortcomings.

Eccentric millionaire Tom Newcliffe (the hilariously hammy Calvin Lockhart) has devised an ingenious plan to realize his ultimate goal of hunting a werewolf. He's invited six guests along with his wife, Caroline (*Ganja and Hess'* Marlene Clark), to his isolated country estate, which has been outfitted with hi-tech cameras and detection systems. The proceedings are monitored in the control room by Calvin's right hand man, Pavel (Anton Diffring). At dinner Calvin announces that someone at the table is a werewolf; never mind how he determined this, since the plot never bothers to explain it. Could it be occult expert Dr. Lungren (Peter Cushing)? Or perhaps the urbane and vaguely sinister Arthur Bennington (Charles Gray)? Newcliffe explains that the touch of silver is enough to kill a werewolf, so they pass a silver candlestick around the table... to no avail. Perhaps the full moon isn't close enough to expose the furry creature in their midst, but soon murder and mayhem abound. Can you guess who the guilty party is during the one minute "Werewolf Break?" See and find out!

Though it bears a superficial resemblance to a particularly insane television movie (no surprise given that director Paul Annett spent the rest of his time on TV shows), *The Beast Must Die* earns points for its imaginative cast, including the always watchable Cushing and a very young Michael Gambon as one of the suspects. While the werewolf's identity is so arbitrary it would even make Kevin Williamson blush, there is one interesting fake out twist worth catching near the end, coupled with the kitschy but fun Werewolf Break device in the best William Castle tradition. The werewolf itself is mostly limited to brief glimpses of a big dog jumping on people on bad day for night lighting, but the killings are brutal enough to make one look back with nostalgia to the days when a PG rating really meant something.

The Beast Must Die has lurked around on video in various versions from Prism and a retitled edition as *Black Werewolf*, though the blaxploitation angle is tenuous at best. Along with the entire Werewolf Break and some gore missing from the TV prints used for all previous masters, the DVD also marks the first letterboxed edition of the film on US video; apart from a few scuffs and scratches on the source print, the transfer looks quite good. It still has the visual texture of a European '70s film, of course, but the improvement over those old VHS tapes is enough to make an Amicus fan breathe a sigh of relief. The mono audio is an adequate presentation, given the strident quality of the original dialogue recording (or maybe it's just Lockhart's voice) coupled with a blaring music score right out of *Starsky & Hutch*. Approach this one more as a murder mystery with campy gadgets and supernatural elements rather than a straightforward horror film.

THE BEAST THAT KILLED WOMEN
Colour, 1965, 60m. / Directed by Barry Mahon / Starring Delores Carlos, Byron Mabe
THE MONSTER OF CAMP SUNSHINE
B&W, 1964, 74m. / Directed by Ferenc Leroget / Starring Harrison Pebbles / Image (US R0 NTSC)

Genre hybrids are always a lot of fun; we've had sci-fi westerns, horror musicals, and spy comedies, to name just a few. Well, at least twice we've also been blessed with monster nudist camp movies. Naturally Something Weird has managed to preserve both of these gonzo treats on DVD, complete with an onslaught of pulchritudinous extras to give you over three and a half hours of

bouncing, fleshy enjoyment. First up is *The Beast that Killed Women,* a senseless delight from exploitation legend Barry Mahon, the guy behind such diverse brain killers as *Cuban Rebel Girls, Censored,* and *Santa and the Ice Cream Bunny.* This time he gives the raincoat crowd a rampaging gorilla terrorizing the grounds of a Miami Beach nudist camp. Basically it comes out at night and either carries a girl off or tosses her in the swimming pool, but the residents are only mildly fearful. Instead they spend their time playing nude volleyball, hanging out in the sun, and even having a round of bareass square dancing. Seriously. The girls don't even bother to put on nightgowns when they sleep; they simply bunk up together to protect each other from the scary gorilla, which will look less than threatening to eagle eyed viewers who have ever seen a furry ape suit. Throw in a scared suburban housewife (Delores Carlos) newly awakening to the joys of nudism, her husband played by sleaze master Byron Mabe, a lot of bored looking guys in boxer shorts, and one stunning Sherilyn Fenn lookalike, and you've got the recipe for a junky good time.

Then it's back to nature for *The Monster of Camp Sunshine,* a black and white oddity that quickly dive-bombed into obscurity and never even merited a legit theatrical release. Nobody seems to have a clue about the real people behind and in front of the camera for this one, which is understandable given the final product. At another nudist camp (this time in New York), the happy and healthy members find their sunny lives turned upside down when Hugo the gardener accidentally chugs some toxic waste from a river recently polluted by a reckless scientist. In the meantime we get to see lots of swimming (both in lakes and pools), naked women walking around in the woods, and laughably bad stock footage, culminating in a mind-bending climax which finds the military launching heavy artillery at the deformed Hugo, scorching a few ill-placed nudists in the process as they roll around on the ground screaming. Can you prove it didn't happen?

The above synopses should be enough to convey the nature of these films, which certainly aren't anywhere close to good but don't qualify as boring, either. *Beast* will probably be the more accessible to most viewers thanks to its lustrous colour palette and gorgeous women, who have that full-bodied covergirl look that seems to have gone out of style now. The transfer is a real knockout, taken from a pristine source and ripe with chroma more suitable to a Vincente Minnelli MGM musical. *Monster* was obviously shot on a shoestring (and a ragged, chewed up shoestring at that), so the black and white print is most likely the only one that even exists. Of course, since this is a Something Weird disc, the movies are just the beginning. Hold on to your hats for a full blown drive-in tribute devoted to the nudist experience, complete with trailers for *Goldilocks and the Three Bares, Nudes on Tiger Reef, Nudist Life, The Beast that Killed Women, Pussycats Paradise,* and *Eves on Skis,* as well as a twisted little Easter Egg hidden on the trailer page. Don't approach that hidden goodie if you're easily offended, however - but then, you probably wouldn't be looking at this disc in the first place if you were. Then there are the featurettes: "Bring 'Em Back Nude," a 1920s short on nudism complete with some startling flashes of pubic hair; "The Expose of the Nudist Racket," a dated and amusing little take on nudism as moral corruption; "Naked Ranch," a weird little western nudism thing that looks more like an experimental film; "Beauty and the Beast," another burlesque bit in keeping with the main feature's killer gorilla; "Back to Nature," a '50s nudist short in the vein of those H.G. Lewis and Doris Wishman features; and the riotous "Nudist Fashion Show," which features bare bosomed lovelies showing off the latest international fashion accessories. Can you bare it?

BEASTIE BOYS: VIDEO ANTHOLOGY

Colour, 2000 / Directed by Nathanial Hornblower, Spike Jonze, Tamra Davis / Criterion (US R1 NTSC) / DD5.1

 With *Beastie Boys: Video Anthology,* the Criterion Collection thrusts the DVD format onto a completely new level, and luckily the content here is creative and bizarre enough to be worth more than a passing glance even for those who don't like music itself, primarily rap with random injections of funk, soul, lounge, jazz, thrash, ska, and pretty much anything else you can name. After sampling just a few of the dizzying options on this disc, it's clear that these energetic clown princes of rap have surrounded themselves with some amazing talent and revolutionized the music video industry.

While it would be impossible to list every highlight and viewing option on this disc, here's a quick overview. The two-disc set compiles eighteen videos (pretty much everything except for the clips from *Licensed to Ill* - sorry, no "Fight for Your Right" here), a handful of which previously appeared in the vastly inferior *Sabotage* disc. Each disc contains two layers: one houses the videos with 5.1 and 2.0 stereo mixes, plus two commentary tracks for every song by

the Beastie Boys, the directors, and other technical crew (including *Being John Malkovich*'s Spike Jonze), transferred at the highest possible bit-rate for maximum image and sound quality, while the second offers the same videos with an awe-inspiring array of features like multiple remixes for each track (some created especially for this collection) and multi-angle options including storyboards, alternate versions, making-of footage, and much, much more. Amusingly, if you pay attention to the audio channel labels on your DVD player, the various commentary and remix options are tagged with hilarious phoney language designations like "Esperanto" and "Serbian." The new 5.1 mixes are genuine demo material, offering a wild soundscape that perfectly complements the barrage of images onscreen, while the commentaries are often uproarious and pull no punches about noting what worked and what definitely didn't in each video.

Especially interesting are at least three of the videos, particularly "Body Movin'," a riotous fusion of footage from Mario Bava's *Diabolik* with newly shot scenes of the Boys enacting a new, action-packed, and surprisingly gory Diabolik adventure. (An alternate G-rated version shot to appease MTV is also included, but most will probably only want to see it once.) Watching the beloved Italian arch-criminal coupled with one of the group's bounciest songs proves to be a great combination, but that's just for starters. The collection's first video, an extended version of "Intergalactic," offers a goofy spin on *Kronos* by way of Japanese monster movies as a giant robot tangles with a big octopus monster and knocks down some structures in the process. The high octane "Sabotage" features the Boys slapping on fake moustaches for a dead on parody of '70s crime shows, complete with freeze-frame credits and characters leaping in and out of cars. (Whatever you do, don't miss the amusing interview with the "cast" of this video in the supplements section.) Some other highlights: "Hey Ladies," a dizzying combination of martial arts and disco mania that must have at least partially inspired Paul Thomas Anderson; the eerie anti-war statement of "Something's Got to Give;" the deliberately ragged, grating, and hilarious camcorder footage of "Netty's Girl" (wholly appropriate to the song, by the way); and "Shadrach," a rotoscoped firestorm of images painted in vivid hues over footage of the song performed in concert. This last video includes some of the most interesting video options, including the original video footage and a superimposed variation with the animation running over its real life counterpart. How on earth they managed to synch up all of the remixes to songs like this is anyone's guess, but kudos to everyone involved for figuring it out. And yes, if you hadn't seen it enough times on MTV already, the video for "So What'cha Want" is here, too. Many of the other videos are mostly straightforward rap style, sung straight into the camera with a few solarizations or optical tricks thrown into the mix, but each one offers its own flavour and could easily win over even the staunchest rap hater. There's no minority bashing, trite concert footage, or hackneyed spouting of social agendas here, just good nasty fun delivered with high energy and enough cutting edge technology to make you wish every band cared about its music and its public this much.

THE BEGUILED

Colour, 1970, 105m. / Directed by Don Siegel / Starring Clint Eastwood, Geraldine Page, Elizabeth Hartman / Universal (US R1 NTSC) / WS (1.85:1) (16:9)

 The most atypical film in the canons of director Don Siegel and jack of all trades Clint Eastwood (who also paired up on *Dirty Harry*), this gothic Civil War melodrama has developed a small but fervent cult following over the years. Universal surprisingly acknowledged this dedication by presenting this gorgeous new transfer, which preserves the dusky hues and sombre lighting schemes essential to creating the proper horrific and romantic mood.

Eastwood plays a hapless Yankee soldier, wounded in battle and near death, who is taken into a cloistered Southern all girl's boarding school. Stupidly, he decides to use his charms on several of the females (ranging from headmistress Geraldine Page to naive young Elizabeth Hartman). The results, to say the least, are not pretty. Whether you find the film provocative and chilling or just downright misogynistic, it's a compelling experience nonetheless and consummately acted, with an uncharacteristically subdued period score by Lalo Schifrin.

The previous fullscreen MCA/Universal laserdisc was presented open frame and was quite lovely itself, with some saturated colour schemes that may not have been what the cinematographer intended. This version pares away some information from the top and bottom of the screen, creating much more focus in several of the group scenes. It's a toss up as to which version is better; both contain the hilarious original trailer, which boasts some of the tackiest come on lines in cinematic history.

BELLE DE JOUR

Colour, 1967, 102m. / Directed by Luis Buñuel / Starring Catherine Deneuve, Jean Sorel / Buena Vista (US R1 NTSC) / WS (1.66:1)

B

 An erotic film from the perpetually bemused Luis Buñuel probably sounded like a crackpot concept at the time, but fortunately he pulled off a surrealist skinflick better than anyone had a right to expect. In this post-Vadim universe European starlets often appeared in various states of undress for high profile art projects, but this one outdoes them all by presenting the astonishing Catherine Deneuve in one of her best roles as Severine, a sexually dysfunctional young wife whose handsome, doting husband, Pierre (*giallo* favourite Jean Sorel), is unable to break through her erotic daytime reveries - which involve such mundane elements as bondage, Victorian horsemen, and pistol duels.

While Pierre's off at work, Severine goes to work at the upscale brothel of Madame Anais (Geneviève Page), where she indulges a series of peculiar fantasies involving funerals, an obsessive gangster with bad teeth (Pierre Clementi), and an odd Japanese gentleman with a mysterious buzzing box. Things get more complicated when friend Pierre Clementi wises up to her double life, the gangster decides to infiltrate her life, and the lines between sex and death, not to mention fantasy and reality, begin to perilously blur.

Despite the sordid subject matter, *Belle de Jour* is never even close to offensive thanks to Buñuel's realization that human sexual impulses are essentially amusing and directly expose everyone's most vulnerable, "honest" sides. On the other hand, love proves to be a very dangerous business, as the ambiguous and haunting conclusion demonstrates. Severine's personality functions as both object and mistress in a most unusual way, as she manipulates situations that would normally be seen as degrading with an attitude that mixes curiosity and compulsion. None of the other actors have a chance against her; while Piccoli's typical urbane charm carries him further than most of the men, Severine is the one who dominates this particular world. Even the volatile Clementi - one of the odder constructs of feminine sexual wish fulfilment - proves to eventually be ineffectual, as the ironic climax proves. Numerous other films later trod through this same territory (most obviously Ken Russell's outrageous *Crimes of Passion*), but none had quite the same style, grace, and subversive wit.

Buena Vista's DVD marks a welcome attempt to raid the overflowing vaults of art house treasures

B

over at Miramax, even if the final product comes up a tad short considering the outrageous price tag. The 1.66:1 transfer is identical to Criterion's previous laserdisc, which marked the first home availability of this title in the U.S. after decades of legal limbo. Colours look a bit faded and unsteady at times, but overall it's a decent enough transfer and captures the strange, autumnal appearance of its colour palette. The awkward English dub track is offered, but only the French version (with optional English subtitles) represents the character accurately. Carried over from the laserdisc are the lurid U.S. trailer and the more elegant 1995 reissue trailer; a new bonus is a thoughtful commentary track by scholar Julie Jones, whose chat represents a nice companion piece to the special edition Buñuel titles available from Criterion. Typical of Disney, an anamorphic transfer has been prepared for use overseas but obviously wasn't considered enough of a priority here.

BESIEGED

Colour, 1998, 92m. / Directed by Bernardo Bertolucci / Starring Thandie Newton, David Thewlis / New Line (US R1 NTSC) / WS (1.85:1) (16:9) / DD5.1

 Though it would have barely registered with audiences during the '70s heyday of Bernardo Bertolucci, *Besieged* has been referred to as a return to form for many viewers missing his visually elaborate character studies like *Last Tango in Paris* and *The Conformist*. While this film bears some similarities to both of those, it marks new territory by presenting a woman as the central and most fully developed figure in the story while leaving the male lead as an object, a cipher in a puzzle of her own creation. While these subdued chamber mind games may not be to everyone's taste, Bertolucci fans in particular should find much to savour here.

After an opening sequence in which her political activist husband is taken away and jailed by an African dictator, the lovely Shandurai (Thandie Newton) flees to Rome and begins studying at a local medical school. To make ends meet she takes a job as a live in housekeeper for Mr. Kinsky (David Thewlis), a withdrawn English pianist and composer who becomes smitten with her. Shandurai is quickly irritated by his numerous gifts but finally makes the ultimate demand on his unrequited love: get her husband out of prison. Surprisingly, Kinsky proves open to the suggestion, but Shandurai soon discovers

that her words carry higher emotional consequences than she realized.

A virtual short subject by Bertolucci standards, *Besieged* really only offers two notable characters and moves quickly (in European terms, anyway) during its brief running time. Newton is a particular standout in a tricky role requiring both independence and submission, while Thewlis is fine in a role that doesn't require much of his usual verbal showmanship. Fabio Cianchetti's remarkable cinematography produces some spectacular simple visuals within the aesthetics of Kinsky's house, featuring a spiral staircase that nicely echoes the spiralling nature of his music. Delicate and beautifully rendered, this was originally planned as a television film in Europe and still betrays its more simplified origins; thus, it's not a major work but a welcome diversion all the same.

While New Line's packaging makes no mention of it, *Besieged* is actually a fully loaded special edition DVD complete with a commentary track by Bertolucci and co-writer Clare Peploe. Bertolucci's accent makes for tough going at times, but he provides some useful insights and manages to inadvertently refute virtually all of the damning (and mostly unjustified) criticisms hurled at the film by Roger Ebert. On a separate track, writer James Lasdun reads his original short story, "The Siege," which provided the basis for the film, and offers some additional comments about the genesis of the story. "A Blind Man Among His Furniture," a 15 minute short subject by Giuseppe Bertolucci about the creation of *Besieged*, is also included, along with the theatrical trailer. Not surprisingly, the transfer itself is a feast for the eyes, filled with warm colour schemes (red, brown, orange) and startling bursts of colour (the initial flower left for Shandurai). The Dolby Digital mix admirably showcases the beautiful music soundtrack but only features a few ambient directional effects.

BENEATH THE VALLEY OF THE ULTRA-VIXENS

Colour, 1979, 93m. / Directed by Russ Meyer / Starring Francesca "Kitten" Natividad, Ken Kerr / CTN (France R2 PAL)

 Lavonna (Natividad) and Lamar Shedd (Kerr) are very much in love but their sex life is frustrating for her due to hubby's penchant for anal sex. Whilst she launches a plan to try and cure him of these desires, Lamar is busy playing away from home in a bid to find a lass who'll willingly submit to his backdoor proclivities. But redemption awaits him just around the corner in the arms of radio evangelist Sister Eufaula Roop (Marie).

Meyer's final (to date) bout of nonsensical no-plot sexual shenanigans is yet another platform for parading frolicsome women with unfeasibly large chests. Some of these ladies, at a pinch, may fuel a fantasy or two but others are more likely to spawn nightmares. Most fearsome of all is the rotund Junkyard Sal (June Mack) who gives Shedd more than he'd bargained for when he attempts his Rear Admiral tactics on her. The wince-inducingly unattractive Natividad takes centre stage for the most part and spends so much time *au naturel* that her wardrobe bill for the entire movie can't have been more than a fiver. Fortunately, for what we must suffer when Natividad or Mack are on screen, Meyer makes amends with the spectacular Anne Marie as Shedd's mega-bosomed saviour Eufaula Roop and scorching Sharon Hill as lesbian dental nurse Flovilla Thatch. There's the usual over the top comic strip violence, the pinnacle of which is reached when Shedd visits homosexual dentist cum marriage guidance counsellor Asa Lavender (a hilarious turn by Robert Pearson); Lavender takes a shine to Shedd and throws a fit when his advances are spurned, taking up a variety of weapons to try and extricate the cowering object of his affections from his hiding place in the closet. Stir in sex in a coffin (propped open, to prevent asphyxia, by a pair of dentures!), Uschi Digard as the incestuous SuperSoul, injured characters oozing myriad colours of blood, Stuart Lancaster with a barrage of absurd dialogue as our Narrator, and even Meyer himself - camera in hand, capturing the action as it unfolds - and you end up with a zany brew that outstays its welcome by at least 15 minutes. However, as mindless mammary movies go, they don't come much bouncier than *Beneath the Valley of the Ultravixens*.

The film is available as a French R2 PAL disc (under the title *Ultra Vixens*) in a 14-chaptered fullscreen transfer with English or French language tracks and subtitles in French alone. The bonus features are a trailer full of rapid-fire clips from a host of Meyer epics, an interactive quiz, and some textual matter on the director and his films. - TG

THE BEYOND

Colour, 1981, 89m. / Directed by Lucio Fulci / Starring Catriona MacColl, David Warbeck / Anchor Bay (US R1 NTSC) / WS (2.35:1) (16:9) / DD5.1, EC Entertainment (Holland R0 NTSC), Vipco (UK R2 PAL), Astro (Germany R2 PAL) / WS (2.35:1) / DD2.0

A few lucky directors have a certain film where all of the elements come perfectly into alignment. Lucio Fulci managed to pull of this feat for an entire quartet, often referred to as his zombie cycle. *Zombie, City of the Living Dead*, and *House by the Cemetery* are all well known and revered among horror fans, but *The Beyond* (*L'aldilà*) is arguably his masterpiece. Oddly enough it was also virtually unknown for many years, with many fans unfortunate enough to be stuck with a brutally edited, rescored version entitled *7 Doors of Death* (released on Thriller Video in the US back in the early '80s). When the original cut of *The Beyond* finally surfaced on Japanese laserdisc, the floodgates opened and the film's reputation went through the roof, even winding up with an unlikely theatrical release from Grindhouse and Quentin Tarantino's Rolling Thunder Pictures on the midnight movie circuit.

During a sepia tone prologue set in 1927 Louisiana, a group of men arrive by boat at the Seven Doors Hotel. They burst into Room 36 and proceed to chain-whip the inhabitant, a painter and warlock named Schweick. Meanwhile a young girl downstairs named Emily (Sarah Keller) reads from an occult text called the Book of Eibon, which erupts into flames as Schweick's face is dissolved with acidic sludge. In 1981 the abandoned hotel is under renovation thanks to the new owner, a relocated New Yorker named Liza (Catriona MacColl). When one of the handymen suffers a bloody accident on the scaffolding, the local doctor, John McCabe (David Warbeck), is called in to keep things under control. A number of bizarre incidents begin to occur beneath and around the hotel, such as constant ringing from the bell in Room 36 and a gruesome fate for poor plumber Joe (Giovanni De Nava). During a car trip along an eerie causeway Eliza first meets Emily, who still looks exactly the same except for her eyes, which have turned a milky white. Other "accidents" at the local morgue and a bookshop indicate that the Book of Eibon holds the key to the hotel's dark secret, with a cryptic gateway to Hell housed somewhere within the property. Ultimately the humid landscape is beset by shuffling zombies, with Liza and John frantically fighting for their lives as they attempt to close that which should never have been opened.

By most rational standards, *The Beyond* can be a confounding experience. The plot has little to do with linear story properties or rational development, and the acting is highly stilted and often awkward. However, any Fulci fan knows that when the filmmaker has kicked into high gear, these are really

B

attributes, not flaws. The lovely and endearing MacColl served as leading lady in three of his best zombie films; apart from being a first rate screamer, she's a terrific protagonist and seems to be enjoying herself. The late Warbeck carved a niche for himself in British and Italian exploitation titles during the '70s and '80s, and his rugged leading man qualities are put to excellent use here as he turns from concerned family physician to pistol-packing defender against the undead. Their characters are more warm and engaging than they really have any right to be, which makes the poetic and thoroughly chilling ending all the more powerful.

If anyone ever questions Fulci's abilities as a filmmaker, kindly direct them to the last 90 seconds of this film. The special effects by splatter maestro Giannetto De Rosi are effectively repellent, with eyes popping from their sockets and faces blending into mush. The legendary, painfully slow tarantula attack sequence is both stomach churning and hilarious, with squeaking arachnids covering one poor victim and casually removing portions of his face with their... uh, teeth, apparently. All of Fulci's most noteworthy collaborators attack this film full throttle, with the amazing Sergio Salvati pumping up the atmospheric lighting across the scope frame and Fabio Frizzi manipulating piano solos and electronics into a tremendous music score. Forget what mainstream critics like Roger Ebert had to say; this film is a heartfelt poem for horror fans and, most importantly, a gory good show.

The distribution history of *The Beyond* was tangled for years, with its DVD acquisition providing even more drama. When Rolling Thunder stepped in, the video rights went to Miramax. Unfortunately their owner, Disney, wouldn't even consider allowing a laserdisc release, despite the massive amount of supplementary material compiled by Grindhouse. The title drifted in limbo for a while after its theatrical run, with a decent Region 2 DVD from EC Entertainment turning up in Holland of all places. Finally the licensors made a deal with Anchor Bay, and years later the DVD finally hit the market. So was it worth the wait? Most definitely. The film itself looks terrific, with the widescreen compositions looking balanced and well judged, while the colours range from appropriately muted to garish and vivid during the gore scenes. The disc offers several audio options: a thunderous 5.1 remix, which offers some wild and amusing separation effects to the rear speakers and increases the scare value immensely; a 2.0 surround version of the same mix; the original mono soundtrack for the more nostalgic viewers; and the original Italian audio track, which is much better than average and invests the film with some welcome

dynamic, emotional shadings. Though the packaging makes no mention of it, the disc also includes optional English subtitles, a very welcome addition.

The most notable special feature here is the commentary track by MacColl and Warbeck, recorded while the latter was on his deathbed. You'd never guess it, though; this is easily one of the best commentary tracks ever recorded and never lets up for a moment. The two actors show a great deal of respect for Fulci and the film itself while poking fun at the filming experience, cracking jokes and making some astonishingly witty observations about the action onscreen. The affection and knowledge shown by this pair cannot be overstated, and it's extremely satisfying that their comments can finally be heard. Check out Warbeck's method of soothing MacColl's queasiness during the tarantula scene for an especially good chuckle.

The DVD also includes the international English trailer (apparently ported over from the Japanese laserdisc master), the Rolling Thunder reissue trailer (with a slightly different opening), a similar German trailer, and a file of cast and promotional photographs and artwork. An alternate colour version of the opening sequence has also been recovered from the German release version, and obviously, it's much more disgusting seeing Schweick's bloody chain wounds and candy coloured face melting in full, MGM-style Technicolor. Necrophagia's music video for a thrash metal song called "And You Will Live in Terror," directed by Jim Van Bebber and featuring clips from the film, is also included but will probably only appeal to a select few out there. Easter Egg hunters out there can also follow the Eibon symbols and see the original US opening for *7 Doors of Death* and a trailer for Fulci's latter day postmodern horror opus, *A Cat in the Brain.*

BEYOND ATLANTIS

Colour, 1973, 91m. / Directed by Eddie Romero / Starring Patrick Wayne, John Ashley / VCI (US R1 NTSC)

 Taking a break from his infamous *Blood Island* series, director/producer Eddie Romero crafted a much lighter film than usual with *Beyond Atlantis*, a strange and often unintentionally hilarious study of the infamous lost continent's amphibious descendants. Despite a few mild splashes of gore and the fantastic subject matter, this is standard, family-friendly drive-in fluff with lots of choice quotable dialogue.

A ragtag band of tourists and low-grade mercenaries including good guy Vic (future *Sinbad* Patrick Wayne) and the scuzzy East Eddie (Sid Haig) lose their way on a sailing excavation and wind up encountering the surviving remnants of Atlantis, where a shipwrecked blonde woman, Syrene (Leigh Christian), has been brought up as their own royalty. According to local custom, she must mate with an outsider, presumably to stave off the ravages of inbreeding, but is uncomfortable with the mating customs of her people. Meanwhile her fellow citizens swim underwater a lot and show off their ping-pong bug eyes.

Not one of the more readily available Filipino titles, *Beyond Atlantis* slipped into the subconscious of an entire generation of impressionable kids and is now back looking even better than it did in theatres. The full frame image is very attractive and appears to be open matte; apart from one or two minor splices, the source material is in first rate condition. The disc also includes the uproarious theatrical trailer, complete with a montage of Syrene being manhandled and repeatedly ordered, "You must mate!"

THE BIG BLUE

Colour, 1988, 168m. / Directed by Luc Besson / Starring Rosanna Arquette, Jean-Marc Barr, Jean Reno / Columbia (US R1 NTSC), Fox (UK R2 PAL) / WS (2.35:1) (16:9) / DD5.1

The first of director Luc Besson's unabashed odes to the sea, *The Big Blue (Le grand bleu)* has existed in so many different versions that its fan base must be relieved to have a "definitive" cut available at last. A financial success almost everywhere except in America, its waterlogged reputation has taken over a decade to recover its shaky theatrical run, primarily thanks to Besson's subsequent high profile career with *La Femme Nikita* and *Leon*, among others.

Based very loosely on the life of real life diver Jacquel Mayol, *The Big Blue* concerns the mysterious link between Jacques (Lars Von Trier regular Jean-Marc Barr) and the call of the "big blue," particularly the dolphins swimming below. From early childhood he becomes close to Enzo (Jean Reno), a fellow free diver. Both of them are capable of controlling their heart rate and breathing, allowing them to sink to unnatural depths. After Jacques' father dies in the ocean, the two friends lose touch. Jacques becomes involved with beautiful, daffy insurance clerk Johanna (Rosanna Arquette), who follows him from Peru to a diving competition in Italy. There, Jacques meets up again with Enzo, the world's diving champ, and their rivalry and friendship become reignited. Johanna and Jacques begin a passionate but difficult affair in which he finds himself unable to commit to her, torn between the solidity of the real world and the spiritual beckoning of the blue water.

Though definitely not a film for everyone, *The Big Blue* is in many respects the ultimate Luc Besson movie. The stunning widescreen cinematography and intense, varied score by his regular composer, Eric Serra, give the film a unique flavour and an eerie resonance despite the threadbare plotline. The entire concept of Jacques' relationship with the dolphins could have been hokey, leading to little more than a TV movie-of-the-week, but Besson's passionate handling of the material manages to pull it off. Not surprisingly he returned to the sea again for *Atlantis*, a free form, plotless film exploring the various wonders of the deep, with Serra performing musical duties again. It would make a perfect companion to *The Big Blue* if it were only easier to find. As for the cast, Barr makes an appealing debut with a difficult role, while Reno continues his string of quirky Besson roles. For cult movie fans, note that Arquette and Griffin Dunne (as her boss) re-team after the underrated *After Hours*, and even Kimberley Beck, the heroine from *Friday the 13th: The Final Chapter*, puts in an appearance.

American viewers first encountered this film in a 118 minute edition, which substituted a Bill Conti score and, unbelievably, tacked on a happy final scene that completely refuted everything preceding it. However, while the Conti score may not be in keeping with the fabric of Besson's vision, it's a beautiful, stirring piece of work, and this alone justifies tracking down the American version as an alternative. Meanwhile in Europe, a 120 minute cut was released to theatres and video with the Serra score intact and several alternate scenes not included in the American print (and vice versa). A Japanese laserdisc provided the first imported look at a truer version of Besson's film, but the real surprise came in 1994 when the European distributor, Fox Video, issued *The Big Blue - Version Longue* on videotape in the UK This 168 minute, letterboxed "extended cut" restored all of the existing footage, with some restored scenes (mostly Arquette's) in French with English subtitles. Finally, Columbia's DVD offers yet a fourth cut of the film, with the French scenes now synched back up into English. This "director's cut" is the same as the British tape in other respects and includes the original Serra score, even isolated as a separate audio track. Bearing in mind the bizarre distribution history, the DVD looks exceptional and blows away all previous video transfers. Colours are rich and stable, with only a few traces of that familiar '80s "hazy" look cropping up here and there. The 5.1 mix does what it can, with some limited split surrounds confined mainly to Serra's score. The sound design is quite beautiful, though, and does a masterful job of pulling the viewer into the story's magical spell. The disc also includes a photo gallery, the US theatrical trailer, and trailers for Besson's *The Messenger* and *Leon*. (What, no *Fifth Element*?)

THE BIG DOLL HOUSE

Colour, 1971, 93m. / Directed by Jack Hill / Starring Judy Brown, Roberta Collins, Pam Grier / New Concorde (US R1 NTSC)

The first and one of the best. If you've ever suffered through those cruddy women in prison movies during a late night television romp, here's a rare example of how it should be done (Jonathan Demme's *Caged Heat* is another). The plot couldn't be simpler: a group of women in prison, led by the resourceful Collier (top-billed Judy Brown), plan an escape. Inside snitch Grear (Pam Grier in her first speaking film role) slips information back and forth to the guards and the evil warden, Ms. Dietrich (a hilarious Christiane Schmidtmer, best remembered for *The Giant Spider Invasion*), in order to get smack for her lesbian lover cellmate. Guards torment and molest prisoners. Prisoners get naked (though not as much as you'd expect for this genre). One evil head guard, Lucian (Kathryn Lodern, the quasi-Bette Davis villainess from *Foxy Brown*) tortures bad girls by tying them to tables and hanging snakes over them. With the aid of guard Sid Haig, the girls eventually the girls stage a big, violent breakout that claims a few lives and leads to a riotous, over the top sequence in the middle of the jungle.

Fast paced and surprisingly well acted, *The Big Doll House* takes itself more seriously than its semi-sequel, *The Big Bird Cage*, and delivers all the usual thrills you would expect, though a few witty lines and some hysterical monologues (the one about the husband and the poolboy is priceless) indicate the filmmakers already knew how to keep their tongues firmly in cheek. As if that weren't enough, you also get a theme song, "Long Time Woman," performed by Pam Grier herself (and later reused in *Jackie Brown*).

The New Concorde DVD follows several other video incarnations, including with a passable release from Embassy and a miserable one under the title *Women's Penitentiary* (which spawned a slew of other retitled women in prison films). The New Concorde version is presented open matte, giving characters way too much headroom in many shots but otherwise a nice presentation. *Big Doll House* was shot on less than optimum materials in the Philippines, thanks to the producer wishes of Filipino schlock experts Eddie Romero and John Ashley (*Mad Doctor of Blood Island*), so this edition is about as good as it's going to look. Sound quality is fine if a bit ragged in spots due to the recording techniques, and the disc is well compressed and contains no noticeable artefacts. This print contains the irritating dubbed-in final line used on reissue prints and all other video versions. Also includes the original trailer and the usual New Concorde coming attractions assortment (*Big Bad Mama, Eat My Dust*, etc.), as well as the usual PR materials about how Roger Corman is such a great guy (but why does his picture have to be on the spine label of every title?).

BIO-ZOMBIE

Colour, 1998, 94m. / Directed by Wilson Yip Wai Shun / Starring Jordan Chan Siu-Chun, Sam Lee Chan Sam / Media Blasters (US R0 NTSC), Mei Ah (HK R0 NTSC) / WS (1.85:1) / DD2.0

Thanks to the likes of *Return of the Living Dead* and Peter Jackson's *Brain Dead*, the gory zombie comedy has actually become a fairly respectable subgenre of the horror film. Though the territory seemed well worn, Hong Kong actually managed to put yet another spin on the subject with the giddy *Bio-Zombie*, a combination of goofball humour and lurching horror that practically backflips over itself to win the audience's approval.

Beginning like a sort of twisted Asian version of *Clerks* (including a jokey credit sequence with a built-in theatre audience), the film follows the misadventures of a pair of VCD bootleggers, Woody Invincible (Jordan Chan Siu-Chun) and Crazy Bee (Sam Lee Chan Sam), who accidentally ram their boss' car into a Chinese government agent who's carrying a soda bottle packed with a dangerous contaminant engineered by Iraq for national devastation. Unfortunately our two anti-heroes dump a load of zombie brew down the agent's throat and toss him in the trunk, which leads to some devastating consequences when they bring him back to the shop. Soon a full scale zombie plague has been unleashed upon their quiet shopping mall, and the only solution is mass zombie destruction.

Okay, so *Bio-Zombie* may not be a sensitive work of cinematic art, but it's one of the more enjoyable horror outings from the end of a decade infamous for nearly burying the genre altogether. Just silly enough to be endearing and graphic enough to keep the gorehounds happy, *Bio-Zombie* in some ways feels like an amphetamine-driven extension of the *Mr. Vampire* films by way of George Romero. The video culture in-jokes are actually quite funny, as our heroes gradually transform from shiftless pirates to butt-kicking bruisers who splatter first and ask questions later. Put your brain on hold and enjoy!

The domestic DVD from Media Blasters appears to be comparable to the region free edition released overseas by Mei Ah, whose logo still remains at the beginning of the print. The non-anamorphic transfer likes nice enough, with solid greens and blues effectively saturating much of the action. Detail looks fine, with only some slight aliasing; the digital noise reduction which plagues many Hong Kong transfers is mostly kept well in check here, most likely due to the recent vintage of the film. The soundtrack contains either the original Cantonese dub (by far the better option) or an L.A.-flavoured English dub track, filled with "dudes" and "whoas." More amusingly, the subtitles can be chosen between a well-written new English translation or, as the menu puts it, "Engrish" subtitles, which carry over the original, chaotically mistranslated subs from the Mei Ah disc. Extras include a handful of lobby cards and trailers for four other Media Blasters titles, but alas, no trailer for *Bio-Zombie* itself. On the other hand, the Mei Ah disc includes an alternate ending option, with Cantonese or Mandarin soundtracks and optional English subtitles. Buckle up and enjoy.

THE BIRD WITH THE CRYSTAL PLUMAGE

Colour, 1970, 98m. / Directed by Dario Argento / Starring Tony Musante, Suzy Kendall / VCI (US R1 NTSC) / WS (2.35:1) (16:9) / DD2.0, TFI (France R2 PAL) / WS (2.35:1) (16:9), Platinum Media Corporation (UK R2 PAL) / WS (1.85:1) (16:9)

The streets of Rome first ran red with blood for many viewers with Dario Argento's directorial debut, *The Bird with the Crystal Plumage*. Cannily featuring a vulnerable American hero and a British female love interest, the film was patently designed to appeal to an international audience while showcasing Argento's seemingly endless reservoir of visual and storytelling abilities. For the uninitiated, the film concerns an American writer, Sam (Tony Musante), who has been staying in Rome with his girlfriend, scream queen Suzy Kendall. One night he witnesses a woman being attacked in an art gallery; the woman survives, and Sam is informed by the police that the assailant is a serial killer slashing his way through the city. Sam feels that he has witnessed something that could lead him to the killer's identity, but he just can't put his finger on it (a narrative device repeated in Argento's *Deep Red* and *Trauma*). Thus, he decides to stay in Rome and do some amateur sleuthing, leading to the expected terrifying results.

Argento never had a stronger plot than this one, which anchors his trademark visual flourishes into a recognizable thematic and human fabric that would later be jettisoned for the candy-coloured fever dreams of *Suspiria* and *Inferno*. Ennio Morricone's groundbreaking, jittery score still manages to eke out every bit of suspense from the murder sequences, and the actors all do a fine job, partial dubbing notwithstanding. For once, the comic relief is actually pretty good, including an unforgettable encounter with an artist who keeps cats for a very unorthodox purpose.

To say the least, *Bird*'s history in theatres and on video has been very tattered. After a reissue under the title *The Gallery Murders*, the film appeared on VHS in America from United/VCI and was concurrently issued by Columbia as a Japanese laserdisc. While the Japanese laserdisc looked more colourful and was uncut, it was only letterboxed at 1.85:1 and suffered from some distracting print damage. The washed out Image/VCI laserdisc of the US print featured a more accurately letterboxed credit sequence but then opened up to an unsatisfying 1.90:1 ratio. Finally the Roan Group released *Bird* completely uncut (featuring a glimpse of one victim's underwear being ripped off and some extra splattery slashing during the stairwell razor murder). The Roan edition also featured much more robust colour and a correct aspect ratio. For its DVD premiere, VCI secured the complete European cut, correctly letterboxed, in an anamorphically enhanced transfer. Though still not 100% free of source damage, the presentation is surprisingly good, with nice colour and a very evocative new surround sound mix that does wonders for the Morricone score. Unfortunately the transitions in and out of the music get a little bumpy, even lopping off the beginning of the memorable line, "All right, bring in the perverts." Interestingly, like the Roan version, this is still partially derived from a US print- note the woman's scream at the end of the opening titles, which was added by the American distributor, and the extra gore appears to have been spliced in (rather badly in the first pressing) from a slightly darker, blurrier print. Extras include the Morricone score also isolated as a kind of jukebox feature with each track separately labelled (though without the alternate cues present on the 1998 Cinevox reissue), apparently yanked from the American vinyl release based on the track titles, as well as the psychedelic US first run trailer.

The UK DVD features a more horizontally compromised transfer (similar to the Japanese laser) in Italian with English subtitles and, like the US prints, is missing the underwear slicing. Extras include the Italian trailers for *Deep Red, Bird*, and *Cat o' Nine Tails*, as well as English trailers for *Demons* and *Demons 2*, a stills gallery, and an odd overdubbed excerpt from the slapdash *Dario Argento's World of Horror 3*. Also available from France in an attractive anamorphic transfer, with French or Italian dialogue tracks.

THE BIRDS

Colour, 1963, 120m. / Directed by Alfred Hitchcock / Starring Rod Taylor, Jessica Tandy, Tippi Hedren / Universal (US R1 NTSC / WS (1.85:1) (16:9), Universal (UK R2 PAL)

The granddaddy of all those horror films about nature running amok, *The Birds* is unquestionably the best. Alfred Hitchcock's gleeful manipulation of his audience has never been more precise than this carefully paced, insidiously frightening tale of Mother Nature lunging back to take a big bite out of humanity. Pampered socialite Melanie Daniels (Tippi Hedren) decides to deliver a pair of lovebirds to the sly Mitch Brenner (Rod Taylor), a man who played a practical joke on her in a pet store. She drives along the California coast to the tranquil Bodega Bay where he spends time with his mother (Jessica Tandy) and sister, Cathy (Veronica Cartwright). When Melanie arrives, a seagull swoops by and cuts her forehead. However, this incident is just the beginning. A farmer turns up dead at his home with his eyes plucked out, Cathy's birthday party is besieged by flocks of malevolent birds, and soon the entire town is filled with fluttering, feathery terror from the skies.

More than a simple creepy campfire yarn, *The Birds* operates as a skilful allegory about people's emotional imprisonment and feelings of helplessness (much like the previous *Psycho*). The traumas endured by Hedren on the film's set have become legendary, and most viewers will agree that her agony resulted in a performance of effective and unforgettable mounting hysteria. Hitchcock's visual colour coding has never been more astute, with the red and green outfits of his female leads providing amusing counterpoint to the startling (but restrained) bursts of bloodshed on the screen. Oddly, *The Birds* contains no background music (apart from a song delivered by children in the film's creepiest scene), with composer Bernard Herrmann instead serving as a consultant for the film's overwhelming soundtrack.

Universal's various video editions of *The Birds* over the years have been a pretty miserable bunch, plagued with chalky colours and blurry image quality. Their DVD is a tremendous improvement in every respect; those grainy prerecords and laserdiscs can now go in the trash. Some of the film was deliberately filmed with either soft focus lenses (Hedren's close ups) or grainy rear projection, so these flaws will always exist; however, the transfer is sharp as a tack and completely satisfying. The disc is outfitted with a number of great extras, including promo newsreels, the hilarious theatrical trailer, Hedren's lengthy screen test (little more than a fashion show really), storyboards, and script excerpts and illustrations for a deleted Mitch/Melanie scene and the legendary unfilmed ending (which would have been a kicker). Inexplicably, the Universal Region 2 release contains the same extras but features a non-anamorphic full frame transfer which, decades before the similar *Jurassic Park*, alternates hard-matted (cropped) special effects shots with open matte footage elsewhere. The letterboxed US DVD looks a little tight on the other hand, but fans should be pleased with either option.

THE BLACK CAT

Colour, 1980, 92m. / Directed by Lucio Fulci / Starring Mimsy Farmer, Patrick Magee, David Warbeck / Anchor Bay (US R1 NTSC) / WS (2.35:1) (16:9) / EC (Holland R0 NTSC) / WS (2.35:1)

Though it will never be a fan favourite on the order of *Zombie* or *The Beyond*, Lucio Fulci's *The Black Cat* fits comfortably within his magnificent run of gothic essays during the early '80s despite its relative absence of graphic gore. Ably proving his skill as a visual director capable of generating atmosphere without buckets of blood, Fulci reportedly shot this one quickly without much passion involved, but as fans of Mario Bava's *Five Dolls for an August Moon* can attest, impersonal and rushed projects can sometimes provide the most interesting results.

A small English village is being terrorized by mysterious deaths all linked by the presence of a black cat belonging to the antisocial professor, Robert Miles (Patrick Magee), who leaves tape recorders in graveyards to capture messages from the dead. One unfortunate man is compelled to smash his car into a bloody, fiery wreck, another plunges onto a series of sharp spikes inside a farmhouse, and a young horny couple suffocates inside an abandoned building. Nosy photographer Jill Trevers (Mimsy Farmer) begins to suspect something unnatural between Miles and his pet kitty after paying them a visit, and she relays her suspicions to out of towner Inspector Gorley (David Warbeck), who has come to investigate the deaths but finds more than he bargained for. Is the true villain here Mr. Miles, who shares an odd psychic bond with his pet, or the sinister black cat itself?

More of a mood piece than a standard Fulci rollercoaster, *The Black Cat* benefits greatly from a wonderful cast of Eurosleaze veterans, including the always watchable Dagmar Lassander (who looked like hell the next year in *House by the Cemetery*) and the perpetually abused and unclothed Daniela Doria. The unusual English setting is wonderfully realized by Sergio Salvati's evocative scope photography, which prowls along the ground, soars over rooftops, and creeps into dark, dusty corners when it's not too busy flashing back and forth between close ups of actors' (and cat's) eyes. Composer Fabio Frizzi takes a break this time, leaving Pino Donaggio to provide a catchy, lyrical score, which remains sadly unreleased to this day.

The story bears little resemblance to the Edgar Allan Poe original apart from the title creature and the claustrophobic, ambiguous finale (lifted semi-effectively from Fulci's earlier *Seven Notes in Black*, aka *The Psychic*), but the gothic mood is well in keeping with the literary master. Watch it back to back with Dario Argento's "The Black Cat" from *Two Evil Eyes* for the full effect (and two contrasting Donaggio scores, to boot). Not all curious fans of European horror will like this film, which moves at a deliberate pace and could be an acquired taste at best, but Fulci fanatics should find enough to savour.

Various companies like Media and Rhino have issued unwatchable pan and scan transfers of this film over the years, while Redemption presented the only bona fide widescreen VHS edition (in PAL), also briefly available on VCD. Anchor Bay's DVD easily eclipses them all with a razor sharp, breathtaking widescreen transfer, with details so sharp you can see each cobblestone. Most of the DVD Fulci transfers have been impressive, but this may be the most welcome and satisfying of the bunch so far. As

with the previous letterboxed version, a thick vertical line appears during a handful of shots on the extreme right of the frame during the opening five minutes, but considering this flaw also appears in the excellent theatrical trailer (included on the disc as well), the glitch was an inherent part of the original negative. The nifty animated menus, complete with cat yowls and Donaggio's main theme, are a nice bonus, and the rather clumsily printed liner notes (craftily hidden on the back of the sleeve) by Travis Crawford offer a nice reappraisal of the film. The previous EC Entertainment DVD contains a fuzzier, non-anamorphic transfer, but does contain a 40-minute Fulci interview, so completists may find both worth hunting down.

BLACK CHRISTMAS

Colour, 1974, 98m. / Directed by Bob Clark / Starring Olivia Hussey, Keir Dullea, Margot Kidder, John Saxon / Critical Mass (Canada R1 NTSC)

Years before he crafted the ultimate comic Christmas film experience, *A Christmas Story*, Canadian director Bob Clark put a completely different slant on the revered holiday with *Black Christmas*, a chilly gem which has been popping up over the years under the titles *Stranger in the House* and *Silent Night, Evil Night*. Though not as well known as many of its American imitators, this film is quite a class act and still manages to scare the living hell out of viewers while all the *Friday the 13th* sequels have faded from memory.

The day before Christmas, the remaining girls at a college sorority and their house mother are getting ready for a long, cold holiday. However, their eggnog-drenched festivities are interrupted by an obscene phone caller whose frightening, distorted voice(s) set the young girls on edge. One of the girls, Claire (Lynne Griffin, later in *Curtains* and *Strange Brew*), is murdered that night, and her body is stored away in the attic by a deranged killer (seen only through point of view shots - later a cliché, but very creepy here). The police, led by John Saxon, investigate the disappearance, which they believe is linked to recent attacks on young town girls. Another sorority girl, Jess (Olivia Hussey at her loveliest), fights violently with her boyfriend, Peter (Keir Dullea), about her decision to have an abortion, and she begins to suspect he may be the killer at large. Meanwhile, the murders continue as Christmas morning passes into night...

Skilfully shot and edited, this film marks the final and strongest entry of Clark's all-too-brief horror career, which also included *Children Shouldn't Play with Dead Things* and the eerie *Deathdream* (and, some argue, continued with *Murder by Decree*). Though it has been imitated countless times (*When a Stranger Calls* in particular), *Black Christmas* holds up thanks to very strong performances (fresh off her turn in Brian De Palma's *Sisters*, Kidder is a particular standout as an asthmatic foul-mouthed party girl) and an unexpected, welcome streak of irreverent humour running throughout the film. Of course, Clark also includes one of his trademark scenes of cops cracking up for minutes on end (repeated famously in his later *Porky's*) and utilizes a marvellous sense of both visual and sound cutting (for example, the Hitchcockian moment when a grieving mother opens her mouth to scream only to cut to a ringing telephone).

The rumbling, abstract score by Carl Zittrer alternates with chilly Christmas carols to create an unsettling soundscape- a Dolby surround remix of this would be unbearably creepy. The killer's voice is one of the most nightmarish ever conjured up on film, prone to screaming and weird shifts in vocal tone that set the viewer on edge within the first five minutes. What really makes this film, though, are the scares. The first attack is a great seat-jumper, and from there Clark delivers one powerful jolt after another. The close-ups of the killer's eyes, reminiscent of *The Spiral Staircase*, are guaranteed to induce chills, and the wintry Canadian setting spotted with colourful splashes of Christmas lights manage to create a shuddery, chilling effect even when the film is viewed in the middle of summer. If it weren't for the bleak, open-ended final plot twist, *Black Christmas* would undoubtedly be recognized more widely as the visceral horror classic it truly is.

First released very briefly on laserdisc from Image during its flood of Warner horror titles, *Black Christmas* has had a chequered history on home video. The matted laserdisc looked fine, composition-wise, and added more to the sides while losing a little from the top and bottom compared to the mediocre VHS version. While Warner has shown little interest in reviving the film on DVD in the US, Canada fortunately came to the rescue with a "25th Anniversary" special edition. (Okay, they missed it by a year, but who's counting?) The image quality is by far the sharpest the film has ever looked, and while the low budget shooting and mediocre film stock are still betrayed by some instability and graininess during a few darker scenes, the presentation is astonishing compared to earlier renditions. As a sticker on the back explains, the company decided to retain all of the available visual information from the film's negative, which means a completely open matte transfer. Apart from an overly spacious amount of headroom, the framing looks just fine and improves significantly over the videotape. The disc also includes a very long, spoiler-crammed trailer under the original title, as well as two short interview segments with John Saxon, who had just watched the film for the first time in decades. His recollections are warm if more than a little sketchy, and he obviously holds the film in high regard. In what may be a DVD interview first, Saxon's tailor receives a prominent credit on the menu screen.

BLACK CIRCLE BOYS

Colour, 1997, 101m. / Directed by Matthew Carnahan / Starring Scott Bairstow, Eric Mabius / Image (US R1 NTSC) / DD2.0

 A strange Canadian film that trades on much of the same goth high school trends found in *The Craft*, this particular film mostly tosses out the standard necessities of these horrific melodramas (preppie bully villains, traumatic humiliation scenes, sexual conquests, etc) in favour of a slow and studied examination of the painful consequences of male bonding. The narrative constantly wobbles between an after school special approach and full blooded horror, but its refusal to push its satanic imagery into anything truly supernatural or demonic may limit its appeal to the blood and thunder gore crowd.

Shattered by the death of his best friend, Kyle (Scott Bairstow) moves with his family to an undefined northern suburb. Isolated from his peers and apparently dedicated only to the fine art of chain smoking, Kyle falls in with a group of headbangers called the *Black Circle Boys*. Led by the unstable Shane (Eric Mabius), who has already been incarcerated and may have killed his own brother, the Boys enjoy hanging out in the woods, doing drugs, and hopping in strangers' swimming pools. Unfortunately the group's cult-like behaviour becomes too much for Kyle, but by the time he decides to back out, it may be too late.

Stronger on acting than logic, *Black Circle Boys* works better as a showcase for its two up and coming male stars than as a thriller. The finale in particular recalls the droning philosophical rants of the similarly shot *Apocalypse Now*, though the resolution - which provides the most novel and ludicrous method of dealing with a murderous Satanist - must be seen to be believed. Mabius does what he can with an unevenly written character, while Donny Wahlberg pops up in a glorified cameo as Greggor, Shane's creepy bisexual mentor. Dee Wallace Stone also drifts through occasionally as Kyle's concerned mom. Interestingly, one fiery murder sequence bears an alarming resemblance to Jim Van Bebber's *My Sweet Satan*, a much more ferocious and potent study of the effects of teen devil worship.

The film's deliberately grainy, colourless photography makes its DVD presentation difficult to judge, but it appears to be primarily an open matte transfer with soft-matted opening titles. The visual textures and detail are good, relatively speaking, though many scenes deliberately pour the shadows on so thick that only flickering candlelight remains visible. The basic surround soundtrack primarily shoves the score and metal music into the exterior speakers, with most of the sound effects and dialogue remained firmly anchored dead centre.

BLACK MAMA, WHITE MAMA

Colour, 1972, 87m. / Directed by Eddie Romero / Starring Pam Grier, Margaret Markov / MGM (US R1 NTSC) / WS (1.85:1) (16:9)

After his fast and successful run of Filipino "Blood" films like *Mad Doctor of Blood Island*, director Eddie Romero switched gears to offer his own spin on the women-in-prison genre. Working from a story co-written by a pre-*Caged Heat* Jonathan Demme, this schizoid production veers from one subplot to another with reckless abandon, all loosely tied together by a plot cribbed from *The Defiant Ones*.

Life behind bars is hell for two prisoners, white Karen Brent (Margaret Markov) and black Lee Daniels (Pam Grier). The inmates can't even take a long, steamy shower without a lesbian guard slobbering over them through a peephole, and let's not even mention the wardens. During a trip in the paddy wagon, an assault from Karen's radical comrades sends the two quarrelling women scurrying off into the jungle bound together by chains at the wrist. At first they indulge in some light bondage cat fighting, but begrudgingly they agree to join forces to survive. Naturally, they do the logical thing and disguise themselves as nuns. While the jailbirds hop on the nearest bus, their escape sends a number of forces in hot pursuit, such as scuzzy gangster Ernesto (Zaldy Zschornack), cowboy bounty hunter Ruben (Sid Haig), and the aforementioned revolutionaries.

The various plot threads finally collide during a bloody showdown at the Filipino docks, where everyone involved is forced to face the music.

Neither the best nor the worst of the '70s WIP films, *Black Mama, White Mama* looks very similar to other Filipino jail epics like *The Big Bird Cage*. The rambling structure results in more than a few pacing lulls, or as Joe Bob Briggs would say, there's an awful lot of plot getting in the way of the story. What makes this film memorable is the presence of Grier and Markov, who teamed up again two years later for another quasi-feminist Italian B-movie favourite, *The Arena*. The two women don't receive as much screen time as one might expect from the title and do far less nudity than the anonymous Asian ladies populating the background; indeed, the stars are almost forgotten entirely for the middle third of the film. The ending is also an unexpected downer that negates much of went before it. Luckily the healthy doses of slapping, screaming, and showering are enough to qualify this as a sleazy good time, worthy of at least a single viewing.

Despite its solid run in theatres throughout the '70s, *Black Mama, White Mama* was infernally difficult to see on home video for many years. A crummy, legally dubious version turned up as part of the *Women's Penitentiary* series before Orion finally went back to the original materials for their overdue VHS version a few years ago. The MGM DVD looks even better, with an anamorphic letterboxed presentation (who'd have ever expected that?) that brings out as much colour and texture as you could expect from a film of this vintage. A couple of very minor source blemishes crop up, but the quality looks great, particularly for the low price, and the sound is crystal clear. The disc includes the US theatrical trailer in a somewhat different form than the one previously included on Something Weird's compilation tape, *Afros, Macks and Zodiacs*.

BLACK NARCISSUS

Colour, 1947, 101m. / Directed by Michael Powell and Emeric Pressburger / Starring Deborah Kerr, Sabu / Criterion (US R1 NTSC), Video Collection (UK R2 PAL)

The surging interest in the dynamic British filmmaking team of Michael Powell and Emeric Pressburger beginning in the 1980s was led primarily by the restoration of *Black Narcissus*, a feverish, erotically charged, but exquisitely tasteful film harmed by numerous altered

B

or censored versions and critical indifference over the years. The situation has now changed, of course, as this film has now been ranked with *The Red Shoes* as one of the team's best films and perhaps their greatest achievement ever in Technicolor photography.

The deliberate story begins when Sister Clodagh (Deborah Kerr) and her holy sisters trek into the wilds of Himalayas, where a former holy palace for concubines is being transformed into a school and clinic for the local Indian children. The studly overseer in a silly hat, Mr. Dean (David Farrar), ignites previously suppressed passions in the sisters, who are also having difficulty coping with the high altitude, the constantly blowing wind, the carnally tempting murals, and a brewing romance between two of their additional charges, a pompous prince (Sabu) and a rejected young peasant girl, Kanchi (Jean Simmons). Sister Clodagh experiences flashbacks to the one man in her life, a suitor back in Ireland who planned to desert her for America, and contemplates the difficulty of maintaining a spiritual life while surrounding by temptation. The oldest of the group, Sister Philippa (Flora Robson), decides to leave following an unfortunate incident involving a young baby and some castor oil, while the mentally unstable Sister Ruth (Kathleen Byron) develops an unhealthy sexual obsession with Mr. Dean, who barely knows she exists.

The concept of physically tempted nuns was strong stuff back in 1947, though compared to the likes of Ken Russell's *The Devils* (with which this bears more than a few passing thematic similarities), *Black Narcissus* is sedate by today's standards, at least in terms of onscreen action. Don't be fooled, however; the film still packs a powerful punch, thanks to the heady intensity of its colour photography and the inexorable slide towards a chilling finale, with a beautifully handled, gasp inducing climax choreographed to Brian Easdale's unsettling score. Cinematographer Jack Cardiff, who also photographed *The Red Shoes* and went on to direct *Girl on a Motorcycle*, deservedly earned an Oscar for his work here; unbelievably, the entire film was shot in Pinewood Studios except for a few handy exterior shots.

Criterion's earlier laserdisc of *Black Narcissus* contained the complete British cut, including all of Kerr's flashbacks and the full "lipstick" scene, with a very attractive transfer. The DVD looks excellent as well, but there wasn't a tremendous amount of room for improvement in the first place. Colours look splashy or subdued when they should, and the tiny details in each amazing matte painting are clearly rendered. The commentary track from the earlier disc by Martin Scorsese and the late Powell has been retained here; though not scene specific, it's enlightening and a joy to hear for film buffs as these two pros discuss the various difficulties in mounting an elaborate production like this with such restrictive means. A rather battered theatrical trailer and some rarely seen production stills are also included, as well as a 27 minute featurette, "Painting with Light." This excerpt from an upcoming documentary by Craig McCall dedicated to Cardiff's cinematography covers everything you could want to known about the visual creation of this film and includes a handy visual demonstration of the three strip Technicolor process, as well as a host of interviews with various crew members and appreciative fans like Scorsese. Far less impressive is the UK disc, featuring a lacklustre pre-restoration transfer.

BLACK SABBATH

Colour, 1964, 93m. / Directed by Mario Bava / Starring Boris Karloff, Mark Damon, Michele Mercier / Image (US R0 NTSC) / WS (1.85:1) (16:9)

The lost art form of the horror anthology doesn't get much creepier than *Black Sabbath*, a trilogy of chilling tales from Italian horror maestro Mario Bava. American horror star Boris Karloff made a rare overseas appearance as host of these tales and provided an unforgettable appearance in the centre tale, one of the most haunting vampire yarns ever committed to celluloid.

Our first episode is "The Telephone," an early giallo (or Italian thriller) in which a voluptuous high class escort girl, Rosy (Michelle Mercier), is terrorized by threatening phone calls. Her vicious pimp, Frank, has just been released from prison and may be responsible, so she calls her former lover, Mary (Lidia Alfonsi), for comfort. Obviously, not everyone survives to see the morning.

In "The Wurdulak," young journeyman Vladimire (Mark Damon) stumbles upon a decapitated corpse along a mountainous road. Eventually he arrives at a desolate home where a frightened family awaits the return of its patriarch, Gorca (Karloff). That night the head of the household shows up, looking quite spooky and brandishing the severed head of a notorious thief and "wurdulak," a vampire who feeds on the blood of his loved ones. As the night passes, the family succumbs one by one to vampirism...

And finally in the film's tour de force, "The Drop of Water," nervous Helen (Jacqueline Pierreux) is called in late at night to prepare the corpse of a recently deceased medium who died during a séance. The ghastly expression on the body's face unnerves Helen, but she still musters the courage to pocket a valuable ring from the dead woman's finger. Meanwhile a fly buzzes nervously around the room, and a repetitive drop of water echoes throughout the room. When Jacqueline returns home, she is terrorized by repeated drops of water... a buzzing fly... and much, much more...

A pure exercise in style that almost makes *Black Sunday* look anaemic, *Black Sabbath* is one of Bava's greatest achievements and a perfect introduction to his style of filmmaking. Originally shown in Europe as *The Three Faces of Fear*, the film was released in the US by AIP under its most famous title in a drastically toned down, altered edition which featured new intros and segues with Karloff, a massive overhaul on "The Telephone" which transformed it into an avenging ghost story, and some mild censorship during the more graphic moments of "The Wurdulak." To make matters worse, the stories' order was shuffled in the following order: "The Drop of Water," "The Telephone," then "The Wurdulak."

The US version is still undeniably effective and has brought about more than a few nightmares among impressionable viewers, but the unadulterated Italian version has been preserved on this DVD. Apart from the obvious substitution of a dubbed Italian actor instead of Karloff's warm, familiar voice, this edition is entirely satisfying and features the original, restrained music score by Roberto Nicolosi instead of the fun but uneven American music by Les Baxter. And of course, the infamous joke punch-line with Karloff at the end is finally back in all its surreal glory. The Image DVD, part of their "Mario Bava Collection," looks infinitely better than any past video edition. The US version has turned up in various incarnations, including a US laserdisc double bill with *Black Sunday*, while Japan and Italy have seen letterboxed editions of the Italian cut.

The anamorphically enhanced DVD looks beautiful, with only a few mild age blemishes detracting from an otherwise full bodied and enchanting presentation. Colours are strong and vivid, while countless bits of background detail are now completely visible. For some reason the original source material contains some mild jittering during the final moments of "The Drop of Water" (which also contain virtually no dialogue, unlike the US version: "...something too terrifying to live through!"). "The Telephone" in particular benefits from the added clarity, with some of Bava's candy coloured lighting schemes now vividly brought to life throughout the entire story. The optional yellow English subtitles are well rendered and appear to be accurate. The disc also includes an amusing Italian theatrical trailer, which cheerfully reveals all of the film's scariest moments and contains the unique pitch line: "Mercy! Scary!" How true, how true.

BLACK SUNDAY

B&W, 1960, 86m. / Directed by Mario Bava / Starring Barbara Steele, John Richardson / Image (US R0 NTSC) / WS (1.85:1) (16:9)

Though technically not the first Italian horror film, *Black Sunday* remains the ultimate example of "spaghetti horror" for most worldwide critics and horror fans. Like other groundbreaking titles ranging from *Frankenstein* to *Psycho*, its elements have become so completely absorbed into the horror movie tradition that it doesn't seem as shocking or unique now as it did in 1960. Fortunately, *Black Sunday* thrives on much more than brutal violence and spooky, fog-enshrouded trees; for his first solo directorial effort, expert cinematographer Mario Bava used all of the cinematic tricks at his disposal to craft an entirely fantastic landscape on film. Using painterly black and white photography and clever camera placement, Bava loosely adapted Nikolai Gogol's short story, "The Vij," into a bewitching dream on film which continues to captivate thirty years later.

In the infamous prologue, the wicked Princess Asa (Barbara Steele) is condemned by her brother to be burned at the stake. Before her death, she proclaims a curse upon the house of Vajda, for which she promptly receives a spiked demon mask hammered into her face. Asa's faithful sidekick, Javutich (Arturo Dominici), is executed as well for his troubles. Two hundred years later, young Dr. Andrej Gorobe (John Richardson), on the way to a medical conference, finds himself in the same village haunted by the malefic influence of Princess Asa. The beautiful young Katia (also Steele), a Vajda descendant, first appears to Andrej while walking two dogs in a graveyard (a great image) and eventually calls Andrej and his mentor, Professor Kruveian (Andrea Checci), into her home to aid her elderly father (Ivo Garrani). As it turns out, the mysterious graveyard is actually the resting place of Asa and Javutich; thanks to some spilled blood and a knocked-over cross during a bat attack on Kruveian, Asa rises from the grave and commands her loyal servant to do so as well. The evildoers proceed to cause havoc in the Vajda castle and wreak their bloodthirsty vengeance, with Asa determined to rule the household that once destroyed her.

Perhaps because of its reliance on established gothic traditions to tell an accessible, linear narrative, *Black Sunday* has been regarded as the Italian horror film for people who don't really like horror films. Though gory at times, it still feels rooted in classic monster tradition with the more subversive aspects (necrophilia, avenging sexuality, religious sadism, and so on) largely left to the viewer's imagination.

Unfortunately, critics usually cite *Black Sunday* as Bava's only "good" film and the benchmark against which all other Italian horror should be measured. At least a dozen of Bava's other films are easily as accomplished and impressive, perhaps even more so, though there's no denying that the alchemy of contrasting elements works here amazingly well. Many of Bava's trademark themes have already become lodged firmly in place: the nest of vipers seething within the confines of the family home; the ability of the dead to exert an inescapable power over the living and confuse such constants as identity and time (see *Lisa and the Devil* for the logical conclusion); and the morbid intermingling of sensuality and death.

In her first horror role, Steele makes a dynamic, fascinating central figure, which understandably became one of horror's most indelible icons. Under Bava's sure hand, she delivers something unearthly that can scarcely be described as a traditional performance.

A rare Bava film to receive high profile distribution and enduring popularity, the film was initially released in Italy under the title *La maschera del demonio*. A translation of this title, *Mask of Satan*, appeared on circulating European prints, but AIP picked it up for US release and retitled it *Black Sunday*. Not surprisingly, some of the gorier images were trimmed down: a few extra seconds of blood and branding during the mask-pounding, a shot of a spike piercing a corpse's eye, and a much longer sequence of a character's face roasting in a fireplace. In addition, a romantic chat between Katia and Andrej wound up on the cutting room floor, and AIP inserted a new, brash music score by Les Baxter onto the soundtrack. (In all honesty, Roberto Nicolosi's more suggestive score is serviceable but hardly the most accomplished work of his career.) Even in diluted form, *Black Sunday* remained very strong stuff, meriting a word of warning at the beginning of the US prints and an outright ban in the UK until 1968. The most complete version available on Japanese laserdisc remained out of reach for most Italian horror fans, while many domestic public domain companies offered a slightly trimmed down version of the European cut or the UK video release from Redemption.

The Image DVD, bearing the original *Mask of Satan* title, is the long awaited answer to many a horror fan's prayers. The print itself is in excellent condition, with only the opening credits sequence displaying any distracting signs of wear. The crisp black and white visuals, enhanced for widescreen televisions, look much better than the prior Image/HBO laserdisc release of the US cut (paired up with AIP's *Black Sabbath*). While completists may want to hang on to the laser for nostalgia reasons, this version should now be considered definitive. The original dubbing, music, and extra footage are all intact, and the most famous visuals now look better than ever: the slow motion carriage ride, the spine-tingling shots of Asa staring up from her crypt, and the gorgeous, Cocteau-like image of Asa's disciples stepping out of the smoking Vajda fireplace, to name but a few.

The disc also includes the original *Mask of Satan* European trailer, which emphasizes the action aspects of the film (and misspells Steele's name, just like the film itself). A handy collection of photos and international poster art features some eye-opening surprises, such as a daylight shot of Dominici with his unused vampire fangs and the film's rarely seen British reissue poster. Also, an interesting note about the original Italian print contains a translation of a scene between Katia and her father, which was nixed from all English language prints.

The greatest point of interest, though, is the running commentary by Tim Lucas; simply put, if there's anything you ever wanted to know about *Black Sunday*, it's probably in here. Basically a feature length audio version of a Watchdog article, Lucas' discussion deftly bounces between cinematic and literary antecedents, thumbnail sketches of all the major participants, and odd bits of trivia and personal observation. For example, the only two films he directly advises viewers to seek out are *Bloody Pit of Horror* and *Viy*, which would make a highly unusual double feature. Lucas includes some startling proposals about directions the film may have taken during shooting, including conjecture about Katia being possessed much earlier by Asa in the film before creative alternate scripting and editing took over. Overall, the wild deluge of facts may be too much for Euro-novices to absorb in one sitting but should keep Watchdogs entertained and enlightened throughout, all the way to the last 90 seconds (in which several minutes' worth of closing thoughts are miraculously stampeded in before the closing titles).

BLACK TIGHT KILLERS

Colour, 1966, 87m. / Directed by Yasuharu Hasebe / Starring Akira Kobayashi, Chieko Matsubara / Image (US R0 NTSC) / WS (2.35:1) (16:9)

While maverick director Seijun Suzuki has become a cult favourite example of Japanese cinema at its most excessive and stylized, *Black Tight Killers* offers an equally dazzling display of pop art compositions, groovy music, and outrageous plot twists, all performed in tongue-in-cheek style by an enthusiastic cast. The title pretty much sets the mood, not to mention opening credits featuring a line of foxy femmes in skin-tight Emma Peel outfits go-go-ing their hearts out on Day-Glo sets out of a '50s MGM musical.

Upon returning from a combat tour as a photographer in Vietnam, Hondo (Akira Kobayashi) goes out for a dinner date with pretty Yoriko (Chieko Matsubara) only to see her abducted by a band of female killers in black tights. The assailants leave behind a dead man whose murder is pinned on Hondo by the police, but fortunately a friend show up to supply him with an alibi. Hondo begins to track down the missing girl and constantly runs into the black-clad assassins, who have a habit of showing up at convenient moments to either help or hinder him. Are they evil pranksters, or is there some deeper conspiracy at work here?

Often hilarious in its whiplash transitions from one exploitable scene to another, *Black Tight Killers* doesn't take itself seriously for a moment but manages to wipe out an astonishing percentage of the cast before the closing credits. Matsubara manages to remain sympathetic and believable even during the most outrageous events, with characters often flying out of windows, prancing around in skimpy outfits, and using ancient secret ninja defence techniques like bubble gum spitting and album hurling. Extra bonus points for the swanky lounge soundtrack, which adds immeasurably to the fun. Austin Powers only wishes he had it this good.

Though not one of the better known Japanese spy film, *Black Tight Killers* has held up well over the years and looks just fine in this print acquired by the American Cinematheque. The punchy colours couldn't look any richer, while the scope framing looks just about right. The master was the only subtitled print in existence (there was no original English language release), so the subs are white and burned-in with touch and go results. Besides, how else are you going to see it? It's basically a sweet and silly little puffball of a movie, but *Black Tight Killers*

offers plenty of fun and action for spy fans, and lots of retro campiness for everybody else. The disc (packaged with extensive liner notes by Chris D. from the Cinematheque) also includes the original Japanese trailer with occasional English pitch lines thrown in to make it more palatable for international viewers.

BLADE

Colour, 1998, 120m. / Directed by Stephen Norrington / Starring Wesley Snipes, Stephen Dorff / New Line (US R1 NTSC), EIV (UK R2 PAL) / WS (2.35:1) (16:9) / DD5.1

A tribute to Hong Kong marital arts and vampire films starring Wesley Snipes doesn't sound like a sure-fire, hit, but against the odds, this adaptation of the intense Marvel Comics cult favourite makes a quantum leap over New Line's prior Gothic comic excursion, *Spawn*; in fact, the dizzying mixture of gory thrills and bone-shattering action makes for ideal pulp entertainment. For once, the avalanche of CGI effects, one-liners, and implausible stunts actually works in the film's favour, creating a delirious, seductive nightmare that simultaneously works as a mindless action popcorn muncher and a perverse slice of bizarre cinema.

Snipes portrays Blade, a heroic vampire hunter whose birth to a woman bitten by a bloodsucker has endowed him with superhuman strength and regenerative powers. On the downside, he also suffers from bloodlust, which is kept in check by his human helper/weapons expert, Kris Kristofferson. After rescuing a beautiful haematologist (N'Bushe Wright) from an attack in a hospital, the two begin a battle against the villainous Deacon Frost (a menacing Stephen Dorff), an upstart vampire hell-bent on reviving an ancient blood god capable of taking over the world.

It would take forever to name all the great little touches in this movie, but the major ones would have to include Traci Lords' unforgettable opening appearance in a very gruesome nightclub event, Eurotrash favourite Udo Kier (in a funny twist on his role in *Andy Warhol's Dracula*) as the head of the vampire council (and whose exit is one of the movie's stylish highlights), Mark Isham's spooky techno-symphonic score (isolated on the DVD with commentary by the composer), and, for once, a very satisfying final scene that actually leaves you hungering for a sequel. For better or worse, *Blade* is also the most relentlessly grisly mainstream film this

B

side of *Hannibal*; how it escaped an NC-17 rating unscathed is a mystery. Once again, New Line has done a terrific job with this Platinum Series edition, featuring a huge array of extras beginning with three featurettes about the origins of *Blade*. Also present are a director's commentary, trailers, and a host of other goodies, including a risible alternate ending. The anamorphic transfer looks very good for an early DVD effort, though the colours are a little more powdery than the theatrical prints. The blistering 5.1 soundtrack never ceases to a home theatre system operating at a fever pitch. The UK disc pares down the extras somewhat from the US disc, most notably leaving off the commentary track.

A BLADE IN THE DARK

Colour, 1983, 109m. / Directed by Lamberto Bava / Starring Andrea Occhipinti, Lara Naszinsky / Anchor Bay (US R1 NTSC) / WS (1.85:1) (16:9), Vipco (UK R2 PAL) / WS (1.66:1)

One of the more violent entries in the Italian slasher cycle of the early '80s, *A Blade in the Dark* attempts to outdo Argento's *Tenebre* in a similar stalk and slash mode that eventually escalates into virtually wiping out the entire cast in the final half hour. Bava's experience behind the camera as assistant director for both his father Mario and for Argento shines through here; amazingly, Blade was only his second film following his promising debut, *Macabre*, and here he cultivates his skills for dealing with irrational fantasy and gore which erupted full force in the later *Demons* films.

Bruno (Andrea Occhipinti), a young composer, is hired by his director friend Sandra (Anny Papa) to score her latest horror film. To get him into the mood, she sends him to stay at a rented villa whose spooky atmosphere will hopefully inspire him to write a truly terrifying score. They both get more than they bargained for, however, when a killer starts stalking the grounds. On his first night, Bruno is startled by a ditzy young woman named Katia (shades of *Black Sunday*!) hiding in the cupboard; the girl dashes off and is quickly slashed to death by an assailant wielding a utility knife. Soon after, another girl who drops by to use the pool winds up disappearing as well. As the suspects begin to add up, even including Bruno's actress girlfriend, Julia (Lara Naszinsky), he begins to put together the pieces of the puzzle and comes to realize that there's more than a passing connection between the film he's scoring and the rising body count in real life.

The true running time for *A Blade in the Dark* (original title: *La casa con la scala nel buio*, or *House of the Dark Stairway*) has long been a matter of dispute among Italian horror followers. The film was originally shot for Italian television (hard to believe considering the extreme gore on display) and planned as four 27-minute instalments. However, the final cut of the film slated for theatrical release, at least in its English language form, wound up at 96 minutes. Essentially the print which appeared on laserdisc from EC Entertainment and earlier on VHS by Lightning Video in the '80s was uncut in terms of being a final "director's cut" for international distribution; however, a somewhat longer version existed only in Italian and has floated through some bootleg tape dealers. While the packaging claims a running time of 104 minutes, Anchor Bay's DVD actually marks the first complete presentation in English of the 109 minute *A Blade in the Dark*; the extra footage doesn't add much in the way of plot development or gore, but it does achieve a more layered, character-motivated approach than the consumer friendly earlier cut. Some of the restored scenes include Bruno making a pay booth call to Julia's boss, more atmospheric night scenes of Bruno exploring the house, a longer build up to the second murder, and several extra red herring bits involving Stanko Molnar as the groundsman, fondling scissors and generally acting suspiciously.

Despite the 16mm origins, *Blade* looks surprisingly good on DVD, some inherent graininess in the original negative notwithstanding. The disc easily blows away the EC laserdisc by several miles, and colours are strong and accurate throughout. The film itself has held up fairly well, thanks mainly to the shocking murder scenes (though the last killing is awfully gratuitous) and an appealing lead performance by Occhipinti, who also appeared in Lucio Fulci's *New York Ripper* and *Conquest* before achieving infamy as the bullfighter who chugs honey off of Bo Derek's navel in *Bolero*. Future horror director Michele Soavi makes a very amusing appearance here and even served as first unit director (hopefully out of costume at the time). The rest of the cast is somewhat less impressive, though this may be due to the ridiculous dubbing ("I love composers; so tell me, how are you in the feathers?" and "Is it possible you're a vacant nerd?" are two of the most oft-quoted offenders). As always, the De Angelis brothers deliver a top notch score, basically a repetitious electronic tune a la *Halloween* that weaves in and out of Bruno's keyboard performances and the murders themselves. Essential viewing for Italian horror fans and beautifully packaged; it's a shame they don't make 'em like this anymore. Extras include a 20 minute "Behind the Blade" interview with Lamberto Bava and writer Dardano Sacchetti, in which they discuss the genesis of the film and the low budget shooting process, and the gory European theatrical trailer.

The non-anamorphic Vipco release in the UK restores the nearly two minutes of bloodshed earlier removed at the demand of the BBFC, but the additional 11 minutes of characters yapping and wandering around hardly constitutes "previously banned footage," as claimed on the packaging.

BLEEDERS (HEMOGLOBIN)

Colour, 1996, 92m. / Directed by Peter Svatek / A-Pix (US R0 NTSC), Int. Licensing (UK R2 PAL) / DD5.1

It's all too fitting that one of the more intriguing horror films of the past few years should wind up going straight to video. This German-Canadian production, which bore the title *Hemoglobin* during its two year tenure sitting on the shelf, quietly slipped into American video stores featuring its cheesy new name and not very subtle box art (squeeze it and watch some fake blood jiggle!), followed amazingly enough by a DVD release. Hiding under the low-grade hype, though, is a thoughtful, strangely poetic tale about the strange lines of human heredity.

Recent émigré Paul Strauss (Canadian actor Roy Dupuis of TV's *La Femme Nikita* and the disturbing *Being at Home With Claude*) travels with his wife (Kristen Lehman) to the small island village of Van Damm's Landing in order to trace his vague, sketchy family tree. Suffering from a strange, unidentified blood disease, Paul and his wife turn to the local boozehound doctor, Rutger Hauer (playing nicely against type and with great restraint), for aid in determining whether his disorder is genetic. It seems the Van Damms, an incestuous family of Dutch smugglers, founded the island but all died mysteriously in a fire 75 years ago. However, Paul exhibits the same traits of blood tampering as the Van Damms, and soon a strange creature chewed up in a local's outboard motor and exhibiting the same odd genetic traits winds up on the doctor's table. Meanwhile, the local cemetery has been unearthed due to the discovery of the local mortician's cheap, cost-cutting coffins; local townie's bodies are missing; and a few of the living have started to disappear...

Boasting impressive production values, sincere performances, and a couple of good, honest scares,

Hemoglobin deserved far better than its cheapo throwaway fate, but at least it fares better on DVD than the miserable VHS version. While most Simitar titles look like bad video bootlegs at best, their full frame transfer here is surprisingly clear and boasts spacious Dolby Surround and Dolby Digital 5.1 mixes, adding considerably to the film's sense of creeping unease and punching up Alan Reeves' evocative synth and guitar score. Unfortunately, the master was done by A-Pix, causing the image to have a weird flat, shot on video appearance similar to their job on Lamberto Bava's *Body Puzzle*, and the dialogue has an artificial digitized quality that most likely was not present in the original film. However, the fact that labels like this are even willing to devote efforts to providing sharp editions of films like this instead of the standard erotic thriller of the week is laudable, and it certainly outclasses the results of substandard companies like Worldvision. A few of the dark scenes betray flaws in the source material (a slight faded strip near the right side of the image, some dusting of grain here and there), but generally this looks much better than would be expected, especially at such a low price. (The later Region 2 release ports over the transfer with a far more attractive cover.)

Horror buffs in particular should enjoy the literate script by Charles Adair, Ron Shusette, and Dan O'Bannon, which features one of the more haunting and depraved (yet subdued) endings in recent memory; in fact, the O'Bannon influence hangs heavily over the film, which exhibits the same Lovecraftian fixations with beasties lurking in dark tunnels, hereditary evil blossoming in the midst of normality, and a quiet New England setting, elements of which turned up in such O'Bannon projects as *The Resurrected* and *Dead and Buried*. While there are a couple of silly moments (the wife wastes no time in having sex with Paul right after he's chowed down on a preserved foetus, and the action during the climax is a little awkward), the story is reverent to its subject matter, fondly recalling the depraved Gothic family horror films of the '60s like *Eye of the Devil, The Shuttered Room*, and *The Dunwich Horror. Bleeders* may not be perfect, but considering the recent drought of decent horror fare, this is a very nice little oasis.

BLIND BEAST

Colour, 1969, 86m. / Directed by Yasuzo Masumura / Starring Eiji Funakoshi, Mako Midori / Fantoma (US R1 NTSC) / WS (2.35:1) (16:9)

A deeply upsetting meeting of the minds between director Yasuzo Masumura (*Giants and Toys*) and legendary gothic horror writer Edogawa Rampo, *Blind Beast* (*Moju*) has become something of a hotly desired title among horror fans after a tantalizing write up in Phil Hardy's *Aurum Encyclopedia of Horror*, followed by the appropriation of its shocking conclusion into a certain widely detested art film in the late '90s. Eventually a new, subtitled edition became available to repertory houses, followed by its quite welcome DVD release. So, how does the film stack up to its reputation?

Accompanied by the strains of mournful chamber music we meet lovely bondage model Aki (Mako Midori), who observes a blind man, Michio (Eiji Funakoshi), obsessively caressing a statue in a museum. Later he shows up as her replacement masseuse and, with the aid of his mother (Noriko Sengoku), abducts the poor girl. She awakens in a darkened warehouse, where the walls and floor are covered with sculpted replicas of eyeballs, breasts, legs... with two giant nude figures as the centrepiece. At first Aki resists her captors, but eventually she and Michio - a sculptor determined to capture her physical and spiritual essence in his craft - commence a mutually destructive relationship based on sex, pain, and obsession, leading to an inevitable, grotesque finale.

Despite the dark and perverse nature of its subject matter, *Blind Beast* contains far more psychological violence than physical. The undeniably effective ending is rendered in an unusual manner of cinematic apostrophe, while the general suffering is delivered more by the actors' primal performances than any brutality directly unleashed on their bodies. This is a long way from the gut-punch gore of earlier Japanese horror like *Jigoku*; instead, *Blind Beast* prefers to burrow into the viewer's psyche by uncovering the potential damage latent in the tension between man and woman. Even the nudity, a long-time staple of "pink" cinema, is depicted in a strange, non-exploitative fashion, particularly as the narrative advances in the third act. Fortunately the experience is leavened by Masumura's astonishing visual approach, which turns each scope composition into a saturated canvas of deep shadows and rich colours. For an interesting double bill, try pairing this one up with the amazing S&M Italian captivity favourite, *The Frightened Woman,* which makes similar use of the same premise and giant sculpted bodies.

Though it has few home video precedents, Fantoma's *Blind Beast* looks about as good as possible for this film. The film elements are clean and

in exceptionally good condition, and while that familiar grungy veneer of '60s Japanese cinema rears its head from time to time, colours and detail are solid where it counts. As with most other comparable titles of its vintage, the mono soundtrack is serviceable but limited; front channel amplification exhibits a little upper end harshness sometimes evident in the original recording. The original Japanese trailer (in scope) is also included.

THE BLOB
Colour, 1958, 86m. / Directed by Irvin S. Yeaworth, Jr. / Starring Steve McQueen, Aneta Corsaut / Criterion (US R1 NTSC) / WS (1.85:1) (16:9)

The small town teenage monster movie par excellence, this goofy and sinfully entertaining chunk of '50s drive-in madness may not be great cinema, but it's hard to resist all the same. A 28 year old Steve McQueen stars as a misunderstood teen named, well, Steve, who's out for a moonlight drive with his sweet girlfriend, Jane (Aneta Corsaut, better known as Helen Crump on *The Andy Griffith Show*). Meanwhile a nearby old man (Olin Howlin) spots a falling meteorite and observes the planetary visitor disgorge a strange blobby substance. Naturally he pokes at it with a stick until the blob hops onto his arm and begins absorbing him. Steve and Jane take the old man to the local doctor's office, where the stellar sludge claims more victims and begins a deadly rampage across the countryside towards town. Nobody believes the frantic teens, who resort to enlisting the aid of their drag racing peers to warn everyone about the creeping, leaping, gliding and sliding villain before it's too late for the entire town and - yes - the world.

Though primitive by today's standards, *The Blob* boasts some unforgettable special effects as the red hunk of massive gelatin runs rampant to the ignorance of those around it. Many other sci-fi films exploited the idea of a formless mass from space, but somehow this is just different. The peppy opening theme song (by an uncredited Burt Bacharach and Hal David, of course), the small town '50s atmosphere, and the intriguing portrayal of teens vs. adults compel the imagination even when the blob itself is out grabbing a smoke for scenes on end. The only major debit is some of the police station sequences, which bog down an otherwise zippy pace. One especially brilliant bit worthy of William Castle finds happy teens in a movie theatre menaced by the blob as it swallows up the projectionist and seeps down along the back walls. Evidently the film impressed an entire generation so much that it has come to represent '50s kitsch, even turning up during the drive-in sequence from *Grease* and inspiring both a campy sequel, *Beware! The Blob* (directed by Larry Hagman) and a respectable, souped-up '80s remake from Chuck Russell.

Someone at Criterion must really, really love this film. It became one of their earliest laserdisc releases in a spiffy widescreen transfer, and now they've updated *The Blob* for a new generation of video collectors with a feature-packed DVD. The film has always looked quite nice and colourful on home video, so the sparkling new anamorphic transfer can best be described as a clearer upgrade of already superior source materials. The image looks spotless and colours have an almost supernatural vibrancy. Note however that many of the actors wear that heavy, orange-tinted make up that results in weird Technicolor shadings found in other '50s titles like *North by Northwest* and virtually everything by Douglas Sirk.

The extras pour in on this disc almost as fast as the blob itself. You get a fold out poster using the same artwork as Criterion's cover, the theatrical trailer, a huge amount of production photos, prop stills, and promotional artwork courtesy of *Blob* collector Wes Shank, and two commentary tracks. (The trailer for Columbia's remake, which was included on the laserdisc, is omitted.) The first commentary features producer Jack H. Harris (*Dinosaurus!*) chatting with the always lively and interesting Bruce Eder. They cover all of the ins and outs of low budget monster moviemaking during that time period, chat about the various cast members, and wax nostalgic about the film's impact on the drive-in and matinee circuits. Then director Irvin S. Yeaworth Jr. (who helmed many Harris projects like *4-D Man*) and Robert Fields (*The Stepford Wives*), who plays Tony in the film, offer their own takes on the shooting experience, with anecdotes involving the location filming in Phoenixville and the various means necessary to convince an audience there's a monster on the loose when the budget doesn't offer much leeway. In short, there's enough here to make even the most ardent Blob-o-phile extremely happy, and those new to the film will find enough reasons to see why it's still worth shouting about.

BLOOD AND BLACK LACE

Colour, 1964, 90m. / Directed by Mario Bava / Starring Cameron Mitchell, Eva Bartok / VCI (US R1 NTSC) / WS (1.66:1)

After more attempts than one could ever want to count, Mario Bava's seminal body count giallo *Blood and Black Lace* has finally been released in a worthy video edition for English speaking viewers. A stripped down, delirious tour of a candy-coloured murder zone, this was really the first film to merge the fashion world with ritualistic murders, and none of its imitators have managed to capture the same level of intensity. Originally released *as Sei donne per l'assassino* (or *Six Women for the Murderer*), Bava's film encountered censorship problems around the world and has been virtually impossible to see in its complete form until now.

In the powerful opening sequence, sneaky model Isabella exchanges a few furtive words with her junkie co-worker outside the Haute Couture fashion salon. She then wanders into the windy night, only to be assaulted by a masked psychopath who disfigures her face with the help of tree bark and strangles her. The murder sets off a chain reaction of terror and suspicion among her co-workers, who fear what she may have written in a recently discovered diary. The salon owner, recently widowed Countess Christina Cuomo (Eva Bartok), and the manager, Max (or Massimo on the Italian track) Morlacchi (Cameron Mitchell), cooperate with the dogged Inspector Sylvester (Thomas Reiner) to untangle the intricate web of drugs, blackmail, and sex which has turned a sleek glamour palace into the stomping grounds for a lunatic. The diary passes through several other hands, all of them swiftly cut down by the ruthless killer, before a double twist ending exposes the nasty truth.

While the storyline may be mechanical in the extreme, Bava uses this rigid structure to weave a series of spellbinding, colourful set pieces much in the style of an MGM musical, with the plot stopping every ten minutes or so for another wild demonstration of virtuosity. Particularly dazzling is an extended chase scene through an abandoned antique shop at night, illuminated by Bava's signature gel lighting and accompanied by Carlo Rustichelli's terrific Latin-influenced score. While most of the performers are simply fodder for their inevitable turn with the killer, Bartok and Mitchell manage to turn in intriguing performances, alternately vulnerable and suspicious, while the women look appropriately lovely in their designer label perfection. For proof of this film's influence beyond the Euro horror market (which spent at least one decade imitating it), look to such relatively recent slasher films as *I Know What You Did Last*

Summer, which cribs the entire antique store sequence almost shot for shot. Accept no substitutes.

The complete history of *Blood and Black Lace* has become an exercise in frustration for many horror fans. The original US prints and first VHS video (from Media Home Entertainment) were trimmed, with the opening murder of Isabella lacking a few brutal seconds of her tree bashing. More significantly, the bathtub murder near the climax of the film was missing several shots of Claude Dantes in a see-through bra, floating dead in the tub as blood begins to seep from her wrists. The Japanese laserdisc was likewise edited but at least WS (a little overzealously at 1.85:1), fairly colourful, and containing the beautiful original European opening titles shot by Bava himself (under the *Six Women for a Murderer* title). Sinister Cinema released a semi-letterboxed edition on video a few years ago, containing the full bathtub murder but taken from a touch-and-go print littered with scratches and speckles. Then came the Roan edition on laserdisc, which included the amusing opening US credits (from Filmation) in very poor shape, with warbly sound, but restored the first murder. Unfortunately the bathtub murder was still cut, causing a severe jump cut as the killer's mask is removed, not to mention a gash in the music; considering that this is arguably the most famous scene in the film (and immortalized uncut in the opening credits of Pedro Almodóvar's *Matador*), this oversight was galling. VCI's DVD rectifies all of these problems, using a beautiful letterboxed transfer prepared for Australian television and grafting on the European credits (along with a mercifully tasteful video-generated title card), which are in slightly inferior condition but still quite watchable. The transfer boasts gorgeous saturated colours and generally good black levels which only become slightly unstable in a couple of scenes during the first reel.

The disc includes the original English dialogue track as well as the Italian and French tracks, with optional English subtitles translated from the Italian (which makes for some very interesting comparisons). Tim Lucas provides a commentary very much in the vein of his previous work on the *Black Sunday* disc; scholarly but never dull, he packs in a tremendous amount of information accumulated from decades of research, including biographical trivia, filming anecdotes, and aesthetic observations guaranteed to enhance one's appreciation of the film. The DVD also includes the original US trailer, as well as virtually identical French and Italian trailers, bonus trailers for *Erik the Conqueror* and the French trailer for *The Whip and the Body*, as well as a video

interview of Cameron Mitchell by David Del Valle (carried over from the Roan laser) and a video interview with Mary Arden. The factual information in the Mitchell interview is highly questionable- Mitchell claims to have made six films for Mario Bava and refers to his filmmaking son as "Umberto" instead of Lamberto. Other goodies include a gallery of photos and promotional art, an isolated soundtrack presentation of four tracks from the original rare Italian vinyl release, and the alternate American credits.

BLOOD FEAST

Colour, 1963, 66m. / Directed by Herschell Gordon Lewis / Starring Mal Arnold, Connie Mason / Image (US R1 NTSC), Tartan (UK R0 PAL)

 Commonly held in high esteem (or contempt) as the first genuine gore film, *Blood Feast* became a grassroots phenomenon and enshrined director H.G. Lewis and producer David F. Friedman in the drive-in hall of fame. Bereft of the qualities that characterize "good" movies, this twisted camp classic instead delivers an avalanche of gruesome dismemberment and howlingly bad acting, resulting in a strangely appealing and tawdry mixture, which has yet to be duplicated.

Sweet little Suzette (*Playboy* Playmate and non-actress Connie Mason) is oh so happy about her upcoming birthday party. Her mother (Lyn Bolton), a dowdy matron whose outfits are more terrifying than anything else in the film, consults a local Egyptian caterer, Fuad Ramses (Mal Arnold). By sheer coincidence, Suzette and her not-terribly-bright cop boyfriend, Pete (Thomas Wood), attend a local class on Egyptian cults and learn about the savage blood rites of the Egyptian god Ishtar (or Eetar, or about ten other pronunciations). Could this have something to do with the vicious murders of young women being committed in this sleepy Florida town? Well, since Fuad is seen wielding his machete from the opening scene, it's clear he's planning Suzette's party as the climax of his "blood feast" to pay tribute to the spray-painted mannequin deity in his restaurant.

Impossible to take seriously on any level, *Blood Feast* compels the viewer simply by topping itself in the gore department. Unlike the *Friday the 13th* films, which mostly tease the viewers with quick and timid flashes of grisly mayhem, Lewis and company, trot out the whole dog and pony show under a spotlight. Legs are hacked off, skulls pulled open, tongues yanked out... and so on. Meanwhile the laughs build up faster than any slasher spoof ("Leg Cut Off!" yells one newspaper headline), while Mal Arnold delivers a hand-wringing villainous performance that actually makes Tod Slaughter look subtle.

A home video stalwart since the dawn of VHS, *Blood Feast* has changed hands so many times it seemed a definitive presentation would be impossible. Luckily the rights fell to Something Weird Video, who wisely chose to inaugurate their DVD line with this irresistible tribute to one of the key '60s horror films. Most obviously, the film looks terrific from start to finish; the gaudy reds and blues in most of the backgrounds have never looked as hypnotic as they do here. Something Weird's previous VHS release was a tantalizing teaser, but this disc is easily the main course. The continuity goofs in Arnold's grey-dyed hair become even more obvious, and the show-stopping tongue tearing looks even more... uh, vivid, than ever.

The soundtrack is about as good as can be expected, given the basic microphone set ups and Lewis'" minimalist" tuba and percussion score. SW's Mike Vraney appears on a very entertaining commentary track in which he manages to coax out amazing tidbits of information from Lewis and Friedman. In fact, it's hard to resist any commentary that kicks off by pointing out *Blood Feast* was edited by Gary Sinese's father! Interestingly, the film's legacy continues on well past the drive-in crowd; even John Waters included affectionate clips from it in *Serial Mom*.

Extras on the DVD include the familiar (and long) theatrical trailer, which includes many of the soppiest highlights, a gallery of H.G. Lewis and Friedman ad mats and poster art, and the bizarre "Carving Magic," a twenty minute educational short by Lewis which features Wood and Harvey Korman (also in Lewis' *Living Venus*) in the tender saga of a married man's quest to become the perfect carver. Given the context of its placement on this DVD, the short becomes far more macabre than intended as the camera lingers obsessively on each succulent slice of animal flesh. Best of all, the disc includes 49 minutes of *Blood Feast* outtakes, previously released on VHS from Something Weird along with unused snippets from its two companion pieces, *Two Thousand Maniacs* and *Color Me Blood Red*. Amazingly, these lost images include some nudity during the opening bathtub sequence and some gore in the climactic garbage truck finale - all accompanied by judicious snippets of the film's score and dialogue. The Region 2 disc is missing both the commentary and nearly half a minute of splatter footage but does contain 11 tracks of the, uh, music score, to use the term lightly.

BLOOD MANIA

Colour, 1970, 80m. / Directed by Robert O'Neill / Starring Peter Carpenter, Maria De Aragon / Rhino (US R1 NTSC)

"Plunge into a night of unspeakable terror!" gasps the cover for *Blood Mania*. At least they got the unspeakable part right. Drive-in and sleaze palace viewers were often suckered in during the early '70s by this low-thrill "psychological thriller" masquerading as a gore film, and now you can relieve the experience of waiting in vain in your very own home with this shiny little disc.

Victoria (Maria De Aragon) is what you might call an unstable girl, though part of the problem may be the company she keeps. Her lust for Craig Cooper (Peter Carpenter), a young doctor, gives her the brilliant idea of coaxing along her father to the grave in order to provide him with money to pay off a nasty blackmailer, Larry (Arell Blanton), who's been keeping secrets about Cooper's abortion service during med school. When Victoria's father (who also happens to be Cooper's boss at the hospital) finally dies, the money and the estate pass on to Victoria's sister instead, triggering a deadly chain reaction.

Blood Mania seems to have the basic ingredients for a trashy good time: the inept animated opening credits which segue into nightmarish footage of a woman running past coloured gel lighting, the labyrinthine plot laced with scuzzy elements like murder and rampant sex, and a slinky female lead whose weird paintings indicate something isn't quite right upstairs. So why is this such a complete bust? The obvious lack of blood would be an obvious starting point, though at least there is one violent killing in the last five minutes. The sex scenes are also extremely drab, with nudity kept to a minimum as characters loll around in bed yapping about the plot. Then there's the cast, made up of actors like Carpenter and the always colourful Alex Rocco (both of whom did better work for Russ Meyer); at least De Aragon is marginally compelling in the most dynamic role of the film. (Trivia note: she's reportedly also the one inside Greedo's costume in the original *Star Wars*.)

Naturally Rhino chose to deliver the best transfer of its budget DVD series for the lousiest movie. Many of their past transfers have been notoriously awful, especially *Galaxina*, but evidently Crown International turned over the original negative for this one. The image quality looks absolutely pristine and vibrantly colourful, with the open matte image far more detailed and blemish free than the old VHS prerecords that used to turn up in mom and pop video stores during the '80s. The hilarious trailer (which tries to make this look much more exciting than it really is) looks equally immaculate, making one wonder exactly what weird twist of fate determines which Grade-Z movies should survive the ravages of time. The mono audio is also spotless and crystal clear, except for the mediocre recording quality of the original that muffles a few lines of dialogue. Press materials announced this film as having an 88 minute running time, but the version that's been circulating for decades has clocked in at 80 minutes. One can only wonder whether anything was ever cut out, but if it was more dialogue, we should all be thankful.

THE BLOOD SPATTERED BRIDE

Colour, 1972, 101m. / Directed by Vicente Aranda / Starring Simon Andreu, Maribel Martin / Anchor Bay (US R1 NTSC) / WS (1.85:1) (16:9)

 Thanks to its title alone, this Spanish entry in the lesbian vampire craze of the 1970s became a 42nd Street and drive-in favourite. Like most European horror films it suffered a number of heavy cuts before reaching the States, but its bizarre imagery and visceral nastiness still gripped viewers well into the home video era. Now fully restored to its original perverse glory, this film will never be perceived in quite the same way again. Forming a sort of sexy, dreamlike trilogy along with Harry Kumel's *Daughters of Darkness* and Roger Vadim's *Blood and Roses,* this nominal adaptation of J. Sheridan LeFanu's oft-filmed "Carmilla" strays far from its source but still captures the twisted essence of the Gothic vampire tale.

Here we have an unstable young bride, Susan (Maribel Martin), who's prone to hallucinating rape attacks while her chauvinist husband (Simon Andreu) is out of the hotel room. She insists they change hotels, so the not quite happy couple winds up at an ancestral home vaguely connected to the husband. They discover historical markers relating to the home's original family, the Karnsteins, and Susan experiences violent dreams involving a strange woman in white. One day while strolling out on the beach, the husband discovers a naked woman (Alexandra Bastedo) buried in the sand, with only her snorkel providing her air. He digs her out and takes her home, where she reveals herself to be Mircalla Karnstein - who, not so coincidentally, is the same woman from Susan's dreams. Repelled by her husband's macho demands, Susan falls under Mircalla's spell and embarks on a spree of bloody mayhem.

In its familiar, censored 80 minute form, *The Blood Spattered Bride (La novia ensangrentada)* is a fascinating but incomplete horrific fantasy laced with unexpected surrealism and nudity. This restoration significantly reinstates a number of graphic sequences, including a jolting amount of frontal nudity and genital-related violence, but it also greatly improves the pacing of the film. Mircalla's memorable discovery on the beach, arguably the highlight of the film, doesn't occur now until an hour into the film, and the character of Carol (Rosa Rodriguez), has been greatly expanded and now plays a vital role in the story's development. Rumours have abounded about various versions of the film, with prints altered to emphasize either the nudity or the gore, and the infamous heart-cutting finale has been the subject of much speculation over the years. It's difficult to imagine the film any stronger than what's on this disc, and the extended ending could be one of those rumours along the same lines as the piranha sequence from *Cannibal Holocaust*. In any case, the film itself will not appeal to all tastes, thanks to the slow pacing and disorienting storyline, but game viewers will be rewarded with a unique vampire tale graced with hefty dollops of eroticism. The strange, jittery music score creates unease from the opening scene, and the evocative imagery of director Aranda (who later helmed the torrid Victoria Abril vehicle, *Lovers*) wouldn't look out of place in one of Jean Rollin's vampire sagas.

Anchor Bay's DVD of *The Blood Spattered Bride* should satisfy the film's fans and looks vastly superior to the muddy, full frame tapes released by companies like MPI over the years. However, the added clarity also emphasizes the film's age, and like many '70s Spanish films, the shadows have a tendency to become brown and muddy in darker scenes. A great deal of restoration efforts obviously went into this title, however, and seeing it look this good is a welcome event for Eurofanatics indeed. The blood in particular during Susan's horrific nightmare is the most vivid you'll ever see on a television screen. Also included is the wacko US combo trailer with *I Dismember Mama*, which has been amazing home video collectors since its inclusion on *Mad Ron's Prevues from Hell* many years ago.

BLOOD SURF

Colour, 2000, 88m. / Directed by James D. R. Hickox / Starring Dax Miller, Katie Fischer / Trimark (US R1 NTSC) / WS (1.85:1) / DD5.1

Cecily (Katie Fischer), a freelance film-maker, and her unscrupulous producer boyfriend Zack (Matt Borlenghi) arrive at a remote island off the coast of Australia to shoot documentary footage of Bog (Dax Miller) and Jeremy (Joel West) engaged in the extreme sport of blood surfing. This plainly insane adrenaline-junkie passtime involves baiting shark infested waters with fish guts, lacerating their own feet and then surfing like hell to escape the voracious shoal of man-eaters. What none of them have realised is that this is also the domain of a deadly saltwater crocodile. Worse yet, their potential rescuer turns out to be unhinged and out to settle a score with the beast. "I guess that's what you call croc teasing," one girl says to another as they defiantly flash their boobs and hurl insults at the 30-foot long reptile struggling to catch up with them. It's a dash of buffoonery in an otherwise relatively taut thriller from Sam Bernard and co-writer/producer Robert R. Levy.

Director James Hickox keeps the action moving swiftly along and the fact that the cast are a largely aggravating bunch naturally adds a degree of satisfaction to watching f/x honcho John Carl Buechler's mean old croc scoff them down. There's a cracking surfy surfin' theme tune from John Manzie and, some dodgy model work and iffy CGI aside, the film has a glossy sheen which is largely due to the idyllic locations lending it production values above its station. The first few killings, being mostly off-screen and relatively bloodless affairs, result in considerable shock value during the last third of the film, which features bountiful explicit bloodshed, inclduing a gruesome impaling and a sequence with the croc biting a man in half that makes Quint's demise in *Jaws* look like an attack by a miffed haddock.

The unusual absence of a standard trailer aside, Trimark's NTSC format release of *Blood Surf* provides a couple of additional goodies, namely a multi-angle facility for storyboard/scene comparisons and some "Bonus Footage". An assembly of a couple of dozen unmatted clips which runs a little over 7 minutes, this is more precisely behind the scenes material as we get to see unfinished effects sequences, preparations for shooting and players occasionally talking to the crew behind camera. This footage is time-coded and unfortunately some of it plays without sound. With 24 chapter stops, the feature itself boasts 5.1 Dolby digital sound and a selection of subtitle options (English, Spanish and French). - TG

THE BLOODSUCKER LEADS THE DANCE

Colour, 1975, 89m. / Directed by Alfredo Rizzo / Starring Femi Benussi, Giacomo Rossi Stuart / Image (US R0 NTSC) / WS (1.85:1) **B**

If this title leads you to expect a gothic, Anne Rice-style fangfest, prepare to be disappointed. Eurosleaze fans may find plenty to gnash on with this irredeemably silly and depraved babes-in-a-castle yarn (previously released in the US during the glory days of Media's Private Screenings label as *The Passion of Evelyn*). Seasoned exploitation pro Alfredo Rizzo appeared to be in a very laid back mood here, as he's content to explore aging castle walls and Italian actresses' undraped forms with equal glee. Besides, you've got to admire a European film set in "Ireland 1902" where the actors aren't all saddled with goofy fake accents.

Gorgeous *giallo* staple Femi Benussi and stalwart Giacomo Rossi Stuart *(Kill Baby, Kill!)* head up a game cast going through the motions of what plays like a particularly perverted Scooby Doo episode, replete with red herrings, gratuitous sex scenes, and a dash of blood here and there to justify the title (including a nasty head in the bed homage to Hitchcock's *Under Capricorn*). The prolonged final explanation manages to put Agatha Christie to shame for sheer wordiness and convoluted twists; you'll need a scorecard by the time it's all over.

As with the other Redemption titles, picture quality is amazingly good considering the film's vintage, despite a few signs of wear and tear at the reel changes. The beautiful colour and fine detail make this one of the most visually pleasing of this batch, and the image is letterboxed at 1.85:1. Contrary to the promises on the packaging, this does not feature a fanged Count with a bad complexion and the disposition of Pol Pot!

THE BLOODY JUDGE

Colour, 1969, 89m. / Directed by Jess Franco / Starring Christopher Lee, Leo Genn, Maria Schell / Redemption (UK R0 PAL) / WS (2.35:1)

A high profile attempt to cash in on the same wave of religious persecution horror so prevalent in the late '60s, Jess Franco's glossy but impersonal *The Bloody Judge* lies somewhere between the lofty aspirations of Michael Reeves'

Witchfinder General and the unabashed sleazy wallowing of *Mark of the Devil*. Filmed luxuriously in scope during Franco's tenure with notorious producer Harry Alan Towers, *The Bloody Judge* was slapped with a ridiculous title change (*Night of the Blood Monster*) and shuffled off to US drive-ins on a double bill with various Hammer titles like *Blood from the Mummy's Tomb*. Unfortunately, this version was also hacked down to receive a PG rating, but DVD owners capable of viewing PAL-compatible discs can now feast on the longer European English language print of Franco's historical opus.

During the reign of King James II, the stern Lord George Jeffries (Christopher Lee) oversees the trials and persecutions of local witches while dealing with the delicate political balances of various warring factions. The waffling Earl of Wessex (Leo Genn) watches it all with a degree of irritation, while his son, Harry (Hans Hass, Jr.), carries on an affair with Mary (Franco regular Maria Rohm), the sister of a condemned witch, Alicia (Margaret Lee). Meanwhile, in proper *Macbeth* fashion, a blind prophet in a cave, Mother Rosa (Maria Schell), frequently intones about the various miseries that will befall the land before a change in power. In the meantime, Jeffries uses his wicked disciple, the hysterically named Satchel (Milo Quesada), to do his bidding and keep all those witches under control.

Rather than presenting Jeffries as an utterly corrupt, self aware brutaliser like Vincent Price in *Witchfinder General*, Franco takes the odd approach of depicting the historically based figure as a man so firm in his beliefs and warped principles that he doesn't comprehend the full damage being inflicted by his gavel. Unfortunately this treatment also makes him a less menacing and compelling figure, despite Lee's usual commanding performance (mostly confined to sitting behind benches and desks). Otherwise the story is pretty much the same as Reeves', with a young couple torn apart by the misguided religious persecutions inflicted by blind justice. Considering this potential and the man behind the camera, though, it's amazing how mild Franco's version is. Extremely talky, *The Bloody Judge* falls squarely with another Franco/Towers production, *Justine*, by playing more like a costume melodrama punctuated with an odd torture scene that seems to have strayed in from a different movie.

The print on the DVD contains a fairly strong, bloody sequence with Alicia's barely covered body being tortured on the rack by Franco stalwart Howard Vernon (in a very funny costume), but aside from a couple of dimly lit bare bottoms, there's no nudity on display here and precious little violence. However, this is the most complete version available... in English, that is. The German edition, *The Witchhunter of Blackmoor (Der Hexentöter von Blackmoor)*, contains many additional topless and torture scenes (primarily with Ms. Rohm), as indicated by the numerous German production stills included with the DVD. The transfer itself is nothing short of miraculous for anyone accustomed to those bad bootlegs over the years. Generously letterboxed and remarkably clean considering its age, the film looks fantastic from start to finish (apart from a couple of unavoidable scratches). The mono soundtrack is fine if unspectacular, with Bruno Nicolai's rich score (possibly the best thing about the film) surviving intact. The disc also includes a dupey-looking US trailer, poster and video art from around the world, and a handful of English stills.

BLOODY PIT OF HORROR

Colour, 1965, 74m. / Directed by Massimo Pupillo / Starring Mickey Hargitay, Walter Brandi / Image (US R0 NTSC) / WS (1.85:1)

And here it is, the world's greatest Italian homoerotic torture film starring a giant fake spider. Originally released in Italy as *Il boia scarlatto*, this depraved mixture of cheesecake, beefcake, and campy torture devices stunned drive-in patrons in the '60s under the title *Bloody Pit of Horror*, promoted as a derivation of the writings of the Marquis De Sade. Whatever literary basis this film may have had goes flying out the window in the first scene, which finds a busload of models and their photographer/mentor (Walter Brandi) crashing a remote, abandoned castle for a glossy photo shoot. However, the castle isn't completely empty; a maniacal former Hollywood actor named Travis Anderson (Mickey Hargitay, husband of the late Jayne Mansfield) has assumed the persona of the Crimson Executioner, a puritanical torturer from the 17th Century bent on punishing interlopers on his property. Driven over the edge by the presence of his former sweetheart among the models, he proceeds to subject the infiltrators to a variety of tortures ranging from the rack to his ingenious "spiderweb."

Though he never really became a movie star in his own right, Hargitay is the real show here. His bizarre career in Italian horror, which led to such oddities as *Delirium* and *The Reincarnation of Isabel*, really started with his stint here, running around barechested in red tights, rubbing his oiled torso and gushing endlessly about his perfect physique. The bland starlets pretty much pale in comparison, prancing around in bikinis but failing to stand out as characters. However, scream queen spotters should look for giallo regular Femi Benussi, who later popped up in *Hatchet for the Honeymoon* and *Strip Nude for Your Killer.*

Though not artfully made, *Bloody Pit* looks for all the world like a sordid '60s comic book sprung to life, its decadent *fumetti* pages spilling one after the other as scantily clad female forms are transfixed in a variety of fetish-oriented tableaux. Add to that a funky, hilariously inappropriate jazz and funk score, and you've got a one of a kind cinematic experience guaranteed to liven any party.

Though it was widely circulated on the public domain market, *Bloody Pit of Horror* shot up a few notches in Euro horror awareness when Something Weird unearthed a longer alternate American print, entitled *A Tale of Torture*, prepared before Pacemaker removed ten minutes of dialogue from the familiar drive-in version. The image quality was adequate at best, but it was a nice recovery all the same.

Something Weird's DVD offers the best of both worlds with a stunningly colourful print of *Bloody Pit of Horror*, perfectly letterboxed and in marvellous condition, with the extra trims included as a supplement. The sound on this film has never been outstanding, but its flaws may be more readily apparent on DVD where the constant layers of distorted recording and background hiss can pull away the trained ear from the pulpy dialogue and screaming. As eye candy, though, this really can't be beat. The disc also includes as astounding little mondo excerpt called "Cover Girl Slaughter," which features several models forced into increasingly outrageous violent poses for book covers, culminating in an unforgettable, Bava-like tracking shot from one setup to the other. Also included are a snippet from *Primitive Love*, a mondo comedy with Hargitay and Mansfield also on DVD, as well as the US theatrical trailer ("My vengeance needs blood!") and a wild compendium of exploitation promotional art accompanied by lurid radio spots.

BLUE VELVET

Colour, 1986, 120m. / Directed by David Lynch / Starring Kyle MacLachlan, Isabella Rossellini, Dennis Hopper / MGM (US R1 NTSC) / WS (2.35:1) (16:9) / DD2.0, Castle Home Video (UK R2 PAL) / WS (1.77:1) / DD2.0

America's king of cinematic weirdness, David Lynch, took his first nightmarish trip through the underbelly of suburbia with *Blue Velvet* before expanding it into the hellish TV landscape of *Twin*

Peaks. All of Lynch's quirky traits are fully formed here: facetious happy small town images, startling and grotesque characters, twisted sexuality, and surreal camerawork, all set to an uneasy collage of '50s pop tunes. Jeffrey Beaumont (Kyle MacLachlan), a college student, returns to his hometown of Lumberton after his father suffers a debilitating heart attack. While walking through a field, the naive Jeffrey comes upon a severed ear, scoops it up in a baggie, and takes the evidence to the police ("Yep, that's a human ear all right"). Overwhelmed with curiosity, Jeffrey convinces plucky high school girl Sandy (Laura Dern) to help him research the ear, which may be connected (so to speak) to a soulful torch singer, Dorothy Vallens (Isabella Rossellini). When Jeffrey boldly decides to sneak into Dorothy's apartment to search for clues, he gets more than he bargained for from the demonic Frank Booth (Dennis Hopper), a foul-mouthed sadist who holds a terrible secret over Dorothy's head.

An unlikely critical hit during the happy era of *Back to the Future*, this bizarre and beautifully composed film sharply divided viewers in its day but has gone on to be regarded by most as one of the decade's finest films. Those expecting a traditional thriller or a shocking horrorfest are bound to be disappointed, as the horror lies mostly in the venomous, profane tirades of Frank rather than the on camera violence, which is actually relatively mild. Kyle MacLachlan makes for an engaging hero in his follow up role to Lynch's grandiose failure, *Dune*, while the supporting cast can hardly be faulted. The late Jack Nance (*Eraserhead*) and Brad Dourif turn up as Frank's cronies... and is it possible for anyone to ever forget Dean Stockwell lip synching to Roy Orbison's "In Dreams?" On the musical end, the film boasts both a quirky score by Angelo Badalamenti and an early vocal performance by Julee Cruise, who later went on to provide vocals for *Twin Peaks* and ethereal solo albums.

MGM's striking DVD is a welcome relief after years of settling for Warner's incorrectly letterboxed laserdisc and a highly unsatisfying, poorly framed Region 2 disc (which at least boasted a new Dennis Hopper interview). The full width of the scope image has finally been restored on the MGM edition, and anamorphically enhanced, to boot, allowing Lynch's striking colour arrangements to survive intact. If you're not watching this film letterboxed, you're simply not watching it at all. Few filmmakers use a widescreen canvas as well as Lynch, and it's completely vital to understanding the impact of this film. The surround audio is often frightening and makes full use of the rear speakers; the initial famous camera plunge into the severed ear, for example, is accompanied by a chilling roar that announces this film will not be an easy ride. The theatrical trailer is also included and reminds viewers of what a tough sell this movie must have been back in '86. A more expanded Region 1 special edition from MGM includes an even newer Lynch-approved transfer and 5.1 remix, along with a new making-of featurette.

BLUEBEARD

B&W, 1944, 70m. / Directed by Edgar G. Ulmer / Starring John Carradine, Jean Parker / AllDay (US R0 NTSC)

One of the key films by cult director Edgar G. Ulmer, this study of romance and madness in turn of the century Paris belongs to the tradition of such costume horrors as *The Lodger* and *Hangover Square*, both of which also presented sympathetic portrayals of their murdering protagonists. Gaston Morrell (John Carradine), a neglected painter, seems to be like every other struggling Parisian artist. However, he has one nasty flaw, namely a tendency of strangling his female models when he's through with them. His next potential victim, the lovely Lucille (Jean Parker), grows close to Gaston but remains unaware of his homicidal tendencies, while the courts and police anxiously try to track down this dangerous Bluebeard in their midst.

In an unexpected move, Ulmer decided to provide extra layers of subtext to his film by making Morrell not just a painter but a puppeteer as well. Thus, an imaginatively shot version of *Faust* performed with marionettes underscores the film's theme of love's deprivation driving a man to dangerous levels of madness. Carradine shines in perhaps his greatest role, though surprisingly he remains offscreen for several long stretches of the story. Because *Bluebeard* was produced by the notorious poverty row studio PRC, its preservation has been largely hit or miss (but mostly miss) over the years. The film's skimpy production values dictated that it be shot on cheap film and badly processed, so a few sequences such as the climactic chase by the Seine suffer from poor exposure and a heavy saturation of grain.

Most viewers have had to content themselves with blurry, unwatchable public domain tapes over the years, but AllDay's DVD presentation is,

relatively speaking, a tremendous improvement. Apart from the inherent flaws in the original film and a badly damaged credit sequence riddled with vertical scratches, the film looks vastly superior in this French-preserved edition, featuring a much richer contrast scale than ever before and a pleasantly steady image. It doesn't shine like a multimillion dollar restoration job, but considering this marginal title has almost slipped into oblivion, the DVD represents a welcome save by AllDay. The disc contains a fascinating inside booklet detailing all of PRC's suggested marketing strategies, as well as a twelve minute documentary, "Bluebeard Revealed," featuring colour footage of the *Faust* production and interviews with principals involved in its production.

BLUEBEARD

Colour, 1972, 121m. / Directed by Edward Dmytryk / Starring Richard Burton, Raquel Welch, Joey Heatherton / Anchor Bay US R0 NTSC) / WS (1.85:1) (16:9)

A campy and compelling train wreck of a film, *Bluebeard* defies categorization by offering up pitch black comedy, campy lunacy, Nazi era intrigue, graphic gore, and plenty of beautiful European women shedding their clothes. On top of that throw in Richard Burton at his hammiest (and tipsiest), and you've got the recipe for an experience guaranteed to confound those who claim they've seen it all.

Sort of an adult spin on the Charles Perrault fairy tale, our story begins with flying ace Baron von Sepper (Burton) celebrating his marriage to the new Baroness, Anne (Joey Heatherton). And yes, his beard really is blue, thanks to warfare chemical exposure. The Baron takes his new bride home where he snaps cheesecake nudie photos of her, refuses to consummate the marriage, and declares he must go off for a trip to Austria. Before he leaves, Anne snoops around and discovers the housekeeper casually brushing the hair of the Baron's mother. This wouldn't be so odd, except Mom is now a skeletal corpse in a rocking chair! Rather than tearing out of the house in a panic, Anne waves goodbye to her hubby and continues to poke around, eventually discovering a secret key that opens a hidden walk-in freezer behind the Baron's portrait. Inside the compartment are the frozen bodies of the Baron's six previous wives, and of course the Baron has just conveniently called off his trip in time to catch his wife in the act. Declaring that he must kill her when dawn arrives, he spends the evening telling her exactly why he killed them all. His marriage to singer Virna Lisi was spoiled when she wouldn't stop singing day and night, so he came up with a novel means of silencing her. Demure nun Raquel Welch admitted to not being a virgin, then spent every hour rattling off the names of her hundreds of lovers. Nathalie Delon failed to entice him by naming all of her body parts and found love in the arms of sex-ed hooker Sybil Danning. Man-hater Agostina Belli found pleasure by kicking Dickie in the crotch and ordering him to whip her. And Agostina Belli failed to react to much of anything, even when he tossed a cat to his pet falcon. Will Anne be next, or can she manoeuvre out of the Baron's clutches before sunrise?

For all its ridiculous excesses, *Bluebeard* is a slick, sumptuous film; the rooms of Burton's lair feature the loudest colours this side of *Suspiria*, the women all wear frilly diaphanous gowns, and Ennio Morricone's outrageous score wavers between gothic organ solos and lush romantic fugues. Much of the film consists of strange banter between Burton and Heatherton, with the latter getting most of the good lines. One example: "You're a monster! You're inhuman! I spit on you, darling!" Blacklisted director Edward Dmytryk was experiencing something of a comeback with films like *The Caine Mutiny*, but one can only wonder what was going through his head when he co-wrote *Bluebeard* and offered it to everyone's favourite drunken Welshman. The contrived twist ending alone is enough to make one wonder exactly what kind of drugs were circulating on the set. They don't make 'em like this anymore, and there's a very good reason why.

Anchor Bay's DVD looks as good as this film ever has, apparently taken from the original spotless negative. The widescreen framing is a welcome relief after USA's discontinued, terribly cropped VHS version, and the mono audio is extremely strong. The vibrant, psychedelic colour schemes come through just fine, though those garish red on blue credits are still punishing to the eyes. The disc also includes the long version of the US trailer, which reveals every single death scene!

THE BODY BENEATH

Colour, 1970, 82m. / Directed by Andy Milligan / Starring Gavin Reed, Susan Heard / Image (US R0 NTSC)

The recent quest among obscure movie fanatics to unearth and re-evaluate fringe filmmakers has brought some previously ignored talents into the light,

but even some of the staunchest cultists can't quite grasp the films of Andy Milligan, the Staten Island auteur whose work possesses a texture and atmosphere unlike any other. His zero budget horror films look like grainy porno loops, peppered with endless scenes of meandering dialogue, random monsters, and graphic scenes of gore designed to keep audiences from scrambling off to the exit doors. This approach obviously won't be to everyone's taste, but for those looking for something a little different, *The Body Beneath* is one of Andy's proudest moments.

The English countryside (and yes, some of it really is England) has been plagued by a series of vampire attacks by aqua-faced bloodsuckers fond of lurking near graveyards. This handiwork all stems from the corrupt Rev. Alexander Algernon Ford (Gavin Reed), who notices that his bloodline is being to thin out. He decides to track down all of the human family relations and, at Carfax Abbey (natch), replenish the vampiric family tree. Ford and his wife, Alicia (Susan Heard), are especially excited to learn that one of the relatives is pregnant, offering an opportunity to start the undead again from scratch and take off to the US for their new stomping grounds.

Unlike many Milligan films, *The Body Beneath* actually has a linear plotline, clearly delineated characters, and a palpable, effective atmosphere aided by the 16mm photography. This is still an Andy epic through and through, with the director also serving as cinematographer, production designer, costumer, and probably even caterer and electrician. Much has been made in recent articles about the seeping through of Milligan's homosexuality into his films, though his sexual politics, if any, are a wild guess at best. Instead he seems to nostalgically evoke the barnstorming Victorian thrillers popularized by the likes of Todd Slaughter, and one could easily see Milligan tackling a project like LeFanu's *Uncle Silas* and other gothic, anti-clerical yarns, if only the resources had been available.

To understand the pure joy of watching *The Body Beneath* on this DVD, remember that Milligan's films were shot on 16mm and blown up - rather cheaply - to 35mm for theatrical screenings, resulting in a dull, washed out, and unwatchable grainy presentation which has been duplicated on almost every video version of his films. This transfer was derived from the original 16mm materials except for the opening credits, which are in noticeably inferior condition. The difference is dramatic to say the least and makes viewing this film a far more pleasurable

B

experience. One can only wonder how other significant Milligan films would fare with this kind of restoration. This print also contains a previously deleted sex scene, during which Milligan's camera sports a bizarre habit of lingering on the nude couple's foot calluses! The colour schemes are surprisingly ambitious by Milligan standards, and at last the vampire women really look a sickly blue and green rather than the bland grey on the previous video versions.

The DVD also includes *Vapors*, a fascinating artefact from the pre-Stonewall days in which two first time visitors to a New York City bathhouse form a brief, fragile connection and vent their frustrations with their own lives. Amazingly candid and downbeat, this makes *Boys in the Band* look positively chipper and cowardly in comparison. The transfer is the same as Something Weird's previous VHS release, apparently taken from the only surviving print which features a black optical strip placed (more or less) over a glimpse of frontal nudity at the end. Who'da thunk this one would ever wind up on DVD? Other extras include a slew of Milligan trailers (*Guru the Mad Monk, Seeds of Sin, The Ghastly Ones, Vapors, The Body Beneath*, and more), all of which demonstrate how cruddy his films looked on the big screen, and a hefty gallery of early '70s exploitation ad mats, all accompanied by Something Weird's usual, inimitable avalanche of tawdry radio spots. Even for Milligan haters, this is essential viewing for historical value alone.

BODY PUZZLE

Colour, 1991, 98m. / Directed by Lamberto Bava / Starring Joanna Pacula, Tomas Arana / Image (US R0 NTSC)

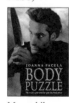

Lovely widow Tracy (*Gorky Park*'s Joanna Pacula) has a problem. Not only has her famous pianist husband Abe died in an auto accident, but someone keeps breaking into her house and leaving severed body parts lying around. Meanwhile a candy store owner is gutted, a poor woman has her hand lopped off in a public bathroom, a young swimmer is castrated, and so on. The investigating police officer, Michael (Tomas Arana), strikes up a hot and heavy romance with Tracy to keep her mind off the rapidly accumulating trophies. Michael's supervising police chief (spaghetti western pro Gianni Garko) tells him to keep his mind on his job; soon Michael concludes that Abe's protégé and probable male lover, unable to cope with the accident, is responsible for the killings. But what's the mysterious link between all of the victims?

A throwback to the delirious Italian mystery films (*gialli*) of the '60s and '70s, *Body Puzzle* was helmed by Lamberto Bava (*Demons*), credited as Larry Louis on the box art but still bearing his real name on the actual print. The serpentine plot involves a few nifty twists (including one "borrowed" from *Body Parts*) and a host of cameo appearances by familiar Italian horror faces like Erika Blanc (*Kill Baby, Kill!, The Devil's Nightmare*) and John Morghen (*Cannibal Apocalypse, Make Them Die Slowly*). Arana and Pacula make for pretty stiff leads, with some of the most unintentionally laughable romantic dialogue in recent memory, but Bava's swift and professional direction manages to keep things under control. Carlo Cordio's throwaway score is overshadowed by the use of classical music played over headphones during the murder scenes (Mussorgsky's "Night on Bald Mountain" here but originally Carl Orff's "O Fortuna" in first run Italian prints).

Like many other horror films, most notoriously Dario Argento's *Opera*, this title was reissued in Italy in a scissored PG-13 level version, *Misteria*; luckily Americans managed to get the full strength cut. Though not as explicitly gory as much of Bava's other work, *Body Puzzle* still contains a few jolting splashes of the red stuff, including one memorable sick sequence in a school for blind children. Though highly implausible, the twist ending delivers a nice change of pace from the usual giallo resolution and should inspire most viewers to go back and retrace how all of the, er, pieces fit together.

Image's DVD looks similar to the earlier laserdisc version licensed through A-Pix. While the A-Pix VHS version was a complete mess, the laser looked fine, with nice dark shadows and crisp sunlit scenery. The DVD is a bit sharper and definitely more affordable, but otherwise it won't come as a drastic revelation for Italian horror fans. The mono sound design is well rendered and dynamic enough to make the absence of stereo less regrettable, and frankly, considering the slick presentation here, there's no reason for any self-respecting Italophile to avoid picking this one up. Incidentally, who on earth is that guy holding a knife on the cover?

THE BOOGEYMAN

Colour, 1980, 83m. / Directed by Ulli Lommel / Starring Suzanna Love, John Carradine

THE DEVONSVILLE TERROR

Colour, 1983, 82m. / Directed by Ulli Lommel / Starring Suzanna Love, Robert Walker, Jr. / Anchor Bay (US R1 NTSC) / WS (1.85:1)

After small oddities like *Cocaine Cowboys* and upon his relocation to America, Lommel turned to the gore genre with *The Boogeyman*, a fun little drive-in favourite that gleefully mixes elements from *Halloween, The Exorcist, The Amityville Horror,* and *Carrie,* among many others, into a gruesome bit of unhealthy and occasionally hysterical horror mayhem.

Lommel's ex-wife, Suzanna Love, stars as a young woman haunted by a childhood memory in which her young brother stabbed their mother and her lover to death. She and her brother return to the traumatic scene, where a mirror in which Love witnessed the carnage has become possessed by the lover's spirit and is wreaking some nasty havoc across the farming community. The outrageous murder sequences had to be intentionally funny, with the celebrated highlight featuring a man skewered through the mouth from behind, after which his girlfriend is bumped by a car door against his face, forming a sort of human shish kebab. Lommel obviously doesn't take the proceedings too seriously and doses it all in heavy red and blue lighting to give it a dreamy, European atmosphere, boosted by the derivative but effective synthesizer score.

Old VHS editions of *The Boogeyman* have been around since the dawn of video, beginning with a fuzzy-looking print from Wizard Video and an improved fullscreen edition a few years ago from Magnum (also released on laserdisc). The original UK release from Vipco hit the video nasties list. In full frame, the movie has a cheesy, made-for-TV appearance that really works against its more ambitious intentions, and the Anchor Bay letterboxed DVD goes some way to correcting that problem. The matting at 1.85:1 crops the compositions down to their original symmetrical intentions, and the increased resolution makes it much easier to watch. Of course, it's still pretty tough to take the movie that seriously (though it's fun as always seeing a latter day John Carradine in a small but memorable role), but it does feature enough of Lommel's trademark emotionally unexpected twists and bizarre visual flourishes to keep genre fans happy.

Far more obscure is *The Devonsville Terror,* a witch persecution horror film Lommel made a couple of years later. Suzanna Love returns as one of three women whose presence in the sleepy town of Devonsville ignites a series of diabolical events recalling a series of heartless witch burnings and tortures 300 years ago. The opening persecution sequence is a classic example of the moody Lommel setup (despite some awfully '80s hairdos and heavy eyeliner for 18th Century women), and occasional moments throughout the film live up to his promise. Donald Pleasence has the token "older actor who knows all" role as a doctor with the pesky problem of tiny worms continually crawling out of his arm (don't ask), and again Love (looking quite different here) does a decent job with the lead. The interesting feminist subtext is never really embellished as well as it could have been, but you have to credit Lommel with trying. The male characters are invariably presented as fascistic jerks whose rage is unleashed when their sexual urges are repressed, not really the most common theme in American cinema. Unfortunately, the finale steals the infamous face-melting from *Raiders of the Lost Ark* to a very uncomfortable degree. In *Video Watchdog,* Lommel professed that this re-enactment was an attempt to expose the inherent fascism of Spielberg's film, but this message is frankly lost entirely in the finished product. Still, it's a moody, sometimes startling film, and while the transfer isn't as crisp and pleasurable as *The Boogeyman,* having a clean letterboxed edition is a welcome addition to any '80s horror library.

BOUND

Colour, 1996, 108m. / Directed by The Wachowski Brothers / Starring Gina Gershon, Jennifer Tilly, Joe Pantoliano / Republic (US R1 NTSC) / WS (1.85:1), Pathé (UK R2 PAL) / WS (1.85:1) (16:9) / DD2.0

Gangland hood Ceasar (Pantoliano), having assisted in the recovery of a fortune in stolen mob money, is awaiting the arrival of boss Gino Marzonne to collect. But Ceasar's duplicitous mistress Violet (Tilly) has conspired with her lover Corky (Gershon) to relieve him of the cash first. They figure that when Ceasar discovers the theft, fearing mob retribution he'll flee, leaving them to quietly disappear $2 million wealthier. Their plans go awry, however, when Ceasar shows more backbone than anticipated; believing he's been set up for a fall by Marzonne's slimy son Johnnie (Chris Meloni) he opts to sit tight and face the music.

Andy and Larry Wachowski's *Bound* is one of the most eloquent erotic thrillers to hit the screen in years. The eroticism is genuinely erotic, the 24-carat thrills spine-tingly thrilling. It runs the emotional racetrack, from the arousing peaks of clandestine sexual encounter between Gershon and Tilly to the dark valleys of alarming violence, most notably a wince-inducing interrogation sequence which culminates in a beaten hoodlum parting company

B

with one of his fingers. A little slow to begin with, it's in the second act that the story really excels, cranking up the suspense to almost unbearable levels, Ceasar's sanity rapidly fragmenting as he digs himself deeper and deeper into a hole from which there's no hope of escape. Pantoliano acts everyone off the screen, which - with stiff(ening) competition from Gershon and Tilly, both of whom positively drip sex appeal - is no mean feat. Embroidered with a fistful of fabulously indulgent, amusingly inventive camera tricks, plus an atmospheric score by Don Davis, *Bound* is rock solid evidence that, in the right hands, meagre-budget cinema - it cost just four and a half million dollars to make - can engender results that put many big-budgeters to shame.

Both Republic Pictures' unrated DVD and the uncut UK release from Pathé are impeccable. The excellent transfers of the movie aside, there's an audio commentary hosted by the Wachowskis with additional input from Pantoliano, Gershon, Tilly, editor Zach Staenberg and Susie Bright (who was "sex consultant" on the movie as well as appearing briefly in the gay bar sequence). It's almost a case of overkill having so many people chattering away at once, but the banter is nonetheless entertainingly chummy and informative, never once broaching uninteresting. Tilly fans take note: Although she and Gershon don't "arrive" until three-quarters of the way in, Tilly positively gushes and more or less dominates from that point forward. There are no visual extras beyond a trailer, which, given that there's mention in the commentary of the existence of a great many bloopers and outtakes, is regrettable. A generous 33 chapter stops allow for easy access to the highlights you'll want to visit time and again; it should be stressed that there are many. Sound options are English or French, with subtitling in English or Spanish. - TG

THE BOYS FROM BRAZIL

Colour, 1978, 124m. / Directed by Franklin J. Schaffner / Starring Gregory Peck, Laurence Olivier, James Mason / Artisan (US R1 NTSC), Carlton (UK R2 PAL) / WS (1.85:1)

A glossy, gory melange of popular box office hits of its day, *The Boys from Brazil* arrived onscreen just in time to follow the dual genres of Nazi horror (*Marathon Man* and the multitude of outrageous Italian SS exploitation films) and supernatural kids (*The Omen, Carrie*). Cleanly adapted from Ira Levin's novel and aimed to

traumatize the same audiences who thrilled to *Rosemary's Baby*, the film never comes close to hitting that plateau of excellence but still delivers the goods on its own modest level.

Ezra Lieberman (Laurence Olivier) is approached by an enthusiastic but not terribly swift young Nazi hunter, Barry (Steve Guttenberg), who jabbers a dubious story about the notorious Dr. Josef Mengele (Gregory Peck) cooking up some kind of genetic conspiracy down in the South American jungles. When Barry turns up dead, Ezra decides to investigate, mostly by visiting the homes of various people related to a string of murders linked to Mengele. Apparently the evil doctor has targeted 94 unlucky married men for death... and oddly enough, all of their children look exactly the same, with jet-black hair and piercing blue eyes, just like a certain infamous German leader.

While it's easy to hate any movie that offered Guttenberg his big break, *The Boys from Brazil* otherwise plays most of its cards right. Peck, enjoying the strangest period of his career, makes an imposing, hammy villain, while Olivier grounds the fantastic tale with his sympathetic, multi-layered portrayal of the aging investigator. Lilli Palmer, the European film star and TV hostess best known to shock fans as the headmistress in the excellent *The House that Screamed*, turns up in a relatively thankless role, while James Mason does the suave, evil henchman routine he also performed in *Salem's Lot*. Film buffs should also look for appearances by the underrated Bruno Ganz (*Nosferatu, Wings of Desire*), who provides one of the big screen's first accurate explanations of cloning, and Walter Gotell, best known as General Gogol in the James Bond films. Jerry Goldsmith contributes a surprisingly elegant, upbeat score, mostly consisting of waltzes and period music to evoke the spirit of a Germany trying to forget its past. Schaffner, best known for his mainstream drama and war films, does an efficient job of delving into the horror genre; while the opening 45 minutes can seem very disjointed and confusing during a first viewing, the film improves considerably as the true nature of the plot begins to unfold. Besides, any film deserves credit for making a gripping, shocking finale that simply involves two men sitting on sofas, surrounded by a pack of Dobermans.

Artisan's DVD duplicates the previous Pioneer laserdisc (but drops the isolated mono music track for some reason); the letterboxed transfer looks cleaner and sharper, not too shabby for a 1978 film. Anyone who grew up watching this (usually heavily cut) on afternoon television will be amazed at the quality of the print, which makes one wonder why other

Hollywood films of this vintage can't look the same. It isn't of the same demo quality as a new 1999 title, of course, but it gets the job done in lieu of a full restoration or 16:9 transfer (which this really should have had). The elegant, creepy animated menus lead the viewer through a long series of informative production notes (focusing particularly on Simon Wiesenthal, the likely influence on Olivier's character), concluding with two long trailers, both of which give away far too much of the story. The British PAL format release from Carlton utilizes the same transfer, without extras.

BRAIN DAMAGE

Colour, 1988, 86m. / Written and Directed by Frank Henenlotter / Starring Rick Herbst, Gordon MacDonald / Synapse (US R1 NTSC) / WS (1.85:1) / DD2.0

 How do you follow up a smash hit cult movie? If that movie is 1982's *Basket Case*, you take what worked in that film and try to make it even better. The result, of course, is *Brain Damage*, an outrageous little gem that ran into trouble when its distributor decided to release it with an R rating in the US. As a result, the film lost two of its most over the top sequences (one involving a club girl getting her brains literally boffed out, and the other featuring a nasty string of brain matter being pulled out of an ear). The watered down version still managed to find an accepting cult audience, especially after its release on video from Paramount, while horror fans managed to track down uncut copies from the UK and Denmark. At least DVD owners can enjoy *Brain Damage* in all its uncut glory, thanks to this labour of love from Synapse (could there be a more appropriate company for this one?).

An elderly woman looks at her bathtub filled up with water and lets out a shriek. Her husband joins her as they frantically ransack their apartment, screaming, "He's gone! He's gone!" Cut to their neighbour, Brian (Rick Herbst, later Rick Herst on *The Guiding Light*), who shares an apartment with his brother, Mike (Gordon MacDonald). Brian wakes up with a strange headache and discovers a crusty, eel-shaped creature lurking in his room. Even weirder, the creature talks and occasionally slips a needle-like appendage from its mouth into Brian's neck, whereby it injects the young man with a psychedelic chemical causing euphoric hallucinations. Brian goes out on a surreal night-time walk

climaxing at a junkyard, where a run-in with a security guard results in the creature scarfing down the guard's brains. Unaware of his new friend's murderous tendencies, Brian blithely ignores both his girlfriend Barbara (Jennifer Lowry) and his brother in favour of spending hours in the bathtub splashing around with his fix-providing pal. After a few more grisly murders, Brian's neighbours eventually catch on and inform him about the history of this creature, called the Aylmer ("You named him Elmer?!"), which has been bought and traded over the centuries. Determined to hold on to his co-dependent prize, Brian refuses to hand over the Aylmer, resulting in tragic and highly surreal consequences.

Surprisingly stylish for such a low budget ($600,000, according to the commentary), *Brain Damage* knowingly winks at other genre titles like *Altered States* and even includes a very funny in-joke for *Basket Case* fans (look closely on the subway). While the basic narrative thread of the film will be familiar for anyone well-versed in other "horror as drug" parables like *The Hunger*, the real joy lies in Henenlotter's curious little detours along the way. The aforementioned nightclub scene remains a jaw-dropping bit of sick cinema, and the finale takes some unexpected turns away from the expected *Basket Case*-style wrap-up. The performers generally do a nice job, with Herbst nicely balancing comical hysteria and genuine pathos. Though uncredited, Zacherley makes a definite impression as Elmer, droning out wisecracks and tormenting Brian with a Tommy Dorsey tune for good measure. *Street Trash* auteur Jim Muro handles Steadicam duties with his usual skill, and Elmer himself, giving Belial a run for his money, makes for a strangely endearing little critter.

Synapse's DVD is everything a horror fan could ask for, featuring the US trailer (and the *Basket Case* one tucked into Henenlotter's filmography for good measure), a beautiful letterboxed transfer (matting off unnecessary information from the full frame 35mm original), and even an isolated score track! The real treat, though, is the commentary by Henenlotter himself, joined by Bob Martin (who wrote the novelization) and *Shatter Dead* director Scooter McCrae. The three casually chat about the making of the film, swapping observations and anecdotes, and basically just make the viewer wish Henenlotter would go make another movie, as it's been way too long since the last *Basket Case*. In the meantime, along with the director's valiant efforts to corrupt audiences around the world through his series with Something Weird Video, this nifty DVD treat will do just fine.

BRAIN DEAD (DEAD-ALIVE)

Colour, 1992, 103/97m. Directed by Peter Jackson / Starring Timothy Balme / Trimark Home Video (US R1 NTSC) / WS (1.85:1) (16:9), Laser Paradise (German R2 PAL) / WS (1.78) / DD2.0

"Your mother ate my dog!" If you haven't seen New Zealand cult director Peter Jackson's splatter-soaked zombiefest, get thee to your nearest video store immediately. *Brain Dead* (retitled *Dead-Alive* in the US due to the odd but interesting Bill Pullman movie of the same name) was essentially the conclusion of Jackson's gross-out trilogy (after *Bad Taste* and *Meet the Feebles*).

Mama's boy Lionel (Timothy Balme) must contend with a number of insane zombie onslaughts after his tyrannical mum is bitten at the zoo by the dreaded Sutran Rat Monkey and turns into a contagion-spreading beastie. With the help of his tarot-following girlfriend, Pequita (Diana Penalver), he uses everything at his disposal, including a very memorable rotary lawnmower, to dispatch the flesh-eating pests.

Brain Dead was originally released in a claustrophobic, pan and scan version (it was shot hard-matted at 1.78:1) on video and laserdisc by Vidmark a few years ago. Aside from being overly soft, the print featured colours so digitally punched up that it practically glowed with pink and shades of lime during the gore scenes; kind of interesting to look at, but that isn't how it appeared in the theatre. (They also issued an abortive R-rated version for Blockbuster, which is almost as amusing in its incoherence as the 92-minute R-rated cut *of The Cook, the Thief, His Wife & Her Lover*). Meanwhile, the Japanese released it under its original title on laser; luckily, this 106-minute version included a few odd but insignificant snippets of footage missing from the unrated American edition. (No entire scenes were cut; the longest deletion is a repeat of Uncle Liz hitting on Pequita during the funeral scene.) The shorter version is much tighter, actually, and is only missing one fleeting second of gore during the finale, in which a zombie is wishboned in half. The Japanese version was also pan and scanned, as well as virtually colourless.

The Trimark DVD marks the best video presentation overall; the colours are rich but not overbearing, and the punchy stereo soundtrack sounds better than ever. Best of all, it's 16:9 enhanced, which provides a much more visually pleasing presentation than any other version. It's still the 97-minute unrated cut, which may or may not be

a good thing, depending on your point of view. It's hard to quibble, really, when it looks this good, and it includes the US trailer as well. The "Red Edition," issued twice by Laser Paradise, contains the complete cut with a more generous 1.78:1 matte. No matter which option you choose, be sure to wear a raincoat when you watch this, 'cuz you'll feel pretty drenched by the time it's over...

THE BRAIN FROM PLANET AROUS

B&W, 1957, 70m. / Directed by Nathan Hertz (Juran) / Starring John Agar, Joyce Meadows / Image (US R0 NTSC)

Though the title could easily apply to those sexy sci-fi spoofs from the 1970s, *The Brain from Planet Arous* appears to have mostly serious intentions despite a plot involving huge floating alien brains possessing John Agar and a dog. A favourite of "bad" cinema retrospectives, *Brain* is compulsively watchable, skilfully made, and boasts nary a dull moment, though it's easy to see why Agar never quite took off as a Hollywood leading man. At least he's moderately likeable and, later in the film, truly terrifying when he laughs maniacally into the camera, his eyes transformed into a horrific, glistening shade of black.

Weird radiation emanating from Mystery Mountain (yes, that really is its name) attracts the interest of nuclear scientist Steve Marsh (Agar), who heads out to investigate with his assistant, Dan (Robert Fuller, who, being the best actor in the film, gets wiped out quickly for his trouble). The two men are assaulted by Gor, a levitating brain from Arous, who zaps Dan and enters Steve's body. Now possessed, the scientist returns home to his girlfriend, Sally (Joyce Meadows); diabolically crazed with a lust for power and sex, Gor/Steve proceeds to make Sally's life hell and plots to bring the worldwide military to its knees. Sally and her father tromp back out to Mystery Mountain where they meet a good brain, Vol, who decides to hide out in the family dog until Gor slips out of Steve's body for some air and becomes vulnerable. Soon it's clear that the only way to resolve this situation will involve a fire axe, some sacrifices from major characters, and the intervention of an alien-inhabited pooch.

Under the pseudonym of Nathan Hertz, regular Ray Harryhausen director Nathan Juran kept a firm grip on this film, making its 70 tight minutes fly by. The special effects are often well below par, particularly the unforgettable spectacle of a hovering Gor, actually a painted balloon on a string. How could you possibly dislike a film like this? In many respects this is simply the ultimate '50s brain movie, and there are certainly enough of those around to choose from. Just check out *Donovan's Brain*, for example, or its closest cousin, the more explicit *Fiend without a Face*. There's just something so compellingly lovable about this film, its zero budget flaws and all, and the underlying sexual weirdness (it ain't called Planet Arous for nothing) should keep film scholars scratching their heads at the meaning of it all.

The DVD print looks terrific, with only a few minor blemishes visible in the opening credits. Otherwise the clarity is sparkling (occasional stock footage notwithstanding), so you can see the wire holding up Gor even more clearly. A much rougher looking theatrical trailer is also included.

THE BRAIN THAT WOULDN'T DIE

B&W, 1962, 84m. / Directed by Joseph Green / Starring Jason Evers, Virginia Leith / Synapse (US R1 NTSC)

 A lunatic entry in the weird subgenre of reanimated head/brain movies, *The Brain That Wouldn't Die* may well be the final word on the subject. Made for about ten cents primarily in someone's basement, this one just goes to show that a depraved imagination and a disregard for the generally accepted rules of cinema can drag the viewer kicking and screaming into territory he never dreamed possible.

Ambitious young doctor Bill Cortner (Jason Evers) has pioneered new techniques of organ experimentation and reanimation, a development that poses a few problems for his colleagues. Bill's medical ethics go flying out the window, so to speak, when he wrecks his car on the way home and his fiancée Jan (Virginia Leith) is decapitated in the process. Bill scoops up the head and returns home, where he brings back Jan's head in a pan during experiments in his basement laboratory. Meanwhile a mysterious creature, the by-product of Bill's scientific mistakes, languishes behind a locked door and develops a psychic link with Jan. Bill goes cruising around for a beautiful body to attach to Jan's cranium, finally settling on an old school acquaintance with a heavy grudge against the entire male gender. It all ends badly, of course.

Largely known to the general public as fodder for *Mystery Science Theatre 3000*, this film has a much longer history with cult movie fanatics who have enjoyed its deranged charms on late night television. Acting is atrocious and over the top, with Leith taking acting honours as the pissed off head who only wants to die. However, it's interesting to note that one year before *Blood Feast*, this film trotted out some amazingly graphic (but hilarious nonetheless) gore effects, such as an infamous arm tearing in which the victim staggers up and down stairs at length and smears blood all over the walls. (Dario Argento, take note.) Of course, AIP released this a couple of years later, so H.G. Lewis still reigns as the official father of the splatter subgenre.

First released by Warners in a mutilated edition that removed all of the bloodshed, *The Brain That Wouldn't Die* has since circulated in a number of public domain editions. Sinister Cinema issued the first uncut edition on VHS on a raggedy looking tape, while Rhino issued its *MST3K* edition on tape and DVD (along with a fuzzy-looking rendition of the uncut print). Synapse's DVD is by far the best of the bunch and looks about as good as a zero budget film of this vintage possibly could. Incidentally, the end credits still bear the film's original pre-release title, *The Head That Couldn't Die*. Also included are the lurid theatrical trailer and a mind-bending gallery of production and promotional stills.

THE BRAINIAC

B&W, 1962, 80m. / Directed by Chano Ureta / Starring Abel Salazar, Ruben Rojo / Beverly Wilshire (US R0 NTSC)

 Thanks to late night television and the usual canny tactics of K. Gordon Murray, that infamous importer of Mexican fantastic delights, *The Brainiac* has become a long cherished gem of sleaze cinema still capable of making jaws drop today. Though the plotline isn't much more than a desexualized rehash of Mario Bava's *Black Sunday* with a hint of sci-fi, the film is so bizarre and compelling that it stands up just fine on its own terms as well.

In the extended prologue sequence set in 1661, the black cloaked members of the Mexican inquisition accuse the decadent Baron Vitelius (Abel Salazar) of consorting with the devil. The Baron laughs off their threats and puts a curse upon the Inquisition's descendants, a decree that takes three hundred years to come to pass. In 1961, a comet streaks through the sky and, upon hitting the earth, unleashes the title creature, a hairy, big-headed incarnation of Vitelius capable of rendering itself

B

invisible and sucking out the brains of hapless victims. In a human disguise, Vitelius holds chic dinner parties for his potential victims, then transforms into his natural state every now and then to suck out their brains via his fork shaped tongue. Naturally he also stashes away some of the leftover brains for later feedings, a practice his servants somehow fail to notice. The flaky Professor Milan (Luis Aragon) and the ingenuous Ronald (Ruben Rojo) and pretty Vicky (Ariadna Welter) try to solve the mystery of the Baron's return, while around them people are dropping like flies with little interference from the dim-witted police.

Alternately unnerving and hysterical, *The Brainiac* is a genuinely surreal experience, just as one might expect from director Chano Ureta (who also helmed the equally worthwhile *The Witch's Mirror*). The moody lighting and gothic atmosphere are thrown askew at every turn by the absurd dialogue (which may been played straight in the Mexican version, for all we know), and the plot contains enough unexpected twists and turns to keep viewers wide awake until the mind-blowing - err, flame-throwing - climax, which includes a nifty nod to *Horror of Dracula* for good measure. Nowhere even close to a "good" film, *The Brainiac* is an acquired taste but well worth the effort.

Beverly Wilshire's DVD is one of their better efforts, which means it's about the same as those battered prints shown on TV. It's a little better than the PD tapes which used to float around from companies like Sinister Cinema, and considering its current unavailability in any format (and bearing in mind BW's apparent collapse), the title is well worth snapping up. Contrast is fairly weak but acceptable, and the print damage is about the same as past video editions. Audio is dull and flat but always understandable, basically equivalent to a videotape. It's a budget label release all the way, right down to the amateurish packaging, but at least in this case you do get your money's worth.

BRANDED TO KILL

Colour, 1967, 87m. / Directed by Seijun Suzuki / Starring Jo Shishido, Mariko Ogawa / Criterion (US R1 NTSC) / WS (2.0:1)

A dizzy, thoroughly wacko hitman yarn, *Branded to Kill (Koroshi no rakuin)* got Suzuki fired from Toho after execs saw the finished print - with good reason. Shot in stark, noirish black and white and crammed from start to finish with goofy visual ideas, the film bears little resemblance to anything else in cinema. Of course, viewer taste will completely dictate a response to this film, which has received both acclaim and disdain since its resurrection from Criterion. At the very least, hardcore foreign film buffs owe it to themselves to check this out and discover a completely unique style of filmmaking.

Hanada Goro (the puffy-cheeked Jo Shishido) has a lot of problems. His hitman career is in jeopardy from stiff competition and uncooperative targets, he can't get over his fetish for the smell of boiling noodles, and a strange girl with a fetish for dead birds keeps showing up to perplex him for no discernable reason. The hits themselves are riotous exercises in black comic timing, with one funny homage to *From Russia with Love* that goes memorably haywire.

Like *Tokyo Drifter*, the transfer appears to be insufficiently letterboxed, though not quite as drastically. The black and white imagery looks crisp and clean, in surprisingly good shape for a Toho film of this vintage (and particularly one so reviled by its owners). The optional white English subtitles below the frame are legible and manage to keep up with the action, delivering the twisty, almost incoherent storyline as well as possible. Suzuki appears in a lengthy video interview to discuss the film's creation and controversial reception.

BRAZIL

Colour, 1985, 142m. / Directed by Terry Gilliam / Starring Jonathan Pryce, Robert De Niro, Katherine Helmond / Criterion, Universal (US R1 NTSC) / Letterboxed (1.85:1) / DD2.0

Having set the standard for comprehensive special editions with their deluxe laserdisc box set of *Brazil*, Criterion replicated the experience into a three DVD package, which offers everything you could possibly want to know about this controversial, stunning film, the most ambitious achievement from former Monty Python member Terry Gilliam. *Brazil* became the thorn in Universal execs' sides when the studio planned to drastically recut the film into a more upbeat experience (the same year a similar fate befell Ridley Scott's *Legend*). Fortunately, Gilliam stood by his film and arranged a clandestine screening whereupon it became a critical cause de celebre and was saved from the execs' scissors. However, the film's longer European cut raised issues as to which version

Gilliam truly preferred; after a seemingly infinite period of tinkering and research, the final "director's cut" (approximately 11 minutes longer than the 131 minute US print) was assembled and released by Criterion. The same edition made its debut on DVD last year in a bare bones version from Universal; however, the film's fans who want the full package in a nice tidy box will want to pick up handsomely packaged rendition, though laser owners will have little reason to upgrade besides the cool-looking DVD sleeve.

In an Orwellian future state (i.e., the present day but thinly disguised with techno trappings), a downtrodden bureaucratic underling named Sam Lowry (Jonathan Pryce before his *Miss Saigon* days) finds himself accidentally thrust into a chaotic clash between the established order and a clandestine terrorist group consisting of Harry Tuttle (Robert De Niro) and Jill Layton (Kim Griest), who bears a striking resemblance to a damsel in distress in Sam's dreams. Meanwhile Sam's mother, Ida (Katherine Helmond) gets continuous facelifts and goes on shopping sprees while his friend Jack (Michael Palin) reassures him about the superiority of the status quo.

Less a linear storyline than a dizzying collision of images and sketches, Brazil expounds upon the surreal world first introduced in Gilliam's short film opener *to Monty Python's The Meaning of Life.* In that sketch, a band of corporate pirates (literally) attacks rival companies through weapons of bureaucracy; here, however, the power of the omniscient governing force retains the upper hand, at least as far as physical domination goes. Startling, grotesque imagery in the Gilliam tradition fits perfectly within the nightmarish logic of a world where paperwork literally smothers and innocents are haphazardly tortured and killed at the mistaken whims of a faceless giant. (See Michele Soavi's *Dellamorte Dellamore* for a similarly paper-driven and self-contained world view.) While Gilliam's abrasive, rapid-fire mixture of black humour and futuristic social horror isn't to everyone's taste, the film is unquestionably a technical triumph in every regard; the visual design, music, acting, and photography are never less than perfect.

Of equal significance, *Brazil* also marks the frenzied pinnacle of a strange and wonderful wave of science fiction and horror films beginning in the early 1980s which flowed against the enforced stream of feel-good, viewer friendly aliens and spaceships forced on audiences during the Reagan/Thatcher era. Though seemingly different on the surface, films like *Brazil, Blade Runner*, John Carpenter's *The Thing*, and on a different tier, *The Hunger* and *Videodrome*, are essentially variations on the same hi-tech, low-communication world in which the human body and spirit are constantly under siege by a malevolent force which eventually turns people against each other and affects their own state of mental well-being. Not surprisingly, all of these films look far more chilling and modern now than when they were released, and in many respects Gilliam's work is the equivalent of the modern Jonathan Swift portion of this world, jabbing and chortling in defiance of a inhuman government gone catastrophically wrong.

As for the quality of the film itself, *Brazil* has never looked better. Though derived from the same materials, the Criterion transfer looks more polished and less grainy than the Universal DVD and, being DVD, features somewhat more dimensional shadows than the laser. This master always looked great, and even without anamorphic enhancement, it's hard to imagine the film getting much better. The shots of neon and planes of glittering metal come off especially well here, and Sam's memorable dream sequences look smooth and luminous.

The extras, however, are what really make the Criterion edition a must have. The 30 minute documentary "What Is Brazil?" kicks things off with an amusing promo piece shot during production of the film, before things turned nasty during distribution, and features some location footage of the striking, unused dream sequence in which Sam is observed by thousands of eyeballs on the ground. A one hour original documentary for Criterion essentially translates the fascinating written account, *The Battle of Brazil*, into visual form by interviewing the key participants in the film's production and subsequent studio clash. Gilliam also appears throughout to introduce other behind-the-scenes snippets, such as an informative (if poorly lit) ten minute talk by composer Michael Kamen about his experience with the film. Storyboards, the trailer, production sketches, and other ephemera round out this second supplement-crammed disc, which takes several hours to sift through by itself. However, at least by this point, the supplement format of DVD - simply slapping everything together on a menu - is less engaging than the guided step by step method of laserdisc, but it's all here for anyone anxious to sift through it.

The third disc closes out with the so-called "Love Conquers All" cut, a radically reedited version shown on syndicated TV, which streamlines Gilliam's dark satire into a toothless, feel-good chunk of eye candy. Fascinating and appalling at the same time, this is one of the most welcome, surreal supplements available on home video and a chilling reminder of just how easily a good film can be sabotaged in the post-production process. Along with *12 Monkeys* and

Criterion's *Time Bandits*, this should be more than enough to tide over Gilliamphiles and continues to stand as a loving testament to a unique and intensely personal work of cinema.

only, though there are selectable subtitles in French and Spanish. The only additional feature is a widescreen trailer that revels in laying out the high levels of nudity and mutilation awaiting punters. - TG

BREEDERS

Colour, 1986, 77m. / Directed by Tim Kinkaid / Starring Teresa Farley, Lance Lewman / MGM (US R1 NTSC) / WS (1.85:1)

A girl attacked by an alien being is confined to hospital, semi-comatose and with no memory of what was clearly a vicious assault. It transpires that she is not the first to encounter the creature and that each of its targets was a virgin. Dr. Gamble Pace (Farley) teams up with Detective Dale Andriotti (Lewman) to track down the fiend responsible. But just as they begin to make headway, the girls waken, their wounds miraculously healed, and depart the hospital in a trance, headed for the catacombs beneath the city.

Not to be confused with 1998's British-made yawn-inducer starring Samantha Janus, writer/director Tim Kinkaid's *Breeders* is a distinct "guilty pleasure" which raises more unintentional laughs than intentional scares. Although some of the f/x are convincingly nasty, the alien monsters are kept largely at glimpse distance, and a good thing too; even TV's *Dr. Who* managed to pull off the man-in-a-rubber-suit ploy with greater aplomb than Kinkaid's team do here. To be fair, it's all entertaining enough for what it is and makes up for a multitude of shortcomings with acres of naked flesh to ogle, and lots of awful acting and bad dialogue to chuckle at. And, clocking in under 80 minutes, at least it doesn't waste any time with pretentious padding. The undisputed highlight in questionable taste comes when a bunch of naked girls are discovered in a Gigeresque alien "nest", writhing ecstatically in what resembles a pool of semen... for no other apparent reason than it looks marvellous! Back in 1985, a still from this sequence published in US horror magazine *Fangoria* caused minor backlash from a few readers and some of those who stocked and sold the magazine. Seemed everyone was perfectly at ease with wall-to-wall photos of splattered brains and severed limbs, but the merest hint of a nipple amidst the carnage and all hell broke loose. Funny old world, isn't it?

MGM's Region 1 offering of the infinitely tacky *Breeders* delivers the film with a 16-chapter breakdown in a 1.85:1 matte. The sound is in English

BRIDE OF CHUCKY

Colour, 1998, 89m. / Directed by Ronny Yu / Starring Jennifer Tilly, Brad Dourif / Universal (US R1 NTSC) / WS (1.85:1) (16:9), Metrodome (UK R2 PAL) / WS (1.85:1) / DD5.1

Chucky, the killer Good Guy doll who first became a national icon with the popular *Child's Play* and became a key player in the Video Nasties ban-spree in Britain, has joined the wave of '80s slasher figures making a comeback in the wake of *Scream*. Amazingly, its jokey title aside, *Bride of Chucky* is the strongest film in the *Child's Play* series, easily laying waste to would-be hip horror dreck like *Halloween: H20* and *Urban Legends*. This is a film made to entertain horror fans, not coddle to them with idiotic teens spouting trendy dialogue, and even more amazingly, it delivers gore in spades.

Years after the last *Child's Play* massacre, Tiffany (Jennifer Tilly) swipes the Chucky doll, formerly possessed by the soul of serial killer Charles Lee Ray, from police storage and revives our pal Chucky (voiced by Brad Dourif, as usual) during a voodoo ritual in her trailer home. After a domestic squabble, Chucky winds up dumping a TV into his former girlfriend's bath and transfers her soul into a female doll. Soon the pair wind up slashing their way on a violent road trip destined for Lee's burial site, where they hope to retrieve an amulet capable of returning both of them to human bodies.

Featuring amusing performances by John Ritter (as a nasty chief of police), Alexis Arquette (doing a goofy Marilyn Manson goth-riff that's a welcome change from his usual catty drag queen persona), and even a cameo by Kathy Najimy, *Bride of Chucky* is a fast-paced, crude, thoroughly unredeeming piece of guttersniping cinema that delivers plenty of squirms and laughs for viewers in a drive-in frame of mind. Tilly and Dourif seem to be having a blast playing off each other and even manage to transform the two bloodthirsty dolls into interesting, romantically tragic figures by the end of the film.

The riotous commentary track with Tilly, Dourif, and writer Don Mancini bears out this impression, as everyone seems to be relaxed and giving 100% all around. Another commentary track with director

Ronny Yu focuses more on the technical and stylistic aspects of the film, and Yu's presence goes a long way to explaining this film's appeal. Along with cinematographer Peter Pau, this team has fashioned a sharp-looking piece of work, drenched in moody lighting and eye-dazzling bursts of colour enhanced by the beautiful widescreen transfer. Graeme Revell, who also scored the mediocre *Child's Play 2*, contributes a serviceable music score that treads a little too closely to Marco Beltrami's *Scream 2* (or, more accurately, Hans Zimmer's *Broken Arrow*) for comfort but still delivers a palpable sense of Elfmanesque diabolical glee. Other extras include the original (tacky) theatrical trailer and "Jennifer's Diary," a humorous account by Tilly of her work on the film, which was previously excerpted in various film publications.

The Region 2 release features a less impressive non-anamorphic transfer but does have one ace up its sleeve: the amusing "Chucky and Tiffany Do London: International Murder and Mayhem."

BRIDE OF RE-ANIMATOR

Colour, 1990, 96m. / Directed by Brian Yuzna / Starring Jeffrey Combs, Bruce Abbott / Pioneer (US R1 NTSC) / Optional WS (1.85:1) / DD2.0

 Largely ignoring the outrageous bloodletting and sexual depravity of Stuart Gordon's original *Re-Animator*, director Brian Yuzna crafted a sequel more focused on his own personal obsessions—namely, lots of grotesque, squishy things palpitating in front of the camera. While it can't hope to surpass the first film in terms of witty dialogue or over the top imagery, on its own terms *Bride of Re-Animator* makes for a brisk, enjoyable hour and a half, and fans should be happy to see most of the characters returning for another round of reanimation and dismemberment.

Six months after the grisly Miskatonic massacre, renegade med students Herbert West (Jeffrey Combs) and Dan Cain (Bruce Abbott) return to the scene and continue their unholy experiments. Using the heart of Megan Halsey, the boys use separate reanimated human body parts to construct an entire woman (tastefully including "the womb of a virgin and the legs of a hooker"). Meanwhile, the severed head of Dr. Hill (somehow still intact after the first film) decides to seek revenge against West, and a snooping police detective prowls around just to make things difficult. As if that weren't enough, Dan's new love, Francesca (Fabiana Udenio, aka *Austin Powers'*

Alotta Fagina), remains blissfully unaware of her beau's morbid pastime.

Pioneer's much-hyped special edition thankfully delivers on its promises, with a wealth of viewing options and supplements designed to keep gorehounds happy for hours. The R-rated theatrical cut and the unrated version are included in full frame, with an optional "theatrical matte" option that superimposes black bars over the image to simulate 1.85:1 framing. In this case, this controversial technique works quite well for the most part, though studios might want to be careful using it in the future. The matte can easily be switched on and off simply by using the DVD remote's subtitle button. As the liner notes explain, the unrated version was culled from a slightly inferior print, and it shows; while passable, the unrated edition looks somewhat smeary and features an unpolished stereo sound mix. The R-rated side improves noticeably on the previous LIVE laserdisc version; furthermore, the Ultra-Stereo soundtrack is much better mixed. Unless you feel like hunting for few examples of alternate footage (the running times are identical), the R version is definitely the way to go; only the finale, in which one character literally goes to pieces, plays out in a far more graphic fashion.

In the extras department, the unrated side includes a half hour making-of featurette, including cast and crew interviews as well as looks at the elaborate special effects. On the R-rated side, look for a "trailer" (actually the video commercial), Dr. West's Casebook (a collection of photos from the film and behind-the-scenes), and best of all, the deleted opening scene of the film, which fills in a number of gaping plot holes. In particular, the fate of Meg after her re-animation and West's escape from those strangling entrails are finally covered; one can only guess why this scene was cut, as it forms a much more logical bridge between the first film and the second Interestingly, this work print scene is followed by a great deal of rough footage shot during its filming from several different angles. Also included is an early deleted sequence in which Dr. Hill's head becomes an attraction at a local sideshow (a nice follow up on West's classic line in the original). Both versions feature two running commentary tracks, one with Combs and Abbott (who sound like good buddies and provide some nice chuckles along the way), and the other with Combs, Yuzna, and virtually the entire effects crew. Both tracks reveal a great deal of nostalgia and enthusiasm for the project, and while it can't really compare to the original, many sceptics may find themselves regarding this film much more fondly after experiencing it in so much depth.

BRIDE OF THE MONSTER

B&W, 1956, 69m. / Directed by Ed Wood, Jr. / Starring Bela Lugosi, Tor Johnson / Image (US R1 NTSC)

Often paired up with *Plan 9 from Outer Space* as the most entertaining of Ed Wood's "so bad they're masterpieces," *Bride of the Monster* offers enough cheap thrills and unintentional guffaws to live up to its creator's legacy. Though known for decades only to lucky late night TV viewers who thought they must have hallucinated the darn thing, the film has since gained recognition thanks to its vivid depiction in Tim Burton's *Ed Wood* and the recent public fondness for camp cinema.

In a desolate marsh, the deranged Dr. Eric Vornoff (Bela Lugosi) has hatched a diabolical plan for domination: breeding supermen through atomic energy. With the help of his lumbering assistant, Lobo (Tor Johnson), Vornoff terrorizes the countryside and even breeds an evil atomic octopus in his backyard. Plucky reporter Jane Lawton (Loretta King) defies the local authorities and decides to investigate, much to her regret.

Anyone who gets a thrill from chintzy paper sets and wooden line readings will have a veritable feast here, as *Bride of the Monster* trots out every monster movie cliché, then pushes each one to new levels of delirium. Lugosi gives his all, relatively speaking, among a cast that often barely manages to keep from cracking up on-camera.

Against all odds, *Bride of the Monster* has been brought to DVD in stunning condition. Never before has it looked even remotely this good, with previously invisible levels of lighting and depth in the sets now completely visible. The fuzz and grain that marred previous versions have completely vanished, leaving smooth and appealing visual textures that actually convey the feeling of a "real" movie. Whether this is in keeping with the Wood spirit, of course, is completely debatable. The soundtrack has also been lovingly remastered, with many of the sound effects and music tastefully spread out to the right and left front channels during 5.1 playback. The familiar theatrical trailer is also included.

THE BRIDE WORE BLACK

Colour, 1967, 107m. / Directed by François Truffaut / Starring Jeanne Moreau, Michel Bouquet / MGM (US R1 NTSC) / WS (1.66:1)

After years of his oft-stated devotion to the films of Alfred Hitchcock, French director François Truffaut finally got around to directing an unabashed homage to the master in 1967 with *The Bride Wore Black (La mariée était en noir)*. This grim ode to thwarted love and revenge reunited Truffaut with his Jules and Jim muse, Jeanne Moreau, who effectively transformed into an avenging angel fuelled by the same romantic passions of the filmmaker's other protagonists.

After being prevented from hurling herself out of a window, the beautiful but grief-stricken Julie Kohler (Moreau) attends a social gathering where she makes the acquaintance of a debonair middle-aged man... and promptly shoves him off the balcony. We then follow Julie as she gradually insinuates herself into the lives of four other men, including a stint as a babysitter for the married Michael Lonsdale (*Moonraker*) and the Artemis figure model of romantically inclined artist Jean-Claude Braily. However, as increasingly elaborated flashbacks reveal, Julie's motives are far more complicated than simple homicide. Her beloved husband, the only man in her life since childhood, was shot down on the wedding steps immediately after their wedding, and now she intends to seek revenge against those responsible. The method in which she accomplishes her mission, however, proves that love is indeed a strange and often dangerous force.

Despite the essentially downbeat subject matter, Truffaut keeps the film light and enjoyable thanks to his usual quirky supporting characters (including his trademark skill with child actors), a deliciously macabre score by the renowned Bernard Herrmann (his second for the director after *Fahrenheit 451*, though they clashed over this project), and the compelling presence of Moreau, who uses her elegance and marvellously expressive face to compensate for the fact that she's clearly too old for the part. The screenplay by Truffaut and Jean-Louis Richard (*Breathless*) was derived from a novel by Cornell Woolrich (under the pen name of William Irish), who also provided the original short story used for *Rear Window*. Truffaut twists the plotline severely to conform to his own cinematic sensibilities, including a completely different resolution. (Note: spoilers ahead!) Woolrich's novel pulls a chilling reversal by revealing that Julie has been tracking down and murdering completely innocent parties, while the bridegroom's death was in fact caused by a different and highly unlikely character omitted from the film. Truffaut's alternative is, in its own way, just as diabolical and in some respects more satisfying, with an ingenious final shot (and sound effect) providing the perfect punctuation.

MGM's irresistibly low-priced DVD of *The Bride Wore Black* is obviously derived from the same master used for their previous widescreen laserdisc edition. Fortunately the original transfer was quite satisfying, and the DVD looks roughly one video generation better in comparison. It also sports the added bonus of removable (and extremely large!) white English subtitles, as well as optional French and Spanish subtitles. Image quality is generally smooth, colourful, and pleasing, with print damage kept to a minimum. The two channel mono audio sounds robust enough, with the combination of Herrmann's score and Vivaldi interludes rendered with all of their musical nuances intact. The DVD also includes the hysterically lurid United Artists theatrical trailer, which makes this look like some kind of sexy spy thriller.

BRIMSTONE AND TREACLE

Colour, 1982, 87m. / Directed by Richard Loncraine / Starring Sting, Denholm Elliott, Joan Plowright / Arrow (UK R2 PAL) / DD2.0

One of the more perverse British cult films from the early '80s, *Brimstone and Treacle* was adapted from by the late Dennis Potter (*Pennies from Heaven*) from his own controversial, banned 1976 television play. Thanks to the presence of pop star Sting (semi-fresh from his first big role in *Quadrophenia*) and featuring a host of solid British actors, this film is truly unlike any other and deserves more than the general oblivion it has found in the last decade.

Prim and proper aging businessman Tom Bates (Denholm Elliott), who writes trite prose for a greeting card company, finds his life turned upside down with the arrival of Martin Taylor (Sting), a charming and supposedly devout young man who insinuates himself into Tom's household. Tom's wife, Norma (Joan Plowright), takes an immediate liking to their young guest, who offers to take care of the couple's bedridden, mentally incapacitated daughter, Patricia (Suzanna Hamilton). However, Martin also conceals a truly diabolical side, though the end results of his wickedness prove to be quite a jolting surprise.

All of the cast members are in top form here, with Sting delivering a surprising and creepy performance he has never matched since this. The film's ambiguous nature proves to be an advantage here, with the twisted and funny last scene causing the viewer to look back on all of the preceding events with a nasty chuckle. The entire concept of evil deeds begetting divine results probably won't turn up on the big screen anytime soon in our politically correct climate, so it's a good thing Potter's typically sharp and witty pen drove the point home with skill the first time. Mention must also be made of the eerie, striking music score, composed by Sting with a little help from Michael Nyman (and judicious pop songs by Squeeze and The Go-Gos).

Though not a stellar DVD release by any means, *Brimstone and Treacle* is a much better offering from the Arrow than their tragic attempt at David Cronenberg's *The Brood*. The image quality is the best available, though the overall transfer is a bit darker than it really should be. Detail is sharply rendered for the most part, and colours appear to be accurate. The stereo soundtrack also features good channel separation, with most of the music split to the exterior channels and dialogue remaining completely centred.

THE BROOD

Colour, 1979, 92m. / Directed by David Cronenberg / Starring Oliver Reed, Samantha Eggar / Opening Edition (France R2 PAL) / WS (1.85:1) (16:9), Arrow (UK R2 PAL)

Frank Carveth (Art Hindle) has placed his unstable wife Nola (Eggar) into the confinement and care of Dr. Hal Raglan (Reed), a psychiatrist whose progressive techniques enable his patients to expunge their hang-ups through a physical manifestation of pent-up rage. After Carveth's small daughter Candice (Cindy Hinds) returns from visiting her mother he is horrified to see bruises and welts on her back; convinced Nola has beaten her, he attempts to put a stop to visitation rights. When Nola's mother and father are murdered by a deformed child-like creature, Carveth begins to suspect that there's a connection between their deaths and Raglan's unorthodox methods of psychiatry.

Set against the backdrop of a bleak winter, *The Brood* will no doubt prove disappointing to those looking for the gruesome scenarios in Cronenberg's then-recent *Shivers* and *Rabid*. The action is more character driven, even touching on poignancy, and although there are some nasty moments woven into the story - prominently a murder with a steak mallet and the alarming beating to death of a playschool teacher in front of a horrified class of children - there's little that competes for the shockingly visceral excesses of those former movies. Hindle is a likeably tenacious hero and diminutive Cindy Hinds gives everyone else in the film a run for their money with a singularly outstanding performance. Reed's psychiatrist is, for him, surprisingly atypical and understated. Eggar on the other hand teeters on over-the-top and has a disarming accusatory stare that freezes the blood. Pick of the crop though is some juicy support from the gloriously oddball Robert Silverman (also in *Rabid, Scanners* and, most recently, *eXistenZ*, all for Cronenberg) as one of Reed's ex-patients, intent on bringing about the doctor's downfall.

The best DVD of Cronenberg's effective little chiller emanates from France on a Region 2 platter under the title *Chromosome 3*. The 1.85:1 matted 17-chapter transfer is excellent, but viewing options are in French, or English with French subtitles only; although technically the subtitles on the latter should be removable, some players are unable to do this. The additional features comprise an interview with Cronenberg and the film's composer Howard Shore (hosted on stage at a promotion in a French Virgin Megastore), a 5-minute collection of film clips and stills from other Cronenberg projects, a filmography, and some observations (in French) from author Serge Grunberg. - TG

[*Note: The full frame UK PAL DVD from Arrow is one of the worst ever released, lifted from a battered VHS tape with tracking problems. Avoid at all costs. - ed.*]

A BUCKET OF BLOOD

B&W, 1959, 67m. / Directed by Roger Corman / Starring Dick Miller, Barboura Morris / MGM (US R1 NTSC)

 The first and best of its kind, Roger Corman's low budget black comedy *A Bucket of Blood* laid the groundwork for cinematic murderers who parlay their bloody craft into artistic acclaim. Though it has been more than outdone in terms of grotesque imagery by similarly plotted films like *Crucible of Terror, Scream Baby Scream,* and especially H.G. Lewis' *Color Me Blood Red,* this one has yet to be topped for sheer effectiveness.

At a dark and smoky cafe, mistreated waiter Walter Paisley (Dick Miller in a rare leading role) envies the acclaim heaped upon the pretentious beatnik poets and painters whose nonsensical creations dazzle the java-sipping patrons. One night

Walter accidentally impales his unpleasant landlady's cat on a knife; to hide the evidence, he simply covers the body in plaster and passes it off as a sculpture called, naturally, "Dead Cat." The local artistic community gushes over Walter's creation, and he even finds approval from the powerful Leonard DiCenzo (Corman regular Antony Carbone) and the lovely object of Walter's affections, Carla (Barboura Morris). Unfortunately Walter finds himself inadvertently responsible for the deaths of several human beings, whose bodies he transforms into more grisly sculptures to build his artistic reputation. How long can Walter carry on this gruesome charade without being caught?

A valuable transition film between Corman's monster marathons of the '50s and his beautifully polished gothic horrors in the '60s (notably the Vincent Price/Poe series), *A Bucket of Blood* has enough visual style and satirical bite to overcome its lack of budget. The beatnik atmosphere is both captured and ridiculed extremely well, complete with a funky pseudo-beat score throughout the entire film. Incidentally, Corman used many of the same sets and cast members after filming to create his infamous three day wonder, *Little Shop of Horrors*, which recycles virtually the same plot. Twenty five years later, he returned to the material again for a middling Showtime remake (called *The Death Artist* on home video) starring Anthony Michael Hall and Justine Bateman, with cameos from Paul Bartel and Mink Stole. It's not awful, but it can't touch the original.

One of the few AIP titles to fall into the public domain, *A Bucket of Blood* has turned up in several unauthorized transfers, most egregiously as part of Slingshot's Roger Corman triple header (along with *The Wasp Woman* and *The Giant Leeches*), all derived from inferior tape sources. Thankfully MGM has come to the rescue with this clean, sharp presentation from the original AIP/Orion master; simply put, you won't see it looking this good outside of a mint theatrical print, if such a thing even exists anymore. The source material is virtually free of any blemishes whatsoever, which will come as a welcome change for most B-movie fans. The only noticeable flaw is a heavy saturation of violently crawling grain during some of the more intense white areas, but all things considered, you can't beat the transfer or the price. Unfortunately, contrary to the back of the packaging, there is no theatrical trailer on the disc.

THE BURNING

Colour, 1981, 87m. / Directed by Tony Maylem / Starring Brian Matthews, Leah Ayres / Dragon (Germany R0 PAL), Vipco (UK R0 PAL)

Five years ago Camp Blackfoot was the site of a prank that went awry and left caretaker Cropsy (David) severely burned. Just up river is Camp Stonewater where a bunch of care-free teenagers are arriving for a summer of sun, swimming and sex. But Cropsy has just been discharged from the hospital where he has undergone failed skin-grafts and counselling for psychological disorders. Clutching a pair of finely-honed garden shears, he heads out to Camp Stonewater to carve up some revenge.

Among countless films to mimic *Friday the 13th*, *The Burning* is one of only a few that actually equalled the source of its inspiration. Knuckle-whitening tension, dazzling Tom Savini mayhem and a classic Rick Wakeman score simmer away to mould it into the ultimate in not-so-happy-camping catastrophes. True there are plot-holes so vast you could paddle a canoe through them, and admittedly all the clichéd nibbles from the stalk'n'slash menu are served up, including that irritating point-of-view camera play that criss-crosses between being the killer and making you think it's the killer when it isn't. But director Maylem handles it all with such zest and intensity that in review its shortcomings don't seem to matter a great deal. The sequence upon which much of the film's notoriety is based - and the one which escorted it into difficulties with British censors - has Cropsy leaping out on a bunch of youths on a raft and in a little over 30 seconds and as many rapid-fire shots, five hapless victims are slaughtered; heads are gashed, chests and necks are gouged and one unfortunate chap raises his hands to protect himself, watching in horror as digits meet blades and scatter like bowling pins. All eyes peeled for Holly Hunter (who later culled a Best Actress Academy Award for *The Piano*) in a minor role. "Don't look, he'll see you. Don't move, he'll hear you. Don't breathe... you're dead!"

Two releases down and we're still waiting for a decent version of *The Burning* on DVD. The region free UK disc from Vipco is unsurprisingly cut; the region free release from Dragon of Germany is at least uncut but its extras are of little or no worth whatsoever. The slideshow stills gallery is a mix of the good (a nice array of lobby cards), the bad (a range of video sleeves that are either too small or pass by too quickly to take in) and the ugly (out of focus pages from a Japanese souvenir brochure). There are a number of textual filmographies supplied, but the promised trailer isn't a trailer at all, rather a compilation of the grisliest moments, amateurishly cut together to approximate the look of

one; rest assured this never played theatrically and to advertise it as a trailer is disgraceful. The fullscreen presentation of the movie - woefully under-chaptered with just 7 stops (only 6 of which actually show on the menu) - boast bold colours in daytime shots, but they become unstable and slightly smeared looking whenever the picture turns dark; given that a large portion of the story takes place at night this is a distinct liability. Sound is available in English or German. - TG

BYE BYE MONKEY

Colour, 1977, 94m. / Directed by Marco Ferreri / Starring Gérard Depardieu, Marcello Mastroianni / Image (US R0 NTSC) / WS (1.75:1)

You know you're in for a weird ride when a movie opens with Gérard Depardieu being consensually raped by a militant feminist theatrical troupe led by Italian cinema starlets Mimsy Farmer (*Four Flies on Grey Velvet*) and Stefania Casini *(Suspiria)*. Sure enough, this is one hour and a half guaranteed to leave most viewers speechless, either in awe or horror. After the aforementioned curtain raiser, aging down and out Luigi (Marcello Mastroianni) stumbles upon the giant dead body of an ape in the middle of a deserted area in New York City (the remnants of Dino De Laurentiis' finale from *King Kong*, so the story goes). Cradled in the dead ape's arms is a young baby monkey, whom the young but jaded Lafayette (Depardieu) decides to adopt as his own baby girl. Lafayette and his American girlfriend (Deborah Foreman look-alike Gail Lawrence) find their already unusual relationship further distorted by this bizarre attempt at parenthood, and Lafayette turns to the quirky Flaxman (James Coco!) for advice about how to deal with what is apparently a collapsing futuristic social state.

Continuing his study of gender roles from such films as *The Ape Woman*, Ferreri's view of humanity here is unlike any other filmmaker's. His perception of the next step of man's evolution is a conciliation between bestial and intellectual, sexual and spiritual, though his own idiosyncratic traits (twisted humour, graphic nudity, and unexpected tragedy) may make the message a bit hard to swallow for the uninitiated. For an interesting double feature, check this out along with Nagisa Oshima's neglected masterpiece, *Max Mon Amour*, in which the nuclear family is splintered by the initiation of a monkey into the human circle.

Image's disc is one of the more attractive in their series of Ferreri releases; though derived from the same Cinecittà print used for the PAL release overseas (which is missing several minutes of footage, including William Berger's entire role!), this has amazingly punchy colours for a mid-'70s low budget European release. Even scenes bathed entirely in strong red lighting fare well, and the English-recorded soundtrack (a rarity for Ferreri) sounds fine. As usual, Philippe Sarde provides a fine, emotionally trenchant music score, and Luciano Tovoli's typically top notch cinematography adds a firm sense of visual style to Ferreri's amusing and often upsetting dissection of mankind's inevitable destructive impulses.

CAFÉ FLESH

Colour, 1982, 73m. / Directed by Rinse Dream (Stephen Sayadian) / Starring Pia Snow (Michelle Bauer), Andy Nichols / VCA (US R0 NTSC)

The only hardcore adult film which gained a substantial "straight" cult following outside the raincoat crowd, *Café Flesh* was the last gasp of mainstream theatrical porn before shot on video productions killed the market in the mid-'80s. While some '70s films like *The Opening of Misty Beethoven* featured lavish production values, excellent writing, and genuine plots, *Café Flesh* pushed the genre even further by incorporating elements of surrealism, avant garde, pop culture, black humour, and science fiction. The result is truly one of a kind and, love it or hate it, this film deserves to be seen at least once.

In a post-nuclear future, the majority of the world's population has been afflicted with an inability to function sexually. Called "Negatives," these morose survivors flock to clubs where they watch the few "Positives" perform sex shows onstage. At Café Flesh, the same crowd goes every night to observe the verbal lacerations of emcee Max Melodramatic (Andy Nichols), while the club's owner, Moms (Darcy Nichols), keeps a tight rein backstage. Two of the regulars, married couple Lana (Pia Snow, aka scream-queen Michelle Bauer) and Nick (Paul McGibboney), ponder why they subject themselves to this madness; however, Lana has a secret. She's actually a Positive but doesn't want to hurt her husband's feelings, so she pretends to be sickened by sexual arousal. Furthermore, as a Positive, she would be forced to leave him and join the circuit as a sex performer, a fate that befalls the innocent, virginal Angel (Marie Sharp). How long can Lana possibly hold out until her secret is discovered?

A bleak, visually striking vision that operates like a neon-lit porn take on *A Boy and His Dog*, this compelling oddity features much better acting and technical credits than audiences could have possibly expected. Those who remain clothed contribute the best performances, with Andy Nichols getting the finest moments in his catchy monologues. He had previously appeared in the excellent *Night Dreams*, produced by *Café Flesh* director "Rinse Dream" (actually Stephen Sayadian, also director of the bizarre *Dr. Caligari*). Satirical writer Jerry Stahl (*Permanent Midnight*) co-wrote the incisive, tight screenplay with Sayadian, with sharp dialogue that sometimes seems far beyond the grasp of the performers. Bauer doesn't exactly set the world on fire with her acting here, and she even seems to use a body double for her climactic sex scene; however, it's odd enough seeing her in a XXX film at all, and just for the record she did the deed for real, sort of, in *Bad Girls*. The outstanding electronic score by Mitchell Froom is so good it was later released in its entirety as a pop album, *The Key of Cool*, and is well worth seeking out.

A popular video title since its initial release from VCA, *Café Flesh* became a high selling title on laserdisc and became an obvious choice for DVD. Fortunately the adult studio has created a dramatically improved new transfer for DVD, with much purer and more stable renderings of the black, hard-edged lighting that consumes all of the film. Some flaws in the source material still show through, not surprising for a title of this vintage, but this is the best it will look outside a movie theatre. And yes, it did play legit theatres (usually at midnight) during the '80s, often with the "money shots" trimmed out at Sayadian's request. Actually, the film wouldn't suffer at all with the omission of its hardcore footage- a rare feat indeed for an adult title. Despite the claims of stereo sound on the back sleeve, the mono audio sounds about the same as the laserdisc, though curiously (and thankfully) the opening female narration has been adjusted to flow in sync with the written crawl on the screen. While a running time of 80 minutes has been reported for the film since '82, it actually runs only 73 minutes. The extras on the disc don't amount to much, mostly a photo gallery and the usual VCA weblinks and title listings; one can only imagine what a commentary track with Sayadian, Bauer, and Stahl would sound like!

CAGED WOMEN

Colour, 1991, 65m. / Directed by Leandro Luchetti / Starring Isabel Libossart / MIA (UK R2 PAL)

Janet (Orive) arrives in South America for a short vacation but immediately falls foul of a corrupt police officer who frames her in a drugs bust. Gaoled in a squalid penal facility, she discovers from another prisoner, Louise (Libossart), that paying male clients are flown in by the governor, then the inmates are turned free into the hostile swampland, only to be hunted for sport, raped and shot dead...

Forget re-runs of *Prisoner: Cell Block H*, if you're seeking a chicks-in-chains epic that truly deserves its WIP classification look no further than *Caged Women* (aka *Caged - Le Prede Umane*). Nothing is neglected in this well above average Italian entry, thus you get wrongful imprisonment, slo-mo hose-downs, inmate molestation, a sleazeball governor (Aldo Sambrell, the only vaguely recognisable player in the show), a lesbian prison wardress (Elena Wiedermann) and a climax in which the prisoners turn on their debauched captors, all wheeled out with gusto for your delectation and delight. With a Lanfranco Perini score backing up the visuals, the softcore sex sequences are slick and arousing, in fact they're more stylishly shot and edited than those in most of the feeble skinflick fare that masquerades as adult entertainment. The female cast are all attractive and spend most of the film sans clothing. The licentious highlight comes when Orive and Libossart, caged on a sun-baked rooftop for some minor indiscretion, are forced to suckle the sweat from each other's bodies in order to survive dehydration; it's exceedingly hot and they're perspiring freely, so the sequence goes on for a very long time! Unexpectedly the ending is a frothy and frivolously upbeat affair in which our heroines are plucked from danger by a helicopter pilot who's immediately rewarded for his gallantry (to the detriment of his flying skills): "I can't find the joystick..."/"We can!".

A disappointingly basic platter from MIA, who have merely reissued on PAL Region 2 DVD (wasting the format's potential entirely by encoding it with just 6 chapter stops) their heavily cut PAL VHS release of some years back. There's not a single extra feature to compensate for this. However, those who favour the movie will deem an upgrade mandatory as the quality of the fullscreen image on disc is a vast improvement over that of the tape. Be aware though, the sleeve erroneously claims a 72-minute running time - in fact it's just 65 - and much of the raunchiest material (including the finale in which Wiedermann is set upon by inmates, strapped to a wooden cross and lashed with her own whip,

only to get turned on by the ordeal!) has been spared us delicate Brits by those kindly denizens of the BBFC. Although there is an uncut Japanese disc of *Caged Women* out there, all the shots of lower frontal nudity have been digitally obscured. - TG

C

CALIGULA

Colour, 1979, 156m. / Directed by Tinto Brass, Bob Guccione, and Giancarlo Lui / Starring Malcolm McDowell, Helen Mirren, Peter O'Toole, John Gielgud / Image (US R1 NTSC) / WS (1.85:1) / DD5.1, Dutch Filmworks (Holland R2 PAL) / WS (1.85:1) (16:9), Penthouse (UK R2 PAL)

The standard against which cinematic sleaze must be measured, *Caligula* has something for everybody: top notch British actors for dramatic weight, a fact-laden script by Gore Vidal, opulent visual design and flashy colours for European film addicts, graphic and plentiful bloodshed for gorehounds, and hardcore sex of every conceivable bent for the raincoat crowd. Obviously this isn't the most comfortable mix, but Caligula still manages to retain a bizarre, shocking fascination two decades after its release. Simply put, there will never be anything like it again, for better or worse.

The young Caligula (Malcolm McDowell), next in line as Emperor of Rome, carries on a flagrant affair with his scheming sister, Drusilla (Teresa Ann Savoy). Caligula orders the death of the corrupt Emperor Tiberius (Peter O'Toole) at the hands of his devoted servant, Macro (Guido Mannari), and ascends to the throne. Caligula gleefully exploits his position in every possible way by engaging in sexual depravity; aside from marrying "the most promiscuous woman in Rome," Caesonia (Helen Mirren), he carries on with Macro's wife, his half brother, and even his horse. After contracting a feverish disease and lingering near death, Caligula's sanity quickly collapses, leading to even more debauchery and butchery as he and his family spiral towards a truly grisly fate.

Designed to compete with the fledgling film efforts of Playboy Productions (who financed Roman Polanski's *Macbeth*), *Caligula* was *Penthouse* publisher Bob Guccione's attempt to break into the movie market with an utterly excessive slap to viewers' sensibilities. For directorial chores he hired Tinto Brass, who had a moderate success with the Nazi sexfest *Salon Kitty*, in the hopes that Brass would be pliable to Guccione's orders. More bizarrely, Guccione recruited novelist Gore Vidal to pen the screenplay, who not surprisingly became appalled when he realized what was being done to his material. Guccione brought over a planeload of *Penthouse* Pets to Italy and filmed a number of hardcore sequences behind Brass' back, including a long lesbian sequence with Lori Wagner and Anneka Di Lorenzo (who sued for career damages and won less than $2 in court) and the notorious ship orgy. Most of the cast members had no idea about the explicit inserts being shot, though the mind still boggles what Mirren and MacDowell thought when they were asked to prance around naked and simulate numerous perverse sexual acts in front of the camera. Peter O'Toole and John Gielgud get off easier thanks to early death scenes, though they too are surrounded by a number of fornicating extras. Ah, the '70s. MacDowell is actually quite good for most of the film, giving a full throttle performance after which his career obviously had nowhere to go. A number of familiar Eurohorror faces turn up along the way, including two future *Tenebre* actors, John Steiner and Mirella d'Angelo, though it's hard to notice anyone else when MacDowell is on the screen. Brass regular Savoy is awful in her large role as Drusilla, though it's doubtful she was hired for her acting talent, and Mirren mostly looks amusing and bewildered by the whole thing.

Originally released at 156 minutes with a self-imposed X rating, *Caligula* was then sliced down to a paltry 102 minutes for an R rating. The latter version, also released on DVD by Image and Penthouse, is quite a different and far more tedious experience, deleting virtually all of the nudity and leaving in long, long stretches of plot with no action whatsoever. The unrated videotape released by Vestron was almost imperceptibly letterboxed at about 1.50:1 and looked pale, grainy, and drab throughout; judging from the 142 minute running time, it was also time compressed, as no actual footage appeared to be missing.

The DVD restores the correct full running time and looks markedly better; on large screen monitors the image quality is very satisfying and looks even richer and smoother than the recent "restored" theatrical reissue. On standard or smaller monitors (about 32" or less), the vast amount of detail may compress poorly and could cause some moiré shimmering during many of the long shots. However, it's still vastly preferable either way to the VHS version, and the letterboxing reveals a number of bizarre details that were previously cropped off (e.g., the physically ill man in the background during the first banquet scene). The Dolby 5.1 soundtrack remix primarily focuses on the music (mostly Prokofiev and Khachaturyan standards) split to the

rear and sides, with an occasional directional effect (lightning, the whirring decapitation machine, and so on) tossed in as well. It's not a spectacular sound mix *per se* but seems very generous considering the movie's pedigree.

The disc also includes a fascinating and often appalling 56 minute documentary about the making of "Gore Vidal's *Caligula*," as it's called here, which was previously included on one of Penthouse's compilation laserdiscs. This bizarre companion piece features Vidal waxing rhapsodic about his depiction of Caligula, intercut with Guccione (in full late-'70s disco lizard regalia) explaining his own motivations behind the film. Behind the scenes footage ranges from set construction to preparation for the hardcore sequences, as well as glimpses of some scenes never included in any final cut (McDowell bashing a senator over the head with a sledgehammer, for example). McDowell and Mirren also appear for quick interviews, with Mirren aptly describing the epic as "an irresistible mixture of art and genitals." Lifted from what appears to be a 16mm source, the documentary looks fine for its age and is quite a welcome bonus.

The attractive package also features some stylish, fully animated menus, and the first pressing of the unrated edition features an additional sampler disc with excerpts from other Penthouse video titles. The two disc Dutch set retains the same extras as the U.S. (except for the bonus Penthouse disc), but with an anamorphic transfer (which still looks rough and muddy, like the film always has) and a mono soundtrack. The U.K. disc only contains the censored version and is best avoided.

CAMILLE 2000
Colour, 1969, 117m. / Directed by Radley Metzger / Starring Daniele Gaubert, Nino Castelnuovo / Image (US R0 NTSC) / WS (2.35:1)

This delicious cocktail of a movie marked a new era for erotic films in general and, most importantly, for Metzger; while he had played around with adapting classic stories into a modern context before (*Carmen, Baby*), here he transformed a classic Alexandre Dumas Fils romance best known as a Greta Garbo tearjerker into a sumptuous, jet-setting tragedy filled with beautiful, self-centred people whose nobler virtues invariably clash with their stations in life.

Apparently, life in the near future will cause cities (Rome, in this case) to be filled only with the rich and decadent. Into this kinky universe stumbles the romantic Armand (Nino Castelnuovo, best known as Pierre in *Umbrellas of Cherbourg* and the *giallo* favourite *Strip Nude for Your Killer*), whose father provides him with a lavish lifestyle in exchange for control over his life. Armand is offered his pick of the ladies for a companion, and against his friends' advice, he sets his sights on Marguerite (the lovely Danielle Gaubert, who tragically died shortly after this was released). A true party girl, Marguerite flits from one lover to another amidst wild parties and bouts of intravenous drugs. Obviously aware that her days are numbered, she resists Armand's desire to form a true relationship, but eventually their passion consumes them. Unfortunately, fate has a few surprises in store for them.

While *Camille 2000* is packed with memorable images and haunting scenes (love those mirrors!), the highlight is undoubtedly a ten minute party sequence in which the voluptuous Olympe (Silvana Venturelli) vies for Armand's affections at a lavish underground party decked out with a gold prison motif; arguably the greatest setpiece in the Metzger canon, the inevitable sex scene is powerful and erotic, tragic and exciting at the same time, with much of its power owed to the fantastic score by Pierro Piccioni, one of the finest of its era. The astonishing locations and production design constantly delight the eye while perfectly evoking the film's period and skewed outlook; likewise, Metzger's keen editing sense is in fine form, particularly in the startling moment when he cuts from a syringe plunging into skin to a close-up of drums being played in a music combo. Metzger also begins to explore the playful cinematic self-awareness (the film begins with a clapboard for *Camille 2000* appearing over the opening shot), which eventually exploded the next year in *The Lickerish Quartet*. Of course, even the most consummate visual style needs something to hang onto, and Castelnuovo and Gaubert, a great screen couple, provide the necessary emotional depth to make the narrative a poignant, even wrenching experience.

The First Run transfer presents the film's Panavision framing perfectly and looks better than ever on the Image DVD. The same transfer was previously available from Audubon Video, which opened the matte up at the top to expose distracting splices and dirt. Metzger's last scope film, *Camille 2000* desperately requires all of the image to really work with an audience, and this is simply the only way to see it. Some print damage is still evident, particularly in the opening two minutes and during reel changes, but the colours are strong if not entirely accurate (the original three-strip Technicolor photography has obviously aged a little). This version also runs much longer than the horrendous VHS release from Magnum Video, which excised the end credits and, strangely, one minute from a very darkly lit, mild love scene in the middle of the film. More oddly, the Magnum and First Run prints conclude with Armand rushing down the steps with Marguerite's friends in a drunken stupor, echoing the film's opening, while the Audubon Video edition contains the same scene earlier (directly after the casino sequence) and simply ends on a simpler, more romantic note at the hospital. Obviously, this difference significantly changes the tone of the film; by placing Armand drunk at the end, the resulting impression is that he has become completely despairing and borderline insane after Marguerite's death. It works either way, but both versions are worth checking out. Like the other First Run titles, the DVD also includes the European release trailer, in this case a collection of stills accompanied by Piccioni's score.

C

CANDY

Colour, 1968, 124m. / Directed by Christian Marquand / Starring Ewa Aulin, Marlon Brando, Richard Burton / Anchor Bay (US R1 NTSC) / WS (1.85:1) (16:9)

In its day, *Candy* was the most scandalous novel by satirist Terry Southern, best known for writing *Barbarella, The Magic Christian*, and *Easy Rider*. His story, an updating of Voltaire's *Candide* for the flower power generation, followed a naive waif through a series of erotic and perverse misadventures, though Southern himself was unable to come up with a finale and turned to Mason Hoffenberg to supply the final demented pages. The book wound up being banned and censored all over the globe, so it was only natural for someone to turn it into a movie. In 1969, *Candy* opened and revealed a crafty way of getting around the controversial subject matter. The Italian/French/American co-production, packed with famous stars, turned the meandering storyline into a trippy, candy coloured comedy with sci-fi and fantastic overtones, complete with a mind-blowing cosmic finale. There really hasn't been another movie quite like it, and for those who can handle cinematic head trips laced with chuckles and gorgeous visuals, this *Candy* is dandy indeed.

Young high school student Candy Christian (*Death Laid an Egg*'s Ewa Aulin), who may be a visitor from outer space, lives a quiet suburban existence with her history teacher father (John Astin). One day the school is sent amok by the arrival of guest speaker McPhisto (Richard Burton), a drunk Welsh poet (what else?) who takes Candy for a ride in his limousine. Their encounter back at her house turns into debauchery, with McPhisto drooling over a mannequin while Candy is ravaged on a pool table by Manuel (Ringo Starr), the family gardener. Since Manuel was saving his chastity for the priesthood, his entire family pursues Candy and her father to the airport, where they catch a ride with military zealot General Smight (Walter Matthau). Again things turn calamitous, leaving Candy and her now comatose father plunging from the plane. At the hospital, Mr. Christian becomes the patient of the celebrated Dr. Krankheit (James Coburn), who vies for Candy's attentions and engages in shouting matches with the hospital administrator (John Huston). With her father now in a coma, Candy tears off into the city streets where she encounters a bizarre assortment of characters, including a gravity-defying hunchback (Charles Aznavour), a fanatical underground film director (*The Bird with the Crystal Plumage*'s Enrico Maria Salerno), and a lecherous Indian guru (Marlon Brando) who services her across the country in a moving truck.

Obviously a plot summary can't capture the dizzy, psychedelic charm of *Candy*, which will please '60s film lovers for its once in a lifetime cast. However, fans of European cult films will also be delighted with the colourful supporting characters, including *Blood and Roses*' Elsa Martinelli as Candy's aunt, Florinda Bolkan (*Don't Torture a Duckling, Flavia the Heretic*) and Marilù Tolo (*Bluebeard*) as Manuel's sisters, and a dubbed Anita Pallenberg as a psychotic nurse. The "out of this world" opening and closing sequences were designed by Douglas Trumbull, who had just completed *2001*, and then there's the catchy, outrageous soundtrack. *Candy* was withheld from home video for decades because of music rights, but now you can hear it all: Dave Grusin's groovy instrumentals, songs by Steppenwolf including "Magic Carpet Ride," and best of all, The Byrds' sweeping closing credits song, "Child of the Universe," which turned up later in stripped down form on their 1972 album *Dr. Byrds and Mr. Hyde*. Incidentally, director Christian Marquand is better known as an actor in such spicy fare as Roger Vadim's *And God Created Woman* and the trashiest movie soap ever, *The Other Side of Midnight*.

Though the packaging doesn't mention it, Anchor Bay's DVD marks not only the first US video release of *Candy* but also the first American availability ever of the uncut European version. Transferred directly from the original negative in Italy, the film looks terrific and boasts an extra six minutes of footage, previously only available on bootleg videotape. Among the highlights are more pandemonium at the hospital, including much more footage with Pallenberg, and a sequence in which Candy is accosted at a bar by some gangsters. The mono audio sounds quite good; try playing it through your front speakers for the full room-shaking effect. While the movie alone would be enough to justify this disc, there are a few nice extras worth noting. The long theatrical trailer is a beautifully edited piece of work, concluding with Ringo's memorable "Viva Zapata!," and the disc also contains some amusing radio spots ("the sweetest movie this side of *Psychopathia Sexualis!*"), talent bios, and a still gallery featuring many behind-the-scenes shots of Aulin relaxing with various cast members.

CANDYMAN

Colour, 1992, 99m. / Directed by Bernard Rose / Starring Virginia Madsen, Tony Todd / Columbia (US R1 NTSC) / WS (1.85:1) (16:9) / DD2.0

 Student Helen Lyle (Madsen), researching a thesis on urban myths, becomes intrigued by the legend of Candyman, a shadowy figure with a hook for a hand who can allegedly be summoned by standing before a mirror and chanting his name five times. Although Helen doesn't believe in such things, a visit to the run-down housing estate which is reputed to be Candyman's domain proves that many people do. When she ignores warnings to leave well alone, people close to Helen begin to die horribly.

A scary and visually striking adaptation of a Clive Barker novella ("The Forbidden") from director Bernard Rose, whose equally stylish (if somewhat less creepy) debut *Paperhouse* is a largely underrated psychological treat. Although the ensuing sequels might have one believe that Daniel Robitaille (aka Candyman) is an unstoppable Michael Myers or Freddie Krueger clone - which, to a point, he became - that's not how he's presented here. An intelligent and imaginative script paints this particular product of (fictitious) urban legend much more profoundly than that. Thus, discarding the two ignoble sequels, viewed as a solo offering, Rose's film is extremely good. It's no rollercoaster of terror, but the unnerving narrative is fleshed out with some decent shock moments and the combined talent both off camera and on makes for a highly entertaining little chiller. Mellifluous-voiced Tony Todd as the titular hook-handed wraith obviously dominates the proceedings, even though we don't see a great deal of him. Virginia Madsen is a convincingly fiery heroine and Xander Berkeley is very plausible indeed as her despicable hubby. Rose's direction and excellent screenplay (which skilfully avoids almost all of the tired slasher movie clichés) aside, Philip Glass's hauntingly melancholy piano melody stays with you long after the final credits have rolled. Regrettably a couple of Brownie points must be docked for the diffusion of a powerful and unexpectedly downbeat denouement with the addition of a ridiculous and ineffectual "shock" coda.

A slightly disappointing *Candyman* package from Columbia Tristar on its Region 1 platter. The 28-chaptered feature can be viewed in either fullscreen or 1.85:1 widescreen format and is in excellent shape, but aside from a slightly grainy trailer that's your lot. Sound selections are provided in English Dolby Surround or French, subtitling is also in English and French. - TG

[Though not immediately noticeable, both the US DVD and British video releases are missing a gory shot from the psychiatrist's murder; only the Columbia US laserdisc is uncut. - ed.]

CANNIBAL FEROX

Colour, 1980, 93m. / Directed by Umberto Lenzi / Starring Giovanni Lombardo Radice, Lorraine De Selle / Image (US R0 NTSC) / WS (1.85:1) / DD2.0, Vipco (UK R2 PAL) / WS (1.85:1), Sazuma (R0 NTSC) / WS (1.85:1) (16:9)

Yikes, this is it! Certainly not the best but perhaps the most appalling of the Italian cannibal movie cycle during the late '70s and early '80s, *Cannibal Ferox* belongs to that horde of disreputable Italian imports which assaulted movie screens and video shelves before the major studios put their foot down. Incidentally, the Latin word "ferox" roughly translates as "ferocious," which should give you some idea of where this movie is coming from. Marketed under the new title of *Make Them Die Slowly*, it soon became a minor media sensation along the lines of *Faces of Death* when Elvira, Mistress of the Dark refused to host its video release from Thriller Video. Soon excerpts were turning up on news programmes to show the depravity being consumed by modern teenagers. Now of course it's a sick and often amusing piece of nostalgia for gorehounds willing to overlook such wretched lapses of taste as real animal killings and laughable latex effects.

In New York, a cadre of tough cops led by Robert Kerman (a veteran of *Cannibal Holocaust* and *Eaten Alive*, aka porn actor Richard Bolla) tracks down a notorious drug dealer named Mike (oft-abused actor John Morghen). Meanwhile plucky NYU grad student Gloria (Lorraine De Selle) ventures into the South American jungle to prove for her thesis that cannibalism doesn't exist. Accompanied by the sympathetic Rudy (Danilo Mattei) and slutty Pat (Zora Kerova, the stage performer in *New York Ripper*), she trudges through the wilderness after their jeep breaks down. Soon they come up Mike and his sidekick, who have had a nasty run-in with a tribe of cannibals who killed Mike's partner. Something doesn't sit quite right with Mike's story, but that doesn't stop Pat from bedding down with the sleazeball for the night. The next morning he encourages Pat to rape and torture a native girl, so obviously he isn't the most sensitive soul in the jungle. Sure enough, the cannibals are out for revenge, and in between bouts of animal fighting and killing, the body parts begin to fly.

While many viewers will undoubtedly be repulsed and amused by the hyperbolic violence on display (a woman suspended on hooks through her breasts, a castration and arm amputation, etc.), *Cannibal Ferox* is also difficult to take seriously thanks to its highly quotable, trashy dialogue. (Fortunately some of the choicer lines have been preserved on Grindhouse's chapter selection titles.) The animal killings are genuinely disturbing and tasteless, disrupting what could have been a simple over the top gutmuncher and pushing it into far more dangerous territory. Unlike Ruggero Deodato's completely serious and more intricate *Cannibal Holocaust*, this trashfest from director Lenzi (who's better suited to *gialli* and *crime* films) makes few attempts at authenticity and wallows around in the gutter like a pro. Add to that a catchy, disco-tinged score by "Budy Maglione" and you've got a midnight oddity unlike any other.

Grindhouse's DVD essentially replicates their impressive laserdisc special edition into a more compact, flashy presentation. The terrific menu screens (pay close attention to John!) take you through a variety of special features, including an on-camera interview with Lenzi, three different theatrical trailers (the US one is the best), and a slew of stills and promotional art. Look for a fun Easter Egg involving a more recent L.A. screening, too. The film itself looks the same as always, with nice saturated colours and accurate widescreen framing.

The image is quite grainy throughout in keeping with its origins but isn't unwatchable, while the English soundtrack has been given a terrific remix into full surround. The jungle scenes constantly buzz with ambient activity, while the music has never sounded better. The original mono Italian track is also included for purists, though the film was obviously designed to be shown with the voices dubbed in English.

The real centrepiece here actually isn't the movie itself but the spectacular, scorching commentary track with Lenzi and Radice who, in their separate recording sessions, offer violently diverging views of the entire production. Lenzi remains proud and complimentary towards his film, while Radice is plainly repulsed and "ashamed" by it, not without good reason. Even for those who despise the film, this feature easily earns the price tag all by itself. While the Grindhouse version offers the most comprehensive study of this peculiar and morally dubious film, the UK DVD from Vipco offers a cut print, trailers, and a photo gallery, while the continental Sazuma disc features an anamorphic transfer (perhaps interlaced from the same master, though it's hard to tell for certain); neither offer the stereo soundtrack or commentary.

CANNIBAL HOLOCAUST
Colour, 1979, 96m. / Directed by Ruggero Deodato / Starring Robert Kerman, Francesca Ciardi / EC Entertainment (Holland R0 NTSC), Vipco (UK R2 PAL) / WS (1.85:1)

 A film radically ahead of its time and still unbearable to watch for many viewers, *Cannibal Holocaust* marks the apex (or nadir, depending on your viewpoint) of the Italian cannibal movie subgenre that flourished through the '70s and early '80s. While most cannibal films can be dismissed thanks to their kitschy play-do special effects and laughable dialogue, this film is a far more challenging and dangerous animal than, say, *Cannibal Ferox*, which sticks firmly to its pulp origins and aspires to little beyond drive-in amusement. Deodato's grim worldview and unremitting nastiness make for a very rough ride whose viciousness remains as potent and startling now, twenty years later.

Four American filmmakers have disappeared without a trace in the Amazon jungle, where an expedition/rescue team led by Professor Monroe (Robert Kerman) goes into the wild to find the lost documentarians. After some tasteless animal atrocity footage and several false leads, the team stumbles upon "The Tree People," a tribe given to such charming practices as raping and killing a woman with a stone dildo as punishment for adultery. Thanks to a gesture of trust involving skinny-dipping, the team is provided with the canisters of film shot by the missing crew, and we switch back to New York City where the footage is screened for appalled financiers.

Despite this inauspicious extended prologue, *Cannibal Holocaust* immediately separates itself from the pack with the footage itself - raw, handheld 16mm images shot from two cameras which follows the four filmmakers, three men and one woman, as they callously tromp through the jungle, committing sexual and violent acts against the "little mud people" and even offing an animal or two in the process. While the actual onscreen killing of animals is completely indefensible, the verisimilitude of these sequences causes the viewer to question the reality of everything else onscreen; the special effects, particularly the notorious image of a woman vertically impaled on a sharp pole, are so gritty and realistically handled that many viewers have taken the found footage as reality. Deodato consistently blurs the line between cinema and actual mondo documentary filmmaking with great skill, brutally tearing viewers' preconceptions about *Mondo Cane*-style practices to shreds. You want to see brutality? Here it is, folks, in its ugly, all too human glory. For once, here's a film that lives up to its claim, and viewers who think they've seen it all will find this to be the closest thing to a genuine emotional "holocaust" ever captured in a fictional film. Love it or hate it, this is an important, vital work in both the horror and mondo genres; no other film has more horrifically captured the feeling of being lost in the middle of the wilderness, surrounded by forces whose only intent is to track you down and kill you. The last fifteen minutes, made even more wrenching by Riz Ortolani's rhapsodic music score, have yet to be topped for sheer gut punch nihilism.

Following a protracted legal battle, *Cannibal Holocaust* was banned in its native country, appeared on video briefly in the UK before being banned as a video nasty, and was never legally released in America at all. Most horror fans first came into contact with this through shoddy Venezuelan bootleg tapes, then through the nice-looking Japanese laserdisc, which distractingly fogged out all of the frontal nudity (quite a lot, in this case). EC Entertainment's DVD is the most satisfying of the bunch, though there's still room for improvement. The letterboxing accurately replicates the film's 1.85:1 exhibition; the framing sequences were shot hard-matted at that aspect ratio, while the found 16mm footage was filmed full frame and matted off on all prints. The theatrical trailer includes a few glimpses of the unmatted footage, though the framing variations probably don't make much difference given the film's haphazard visual composition. The film clocks in here at about 91 minutes, roughly 5 shorter than the longest prints, but this appears to be due to time compression as nothing has been cut. Ortolani's score is isolated on the analogue tracks (probably lifted from the Lucertola Media CD), and Deodato appears for a brief interview. A few stills from the notorious "piranha bait" scene, reportedly never completed, appear as a supplement; it's hard to imagine why this scene has been considered so controversial over the years, since it doesn't look even remotely close in shock value to the other cannibal segments in the film. EC has made the film available both in a flat (non-16:9) uncut edition and a remastered 16:9 transfer, though inexplicably the latter is shorn of five seconds from the "Road to Hell" sequence. For the more easily offended, the UK disc features a censored and essentially worthless print excising most of the more extreme imagery, while a DVD from Grindhouse has been in the works after a U.S. theatrical midnight run but has not materialized as of this writing. Proceed at your own risk.

CANNIBAL MAN

Colour, 1971, 98m. / Directed by Eloy de la Iglesia / Starring Vicente Parra, Eusebio Poncela / Anchor Bay (US R1 NTSC) / WS (1.85:1) (16:9)

Nothing promises a rollicking good time like a movie opening up with a graphic slaughterhouse tour. A brutal and strangely melancholy film, *Cannibal Man* (or technically, *The Cannibal Man*) begins with humble cow butcher Marcos (Vicente Parra from *Soft Skin on Black Silk*) contentedly chomping away on a beefy sandwich and hanging out at a bar where a TV commercial proclaims "It's good because it's got meat!" Marcos hops into a cab along with his girlfriend (Emma Cohen) but gets into a spat with the driver and kills him in a rage. He ignores his girlfriend's insistence that he goes to the police and finally strangles her just to keep her quiet. Pretty soon almost everyone he knows stumbles across evidence of the crimes and has to be added to the rising body count, with the unfortunate result that Marcos' apartment becomes awfully crowded. Hmm, could his job possibly be the

answer to his problem? Meanwhile his sympathetic gay neighbour (Pedro Almodóvar regular Eusebio Poncela) observes everything from afar and makes a surprising offer...

One of Spain's more notorious exports, *Cannibal Man* was originally *titled La semana del asesino* (or *The Week of the Murderer*, since he kills once a day) and circulated in Europe under a more subtle title, *Apartment on the 13th Floor*. Director Eloy de la Iglesia was one of the major directors to push Spanish censorship boundaries with this film and a number of powerful gay-oriented films like *El Diputado, Los placeres ocultos, El Sacerdote,* and the unforgettable *Colegas*, all of which eventually found an audience on video. While *Cannibal Man* certainly doesn't skimp on the red stuff, it's ultimately not as graphic as the late '70s splatter epics and quite different from the flamboyant bloodletting of Italian thrillers around the same time. The fetid atmosphere of decay and frustration is overpowering, with the most horrific use of a single apartment since Roman Polanski's *Repulsion*. The social implications of a Spanish society which ultimately cannibalizes itself are hardly subtle, but it's this kind of treatment that allowed directors like Iglesia, Jess Franco, and many others to flourish under their new government.

Anchor Bay's DVD looks fine under the circumstances, though this film will never be visually glossy. The grimy colours and grainy film stock are transferred in all their original grindhouse glory, while the dubbed English audio (why?) isn't too harsh on the ears. A Spanish print would have been preferable, but presumably this is all the distributor, Atlas, was willing to offer. The disc also includes a nondescript English-language theatrical trailer (and yes, it did briefly play US movie houses in the early '70s). Phil Hardy's *Aurum Encyclopedia of Horror* reports an original running time of 120 minutes, but as with *Autopsy*, this could be misinformation passed on by the original press materials.

THE CANTERBURY TALES

Colour, 1971, 110m. / Directed by Pier Paolo Pasolini / Starring Laura Betti, Tom Baker / Image (US R1 NTSC), BFI (UK R2 PAL) / WS (1.85:1)

The late Pier Paolo Pasolini's second film in his "Trilogy of Life" series, *The Canterbury Tales*, at least ranks as the most ribald and coarse entry in this literary cycle. While *The Decameron* and *The Arabian Nights* based their sometimes shocking imagery on the events in the stories themselves, Pasolini felt compelled to embellish these Chaucer stories (which everyone probably remembers from school) with a number of explicit incidents. While the infamous "Miller's Tale" obviously didn't need much elaboration in the raunchiness department, the other stories, while true to their origins, have been fleshed out (with Pasolini himself playing Chaucer!) to include S&M and other unexpected "modern" touches. Whatever your opinions about the merits of the film (and most critics don't acknowledge many), these discs are, like the other trilogy instalments, probably the best we'll see.

Derived from the archival MOMA print, this likewise bears occasional signs of wear (some speckling here, a splice there), and the added clarity of the DVD format makes the low budget's limitations even more obvious. However, if you're a Pasolini completist, there's no excuse not to pick this up. The strange collection of actors includes everyone from *Dr. Who*'s Tom Baker (doing a highly unnecessary nude scene) to Italian super-bitch specialist Laura Betti (*1900, Bay of Blood*), not to mention Josephine Chaplin, of all people. The result is a bizarre aural clash between authentic English voices and some wildly anachronistic faux-Cockney accents given to blatantly Italian actors; the results are highly inconsistent. (It is worth noting that Image's disc is of the original English-language version, whereas the BFI's U.K. disc contains an Italian-dubbed version.) If you're looking to shock your friends who think they've "seen it all," don't miss the film's now-legendary final minutes in hell; no description could possibly do this over-the-top sequence justice.

THE CAR

Colour, 1977, 96m. / Directed by Elliot Silverstein / Starring James Brolin, Kathleen Lloyd / Anchor Bay (US R1 NTSC) / WS (2.35:1) (16:9) / DD5.1

For some reason filmmakers around the middle and end of the '70s were obsessed with cars. You want comedies? *Smokey and the Bandit. The Cannonball Run.* Horror? *Duel. The Hearse..* Heck, even *Death Car on the Freeway*. It was inevitable that someone would eventually do a movie called *The Car*, and the results are exactly what you would expect: a big driverless old car from hell (literally) careens around the desert and causes mayhem. And there's your plot.

Thanks to late night TV (usually cut to shreds), *The Car* has actually built up a sizable cult following over the years, and obviously someone at Anchor Bay must really love it judging from the relatively spectacular treatment it receives here. While Universal shunted the film off to the sidelines for decades, fans who shouted for *The Car* got a DVD that presents this goofy little gem in all its glory. Don't be fooled by the critical raves on the packaging which call this film "existentialist" and liken it to Ingmar Bergman(?); this is horror schlock territory all the way.

Sheriff Wade Parent (James Brolin, doing a warm up for *The Amityville Horror*) becomes appalled when both visitors and residents in his small desert town are ploughed down by the aforementioned malefic car, which emits a really annoying honk after each kill. He even begins to fear for the safety of his girlfriend, Lauren (Kathleen Lloyd, doing her best Paula Prentiss impression), and his kids, Kim and Kyle Richards (who appeared separately in damn near every '70s movie all the way from *Escape to Witch Mountain* to *Halloween*). The cops become especially concerned after one of their own, John Marley (best known for waking up with a horse's head scene in *The Godfather*), gets offed by the car, along with John Rubinstein, who makes the most of his one scene by chewing all the scenery in sight.

What sets *The Car* apart from all the killer shark/bear/tarantula/bulldozer movies of the period is its tendency towards unpredictable, nihilistic plot twists, with one kicker two thirds of the way through that should stop most viewers in their tracks. (Don't watch the trailer first!) The film spends a lot of time etching its characters, such as recovering alcoholic cop Ronny Cox, which makes it a bit richer and more interesting than standard direct to video horror today, and the expert widescreen lensing by Gerald Hirschfeld perfectly captures the arid locations and gives the car itself a convincing sense of demonic fury. On the other hand, Leonard Rosenman's clunky score overstates most of the horrific moments and pounds viewers on the head when it should simply creep up behind them.

Not surprisingly, the DVD itself is close to flawless. While a pointless pan and scan transfer has also been included, the anamorphic letterboxed version is really the only way to watch this. Gorgeous hues, no noticeable artefacts, and a killer Dolby 5.1 remix make this quite a nice showpiece - and the menu screens are extremely amusing.

CARMEN, BABY

Colour, 1967, 90m. / Directed by Radley Metzger / Starring Uta Levka, Claude Ringer / Image (US R0 NTSC) / WS (2.35:1)

A vivid, stylish retelling of the familiar story made popular in Bizet's opera (but derived from a novel by Prosper Merimee), *Carmen, Baby* was Radley Metzger's first film in colour, a device he utilized to the hilt. Eye-popping reds and blues dot the screen everywhere from Carmen's solid hue dresses to the luminous sea surrounding the port town in which the story is set. In Metzger's most famous sequence, he slowly films an entire love scene by panning back and forth through a series of perfectly arranged, multicoloured wine bottles. (Russ Meyer later mocked this familiar setpiece in Re: Search's *Incredibly Strange Films*.) Though not as audacious or intense as the masterpieces which would immediately follow, this film marks an important step in Metzger's development as a director and in some respects plays like a rough draft for the similarly themed *Camille 2000*.

Carmen (Uta Levka), a popular "working girl" of the streets, is arrested by a young, wet-behind-the-ears police officer, Jose (Claus Ringer). The villagers explain that Carmen may do as she pleases; for example, she often helps herself for free from the food stands in the town square as long as she later provides some special compensation of her own. Jose lets Carmen go, even after she incites a brawl, much to the rage of his superior officer. For his carelessness, Jose receives a month in jail but finds the time worth it. Smitten with Carmen, he begins to pursue her despite her wanton ways and irrational belief in astrology. In one memorable sequence (whose suggestiveness was created entirely in the editing room, according to Metzger), Carmen does a particularly dirty dance with a Chianti bottle that must be seen to be believed. The two attempt to forge a relationship, but alas, Carmen refuses to be controlled, realizing she is destined for nothing but tragedy.

Because Levka was in the early stages of pregnancy at the time, she does virtually no nudity, forcing Metzger to come up with creative ways to generate heat while showing very little. Coupled with his first really structured narrative, the results forced him to expand as an artist and as a result produced the blend of classical storytelling and inventive visual elegance with which he has become associated. As the free-spirited Carmen, Levka is one of Metzger's best heroines, completely blowing poor, bland Mr. Ringer off the screen. The attractive settings and Mediterranean architecture make for some dynamic eye candy as well, while cinematographer Jura continues to prove himself adept at creating striking widescreen compositions.

Though profitable during its theatrical run, *Carmen, Baby* remained unavailable on video until Audubon released a VHS version in 1994. Though the anamorphic imagery was cropped to fullscreen, the incredibly saturated candy colours were a joy to behold. The new edition prepared by First Run and released on DVD by Image features more subdued colours but thankfully restores the full scope aspect ratio, more than compensating for the loss. The print is in solid shape despite a few minor scuffs and specks during reel changes, and sound quality, while not startling, is clear and intelligible. Overall this is the most satisfying presentation of the film to date, but completists will probably want to hold on to the old Audubon version as well. The DVD also includes the original, very long trailer.

CARNAL KNOWLEDGE

Colour, 1971, 98m. / Directed by Mike Nichols / Starring Jack Nicholson, Art Garfunkel, Candice Bergen, Ann-Margret / MGM (US R1 NTSC) / WS (2.35:1) (16:9)

Not exactly what people expected from the man behind *The Graduate*, the controversial *Carnal Knowledge* belongs with the ranks of *Last Tango in Paris* and *Deep Throat* as one of the films that helped to shatter the sexual censorship taboos of the early '70s. The difference here, of course, can be found in the fact that the supposedly "pornographic" content of the film lies almost entirely in its dialogue; only a few seconds of the film contain any actual nudity or sexual activity. Nearly thirty years after its initial release, long after the furore has died down, the film still manages to shock and disturb; while it may not be as easy to take as other films from its director and stars, *Carnal Knowledge* could very well be their finest hour.

Two college roommates, Jonathan (Jack Nicholson) and Sandy (Art Garfunkel), candidly share stories about their sexual fantasies. At a college mixer function, Jonathan urges Sandy to go after Susan (Candice Bergen). However, Jonathan later goes after Susan himself, and both men lose their virginity with her. From this point on, both Jonathan and Sandy experience one dysfunctional relationship after another, with Jonathan in particular building up a reservoir of resentment and distrust toward the female gender. His relationship with Bobbie (Ann-Margret), a declining sex kitten, results in her becoming a housebound wretch who cries for marriage to justify her existence, while Sandy dates gradually younger women in an attempt to deny his shortcomings as a man.

Obviously not a feel-good movie, *Carnal Knowledge* is nevertheless laceratingly witty and stunning well acted. Nicholson has never been better, but everyone else is up to his level. Ann-Margret finally proved she could really act and opened up several new doors for her '70s work (*Joseph Andrews, Tommy*), and Candice Bergin finally got to flex her acting muscles after wallowing in truly bizarre Hollywood exploitation films (*The Hunting Party, Soldier Blue, The Day the Fish Came Out*). Finally, Garfunkel made the complete transition to actor in what would prove to be a very unusual career, climaxing (in a manner of speaking) with Nicolas Roeg's *Bad Timing*. Therefore, while this film may be classified most obviously as art, it offers quite a few pleasures for sleazemongers as well. And don't forget Rita Moreno's incredibly surreal cameo in the last scene, one of the most unsettling finales of the decade.

Nichols displays a sure cinematic hand throughout and makes some surprising choices along the way. He approaches Jules Feiffer's script (originally a play and actually produced on the stage many years later) as a kind of scientific experiment, avoiding any kind of music score apart from a few bland source tunes in the background. Giuseppe Rotunno's elegant widescreen photography gives the proceedings a Sartre-inspired ambience in which the world seems to have been pared down to a few pathetic players, only one of whom is even dignified with a last name. The clean, precise lighting ranges from icy white (the ice skating sequence, the last scene in Sandy's apartment) to rich, dusky shades of brown and gold (the college and Bobbie sequences); these startling visual contrasts echo the characters' inability to reconcile their romantic fantasies with the reality of their fellow human beings.

MGM's DVD presentation of *Carnal Knowledge* improves significantly on the Criterion laserdisc, thanks to a subtle, dusky anamorphic transfer. It still looks like a '70s film, obviously, but this is a film best experienced letterboxed or not at all - and it's never looked better than it does here. A few hints of grain and some fluctuating shadows are the only noticeable flaws in the source print, which is in excellent condition. The mono audio is clear and definitely acceptable, since it consists almost entirely of dialogue. No trailer is included, but the booklet enclosure features some nice factual tidbits, mostly related to the film's legendary courtroom battles beginning in Albany, Georgia and ending in the Supreme Court.

CARNIVAL OF SOULS

B&W, 1963, 79/84m. / Directed by Herk Harvey / Starring Candace Hilligoss, Sidney Berger / Criterion (US R1 NTSC), Image (US R1 NTSC), MPIC (UK R2 PAL), Koch, Diamond (US R0 NTSC)

 One of the few lucky low budget horror films to escape oblivion, Herk Harvey's low budget Kansas miracle, *Carnival of Souls*, became a cult classic entirely through word of mouth and late night TV screenings. When public domain copies began trickling onto the video market, demand for the film reached a fever pitch, which resulted in a highly unlikely but welcome theatrical release in 1989. So, does the movie itself deserve all this attention? Absolutely.

During a foolhardy drag race across a rickety wooden bridge, a carload of young women plunges off into a deep river. While officials drag the waters for bodies, one of the women, Mary Henry (Candace Hilligoss), emerges onto land. However, when she travels to a nearby town to accept a job as a church organist, Mary is haunted by the presence of a ghostly man who seems to be strangely connected to an abandoned old pavilion. Mary becomes increasingly disconnected from her surroundings, with ghouls appearing at inconvenient moments, seemingly beckoning her back towards a watery grave.

Though virtually no one involved in *Carnival* went on to a real film career (though Hilligoss did turn up in *Curse of the Living Corpse*), this film exhibits an astonishing command of the film medium, particularly for a first feature. The imaginative use of black and white photography, shadows, sound effects (or the absence thereof), and film speed create an off kilter, creepy atmosphere that clings to the viewer's psyche long after the melancholy final shot. The fact that the entire film is scored with an organ (kudos to Gene Moore) adds to the sense of unease that escalates throughout its brief running time.

While nothing can compare to seeing *Carnival of Souls* in a movie theatre (preferably a nearly empty one), Criterion's DVD special edition comes as close as possible in a home environment. Almost absurd in its avalanche of supplementary material, this set should keep horror fans busy for many, many hours as they explore this odd fusion of art house surrealism and bare knuckle horror. The 79 minute theatrical cut (prepared by the distributors back in '62) is presented first, and the visual quality is remarkable. Image quality is clean and almost three dimensional throughout, with a number of visual details difficult to spot even in theatrical prints. This disc also includes 45 minutes of outtakes (some of them funny, some random and tedious), the rarely seen theatrical trailer, and two Kansas-produced TV documentaries, "The Carnival Tour" (a survey of the film's locations today) and "The Movie That Wouldn't Die," a look at the film's resurgence, complete with footage of Harvey, Hilligoss, and many other actors and technicians at a 1989 screening. A brief illustrated history also explains the odd history of Salt Lake City's Saltair pavilion, which figures so prominently in the film's climax.

Now, on to disc two. This expanded "director's cut" features approximately five minutes of footage trimmed from the original theatrical cut and is the one most widely seen by viewers today. This edition was first released on VHS by Sinister Cinema, then did the theatrical circuit before appearing on laserdisc from Image. The extra material is interesting and nice to have, though the theatrical cut actually features better pacing. Watch them both and judge for yourself. The video quality here is noticeably downgraded from the first disc and looks almost identical to the laserdisc. It still looks quite nice, but the advances in transfer technology over the past few years are still plainly evident when comparing these two discs.

The real coup here is a running commentary by the late Harvey and screenwriter John Clifford (presumably prepared but not used for a prior video or laserdisc edition), which feels as expected like a primer on how to make a crafty and effective local shocker with virtually no money. Supplements here include a survey of the Centron Corporation, for which Harvey and most of his crew worked for several decades, with an hour long sampler of Centron educational and industrial films thrown in for good measure. (Shades of the Latent Image spots on Elite's *Night of the Living Dead* laserdisc!) Tom Weaver's interviews with the principal creators (including Hilligoss) answer even more questions not covered in the understandably choppy commentary. Obviously a thorough and dedicated labour of love, this *Carnival of Souls* is jaw dropping in its exhaustive study of a film few people even acknowledged merely a decade ago.

A bare bones version for casual collectors is also available in the US from Image as part of the Wade Williams Collection, though without the advertised "SuperPsychorama" feature from Williams' VHS in which the zombies were colour tinted! However, this doctored version was available as a bonus DVD in the January 2002 issue of the UK's *Total Film* magazine. A handful of public domain companies have cashed in as well, but these are best avoided.

CARRIE

Colour, 1976, 99m. / Directed by Brian De Palma / Starring Sissy Spacek, Piper Laurie, Nancy Allen / MGM / WS (1.85:1) (16:9) / DD5.1

 Introverted loner Carrie White (Spacek) is picked on at school by spiteful kids and teachers alike, whilst at home she's browbeaten by her domineering religious zealot mother (Laurie). With the onset of womanhood, Carrie becomes increasingly aware of her burgeoning gift for telekinesis. The worm is about to turn.

25 years on from its initial release Brian DePalma's *Carrie* - among the more successful transitions from page to screen of a Stephen King novel - continues to hold its own alongside most modern day shockers. Due in no small part to the outstanding acting of Oscar nominees Spacek and Laurie, it's a potent evocation of brooding evil and heartbreaking poignancy. DePalma is a master at extruding maximum audience agitation - the sequence in which Carrie is set to fall victim to the ultimate humiliation is drawn out to unbearable length - and he sustains the squalling tension right up until the oft-aped but never bettered finale, when he shanghais us with an expertly served jolt. Amy Irving (who returned for the belated sequel) and in particular William Katt are likeable as the only people who display any compassion towards the ugly duckling. Nancy Allen and a youthful John Travolta are the cruel reprobates who pay the piper for scheming against her. Regular DePalma collaborator Pino Donaggio submits a beautifully opulent score. The image of a blood-drenched, wide-eyed Spacek maiming and pulverising everyone in sight amidst the inferno that was formerly the high school prom, is an enduring icon of terror cinema and one that won't fast be forgotten.

MGM supersede their previous DVD release of *Carrie* (which included only the film and its trailer) with a special edition disc chock full of goodies. The highlight is a pair of documentaries with a combined running time of almost 90 minutes, in which most of the key participants reflect upon and discuss the film at length; Travolta, however, is a conspicuous truant - too big these days to acknowledge his Thespian roots? There's a segment discussing the short-lived *Carrie* musical stage production, a trailer, some textual comment and a pleasing slideshow format gallery of photos and lobby cards. The film's original opening sequence would have made for a worthy inclusion as a "deleted scene", although it is at least represented by a number of excellent stills. The 32-

chaptered film itself appears on first inspection to be a little soft, though it's always had an ethereal look to it and has seldom, if ever, looked quite as nice as it does here. Language options are provided in English 5.1 stereo surround or English, Spanish and French mono, with subtitling in French and Spanish. - TG

CASINO ROYALE

Colour, 1967, 126m. / Directed by John Huston, Ken Hughes, Val Guest, Robert Parrish, Joe McGrath / Starring Peter Sellers, Woody Allen, David Niven / MGM (UK R2 PAL) / WS (2.35:1)

Sir James Bond (Niven) is called out of retirement to foil a SMERSH plot to take over the world, only to discover that the man running the operation is none other than his own nephew Jimmy Bond (Allen), aka Dr. Noah. "We'll run amuck... if you're too tired we'll walk amuck" says Woody Allen to Daliah Lavi in one of *Casino Royale*'s few amusing scenes. If only the creators hadn't been allowed to run amuck they might have conjured up something decent. That they had in their hands Ian Fleming's first 007 novel (pure gold-dust in terms of cinematic rights) and turned it into this slapdash abomination is mind-boggling. Using Fleming's own work to spoof the success of the official Bond series wasn't the sharpest idea to begin with, but *Casino Royale*'s five directors, three writers and kaleidoscope of stars barely manage to muster a decent joke between them. The nucleus of the problem isn't just serious comic deficiency syndrome either, it's more pressingly a lack of coherent narrative, not so much that the myriad of ancillary plot threads confuse the issue, rather that ancillary threads are just about all there is; with each director having a different take on what the film should be, it lurches unevenly from one haphazard setpiece to the next with no apparent sense of direction whatsoever. Characters are introduced and then disappear without trace, only to re-emerge during the final rumpus, leading one to conclude that great chunks of their material were lost to the mythical cutting room floor. Only towards the end, and the belated introduction of Allen's character (the only reason for bothering with this pap), does a hint of purpose trickle into view, but by then it's too late and fails to raise the proceedings above what is essentially a vehicle for a gathering of high profile celebs - including David Niven, Orson Welles, Peter Sellers, Ursula Andress, Deborah Kerr, Barbara Bouchet and walk-ons from the likes of George Raft,

William Holden, Jean Paul Belmondo and Peter O'Toole - to royally humiliate themselves. Unquestionably one of the most shameful wastes of talent and money in cinema history.

MGM avoided the special edition treatment for this bastard cousin of the official 007 series, which is a shame because, hindsight being a wonderful thing, the time is ripe for a retrospective piece assembling the surviving participants and allowing them to air their thoughts about this profligate disaster. This jarring oversight aside, the 16-chapter transfer on the Region 2 platter is as crisp and clean as any of their "proper" 007 entries, and in spite of the appalling lack of continuity which leads one to suspect something's missing, this is the full enchilada; although a version with the missing footage restored would do wonders for its coherency, I'm not sure the world will ever be ready for a four-hour version of *Casino Royale*! The only additional feature is a pair of trailers (one letterboxed, the other fullscreen pan & scan and suffering from hideous cropping). Mono language options are English, French, German, Italian and Spanish, and subtitling is provided in all of the above plus Dutch, Swedish, Finnish, Norwegian and Danish. - TG

THE CAT AND THE CANARY

Colour, 1978, 98m. / Directed by Radley Metzger / Starring Carol Lynley, Honour Blackman / Image (US R0 NTSC) / WS (1.66:1)

Something spooky is going on at the Glencliff Manor. In 1933, twenty years after the death of rich old Cyrus West, his relatives have gathered on a dark and stormy night for the reading of his will. With the aid of reliable Mrs. Crosby (Wendy Hiller), Cyrus himself (Wilfrid Hyde-White) appears to his heirs via celluloid and at long last reveals the distribution of his wealth. Some, namely the sweet and innocent Annabelle West (Carol Lynley), are overjoyed by the news, while others, like the bitchy Susan Sillsby (Honour Blackman), are less than enthusiastic. Trapped in the house overnight by the storm, the guests are informed by a mysterious visitor that a madman has recently escaped from a nearby asylum. Nicknamed "The Cat," this lunatic uses claw-like appendages to attack his victims... and he may very well be hiding in the house.

A virtuoso adaptation of the classic 1922 play (most famous as a silent adaptation to film by Paul Leni in 1927), this underrated horror film, Metzger's only outing in the genre, would have a much better reputation had not been associated with all of the remakes and sequels prevalent in the late '70s. The Agatha Christie movie trick of using lots of notable British stars works extremely well here, with Blackman (Pussy Galore herself) taking top acting honours. Olivia Hussey looks nice but generally has little do as Blackman's presumably lesbian lover, and Lynley does fine as the naïve innocent heir (though both she and good guy Michael Callan seem a few years too old for their roles). The real stars of the film, though, are Metzger and the house; he obviously has great fun deploying every old dark house trick in the book and frequently plays with the conventions of cinema (particularly the will reading sequence and the delightful end credits). Beautifully shot and edited, the film soaks in spooky atmosphere, perfect for viewing on a dark, rainy evening, and good luck guessing the murderer's identity. A real pleasure from start to finish.

Like most of the Metzger titles, this one shows some signs of wear, including more than a few speckles, but looks far superior to the awful, long unavailable VHS edition from RCA Columbia back at the dawn of home video. Letterboxed at slightly more than 1.66:1, the image quality looks fine but appears to be missing mild slivers on the left and right edges of the screen. In any case, it's great to finally have this back on video, and even viewers unfamiliar with Metzger's other films should find plenty of entertainment here.

A CAT IN THE BRAIN (NIGHTMARE CONCERT)

Colour, 1991, 93m. / Directed by Lucio Fulci / Starring Lucio Fulci, Brett Halsey / EC Entertainment (Holland R0 NTSC), Astro (Germany R2 PAL) / WS (1.66:1)

While Wes Craven has been mining the veins of postmodern, reflexive horror in America with New Nightmare and the Scream saga, Lucio Fulci got there first with A Cat in the Brain, aka Nightmare Concert, in which Fulci plays a director named, hmmm, Lucio Fulci, who drives around experiencing macabre visions during the shooting of his latest film. Fulci likens this experience to a cat clawing inside his head, shown literally in graphic detail as a furry kitty puppet flopping around in gooey cerebral matter. Fulci consults a psychiatrist (David L. Thompson) who decides to let horror films take the rap for his own murderous urges. The psychiatrist goes out and kills a string of young women, while Fulci thinks he is responsible for the crimes.

One of the most deranged films in the Italian horror canon, Cat has sharply divided Fulci fans on virtually every level. Cheaply shot on 16mm and blown up to 35, the narrative consists largely of excerpts from other films (particularly Fulci's A Touch of Death and Ghosts of Sodom) intercut with new Fulci scenes. Since actor Brett Halsey (infamous from Fulci's S&M drama, The Devil's Honey) appears in several different clips from different films, the experience is not unlike Plan 9 from Outer Space as his appearance changes from scene to scene. Newcomers to Fulci will definitely wonder what the fuss is about: the acting is uniformly terrible, the visuals are cheesy at best, and Fabio Frizzi's score awkwardly mixes new Muzak compositions with excerpts from his past glory days (The Beyond, etc.). Scene for scene, this may be Fulci's goriest film, and this aspect alone has earned it some fan loyalty; on another level, it's a bizarre cry for understanding, as Fulci appears to be exorcising demons and coming to terms with the nastier pitfalls of his chosen profession. Many people will be turned off by the nonlinear and often maddening collision of nonsensical scenes and misogynist gore, but it's an interesting film nonetheless.

The print used for the EC Entertainment disc is comparable to the Box Office Spectaculars / Grindhouse laserdisc and definitely cleaner than the Japanese one. The English dubbing sounds more canned than usual, with poor recording resulting in some voices trailing off beyond the point of coherence. The US laserdisc includes the original trailer, a gallery of stills and promotional Fulci artwork, and a very lengthy and endearing video segment of Fulci at the 1996 Fangoria's Weekend of Horrors, while the EC disc contains the trailer. A newly mastered 16:9 US edition in both English and Italian is forthcoming at the time of this writing from Image..

THE CAT O' NINE TAILS

Colour, 1970, 112m. / Directed by Dario Argento / Starring James Franciscus, Karl Malden, Catherine Spaak / Anchor Bay (US R1 NTSC) / WS (2.35:1) (16:9) / DD2.0, TFI (France R2 PAL) / WS (2.35:1) (16:9)

While strolling at night with his niece, Lori (Cinzia De Carolis), a blind retired reporter named Franco Arno (Karl Malden) overhears a conversation involving blackmail in a nearby car. Following a

break-in at the prestigious Terzi Institute for genetic research, one of the leading researchers winds up decapitated by a passenger train the next morning. Coincidentally, the victim happened to be a participant in the blackmail discussion, so Arno teams up with scrappy newsman Carlo Giordani (James Franciscus), both of whom get more than they bargained for. Carlo gets close to Anna (Catherine Spaak), the mysterious daughter of the institute chairman, while Arno chases down several clues of his own. Meanwhile Carlo's photographer friend, Righetto (Vittorio Congia), has a close encounter with a garrotte wielding killer who continues to strike again and again, determined to cover up a most deadly secret.

After scoring a smash hit with his first film, *The Bird with the Crystal Plumage*, director Dario Argento quickly attempted a reprise by expanding that trendsetting *giallo*'s formula of Americans in Italy rubbing shoulders with the criminal element and a psychopathic killer. However, *The Cat o' Nine Tails* failed to capture the critical and commercial appeal of that first hit, thanks to its abrasive insistence on refusing to conform to expectations. Romantic subplots, whodunit elements, and standard three act plotting are all tossed out the window with a glee bordering on the sadistic, allowing Argento instead to experiment wildly within the template of a murder mystery in which form and style coexist most uneasily. After this film Argento returned one year later with the even more troubling *Four Flies on Grey Velvet* before launching onto a different plane entirely with two successful hits in a row, *Deep Red* and *Suspiria*. While *Bird* featured several quirky moments which diverted temporarily from the main storyline, *Cat* fractures itself entirely into a series of bizarre incidents. A mysterious locket, a champion cursing pro from the underworld, a deadly gay love triangle, chromosome experiments on murderers, a razor-happy barber, and a speedy police chase through a parking deck are just a few of the odd tricks up Argento's sleeve. Though the tone of the film is oddly antiseptic and jagged, the characters are among Argento's warmest, with Franciscus and Malden making a most appealing pair of sleuths. The violent finale deliberately subverts viewer expectations by operating less as a whodunit than a nasty piece of narrative machinery which leaves its characters, innocent or not, emotionally or physically scarred for the rest of their lives. Ennio Morricone's score performs a similar function, beginning with a soft and sweet lullaby theme before plunging into some of

his darkest, strangest jazz improvisations, with shots of the killer's eyes punctuated by disturbing musical clicks, yowls, and thuds. Cat also finds Argento experimenting more with the possibilities of editing to layer his narrative, such as the obvious example of subliminal flashes used to indicate an upcoming scene or recap an important piece of information. He later expanded on this technique in *Four Flies* (particularly the memorable finale) and, most effectively, in the celebrated visual and verbal echoing of *Deep Red*.

Along with the still MIA *Four Flies*, *Cat* was one of the hardest Argento films to see for many years in anything resembling its original form or a decent print. An RCA Japanese laserdisc came to the relief of some collectors; letterboxed at approximately 2.00:1 and sporting an odd gold-ish tint, this was the best option available compared to, say, the slaughtered TV print offered by Bingo Video (which cut over 22 minutes of the comic elements, not to mention nudity and violence). (Note: Like Bird, Cat was rated GP for its theatrical US run, which just goes to show how out of whack the MPAA has gotten in the last thirty years.) Bearing these factors in mind, along with the bootleg Diamond DVD which is better left undiscussed, Anchor Bay's disc of *Cat* looks as good as one could expect. Apart from the noticeably scratchy credits which appear to be spliced in from another print (and disappointingly clip off the opening few seconds of Morricone's theme), the source material looks much more vibrant and colourful than most Argento fans could have anticipated. Gone is that sickly yellow wash we've all come to know and tolerate; here the colours are natural, bright, and quite appealing, particularly the striking odd splashes of red in the background decor.

The surround audio is limited mostly to Morricone's score, which has been re-channelled to the front speakers; even the car chase plays out almost entirely in mono. The disc also includes surround tracks in Italian and French- without subtitles or captions, alas. However, an English subtitle track is activated to translate some onscreen text (newspapers, identifying building plaques, etc.) in Italian, as opposed to the Japanese laser, which used awkwardly inserted English language footage (with much paler colour) instead.

Extras include "Tales of the Cat," a standard, recently shot featurette in which Argento, Morricone (!), and co-writer Dardano Sacchetti offer a thumbnail version of the circumstances which led to the film's creation, complete with even-handed views of its successes and faults. The promotional material is at least as interesting; an immaculate international trailer features a delirious mixture of footage and tinted stills to create a genuinely appealing promotional piece. It was obviously reworked to lesser effect for the US trailer and TV spots (in much more battered condition), which spoil the visuals with some unconvincing verbal hype. Finally you get some appreciative liner notes (sadly buried on the back of the cover jacket), a gallery of posters and stills, and two radio promos featuring some highly unorthodox soundbites from the two stars.

CAT-WOMEN OF THE MOON

B&W, 1953, 64m. / Directed by Arthur Hilton / Starring Sonny Tufts, Victor Jory / Image (US R0 NTSC)

For those of you who like to keep track of that peculiar strain of science fiction movies about distant worlds inhabited by sexy women, *Cat-Women of the Moon* is most likely the one that started it all. Sure, things got loopier with the likes of Doris Wishman's *Nude on the Moon*, but on the other hand this one comes complete with giant immobile spiders (yup, the same ones used in *Missile to the Moon*), alien catgirls doing interpretive dances in black leotards, and music by the great Elmer Bernstein back when he was slumming with the likes of *Robot Monster*. What's not to love?

A band of astronauts led by the unlikely pair of Laird (Sonny Tufts) and Kip (Victory Jory) head into space with the assistance of one female, Helen (kittenish western staple Marie Windsor). As they approach the moon, Helen goes ballistic and causes the ship to crash, leaving the astronauts to explore the sinister caves of their strange new world. After an ambush by space spiders, the visitors are taken to the architecturally questionable lair of the moon women, whose feline attributes are mainly confined to their exotic make-up and slinky dance routines. Naturally it turns out that Helen fell under the women's telepathic control as they neared the moon, and in fact they plan to hijack the ship for their own nefarious purposes. Can Helen resist their cunning psychic powers? Can the men stay out of the tempting clutches of the cat-women? Watch and find out!

Like *Robot Monster*, this film was shown in both flat and 3-D editions. However, director Arthur Hilton (whose career pretty much slammed to a halt with this one) fails to exploit the 3-D device at any point, even during the spider footage. Anyone who has tried to sit through Rhino's awful 3-D VHS edition (which looks like 2-D, only fuzzy and a lot more annoying) will be thankful that the Wade

Williams/Image DVD is instead taken from an immaculate, razor sharp 2-D print. The quality is much better than you would ever expect, easily outclassing the other past tape versions. Just savour every little detail, from the outer space matte paintings to the strings holding up the spiders to the shimmering bits of decor in the cat-women's foyer. The mono audio is also crisp and free of any noticeable defects. The disc also includes the lurid original theatrical trailer, which offers a nice thumbnail description of the entire film. Come on, you know you want it.

CAVE OF THE LIVING DEAD

B&W, 1964, 86m. / Directed by Ákos Ráthonyi / Starring Adrian Hoven, Karin Feld / Image (US R0 NTSC) / WS (1.77:1)

Completely unrelated except for their concerns with Gothic horror and the fact that they wound up on a strange, obscure double bill together thanks to producer Richard Gordon, *Cave of the Living Dead* and *Tomb of Torture* hit DVD in a manner similar to their companion arrivals on VHS back in the '80s. Luckily the prints used here are vastly superior and fully capture the spooky, engaging ambience of a drive-in experience which has now drifted off into the mists of time. Originally titled *Der Fluch der Grunen Augen (The Curse of the Green Eyes)*, the retitled, dubbed edition of *Cave of the Living Dead* easily betrays the influence of both Mario Bava's *Black Sunday* and the Edgar Wallace *krimi* rising to public acceptance in Germany.

Our hero, world weary cop Frank Doren (Adrian Hoven of later Jess Franco and *Mark of the Devil* fame), is called in to investigate a peculiar string of murders in which each female victim's demise is accompanied by a power outage for one hour. The villagers inform him that a vampire is responsible for the malefic handiwork, and indeed another victim (Erika Remberg from *Circus of Horrors* and *The Lickerish Quartet*) falls prey that evening. Various clues and a consultation with a local "witch" lead Doren to associate the crimes with the mysterious Professor von Adelsberg (Eurosleaze favourite Wolfgang Preiss), whose estate is linked to a nearby grotto housing a terrible secret.

Despite the sometimes clumsy dubbing, *Cave of the Living Dead* is an efficient and often stylish example of '60s gothic horror. The groovy music score, dead serious performances, and occasional

C

gruesome effects kick the plot into gear whenever interest starts to flag, and both mystery and monster buffs should find plenty here to enjoy on a dark evening. The DVD looks exceptional, with accurate framing, perfectly rendered black and white gradations, and only some occasional print damage betraying its neglected status all these years.

CECIL B. DEMENTED

Colour, 2000, 88m. / Directed by John Waters / Starring Melanie Griffith, Stephen Dorff / Artisan (US R1 NTSC) / WS (1.85:1) (16:9) / DD5.1

 It's all too appropriate that most critics were appalled and confused by *Cecil B. Demented*, the most difficult and brutal John Waters film since *Female Trouble*. A far cry from the twisted but ultimately uplifting family studies in recent years (and yes, that includes *Serial Mom*), this razor sharp act of parody (both of Waters himself and the Hollywood system) takes the concept of sacrificing one's life for art to the most ridiculous extremes imaginable.

At the Baltimore premiere of her latest feel good romantic comedy, Some Kind of Happiness, fading Hollywood starlet Honey Whitlock (Melanie Griffith) is abducted at gunpoint by a band of cinematic terrorists. The leader, a raving underground filmmaker named Cecil B. Demented (Stephen Dorff), forces Honey to perform in his latest *cinéma vérité* masterpiece, whose crew sports tattoos of filmmakers like William Castle, H.G. Lewis, Almodóvar, and so on. Gradually Honey comes to sympathize with her captors' radical sensibilities and decides to bring down a corrupt system that would foist something like *Patch Adams: The Director's Cut* and a sequel to *Forrest Gump* on the American public. Some of the more colourful characters include revolutionary ex-porn star Cherish (Alicia Witt, who steals the film with her Christmas story), drug addict Lyle (Adrien Grenier), and disgruntled heterosexual hairstylist Rodney (Jack Noseworthy). Demented's spontaneous film shoots result in more than a little bloodshed, but his conception for the grand finale goes far beyond what Honey could have ever expected.

Like all Waters films, much of the fun in *Cecil B. Demented* lies in the incidentals. Many of his stock players make hilarious cameos, including Mink Stole, Patty Hearst, and Ricki Lake, while the requisite celebrity appearances go to Kevin Nealon and Eric Roberts. Griffith proves to be a good sport

in her most interesting role since *Body Double*; she may not have redeemed herself after years of crud like *A Stranger Among Us*, but at least she's willing to joke about it. Dorff's portrayal is more difficult to assess, as he comes off as manic and overdone during an initial viewing. However, revisiting the film uncovers some delicious nuances in his performance, including some well timed reaction shots impossible to catch the first time around. The overall concept of the film is obviously vintage Waters, and while some of his conceptual touches don't quite work (for example, why would Demented pay homage to a hack like Otto Preminger?), the giddy audacity of it all and the steady stream of surprises should keep even the savviest film buffs on their toes.

The theatrical presentation of Cecil B. Demented was one of the ugliest in recent memory thanks to Artisan's washed out, grey looking prints. The DVD is nothing short of a revelation by comparison and drastically alters the entire tone of the film. Gaudy colours punctuate almost every scene, from the vibrant lavender and red lighting of Demented's headquarters to the hellish contrasts of orange flames and blue backlighting during the finale. The improved colour palette provides a much more lively, aggressive texture for the film, and the anamorphic transfer looks terrific. The cacophonous soundtrack throws in everything from Moby to hardcore punk to Liberace, so expect the 5.1 mix to keep your speakers busy. For a one time hater of Dolby sound, Waters has certainly embraced it in recent years.

Anyone who has experienced Waters' gut-busting commentaries for *Serial Mom, Pecker*, *Polyester* and *Pink Flamingos* should know what to expect here. One of the best commentators around, he dishes out one witty observation after another and offers nothing but praise for most of his collaborators. As he did with Kathleen Turner, Waters praises Griffith for her willingness to go along with his crackpot cinematic designs. Let's hope his long held wish to get Meryl Streep in one of his films comes to pass before too long.

The disc also includes two theatrical trailers, a "critics are raving" TV spot, and a 22 minute episode of Comedy Central's *Canned Ham* which finds Waters lounging around a pool with Dorff, Witt, and Stole, chatting about the making of the film. Despite the Comedy Central logo in the corner, this is obviously a pre-broadcast version due to the heavy amount of uncensored profanity left in the film clips. Once again Waters is a stitch here, and while everyone has good things to say, Witt seems to be the bubbliest of the group.

THE CELL

Colour, 2000, 107m. / Directed by Tarsem Singh / Starring Jennifer Lopez, Vince Vaughn, Vincent D'Onofrio / New Line (US R1 NTSC), Entertainment in Video (UK R2 PAL) / WS (2.35:1) (16:9) / DD5.1

Demented necrophiliac killer Karl Stargher (D'Onofrio) has a penchant for slowly drowning his victims in a watertight cell, then bleaching the corpses to look like dolls before molesting them. Moments before the police move in to arrest him, Stargher suffers a seizure which leaves him comatose. Knowing that his latest victim is still alive, FBI agent Novak (Vaughn) turns to child therapist Catherine Deane (Lopez), who, via a revolutionary hi-tech process of conscience transference, is able to enter the minds of her patients. With the clock ticking on the life expectancy of Stargher's captive, Deane agrees to enter his mind to try and discover where she has been locked away.

Generally reviled by critics upon its initial release - and understandably so, for there's some most unpleasant business going on here - The Cell is a 24-carat example of style over substance. On one hand a standard, albeit fairly taut, cop/serial killer thriller, it's in the mind transfer sequences when Deane enters Stargher's twisted mind that the film becomes an out of control rollercoaster platform for director Singh's outrageous imagination. Grotesque clockwork corpses, child abuse, repellent disembowelling and a living vivisected horse only scrape the murky surface of the horrors that Deane encounters as she moves deeper and deeper into Stargher's decayed conscious, each stratum more disturbing and bizarre than the last. Singh shows little interest in character development and the protagonists are very much one-dimensional, their activities merely a cipher to each new multi-layered dreamscape. Love it or loathe it, there's no disputing that this is a visual smorgasbord second to none.

Divided into 22 chapters, New Line's Region 1 disc is a veritable fiesta of goodies. The 2.35:1 image preserves its original theatrical look and is richly textural. There are 5.1 surround and 2.0 stereo surround sound options, with subtitling in English only. Along with one enthusiastic commentary from director Singh and a second from members of the production team, there are six multi-angled f/x sequences, an 11-minute behind the scenes documentary (which is actually little more than a bunch of sycophantic faces heaping praise upon their director), eight deleted scenes with optional Singh commentary, two trailers, the isolated score (though Howard Shore's suitably dark work isn't especially aural friendly), filmographies, a rather pointless empathy test and a map of the brain. For those who care, there are also several DVD-ROM extras.

Although the Region 1 release is probably the preferable choice, the Region 2 disc differs in a number of respects that will tempt the discerning Cell enthusiast to consider the additional purchase. The R2 feature includes an extended sequence of Stargher in the hoist as he masturbates over the bleached corpse of his victim. This extremely disquieting material was only ever intended for the European cut and it's nice to see it got past the BBFC's pruning shears intact; although missing from the R1 feature, it is presented on that disc as a deleted scene. There is also one additional, if unremarkable, deleted scene on the R2 platter, being an expansion of the police briefing. On the down side, the R2 release is devoid of the second commentary available on R1. And, strangest of all, the self same deleted scenes - presented as quality finished footage on R1 - are, on R2, washed out, blurry and plastered with running time codes and 'Property of New Line Cinema' captioning. - TG

THE CEMENT GARDEN

Colour, 1992, 104m. / Directed by Andrew Birkin / Starring Andrew Robertson, Charlotte Gainsbourg / New Yorker (US R1 NTSC) / DD2.0

A deeply strange and hypnotic film, The Cement Garden is one of those films best discovered by adventurous viewers, since few are likely to recommend it to any casual friends. Translating the stark, perverse prose of writer Ian McEwan (The Comfort of Strangers) to a visual medium, director Andrew Birkin (brother of actress and pop chanteuse Jane Birkin) uses potentially shocking story elements to craft an experience which truly resembles nothing else ever filmed.

A British family living in a bland rock house away from the city finds its daily patterns upset by the oldest two children's passage into adolescence. Julie (Charlotte Gainsbourg, daughter of Jane and the late Serge Gainsbourg) uses her developing feminine wiles to control her three siblings, while next in line Jack (Andrew Robertson) passes the time pleasuring himself in front of a mirror. While paving over the backyard with cement, their father collapses from a heart attack and dies on the spot. The mother (Sinead Cusack) becomes bedridden and loses her will to live, warning the children of being shipped off to an orphanage before following her husband to the grave. The kids do the only natural thing, of course: wrap up the body, drag it down the basement, and encase it in a metal locker filled with cement. Without any adult guardians, the four children set up their own social system and live off of their parents' bank account, which had been signed over to Julie's name. For support Julie takes on a much older boyfriend, the slimy Derek (Jochen Horst), who begins to suspect something is not at all well within the household. As if that weren't enough, Jack's sexual longings for his sister begin to intensify, and she may feel the same way, too...

Pared down to its bare essentials, *The Cement Garden* is primarily a showcase for Birkin's striking visual style and the excellent performances by the two leads. The film plays with the concept of androgyny like nobody's business, from Julie and Jack's gender-switched haircuts and asexual (often exposed) bodies to the cross-dressing youngest child, Tom (Ned Birkin, the director's son). It all looks amazing, with pitch perfect editing and amazing dreamlike imagery right out of a fairy tale. Watch it on a double bill with *Jack Be Nimble* for an even greater impact.

New Yorker's DVD of *The Cement Garden* is, like the cable and VHS versions, derived from an open matte master which may still be very slightly cropped from 1.66:1. The compositions look fine, though, and the disc is transferred at an extremely high bit rate, yielding excellent image quality from what could have been a technical nightmare. The dark shadows and delicate clouds of dust that fill the basement scenes look just fine, and only some unavoidable hints of grain in the original print offer any distraction. The Dolby Surround audio is fine, with most directional effects limited to the fine early score by Edward Shearmur. The disc also includes the US trailer (nicely edited but a little misleading) and some interesting cast/crew bios; the one for Andrew Birkin is a particular standout, with some amazing tidbits of obscure trivia.

CENTRAL PARK DRIFTER (GRAVEYARD SHIFT)

Colour, 1987, 81m. / Directed by Jerry Ciccoritt / Starring Silvio Oliviero, Helen Papas / Media Blasters/Shriek Show (US R1 NTSC)

Though the cover tags this glossy vampire flick as *Central Park Drifter*, it's actually a 1987 film called *Graveyard Shift*, presumably retitled for its DVD debut to avoid confusion with the 1990 Stephen King

abomination. A staple of video stores during the format's early days, this odd blending of fang-gnashing, light erotica, romance, and urban blight still holds some interest in an overcrowded genre, and while the actual presentation leaves much to be desired, fans of cinematic bloodsuckers may still find it worth a look.

The generic plotline concerns a taxi driver named Stephen Tsepes (Silvio Oliviero), who uses job to procure women as food for his vampiric habits. In between Scorsesian forays through the city's mean streets, Stephen turns the occasional despairing lady into a creature of the night who crashes swanky high society parties. The repetition of Stephen's existence is disrupted by Michelle (Helen Papas), a producer who awakens emotions inside his undead heart. Meanwhile, the escalating body count from Stephen's disciples has the police hunting down a scapegoat. If you've seen any other post-'85 vampire erotica like Roger Corman's *Dance of the Damned*, you can probably guess where it all heads after that.

Extremely skimpy on substance, *Graveyard Shift* instead tries to pump out as much style as possible on an impoverished budget. Poised somewhere between MTV, French cable porn, and Dario Argento, the film's visual style is so relentless and strange that it compensates somewhat for the film's numerous technical failings, particularly the badly post-synched dialogue. Oliviero is a refreshing change from the standard lonely, *Tiger Beat* friendly vampire hero; instead he could have easily stepped out of an Abel Ferrara movie.

Fans of blood and boobs will find plenty of distractions here, as every ten minutes or so finds another fleshy coupling turning nasty with a flash of someone's pointy choppers. *The Hunger* this ain't, but *Graveyard Shift* is an adequate way to kill an hour and a half and, perhaps because of its '80s trappings and weird fusion of genres, remains more interesting than today's direct to video horror fare.

Though its colourful visuals cry out for a top of the line digital transfer, Graveyard *Shift* has instead been ported over to DVD from a lousy master that looks at least as bland as the VHS edition, released over a decade ago. Video noise, smudgy colours, and some distracting wavy patterns visible in dark black areas are only the beginning of this transfer's problems; surely a better element must exist somewhere. The mono soundtrack is likewise flat and unimpressive. The real selling point for this disc, which is otherwise light on extras, must surely be the trailers for other Shriek Show titles, including gory Euro trailers for Joe D'Amato's *Beyond the Darkness* and Andrea Bianchi's marvellous schlock gem, *Burial Ground*, as well as what appears to be a rough edit of a promo for Lucio Fulci's *Demonia*.

CHAINED HEAT

Colour, 1983, 95m. / Directed by Paul Nicholas / Starring Linda Blair, John Vernon, Sybil Danning / MIA (UK R2 PAL)

There are good movies. There are bad movies. And then there's *Chained Heat*, a women in prison epic so stupefyingly out of whack from its opening frames that words can't describe it. Only the shakiest thread of a plot runs through this insane, darkly lit chunk of exploitation excess, crammed to the corners with a cast of drive-in veterans and every possible cliché you can imagine, driven to its silliest extremes. Steamy showers, prison riots, rapist guards, evil wardens... yup, it's all here, but you've never seen it like this.

Sweet little Carol (Linda Blair, doing nudity for the first time) is on her way to the slammer for a few months after accidentally running someone over with her car. The world behind bars is controlled by two gangs, one white (led by the amazing Sybil Danning as Ericka) and one black (led by Cleopatra Jones herself, Tamara Dobson, as Duchess). Carol rebuffs Ericka's advances in the shower (where you can also catch a full frontal appearance by Russ Meyer vet Edy Williams), leading to heightened tensions and more than a few ladies being tossed into solitary. Meanwhile the corrupt warden (John Vernon, who's no stranger to embarrassment) tapes homemade porn flicks with his female prisoners in his office jacuzzi (huh?). "Don't call me warden, call me Fellini," he purrs to one unlucky lady as the film stumbles towards its unlikely climax. Then there's the stern prison matron (Stella Stevens) and the drug-and-hooker dealing guard Lester (Henry Silva), both of whom become involved before Carol decides to blow the lid off the whole corrupt system.

While it's hard to pick a highlight in a film so packed with hilarious moments of sleaze, one can only wonder what Blair (not at her slimmest here) was thinking as the filmmakers primped her up as a luscious sex symbol. Her shower scene with Danning has become the stuff of legend, and rightfully so, but virtually every scene will have viewers clutching their heads trying to make sense of it all. The British DVD of Chained Heat from MIA is an improvement over the ancient, unwatchable Vestron VHS edition, but not by much. The full, open matte image has been exposed, causing distracting switches between full frame and hard matted (1.85:1) scenes. Reportedly the Japanese edition was matted off all the way through, which would have been preferable considering the boom mike here is visible bobbing around in almost every scene. Of course, this recurring glitch just adds to the surrealist hilarity that is *Chained Heat*, and many of its fans have grown to love that little orange microphone more than many of the performers. The image is still dark and muddy, just as it always has been, and the compression is really poorly handled. Ghosting, streaking, and jittering are evident in most panning shots, or even when someone simply walks across the frame. Casual viewers may not notice, but DVDphiles will be in agony. The enhanced clarity of DVD also brings out some annoying flaws in the print, including numerous thin guitar string scratches that last for minutes on end. Approach at your own risk.

THE CHANGELING

Colour, 1980, 118m. / Directed by Peter Medak / Starring George C. Scott, Trish Van Devere, Melvyn Douglas / HBO (US R1 NTSC) / WS (1.85:1) (16:9) / DD2.0

Now this is how you do a scary ghost story. While American theatres were deluged with blood and thunder FX spectacles, this Canadian chiller quietly slipped in and managed to scare the daylights out of unsuspecting audiences. The subject matter harks back to the great turn of the century English ghost stories which used suggestion and elegant plotting to chill the reader, and thanks to its earnest performances and numerous hair raising sequences, *The Changeling* hasn't dated one bit over the past twenty years.

A typically excellent George C. Scott stars as John Russell, a classical composer and university instructor who rents a sprawling mansion from the local historical society while he works on his latest opus. Still recovering from the shocking death of his wife and child, he doesn't quite know how to take it when the house shows signs of being haunted. Loud pounding noises emanate from within the walls every night, windows mysteriously shatter, and the discovery of a hidden room unearths a music box with a chilling connection to John's latest piece. With the help of society worker Claire (Trish Van Devere, Scott's real life wife), John arranges an unusual séance, which finally allows direct contact with the spirit inside the house. The dark secrets ultimately lead John to a prominent senator (Melvyn Douglas) and a bloodcurdling final act.

Along with the excellent *The Ruling Class*, this film marks a high point for erratic Hungarian director Peter Medak, who more recently fettered himself away on *Species II* and several TV shows. Here he displays style to burn, with some dazzling mobile cinematography and a fine eye for atmospheric detail. The simple image of a cobweb-covered child's wheelchair becomes an unforgettably sinister apparition, and even something as simple as a piano key striking by itself can cause a jolt. Then of course there's "the ball"... but viewers will be better off discovering that one for themselves.

Despite claims on some posters that this film was shot in scope, *The Changeling* was filmed hard-matted at 1.85:1 and has suffered terribly on video over the years. The drab, nearly unwatchable laserdisc from Vestron and the cassettes from HBO conveyed none of the rich, burnished textures in the house or the vibrant, eerie blues of many scenes which take place at twilight. The HBO DVD finally gets it right, with a beautiful anamorphic transfer from an unblemished print. Bear in mind that a couple of scenes, notably the opening credits, were shot with zoomed-in lenses, so some fuzziness and graininess can pop up a couple of times in the original source. Otherwise this is as sleek and smooth as this film could possibly look. The surround audio is also an improvement over the laserdisc, with sharper channel separation and much more fidelity to the striking Rick Wilkins score. No extras apart from some cast and crew bios, but with a film this good, the presentation itself more than warrants the price tag. Turn down the lights, curl up under a blanket, and prepare to shiver.

CHAPPAQUA

Colour, 1966, 82m. / Directed by Conrad Rooks / Starring Jean-Louis Barrault, Conrad Rooks / Wellspring (US R1 NTSC)

Chappaqua, as our drug-addled protagonist Russell Harwick (Conrad Rooks) explains, is a small town in New York where he grew up in an innocent environment heavily populated with Indians. What this has to do with recovering from rampant alcoholism and drug abuse is anybody's guess, but it must mean something to Rooks, the son of the Avon Corporation's CEO and writing buddy of numerous famous members of the beat generation. Apparently Rooks got a chunk of cash from dad and decided to make a film about his own drug treatments in Switzerland (relocated to France in the film). In the film, he relates his experiences and hallucinations to a doctor (Children of Paradise's Jean-Louis Barrault) as he undergoes a mysterious "sleep treatment." As far as autobiographical self-confessions go, this is about as sincere as *John Wayne Bobbitt: Uncut*, but '60s buffs will get a big kick out of seeing William S. Burroughs appear as Opium Jones, the head of the institute, and a quick cameo by Allen Ginsberg. While Rooks may not be a coherent filmmaker, at least he had the sense to hire the best talent he could find. Talented indie cinematographer Robert Frank (who also lensed the notorious Rolling Stones documentary *Co*ksucker Blues*) does some beautiful work here; the film alternates at random between colour and black and white footage a la A Man and a Woman (most but not all of the colour footage relates to Rooks' hallucinations), but Frank really shines during the haunting black and white sequences. Rooks' thespian skills really defy description, though it's unlikely someone would deliberately give such a bad performance. In any case, he does deliver some occasionally startling moments, such as his arrival at the clinic when he drops to the floor in front of a desk and suddenly finds the surface turned to ice - and he hallucinates a man suddenly doing figure eights around him. Of course, his first appearance is memorable, too, at a New York acid party where the Fugs stomp on sugar cubes spelling out the letters "LSD" and an eye-rolling Rooks sprawls on the floor and licks up the residue. Rooks also provides some terrific mid-'60s footage of 42nd Street, and watching all of the trash theatre marquees floating by provides a lot of fun ("Hey, it's *Olga's White Slaves!*"). Unfortunately, the good moments are seriously hampered by Rooks' bratty, self-indulgent ranting and some awfully stupid hallucinations (in one he's a vampire who attacks a woman at a party and winds up sprawling her on a table and covering her with fruit!). Clarity is definitely not the order of the day, but Rooks does manage to pull off a genuinely haunting final scene that almost makes the whole trip worthwhile (and probably explains how this won the Silver Lion at Cannes).

Chappaqua may be a series of magnificent, visionary images encasing a core of pure swill, but Fox Lorber's DVD is one of their best to date. The film was apparently shot on 16mm, but it looks exceptionally clear for its vintage with no noticeable digital artefacts. The percussive Ravi Shankar score (released on two separate albums with some spoken word performances by Burroughs) sounds fine, though a stereo mix would have been very effective (okay, wishful thinking, but...). The film's running time has been a subject of some dispute; apparently the press materials at Cannes promoted this as 92 minutes, though theatrical prints run 82 (as does the DVD). Other sources report cuts as short as 75 minutes which deleted the tame female nudity and other bits of potentially offensive material. Since Rooks himself supervised the transfer and owns the film, the current running time seems the most likely. The DVD also includes the video release promo clip (passed off as a trailer for some reason). Incidentally, Rooks' obvious obsession with other cultures probably inspired his second (and only other) film, a 1973 adaptation of Herman Hesse's *Siddhartha* (available on DVD from Milestone).

CHARADE

Colour, 1963, 114m. / Directed by Stanley Donen / Starring Cary Grant, Audrey Hepburn, Walter Matthau / Criterion (US R1 NTSC) / WS (1.85:1)

A witty, elegant thriller bent on beating Alfred Hitchcock at his own game, *Charade* is something of a departure for director Stanley Donen, best known for his glossy MGM musicals. Cary Grant, returning to *North by Northwest* territory, here steps aside for the main character (a radiant Audrey Hepburn), the innocent plunged into a world of espionage and murder. While *Charade* could have easily become a bland spy knockoff, every element works perfectly: Grant and Hepburn's chemistry, the witty and startling screenplay, the gorgeous Parisian locales, and of course, Henry Mancini's catchy, infectious score. For anyone who has yet to become acquainted with this sparkling little gem, consider Criterion's DVD a perfect introduction.

After her husband dies in a mysterious train accident, Regina Lambert (Hepburn) finds a number of weird people congregating at the funeral and tormenting her with weird, veiled threats. A local treasury agent (Walter Matthau) informs Regina that her husband stole a horde of Nazi gold along with three other men; unfortunately, the other men never got their cut and are now determined to recover it. Enter Cary Grant as a charming but mysterious man who seems to protect Reggie but changes his name more often than his clothes. Regina begins to fall for the handsome stranger, but can he be trusted?

Though successful during its theatrical release, *Charade* has been largely ignored in the decades. Film buffs often place it on their list of "hidden treasures," and newcomers usually remarks, "Wow! What a great movie; why haven't I ever heard of it?" Part of the blame may lie with Universal, who forgot to include the necessary copyright information on the actual print and allowed it to fall into quasi-public domain territory. Thus, every hack video distributor released substandard cheap videotapes and DVDs onto the market, where the sleek photography simply turned to mud. An attractive, legitimate Universal videotape was briefly released but, at a higher price, simply couldn't complete with all the $10 specials lying around, though at least most cable stations in recent years have shown clean, viewable prints of the film. Not surprisingly, Criterion's DVD blows away all of the other renditions with a vivid, clean widescreen transfer, in very close to immaculate condition apart from the speckly opening Universal logo. Colour plays a tremendous role in the film ranging from clothing to set design, and the vibrant DVD makes an excellent showcase for Donen's keen visual sense. The sound is fine but a little disappointing considering the improvement in the image; in particular, Mancini's dynamic opening title cue (accompanied by Maurice Binder's terrific credits) could use some more punch, even in straight mono.

The film itself still holds up incredibly well, with Grant and Hepburn at the peak of their craft and pros like Matthau, George Kennedy (sporting a pre-Live and Let Die mechanical arm), and James Coburn doing excellent supporting bits. For such a "frothy" title, the violence is surprisingly strong and graphic at times, though never offensive or overwhelming. The DVD includes commentary by Donen and screenwriter Peter Stone, who largely cover the location shooting and contributions made by the various participants in the film, as well as the delightful original US trailer.

CHEEKY (TRASGREDIRE)

Colour, 2000, 92m. / Directed by Tinto Brass / Starring Yuliya Mayarchuk, Jarno Beradi / Arrow (UK R2 PAL), Univideo (Italy R2 PAL) / WS (1.66:1) (16:9) / DD5.1

Tinto Brass' *Cheeky* (*Trasgredire*) comes off like a sweet-natured hybrid between his elegantly mounted skinfests and a slick Penthouse video. The narrative jumps back and forth between London and Venice, as sexy young Carla (Yuliya Mayarchuk) saunters through the British streets hunting for an apartment she can share with her boyfriend, Matteo (Jarno Beradi). While absence may make the heart grow fonder, it also lands both lovers in a lot of trouble as they're tempted by a parade of potential conquests. Which will win out... the heart or the loins? Buoyed by yet another infectious Pino Donaggio score, *Trasgredire* is good, ribald fun, neither his best nor his worst film. Interestingly, his fanny fetish seems to be receding with this film, as he lavishes more intention on the comparatively slimmed down female star's athletic figure. It's also notable as one of his few films to partially drop male "prosthetics" in favour of the real thing.

The Italian DVD is by far the most successfully presented Brass film on DVD thanks to a stunning, colourful anamorphic transfer and a rich 5.1 mix, all of which make one wish his earlier films could have received the same treatment. The original Italian and dubbed English audio tracks are included, along with the Italian theatrical trailer. The Arrow DVD features the English dub, the Italian trailer, a flat widescreen transfer, and the same Brass interview used on their earlier titles.

CHERRY FALLS
Colour, 2000, 92m. / Directed by Geoffrey Wright / Starring Brittany Murphy, Michael Biehn, Jay Mohr
TERROR TRACT
Colour, 2000, 96m. / Directed by Lance W. Dreesen & Clint Hutchison / Starring John Ritter, David DeLuise, Bryan Cranston
USA (US R1 NTSC) / WS (1.85:1) (16:9), EIV (UK R2 PAL), Filmax (Spain R2 PAL) / WS (1.85:1) / DD2.0

As if we didn't already know that studios have completely lost any idea how to handle a horror film, the soon to be defunct USA dropped the ball by sending two worthy, witty, gore-filled entries straight to video while cruddy *Scream* knockoffs populated the multiplexes. While neither are classics by any stretch, *Cherry Falls* and *Terror Tract* make for a solid evening of creepy viewing and could have been quite successful had they been released in a more permissive age.

First up is *Cherry Falls*, the controversial American debut for critic turned director Geoffrey Wright (*Romper Stomper*). Essentially a reversal of the promiscuity equals death mantra of '80s slasher films, this isn't exactly a spoof; in fact, it somehow captures the exact atmosphere of films like *My Bloody Valentine and He Knows You're Alone,* which

may seem alien to entire generations of horror fans. In the opening sequence, a young virginal pair of teens preparing to go all the way find their plans interrupted by a knife-wielding assailant outside their car. The case is handled by Sheriff Marken (Michael Biehn), whose daughter, Jody (*Clueless'* Brittany Murphy), goes to the victims' high school. The English teacher, Mr. Marliston (Jay Mohr), tries to help the students cope with the tragedy, which is quickly followed by another brutal slaying. The murders are all connected by one element: the word "virgin" carved into the victims' flesh. Soon Jody has a close encounter with the maniac, apparently a gaunt woman with long black, streaked-streaked hair. When word breaks out across the school about the killer's modus operandi, the students come up with a novel, perverse method of removing themselves from consideration as the next victims.

Originally slated for a 2000 theatrical release, *Cherry Falls* became a major problem for USA after it was repeatedly slapped with an NC-17 rating. Rumours abounded on the Internet about graphic footage supposedly removed during the ratings submission process; even worse, after countless aborted theatrical dates, the film finally showed up first in America on the USA Network in an incoherent, butchered version devoid of almost all bloodshed. At least *Cherry Falls* has other strengths, such as Wright's strong visual sense, an engaging central performance from Murphy, and a habit of throwing in strange, kinky grace notes in the least expected sequences, such as a toe fetish semi-sex scene and the unforgettable exclamation, "It's a hymen holocaust!" On the other hand, the killer's identity comes as no surprise whatsoever, though it does offer a bizarre visual punchline. When USA ran a test screening of the film immediately before its first MPAA submission, *Cherry Falls* was not drastically different from the version ultimately used for the DVD. Primarily this R-rated cut substitutes some alternate shots during a few brutal flashes of violence; for example, an early series of subliminal flashes depicting a young girl being crucified to a tree replaces a gruesome close up of her wrists being nailed with a different shot of her screaming instead. Fleeting trims amounting to only a few seconds in total were performed on the discovery of another body "overhead" and during the climactic assault, while the opening murder features some awkward frame skipping to soften the scene's impact. In short, the differences are marginal at best and hardly justify the fracas raised about the NC-17 rating. Apparently discouraged by the failure to turn *Cherry Falls* into viable theatrical material, USA has rushed it onto disc with little care. The 16:9 transfer looks fine, with solid colours and good black levels, but the surround soundtrack is simply terrible. Dialogue is muffled and poorly mixed, while the surround effects are harsh, muddy, and far too loud. Even through basic television playback, the audio comes off poorly and feels wildly unbalanced. Amazingly, the disc doesn't even contain the theatrical trailer that ran in some theatres before USA's Halloween release plan was yanked. The similarly censored UK and Spanish discs feature six minutes of cast/crew interviews and a four minute B-roll of trims.

If *Cherry Falls* is a throwback to gimmicky '80s slashers, *Terror Tract* jumps back to the hoary days of horror anthologies before the days of *Tales from the Crypt*. Reminiscent of '80s multi-story horror confections like *Creepshow* and *Nightmares*, as well as their Amicus antecedents from the '70s, this amusing and frequently surprising sickie in many outdoes its companion film. For once the framing story is a real grabber, with John Ritter starring as Bob Carter, a desperate real estate agent trying to persuade a young couple (Allison Smith and David Deluise) to buy a house in a seemingly normal neighbourhood apparently rife with violence and supernatural events. In each of the three houses he shows, Carter relates the horrifying story of the past owners. The first and weakest story concerns a woman, Sarah Freemont (Rachel York), whose husband learns of her adulterous affair with the local stud, Frank (Carmine Giovinazzo). Hubby's gruesome retribution backfires, but Sarah and her lover's attempts to dispose of his body don't quite work as planned. The second and most blackly humorous yarn features Bryan Cranston (the dad from *Malcolm in the Middle*) as a father driven to the brink by his daughter's pet monkey, Bobo, who has developed a nasty habit of offing anyone who stands in its way. In the third and most frightening tale, Sean Goodwin (Will Estes) has developed the ability to witness terrifying murders before they happen through the eyes of the Granny Killer, who wears a creepy old lady mask. Sean relates his plight to a psychiatrist (Brenda Strong) who begins to believe Sean may be the killer himself...

Better than anyone would ever a right to expect, *Terror Tract* unquestionably delivers the shocks and features some great nods to past horror films ranging from *Monkey Shines* to *Dressed to Kill*, though the show-stopping final scene is really a delirious feat all its own. The opening sequence, in which a succession of animals prey on each other around the neighbourhood, is a fun throwback to the days of *Cat's Eye*. Horror fans should especially enjoy the last story, a gruesome piece of audience manipulation with a nifty little sting in the tale. Luckily USA's

transfer of this film is substantially better than *Cherry Falls*; the surround audio is quite satisfying, while the image is sharp, clear, and pleasing to the eye. It's a shame virtually no one outside of overseas screenings and film festivals ever had a chance to see either of these films as intended, but at least they're available to home viewers as a reminder that decent horror films are still being made; they're just much harder to find.

THE CHILD
Colour, 1977, 86m. / Directed by Robert Voskanian / Starring Laurel Barnett, Rosalie Cole
I EAT YOUR SKIN
B&W, 1964, 84m. / Directed by Del Tenney / Starring William Joyce, Heather Hewitt / Image (US R1 NTSC)

 A young woman is hired as private tutor for a strange little girl living in a remote house in the woods. Once installed there, she discovers that Rosalie, her young charge, is in contact with mysterious creatures from the cemetery nearby. Various relatives and neighbours are bumped off by the monsters before the evil child turns her attentions on her new teacher. Soon the woman is fleeing for her life as Rosalie's "friends" attack.

If you like the zombie subgenre it's definitely worth checking out *The Child*, a movie with a mid-seventies amateur feel, which unleashes some nerve-rattlingly aggressive cadavers into the action in the last twenty minutes, and packs the rest of the running time with strange music, tilted camera angles and warped acting. There's no attempt at realism - dry ice wafts into shot as soon as the heroine crashes her old-fashioned car at the start of the film. The rhythm of the story has that delightfully wayward quality of 1970s exploitation, where weird digressions lurk at every turn. The old lady who should be a minor character hogs the script with an eccentric non-actorly performance. The camera tilts like a sick sailor. The music is Liberace vamping for Bela Lugosi's stage show, accompanied by a drunken scorpion on synthesizer. The plot and characters are almost non-existent (the lead female has "problems" but thankfully we don't hear too much about them). It's like a fever dream and refuses to become a normal movie. Watch it late at night and offer a prayer for the lost art of exploitation cinema before you turn in.

The presentation of this film is a mixed bag. Strong, clear colour and solid blacks in some scenes

C

contrast with rather murky, grainy footage elsewhere (mostly due to the film's low budget origins). A muted audio presentation and some unwelcome speckling on the print also hold it back from being an ideal version. The sound isn't distorted and remains noise-free with the volume turned up, but it's still a bit dull, probably because of over-zealous equalization to remove high-end noise at the mastering stage. The swarms of white speckles that appear during one of the film's most exciting sequences are particularly unfortunate, but despite these flaws the film is presented well enough to be worth picking up. As this is a personal favourite of mine, I wish it could have been as immaculate as Something Weird's H.G. Lewis transfers, but you can't have everything!

The biggest "extra" is another feature, 1964's *I Eat Your Skin*, written, produced and directed by Del Tenney. Whilst laying low on a remote tropical island, a playboy journalist and his current squeeze encounter a mad scientist intent on transforming the natives into an army of the undead. Seven years after it was made, under the title *Voodoo Blood Bath*, this shelved zombie flick was retitled by exploitation legend Jerry Gross to accompany the extremely gory *I Drink Your Blood* on a classic drive-in double bill. Although it fails to live up to the specifics of such a wonderfully hideous title, it turns out to have charm anyway, and even a few scares in the form of some alarming zombie attacks. Despite a few talky patches, the leading cast are pleasant and at 79 minutes there's enough action to sustain a casual viewing. Like many of the second features on these Something Weird discs, the print is a touch worn in places. However, there's nothing that really hinders enjoyment, unless you demand perfection for even the most fleeting of pleasures. There are no digital artefacts and the contrast is acceptably clear, what flaws there are being due to the age of the print and the cheapness of the original production. Also includes the theatrical trailer for *The Child* and other Harry Novak productions, two educational shorts ("The Outsider" and "The ABC of Baby Sitting"), and a gallery of horror drive-in exploitation art with radio spots. - ST

CHILD'S PLAY

Colour, 1988, 87m. / Directed by Tom Holland / Starring Catherine Hicks, Chris Sarandon / MGM (UK, Germany R2 PAL) / WS (1.85:1), MGM (US R1 NTSC) / DD4.0

Though television series like *The Twilight Zone* and *Night Gallery* had exploited the concept for years, horror films never really successfully exploited the

killer doll concept until *Child's Play*. Of course, there were fringe efforts like the ventriloquist's dummy movies (*Dead of Night, Devil Doll, Magic*) and TV movies like *Trilogy of Terror,* but once little Chucky started hacking his way onto the screen, slasher cinema was never the same.

Vicious serial killer Charles Lee Ray (Brad Dourif), is hunted down by police to a Chicago toy store where, after being severely wounded, he performs a strange voodoo ritual involving one of the popular Good Guy dolls. Ray is finished off by the police, and life goes on as normal. Enter Karen Barclay (Catherine Hicks), a single mom trying to make ends meet and provide some food on the table for her young son, Andy (Alex Vincent, a pretty good child actor). Andy dearly wants a Good Guy doll for his birthday, but Karen can't come up with the money to pay full retail price. However, an opportunity to buy a slightly damaged black market Good Guy doll presents itself, and Karen seizes the opportunity. Overjoyed with his gift, Andy spends all of his time with the doll, which seems to be giving the boy some strange ideas. Pretty soon, following a brutal murder in their apartment, Karen begins to believe Andy's claims that Chucky is alive - and not such a good guy after all.

The only other notable genre film by *Fright Night* director Tom Holland, *Child's Play* kicked off an entire franchise of Chucky movies (and was even outdone by the gloriously wacko *Bride of Chucky*). Brad Dourif's sardonic delivery of Chucky's lines makes him one of the more personable screen psychos, and all of the cast members, including former bloodsucker Chris Sarandon as the investigating police detective, do an efficient and believable job. Though hardly a classic, the film offers some good thrills and at least one genuine shudder when Karen first learns Chucky's secret. Unfortunately, some last minute cutting and tinkering left quite a few scenes ragged and incoherent, particularly Andy's birthday morning chat with Karen and the incident with Chucky and the voodoo practitioner. Still, at less than 90 minutes, it's a quick, breezy, and fun ride, with some nice effects work by *Tales from the Crypt*'s Kevin Yagher (it looks a bit dated now but really packed a punch in its day). All of the usual slasher conventions are present and accounted for (countless false endings, ridiculous gore, morbid one-liners, etc.), but the script manages to wring a few new twists out of an old horror rag. Incidentally, the original writer, Mancini, and Lafia had a number of disputes with Holland about his rewrites and alterations to the script during shooting; judging from the less than stellar results of Lafia and Mancini's *Child's Play 2,* it may have been just as well.

Despite its relatively high slot in the modern horror pantheon, *Child's Play* has been given a relatively lacklustre incarnation on DVD. MGM's transfer looks like a sleeker, more defined rendition of the same open matte master used for their laserdisc. The clarity and compression job are fine, but it still has that vaguely grungy late-'80s video look that could have probably been avoided with a little studio expense. The US version is slightly open matte with a little missing on the sides, while the Region 2 counterparts are non-anamorphic hard matted. The theatrical Dolby surround mix sounds about the same, with Joe Renzetti's thunderous score shrieking nicely from all of the channels. Don't expect a demo piece, though. Also includes the original theatrical trailer.

CHILDREN SHOULDN'T PLAY WITH DEAD THINGS

Colour, 1972, 88m. / Directed by Bob Clark / Starring Alan Ormsby, Valerie Munches / VCI (US R1 NTSC) / WS (1.85)

Horror fans can't seem to agree on this one. A textbook example of a cult movie designed for fans, *Children Shouldn't Play with Dead Things* consistently divides its audience between those who respond to its morbid humour and low budget creepiness or just simply find it cheap and irritating. Set entirely during one night on a remote island, this tongue in cheek horror opus from Bob Clark (*Black Christmas, Deathdream*) is admittedly very difficult to warm up to if you're not in the mood; for best results, try watching it after midnight with plenty of beer and popcorn on hand, preferably in the company of other people looking for a few lowbrow chuckles and scares.

Alan (producer Alan Ormsby, later responsible for writing the ill-advised remake of *Cat People*), an egomaniac theatrical director, escorts several struggling hired actors (his "children") to a remote island where they can perform a satanic ritual. It all turns out to be one big, sick lark involving some tasteless practical jokes in which they dig up a corpse (nicknamed "Orville") and read spells which will supposedly bring him back to life. The omnisexual Alan also arranges for his two flamboyantly gay pals to run around in cheap costumes and scare the folks for no apparent reason other than his own twisted

private amusement. Unfortunately, as it turns out, the black magic spells really do work. The corpses begin to rise in a particularly foul mood, and Alan finds his callous witticisms useless in the face of the clutching, rotting hands of the undead.

In essence *Children* operates like an E.C. Comics tale stretched out to feature length, with thoroughly obnoxious, vile characters who all get their just desserts. Whether Ormsby intended his portrayal to be utterly grating or simply gave a bad performance, the character of Alan is the true villain of the film and stoops to a low during the final scene that even makes the zombies pause for a second (a great moment!). Despite its flaws, *Children* features a terrific concluding half hour in which the horror finally takes over completely. Clark generates a truly chilling atmosphere throughout, but once the dead start to walk, things get very, very creepy.

This restored edition of *Children* originally appeared on laserdisc from Phantom Video, a fledgling company who unfortunately had to discontinue its pressing immediately due to an unforeseen rights issue. VCI has used the same materials here, and the transfer looks more colourful but is plagued with unstable blacks and a dodgy compression job. The film will never look pristine due to its impoverished budget and deliberately hazy look, at least this easily blows away the horrible MPI video and washed out TV prints that have been floating around for years. The DVD goes one better on the laser by also including a gallery of lobby cards and promotional art. Shame about the packaging, though.

CHRISTINE

Colour, 1983, 91m. / Directed by John Carpenter / Starring Keith Gordon, John Stockwell, Alexandra Paul / Columbia (US R1 NTSC) / WS (2.35:1) (16:9) / DD2.0

A rock solid improvement over Stephen King's interesting but fatally overlong novel, *Christine* may not be the scariest John Carpenter film by a long shot but is certainly among his sleekest. While the trend has been to dismiss most of the King adaptations in the '80s as trash, critics are fortunately beginning to now reassess most of these neglected titles (*The Dead Zone, Creepshow, Cat's Eye*, etc.), and *Christine* is perhaps the most overdue for some respect.

After a brief, amusing prologue in which we see the title car, a 1958 cherry red Plymouth Fury, being wheeled off the assembly line and already causing mayhem, the film concerns a circle of high school friends in 1979. Arnie (Keith Gordon, doing an excellent job), a laughable nerd, and Dennis (John Stockwell, doing an adequate job), a clean cut jock, are unlikely friends whose bond is tested by two new arrivals: Arnie's renovated new car, Christine, and a new girl at school, Leigh (*Baywatch*'s Alexandra Paul). Thanks to the malefic influence of his car, Arnie becomes darker, cooler, and more dangerous, attracting Leigh but putting her in danger when the car itself becomes jealous. One night Christine is trashed beyond recognition by a group of bullies, but when the vandals begin to die one by one, Dennis and Leigh begin to suspect that their friend may be under an evil influence or perhaps a murderer himself.

While the device of a killer car had already become hoary by this point, Carpenter injects the concept with a dose of simple but extremely effective special effects, which are far more effective than the avalanche of CGI the story, would probably receive today. All of Carpenter's scope films rely heavily on each inch of the frame for maximum effectiveness, and *Christine* is no exception. The careful arrangements of characters on the screen (usually with the dominant personality for the scene in the foreground) makes the pan and scan version included here quite useless; fortunately, the splendid new widescreen transfer is close to perfect and a t.emendous improvement over the sick, chalky-looking letterboxed laserdisc a few years ago. The surround soundtrack doesn't rip forth like more recent mixes but does get the job done; frankly, it's nice to see this film in such good shape after years of bad video transfers and sub-par TV screenings. Sleaze fans should get a kick out of seeing Roberts Blossom from *Deranged* in a chilling cameo as Christine's prior owner, and look for Kelly Preston, aka Mrs. John Travolta, as Dennis' girlfriend. Only debits: no trailer or Carpenter commentary, and an awfully cheap-looking, ugly cover design that looks like a bad imitation of the poster for 1958's *Diabolique*.

C.H.U.D.

Colour, 1984, 96m. / Directed by Douglas Cheek / Starring John Heard, Daniel Stern, Kim Greist / Anchor Bay (US R1 NTSC) / WS (1.85:1) (16:9)

One of the more beloved horror titles of the '80s thanks to its omnipresent TV spots ("Cannibalistic Humanoid Underground Dwellers!"), *C.H.U.D.* will never be mistaken for a great movie, but the prospect

of seeing established actors in a Larry Cohen-style exploration of monsters rampaging through '80s urbania is simply too bizarre to resist.

Picking up from the *Raw Meat* concept of homeless people inhabiting the subway tunnels of our major cities, *C.H.U.D.* turns these subterranean vagrants into mutated beasties thanks to a chemical leak. New York City is under siege. People are vanishing at an alarming rate, even to the extent of being snatched into the ground through handy manhole covers. A soup kitchen cook (Daniel Stern) decides to snoop around to see where all the bums are going, while photographer George Cooper (John Heard) gets a similar urge to snoop around the sewers, much to the disdain of his girlfriend (Kim Greist). The police have decided to cover up all of the disappearances, but thankfully our underdog forces decide to join up and uncover the dark, deadly secret of the C.H.U.D. (And incidentally, that acronym stands for something entirely different than the ads would have you believe.) Amazingly, both Heard and Stern managed to survive the mutant onslaught to team up again for something even more horrifying - the first two *Home Alone* movies.

Dark, dingy, and utterly strange, *C.H.U.D.* is just deranged enough to hold your attention on a slow evening. The whole New York conspiracy angle is less than gripping, but the actors jump into their roles with undeniable enthusiasm; Stern in particular seems to make the most out of a potentially dull part. However, Greist (fresh off Terry Gilliam's *Brazil*) has the film's best moment in a shower, which must be experienced to be believed. The worst thing that can be said about *C.H.U.D.* is the fact that it spawned perhaps the most agonizing sequel known to mankind, *C.H.U.D. II: Bud the Chud*, which will never, ever see the light of DVD if Anchor Bay has any mercy at all.

Given that it looked pretty cruddy even in theatres, *C.H.U.D.* fares just fine on DVD (though astoundingly, its tagline is hilariously misspelled on both the front and back covers). Numerous television screenings incorporated some cutting room floor footage, and this disc contains the longest possible cut of the film. A memorable diner sequence with John Goodman and Jay Thomas, which capped off the original version, has now been shifted to the one hour mark, where it makes more sense structurally but deprives the film of a punchy payoff at the end. The 1.85:1 framing looks fine, removing much of the dead headroom from the earlier laserdisc and VHS editions, while the mono audio is fine if unremarkable. The disc includes some amusing animated menus leading the viewer to the extras, including copious make up test shots and still, the punchy trailer, and a hilarious Easter Egg accessible by clicking on the C.H.U.D.'s glowing eyes. To appreciate it, though, be sure to first check out the commentary track, which features a lively round of discussion with Stern and Heard (yes, they really did agree to talk about this one), along with director Douglas Cheek. (Hint: listen to their comments during the shower scene.) Stern is the most zealous of the bunch, but everyone chips in with bits of trivia and funny anecdotes. All of you closet *C.H.U.D.* fans out there will be more than pleased.

CIRCUS OF HORRORS

Colour, 1960, 91m. / Directed by Sidney Hayers / Starring Anton Diffring, Jane Hylton / Anchor Bay (US R1 NTSC) / WS (1.66:1) (16:9)

 Usually lumped together with its equally disreputable Anglo Amalgamated cousins from 1959-60, this combination of surgical terror and big top mayhem is the most outrageous and pulpy of the bunch. Attractively mounted and undeniably executed with gusto, *Circus of Horrors* doesn't even attempt to artistically dissect the human psyche (like *Peeping Tom*) and dress up its catalogue of killings with mundane, posh settings like *Horrors of the Black Museum*. Instead you know you're in the hands of lunatics right from the opening scene, in which ambitious plastic surgeon Dr. Schueler (Anton Diffring) suffers the threat of jail and professional ruin after a botched operation on one of his female patients. Along with his assistant, Angela (Jane Hylton), the good doctor hightails it to the French countryside, where he goes into hiding by shaving off his beard and gaining the confidence of a down and out circus owner (Donald Pleasence), whose disfigured daughter, Nicole (*Brides of Dracula*'s Yvonne Monlaur), stands to gain much from his skill with a scalpel. The drunken host winds up falling prey to his own circus bear, leaving the doctor to take over the circus. Flash forward a couple of years; the circus has become a rousing success under the supervision of "Dr. Rossiter," with the repaired Elissa now starring in a daring high wire act. However, things get sticky when the tempestuous Magda (Vanda Hudson), the more vulnerable half of a knife throwing act and Rossiter's occasional bedmate, decides to leave the show despite all he's done to make her beautiful and promote her career. Naturally her performance that night does not go smoothly. As the police investigate, bitchy starlet Elissa (*The Lickerish Quartet*'s Erika Remberg) becomes the latest potential target of the doctor's wrath... and many more could meet violent ends under the circus tent, where every crouching lion and daredevil trick promises certain death.

Like other prime screen villains of the period like Michael Gough and Peter Cushing, Diffring has a field day as the wicked but all too human surgeon whose decent intentions never lead to positive results for his patients. The abundance of circus footage works better here than in similar efforts like *Berserk!*, mainly thanks to a pervading tone of perversion and depravity seething underneath the glossy surface. Ace cinematographer Douglas Slocombe (a veteran of all the Ealing classics) turns each scene into a riot of colour and action, while the direction, writing, and editing keep things moving at a feverish clip until the appropriately delirious (and wholly improbable) finale. The unsettling juxtaposition of women prancing around in cheesecake outfits, sometimes with physically deformed faces for contrast, with gimmicky murders proves to be more than a basic exploitable factor; here it's the film's entire reason for being, and on this ignoble but efficient level it succeeds completely. Then of course there's the terrifically gooey Lawrence Welk theme song, "Look for a Star," which became something of a standard at the time and will spend many days afterward bouncing around in viewers' heads.

Yet another casualty of HBO's horror catalogue acquired through Thorn/EMI, *Circus of Horrors* has fared terribly on home video thanks to an ugly, washed out transfer that could have only been worsened if the film had been cropped from a wider aspect ratio. This edition, available for years on VHS and even a double feature Image laserdisc with the AIP cut of Mario Bava's *Baron Blood*, has thankfully been eclipsed by the Anchor Bay DVD. The vibrant and pristine source material makes for a much more enjoyable viewing experience, and the 1.77:1 framing looks fine. The slightly tight opening credits indicate a possible 1.66:1 presentation in Europe, but the Anglo Amalgamated credit still fits on the screen without any cropping. In any case, the framing of the film itself doesn't appear compromised.

Incidentally, rumours have abounded for years about shots cut from the film, and Hayers confirmed on more than one occasion that the knife-throwing scene was indeed filmed with a shot of the blade puncturing the actress' neck. However, this shot has never been included in any distributed prints at the behest of the British censor, leaving only an aftermath view, which turns the audience's reaction and the editing of the scene into pure nonsense. Whether this footage still exists in a vault somewhere, of course, is anyone's guess. Otherwise the film, as lurid and violent as it may seem, isn't all that gory and derives most of its punch from the sheer weirdness of its visuals. The mono audio is also much more robust than the HBO version; just check out that opening circus fanfare. Extras on the disc are limited but satisfying, all things considered. The strange British trailer (in colour) is included, though oddly the wilder American one (prepared by AIP) - which has surface don several PD compilations - is not. However, you do get three TV spots (in B&W), a Diffring filmography, a poster and still gallery, and best of all, the complete, undiluted "Look for a Star" playing out in its entirely over the extras menu. So much for shelling out big bucks for that out of print vinyl release...

CITIZEN X

Colour, 1995, 103m. / Directed by Chris Gerolmo / Starring Stephen Rea, Donald Sutherland / HBO (US R1 NTSC)

Forensics specialist Viktor Burakov (Rea) is placed in charge of the hunt for the deadliest serial killer in Soviet Russia's history. Expected to turn results, yet foiled every step of the way by the politically motivated bureaucracy of the very people demanding them, Burakov finds an ally in Colonel Fetisov (Sutherland). Together, as the years pass and the bodies mount up, they strive methodically towards capturing "Citizen X".

Though lacking some additional suspense factor by revealing the identity of the killer early on in the story, this is nonetheless a gripping and intelligent dramatisation of actual events that took place in Russia throughout the 1980s. Rea delivers a masterful realisation of compassion and despair as the iron-willed Burakov, whilst Sutherland is subtly brilliant as the anti-bureaucratic Fetisov. There's staunch support from Max Von Sydow in a small but pivotal role as the psychiatrist who draws up a profile of "Citizen X" and succeeds in breaking him through gentle coaxing, and Joss Ackland as the loathsome Party Chairman. Top Brownie points, however, go to Jeffrey DeMunn as malignant killer Andrei Chikatilo; with little dialogue, his is a performance through eyes and facial expressions, projecting inner turmoil with more conviction than words could ever have mustered. Though never quite made an object of sympathy, the film does dally briefly with the tragic circumstances behind his compulsion to kill and although one has to despise him there's also a degree of understanding for the man who's as disgusted with

what he has become as we are. His murders, being as the victims are primarily children, are extremely disturbing events and thankfully never depicted too graphically. The story highlights the abject stupidity of the Soviet system at the time and how red tape added years and countless more bodies to the solving of the case. Though shot in Hungary, the grim depiction of shabby and oppressive architecture captures to perfection the feel of the 1980s Soviet Union. The denouement, though sombre, is at the same time jubilant. Don't be deterred by the knowledge that this was made for TV; it's a fascinating and absorbing film guaranteed to keep you glued until the final credits roll.

HBO's DVD presentation of *Citizen X* is a fullscreen affair of premium quality, but where extra materials are concerned it's as desolate as pre-Perestroika Russia - some textual matter and that's it. Divided into 9 chapters, the film is presented with a choice of English or French dialogue and subtitling in French. - TG

THE CITY OF LOST CHILDREN

Colour, 1995, 112m. / Directed by Marc Caro & Jean-Pierre Jeunet / Starring Ron Perlman, Daniel Emilfork / Columbia (US R1 NTSC) / WS (1.85:1) (16:9) / DD5.1, EIV (UK R2 PAL) / WS (1.85:1) / DD2.0

For a successor to their outlandish French art house hit *Delicatessen*, the visually gifted pair of Marc Caro and Jean-Pierre Jeunet (*Alien: Resurrection*) went even further over the top with a surreal, self-contained fantasy related almost entirely from children's viewpoints. The end product, *The City of Lost Children*, divided audiences who either found it captivating and imaginative or shrill and overblown. Regardless, the aesthetic artistry invested in every single frame of this film is consistently breathtaking, and for anyone inclined towards the films of Terry Gilliam and David Lynch, *City of Lost Children* provides enough delights on every possible level to reward multiple viewings.

The sad, lonely, self-absorbed Krank (Daniel Emilfork) lives on a self-constructed laboratory where he keeps the talking brain Ervin (voiced by Jean-Louis Trintignant!), thriving in a jar. Accompanied by a series of clones (all played by the fantastic Dominique Pinon), Krank spirits away small children to his oceanic home and uses a device to steal their dreams, since Krank was not created with the capacity to dream himself. A spirited young girl, Miette (Judith

Vittet), notices the disappearances of her peers, including her surrogate brother, Denree. With the help of the simple but strong One (Ron Perlman), Miette winds her way through the nocturnal city and tries to track down the insidious abductor.

Crammed with bizarre incidental characters and events along the way, *City* thrives more on its little details than the basic storyline. The famous teardrop scene alone is easily worth the price of admission, recalling the earlier cause and effect showpiece in *Delicatessen*. In fact, much of *Children* feels like a green-washed, elaborate second draft of its predecessor, with the romantic anchor of the first film replaced by protection of a child in this one. The filmmakers display an endless amount of inventiveness throughout almost to the point of complete overload, with Angelo Badalamenti's heart-tugging score and the sincere performances always managing to keep events from spinning off into the completely avant garde. Interestingly, the casting of Fellini regular Emilfork (also in *The Devil's Nightmare*) aptly pegs Jeunet and Caro as the sci-fi Fellinis of the '90s, with their emphasis on eye-popping décor and unusual, fascinating human faces.

Columbia's earlier widescreen laserdisc of *City* looked fairly good, but the DVD is a tremendous improvement. Razor sharp throughout, even during those tricky scenes drenched in darkness and fog, this has obviously been handled with a great deal of care and affection. The DVD is actually closer to a special edition than the packaging might indicate, with a welcome costume gallery provided to highlight the stylish Gauthier designs and a running commentary with Jeunet and Perlman, who provide plenty of anecdotes about the elaborate, difficult process of making the film and the sacrifices made along the way. Presented in French with optional English subtitles (or the English dub track, which is adequate but not very satisfying), this film should deservedly continue to amass a following in years to come, and this edition should make that task even easier. On the other hand, the UK disc contains only an English dubbed option(!), with extras limited to a paltry filmography and image gallery.

CITY OF THE DEAD (HORROR HOTEL)

Colour, 1960, 76m. / Directed by John Llewellyn Moxey / Starring Patricia Jessel, Christopher Lee / Elite, Troma (US R0 NTSC) / WS (1.80:1), VCI (US R0 NTSC) / WS (1.78:1) (16:9)

Rarely cited as a top rung horror masterpiece, *City of the Dead (Horror Hotel* had the misfortune of being released during what is arguably the best year ever

for cinematic horror, 1960. Two of its contemporary heavyweights, *Psycho* and *Black Sunday* (both of which this film strongly resembles in unusual ways), went on to influence a whole decade of US and European filmmaking, while *Horror Hotel* quietly crept off and scared the bejeezus out of unsuspecting TV viewers. If you haven't seen it, do so now! And if you have, well, there's no excuse for not owning at least one of its incarnations on DVD.

During the Puritan era a ferocious witch named Elizabeth Selwyn (Patricia Jessel) is dragged out into the town square of Whitewood and condemned to be burned at the stake. Before perishing she utters a curse upon the township and vows to seek revenge. Centuries later, Professor Driscoll (Christopher Lee) teaches a course on witchcraft and captures the imagination of Nan Barlow (Venetia Stevenson), a perky young college student. Nan decides to use her vacation time to go to Whitewood for her senior paper research project, against the judgment of her boyfriend, Bill (Tom Naylor), and her brother, Richard (Dennis Lotis). Driscoll, a native of Whitewood, suggests that Nan stay at the Raven's Inn. After a strange and spooky nocturnal drive during which she picks up a mysterious hitchhiker, Nan arrives at Whitewood and takes her room at the inn, run by Mrs. Newlis - who bears a striking resemblance to a certain deceased witch. Nan borrows a book from the lovely local librarian (Betta St. John) and settles in for some good, solid fact-finding. When Nan fails to return on time, Bill and Richard fear she might be in trouble and go to Whitewood to find her. What they discover is far more insidious than they could have ever imagined...

Though probably intended to cash in on the growing cycle of Hammer horror hits, even down to recruiting Christopher Lee into the cast, *Horror Hotel* is a different kind of animal. The New England setting consists mainly of fog enshrouded studio sets, while the British cast adopts American accents of wildly varying degrees of success, but these quirks actually work in its favour. The overwhelming atmosphere and constant nightfall are genuinely creepy, and the weird clash of modern scepticism and ancient mysteries provide an engaging conflict for the unpredictable storyline. Much has been made of a plot twist at the end of the first act, but the finale is no less impressive, with a race against time performed in a graveyard populating by chanting demonic figures. Incidentally, five years later co-producers Milton Subotsky and Max Rosenberg would go on to co-found Amicus Pictures, a fascinating Hammer competitor responsible for such moody gems as *From Beyond the Grave* and *Asylum*. Needless to say, Amicus fans will find many of their favourite elements already in place within this astonishing film.

A surprising early success on laserdisc for Elite Entertainment, *Horror Hotel* was a natural choice for them to release in their first wave of DVD titles during the late '90s. Their transfer came from a relatively good 16mm print, which suffered only from a five minute stretch of guitar string scratches and, overall, dull black levels. The Roan Group issued another DVD through Troma derived from purportedly the only surviving 35mm elements but suffered from extensive damage. The Roan edition boasts sharper detail and stronger blacks, but it's also too dark in some scenes (the opening credits are completely impenetrable) and suffers from heavy speckling and scratches at several points. The compression is better than the early effort by Elite, an interesting comparison to show just how far the art of DVD has come in a couple of years. The Elite disc also contains a smudgy looking trailer, while the Roan one omits the trailer in favour of an engaging on-camera discussion by Christopher Lee about the making of the film. The first pressing of the Roan version also includes a very odd and unfortunate Easter Egg involving Lee, but most copies were quickly withdrawn.

The VCI edition under its original UK title arrived later and stands as the definitive version to date, with a richly detailed, sharp transfer that easily qualifies as immaculate. Lee also participates in this version through both a commentary and video interview, along with a nifty video chat with Moxey and Venetia Stevenson, who still looks quite lovely and charming. The US trailer is presented with new digital title cards for some reason.

CITY OF THE LIVING DEAD

Colour, 1980, 93m. / Directed by Lucio Fulci / Starring Christopher George, Catriona MacColl / Anchor Bay (US R1 NTSC) / WS (1.85:1) (16:9) / DD5.1, EC Entertainment (Holland R2 NTSC), Vipco (UK R2 PAL), Astro (Germany R2 PAL) / WS (1.85:1)

 Following the wild success of *Zombie*, outrageous Italian horror director Lucio Fulci next splattered blood on the drive-in screens of America with this Gothic feast of zombies and the supernatural, known to most folks as *The Gates of Hell*. Though a few minutes of transition dialogue were trimmed, the film's splashy thrills remained intact and earned it a heavy fan base at the dawn of home video. In the most famous scene, an unfortunate simpleton (Giovanni Lombardo Radice, aka *Make Them Die Slowly*'s John Morghen) has a nasty encounter with an electric drill, a sequence that raised the hackles of British censors and landed the film in trouble around the world.

Father Thomas, the local parish priest in Dunwich (another Fulci nod to Lovecraft, get it?), hangs himself in the local cemetery, unleashing a series of uncanny events on the small, desolate town. Corpses rise, worm-infested bodies pop up, glass explodes and punctures bleeding wounds into walls, and a teenage girl (Daniela Doria, also abused in Fulci's *The Black Cat*) regurgitates her intestines, much to the horror of her boyfriend (director Michele Soavi in an early acting bit). Meanwhile in New York, a psychic, Mary Woodhouse (Catriona MacColl), experiences a vision of the Dunwich horror during a séance and falls into a deathlike trance. She is narrowly saved from being buried alive by an aggressive reporter (Christopher George), and they drive to Dunwich to stop the escalating evil before it reaches full force on All Saint's Day.

While this all may sound like a mindless gorefest, *City of the Living Dead* is much more than the sum of its gooey parts. From the late 1970s to 1982, Fulci assembled a stunning crew for his zombie-centric horror films, culminating in his masterpiece *The Beyond*. Thanks to Sergio Salvati's magnificent cinematography, Gino de Rossi's skincrawling special effects, and Fabio Frizzi's haunting score, the film works up a feverish series of incidents which provide a heavy visceral kick missing from Fulci's later comeback efforts. The game cast does quite a job, with the lovely MacColl in first of three memorable lead roles for Fulci and blonde starlet Janet Agren (*Eaten Alive!*) turning up as a neurotic Dunwich resident. On a narrative level, *City* makes no sense at all (especially the last 30 seconds), but if you're willing to just kick back and go along with Fulci's demented fever dream, it's quite a ride.

For horror fans, Anchor Bay's DVD is the long awaited answer to a lot of prayers. Previous versions of *City* have been extremely grainy and usually cut, though the Japanese laser and EC Entertainment laser and DVD releases were the best of the bunch. The Anchor Bay DVD presents the complete English version, and the image quality is greatly improved. The eerie prowling camera shots of the town streets at night look smooth and ominously rich, and of course, the show-stopping drill scene can be experienced in all its widescreen glory. The film has always had a grainy, gauzy appearance which still lingers here; everything from cheap film stock to bad lab work has been cited for this flaw, but fans have grown to accept it as just another part of the film's weird, disjointed anatomy. The original European English-language trailer is included, and the audio has been given a spacious 5.1 overhaul which nicely separates the Frizzi music and some of the punchier sound effects to the outer speakers. Considering the high number of jolting, manipulative sound effects, this could well be the scariest audio remix in DVD history. For you '80s sleaze fans, there are also some amusing radio spots for its amazingly unlikely American theatrical run.

A CLOCKWORK ORANGE
Colour, 1971, 137m. / Directed by Stanley Kubrick. / Starring Malcolm McDowell, Patrick Magee / Warner / WS (1.66:1) / DD5.1

Hands down the most contro-versial film in the Kubrick canon, *A Clockwork Orange* was only recently permitted in England and has gone through more censorship hassles than the entire works of Lucio Fulci put together. That said, time has been extremely generous to this film, which provides both an amusing portrait of its own era (the mod clothes and hairstyles, outrageous lounge-inspired art direction, throbbing electronic music) and a prescient vision of how the future will only exacerbate the savage versus civilized conflicts inherent in mankind.

While Kubrick's previous *2001* presented a central character rendered inert by his surroundings, here the viewer is given Alex (Malcolm McDowell), a dynamic, intelligent, and often witty psychopath who performs any antisocial action dictated by his whims - beatings, robbery, rape, and murder. Significantly, many critics made the bizarre assumption that because Alex narrates the film, Kubrick must agree with what our "humble narrator" is saying. Thus, according to this train of thought, classical music, artwork, and women in general are corrupt objects worthy of mistrust at best. The film's extremely potent streak of humour also belongs to Alex and reinforces the message that a twisted member of society is not so far removed from normality as is so often assumed. On a more superficial level, *A Clockwork Orange* is also a supremely well-crafted piece of entertainment, slickly acted and performed, often disturbing, and

strangely enough, nowhere remotely as explicit as its reputation has suggested. Like *The Texas Chainsaw Massacre*, most of the violence is brutal and often difficult to watch but committed from a great distance or off-camera, allowing the viewer's imagination to unpleasantly fill in the blanks. Oddly, Anglophile Kubrick omitted the final chapter from Burgess' novel in his adaptation (presumably because he only read the US printing), which would have ended the film on a more sincere and positive note.

Though derived from the same materials used for Warner's widescreen laserdisc, the DVD *of A Clockwork Orange* looks markedly better, with smoother colours and less video noise. Like the laser reissue, this is actually the original X-rated print with the entire "William Tell Overture" sequence, which was visually altered to obtain an R rating upon the film's theatrical reissue. It may not be first-rate demo material, but the DVD gets the job done and conveys the film's wild visual schemes relatively well. The 1.66:1 framing reveals more at the top and bottom than the theatrical version, while a few sequences (the opening titles, newspaper headlines, etc.) are hard-matted at 1.85:1 as originally shot. The DVD also includes the 1971 theatrical trailer, which may give Japanese seizure cartoons a run for their money.

COBRA VERDE
Colour, 1988, 110m. / Directed by Werner Herzog / Starring Werner Herzog, King Ampaw / Anchor Bay (US R1 NTSC) / WS (1.78:1) (16:9) / DD5.1

The alarming decline in American arthouse cinema after the '70s is unmistakable when one considers that latter day projects by Fellini, Kurosawa, Antonioni, and other masters remained either unreleased or thrown away in minor showings many years later outside their native countries. Most incredibly, the final Werner Herzog film starring Klaus Kinski, *Cobra Verde*, never saw the light of American projectors outside of a few isolated film festivals, leaving film fans the only option of seeking out bootleg videotapes to satisfy their curiosity. Fortunately the film has now resurfaced in pristine condition, and while it isn't quite the delirious accomplishment of *Aguirre* or *Fitzcarraldo* (how could it be?), this one comes very close at times and serves as a fitting coda to one of the cinema's more unusual partnerships.

Francisco Manoel da Silva, an infamous bandit and rebel known as Cobra Verde (or "green snake"), finds a profitable stint as the slave overseer for a

Brazilian plantation owner. Naturally Francisco impregnates his boss' daughters - never a smart career move - and is sent off to the desolate western coast of Africa on a seemingly deadly mission to reopen the slave trade in that area from the treacherous King of Dahomey. Naturally things don't go as planned, with our antihero winning the loyalty of a huge tribe of female warriors in an uprising against the King in what can only be termed a topless version of *Zulu*. As expected, Francisco winds up confronting nature itself and his own internal demons in the unforgettable final act.

The DVD of *Cobra Verde* is just as impressive as Anchor Bay's other Herzog titles, with a splendid widescreen transfer which accurately captures the delicate colour palette used in the film's artful cinematography. A lengthy opening conversation lit only by a single flickering candle is just one of the many carefully lit scenes which could have been disastrous on DVD, but the results are impressive and quite natural in appearance. The 5.1 remix simply tweaks the already existing Dolby Stereo master instead of creating a new mix from scratch; considering this is also a relatively recent film in this particular collection, the results are more pristine and could easily be mistaken for a film made only a year or two ago.

Herzog once again returns for a lively commentary track in which he discusses his final cinematic hour with Kinski, who was becoming quite impossible by this point and was evidently not up for another round with the demanding director. Unlike *Fitzcarraldo*, this was actually filmed in German, so the decision to lavish the 5.1 treatment only on the German track makes sense. Unlike landmark works such as *Nosferatu* or *Heart of Glass*, this score by Popol Vuh has rarely been heard but is extremely effective in creating an otherworldly sense of space and time. The English dub track in 2.0 surround is generally a mess, with the native sequences presented with subtitles and Kinski's dialogue sequences sloppily dubbed. Stick with the subtitled version by all means. The disc also includes the original German trailer, a fair approximation of the film itself.

COFFY

Colour, 1973, 88m. / Directed by Jack Hill / Starring Pam Grier, Booker Bradshaw / MGM (US R1 NTSC) / WS (1.66:1)

Following their successful pair of women's prison yarns, *The Big Doll House* and *The Big Bird Cage*, director Jack Hill and rising star Pam Grier moved from Roger Corman to Samuel Arkoff's American

International Pictures for two of the finest black action films ever made, *Coffy* and *Foxy Brown*. These stylized comic books for the silver screen presented strong heroines, fast and brutal action, snappy and often uproarious dialogue, and an uncanny knack for rousing the audience to cheers at least once every five minutes. Though blaxploitation was mostly ignored during the '80s, its resurgence thanks to the support of fans like Quentin Tarantino and the easy accessibility of home video have given these classics far more exposure than their inner city and drive-in runs back in the '70s.

In *Coffy*, Grier portrays the title character, a nurse who decides to tear down the drug network that left her little sister an emotionally devastated junkie. The film opens with a rousing set piece in which Coffy, disguised as a hooker, deals out justice via shotgun and syringe, and then returns home to the loving arms of her straight and narrow boyfriend, Howard (Booker Bradshaw). Coffy's detective work leads her to the outrageous drug dealing pimp, King George (Robert DoQui), who comes complete with his own theme song and a stable of sexy call girls. Coffy poses as a Jamaican whore (yes, really) to get closer to King George and discover his insidious connections. After a series of catfights, double crosses, and baddie bashing, Coffy eventually uncovers the horrible, tragic truth behind drug dealing circuit.

In this film, everything simply works perfectly. Grier is at her best, supplying plenty of high kicking, gun blasting, and skin baring, while Hill clearly put all of himself into the screenplay and direction, both of which are more slick and insightful than the average viewer would ever expect from an exploitation film. The story moves along at a fast clip and even finds room for a terrific turn by Hill regular Sid Haig as ruthless Russian "Omar," while the always intriguing Alan Arbus (*Greaser's Palace*) turns up to represent the corrupt white side of the drug trade. Of course, the film wouldn't be complete without that funky, catchy score by R&B artist Roy Ayers... but be warned, the theme song will stick in your head for days.

Coffy was first released on VHS by Orion, whose full frame transfer was completely open matte and looked quite good at the time. A laserdisc edition briefly appeared before passing over into MGM's "Soul Cinema" collection. Luckily the new DVD is even better, with a crisp new transfers boasting marvellous colour saturation. The films' '70s origins are still evident by some grainy looking night scenes and a few minor speckles in the prints, but overall the presentation is quite impressive. The mono audio is also tremendously improved, with greater dynamic range and less background hiss than the Orion master. Contrary to the packaging, which cites an aspect ration of 1.85:1, *Coffy* is actually 1.66:1, leaving a comfortable amount of headroom without the distracting empty spaces evident on the Orion version. The disc also includes the theatrical trailer and a Jack Hill commentary, which ties in nicely with his one on the Foxy Brown DVD.

COLD EYES OF FEAR

Colour, 1970, 91m. / Directed by Enzo G. Castellari / Starring Giovanna Ralli, Fernando Rey / Image (US R0 NTSC), Redemption (UK R0 PAL) / WS (1.85:1)

 Cold Eyes of Fear will leave newcomers to Eurotrash scratching their heads in bewilderment. The impossibly convoluted tale (ostensibly an entry in the era's *gialli*, or thrillers) involves the usual brutality, nudity, and a madman causing mayhem in London, so the very Italian-looking cast is dubbed with highly improbable, phoney British accents. Gianni Garko, best known for his spaghetti western role as "Sartana" and his turn in Lucio Fulci's *The Psychic*, is the innocent protagonist, while Euro-sex veteran Frank Wolff (as the maniac out for vengeance) and Luis Buñuel favourite Fernando Rey (who spends the bulk of his part sitting at a desk) wallow around in the depravity like seasoned pros.

Enzo G. Castellari, best known for his low-budget sci-fi and Fabio Testi gangster movies, does a fine job of sewing all of the necessary exploitation elements together while understandably failing to fret about such things as rationality and coherence. In fact, the film often feels more like an off-kilter crime film than a real giallo, a fact borne out by some oddball Castellari touches like a lengthy gang fight thrown into the middle of the film for no apparent reason. The free-form Ennio Morricone music adds appreciably to the film's off-kilter sleaze ambience (though a number of cues were lifted wholesale from his other scores of the period).

Overall the print looks much better than most other films of its vintage, with punchy colours, fine detail, and no noticeable compression defects. Of course, the occasional print flaw pops up here and there, and this version does display a few strange quirks (no opening title card, for instance, and the final shot looks like it was culled from a totally different, third-generation video source). While the

audio is clear, the dialogue sound elements seem to have suffered with age and sound like they were recorded on old vinyl. The original ads boasted this was filmed in "70 mm Techniscope," but the 1.85:1 letterboxing looks about right (notwithstanding some slight grazing on the side of the credits). The trailer, apparently designed for an abortive US release under the title *Desperate Moments* (apparently a nod to the film's more than passing resemblance to *The Desperate Hours*), follows the feature. The UK disc from Redemption also adds on a gallery of posters, video art, and fotobuste.

COLOR ME BLOOD RED

Colour, 1965, 79m. / Directed by Herschell Gordon Lewis / Starring Don Joseph, Candi Conder / Image (US R1 NTSC), Tartan (UK R0 PAL)

 The finale to H.G. Lewis and Dave Friedman's "Blood Trilogy" proved to be a more troubled affair, resulting in the end of a successful run of films on the US grindhouse circuit. A cockeyed entry in the crazy artist subgenre of '60s horror (including *A Bucket of Blood*, *Portrait of Terror*, and, by extension, *Little Shop of Horrors*), this odd film only features a few mild, intermittent flourishes of the outrageous gore which characterized the duo's previous two hit films. On the other hand, the filmmakers' skills and the acting (no doubt due to Connie Mason's absence) had markedly improved, resulting in an odd curio which will appeal primarily to diehard Lewis and Friedman fans.

Perpetually aggravated artist Adam Sorg (Don Joseph) can't seem to find the personal satisfaction and public recognition he craves for his paintings. However, a little mishap puts a bright idea in his head - namely, human blood makes for a really great shade of red. When his own precious fluids begin to run dry, Sorg turns to his girlfriend, who dies during a domestic squabble. Now stark raving mad, Sorg sacrifices everything for the sake of his art, though at great expense to nearby neighbours and tourists.

Filmed along a series of attractive seaside Florida locales, *Color Me Blood Red* benefits greatly from its unusual setting and the edgy, deliberately paced depiction of growing dementia, which anticipates such nihilistic works as *Driller Killer*. However, newcomers would do best to try the other two films in the trilogy first, as they offer a more accessible and quickly paced example of the Lewis style. The fact that the film was eventually forced through post-production without its creators' involvement may account for its inconsistencies, which is largely borne out on the DVD commentary track by Lewis, Friedman, and Mike Vraney. Obviously coming down from the giddy high of *Blood Feast* and *Two Thousand Maniacs!*, the two grand gentlemen of exploitation take the opportunity to expand upon their working relationship at the time and the factors which were involved in their close union and ultimate separation.

The most claustrophobic and visually subdued of Lewis' gore films, this title looks quite good under the circumstances. The brown interior scenes and bright ocean shots look clear, though some problems with the film stock result in a loss of detail during certain darker portions of the film. The opening scene in particular looks the worse for wear, but this has always been the case. Simply put, it's unlikely a better version of this film will ever surface.

The DVD also includes the original trailer ("a study in the macarrb!" growls the announcer during one unintentionally goofy moment), which predates *Last House on the Left* by several years in its "only a movie" campaign. A ten minute reel of outtakes from the Something Weird vaults is also included, mostly consisting of alternate footage from the outboard motor disembowelment scene (later duplicated in *I Spit on Your Grave*). An uncut version is also available in a trimmed down package (no commentary, for one) in the UK from Tartan.

COMBAT SHOCK

Colour, 1986, 91m. / Directed by Buddy Giovinazzo / Starring Rick Giovinazzo, Veronica Stork / Troma (US R1 NTSC)

Contrary to the title and the cover art, which depicts a Rambo-style Vietnam bloodbath, *Combat Shock* is completely unlike any other film released by Troma and should surprise folks accustomed to dreck like *Troma's War* and *Surf Nazis Must Die*. The reason for this, of course, is that Troma's instincts as distributors who pick up small indie productions surpass their skills as filmmakers (so far). Unfortunately, while *Combat Shock* has amassed a decent cult following over the years, it has also drawn a lot of fire for its misleading advertising (try imagining the face of a Steven Seagal fan who rented this hoping for a little mindless gunplay).

A down in the dirt, thoroughly depressing and uncompromising work, *Combat Shock* demands that its audience accept the film on its own terms, though whether each individual viewer is willing to go along

for the ride is completely a matter of personal taste. Love it or hate it, there's no denying that this bitter little pill has far more on its mind than the entire Toxic Avenger series put together. Originally shown on the festival circuit under the title *American Nightmares*, this film fell afoul of the MPAA who, not surprisingly, objected to the very graphic violence (which is justified by the plot but certainly hard to take). Rumours immediately spread through the horror fan networks about explicit footage cut from the film on a scale that rivalled *Last House on the Left*, particularly surrounding the infamous "baking" scene at the end. Now that Troma has finally issued the complete version, fans can judge the entire work for themselves. Running six minutes longer, this print is definitely bloodier but not much more explicit that what was shown in theatres. The extra carnage consists of very moist bullet squib effects, though the most squirm-inducing scene involving a junkie dosing up via an arm wound is mercifully about the same. Thankfully, the baking scene still remains left to the audience's imaginations, which have already been battered and bruised by that point anyway.

Described by Giovinazzo as a cross between *Eraserhead* and *Taxi Driver*, the film follows a few sordid days in the life of Frankie (Buddy's brother Rick, who also did the unsettling electronic score). A traumatized Vietnam vet now saddled with the pangs of poverty in New York City, Frankie tries to cope with the burdens of his pregnant wife, who sits around watching static on TV all day, and his newborn baby, mutated by the after-effects of Agent Orange into something resembling a smushed grey Muppet. Drug dealers, underage hookers, and junkies fill the daily scene of Frankie's life, and his increasingly disturbing flashbacks to Vietnam continuously set him on edge and drive him to the brink of a nervous breakdown. Bloodshed erupts, of course, but anyone expecting the gung-ho cathartic vigilantism of *The Executioner* is going to be in for a nasty surprise.

As usual, Troma's DVD is quite a blast. Aside from the usual Troma hard sell plugs and an intro by Lloyd Kaufman, this also features an impromptu camcorder chat with Kaufman and Giovinazzo, as well as handful of trailers and some promotional stills. The real fun, though, lies with the running audio commentary track by Giovinazzo, who makes for surprisingly warm and entertaining company along this rough road. He offers numerous funny anecdotes about the film (especially his efforts to make Staten Island look like Vietnam!) and discusses its bizarre production and censorship history, as well as his little visual filmmaking tricks (like the great idea of projecting the Vietnam flashbacks onto Rick's face). Giovinazzo is joined by notorious German director Jörg Buttgereit (*Nekromantik, Der Tödesking*), obviously a big fan of the film and provider of some often hilarious observations in his thick accent ("Ya, I vas vondering aboot dat, all de blood..."). (Check out the similar special edition for *Killer Condom* for even more Buttgereit commentary fun.) In the meantime, hopefully Giovinazzo's other recent projects will see the light of home video or, wishfully thinking, a theatre screen.

The actual transfer of *Combat Shock* is most likely the best we'll see and is often very good during the interior scenes. Dark shots and some exteriors are marred by grain due to the 16mm origins, though the full frame presentation far surpasses the smudgy R-rated cut released by Prism back in the late '80s. Don't expect demo material here, obviously, but if you love the film, you'll be more than pleased- and it's a thankful improvement over Troma's recent EP-speed VHS version, too. Quite a bummer ride, *Combat Shock* nevertheless offers some food for thought and once again shows Troma in top form in the DVD special edition department.

COMIN' AT YA!

Colour, 1981, 91m. / Directed by Ferdinando Baldi / Starring Tony Anthony, Victoria Abril / Rhino (US R1 NTSC) / WS (2.35:1)

 For anyone who ever wondered how that mini-trend of 3-D movies in the early '80s got started, here's the answer. Before *Jaws 3-D*, before *Friday the 13th Part 3-D*, there was *Comin' at Ya!*, a spaghetti western shot for about ten cents that wound making a bundle at the box office. In fact, its star, the bland Tony Anthony, even made a follow up *Raiders of the Lost Ark* 3-D rip-off, *Treasure of the Four Crowns*. Kitschy, silly, and often just simply strange, *Comin' at Ya!* isn't very good, but for those nostalgic or curious souls who haven't been able to see it in the years since its theatrical run, Rhino's DVD offers a fair approximation of this unique experience.

Honourable gunslinger H.H. Hart (Anthony) is interrupted during his wedding to the lovely Abilene (Victoria Abril) by a pair of grotesque, lecherous brothers, Pike (Gene Quintano) and Polk (Richardo Palacios). The villains steal his bride and even cart off a few other women from town, then dump the ladies in the desert. Hart goes in hot pursuit, engaging in numerous fisticuffs and shootouts along the way.

Completely undistinguished in terms of filmmaking or plotting, *Comin' at Ya!* at least features some of the strangest 3-D effects of all time. During the opening credits alone, beans spill all over the camera, bullets fire at the audience, and hands reach out for the viewer's face. Not enough? How about guys falling downstairs (in slooooow motion), spinning fiery pinwheels (for the five minute recap at the end), bats, spiders, scurrying rats, flaming arrows (the best part), and even a baby's bare bottom! Some of the Leone-style scope photography looks nice, too, and Carlo Savina contributes a spare, elegiac score that probably deserved a better film. Also, fans of Spanish starlet Abril (*Tie Me Up! Tie Me Down!, High Heels*) will be interested in seeing one of her earliest roles before she became a European celebrity.

Unfortunately, though nicely letterboxed (though maybe zoomed in a bit too much considering the tight framing of the opening Filmways logo), the Rhino DVD can't replicate the polarized (grey lenses) 3-D experience from the theatrical prints. Instead, viewers get a standard red/blue presentation, which distorts much of the colour photography and causes some unfortunate blurring and loss of detail in the process. The print quality itself is satisfying, however, and the 3-D effects manage to survive intact. Considering the circumstances, though, it would have been preferable to have a standard colour, 2-D variant for people who might actually want to see what the film really looked like. Incidentally, the glasses enclosed with this DVD were folded backwards; the red lens should be over the right eye. Also includes the corny, amusing US trailer, which features no footage from the actual film but instead offers a "live" demonstration of how 3-D actually works... sort of!

THE COMING OF SIN

Colour, 1978, 84m. / Directed by José Larraz / Starring Patricia Granada, Lydia Zuaso / Pagan (UK R0 PAL) / WS (1.78:1)

The Coming of Sin

A perverse little number from the erratic but always interesting José Larraz (*Vampyres*), this rarely seen, low budget blend of exploitation and art is best known to fans of Euro sleaze under its more colourful theatrical release title, *Violation of the Bitch*. For its first DVD release, Pagan translated the original Spanish title, *La visita del vicio* (or more literally, *Vice's Arrival*), as *The Coming of Sin*. Under any name though, it's a twisted, often mystifying daydream filled with erotica and surrealism.

Beautiful amateur painter Lorna (Patricia Granada) passes her sunny days dabbling with a paintbrush and burying herself in the family library. Life changes dramatically with the arrival of Triana (Lydia Zuaso), a dark-haired girl from a gypsy clan who comes to stay indefinitely and sparks a gradual, torrid relationship with Lorna. However, Triana's dreams are haunted by images of a naked man (Rafael Machado) on horseback, a premonition which comes true one day while she strolls through the woods surrounding a nearby lake. The mysterious man, who never seems to wear much, attempts to rape Triana, who runs home and tells Lorna about the weird naked guy living with his horse out in the wild near their house. Lorna goes to investigate while Triana's fantasies continue, including one which finds her naked inside a giant horse about to be... uh, straddled, apparently. Soon the mystery man directly intrudes on their lives, beginning an unholy triangle of lust that culminates in a dark reversal of fortune.

Though undeniably rough around the edges, *The Coming of Sin* is a strangely compelling alternative to the usual plotless European sex films of the period. The non-actors were evidently hired more for their looks than their thespian skills, and they make for adequate pawns in Larraz's little mind game. On the other hand, the awkward dubbing reliant on forced British accents makes for some nasty ear punishment.

As with his other kinky countryside yarns like *Vampyres* and *Symptoms*, Larraz relies on soft focus photography and elegant camera movements to counterpoint the often extreme and bizarre activity onscreen, including some fairly graphic and fleshy sex scenes. An even stronger variant with hardcore inserts made the grindhouse rounds under the title of *Sex Maniac* and has turned up on the bootleg video circuit (as well as an Italian PAL VHS release as *Sodomia*), but this unofficial bastardization of Larraz's film is best avoided. On the other hand, the international version under the *Violation* title, originally released in Holland and other European countries before hitting the video dupe market, was dramatically shorter than Larraz's preferred cut, clocking in just at 70 minutes. This cut eliminates several crucial scenes in their entirety and alters the opening credits to play out over a later scene.

The Pagan DVD represents the closest approximation of Larraz's original intentions. The BBFC lists a deletion of 1 minute and 15 seconds to obtain an "18" certificate, a punishment given to Triana's rape scene, which is still quite explicit but contains a strange jump in the audio, abruptly cutting off the music. Nothing from the other English language video editions is missing, and the added material is quite valuable. Image quality is quite good considering the softness of the source; the gauzy appearance reveals some compression problems, but the clarity of the image and nicely defined pastel colour schemes make up for it. The letterboxing also adds some much needed breathing room to Larraz's claustrophobic close ups, which come off as oppressive and clumsy on earlier cropped video editions. The DVD also includes a photo gallery and a thirty minute interview with Larraz, apparently the complete unedited version of his discussion excerpted in his episode of the worthy Channel 4 series, *Eurotika!* Candid and often quite funny, he discusses his career at great length, and the disc offers chapter indexes to each film and subject.

COME PLAY WITH ME

Colour, 1977, 90m. / Directed by George Harrison Marks / Starring Mary Millington, Alfie Bass / Medusa (UK R2 PAL)

A pair of banknote counterfeiters (Marks and Bass) do a runner with a perfect set of plates. They take refuge from their mobster employers at a health farm, which, to attract business, has just employed a pack of nymphets. Without doubt the most famous British sex film of the 1970s, or any other era, *Come Play with Me* is the baby of famed purveyor of soft porn, George Harrison Marks. An Ealing-flavoured comic caper with a hearty dollop of sexy sauce, its renown stems primarily from the fact it was the film that propelled sex queen Mary Millington into the collective conscious of Britain's male populace. Her actual input is negligible; although her name appears before the title card at the outset, more honestly indicative of her participation is her placing on the closing credits (name number 38 on a cast list of 39). Despite this - and the fact she's a little overshadowed by some of the other girls (Mireille Alonville, Suzy Mandel, Anna Bergman and Penny Chisholm) - for many, almost a quarter of a century later, Millington remains the sole reason for tuning in.

Marks not only directed *Come Play with Me*, but produced, co-wrote and starred in it too (sporting spectacles, goofy teeth and a terrible wig), and there's no denying he had an eye for a pretty face; if not particularly natural in front of the camera or gifted in the delivery of dialogue, the girls are (mostly) very attractive indeed. The remaining cast is a veritable who's who of third rate comics (Henry McGee, Norman Vaughn, Cardew Robinson, Bob Todd), washed-up Brit stalwarts (Derek Aylward, Michael Balfour, Tommy Godfrey, Milton Reid) and marginally higher profile players who should probably have known better (Ronald Fraser, Irene Handl, Alfie Bass). Yet the whole show is so amiably quaint - Marks even drops a song'n'dance number into the proceedings! - that it's intoxicatingly agreeable. Several of the extremely lightweight sex scenes were shot twice, the stronger takes utilised in a scarcely seen version destined for more liberal continental territories. Millington's follow-up, *The Playbirds*, proved to be a far better showcase for her limited but undeniably appealing talents.

The quality of Medusa Pictures' Region 2 fullscreen DVD is far better than one might expect given the age and the low-budget nature of the production. The 22-chapter-encoded film is in remarkably good shape with bright, vivid colours that only occasionally show evidence of instability. It is, naturally enough, the non-explicit UK version . The only extra feature is a 6-minute featurette entitled "Mary Millington 1946-1979 Prologue," apparently made some time shortly after her death. Comprising a lugubrious commentary and a few clips from *Come Play with Me* and *The Playbirds*, as a tribute to the woman whose allure captivated millions it's rather short and uninspired, and the motivation behind its original construction is uncertain. It's just a shame that the rights to include the Channel Four television documentary about her life could not have been secured. - TG

CONAN THE BARBARIAN

Colour, 1982, 129m. / Directed by John Milius / Starring Arnold Schwarzenegger, James Earl Jones / Universal / WS (2.35:1) (16:9)

"What is best in life, Conan?" "To crush ya enemies, have them brought before you, and to hear the lamentations of their women." Well, what else can you say about this one? John Milius' ultra-macho "guy movie" version of our primeval past was Arnold Schwarzenegger's first big Hollywood starring role and really kicked off the whole sword 'n' sandal subgenre that cursed viewers for most of the early '80's. I really can't put down any movie that has Arnold punching out a camel, so let's just say that if you love the movie, you'll probably want the DVD.

The slim storyline concerns little Conan, whose parents are viciously murdered by the evil Thulsa Doom (James Earl Jones). After years spent building up a muscular bod in slavery, Conan is set free and joins up with thieves Gerry Lopez and Sandhal "I don't do nudity (unless I get paid well)" Bergman to infiltrate Doom's cult headquarters. After encounters with wacky wizard Mako and Norse king Max Von Sydow, Conan lays waste to Doom's followers and engages in several brutal battles.

Universal first released this film with the same lousy transfer as the one for their laserdisc, meaning the colours were unstable and the image was overly littered with grain. Fortunately the "Collector's Edition" (available in Regions 1, 2, and 4) looks even better than the theatrical prints, with a surprisingly smooth texture. The Dolby Digital stereo is fine, with Basil Poledouris' magnificent score sounding robust and lively as usual, though a little redirection might have given the sound effects more presence. All in all, it's about as good as you would expect considering the film's history.

The bonuses include the original US trailer, a Milius/Schwarzenegger commentary (which offers less than you might imagine), a "Conan Unchained" featurette containing interviews with the principals, and a wide selection of notes and image galleries. Incidentally, *Conan* was trimmed of several minutes of gore and brutality before its release due to an X rating from the MPAA, and it would be nice someday if MCA would put out the money to have this film restored to its intended length. However, the special edition does contain some significant added footage, including more of a resolution concerning the abducted princess.

THE CONCRETE JUNGLE

Colour, 1982, 95m. / Directed by Tom DeSimone / Starring Jill St. John, Tracey E. Bergman / MIA (UK R2 PAL)

After the '70s heyday of Roger Corman and Filipino women in prison films, the genre seemed to have run itself into the ground by the decade's end. However, much to everyone's surprise, a second wave began in the early '80s, starting with the accomplished *The Concrete Jungle*. Though later eclipsed by its trashier successors like *Chained Heat* and *Reform School Girls*, this pivotal film is one of the more endearing of its kind, and unlike most of its ilk, you might be able to respect yourself in the morning after watching it.

Sweet young Elizabeth (soap actress Tracey E. Bergman) gets busted at the airport when her two-timing boyfriend, Danny (*Foxy Brown*'s Peter Brown), stuffs baggies of cocaine into her skis. The corrupt warden, Fletcher (Jill St. John), doesn't make life easy for the new arrival, who gets the nickname "Cherry" from the head honcho inmate, Cat (the amazing Barbara Luna). Cherry's daily grind of scrubbing toilets changes when Cat gets her a job in the laundry room; unfortunately Cat expects her favours to be returned and runs a drug ring under Fletcher's supervision. After Cherry accidentally witnesses Cat's murder of junkie Margo (Niki Dantine), tensions rise and Cherry begs Danny to get her released.

Though it could have been a formulaic disaster, *The Concrete Jungle* rises well above expectations thanks to dynamic performances from most of the cast and assured, slick direction from Tom DeSimone, best known for *Hell Night* and the unlikely 3-D gay porn fantasy, *Heavy Equipment*. Apart from a bizarre topless mud wrestling riot near the end, the film rarely veers into camp and instead makes the characters compelling enough that offer some emotional investment in the finale. It's no masterpiece to be sure, but for an example of babes behind bars drive-in fare, this is one of the best offerings around. And look fast for *I Spit on Your Grave*'s Camille Keaton as one of the inmates, too!

While their transfers are very touch and go on DVD, MIA has done a nice job with their British release of this difficult to find title. The open matte transfer looks great, with vivid colours and clean, crisp print quality. No VHS edition has ever looked this good, and unlike *Chained Heat*, you don't see boom mikes playing peek-a-boo at the top of the screen either. The audio for this film has always been too muffled for its own good, and sadly the problem hasn't been corrected here. Turn up the volume, though, and it sounds dull but acceptable.

THE CONVENT

Colour, 2000, 76m. / Directed by Mike Mendez / Starring Adrienne Barbeau, Joanna Canton / Trimark (US R1 NTSC) / WS (1.85:1) / DD5.1, Metrodome (UK PAL R2) / DD2.0

With the notable exception of Peter Jackson, the gory party movie became an endangered species after the 1980s. For all of you who long for the glory days of *Night of the Creeps*, *Waxwork*, and *Demons*, welcome to *The Convent*,

a much needed break from the flood of serial killer "thrillers" and *Scream* imitations. This wild, trashy, and often uproarious splatterfest was picked up by A-Pix for American distribution but was left homeless when that company folded at the end of 2000. Therefore, Great Britain and Germany now remain the easiest places to see this cult favourite in the making.

After an unforgettable, outrageous prologue set to Lesley Gore's "You Don't Own Me," which will remain undescribed here to avoid spoiling any surprises, the film begins in fairly standard fashion as a gang of sorority and fraternity members decides to spend the evening painting their letters on an old convent supposedly haunted for the past forty years by the ghosts of massacred nuns. The sorority's "good" member, Clarissa (Joanna Canton), brings along her former best friend, goth punker Mo (Megahn Perry), along for the ride. After stopping for a moment at the house of the town recluse, Christine (Adrienne Barbeau), who supposedly spent time in an asylum following the convent tragedy, the college students arrive at the convent and pass the time by making out, smoking dope, and chasing after a dog named Boozer. Unfortunately their playtime is interrupted by the arrival of two campus cops (including rapper Coolio in a glorified cameo), leaving Mo alone to fight against an incompetent quartet of wannabe Satanists. When the others return to fetch Mo at the convent, all hell begins to break loose as the demonic nuns invade the bodies of their victims, painting the walls with blood and preparing for the ultimate sacrifice. Clarissa flees to seek help from Christine, who reveals the truth behind the convent in an extended flashback (easily the film's most hysterical sequence) and agrees to return for another round of devil bashing.

Though it certainly has its share of dumb moments, *The Convent* speeds on like a rollercoaster during its compact 76 minute running time, with enough profane quips from Ms. Barbeau, spirited performances from everyone else, and bucketloads of multi-coloured splatter to remind you just how anaemic most horror fare has become lately. From the gaudy electronic score to the goofy shock ending, this would fit perfectly with *any Evil Dead* festival, provided that expectations are kept reasonable.

The DVD from Metrodome looks fine, with the open matte transfer exposing huge amounts of open space at the top and bottom of the frame, while the Trimark edition mattes it off at 1.85:1 (non-anamorphic) for more balanced compositions. Colours are vivid throughout and often tread into day-glo territory, while the thunderous soundtrack makes excellent use of split channel effects, particularly in the US 5.1 version. The surround speakers remain constantly active, so be sure to turn it up loud and enjoy. The Metrodome disc also includes a spoiler-filled UK trailer (promoting it as "Nuns, Guns, and Gasoline," a very similar tagline to the US poster for *Cemetery Man*), matted off at 1.85:1 and looking much worse than the film itself, as well as a few cast bios, while the Trimark disc contains a smattering of deleted scenes, two audio commentary tracks, and cast and crew interviews.

THE COOK, THE THIEF, HIS WIFE & HER LOVER

Colour, 1989, 124m. / Directed by Peter Greenaway / Starring Helen Mirren, Michael Gambon / Anchor Bay (US R1 NTSC) / WS (2.35:1) (16:9) / DD2.0

 The finest film by Peter Greenaway and arguably the most significant, devastating work of English-speaking cinematic art released in the '90s, *The Cook, the Thief, His Wife and Her Lover* still hasn't received its full due. The firestorm that surrounded its release (and in tandem with *Tie Me Up! Tie Me Down!* ultimately led to the creation of the NC-17 rating) made the title a catchphrase for daring adult entertainment, which this certainly is, but the film also marks a tremendous step forward for Greenaway as an artist. The film marks a fluid bridge between the quirky, small scale exercises in human foibles like *Drowning by Numbers* and the more lavish, unabashed studies in excess like *Prospero's Books* and *The Baby of Macon*. For all his achievements, *The Cook* is still his finest hour and an essential part of any self-respecting film buff's education.

The newly opened Le Hollandais restaurant is immediately beset by problems. The obnoxious gangster owner, Albert Spica (Michael Gambon), has his thugs beat up a debtor in the parking lot behind the building while the soft spoken head chef, Richard (*Diva*'s Richard Bohringer) tries to cope inside the kitchen with cluttered signs, power outages, and Albert's offer of questionable spoiling food delivered outside in trucks. Albert's wife, Georgina (Helen Mirren), tolerates his verbal and physical abuse by quietly stealing away for a smoke in the bathroom, but that night she catches the eye of one bookish customer, Michael (Alan Howard). The two begin an illicit affair which continues each night, forcing them to copulate in the restroom and among the stored food. When their infidelity is inevitably discovered, the four characters experience a violent, vengeful chain of events of Jacobean proportions.

Most obviously, *The Cook* is one of those rare films in which everyone involved is at the absolute top of their game. The actors have a ball with their meaty roles, though obviously Gambon and Mirren get the juiciest moments, and Greenaway's combination of aching human drama and stunning aesthetic visuals has never been more potent. His regular cinematographer, Sacha Vierney, conjures up some jaw-dropping camerawork, which carries the viewer on gliding wings through each massive room of the restaurant, where the characters' Jean Paul Gauthier clothes change through each doorway to match the decor. Michael Nyman, Greenaway's frequent composer at the time, also provides one of his finest scores, highlighted by the unforgettable twelve minute "Memorium" which plays out at different intervals over the one week period (visually designated by different dinner menus for each calendar day).

Many critics at the time were tempted to read the film as a savage critique of Thatcher's callous financial policies in Great Britain during the eighties, but the film's impact goes well beyond such a specific social reading; one could easily apply this scenario to any oppressive political climate even during the present day. Incidentally, fans of British comedies should keep their eyes peeled for two very prominent future cast members of the hilarious *Vicar of Dibley* among the regular diners. *The Cook* epitomizes the kind of edgy fare Miramax used to corner the art film market before their regrettable consumption by Disney. Though unrated in theatres, it was eventually branded with an NC-17 by the time of its video release thanks to a licensing deal with Trimark.

The VHS editions ranged from an uncut letterboxed version (also released on laserdisc) to a laughable R-rated cut, which excised half an hour of footage. The world's largest and most despised video chain (and we all know who that is) originally stocked the NC-17 version before yanking it and having the tapes destroyed, with the R-rated alternative eventually becoming the most widely known edition. That's a shame, though oddly enough, the bowdlerized cut is in many ways more perverse because of what it implies rather than shows. For example, the stunning final scene doesn't actually show what one character eats, leaving the viewer with an impression more foul than what Greenaway originally filmed. Though the spacious scope visuals of *The Cook* are essential to appreciating the film on any level at all, the letterboxed laserdisc looks woefully inadequate compared to Anchor Bay's magnificent DVD. The anamorphic transfer corrects the aspect ratio, which was squeezed horizontally on the laserdisc, smushing out everyone's heads in the process, and the colours and black levels are drastically improved. The hellish reds of the dining room interior have now been properly restored, so forget the laser's comparatively murky, dull shades of brown and beige. Simply put, toss those laserdiscs out and get this instead; the upgrade is most definitely worth it.

The surround audio on the laserdisc was always very strong, and the DVD sounds identical, with Nyman's piano and string heavy music giving the rear speakers a very hefty workout. While this film easily deserves a full blown special edition someday, this DVD is more than satisfactory for the time being. Apart from the terrific transfer, the disc includes two international trailers (with any studio credits conspicuously absent). One runs a little over three minutes and features some very effective manipulation of voiceovers and dissolves, while the second trailer trims down the same basic idea to about a minute and a half.

THE CORRUPTOR

Colour, 1999, 110m. / Directed by James Foley / Starring Mark Wahlberg, Chow Yun-Fat / New Line (US R1 NTSC) / WS (2.35:1) / DD5.1

 Neither the best of the recent cycle of Asian-influenced action films nor the worst, *The Corruptor* features Mark Wahlberg (uh, as opposed to Marky Mark) reteaming with director James Foley after their underrated domestic shocker, *Fear*. While Wahlberg's earlier action entry, *The Big Hit,* was one of the more irritating hyper-action efforts in recent years, he's mercifully in better hands here but really can't hold a candle to the screen presence of his co-star, Chow Yun-Fat. Danny Wallace (Wahlberg) is a moderately experienced cop assigned to Chinatown under the supervision of Nick Chen (Chow Yun-Fat), a cop who used his Triad connections to rise to the top. Unfortunately, a gang war between the Triads and the younger Fukienese Dragons is threatening to tear Chinatown apart, and Danny finds himself caught in the middle. The leader of the Dragons, Henry Lee (Ric Young) (the titular character), manipulates the political alliances within the community, causing Danny to question the integrity of Nick, who is torn between his social ties and his conscience.

While the first half of the film is a fairly engaging but traditional good cop/bad cop scenario, a mid-story twist raises the stakes considerably and really kicks the film into high gear. Most of the action sequences work well, though they never come close to attaining a John Woo level of intensity thanks to Foley's propensity for *NYPD Blue*-style zooms and rapid shock cutting. Chow Yun-Fat makes a credible, interesting flawed hero, indicating with both this and *The Replacement Killers* that he may very easily make the transition to an English language superstar. Carter Burwell's jagged, techno-laced score enhances the proceedings nicely but obviously doesn't function quite as well on its own, though New Line has thoughtfully isolated the entire score with Burwell commentary on one of the audio tracks.

Not surprisingly, the entire DVD package is top notch and lives up to New Line's already stellar reputation. The anamorphic transfer looks terrific and does an effective job of rendering this dark, gritty-looking film without any distracting video noise. The sound mix is completely organic and renders the gunshots, ambient street noises, and thudding music with plenty of ferocity, while Foley's commentary elaborates on everything from Chinese-American culture to the technical ins and outs of urban film shooting.

The accompanying documentary, "From the (Under)Ground Up," covers virtually every aspect of the film and is far from your standard studio promotional piece. Oddly, the various segments of this documentary have been splintered apart as separate sections of the DVD; thus, the extended unrated version of the car chase (and it definitely is unrated!!) is a self-contained six minute chapter, as are several other interview sequences; thus, a slight pause occurs when moving from section to section. Even the trailer is thoroughly dissected, with two earlier drafts shown before the completed one. In virtually every respect, New Line has continued to set the standard once again.

COUP DE TORCHON

Colour, 1981, 128m. / Directed by Bertrand Tavernier / Starring Philippe Noiret, Isabelle Huppert / Criterion (US R1 NTSC) / WS (1.78:1) (16:9)

The tradition of film noir has long been a favourite subject of French directors like François Truffaut and Jean-Pierre Melville, and while he's best known in the US for benign dramas like *A Sunday in the Country*, Bertrand Tavernier has occasionally gone

to that well, too. His most successful crime drama remains *Coup de Torchon (Clean Slate)*, a scathing, black comedy adaptation of Jim Thompson's hard-boiled novel, *Pop. 1280* (published in France as *Pop. 1275*, much to Tavernier's amusement on this disc). Transposing the Thompson narrative from the Depression-era rural South to 1930s French Africa, the film begins with dejected and widely ridiculed police chief Lucien Cordier (Philippe Noiret) resting under a tree as he watches a group of African boys suffering underneath the merciless sunlight. An eclipse begins, frightening away the lurking vultures overhead, and Cordier builds them a fire. He then returns home to his openly contemptuous wife, Huguette (a frumped-up Stephane Audran), and goes about his daily routine which finds law abiding townspeople and the shady underworld alike mocking his lack of power. Spurred on by the erotically charged presence of a new arrival named Rose (Isabelle Huppert), Lucien realizes his position allows him a dangerous amount of immunity to the law...which comes in handy when he turns to murder. And then he does it again...

While Jim Thompson adaptations briefly became a hot property in the '90s thanks to *The Grifters, After Dark My Sweet*, and a remake of *The Getaway*, Tavernier's film makes a deliberate effort to capture the sardonic, multi-layered nature of the late novelist's difficult prose. Each character seems to have ten different thoughts running through their minds in each scene, and Noiret does a magnificent job of gradually transforming from a bumbling schmuck into an all too human monster. Huppert has less to do but looks terrific all the same, while Audran (best known for her films with husband Claude Chabrol) is pitch perfect as usual. Composer Philippe Sarde provides one of his best scores, a poignant mixture of jazz and orchestra with some odd atonal flourishes, and the parched cinematography manages to be elegant and sweaty at the same time.

Criterion's anamorphically enhanced DVD is a tremendous improvement over their gritty looking laserdisc; colours are more robust and detail levels are quite impressive. Some dark scenes are still grainy due to the original source material, but apart from a mint quality opening night screening, this film couldn't look much better. The optional English subtitles have also been tweaked to improve both clarity and grammar over prior editions. The disc also includes the US theatrical trailer (which passes this off as a crime story, a comedy, and a romance - pretty accurately), a 20 minute video interview with Tavernier (who offers some nice insights into the adaptation process and the bizarre location shooting), and an alternate ending (narrated by Tavernier) which finds the memorable public dance finale culminating in the arrival of men in gorilla suits! Hmm, wonder why they cut that one?

C

THE CRAFT

Colour, 1996, 101m. / Directed by Andrew Fleming / Starring Fairuza Balk, Robin Tunney, Neve Campbell / Columbia / WS (1.85:1) (16:9) / DD5.1

New girl in town Sarah Bailey (Tunney) chums up at school with Bonnie (Campbell), Rochelle (Rachel True) and Nancy (Balk). The quartet share a fascination with witchcraft and discover that when they pool their limited energies they are able to summon up a powerful force which, in the wrong hands, could prove deadly...

On face value *The Craft* is a conventional cautionary tale of how power corrupts, that attaining all you desire can erode your cognizance of the things that really matter, and most specifically that you shouldn't mess with things you don't understand. Director Andrew Fleming toys with familiar teenage angst thematics, initially by having his coven of witches use their powers for the sort of petty wish fulfilment that viewers can identify with, be it putting pay to the school bully, or retaliating against an ex-boyfriend. This approach keeps the proceedings fairly even keeled and lays foundation for a degree of believability. Special effects are employed conservatively in the early part of the story, building to climactic gross-'em-out overload in the last couple of reels. Tunney is particularly good as the altruistic white witch of the coven, whilst Balk (the innocent little thing who returned to Oz a decade earlier) is magnificently satanic as the trailer trash Goth who goes clean off the rails; there's something hypnotic and penetrating in her eyes that conveys genuine instability.

Probably of greatest appeal to a younger audience, *The Craft* never quite takes on the mantle of being out and out scary. However, it boasts a taut script, good performances from an attractive cast, some tasty effects, excellent cinematography - the sequence in the glade in which the girls first exercise their gifts is beguiling - and a choice rock soundtrack, resulting in one of the best witch-bitch movies of the past few decades.

Marked by 28 chapters, Columbia's release delivers an excellent quality 1.85:1 matted presentation of *The Craft* with a number of interesting additional features. These include a commentary from director Fleming, an original behind-the-scenes featurette (not on the Region 2 version), a 25-minute retrospective, a selection of trailers (along with *The Craft*, a number of other genre titles are previewed), an isolated score, and best of all a selection of deleted scenes, all of which would have been worthy inclusions in the final edit. The language choice is English 5.1 Dolby Digital, English Dolby Surround, French, Spanish or Portuguese, with subtitles in these same four languages plus Chinese, Korean and Thai. - TG

CRASH

Colour, 1996, 111m. / Directed by David Cronenberg / Starring James Spader, Holly Hunter / New Line (US R1 NTSC), Columbia (UK R2 PAL) / WS (1.78:1) (16:9) / DD2.0

Maligned by Ted Turner, ignored by American audiences, and a general offence to many of the attendees at Cannes, David Cronenberg's *Crash* has been so overshadowed by the political and critical turmoil surrounding it that the actual film's voice has been drowned out in the process. If you like Cronenberg, you'll love the film, which is a quantum leap in maturity and quality over the flat *M. Butterfly*. While the sight of James Spader sexually assailing a gash in Rosanna Arquette's leg may not appeal to every sensibility, this is a challenging and often rewarding ride if you're willing to go along with the filmmaker's own unique, marvellously depraved point of view.

Based on J.G. Ballard's scandalous counter-culture novel, *Crash* revolves around James Ballard (Spader), a director who suffers a near-fatal car crash when he collides with doctor Holly Hunter. The two find themselves aroused by the experience, and she introduces Ballard to a bizarre subculture dedicated to re-enactments of famous celebrity car crashes (Jayne Mansfield, James Dean, etc.). The group's leader, Vaughn (the always fascinating Elias Koteas), orchestrates a series of fleshy auto escapades involving his protégée, Rosanna Arquette, and Ballard's spacey, erotically insatiable wife (Deborah Kara Unger, *The Game*). One of the film's most notorious scenes, a mild sex scene between Spader and Koteas, was primarily responsible for driving audience members away, but there's much stronger stuff on display. The eerie, unresolved finale ("Maybe the next one") amazingly manages to

wrap up the dreamlike proceedings on a satisfying note that will leave a strange mood hovering in your mind long after the film is over.

While no video presentation can really replicate experiencing *Crash* in the theatre (after which audience members had to drive home), DVD is about as close as you can get. Though supervised by Cronenberg, the Criterion Collection laserdisc was a visual mess, smeary and dull, with poor detail. The anamorphically enhanced DVD is a feast for the eyes, filled with glittering planes of glass and metal and suffused with unearthly shades of blue and silver. There's simply no comparison. The US DVD also has the option of playing the film's R-rated cut, which causes momentary pauses in the film's playback as it skips over the most graphic bits. Aside from basic curiosity, however, it's hard to imagine why anyone would want to see this watered-down Blockbusterized edition. Likewise, the Dolby Digital soundtrack is expansive and chilling, with Howard Shore's unnerving experimental score swelling from each speaker and drowning the ears in uneasiness and lust. Unfortunately, aside from the US trailer, the DVD features none of the Criterion bonuses (feature length commentary by Cronenberg, the original and superior Canadian trailer, and a making-of featurette), so completists will unfortunately want to get both. If you just care about the movie, though, the DVD is definitely the best (and most affordable) way to go.

CREEPSHOW

Colour, 1982, 120m. / Directed by George A. Romero / Starring Hal Holbrook, Adrienne Barbeau / Warner (US R1 NTSC) / WS (1.85:1) (16:9) / DD2.0

"Five jolting tales of terror!" promised the teaser posters for *Creepshow*, the landmark collaboration between director George A. Romero *(Night of the Living Dead)* and Stephen King. Of course, most viewers didn't really expect what they got: a loving, colourful homage to the twisted and controversial E.C. Comics of the '50s, which featured nasty people getting their just and gory desserts. Of course, *Creepshow* also kicked off the '80s horror anthology wave on television, which began with Romero's *Tales from the Darkside* and continued with HBO's *Tales from the Crypt* (not to mention *Freddy's Nightmares* and *Friday the 13th: The Series*, but that's another story). *Creepshow* also spawned its own sequel, which couldn't come close to the level of gruesome wit displayed here. The entire film revolves around a horror comic book discovered by an angry father (Tom Atkins) in his son's room. After tossing out the book, viewers are treated to each story, introduced and punctuated throughout with stylized framing devices, wipes, dialogue balloons, and garish backgrounds.

In "Father's Day," a family of bickering rich snots, including the murderous Aunt Cordelia (Viveca Lindfors), gathers to honour Father's Day in memory of their late patriarch, Nathan. Featuring a young, disco dancing Ed Harris (also in Romero's *Knightriders*), the clan meets a grisly end one by one as Nathan (played by *Martin*'s John Amplas, though you'd never recognize him!) rises from his grave and demands, "I want my Father's Day cake!"

Next up is "The Lonesome Death of Jordy Verrill," the anthology's weakest link, in which Stephen King himself appears as a redneck who discovers a smouldering meteorite in his backyard. Dumb Jordy pours water on the smoking rock, which cracks open and spews out a glowing green goo. After touching the weird fluid, Jordy finds himself slowly being consumed by a weird kind of weedy fungus and resorts to extreme measures to relieve himself of this itching, growing affliction.

Things really kick into gear with "Something to Tide You Over," featuring a smoothly menacing Leslie Nielsen as a millionaire who's less than pleased with the infidelity of his young wife (*Dawn of the Dead*'s Gaylen Ross). Nielsen decides to put his private beach to use by burying Ross and her lover, Ted Danson, up to their necks in sand and watching via closed circuit television as the tide swallows them up. All goes according to plan... until night falls.

"The Crate," a gloriously over the top showcase for Hal Holbrook and Adrienne Barbeau, features this memorable pair as a university professor and his shrewish wife. When a janitor discovers a mysterious crate in the college basement and gets consumed by the creature inside, Holbrook and his colleague, Fritz Weaver, decide to clean up the mess and deal with this uncanny find. However, Holbrook also devises a plan for the crate that doesn't involve going to the police- but does involve an encounter between Barbeau and the fluffy monster inside.

Finally, "They're Creeping Up on You" (an extremely apt title) presents E.G. Marshall as a pathologically clean, racist recluse who contains his financially secure existence within his antiseptically clean penthouse. Unfortunately, a roach manages to sneak its way in. And another. And another...

Creepshow makes for a fine presentation from Warner in both a full frame (unmatted) version and

an anamorphically enhanced widescreen transfer, which for some reason is framed slightly tighter than the earlier laserdisc release. Both versions look vibrant, with Romero's super-saturated colours bursting off the screen. Some very minor flaws in the print itself are apparent upon close inspection, but *Creepshow* won't look any better outside of a theatre. While the unmatted side looks balanced, the widescreen version is more effective as it focuses the compositions more tightly and removes some extraneous, distracting information at the top and bottom of the screen during the transitions between stories. The Dolby Surround soundtrack features some nice directional effects ranging from thunderclaps to John Harrison's imaginative, creepy score (well deserving of a CD release in the US), which is typically seasoned with some of Romero's beloved mono library music cues. The fun theatrical trailer, done in the comic style of the film, is also included, both matted and full frame, and looks surprisingly good. A fine presentation, particularly at that price, and even fans who already have the laser should definitely consider picking this one up.

CREEPSHOW 2

Colour, 1987, 92m. / Directed by Michael Gornick / Starring Lois Chiles, George Kennedy / Anchor Bay (US R1 NTSC) / WS (1.85:1) (16:9), Cinema Club (UK R2 PAL)

While the original *Creepshow* wasn't exactly a critical darling, its stock increased rapidly when George A. Romero and Stephen King nominally returned to the same well with *Creepshow 2*, which pares down the five story format of the first film to three here. At the time of its release, the movie didn't really work and felt like a wobbly attempt to make a few bucks without the love for E.C. Comics found in the original. Over a decade later... well, it still isn't a great movie, but it does make an interesting footnote to the end of theatrical independent horror movies playing at multiplexes around the US.

The framing device this time is more complicated, with Tom Savini appearing in heavy make up as "The Creep," dispensing *Creepshow* comic books from his truck to an eager young boy longing to buy some giant Venus Flytraps. The boy's story then turns into a cartoon, juggled back and forth with animated footage of the Creep narrating the stories in a castle. (So yes, at the end of the film we have to back out of three separate framing stories... quite awkward.)

First up is "Old Chief Wood'nhead," which stars George Kennedy and Dorothy Lamour as a couple of shop owners near Indian territory in the desert. Despite their failing business, George keeps up good relationships with the natives and takes care of the large wooden Indian adorning the front of his store. When the chief of the local tribe rewards George for his service with some precious jewels, the chief's son and his delinquent friends crash the store, intending to grab some quick cash for an escape to Hollywood. However, the wooden Indian outside has other plans...

The second and most memorable story, "The Raft" (adapted from King's short story), features four pot smoking teens hopping onto a large raft aloft in an isolated lake, only to find themselves surrounded by a large carnivorous mass resembling an oil slick. Though light on story, the tale moves along at a nice clip and features some memorable horrific highlights, including a terrific sucker punch climax.

Finally, the most oft-quoted episode, "The Hitchhiker," stars *Moonraker*'s Lois Chiles as Annie Lansing, an adulterous woman whose speedy post-coital trip back to her husband is interrupted when she accidentally runs over a road worker. She then takes off instead of calling the police, only to be continually harassed by the decaying human roadkill, who keeps popping up and chiming, "Thanks for the ride, lady!"

Unlike the colourful and stylized first film, *Creepshow 2* feels more like three episodes of Romero's *Tales from the Darkside* strung together and spiced up with extra nudity and gore. Each one could have been trimmed by about ten minutes, but horror fans should find enough to eke out some entertainment value on a slow evening. Chiles delivers the only truly memorable performance, with her nastiness alternating with hilarious panic as the gory hitchhiker turns her drive into a living hell. Director Michael Gornick does a professional if unexceptional job; in fact, everyone performs adequately except for composer Les Reed, whose droning, perky synth score really should have been scrapped, and the animators of the linking story, which looks ragged even by Scooby Doo standards.

Anchor Bay's disc looks about as good as one could expect; the film has always looked rather flat and pallid, but the colours and detail are fine. The letterboxing is tighter on the top and bottom than the open matte New World tape and looks all the better composed for it. Extras include the theatrical trailer - which casually spoils the endings of all three stories! - and a gallery of behind-the-scenes photos, include a nice chummy image of Chiles and King

(who has a longer-than-usual cameo in the film as a trucker). The cropped, fullscreen UK disc includes only the trailer.

CRIMES OF PASSION

Colour, 1984, 113m. / Directed by Ken Russell / Starring Kathleen Turner, Anthony Perkins / Anchor Bay (US R0 NTSC) / WS (1.85:1) (16:9)

Bobby Grady (John Laughlin) and his wife Amy (Annie Potts) find they no longer have anything in common. Through his work Bobby crosses paths with businesswoman Joanna Crane (Turner) and discovers that she moonlights with a sordid and soul-destroying double life as prostitute China Blue. In each other Bobby and Joanna find comfort, for him the passion that is missing from his marriage, for her the heady flush of finding true love for the first time. But into the fray comes a psychotic preacher, Peter Shayne (Perkins), who has seen in China Blue the salvation he seeks for his own depravity.

It's difficult to decide who steals the show here; Kathleen Turner as successful business woman cum deliciously tarty whore, or Anthony Perkins, sweating profusely whilst spouting religious rhetoric and liberal profanities as a character that would even give Norman Bates the collywobbles. Producer Barry Sandler's script is occasionally a little contrived but it bristles with wit and provides the assembled thesps - Turner in particular - with some sharp one-liners and wickedly barbed put-downs: "We may run out of Pan-Am coffee..." purrs China, kitted out for a client as a nymphomaniac airline hostess, "...but we'll never run out of TWA tea." Sure, it's as old as the hills, but Turner's raunchy delivery is one of many moments in the movie to be relished. As is the humorous delve into the little black bag that Shayne keeps at his side - among the apparatus within is an AutoSuck ("...and it swallows!") and a Beat-Me-Eat-Me Liquorice Whip ("The taste that leaves it's mark forever"). Accompanied by a triumphant score from Rick Wakeman (who puts in a one-shot on-screen cameo), *Crimes of Passion* is as stark a probing of the murky backwaters of sexual deviancy and dark desires of the human animal as you're ever likely to encounter. In a nutshell, a film to be treasured. "Ready when you are CB!"

Anchor Bay's original DVD release of CRIMES OF PASSION was an uncharacteristically frugal offering without a single bonus feature. Fortunately their 2002 reissue made restitution. As well as a hugely entertaining Barry Sandler/Ken Russell commentary and a trailer, it includes a 20-minute collection of deleted scenes (with optional Sandler commentary), none of which would have improved the final cut to any discernible degree but most of which offer juicy dialogue exchanges and make for worthy supplemental inclusion.

The feature itself is in beautiful shape, matted to approximately 1.85:1 and divided by 29 chapter stops. Where the British VHS release succumbed to the censor's shears - most notably in the sequence when China buggers a police officer with his own night-stick - Anchor Bay's disc is uncut. More than just uncut, in fact, for several additional minutes of previously unseen footage has been restored to make this a longer version of the film than has ever been seen before. - TG

CRIMINAL LOVERS

Colour, 1999, 91m. / Directed by François Ozon / Starring Natacha Régnier, Jérémie Rénier / Strand (US R1 NTSC) / WS (1.85:1), Paramount (France R2 PAL) / WS (1.78:1) (16:9) / DD2.0

Psychosexual undercurrents in fairy tales have been dissected by artists and critics for years, so it's no small compliment to say that *Criminal Lovers* manages to find a novel spin on such a shop-worn concept. Serenely and ironically detached but passionate and horrifying in equal measure, this second feature length effort from Ozon continued to boost his reputation as one of France's most promising and gifted directors, a stance he has since proven in his future works.

Sexual tease and latent sadist Alice (Natacha Régnier) enjoys a close but nonsexual relationship with Luc (Jérémie Rénier), her compliant classmate who allows her to manipulate his emotions thanks to his unfulfilled capacity for desire. Alice talks him into murdering a fellow student, Saïd (Salim Kechiouche), who may or may not have raped and humiliated Alice earlier at school. The brutal stabbing leaves an inconvenient body which the teens cart off into the woods, where they immediately lose their way after a speedy burial. Their criminal activity has been monitored by a sinister woodsman (Miki Manojlovic) who traps them in his cabin when they sneak in to pilfer some food. Alice remains locked down in a rat-infested basement, while Luc is occasionally brought up for mealtime conversation and bathing privileges. The woodsman

professes to be an ogre who feeds on plump little boys and lean little girls, but his designs ultimately prove to be far more complicated. Meanwhile through flashbacks the twisted story of Alice, Luc, and their victim unravels through a series of poetic diary entries and disturbing revelations, culminating in a surreal finale which transforms them all.

Spinning off from the idea of two young people on a crime spree, *Criminal Lovers* is surprising and engaging enough to support Ozon's often wild flights of fancy, most of which are designed to shock or amuse... or, most likely, both. His previous film, *Sitcom*, traded on the domestic perversions pioneered by John Waters, but here the formula is something more novel and striking. The forest setting contrasts effectively with the stylized flashbacks, and even a simple shoplifting jaunt through a department store becomes a dreamy tangent thanks to the elegant camerawork and crafty, restrained use of music.

Though the characters remain ciphers at heart, Régnier takes top acting honours for her seductive turn as Alice, a complex performance which turns a potentially facile and hateful character into a troubled, fascinating girl whose sexual desires trigger a wholly irrational and dangerous penchant for murder. Film buffs will also have fun spotting references to other similarly themed films, the most obvious being Charles Laughton's *Night of the Hunter* (which is quoted almost verbatim twice during the last five minutes), though the film manages to retain its own identity and agenda throughout without resorting to overdone winking at the audience. Well, except for maybe the forest animals near the end...

The striking visuals of *Criminal Lovers* are captured well enough by Strand's passable if somewhat lazy DVD, which features no relevant extras (apart from a few other alternative themed trailers). The non-anamorphic transfer and non-removable subtitles will probably irk those used to the Criterion treatment, with good reason, but the video quality is extremely sharp and colourful. The English subtitles are large enough and easy to read, while the surround soundtrack burst to multi-channelled life on those few occasions when the film calls for it. For some reason the opening shot displays some jarring compression flaws in the wallpaper behind Luc, but mercifully the rest of the disc looks just fine. The PAL French disc features a terrific anamorphic transfer with optional French or English subtitles, along with a most unusual bonus feature: a new edit of the film which places all of the events (with one exception) in chronological order, though do to the elimination of repeated footage, it now runs a mere 76 minutes! For some reason this is the only Ozon French DVD release without a commentary track.

C

CROCODILE

Colour, 2000, 92m. / Directed by Tobe Hooper / Starring Caitlin Martin, Harrison Young / Trimark (US R1 NTSC) / WS (1.85:1) / DD2.0

Tobe Hooper's *Crocodile* is a film so completely awful, so misguided and catastrophically painful, it really makes you wonder how bad something has to be before a studio decides to leave it on the shelf where it can't do any more harm. Apparently Hooper was the logical directing choice for this monster mash manqué because, well, he did the killer croc routine before in *Eaten Alive*, and if it kind of worked once... Alas, even those bemoaning the latest postmodern teen slasher flick will run for cover from this one, which makes *Lake Placid* and *Anaconda* look like models of rich characterization and clever plotting in comparison.

The plot concerns... uh, well... there are these obnoxious, brain dead college students, though how they stumbled into any US institution of learning is never explained. Taking time out from chasing each other and partying to awful pop tunes on their trawler, they stomp through the marshy wilderness, float around on inner tubes, and accidentally wreck a nest of croc eggs. Naturally the CGI crocodile isn't happy and starts wreaking sleep inducing, computer-generated mayhem, despite the noble efforts of the yokel croc raiser and the police. People scream. People run. And that's about it. While even the lowest Z-grade monster movies usually possess some degree of charm, *Crocodile* seems determined to alienate its fan base from the opening scene by throwing in vapid, aggressively irritating characters, acted with the absolute minimum of charm by an indifferent cast. If you're brave enough to tackle this film, keep a couple of six packs handy to dull the pain and watch it with some friends who can at least heckle the crocodile.

The DVD from Trimark looks appropriately glossy and reminiscent of a music video, which isn't necessarily such a good thing. Ditto for the surround audio, which pumps tunes from the rear speakers without making much of an impression. A Tobe Hopper commentary track (likely filled with profuse apologies) has been promised for the final release but was not included on Trimark's DVD screener. Don't say you weren't warned.

THE CROW

Colour, 1994, 101m. / Directed by Alex Proyas / Starring Brandon Lee, Ernie Hudson / Buena Vista (US R1 NTSC), EIV (UK R2 PAL) / WS (1.85:1) (16:9) / DD5.1

An eerie work of horror both on screen and in real life, *The Crow* was notorious before its release as the film whose shooting claimed the life of Brandon Lee, Bruce Lee's son, due to a firearms accident. The film was completed using digital effects and a body double for some uncompleted shots, and fortunately the final result managed to overcome its reputation to emerge as one of the most significant comic adaptations ever filmed. Years after its release, the film can now be more clearly assessed as a groundbreaking work of cinematic art, even if the long overdue special edition from Miramax/Dimension leaves something to be desired.

Set in one of those perpetually dark, rainy cities, *The Crow* begins with the murder of musician Eric Draven (Lee) and his fiancée, Shelly, on Devil's Night, October 30. The perpetrators are Top Dollar (Michael Wincott) and his motley crew of criminal henchmen, including T-Bird (*The Warriors'* David Patrick Kelly) and Grange (Tony Todd). Albrecht (Ernie Hudson), one of the investigating officers, tries to help the dead couple's young friend, Darla (Anna Levine), cope with the tragedy. One year later, a crow from the netherworld summons Eric from the grave to avenge the evil deed, and he dons black and white stage make up as well as a black body suit before embarking on his violent quest for retribution. Seemingly impervious to physical harm, he picks off his enemies one by one while grieving for his lost love and maintaining some semblance of contact with the friends he left behind.

Director Alex Proyas, who followed this up with the equally flashy but far less satisfying *Dark City*, does a magnificent job of transferring James O'Barr's series of graphic stories to cinematic life. For once the grungy cinematography, music video editing, and hyperkinetic violence which have been beaten to death in countless neo noir films clicks perfectly here, most likely due to the dovetailing subject matter involving death, loss, and emotional disconnection. While Lee isn't exactly called upon to do any tremendous acting, he's a gripping presence in the film and maintains a sense of purpose and emotional anguish during his action sequences. The musical combination of goth rock and Graeme Revell's dense, haunting score is also a textbook example of how to make a Top 40 friendly soundtrack without tearing up the fabric of the film. Two cinematic sequels and one television series followed this, but none could come close to duplicating the original's impact.

The first DVD of *The Crow* was something of a mess, carrying over the old letterboxed laserdisc transfer to disastrous effect. This much-needed anamorphic upgrade looks much closer to the theatrical experience, but bear in mind that the original film was shot with strange, colour saturated shadows and some intentional grain. The juiced up Dolby Digital 5.1 and DTS tracks sound terrific; nary a scene goes by without some wild directional effects swooping through every speaker, but the separation is integrated well without jarring the viewer from the film itself.

Inexplicably, this special edition of *The Crow* has been spread out to two discs, perhaps to accommodate the extra audio information on the film itself. First up is a decent commentary track by producer Jeff Most and screenwriter John Shirley, who offer some insights into the process of adapting a comic and the technical challenges posed by the production. The absence of Proyas and co-writer David Schow is sorely felt, however, and much material feels left uncovered. The second disc contains a standard 20-minute promotional featurette, including interviews conducted on the set with Lee, Todd, Kelly, and other cast members. The disc also features a camcorder interview with O'Barr (recorded in his basement in 2000) and a handful of extended scenes, including the truncated arcade fight from the beginning of the film. A "deleted scenes montage" cobbles together about five minutes of random trims from the film, though the infamous deleted Skull Cowboy sequence with Michael Berryman is conspicuously absent. Several galleries run through some unused poster designs, "production design stills" which look like a combination of storyboards and O'Barr's artwork, and some more standard storyboards. PC DVD-Rom users can also access the film's screenplay to run concurrently with the movie, as well as a trivia game and an option to view the film with a series of pop up quotes and factoids, similar to Universal's trivia gimmick on the *Bring It On* DVD (but less smoothly integrated here).

It's an interesting package, but considering the potential for supplements with this film, the extravagance of a two disc set promises more than it actually delivers. Apart from some of the more obvious deleted footage still MIA, the disc doesn't even include any of the film's striking theatrical trailers or TV spots. Too bad, but at least they finally

got the transfer right. Also available in a box set with the two sequels, which are recommended only to die hard *Crow* fans.

CRUEL INTENTIONS

Colour, 1999, 97m. / Directed by Roger Kumble / Starring Sarah Michelle Gellar, Ryan Phillippe, Reese Witherspoon / Columbia / WS (1.85:1) (16:9) / DD5.1

 Campy, ludicrous, and unabashedly over the top, *Cruel Intentions* is either a dim-witted '90s defacing of a classic tale or a shrewdly conceived, bitchy twist on all the recent teen literary adaptations - or perhaps both. Regardless, this sinfully entertaining film is rarely dull and definitely takes the cake for the largest number of "I can't believe I just heard that" lines for the year.

Sarah Michelle Gellar and Ryan Phillippe, last seen together as obnoxious hook fodder in *I Know What You Did Last Summer*, team again as Kathryn Merteuil and Sebastian Valmont, diabolical stepsiblings who derive pleasure from sadistic sexual power plays in their upscale high school environment. Sebastian's next conquest in the making is virginal Annette Hargrove (Reese Witherspoon), whose recent *Seventeen* manifesto promoting chastity makes her a perfect target. Kathryn doubts Sebastian's confidence and makes a deal - if he fails to bed Annette, he hands over his car to Kathryn; if he succeeds, Kathryn will fulfil all his sexual desires.

Anyone familiar with the hit play *Les liaisons dangereuses* or its successful 1988 film adaptation with Glenn Close and John Malkovich will immediately recognize this scenario, which also spawned another version from Milos Forman (*Valmont*). However, *Cruel Intentions* most closely resembles the 1960 Roger Vadim version, which transposed the story into the modern setting of capricious Europeans on holiday and slathered the proceedings with layers of infectious jazz music. Here, first time director Kumble (who earned his chops doing theatre) uses a blend of pop songs and Ed Shearmur's weird, wispy techno score (replacing John Ottman, which could have been interesting) to create an Upper East New York populated by rich, bored kids who have nothing better to do than screw with each other's heads. It's not a particularly daring concept, but the rude and often scathing sexual chitchat keeps things interesting, as well as the

C

occasional odd surprise like Gellar doing an impromptu open-mouthed liplock with Selma Blair. Most of the cast seems to be in the joke, with Witherspoon doing a nice job as always and Gellar camping it up with her heaving breasts and acidic *bon mots*. Unfortunately, Phillippe really isn't up to the task of playing Valmont; in fact, he rarely seems up to the task of acting at all and seems determined to become the Ryan O'Neal of the '90s. Not a great film by a long shot, but expect this one to show up on a lot of guilty pleasure lists in years to come.

Columbia's DVD trots out as many extras as you could imagine for this film, beginning with Kumble's feature length audio commentary (along with *Jawbreaker*, this could be the most overly serious commentary ever recorded for a nasty teen film). Six deleted scenes are the real highlight here, one of which (the "war" scene) absolutely should have been retained to clarify some major plot points (Kumble claims it was excised because it killed audience sympathy for Valmont - huh!?!). The first deleted scene, while extraneous, is a real howler and could have been the highlight of the movie. The package rounds out with two music videos, a studio-produced "Making of" featurette, and Creative Intentions, a look at the film's quasi-perfume commercial production design. The film itself looks terrific and the Dolby Digital remix presents the soundtrack in all its Top 40 glory.

CRY OF THE OWL

Colour, 1987, 100m. / Directed by Claude Chabrol / Starring Christophe Malavoy, Mathilda May / AllDay (US R0 NTSC) / WS (1.66:1)

 Due to an unfortunate set of circumstances, Claude Chabrol's moody thriller *Cry of the Owl (Le cri du hibou)* was largely ignored after its marginal theatrical release. A specialist in the psycho-logical suspense genre, Chabrol has been mining into the darkest corners of the human psyche since the early days of the French New Wave, and this film continues the tradition. Many films have tried to ape Chabrol's style (most obviously *With a Friend like Harry*), but there's really only one original. Estranged from his wife and finding solace in the countryside, morose draftsman Robert (Christophe Malavoy) discovers his voyeuristic side while lingering in the backyard of his beautiful neighbour, Juliet (*Lifeforce*'s naked space vampire, Mathilda May). Much to his surprise, Juliet doesn't mind his Peeping Tom practices; in

fact, she finds him a refreshing alternative to her boorish boyfriend, Patrick (Jacques Penot), and comes to regard Robert as death personified. Robert is less than amused, however, insisting he isn't death... and yet the Vichy countryside is soon populated with far more corpses than normal.

A clean, spare work of storytelling and filmic craftsmanship, *Cry of the Owl* seems like a film out of its time; you'd never guess it was a late 1980s title, so snugly does it fit with '60s Chabrol fare like *This Man Must Die* and *Les Biches*. The tricky narrative from a novel by Patricia Highsmith (*The Talented Mr. Ripley*) hums along with mechanized perfection, and all of the actors perform ably as pawns in this increasingly bewildering labyrinth of double crosses and murder. The oblique, haunting final shot - open and yet perfectly satisfying at the same time - perfectly sums up Chabrol's approach, which suggests endless gulfs of emotional darkness yawning beneath all of his complacent characters. Though his work is fairly well represented in his homeland, Chabrol has not fared nearly so well outside of France.

Though *Cry of the Owl* was released on UK home video and made the rounds elsewhere as a bootleg title, its American VHS plans were thwarted when New Yorker apparently dropped the ball and lost it due to a legal snafu. After languishing in obscurity for well over a decade, the film was recovered by AllDay, whose transfer looks about the same as the British edition. The non-anamorphic framing looks fine, though the image quality is dated and benefits from some darkness adjustment via television or DVD player. The English subtitles are non-removable. Along with a still gallery, the disc also includes a feature commentary by Ric Menello (with an extended cameo appearance by AllDay's David Kalat), which dissects both this film's tangled history and Chabrol's place in the French New Wave, the history of suspense directors, and the pantheon of great directors worldwide. It's an informative discussion and will probably be useful to both newcomers and seasoned fans alike.

CRY UNCLE!

Colour, 1971, 87m. / Directed by John G. Avildsen / Starring Allen Garfield, Madeleine Le Roux / Troma (US R1 NTSC)

Years before he went on to acclaim with *Rocky* and *The Karate Kid* (and disdain with *Rocky V* and *The Karate Kid III*), director John G. Avildsen was way, way out of the mainstream. After directing the controversial *Joe*, he actually made a movie for

Troma - and it's one of the best moves that company could have made. The result, *Cry Uncle!* (known in England as *Super Dick!*), is an X-rated private eye spoof starring potbellied character actor Allen Garfield (*The Stunt Man*) in a veritable avalanche of nudity and sick humour that makes *There's Something about Mary* look genteel in comparison.

Private investigator Jake Masters (Garfield) can't seem to keep his hands off women - and, in perfect keeping with the logic of this film, they can't stay away from him, either. ("If you weren't such a good lay, I'd kill ya," snaps one especially jaded character.) Called in to work for a millionaire falsely accused of murdering a young amateur porn actress, Jake winds up teaming with Cora Merrill (Madeleine Le Roux, sort of like an uninhibited young Eileen Brennan), a high-class hooker. Jake's investigation takes him to back alley flophouses and corrupt suburbs populated by a head-spinning assortment of depraved lunatics, leading to an infamous (and darkly funny) necrophilia scene that became this film's primary claim to fame.

Though not as fall-down funny as it could have been, *Cry Uncle* has held up fairly well over the years. In a rare leading role, Garfield really runs with the opportunity and makes for a very funny, sleazy protagonist, adept at both verbal and physical comedy. Amazingly, the film has lost little of its shock value over the years, with heavy amounts of full frontal nudity (including Garfield, alas) and even some brief hardcore footage shown in negative during a stag film.

Troma's DVD is one of their better-looking efforts to date, with excellent clarity for an early '70s zero budget film. Colours are consistently accurate and robust, though one flaw in the film - a vague yellowish tinge during process shots like wipes and split screens - cannot be avoided. The opening titles are letterboxed at approximately 1.75:1, while the rest of the film unfolds with the matte removed, exposing lots of extraneous headroom (and nudity) throughout. The mono sound quality is fine and distortion free. As usual, Troma has decked out this film with tons of extras, including some funny on-camera interviews and, even better, feature length commentary with Avildsen and Garfield. Both men make for very humorous and pleasant company; Garfield in particular manages to fling out hilarious off the cuff remarks whenever things get threaten to slow down. Some fascinating tidbits emerge along the way, such as the fact that *Cry Uncle!* is a

favourite of both Robert Redford and Oliver Stone! Soap opera fans should look for the film debut of Debbi Morgan, who later went on to acclaim in *Eve's Bayou*, as a trashy young naked prostitute in bondage; the fact that she went straight from this to *Mandingo* and then to *General Hospital* makes for one of the strangest career trajectories ever. Paul Sorvino also turns in an early appearance as a chain-smoking cop who can't stop coughing. The only real irritant is the DVD menu screens, all of which make repeated use of the grating theme song; it wears out its welcome after about twenty seconds. All in all, if you like your '70s comedy raunchy and on the weird side, it's hard to go wrong with this one, and Troma has every reason to be proud.

CUBE

Colour, 1997, 90m. / Directed by Vincenzo Natali / Trimark (US R1 NTSC), Alliance (Canada R1 NTSC), Cinema Club (UK R2 PAL), Feature Film Project (Australia R4 PAL) / WS (1.85:1), Seven Sept (France R2 PAL) / WS (1.85:1) (16:9) / DD2.0

If David Fincher decided to direct a *Tales from the Crypt* episode channelled through the spirit of Rod Serling, the result would probably come out a lot like *Cube*, an entertaining if derivative morality tale which seems to be stressing the messages, "Be kind to thy neighbour" and "Pay close attention to math class." Of course, the film's primary concern is miles and miles of eye-popping art direction and glossy hi-tech gore (a la *Hellraiser* and *Hardware*), all bathed in delicious candy coloured lighting (think Roger Corman's *Masque of the Red Death* room colour schematics as designed by Dario Argento). So, it's not the most original movie in the world, but if you're tired of jokey teen slashers, this is a nice reminder of how shocks can be dished out with intelligence and skill.

The everyman tale begins with several people awakening to find themselves trapped in a series of rooms - perfect cubes - linked by a series of metal doorways. Unfortunately, some of the rooms are booby trapped with invisible, vicious devices capable of burning off a victim's face or chopping him into tiny square pieces. The confused protagonists include a free clinic doctor, a math student, an escape artist, a mentally handicapped guy, and a borderline fascist leader; how their skills come into play as they fight for survival forms the primary motivating force of the film. The simplistic statements about mankind's inherent destructive nature are less interesting than

C

the elaborately designed body count scenarios, which lend the film an astonishing amount of tension in several sequences. Of course, how willing you are to put up with a riddle that essentially never solves itself will determine how well you make it through the 90 minutes, which will be a rough ride for anyone expecting clear answers and happy endings. The acting is generally fine, with David Hewlett (*Scanners 2*) providing the most familiar face for genre fans.

Trimark's sharp widescreen transfer and disoriented Ultra Stereo soundtrack are rendered about as well as possible for a low budget effort like this, and the extras make it quite a bargain. Aside from running feature commentary by the filmmakers, the disc also includes production art, three insignificant deleted scenes, and interesting cube designs, as well as the nifty US trailer. (Too bad they couldn't do more with the menu screens - considering the film's subject matter, the possibilities were limitless.) If possible, however, don't watch the trailer before the film, as it contains a couple of irritating spoilers. Several times during the commentary, the director refers to *Cube* as simply a science-fiction film, but this isn't really an accurate definition; it's really an art horror film for the mathematically inclined, and in theory, none the worse for that.

The Canadian and British counterparts do not feature the extras but offer an affordable option for those seeking the film itself, while the Australian disc is comparable to the US release; on the other hand, only the French DVD (with non-removable subs on most players) offers an anamorphic transfer, along with a similarly themed short film, "Elevated."

CUL-DE-SAC

B&W, 1966, 111m. / Directed by Roman Polanski / Starring Donald Pleasence, Françoise Dorléac / Pioneer (Japan R2 NTSC) / WS (1.66:1)

 For a follow up to his acclaimed horror-art classic *Repulsion*, director Roman Polanski decided to go for a lighter tone... but not by much. Rarely seen and virtually ignored since its release, *Cul-de-sac* is a blackly amusing comedy of manners mixed with the traditions of hostage crime dramas, all filtered through the quirky sensibilities of Polanski and co-scenarist Gerard Brach. Blessed with one of his best casts and a sterling crew behind the camera, this may not be a film for all tastes (what Polanski film is?), but lovers of the offbeat will cherish this poisonous little treat.

Two robbers on the run after a botched job, Richard (Lionel Stander) and the mortally wounded Albert (Jack MacGowran), finally come to a halt along the English coast. They take refuge in a decaying castle inhabited by a submissive Englishman, George (Donald Pleasence), and his authoritative and alluring French wife, Teresa (Françoise Dorléac). However, our innocent couple doesn't go along with the standard thriller pattern of playing the helpless victims, and soon matters escalate strangely and hilarious out of hand.

From the disorienting opening sequence, which finds the criminals' car stranded out in the middle of nowhere, *Cul-de-sac* finds sinister amusement in leading its audience along on a path that fittingly seems to lead to a dead end. The fun lies in what happens along the way, with Pleasence shining in one of his best and most atypical roles. Everyone else is up to his level, though, with MacGowran amusingly making the most of his few, agonized lines; he would team up with Polanski again for *The Fearless Vampire Killers*. Celebrity spotters should keep their eyes open for a bit part by a young Jacqueline Bisset, speaking her first lines ever onscreen. The late Polish jazz composer Krzysztof Komeda, who went on to fame scoring *Rosemary's Baby*, pitches in with a catchy, sparse series of musical motifs which assure the viewer that this is indeed a comedy, all surface appearances to the contrary.

Though almost impossible to find in the United States, *Cul-de-sac* has been given a much more respectable treatment in Japan. Pioneer's DVD is a joy to behold from start to finish, apart from some damage during the company logos and part of the opening credits. The print used is nearly pristine and features excellent contrast (even better if you have a black enhancement control on your player), while the audio is crisp and clear throughout. The Japanese subtitles can be turned off, allowing English-speaking viewers to experience this little gem without any distractions. The disc also includes a trailer reel composed of edited European previews for *Repulsion, Cul-de-sac*, and *Knife in the Water*, all available on Japanese DVD.

THE CURIOUS DR. HUMPP

Colour, 1967, 87m. / Directed by Emilio Vieyra / Starring Aldo Barbero, Ricardo Bauleo / Image (US R0 NTSC)

If it weren't for the avalanche of bare flesh on display, *The Curious Dr. Humpp* would occupy a fond place in viewers' hearts as the epitome of great

"bad" movies, which of course means it's not really bad at all. Fast paced and thoroughly delirious, this film became one of the banner titles in Something Weird's "Sexy Shockers from the Vault" series courtesy of Frank Henenlotter, and with very good reason. Every scene brings a new delight, be it a loopy line of dialogue, an outrageous act of monster depravity, or an undraped Argentinean lass strutting her wares before the camera.

Originally titled *La venganza del sexo*, this film was retooled significantly for its US release thanks to inserts (shot in the US by distributor Jerry Intrator) of orgies and other dalliances for added salacious content. The film was already saucy enough, but the new footage really sends it over the top. The various scenes revolve around a mad scientist named Dr. Humpp (Aldo Barbero), whose genius and joie de vivre are fuelled by a potion derived from human orgasms. When his supply of horny couples runs dry and his sardonic talking brain in a tank can no longer offer advice, the doc resorts to his unforgettable blank-faced monster (a la Dr. Orlof) to abduct virile subjects for his ungodly experiments. One of these unwilling subjects is George (Ricardo Bauleo), a reporter trying to uncover the method behind the doctor's madness. In between non-consensual humping sessions, George devises a plot to hurl the madman's plans back in his face.

Sort of the Argentinean equivalent to Jose Mojica Marins (aka "Coffin Joe"), director Emilio Vieyra carved a niche as the director of outlandish horror-oriented nudies like this and *The Deadly Organ*, whose trailer and promo spots are also included on this DVD. Thanks to Something Weird, at least his one unqualified masterpiece of the perverse can be enjoyed by an astonished public, and the man certainly knows how to turn out a gorgeous black and white film regardless of subject matter. The DVD transfer looks sharp as a tack, even better than the SW tape lifted from the negative (!) of the spicy US cut, and it's doubtful the English dubbing removes many of the nuances from the original language track. Besides, the sheer volume of quotable lines makes it ideal for sampling on your computer or answering machine. You also get the film's US trailer and the marvellous original Argentinean credits, complete with animated titles in the vein of *The Fearless Vampire Killers.*

Three oddball shorts are also tossed into the brew, including one explicit little number called "The Girl and the Skeleton" that would make Bob Guccione very, very happy. The other shorts are "My Teenage Fallout Queen," sort of a proto-video by George McKelvey that must be witnessed to be believed, and "Rasputin and the Princess," another one of those trademark monster nudie snippets from the pre-hardcore days. Finally there's the trademark gallery of exploitation art with yet another new assortment of radio spots guaranteed to have you longing for the good ol' drive-in days.

THE CURVE (DEAD MAN'S CURVE)

Colour, 1997, 92m. / Directed by Dan Rosen / Trimark (US R1 NTSC), Tartan (UK R2 PAL) / WS (1.85:1)

The old urban legend (or campus legend, if you will) goes that if a student's roommate commits suicide, he gets a 4.0 grade point average for that semester to aid in coping with the grief process. While nobody seems to know how this little tale got started, it does get a thorough work-over in *The Curve* (formerly known under the catchier title, *Dead Man's Curve*), a tricky if flawed thriller that delivers some nice twists and good performances for viewers willing to overlook some of its more self-indulgent moments. Interestingly, this shot-in-Baltimore film sat on the shelf for almost two years while its distributor decided how to handle the release of a very similarly themed film, *Dead Man on Campus*, which turned out to be a crushing dud in every respect. Thankfully, *The Curve* (which was shot earlier) is significantly better and doesn't really deserve its half-hearted straight-to-video treatment.

Two college friends, Tim (Michael Vartan) and Chris (Matthew Lillard, who actually makes Nick Cage look restrained in comparison) devise an elaborate plot to throw their third roommate, the boorish Rand (Randall Batinkoff), off a cliff and establish the death as suicide. However, things don't go as planned when Rand's body disappears, and a police investigation begins to close in a little too close to home. Tim already finds himself beginning to crack under the pressure of trying to get into Harvard grad school, not to mention sexual performance problems with his girlfriend (*Felicity* herself, Keri Russell, who does one scene in here her goody-goody TV persona would never allow). Tim discusses his problems with school shrink Dana Delaney, who begins to suspect that perhaps the boys have been up to no good.

Considering the film's low budget and its first time director status (Rosen also wrote the screenplay for overrated indie favourite *The Last Supper*), *The Curve* generally works well as a Gen X twist on Alfred Hitchcock's *Rope*. The sardonic humour and plot twists manage to replace the expected cheap scares and gore you would normally expect, though Rosen throws in a few too many lame jokes about The Smiths (yes, they're a downbeat band, we get it, ha ha) and resorts to that well worn cliché, the barbaric cops who seem to do everything wrong. However, while the film is a bit tough to get into, the generally good performances and unexpected turns manage to salvage what could have been a by the numbers potboiler.

All of the characters are generally unsympathetic jerks and spineless doormats, but this becomes the primary theme of the film: today's cutthroat society has forced people into predatory lifestyles even before they enter the job pool. The last ten minutes are particularly good, though "Psych" would have been a better final line than what the filmmakers chose. Of course, it's also great fun watching the up and coming cast members backstabbing each other for an hour and half; Vartan and Russell are especially interesting to watch in light of where their careers have taken them now. All in all, a pretty good shot, and recommended with reservations.

DARIO ARGENTO'S WORLD OF HORROR

Colour, 1985, 71m. / Directed by Michele Soavi / Synapse (US R1 NTSC)

 Even non-fans of Italy's most famous and stylish director should be entertained by this thorough, affectionate look at the ins and outs of European horror filmmaking. Generous film clips and amazing behind-the-scenes footage combine under the sure hand of first-time director Soavi (who went on to helm *Dellamorte Dellamore* and *The Church*) to create a lively, blood-spattered tribute to an art that seems to be falling by the wayside.

Synapse did their best with the problematic original materials, and while it's great that this is finally back on the market after over a decade in video moratorium hell, the transfer to our eyes looks about the same as the old Vidmark release on VHS and laserdisc. This is probably due to the fact that this was made on 16mm anyway, so it's probably never going to look sparkling and crisp; as it is, the colours are fine despite the inherent picture softness.

The extras are surprisingly skimpy, limited mostly to an Argento filmography. Too bad they couldn't pair this up with Luigi Cozzi's more disjointed but worthy sequel, *World of Horror 2* (aka *Master of Horror*), which was made five years later. More Argento documentary madness can be found in the Channel 4 production of *Dario Argento: An Eye for Horror*, available as a standalone from Image in the US or on the British Region 2 release of Argento's *Sleepless*.

THE DARK CRYSTAL

Colour, 1982, 93m. / Directed by Jim Henson & Frank Oz / Columbia / WS (2.35:1) (16:9) / DD5.1

 The last thing anyone expected from the creator of *The Muppets*, Jim Henson's *The Dark Crystal* was its creator's ambitious bid for status as a serious filmmaker and a pioneer in fantasy storytelling. While the film failed to find a large audience during its theatrical release, many of those who did manage to see it never forgot the completely fresh, exciting new world created entirely through puppets and creative art design. Like most of the overlooked entries in cinema fantastique for the amazing year of 1982, this film has found a steadily growing audience over the years more receptive to its complex, challenging attempts to depict the relationship between good and evil.

In an undefined land and time, a race of beings use a large, purple crystal as their source of power and knowledge. When the crystal is cracked, strife and conflict appear; according to a prophecy, the crystal will one day be healed by a race called the Gelflings. Fearful, the evil Skeksis arrange to slaughter all of the Gelflings they can find, but an infant named Jen escapes and is raised by the gentle Mystics. When Jen grows older and his master dies, he accepts his mission and, much to his surprise, encounters another of his kind, Kira, to aid his quest.

Obviously indebted to the writings of Joseph Campbell, the story by Henson and script by David Odell (*Cry Uncle!*) has been criticized for being both too facile in its depiction of the heroes and too complex and frightening for children. However, this difficult balancing act reveals exactly what this film is trying to accomplish - present naive, childlike protagonists thrust into a bewildering and dangerous set of circumstances they don't understand. Indeed, *The Dark Crystal* is not really a children's film per se, though virtually anyone of any age can enjoy it. The film's greatest asset, its fascinating and realistic environment, teems with a mind-blowing array of creatures, proving once and for all how off base George Lucas was with his digital menagerie in *Star Wars: The Phantom Menace*. The film also boasts an amazing early score from Trevor Jones (right after *Excalibur*), now isolated separately on the DVD to placate fans longing for a CD release.

The *Dark Crystal* first appeared on laserdisc from HBO/Image as a deluxe collector's edition: letterboxed, surround sound, with trailers, a brief deleted Skesis funeral scene, and a fascinating one hour television documentary, *The World of the Dark Crystal*. The latter extra feature, which contains extensive footage of Brian Froud and Henson at work designing the creatures, was really the *piece de resistance* for this set, which was excellent for its time but hampered by inaccurate 2.0:1 framing. Disney subsequently reissued the film on laserdisc with an improved, more accurate widescreen transfer but no extras.

Fortunately, the best of both versions and much more has been gathered by Columbia for its special edition on DVD, boasting a sparkling new anamorphic version of the film which easily blows all of the other ones away. Perfectly letterboxed and invigorated with a spacious new 5.1 remix, this *Dark Crystal* finally resembles the theatrical experience and should win over plenty of new fans. The fun doesn't stop there, though; aside from the aforementioned documentary and isolated score, the DVD includes a wealth of outtakes and rough-cut footage, demonstrating the process through which the characters were created. Especially amusing is an early version of Aughra's first scene, in which she is voiced by Frank Oz in Yoda mode instead of Billie Whitelaw (*The Omen*), who provided her voice in the final cut. Columbia has also provided optional subtitles from the final film within these sequences to demonstrate how much the dialogue changed during the dubbing and editing process. Aside from a handful of American and European trailers and TV spots, the DVD also includes the trailer for *Labyrinth* and a video promo for Henson's *The Storyteller*.

THE DARK HALF

Colour, 1993, 123m. / Written and Directed by George A. Romero / Starring Timothy Hutton, Amy Madigan / MGM (UK R2 PAL) / WS (1.85:1) (16:9), MGM (US R1 NTSC) / DD4.0

Following the lacklustre commercial reception for *Monkey Shines*, George Romero surprisingly decided to stay on to direct an adaptation of *The Dark Half*, his second shot at Stephen King

following the anthology *Creepshow*. Unfortu-nately, while the film was completed in 1991, it sat on the shelf for two years due to Orion's financial difficulties. Ironically, *The Dark Half* has now become one of the first titles ushered through to DVD by MGM after acquiring Orion's back catalogue, and horror fans who missed it during its fleeting theatrical run and long discontinued video release should have no problem discovering it now.

In the extended prologue, young Thad Beaumont discovers the joys of short story writing and spends his days churning out one tale after another on his new typewriter. Unfortunately, the narrative rush also provokes some splitting headaches, which result in him passing out on the way to school. Doctors perform emergency surgery in which they discover the remains of an unborn twin absorbed into his brain - a little bit of eye here, some nostril there. For some reason, Thad's talent has caused the previously dormant cannibalized foetus to continue growing, and as the doctors remove it, several hundred sparrows begin flapping outside the windows...

Flash forward to Thad as an adult (Timothy Hutton). Now a successful novelist, teacher, and father, he is approached one day by an admirer who claims to know that Beaumont, a respected but not profitable novelist, is also writing sleazy junk novels under the name George Stark. Thad reacts violently to the blackmail attempt and, at the urging of his wife, Liz (Amy Madigan), goes public with the news. He even arranges a publicity stunt in which he kills off and "buries" Stark. Liz expresses relief, claiming that Thad exhibited a nasty, Jekyll and Hyde personality when he worked on the Stark novels. When the blackmailer ends up dead, however, Thad finds himself the number one suspect... and he begins to suspect that Stark hasn't completely been a figment of his imagination.

As usual, Romero exhibits a high degree of skill and control over the material, with skilfully handled shock sequences and a knack for bringing realism to seemingly bizarre, surrealistic imagery. A fine stable of actors further help in lending credence to the unlikely story, with Hutton doing a typically top-notch job in two roles and Madigan, somewhat underused, making a sympathetic wife. Michael Rooker (*Henry: Portrait of a Serial Killer*) turns in a fine performance as Alan Pangborn, King's recurring sheriff character, and Julie Harris (*The Haunting*) even turns in an amusing cameo. An early, effectively creepy score by Christopher Young (*Hellraiser*) provokes genuine goosebumps thanks to its subliminal manipulation of strings and children's choir to chilly effect.

What prevents *The Dark Half* from becoming a completely successful film, alas, is what usually makes a film work: its extreme fidelity to the source novel. Not one of King's more coherent works, the storyline throws in numerous disparate elements and refuses to explain many of them, even on the level of nightmare logic. Romero was no doubt drawn to the theme of a man's rage becoming externalized (earlier explored in *Monkey Shines*), but the problem here is that no distinct pattern emerges to explain Stark's physical existence. Thad still exhibits signs of a psychological split, and the entire use of the sparrows seems like yet another King *deus ex machina* thrown in to create an effective image at the expense of narrative. King himself experienced a similar situation when his nom de plume, Richard Bachman (*Thinner*), was exposed by an avid fan, and no doubt he felt he was exorcising his frustration through this book. However, as with his other semiautobiographical works like *Misery* and *It*, self-indulgence tends to sap away the real potential of the material. Had Romero dug deeper into the roots of King's nightmare vision and attempted to unearth the frenzied psychological patterns underpinning it, he might have had a real masterpiece on his hands. However, what remains is still quite effective on its own terms and makes one wonder what Romero could have accomplished had he chosen a better realized King novel.

MGM's US open matte edition of *The Dark Half* appears to be taken from the same source materials used for the Orion laserdisc, albeit with a cleaner transfer and better colour delineation. However, it still looks like an early '90s video transfer thanks to some murky shadows and occasionally smudgy background detail. On the other hand, the UK disc from the same studio boasts a fresh new anamorphic widescreen transfer; why is anyone's guess. The basic surround mix delivers both the music and shock sound effects (complete with plenty of flapping wings) with no noticeable distortion, and since a 5.1 mix seems extremely unlikely in the near future, it will do just fine for now.

DARK ODYSSEY

B&W, 1957, 95m. / Directed by Radley Metzger and William Kyriakis / Starring Athan Karras / Image (US R0 NTSC)

Radically different from anything else in Radley Metzger's filmography, *Dark Odyssey* transplants the elements of Greek tragedy into a modern

American setting and reaffirms that lying beneath his impeccable skills as a stylist is an assured dramatist as well. The early score by Laurence Rosenthal, who later hit the big time in Hollywood, is a fine model of dramatic underscore with some definite traces of an Alex North influence. Extremely serious, deliberately paced, and surprisingly moving at times, *Dark Odyssey* reveals an early, rarely seen side of Metzger.

Yianni Martakis (Karras), a sailor immigrant in New York, is on a mission to find and kill the man who raped his sister. Along the way he becomes entangled with the sweet, unassuming Niki Vassos (Jerrems), and must decide whether he should forget his path of vengeance and perhaps begin living a normal life. Beyond the simple eye for an eye plot, however, is an interesting look at Greek culture in New York circa the late '50s, with a heavy emphasis on family dynamics. While this isn't really a sensual film (except in perhaps a twisted Tennessee Williams kind of way), the clashes of rugged masculinity and fiery femininity make for some unusual interactions here. Karras in particular gives an effective performance, deliberately starting out bland and dogged but becoming more complex and delicately shaded as the story progresses. The location shooting starkly depicts New York in terms far more gritty than a Hollywood effort would have dared and in some ways would make an interesting double bill with *West Side Story*.

The Image DVD, culled from the same transfer as the First Run VHS release, looks significantly less grainy and features much deeper blacks in the image. The black and white elements are remarkably clean, and the film is presented full frame in what appears to be close to its original aspect ratio (the credits are very slightly cropped but probably just needed to be windowboxed). Strangely, a few scenes on all versions contain some horizontal streaking from the edges of the screen, particularly during daylight sequences (the opening is the most noticeable), but since this could very well be the only complete print in existence, this version is the only game in town. Though the packaging makes no note of it, the film is followed by a trailer for the film's truncated theatrical reissue under the title *Passionate Sunday*.

DARK STAR

Colour, 1974, 83/68m. / Directed by John Carpenter / VCI (US R1 NTSC), Fabulous Films (UK R2 PAL) / WS (1.85:1)

For anyone who's ever gone to a sci-fi convention and had to sit through a numbing parade of shoestring zero budget space epics, *Dark Star* is an example of how to do it right. Boosted by clever scripting, imaginative special effects, and a truly unique atmosphere, this first effort by director John Carpenter and writer Dan O'Bannon (who acts here and went on to write *Alien* and the underrated *Dead and Buried, Return of the Living Dead,* and *Bleeders*) managed to beat the odds and find a theatrical release. Like George Lucas' *THX-1138,* this was expanded from a student project at UCLA, though in this case they simply tacked on extra scenes to the existing project (blown up from 16mm) instead of remaking it.

Dark Star has been most widely available in its theatrical 83 minute cut, though a "Special Edition" on VHS and laserdisc presented the 68 minute original variant with the extra scenes tacked on to the end. The VCI DVD presents both versions through seamless branching; when playing the shorter version, the DVD player simply skips past the cut scenes, causing a fleeting pause during the film's playback. Despite the filmmakers' objections, the extra scenes aren't overly detrimental to the film's pacing, so the smoother playback of the full cut is generally a more satisfying experience. The transfer is about the same as the laserdisc (this will obviously never look like *Terminator 2,* for obvious budgetary reasons), but the film has been given a surprisingly good Dolby Digital 5.1 sonic overhaul, with Carpenter's bizarre score (a mixture of electronic space-age drones and Country and Western!) constantly swirling in the rear and side channels. Much like the stereo boosts given to *Evil Dead, Phantasm,* and *Texas Chainsaw Massacre,* this lavish treatment may seem excessive given the film's humble roots but generally makes the film more exciting and startling even to returning viewers. On the other hand, the UK disc is especially harsh on the eyes and best avoided.

Basically an elaborate satire of Stanley Kubrick's *2001: A Space Odyssey* and *Dr. Strangelove,* the film opens on the titluar ship, where four astronauts have succumbed to boredom and borderline insanity after years spent drifting aimlessly in space. They pass the time by destroying "unstable planets" with talking bombs, tormenting each other with insults, reading comic books, and dealing with the occasional near-fatal disaster. In the film's most justifiably famous sequence, O'Bannon attempts to hunt down an alien he brought on board

(because "we needed a mascot") and finds himself trapped in a very long open elevator shaft. Though the huge beach ball alien is a goofy sight, the sequence is a perfect marriage of suspense, uneasy humour, and clever composition and editing, trademarks which also distinguish the film as a whole. The '70s trappings, such as rampant facial hair, uncontrolled sideburns, and hysterically dated "technology" on the ship, actually make the film more endearing; if you've ever wanted to go make a sci-fi film in your own backyard, this is the movie to inspire you.

DAUGHTER OF DR. JEKYLL

B&W, 1957, 71m. / Directed by Edgar G. Ulmer / Starring Gloria Talbott, John Agar / AllDay (US R1 NTSC) / WS (1.85:1)

In the wake of Universal's classic monster films, horror filmmakers during the 1950s desperately scrambled to cobble together as many monster hybrids as possible to compete with the rival alien invaders stomping the local silver screens. Thus we got oddities like *I Was a Teenage Werewolf* and *Blood of Dracula,* among many others. However, *Daughter of Dr. Jekyll* is easily one of the oddest and most endearing of the bunch. Critics have attempted to tie its surreal logic to other films by cult director Edgar G. Ulmer, particularly *The Black Cat,* but perhaps the best way to experience this berserk little gem is on its own terms without any preconceptions.

In an unforgettable curtain raiser, the audience is informed that the murderous, werewolf like doctor of Robert Louis Stevenson's story has been dispatched for good, only to have a furry version of Hyde turn to the audience and ask, "Are you sure?" That's about it for the literary source, since Hyde of course was not a werewolf. Flash forward several decades to the Jekyll ancestral home, where lovely Janet Smith ('50s scream queen Gloria Talbott) arrives with her boyfriend, George (John Agar). All seems well at first, but Janet is appalled when she learns the details of her father's experiments from her former guardian, Dr. Lomas (John Shields), and fears her own genetics might be tainted by his madness. Sure enough, the countryside is soon bloodied by gruesome murders committed by a werewolf-like creature who, according to reason, can only be killed by a stake through the heart (?). Is Janet responsible, or is there actually some darker fiend at work?

Despite the notorious sarcastic remark of critic Andrew Sarris ("Anyone who loves cinema must be moved by *Daughter of Dr. Jekyll*"), which is even emblazoned on the DVD's back sleeve, Ulmer's low budget tribute to Universal horrors is not without its charms and boasts some hilarious technical gaffes which somehow make it even more fun. On the verge of her most memorable role in *I Married a Monster from Outer Space*, Talbott is excellent and beautiful as always, while Agar's legendary half-hearted performance lives up to its reputation. Ulmer uses the decrepit sets and overactive fog machines with his usual high degree of skill and cunning, making this a constantly eye-catching film even when it doesn't quite make sense. Mystery Science Theatre 3000 fans may not find all of the inept chuckles they were hoping for, but true blue horror fans should find this makes a dandy evening's diversion and firmly belongs in every creature feature library.

While AllDay has had some successful ventures with the earlier entries in their Edgar G. Ulmer Collection like *Bluebeard* and *Strange Woman/Moon over Harlem*, those restorations could not possibly prepare anyone for the remarkable appearance of *Daughter of Dr. Jekyll*. The 1.85:1 framing works amazingly well here, lending the film a sense of composition and visual savvy completely missing on the old, cramped VHS version from Key Video.

Taken directly from the original negative materials, this transfer is as fresh and sharp as any title of its vintage, with only an occasional mild scratch or stain to betray its B-movie origins. A powerful mono audio track can be played normally or with the music and effects track isolated, which should make for good creepy fun during a Halloween party. That's just the beginning, though. You also get the fun if unspectacular theatrical trailer and two interview segments. "At Home with John Agar" offers a ten-minute chat covering his career and experiences with Ulmer, though the two didn't exactly become fast friends during the film's shooting. More eye-opening is a fifteen minute video interview with Ulmer's daughter, Arianne, who offers a fascinating account of the legal wranglings she endured while trying to track down and preserve this particular title. Oddly enough no mention is made of this film's alternate TV version, which was padded out and included snippets from *Frankenstein 1970* during the heroine's memorable nightmare sequence. An extensive gallery of stills and poster art is also included, with a few bits of artwork for this film's double bill with *The Cyclops* (also starring Talbott). Check your personality at the door and enjoy.

DAUGHTERS OF DARKNESS

Colour, 1971, 100m. / Directed by Harry Kumel / Starring Delphine Seyrig, John Karlen / Anchor Bay (US R0 NTSC) / WS (1.66:1)

Years before *The Hunger*, the '70s were a hotbed of European lesbian vampire romps ranging from Hammer's *The Vampire Lovers* to the more Catholic *Blood Spattered Bride*. However, the 1971 Belgian arthouse favourite *Daughters of Darkness* (originally titled *Le rouge aux levres*, or *The Red Lips*) is a somewhat different animal. Surrealist director Harry Kumel, a contemporary of European émigrés like Von Sternberg, conjured up a dark, magical brew spilled over with haunting imagery and strange, dreamlike plot twists, all revolving around his ethereal vampiress, Delphine Seyrig (*Last Year at Marienbad*). In fact, Seyrig may be the greatest of all female screen vampires; her world-weary persona - sort of Marlene Dietrich after lingering in a sarcophagus a few years too many - dominates every frame in which she appears.

Recently married Stefan (John Karlen of *Dark Shadows* and *Cagney and Lacey* fame) and Valerie (Danielle Ouimet) find themselves staying at a deserted, off-season hotel along with the travelling Countess Elizabeth Bathory (Seyrig) and her beautiful lesbian companion, Ilona (Andrea Rau). Soon Bathory sets her sights on seducing Valerie away from her brutal husband, who has more than a few nasty skeletons tucked away in his closet.

Originally chopped down by over 10 minutes and re-edited (both visually and musically), *Daughters of Darkness* has been restored to its original European running time for this dazzling new transfer. Aside from a great deal of extra nudity, this print also allows the film adequate time to weave its spell, with Kumel's languorous fades to red at the end of many scenes finally reinstated. While budgetary limitations show through in a little grain here and there, the picture quality easily blows away all previous versions. The letterboxing crops a little off the top and bottom of the image compared to the fullscreen VHS editions from companies like Sinister Cinema and VCI, but this framing adds considerably to the film's dizzy sense of composition. The Roan laserdisc and Anchor Bay DVDs look about the same, quality-wise, and contain an amusing running commentary with Karlen and David Del Valle in which the actor provides some fascinating, often shocking anecdotes about the shooting of the film. It's a shame Kumel only made one more feature film (the elusive

Malpertuis) before semi-retiring, only to appear every now and then for minor television work. In any case, he did create one true, indelible masterpiece, an essential title for horror and arthouse collectors alike.

DAWN OF THE DEAD

Colour, 1978, 128m. / Directed by George A. Romero / Starring David Emge, Ken Foree / Anchor Bay (US R1 NTSC) / WS (1.66:1, 1.85:1), Dutch Filmworks (Holland R0 PAL) / WS (1.75:1), BMG (UK R2 PAL)

 Either adored or reviled by critics on its initial release (which broke box office records in Europe and Asia), *Dawn of the Dead* was one of the first unrated, explicitly gory films to become a smash hit in the US and paved the way for more blood-soaked mayhem to follow. Of course, Romero's classic also contains its fair share of social subtext beginning with the familiar shopping mall setting. However, the analysis continues far beyond simple American consumerism, with militarism, the institution of marriage, and the consequences of a repetitious, deadening lifestyle all coming under fire. Oh, yeah, and it has some pretty amazing Tom Savini effects, too.

Presumably picking up after the zombie plague from *Night of the Living Dead* has engulfed the nation, *Dawn* picks up during a technical crisis at a local television station and introduces its four protagonists: couple Stephen (Emge) and Fran (*Creepshow*'s Gaylen Ross), Roger (Scott Reiniger), and Peter (Foree, another strong black Romero hero). While the ghettos turn into a zombie and military bloodbath, the quartet escape and find shelter in a shopping mall where they quarantine themselves into a blockade of shops and desolate storage areas. All goes well, if somewhat boringly, until a frisky group of bikers decide to invade the mall...

Anchor Bay has unveiled no less than two incarnations of Romero's masterpiece, and while the "US Theatrical Cut" might seem inferior by missing about 12 minutes from the 140-minute "Director's Cut," both versions are well worth owning. Numerous publications have documented the minute changes between these two cuts, as well as the European version, *Zombi*, supervised by exec producer Dario Argento. However, for a casual and entertaining viewing experience, the "US" cut, which has been most familiar to audiences over the

years, remains the superior edition. The longer edition may be more purely Romero, but this movie just isn't the same without that blast of Goblin music over the main titles. Also, the 128 minute version simply moves faster; the director's cut embellishes more and rewards fans with greater insight, but for the uninitiated, it simply drags.

While the Director's Cut version released on laser (Elite) and DVD (Anchor Bay) looks passable, Anchor Bay's DVD of the standard cut is a knockout, easily blowing away the prior releases from HBO Video and Republic. In fact, the crispness of detail outdoes any version of *Dawn* to date, period, and the colour saturation looks much purer and richer than could be expected from such a low budget film.

Both Anchor Bay DVDs contain the same theatrical trailer, while the Elite special edition laser contains more extras (not as thorough as their *NOTLD* but fun nonetheless). The 128 minute Anchor Bay DVD also includes an amusing circa-'78 TV spot for the Monroeville Mall and a few extra scenes from the alternate *Zombi* cut (but none of the extra gore footage from the climactic attack sequence, alas). Also, the less severe 1.66:1 matting on the shorter cut makes it easier on the eyes; oddly enough, some alternate footage from the longer cut is still present from time to time, technically make this some sort of digital mutt.

A long promised Anchor Bay special box set containing all of the possible extras and existing cuts will hopefully materialize in the near future but has not as of this writing been announced. Those pining after the full Argento version (a hell of a lot of fun in its own right) can also pick up the lavish Dutch set, which contains the longer Romero cut (letterboxed somewhere between the two Anchor Bay transfers), Argento's edit, and the *Document of the Dead* documentary. Those who prefer their *Dawn* diluted can also try the UK disc, which has been shorn of a few gory shots.

DAWN OF THE MUMMY

Colour, 1981, 88m. / Directed by Frank Agrama / Starring Brenda King, Joan Levy / Laser Paradise (Germany R0 PAL)

 This lovably dopey splatter film could only have come from the early '80s, when the dying throes of disco and the influx of gore-soaked European horror films produced some truly strange animals indeed. While the title promises a spirited, gory romp in the tradition of George Romeo, this low budget New York production (partially shot in Egypt) comes a lot closer to Lucio Fulci territory instead.

In the sticky prologue, a member of Egyptian royalty is graphically mummified (complete with organ removal) and placed into a pyramid crypt along with his slaves, who are entombed without body wrapping. About 3000 years or so later, some jewel thieves break into the pyramid and awake the mummy, along with his now zombified servants. A visiting cadre of Americans stumbles into the pyramid for a photo shoot, but the models are more concerned about the state of their toenails than the rampaging dead lurking in the darkness. Pretty soon the nearby Egyptian village is overrun by zombies, who pillage the natives in a riotous orgy of eye gouging and entrail-munching before the ridiculous climax.

Okay, so it ain't fine art by any stretch of the imagination, but *Dawn of the Mummy* can be loads of fun as long as you keep popcorn and some alcoholic refreshment handy. The long, slow stretches of dialogue in the middle at least offer some unintentional laughs, but most gore fans will definitely want to stick around for the big finale. The catchy, kitschy disco-on-the-Nile score is pretty amazing as well; did anyone actually buy the soundtrack album back in '81? Someone needs to do a CD reissue, pronto.

Laser Paradise's PAL release on DVD marks the first availability of *Dawn of the Mummy* in many years, with most horror fans only encountering it through the rare, poorly transferred Thorn/EMI VHS version. Relatively speaking the DVD definitely looks crisper, but this film always had the appearance of being projected on a strip of dirty burlap and suffers from pale, lifeless colours and shadows. In lieu of a full scale restoration this is a watchable alternative, but don't expect much.

THE DAY THE EARTH CAUGHT FIRE

B&W/Tinted, 1961, 99m. / Directed by Val Guest / Starring Edward Judd, Janet Munro / Anchor Bay (US R1 NTSC) / WS (2.35:1) (16:9), Network (UK R2 PAL) / WS (2.35:1)

One of the best films Hammer Studios could have made, *The Day the Earth Caught Fire* is an imaginative, resourceful science fiction yarn about what might happen if the Earth wound up spinning out of its orbit towards the sun. Eschewing the ludicrous soap opera situations and bombastic effects which crippled efforts like *Meteor* and *When Time Ran Out*, this depiction of doomsday pulls no punches and offers no easy answers, instead leaving the viewer with an uneasy but not hopeless feeling about what might happen with each coming sunrise.

In the orange-tinted opening sequence, reporter Peter Stenning (Edward Judd) sits at a desolate counter, recording for dubious posterity the story of how the world became a heat-lashed wasteland. It all began when his day-to-day job at the newspaper office was disturbed by the realization that something might be tying together an increasing number of "small" worldwide catastrophes. With the aid of a co-worker (Leo McKern) and a government worker, Jeannie (the shapely Janet Munro), who possesses some valuable information, Peter sets out to expose the truth to a humanity unaware of its numbered days. Apparently the simultaneous detonation of nuclear bombs by the US and the Soviet Union at opposing poles on the planet has disrupted the Earth's orbital pattern, leading it on a fiery path directly to the sun. As mankind gradually descends into barbarism and panic, only one possible solution emerges...

The clever juxtaposition of black and white scope photography, restrained colour tinting, stock footage, and resourceful special effects ably supports a surprisingly powerful storyline. The characters are all literate, interesting people, spouting out dialogue that would make Howard Hawks proud while rendering credibility to the disturbing premise (which was condensed to an equally nightmarish degree in a *Twilight Zone* episode, "The Midnight Sun"). Munro lingers longest in the memory thanks to one particularly sweaty scene, but everyone pulls off their parts with nary a false note.

British science fiction has often been discredited by the general public in the wake of the (too) many Dr. Who cash-ins and copies; this film, along with its spiritual companion pieces like the Quatermass films and *Journey to the Far Side of the Sun*, proves that thought provoking sci-fi doesn't have to mean boring. Finally, the last shot is, in its own lingering, unresolved way, quite perfect. Long a victim of butchered pan and scan broadcasts, *The Day the Earth Caught Fire* has regained all of its much needed visual sweep with this beautiful anamorphic transfer from the vaults of Canal Plus. The dialogue isn't remotely as sharp and often descends into purely muffled earstrain, so be prepared to switch on those very welcome closed captions if necessary.

Though it wouldn't seem a likely candidate for a full blown special edition, Anchor Bay has packed the disc with enough extra goodies to make it a welcome purchase beyond the obvious pleasures of the film itself. Director Val Guest (*The Abominable Snowman*) appears for another commentary track, hosted by Ted Newsom, in which he points out many of the locales and actors used to bring verisimilitude to a story that must have seemed unbelievable at the time. The menu screen also leads to a varied gallery of still and promotional images, as well as a theatrical trailer and ragged TV spots, while the liner notes by Mark Wickum offer a nice sketch elaborating on Guest's place in the British sci-fi pantheon. Read them before sampling the commentary for a good introduction to one of the most fruitful periods of English language cinema, long before the vapid, thunderous days of big budget science fiction blockbusters.

DEAD AND BURIED

Colour, 1981, 92m. / Directed by Gary Sherman / Starring James Farentino, Melody Anderson / Dragon (Germany R0 NTSC) / WS (1.66:1)

Melancholy and twisted, *Dead and Buried* has gradually earned its sleeper reputation over the years but still hasn't received the kind of credit it deserves. This peculiar blend of small town menace, zombies, voodoo, and jolting plot twists still packs a punch today long after its slasher brethren have faded into the woodwork, and the shock ending will definitely linger in your memory long afterward.

The film opens along the coastline of Potter's Bluff, where a photographer (Christopher Allport) has stopped to snap a few nature shots. A beautiful young woman (Lisa Blount) strikes up a conversation with him and asks whether she could be a model. The photographer offers to take her photograph, and she responds in an unusually seductive manner. Unfortunately, their romantic idyll is shattered when a group of strangers suddenly appear, tie up the hapless photographer, douse him with gasoline, and set him ablaze while recording his death throes via photographs and film. Later the town sheriff, Dan (James Farentino), is called in to investigate a car crash, which has left its victim burned beyond recognition. Dan begins to suspect that the burning occurred outside of the accident, a theory he attempts to sell to the quirky local coroner, William Dobbs (Jack Albertson in his last screen role). Dan's tranquil home life with his beautiful wife, Janet (Melody Anderson), becomes strained as Dan is convinced

that a mounting number of gruesome accidents could be related to the occult. Even worse, the victims have a nasty habit of coming back to life... and taking their place among the townspeople.

Written and performed with unusual subtlety, *Dead and Buried* cannily uses its TV-friendly cast to gradually undermine viewers' expectations. The film has earned a reputation for its graphic gore and came under fire in the UK, though Stan Winston's gruesome effects actually occupy a relatively small amount of screen time. In fact, the most memorable violent effect involves a simple syringe and no blood whatsoever. The violence never overwhelms the compelling storyline, which gradually tightens to a delirious final act. Genre fans in particular should look for an early role by Freddy Krueger himself, Robert Englund, and a haunting music score by Joe Renzetti , who later went on to *Child's Play* and several Frank Henenlotter films. Oddly enough, this film also marked a directorial comeback for Gary Sherman, who had vanished for ten years after the magnificent British shocker, *Death Line* (aka *Raw Meat*). Unfortunately his career quickly went downhill, distinguished only by the memorable drive-in favourites *Vice Squad* and *Wanted: Dead or Alive*. Perhaps twenty years after this film he'll try his hand at big screen horror again.

Dead and Buried had the extreme misfortune of being released on VHS by Vestron, whose shoddy early transfers hit rock bottom here. Almost completely devoid of colour, this tape sabotaged the film's carefully modulated misty atmosphere and completely removed the upper and lower matte on the image, exposing safety clips holding up the black and white photograph during the opening credits, among other goofs. Dragon's DVD restores the film's 1.66:1 framing and looks much better, though the transfer itself still leaves a lot to be desired. The heavy doses of grain and overworked digital noise reduction distortion make for a less than satisfying picture, but at least the original colour schemes are back in place. *Dead and Buried* has never looked better... but that ain't saying much. The mono audio is a little clearer than the tape but still sounds more muffled and distorted than it probably should. The disc includes optional German and Dutch subtitles, as well as a spoiler-filled, awful looking German trailer. Don't let these flaws dissuade you, however; see this movie any way you can.

THE DEAD ARE ALIVE

Colour, 1972, 101m. / Directed by Armando Crispino / Starring Alex Cord, Samantha Eggar / Eurovista (US R0 NTSC) / WS (2.35:1)

The first of two Italian thrillers directed by jack-of-all-trades Armando Crispino, *The Dead Are Alive* is better known to giallo fans under the more evocative but equally misleading title of *The Etruscan Rises Again*. Sporting the usual international cast, a few gory murders, and a labyrinthine plot that frequently rises to the level of pure hysteria, this is '70s shocker filmmaking at its most typical, though newcomers to Eurosleaze may be left scratching their heads half an hour into the story.

Jason (Alex Cord), an American photographer, has arrived at the excavation site of a series of Etruscan tombs tagged for archaeological study. His arrival sparks a reunion with his ex-wife, Myra (Samantha Eggar), who has become involved with a much older but equally temperamental conductor, Nikos Samarakis (John Marley). The Etruscan dig is disrupted when two interloping teenagers are brutally clubbed to death (a scene highly reminiscent of Dario Argento's *Four Flies on Grey Velvet*, only bloodier), and the bodies are arranged in a strange fashion suggesting the ancient sacrificial rites of Tuchulcha, an Etruscan god whose face adorns the tomb's walls. The murders continue, accompanied all the while by startling bursts of loud choral music, as Jason scrambles to deal with his feelings toward Myra and unravel the mystery in the process. Meanwhile Nikos prepares for an elaborate musical show to celebrate the ancient Festival dei Due Mondi, whose timing coincides with another violent turn of events.

Though less explicit and outrageous than *Autopsy*, Crispino's second horror outing, this film shares with its successor a batch of dysfunctional and often unlikeable characters, a gimmicky supernatural conceit designed to divert suspicion from an all too human murderer, and a melancholy, poetic finale. Though hardly an outstanding entry in the giallo sweepstakes, the proceedings are enlivened by the unusual settings, some earnest performances (with Marley in particular leaving the scenery torn to shreds), and a beautiful score by *Mondo Cane*'s Riz Ortolani. The murders are appropriately brutal for the time without resorting to explicit knifings, and for once in this genre, the male victims outdistance the female ones. Complete with an unusually good American dialogue track with voices from most of the original actors, *The Etruscan Rises Again* was briefly released in the US under its alternate title by National General Pictures, who also distributed the American edition of Argento's *The Cat o' Nine Tails*. The film has been infernally difficult to see ever since, with many European prints (particularly the one prepared for co-financier Germany) missing both violence and crucial plot points, including one of Marley's better tantrums. Even uncut prints (such as the Dutch video edition entitled *Overtime*) have been terribly cropped, destroying the original scope compositions.

A scope 16mm print was transferred to video by Luminous Film and Video Wurks, who now carry the same transfer on DVD through the banner of Eurovista. To start off with the good news, the horizontal letterboxing looks just about right and is even slightly windowboxed to provide as much image as possible. The colours are relatively strong and stable, and for what it's worth, this is by far the best the film has ever looked on home video. However, the picture is also a bit soft, and the print has suffered from some distracting damage, including numerous scratches, awkward splices (particularly during the opening credits), and a recurring tiny tear in the lower left corner which lasts throughout the entire film. Also some scenes appear to be oddly misframed, likely a flaw from the original source, with the top matte coming in far too low at times and covering up the upper half of people's heads. The picture is also squeezed out horizontally a bit too much, with the framing actually measuring out closer to 2.45:1.

The audio is scratchy and muddy at times, but dialogue remains intelligible throughout. More inexplicably, the first few seconds of the opening shot are missing, and while trying this disc out on four different players, the film abruptly freezes and returns to the main menu just before the end credits kick in. To watch the credits, you must either fast forward for a moment past the final shot of the film or access them directly from the scene selection menu. Toshiba owners should also note that the disc freezes up on the opening Eurovista logo; you have to access "Title 1" on your remote to go to the film rather than going to the menu or hitting "Play." Extras include a black and white "Terror Times" booklet reproducing the original US press kit, a gallery of international lobby cards and video art, and some sketchy talent bios. Worth picking up for Eurocult completists, but be aware of what you'll get.

DEAD CALM

Colour, 1989, 95m. / Directed by Phillip Noyce / Starring Nicole Kidman, Sam Neill, Billy Zane / Warner / WS (2.35:1) (16:9) / DD2.0

A breakthrough film for almost everyone involved, *Dead Calm* only lasted briefly in theatres but won a loyal audience on home video and cable. Nicole

Kidman became a familiar face, Billy Zane (*Titanic*) played the first of his gonzo nautical villains, and director Phillip Noyce (the Harrison Ford/Tom Clancy films) finally had a hit after toiling in cable TV and unseen art house projects. The fuss is easy to understand, as *Dead Calm* remains a taut if imperfect little thriller and a compelling stylistic exercise, filled with gorgeous widescreen scenery and earnest performances.

Essentially an updating of the Orpheus myth filtered through Roman Polanski's *Knife in the Water*, the film introduces a married couple, John (Sam Neill) and Rae (Nicole Kidman), out boating in the Pacific Ocean to recuperate from the death of their son in a violent car accident. One day John spies a man in a small lifeboat rowing towards them from a distant ship. The stranger, Hughie (Billy Zane), tells them that his boat is sinking and that he is the only survivor. John takes off to investigate the seemingly deserted ship, which is gradually sinking, and uncovers a horrific secret. Meanwhile the charismatic but quite insane Hughie stalks and terrorizes Rae, who must use all means at her disposal to regain the ship and rescue her husband from a watery death.

As might be expected from the presence of George Miller (*Mad Max*) behind the scenes, *Dead Calm* is a very riveting film for anyone who can tolerate the claustrophobic settings and threadbare plotline. Few surprises actually emerge during the film, but the pleasures lie mostly in watching the performers interact. Kidman is a particular revelation, with her fiery hair and porcelain features making her an ideal heroine. Some of her decisions during the film are astonishingly stupid (tying up and subduing Hughie on several occasions rather than simply killing him, for example), but it's to Kidman's credit that the character always works and never loses audience sympathy. Neill has little to do after the first twenty minutes besides scrambling around in the water, but he's efficient and appealing as always. The underrated Graeme Revell contributes an astonishing score filled with tribal percussion and eerie soprano voices; its unavailability on CD is a true crime. The film's only glaring flaw is its essential lack of depth, a factor that could have been avoided with a denser screenplay. Originally slated and partially filmed as an Orson Welles project with Laurence Harvey back in the 1950s, the story (from a Charles Williams novel) contains some tantalizing basic ideas, such as Rae (the Eurydice figure) fighting Hughie ("death")

while her husband literally goes into the "underworld" (the watery ship) to find the truth. Had the filmmakers sacrificed one or two chase scenes in favour of character development, *Dead Calm* could have been a masterpiece, but what remains is still more than worthwhile.

Warner's long delayed DVD spawned a number of rumours since its initial announcement, mostly involved scenes cut from the final assembly and a commentary track. Alas, the DVD is virtually bare bones, with only the US trailer as any kind of bonus. Fortunately the transfer itself makes up for this loss, as Warner has gone to quite a bit of trouble improving on their dismal laserdisc release. Issued back at the dawn of letterboxing, the laser featured a heavily compromised 1.85:1 transfer of this scope film, but the DVD thankfully restores the entire width of the picture. Given the careful and expansive compositions used throughout, this presentation is crucial to enjoying *Dead Calm*, and the brilliant bursts of colour throughout look fresh and free of any distortion. The soundtrack is still straight Dolby Surround, but the startling channel separation offers a few nifty showcases for audiophiles, especially all of the flare-shooting scenes.

THE DEAD HATE THE LIVING!

Colour, 1999, 90m. / Directed by Dave Parker / Starring Eric Clawson, Jamie Donahue / Full Moon (US R1 NTSC) / DD2.0

After Kevin Williamson and company drove the slasher movie into the ground with the postmodern hipster antics of *Scream*, the folks at Full Moon evidently decided to do the same thing to Lucio Fulci zombie movies. Relatively speaking, *The Dead Hate the Living!* is the best film the fantasy-oriented studio has released since the heyday of Stuart Gordon, but it suffers from the same problem which plagues such "homages" as *The Faculty*- namely, making constant references to the films or books you're ripping off doesn't make the theft any less irritating.

A group of less than brilliant no budget filmmakers have broken into an abandoned hospital to shoot a horror opus about horny zombies, or something like that. The director, David Poe (Eric Clawson), has brought along his two feuding sisters, Shelly (Wendy Speake) and Nina (Kimberly Pullis), both of whom have been promised the lead role (which apparently consists of stripping down to her skivvies and having her head ripped off). The blonde production assistant, Topaz (Jamie Donahue), has a crush on David but hasn't had a chance to make her move, while David's best buddy, Paul (Brett Beardslee), is immersed in his avalanche of gory latex effects and a not so secret longing for Shelly. While scouting around the hospital, Topaz discovers a cavernous basement filled with preserved human organs and a large black coffin/gate/sculpture thing containing the dead body of Dr. Eibon (Matt Stephens) (Eibon, as in the book from The Beyond, get it?). Suddenly the film turns into a cross between *Stagefright* and *Children Shouldn't Play with Dead Things* when the director decides to use the body in his film, a stupid move which naturally unleashes a doorway to a netherworld filled with shuffling zombies (well, half a dozen of 'em anyway). As the crew dies horribly, David realizes his pet film project may be in serious danger.

Good news first: *The Dead Hate the Living* is rich in atmosphere and thankfully doesn't skimp on the gore. In fact, the red stuff pours enough to make one wonder how on earth it got that R rating on the back of the box. The actors are all pretty competent, by and large, though the wiseass dialogue doesn't really allow much room to stretch. The effects range from impressive (one zombie's fate near the end in particular) to appalling (some horrendous CGI fire effects), but anyone used to Fulci's oatmeal on the face treatment should be amused. However, the sheer avalanche of cutesy horror references ("What would Bruce Campbell do?," "You'll be the next David Warbeck," "Make them die... slowly," "Gino De Rossi, eat your heart out") often swallows up the film and destroys any attempts at spookiness. More jarringly, the ending swipes the finale scene from Fulci's *The Beyond*, almost shot for shot. Sure, the resemblance is intentional, but that doesn't make it any less annoying. The "fanboy" crowd already knows their spaghetti cinema, thank you very much, and doesn't need to be reminded of it every two minutes.

Full Moon's lavish DVD of *The Dead Hate the Living* indicates they're quite aware this film is a cut above your average *Subspecies* sequel. The transfer looks fine but a tad on the pale side, while the colourful Argento-style lighting (rapidly becoming an indie horror cliché) looks nicely saturated. The surround sound is mostly limited to isolated sound effects (squishing, gunshots, etc.) and a kitschy retro punk/metal soundtrack, presumably meant to go along with Dr. Eibon's distracting and non-menacing resemblance to Rob Zombie. The disc includes a nice audio commentary which is often entertaining and informative about horror filmmaking than the movie itself, as well as the

typically affectionate "Videozone" making-of sequence. Other bonuses include music videos (with the ever present Penis Flytrap), a surprisingly weak trailer, production info and photos, and cast/crew reminiscences. A better effort than a lot of major studio product, to be sure, and a nice treat for horror fans looking for a little zombie action.

DEAD WATERS (DARK WATERS)

Colour, 1994, 93m. / Directed by Mariano Baino / Starring Louise Salter, Venera Simmons / York (US R1 NTSC) / DD5.1

For a very brief period in the mid-'90s, director and acknowledged Dario Argento worshipper Mariano Baino was touted as the next big thing in Italian horror based on the strength of his striking short film, "Caruncula." The hype dried up just about immediately when Baino's first full length feature, *Dark Waters*, hit European cinemas and sent most audiences into a stupor. Years later the film went straight to video in the US under the title of *Dead Waters*, where it failed to cash in on the growing wave of Euro horror mania. However, viewers in a forgiving frame of mind may want to take a look at one of the odder late moments in Italian horror before the industry finally caved in on itself.

In the puzzling prologue, an isolated religious establishment on a stormy island is beset by problems originating from a stone medallion. Nuns trudge through the landscape carrying fiery crosses, a young girl is repeatedly stabbed until the water runs red with her blood, and a priest trapped in an underground flood meets the wrong end of a broken shaft of wood. Flash forward twenty years later, as young Elizabeth (Louise Salter) arrives at the aforementioned island to discover why her father has been sending payments to the nuns ever since her mother's premature death. The Mother Superior and her charges prove less than helpful, so Elizabeth takes to the library to find out the horrible secrets that have left her with nightmarish flashbacks involving a long lost sister. Meanwhile the occasional malicious nun tries to shove her out a window or stab her, leaving Elizabeth more determined than ever to uncover the diabolical secret that ties her to this wicked order of homicidal nuns.

From the opening moments, *Dead Waters* tries its best to overwhelm the viewer with rich, suffocating visuals. The opening half hour is almost entirely devoid of dialogue, leaving the viewer to piece everything together with a series of visual clues equally inspired by Argento, Jodorowsky, and even Michael Mann, whose *The Keep* is aped right down to the droning, Tangerine Dream-inspired synth score. Unfortunately the pace is agonizingly slow and the actors walk through their roles in a somnambulist fashion. Gore fans will find a few scattered thrills, such as an extended entrail-pulling that seems to have wandered in from another film, while the parallels to the works of another more direct Argento disciple, Michele Soavi, are often amusing to tally up. Just think about *The Church* and *The Sect,* which were equally incoherent but a whole lot more fun.

York's DVD improves only slightly upon their VHS edition, which appears to be very mildly cropped from the 1.66:1 original to no damaging effect. The image quality is gritty but clear, while the low budget produces a grainy visual texture kept under control for the most part throughout the transfer. Don't expect a whole lot, but it could have been worse. On the other hand, the soundtrack is simply bizarre. The two channel stereo tracks have been remixed into 5.1 so everything is sent to the rear speakers, including dialogue. For best results, those with Dolby Digital receivers would be advised to switch to normal two channel stereo playback for this one. The English dialogue (which appears to have been recorded largely on the set, oddly enough) is clear and intelligible enough throughout. No extras to speak of- not even chapters or a menu.

THE DEAD ZONE

Colour, 1983, 103m. / Directed by David Cronenberg / Starring Christopher Walken, Brooke Adams / Paramount (US R1 NTSC), MIA (UK R2 PAL) / WS (1.85:1) (16:9) / DD5.1

Hurled into a five-year coma after a terrible motoring accident, Johnny Smith (Walken) wakes to find his youth, his job and his fiancée (Adams) all gone. He also has to come to terms with the fact he has psychic abilities - largely dormant before the crash, yet now overwhelmingly prevalent - that enable him to sense disaster, be it past, present or in the future. Having helped the police track down a deadly killer, Johnny realises the true extent of his powers and opts for a reclusive lifestyle away from the probing eyes of his fellow man. But when he learns of a future cataclysm, he must decide whether he has the right to intervene and alter that which will otherwise devastate the entire world.

David Cronenberg's films tend to fall into two very distinct categories. On one side we have the skilfully crafted eminence of *Shivers, Crash, The Brood, Rabid,* and *eXistenZ*, on the other the ineffectual ennui of *Scanners, Naked Lunch, Dead Ringers* and *Videodrome. The Dead Zone* not only falls into the former category, being the director's most palatable mainstream offering yet, but with the possible exception of *The Green Mile* it also happens to be the finest adaptation of a Stephen King work.

Always good value for money, Christopher Walken's performance here is quite breathtaking. Ably supported by a stellar cast - primarily Herbert Lom, Tom Skerritt, Anthony Zerbe, Martin Sheen and Brooke Adams - this is the stage upon which he plied his trade with more gusto than in any of his other diverse roles to date. Eagle-eyed Cronenberg apostles will no doubt spot appearances by Nicholas Campbell (*The Brood*), Peter Dvorsky (*Videodrome*), Les Carlson (*The Fly*) and Cindy Hines (*The Brood*).

In summation *The Dead Zone* isn't so much frightening as it is bitterly sad. Michael Kamen's sumptuous score adds ambience to the emotional highs and lows, as everything Smith knew is wrenched away from him and his life becomes a tragic downward spiral towards eventual self-destruction. Much as King's novel was two distinctly different tales, so the film is almost two different films, with only Walken and Adams as the thread connecting them. The first half establishes Smith's accident and the turmoil born thereof, before scattering serial killer fibres into the mix. At mid-point it veers off in another direction and becomes a gripping political thriller. Yet both halves complement each other extremely well and the whole is such a satisfying viewing experience that one is compelled to return to it again and again.

Cut from the 1985 British Thorn EMI release, the nastiest moment in *The Dead Zone* comes when the Castle Rock Killer is cornered and takes his own life with a pair of scissors. The excision of the "pay off" resulted in a grating jump on the soundtrack and made for a clumsy looking conclusion to the tension Cronenberg so skilfully ekes out of the lead up. Fortunately the scene was reinstated when the film was reissued budget price by MIA Video a few years ago (and subsequently reissued on DVD), but the overall calibre of that version was unsatisfactory.

Paramount's beautiful quality DVD makes up for the years of neglect that the film has endured in various incarnations by yielding a flawless, uncut print matted to its original theatrical ratio. Broken into 16 chapters, the sound is available in English 5.1 surround, English Dolby surround or French mono, with optional English subtitles. For a film that cries out for director commentary or a retrospective documentary, it's a little discouraging that the only extra included is a trailer. - TG

D

DEADBEAT AT DAWN
Colour, 1987, 80m. / Directed by Jim Van Bebber / Starring Jim Van Bebber, Marc Pitman / Synapse (US R1 NTSC)

A leading entry in the gutter-gore sweepstakes of the glorious 1980s, *Deadbeat at Dawn* quickly joined the company of films like *Combat Shock* and *Street Trash*, all very low budget films distinguished by their imaginative camerawork and extreme, hyperbolic violence. While director and star Jim Van Bebber had been cutting his teeth on short films for ten years, he decided to produce his 16mm street gang opus as a feature that ironically proved to be his only completed full-length film to date.

The storyline itself consists of virtually every cliché from the late '60s or early '70s mob or gang film of your choice, then tossed into a blender. Goose (Van Bebber), the leader of a gang called the Ravens, decides to call it quits thanks to the urging of his occult-fixated girlfriend (Megan Murphy). When he learns that his boys are soon to be joined with a rival gang called the Spiders (or the Spyders, depending on which graffiti you read), Goose thinks the time is right - at least until Murphy turns up dead despite his efforts to protect her. Determined to seek revenge and live his life without fear, Goose locks horns with his evil rival, Danny, and unleashes a torrent of street fighting and kung fu fury on his enemies.

Adopting a visual style straddling somewhere between the crimson-drenched fever dreams of Kenneth Anger and the grimy colour-coding of a Harry Novak soft porn film, *Deadbeat at Dawn* deliberately grates on the viewer's senses and probably won't demand repeated viewings from all but the most devoted cult film fans. However, when the action does kick in, Van Bebber delivers some amusing thrills built on dismemberment and spewing bodily fluids. Unfortunately, the fights themselves fall somewhat short of their Hong Kong and AIP models, with some clumsy tossed punches and missed kicks constantly assuring the viewer that it's only a movie. However, with this can't-miss combination of sex, action, gore, and black humour, the film's cult reputation is easy to understand and

does merit its lavish treatment on DVD. Long unavailable on video outside of the bootleg circuit (and completely banned in Britain, not surprisingly), *Deadbeat at Dawn* looks much better than expected on DVD. Already a notorious release, the disc came under public fire from its director, but it's hard to comprehend his problems with its presentation. The image quality looks extremely crisp and clean for 16mm, with even the most heavily drenched colours shining through for the most part. The mono audio does what it can, considering the film always sounded like it was preserved on a tape recorder. Van Bebber offers up a commentary track for the entire film (and, unadvertised, on several of its supplements), joined at various points by producer Michael King, actor Marc Pitman, and cult enthusiast David Gregory, among others.

Whatever faults the film itself may have, the DVD itself is really beyond reproach, offering a host of both obvious extras and a few hidden treats as well. "My Sweet Satan," a 20-minute short film from 1992, is actually a more impressive piece of work than the main feature, offering a harsh and unsettling portrayal of the Satanic youth panic, which became an American media hot spot for a few years. A very long Van Bebber filmography lists everything from his first short home movie all the way up to his notorious unreleased epic, *Charlie's Family*, which for some reason features a release date of 1999 (wishful thinking, alas). Other bonuses include two minutes of outtakes (mostly alternate camera angles of the fight scenes), the faux trailer for *Chunkblower* (a nonexistent gore film by Van Bebber), and a sample of the director's work for Skinny Puppy, the "Spasmolytic" video and an album commercial. Unfortunately, the unsettling "Road Kill" (included on a previous Film Threat VHS compilation of Van Bebber's work and available as part of a UK R2 PAL DVD with "My Sweet Satan," a Necrophagia music video, and a few shorts) is noticeably absent here, due to legal reasons.

DEADLY WEAPONS
Colour, 1973, 75m. / Directed by Doris Wishman / Starring Chesty Morgan, Harry Reems / Image (US R0 NTSC)

One of those astounding '70s drive-in movies that made even the most jaded 42nd Street viewers stop cold in their tracks, *Deadly Weapons* introduced the world to Chesty Morgan (actually Polish-born Lillian Wilczkowsky, credited here as Zsa Zsa). Chesty's eye-popping 73-inch bustline catapulted her to cult icon status despite the fact that she couldn't act worth a lick, even with dubbing. Coupled with the, er, unique cinematic stylings of director Doris Wishman (who displays her usual fondness for losing focus and wandering the camera across random items of furniture), *Deadly Weapons* is truly a sight to behold.

Despite the fact that he's a member of the mob, good old Larry seems to be the perfect match for his busty advertising exec girlfriend, Crystal (Chesty, natch). After secretly tucking away an incriminating list of names while performing his duties, Larry instigates a string of violence which leads right up to his doorstep right after he proposes to Crystal. Luckily she hears his murder over the phone and picks up a few details of the killers' plans to hide out through their burlesque connections. Naturally Crystal poses as a stripper and uses her enormous womanly gifts to smother the jerks (including *Deep Throat*'s Harry Reems) responsible for offing her fiancé. Of course, even Crystal can't anticipate the big twist ending Doris has hidden up her sleeve.

More of a visually trashy '70s experience than a coherent narrative, *Deadly Weapons* wallows in appalling fashion, glittery nightclub decor, garish lighting, and jarring post synch dubbing that sounds like broadcasts from a different galaxy. Chesty's legendary acting ability consists of one single, confused expression, making it impossible to tell her moments of happiness and rage apart.

What's not to love? A home video staple that has enlivened dull parties for years (with one edition even hosted by Joe Bob Briggs), *Deadly Weapons* is a natural for any sleaze lover's DVD collection. The image quality looks exactly the same as it always has - colourful but grainy and muddy, just how it looked in the theatre. The open matte, full frame image looks fine, considering the arbitrary camera placement that became Ms. Wishman's trademark. And yes, some of those scenes really do drift out of focus; that's not the DVD's fault. The disc also includes a long, very revealing theatrical trailer, as well as promotional art and a spot for Chesty's big follow up epic, *Double Agent 73*.

DEATH RACE 2000

Colour, 1975, 79m. / Directed by Paul Bartel / Starring David Carradine, Sylvester Stallone / New Concorde (US R1 NTSC), Universal (UK R2 PAL)

Score 100 points for this fast paced drive-in masterpiece, a rare example of a B-movie outdoing the big budget Hollywood product it's trying to imitate.

Back in the mid-'70s, Roger Corman made a minor cottage industry out of women in prison and horror films thanks to his wild and wonderful New World Pictures. One of the high points, *Death Race 2000*, was intended to ride on the coattails of the ponderous MGM sci-fi/action/sports epic, *Rollerball*; what director Paul Bartel (*Eating Raoul, Private Parts*) delivered was a minor masterpiece of bloody social satire.

In the far off year 2000, America has become a bloodthirsty fascist state where fans gather for the "Death Race," in which outrageous contestants race their cars across the country and earn points for the number of pedestrians they hit along the way. The elderly and children earn the highest points, of course. The government's racing wunderkind, Frankenstein (David Carradine), is a biomechanically reconstructed superstar in competition with the bitter Joe Viturbo (a young Sylvester Stallone). Other competitors include Calamity Jane (Bartel regular Mary Woronov of *Rock 'n Roll High School*) and Matilda the Hun (Roberta Collins of *Caged Heat*). However, some Americans, including Frankenstein's new navigator (Simone Griffith), have joined a growing resistance determined to bring down the death race and overthrow the President.

Of course, the main purpose of the film is to supply plenty of action, blood, and laughs, and it delivers these by the bucketful for a very speedy 79 minutes.

Through a legal snafu involving the hand-drawn title cards, *Death Race 2000* slipped into the world of quasi-public domain titles and even surfaced at the dawn of DVD in a passable print. However, this official release by Corman's New Concorde is by far the sharpest edition ever available. The full frame transfer was obviously intended to be shown matted off at 1.85:1 (there's a lot of headroom in most of the shots), and the colour and detail are terrific considering the film's utter lack of budget.

Trash movie fans will be delighted by a number of familiar faces, including Italian horror regular Harriet White (*The Horrible Dr. Hichcock*), *Cagney & Lacey*'s Martin Kove, Bartel himself as a doctor, and a quick bit by director John Landis as a mechanic. The exciting cinematography by Jonathan Demme's favourite cameraman, Tak Fujimoto, clearly indicates his growing talent, and Bartel's swift, efficient, and very funny direction foreshadows his later black comedy masterpiece, *Eating Raoul*. The DVD also includes the Leonard Maltin interview with Corman included on the

D

earlier VHS sell-through release, as well as trailers for this film as well as *Big Bad Mama, Eat My Dust,* and *Grand Theft Auto.*

DEATHSPORT

Colour, 1978, 89m. / Directed by Nicholas Niciphor and Allan Arkush / Starring David Carradine, Richard Lynch / New Concorde (US R1 NTSC)

Deathsport may not be the dumbest film ever produced by New World, but it certainly does try. A threadbare, queasy mishmash of *Death Race 2000, Zardoz,* and *Robot Monster,* this is the kind of poorly written junk in which characters refuse to speak with contractions ("I can not go there, and you must not tell him or it will be terrible"), while they have apparently managed to progress technologically while regressing fashion-wise to skimpy caveman gear and silver lame pants. '70s drive-in junkies and fans of controlled substances may find some entertainment value here, but all others should approach with caution.

A bunch of powerful leaders called "statesmen" make a habit of picking up athletic stragglers from the desert, then forcing them to participate in Deathsport, a vaguely defined activity in which deadly motorcycles chase people around in circles. One unlucky participant, Kaz Oshay (David Carradine), happens to be the son of some kind of psychic leader, and he manages to stage a couple of daring jailbreaks in between violent Deathsport matches. Tagging along with him is the lovely young Deneer (Claudia Jennings), while the diabolical and insane president (John Himes) sends the evil Ankar Moor (Richard Lynch), a codeless bounty hunter, after the duo. More mayhem ensues. Lasers fire all over the place. Motorcycles chase more people around. The audience suffers.

While all of Roger Corman's '70s productions were shot for very little money, *Deathsport* looks more ragtag than most. Without the cheeky, gory satire of *Death Race 2000,* it plays far too seriously, with all of its laughs coming from the stilted dialogue, bad stunts, and punishing visual decor. While the talented Allan Arkush (*Rock 'n' Roll High School*) started the production, chores were picked up by Nicholas Niciphor, using the pseudonym of Henry Suso. Possibly recognizing that he was saddled with a sinking ship, Roger Corman stepped in to complete the film himself, and the ragged production history immediately shows through.

Carradine looks distracted and humiliated throughout, though at least the target audience gets lots of gratuitous frontal nudity from Jennings (*Gator Bait*), the famous *Playboy* Playmate who died in a car wreck shortly after this film was completed. Her role doesn't call for much, but at least she's fun to watch and performs like Meryl Streep compared to some other Playmates-turned-actresses (e.g., Barbi Benton). Andy Stein's droning synth score slathers every scene in a dreary mishmash of electronic garble and doesn't even qualify as good '70s camp.

As lacking as the film itself may be, New Concorde' DVD looks surprisingly good. The transfer is most likely open matte, though the film was lensed so poorly it's hard to tell. The opening credits display some nasty print damage, but the rest is in excellent shape and features the same razor sharp clarity and colour definition of their *Death Race 2000* release. The packaging promises a theatrical trailer and a Roger Corman interview with Leonard Maltin, neither of which materializes on the actual disc. A shame, really, as it would be interesting to see Corman try to remember anything noteworthy at all about this movie. The Universal UK disc is identical to the US release.

DEATHSTALKER II: DUEL OF THE TITANS

Colour, 1987, 89m. / Directed by Jim Wynorski / Starring John Terlesky, Monique Gabrielle / New Concorde (US R1 NTSC)

Legendary warrior Deathstalker (Terlesky) meets waiflike prophetess Evie (Gabrielle) who is really a banished princess returning to her kingdom. The Sorcerer Jerak (La Zar) has replaced her with a wicked clone and Deathstalker vows to help Evie reclaim the throne. Cheap sets, cheap effects, cheap performances and even cheaper gags. There's no mistaking we're in Jim Wynorski country. Though less interesting of late, there was a period during the late 80s and early 90s when he was capable of transforming shoestring budgets into relatively splashy yarns. *Deathstalker II* is one of them, a fast-paced *Conan* rip-off steeped in lame wit. John Terlesky makes for an affable hero and there's an early turn by Monique Gabrielle (who went on to appear in a slew of Wynorski titles) who may have limited performance skills but is certainly easy on the eye. John "*Beyond the Valley of the Dolls*" La

Zar, however, is rather disappointing and makes for nowhere near as good a villain as one might expect. Wynorski loads his micro-epic with plenty of action, including a zombie attack, a sparring match in which pro-female wrestler Queen Kong gives Terlesky a pounding, encounters with tribes of Amazon warriors, and endless swordplay padding (much of it lifted from the original *Deathstalker*). Chuck Cirino's theme music becomes ever more annoying as it's trotted out in a variety of arrangements, though acknowledging its overuse there's a nice moment when Gabrielle turns to a minstrel strumming on his lute and screams "Don't you know another tune?!" Good humoured mediaeval fantasy adventure for none too demanding audiences, *Deathstalker II* even rewards the patient with a bunch of out-takes during the closing credits.

New Concorde continue their economic use of the term "digitally remastered"; if this Region 1 DVD of *Deathstalker II* has been so treated then I'm an Amazon princess. Print damage, traces of dirt in the frame and patches of excessive speckling are all in evidence throughout the 20-chapter feature. It's not so much that the film warrants an expensive clean-up job, but if you're going to claim it, do it! The incurably enthusiastic Wynorski holds court during an audio commentary which includes the welcome musings of actor Terlesky (who shares some comical anecdotes) and the rather pointless presence of actress Toni Naples (who does not). Wynorski is impeccably honest and seems to take pleasure in drawing attention to the picture's foibles. The print used for the DVD is uncut and he also points out scenes that are first-time viewing for American audiences. This "restored" material will already be familiar to those who've seen the British New Dimension cassette release, although that was missing some 20 seconds of footage, a few seconds for violence but most obviously a section of the scene in which Gabrielle is molested by rampant guards; all this material is intact on the DVD. Cast and crew biographies plus the film's trailer (along with those for *Deathstalker* and the similarly themed *Barbarian Queen* and *Barbarian Queen II*) comprise the only other bonus materials. - TG

THE DECAMERON

Colour, 1970, 107m. / Directed by Pier Paolo Pasolini / Image (US R1 NTSC), BFI (UK R2 PAL) / WS (1.85:1)

The first Pasolini film to hit the DVD market, *The Decameron*, is a bawdy adaptation of Boccaccio's famous moral tales. The US edition from Image

sports a great reproduction of the US poster art on the cover and is pretty much the same transfer as the long unavailable laserdisc release; both are now unavailable. The same transfer later appeared in the UK from the BFI, with optional English subtitles. The print is acceptable but a bit coarse; the sound is scratchy and easily betrays the film's impoverished budget. It's strange that a better print can't be found in Italy (and perhaps including a few of the notorious scenes that were excised prior to its general release); however, completists will be thankful this exists at all.

The film itself has aged rather well, combining the raucous humour and elegance that would mark the later *Canterbury Tales* and *Arabian Nights*, respectively. Sexual content is the lowest of this "Trilogy of Life," confined mainly to some relatively chaste frontal nudity and a few naughty jokes. Newcomers would do well to start here.

DEEP BLUE SEA

Colour, 1999, 105m. / Directed by Renny Harlin / Starring Thomas Jane, Saffron Burrows, LL Cool J / Warner (US R1 NTSC, UK R2 PAL) / WS (2.35.1) (16:9) / DD5.1

A rare summer popcorn movie that really delivers, *Deep Blue Sea* may not be high art but it's definitely a lot of fun. Deftly merging horror with his spectacular flair for action setpieces, director Renny Harlin has crafted a slick, suspenseful, and satisfying slice of hokum that also packs a strong wallop on DVD.

A wealthy investor (Samuel L. Jackson) flies out to a remote ocean-bound research facility, where his funds are supporting a potential cure for Alzheimer's derived from shark brain proteins. The lead scientists, Dr. Susan McAlestar (Saffron Burrows) and Jim Whitlock (Stellan Skarsgård), demonstrate the elaborate methods by which they have developed "super sharks" to provide the protein, thanks to the aid of paroled shark wrangler Carter (Thomas Jane). The experiments prove to be a success, but disaster strikes when one shark manages to escape and deliver a crushing blow to the facility, sending it rapidly sinking underwater. Together the three test sharks invade the watery lab and begin chowing down on the residents until only a handful of survivors remain, struggling to get back to the surface in one piece.

Though hardly an actor's showcase, *Deep Blue Sea* benefits from some strong bits of character acting, particularly Jackson's hilarious spin on the know-it-all millionaire (his "big scene" in the middle of the film is one of the year's best). Burrows' distracting resemblance to Harlin's wife, Geena Davis, may be a tad difficult to ignore, but she successfully walks the line between sympathetic researcher and callous God-player, while Jane goes through the action hero motions with great physicality. Trying to pick out who will die (and when) proves to be nearly impossible with this film, which throws some terrific unexpected curveballs throughout its running time and barely pauses for air. The animatronic and CGI shark effects range from outstanding to more than a tad hokey, but these beasts are quite fearsome and great fun to watch; the opening twist on Jaws proves that all of the filmmakers know their stuff and aren't afraid to play around with conventions.

As usual, Warner has delivered a fully loaded DVD with enough extras to easily kill off an entire evening. The film itself looks dazzling in an anamorphic transfer that beautifully showcases the title colour, while the explosive Dolby Digital 5.1 mix constantly pumps each speaker full of information from start to finish. This is simply a reference disc all the way and should please even the staunchest home theatre enthusiast.

Extras include several deleted scenes, all of which add tremendously to the depth of the characters. Skarsgård in particular lost some of his finest moments from the completed cut, and at least his decision to do this film in the first place now makes more sense. Bellows also becomes more finely shaded thanks to an early birthday speech that elaborates on her personal motives. The deleted footage appears to be lifted from a fuzzy work print and unfortunately is in very rough shape, but it's a welcome addition in any form. Also included is a by-the-numbers but welcome featurette on the shark special effects, some standard behind-the-scenes footage, production notes and photos, and the theatrical trailer. Oddly, the film's notorious original ending (in which one pivotal character's survival was nixed by bloodthirsty test audiences) is not included.

DEEP RED

Colour, 1975, 126m. / Directed by Dario Argento / Starring David Hemmings, Daria Nicolodi, Anchor Bay (US R1 NTSC) / WS (2.35:1) (16:9) / DD5.1, Platinum Media Corporation (UK R2 PAL) / WS (2.35:1)

The final word in stylish murder mysteries, Dario Argento's *Profondo Rosso (Deep Red)* broke out of the cinematic horror gutter and became a bona fide classic around the world. Apart from Mario Bava, no one had managed to create such an ingenious combination of visual style, devilish plotting, and a gripping soundtrack; indeed, this is not only perhaps Argento's greatest film, but also one of the highlights of Italian cinema as a whole.

At a parapsychology conference in Rome, German psychic Helga Ullman (Macha Meril) finds her public demonstration disrupted when she senses the presence of a psychotic killer in the audience. "You have killed, and you will kill again," she proclaims, pointing out into the audience. Soon after, she is brutally killed in her apartment, an act witnessed from afar by a British pianist, Marcus Daly (*Blow Up*'s David Hemmings). Spunky reporter Gianna Brezzi (Daria Nicolodi) realizes Marc's value as an eyewitness but cannot protect him as the killer continues cutting a bloody path right to Marc's door. Through some amateur detective work, our neurotic hero deduces the killings may be related to an abandoned, supposedly haunted old house on the outskirts of town.

Deep Red is one of those few, fortunate creations in which every element seems to fall perfectly into place. Argento at the height of his powers is enough of an asset, but the film also has engaging, first rate performances from Hemmings and Nicolodi, a groundbreaking and often imitated rock score by Goblin (go buy the CD!), brilliant mobile camerawork, and enough shocks to keep the most jaded horror fan on the edge of his seat. Many of the film's gory set pieces have been copied over the years, with John Carpenter starting the trend with *Halloween* (the sofa/knitting needle scene) and *Halloween II* (the scalding bathtub murder).

Trying to assemble a "complete" official version of *Deep Red* has been a daunting task over the years. Most English-speaking viewers first saw a drastically cut 98 minute version, sometimes under the title *The Hatchet Murders*. This edition turned up horribly panned and scanned on VHS from HBO, but soon after a letterboxed Japanese laserdisc turned up under the title *Suspiria 2* (though this film was made first!). The Japanese cut, running 105 minutes, contained several extra gory shots and a comic relief sequence with Hemmings and Nicolodi riding in the latter's junky car. Italian video offered an uncut, two hour version without subtitles; this version contains no extra gore or plot information, but a great deal of extra local colour and comic/romantic interplay.

Anchor Bay's DVD assembles all of the extant English language footage (and yes, the film does work better in English) with the extra Italian scenes for the closest thing to a definitive *Deep Red* we will probably ever see. The image quality here is an enormous improvement over all other existing versions, with a number of previously obscured details now perfectly visible. For example, the viewer can now see four separate, significant images of fluid seeping from character's mouths during violent moments, one of the many subtle recurring motifs throughout the film. A major clue early on in the film is also much easier to see, as is the revelation concerning that creepy fresco. While the film's closing credits were prepared both in Italian and English ("You have been watching *Deep Red*!"), the DVD includes a new variant with the English credits rolling over a still shot of Hemmings' face. It's a perplexing alteration. As for audio, the mono soundtrack has been remixed to 5.1, with admirable results. The music carries most of the load for the exterior sequences, with only a few sound effects making their way to the rear channels. A few sequences that would seem to call out for the 5.1 treatment, such as the gruesome garbage truck scene, remain almost entirely dead centre. The Italian dialogue is presented with subtitles during the additional scenes for the English soundtrack, while the Italian-only version may be played with subtitles throughout. The disc includes two theatrical trailers: one for the US and the original Italian (which includes some intriguing still photos). Argento appears for an interview segment in which he's joined by Goblin band members and co-writer Bernardo Zapponi.

The subsequent UK DVD release features only the Italian language version with English subtitles and, like the previous Redemption VHS, omits the shots of the pinned lizard and fighting dogs. On the other hand, it does contain the original end titles with Hemmings' face and hands continuing to move, and adds on the same extras found on Platinum's release of *The Bird with the Crystal Plumage*.

THE DEFILERS

B&W, 1965, 65m. / Directed by Lee Frost / Starring Byron Mabe, Jerome Eden

SCUM OF THE EARTH

B&W, 1963, 71m. / Directed by Herschell Gordon Lewis / Starring Thomas (Sweet) Wood, Allison Louise Downe
Image (US R0 NTSC)

Ah, the roughies of the 1960s. Filled with antisocial behaviour, sexual deviance, and mixed messages galore, these forays into the underbelly of the human psyche pushed the softcore "adults only" quickie into truly dangerous territory. Two of the finer examples of this grungy chapter in the grindhouse history have been archived together by Something Weird for another memorable DVD drive-in double feature, complete with trailers and loony goodies bound to make the discerning sleaze fan sit up and take notice.

The first film on the roster is *The Defilers*, which opens up with a dialogue-free sequence in which two spoiled louts (Byron Mabe and Jerome Eden) escort their two girlfriends for some nocturnal fun and frolicking on the beach. "There's only one thing that makes this worm-infested life worthwhile," Mabe philosophizes. "Kicks - kicks!" Apparently his slightly more conscientious friend agrees, and while Mabe isn't busy giving his girlfriend some suspiciously willing lashes with his belt, the two buddies decide to have some fun by kidnapping a sweet young thing (Mae Johnson) fresh off the bus in Los Angeles. After some terrific footage of Hollywood Boulevard in all its 1963 glory, Johnson settles into a hotel room and promptly winds up escorted to the Valley by our two anti-heroes, who drag her off to a basement and keep her prisoner as their own personal love slave. They continue their partying and country clubbing above ground, descending now and then for a little fun and games with their new captive. Of course, this not so idyllic existence can't go on forever, and it all ends on an appropriately hysterical and gory note.

"You're damaged merchandise, baby, and this is a fire sale!" snarls one of the pornographers in *Scum of the Earth*, a mostly blood-free collaboration by that unbeatable *Blood Feast* team, H.G. Lewis and David F. Friedman. Less grungy but far more hilarious than Friedman's *The Defilers*, this heavy breathing twist on Ed Wood's *The Sinister Urge* reveals what cheesecake photographers really do to snag pretty girls in front of their cameras. The latest victim is the impossibly naive Kim (Sherilyn Fenn look-alike Vickie Miles, aka Allison Louise Downe), who's trying to save up for college and agrees to earn a few extra bucks with the help of kindly photographer Harmon (Thomas Wood, aka Bill Kerwin, billed here as "Thomas Sweetwood" and sporting a bizarre skunk hairdo). Along with scuzzball Larry (Fuad Ramses himself, Mal

Arnold), Harmon talks his girls into compromising positions where they remove their tops and perform acts best left implied, some involving hairy and horny strong-arm Ajax (nudist camp vet Craig Maudslay, Jr.). Larry scoffs at the constant threats to go to the police: "You got nothin' on me, daddy-o; I'm a minor!" (never mind that he looks way past thirty). However, Kim proves to be more trouble than she's worth, particularly when the porn peddlers force her to do a "nature study" with equally tortured modelling veteran Sandy (Sandra Sinclair) and another girl, in which they're coerced into - horror of horrors - posing in their bathing suits while waving party hats and baseball bats. Murder and mayhem ensue, with a frantic oceanside finale containing a most unexpected colour homage to Alfred Hitchcock's *Spellbound*.

Though both films run barely over an hour each, they certainly pack in enough entertainment value to fuel a dozen Oliver Stone epics. Scum in particular weaves in and out of a surprising number of subplots and supporting characters (never mind the atrocious acting), while both features sport that wonderfully shadowy, atmospheric black and white photography that made these disreputable quickies look far more polished than their budgets would allow. Lewis fans in particular will enjoy seeing most of the "Blood Trilogy" regulars popping up and giving their usual stilted performances, laced with insane and endlessly quotable dialogue.

As per Something Weird's standards, these features look exceptionally good for their age and probably couldn't get much better. *The Defilers* is virtually in mint condition, with perfect contrast levels and nary a flaw to be found. *Scum* looks a bit more battered, though the image quality itself is quite good. Sound on both is consistently clear and satisfying, with every dramatic pause and whip of lashing leather perfectly intact.

Of course, the movies are just half the fun. Playing the drive-in option on the DVD assaults the viewer with hilarious promos, kicking off with Julie Andrews' unforgettable endorsement for the new MPAA ratings system and including such delicacies as a sex hygiene book pitch, concession stand shorts, a short subject entitled "Intimate Diary of Artists' Models" (reteaming the irrepressible Ajax and Sandy), and a snippet from Barry Mahon's *Naked Fury*. Then there are the trailers, which alternate between knee-slapping hyperbole and shocking lapses of taste. Reel and gasp to the delights of *Aroused!, Confessions of a Psycho Cat, Banned, Sex Killer, Sock It to Me Baby, The Curse of Her Flesh, The Ultimate Degenerate, The Pick-Up,* and best of all, the absolutely delicious *All Women*

Are Bad ("...and this is the film that proves it!"). There's even a particularly smutty Easter Egg hidden on the trailer menu screen, so brace yourself for hours and hours of good, scuzzy fun.

DELIVERANCE

Colour, 1972, 109m. / Directed by John Boorman / Starring John Voight, Burt Reynolds / Warner (US R1 NTSC, UK R2 PAL) / WS (2.35:1) / DD5.1

Both a riveting action film and an intelligent example of how to translate a novel onto the big screen, *Deliverance* remains the definitive study of wilderness terror. Director John Boorman, who seems to make a specialty of dabbling wildly in every genre he can find, seemed an unlikely choice given his track record of gritty Lee Marvin films (*Point Blank, Hell in the Pacific*), but this turned out to be his finest film of the 1970s.

Four Atlanta businessmen - Ed (Jon Voight), Lewis (Burt Reynolds), Bobby (Ned Beatty), and Drew (Ronny Cox) - decide to spend the weekend in the North Georgia mountains shooting the rapids along the (fictitious) Cahulawassee River. They first encounter some creepy inbred rednecks and attempt to bond through a little banjo duel, and then head off in their raft for some carefree excitement. They get a little more than they bargained for, however, when two vicious locals ambush them in the woods and, the most notorious sequence, threaten Ed and Bobby's manhood. The mountain men and the city folk wind up in a harrowing battle for survival, with Ed finding himself resorting to his most savage instincts in order to survive.

The intensely descriptive novel by poet James Dickey has long been a staple of Southern reading courses, even in high school (believe it or not), and while Boorman and Dickey experienced quite a few squabbles during the shooting, the results could not have been better. Dickey's eloquent prose transforms into beautifully shot, realistic white water sequences and gut-wrenching suspense passages; likewise, the actors are all at the top of their form, with Reynolds finally proving he had more going on in his head than a simple wiseguy grin. Voight in particular had a lot to live up to following *Midnight Cowboy*, and his performance here makes his inferior assignments afterwards all the more regrettable. Interestingly, aside from occasional passages of banjo music and some ambient electronic gurgling, the film is virtually devoid of music, lending it a harshness and immediacy never duplicated. Many films attempted to duplicate this film's success, and its influence can be found all the way from *Southern Comfort* to *The Blair Witch Project*. This is the film that makes anyone think twice before wandering off in the woods.

Warner's Region 1 DVD looks similar to their earlier letterboxed laserdisc release, albeit with improved resolution thanks to a refurbished anamorphic transfer. Though a cropped edition is included for those who only want half of the action, the scope presentation is really the only option given cinematographer Zsigmond's penchant for using the entire frame and deftly operating a mobile camera during the rafting and chase scenes. Though the film still has a few remnants of that dull early '70s film look thanks to some apparently inferior film stock and the green and brown colour schemes, it's hard to imagine this looking much better.

The soundtrack has been given a complete 5.1 audio remix, and as with most Warner releases, the results are extremely impressive. Though this isn't an audio powerhouse in the traditional sense, the channel separation encompasses everything from the terrifying rush of river water to the faint ambient sounds of forest wildlife. The DVD also includes the memorable original trailer and, even better, a fascinating ten minute educational documentary produced during the shooting about the relationship between Boorman and Dickey. Only complaint: a commentary track by Boorman would have been extremely welcome (imagine the stories he could tell!). The Region 2 disc is missing even these sparse extras.

DELLAMORTE DELLAMORE

Colour, 1994, 105m. / Directed by Michele Soavi / Starring Rupert Everett / Medusa (Italy R2 PAL) / WS (1.85:1) (16:9), Laser Paradise (Germany R0 PAL) / WS (1.85:1) / DD2.0

That rarest of beasts, a '90s Italian horror film that actually received a (belated) theatrical release in America, *Dellamorte Dellamore* (literally *Of Love, Of Death*) had all the makings of a major cult item but instead has been quietly startling viewers on art film cable channels under the clumsy title of *Cemetery Man*. Director Michele Soavi (*Stage Fright, The Sect*) obviously continued to hone his craft as a filmmaker with each project, thanks in no small part to his work with Terry Gilliam on *The Adventures of Baron Munchausen*;

hopefully he will eventually come back out from his self-imposed retirement and continue to amaze us all.

The twisty narrative, lifted from a novel by *Dylan Dog*'s Tiziano Sclavi, concerns a sheltered cemetery keeper, Francesco Dellamorte (Rupert Everett), who guards the gothic resting place for the dead in the small town of Buffalora. Accompanied only by his monosyllabic, mentally deficient helper, Gnaghi (the amazing François Hadji-Lazaro), our hero must deal with the living dead, who rise from their graves within seven days after being buried, by shooting them in the head. A beautiful and mysterious young widow (Anna Falchi) comes to visit one day, and afterwards Francesco's life is never the same.

As philosophically rich and sensually aware as it is filled with zombie-blasting mayhem, *Dellamorte Dellamore* is truly unlike any other film in European cinema. Everett delivers one of his best, non-campy performances; his morose, sarcastic, yet oddly romantic hero is truly a representative figure of our "jaded" modern times, while the stunning Falchi deservedly earned a cult following for her memorable three (!) roles. Thanks to his apprenticeship with the likes of Dario Argento and Joe D'Amato, Soavi's gift for surreal imagery reaches its apex here; the first twenty minutes alone is a masterpiece of visual storytelling, and the jarring, haunting final scene cannot be easily forgotten. Composer Manuel De Sica (*The Garden of the Finzi Continis*) contributes an atypical electronic score that integrates perfectly within the film's bizarre, dreamlike texture. Not a film for all tastes, to be sure, but it's easily the most significant Italian horror title of the past decade.

The most widely seen version of this film, the *Cemetery Man* US videotape and laserdisc transfer released by Fox, is a nearly unwatchable mess, badly cropped on all sides of the screen and annoyingly fuzzy, to boot. The previous Japanese laserdisc was letterboxed more accurately and sported a nice surround track but suffered from pasty, washed out flesh tones. Both of these were supplanted by Laser Paradise's "Red Edition" of *Dellamorte Dellamore*, which more closely approximates the theatrical experience. More information is visible on all sides of the image even compared to the letterboxed Japanese disc, and the flesh tones are much richer and more dimensional. The audio is about the same, with the music in particular often overpowering the rear and front speakers. The disc also includes an amusing German trailer as well as an assortment of trailers and clips for titles like *Stage Fright, Brain Dead*, and *Army of Darkness*.

DEMENTIA

B&W, 1953, 54m. / Directed by John J. Parker / Starring Adrienne Barrett, Bruno Ve Sota / Kino (US R1 NTSC)

Standing with *A Bucket of Blood* as a rare successful example of "beat" horror, *Dementia* earned its place in most history books as the movie those teenagers are watching during the theatre sequence of *The Blob*. More seasoned horror buffs came to know it primarily through word of mouth and murky looking bootleg tapes as an avant garde curio, which provoked the New York censors into fits. More bizarrely, it was slightly trimmed down, slathered in leering ooga-booga narration by Ed McMahon (yes, that Ed McMahon), and retitled *Daughter of Horror*, where it terrorized a few unsuspecting drive-ins, caused a few sleepless nights, and vanished off into the ether. Against all odds, Kino has resurrected *Dementia* in both its original form and its better known *Daughter of Horror* variant, and surprisingly enough, the results exceed one's expectations.

Devoid of dialogue, our expressionistic tale begins in a fleabag hotel room where the Gamine (Adrienne Barrett) tosses and turns in a feverish delirium. Decked out in black (plus a shiny medallion) and carrying a switchblade knife, she emerges into the dangerous city streets where the past and present intermingle. Many of the citizens lack faces, and one particularly spooky man escorts her to the cemetery where she relives a traumatic incident involving parental molestation and murder. She then winds up in the clutches of the Rich Man (Bruno Ve Sota), who drags her around to swanky nightspots and indulges in one of the more memorable late night meals in celluloid history. A scuffle ensures which finds our confused heroine running for her life, performed an impromptu amputation (in full public view), jamming out with Shorty Rogers and His Giants at a jazz club, and eventually spiralling into hysteria. Or does she...?

The difference between the two versions of *Dementia* on this DVD lies primarily in the narration, which turns a free form essay in madness into a campy, trashy delight in the vein of Ed Wood circa *Glen or Glenda?*, albeit with slick cinematography. The original is no laughing matter, however, and somehow manages to pull off that tricky balancing act between art and sleaze; in fact, from the similar starfield opening to the German Expressionist lighting and sets, this would make a dandy double feature with *The Night of the Hunter*.

Special kudos should also go to the elaborate musical team, consisting of a non-stop score by George Antheil, musical direction by the great and sorely missed Ernest Gold, and eerie abstract vocals by Marni Nixon, who dubbed some of the most high profile female actresses in '50s musicals.

For a film of its vintage, *Dementia* has survived surprisingly well. Apart from a few speckles and blemishes, the original version looks marvellous, with beautiful dark shadows and pure, clean grey scales. The notes on the box explain this was derived from the original negative, while *Daughter of Horror* was lifted from a rather good 35mm film print. The extras answer virtually any questions one could have about the film, thanks mainly to a lengthy and fascinating essay entitled "Dementia: A Case Study," delineating the violent censor battles and bizarre distribution back story. Other goodies include a *Daughter of Horror* trailer, a hilarious pressbook (check out those promotional suggestions), and a gallery of photographs. Obviously you should know what you're getting into before showing this to any family and friends, but *Dementia* is one wild ride worth taking.

DEMENTIA-13

B&W, 1963, 75m. / Directed by Francis Ford Coppola / Starring William Campbell, Luana Anders / Troma (US R1 NTSC) / WS (1.50:1), Koch, Madacy, United American (US R0 NTSC)

Long before making a splash with *The Godfather*, Francis Ford Coppola was part of the stable on up and coming talent supervised by Roger Corman for American International Pictures during the 1960s. Though he started out with innocuous nudies like *The Bellboy and the Playgirls*, Coppola soon proved his worth against seemingly impossible odds with *Dementia 13*, one of the most memorable *Psycho* knockoffs. With the aid of clever casting, imaginative photography, and some genuine seat-rattling shocks, this zero budget quickie became a late night TV favourite and has haunted viewers for nearly four decades.

During a nocturnal rowboat trip, crafty Louise Haloran (Corman favourite Luana Anders) is appalled when her manipulative husband, John, drops dead from a heart attack. Since Louise hasn't been written into John's lucrative family will, she dumps his body over the side (along with his gurgling transistor radio) and types out a note alerting John's mother that she will be coming over to the family estate in Ireland for a little visit. The Haloran estate welcomes Louise with open arms, particularly when she poses as a psychic with an ability to contact the spirit of John's long dead sister, Kathleen. The family matriarch (Ethne Dunn) proves the most susceptible to Louise's manipulations, but John's brothers, Richard (William Campbell) and Billy (Bart Patton), may not be so easily swayed. Then there are the other parties involved, such as the family doctor, Justin Caleb (the always fascinating Patrick Magee), and a weird groundsman with a penchant for hunting at night. Suddenly shocking axe murders begin to proliferate at Castle Haloran, and some dark, gruesome family secrets are soon revealed.

Simply put, *Dementia 13* is a horror film that either grabs you right away or doesn't. The rich, atmospheric opening sequence (in which both characters seem to be floating in a black void) is just the first of many memorable sequences; thanks to Coppola's visual skill, even a simple visit to a child's bedroom at night becomes a visual tapestry of macabre faces and menacing shadows. The film's real *tour de force* (and most direct borrowing from *Psycho*) occurs a third into the film; this lyrical, horrific set piece is still one of Coppola's finest hours but can't really be discussed further without destroying the story. On the other hand, the killer's identity isn't really much of a stunner, but the plot still contains enough novel twists and turns with each character to keep the viewer riveted to the screen. Kudos as well to composer Ronald Stein (*The Haunted Palace*), who produced what is arguably his finest work ever with a chilling combination of harpsichord, strings, and percussion.

Due to a legal snafu with the opening animated title card, *Dementia 13* wound up falling into the public domain and has suffered from some of the worst transfers in home video history. The delicate black and white photography has more often looked like a blurry mess on VHS, so it was with great anticipation that Roan announced a widescreen laserdisc release back in the '90s. Their efforts should be evaluated with a little historical perspective; while Corman undoubtedly must possess superior print material somewhere in his vaults, the Roan edition, while undeniably flawed, was at least a step up from any other option out there at the time. Distracting print damage is evident throughout, the image is smudgier than titles made decades before it, and God only knows what the original aspect ratio is supposed to be (the disc claims to be 1.66:1 but measures out closer to 1.50:1). The mono audio is a little cleaner than the tape counterparts, but some of the dialogue is still muddier than it should be. More immediately pleasing are the extras, including the theatrical trailer (containing glimpses of Monte Hellman's 'hypnotist' prologue for the film, which is missing from virtually all currently circulating prints), a feature audio commentary from Campbell detailing the location shooting and various people involved with the production, and a digital counterpart to the "D-13" test (a psych evaluation from the theatrical run) originally reproduced as an insert with the laserdisc.

DEMONIA

Colour, 1988, 84m. / Directed by Lucio Fulci / Starring Brett Halsey, Meg Register / Media Blasters (US R1 NTSC), Astro (Germany R2 PAL) / WS (1.66:1)

An ambitious but ultimately failed attempt to recapture the mood of Lucio Fulci's gore-drenched gothic masterpieces from the 1980s, *Demonia* is arguably the most frustrating of the director's attempts to recharge the Italian horror industry. Less demanding than *A Cat in the Brain* and certainly more compelling than *Zombi 3,* this is an odd footnote in its creator's career but a fairly worthwhile outing for less discriminating fans of onscreen bloodshed.

Our supernatural yarn begins appropriately with an extended historical flashback in which a group of Sicilian nuns winds up crucified and burned by locals in a cave underneath their convent. The ordeal is relived as a dream by Liza (Meg Register), an archaeologist who goes on a dig in the same area with Professor Evans (Brett Halsey). Liza discovers the walled-in skeletal remains of the nuns, which leads to a series of inexplicable and gruesome deaths. A fellow researcher winds up harpooned and decapitated, a spike trap wipes out a pair of Irish diggers, and Liza is pulled deeper into a centuries old mystery, which has returned to take its toll on the present.

The structure of *Demonia* closely follows the models of such favourites as *The Beyond* and *City of the Living Dead*, but the sense of irrationality and foreboding that characterized those masterpieces is awkwardly fumbled here. The lacklustre performances, flat cinematography, and watery electronic music sap away most of the potential suspense, but on the positive side, Fulci does cut loose with a few anarchic gore scenes to goose viewers awake. In the most memorable (and puzzling) of these, one character is wishboned in half while tied between two trees, a sequence done earlier (and more convincingly) in Ruggero Deodato's *Cut and Run.*

The most extended death finds a poor soul impaled through the neck with a meat hook and his tongue nailed to a table for good measure, but the effects keep it from reaching the delirious heights reached by the likes of FX maestro Gianetto de Rossi. Oddly, the most shocking and memorable moments comes during a mid-film flashback, in which a simple knife to the throat during the throes of lovemaking is filmed in a very unexpected fashion. Finally, the puzzling finale seems to follow *City*'s example but comes off even more confusing in the process.

Media Blasters, a company best known for its Japanese anime and fantasy film releases, made a solid attempt at entering the Eurohorror DVD sweepstakes with the first North American video release of *Demonia*. The DVD finally offers fans the chance to appraise the film outside of a fuzzy, third generation VHS bootleg, and overall it's hard to imagine the film looking much better. Apart from some grain and flickering dirt during the opening sequence and a few mist-laden moments in the crypt, the transfer and presentation is fine. Considering the budget, the film may have been shot in mono originally (though the lack of official video releases makes this hard to verify); assuming it was originally mixed in single channel sound, the audio is fine apart from the painful dubbing.

The disc comes with as many extras as one could expect for an essentially unreleased film. "Fulci Lives!" is a four minute camcorder documentation of the director at work on the tree scene, as he stands around answering questions about his recent work. Interestingly, he pegs *Aenigma, House of Clocks*, and *Sweet House of Horrors* as his favourites. A print interview offers a chat with Brett Halsey (who appeared in several other Fulci films during this period, most significantly *The Devil's Honey*), and the disc is rounded out with a Fulci biography and, printed on the back of the chapter listing, a Fulci filmography.

THE DEMONIACS

Colour, 1973, 95m. / Directed by Jean Rollin / Starring Joelle Coeur, Lieva Lone / Image (US R0 NTSC) / WS (1.66:1)

Director Rollin's first serious attempt to venture outside the parameters of his famous erotic vampire tableaux, *The Demoniacs (Les demoniaques)* finds him working with a stronger plot and assortment of characters than usual. In the memorable opening, a quartet of pirates led by the evil, hysterical Tina lure a ship onto the rocks and molest two young girls who managed to flee from the wreckage. The young blonde girls are left for dead, but during a heavy night at the local tavern, one of the pirates experiences *Macbeth*-style visions of the beautiful victims, their hands and eyes stigmatized with blood. He flees to Tina, who leads the wreckers back to the scene of their crime. The two girls are still there, barely alive, and escape to the haunted ruins of a church where a powerful spirit resides inside a cell. After meeting the spirit's handmaiden (a woman dressed as a clown, which makes no sense but looks very striking), the girls release him and engage in some sins of the flesh. In gratitude, the spirit grants them supernatural powers which, until dawn, will allow them to seek retribution against their attackers. The girls embark on their tragic quest, which culminates in a haunting and strangely poignant beach finale.

Rarely seen in English but briefly released in a shortened version by Something Weird Video as *Curse of the Living Dead*, *Demoniaques* found most of its audience through blurry, bootleg SECAM-converted tapes. To say the least, the new edition from Image and Redemption is a complete revelation. The source materials used here are absolutely immaculate, without any noticeable dirt or print damage whatsoever, and the colour and detail quality are never less than striking. The mild 1.66:1 framing exposes all available picture information and looks ideally placed.

Like all of Rollin's films, the formal visual design plays an important role, and here he plays with the conventions of serials and pirate dramas (Fritz Lang's *Moonfleet* is an acknowledged influence, but traces of Jamaica Inn show up as well). The delightful opening features a voiceover introducing the characters over superimposed shots of the actors, a device indicating that Rollin will be venturing into slightly different territory. However, the expected nudity, violence, and bizarre imagery are still in rich supply, with Rollin crafting some highly memorable sequences thanks to the eerie ruins and the strange beach scenery, punctured with the torn and ragged wooden remains of crashed ships. The performers are also allowed opportunities to exhibit more personality than usual, with the villains making a memorable bunch, especially Tina's scene-stealing "kill them!" rants.

Rollin's trademark visual fetish motifs are all present, including the mute blonde twins who were later turned up in various performer guises in *Requiem for a Vampire, Phantasmes*, and *Two Orphan Vampires*. A few moments are slightly spoiled by the rushed production, such as one strangely edited death in which a character's throat is slashed by falling on a ridiculously huge liquor bottle, but for the most part, this is a solid introduction to Rollin's style and a satisfying demonstration of his strengths as a director. The optional subtitles are always legible and well chosen, though for some reason the use of "merde" receives some amusing euphemisms (e.g., "bloody hell!"). The original French trailer is also included.

DESECRATION

Colour, 1999, 87m. / Directed by Dante Tomaselli / Starring Irma St. Paule, Christie Sanford / Image (US R0 NTSC) / WS (1.85:1) / DD2.0

Appropriately, the New Jersey horror film *Desecration* opens with a prominent then studio director Alfred Sole, whose *Alice, Sweet Alice* offers a similar horrific study of Catholic iconography. In this case, however, first time helmer Dante Tomaselli offers an overtly supernatural fever dream, consisting of one delirious set piece after another with only the vaguest shred of a narrative.

Haunted by the mysterious death of his mother years earlier and his rigid education at a Catholic school, young Bobby (Danny Lopes) already leads a decidedly abnormal existence. One day he accidentally kills one of the nuns by flying a model plane into her head (don't ask), an event which unleashes all kinds of weird, demonic forces around him. A fellow student plunges into a sylvan hole, which promptly vanishes, nuns' faces contort into hideous deformed visions of evil, and mom herself pops up to invite poor Bobby straight to Hell.

Filled with an obvious love of avant garde film ranging from David Lynch (an *Eraserhead*-inspired dream sequence) to Maya Deren (*Meshes of the Afternoon*), Tomaselli's pet project began life as a short film, part of which is included on the DVD. Many of his horrific interludes pack a powerful surrealist punch, such as the nightmarish, Rollin-inspired images of nuns screaming and morphing behind a wrought iron gate. The pace lags somewhat during protracted dialogue scenes with Bobby's elderly guardian (Irma St. Paule), but the film also wrings chills from unexpected sources, such as a seemingly kindly priest flashing a terrifying, malefic smile while standing behind Bobby's back.

Though filmed on a low budget and sporting flat, cleanly lit visuals without too much flash or depth, *Desecration* has been given an admirable DVD transfer and offers a generally satisfying viewing experience. The 1.85:1 framing is flattering, though a few tightly composed shots indicate some extra visual space may be obscured (1.66:1 might be more accurate). The straight Dolby Surround track contributes a great deal to the film's creepy, often subliminal directorial tricks, so multi-channel viewing is highly advised to savour the strange ambient noises flooding through even the most perfunctory scenes.

DESTINATION MOON

Colour, 1950, 92m. / Directed by Irving Pichel / Starring John Archer, Warner Anderson / Image (US R0 NTSC)

Neither as well known nor revered as high pedigree science fiction classics like *War of the Worlds*, *Destination Moon* will always have a place in the history books as the one that started it all. Based on the novel *Rocketship Galileo* by the legendary Robert A. Heinlein (who co-wrote the screenplay), this film captured the imaginations of many impressionable kids during its initial run and became even more famous when it later, eerily paralleled the actual first moon landing shown on worldwide television.

Forced into a clandestine plan to complete a rocketship for the first exploration of the moon, three men - a scientist (Warner Anderson), an aircraft industrialist (John Archer), and a space expert (Tom Powers) - arrange to carry out their dream. A number of obstacles arise along the way, but that's nothing compared to the challenges they face in the cold recesses of space, where the astronauts must face a difficult and life-altering decision in order to reach home. Alternately fascinating, suspenseful, and dated, *Destination Moon* is more than a simple sci-fi artefact of its era. Legendary sci-fi and fantasy producer George Pal first made a name for himself with this title, arguably the most grounded entry in his string of successful entries in fantastic cinema. Not surprisingly, the acting is nothing special but gets the job done, while the special effects pleasingly look like they could have jumped right off the cover of a space age lounge album.

Appropriately, the first major space age sci-fi film in America was lensed in eye-popping Technicolor, and the DVD presentation offers the best opportunity to savour its unique charms. Luminous shades of red and blue often suffuse the screen, and the clarity of the image and print quality are well above the dupey video copies circulating for years. As with many '50s titles, the flesh tones have gone a little orange in some scenes, but this problem is easily overlooked considering the overall quality of the presentation. The mono audio fares even better, with none of the usual distortion and hiss associated with films of this vintage. The theatrical trailer is also included.

THE DEVIL RIDES OUT

Colour, 1968, 96m. / Directed by Terence Fisher / Starring Christopher Lee, Charles Gray / Anchor Bay (US R1 NTSC) / WS (1.78:1) (16:9) / DD5.1

The Devil Rides Out represents everything good about Hammer Films in its heyday. Long before the subject of Satanism became didactic, one-sided fodder after the success of *Rosemary's Baby* and *The Exorcist*, this excellent chiller offered a truly compelling and intelligent conflict between the forces of light and darkness in which the viewer cannot help but side completely with the former.

Wisely cast against type, Christopher Lee has one of his finest roles as the Duc de Richleau, an urbane gentleman whose knowledge of the black arts comes in handy when his good friend Simon (Patrick Mower) falls under the hypnotic influence of diabolical priest Mocata (Charles Gray). Simon fails to show up for a reunion with Richleau and another friend, Rex (Leon Greene), so the two barge into his home and ruin plans for a black mass by dragging Simon off with them. Unfortunately Simon escapes, and our heroes must resort to tracking down a mysterious and beautiful woman, Tanith (Nike Arrighi), who is destined to join Simon at an upcoming baptism into Satan's service. Richleau and Rex disrupt a woodland devilish orgy attended by the Goat of Mendes, one of the devil's incarnations, and spirit away Simon and Tanith to a remote country home. Naturally Mocata comes a-calling and, when turned away by the lady of the house, promises to send his forces to gather those who have been promised to him...

Obviously *The Devil Rides Out* is primarily Lee's show, and he's exactly the man anyone would want on their side in a battle against evil. However, future James Bond bad guy (and Time Warper) Charles Gray is also outstanding as Mocata, a fearsome and crafty adversary who avoids putting himself in any physical danger. He will be missed. Special notice should also be given to Sarah Lawson,

who twists the potentially drab character of a protective upscale mother into a strong, fascinating woman perfectly capable of dealing with monstrous forces invading her home. Credentials behind the scenes are equally up to par, with the legendary Richard Matheson (*I Am Legend*) skilfully adapting Dennis Wheatley's occult novel (while wisely retaining the 1930s setting) and director Terence Fisher obviously using all of his formidable directorial skills to deliver some of horror's best setpieces. The suspenseful and frightening passage in which our heroes are confined within a holy circle and assaulted by demonic forces is as good as '60s horror gets.

Anchor Bay's DVD was a long time coming, several years after Elite's briefly available laserdisc edition. The anamorphically enhanced image is excellent, much cleaner and more colourful than the drab TV prints fans had to endure for decades. James Bernard's powerhouse music score sounds terrific in the disc's 5.1 audio mix, which often threatens to overpower the comparatively quiet dialogue in the centre speaker. Ambient directional effects are sparingly used but effective, particularly the unforgettable Angel of Death scene. Lee and Lawson also appear for an interesting commentary track; it's obvious they hold a great deal of affection and admiration for the film, and their warm recollections are a welcome addition to anyone's respect for their accomplishments. Also included are the original UK and US theatrical trailers, which are identical except for the title change. In America the film was titled *The Devil's Bride*, with the title card stupidly altered to feature a satanic goat image over a Star of David! The British version on this disc also contains some extra bloodletting during a goat sacrifice and some extremely mild swearing. Still, it's amazing this was actually given a G rating back in '68. Another episode of *World of Hammer* is included as well, this time focusing on the studio's general output as narrated by Oliver Reed as usual.

THE DEVIL'S NIGHTMARE

Colour, 1971, 93m. / Directed by Jean Brismee / Starring Erika Blanc, Jean Servais / Image (US R1 NTSC), Salvation (UK R0 PAL) / WS (1.66:1)

The Belgian/Italian Gothic gem, *The Devil's Nightmare*, has been circulating on video under so many titles and variant cuts that it would be impossible to list them all. The primary reason for the film's cult rests with the presence of sultry Erika Blanc, a drop-dead gorgeous '60's and '70's scream queen who really outdoes herself here as a scantily clad succubus.

The wacko plot finds her decimating seven tourists (partially representatives of the seven deadly sins, which has led some folks to call this a precursor to David Fincher's *Se7en*!). The murders themselves are pretty weak tea, with the bloodshed more in line with those old dark castle chillers like *Castle of Terror*, so the fun really lies in the film's giddy disregard for restraint and logic. Characters ogle each other, their food, money, and the castle setting with wild abandon, as the film's nominal hero, a priest, looks on oh so solemnly. Daniel Emilfork, one of Fellini's trademark oddball actors, makes an appearance as a sinister coachman, and Alessandro Alessandroni virtually steals the film with his insane, electric-guitar-tinged score.

The print quality (pleasingly letterboxed at about 1.66:1) is by far the best we'll see anytime soon; though some signs of wear show up during the main titles and around the reel changes, the picture quality and clarity are very satisfying. Furthermore, this print contains a hysterically prolonged, heated lesbian sequence that stops the film in its tracks early on. Though the packaging fails to note it, the DVD (and the earlier laser release) contains the original Italian soundtrack on the second audio channel. It's great fun, as this version contains a far more pronounced music score and some odd variations in the dubbing of dialogue. The film is followed by a brief US theatrical trailer. The UK Redemption disc contains only the English language dialogue track but does throw in a gallery of twenty stills, ten posters, and five video covers, and sports a somewhat cleaner and more stable transfer.

THE DEVIL'S RAIN

Colour, 1975, 85m. / Directed by Robert Fuest / Starring Ernest Borgnine, William Shatner / VCI (US R1 NTSC) / WS (2.35:1)

 Ah, the wonders of movie salesmanship. Thanks to a completely wacko cast and an ending touted in the ads as "absolutely the most horrifying ending of any motion picture ever" (altered on the video to "amazing" instead of "horrifying"), *The Devil's Rain* became a familiar staple in US drive-ins and on late-night TV. Not surprisingly, a bit part by John Travolta (as "Danny") before he became the world's most famous Sweathog helped this one milk out even

more bucks through endless reissues, and on some venues he even supposedly got top billing (a la Brooke Shields in *Alice, Sweet Alice*). Even today, many horror fans still feel nostalgic about this shaggy little beast of a film, which marked a rare American outing for British director Robert Fuest (best known for the TV series *The Avengers* and the *Dr. Phibes* films with Vincent Price).

The surreal, often disjointed plot follows a group of Satanists holed out in rural America. While their powers have reached unprecedented heights wherein they can actually destroy their victims through the weather (thus the title), their leader, a reincarnating "minister of Satan" named Jonathan Corbis (Ernest Borgnine), is not satisfied. He intends to deliver a number of souls (kept locked in a glass container) promised to Satan, inscribed by blood in a book which was taken from the cult three hundred years ago and secreted away by a treacherous member. The cult's terrorizing of the traitor's descendants, the Prestons (an unlikely country family consisting of Ida Lupino, William Shatner), comes to a head when Lupino is converted into an eyeless minion of Satan and Shatner winds up dragged into the cult's chapel for unspeakable rituals. Luckily, Shatner's younger brother, Tom (Skerritt, that is, looking like he did a little too much partying on the set), comes to the rescue after Tom's wife, Julie (Joan Prather), uses her convenient ESP abilities to hone in on the diabolical menace. Corbis' evil ultimately pays its price in the infamous, lengthy finale, which features most of the cult members reduced to mounds of slimy goo. (not much of a plot spoiler since this scene was splashed all over the posters and video art.)

Sporting amusingly weird and colourful special effects, *The Devil's Rain* isn't exactly an epic work of pioneering horror, but it does kill an hour and a half rather nicely. Unintentional chuckles abound; watch for Travolta yelping "Blasphemer! Blasphemer!" and having his face dribble off - does the Church of Scientology know about this one? - and Borgnine even metamorphoses into a goofy-looking ram (complete with horns). Even the founder of the Church of Satan and author of *The Satanic Bible*, Anton LaVey, puts in an appearance as a cultist and served as a consultant on the film (a service he also performed on *The Car*, another guilty favourite). Wild stuff, to be sure, and not unlike another fun '70s rural horror vehicle with Shatner, *Kingdom of the Spiders*; oddly, both films boast extremely horrific imagery that managed to squeak by with PG ratings. Ah, the good old days.

VCI's DVD looks about the same as their scarce letterboxed laserdisc released through Image several years ago, albeit a little more digitally tweaked. The print is in very good condition, and while the film itself will always be hampered by its low budget and scrappy production shooting, this actually looks much better than its appearances through drive-ins and late night TV. The evocative scope photography (in Todd-AO - how often do you see that on a horror movie?) makes excellent use of shadows and weird spatial compositions, though most general circulating prints were chopped off to 1.85:1. The DVD presents the full image, thankfully, with some appropriately bright, gaudy colours throughout, and includes a brief photo gallery and a tacky US reissue trailer that spoils some of the ending's highlights. For some reason, the scene selection menu doesn't exist.

DIAMONDS ARE FOREVER

Colour, 1971, 125 m. / Directed by Guy Hamilton / Starring Sean Connery, Jill St. John / MGM / WS (2.35:1) (16:9)

South Africa's diamond industry is taking a pounding through an excess of smuggling activity. James Bond (Connery) poses as a two-bit runner to infiltrate the coalition believed to be responsible, which leads him into a SPECTRE scheme to blackmail the world with the threat of decimation from an orbiting satellite armed with a powerful laser beam.

As the first Bond I saw way back in '72, I've a soft spot for *Diamonds Are Forever*, though it's far from the best. After a one-film hiatus, Connery returns to 007 pastures and kicks off the action by avenging the death of Mrs. Bond at the climax of OHMSS. Yet the film fails to capture the hard-hitting essence of some of his earlier appearances. The plot turns become increasingly outlandish as Bond jets from Amsterdam to Las Vegas to a not particularly vigorous showdown on a oil rig off the California coast. Jill St. John is insipid as Tiffany Case, Charles Gray is far too gentlemanly as Blofeld (particularly in the wake of Telly Savalas's superior crack at the part in the previous film), and having two homosexual hitmen (Putter Smith and Bruce Glover) might have been daringly innovative for the time, but their camp behaviour gives rise less to a sense of danger than it does laughs. Buxom Lana Wood as the insouciant Plenty O'Toole ("Named after your father, perhaps" quips Bond) is a standout, though misjudged cutting renders her demise all but unintelligible. In fact, the plot never manages to surmount several illogicalities cultivated by irrational editing

decisions. Regardless of this, there's a flashy car chase through Vegas, a super let's-see-you-get-out-of-that pulse-racer with Bond (trapped in a coffin) being cremated, a fun passage where our man sabotages a practice moonwalk and makes off in a moon buggy across the Nevada desert, a trip through an oil pipeline on a welding machine (surpassed in terms of excitement when the concept was revived for *The World Is Not Enough*) and a nice bit of business with Bond mountaineering up to the inaccessible penthouse suite of a Vegas hotel.

MGM's special edition DVD does *Diamonds Are Forever* proud. Having worked its way through various video and laserdisc incarnations, the 32-chapter encoded letterbox format movie here looks as perfect as it's ever likely to, hopefully rendering future re-purchase unlikely. It's also nice to note that the Maurice Binder credits sequence on the print utilised is the saucier of two existing versions, briefly revealing parts of the female anatomy obscured in an alternative set prepared for less tolerant territories (which, back in the early 70s, included the UK). A feature-length commentary from director Guy Hamilton and members of the crew and cast is accessible. The half-hour retrospective involves many of the film's participants and includes footage deleted from the release print of the movie. A 45-minute documentary overviews the life of famed producer Albert R. Broccoli. There's also a pair of trailers, five TV spots and three radio spots. Four deleted scenes round out the package, among them a Sammy Davis Jr. cameo in the Vegas casino and a couple of Plenty O'Toole sequences, the inclusion of at least one of which would have clarified the logic behind her murder. The sound is in English only, with a choice of French or Spanish subtitling - TG

DIARY OF A CHAMBERMAID

B&W, 1964, 98m. / Directed by Luis Buñuel / Starring Jeanne Moreau, Michel Piccoli / Criterion (US R1 NTSC) / WS (2.35:1) (16:9)

As he comfortably settled into middle age, director Luis Buñuel found himself moving deftly from one cinematic phase to another, slipping his anarchic surrealist touches into stories the general public could accept and enjoy. Though not as overtly scandalous as such classics as *Belle de Jour*, *Diary of a Chambermaid* finds the master ripping apart bourgeois conventions with unexpected humour and bizarre imagery. At a provincial high society home in 1930s France, wide-eyed domestic Celestine (French New Wave icon Jeanne Moreau) arrives to serve for the seemingly normal Monteil family. Naturally things are not even remotely what they seem, as each man from the foot fetishist aging patriarch to the gun-toting husband (Michel Piccoli), whose frigid wife (Françoise Lugagne) is Celestine's only real challenge. The estate is rocked when a young girl is found raped and murdered in the woods, and persecuted, fascist handyman, Joseph (Georges Geret), is accused of the crime. Celestine does a little private investigation to uncover the truth... though in typical Buñuel fashion, her motives may not be all that they seem.

One of the most formally beautiful films in the director's canon, *Diary of a Chambermaid* feels on the surface more like a comedy of manners *a la* Jean Renoir. However, those odd little touches clearly betray the hand of the real author: ace hunter Piccoli blasting a butterfly off a flower, Moreau letting one of her admirer's rhapsodize over her black leather boots, and the brief but chilling image of the young murder victim, her bloodstained legs adorned with snails. Moreau is wonderful, displaying a wicked blend of sensuality and wry humour, which nicely counterbalances Piccoli's trademark blend of urbane perversity. Buñuel didn't shoot many of his films in scope, but he proves quite adept with the framing here, making one wonder what he could have accomplished had he pursued the format any further.

Criterion's DVD of *Diary of a Chambermaid* is even more of a stunner than their already superlative job on *The Discreet Charm of the Bourgeoisie*. The restored source material is immaculate and almost three dimensional in its clarity, with nary a scratch, scuff, or compression flaw to be seen. Past VHS releases both pan and scan and letterboxed look simply anaemic in comparison. The disc also includes a fetching French trailer in which a noncommittal Moreau is interviewed over clips from the film; other bonuses include a nostalgic video interview with Jean-Claude Carriere (who wrote many of the director's French projects) and a printed 1970s interview with Buñuel in which he discusses this film in typically elusive fashion.

DIE SCREAMING MARIANNE

Colour, 1971, 96m. / Directed by Pete Walker / Starring Susan George, Barry Evans / Image (US R0 NTSC)

Director Pete Walker's first departure from saucy sex comedies, *Die Screaming Marianne* in some ways prefigures his more bloodstained shockers to

come but falls more into the Hitchcockian thriller category. Though devoid of nudity and containing only one quick instance of bloodshed, the film is a generally absorbing yarn, good for passing a slow afternoon and particularly interesting for the basic ideas, which would be fleshed out, in Walker's later masterpieces.

Poor Marianne (Susan George) is on the run. Abandoning her job as a go go dancer in Portugal, she hitches a ride with sleazy Sebastian (Christopher Sanford), who asks her to marry him after they've been shacking up in London for two weeks. She reluctantly agrees but, due to a bizarre twist, winds up legally tied instead to Sebastian's more wholesome and handsome friend, Eli (late British sex comedy staple Barry Evans). It turns out Sebastian's motives have been less than honourable, as he's been scheming to return Marianne to her corrupt ex-judge father (*A Lizard in a Woman's Skin*'s Leo Genn), who lives in exile in a Portuguese hacienda with Marianne's homicidal, incest-loving half sister, Hildegarde (Judy Huxtable). Marianne and Eli become lovers while Sebastian and Marianne's family scheme to get her back before her twenty-first birthday, at which time she will gain access to a mysterious bank account set up by her late mother. Double crossing, murder, mayhem, and steam baths ensue.

The lurid title might lead Walker fans to expect a hyper-sleazy slice of sex and violence, but instead *Die Screaming Marianne* moves at a low boil rather than a fever pitch. The cast is great fun to watch, with Evans and George making a surprisingly engaging couple, and Walker regular Anthony Sharpe (who later took the reins in the magnificent *House of Mortal Sin*) pops up as, of course, a minister. Only Genn's performance proves to be a major distraction, thanks to his annoying habit of incoherently mumbling his lines right down his chin. The first hour is the most enjoyable, thanks to the swinging London scenery, the jazzy score, and Walker's gaudy optical tricks, including split screen and bizarre wipes. The last half hour stumbles somewhat after everyone's motives have been exposed, leaving the bad guys to chase George around in circles until the 90 minute mark has been reached. The script also tries to gloss over a few nasty holes; in particular, George's escape from one near death situation is left annoyingly vague. Furthermore, Evans expresses surprise no less than three times upon learning that the judge is George's father, for no good reason whatsoever. Structural problems aside, Walker at least manages to keep the story under control and, in his typical fashion, winds things up on a bitter, ironic note.

Relatively speaking, the DVD from Image looks vastly superior to any past transfer of this film. The low budget and '70s film stock show through in some visible film grain and some bizarre splices which were apparently part of the original film assembly, but the clarity and intensity of the colours are quite satisfying. Just check out those saturated reds during George's memorable frenzied dance over the opening credits, which looked almost unwatchable on the Unicorn VHS version several years ago. Incidentally, this also marks the first appearance of the uncut version in the US; the Unicorn tape bluntly dropped almost all of the third reel, including Sebastian's first dinner with the judge, rendering most of what follows nonsensical and barely running over 80 minutes in length. As usual, Walker shot the film open matte, and the split screen sequence clearly indicates compositions intended to be masked at 1.66:1. The extra information proves to be slightly distracting, as when George's bra is clearly visible while she's supposed to be taking a bubble bath.

THE DIRTY GIRLS

B&W, 1965, 78m. / Directed by Radley Metzger / Starring Reine Rohan, Denyse Roland / Image (US R0 NTSC) / WS (2.35:1)

Though Radley Metzger made his directorial debut with *Dark Odyssey*, the first film to actually feel like a "Metzger movie" was *The Dirty Girls*, the one that really started it all. Handsomely mounted on a low budget and filmed on location throughout Europe, this amusing and sometimes startling film derives its inspiration from the hilarious mondo movies of the '60s (thanks to a solemn, breathy male narrator) and naughty French art films. Clearly not meant to be taken seriously on any level, the film revels in viewers' conceptions of high class prostitution as a mysterious, glamorous profession in which girls can break taboos and satisfy every carnal urge without consequence. Modern P.C. audiences may not be able to understand the angle used by films like this, but Metzger devotees and European film fanatics will most likely feel otherwise.

The narrative, to use the term loosely, bounces between two popular ladies of the evening. The first, Monique ("a hundred women rolled into one!"),

plies her trade in Paris and meets her clients through a local bar. The second, Garance, cavorts through Munich looking for love in all the right places. Between the two of them, the lucky viewer gets to experience a number of forbidden delights, including some light S&M and a swimming pool orgy at which a bored millionaire dangles a piece of diamond jewellery from a fishing rod over the wet partygoers. One of the girls makes out against a mirror ("The forbidden act of self love!" as the trailer puts it), and a mild near-rape threatens to put a stop to Monique's happiness. Structurally, none of this really goes anywhere fast, but it's great fun to watch, leading to an unexpected and amusing shower stall finale that caused quite a stink in its day.

First Run's scope transfer of *The Dirty Girls*, released by Image on DVD, improves in every way over the pale, fullscreen VHS version from Audubon. Though not entirely free of occasional mild print damage, the source material is much cleaner and actually makes it much easier to tell the fresh Metzger footage from the stock city shots which occasionally serve as chapter markers in the story. The DVD also includes a very splicy trailer and, amazingly, a six minute reel of nudity-filled scenes clipped from the final release print.

The cut released to theatres and present on the DVD contains little explicit nudity, and the restoration of this footage indicates just how far the filmmakers were willing to go if necessary. Probably not the best title for Metzger newcomers to start with, *The Dirty Girls* will more likely provide continued amusement and entertainment for viewers interested in seeing the genesis of the director's unique, striking cinematic style.

THE DISCO GODFATHER

Colour, 1979, 93m. / Directed by J. Robert Wagoner / Starring Rudy Ray Moore, Carol Speed / Xenon (US R1 NTSC)

Rudy Ray Moore (*Dolemite*) returned to his beloved urban milieu with *The Disco Godfather*, also released on video as *The Avenging Godfather* and - the best of both worlds - *The Avenging Disco Godfather*. Moore really shines as Tucker Williams, the dancing king DJ "godfather" mixmaster at the popular Blueberry Hill nightclub. His routine involves spinning wax and rapping hilarious catch phrases for the crowd. One night his nephew, Bucky (Julius Carry), comes to the club hopped up on "PCP! Angel Dust! The new psychedelic drug of the '70s!" and winds up in a hospital with lots of other drug-damaged wrecks. After a helpful lecture by a doctor on the dangers of hard drugs (including one jaw-dropping flashback), Tucker decides to wage war on the drug community, kickboxing and bitchslapping his way into your heart. Meanwhile viewers also get to experience first hand the horrors of PCP, which consists of weird psychedelic visions involving an African demon woman and a day-glo skeleton (these sequences obviously influenced the last segment of *Tales from the Hood*).

A dimly lit film, *Disco Godfather* looks as good as it ever has but was obviously a nightmare to transfer to DVD. The low budget obviously prevented any real depth in the shadowy photography, so a few murky shots actually looked that way in the theatre. Overall, though, the flashing lights and sequins look just great, and simply having this title at all is pretty miraculous. Considering what they had to work with, Xenon has done a decent job. Also available as part of a Dolemite box set, containing all of Moore's films with flashy poster art on the covers.

THE DISCREET CHARM OF THE BOURGEOISIE

Colour, 1972, 101m. / Directed by Luis Buñuel / Starring Fernando Rey, Delphine Seyrig / Criterion (US R1 NTSC) / WS (1.85:1) (16:9)

 Most of the world's great filmmakers seem to mellow with age, but fortunately the best simply improve like a fine wine. Take for example the master surrealist Luis Buñuel, who continued to produce masterpieces through the age of 77 and even garnered an Academy Award for Best Foreign Film in 1972 with *The Discreet Charm of the Bourgeoisie,* a slippery and often hilarious black comedy which offers a teasing flipside to his earlier "dinner guests trapped in a house" classic, *The Exterminating Angel.* As with all Buñuel films, this may not be to everyone's taste, but those who are game will find it quite a delectable dish.

In the early evening, a group of wealthy guests arrive at the home of Alice (Stephane Audran, Claude Chabrol's muse), who is startled to find them ready to eat dinner. Her husband is away, she claims, and she thought the dinner was scheduled for the following night. Reactions range wildly: bemused indifference from the optimistic Madame Thevenot

(*Daughters of Darkness'* Delphine Seyrig), pragmatic determination from drug dealing diplomat Don Rafael (Fernando Rey), and snotty irritation from the petulant Florence (Bulle Ogier). Everyone clambers outside to a nearby restaurant, where they are seated next to a cloistered room lit with candles. An alarmed Alice discovers that the restaurant owner's dead body has been laid out next to their table with the waitstaff, and kitchen help are waiting for the undertaker. Needless to say, no one eats. During a luncheon appointment, the bourgeoisie's plans are interrupted again when hostess Alice's adulterous urges send her scurrying off for some love in the bushes; another incident at a restaurant is interrupted when a young solider sits down to relate a bizarre, gruesome, and darkly humorous ghost story involving his childhood; and the diplomat's dinner is interrupted by terrorists, government officials, and other minor distractions. Interlocking stories pile upon each other until the line between reality, dreams, and fantasies becomes indistinguishable... but as always, appetites for food, sex, and emotional satisfaction remain constantly, comically thwarted.

While the director's surrealist roots are quite in evidence, including the repeated supernatural elements and bizarre injections of gunplay and sexual tomfoolery, his outlook on humanity had obviously become more benevolent over the years. As mirrored in the recurring image of the protagonists walking down a country road, his flawed characters persist in their own private missions and refuse to give up despite the bizarre curveballs life has in store for them. Add to that a dream cast of European professionals, led by the always magnificent Fernando Rey (also in Buñuel's *Tristana* and *That Obscure Object of Desire*), and you have a wonderfully strange piece of world class cinema whose message can adapt perfectly from one generation to another without losing any of its resonance. Likewise, the wry humour has lost none of its potency; for instance, the recurring gag of a priest who enjoys dressing up as a gardener can still induce uncontrollable giggling on repeated viewings.

Criterion's two disc set of *The Discreet Charm of the Bourgeoisie* marked the long overdue debut of Buñuel on American DVD and fortunately they did this classic justice in every respect. While the film's age is evident during the grainy, hazy opening credits, the rest of the presentation is absolutely pristine in every respect, almost three dimensional in its razor sharp clarity and beautifully rendered colours. The previous laserdisc from Orion was a dull, cropped atrocity, while mildly letterboxed

(1.60:1) prints aired briefly on the Independent Film Channel. The Criterion version bests them all by a wide margin, and the framing looks ideally suited for Buñuel's elegantly composed set pieces. The optional, yellow English subtitles are also a tremendous improvement and more accurately reflect the rapid fire puns and *bon mots* dropped by the characters as they bound from one table to another. The first disc also contains the original French theatrical trailer with optional subtitles along with a twenty five minute documentary, *El Naufrago de la Calle de la Providencia* (or *The Survivor on the Street of Providence*), a 1970 homemade film by his friends Arturo Ripstein and Rafael Castanedo. Essentially a loving portrayal of the master at home, this treat focuses on his love of mixing martinis (!) and his obvious affection for his fellow man despite the oppressive institutions of politics and organized religion. (And yes, you get the martini mix recipe, too.)

Disc two contains a recent 98 minute documentary, *Regarding Buñuel*, which was apparently produced for European television. Virtually everything you could possibly want to know about the director is contained somewhere in here, from his birth to his career highlights and all of the troubles in between, including his flight from Spain. Various friends, family connections, and actors (including Michel Piccoli and Angela Molina) offer their own insights into the legendary filmmaker, who had a knack for delivering perfect, unbelievable jokes with a deadly serious poker face. How very appropriate.

DISTURBING BEHAVIOR

Colour, 1998, 84m. / Directed by David Nutter / Starring James Marsden, Katie Holmes, Nick Stahl / MGM / WS (1.85:1) (16:9) / DD5.1

 The unkind year of 1998 saw a number of potentially promising films like *54* and *The Avengers* bite the dust due to studio butchery and reshooting that left the final products dog-eared and incoherent. However, *Disturbing Behavior* is perhaps the saddest case because it was, by all reports, a pretty good movie to begin with when it was delivered to MGM. Unfortunately, the powers that be decided it would be a good idea to hack the almost two hour film down to a sparse 84 minutes and market it towards the *Scream* crowd. Not surprisingly the film failed, due in no small part to the fact that an untrained eye couldn't tell its

trailer apart from other post-modern slasher clones that seem to be breeding like bunnies. While MGM prohibited director David Nutter (who cut his teeth on some of the more stylish and emotionally dense episodes of *The X-Files*) from preserving his director's cut on DVD, they did allow the inclusion of eleven scenes as a supplement. Apparently since this footage only involved such trivial matters as character motivation and explanation the film's plot, it obviously didn't warrant inclusion in the final product. Nutter's commentary throughout the film and the deleted scenes eulogizes the remains of his film without directly bashing MGM, but it's pretty clear that the studio screwed up, big time. Until the release of a true director's cut, however, this is a fascinating look at just how much a movie can be transformed after the filming process is completed.

New kid Steve (James Marsden) arrives in the sleepy town of Cradle Bay, once a haven for juvenile delinquents. Now the high school is dominated by the Blue Ribbons, a group of sunny, preppy types who have a strange habit of becoming violent when their hormones kick in. Aside from closet intellectual janitor William Sadler, all of the adults are oblivious to what's really going on. After his druggie pal Gavin (Nick Stahl) is suddenly converted into a letter-jacket wearing lobotomy case, and with the help of love interest Rachel (*Dawson's Creek* ingénue Katie Holmes), Steve tries to uncover the chilling secret behind the transformation of his classmates.

Common cult fan tendency is to rate mistreated films as flawed classics, and while *Disturbing Behavior* is better than its critical reception might indicate, it is also obviously not a perfect film. Even with the extra half hour, the storyline itself too obviously replicates other titles. Most obviously, several critics pointed to *The Stepford Wives* (though its second made-for-TV sequel, *The Stepford Children* would be more appropriate), but other films rear their heads, too, such as *A Clockwork Orange* (copied almost identically in Marsden's brainwashing treatment) and, as the title implies, Michael Laughlin's 1981 cult favourite, *Strange Behaviour*, which also involved a doctor in a small town performing wacko behavioural experiments on teenagers who wind up turning violent.

Thematically speaking, the story provides less insight into the high school caste system than any given five minutes of *Heathers*. On the other hand, the film boasts extremely crisp, assured direction by Nutter, an elegant and haunting score by Mark Snow, and rich, atmospheric cinematography by John Bartley. The performances are somewhat difficult to judge considering the heaps of character development left on the cutting room floor- Holmes has little to do in the final version but show off her nose ring and use the word "razor" a lot. On the other hand, the previously unseen confrontation and love scene between her and Marsden reveals that both of them were trying to invest their characters with more depth than might immediately be apparent. Acting honours easily go to Stahl, who somehow transforms yet another knock off of *Fright Night*'s Evil Ed character into a tragic adolescent trapped by his own intelligence. In fact, the film's original, far superior ending (also included in the supplements) confirms the film's intent as a sort of modern day paranoid fable.

The film works best if approached as a horror film only in the sense that it deals with uncanny events visited upon people attempting to go about normal lives. The absence of cheap scares and gore frustrated most audiences looking for a knife-happy thrill ride, and the relentless onslaught of grunge songs (will this trend ever end?) seems like a desperate attempt to convince viewers that they're really watching a hip, trendy scare flick. What we have instead is something a bit more interesting, and had it been promoted more honestly (catering more towards *X-Files* fans, for example) and allowed to retain its own logic and characterization, *Disturbing Behavior* may have had a fighting chance.

DIVINE TRASH

Colour, 1998, 96m. / Directed by Steve Yeager / Wellspring (US R1 NTSC) / WS (1.85:1)

 As the title implies, this 1998 documentary focuses on the creative period in which pioneering underground John Waters joined forces with his larger than life muse, the drag queen Divine, for a series of shocking films ranging from *Mondo Trasho* to the immortal *Pink Flamingos*. While Waters has already been profiled in-depth several times on programs like *The Incredibly Strange Film Show*, Steve Yeager's feature-length documentary tops them all by including a great deal of footage he filmed during the production of *Pink Flamingos*, as well as interviews with all of the surviving principal players. Following the same basic narrative flow as John Waters' book *Shock Value*, this fast paced and skilfully edited account derives much of its humour from Waters himself. He recounts many of the most famous anecdotes surrounding the film (the trailer inferno and the showstopping doggie doo finale,

among others), peppered with amusing biographical information. His parents and friends chime in with their own recollections, while Dreamland Studios veterans like Mink Stole, Mary Vivian Pearce, Paul Swift, Pat Moran, and Vincent Paranio reminisce about the good old days when they spent hours filming in the freezing Baltimore woods. Interviews with Divine's mother and close friends also paint a tender portrait of the world's most famous and influential cross-dressing performer (who's aptly described as "a drag terrorist"), while 1972 interview footage with Divine, Waters, and the late David Lochary paint a revealing portrait of the enthusiastic, drug-addled state of mind during the shooting. Yeager's film leaps beyond the already gripping details of Waters' film productions and places his work in its historical and artistic context as well. Filmmakers including his influences (Herschell Gordon Lewis, the Kuchar Brothers) and his admirers (Jim Jarmusch, Richard Kern, David O. Russell) offer their own perspectives on Waters' work and the underground movement in general, spiced up with tantalizing clips from such hard-to-find gems as *Sins of the Fleshapoids* and *Flaming Creatures*. Of course there are plenty of clips from Waters' films as well, from an unfinished short film inspired by *The Wizard of Oz* through *Female Trouble*. Most of the graphic highlights of his career are implied rather than shown, such as the legendary singing sphincter, but there is a jolting bit of near-hardcore footage from a Swedish sex education film.

Originally excerpted years ago as a work in progress on Criterion's *Pink Flamingos* laserdisc, *Divine Trash* has been brought to DVD in high style. The image quality varies due to the condition of the film clips, but the recent footage looks excellent and razor sharp. The 1.85:1 letterboxing imposed on the picture doesn't add much to the aesthetic value and often crops off people's heads during the 16mm film snippets. The mono audio is quite strong, with a funky trash-lounge score by Dan Barto running smoothly through the entire film. No extras apart from a few skimpy bios, but even with no frills the documentary easily earns its place in any Waters fan's library.

DJANGO

Colour, 1966, 90m. / Directed by Sergio Corbucci / Starring Franco Nero, Loredana Nusciak / WS (1.66:1) (16:9)

DJANGO STRIKES AGAIN

Colour, 1987, 83m. / Directed by Ted Archer (Nello Rossati) / Starring Franco Nero, Donald Pleasence Anchor Bay (US R1 NTSC) / WS (1.66:1) (16:9)

For spaghetti western fans, the name "Django" has become a legendary catchphrase. For everyone else, it regrettably means very little. A contemporary of Sergio Leone's legendary *Dollars* films with Clint Eastwood, *Django* is a much dirtier, rougher piece of work, which also injects conventions of Japanese cinema and pulp novels into the western framework. Perhaps due to its difficult title, *Django* never broke out of cult status in America but spread like wildfire over Europe, kicking off a host of tangentially related imitators that continued into the 1980s.

In the legendary, iconic opening sequence, Django (Franco Nero) appears as an unassuming yet oddly sinister figure trudging through a muddy western town. Clad in a dirty coat and dragging a coffin behind him, he quickly makes enemies with a diabolical fallen Major and rescues a tied up young woman in peril. Staying near a saloon/brothel in town, our antihero finds himself in the middle of a war between the Major's faction of vigilantes and a band of Mexican revolutionaries, who have become more than a little curious about what Django's hiding in his coffin.

Despite its lack of polish or artistic ambitions, *Django* grabs the viewer's attention through the sheer stark force of its imagery and the unremitting nastiness of its violence. The infamous ear slicing scene alone should have been enough to leave mid-'60s audiences catatonic with shock, but the entire film really rolls around in the dirt and still packs a punch. With his grungy clothes and unshaven appearance, Nero makes a good laconic leading man; it's easy to see why he went Hollywood for a brief period after this film.

Anchor Bay's lavish DVD set presents *Django* in a slightly more generous 1.66:1 letterboxed transfer compared to the marginally letterboxed versions previously issued (but long unavailable) on US video. The anamorphically enhanced image quality looks excellent throughout, with only a few minor scuffs on the source material. The brownish and orange tinge present through much of the film is intentional and inherent in all existing versions. The sound quality reflects the limited capacity of the dubbing studio used for the English version, which is dubbed far more atrociously than the Leone westerns. Luis Bacalov's too-catchy score survives intact, but the dialogue still sounds trapped in a vacuum and rarely comes close to approximating anyone's lip movements. The box set also includes a spectacular full colour booklet detailing the history of the official and unofficial Django films, complete with an eye-popping array of Italian poster art. A fine piece of scholarship and a handy guide for spaghetti western fanatics, this is almost worth the inflated price by itself. Extra supplements include a trio of brief theatrical trailers (all pretty much the same in tone), a recent Franco Nero interview in which the well preserved actor fondly discusses his legendary role, and a terrific "Django shooting game" the viewer can play with the DVD remote control. A remastered edition with additional footage and the original Italian soundtrack has also been prepared for US release at the time of this writing.

Packaged with the *Django* set comes a much more obscure companion feature, *Django Strikes Back*, in which Franco Nero reprises his role twenty years later! Originally released in Italy as *Django 2: Il Grande Ritorno*, the film was never widely released; even the US didn't receive it as a straight to video title. While the character may be the same, the jungle setting, low budget '80s photography, and massive rapid-fire gunplay put this more in the league of Italy's *Rambo* knockoffs, such as the *Indio* series. Adding to the peculiarity of the project is a Laura Gemser-style bondage queen figure and some increased salacious sexual material, far more blatant than what was suggested in the first film. Of course, the character of Django seemed more interested in pleasures of the flesh than the average "Man with No Name" spaghetti western hero, so this may have been a logical step forward. After years of living in solitude as a monk, Django is called back into service to rescue his daughter from the clutches of the evil Christopher Connelly (sporting a funny Udo Kier accent), who is running a steamer through the South American jungle. Along the way he meets the peculiar Gunn (Donald Pleasence) and a host of other bizarre characters before finally breaking out his trusty Gatling gun.

While it's always good to see Nero back in action, *Django Strikes Again* never catches fire like the original film. The constant waffling between genres, coupled with Ted Archer's flat direction, makes it more of a passable action piece than a true return to form, but its long overdue release is certainly welcome. Like its predecessor, the film has received first class treatment from Anchor Bay, who even included a subtitled five minute Italian prologue scissored from the English print prepared for export. Basically an amusing vignette with two old-timers trying to recall the name of "that guy with the coffin" before being blown away, this kicks the film off on a better note than simply jumping into the main titles. Aside from the slightly dupey opening, the image quality is very good, if a bit murky during the night scenes. The English surround soundtrack features most of the performers' original voices, a very welcome touch, but features a rather primitive sound mix with some sloppy channel separation (ditto for the alternate Italian track). Considering what they had to work with, though, the DVD sounds just fine, and Gianfranco Plenizio's electronic score is surprisingly catchy and effective throughout. Also included is the trailer and another brief Franco Nero interview in which he discusses the genesis of the sequel. Both films feature some terrific animated menus, including hilarious faux-Spanish menu options and nifty bullet-ripping effects.

DOCTOR OF DOOM

B&W, 1962, 77m. / Directed by Rene Cardona / Starring Armando Silvestre, Lorenza Velazquez / Beverly Wilshire (US R0 NTSC)

 The first big female wrestling film from Mexico is arguably the best, despite the cult popularity later heaped upon *The Wrestling Women vs. the Aztec Mummy* (also directed by trash maestro Rene Cardona). In fact, the story worked so well that Cardona and his colleagues essentially remade it over and over again, most blatantly as the more explicit *Night of the Bloody Apes*. Watch both for a truly hazardous double feature.

The female wrestling community is shaken when the scientist sister of Gloria Venus (Lorena Velazquez) is abducted by a mad hooded scientist, whose brain experiments have produced a mad, ape like creature named Gomar. Gloria and her colleague/friend, Golden Rubi (Elizabeth Campbell), decide to investigate and help their policemen boyfriends (including Armando Silvestre, later in Bloody Apes) uncover the dastardly conspiracy. What follows is a rapid-fire succession of confrontations between the rasslin' babes and the doctor's minions, including a near death torture chamber melee. Naturally the scientist proves to be far more indestructible than anyone anticipated, as he reappears in a new guise as a wrestling manager and unleashes yet another formidable, scientifically enhanced foe against our heroines.

Originally entitled *Las luchadoras contra el médico asesino*, this film has been a drive-in and late night TV staple for years under a variety of titles. Most recently it turned up on VHS in a musically doctored form *as Rock 'n' Roll Women vs. the Aztec*

Ape, though the original AIP version, *Doctor of Doom*, comes closest to the original dubbed glory intended by K. Gordon Murray. The film moves quickly and boasts a number of hilarious highlights, including an educational female wrestling demonstration that must be witnessed to be believed. On top of that you get voluptuous women, a midget wrestler, a gang of masked baddies, and the aforementioned flesh-eating ape monster. Then there's the outrageous climax, which is simply best experienced without any prior description to be properly appreciated.

The budget priced Beverly Wilshire DVD contains a somewhat scratchy but passable TV print, which looks pretty similar to the soft presentations broadcast for years. In lieu of a full scale restoration someday, this version will do just fine and makes for a passable introduction. The quality actually gets better as it goes along, with the scratches and dirt minimizing more and more with each reel. Obviously penned quickly by someone who knew nothing about the film, the liner notes on the back are exceptionally bizarre: "Life is so short. No wonder there are individuals that try and find ways to extend it. But what makes a perfect candidate to receive this gift? Is it really a gift... or a curse? Could the one who tries by the real doctor of death? [sic] The real question is... who really wants to live forever?" Yes indeedy!

DOLEMITE

Colour, 1975, 90m. / Directed by D'Urville Martin / Starring Rudy Ray Moore, D'Urville Martin / Xenon (US R1 NTSC)

 If the name Rudy Ray Moore doesn't mean anything to you, prepare to be amazed. Back in the '70s, "blaxploitation" (a genre which actually wasn't always exploitative but was signified by a prominent use of black actors and filmmakers in various genres, mostly horror and action) flourished in drive-ins and urban theatres thanks to studios like AIP and MGM. On the really wild side, though, some maverick films slipped through that defied even this new genre, off the wall oddities like *Welcome Home Brother Charles (Soul Vengeance)* and, most notoriously, *Dolemite*. Rudy Ray Moore, a stand up comedian, created the "Mack" character of Dolemite, a crafty, foul-mouthed crime boss stud who raps stories to the masses and kicks serious butt whenever he gets the urge. In 1975, Moore brought Dolemite to the screen... and the rest, of course, is history. The virtually nonexistent plot kicks in when our antihero is released from prison and comes home to find out that his rival, Willie Green (director Martin), has muscled in on Dolemite's territory and completely corrupted the neighbourhood. With the help of nightclub goddess Queen Bee (Lady Reed, a fellow stage performer who appeared on several of Moore's albums) and an interracial gang of karate-trained hookers (seriously!), Dolemite decides to bust some chops. After taking out some corrupt white mobsters, Dolemite hunts down Green himself for the big bullet-spraying, chop-socky showdown, but not before bedding a few of his girls along the way.

Technically inept and amateurishly acted, *Dolemite* fails on virtually every level on which a movie is supposed to work, but that's really part of its charm. With no previous acting experience, Moore seems to be reading cue cards throughout and usually throws his punches and kicks several feet away without ever connecting with his opponents. Put simply, this is one great party movie: Moore's nasty rap numbers, his nonsensical and profane putdowns, and heavy doses of comical sex and violence make for one seriously fun and highly bizarre ride.

While imperfect, Xenon's DVD transfer is light years ahead of those cruddy old VHS copies. The print bears an R rating card at the beginning, though supposedly a slightly different X-rated cut circulated in a few theatres during the movie's initial run. In any case, it's hard to imagine what was cut, though a few lines do appear to be missing (in a film edited so randomly, it's hard to tell for sure). The image quality is surprisingly clean and sharp, with nicely saturated (and often tacky) colours and a relatively clean soundtrack (let's face it, this will never be a THX title). If you ever wanted to rap along with "The Signifying Monkey," this DVD is the answer to your prayers, as it contains the complete words for both the full routines in the film, as well as snippets from Xenon's recent *Legend of Dolemite* (a self-promoting documentary) and *Shaolin Dolemite* (basically awful footage of Moore spliced into a kung fu film). Wacko fun all around.

DON'S PARTY

Colour, 1976, 90m. / Directed by Bruce Beresford / Starring Ray Barrett, Clare Binney / Wellspring (US R0 NTSC)

Don and Kath Henderson, a typical Australian middle class couple, invite their friends for a dinner

and cocktail party to watch the nation's much-anticipated election returns. Unfortunately, as the booze and tension begin to set in, the genteel group becomes catty and eventually violent, leading to brawls, skinny-dipping, sexual dalliances, and other antisocial activities. Adapted by writer David Williamson from his stage play, this acerbic black comedy retains the intimacy and bite of a theatrical production combined with the liberties provided by the evolution of '70s cinema: profanity, frontal nudity, and political subtext (incidentally, the political party terms are reversed in Australia - right is liberal, left is conservative). More significantly, this marks a bridge in the filmic career of Bruce Beresford, who had previously cut his teeth on satiric sex comedies like the Barry McKenzie films. Here Beresford's raunchy history still shines through but is integrated into a more socially relevant whole as Don finds his party disintegrating into a backbiting mess. Later Beresford went on to more commercial, mainstream statements like *Driving Miss Daisy* and *Paradise Road*.

The late John Hargreaves serves nicely as the audience identification figure here, while sharp-eyed Aussie cinema followers will enjoy spotting Jeanie Drynan, years before she played the tragic mom in *Muriel's Wedding*, as Kath. Late night Cinemax veteran Graeme Blundell, who slummed his comedic talents in soft porn comedies like *Alvin Purple* and *Pacific Banana*, turns in an atypically brash and edgy performance as the conservative Young Turk of the group.

Wellspring has done a satisfying job of bringing *Don's Party* to DVD in all its shag carpet glory; the full frame image doesn't appear to be missing anything significant, indicating this was shot for 1.66:1 exhibition at the widest. The detail is much improved from the ragged, blurry prints that have passed around on these shores; the kitschy '70s Aussie fashions and art direction now look bright and vivid, though the transfer is a bit too light and benefits from TV monitor or player adjustment. The mono soundtrack is clean if unspectacular, with no significant noise or distortion. No extras, and the DVD features a very strange, vague martini design on the cover.

DON'T LOOK IN THE BASEMENT

Colour, 1973, 89m. / Directed by S.F. Brownrigg / Starring Rosie Holotik, Jessie Kirby / VCI, Diamond (US R1 NTSC)

"To avoid fainting, keep repeating to yourself, 'It's only a movie... only a movie...'" Wait, isn't that the tagline from *Last House on the Left*? Yep, but that didn't stop the distributors, Hallmark, from recycling the come-on line from their earlier Wes Craven/Sean Cunningham drive-in hit. In fact, the posters even claimed *Basement* was "from the makers of *Last House on the Left*" - oh, well. Nevertheless *Basement* amassed a small but devoted following over the years. Though little more than splattered paint, the heavy gore quotient manages to sustain interest throughout, and fans of Jack Sholder's excellent *Alone in the Dark* may be intrigued to see an earlier horror treatment of the same theme. On a technical level, this one makes H.G. Lewis look like Dario Argento, but a few clever touches here and there and a suitably claustrophobic final twenty minutes should make this worth a look for viewers in an undemanding mood.

Following a disorienting precredits sequence in which a doctor and nurse are dispatched by their patients, Nurse Charlotte Beale (Rosie Holotik) arrives at a secluded, privately run Florida psychiatric institute. The inmates are now under the control of Dr. Masters (Annabelle Weenick), following the axe murder of the prior doctor by one of the patients, "Judge Oliver W. Cameron." Dr. Masters explains that the doctors and patients consider themselves to be one big family and don't even have locks on the doors for protection. Smart, eh? Charlotte roams around and makes the acquaintance of the various inmates, beginning with Mrs. Callingham, who warns Charlotte of impending danger and incessantly quotes William Allingham's "Faeries" ("Up the airy mountain / Down the rushing glen..."). Mrs. Callingham winds up with her tongue cut out for her trouble, but the others are no less peculiar. Sam, rendered imbecilic by a lobotomy, slurps on popsicles and plays with toy boats all day. Allyson, a raging nymphomaniac, just wants to be loved no matter what. Sergeant Jaffee, believing he's still in the middle of a war, presides over his neighbours night and day. Unfortunately, after the death of a visiting telephone repairman and a few other peculiar incidents along the way, the truth begins to emerge, and Charlotte finds herself fighting for her life.

Not surprisingly, VCI's DVD presentation is highly imperfect, given the fact that this was shot for zero money in the middle of Florida on 16mm. The clarity is fine, though some of the colours look a little too reddish for comfort in some shots. The replaced title card indicates this may have had a different title at one point or perhaps just kept changing distribution hands. However, the source material is generally clean, and the sound is rendered accurately enough so that you can actually hear the camera running in a few scenes. No trailer for the film itself is included, but the usual promo reel for other VCI titles is present and accounted for.

DON'T LOOK NOW

Colour, 1973, 105m. / Directed by Nicolas Roeg / Starring Donald Sutherland, Julie Christie / Arthaus (Germany R2 PAL), Studio Canal (France R2 PAL) / WS (1.85:1) (16:9)

Though still held in high esteem (including an appearance in the BFI's top ten British films of all time), *Don't Look Now* has been largely distanced from the controversy it stirred up in the 1970s. Arguably the most commercial and, in many respects, completely satisfying film by the erratically brilliant Nicolas Roeg (*The Man Who Fell to Earth*, *Performance*), this stylish and provocative psychic chiller has lost little of its power to challenge, shock, and amaze.

In the perfectly edited opening sequence, art restoration expert John Baxter (Donald Sutherland) and his wife, Laura (Julie Christie), find their idyllic English country afternoon shattered by the accidental drowning death of their young daughter, Christine. John experiences an unsettling vision during the tragedy, which proves to be a portent of things to come. Flash forward to Venice, where John has been brought in to work on a precious holy fresco. During lunch at a restaurant they are approached by a blind English medium, Heather (Hilary Mason), who informs them that their daughter is expressing happiness and messages of reassurance from the afterlife. Gradually the couple attempts to heal the damage wrought by grief, but the streets of Venice are haunted by a series of gruesome murders, the bodies found drifting in the canals. Furthermore, John's visions have begun and may be related to the strange figure in a red coat lurking in Venice's darkest corners. Is it Christine sending him a warning... or something more sinister?

Like most of Roeg's films, *Don't Look Now* is both a sensory and emotional experience that can be interpreted on several different levels. Most superficially, this is a romantic ghost story with a genuinely shocking surprise finale, truly one of the genre's most nightmarish climaxes. On a deeper level it's a meditation on the tricky nature of perception and fate, where human destiny can be thwarted by a simple misreading of the signs hidden in everyday reality. Christie and Sutherland are both at their peak here, matched all the way by Roeg's impeccable sense of visual composition and a dizzying series of symbols which somehow manage to coalesce perfectly at the end, even if they don't all quite make rational sense. The lyrical score was composed by Pino Donaggio who, so the legend goes, was picked when the film's producer had an inspired vision while spotting the composer on a gondola during location scouting in Venice.

When *Don't Look Now* first opened, much of the publicity centred around a steamy, memorable love scene between Sutherland and Christie, brilliantly intercut with intimate shots of the couple preparing to go out on the town afterwards. Rumours began flying that the performers had actually gotten carried away and made love for real during shooting, and the sequence was at least partially blamed for Warren Beatty dumping Christie around the same time. Furthermore, various sources reported that Roeg had shot additional explicit footage that never made it into the final cut, though even Roeg himself at one point dismissed this claim as a falsehood. Well, surprise! This newly restored version released on DVD in Europe, prepared in conjunction with the BFI and Canal Plus, contains a completely different and much more explicit cut of the love scene, with a few fleeting shots that would never have come close to earning an R rating even in the lenient '70s. One particularly startling crotch to grinding crotch shot could have been enough to send Beatty into a furore.

Arthaus' anamorphically enhanced transfer looks terrific, with rich, vibrant colours that put the overly bright, pasty domestic laserdisc to shame. The framing only adds a slight amount to the sides while removing a bit from the top of the frame, but the compositions look much more balanced than previous transfers. The disc (which bears the title *Wenn die Gondeln Trauer tragen*) features optional German and English soundtracks, as well as optional German and English subtitles. The English subs come in particularly handy, as they translate much of the Italian and traditional Latin dialogue which remained mysterious in all previous versions. The disc also includes the original British Lion theatrical trailer, which is nearly similar to the one prepared by Paramount. The same transfer is also available on French DVD (as *Ne vous retournez pas*), but the subtitles cannot be deactivated from the English language version on most players. Good, creepy fun all around, and well worth the investment for horror fans and art house buffs alike.

DON'T MESS WITH MY SISTER

Colour, 1985, 85m. / Directed by Meir Zarchi / Starring Joe Perce, Jeannine Lemay / Elite (US R1 NTSC) / WS (1.85:1) (16:9)

 You'd have to be psychic to guess this film came from the director of *I Spit on Your Grave* which, while no classic, at least remained interesting and appeared to be conveying some kind of statement about rape and vigilante justice, however misguided. On the other hand, *Don't Mess with My Sister* seems determined to squash viewer expectations at every turn by denying anything resembling entertainment, instead tossing away scene after scene of actors emoting, fighting, and driving aimlessly for no good reason.

The sister of the title is Clara (Jeannine Lemay), whose disgruntled lunkhead Italian-American husband, Steven (Joe Perce), works as a bookkeeper for her junkyard-owning brothers. Steven plans for something bigger and better by going to night school and escaping his loveless marriage, but his dreams are threatened when he becomes fixated on bleach blonde belly dancer Annika (Laura Lanfranchi), a stripper who does her own lacklustre dance of the seven veils without removing much clothing. Steven's passion rises after she does a stint at his birthday party. One of Annika's lecherous clients turns nasty, so Steven jumps in and engages in some assault and battery, which she repays by taking him to bed. Naturally Clara's kin aren't too happy about their brother-in-law's behaviour, leading to a junkyard showdown.

All of this really sounds more exciting than it plays, but Elite's DVD gives this film the deluxe treatment all the same. The transfer looks about as good as an inept Abel Ferrara knockoff possibly could, with the 1.85:1 framing matting off extraneous information from the top and bottom. Colours look bright and stable throughout. The disc also includes a leering theatrical trailer (which again looks a lot more interesting), along with 10 very, very long minutes of deleted scenes, which are presented full frame and mostly expand on footage already present in the movie. Don't expect bottom of the barrel *MST3000* thrills here, folks; this one is highly recommended only as a sleep aid.

DON'T TORTURE A DUCKLING

Colour, 1972, 102m. / Directed by Lucio Fulci / Starring Florinda Bolkan, Barbara Bouchet / Anchor Bay (US R1 NTSC) / WS (2.35:1) (16:9)

While many Italian murder mysteries (or gialli) involve black-gloved killers stalking women in the big city, Lucio Fulci's *Don't Torture a Duckling (Non si sevizia un paperino)* turns the formula completely inside out to produce a violent, sweltering masterpiece of regional and religious oppression. Don't expect to see any shuffling zombies or gory power drills in this one, folks.

In a small village in southern Italy, young preadolescent boys are turning up dead from strangulation. Evidence points to a number of possible suspects, especially the local "witch," Martiara (Florinda Bolkan), whose voodoo practices and possible insanity make her a likely candidate. But what about Patrizia (Barbara Bouchet), the bored city girl hiding out after a drug scandal, who now passes the time by flaunting her naked body in front of children? The local Catholic Church, headed by young Don Alberto (*The Psychic*'s Marc Porel) and his mother, Aurelia (Irene Papas), tries to keep the population under control, but even the local police are baffled by the case. A reporter from the north, Andrea (Tomas Milian), comes to investigate and recruits Patrizia to discover some genuinely ugly truths about the quiet provincial town.

Virtually unseen outside Italy since its release, *Don't Torture a Duckling* is one of the crucial films in the Fulci canon. He once again displays the precise control of the giallo format found in the previous *A Lizard in a Woman's Skin* and *One on Top of the Other*, but he also introduces a number of elements which would reappear prominently throughout his later work. The film's theme of innocence preserved through murder, coupled with the prominent use of Donald Duck as a plot device, later appeared in the much nastier *New York Ripper*, while the memorable face-smashing finale dovetails nicely with its identical appearance at the beginning of Fulci's next film, *The Psychic*. However, *Duckling*'s most memorable sequence, in which a main character is subjected to a horrific fate involving chain-whips, is so effective that Fulci repeated it during the prologue of *The Beyond* and returned to the concept of provincial vigilantism in *City of the Living Dead*.

Duckling is much more than a simple blueprint for Fulci's themes and obsessions though; on its own terms the film is a singular accomplishment, a chilling horror film and social thesis flooded with sunlight, punctuated with odd scenes of dark rainfall. This contrast is reflected in the magnificent score by Riz Ortolani, which oscillates between chilling atonal suspense music and the deliberately syrupy, haunting main theme, which appears ironically in several key scenes. The acting is also among the best in a Fulci film, with Bolkan in particular delivering a tour de force performance as the mistreated outcast. One of the many Euro starlets who blossomed in Italian thrillers, Barbara Bouchet never looked better and has an undeniably memorable entrance in the film.

Long available to collectors via dupes of a half-WS (1.85:1) transfer from Dutch video, *Don't Torture a Duckling* has long been overdue for a decent video presentation. Thankfully, Anchor Bay's DVD does justice to the film's expert scope photography and unorthodox colour schemes. This still looks like a '70s title, which means some visual grain and film stock inconsistencies from time to time, but it's hard to imagine this looking much better. Though much of the film was filmed with English dubbing in mind, some of the voices are a little jarring considering the rural nature of the characters. Otherwise the audio is fine, but in this case an alternate Italian track might have been welcome (as opposed to titles like *Shock* where it makes little difference at all).

DON'T TOUCH THE WHITE WOMAN!

Colour, 1974, 109m. / Directed by Marco Ferreri / Starring Marcello Mastroianni, Catherine Deneuve / Image (US R0 NTSC) / WS (1.75:1)

This movie is bonkers! Marco Ferreri's bizarre modern "western," *Don't Touch the White Woman (Touche pas la femme blanche)*, was never given an official US release and barely ran in the UK; it's easy to see why. Taking political commentary to radical extremes, Ferreri presents the familiar story of Custer's Last Stand, now set in mid-'70s Paris. Some characters wear period clothes, while others are garbed in sweatshirts or business suits. Indians remain in native clothes and wander around the outskirts of Paris while Custer (a fabulously self-indulgent performance by Marcello Mastroianni) plots their extermination. Characters constantly refer to President Nixon (whose portrait appears with amusing frequency in the background) as the force behind the white men's plot, making this a sort of twisted allegory for American colonial corruption extending into the Watergate era. Last but not least, the whole disorienting experience climaxes with an elaborate, spectacularly gory recreation of Little Big

Horn that comes off like *Soldier Blue* reinterpreted by Mel Brooks at the end of *Blazing Saddles*.

General George Armstrong Custer is called in to lead the American troops in a mission decreed by God to wipe the Indians from their native land and claim the territory for the white men. A patriotic, well to do young woman (Catherine Deneuve) flirts with Custer and eventually goes to his bed the night before battle, while Custer's disgruntled Indian sidekick (Ugo Tognazzi, a Ferreri regular) constantly attempts to make passes at Deneuve and picks up white prostitutes to satisfy his strange porcelain lust. Custer often utters the title phrase to discourage his "lowly" Indian, leading to a sick little punchline during the finale. Meanwhile, Custer is antagonized by the flamboyant Buffalo Bill (a scene-stealing Michel Piccoli), and French singers continuously warble C&W tunes in the background to add to the surreal effect.

Obviously this is not a film for all tastes; even viewers accustomed to Ferreri's bizarre pacing and visual quirks may find this tough going, as the film outstays its welcome by a good 15 minutes at least. However, from a satirical standpoint, *Don't Touch* is a fascinating, idiosyncratic work that could only have come from France in the '70s. The cast seems to be having a ball, though Deneuve has far too little screen time. Philippe Sarde's eccentric score, which ranges from romantic to incredibly disturbing, is unlike anything else in his musical canon.

Image has done as good a job as can be expected with this film, which is presented full frame except for the letterboxed (1.75:1) opening and closing titles. Aside from a few close ups, the cropping does little damage to the film, and the colour is surprisingly vivid and clean. The yellow subtitles are burned onto the image, unfortunately, and are consistently clear and legible. While this film has probably not been preserved under ideal conditions over the years, the Dolby Digital mono soundtrack is surprisingly sharp.

DOUBLE AGENT 73

Colour, 1974, 73m. / Directed by Doris Wishman / Starring Chesty Morgan, Frank Silvano / Image (US R0 NTSC)

 For her second big screen adventure Chesty Morgan plays Jane, aka Agent 73, who's called in from an idyllic vacation (at a nudist camp!) to track down a nefarious drug dealer known as Toplar. In order to accomplish her

assignment, Jane allows her superiors to implant a camera in her left breast. Every time she snaps her pendulous boob, a shutter and a flash go off. (The technical rationale behind all this is never explained, nor would it need to be in a Wishman film.) The point of all this is to take pictures of a dangerous circle of criminals and deduce from a telltale scar which one is the leader. Of course, Jane is further motivated by the fact that the camera will explode if she doesn't return to her boss' office in time. Ouch!

A fitting sequel in every way, *Double Agent 73* reveals absolutely no improvement whatsoever in Chesty's acting ability. Wishman gallops gamely through the sick storyline with the gusto of a pro, often trailing her camera off to gaze hypnotically at Chesty's horrific outfits and platform shoes, not to mention the usual random items of furniture. Astounding. Chesty doesn't really use her "weapons" in action this time, but the sheer lunacy of the premise more than makes up for it.

Like *Deadly Weapons*, this DVD is a bit more crisp and colourful than the past VHS editions but, like most grindhouse '70s films, will never look all that dazzling. The disc includes both Chesty trailers and some hilarious artwork that must be seen to be believed. Unfortunately, Chesty quickly retired from Z-movie acting after this pair of classics; apart from a brief appearance in Fellini's *Casanova*(!), she did the strip club circuit and eventually retired. The world will never be the same.

DOUBLE SUICIDE

B&W, 1969, 83m. / Directed by Masahiro Shinoda / Starring Kichiemon Nakamura, Shima Iwashita / Criterion (US R1 NTSC)

 Though few will probably qualify it as a pleasurable viewing experience, *Double Suicide (Shinju ten no Amijima)* is a technically startling, compelling aesthetic experience. The title itself gives away the finale, so the tragic inevitability of the story keeps the viewer at an emotional distance while experimental director Masahiro Shinoda toys with the cinematic possibilities of filming a *bunraku* (Japanese puppet play). This art form allows the puppets to be manipulated by kurago (puppeteers dressed entirely in black), a convention kept to unsettling effect within the film itself.

After a prologue in which the play is established and the director establishes over a phone how he wants the proceedings conducted, human actors take over to tell the story of Jihei (Kichiemon Nakamura), an established and respected paper mill baron whose contended family with a wife (Shima Iwashita, the director's wife) and children is disrupted when he begins an affair with Koharu (also Iwashita), a prostitute. For months he vows to buy her freedom but finds himself unable to do so, while his father-in-law demands an immediate divorce and the removal of his children. Rejected by society, the two lovers flee together to continue their love, but Jihei realizes their only solution to their problem lies in the afterworld. Koharu proves reluctant to take her own life, but the powers of fate cannot be denied.

Based on a 1720 play by the renowned Monzaemon Chikamatsu entitled *Double Suicide at Amijima*, this disturbing film manages to be wrenching and curiously hypnotic at the same time. The stark black and white photography provides a subtle interplay of visual surfaces and the contrasts of fabrics and backdrops, while the frame often splits into beautifully composed juxtapositions of diagonal, vertical, and horizontal planes, a technique carried to its natural conclusion during the violent finale which finds the lovers' bodies splayed against each other. Special note should also go to the minimalist score by Toru Takemitsu, a far cry from his more familiar work for Kurosawa.

Criterion's DVD has been mastered from the same full frame source used for their previous laserdisc and tape editions, though it looks slightly crisper and features more robust contrast. The optional English subtitles are identical and remain easy to read throughout. Some minor grain is evident during some of the stronger white areas onscreen, but this has existed in all previous transfers, too. The disc's only extra consists of a thoughtful 1970 printed essay by feminist critic Claire Johnston, which accompanied the film's surprising US theatrical art house release.

DR. JEKYLL & SISTER HYDE

Colour, 1971, 97m. / Directed by Roy Ward Baker / Starring Ralph Bates, Martine Beswick / Anchor Bay (US R1 NTSC) / WS (1.85:1) (16:9)

Dr. Jekyll (Bates) is developing an antidote to common diseases and stumbles upon a formula that transforms him into a woman. Taking on the persona of his "sister" Mrs Hyde (Beswick), in order to sustain the duality Jeckyll needs female hormones - the fresher the better. But the symbiosis quickly sours as the malevolent Hyde

proves the dominant half of the partnership. More than just a kinky twist on the classic Robert Louis Stevenson tale, director Roy Ward Baker's highly original film is also laced with dollops of Burke & Hare and Jack the Ripper, the upshot being one of Hammer's most evocative latter-day chillers. *Avengers* supremo Brian Clemens provides the imaginative and witty script - "My brother hasn't been himself of late" - which, consciously or otherwise, touches on latent homosexuality with Jeckyll (as Hyde) seducing medical colleague Professor Robertson (Gerald Sim) and upstairs neighbour Howard Spencer (Lewis Fiander), albeit for different reasons; the former is a precursor to slaughter, the latter purely for recreational purposes. There are splashes of violence commensurate with Hammer's finest shock moments of the period including a stiletto through the throat, but the Kensington Gore is largely sidelined in favour of strong character development and intelligent storytelling. The transformations are staged in cost-cutting effects-free mode - with the exception of one time-lapse sequence, they're mostly cheating cut-aways - but still reap effective results. The late Ralph Bates is excellent as the pitiable victim of a quest for knowledge, Martine Beswick better still as his *bête noire*. One to be relished.

Anchor Bay deliver the goods yet again with their Region 1 DVD, its only shortcoming being the truancy of the retrospective documentary that the material commands. Yet being as this is a failing common to their Hammer releases, it isn't all that surprising. The commentary from Baker, Beswick and Clemens is entertainingly informative, and there's a nice slideshow-style gallery of stills and poster art that unfolds to the accompaniment of David Whitaker's theme music. An atmospheric British release trailer, and two radio spots (which play out over a selection of ad mats) sweeten the deal. The 25-chapter encoded print of the film is presented with a choice of English or French sound and displays only the most negligible traces of wear. - TG

DR. NO

Colour, 1962, 111m. / Directed by Terence Young / Starring Sean Connery, Ursula Andress / MGM / WS (1.78:1) (16:9)

When the British government's Jamaican operative and his secretary vanish without a trace, James Bond (Connery) is dispatched to investigate. Once there his suspicions are aroused by the activities on a nearby private island of reclusive Chinese scientist

Dr. No (Wiseman). The first, but by no means the best Bond, from the opening shot through the gun barrel and the ensuing twangy theme music - both of which would become trademarks of the series - this is still provocative stuff. Terence Young, who famously imbued Sean Connery and his screen persona with a measure of his own sophistication and panache, pitched Bond's introduction perfectly (at the gaming tables of a smoky London casino in the early hours of the morning) and a cinematic legend was born. The script is relatively faithful to Ian Fleming's novel - a facet that would alter dramatically in later films, some of which threw out everything but the title - and Dr. No has a daringly sadistic edge for its day, something else gradually whittled away over the years; John Kitzmiller gets a broken flashbulb scraped across his face (and is later incinerated by a flame-thrower), Connery shoots dead oily Anthony (Dial M for Murder) Dawson in cold blood, and he himself takes a beating from some thuggish guards (one of whom is actor Milton Reid, back 15 years later for The Spy who Loved Me). The scene in which Bond is disturbed in the night by a lethal arachnid beneath the bedclothes is one of the most famous in the series, even though the sheet of glass separating the spider from Connery's valuable skin is patently obvious. Joseph Wiseman is great as the titular steel-handed scientist, toppling American test missiles from his hostile island retreat, though he doesn't make an on-screen appearance until a little over 20 minutes from the end. Leading lady Ursula Andress (wearing that bikini) doesn't perform her famous stroll out of the surf until halfway through either, not that Bond's libido suffers; within the first hour he beds both Eunice Gayson and Zena Marshall. Boasting a hi-tech glossiness that set the tone not only for the Bonds that followed but for hundreds of imitators too, Dr. No is as enthralling today as ever it was.

The special edition DVD from MGM is unsurprisingly the film's finest platform yet. Divided by 32 chapter-stops, the 40-year-old movie is practically flawless; but for the sartorial trend and the hairstyles (always give-away factors in the dating game), the clarity of the print is such that you might believe it was shot last year. A lengthy (42 minute) documentary delves into its production and a second, shorter programme turns its attention to director Terence Young, who ended up making what many consider to be the best three films in the series. A commentary features soundbites of Young and members of the cast and crew. Additionally there's a 9-minute b/w US TV featurette from 1963 (frankly very dull), six radio spots, four trailers (two of which were cobbled together for reissue double bills with From Russia with Love and Goldfinger), two TV spots (again for its billing with Goldfinger) and a gallery of production photos and artwork. Languages and subtitling options are available in English, Spanish and French. - TG

DR. PHIBES RISES AGAIN

Colour, 1972, 88m. / Directed by Robert Fuest / Starring Vincent Price, Robert Quarry, Fiona Lewis / MGM (US R1 NTSC) / WS (1.85:1) (16:9)

Like most sequels, Dr. Phibes Rises Again faced an uphill battle to outdo its already outlandish predecessor. Luckily AIP had the same director and lead actor handy, so they simply decided to provide more of the same, and while this second outing for the murderous doctor falls slightly short of the mark, it makes a dandy companion piece to the original all the same.

Months after the surreal embalming finale of The Abominable Dr. Phibes, our faceless antihero (Vincent Price) is returned to life in his underground lair when a special position of the moon sets into a motion a series of contraptions fill him back with blood. Summoning his lovely assistant Vulnavia (Valli Kemp) from the netherworld, he plans for a lavish expedition to Egypt in order to revive his wife, Victoria (Caroline Munro), in the mystical River of Life. Unfortunately his art deco palace has been vandalized and his precious holy papyrus scrolls stolen by his archrival, Biederbeck (Robert Quarry), who intends to find the River himself. After creatively dealing with Biederbeck's bodyguard / manservant (exploitation veteran Milton Reid), Phibes and Vulnavia are finally off to sea, along with Biederbeck, his seductive ladyfriend Diana (Fiona Lewis), and even Peter Cushing in a throwaway bit as the ship's captain. Of course, obtaining the scrolls also necessitates the removal of Biederbeck's assistants, so Phibes returns to his murderous ways thanks to some handy gadgets, the most memorable of which involves a load of scorpions.

In comparison to the first film, this Phibes outing feels more rambling and hastily put together. The murders are still outrageously nasty fun, but the lack of a coherent pattern like the original's ten plagues removes some of the cheeky suspense. The return of Peter Jeffrey's Inspector Trout also feels more than a little contrived, though he does provide the film with a couple of its funniest moments. As for the completely successful elements, the sandy locales are a marked change of pace from the glossy surrealism of the first film, while John Gale provides an excellent score, which perhaps surpasses the already wonderful original. The opportunity to watch newer horror blood like Quarry and Lewis act opposite Price (and Kemp, an exceptionally lovely new Vulnavia) is also tremendously appealing, particularly thanks to the nice conceit of having a villain going against Phibes instead of another sympathetic doctor.

MGM's DVD isn't as dazzling as their transfer of the first film, but then this one's appearance has always been a bit softer and more muted. The bulk of the print looks excellent, better in fact than the previous Vestron and Orion editions, though some damage creeps through now and then. Don't panic when you see the mediocre quality of the clips at the beginning; they've always looked like that. As with the first *Phibes*, the letterboxing loses almost as much from the top and bottom as it gains on the sides, but the compositions looks nicely balanced. Of course, the "music edited for home video" disclaimer on the box notwithstanding, the big news here is the long awaited restoration of Price's victorious rendition of "Somewhere over the Rainbow" during the final scene, which was substituted rather poorly in all previous home video and TV editions. It's about time! The disc also includes the original theatrical trailer ("He lives!"), which as usual is a lot of fun.

DR. STRANGELOVE, OR HOW I LEARNED TO STOP WORRYING AND LOVE THE BOMB

B&W, 1964, 93m. / Directed by Stanley Kubrick / Starring Peter Sellers, George C. Scott / Columbia, Warner / WS (1.66:1)

General Jack D. Ripper (Sterling Hayden) has a problem: he thinks Communists have tainted the US water supply and corrupted his precious bodily fluids. The solution? Bomb the country off the map, of course. Of course, US President Merkin Muffley (Peter Sellers) is none too pleased when Ripper sends a bomber off to the USSR, and the world leaders attempt to resolve their differences over the phone. The Soviet leaders threaten to detonate a mysterious Doomsday Device in retaliation, and it's up to Britain's Captain Mandrake (Sellers again) and the questionable

advice of a former Nazi, the wheelchair-bound Dr. Strangelove (Sellers... uh, again), to perhaps avert a worldwide disaster.

One of the most enduring products of its era, *Dr. Strangelove* finds Kubrick using a surgeon's precision to find the uneasy humour in what started out as a straight nuclear terror novel, Peter George's Red Alert. The result, often termed a "nightmare comedy," has withstood the test of time despite its timeliness (anyone who never experienced the Cuban Missile Crisis probably won't experience the exact queasy effect this film was intended to cause).

Typically, the film is extremely slow-paced for a comedy, often lingering on several straight scenes in a row before exploding again into a moment of unexpected laughter, usually courtesy of Sellers' three dynamic performances. In fact, Sellers is so astonishing that many scenes without him feel bland in comparison, and this may be the film's only real weakness. As usual, the crew behind the scenes does a top flight job, particularly the eye-popping production design by Ken Adam (responsible for the most memorable villain hideouts in the James Bond films) and Laurie Johnson's militaristic score. Best of all, the ending still packs a punch, and it would have been amazing to see this during its first run in American theatres.

Like the Criterion laser, Columbia's DVD of *Strangelove* is struck from Kubrick's personal print of the film and switches between full frame (open matte - nothing is missing) and soft-matted 1.55:1. Kubrick's oft-expressed displeasure at the presentation of this film in theatres begs the obvious question of exactly how he did intend to have it shown, but apparently this version is what he wanted. As with most Columbia DVDs, the transfer has been performed with a great deal of care and, aside from the ragged opening titles, looks very good. None of the extras from the Criterion edition are retained here, but the special edition version under the Columbia banner adds a host of new goodies, including trailers, a bizarre split screen interview with Peter Sellers and George C. Scott, an image gallery, and two informative documentaries, "The Art of Stanley Kubrick: From Short Films to Strangelove" and "Inside the Making of *Dr. Strangelove*." The same disc is carried over by Warner into its UK Kubrick box, but only the bare bones DVD is present in its US counterpart.

DRACULA

B&W, 1931, 75m. / Directed by Tod Browning / Starring Bela Lugosi, Helen Chandler / Universal (US R1 NTSC)

A legendary film whose reputation has arisen almost entirely thanks to its lead performance, *Dracula* may not bear much resemblance to the Bram Stoker source novel but nevertheless has rightfully earned its status in the horror classic pantheon. Much of the criticism of the film still holds true- the Transylvania sequences are masterful, while the London ones can induce sleep- but for sheer iconic value, *Dracula* has yet to be surpassed.

In familiar fashion, the tale introduces Renfield (Dwight Frye), a real estate agent on his way to the castle of Count Dracula (Bela Lugosi), who welcomes his guest in a most peculiar fashion. Renfield deduces after some time that he should probably escape or lose his life, but by the time he returns home he's out of his mind and winds up in an asylum. However, the Count has purchased Carfax Abbey, a decaying property in London, through which he insinuates himself into British society and begins to prey on the local denizens. The wily Dr. Van Helsing (Edward Van Sloan) unravels the mystery and realizes that the lovely Mina (Helen Chandler) is next on the Count's list; only by resorting to time-worn methods of battling evil can the doctor defeat this evil creature of the night.

Unlike Francis Ford Coppola's pseudo-operatic take on the novel, this *Dracula* remains romantic more through implication than plotting. Lugosi's piercing eyes and strange, elegant demeanour make him a truly imposing figure, one which he was clearly born to play. As magnetic as this vampire may be, the viewer is never allowed to forget what he truly is. While the majority of the film is extremely stagy (good as he is, Van Sloan has more than his share of awkward moments), the film still manages its share of dreamy, nightmarish moments, thanks primarily to Freund's graceful camerawork and a genuinely crazed performance from Frye as the crazed, insect-scarfing Renfield. While James Whale's *Frankenstein* used powerful imagery to compensate for the relative quietness of its soundtrack, *Dracula* has always seemed terribly sluggish due to a complete absence of background music.

Universal's DVD includes the option of playing a new Philip Glass score, performed by the Kronos Quartet; as revisionist as this may sound, this audio option actually helps the film's pacing in many respects. The hypnotic, austere quality of the music especially boosts the stagnant second half, though the tone of Glass' compositions is obviously an acquired taste and will not appeal to everywhere. Sadly, the image quality is the least impressive of the Universal monster releases. While their laserdisc of the "restored version" of the film, complete with some spooky background noises deemed too intense for 1931 viewers, looked much better than those old TV broadcasts, the DVD appears to be culled from a standard general circulation print. The quality still outclasses almost every film of this vintage, but compared to the astonishing restoration performed on *Frankenstein*, it's odd that *Dracula* would look so lacklustre. At least the restored sound effects are still intact, so you can hear every squeaking rat and howling wolf as originally intended.

As usual, the bonuses are top notch: David J. Skal contributes both a lively and educational commentary track (which compresses an amazing amount into 70 minutes) and a *Dracula* documentary, which follows the same path as the other monster featurettes. The story's history and its path to the screen receive most of the attention, with occasional juicy vignettes thrown in to keep things interesting. A typically rough-looking theatrical trailer and the usual photo gallery (most of which will be familiar to *Famous Monsters* readers) round out the usual supplements. However, Universal has gone the extra mile of including the legendary alternate Spanish version, which was shot on the same sets but with different actors in Spanish. More protracted and "European" in tone, the Spanish version features much stronger visual fluidity but lacks the forceful personas of Lugosi and Van Sloan. In purely cinematic terms, though, the Spanish *Dracula* easily wins on a scene-for-scene basis. The impressive restored transfer is identical to the VHS release several years ago, with the same introduction by the film's female star, Lupita Tovar. An impressive package, this *Dracula* may not be perfect but certainly delivers on its promise for an admirably low price tag.

THE DRAUGHTSMAN'S CONTRACT
Colour, 1982, 107m. / Directed by Peter Greenaway / Starring Anthony Higgins, Janet Suzman / Wellspring (US R1 NTSC) / WS (1.66:1)

The only Peter Greenaway film designed to specifically evoke a certain British time period, *The Draughtsman's Contract* appears on the surface like some twisted Restoration comedy filled with scheming aristocrats and clever turns of phrase. One of the most enthusiastically received and controversial feature debuts of the early '80s, this remained Greenaway's most high profile effort for eight years until *The Cook, the Thief, His Wife and Her Lover* secured his position in the art house pantheon. However, *Draughtsman* actually has much in common with his later work, ranging from the bizarre background details, such as a nude living statue, to the brutal, jarring twist ending.

At a gossipy dinner party, an arrogant young draughtsman, Mr. Neville (Anthony Higgins), is enlisted by the middle-aged Mrs. Herbert (Janet Suzman) to execute twelve drawings of the Herbert estate as a surprise gift for her loutish husband, who is usually away on business. In exchange, Mrs. Herbert will go along with Mr. Neville's sexual demands, once for each drawing. Mrs. Herbert's daughter (Anne-Louise Lambert) becomes more than a little intrigued by the arrangement and enters into a similar bargaining position with Neville, whose fussiness with the layout of each drawing compels him to chase sheep away from the scenery and demand passers-by to wear the same clothing each day. However, some inconsistencies in the day to day arrangement of seemingly familiar objects, such as linen and open windows, cause Neville to wonder whether Mr. Herbert is actually away on business... or perhaps is no longer among the living.

As with many Greenaway films, all of the characters are more pieces of a diabolical mind puzzle than living, breathing human beings, bereft even of first names, and the cast gamely acts accordingly. As Neville, Higgins (also in *Vampire Circus* and *Flavia the Heretic* under the name Anthony Corlan) has one of his most memorable roles and finds the humour in an essentially repellent character. Without giving too much away, the various layers of the narrative may prove off-putting to viewers who expect to find some redeeming qualities unveiled at the end of the film; there will be no redemption or clever moralizing here. As a document of a historical period, *Draughtsman* is remarkably convincing, particularly considering its virtually nonexistent budget.

The costumes, scenery, and stylish lighting manage to equal *Barry Lyndon* with a fraction of the resources, while Greenaway's intricate and biting script should keep English majors chortling with delight. Interestingly, his original festival cut of the film ran a full three hours and reportedly contained a number of crucial plot points and explanations which would up on the cutting room floor, including a rationale for the living statue. Unfortunately, this version has not been screened since 1982 and may have been lost forever (if it doesn't exist in one of Greenaway's vaults somewhere). As far as the standard theatrical version goes, however, Wellspring's DVD is by far the best. MGM issued a dismal VHS version back in the early '90s, apparently lifted from a muddy 16mm transfer and cropped on all four sides. The DVD restores the full breadth of the compositions, which is crucial with this title, and more significantly presents the delicate colour schemes as originally intended. Michael Nyman's ingenious, Purcel-inspired score sounds very good for straight mono, and dialogue is clear and intelligible throughout. No trailer is included, a regrettable absence; it would be interesting to see how United Artists and Channel Four pitched this in theatres.

D

DREAMSCAPE

Colour, 1984, 99m. / Directed by Joseph Ruben / Starring Dennis Quaid, Kate Capshaw / Image (US R1 NTSC), MIA (UK R2 PAL) / WS (1.78:1) (16:9) / DD5.1/DTS

 The first of a long string of dream-related horror and science fiction movies during the 1980s, *Dreamscape* plays like a more family-friendly alternative to Wes Craven's *A Nightmare on Elm Street*, which also involves people being murdered in their dreams by a man equipped with finger blades. Sporting a great cast of cinema vets mingling with up and coming '80s stars, this film became a familiar staple on cable TV and home video, where it won over a loyal audience of future Generation X-ers before disappearing inexplicably until its DVD revival.

A government-funded group of scientists involved in dream studies led by Dr. Novotny (Max Von Sydow) tracks down one of the psychic community's former star pupils, Alex (Dennis Quaid), who lives a vagabond existence picking up money at horse races. Under Novotny's guidance, Alex is introduced to a process by which he can enter the dreams of sleeping patients and uncover the sources of their subconscious problems. Novotny's assistant, Jane (a pre-*Temple of Doom* Kate Capshaw), sparks some immediate chemistry with Alex but keeps her distance for professional reasons. Meanwhile the project's secret "benefactor," sinister government bigwig Bob Blair (a none-too-subtle Christopher Plummer), makes veiled threats to Alex and spends his efforts coaching another dream-skilled psychic, the creepy and unstable Tommy Ray (David Patrick Kelly). Soon Alex begins to put the pieces together and learns that the entire dream studies may have some connection to Blair's relationship with the US President (Eddie Albert), who has been experiencing traumatic nightmares involving nuclear destruction...

A clean, efficient, and enjoyable popcorn-muncher, *Dreamscape* was the first mainstream effort for director Joseph Ruben, who had previously cut his teeth on drive-in fare like *The Pom Pom Girls*. Here he injects some of the Hitchcock references (such as the Thornhill Institute), which would later appear more obviously in his best film, *The Stepfather*, and to a lesser degree in his later thrillers like *The Good Son* and *Sleeping with the Enemy*. Here he shows a comfortable hand with a complex storyline and a hefty cast of characters, all of whom remain vivid and mostly believable. Capshaw and Quaid are especially appealing in their early roles, and it would have been interesting to see them reteam in another film down the road. A few elements of the film have become unavoidably dated over the years, particularly the synth-heavy Maurice Jarre score (though not as embarrassing as his abrasive work on *No Way Out*), though the special effects, such as the great stop motion snakeman, are a pleasant reminder of how lucky this film was to be made before the onslaught of computer-generated digital effects. Here the effects still manage to serve the story, which takes some odd turns every few minutes and climaxes with a genuinely nightmarish train sequence that scarred an entire generation of impressionable kids. Best known in the history books as the film that tied with *Red Dawn* by one week as the first movie to be released with a PG-13 rating, *Dreamscape* was actually trimmed slightly to avoid an R rating and underwent even more censorship in Britain, where shots involving those pesky, illegal nunchukas were removed. The longer "European" version features some additional groping during the Quaid/Capshaw sex dream and slightly more gore during the memorable snakeman nightmare sequence (which still packs quite a punch), though it doesn't make much difference either way.

The DVD, from an original interpositive according to the packaging, is the standard PG-13 version and looks much better than other video incarnations. The letterboxed image appears to expose all of the available frame, while colours and detail are especially strong for a mid-'80s title. A few effects shots are almost too clear for comfort, such as the first dirt-ridden process shot of Quaid during the skyscraper nightmare, but this just comes with the DVD territory. The new Dolby Digital 5.1 and DTS audio mixes both sound fine considering the age limitations on the source; some scenes play almost in mono or barely surround, while others erupt into full directional life, particularly the crucial dream sequences. The straight 2.0 surround track fares surprisingly well in comparison, and viewers may wish to compare them and choose their own preference. Also included is a running commentary track by members of the production team, including producer Bruce Cohn Curtis, writer David Loughery, and FX master Craig Reardon, which covers the film's origins and how the dreams were designed to accommodate the technical possibilities of the period. Other goodies include some brief snakeman test footage and an amusing "Monster!" feature on the main menu, which incidentally is very nicely designed and a perfect reflection of the film's mood.

DRESSED TO KILL

Colour, 1980, 105m. / Directed by Brian De Palma / Starring Michael Caine, Angie Dickinson, Nancy Allen / MGM (US R1 NTSC) / WS (2.35:1) (16:9) / DD5.1

 It's difficult to imagine a horror-thriller more purely enjoyable than this high peak of Brian De Palma's career, a gleeful joyride of a film that continues to reward after countless viewings. Though it received a mixed critical response amidst a huge turnout from the public, the film has gone on to be considered one of the '80s' most accomplished directorial feats and contains enough terrific set pieces to fuel a hundred *Basic Instincts*. Much of the fun lies in the insidious surprises tucked into its plot, on the surface a playful riff on *Psycho*.

Angie Dickinson stars as Kate Miller, a New York housewife whose steamy, violent fantasies offer some relief from her unsatisfying sex life with an inattentive husband. While her son, Peter (Keith Gordon), toils away in his room on science projects, Kate goes to see her analyst, Dr. Elliott (Michael Caine), and spends an afternoon at the Metropolitan Museum of Art, where she engages in an extended bout of flirting with a handsome stranger. To reveal more would be unthinkable, but other characters gradually work their way into the storyline, including plucky Park Avenue hooker Liz (Nancy Allen, Mrs. De Palma at the time) and a mysterious, tall blonde with an unhealthy fondness for straight razors.

After experimenting with a variety of cinematic techniques like split screen, sound layering, visual storytelling, and other forms of audience manipulation in his earlier films, De Palma was finally ready to pull out all the stops with this feverish rollercoaster ride. Nary a second is wasted as the viewer is swerved through New York on what amounts to a dark tour of human sexuality, where few people are what they seem and logic is ignored in favour of immediate sensation. At the time the film's combination of erotic visuals and visceral violence was protested by many critics and feminist groups, though the subsequent wave of erotic thrillers has shown just how difficult De Palma's balancing act really was. The sex and violence are essentially tools for a much larger directorial intent to please the viewer at any cost, and even the triple whammy ending (which could have been infuriating in lesser hands) comes off instead as yet another delicious flourish, the icing on an already sinfully rich cake.

All of the actors seem to be enjoying themselves immensely, particularly during the rapid fire banter between Allen, Gordon, and police detective Dennis Franz, whose laughably huge collars are the only element of the film to suffer with age. Best of all is the sumptuous score by Pino Donaggio, one of the finest accomplishments in a criminally underrated career. Both men had come fresh off the low budget student film project, *Home Movies*, and had obviously recharged their batteries for a full throttle exercise that often approaches the operatic.

Fans of the Donaggio score will particularly appreciate the new 5.1 mix accorded to the film by MGM, whose DVD is the most satisfying in a long and tangled theatrical and home video history. The film was shot in 2.35:1 Panavision and recorded in mono, and in order to garner an R rating, several snippets of nudity and latexy gore were removed from the opening shower fantasy, the infamous elevator scene, and the final climax. Also, some of Allen's dialogue during the erotic speech in Caine's office was redubbed. The uncensored "European" cut of the film surfaced on Warner Home Video in the very early days of VHS, but the brutal panning and scanning destroyed much of the film's effectiveness. Meanwhile Vestron retained laserdisc rights and released two versions, both R-rated: pan and scan and a later letterboxed edition, sapped of virtually all colour, which squeezed the entire frame into a cramped 1.85:1 aspect ratio. The rights then passed to Orion, who issued an "unrated," correctly letterboxed version through Image on laserdisc; though the film was complete in terms of running time, Allen's dialogue was still softened. At the same time the film turned up on VHS again from Goodtimes, in its R-rated form licensed from Orion. The company's dissolution turned the rights over to MGM, and while the R-rated version turned up on

DVD first in a letterboxed, optically censored disc from Japan, the American MGM DVD is the closest thing possible to a definitive edition.

In another hilarious nod to the inexplicable ratings policies of Blockbuster, the DVD carries a prominent R rating on the back and then discreetly lists "Unrated Version Option" among the special features listing. Using seamless branching, one can either watch the complete Euro cut or the R-rated version. The new, anamorphic widescreen transfer looks better than previous incarnations, of which the Orion/Image disc was the best of the bunch. More visual information is exposed on all edges of the frame, and the rich, striking colour design has never looked better. Attentive viewers should pay attention to every inch of the widescreen compositions, as De Palma tucks neat little details into the background, which may not be apparent the first time around. Watch out for people in the background in particular. The audio options include the aforementioned 5.1 mix (nicely recreated from the music and effects tracks and well suited to the film's overheated tone), the original mono mix, and a very funny French track, not to mention French and Spanish subtitles and, amazingly, the film's first presentation with closed captions.

A fully loaded special edition, *Dressed to Kill* contains all the supplements a fan could want (well, except for maybe a Donaggio interview and isolated score). "The Making of *Dressed to Kill*" features interviews with De Palma, Dickinson, Allen, Gordon, Franz, and producer George Litto, all of whom offer completely individual anecdotes about the making of the film. De Palma provides the structuring voice of the piece, though as with his appearance on the *Obsession* documentary, it's apparent he feels more comfortable behind a camera than in front of one. Interestingly, little attention is given to the radical transformation the film underwent during its various drafts, beginning as a vignette in a proposed De Palma film of *Cruising* to the finished form today. Check out the discontinued but easily available paperback novelization by De Palma for a peek at an earlier, fascinating draft of the story. Allen seems to have the best memory for the production, though everyone offers something of value. And don't miss Dickinson's surprise use of one of the film's props during the end credits.

Two featurettes cover the censorship aspects of the film, one comparing the variant unrated, R, and bastardized TV cuts, and the other ("Slashing *Dressed to Kill*") recounting the protests and violent reactions during its release as well as the MPAA scandal, one of the first of many. "An Appreciation by Keith Gordon" features the actor/director recounting his own experiences with the film and, as with his appearance on the *Jaws 2* disc, explaining how it influenced his later career choice. Other extras include the spoiler-packed theatrical trailer, two galleries of promotional photographs and the terrific advertising art both used and rejected, and the usual "collectible booklet," which appears to have been hastily prepared and incorrectly lists *Body Double* as De Palma's next film.

DRILLER KILLER

Colour, 1979, 96m. / Directed by Abel Ferrara / Starring Jimmy Laine (Abel Ferrara) / Cult Epics (US R1 NTSC), Visual Entertainment (UK R2 PAL), Opening Edition (France R2 PAL)

One of the key titles in the notorious "video nasty" panic in Britain, *Driller Killer* has, like *I Spit on Your Grave*, risen to infamy based almost entirely on its title alone. While video box covers and lurid posters for the film promised a maniac stalking semi-clad nubile beauties, this depiction couldn't possibly be more misleading. In fact, this extremely low budget artsy film spends most of its running time etching a despairing, *Taxi Driver*-like portrayal of scuzzy New York life during the late '70s, and all of the victims killed onscreen are male. Not surprisingly, teens who checked this one out on video expecting cheap splatter thrills were often crushingly disappointed.

Reno (director Abel Ferrara), a starving artist, lives in a squalid New York apartment surrounded by drunken derelicts, one of whom happens to be his father. Plagued with nightmarish visions and barely able to keep any food in the fridge, Reno tenuously clings to sanity thanks to the presence of his girlfriend, Carol (Carolyn Marz), who is currently separated from her husband and also has a live-in lesbian lover, Pamela (Baybi Day). Reno works desperately on a huge painting of a buffalo which he hopes will earn some money from a flamboyantly gay art rep, but his concentration is shattered when a punk band moves next door and plays all day and night. Pretty soon Reno snaps and starts darting around the nocturnal city streets, picking off the occasional bum with his electric hand drill.

An interesting cult item, *Driller Killer* was the first semi-legitimate effort from director Abel Ferrara (who had earlier directed and acted in the hardcore *Nine Lives of a Wet Pussy* and crafted a Keith Richards short film). Though the result is flawed, at least it's more imaginative and vibrant than some of

Ferrara's later work, such as *Dangerous Game*. On its own terms, *Driller Killer* offers occasional stylish moments, a quirky sense of humour, and some very potent atmosphere but would have probably vanished into oblivion were it not for Ferrara's dazzling follow up film, *Ms. 45*, which explores much of the same territory from a female perspective. Only two scenes qualify as graphically violent but are relatively tame compared to the splashier '80s horror trends; in fact, Ferrara's pizza eating habits are far more repulsive.

Shot on 16mm during the weekends over a period of almost two years, *Driller Killer* has never looked too great, and it still doesn't on the Cult Epics DVD. It's cleaner and smoother than the VHS versions during the daylight scenes, which unfortunately comprise about 5% of the film; otherwise, the murky photography and uneven film development processing will never be too visually appealing. The opening sequence in particular looks smudgy and dark, but at least Ferrara's stylish quirks and inventive use of colour emerge throughout. Had this been a standard priced horror title, fans would have little room to complain, but considering the hefty price tag, a few consumers may be justifiably upset. Ferrara provides a highly unique commentary in which he says "uh oh" about five thousand times and makes weird, growling comments about all of the actresses in the film. He does offer a few interesting nuggets of trivia about low budget shooting during that period, but mostly he rambles off slurred reactions to the onscreen events and repeatedly criticizes his own work ("Let's see if this scene can go on half an hour longer;" "Hey, there's a good shot, for once"). Not exactly the best way for an auteur to build enthusiasm for his work, eh? The DVD also includes a thorough Ferrara filmography and a 30 second trailer that includes one shot (a close-up of Reno saying "it's only a window, Dalton") that isn't in the actual film. The censored UK DVD offers the same extras, minus some splatter. The anamorphically enhanced French DVD is really the only visually appealing option, and it also throws in a blood-drenched trailer, the aforementioned commentary, audio options in English or French, and optional subtitles in French, Dutch, or Spanish.

DRIVE-IN DISCS VOL. 1
ATTACK OF THE GIANT LEECHES

B&W, 1960, 62m. / Directed by Bernard L. Kowalski / Starring Ken Clark, Yvette Vickers
THE SCREAMING SKULL
B&W, 1955, 66m. / Directed by Alex Nicol / Starring John Hudson, Peggy Webber
Elite (US R1 NTSC) / WS (1.85:1) (16:9)

Already a mythologized piece of Americana lore after recently passing into extinction, the drive-in experience is difficult to explain to those who never had a chance to sit out and watch a good, juicy B-movie under the stars. However, the souped-up technological thrills of the DVD format have inspired more than a few folks to recreate the experience, including several public domain double and triple headers as well as a dizzying series of Something Weird double bills, complete with ad pitches and trailers. Elite Entertainment tosses in its two cents with the ambitiously titled *Drive-In Discs #1*, pairing up the beloved grade-Z monster romp *Attack of the Giant Leeches* (given its familiar shortened name, *The Giant Leeches*, on the packaging) with a more restrained spooky mystery, *The Screaming Skull*. So, does the disc itself live up to its potential? Let's find out...

A heavy breathing attempt to inject monsters into the backwoods, poor white trash genre, *Giant Leeches* kicks off with lonely boater Lem spotting a huge, sucker-covered black creature darting through the swamp water near his shack. He hurries to the local watering hole to tell his tale, where the lusty, married Liz (*Attack of the 50-Foot Woman*'s Yvette Vickers) is making the moves on Cal (Michael Emmet). Nobody wants to believe Lem's story, but soon he and other townsfolk fall prey to the slimy monsters, who drag their victims off to a watery cave to be, well, sucked to death. Good guy lawman Steve (Ken Clark) and his sweetie, Nan (Jan Shepard), lead expeditions into the swamps, where bloodless bodies have begun to drift up. Can the leeches be stopped before the entire town becomes a midnight snack?

Pure trash from start to finish, *The Giant Leeches* is terrifically entertaining. Vickers really steals the show, prancing around in skimpy clothing (or, more precisely, glorified undies), licking on lollipops and eventually becoming screaming, wide-eyed leech fodder. Producer Gene Corman doesn't skimp on the cheap thrills (and yes, his brother Roger was an executive producer), and the scuba-diving leech costumes (which change from sucker-covered suits to guys apparently covered in trash bags) are among the more peculiar entries in the '50s monster sweepstakes. The fabled leech feeding scene is a particular highlight and surely scared the bejeezus out of more than a few impressionable kiddies at matinee showings. At least in visual terms, *The Screaming Skull* is a classier affair thanks to slick cinematography by Roger Corman's gifted cinematographer, Floyd Crosby, and some effective gothic atmosphere. Ignore the vapid story, which finds shifty Eric Whitlock (John Hudson) returning to his familial estate after the mysterious bludgeoning death of his first wife. Eric's new bride, Jenni (Peggy Webber), is more than a tad distraught over the ghostly events taking place in the house, with skulls popping up in the unlikeliest of places as she battles insomnia by wandering the property in a diaphanous nightgown. Not surprisingly, there's a decidedly non-supernatural explanation behind it all... or is there?

Though painfully light on actual shocks, *The Screaming Skull* is still entertaining enough thanks to its overwrought acting and a bravura final act, which finds the main characters (and the viewer) pelted by skulls lurching out of closets, hallways, and swimming pools. It ain't art, to be sure, but the whole thing amuses in a sub-William Castle manner, and *Mystery Science Theatre 3000* viewers will remember it from one of the program's more memorable episodes. In addition to the films, Elite has decked out this disc with a slew of gorgeously preserved intermission reels and concession stand ads. Aside from the familiar "Let's Go Out to the Lobby" promo, you also get ads for "Chilly Dilly" pickles, trailers for films like *The Wasp Woman*, and a couple of public domain Max Fleischer cartoons featuring Popeye and Betty Boop. All of this archival material looks great and appears to have undergone quite a bit of restoration.

Unfortunately, that brings us to the real problem with this disc. Most fans would probably like to pick this up for the films themselves, and they simply look wretched. *The Giant Leeches* has never fared too well on video (including Slingshot's earlier PD release of it with *A Bucket of Blood* and *The Wasp Woman*), but the cruddy compression job (with all of this material smushed onto a single DVD layer) leaves the pasty image riddled with artefacts of every conceivable nature. The washed out opening scene is unwatchable, and it just gets worse. Reasonably crisp editions of *The Screaming Skull* have been floating around for years, so its presentation here is even more of a shock. Some poorly applied noise reduction has left the image soft and dull, but the jagged surfaces of objects shimmer and strobe all over the screen. The contrast is also overdone, leaving everything a stark black or white, with skin tones erupting into glaring chalky hazes throughout. Also, apart from the two cartoons, everything has been letterboxed at 1.85:1. While the gimmick of 16:9 enhancement sounds nice, trying to crop off what looks like a VHS transfer of a 16mm source proves disastrous, leaving the original full

191

frame compositions cramped and uncomfortable. Most of the credits still miraculously remain onscreen, but this really isn't how these films were meant to be framed. The attitude here appears to be that the ephemera surrounding the drive-in experience is more important than the films themselves, so the main features have been simply thrown in with little regard for their target audience. The disc also includes an alternate track in "Distorto," which presents a 5.1 audio replication of the drive-in experience. Basically this means lots of split channel effects of car doors slamming, crickets chirping, and girls asking boys to go grab a Coke. This leaves the program audio itself gurgling from the front left channel, just like a drive-in speaker attached to your car. The ambient effect is fun for a few minutes, but the potential for a genuinely creative or comic scenario here was really blown. Imagine all the things that really went on at drive-ins, and you'll get the idea of where they could have gone with this one. A second drive-in disc pairing up *The Giant Gila Monster* and *The Wasp Woman* essentially offers more of the same.

THE DUNWICH HORROR

Colour, 1970, 88m. / Directed by Daniel Haller / Starring Sandra Dee, Dean Stockwell, Ed Begley / MGM (US R1 NTSC) / WS (1.85:1) (16:9)

Though MGM's packaging desperately tries to pass this film off as a satanic thriller in the vein of *Rosemary's Baby*, this second H.P. Lovecraft adaptation from art director turned auteur Daniel Haller (*Die, Monster, Die!*) is actually another flawed attempt to capture the unimaginable, cosmic gods of Lovecraft's literature on film. While the placement of giggling good girl Sandra Dee in such a milieu could have been disastrous, she actually makes a fairly credible horror heroine; the film's weakness in fact lie elsewhere, making it a fascinating if ultimately not quite satisfying visual feast combining psychedelia with gothic excess.

Vaguely creepy Wilbur Whately (Dean Stockwell) appears at Miskatonic University to raid the archives for the Necronomicon, a tome containing details and summoning instructions for an ancient race of gods known as the Old Ones. Lovely student Nancy (Sandra Dee) also catches Wilbur's eye, though not for reasons one might suspect; in fact, he attempts to steal the book and plans to use Nancy in a recreation of a ritual which

led to Wilbur's supernaturally tainted birth. Meanwhile Wilbur's unseen twin brother, locked up within the confines of the Whately estate, becomes increasingly impatient for the arrival of its creators, and Nancy's decision to accompany Wilbur to the less than hospitable hometown of Dunwich results in a stormy, violent finale which finds our warlock anti-hero facing off against the resourceful Dr. Armitage (Ed Begley), the only man capable of halting Wilbur's occult rituals.

More of a visual artist than an assured storyteller, Haller imbues *Dunwich* with a strong, off-kilter atmosphere of ancient evil seeping within the very stones and earth of New England, perhaps in a manner even more palpable than that of his mentor, Roger Corman (who stayed on as executive producer). Even Corman's regular composer, Les Baxter, turns up to provide an insanely catchy music score, most memorably accompanied by animated opening credits. Sadly long out of print after a brief appearance on vinyl, the music alone may be enough to draw in both horror fans and lounge music buffs.

After the ultimately lukewarm reception of this film (along with the similarly flawed *The Shuttered Room*), Lovecraft adaptations seemed to have become extinct until Stuart Gordon injected new life with his delirious *Re-Animator*, which ushered in a brief but welcome new renaissance for America's second most respected writer of classic horror/fantasy.

Originally rated M and re-rated PG under the new MPAA system, *The Dunwich Horror* made its first video appearance in a murky, open matte transfer from Embassy. Those cheaply produced tapes didn't last on most shelves for very long, but perhaps it was all for the best. When the rights passed over to MGM, the studio released a VHS edition containing a minute of previously unseen footage trimmed before the film's theatrical run. Consisting of various female nude shots (including one partially undraped body which could be Dee or a body double, though the dubious MGM "Fun Facts" on the box claim it was really her), the restored footage made this one of the most eagerly anticipated DVD titles.

Fortunately the extended version (with a new R rating) has remained intact on DVD, where it now sports a lustrous anamorphic transfer as well. The framing looks a little tight on top at times, but generally the compositions seem balanced and don't lose anything in the wider aspect ratio. The disc also includes the original AIP theatrical trailer, which indicates what a tough sell this movie was back in 1970.

EATEN ALIVE (DEATH TRAP)

Colour, 1976, 88m. / Directed by Tobe Hooper / Starring Neville Brand, Mel Ferrer, Carolyn Jones / Elite (US R1 NTSC) / WS (1.85:1) (16:9), Diamond (US R0 NTSC), Vipco (UK R0 PAL)

Following the unexpected success of *The Texas Chainsaw Massacre*, director Tobe Hooper decided to switch cinematic locales from the arid landscapes of Texas to the sultry bayous of Louisiana. In *Eaten Alive*, also known on the drive-in and horror grindhouse circuit under such titles as *Horror Hotel, Starlight Slaughter*, and *Death Trap*, Hooper cranks up the sick humour with which he discreetly laced his first film. Unfortunately, few bothered to see or remember *Eaten Alive*, thanks to bad distribution and its notable departure from the *Chainsaw* method of guerrilla horror filmmaking.

At a sleazy brothel run by Miss Hattie (Carolyn Jones), a newly arrived hooker (Crystin Sinclaire) with a bad wig decides she doesn't want to cooperate with horny cowpoke Buck (a very young Robert Englund, who delivers the hilarious opening line). The naive girl gets kicked out and winds up at the Starlight Motel, where the owner, Judd (Neville Brand), welcomes her with a particularly grisly form of hospitality. Soon after, a family comes to stay for the night. The father, Roy (William Finley), gets extremely peeved when the family dog gets eaten by Judd's pet crocodile. When Roy tries to take a shotgun to the hungry croc, Judd pulls out his trusty scythe and takes care of his rude guest. Roy's daughter, Angie (a pre-Halloween Kyle Richards), soon winds up orphaned, but more company arrives in the form of the hooker's father, Harvey (Mel Ferrer), and sister, Faye (Marilyn Burns). As the unhinged Judd tries to cover up his ghastly crimes, events soon spin wildly and violently out of control.

While *Texas Chainsaw* earned respect for depicting violence almost entirely through suggestion rather than graphic bloodletting, Hooper pulls out all the stops here. People munching, dog munching, slashings, and shootings are all splashed across the screen, but fortunately Hooper keeps his tongue in cheek by depicting the murderer as a quirky, wooden-legged backwoods yokel who elicits as many nervous chuckles as screams. Filmed almost entirely inside a single set, the film makes good use of its claustrophobic environment and some surreal, stylish visual touches, though mainstream horror fans may find the pace too slow and erratic to build much momentum. The actors generally do a good

job, with movie tough guy Brand gleefully chomping the scenery (this was during his odd drive-in period, which also included *Psychic Killer*). And once again, Hooper and Wayne Bell have crafted an unnerving musique concrete score that drives up the suspense as much as the events onscreen.

Priced as a bargain public domain level title, the first DVD release of *Eaten Alive* from Diamond sinks well below normal professional standards - quite unwatchable, in fact, suffering from a substandard compression job which causes many colourful background walls during the film to crawl like ants. Luckily it's eclipsed by the Elite version, which still suffers from some print damage but looks much cleaner and more colourful. The anamorphic widescreen framing looks dead on, and the well balanced night scenes look better than during the film's original drive-in run.

ECSTASY OF THE ANGELS

Colour/B&W, 1972, 88m. / Directed by Koji Wakamatsu / Starring Ken Yoshizawa, Rie Yokoyama / Image (US R0 NTSC) / WS (1.66:1) (16:9)

Ecstasy of the Angels (Tenshi No Kokotsu), a jarring exercise in experimental cinema from the director of *Go, Go Second Time Virgin*, was also shown as *Angelic Orgasm*, which should tell you something. While *Go, Go* features a somewhat linear narrative to couch its more bizarre flights of fancy, this film dispenses with conventional storytelling to plunge into a melange of political dissertations, rough and violent sex, explosions, and swanky nightclubs.

A band of military radicals passes its time by hanging out at a club, engaging in sweaty lovemaking, and plotting the infiltration of foreign military bases to obtain weapons. Known only by their code names lifted from days of the week, they become increasingly paranoid when their latest scheme is thwarted by an explosion, leaving them fighting a rival group and ripping each other apart. In the most extended and unpleasantly memorable sequence, a villainous man in sunglasses leading the rival group attempts to learn the whereabouts of a secret arsenal by impaling a woman's thigh with a pencil while her boyfriend is pummelled in the background... and it only goes downhill from there.

Though it certainly looks and feels like an exploitation picture, *Ecstasy of the Angels* clearly has much more on its mind. The infusion of radical

E

politics into the head-spinning assault of nudity and gore makes for a very odd experience, and the rapid shifts in time, film stock (black and white alternating with colour), sound effects, and character affiliations make this a dense, difficult hour and a half. Many scenes appear to be constructed simply to make the viewer ponder, "What the heck was that, and what is this movie about?" Whenever things threaten to spin completely out of control, however, Wakamatsu manages to throw in another round of sex and violence to hold one's interest before he barrels forward to another downbeat, poetic ending.

The film transfer of *Ecstasy of the Angels* looks just fine given the age and nature of the film; though lacking the visual formality of *Go, Go Second Time Virgin*, the film still contains some stunning cinematography and a surreal, hypnotic editing scheme. The permanent subtitles appear to capture the essence of the dialogue, which comes in erratic bursts, and the mono audio sounds perfectly clear if unspectacular. The disc contains extensive, informative liner notes by the American Cinematheque's Chris D. and a shot-on-video interview with Wakamatsu.

THE EDUCATIONAL ARCHIVES
Fantoma (US R1 NTSC)

The onslaught of home video wiped out the use of 16mm classroom films in most schools after the early 1990s, but anyone should be able to relate on some level to Fantoma's pair of entries in *The Educational Archives*. The scratchy educational film has recently been transformed by nostalgia into a symbol of naiveté and kitsch, rubbing kids' faces in lurid subject matter while wagging a finger and telling how awful, awful it all is. While the more notorious of these films took more than a page from the *Reefer Madness* school of cinema by exaggerating their subjects to the point of absurdity, these offerings from Fantoma are more quaint and grounded in reality, offering education with an entertaining little twist.

Volume One, "Sex & Drugs," starts out a little misleadingly with the bizarre "LSD: A Case Study," which amounts to swirling colours splashed over a *La Jetée*-style montage of narrative photos as the female narrator finds her acid trip disrupted by a talking troll hot dog. Really. Things settle down after

that with other "Case Study" films devoted to heroin, barbiturates, and amphetamines (aka speed), all attempting to interpret their testimonials in visual terms. Other gems include "Human Growth," in which a sitcom friendly son and daughter on the brink of puberty go to school and learn the very vague facts of life; "Narcotics: Pit of Despair," a goofy anti-beatnik rant in which a man is lured into dope by his dropout friend; "Know for Sure," a black and white cautionary tale about syphilis; "It's Wonderful Being a Girl," in which a mom and daughter have a little heart to heart about tampons (interspersed with an unintentionally hilarious talk about periods around the swimming pool); "Marijuana," the notorious Sonny Bono clip in which the late politician (in bad Sgt. Pepper garb) offers some half-hearted words of advice against the evil weed; "Social-Sex Attitudes in Adolescence," a broad overview of sexual activity during the '50s with straight faced narration by Lorne Green; "LSD: Insight or Insanity," a pretty typical late '60s anti-acid diatribe with Sal Mineo cashing his paycheck; and finally the bizarre, thoroughly unexpected "The ABC of Sex-Ed for Trainables," which kicks off with a female teacher urging a conference room of teachers to rattle off slang terms for the male member, followed by a study of how to broach the subject of the birds and the bees with the mentally impaired. Revealing, bracing stuff, and an appropriate close to a fascinating disc.

Though the title of "Social Engineering 101" for Volume Two might sound a bit more bland, have no fear; the fun's just starting. In "Lunchroom Manners," a kid is scared straight from being rude at the lunch table after seeing a puppet show about the pushy, inconsiderate Mr. Bungle. More disturbing is "Soapy the Germ Fighter," in which a dirty young boy's sleep is ruptured by the presence of a giant, creepy talking bar of soap with arms. "Appreciating Our Parents" explains why mom and dad are so dysfunctional, showing that bread winning and house care can be enough to lead to borderline child neglect. In "Shy Guy," *Bewitched*'s Dick York awkwardly plays an introverted radio geek who tries to ingratiate himself to his classmates by silently observing their behaviour and imitating them. And according to the film, this is a good thing. The short "Why Doesn't Cathy Eat Breakfast?" is almost Godardian in its utter refusal to offer any kind of coherence or point, instead focusing on a young girl who just won't eat the most important meal of the day. Turn off the projector and discuss! "Right or Wrong?" promises a stark, black and white hell for those who make the wrong choice in basic ethical decisions, such as returning lost objects or being a tattle tale. The B&W parade continues with "Personality and Emotions," in which friends, brothers, and sisters are shown interacting in all the right and wrong ways. (Interestingly, this one probably holds up the best out of the bunch thanks to its non-reliance on period stereotypes and lingo.) "Why Vandalism?" would make a good companion piece to stuff like *The Violent Years* and *Jacktown* as it demonstrates the threat of hooliganism and tries to get to the bottom of this emotionally troubling phenomenon. Surrealism rears its head again with Mr. Chalky teaching fascist "Manners in School" to a pushy kid who really should know better. Finally, "The Outsider" - basically a gender twist on "Shy Guy" - finds a normal looking girl coping with that certain disconnected feeling at school, only to slowly work her way back in as a productive member of society.

Lovingly compiled and presented, these are all above average examples of the educational film format and rarely offer the tedious stretches of banal lecturing which marred the worst examples. Don't expect to relive that feeling of eyelids drooping down onto your desk while watching these programs, thank God. The time periods range from the early '50s to the '70s, but the tone and approach stays about the same regardless. How effective these films were in the end is subject to debate, but at least they gave several generations of kids fond memories and a certain favourite film they no doubt carry around with them to this day. As expected, image quality depends entirely on the source material from one film to the next. Some feature jumps, scratches, blotches, or faded colour, but all are watchable and look at least a step or two above your standard 16mm print that's been circulating through dozens of classrooms. Since the entire disc could be considered a huge batch of extras, the only real ancillary materials are a pair of amusing classroom filmstrips and informative, brochure-style liner notes by avgeeks.com's Skip Elsheimer. Another two volumes are also available, covering driver's education and job safety. Let the 16mm madness begin!

EDWARD SCISSORHANDS

Colour, 1990, 105m. / Directed by Tim Burton / Starring Johnny Depp, Winona Ryder / Fox (US R1 NTSC, UK R2 PAL) / WS (1.85:1) (16:9) / DD4.0

Edward (Depp) is the Frankensteinian creation of a kindly inventor (Vincent Price) who resides in a castle overlooking Suburbia. When the old man dies before completing his work, Edward is left with a

temporary collection of knives and scissors where there would soon have been hands. Rescued from the solitude of the castle by Avon lady Peg Boggs (Wiest), Edward attempts to adapt to a normal life by turning his blades first to topiary and then hairstyling. But the admiration he enjoys as someone "different" doesn't last long, and once the rot sets in his new found life quickly sours.

Tim Burton appears to have an affinity for social outcasts - the Dark Knight (*Batman* and *Batman Returns*), Vincent Molloy (in his supreme animated short, *Vincent*), Jack Skellington (*The Nightmare Before Christmas*) and even to a degree Ed Wood (in the bitter-sweet biopic of the same name). Together with actor Johnny Depp he created the superlative pariah and an almost flawless masterpiece with the sentimental fairytale *Edward Scissorhands*. Woven into its fantastical framework is an extremely touching almost-romance between Depp and Ryder that's doomed before it even begins. Indeed, Depp's performance evokes such empathy that the cloying sense of despair over his fate at the picture's conclusion is tangible to the point that multiple viewings do nothing to diminish its potency. Frequent Burton collaborator Danny Elfman's enchanting score peaks during a stunning Burton visual coup when Ryder twirls in slow motion, the air filling with shimmering crystals as Depp fiercely carves away at an ice sculpture. Sheer magic.

Fox's "10th Anniversary Edition" DVD serves Burton's ultimate fantasy extravaganza well, with a lush transfer that preserves in pin sharp detail the snow-sprinkled vistas, the succulent greens of Edward's garden and the searing blue skyscapes above.

Divided into 24-chapters and with sound options in English 4.0 Surround, English Dolby Surround or French Dolby Surround (with subtitling in either English or Spanish), there are a number of extras, though nothing nearly as exciting as the sleeve listing might lead one to expect. There are two commentaries, one from Tim Burton and another from Danny Elfman, plus a couple of trailers and a small collection of TV spots (some of which are dubbed in Spanish). The featurette and soundbites are little more than brief interview excerpts with cast and crew. However, it's the gallery of concept art that proves most unsatisfactory of all; given the wealth of materials that must exist, it comprises just six (yes, six!) of Burton's drawings and is wholly unrepresentative of the man's unique talents. Recommended for the presentation of the movie

E

alone, provided you don't expect too much from the extras you won't be disappointed. - TG

Note: The UK Fox disc contains the same extras but is missing 15 seconds of footage, removed in order to obtain a PG certificate. - ed.

81/2

B&W, 1963, 138m. / Directed by Federico Fellini / Starring Marcello Mastroianni, Claudia Cardinale / Criterion (US R1 NTSC) / WS (1.85:1) (16:9)

 If you think of the Federico Fellini filmography as a series of college courses, *8?* is Calculus III - the difficult, towering, but rewarding hurdle after which everything else feels utterly simple. Is it a work of towering brilliance or a self-indulgent, rambling spectacle? Well, both of course, and that's most of the fun. Burned out by the hectic pace of maintaining his status as a celebrity director, Guido (Marcello Mastroianni) finds temporary release by drifting off into fantasies, the first of which finds him ascending into the clouds during a traffic jam. Guido seeks solace and rejuvenation at a remote health spa for the rich and privileged, where he continues to encounter journalists, his producer (Guido Alberti), and most inconvenient of all, his aloof wife, Luisa (Anouk Aimée), and his sultry mistress, Carla (Sandra Milo). His flights of fancy continue as he flashes back and forth between past, present, and future, his childhood memories sprinkled with outrageous exaggeration and moments of pure surrealism: a towering buxom beauty, a horde of women (including Italian horror icon Barbara Steele) submitting to his will as he whips them into shape, and the angelic epitome of inspiration, Claudia Cardinale herself. Meanwhile his producer initiates preparations for a massive science fiction film, the antithesis of the pure and honest film Guido longs to make.

Along with *La Dolce Vita*, this film personifies what people associate with the term "Felliniesque." Buxom women bouncing across the screen, eccentric people gallivanting through fields and carnivalesque settings, and bizarre fantasy sequences pepper this sprawling foray into the mind of a director unsure of how to progress with his next film. Of course, it's no secret that this subject was exactly the problem Fellini himself had at the time, making this an elaborate game of mirrors in which Fellini and his cinematic alter ego become difficult to separate. Everyone involved operates at the top of their form here, from all of the women (who seem to appreciate

being at the centre of Fellini's attention when his camera turns to them) to Nino Rota's buoyant score, easily one of his best. Criterion's earlier laserdisc of *81/2* looked fairly good, considering, and certainly beat out the more widely seen English dubbed edition from MPI, which was washed out and barely letterboxed at 1.55:1. The dubbing *per se* actually wasn't that bad, since Fellini as usual had all of the Italian dialogue looped in later with only scant regard for the actors' lip movements anyway. In either English or Italian, you're not hearing the actors' voices. (His later films, most notably *Satyricon* and *Casanova*, actually hold up better in their English dubbed versions, which are sadly the lesser seen variants.) The DVD looks almost immaculate, with only some vague fluttering in dark areas inherent in the original film offering any distraction from the amazing, beautifully lit black and white visuals.

More than just a presentation of the movie, the DVD is also a handy crash course in Fellini in general. A commentary track (apparently edited together from two different locales) features Fellini critic and colleague Gideon Bachmann and NYU film professor Antonio Monda dissecting the film and placing it in context within the director's career. The track starts uneasily, as most of the discussion points out to the viewer clues to differentiate between the dream sequences and reality (which also drains out a lot of the fun from the film), but gradually the commentary becomes looser and less focused on picking apart what everything in the film might mean. Other extras on the first disc include an engaging seven minute intro by Terry Gilliam (which oddly doesn't play before the film itself and must be selected separately), an illustrated booklet of Fellini essays (including snippets from his autobiography), and the kinky American theatrical trailer (prominently pushing distributor Joseph Levine, as usual). Disc two offers much more, including "Fellini: A Director's Notebook" (a 52 minute autobiographical study detailing his work habits), the 48 minute "Nino Rota: Between Cinema and Concert" a tribute to one of Italy's most esteemed musical talents; a large selection of production and promotional photographs; and interviews with Milo, director Lina Wertmuller, and Vittorio Storaro (a disciple of this film's brilliant cinematographer, Gianni di Venanzo).

81/2 WOMEN

Colour, 1999, 122m. / Directed by Peter Greenaway / Starring John Standing, Polly Walker / Universal (US R1 NTSC) / WS (1.66:1) (16:9) / DD2.0

Continuing his pattern of alternating critically praised arthouse projects with alienating personal studies, the controversial Peter Greenaway followed his unexpectedly popular *The Pillow Book* with *81/2 Women*, a playful and thoroughly obscure compendium of art history, fetishism, film history, and globe-hopping comic debauchery. The results pleased few, but Greenaway fanatics will find it more rewarding than newcomers despite its glaring flaws.

Following the death of his wife, Philip Emmenthal (John Standing) finds his structured world falling apart. He seeks solace in his Swiss estate with his son, Storey (Matthew Delamere), who runs a string of pachinko gambling parlours in Japan. After seeing Fellini's *81/2* at a repertory theatre, they devise a strange means of grief therapy and sexual release by turning the Swiss home into a brothel for one year. Between the two countries they recruit eight and a half highly unusual females for their experiment (and yes, the half woman is exactly what you think, as tasteless as that concept may sound). Among the women: Griselda (Toni Collette), a butch Swedish accountant who escapes conviction for embezzlement and takes up a fantasy existence as a nun; Beryl (Amanda Plummer), a horse enthusiast with a neck brace whose greatest love is her giant pet pig; Palmira (Polly Walker), an open society whore who gives her body to Philip but sparks anguished desire within Storey; and many others, including a compulsive Japanese gambler and an overly fertile Italian. Gradually the ongoing process of the life cycle decreases their number, and Philip and Storey find that escaping into fantasies can yield only temporary rewards.

In his original screenplay for this film, Greenaway assembled a wild concoction of homages to Fellini and Godard, with each women corresponding to both a Fellini film and a popular erotic trope in art history. This analogy is mostly scrapped in the film, which still includes portions of the screenplay itself as superimposed title cards but comes off as more disjointed and ultimately perplexing. Storey's bizarre ability to predict and even cause earthquakes results in a weak punchline, with the final tender moments of the story strangely muted and lacking in much emotional or aesthetic resonance. Most damningly, this film suffers even more than *The Pillow Book* or *The Baby of Macon* from the absence of composer Michael Nyman. If the two men can't patch things up, Greenaway needs to find another composer, and quickly, to fill the strange aural void left within his recent films. On the other hand, like other Greenaways, *81/2 Women* is often rapturously beautiful to watch, with Sacha Vierney's camerawork as steady and painterly as ever. Many of the comic scenes are unforgettable, with some especially funny banter between the father and son keeping things more lightweight than might be expected. Especially amusing are Collette's last few scenes, which are not easily forgotten. As with *Prospero's Books*, one can only wonder how on earth this film got away with an R rating considering the avalanche of nudity on display (including Plummer, alas), though the relative lack of actual sex scenes may be the reason.

Greenaway films depend heavily on a good presentation due to their meticulous visual arrangements, and the DVD of *81/2 Women* looks particularly outstanding on video. The colours here are truly amazing to watch, particularly during the eye candy compositions of the pachinko scenes and a few of Greenaway's trademark pastoral landscape shots. A couple of zoom shots, particularly the very first image of the movie, reveal some visual limitations within the original film, but overall this looks better than the theatrical prints and benefits from a more generous 1.66:1 framing, with slight windowboxing on the sides during anamorphic playback. The surround audio is fine considering there isn't much going on, sonically speaking. The disc also includes the US theatrical trailer in fullscreen, an appropriately bizarre and intriguing piece of promotion.

THE ELEMENT OF CRIME

Colour, 1984, 104m. / Directed by Lars von Trier / Starring Michael Elphick, Me Me Lai / Criterion (US R1 NTSC) / WS (1.85:1) (16:9)

Long before he became one of the great modern *enfants terribles* of filmmaking with *Breaking the Waves*, *The Idiots*, and *Dancer in the Dark*, Danish director Lars von Trier already had talent to burn in his first film, *The Element of Crime* (or *Forbrydelsens element* in its native country). Like most of his films, this is definitely a love it or hate it project, with a visually dazzling appearance and deliberately sluggish pace that will leave uninitiated viewers begging for mercy after 15 minutes. For those who like von Trier or edgy world cinema, *The Element of Crime* is required viewing, but others definitely will want to rent before they buy. Seasoned, world weary retired cop Fisher (Michael Elphick) sits beneath the unsettling gaze of an obese, foreign therapist (Ahmed El Shenawi), who uses hypnosis to coerce Fisher into relating the horrific tale of what happened to him in Europe. Told in flashbacks with constant voiceovers, the story follows Fisher from his complacent residence in Cairo to his old stomping grounds in a post-apocalyptic Germany, where some unnamed disaster has left the world bathed in perpetual darkness and drenched in polluted, shimmering lakes. Fisher consults an esteemed criminologist and former detective, Osborne (Esmond Knight), who has written a detailed procedural work called *The Element of Crime*. According to the book, a detective can retrace a killer's steps and, by inhabiting the criminal's environment, discover everything he needs to know about the culprit. Fisher decides to use the book as his model for hunting down Harry Gray, the primary suspect in a gruesome series of slayings dubbed "The Lotto Murders," because the victims were all young female lottery ticket sellers who wound up strangled and disfigured with broken bottles. Fisher begins at the site of the first murder and works his way through the seedy local populace, encountering surreal characters and visual tableaux along the way. He hooks up with a prostitute named Kim (Me Me Lai, the star of *Jungle Holocaust* and *Man from Deep River*!) and takes her along on his journey, stopping occasionally to have sex with her in hotel rooms and atop Volkswagens. ("I'm going to screw you back to the Stone Age," he charmingly claims at one point, to which she later adds, "I want you to screw God into me.") Fisher feels himself closing in on his prey, but he soon comes to fear that his own soul may be disintegrating in his quest for the truth about the criminal mind.

While the plotline isn't much more than a retread of Thomas Harris' *Red Dragon* by way of *Blade Runner* postmodern film noir, von Trier's astounding visual sense turns the most mundane scenes into fascinating, multi-layered visuals. His most brilliant moments find the camera trailing over characters dangling near the edge of an abyss, as when Fisher languishes in a drunken haze by a stone precipice or Kim lies beneath an arrangement of glowing yellow lights. In fact, most of the film stock was manipulated into a hellish sepia tone, rendering unnatural shades of gold and orange over every scene except for occasional dramatic interruptions of electric blue (usually light bulbs or TV screens) or, more rarely, red. This technique could have been a childish stunt, but it works beautifully here and produces a sense of unease that never lets up. In a sense this feels like a dry run for his third film, the masterful *Europa* (or as Miramax christened it in the US, *Zentropa*, available as a widescreen DVD in Spain), which also opens

with the audience being lulled into hypnosis and sports a lab-manipulated use of monochromatic footage alternating with colour. Sharp eyed viewers should also look for a cameo by von Trier as a skinhead hotel clerk referred to by Fisher as the "Schmuck of Ages."

Apart from scarce arthouse screenings, for over a decade most viewers could only see *The Element of Crime* in a horribly muddy, cropped VHS edition from Unicorn. The Criterion edition looks infinitely better, and what was most likely a transfer technician's nightmare has resulted in a beautifully nuanced image with appropriately rich and black shadows. Don't panic when the film comes on; it really is supposed to look that way, and the film's look obviously influenced such later films as *The City of Lost Children* and pretty much everything by David Fincher. The mono soundtrack is fine, though the English dialogue can get muddy thanks to the international cast and oppressive sound mix. Thankfully Criterion has included optional English subtitles, which come in handy throughout the film.

The disc also includes the original European trailer, which blows several key moments late in the film, and a terrific 54 minute documentary, Stig Björkman's "Tranceformer: A Portrait of Lars von Trier," which features in depth interviews with von Trier and his long-time collaborators. From early family home movies to short film projects to his features up to *Breaking the Waves*, this is everything you could want to know about the controversial filmmaker. Especially interesting are mint quality clips from the rarely seen *Epidemic*, his second film, and some great behind the scenes footage from *Breaking the Waves*. (Funniest moment: Jean-Marc Barr's observation before shooting his shower stall scene with a naked Stellan Skarsgård.) There may not be a particularly groundbreaking message by the time it's all done, but at least you get a thorough, sometimes contradictory portrait of a cinematic voice that cannot be ignored.

THE ELEPHANT MAN
B&W, 1980, 125m. / Directed by David Lynch / Starring Anthony Hopkins, John Hurt / Paramount (US R1 NTSC) / WS (2.35:1) (16:9) / DD5.1, Pioneer (Japan R2 NTSC) / WS (2.35:1) / DD2.0, Momentum (UK R2 PAL) / WS (2.35:1) (16:9) / DD2.0

The least likely film imaginable to follow the abrasive midnight hit *Eraserhead*, David Lynch's *The Elephant Man* was the director's unorthodox entry into the Hollywood system by way of a black and white biopic featuring British actors which, against the odds, became a critical and commercial favourite. Along with *The Straight Story*, this film is one of Lynch's most accessible and, believe it or not, can be enjoyed by viewers who normally wouldn't come anywhere near his more avant garde experiments.

Based with a few embellishments on the true story of John Merrick (John Hurt), a deformed 19th Century man afflicted with the debilitating Proteus Syndrome, *The Elephant Man* focuses on his relationship with Dr. Frederick Treves (Anthony Hopkins), a respected physician. Treves first encounters Merrick on the sideshow circuit, where the "freak" is paraded before awestruck patrons by exploitation peddler Mr. Bates (Freddie Jones), who claims Merrick's title of "The Elephant Man" originated after Merrick's mother was tramped by a circus elephant during pregnancy. Treves brings his discovery to the attention of his fellow doctors and attempts to integrate John into some semblance of a normal lifestyle, providing some of the self esteem that has eluded him all his life.

While *The Elephant Man* is obviously a poignant and intelligent film, its impact is increased considerably by Lynch and his fellow contributors behind the camera. Cinematographer and occasional director Freddie Francis, one of the greatest cameramen who ever lived and a master of using the anamorphic frame, creates a stunning series of visual tableaux using black and white to reproduce images from Victorian photographs.

Though many sequences are still firmly entrenched in Lynch's experimental background, such as the nightmarish opening sequence and the striking cosmic finale (duplicated to equally touching effect in *The Straight Story*), for the most part Lynch restrains himself to focusing on the odd little details which form this universe, as alien in its own way as the surreal underbelly of Lumberton in *Blue Velvet*. He also receives excellent support from his once in a lifetime cast, featuring vets like John Gielgud and Wendy Hiller rubbing shoulders with the remarkable Hurt and Hopkins, as well as lone Yank Anne Bancroft as Mrs. Kendall (whom Merrick apparently never met in real life). Oddly enough this film was the first major release for Brooksfilms, Mel Brooks' production company, which went on to fund such titles as *My Favourite Year* and David Cronenberg's *The Fly*. This also explains why Brooks' regular composer, John Morris, turns up to provide such a remarkable score here.

Paramount's DVD offers the most attractive presentation of the film, with a cleansed and scrubbed anamorphic transfer and a suitably unnerving 5.1 audio mix. Pioneer's Japanese DVD, the first edition to be snapped up by collectors, suffers from a heavy amount of NTSC aliasing, and moiré patterns crops up during a few sequences. It also features the original theatrical surround mix, as does the more pleasing UK anamorphic PAL release from Momentum, which also boasts a handsome illustrated book inside the packaging. Only the US disc contains a new half hour featurette in which Hurt, Brooks, and company reminisce about the making of the film; unfortunately, as pleasant as these gentlemen are, they can only barely compensate for the notable absence of Hopkins and Lynch. A new interview with make-up artist Christopher Tucker and the original theatrical trailer round out the package.

EMBRYO

Colour, 1976, 104m. / Directed by Ralph Nelson / Starring Rock Hudson, Barbara Carrera / Passport (US R0 NTSC)

Embryo is the kind of perverse all-star schlock they just don't make anymore. As fascinating as a prolonged and expensive car wreck, this film is so odd, so completely removed from the normal standards of human cinematic behaviour, it really must be seen to be believed. Our well-intentioned scientist hero, Dr. Paul Holliston (Rock Hudson), devises a method of growing foetuses outside of the womb, along with the help of his moral conscience, Martha (Diane Ladd). After running over a dog during a rainstorm, he decides to take the dying pooch home and remove its foetus for scientific experiments. Sure enough, he's got a test tube Doberman on his hands... so hey, why not try it on a human foetus, too? The result of his next experiment is the beautiful and super-intelligent Victoria (Barbara Carrera), the perfect female companion. Unfortunately, contrary to Dr. Holliston's assumptions, genetics turns out to be a very tricky and nasty business.

Horror and science fiction films turned out to be a refuge for waning Hollywood stars in the '70s, most notably with Gregory Peck lending his expert thespian skills to *The Omen* and *The Boys from Brazil*. Unfortunately poor Rock is a long way from Douglas Sirk movies here, as he's forced to over-emote and spit out reams of scientific babble while drooling over an understandably confused Ms. Carrera. The film's highlight is a goofy high society party sequence in which Carrera squares off against temperamental master chessman Roddy McDowell, whose overacting will leave unprepared viewers in a state of shock. Look fast in the same scene for that perennial '70s media staple, Dr. Joyce Brothers, and don't miss the unbelievable finale.

While not all films could possibly command the deluxe treatment of, say, a Criterion special edition, *Embryo* at least deserves better than its DVD release here. Passport's disc manages to give the Arrow DVD of *The Brood* a solid run for its money as the absolute worst ever pressed; the image isn't even up to snuff compared to an EP-speed copy off of cable. Detail is completely lacking, shadows are washed out to a dull grey, the image is clumsily cropped from 1.85:1 without scanning, and video dropouts even litter the image on more than one occasion. The audio isn't any better, constantly buried under a sea of hiss and distortion. Ugh. The packaging lies and promises a theatrical trailer and "Dolby Surround Sound," neither of which materialize. Of more interest is a mini-program entitled "And God Created Woman," which compiles trailers for films like *Cat People* (both versions), *The Bride*, *Frankenstein Created Woman*, and a few other killer she-creature titles.

EMMANUELLE

Colour, 1974, 94m. / Directed by Just Jaeckin / Starring Sylvia Kristel / Wellspring (US R0 NTSC), Momentum (UK R2 PAL) / WS (1.66:1)

Ah, the '70s. A time when a film like *Emmanuelle* could make a fortune in the theatres. Though the erotic value of this notorious French drama doesn't pack much of a punch after decades of softcore fumbling, it's nice to see what a curious little film this really is. Shot in the spirit of a very expensive, skilful perfume ad, this at least works as trashy eye candy, a quality completely lost in the long unavailable, horrendous prints on home video from companies like RCA/Columbia.

The plot (pardon the term) concerns Sylvia Kristel as a restless young wife who explores her sexuality while visiting Thailand. She takes a female lover, learns the erotic art of love with the help of a dirty old man in a nice suit, and eventually becomes a complete exhibitionist. The movie never really says whether this is a good thing, but apparently a lot of people thought so judging from the positive response this received. Political correctness aside, *Emmanuelle* remains a professionally crafted work of Eurotrash, though exactly what sets it apart from other similar films of the era may not be obvious.

Wellspring's DVDs have received a lot of criticism, but they have done a nice job here. The transfer is clean, bright, and colourful, and the letterboxing clarifies a number of well-composed camera set-ups. Best of all, you can finally watch the film in French with (optional) English subtitles or in the familiar, atrociously dubbed English version. Just getting to hear both versions of Pierre Bachelet's kicky theme song is worth the price of admission alone. The later British disc (with a much better cover but missing 38 seconds of rough sex) offers even more languages (German, Italian, and Spanish) and a jaw-dropping 11 subtitle options (Danish, Dutch, English, Finnish, German, Italian, Norwegian, Portuguese, Spanish, Swedish and Turkish!), as well as the steamy trailer.

EMMANUELLE 2

Colour, 1975, 87m. / Directed by Francis Giacobetti / Starring Sylvia Kristel / Wellspring (US R0 NTSC), Momentum (UK R2 PAL) / WS (2.35:1)

Emmanuelle (Kristel) returns to Hong Kong to be with husband Jean (Orsini), whereupon she embarks on a series of extra-marital escapades, with the knowledge, blessing and occasional involvement of her ever so obliging hubby. In particular they both have their hearts set on bedding the beautiful virgin Anna-Maria (Rivet).

At the risk of slaughtering something of a sacred cow, aside from the fact that Just Jaeckin's original *Emmanuelle* brought softcore erotica to mainstream audiences en masse, it was a mind-numbingly dull film. *Emmanuelle 2* is superior on every count to its predecessor. On her second outing as the titular seductress, Sylvia Kristel's performance is far hotter than the first time round; the erotic bits are infinitely more arousing; the supporting ladies - among them Catherine Rivet, Caroline Laurenc and Laura Gemser (the latter in a soapy lesbian massage sequence that predates her taking on the role of Emmanuelle herself for a string of substandard B-graders) - are much sexier than before; Francis Giacobetti's direction is more involving than Just Jaeckin's; and Francis Lai's score has oodles more allure than his co-written score (with Pierre Bachelet) for the original. And never before has there been a finer endorsement of the therapeutic benefits of acupuncture!

Warning: Fox Lorber's Region Free US DVD - until recently the only version available to disc-seeking Kristel enthusiasts - falls short of perfection on several counts. Not only does it suffer from muted colours, in spite of the sleeve claim of a 92 minute running time (which deceitfully adds 6 minutes to the true running time) it's cut; most noticeably the sequence in which Emmanuelle watches an erotic Japanese animation is shorn of almost a third of the original footage. Where this sequence was presented intact (albeit compromised by fullscreen presentation) in the UK's original Thorn EMI cassette release, it was truncated to the point of virtual extinction in the reissued tape from 4 Front. What a surprise then to discover that when the film hit DVD in Britain, it was more complete than either the US disc or the UK tape. As with its lacklustre American cousin, Momentum Pictures' disc is sleeve-titled *Emmanuelle 2* but screen-identified *Emmanuelle L'Antivierge*, though the widescreen picture here is pin-sharp and colourful beyond description. It also comes up trumps in the sound division, giving one the options of either scoffing at the shoddy English dubbing or jettisoning it in favour of the original French soundtrack with English subtitles. Additionally one has audio options in German, Italian and Spanish, with subtitling in no less than 11 languages. There are a more than adequate 20 chapter stops. With the only shortcoming being in the supplement department - just a (French language) trailer - Momentum's DVD is the best treatment of this superior slice of 70s erotica to find its way onto the market and it should be pounced on and devoured with gusto. - TG

THE EROTIC ADVENTURES OF ZORRO

Colour, 1972, 102m. / Directed by William Allen Castleman & Robert Freeman / Starring Douglas Frey, Robyn Whitting / Image (US R0 NTSC)

 Another saucy take on a familiar American legend, *The Erotic Adventures of Zorro* drops the viewer right into the middle of pre-statehood California, where no-good racketeers control the land and exploit the Mexican people (as opposed to now, of course, where everyone is treated fairly and equally...). In the tradition of his earlier softcore romps, producer David F. Friedman piles on the jokes as fast as the skin, though the increasing explicitness of the era

(on the eve of *Deep Throat*) causes this film to crank up the explicitness several degrees. It's still not quite hardcore, but that's not for lack of trying.

The local people are currently held in a reign of terror by tax-happy Luis Bonasario (Friedman regular Jude Farese). His exploitation ranges all the way to ravishing the local ladies along with the corrupt Sgt. Latio (sexploitation legend Bob Cresse), who dispenses one liners even during his hyperbolic sex scenes. At the behest of his father, expert swordsman and ladies' man Don Diego (Douglas Frey) arrives in town from Spain and poses as an outrageous homosexual to divert the evildoers' attention from his true identity: Zorro, defender of the people. Diego falls for Bonasario's niece, Maria (Robyn Whitting), who has developed quite a crush on the masked hero. Will he save the day? And more importantly, will he become monogamous?

As with most Friedman productions of the era, *Zorro* is extremely well mounted, wittily scripted, and lots of fun for those who are game. The film takes about half an hour of plotting before the plentiful sex scenes begin, but luckily the performers are all skilled enough to make their dialogue engaging enough on its own. The sets and costumes all look like the real thing, at least as convincing as any "real" Zorro movie (and yes, that includes the Antonio Banderas one). Oddly enough, for such a ghettoized film, this *Zorro* has been imitated a lot of the years, including a much-noted similarity to 1980's *Zorro, the Gay Blade*, which lifts many plot points and jokes in their entirety. At least Hollywood hasn't gotten around to copying *The Long Swift Sword of Siegfried...* yet.

Not surprisingly, this Something Weird special edition looks quite spectacular, with sharp print quality and almost-Technicolor hues providing plenty of eye candy. Though this is one of Friedman's longest films, the excellent presentation makes it fly by in what seems like minutes. The commentary track with Friedman and Something Weird's Mike Vraney is a rollicking good time as usual, filled with anecdotes about the grindhouse business and trying to sell a softcore item in an increasingly competitive market. Also included is the very explicit theatrical trailer, another trailer for *Siegfried*, a gallery of Friedman posters and ad art, and a short called "Scarred Face" which is a lot of fun and belongs on here as well as anything else.

ESPRIT D'AMOUR

Colour, 1983, 89m. / Directed by Ringo Tam / Starring Alan Tam, Joyce Ngai / Mega Star (HK R0 NTSC) / WS (1.80:1)

After a young woman, Siu Yu (Ngai), slips and falls to her death from the roof of an apartment building, insurance investigator Koo Chi Ming (Tam) is assigned to determine whether it was an accident or suicide. Under specific instructions from his unethical employer to reach a verdict of the latter in order that there needn't be a pay-out, Koo is visited by Siu Yu's ghost to make sure that he reaches the right decision. The pair strike-up a friendship and fall in love, much to the chagrin of Koo's parents and girlfriend (Cecilia Yip), who hire an exorcist to be rid of Siu Yu once and for all.

Director Ringo Tam's enchanting tale casts pop singer Alan Tam as the spirit-smitten Koo, handling with equal aplomb the demands of both the lighter material in the story's middle third and the darker moments as romance crumbles to tragedy. Exquisite Joyce Ngai (aka Ni Shu Chun) is perfect as the doll-like Siu Yu, impishly taunting Koo to the borders of insanity and then melting into a love that transcends the barriers of death. Alan Tam also provides vocals on the end-credits rendering of Tang Siu Lam's haunting melody (heard recurrently throughout the story), which plays out over a heart-rending shot of Koo, everything lost, stood alone in the pouring rain. If I were asked to recommend to anyone a single Hong Kong film from the last twenty years, *Esprit d'Amour* would, without hesitation, be it. Seek out and savour.

A more than welcome entrant into the DVD arena, the 1.80:1 matted transfer is divided into a somewhat inadequate 9 chapter stops. The print is a little faded in places but fortunately not sufficiently as to harm the thoroughly rewarding viewing experience of Ringo Tam's thoroughly engaging narrative. The transfer boasts Dolby Digital 5.1 surround sound. Mega Star's disc includes a slightly scratchy trailer, plus star profiles and filmographies, and trailers for a small handful of Media Asia titles. Cantonese or Mandarin languages are available, with half a dozen subtitle options. The sleeve notes are in both Chinese and English. - TG

EVEN DWARFS STARTED SMALL

B&W, 1971, 96m. / Directed by Werner Herzog / Starring Helmut Döring, Gerd Gickel / Anchor Bay (US R0 NTSC) WS (16:9)

The very definition of a weird movie right to its core, Werner Herzog's *Even Dwarfs Started Small (Auch Zwerge haben klein angefangen)* is gloriously,

riotously insane and politically incorrect. Sporting a cast consisting entirely of little people (think *Terror of Tiny Town* via Godard), the film posits a world populated entirely by dwarfs and midgets where all of society's rules begin to break down in favour of a new world order. A linear plotline would be impossible to describe, but *Even Dwarfs* focuses primarily on an institution where the dwarfs and midgets have begun a war between each other. The escalating insanity consumes their supervising wardens and the animals surrounding the institute. Chickens are tossed through windows, the dwarfs mount a huge dead pig, a monkey is crucified to boards (an image memorably duplicated by Nine Inch Nails), cars are decimated and torched, and in the unforgettable final scene, Hombre, the happiest of midgets, chortles hysterically for several minutes on end as he waits for a camel to relieve itself.

A completely bizarre entry in Anchor Bay's legacy of Herzog titles, *Even Dwarfs* will appeal far more to his experienced fans than the casual viewer. Shot in grainy black and white and presented in its original full frame aspect ratio, the film looks similar to other semi-comical monochromatic nightmares as *Begotten, Eraserhead, Rape of the Vampire,* and *Tetsuo the Iron Man.*

The DVD has been respectfully handled and features optional, easily legible English subtitles, as well as a running commentary track by Herzog with actors Crispin Glover (who also contributed the inner liner notes) and Norman Hill. Obviously a labour of love, the commentary is more edgy and nostalgic than Herzog's other discussions as he recalls the outlandish circumstances surrounding the making of the film. The infamous cactus patch episode is well covered, but there are plenty of other surprises lurking inside, too. Approach with caution, but for those with open minds, *Even Dwarfs Started Small* easily lives up to the confusing, peculiar promise of its title.

THE EVIL DEAD

Colour, 1982, 85m. / Directed by Sam Raimi / Starring Bruce Campbell, Ellen Sandweiss / Elite Entertainment (US R1 NTSC) / DD5.1, Anchor Bay (US R1 NTSC) / DD2.0, Anchor Bay (US R1 NTSC, UK R2 PAL) / WS (1.85:1) (16:9) / DD5.1

Several horror publications and fans have dismissed Sam Raimi's first film, *The Evil Dead*, as an amateurish rough draft of his later Three Stooges-inspired sequel, *Evil Dead 2*, but the two films really have little to do with each other aside from plot similarities. *Evil Dead* is a pure, gut-wrenching horror experience, an unrelenting roller coaster ride, peppered with laughs at its outrageousness but definitely not a comedy. Some of the finest seat-jumping moments ever put on film are here, not to mention enough gore to stand up respectably next to later blood-drenched epics like *Re-Animator*. On top of that this is one great-looking movie, which uses its paltry budget to spin out an eye-popping series of beautiful, startling images accompanied by a great, disorienting soundtrack. A modern classic among classics that just gets better with age.

Five college buddies drive out to the middle of Tennessee to stay in a remote cabin and uncover a reel to reel tape recording which invokes an evil spirit. One by one, the not particularly swift humans are possessed by the malevolent force and do gruesome things involving pencils and knives. The one survivor, Ash (Bruce Campbell), is tormented, abused, and doused with more red gushing fluid than any other horror hero in history, while Raimi's restless camera zooms, swoops, and glides in a series of virtuoso scenes which render the "plot" virtually nonexistent. Simply put, without this film, there would be Coen Brothers and, most likely, no Hong Kong fantasy films, and its influence continues to shine today.

The Evil Dead first appeared on video in a muddy, lifeless VHS edition from HBO Video and a sharp, colourful Japanese laserdisc. After years on moratorium, Elite Entertainment licensed the film and performed a new transfer under Raimi's supervision. The CLV laserdisc, CAV special edition laserdisc, and DVD special edition all contain the same transfer; it looks fine, with good detail, and definitely improves over the HBO version. Furthermore, the Dolby Digital 5.1 remix on the laser and DVD is a house-shaker, delivering Joseph Lo Duca's shrill, nerve jangling score far more clearly than any other edition.

The special editions also feature a commentary track by Sam Raimi and producer Robert Tapert, with Bruce Campbell doing his own solo track. The commentary is lively and interesting, with Campbell even riffing on what he expects Raimi to say on the other audio track. The same tracks also appear on Anchor Bay's widescreen DVD edition, packaged both in a standard and as a rubber-bound "Book of the Dead" featuring an additional documentary on the film's UK distribution and complicated video history. Both discs contain the theatrical trailer, a still photo gallery, and an amusing 18 minutes of rough takes of the "evil dead" in action.

Anchor Bay earlier released a no-frills edition (with five separate disc designs) for buyers who only wanted the movie at a lower price; in many respects the first Anchor Bay DVD is the best presentation of the lot as it features the most vivid colours and gorgeous, deep shadows and textures throughout; the opening shot across the lake has a beautiful, glassy sheen missing entirely from all other versions, and of course, the blood flows much redder than ever before. Just compare the early shot of a blood-coloured strawberry shake being blended, which looks vibrant and pure on the first Anchor Bay disc but looks a muddy brown on all of the others. The imposed matting on the second Anchor Bay version is mostly distracting, lopping off the tops of actors' faces during deep focus shots and generally tossing composition out the window throughout the climax. At least it reinstates the now infamous shot of lightning striking a tree, which was removed from the Elite and first Anchor Bay discs at Raimi's insistence. Early press releases for the "Book of the Dead" also announced the inclusion of "Within the Woods," a 26-minute trial run for this film in which Campbell himself becomes the possessed villain thanks to an Indian curse(?). Legal entanglements prevented its release, leaving only unwatchable bootlegs floating among horror fans. The one area in which Anchor Bay's latest rendition undeniably beats the others is packaging; the book itself is a wonderfully macabre marketing device and looks quite sinister sitting on one's shelf.

EVIL DEAD TRAP

Colour, 1988, 102m. / Directed by Toshiharu Ikeda / Starring Miyuki Ono, Fumi Katsuragi / Synapse (US R1 NTSC) / WS (1.85:1), Japan Shock (Holland R0 NTSC)

Proving that even the most trite genre elements can still work in the right hands, *Evil Dead Trap (Shiryo no wana)* leaves no slasher convention and stylish flourish unturned as it provides a ruthless catalogue of slasher mayhem. Something of a cult favourite on the bootleg video market for the past decade, the film certainly isn't high art but serves its purpose as a fast moving party film, randomly dishing up graphic and imaginative gore under the most visually impressive settings possible. First of all, don't let the title fool you. Despite the *Evil Dead* reference, there are no rampaging demons or skeletal apparitions to be found.

Late night talk show host Nami (Miyuki Ono) makes a living showing "reality program" videotapes sent in from various viewers. One day she receives a tape featuring the stalking and gruesome mutilation of a young woman, who eventually receives a blade in the eyeball for her troubles. As a publicity stunt, Nami and her crew decide to track down the location in the tape, which leads them to a creepy, seemingly abandoned warehouse containing endless corridors with blue lighting schemes out of *Suspiria*. One by one the interlopers are picked off in outrageously contrived methods by a raincoat clad madman, who uses crossbows, lariats, and other nasty weapons in his vicious series of literal death traps. Eventually the film narrows down to the standard showdown with the killer, which tosses in a supernatural twist and an inexplicable final sting, ending the film on a blood-soaked note.

If you're a gore fan, there's really no excuse for not having *Evil Dead Trap* in your collection. The body count technique becomes utterly hyperbolic here, as director Toshiharu Ikeda and screenwriter/comic book legend Takashi Ishii (who later directed the magnificent *Gonin*) keep the Argento and Fulci homages coming at a fast clip and dispatches characters with a viciousness bordering on the operatic. Oddly enough, the previous year's *Stagefright* from Michele Soavi features some astonishingly similar sequences, including fast, shaky, ground level shots from the killer's point of view and a rain-soaked murder outside a car, though whether the filmmakers could have possibly imitated a film so recent is questionable at best.

Previously released on DVD in Holland from Japan Shock, *Evil Dead Trap* has been given quite a impressive visual overhaul Stateside, with the original Japanese version presented with optional English subtitles. The image quality is especially good for a low budget '80s film, with eye-popping bursts of colour throughout and all of that nice grainy detail in sharp focus. The mono soundtrack sounds about the same as it always has, with the bald-faced Argento/Frizzi "homage" music score coming through clear enough. Extras include the Japanese theatrical trailer (which has already graced more than a few grey market sell through collections but looks better here), some hilariously repetitious animated menu screens, and a commentary track with Ikeda and special effects maestro Shinichi Wakasa that can only be described as surreal. This one's up there with *Driller Killer* on the unintentional humour scale, featuring the most rigid and unconvincing "spontaneous" observations ever recording. Both participants giggle and shatter their sentences into indecipherable fragments, with pronunciations that set back political correctness about forty years. Synapse even included a disclaimer inside the packaging that the commentary isn't up to their usual standards, but thank God they decided to include it anyway. This one's a real keeper; amaze your friends with the movie, then send them over the edge with the commentary.

EVIL SPAWN

Colour, 1987, 78m. / Directed by Kenneth J. Hall / Starring Bobbie Bresee, Drew Godderis / Ventura (US R1 NTSC) / WS (1.85:1)

 Al Adamson, one of the more infamous drive-in directors during the late '60s and early '70s, made a career of assembling patchwork quickies from bits of footage involving fading horror stars mingling with at least two or three different plotlines which clumsily converge at the end. The spirit of Adamson remains alive and well in *Evil Spawn*, an endearing mess of a film which began with some random dialogue footage by John Carradine for a project entitled *Frankenstein's Brain*, directed by Fred Olen Ray. Eventually the scenes wound up in *Evil Spawn*, a tongue-in-cheek monster romp filled with amusing Argento-style lighting, delicious overacting, and of course, nudity and gore. The film later resurfaced in radically reedited form with newly shot footage as *The Alien Within* and also did the rounds under the name *Evil Spawn* as well, leaving many trash fanatics scratching their heads.

Short-lived scream queen Bobbie Bresee (best known for the jaw-dropping *Mausoleum* - where's that DVD?) stars as Lynn Roman, a fading silver screen star who believes her career might be revived by taking an experimental serum pioneered by a late scientist, Dr. Zeitman (Carradine). Unfortunately these nasty alien microbes infiltrating Lynn's body turn her into a towering, bug-like monster whenever her passions are aroused, causing her to go on a murderous rampage. Despite her newly youthful appearance, Lynn still can't get a job, leading her to increase her fix dosage and wipe out such innocent parties as her youthful assistant, Elaine (Pamela Gilbert), whose extended skinny-dipping and subsequent gory demise form the film's highlight.

Can this actress gone bad be stopped before Hollywood is wiped out entirely?

A pure work of trash from start to finish, *Evil Spawn* doesn't even try to pretend it's anything besides a fast paced, senseless romp. A far cry from the squealing girls who pass for scream queens these days, Bresee is well cast as an older woman trying to make it in a cutthroat business; had her plight been explored a little more thoroughly, this could have been a fascinating '80s answer to Roger Corman's *Wasp Woman*. As it is, viewers will just have to make do with the bizarre editing, amusing special effects (which include Bresee barfing white goo into the camera and sporting plastic monster teeth), and the kitschy electronic score, which will make any '80s cable viewer feel right at home.

Previous VHS editions of *Evil Spawn* have looked like total garbage, so at least the Retromedia disc is a step up to watchable. The variety of film stocks and limited technical resources cripple the ambitious colour design, which features some surprisingly vivid bits of expressionistic lighting, but the wider framing allows additional information on the sides, making this at least an acceptable presentation. The disc includes a Nite Owl Theatre romp with Fred Olen Ray, complete with naked girls cavorting through the set; the extra materials include longer outtakes of the Carradine footage and some production photographs of the original monster design, which was jettisoned when Ray turned over the reins on the project. Also included for posterity is the bizarre theatrical trailer, which tries to pass this off as a Carradine sci-fi film.

EXCALIBUR

Colour, 1981, 140m. / Directed by John Boorman / Starring Nigel Terry, Nicol Williamson / Warner (US R1 NTSC, UK R2 PAL) / WS (1.85:1) (16:9) / DD5.1

After the less than enthusiastic reception given to his efforts in science fiction (*Zardoz*) and horror (*Exorcist II: The Heretic*), John Boorman decided to tackle a most challenging task: the screen's most intelligent, accurate treatment of the King Arthur legend. Luckily, the film succeeded after a considerable amount of work and quickly established itself as both a cult hit and a commercial favourite. While Boorman injected the film with an appropriate amount of sex and violence without going overboard, Warner also prepared a PG edition for matinee revenues and day screenings on HBO; of course, everyone who grew up watching that version is usually startled by the R-rated original.

With the aid of Merlin (Nicol Williamson, in one of his best performances), Uther Pendragon (Gabriel Byrne) infiltrates the castle of his rival and impregnates his wife, Igrayne (Boorman's daughter, Katrine). Her son, Arthur (Nigel Terry), grows up as a humble farmhand but becomes King of England when he successfully pulls the magical sword Excalibur from the stone in which it has been imprisoned. Arthur marries Guinevere (Cherie Lunghi), who then begins an affair with Arthur's finest knight, Lancelot (Nicholas Clay). Meanwhile Arthur's half sister, Morgana (a great Helen Mirren), aspires to be a great magician and manipulates both Merlin and Arthur into some unspeakable acts that could destroy the kingdom.

Constructed like an elaborate dream, *Excalibur* can be a bewildering experience on first viewing even for those familiar with the Arthurian legend. While Boorman adheres faithfully to Malory's *Le morte d'Arthur*, the shifts of character focus cause the narrative to move in some unexpected directions. For example, the quest for the Holy Grail involves none of the significant players but stands as perhaps the greatest sequence of the film. Of course, then there are the battle sequences - gritty, bloody, and powerful accomplishments which obviously influenced such later films as *Braveheart* and *The 13th Warrior*. Not a film for all taste, particularly the prudish, this is nonetheless a testament to its director's ability to combine artistic achievement with lavish entertainment.

The DVD from Warner is bound to provoke some controversy among DVD-philes. First of all, most of the night scenes in the film have always looked very grainy and will continue to do so. That said, the DVD is a tremendous improvement over the previous LD renditions; the reflective metallic surfaces, ghostly candy-coloured lighting, and misty landscapes all look magnificent. The 1.85:1 framing shears a shred of information from the top of the earliest fullscreen presentations and adds considerably to the side, apparently Boorman's choice when preparing the master. The 5.1 remix sounds fine if generally unspectacular, given the limited thin range of the original audio materials technicians had to work with. Trevor Jones' atmospheric score sounds better than ever, though, even if it's upstaged by the definitive cinematic use of Carl Orff's *Carmina Burana* (as well as a few judiciously placed Wagner excerpts). Boorman himself contributes a fine, intelligent commentary in which he primarily focuses on the difficulties of literary adaptations and the various pitfalls and triumphs experienced during the location shooting. In fact, the only real quibble with the DVD is the tacky cover design; the gorgeous original poster art has been replaced by misleading, sunny artwork better suited to Warner's *Camelot*. Strangely, Boorman's commentary track is missing from Warner's UK version.

EXISTENZ

Colour, 1999, 98m. / Directed by David Cronenberg / Starring Jennifer Jason Leigh, Jude Law / Alliance (Canada R1 NTSC), Buena Vista (US R1 NTSC), Momentum (UK R2 PAL) / WS (1.78:1) (16:9) / DD5.1

David Cronenberg's most viewer-friendly film since *The Fly* tackles the potentially trite subject of virtual reality in his usual off-kilter, probing style. Featuring one of his strongest casts and his usual behind-the-scenes conspirators at the top of their form, *eXistenZ* makes for both a relatively safe introduction for newcomers and a kicky diversion for fans of his similar *Videodrome*.

During a sneak testing session for her newest game, *eXistenZ*, virtual design goddess Allegra Geller (Jennifer Jason Leigh) falls victim to an assassination attempt that goes awry. Protected by her company's jittery public relations agent, Ted Pikul (Jude Law), she flees to the countryside where the two enter her game to uncover the dark secrets behind the assassination plot. As the film shifts in and out of reality and the virtual scenario, the two become increasingly confused about their own surroundings and identities.

Anchored by two solid lead performances, Cronenberg's quirky chamber piece deliberately toys with viewers' expectations right from the beginning. The expected hi-tech hardware is replaced by flesh game pods and umbilical connections into players' spines, while blatantly phoney and arch performances are exposed to be precisely that. The twisty narrative constantly threatens to veer into incoherence but always stops short to reveal one more jolting surprise, and the director's often overlooked sense of humour is well in evidence here. Leigh provides one of her most fetching performances and has never looked better, while Law skilfully adapts to the transformative needs of his role to prove his standing as one of the new acting generation's most promising talents. The excellent Sarah Polley and Christopher Eccleston are virtually tossed away in small parts, but Ian Holm, Willem

DaFoe, and the rest of the crew have juicier parts to tackle. As usual, Howard Shore's moody, experimental score nails each scene perfectly, while Peter Suschitzky manages to equal the evocative cinematic imagery he conjured up in *Crash*.

First released in a basic US DVD edition from Buena Vista with only the US trailer as a bonus, *eXistenZ* has been given a much more elaborate treatment in its Canadian and English variations from Alliance and Momentum, respectively. The anamorphically enhanced transfers of all the discs look very similar, with the non-US versions boasting a slightly less "digitally filtered" look. The special editions feature no less than three running commentaries; Cronenberg provides the first and most entertaining, which points out a number of small touches that would escape the casual viewer. Suschitzky and special effects supervisor Jim Isaac discuss their own involvement on separate tracks and essentially provide every scrap of technical information imaginable about the film, augmented with a few nifty references to Cronenberg's past work. "The Invisible Art of Carol Spier," a 53 minute documentary dedicated to the film's production designer (and a Cronenberg regular), features behind-the-scenes footage and interviews covering her diverse career, with a special emphasis on *eXistenZ*. The Canadian trailer strongly resembles the one designed by Miramax, with a techno-music finale, but the alternate French-language Canadian trailer also included on the Alliance disc features completely different editing and music cues lifted from *Scream*.

EXORCISM

Colour, 1974, 94m. / Directed by Jess Franco / Starring Jess Franco, Lina Romay / Synapse (US R0 NTSC) / WS (1.66:1) (16:9) / DD2.0

Though the title conjures up images of a dubbed *Exorcist* imitation replete with levitations and chanting priests, this early '70s concoction from Jess Franco is actually something far more personal and unsettling. Though his earlier work was certainly no stranger to combining sex and violence in abnormally high doses, *Exorcism* (or as it was known in its first European incarnation, *Exorcismes et Messes Noires*) pushes the director into non-commercial territory by serving up one helping of depraved activity after another, linked by only the thinnest connective tissue of a plotline.

The film begins with a protracted eight minute sequence, not so subtly derived from *Succubus*, in which a nude Lina Romay, transfixed to a wooden cross, is tortured by elegant blonde Catherine Lafferiere, who knifes a dove and smears her victim with its blood. However, this display is merely pretend, a theatrical mass performed for an appreciative, decadent nightclub audience. However, so-called priest and recent mental patient Mathis Vogel (Franco) finds these displays representative of a demonic disease spreading throughout society, and he means to purge these demons at any cost. He writes stories for a local publication (where Romay happens to work as a secretary and dabbles in lesbian affairs during her off hours), but his real crusade involves the purgative deaths of corrupt souls. Meanwhile the police investigate the insidious crimes with the aid of a virile writer (*The Midnight Party*'s Pierre Taylou) from Franco's office, leading to a final showdown over the future of Romay's soul.

Set in a dark, deadly Paris seemingly populated exclusively by selfish, deluded nutcases, *Exorcism* works best as a look at the dark side of the free, swinging attitudes popular at the time. Swingers clubs, orgies, and even one on one bedroom encounters have a tendency to hide nasty secrets; it actually makes sense that Vogel's deranged conception of himself as a sexualized angel of death could spring from this environment, but Franco clearly keeps the line drawn between fantasy and reality. Though produced as a hard mixture of simulated sex and violence, the Eurociné film was reissued with hardcore inserts (some performed by Franco himself, according to a *Video Watchdog* interview with company head Daniel Lesouer), which actually made the film even less erotic.

The most widely seen version, *Demoniac*, appeared on US video from Wizard in a heavily butchered version and actually represents an alternate 1979 edition with newly filmed plot exposition and additional sequences of Franco wandering around Paris. The "uncut" version of this variant, entitled *The Sadist of Notre Dame*, made the rounds in Europe and turned up somewhat more completely on video in Ireland courtesy of Redemption. Now the "producer's cut" of this film from Eurociné has made its way to DVD courtesy of Synapse in what could be considered the most coherent of all possible versions. Cobbling together the export *Exorcismes* version with some additional footage from the vaults (some of which seems to have been prepared for *Sadist*, judging from the dialogue about Vogel's mental history), the disc contains the hardest possible footage without resorting to the jarring XXX inserts (which also marred the hard porn release of Franco's *Female Vampire*). Apart from the virtually non-stop nudity, this cut also contains the full entrail-ripping murder scene in which Vogel graphically knifes open one of his victims. In short, this is essential viewing for those interested in Franco, but some newcomers may be left scratching their heads as the film veers from one extreme to another. The only unquestionable failing of the film is its dialogue track, which was apparently recorded without sound and poorly dubbed in every possible language. The English version here is as sloppy and grating as it always has been, but Franco fanatics should know exactly what to expect.

Long available in a countless number of video editions both authorized and bootlegged, *Exorcism* has never looked better than it does here. Forget those colourless, badly edited dupes; the print material here is detailed and features nicely delineated black shadows with vivid colour saturation, essential to an appreciation of the film's seedy, menacing texture. Some damage to the original film crops up during the opening sequence, which features some scratches and jumps throughout the credit sequence, while some of the original edits between shots were evidently done quickly on the cheap based on some noticeable shifting and jumping. The text for the credits seems to be equally careless, with inconsistent fonts (some not even properly placed on the frame) giving the false indication that something might be wrong with the film's framing. However, the anamorphic transfer itself (framed at the original European aspect ratio of 1.66:1) appears to be faultless and the mono soundtrack (sporting a nifty, sinister organ score) appears to be cleanly pulled from the negative, making this one of the most welcome and satisfying of Franco's DVD releases to date. Of course, the big news for this disc is the first ever Franco commentary, which is about as strange, fascinating, and erratic as one could possibly hope. His English hasn't improved much over the years, but his comments moderated by current producer Kevin Collins are generally intelligible with close listening and an understanding of the questions from the adept moderator. Occasional lapses into silence are filled in with the film's soundtrack; however, Franco finds enough to say about the actors and the filming to make the experience worthwhile. Other extras include a lengthy theatrical trailer (under the *Demoniac* title), an alternate four minute version of the opening scene with both women fully clothed, a still gallery, and a nifty two-sided Amaray sleeve offering dual artwork options.

THE EXORCIST

Colour, 1973, 122m. / Directed by William Friedkin / Starring Ellen Burstyn, Linda Blair / Warner / WS (1.85:1) (16:9) / DD5.1

Still the most financially successful horror film ever made, *The Exorcist* amazingly continues to shock, disturb, and provoke debate as intensely as the original uproar caused on its release in 1973 - though its theatrical reissue oddly provoked as many giggles as it did scares. Fortunately, Warner has finally treated this nerve-jangling possession drama with the respect it deserves with *three* DVD releases to date; unfortunately, all versions are necessary for a full appreciation of the film.

The first DVD edition, containing only the film and a TV teaser, is the most faithful presentation of the actual movie. While all contain Dolby Digital 5.1 mixes of varying effectiveness, notoriously letterbox-phobic director William Friedkin apparently decided to do some visual tweaking on the 25th Anniversary version before placing his seal of approval on a widescreen transfer. Aside the replacement of the familiar red Warner logo at the beginning (too bad- along with *A Clockwork Orange*, this was the most memorable use of the studio's card during the '70s), Friedkin followed in the dubious footsteps of John Badham's colour draining on the 1979 *Dracula* by rendering the dream sequences and hallucinations(?) involving Damien Karras' mother in virtual black and white. Gone is the dusky, eerie yellow of the image of her standing at the subway steps; now, it simply looks lifeless. Also, Karras' final transformation has been digitally altered to look smoother than the simple jump-cut from demon to human in other prints.

So, to put it simply, if you just want to see the original movie, buy the first DVD. On the other hand, the 25th Anniversary version contains a wealth of fabulous extras. *The Fear of God*, an already legendary documentary by the BBC on the making of the film, is obviously the centrepiece; aside from containing numerous snippets of footage deleted from the film (including the notorious "spider walk" sequence), this expertly constructed 75 minute documentary (edited down on the VHS and laser editions) contains interviews with all of the living principal cast and crew. Not surprisingly, attention is devoted to the true story which purportedly influenced writer William Peter Blatty, and everyone spins the usual eerie stories about the mysterious deaths and mishaps that occurred during the

shooting. The real fire, though, comes from the interaction between Friedkin and Blatty, whose clashes on the film became the most publicized of the era. Their commentary during the film itself remains polite and observant, but the documentary (and a few interview outtakes also thrown in for good measure on their own) show these volatile creators at the height of their bantering, peacock-strutting best (just count every time Friedkin explains that viewers take away from the film whatever they bring to it).

Other bonuses include three theatrical trailers, four TV spots, the original unused ending (verbatim to the one in the novel), and surprisingly, a letter-boxed, beautifully edited trailer for the infamous *Exorcist II: The Heretic*. This smashing piece of advertising makes one wonder if perhaps Warner would consider doing a DVD edition of this flawed, unintentionally hilarious, but fascinating film, containing both the original director's cut and the alternate re-release version. Any takers?

Then there's the matter of *The Exorcist: The Version You've Never Seen*, an expanded and heavily doctored version which adds new subliminal flashes of "Captain Howdy," elaborate (and loud) sound effects, and several chunks of additional footage. The spiderwalk sequence (with different footage from the aforementioned documentary) is quite chilling on its own, but wrecks the narrative with its placement; any doubt about Regan's involvement in the sinister events is now completely wiped out, and Burstyn's subsequent denial just seems idiotic. The best addition involves a quiet moment between Karras and Merrin on the stairs, but for the most part the changes are superfluous at best (and in the case of the extended ending, disastrous). Warner's DVD offers a nice video and audio presentation of this controversial retooling, which eventually pitted the studio against Friedkin and Blatty in a nasty lawsuit. Friedkin's commentary this time around is entirely expendable as he comments on the action without offering much insight; other extras include four TV spots, two radio spots, and two trailers for the new edition (one of which was famously banned by the MPAA for being "too intense").

EXORCIST III

Colour, 1990, 110m. / Directed by William Peter Blatty / Starring George C. Scott, Ed Flanders / Warner (US R1 NTSC) / WS (1.85:1) (16:9) / DD5.1

A strange, strange little movie, *Exorcist III* found author William Peter Blatty returning to the director's chair following his cult favourite *The*

Ninth Configuration, though the experience here was equally compromised by studio tampering. Adapting his more streamlined novel *Legion* and completely ignoring John Boorman's *Exorcist II: The Heretic*, Blatty demonstrated a sure hand with his material and, deep flaws aside, the film still retains a compellingly hypnotic power in many scenes.

Fifteen years after the exorcism of Regan MacNeill, Lieutenant Kinderman (George C. Scott) has continued to maintain a friendship with Father Dyer (Ed Flanders). Both men are vaguely haunted by their experience with Damien Karras (Jason Miller), the priest who gave up his own life to save the young Regan, but have moved on with their lives. However, Georgetown is now rocked by a series of perverse, religiously oriented slayings, which reveal an impish and devious killer at work. The circumstances of the crimes eerily parallel the modus operandi of the Gemini Killer (Brad Dourif), who died the same night as Regan's exorcism. Could the two be related? And what about the anonymous mental patient who at varying points seems to resemble both Karras and the Gemini Killer?

The reshooting and cutting of *Exorcist III* (titled *The Exorcist III: Legion* even in the trailers) was well publicized even before its release. Most of the problems centred around the finale, for which executives decided an exorcism had to be present in the film to justify the title. Thus, poor Nicol Williamson stumbles around and performs a very sticky exorcism for no apparent reason, leading to the incredibly abrupt final shot. Fortunately, many other sequences display Blatty at his best: the eerie opening sequence in a deserted church, the murder of a priest in a confessional, and best of all, the heart-stopping shock moment involving a nurse left alone at night. Scott's character is very oddly written (the "fish" scene is beyond description), but he does well under the circumstances. Star watchers will have fun spotting numerous bit parts by everyone from Samuel L. Jackson to Fabio (yes, that Fabio) in a very weird dream sequence in heaven, while horror buffs will enjoy seeing Zohra Lampert *(Let's Scare Jessica to Death)* as Mrs. Kinderman and the notoriously difficult Viveca Lindfors (*Creepshow, The Bell of Hell*) as a possessed agent of the devil.

Warner's basic DVD of this film is still more than many horror fans could have expected, given its relative obscurity in the shadow of the original film. The anamorphic transfer is far cleaner and smoother than the Fox VHS and laserdisc editions, with information added to the sides and a little trimmed from the top. The highly manipulative soundtrack really benefits from a good sound system, with demonic whispers and subliminal mutterings often flitting in the background of the most mundane scenes. The suggestive, memorable theatrical trailer is also included.

EYE OF THE NEEDLE

E

Colour, 1981, 112m. / Directed by Richard Marquand / Starring Donald Sutherland, Kate Nelligan / MGM (US R1 NTSC) / WS (1.85:1)

A striking adaptation of Ken Follett's popular espionage novel, *Eye of the Needle* is one of those fortunate early 1980s films that stands the test of time. Unlike many World War II thriller, both the book and film focus as much on character development and atmosphere as the traditional mechanisms of warfare, making this a satisfying tale on several different levels.

One of Nazi Germany's deadliest agents, The Needle (Donald Sutherland), has been posing as Faber, an unassuming Englishman near London, during the early years of World War II. Equipped with photographs that prove the Allies' intention of storming Europe through Normandy, Faber is instructed by one of his contacts to rendezvous with a U-Boat and personally deliver his evidence and testimony to Hitler. With British Intelligence in hot pursuit, Faber must escape from the train taking him to his destination and instead steals a boat, which he promptly steers into a violent storm. Shipwrecked and washed up on Storm Island, Faber makes his way to the isolated home of Lucy (Kate Nelligan), a wife and mother who lives with her embittered husband, David (Christopher Cazenove), who lost his legs in a car accident on their wedding day. Not surprisingly, Lucy quickly begins a passionate affair with the mysterious stranger, unaware of his true identity and his plans to notify the Germans of his location.

Though it could have easily been a trite melodrama, *Eye of the Needle* is boosted considerably by the two lead performances. Sutherland's performance at first seems ice cold and aloof, but in the second half he reveals some fascinating shadings to his character, particularly during the lengthy standoff between him and Lucy. As poised and charming as any Golden Age Hollywood star, Nelligan has never looked prettier and makes a fine, sympathetic heroine. Thanks to its austere cinematography and a rich symphonic score by the always reliable Miklos Rozsa, the film evokes classic '40s thrillers while injecting modern levels of startling violence (the axe scene will have viewers cringing) and tasteful nudity. Director Richard Marquand, best known for helming the weakest *Star Wars* film (at the time), *Return of the Jedi*, performs the same competent duties as his later and similarly plotted *Jagged Edge* while maintaining the strong and uniquely lonely British atmosphere from his wild 1979 horror excursion, *The Legacy*. Along the way he and screenwriter Mann also include some sly nods to Sam Peckinpah's *Straw Dogs* and Claude Chabrol's *Le Boucher*, among others, while firmly establishing the film's own identity throughout. The film isn't perfect - the last scene is a little rushed and abrupt, and a subplot involving Ian Bannen promises to go somewhere but never does - but it certainly deserves a look and offers a showcase for almost everyone involved at the peak of their craft.

MGM's DVD of this United Artists title is a dramatic improvement over the old, fuzzy VHS editions familiar to most viewers. While the source materials present some inherent problems, most noticeably the heavy grain, which suffuses a couple of sky, shots, the print is extremely clean and offers satisfying levels of detail. The robust mono audio track compensates for the lack of multi-channel sound, with the score in particular offering a dynamic range previously unheard outside a movie theatre. The memorable theatrical trailer is included, as well as the usual printed production notes.

EYES OF LAURA MARS

Colour, 1978, 104m. / Directed by Irvin Kershner / Starring Faye Dunaway, Tommy Lee Jones / Columbia (US R1 NTSC, UK R2 PAL) / WS (1.85:1) (16:9)

 Writer/director John Carpenter has always been open about the influence of Italian horror films on his own work, so it shouldn't come as much of a surprise that his script for *Eyes of Laura Mars* plays like a pastiche of every major *giallo* prior to 1978. The chic fashion house settings and brutal model killings from *Blood and Black Lace*, the psychic premonitions and obsessive mirror imagery of *Deep Red*, and the sexy slasher set pieces from dozens of Lucio Fulci and Sergio Martino efforts are in abundance here, all dressed up in New York '70s disco chic and a trendy cast. The end product is glossy junk - even Carpenter more or

less disowned it - but you'll never see a film like this in American theatres again.

Controversial photographer Laura Mars (Faye Dunaway) wakes up from a frightening dream in which she witnesses the murder of an acquaintance from the killer's point of view. Laura's latest book of sexy, violent photos, *Eyes of Mars*, also figures prominently in the dream, which climaxes with the victim's eyes being gouged offscreen by an icepick. At a media-heavy gallery opening of her work, Laura meets police detective John Neville (a boyish Tommy Lee Jones) whose contempt for her craft doesn't prevent him from being immediately attracted to her. Neville notices that some of Laura's more sadistic photos bear an uncanny resemblance to actual crime scenes in the wake of a serial killer, and apparently her visions have actually been inspiring some of her work. When two of Laura's models turn up dead as well, she and Neville attempt to pinpoint the lunatic. Is it Laura's slimy ex-husband, Michael (Raul Julia)? Her nutty chauffeur (played by a nutty Brad Dourif)? Or her weird agent (Rene Auberjonois)? In the best giallo tradition, the killer's identity is completely arbitrary and comes complete with an absurd, improvised "why I did it" speech that must be heard to be believed.

Originally intended by producer Jon Peters as a vehicle for his girlfriend (at the time), Barbra Streisand, this film went through many permutations over a two year period. Babs contributed the hard rock theme song, "Prisoner" (which is at least more tolerable than "Evergreen"), but dropped out of the leading role to do *The Main Event* instead. (You decide which career move would have been better.) Carpenter's screenplay, originally titled *Eyes*, went through extensive rewrites by *Straw Dogs'* David Zelag Goodman, who tossed out many red herrings and fleshed out the love story angle. Hot off her Oscar win for *Network*, Dunaway stepped in as Laura Mars and delivered her usual over the top performance. Improvisation isn't exactly the most appropriate acting technique for a formal, rigorous thriller, and the results here are frankly disastrous. Dunaway and Jones' ad-libbed love scene in Central Park has justifiably become the stuff of camp legend and is guaranteed to make viewers question their own sanity. The film's trash value has increased immensely over the years, with a relentless disco score pounding behind every photo shoot and enough bad hair and fashion on display to remind everyone that the '70s did indeed have a dark side.

Columbia's DVD of *Eyes of Laura Mars* may not be labelled as a special edition, but it definitely delivers the goods. The glittering new anamorphic transfer looks superb, easily eclipsing the dull, over-bright widescreen laserdisc. A few darker scenes reveal that '70s cinema bugaboo, grainy shadows, but the source material appears to be in pristine condition. The open matte, full frame version on Side B exposes more visual information on the top and bottom, usually turning the visuals into bland TV movie set ups. The memorable opening shot of Dunaway's eyes is far too unmasked, turning this into *The Nostrils of Laura Mars* as well.

Director Irvin Kershner, best known for helming *The Empire Strikes Back*, provides an interesting but dry audio commentary. The beginning is unpromising with a simple blow by blow description of what's happening onscreen, but he eventually becomes comfortable enough to discuss the background of the film and the various personnel involved. More immediately compelling is an eight minute featurette in which stills from the films (including Helmut Newton's gloriously sleazy fashion photos) are accompanied by audio of the disc's producer, Laurent Bouzareau, listing the many differences between Carpenter's screenplay and the final film. Also included is a promotional featurette, Visions, basically a montage of behind the scenes footage and film clips designed to promote the film's theatrical release.

EYES WIDE SHUT

Colour, 1999, 156m. / Directed by Stanley Kubrick / Starring Tom Cruise, Nicole Kidman / Warner (US R1 NTSC; UK R2 PAL) / DD5.1

 Not one to go out with a whimper, Stanley Kubrick spent a ridiculously protracted amount of time bringing his final opus, *Eyes Wide Shut*, to the screen, even delivering the final cut mere weeks before his death in 1999. An escalating series of rumours promised a feast of eroticism and taboo-breaking, while critics refrained from discussing any significant aspects of the plot. Of course, as it turns out, the film is anything but titillating (at least in the conventional sense), and no amount of plot description could really sabotage the surreal spell evoked by Kubrick's typical cool, sharp visual precision.

Set in an artificial New York filled with twinkly Christmas lights and dreamy, soft focus abandoned streets, the film begins with Dr. Bill Harford (Tom Cruise) and his wife, Alice (Nicole Kidman), attending a lavish Christmas party hosted by Victor Ziegler (Sydney Pollack). During the party, both husband and wife are vaguely tempted by members

of the opposite sex, which prompts Alice back at home to deflate Bill's pompous self-assured concept of their marriage by telling him in detail about an affair she almost had. Images of Alice's infidelity plague his mind, leading Bill to embark on a voyeuristic journey of self-discovery which takes him through the dark back roads of the city and the outlying suburbs, where sex and death lurk closer together than he had believed.

A film seemingly detached from time itself, *Eyes Wide Shut* prompted criticism in many quarters, ranging from its slow pace (a Kubrick trademark) to its reliance on '60s mentalities of marriage and psychology. When isolated as a dreamlike experience on its own terms, the film (adapted by Kubrick from the novel *Traumnovelle* by Arthur Schnitzler) offers its own rich rewards, particularly on repeated viewings. Like Radley Metzger's very similar *The Lickerish Quartet,* Kubrick's opus manipulates the filmic conventions of time, setting, and erotic imagery to stimulate viewers into questioning their own position as an audience. This prospect becomes more troubling as the film progresses, with the now infamous masked orgy sequence (a sort of cross between Jean Rollin and *Story of O*) and its tragic aftermath forcing the viewer to connect the dots and decide exactly how the protagonist fits into the whole puzzle. For such a seemingly chilly film *Eyes Wide Shut* contains a fair amount of humour, often derived from Cruise's flippant display of his medical I.D. card and increasing bewilderment at his surroundings; in addition, the hilarious final line offers an unexpected tip of the hat to Ken Russell's *Crimes of Passion,* of all things.

Few films have been more problematic during both their theatrical and home video releases. A storm of controversy erupted when Warner Bros. opted to use CGI imaging to obscure some of the more, er, vigorous portions of the orgy scene, thus allowing US viewers to gaze on awkward-looking computerized mannequins instead. However, the uncensored version played widely outside the US, leading most to speculate that the DVD would be the original version. Alas, 'twas not to be. The US disc of course is still censored, an inexplicable decision which Warner has attributed to both respect for Kubrick's "vision"(?) and the necessity to avoid releasing unrated product. Of course, Warner has already released unrated DVDs (*True Romance,* anyone?) with no retail backlash whatsoever, so one can only wonder what on earth was going on here. Luckily the "European" cut is available on the Warner UK DVD, looking just as crisp and colourful as its US counterpart. The heavy grain that was so evident in the theatrical prints is noticeably lessened here, and the supplements are identical on both versions (separate Cruise/Kidman/Steven Spielberg interview snippets and two TV commercials). While British prints were aurally manipulated to remove a troublesome Buddhist chant from the orgy scene, the DVD thankfully reinstates the original music. However, a now legendary goof (a crew member's reflection glimpsed in the metal of a shower door early on in the film) has been digitally removed, for better or worse.

One odd historical note: this is the first Kubrick film since *2001: A Space Odyssey* to use multi-channel sound; not surprisingly, he anchors most of the film dead centre, with music directed to the surround speakers. The framing issue of the home video of *Eyes Wide Shut* has also caused some grumbling; the full frame image exposes the full camera negative, according to Warner, though anyone who saw the first trailer knows that the familiar nude mirror scene with Kidman and Cruise was zoomed in for the theatrical prints (and thus, the video). Otherwise the image offers far more headroom than the 1.85:1 version screened in theatres and looks comfortable throughout. Simply put, both versions look fine, but Kubrick fans and American purists with compatible players would be well advised to seek out the British DVD over the Region 1 disc; it does make a difference.

FADE TO BLACK

Colour, 1981, 101m. / Written and Directed by Vernon Zimmerman / Starring Dennis Christopher, Linda Kerridge / Anchor Bay (US R1 NTSC) / WS (1.85:1) (16:9), MIA (UK R2 PAL)

Neither as awful as some critics griped on its original release nor as remarkable as its champions have proclaimed, *Fade to Black* contains enough fascinating and creative elements to overcome some irritating structural and thematic flaws, providing an enjoyable and occasionally impressive film at least worth an evening's rental. Shot for little money and a moderate success on the drive-in and shopping mall circuit, the film made an impression thanks to its occasionally nightmarish imagery and a very memorable trailer (thankfully included here).

Eric Binford (*Breaking Away*'s Dennis Christopher), a wimpy movie buff, lives a pathetic existence in which he's browbeaten by his aunt, mocked by his co-workers, and unable to get a date.

He constantly watches one movie after another, including such favourites as *White Heat* and *Kiss of Death*. He finally meets the girl of his dreams, Marilyn (Linda Kerridge in a very nice performance), who looks an awful lot like a similarly named dead blonde celebrity. When things with Marilyn don't work out, matters go from bad to worse. Eric sinks into a world of complete cinematic dementia and acts out his most familiar violent fantasies, dressing up as characters ranging from Richard Widmark to Karloff's mummy and Lugosi's Dracula.

A bizarre mixture of *Maniac, Taxi Driver*, and *The Monster Squad*, the film benefits primarily from Christopher's convincing, creepy, yet essentially sympathetic performance, though the unappealing scene in which he abuses himself to a fantasy of Kerridge crooning "Happy Birthday, Mr. President" may test most viewers' sensibilities. Craig Safan's nerve-jangling score ranks with some of his best work of the period; too bad he doesn't still do so many horror movies. What keeps the film from completely succeeding is the essential message than excessive film mania causes a tendency to react violently and indulge in gruesome activities - precisely the same activities in which the film wallows and tries to turn a profit. For all its skilful writing and sincere delivery, this essential contradiction never resolves itself and ultimately leaves a feeling of emptiness rather than utter terror.

Anchor Bay's DVD sports no extras besides the trailer and a genuinely wild animated menu screen, but this should be enough to satisfy fans. The image quality looks fine though unremarkable; the obviously less than prime film stock combined with the urban setting don't exactly make for a visually dazzling setting. The framing mattes off extraneous information from the previous Media VHS version while adding a little to the right and left sides; compositions really look fine either way. Definitely not for all tastes, *Fade to Black* continues to leave horror fans split down the middle but still manages to retain a strange fascination and morbid effectiveness even after dozens of other wacko serial killers in its wake.

THE FALL OF THE HOUSE OF USHER

B&W, 1928, 66m. / Directed by Jean Epstein / Starring Marguerite Gance, Jean Debucourt / AllDay (US R1 NTSC)

Believe it or not, the year 1928 produced two groundbreaking, avant garde adaptations of Edgar Allan Poe's "The Fall of the House of Usher." In

America, James Sibley Watson, Jr. directed a 14 minute short film without intertitles, loosely using the Poe story upon which to construct elaborate editing schemes and eerie, off-kilter visuals. This version was preserved on DVD in Image's monumental *Treasures from American Film Archives* box set, and AllDay has provided a DVD of its remarkably similar French sister film, *La Chute de la Maison Usher*, directed by experimental stylist Jean Epstein. Luis Buñuel, a regular Epstein collaborator, signed on as assistant director but walked out over interpretive issues; the two never worked together again. Though similar to Poe's story in essence, Epstein's film takes drastic liberties with the particulars, proving that movie audiences have been getting watered down renditions long before the days of Hollywood.

Allan (Charles Lamy) undergoes a lengthy, difficult journey, stopping off in a superstitious village to seek directions to the house of Usher. Finally he arrives to find his friend, Roderick (Jean Debucourt), distraught over the degenerative illness afflicting his wife, Madeleine (Marguerite Gance, wife of Napoleon director Abel Gance). A doctor (Fournez Goffard) also lives on the premises to tend to Madeleine's "condition," while Roderick passes the time by preserving her beauty on canvas before she fades away entirely into a cataleptic trance from which she may never awake. Tragedy eventually strikes... but the horror is far from over.

From a visual standpoint, *Usher* is an absolutely remarkable film crammed with one breathtaking surprise after another. The elaborate outdoor funeral procession superimposed with flickering candles, the appearance of Madeleine cloaked in a diaphanous shroud, and several eerie, floor level tracking shots tearing down the hallways amidst flurries of windblown leaves are just a few of the highlights borne from Epstein's lens. Unfortunately horror fans will have to throw out any preconceptions about the Poe story to accommodate Epstein's narrative, which throws out the entire implied incestuous angle by making Madeleine the wife instead of the sister, thus requiring a wholly unconvincing happy ending out of left field. At least Epstein acknowledges his manipulations by incorporating some nice references to other Poe tales, most notably "Ligeia" and "The Oval Portrait," while the decaying atmosphere of the house itself is wonderfully gothic and oppressive.

AllDay's lovingly prepared DVD presents what appears to be the only acceptable surviving film material, prepared in 1980 with French intertitles and spoken English translation. The accompanying music score is in many ways worth the price tag all by itself; a chilling and often beautiful quasi-medieval accompaniment laced with mandolins and dulcimers, this lies somewhere between Dead Can Dance and *The Name of the Rose*, adding immeasurably to the film and crafting a haunting listening experience in its own right. Overall, despite its shortcomings, the Epstein Usher is a fascinating, worthy adaptation of a familiar tale, and fans craving a hefty dose of surrealism with their Poe should be delighted with its eerie charms.

F

THE FALL OF THE HOUSE OF USHER

Colour, 1960, 80m. / Directed by Roger Corman / Starring Vincent Price, Mark Damon / MGM (US R1 NTSC) / WS (2.35:1) (16:9)

The one that started it all. While Roger Corman had been churning out drive-in quickies for several years and Vincent Price had earned his horror matinee idol status with William Castle gems like *House on Haunted Hill*, both men earned an entirely new level of respectability and popular acclaim with *The Fall of the House of Usher* (or, as most prints and marquees simply called it, *House of Usher*). Surprisingly close to the original Edgar Allan Poe story, this was one of the AIP studio's biggest hits at the time and set off a long, fruitful series of Corman/Price gothics, mostly based on other Poe stories.

Philip Winthrop (*Black Sabbath*'s Mark Damon) arrives at the foggy, foreboding estate of Roderick Usher (Vincent Price), a morose, obsessed man whose sister, Madeleine (Myrna Fahey), is destined to be Philip's bride. As Roderick explains, the Usher bloodline is cursed, and Madeleine has been afflicted with cataleptic trances, which will one day soon prove to be her doom. Philip dismisses Roderick's claims, but then Madeleine seems to pass away and is interred in the family crypt. However, death is hardly the end for poor Madeleine and her possibly mad brother...

Exquisitely mounted on a deceptively low budget, *House of Usher* is a colourful feast of macabre, overripe imagery, slim on plot but heavy on atmosphere. All of the ground rules for further Poe films are clearly laid out here, making this the horror equivalent of *Dr. No*. Floyd Crosby's expert scope photography, Price's brooding central performance, and Les Baxter's brash, emphatic music all combine for a cinematic experience which proved to be one of the most influential of its decade. While Corman later outdid this one in future entries, *House of Usher* holds up extremely well apart from the hamstrung special effects which render the final nightmarish inferno a tad less convincing than one might hope, even for 1960.

Until the long overdue widescreen laserdisc from Image/Orion, most viewers had to content themselves with horrifically cropped video editions of *House of Usher*, which rendered the cinematography incomprehensible. The laser was a gem for its time, and the anamorphically enhanced MGM DVD is even better. Marvellously saturated colours and a very smooth compression job make this a joy for the eyes, and while the source material exhibits a few more signs of wear than the virtually immaculate laser, the enhanced clarity makes it more than an even trade. The mono audio is clear and stable, though a bit lower than normal. Apart from the new transfer, fans of the series will be overjoyed with the addition of the US theatrical trailer and a feature length commentary by Roger Corman, who affectionately recalls the details of getting the film produced under the Nicholson/Arkoff regime of AIP and the methods he used to craft a sumptuous visual appearance with limited resources.

FALLEN

Colour, 1998, 127m. / Directed by Gregory Hoblitt / Starring Denzel Washington, Embeth Davidtz / Warner / WS (2.35:1) (16:9) / DD5.1

Denzel Washington is in unusually subdued form in this unnerving chiller, which died too quickly at the box office but offers several points of interest. Many viewers were put off by the deliberate pace and grim finale, but if you know what you're getting into and don't expect something along the lines of *Ricochet*, there's plenty to savour here, including one of the creepiest chase scenes ever filmed.

Washington stars as Detective John Hobbs, whose capture of a serial killer turns into a nightmare after the criminal's execution. His soul appears to be passing from one body through another across the city, replicating his crimes and moving in closer to Hobbs' own personal life. The transfer of this difficult, darkly shot film is immaculate, filled with rich browns and golds, and the (very loud) sound mix should have home theatre owners leaping for joy. Full running audio commentary (focused mainly on the logistical and economic aspects of the production) with the producer and director, as well as the trailer, round this out as a satisfying presentation of an underrated film.

FANDO AND LIS

B&W, 1967, 96m. / Directed by Alejandro Jodorowsky / Starring Tamara Garina, Sergio Kleiner / Fantoma (US R1 NTSC) / WS (1.66:1)

Outrageous. Shocking. Insane. For years these words have been applied to many directors, but none more so than Alejandro Jodorowsky. A mercurial talent who turns up with a film every seven or eight years, he first came to prominence around the world with *El Topo*, the first genuine midnight movie, in which the director also appeared onscreen as a gunfighter clad in black leather embarking on a mystical journey through the desert. Of Jodorowsky's subsequent projects, only the brilliant *Santa Sangre* really came close to striking the same nerve in America. However, his fans can now sample the earliest surviving example of his work with *Fando and Lis*, his first real film (not counting a filmed mime project called "The Severed Head"), which was buried after its release following a stormy reception at the Acapulco Film Festival and its subsequent disposal by international distributor Cannon Films.

Designed like a confrontational road movie, *Fando and Lis* begins with the two title characters embarking on a quest to find the mythical city of Tar, a kind of utopia Fando's father used to speak about years ago. Though crippled, Lis has no problem with the trip as long as Fando carries or pushes her through the rough terrain. Along the way they encounter a number of bizarre sights, including a group of orgiastic mud wallowers, blood-sipping vampires, transvestites, and amateur musicians. Fando and Lis also undergo some internal changes of their own, including a memorably body painting session that spins wildly out of control and a climactic scene involving pigs that will leave most viewers gasping with disbelief. (Pasolini, however, would have been proud.)

Jodorowsky shot the entirety of the film on spare weekends, following a one page draft based upon the Fernando Arrabal play, which he and his troupe had been performing for several months. Not surprisingly, the results confounded most critics, and the explicitness of its imagery (particularly for '67) didn't exactly please the censors, either. Jodorowsky claims that all of the violence and blood in the film was real (apparently including - shudder - the vampire scene), a trend he later continued by raping his co-star on camera in *El Topo*. (Oddly, the actress in question has never really spoken out about her reactions to this scene.) *Fando* is most definitely a product of its time, revealing influences of filmmakers like Buñuel, but also contains some interesting precursors of later early '70s films. Most obviously, Michelangelo Antonioni's *Zabriskie Point*, filmed in 1970, mirrors Fando in a number of eerie respects, ranging from the aforementioned orgy (very similar to *Zabriskie*'s desert couplings) to the entire concept of a disconnected young couple embarking on an anti-establishment voyage of self-discovery through the desert. Seen over thirty years later, *Fando and Lis* will strike viewers as either a magnificent metaphysical journey or a load of quasi-mystical baloney, depending on one's point of view; in either case, it's a fascinating work and definitely worthy of preservation.

The DVD of Fantoma carries a steep price tag but more than delivers. The film itself, taken from the original negative, looks fantastic, with only some very minor occasional blemishes on the emulsion. Some of the brighter sunlit scenes have a slight strobing quality, which may have been a flaw with the original film, but the contrast and depth of detail are extremely satisfying. Accurately framed at 1.66:1, the film is presented in Spanish with optional English subtitles; more astonishingly, Jodorowsky's dense, multi-layered commentary track in English is also presented with optional subtitles, due to his thick accent.

The film itself is only the beginning, though. The DVD also contains the complete 87 minute subtitled version of *The Jodorowsky Constellation (Le Constellation Jodorowsky)*, a 1995 documentary for French television most widely circulated in a truncated one hour edition. While reading about Jodorowsky can be unnerving (he's "talented to the point of madness," as the documentary puts it), on film he actually seems personable and witty, a far cry from his brutal *El Topo* persona years ago. The documentary covers every imaginable aspect of his career, beginning with his education in mime (Marcel Marceau appears to share a few anecdotes), his creation of the "Panique" anti-surrealist theatrical movement, his successful comic book career, and most thoroughly, his current "psychomagic" seminar presentations. The films also receive a huge amount of attention; completists will be happy to see letterboxed, uncensored clips from both *El Topo* and *The Holy Mountain*, while Peter Gabriel appears to discuss his encounters with Jodorowsky and the profound influence *El Topo* had upon his music. Best of all, Jodorowsky provides a look at the original sketches and storyboards for his elaborate, unproduced version of *Dune*, later picked up by David Lynch. He also discusses the "failure" behind such completed projects as *Tusk* and *The Rainbow Thief* while spinning out a few diverting stories along the way. A very illuminating (so to speak) and worthwhile film, this is an ideal companion piece.

THE FANTASTIC FILM WORLDS OF GEORGE PAL
Colour, 1985, 93m. / Directed by Arnold Leibovit / Image (US R0 NTSC)

During the science fiction and fantasy boom of the 1950s, few names could compare with George Pal. In many ways the pioneering visionary in the ways we view outer space and fantastic creatures on the screen, he turned out a string of masterpieces as both director and producer, using his experience with puppeteering and special effects to bring previously unimaginable sights to stunned audiences around the world. This informative and extremely entertaining documentary takes a thorough look at Pal's career, from his early days in Hungary and Germany making European shorts with various types of puppets combined with simple techniques involving painting and glass. His transition to Hollywood following the rise of Nazism allowed him to bring his Puppetoons to audiences of impressionable children, but the move to live action proved to be even more fruitful. His groundbreaking *Destination Moon* presented a heightened new realism for cinematic space travel, and he soon realized that science fiction could become a tremendous box office draw. His literary adaptations remain loved by audiences today: *The War of the Worlds, The Wonderful World of the Brothers Grimm, 7 Faces of Dr. Lao, The Time Machine, tom thumb*, and his last film, the pulpy *Doc Savage: Man of Bronze*.

The Fantasy Film Worlds of George Pal assembles a who's who of Hollywood filmmaking, combining actors who worked on Pal's productions (such as Rod Taylor, Tony Randall, and Barbara Eden) to admirers like Joe Dante and Ray Harryhausen (who worked with Pal along with animation legend Willis O'Brien). The clips from Pal's early works are especially tantalizing and could have gone on much longer; "Sleeping Beauty" in particular looks like a dazzler. Unlike standard Hollywood biographies, this one keeps up a rapid pace and keeps a steady flow of fascinating clips and home movies to provide a solid, well rounded portrait of a man who loved entertaining people in any way possible.

The Image DVD looks quite good for a mid-'80s documentary, with strong colours and no noticeable compression flaws. The contrast level and clarity vary wildly from clip to clip, for obvious reasons, but such is the nature of an archival beast. The mono audio also gets the job done quite well for its age. The disc also includes a host of Pal-related extras, such as promotional material for many his films from *Destination Moon* to *Doc Savage*, as well as more interview footage deleted from the final cut, some additional home movies, some warm and intriguing comments from Puppetoon veterans, and a peek at the newsreel premiere footage for Brothers Grimm. In short, no fantasy film buff should be without this disc, and hopefully his entire catalogue will one day be available to perfectly complement this love letter to one of the 20th Century's most significant creative talents. Pal's *The Puppetoon Movie*, which contains several of the works glimpsed here in their entirety, is also available from Image on DVD.

THE FANTASTIC NIGHT

B&W, 1949, 90m. / Directed by Marcel L'Herbier / Starring Fernand Gravey, Micheline Presle / Image (US R0 NTSC)

A unique attempt to fuse the magical poetic approach of Jean Cocteau into a standard romantic fable, *La nuit fantastique (The Fantastic Night)* has largely fallen into oblivion as one of the post-WWII attempts by French cinema to find its voice. In retrospect, however, it offers a fascinating and often startling example of the methods through which artistry and mainstream entertainment can interact.

Haunted by visions of a beautiful lady ghost leading him through the city, Denis (Fernand Gravey) experiences a strain on his waking hour relationship with his haughty, unfaithful fiancée, Nina (Saturnin Fabre). Denis feels that his heart cannot be totally faithful to Nina, as this figment of his imagination appears to hold some mysterious destiny in store for him. One night, the beautiful woman, Irene (Micheline Presle), awakens Denis and leads him to a restaurant for dinner with her fiancé and father. Denis believes he is still dreaming but goes along with the flow of events, which segue to a surreal magic show and an encounter in an asylum. Irene possesses a secret fortune that has become the target of some con men, and only Denis can rescue her from a plot more intricate than he could have imagined.

An obvious attempt to apply the Hollywood gloss of David O. Selznick to a supernatural love story in the best European tradition, La Nuit Fantastique is a curious artefact marred primarily by its insistence on verbal humour to deflect any of the uneasy aspects within the supernatural subject matter. However, the romantic elements are handled more successfully, and the elegant images of translucent ghosts haunting the Parisian streets are well realized. Avant garde director Marcel L'Herbier, who helmed the 1930 version of Gaston Leroux's *Perfume of the Lady in Black*, creates an intoxicating atmosphere of dreamlike beauty thanks to gorgeous, well-rounded black and white photography, while resistance fighter Gravey makes a personable and charming hero.

The elements used for this DVD are in remarkably good shape, with only a few jagged splices during the opening credits and the final reel betraying its age. The image is often breathtakingly detailed and filled with rich contrast levels, both of which are crucial for an appreciation of the film's painterly images. However, the soundtrack is even more impressive; it's one of the most robust and razor-sharp mono audio tracks ever presented, especially remarkable for a film of this vintage. The optional, yellow English subtitles are well rendered and consistently accurate.

FAREWELL MY CONCUBINE

Colour, 1993, 171m. / Directed by Chen Kaige / Starring Leslie Cheung, Zhang Fengyi / Buena Vista (US R1 NTSC) / WS (1.85:1) / DD2.0

One of the breakthrough art house hits of the early '90s, Chen Kaige's *Farewell My Concubine (Ba wang bie ji)* was a surprise hit for Miramax, presumably as the film adopted the powerful aesthetics established by Zhang Yimou (*Raise the Red Lantern*) into a sweeping, Western-friendly epic format. Perhaps not surprisingly, this film also encountered a great deal of controversy in its homeland when first released, but went on to garner several awards, including Cannes and a Best Foreign Film Academy Award nomination. Considering the film's volatile subject matter, this was no mean feat.

Charting the history of twentieth century China into its current status as a Communist nation, the film elegantly weaves together historical fact with the fictional story of two young men. Raised within the brutal confines of an opera training school, the two first meet as boys but hold on to their friendship in adulthood. Dieyi (Leslie Cheung) triumphs in female roles on the stage and harbours secret longings for his friend, Duan Xiaolou (Zhang Fengyi), who finds equal acclaim in their regular performances of the opera Farewell My Concubine. Much to Dieyi's consternation, Xiaolou becomes involved with the lovely but manipulative ex-prostitute Juxian (Gong Li), whose presence threatens to tear them apart. Meanwhile, the increasingly intolerant political climate grips all three of them into an inextricable web of intrigue and treachery from which not all of them will manage to survive.

In an unexpectedly gracious gesture, Miramax has included, for the first time in America, the full 171 minute edition of *Farewell My Concubine* for its DVD debut. The original US and UK editions ran 16 minutes shorter, with much opera performance footage and some subtle gradations of character development falling under the editor's scissors. Some potentially NC-17 level material was also lost, including some gruesome bloodletting and a disturbing, borderline paedophilic sequence involving urination. The uncut version was released overseas by several different companies on laserdisc, DVD, and VCD, and apparently Miramax realized that the truncated version would be a pointless insult to their target audience.

While some newcomers to the film may squirm during some of the opera sequences, which can sound harsh and unnatural to some untrained Western ears, the expanded length restores much of the epic scope to the film and adds to the creative resonance that binds the two male leads. Each of the three primary performers is in top form, with the always reliable Leslie Cheung making the strongest impression as the fragile, emotionally unstable "concubine." Gong Li looks beautiful and delivers a forceful performance as always, while Zhang Fengyi is both commanding and compassionate in another memorable turn equal to The Emperor and the Assassin, also for director Chen Kaige (*Temptress Moon, Yellow Earth*). Chen doesn't simply bask in standard epic filmmaking methods, however; his skilful manipulation of recurring masking imagery, coupled with excellent use of mirrors, makes the film as psychologically beguiling as it is visually dazzling.

Apart from the typically asinine liner notes, Miramax's DVD is a consistently satisfying presentation. Crisp, colourful, and pleasingly film-like, the letterboxed image improves considerably upon their older LD release, and the standard Dolby Surround soundtrack has been left intact. It's not much of an aural powerhouse except for devotees of Chinese opera, but the audio gets the job done nicely and features a few directional effects (mostly involving gunshots and the orchestral score). The framing sequences with both men in costume standing in smoky spotlights look as grainy and problematic as ever, which could be easily mistaken for artefacting on DVD, but the rest of the film looks exceptionally vivid. No extras are included aside from 20 chapter stops (very skimpy for a film of this length).

FASCINATION

Colour, 1979, 83m. / Directed by Jean Rollin / Starring Brigitte Lahaie, Franca Mai / Image (US R1 NTSC), Metrodome (UK R0 PAL) / WS (1.75:1)

Mark (Lemaire), having pulled off a robbery, double crosses his compatriots and makes off with the booty. Understandably peeved, the shabby bunch of miscreants gives chase and eventually corners him in an old chateau. His escape cut off, Mark finds himself in the company of the sole two occupants of the house, Elisabeth (Mai) and Eva (Lahaie). After first bullying the women, Mark soon befriends them when they offer him sanctuary until nightfall when darkness will facilitate his escape. They seal his unwitting detainment by piquing his curiosity over the impending arrival of a mysterious group of acquaintances.

Renowned primarily for a succession of cheap and lusty vampire yarns throughout the '60s and '70s, it was only when Rollin stepped beyond the confines of well-trodden fang territory that he forged some of his finest work. *Fascination* may not be his best, but it's certainly his strangest and is as compelling a 90 minutes as you're likely to spend in the company of Monsieur Rollin. Centring on the activities of a clique of blood-supping bourgeoisie, paucity of plot is no stranger for the director, such minor things invariably playing second fiddle to the visual framework. In this latter respect *Fascination* excels. Pleasingly absent are the cheap prosthetics that encumber some of his other cinematic submissions - in fact there's a startlingly realistic stabbing - and we also get the best line of dialogue to emanate from any Rollin escapade: "Blood is the life which

flows in you, but it's also death when it escapes."
And, of course, there's Brigitte Lahaie. That Rollin
cast her in no less than four of his movies says more
than a little about her ability to captivate the male
ardour. Lahaie possesses an indefinable magnetism,
a sexual allure that enables her to effortlessly
dominate the screen.

From the evidence delivered us over the years,
it's fair to say that Rollin has more than a passing
interest in lesbianism (all say "Yeah"!), and the
intimacy between Lahaie and Mai in this film is
more provocative than anything he has done before
or since. Moments such as the all too brief framing
of Lahaie outside the chateau - the setting sun
twinkling through the trees and playfully dancing in
her hair - and a woman dipping her finger in blood
and rubbing it teasingly around her pouting lips are
the icing on the cake, and can be chalked up among
most arresting visual coups of Rollin's entire *oeuvre*.

Image Entertainment's DVD treats Rollin's last
film of the 1970s very well indeed. Along with a
splendid film transfer, matted to 1.66:1, the extras
comprise a French language trailer, a Rollin filmography and a gallery of stills and poster art. The film
is in French with optional English subtitles. - TG
*The UK DVD release features an identical transfer
along with galleries of posters, video art, and stills,
but inexplicably the BBFC ordered a 1 second cut to
the trailer! - ed.*

FATAL FRAMES

Colour, 1996, 125m. / Directed by Al Festa / Starring
Stefania Stella, Rick Gianasi / Synapse (US R1
NTSC) / WS (1.85:1) / DD2.0

While the *giallo* appeared to more
or less die out in the early '80s,
some Italian directors still seem
determined to resurrect the format.
The loopiest attempt by far must
be credited to Al Festa, the multi-
talented director and songwriter(!)
who fashioned this star-studded slashfest as a
vehicle for his unique looking chanteuse wife,
Stefania Stella (playing herself, of course). The
results are truly unlike anything else ever committed
to film, and Synapse's wild DVD presentation does
this rabid gem full justice.

Following a puzzling black and white prologue
in which a young boy stumbles upon his
grandfather(?) watching a scratchy snuff movie, we
jump to the present day where hot shot music video
helmer Alex Ritt (Rick Gianasi) is recruited to direct
the latest music clip, "Eternal City," for up and

coming Roman singing sensation Stefania Stella. An
American ballet dancer working on Stella's music
videos goes out with Alex for a date which turns into
bloody mayhem as she's slain by Rome's notorious
"video killer," a maniac who cuts up women and
videotapes the results for the police. The inspector in
charge (David Warbeck) is mystified by the killings,
which have become more entwined with the career
of Stella. As Alex and his seductive employer find
their relationship becoming more than just business,
he also seeks the aid of a colourful gallery of
characters, including an aristocratic psychic
(*Suspiria*'s Alida Valli), an American criminology
expert (Donald Pleasence), and a crusty old historian
(*Phantasm*'s Angus Scrimm) who may hold the key
to unlocking the deadly crime wave.

While Festa seems to think he's making a '90s
version of *Deep Red*, his attempt to ape that film's
running time (over two hours) seems more like
excess here than a richly detailed tapestry. Stella's
hilarious music videos provide even more padding
than the meandering storyline can possibly bear, but
this ramshackle construction actually makes *Fatal
Frames* oddly compelling in a train wreck sort of
way. Besides, it's astonishing to see so many horror
genre pros in one film, though most of them are
hardly in their prime here. Indeed, it's sad to reflect
how many participants have already passed away.

Since *Fatal Frames* is still a relatively recent
film, it's hardly surprising that Synapse's DVD
looks and sounds terrific. The vivid use of colourful
lighting (however illogical) comes through just fine
without any distortion; just check out those pulsating
blues and reds. However, the movie itself is just the
beginning. While Synapse already took the cake
with the goofiest audio commentary ever recorded
for *Evil Dead Trap*, this disc actually manages to
equal (and possibly even surpass) that achievement.
Festa and Stella provide a very dense commentary
track complete with spooky reverb effects and
moody synth music for the entire 125 minutes of the
movie! Though many of their remarks are rendered
incoherent by the combination of these audio effects
and their thick accents, the little facts about the
movie that do come through are generally
interesting, particularly Festa's accounts of location
shooting in Rome. As for Stella... well, she's about
the same as she is in the movie.

Other goodies in this psychotic grab bag include
two Italian trailers, one American trailer (pretty
much the same), a reel of deleted scenes (including
an odd post-coital spat between Stella and Gianasi),
a behind-the-scenes featurette touting Festa as the
great new hope of Italian horror, and some talent
bios with a very unorthodox layout. Of course this

just wouldn't be complete with some Stefania Stella music videos, which are basically condensed versions of the various snippets and video shoots through the feature. Now you too can astonish party guests by showing them "Alibi" and "Eternal City;" they may never speak to you again.

FAUST

B&W, 1926, 116m. / Directed by F.W. Murnau / Starring Emil Jannings, Gosta Ekman / Kino (US R1 NTSC) / DD2.0

 One of the great pioneers of German silent cinema, F.W. Murnau has become almost exclusively associated in recent years with his influential vampire classic, *Nosferatu: A Symphony of Horror*. However, his astounding grasp of the visual medium of film is also evident in his other masterpieces, such as *Sunrise, The Last Laugh*, and the sadly underappreciated *Faust*, his final film made in Germany before the rise of Nazism sent him packing for Hollywood.

The familiar Wolfgang von Goethe tale of a man selling his soul to the devil serves as a loose springboard for Murnau's phantasmagoria of narrative strands and visual indulgences. The moral saga begins in the heavens, where the divine powers negotiate with Satan (Emil Jannings), aka Mephisto, over the fate of humanity. Eventually a deal is struck in which an archangel agrees to relinquish humanity to the powers of darkness if Mephisto can gain control of the soul of Faust (Gosta Ekman), an elderly professor and alchemist. The devil appears in a number of guises as he talks Faust into signing a contract, exchanging the human's soul in exchange for youth and material goods. Mephisto even takes him flying over the village and mountains on an exotic aerial tour, not to mention an introduction to the beautiful Gretchen (Camilla Horn) with whom Faust falls immediately in love. Along the way the film diverts into scenes of fanatical religious fervour, tragedy, and supernatural horror, before Faust and Gretchen confront their fates in the pyrotechnic finale.

Though not critically regarded as highly as *Nosferatu*, *Faust* is about as exciting as silent cinema can be and would make a fine introduction for those who normally insist on a dialogue heavy soundtrack. The striking opening images of skeletal horseback riders plunging through the clouds are just the beginning of an astounding stream of marvellous visionary concoctions. Not to be outdone by special

effects, Jannings (*The Blue Angel*) nearly blasts through the roof with his dynamic, often hilarious portrayal of Mephisto, a charismatic and terrifying apparition. Whether dishing out quirky flourishes with his hands or, in the most audacious image, looming high in his black cloak to bring the plague onto a small German village, Jannings is simply unforgettable and makes his "human" co-stars quite dull in comparison. (Keep an eye out as well for Gretchen's brother, played by William Dieterle, future director of *Portrait of Jennie* and *The Devil and Daniel Webster*.) The film only makes one significant misstep by tacking on a trite, unnecessary celestial epilogue after already reaching a perfect, wrenching closing shot during the climax; however, moral watchdogs at the time probably insisted on a clear-cut moral message at the end lest viewers feel too alarmed by the preceding events.

Derived from an original English language print, Kino's transfer of *Faust* lives up to their previous collaborations with David Shepherd. Image quality is quite good and detailed, and while some of the unavoidable ravages of time are still in evidence, this is much better than any of the (quite scarce) VHS editions. An excellent orchestral score by Timothy Brock and the Olympia Chamber Orchestra is one of the most effective in recent memory, delicately accentuating the action without any jarring electronic flourishes or pretentious "old timey" inflections to the music. The disc also contains a terrific gallery of behind-the-scenes photographs, including some hilarious shots of Jannings preparing for his role, often only half covered in make up on his face and body. In an ideal world, an even deeper look into the film's delirious special effects would have been welcome, but the final work certainly speaks well enough for itself.

FEMALE CONVICT SCORPION

Colour, 1972, 88m. / Directed by Shunya Ito / Starring Meiko Kaji / Image (US R0 NTSC) / WS (2.35:1) (16:9)

 A female prisoner movie unlike any other, *Female Convict Scorpion: Jailhouse 41* dispenses with many of the women in prison clichés and goes straight for the jugular. Based on a popular comic book series, this is actually the second film in a volatile string of films following the exploits of virtually silent inmate Sasori ("Scorpion"), a resourceful outsider who stands by and watches her enemies fall into their own traps, striking out herself only when they least expect it. While trapped in solitary confinement with only a sharpened spoon to whittle away the hours, Scorpion is interrupted and dragged out into the prison courtyard by the brutal warden (whose left eye she has already claimed in a previous skirmish). The visiting officials are appalled when the female prisoners revolt thanks to another attack by Scorpion, and the woman are all punished by going on a gruelling work detail. The fellow prisoners don't take very kindly to Scorpion's efforts, but they all band together to stage a rousing escape which sends them fleeing into the wilderness. They seek refuge for the night near a dilapidated shack where an old woman relates each woman's tragic criminal history. This is soon followed by a surreal morning in which the fugitives hijack a bus and embark on a final, outrageous attempt to flee the warden's clutches.

Written words cannot adequately do justice to the dizzying spectacle of this film. The expansive camera compositions from Japanese ghost stories mingle with the furious violence of European crime dramas and the vibrant, unnatural candy colours of Mario Bava, tossed in with stylized, aesthetic violence most akin to a fusion of Dario Argento and Sam Peckinpah. The Tohoscope frame constantly erupts into split, swirling imagery, which keeps the viewer's eye entranced from one edge of the frame to the other, and the delirious soundtrack (a mixture of fuzz guitar and two catchy theme songs) perfectly captures the balance between gritty tragedy and over the top, hilarious excess. Many characters exhibit a surprisingly black sense of humour, with each female prisoner firmly establishing her own identity in a society that could not possibly care less about her fate; along with *Diabolik*, this is the closest thing to a bona fide filmed comic book you'll ever see. The beautiful and striking Meiko Kaji, who went on to play the more famous Lady Snowblood, makes for an imposing, sympathetic, and sometimes frightening anti-heroine, whose long hair and rigid demeanour make her a compelling distaff equivalent to Clint Eastwood's Man with No Name.

The American Cinematheque thankfully rescued this gem from oblivion (along with a horde of other worthy Japanese exploitation items), and the only existing subtitled print has provided the master for this DVD release. For a film with little acknowledged historical value, the print is thankfully in good shape with only a few unavoidable blemishes across the colourful 16:9 transfer. The white, burned-in subtitles can be indistinct at times, but it looked this way on the big screen, too. Don't look for a demo piece to show off modern DVD technology; the real star of this disc is the film itself, and anyone interested in cult cinema simply needs to have this movie. The disc also includes the operatic trailer, which focuses on the film's more gruesome moments.

FEMALE VAMPIRE

Colour, 1972, 101m. / Directed by Jess Franco / Starring Lina Romay, Jack Taylor / Image (US R1 NTSC) / WS (2.35:1) (16:9)

The movie that most clearly separates director Jess Franco's career between the '60s and '70s, *Female Vampire* has been known under such a bewildering number of titles and alternate versions that few people have any idea which print could remotely be considered "definitive." Franco filmed a horror-oriented edition, *The Bare Breasted Countess*, in which his vampiric heroine feeds from her victim's necks, while the more erotic and potent variation presented here finds her aiming well below the waistline with her human prey. Either way it's an intoxicating film for those familiar with the European exploitation game and a maddening exercise in sensual excess for those who aren't.

Wearing only a black belt, boots, and a cloak, the mute and often nude Irina Karlstein (Lina Romay) strolls dreamily through a forest and approaches a hapless man at a nearby farmyard. What begins as a heated sexual encounter quickie turns nasty as her oral services literally drain him of life, killed at the height of passion. Back at her mountainside home, Irina indulges in all manner of perversions with her muscular servant (Luis Barboo), a few handy throw pillows, a bedpost, and an unlucky number of visitors. Meanwhile a visiting writer (Jack Taylor) becomes obsessed with his visions of Irina, whom he comes to regard as his destiny. Their eventual face to face encounter ignites a passion that can only reach one kind of climax: death.

While Franco himself pops up as the investigating Dr. Roberts (and teams up with a guy named Dr. Orloff, of course), the majority of *Female Vampire* is a virtually plotless study of overlapping visual images. The Mediterranean beach setting produces some uncannily weird results, with Irina's drives and the desolate seascapes producing a vampire film unlike any other (except perhaps *Vampyros Lesbos*, which introduced some of the nautical/vampire motifs earlier). Much of the film's power lies in the haunting jazz score by Daniel White, who scored many of Franco's finer films from this period, and the scope photography so often devastated in sloppy pan and scan transfers aids immeasurably in creating the film's all-consuming atmosphere of tragic lust.

Most video collectors encountered the vampire version as *Erotikill* from Wizard Video, while the naughtier cut was released as *Loves of Irina* from Private Screenings. The latter version was missing several sequences, particularly most of the explicit dungeon encounter with Monica Swinn. A third version entitled *Les Avaleuses* (or *The Swallowers*) featured crude hardcore footage of Romay (filmed much later) performing her skills on a variety of anonymous actors; virtually unwatchable and sloppily assembled, this cut is the least effective of the three. The EuroShock DVD of *Female Vampire* retains the ideal "sexy" cut of the film but sports a few oddities of its own. The dungeon footage and the entire ending are fully intact; the only discrepancy lies with Romay's oral servicing of Ramon Ardiz (her ex-boyfriend, incidentally), which contained some glimpses of semi-hardcore fellatio in the Private Screenings and Redemption Benelux versions. This edition contains only profile shots of the scene, while the music continues uninterrupted. Otherwise the print is identical in content and is by far the best this film has ever looked.

Transferred from he original materials in the Eurociné vaults, this film has never looked remotely this good anywhere else, with beautiful detail, accurate letterboxing, and rich colours. The level of detail is quite explicit, with some formerly obscured details of Ms. Romay's anatomy now, shall we say, unquestionably visible to the naked eye. The disc also includes all of the alternate Erotikill scenes, in which Romay shows off her ability to retain blood on her voluptuous lips, and the original French language theatrical trailer.

FIEND WITHOUT A FACE

B&W, 1958, 74m. / Directed by Arthur Crabtree / Starring Marshall Thompson / Criterion (US R1 NTSC) / WS (1.66:1) (16:9)

For those of you who thought '50s monster movies couldn't be scary or disgusting, we kindly submit *Fiend without a Face*. Though it comfortably fits the formula of nearly every Cold War era sci-fi/horror fusion (exemplified by Howard Hawks' *The Thing from Another World*), this sick little cult favourite goes so far over the boundaries of good taste one can only wonder how

matinee kids managed to handle it without going into mass hysteria. Thankfully someone at Criterion must have been bowled over by this one during a youthful encounter, since the usually highbrow company has given *Fiend* the red carpet treatment on DVD.

When we begin, a soldier at an isolated military base discovers a dead body sprawled out in the woods. The victim's sister, Barbara (Kim Parker), works as a scientific assistant for the military. Recent experiments involving nuclear power and its transmission to improve the use of fighter planes have left the base bereft of power, and locals seem to be dying off mysteriously with horrified expressions on their faces. Good guy Major Jeff Cummings (Marshall Thompson) decides to investigate the deaths, which all share one thing in common: the victims' brain and spinal cords have been sucked away! Eventually the truth comes to light when the elderly Professor Walgate (Kynaston Reeves) explains that these beasties are "thought creatures" - invisible parasites that feed on human grey matter. As pandemonium escalates, the survivors attempt to make these monsters visible. Do they succeed? Well, the poster gives it away, so yes, the last twenty minutes or so finds our heroes boarded up in a house fighting slimy flying brains, complete with antennae and little vine-like appendages, which use their spinal cords to wrap around people's throats and open their skulls.

Not only is this amazingly strong stuff for the '50s, but the viewer is also treated to numerous shots of the stop motion brains exploding in rivulets of gore during contact with a bullet or an axe. One could probably make a case for *Fiend* as the influence for later boarded up monster favourites all the way from *The Birds* to *Night of the Living Dead*, but even without these cultural references, it's extremely effective once the story kicks into high gear. The first two acts are reasonably compelling and creepy, with Thompson and Parker no more than merely adequate as the romantic leads, but the build up gives no indication of the splattery mayhem to come. As with his only other significant genre entry, 1960's *Horrors of the Black Museum*, British director Arthur Crabtree demonstrates an indisputable flair for defying audience expectations and delivering explicit shocks that seemingly burst out of nowhere. The animated brains aren't too shabby, either, though modern audiences may find the whole thing unintentionally hilarious as well.

Though released theatrically in the US by MGM, *Fiend without a Face* surfaced on home video from Republic and even turned up in a short-lived laserdisc edition. This edition suffered from some heavy print damage during the first 45 minutes, particularly during the outdoor scenes, but otherwise it looked fine. Criterion's DVD reveals that this damage was an inherent part of the original source material; even with the application of digital technology, the speckles and stains are still evident. At least the print is appreciably sharper and boasts much richer contrasts; it's probably safe to say that this is the best *Fiend* will ever look without a multimillion dollar touch up job. The last half hour looks immaculate and razor sharp, while the 1.66:1 framing (anamorphically enhanced with slight windowboxing on the sides during 16:9 playback) appears well balanced throughout.

The disc includes a feature length discussion by film historian Tom Weaver with producer Richard Gordon, in which they cover everything from the original, radically different short story (by Amelia Reynolds Long) to the various histories of the cast members to the reasons an oft-proposed remake would never work. In a gesture similar to their treatment of *The Blob*, Criterion has also outfitted the disc with a host of promotional and supplemental goodies; the terrific animated menus take you to a written illustrated essay, a gallery of posters and promotional stills (also playable as a continuous featurette with Gordon commentary - check out the *Fiend without a Face* Resin Model Kit!), and a gallery of contemporary newspaper ads. Other films from Gordon are represented by trailers for such favourites as *The Haunted Strangler, Corridors of Blood*, and *The Atomic Submarine.*

FIGHT CLUB

Colour, 1999, 139m. / Directed by David Fincher / Starring Brad Pitt, Edward Norton, Helena Bonham Carter / Fox (US R1 NTSC, UK R2 PAL) / WS (2.35:1) (16:9) / DD5.1

Widely touted as the special edition to end all special editions, Fox's *Fight Club* is such a massive undertaking of design and technology within the DVD format that the film itself could easily get lost in the shuffle - which, considering the film's theme, might not be entirely inappropriate. A canny distillation of Generation X anxiety into a barbed anti-consumerist package, *Fight Club* desperately strives to be as uncommercial and brutally uncompromising as possible and, for the most part, succeeds.

Plagued by insomnia and dissatisfaction with his numbing day to day life, our nameless narrator (Edward Norton) resorts to attending crisis therapy groups for testicular cancer, blood disorders, and so on in order to get the cathartic rush he needs for a good night's sleep. Unfortunately his happiness is thwarted by Marla (Helena Bonham Carter), another posing squatter who sits in on support groups and feigns illness. During a plane ride our jittery protagonist encounters a strange man named Tyler Durden (Brad Pitt), a soap salesman and amateur philosopher who comes to Norton's aid when his apartment is blown to smithereens. Now homeless, he shacks up with Tyler in a decrepit abandoned house where they form a twisted form of marital bliss, with Tyler occasionally bringing Marla over for nights of marathon sex. One night outside a bar Tyler provokes our narrator into starting a fight, for no good reason other than the basic primal male aggression of it all. Other spectators soon gather around and show interest, leading Tyler to come up with a brilliant idea: start a fight club! The gang sets up their club in a basement where Tyler decrees a series of rules for each member to follow. Unfortunately, this new quasi-fascist regime ultimately turns out to be even more restrictive and dangerous than the corporate controlled world on the surface.

As with director David Fincher's other films like (*Alien 3, Seven* and *The Game*), this trip into modern man's tattered psyche is characterized by dark, tenebrous colour schemes and a jarring plot twist which gains in significance on repeated viewings. Fincher and screenwriter Jim Uhls admirably swerve Chuck Palahnuik's novel into turn of the century relevance by assaulting the viewer with images of the human body constantly under mutation. The '90s generation, according to the film, is a tamed and twisted version of male sexuality, where the men sprout breasts during testosterone therapy, Tyler pushes his aggression in family's faces by splicing images of genitalia into prints of Disney movies, and betrayal to one's pack is rewarded with rubber band castration. Likewise, women are best dealt with here by keeping them at arm's length; the most intimate and unaffected contact the two men encounter with female flesh during the body of the film comes when they haul around bags of liposuction residue. Unfortunately, this is where the film ultimately paints itself into a corner during the final sequence, which tries to have it both ways (nihilistic and oh so sardonic vs. romantic and optimistic) but, like *Seven*, is a whole lot less profound than it thinks it is.

The strength of *Fight Club* lies in its firm grounding in recognizable situations gone hilariously berserk, such as Norton's unforgettable "resignation" scene in his boss' office (which also appeared in a very similar but less bloody form in the identically themed *American Beauty*). As for the violence itself, the film's critics, including a much publicized and amazingly ill-informed editorial in *The Hollywood Reporter*, presumably (a) didn't bother to watch the film all the way through or (b) didn't notice that the actual fighting takes up about 10 of the film's 139 minutes. The title is a metaphor; it's not a description.

Fox's avalanche of special features on the DVD makes it well worth purchasing even for those who don't love the film itself. The four commentary tracks (including Fincher, Pitt, Norton, Carter, and virtually every major creative and technical person involved) make for engaging listening in tiny doses but also contain long, long stretches of tedium; cutting one or more of the tracks down and editing it with another might have been a good idea. Very few of the comments actually relate to the onscreen action and often overlap with the same observations from someone else. However, this is really the only weakness in an otherwise staggering package. Deleted scenes, hilarious public service announcements, trailers, a music video, Internet spots, galleries, behind the scenes featurettes, the requisite Easter Eggs, and so much more will keep you browsing for hours on end. (The UK release features identical extras but was trimmed by 4 seconds thanks to the BBFC.)

The transfer itself looks very good, but most viewers' attention will be seized by the blistering, highly aggressive 5.1 soundtrack. The opening music alone roars to life with sharply divided signals in every channel, and the soundtrack thereafter rarely pauses to let the ears pause for rest. Of course, the irony of two hours of guerrilla, anti-consumer ravings packaged in a slick, mammoth technological product from a major studio cannot be ignored and, perhaps, speaks volumes about the modern DVD experience in itself.

FINAL DESTINATION

Colour, 2000, 98m. / Directed by James Wong / Starring Devon Sawa, Ali Larter / New Line (US R1 NTSC), EIV (UK R2 PAL) / WS (1.85:1) (16:9) / DD5.1

One of the more crucially misunderstood horror films in recent memory, *Final Destination* could easily be mistaken for an average teen slasher flick (right down to the *Scream*-like face collage poster). However, *X-Files* director James Wong followed the lead of another vet from the show, David Nutter (*Disturbing Behavior*), by using his teen cast to cloak a satirical riff on classic horror films, with far greater success in this case. Laced with effective jolts, a dense atmosphere of paranoia, and a mordant sense of humour, this is a *Destination* well worth reaching.

After boarding a plane with his classmates for a trip to Paris, Alex Browning (Devon Sawa) experiences a horrific vision of the aircraft exploding shortly after takeoff. Alex's hysterical reaction gets him thrown off the plane, along with five other students and one teacher. Sure enough his prediction comes true, attracting the attention of two FBI agents who think Alex may have been involved. Shortly after the school's memorial service, Alex's friend and fellow survivor Tod Waggner (Chad Donella) meets a grisly end, seemingly by accident or suicide. Numerous eerie coincidences and visual clues, along with an informative lecture on death by coroner Tony Todd (*Candyman* himself), tip Alex off that death is swerving back around to claim those who were meant to die in the crash. While the arrogant Carter (Kerr Smith) refuses to believe Alex, outside girl Clear Rivers (cue groans- played by *House on Haunted Hill*'s Ali Lartner) believes Alex as he searches for the underlying pattern to the bizarre deaths before it's too late.

On its most superficial level, *Final Destination* operates well as a rollercoaster of unexpected thrills, filled with spooky little touches and at least one marvellously contrived seat-jumper moment best described as a gory twist on *Cat People*'s most famous scare. Sawa makes an effective and vulnerable hero, proving along with *Idle Hands* that he's a much more likely candidate for horror stardom than reluctant fellow thespians like Neve Campbell and company. The script is also peppered with terrific references for film fans, reaching well beyond the cutesy device (lifted from *Night of the Creeps*) of naming its characters after classic horror personalities (Browning, Waggner, Schreck, Hitchcock, Murnau, Chaney, Dreyer, and God help us, even a "Val" Lewton).

The influence of British horror hangs heavily over the film, acknowledged by unexpected cameos from the looming eagle statue from *Burn, Witch, Burn!* and the nocturnal train track scene from *Night of the Demon* - incidentally, both films about characters contriving to outwit the supernatural forces of death. These are subtle echoes of horror's past, however, and not the postmodern smoke and mirror tricks that consumed most horror films in the '90s. *Final Destination* plays its material very straight for the most part and is all the better for it.

As expected, New Line delivers a top notch DVD with a razor sharp widescreen transfer. The sound mix is often quite harrowing, from the plane explosion to the subtle manipulation of Shirley Walker's creepy score (graciously isolated on a separate track with commentary by the personable composer). You also get three deleted scenes including the infamous original ending, which was reshot months later for a more crowd-pleasing (if somewhat irrational) grace note to end the film. The other cut scenes tie in with the original ending as well, and their inclusion is of great value for fans of the film. On two other commentary tracks you can listen to Wong, producer and co-writer Glen Morgan, writer Jeffrey Reddick, and editor James Coblentz expound on the shooting and post-production of the film, while Sawa, Smith, Donella, and Kristin Cloke reminisce more loosely about their experiences in front of the camera. Both are entertaining and filled with nifty little anecdotes, with little dead space for attention to lag. Then it's on to the featurettes, including the marvellous "The Perfect Souflee," a behind-the-scenes look at New Line's test audience procedure and how profoundly it impacted the creation of the film. Accolades all around for this one. Premonitions takes a dip into real life psychic phenomena courtesy of Pam Coronado, who uses her sensory gifts at police crime scenes. Also included are the theatrical trailer (an unusually effective and spoiler-free piece of work, and a good model for other studios to follow), as well as cast/crew bios and two games, "Death Clock" and "Psychic Test," both of which pretty much speak for themselves. The UK disc retains most of the extras but drops the second commentary track.

FIST OF FURY

Colour, 1972, 110m. / Directed by Lo Wei / Starring Bruce Lee, Nora Miao / Media Asia (HK R0 NTSC) / WS (2.35:1) / DD5.1, Fox (US R1 NTSC) / WS (2.35:1), Hong Kong Legends (UK R2 PAL) / WS (2.35:1) (16:9)

The best of Bruce Lee's Chinese films, *Fist of Fury* (retitled *The Chinese Connection* for English language distribution) was his second starring vehicle following the smash hit starring debut, *The Big Boss* (called *Fists of Fury* in the US - got that?). More political and serious than its predecessor, *Fist of Fury* serves as an unabashed showcase for Lee's awe-inspiring marital arts skills

and, along with the nearly perfect *Enter the Dragon*, also provides a nice introduction to his work. The original Cantonese title of the film, *Jing we men* (loosely translated as *Doorway to Martial Arts Excellence*), conveys one of the essential concepts of the film (and Lee's entire career, in fact); the important role of education and its effects on society.

Set in Shanghai during the oppressive rule of the Japanese, the narrative begins with Chen Zhen (Lee) arriving at his old martial arts school where he learns that his teacher has been murdered. Chen breaks down at his master's funeral and determines to uncover who was responsible. Not surprisingly, after some moderate detective work and some testy interrogation, he traces the poisoning death to a Japanese school, thus allowing Lee and director Lo Wei to present some amusingly violent allegories for the culture clash. Chen keeps his rage pent up out of respect for his master until he begins to uncover the truth, causing him to suddenly explode in a violent, howling rage, killing a few men in the process. Chen goes on the run, though the innocent Nora Miao tracks him down in the woods and tries to help him deal with his quest for vengeance. The final third of the film, in grand Lee style, finds him infiltrating the Japanese school and going hand to hand with a number of powerful foes, including a sinister Russian, Petrov (played by Lee student Robert Baker and dubbed in the Cantonese version by Lee himself!).

Though not a particularly stylish nor technically accomplished film, *Fist of Fury* holds up extremely well thanks to Lee's powerful screen presence and the elaborate social subtext. Lee's bottled up fury for the opening half hour forces an audience to become increasingly agitated and excited, waiting for him to burst into action, and indeed he does. Lee also provides his first trademark scene with nunchakas, those ultra-lethal implements of certain death banned for two decades on cinema screens in the UK (as opposed to guns and chainsaws, which are okay.) American viewers accustomed to post-*Death Wish* portrayals of solo vengeance in film will be jarred by the finale, which continues well past the standard climax to offer a thought provoking commentary on nobility and sacrifice.

Fist of Fury has been released under its export title twice already on DVD, from Goodtimes (passable) and, as part of its Bruce Lee box set, from Fox. The bare bones Fox edition presents the same crisp but scruffy-looking dubbed laserdisc transfer from several years ago, using Columbia's master from all those familiar reissued drive-in and urban screenings. Media Asia has shown much more respect for the film, which is presented in a similarly letterboxed but brighter edition. The soundtrack in Cantonese, Mandarin, and English has been remixed quite well in Dolby Digital 5.1. Though the Morricone-style music is spread a little thin with such wide separation, the fight scenes and ambient effects should satisfy any martial arts film fans who wanted more after Warner's spectacular *Enter the Dragon* remix. Weapons swish through the air, punches reverberate between the audio channels, and body blows and flying kicks constantly pan from left to right, back to front. Very nicely done.

Media Asia has also lavished a number of extras on this DVD, which is housed in a CD-style silver cardboard long box with a Bruce Lee zipper hip pouch(!). All of Bruce's Chinese trailers are accessible from the fun animated menu screens: *Fist of Fury* (amusingly accompanied by Strauss' "Thus Spracht Zarathustra" and Bernard Herrmann's love theme from *Vertigo!*), *The Big Boss, Game of Death*, and a very interesting Cantonese trailer for *Enter the Dragon* which offers a fascinating comparison with Warner's promotion of it in the US. A few brief outtakes from *Game of Death*'s fight scenes are also thrown in for good measure. Most surprisingly, Media Asia also supplied two commentary tracks, in Cantonese by Donnie Yan and in English by British Hong Kong Action Cinema author Bey Logan, who incidentally portrayed Petrov in a TV remake of *Fist of Fury*. Logan, who obviously did quite a bit of preparation beforehand, manages to keep the commentary speedy and interesting throughout, with some useful insights into Chinese culture and colour symbolism within the film, the Japanese and Western influences on the film's music and editing, and the complex relationship between Bruce Lee and Lo Wei, who never worked together again after this film. Logan also pauses along the way for a few amusing personal observations, such as his assessment of Nora Miao's silly hairdo and a (hopefully joking) reference to Steve Martin. The disc is subtitled in the usual nine languages, Media Asia style; the English subtitles are large and readable, though sometimes inaccurate. This option is far more preferable than the familiar dubbed version, which has always sounded flat, irritating, and out of synch. Though *Fist of Fury* was dubbed in post-production in all languages, the Cantonese version is the most enjoyable as it offers Lee's character voice with the clearest audio and is still synched with his onscreen dialogue. The Mandarin track sounds less robust and a little noisier, often slipping out of synch with the lip movements. Unlike many Media Asia titles, *Fist of Fury* and the other Bruce Lee titles are not as readily available from general retailers in the United States but can be obtained from Chinese video dealers and online Asian DVD services. The British release from Hong Kong Legends is a also stunner, being 16:9 enhanced, uncut and packed with extras.

A FISTFUL OF DOLLARS

Colour, 1964, 99m. / Directed by Sergio Leone / Starring Clint Eastwood, Marianne Koch / MGM (US R1 NTSC, UK R2 PAL) / WS (2.35:1)

"It's the first film of its kind... and it won't be the last," intones the trailer for Sergio Leone's *A Fistful of Dollars (Per un pugno di dollari)*. Truer words were never spoken. Thanks to this modest little Italian western, which took three years to find success on American shores, the '60s and '70s were flooded with hundreds of "spaghetti westerns" featuring a mixture of Italian and American actors reinventing a genre Hollywood had long thought dead. While entertaining and stylish enough on its own terms, *Fistful* actually improves after viewings of Leone's other films so latent images and recurring motifs can be better appreciated. For example, his imaginative use of props, close ups, and unorthodox pacing (long quiet stretches punctuated by unexpected violence) truly came into their own in his later films, but it all started here. Like *Dr. No*, the first film may not precisely be the best, but it does command a great deal of respect and still holds up just fine.

The plot, acknowledged as a close derivation from Akira Kurosawa's feisty *Yojimbo*, features Clint Eastwood as "the man with no name" (actually, it's Joe), a mythic, fast drawing gunslinger who arrives in a town divided between two warring factions. After sampling the local colour, Eastwood devises a plan whereby he sells his services out to both sides, causing them to kill each other off and leave the town a whole lot cleaner in the process. Of course, the nastiest of the bunch, Ramon (Gian Maria Volante, also in the follow up, *For a Few Dollars More*), is still left standing and faces a thrilling, iconic showdown with Eastwood in the centre of town.

Fistful already contains the crucial elements spaghetti western fans savour: violent shootouts, quirky humour (Eastwood's mule speech near the beginning is a classic), and a trailblazing music score by Ennio Morricone (yep, the whistling is in here, too).

Though this is the beginning of the *Dollars* series, MGM chose to release *Fistful* on DVD last, leading fans to hope it would receive the same refurbished treatment accorded to *The Good, the Bad, and the Ugly* and *For a Few Dollars More*. However, the non-anamorphic DVD looks similar to but slightly sharper than the laserdisc - a satisfying transfer, but it probably could have been improved up to the level of its companion films. As with many of MGM's digital video transfers for laserdisc, some of the extremely detailed landscape shots display more aliasing than they should, but overall anyone who passed on the laser should be happy with this release. The scope framing appears accurate, and the dusky shades of brown and red, which predominate the film, are free of noticeable distortion. However, anyone who already has the laser won't find any surprises here aside from the inclusion of the trailer, inexplicably left off the earlier release. The sound quality is adequate but has obviously not borne the ravages of time, with some of the quiet scenes containing a faint level of crackling and distortion.

Incidentally, this is the longer European cut of the film, with approximately three minutes of gunfire and dialogue trimmed from US prints; perhaps someday MGM will also recover the notorious phoney prologue shot by Monte Hellman with Harry Dean Stanton added for a '70s US television screening.

FITZCARRALDO

Colour, 1982, 157m. / Directed by Werner Herzog / Starring Klaus Kinski, Claudia Cardinale / Anchor Bay (US R1 NTSC) / WS (1.85:1) (16:9) / DD5.1

 In a career filled with unforgettable, potentially destructive performances, none can compete with the sight of Klaus Kinski in *Fitzcarraldo*. Kinski stars as Fitzgerald, a strong-willed and possibly insane opera devotee and rubber baron. Thanks to his powers of persuasion, his lover, Molly (Claudia Cardinale), agrees to front the money from her "respectable" prostitution career for a large steamer. Fitz plans to drag this ship through a South American jungle to establish himself in a previously isolated territory near Iquitos, Peru. Unfortunately, his task involves hauling the gargantuan steamer up a huge mountain, a seemingly impossible feat he accomplishes through the local Indians (who dub him "Fitzcarraldo"). From the opening scenes, Kinski manages a difficult balancing act, which conveys his insane passion for opera (his impassioned plea outside the opera house when he and Molly arrive late to see Enrico Caruso) and the ultimately tender motivations behind his lunatic venture.

As with his other Herzog titles, much of this mania was reportedly genuine, as the director and star clashed on this production even more than the infamous *Aguirre: The Wrath of God*. Various stories abound regarding the injuries and deaths of many participants in the film, with Herzog and Kinski supposedly even squaring off and plotting to murder each other before the film's completion. Much of this turmoil was documented in the astonishing *Burden of Dreams*, Les Blank's shattering documentary following the production of the film (whose original stars included Jason Robards and Mick Jagger!). Sadly, this documentary could not be included on the DVD but would have made a perfect companion piece, despite (or because of?) its portrayal of Herzog as a raving lunatic best put out of his misery. Herzog has obviously come back down to earth quite a bit in the following years, and as with Anchor Bay's *Nosferatu*, he provides a rational, ingratiating commentary that understandably soft-pedals some of the more outrageous behind-the-scenes tales. (His producer, Lucki Stipetic, joins on the track as well.)

Fitzcarraldo abounds with stunning, slowly paced imagery, which will either captivate audiences or bore them to tears, depending upon one's personal tastes. For the patient, the film offers a number of rich rewards, culminating in the unforgettable dual climaxes (one physical, the other emotional), which rank as some of Herzog's finest filmmaking ever. Progressive rock group Popol Vuh provides yet another hypnotic, unforgettable score, laced as usual with opera and classical selections, and the entire cast ranging from professionals to memorable Indian amateurs seems entirely convincing throughout.

Anchor Bay's DVD appears to be mastered from the same elements used for the PAL British laserdisc, though anamorphically enhanced. This bonus aside, the image quality isn't quite as impressive as *Nosferatu* but still way ahead of the old cropped VHS version from Warner. Many scenes look a tad more washed out and grainy than they should, but the majority of the film is satisfying to watch and offers few complaints.

The original English track and German dub track are included, both tastefully remixed in Dolby Digital 5.1, with English subtitles. Purists can be forgiven for assuming that the film was shot in German, but the English track reveals that Cardinale was speaking her lines in English, while Kinski's voice is also in sync throughout. A moderate selection of production and promotional stills are also included. In the end, for a film whose very title has become synonymous with lunacy, its treatment on DVD reveals a great deal of respect and careful planning, which has certainly paid off.

FIVE DOLLS FOR AN AUGUST MOON

Colour, 1970, 79m. / Directed by Mario Bava / Starring William Berger, Edwige Fenech / Image (US R0 NTSC) / WS (1.85:1)

 Italian horror legend Mario Bava's oddest murder mystery, *Five Dolls for an August Moon*, is a film more often discussed than actually seen. Never released theatrically in America (unlike its blood-soaked counterpart, *Twitch of the Death Nerve*) and often condemned by no less than the director himself, the film has gained back some critical ground in recent years due to its relentless parade of eye candy and easygoing, loungy atmosphere. This is more of a tasty little bon bon for seasoned Eurofanatics than a suitable entry into Bava's candy coloured cinematic fairy tales, so don't necessarily expect to fall in love with it on first viewing... though many have, and with good reason.

The circuitous plotline follows a group of people isolated at an ultra-modern beach house on an island, where the well-to-do guests revel in jazzy, twisted party games when they're not too busy trying to wrench a secret new chemical formula from its inventor, Gerry Farrell (William Berger). Though everyone is ostensibly paired off with a partner, flirting and infidelity become the order of the day until someone decides to resort to murder... and one by one, the guests' bodies wind up stashed in plastic wrapping and hung in the meat freezer. As the body count rises, tensions and distrust lead to fistfights, suicides, and an ironic final twist.

The breezy and meandering tone of *Five Dolls* can be a strange sensation at first, as the film bizarrely avoids graphic violence and instead presents each corpse as a tableaux discovered by the characters; whether sprawled on the beach, floating in a bathtub, or most memorably lashed to a tree and transfixed with a knife, each body becomes a mounting black joke as the soundtrack pulses with Piero Umiliani's delicious, feverish beat score. Though each actor is basically cast as a familiar "type" (the scheming wife, the snotty businessman, the swarthy gigolo), everyone looks terrific and seems to be having a good time. Chief among these is frequent Sergio Martino giallo muse Edwige

Fenech, who steals the opening party sequence by dancing with wild abandon, slurping down cocktails, and generally kicking off the proceedings with an air of wicked good humour. Though his heart was supposedly not in the project, Bava nevertheless invests the *Ten Little Indians* style narrative with some terrific flourishes, such as the languorous shots of lovers passing cigarettes with their toes in bed and the oft-admired, astounding montage of a dish of marbles scattering down a flight of stairs and splashing into a victim's tub.

The only widely circulated English edition of *Five Dolls* came on British VHS courtesy of Redemption, but the Image DVD proves to be worth the wait. Vibrantly colourful and well framed at 1.85:1, the transfer has been lifted from a nice, almost immaculate print and features both the English-dubbed soundtrack (more or less in sync with the multinational actors but rather tinny sounding) and the more poetic Italian dialogue track, complete with newly translated, optional English subtitles. Furthermore, the print contains an extended end credits sequence omitted from all previous video transfers along with the familiar playout music following the end credits. Also, Italian soundtrack fans should pay close attention to the menu screens... Obviously supplements for this barely distributed film are limited, but the disc does come with informative liner notes from Tim Lucas filled with the usual amusing anecdotes, as well as other Bava trailers and filmographics for Bava, Fenech, and Umiliani.

FLESH

Colour, 1968, 89m. / Directed by Paul Morrissey / Starring Joe Dallesandro, Patti D'Arbanville / Image (US R1 NTSC)

 Flesh, the first feature-length collaboration between Morrissey and Warhol, features exhibitionist Factory studboy Joe Dallesandro in his underground star-making role as a hustler who experiences various walks of life in NYC circa 1968. Many viewers will find this film shocking and almost impossible to deal with, thanks to the fact that it was shot and edited entirely in-camera (in other words, what you see in the movie is exactly what they shot, in sequence- meaning lots of very, very long shots, jump cuts, etc.). Obviously the unavoidable grain in the cheap film makes this less than ideal for DVD consumers looking for the next audio/video demo title, but *Flesh* has never looked

F

better than it does here (and certainly clearer than the old Mystic Fire videotapes). The punchy colour and clarity manage to make the scruffy 16mm origins more forgivable, and while the film itself is less interesting than some of its follow up features (*Trash*, *Lonesome Cowboys*, etc.), this belongs on any midnight movie follower's shelf.

FLESH FEAST

Colour, 1970, 72m. / Directed by Brad Grinter / Starring Veronica Lake, Phil Philbin / Beverly Wilshire (US R0 NTSC)

One of the most interminable schlock films around, *Flesh Feast* makes Al Adamson look like a model of filmmaking savvy in comparison and would be completely forgotten if it weren't for the presence of Hollywood icon Veronica Lake, making an ill-advised comeback attempt as a scientist obsessed with maggots. Shot mostly around Miami, Florida (or, more accurately, a series of motel rooms in Miami), the film is 99% pointless yapping by the inept cast, with the other 1% consisting of Veronica toying with her precious wriggly friends and unleashing them on Nazi baddies.

The story, such as it is, presents Lake as Dr. Elaine Fredericks, who uses larvae in a series of vaguely defined experiments to find the modern fountain of youth. A series of visitors from South America begin to cause trouble, abducting various people at the airport and arranging for Fredericks to perform her magic on a mysterious visitor named Max Bauer. Naturally these turn out to be neo-Nazis with a fiendish plot to unleash Der Fuhrer on an unsuspecting world, but with the aid of newspaper editor Ed Casey (Phil Philbin), who's investigating the bizarre death of one of his reporters who was trailing an arms dealer, and Ed's assistant, Kristine Powell (Heather Hughes), our semi-deranged heroine finds a way to reveal her true motives.

Completely devoid of such burdens as suspense, characterization, or any real reason for being, *Flesh Feast* earns its place in the history book solely for its fascination with "living, crawling maggots" and the oddly compelling spectacle of a nearly unrecognizable Lake overacting like mad actually makes one nostalgic for Dana Andrews in the comparatively high class *The Frozen Dead*. Director Brad Grinter continued to bless grindhouse viewers with his talents in such further epics as 1971's *Blood Freak*, the world's strangest mutant turkey movie, but never

again was he allowed to trash a fading star's reputation to such a disturbing degree.

As bad as it is, *Flesh Feast* might at least be bearable with a decent transfer, which it certainly didn't receive here. The Beverly Wilshire DVD appears to be mastered from an EP-speed VHS dupe of the long out-of-print World Video edition and, along with *Galaxina*, could be the worst release so far in the format's relatively brief history. Contrast is nonexistent, dropouts litter the screen, focus is smudgy and blurry, and colours are pasty and washed out. If you really must see this film and can find absolutely no other way to do it, then maybe the disc will be worth the eight or nine bucks it goes for in some outlets, but otherwise, steer clear!

FLESH FOR FRANKENSTEIN

Colour, 1973, 95m. / Directed by Paul Morrissey / Starring Udo Kier, Joe Dallesandro / Criterion (US R1 NTSC) / WS (2.35:1)

The Baron (Kier), preparing a male companion for his already assembled female zombie (Delila Di Lazzaro), sets out with his gofer Otto (Arno Juerging) in search of one final component. Finding just what he wants atop the shoulders of a handsome shepherd (Srdjan Zelenovic), he decapitates him and makes off with the head and its "perfect nasum". The deceased's friend (Dallesandro) finds employ as a servant at the Baron's castle and, discovering what the madman has done, sets about curtailing his crazed research.

A priceless serving of comic-horror cinema from Paul Morrissey, the director who also gave us the infamous *Blood for Dracula*. With its wicked streak of black humour, and strewn with some of the most sickening imagery ever committed to film, *Flesh for Frankenstein* is actually so unrelentingly flagrant that one can't do anything but laugh. The Baron is played in the face of major league insanity by the magnificent Udo Kier who conveys a sparkling air of probity and delivers his absurdly nihilistic dialogue with the utmost conviction. His shared scenes with the creepy, bug-eyed Arno Juerging are to be relished. By contrast, Morrissey favourite Joe Dallesandro (who spends as much time servicing Monique Van Vooren as he does serving dinner) isn't unlike Sam "*Flash Gordon* 1979" Jones to look at and speaks his lines with the amusing insincerity of Buster "*Flash Gordon* 1936" Crabbe; you can't help but wince at his sheer awfulness. Breathtakingly gorgeous Dalila Di

Lazzaro's doll-like beauty manages to eclipse the distraction of her grotesque body-scarring, lovingly applied by effects wizard Carlo Rambaldi... yes, the same chap who went on to create Spielberg's *E.T.*! In spite of the fact that the blood'n'guts sequences are so outrageous as to be comical, one still needs to have a strong stomach to sit through the post-mortem menu of livers, lungs, and all manner of (thankfully unidentifiable) intestinal matter, all thrust in your face with gleeful abandon... quite literally if you're fortunate enough to catch the film in its original, rarely seen 3-D format.

As classy a package as one has come to expect from Criterion Collection releases, *Flesh for Frankenstein* reaches DVD in a replica of the company's earlier laserdisc pressing. Minus the 3-D technique, the 2.35:1 matted, 31-chapter-encoded print of the film is presented in all its demented, uncut glory with a palette of searingly vivid colours. A feature-length audio commentary is provided by Kier and Morrissey, hosted by author/critic Maurice Yakowar. The star and his director offer up a wealth of informative anecdotal material, but the scholarly observations proffered by Yakowar are patronisingly trite; this unwelcome form of highbrow dissection and critique - proffering "meaning" behind certain camera angles and images, where in fact there is none - is tiresome and conceited, and has infected a number of genre titles, among them some of the works of Mario Bava. Although the absence of a trailer is regrettable, Claudio Gizzi's beautiful, melancholy score provides the backdrop to a joyous slideshow presentation of still images, the undisputed highlight of which is a shot of Srdjan Zelenovic (who remains stone-faced throughout the movie) laughing it up on set. - TG

FLESH GORDON

Colour, 1972, 86m. / Directed by Michael Benveniste and Howard Ziehm / Starring Jason Williams, Suzanne Fields / Hen's Tooth (US R1 NTSC) / WS (1.66:1), EIV (UK R2 PAL) / WS (1.85:1)

A breathtakingly stupid cult item, *Flesh Gordon* rose to prominence as a midnight and college campus hit around the same time as other word of mouth hits *like A Boy and His Dog* and *El Topo*. Unlike those films, however, *Flesh* can't really be defended as a work of cinematic art, nor does it even try. Instead the filmmakers chose to do a goofy, corny, sexually outrageous tribute to the old Flash

Gordon serials, complete with up-to-date special effects, kitschy costumes, and godawful acting. Of course, in the right frame of mind, it's also a huge amount of fun despite some slow stretches, laced with a few memorable lines of dialogue and surprisingly ambitious visuals.

A mysterious attack of sex rays is sending the Earth into pandemonium. According to a venerable scientist (John Hoyt), these rays are being sent from another planet and cause earthlings to collapse into an uncontrollable sexual frenzy. When a plane flight is sabotaged by these rays, two passengers, Flesh (Jason Williams) and Dale Ardor (Suzanne Fields), manage to escape and find themselves at the remote home of Dr. Flexi Jerkoff (Joseph Hudgins), an eccentric scientist. Jerkoff informs the newcomers that he has designed a spaceship by which he will thwart the evil plans of the planet Porno, which is responsible for the attack. The trio take off and, upon arriving at Porno, wind up in the court of the wicked Wang the Perverted (William Hunt). Emperor Wang devises a number of grisly tortures for the earthlings, but Flesh manages to escape with Princess Amora (Mycle Brandy), who ravishes him on her ship. A number of further misadventures ensue, with Dale attacked by a gang of lesbians led by the hook-armed Chief Nellie (Candy Samples) and Jerkoff discovering the Power Pasties by which he can defeat Wang's army. With the help of Prince Precious (Lance Larsen) and his tribe of gay forest men, Flesh and his friends return to Wang's castle and stage a daring attack.

Rumours have abounded about *Flesh Gordon* since its initial release. Producer Bill Osco and co-director Howard Ziehm had first struck gold *with Mona, the Virgin Nymph,* the first narrative hardcore feature film, and originally *Flesh Gordon* was conceived as a $25 million porn epic. When it was released with an X-rating and nary an explicit close-up to be found, audiences assumed that a stronger version existed somewhere. However, as anti-erotic as the final product may be, *Flesh* is still definitely not for kids, considering the heavy amounts of frontal nudity, lewd puns, and softcore sex. (However, a couple of distant, fleeting hardcore moments can be spied during the orgies in Wang's palace.) In the late '70s and early '80s, a softer R-rated version circulated through theatres, with virtually all frontal nudity trimmed out (the result played like a dull *Saturday Night Live* skit). The 78 minute X-rated cut appeared on home video from Media in a blurry, badly cropped edition that nevertheless won over a new legion of fans, followed by the same transfer on laserdisc from Image. Unfortunately, *Flesh Gordon* went into moratorium hell for over a decade after Media's disappearance, only to resurface from Hen's Tooth Video with a widely touted extra ten minutes of restored footage. Many fans gathered that these extra scenes would be hardcore, but in fact this footage consists of many minor trims made by Ziehm after the film's premiere to speed up the pace. There is some additional nudity, but mostly the unseen material consists of extra dialogue, more establishing shots, and a few transition scenes, particularly with the forest people. It makes for a better paced and less exhausting film, but don't expect anything terribly revealing.

The technical production of *Flesh Gordon* was extremely complicated, but basically, it was mostly shot in 16mm, with the stop motion effects added when it was blown up to 35mm. Thus, the 16mm negative (assuming it still exists) would be useless. The Hen's Tooth transfer is culled from the longer 86 minute premiere print (35mm), letterboxed at approximately 1.66:1. Though the film isn't well framed by any means, the extra vertical information makes it less claustrophobic and adds some aesthetic value to the amusing comic book opening titles. The effects sequences look the best, featuring some terrific work from Jim Danforth (whose name is spelled backwards in the credits) and a number of other soon-to-be-prominent FX artists. Highlights include a *Jason and the Argonauts*-style beetleman attack, a blinking penisaurus, and a great, hilarious clambering monster (voiced by an uncredited Craig T. Nelson!) reminiscent of Harryhausen's beloved Ymir. The film itself has always looked pretty rough, with lots of grain and washed out colour, and the DVD isn't really any different. Turning down the brightness control on the TV helps it out, though, and reduces the grain considerably. While the film's fans will be accustomed to this appearance and probably don't expect much, anyone looking solely for a great visual experience would be well advised to look elsewhere.

The disc includes the original theatrical trailer (which de-emphasizes the sex, oddly enough) and, astonishingly, a commentary track by director Ziehm. Thankfully, Ziehm answers a number of nagging questions about the film, and while he often seems to be reading notecards and never comments directly on the film's action, he delivers a number of fascinating and sometimes shocking anecdotes. He blasts the shoddy and manipulative techniques of Osco (who also released the porn musical *Alice in Wonderland* before winding up in jail) and co-director Michael Benveniste, who was fired off the film. While the orgy scenes in the film were obviously performed for real (including a mentioned gay orgy that never materialized in the final product), only one sequence, with Flesh and Amora, was actually lensed as a full hardcore sequence. However, legal wrangling in California resulted in all of the graphic footage being chopped out of the negative and confiscated by the local government, never to be seen in a final edit of the film. For anyone who claims the initial release of the film was XXX, it just ain't so. Ziehm also relates the numerous special effects hassles, the budgetary nightmares, the loss of the original assembled negative, and his own early experiences doing porn features and stag loops, including some personal details that may have been better left unsaid. Ziehm's chat is a frank, unashamed, and very welcome contribution to the film, often more startling and graphic than the film it accompanies. The featureless British DVD release features a more severely matted transfer of a BBFC censored cut.

FOR YOUR EYES ONLY

Colour, 1981, 128m. / Directed by John Glen / Starring Roger Moore, Carole Bouquet / MGM (US R1 NTSC, UK R2 PAL) / WS (2.35:1) (16:9) / DD5.1

When a spy ship carrying an ATAC - a valuable piece of government hardware - sinks off Corfu the British rush to retrieve it before the Russians move in. Their first emissary locates the site of the wreck but is murdered, so James Bond (Moore) is sent in and teams up with the man's daughter, Melina (Bouquet), to locate her father's killer and salvage the device.

Former 007 editor/2nd unit director John Glen cooks up a Bond that matches *The Spy Who Loved Me* as the best of the Moore septet. Smarting from criticism levelled at *Moonraker*, the team went back to basics for a good old fashioned slice of espionage inspired once again by the Ian Fleming novels. With this mandate came a freshness to commodities peddled to audiences numerous times before, the subsequent ski action, car chases and underwater combat proving more gratifying than ever. The film is also bookended by two of the finest action sequences in the series. The pre-titles is a corker, played out in the skies over an abandoned London gasworks; it's better than the backdrop might suggest, with an electrocuted pilot, a helicopter remote-controlled by perennial 007 nasty Blofeld, and Bond clinging precariously to the outside as it swoops over the industrial stacks. The finale has our man booted off the ledge of a rocky peak and plummeting hundreds of feet with only a spindly rope to save him.

Carole Bouquet is among the loveliest Bond ladies and has the most gorgeous eyes imaginable. Lynn-Holly Johnson is teenage nymphomaniac ice skater Bibi Dahl (a sneakily appropriate corruption of Baby Doll?), whom a cautious Bond amusingly defers bedding; he buys her an ice cream instead! Julian Glover and Topol slug it out for top villain slot and it's a nice touch that we don't learn which of the pair is the real scoundrel until well into the story. Others among the premium cast - an inordinate number of whom died young - include Michael Gothard as smooth and silent executioner Locque, Charles Dance (with barely a line of dialogue to call his own) as one of his gunmen, Cassandra Harris (Mrs. Pierce Brosnan until her premature death) as another 007 bedtime conquest, Jack (*New York Ripper*) Hedley as the murdered British envoy, Jill Bennett as a skating coach with more than a professional interest in her pupil, and fleetingly glimpsed model Tula Cossey (the Bond babe later revealed to be sex-changed Barry Cossey). The final scene with Janet Brown and John Wells as Margaret and Denis Thatcher is dreadfully misplaced but wickedly funny just the same.

Comprising a generous 56 chapter marks, the print of *For Your Eyes Only* on MGM's Special Edition disc is excellent. The remainder of the disc lives up to the quality of the feature, boasting not one but two commentaries (the first with director John Glen and members of the cast, the second with executive producer/co-writer Michael G. Wilson and a number of the crew). Additionally there's an excellent documentary, a gallery of stills, four trailers, two radio spots, two short animated storyboard sequences and the promo video for Sheena Easton's theme song (in actuality the film's titles sequence without the titles, unveiling a few glimpses of the female form usually obscured by people's names) A choice of English or French sound and subtitling is available. - TG

FORGOTTEN SILVER

Colour/B&W, 1996, 53m. / Directed by Peter Jackson & Costa Botes / Starring John O'Shea, Margeurite Hurst / First Run (US R1 NTSC) / DD2.0

This departure of sorts for New Zealand's greatest current cinematic export, Peter Jackson *(The Lord of the Rings)*, allows him to apply his gusto and visual wizardry to a film more gentle and heartfelt than all of his other work put together. While *Heavenly*

Creatures displayed a more humane and character-driven side than one might guess from the splattery likes of *Brain Dead*, the unorthodox structure of *Forgotten Silver*, along with the added factor of a co-director in the form of Costa Botes, produces something entirely new and magical. It's impossible to discuss *Forgotten Silver* without giving away some crucial elements of both the story itself and the factors behind its creation, so if you're simply curious, just know that this is a terrific film and can be shown to virtually any member of the family. Furthermore, fans of experimental cinema, silent classics, and cinematic virtuosity will be especially gratified by what everyone involved has achieved here. Okay... now you've been warned. Shall we proceed?

The one hour pseudo-documentary begins with Jackson and Botes being invited to the relative of Colin McKenzie, an obscure New Zealand filmmaker from the early days of celluloid who has been relegated to footnote status in most reference books. Leonard Maltin, Miramax's Harvey Weinstein, and actor Sam Neill all appear throughout to offer their own observations on McKenzie and the ramifications of the directors' discovery of McKenzie's legacy, a massive amount of films and historical documents capable of changing the entirety of film history itself. The ambitious McKenzie had movies in his blood from an early age, when he used a steam engine to power a projector, ran his camera with a bicycle, invented the tracking shot, and got into trouble for stealing an unholy amount of eggs. Before anyone else he developed colour film, talking pictures, the close-up, and the massive biblical epic. Unfortunately the bizarre quirks of world history and financial unpredictability conspired against McKenzie, who found the love of his life thwarted (at least temporarily), his dream project of *Salome* nearly sabotaged by shaky backers, and his career compromised by his creative involvement with a slapstick comedian.

As Jackson unabashedly admits on this DVD, *Forgotten Silver* is essentially "a great big lie," a delicious hoax that perfectly imitates the advances of cinema for the past one hundred years. The clips of McKenzie's films are dead on, with enough humour to provoke a chuckle but never going overboard to call into question the story's authenticity. In fact, while McKenzie and his cohorts never existed, it's astonishing how much pathos is evoked during the final few minutes; the powerhouse of a punchline ends the film on a perfect, bittersweet grace note. Not to be overlooked is the magnificent imitation of a silent epic, with McKenzie's *Salome* brilliantly encapsulated during its long delayed premiere which contains some striking visuals not too far removed from some of the genuine pioneers of silent cinema.

First Run's DVD looks essentially the same as their VHS version, which was sharp enough already. This still looks like a television program, no better or worse, and makes for a fine presentation. The real treat here is the extra material, including several bits of deleted footage (interviews with Maltin, Jackson and Botes hiking through the New Zealand jungle some more, and so on), a running audio commentary with Botes (vaguely identified as "director's commentary" on the packaging), and a 22 minute behind the scenes documentary entitled "Behind the Bull," containing a wealth of information about the production of the film. Some of the treats here include undoctored McKenzie footage before the lab work, interviews with Jackson and Botes, FX designs, and much more.

4D MAN

Colour, 1959, 85m. / Directed by Irvin S. Yeaworth, Jr. / Starring Robert Lansing, Lee Meriwether / Image (US R0 NTSC)

A strange and belated major studio effort to cash in on the '50s sci-fi craze, *4D Man* subverts many of the already established traditions of its genre and has aged far more interestingly than the average drive-in fare. Boosted by decent production values and a bizarre, wall-to-wall jazz/lounge score, this one has been grabbing the attention of late night TV viewers for years, with good reason.

After a lab fire resulting from his experiments, scientist Tony Nelson (James Congdon) decides to visit his older brother, Scott (Robert Lansing). Also a scientist, Scott is incensed when Tony woos away Scott's girlfriend, Linda (Lee Meriwether). Seeking revenge, Scott steals Tony's new scientific discovery, which allows an object to pass through solid matter. Unfortunately, Scott gets caught in the middle of a transmission and is imbues with the ability to pass through solid matter himself. Whenever Scott passes through a wall or a piece of furniture, he ages instantly, but when he passes through another human being, he absorbs their life force and becomes younger at their expense. The

powers of such an ability become too much for Scott's mind to handle, and he quickly becomes a very deadly threat to society at large.

Most notable to many TV fans for an appearance by Patty Duke at age 12, *4D Man* features all the vivid Technicolor sheen of a Ross Hunter production like *Imitation of Life* thanks to its support from Universal. Reasonably well acted and filled with surprises, the film may not change anyone's life, but it hums along just fine and makes for a great evening's entertainment for the discerning sci-fi buff. The elements used for the DVD are generally in good shape, with robust Technicolor hues in the best '50s tradition and some unavoidable patches of muddiness and grain, which are at least less noticeable than past transfers.

FOUR DIMENSIONS OF GRETA

Colour, 1972, 85m./ Directed by Pete Walker / Starring Tristan Rogers, Karen Boyer / Salvation (UK R0 PAL)

Before he briefly became Britain's most significant horror filmmaker in the 1970s, Pete Walker earned a decent living cranking out frothy sex comedies like *Cool It Carol* and *School for Sex*. More techni-cally polished and elaborate than, say the British Confessions of... series, these films aren't particularly outstanding works of exploitation but do hold their own within their limited genre. One of the odder entries, *Four Dimensions of Greta,* threw in the added gimmick of four 3-D flashbacks (filmed in black and white with the old red and blue glasses routine), a device Walker used to more grisly effect the same year for the finale of *The Flesh and Blood Show.*

On an airplane, dutiful German reporter Hans Wiemer (popular TV soap actor Tristan Rogers) pulls out a photograph of a beautiful blonde woman and ponders his current circumstances. Recruited by his publishing magnate boss over dinner for a "business trip" to London, Hans has actually been asked to track down the missing Greta, who has apparently been swallowed up without a trace by the swinging scene of London. Hans reluctantly leaves his idealistic girlfriend and, upon his arrival in the big city, promptly descends into a world of swinging underground clubs populated by topless dancers and easy girls willing to share their stories about the saucy, naughty Greta. The first tale, told by a chunky naked woman stuck to a piece of clear inflatable furniture, depicts Greta as a freewheeling slut who scared the other girls with her joie de vivre. Then the requisite savvy black swinger tells her own tale about working with Greta at a strip joint where the title character performed a bizarre nude routine involving lots of billowing white blankets. Then it's on to the maimed Roger (ubiquitous British sex comedy star Robin Askwith), Greta's purported boyfriend, who offers a much more loving, wholesome take on their relationship. Greta's "fourth dimension," according to one of her older acquaintances, was trading her charms (including massages) to tease men and provoke them into fistfights. Eventually Hans sorts out the truth, and with the help of Roger and a little tedious slapstick action all eventually becomes right with the world again.

While the idea of 3-D sex films sounds too tawdry and surreal to resist, few films have actually made good use of the concept. *Greta* is no exception, with only a broken bottle and the occasional bare breast thrust into the camera during the four flashback scenes. Most of the 3-D footage looks more stagebound than the rest of the film, whose gaudy club scenes and abundant displays of frontal nudity would have been better chosen to come leaping out into the audience's lap.

Fans of '70s kitsch will have a ball with the post-mod fashions, tons of hipster lingo, and the goofiest phoney German accents ever recorded on film (and yes, that includes The Producers). The music score ranges from an outrageously tacky theme song to a fairly decent instrumental score, though it never scales the delirious musical heights achieved by continental sex comedies around the same time in France and Italy. The extras, which can be a little daunting to track down, include a US theatrical trailer (apparently, yes, it did play outside the UK) and a smattering of stills and theatrical posters.

As with Walker's other films, Greta was shot open matte with an eventual matting job between 1.78.1 and 1.85:1 planned for its theatrical presentation. The full frame DVD looks fine overall, though the print reveals some distracting battering and staining during the next to last reel. Colours are fairly dull throughout most of the film, but the occasional vivid splashes of red and blue lighting reveal this was probably intentional. The 3-D effects work about as well as most other DVD attempts; it's passable but not as effective as the theatrical experience. The glasses included in the box must be held in front of your eyes at all times and can't be propped, making one thankful for the relative brevity of the 3-D scenes. No extras apart from a filmography.

FOUR OF THE APOCALYPSE

Colour, 1975, 104m. / Directed by Lucio Fulci / Starring Fabio Testi, Lynne Frederick / Anchor Bay (US R1 NTSC) / WS (1.85:1) (16:9)

Though ostensibly a western, the grisly and bizarre *Four of the Apocalypse* fits more snugly with director Lucio Fulci's gothic horror outings than most of his other work outside the genre. Many of the collaborators who would shape some of Fulci's most nightmarish visions, such as composer Fabio Frizzi and cinematographer Sergio Salvati, demonstrate how significant their contributions were even this early in the game, and for once, Fulci seems to be sufficiently engaged in the proceedings to experiment with his visuals and narrative form in some unexpected ways. Though possibly a difficult place to start for newcomers, *Apocalypse* is a must see for Fulci fanatics and proves once again that his grisly excesses were grounded in a firm stylistic approach.

In the late 1800s, con artist Stubby Preston (Fabio Testi) arrives in Salt Lake City and promptly winds up tossed overnight in prison, with his marked cards consigned to a fireplace. In the cell he meets three fellow misfits: young pregnant hooker Bunny (*Schizo*'s Lynne Frederick), town drunk Clem (Michael J. Pollard), and delusional slave Bud (Harry Baird), who has an unusually friendly relationship with cemeteries. A brutal attack by masked gunmen leaves the town back under the thumb of the law, so the sheriff (*Zombie Holocaust*'s Donal O'Brien) ejects them from town into the desert. Along the way to a new destiny they meet Chaco (Tomas Milian), who seems like a nice guy until he gets everyone stoned on booze and peyote, then proceeds to blow out Clem's kneecaps and rape Bunny while Stubby and Bud are tortured and left tie to the ground. The four manage to escape and resume their trip to the Promised Land, only to encounter something far different from what they expected. After a number of sacrifices and tragedies, fate finally allows events to come full circle as Stubby decides to seek revenge against Chaco.

Spaghetti western fans expecting cool, mysterious gunmen shooting in out against mythic landscapes will be shocked by this downbeat, deliberately paced portrayal of the West as a merciless land capable of swallowing men's souls without leaving a trace. The criminally underrated Testi is excellent in the lead role, which allows him to transform both physically and emotionally several times throughout the course of the sprawling narrative. However, Milian also swipes his precious minutes of screen time as the memorable villain, a nightmarish figure whose sadism hits a fever pitch when he skins off one unlucky victim's stomach and pins a sheriff's star into his flesh of his chest. The always eccentric Pollard (best known for *Bonnie and Clyde*) really doesn't have much to do; he made a much stronger impression as a western figure in 1972's rarely seen oddity, *Dirty Little Billy*. Like many other '70s spaghetti western scores (most obviously *Keoma*), this one sports a freakish mixture of vocals and experimental instruments interrupted by crooning folk tunes which are, shall we say, best appreciated as irony.

The back cover for Anchor Bay's DVD of *Four of the Apocalypse* promises the inclusion of footage deleted from all circulating prints of the film, with the reinstated dialogue in Italian with optional English subtitles. These scenes include the aforementioned Chaco torture routine as well as a greatly expanded version of Bunny's rape (though only the former contains subtitled dialogue).

The only previous English language release in Japan looked watchable despite these studio-imposed cuts, but the DVD's quality is tremendously improved. Though detail is hampered by some of Salvati's soft focus compositions, particularly during the misty opening scene, the transfer looks as good as one could expect, with accurate colour reproduction. The only significant debit is a tiny vertical line running through a few scenes near the right side of the screen, similar to the flaw in the negative of Fulci's *The Black Cat*. The film can also be played with its entire Italian language soundtrack, though alas no English subtitles are provided. The Italian track contains several notable variations from the English version, including the (thankful) absence of an opening narration.

Extras include the nicely edited English language European trailer, cast and crew bios (including some illuminating anecdotes about Testi), and a compact but informative featurette, "Fulci of the Apocalypse," in which Milian (in English) and Testi (in Italian) reminisce about working with the notorious director, whose questionable behaviour is one of the primary focuses. Milian also offers some hilarious stories, expanded further into an Easter Egg on the special features menu.

FOUR SIDED TRIANGLE

B&W, 1953, 81m. / Directed by Terence Fisher / Starring Barbara Payton, John Van Eyssen / Anchor Bay (US R1 NTSC)

The first true science fiction film from England's Hammer Films, *Four Sided Triangle* has never been much of a critical darling; even Leonard Maltin gave it a "BOMB." However, its quiet merits have become more appreciated among film cultists, and fans of director Terence Fisher in particular should find that there's much more here than meets the eye.

The oddly structured yarn begins with Dr. Harvey (James Hayter) relating his lifelong observations of three people, Bill, Robin, and Lena, who were an inseparable trio as children. However, Lena went off and became unhappy with her life, causing her to return to the village of her youth and contemplate suicide. However, her faith in life is partially restored when she reunites with Bill (Stephen Murray) and Robin (John Van Eyssen), both of whom have developed a "reproducer" capable of creating an exact copy of physical matter. Lena becomes their assistant and steals the heart of Bill, who plans to reveal his romantic intentions to her. However, that night Lena and Robin announce their engagement, and Bill is crushed. When Robin leaves for a few days, Bill talks Lena into an unorthodox solution: with the help of the reproducer, Bill can create an exact duplicate of Lena, thus solving their romantic problems. The experiment seems to go as planned, but...

With its emphasis on human relations and small village atmosphere, *Four Sided Triangle* is one of the more personable '50s sci-fi films, sort of like a cloning variation on *Our Town*, complete with the first person narrator who addresses the audience. None of the actors are really spectacular, though Payton (*Bride of the Gorilla*) does an adequate job in her dual role. The real star is Fisher, whose economic storytelling and precise visual flair gives the story more drive and urgency than the average B-movie programmer. However, the script suffers from a few faults even this master filmmaker cannot surmount, such as a trite "don't mess with Mother Nature" message justified by an irritatingly arbitrary, tragic finale.

Anchor Bay's DVD utilizes the same beautiful transfer from the original British negative found on the earlier Roan laserdisc, and here it's even sharper and more lustrous. Those shiny test tubes and blinding flashes of light never looked better. The mono audio has also been carefully cleaned up, resulting in a distortion-free soundtrack punctuated by a sometimes bombastic music track. The only extra is another half hour instalment in the British

TV overview series, *World of Hammer*, this time devoted to the Hammer Frankenstein films. This choice is oddly appropriate, as *Four Sided Triangle* introduces many themes and visual motifs which would later surface in Fisher's masterful and underrated *Frankenstein Created Woman*. And whatever you do, don't read the liner notes on the back of the box before viewing the film!

FOUR TIMES THAT NIGHT

Colour, 1969, 84m. / Directed by Mario Bava / Starring Brett Halsey, Daniela Giordano / Image (US R0 NTSC) / WS (1.78:1) (16:9)

Still basking in the giddy comic book haze of his sublime *Diabolik*, director Mario Bava branched out away even further from gothic terrors with *Four Times That Night (Quante volte... quella notte)*, a loose and breezy sex farce which borrows its structure from Akira Kurosawa's *Rashomon*. Bava rises to the task quite well and brings his trademark visual skills into play for some dazzling little flourishes throughout the film, making it a diverting little bon bon in a career lined with masterpieces.

Pretty young Tina (Daniela Giordano) finds her afternoon dog walk disturbed by sports car driving lothario Gianni (*Return of the Fly*'s Brett Halsey), who asks her on a date. Despite her convent breeding, Tina agrees to see him that night but returns home much later than planned with her dress torn. In flashback, Tina frantically tells her mother about the evening, which begin with a trip to a nightclub and escalated into Gianni's frantic rape attempt while dressed in leopardskin underwear. However, the next day Gianni, sporting a nasty scratch on his face, tells his buddies a quite different story in which Tina was actually a sex mad panther who demanded hour after hour of satisfaction. Back at Gianni's apartment, the lecherous doorman (Dick Randall) offers yet another variation of the story, in which Gianni, a manipulative homosexual, lured Tina in for an evening of debauched sexual antics (partially involving *Twitch of the Death Nerve*'s skinny-dipper, Brigitte Skay). Of course, the fourth version - the whole story, natch - proves to be an entirely different affair.

A colourful pop art feast for the eyes, *Four Times That Night* allows Bava's camera to run rampant and soak in every detail of the mod clothing and sets. Though working with a miniscule budget, the director turns simple settings like a shower or a bedroom into visual playgrounds of bold primary colours and catchy geometric shapes, while inflatable furniture, rope swings, tinted drinking glasses, and wallpapered photo collages become props for each character's Freudian delights. The sexuality itself is limited by today's standards, with a few bare breasts and coyly concealed fumblings making this a quaint reminder of the innocence of pre-Emmanuelle erotic cinema. More importantly, the film is genuinely funny, alternating hilarious verbal wit (particularly Tina's self-empowering claims while locked in the bathroom during the first episode) with physical comedy in the best tradition of an English bedroom farce. The funky lounge score by Coriolano "Lallo" Gori adds to the fun and foreshadows Piero Umiliani's similar work on Bava's similar cotton candy exercise, *Five Dolls for an August Moon* in 1970.

Rarely seen in any form, this film has become something of a holy grail for Bava completists. Some video dealers have circulated a smudgy tape version of the barely released English dubbed edition, which dumbs down the dialogue and brutally crops Bava's compositions. Therefore the Image DVD is a welcome restoration of a film few even know to look for, and the print by and large is in satisfying shape. Only the animated opening credits (an amusing cartoon twist on a Rorsach test, appropriately enough) and the first scene suffer from notable damage, while colours are always vibrant and clearly rendered. The Italian dialogue fares much better than the English version, while the subtitles convey the puckish, rapid fire exchanges surprisingly well. The disc also comes with extensive liner notes from Video Watchdog's Tim Lucas, who provides plenty of historical tidbits to make this an even more cherished and significant release.

THE FOURTH MAN

Colour, 1983, 103m. / Directed by Paul Verhoeven / Starring Jeroen Krabbé, Renée Soutendijk / Anchor Bay (US R0 NTSC) / WS (1.85:1) (16:9)

Perhaps Paul Verhoeven's most completely satisfying film, *The Fourth Man* is the closest of his Dutch productions to his later stylized, fearless Hollywood titles, which run the gamut from acknowledged modern master-pieces (*Robocop*) to bafflingly surreal misfires such as *Showgirls*. Drawing on a seemingly endless reservoir of influences, ranging from Nicolas Roeg to Christian iconography and bisexual chic, Verhoeven and his usual stable of actors and crew members have ultimately concocted a diabolical black comedy about the dangers of the creative process and the even greater perils of blindly following one's libido.

An alcoholic writer named Gérard Reve (Jeroen Krabbé), incidentally named after the source novel's author, stumbles out of a DT-laden stupor and leaves his male companion in Amsterdam to embark on a train trip to Flushing. Along the way he encounters a handsome man (Thom Hoffman) at a magazine stand and experiences horrific hallucinations during the ride while observing a blue-clad Madonna and child. Upon his arrival, he is escorted by beautiful beautician and literary groupie Christine (Renée Soutendijk) through his speech and eventually winds up spending the night at her house. After seeing a photo of her boyfriend, Herman (who happens to be the young man from the station), Gérard craftily goes to bed with his female chaperone and feigns psychic powers so that he may have a chance at getting Herman for himself. However, Gérard's terrifying visions continue and become more intense, particularly when he learns that Christine has had three husbands... all of whom may have died under violent circumstances. Who will be the fourth man?

Though released in the '80s, The Fourth Man feels for all the world like an audacious '70s art film, loaded with symbolism and intricate plot threads that require the viewer's imagination for any full sense of closure. The final fifteen minutes in particular leave the story open to a number of interpretations, a trick Verhoeven tried to pull off again with less impressive results in Basic Instinct, a more literal lesbian twist on the same story.

Though still powerfully erotic, the film has lost much of its shock value (attributed at the time to plentiful frontal nudity, gore, and one unforgettably jolting bit with a pair of scissors), thanks to wider familiarity with European horror and erotica in the wake of home video. Fortunately the performances, writing, and photography are of such a striking calibre that the film has not dated at all; in particular, Krabbé's devilish, neurotic performance makes one wonder why no one has used him even remotely as well in America. And for those interested in the early career of Jan de Bont before he hit it big as the cinematographer of Die Hard and the director of Speed (and, um, a few other movies we won't mention here), this is the first of his Verhoeven contributions that really shows what the man could do with a camera. From the moody opening shot of a spider straddling the top of a crucifix to the neon-saturated interiors of Christine's house, this is first rate eye candy all the way.

A surprise art house success in America, The Fourth Man has been reissued in several different versions over the years. Media's VHS release featured a very hazy cropped transfer with a passable but awkward English dub job, while those longing for a subtitled print were finally rewarded with a laserdisc release from Image as part of its Cinematheque line a few years later; though mildly widescreen (about 1.55:1), the print suffered from white subtitles which tended to vanish against white objects like Christine's car at the bottom of the screen. Compared to such flawed company, Anchor Bay's disc can't help but be an improvement, and indeed there's little to complain about here. The audio is significantly cleaner and more clearly defined than the laserdisc, which muffled Loek Dikker's atmospheric score into a dull rumble, and the yellow English subtitles are a vast improvement in both speed and readability. The anamorphic 1.85:1 presentation adds information to the sides while losing a sliver from the top and bottom, but it looks well composed and about as vibrant as one could hope for, despite some graininess inherent in the original source materials.

Also included are the European theatrical trailer (too bad there isn't a US one for comparison) and talent bios for Verhoeven, Krabbé, and most interestingly Soutendijk, whose transcribed comments make for an interesting counterpoint to her all too brief filmography.

FOXY BROWN

Colour, 1974, 94m. / Directed by Jack Hill / Starring Pam Grier, Peter Brown / MGM (US R1 NTSC) / WS (1.85:1) (16:9)

 The following year after Coffy, director Jack Hill and star Pam Grier were back with a film originally conceived as a sequel entitled Burn, Coffy, Burn. More outrageous and loosely structured than its predecessor, Foxy Brown continues the vengeance motif as government agent and drug informer Michael (Terry Carter) emerges from facial reconstruction surgery to the delight of his girlfriend, Foxy (Grier). Unfortunately Foxy's no-good smack dealing brother, Link (Antonio "Huggy Bear" Fargas), sees through Michael's new visage and, eager to earn his way back into the underworld's favour, snitches the secret to evil drug baroness Katherine Wall (Katheryn Loder), who also runs a hooker ring with her two-timing boyfriend, Steve Elias (*Kitten with a Whip*'s Peter Brown). When Michael turns up dead at her doorstep, Foxy forces the truth out of Link and poses as a hooker (again). When her cover is blown by a stunt she pulls on a judge during a three way with fellow prostitute Claudia (Juanita Moore), Foxy gets dragged off to a farm for some hardcore punishment. However, as Katherine and her cohorts are about to find out, hell hath no fury like a Foxy scorned.

While it may not be as "good" as *Coffy* in the traditional sense, *Foxy Brown* is a delirious experience completely unto itself. The delicious 007-style opening credits (accompanied by Willie Hutch's crackerjack theme song), the gaudy clothes, the snippy and campy one liners, and the world's finest lesbian bar fight are just a few of the pleasures on display here. The final five minutes will leave even the most hardened exploitation vet slack-jawed in amazement, but we wouldn't dream of spoiling any of its surprises here. Just watch the movie for yourself and witness drive-in black action madness at its absolute finest. Or as Link says, "That's my sister... and she's a whole lotta woman."

Foxy Brown looks quite attractive in its DVD incarnation, which follows previous versions from Orion on VHS and laserdisc. The anamorphic treatment boasts a very pleasing, smooth visual texture that blows away the laserdisc by comparison. While the 1.85:1 letterboxing preserves the film's theatrical appearance, the framing will look extremely tight for those accustomed to the previous open matte framing. In particular, Ms. Grier's afros have a tendency of vanishing beneath the upper matte, and the modified compositions turn the opening credits into an even more blatant celebration of Grier's bouncing breasts.

As with *Coffy*, the disc includes the theatrical trailer (identical in quality to their earlier edition on the *Switchblade Sisters* DVD), as well as audio commentary by Hill. In keeping with his numerous other commentaries, he's very laid back and extremely informative, recalling even the smallest bit players and discussing the ins and outs of fast, affordable moviemaking. Obviously he devotes much speaking time to Grier and Haig (who appears in a funny extended cameo as a "plane driver") while doing an efficient job of placing the films in context both in terms of his career and the state of exploitation moviemaking at the time. Thank goodness MGM saw fit to deck these films out with the extras they deserve, and it's gratifying to see these much maligned entertainment being treated as well as famous Hollywood productions.

FRANKENSTEIN CREATED WOMAN

Colour, 1967, 92m. / Directed by Terence Fisher / Starring Peter Cushing, Susan Denberg / Anchor Bay (US R1 NTSC) / WS (1.78:1) (16:9)

 An unusually eccentric and poignant instalment in the Hammer Frankenstein cycle, *Frankenstein Created Woman* deliberately avoids the shambling, stitch-heavy monsters of previous films. Instead the incomparable Terence Fisher focuses his camera on the psychological consequences of a tormented soul coping not only with another body, but another gender as well. Incidentally, the title was supposed to be *...And Frankenstein Created Woman*, but religious organizations were none too supportive.

After being revived from suspended animation, the fearless Baron Frankenstein (Peter Cushing) continues his experiments with the aid of two assistants. One of his cohorts, the volatile Hans (Robert Morris), gets into trouble at the local tavern, where his disfigured girlfriend, Christina (*Playboy* pinup Susan Denberg), endures the taunts of the locals. Following an accidental death, Hans is charged with murder and executed by guillotine, all under the watchful, horrified eyes of Christina. The Baron decides to use Hans' body as the guinea pig in a new experiment involved the transference of souls, with Hans now inhabiting the vessel of a facially restored Christina. Unfortunately Hans' psyche dominates Christina and sends her on a vengeful rampage of murder, in which she receives her orders from her dead love's imaginary severed head! The Baron soon understands the disastrous results of his experiment and attempts to rectify the matter before it's too late.

One of the last Hammer films to emphasize subdued gothic horror instead of bare breasts and gushing blood, *Frankenstein Created Woman* treats its lurid subject matter with a sombre tone in keeping with Fisher's other tales of thwarted romance like *Phantom of the Opera*. Cushing is excellent as always, revealing a more multifaceted and even compassionate Frankenstein compared to the callous monster found the following year in *Frankenstein Must Be Destroyed!* Though not a dynamic Hammer figure on a par with Barbara Shelley or Ingrid Pitt, Denberg holds her own on the screen despite her fully clothed appearance throughout the film. (Her legendary bikini shots with Cushing for the film were done for publicity purposes only.) The usual Hammer/Fisher crew is present and performing at full speed, with Arthur Grant handling photography chores with his usual colourful precision and composer James Bernard turning out another top notch score, much more tonal and romantic than his usual work. The concept of a man struggling within a woman's body provides some unusually perverse touches, such as Christina/Hans seducing one potential victim during a picnic; in some respects this could be seen as a dry run for the more lurid '70s variation, *Dr. Jekyll and Sister Hyde.*

Anchor Bay's DVD of *Frankenstein Created Woman* looks easily up to par compared to the rest of their Hammer discs. Picture quality is first rate and does justice to the film's elegant, often subdued colour schemes, while the mono audio captures every nuance of the music score. The disc also includes the hyperbolic UK theatrical trailer, as well as a combo trailer, two TV spots, and the *World of Hammer* episode devoted to "Frankenstein." And don't miss those priceless menu screens.

FRANKENSTEIN'S CASTLE OF FREAKS
Colour, 1973, 90m. / Directed by Robert H. Oliver (Dick Randall) / Starring Rosanno Brazzi, Michael Dunn / Image (US R0 NTSC)

 Sleaze producer extraordinaire Harry Novak made a living introducing the grindhouse crowd to such deliciously deviant gems as *The Sinful Dwarf, The Toy Box,* and Jean Rollin's *Requiem for a Vampire.* One can only wonder how on earth he planned to cash in with *Frankenstein's Castle of Freaks,* an Italian import originally titled *Il castello della paura (Terror Castle).* This wacko fusion of Paul Naschy style monster battles and leering cheesecake sits uncomfortably between genres, and for that reason alone it makes for compelling, one of a kind viewing. The fact that it stars the lead from *South Pacific* doesn't hurt, either.

The seemingly normal but deranged Count Frankenstein (Rosanno Brazzi) - apparently no longer a Baron - seizes a once in a lifetime opportunity when Neanderthals are discovered in a nearby cave. He uses a caveman body to create a new monster called Goliath (Loren Ewing), which promptly develops an interest in Frankenstein's female companion (Simone Blondel). Meanwhile the castle dwarf, Genz (Michael Dunn), becomes peeved at the attention lavished on the creature and, pouting away, takes off to the countryside. There, Genz recruits another Neanderthal named Ook (played by *Starcrash's* "Boris Lugosi," aka

Salvatore Baccaro) and arranges a battle between titans back at the Frankenstein castle.

Though the DVD carries no MPAA rating, the trailer included boasts a PG card. If this is accurate, the ratings board was definitely more lenient in the '70s, as this contains just enough female skin to please the Playboy crowd without drawing attention completely away from the monsters. There's nothing all that sexual about the film, which may account for its more family friendly status among the Harry Novak canon of '70s sickies. The print quality is wonderful, with some highly saturated colour lighting and voluptuous fabrics filling most of the interior shots. There's nary a scratch or tear in sight, too. Apart from the trailer, the viewer also gets two shorts, "The Monster and the Maiden" (in which Frankenstein's monster cavorts with a scantily clad miss) and "Frankenstein and the Naughty Nurse," which... well, the title pretty much says it all. The usual comprehensive gallery of exploitation ad mats and radio spots rounds out a nice package.

FRANTIC
Colour, 1988, 120m. / Directed by Roman Polanski / Starring Harrison Ford, Emmanuelle Seigner / Warner (US R1 NTSC), Warner (UK R2 PAL) / WS (1.85:1) (16:9) / DD2.0

 The perverse opposite of its title, *Frantic* is director Roman Polanski's dreamy, stylish entry in the Hitchcockian suspense genre, and as usual he fills out the storyline with his usual delightful touches and eccentric characters. Anchored by a solid central performance by Harrison Ford as the sympathetic Yank lost in the haze of Paris, this thriller wisely focuses more on atmosphere and character development than on gun battles and car chases.

After arriving in Paris for a conference, an American doctor, Richard Walker (Ford), is horrified when his wife, Sondra (Betty Buckley), disappears without a trace from their hotel room. The local police prove to be of no help whatsoever, but soon Richard deduces that a tragic mix up has resulted in his wife being abducted by the Parisian gangster/drug underground. With the aid of a mysterious young waif named Michelle (Polanski's wife, Emmanuelle Seigner), Richard decides to confront the evildoers on his own terms, but perhaps at the expense of several lives.

In the first of her memorable appearances in her husband's films (also including *Bitter Moon* and *The*

Ninth Gate), Seigner makes an indelible impression and gives Ford a run for his money. Critics have often taken shots at her acting ability, but there's no denying that she's beautiful to look at and fits her Polanski roles quite well. Ford looks appropriately dazed and vulnerable throughout, a surprising choice considering this film landed in the middle of his Indiana Jones heyday. Perhaps best of all, the legendary Ennio Morricone contributes a spectacular, vertigo-inducing score that lends an unearthly tone to even the most ordinary dialogue scenes.

While Warner has issued *Frantic* on DVD in both the United States and England, the two versions are quite different. The American edition, part of their bargain budget line, is a grainy rehash of their old VHS/laserdisc transfer. The image quality is colourful but annoyingly grainy; even worse, the hard-matted image has been cropped on the sides and has even lost some information on the top and bottom! This claustrophobic edition may be cheap, but it does little justice to the film's visual artistry. (To add insult to injury, the closing credits are perfectly letterboxed and look beautiful.) The Region 2 release in Great Britain looks much better, with accurate 1.85:1 anamorphic letterboxing and a merciful decrease in the amount of grain. The surround soundtrack is comparable on both versions, and neither disc contains any bonus material.

FREEWAY

Colour, 1996, 102m. / Directed by Matthew Bright / Starring Reese Witherspoon, Keiffer Sutherland / Republic (US R1 NTSC), VCI (UK R2 PAL) / WS (1.85:1) / DD2.0

Illiterate and foul-mouthed reprobate Vanessa Lutz (Witherspoon) arrives home from school one day to find her prostitute mother and lecherous slob of a stepfather arrested on drugs charges. Rather than submit to foster care, Vanessa takes off in search of her Grandmother. When her car breaks down on the freeway, she's picked up by Bob Wolverton (Sutherland), an apparently clean cut child counsellor but actually a paedophile serial killer. What Wolverton doesn't realise is that he's crossed swords with a girl who's even less sane than he is.

Certainly not for the faint-hearted, I can't recall ever sitting through any other film quite as weird as Matthew Bright's *Freeway*. A severely twisted and macabre fairytale taking its cues from the Grimm's

"Little Red Riding Hood" - Sutherland even dresses up as Grandma to await the arrival of an unsuspecting Witherspoon - this is pure trash of the highest calibre, brimming with midnight black humour and unpleasant characters and imagery. If you imagine that Quentin Tarantino had written the script and handed it to John Waters to direct, you'll get a good idea of what to expect; hilarity and repugnance in equal measure. Witherspoon delivers an A1 performance as the street-smart kid from the wrong side of the tracks, giving her would-be murderer a far tougher ride than he'd bargained for. Sutherland meanwhile is suitably smooth and oily as the big bad Wolverton, all demented leers and sadistic drooling. There are entertaining turns from Amanda Plummer, Dan Hedaya and Sydney Lassick. Backed by a quirky, off the wall Danny Elfman score, *Freeway* will undoubtedly alienate some with its dubious subject matter, but it's worth a look if only to see Brooke Shields doing the world a favour by blowing her brains out with a shotgun. The belated sequel substituted names for unknowns with stupefying inferior results.

While the British disc release of *Freeway* suffers from minor BBFC tampering in its more extreme moments, Republic Pictures' Region 1 release delivers an uncut 1.85:1 matted print with a generous 40 chapter points. Regrettably it doesn't include the 15+ minutes of behind the scenes footage and cast/crew interviews on its Region 2 counterpart, its extras instead comprising a standard trailer and a feature commentary from director Matthew Bright. The sound is in English only with subtitling in English and Spanish. - TG

FREEWAY 2: CONFESSIONS OF A TRICKBABY

Colour, 1999, 97m. / Directed by Matthew Bright / Starring Natasha Lyonne, Vincent Gallo / Edge/Full Moon (US R1 NTSC), Tartan (UK R2 PAL) / WS (1.85:1) / DD2.0

15 year-old Crystal (Lyonne) is a faux prostitute who specialises in coaxing and then beating up and robbing her would-be "tricks". Cyclona (Maria Celedonio) is a psychotic lesbian convicted of murdering her entire family. Imprisoned together and facing 25 years to life for their crimes, the pair forges an unstable alliance and bust out of jail. However, Crystal soon realises that Cyclona is out of control, a deadly killer driven by hallucinations and voices compelling her to kill.

Leaving a trail of violence and destruction in their wake, they head for Mexico where Cyclona believes they will find sanctuary with her childhood guardian Sister Gomez (Gallo).

A lewd, dark and disturbing movie from Matthew Bright, which doesn't warrant the *Freeway 2* part of its title at all, since it bears no relation whatsoever to his former superior movie. Tenuously based on the fairytale "Hansel and Gretel", the director crowbars in enough taboos - incest, substance abuse, lesbianism, bulimia, necrophilia, projectile vomiting, child pornography and a transvestite nun! - to fill a dozen movies, but rather than being inventive the results are turgid and offensive in the extreme. In fact I can't think of another movie that lays out such a singularly grotesque and unappealing collection of misfits; even our felonious antiheroines are repellent and unsympathetic, without a single redeeming quality between them. This is the sort of film that actors appear in strictly for the cash, only to omit it from their CV and refuse ever to speak of it. So just why John Landis agreed to a cameo is an enigma beyond comprehension. Where *Freeway* is solid sleazy fun, *Confessions of a Trickbaby* is gloomy and depressing garbage; the sporadic oasis of inspiration dotted throughout deserts of sub-mediocrity just don't cut the mustard. By all means take a dip into its unsavoury cesspool out of morbid curiosity, but just don't claim afterwards that you weren't warned.

Unlike the original *Freeway*, *Freeway 2: Confessions of a Trickbaby* was surprisingly left intact for its UK release, and the respective US and UK DVDs present the film in all its sordid glory in a 1.85:1 matte with an adequate 19 chapter stops. Aside from a trailer, some cast filmographies and a batch of promotional materials for other Full Moon product, there are no additional features. Whereas director Bright recorded a commentary for his original film, he has not done so here; a shame, for it would have been intriguing to hear what he has to say about this thoroughly vile and dismal offering.
- TG

FRENZY

Colour, 1972, 116m. / Directed by Alfred Hitchcock / Starring Jon Finch, Barry Foster / Universal (US R1 NTSC, UK R2 PAL) / WS (1.85:1) (16:9)

London has become the stalking ground of a brutal sex killer known as "The Necktie Murderer". After the owner of a marriage bureau, Brenda Blaney (Barbara Leigh Hunt), is found murdered, her down-on-his-luck ex-husband Richard (Finch) is wrongly

suspected by police of being the killer. As the evidence against him mounts up, he goes into hiding, abetted by two trusted friends, barmaid Babs Milligan (Anna Massey) and jaunty Covent Garden fruiterer Robert Rusk (Foster). With *Frenzy* the Master of Suspense unveiled a thriller that polarised his fans and drew accusations of misogyny from some quarters. In actuality the film is no more misogynistic than, say, *Psycho*, it's merely that 1972 tolerated more graphic an account of murder than 1960. It's true, the rape and murder of Barbara Leigh Hunt is exceptionally unpleasant - in fact it's one of the nastiest ever filmed - but it achieved its notoriety without being gratuitous or resorting to cheap exploitation tactics.

As with most classic Hitchcock, this isn't a whodunit as much as a howishegonnagetdunforit, indeed we know virtually from the outset that the killer is Foster's character, Bob Rusk. Shot entirely in the UK, *Frenzy* was a return to form for the director after the less than astounding *Topaz* and *Torn Curtain*. Anthony Shaffer infuses the script with some nice little moments of macabre humour, most notably Rusk's attempts to retrieve a damning piece of evidence from the clenched fist of a rigor-mortis-ridden victim. However, it was a definite mistake to make Finch's hero so contemptible and Foster's killer so infinitely more amicable - it's an experiment that didn't pay off, for it's hard to care a great deal when Finch is banged up for the murders he didn't commit. Alec McCowen's mildly comic but nonetheless methodical police inspector, stressed by his wife's experiments in gastronomy, is a treat and counterbalances some of the more lurid elements of the plot. And there's some amusing Hitchcockian observational comedy to be found in the interplay between the man and wife-to-be outside the marriage bureau. There are some outstanding visual and aural nuggets littered throughout too; for an example of the former, look no further than the much talked-about reverse track from Rusk's apartment, down the stairwell and back out of the door into the bustle of Covent Garden market - the juxtaposition of the heinous crime we know is being committed in that room against the mundane normality of the activities outside is a touch of sheer genius. Quintessential Hitchcock.

Just shy of its 30th anniversary, Hitchcock's penultimate film has been treated with its deserved respect on Universal's flawless DVD release (which is featureless in its UK incarnation). The 1.85:1 matted feature is divided by 18 chapter points and offers sound in English or French, with subtitles in English or Spanish. The extra features on the disc are a real delight. First and foremost there's a 45 minute documentary which charts the film's production, including, among much else of note, recent interviews with Foster, Finch, Massey and Shaffer, a trove of fascinating and remarkably well preserved behind the scenes footage of Hitchcock at work on the streets of London, and even snatches of Henry Mancini's rejected score (which was supplanted by Ron Goodwin's outstanding contribution). There's also a trailer, which opens with Hitch floating on his back down the River Thames, an expansive gallery of still images, and some production notes. No serious collector can afford to be without this disc. As the ignominious Bob Rusk would put it - "Lovely"! - TG

FRIDAY FOSTER

Colour, 1975, 90m. / Directed by Arthur Marks / Starring Pam Grier, Yaphet Kotto / MGM (US R1 NTSC) / WS (1.78:1)

After the successful run of *Coffy* and *Foxy Brown* in drive-ins and urban areas, AIP quickly pushed along two more vehicles for the reigning queen of black action cinema. Unfortunately they neglected to retain director Jack Hill, who knew exactly how to tailor the mayhem around Grier's dazzling looks and personality, so the subsequent 1975 efforts fell short of the mark. In *Friday Foster* Grier portrays the title character (of course), lifted from a '70s comic strip. This slinky magazine photographer arrives at the L.A. airport to cover the arrival of bigwig Blake Tarr (Thalmus Rasulala) and winds up taking incriminating shots of an assassination attempt. Unfortunately this incident is just the beginning of an insidious plot to wipe out prominent black public and private figures. To save her life and do what's right, Friday enlists the aid of her cop boyfriend (Yaphet Kotto) and weaves her way through a colourful gallery of suspects and alliances from L.A. to Washington, D.C., including flamboyant fashion diva Madame Rena (Eartha Kitt), dirty white politician Enos Griffith (Jim Backus), and the jive-talking Fancy Dexter (*The Love Boat*'s Ted Lange - yes, you get to hear Isaac swear!).

Though fairly low on action, *Friday Foster* is breezy, disposable fun, with Grier obviously enjoying the opportunity to act in one of the greatest acting ensembles ever for a blaxploitation film.

Every scene reveals another familiar face, with the incomparable Godfrey Cambridge stealing all of his screen time during Friday's unforgettable sojourn to a gay bar. Unfortunately, apart from the obligatory topless love scene, the sleaze factor here is alarmingly low; instead director Arthur Marks (*J.D.'s Revenge, Monkey Hustle*) goes for a slick visual look that now resembles an average made-for-TV movie. At least Pam does get one classic ass-kicking moment: "I'm delivering the milk!"

Friday Foster is non-anamorphic and looks better than its previous Orion versions, albeit still a bit soft with dullish colours. However, the print is once again clean and looks accurately letterboxed.

FRIDAY THE 13TH

Colour, 1980, 90m. / Directed by Sean Cunningham / Starring Betsy Palmer, Adrienne King / Paramount (US R1 NTSC) / WS (1.85:1) (16:9)

Unlike the *Nightmare on Elm Street* series, the notorious *Friday the 13th* films didn't simply spawn serial killer extraordinaire Jason Voorhees full fledged within the first film. Instead, the first four *Friday* films, deeply flawed as they are, form a kind of unholy evolutionary scale chronicling the development of a horror icon. From this perspective, the first film may come as a rude shock for anyone expecting a guy in a hockey mask hacking up unsuspecting teenagers.

Following a vague prologue in which a pair of horny camp counsellors are killed by someone or something unseen, the film picks up in the "present day" with a young girl, Annie, hitchhiking her way to Camp Crystal Lake, where she is to begin working for the summer. Unfortunately, her driver turns nasty and slits her throat in the middle of the woods. Cut to Camp Crystal Lake itself, where a truckload of counsellors in training are preparing for the reopening of the notorious, cursed summer camp. As night falls, the bored teens resort to strip poker and other adolescent activities to pass the time, but strangely enough, they seem to be vanishing one by one. Soon the requisite virginal member of the troupe, Alice (Adrienne King), finds herself going face to face against the killer in a brutal fight to the death.

Friday the 13th personifies every convention of the early '80s slasher genre: fresh young victims, gory (but not lingering) killings, and plenty of cheap, moody scares. Though artistic craftsmanship is hardly the name of the game here, director

Cunningham (*House*) displays a reasonable ability to wring the maximum amount of tension out of a basic "afraid in the dark" situation. Furthermore, the film packs some extremely effective jolts, particularly the *Carrie*-inspired last minute shocker that left many viewers ejecting several feet above their theatre seats. None of the actors, including a young Kevin Bacon, have much to do but make a fairly amiable group, and for once this slasher prototype actually takes its time between slaughters to build up some sense of characterization. This method may seem boring to jaded viewers brought up on hyperactive slasherthons (particularly the film's middle third, in which virtually nothing happens), but for anyone who wants to see where the genre got its start, this and *Halloween* are the places to start.

Watchable video editions of *Friday the 13th* have been few and far between over the years. Paramount's original US video master was simply terrible, cropped distractingly from the 1.85:1 theatrical prints and sadly lacking in any colour or black scale. The Warner Brothers Japanese laserdisc and VCD release featured a fullscreen transfer with much additional image on all four sides of the screen, but more intriguingly, Tom Savini's splashy gore effects ran on for an additional few seconds during three murder scenes. Though limited to a few frames in some cases, Annie's throat slashing, a facial axing, and one infamous spear through the bed gag contained enough additional explicitness to send gorehounds buzzing with excitement.

When Paramount announced the title for DVD, anticipation waned when the standard R rating was cited for the print. However, at least the first murder remains uncut, surprisingly enough, and the axing sequence (a mere handful of frames) doesn't matter much one way or the other. The spearing - easily the most viscerally horrifying moment in the film - is the only noticeable loss. However, the transfer itself compensates; nicely framed with all vertical information intact, this anamorphic presentation outclasses every previous version in all departments. Though some signs of cheap early '80s photography pop through here and there, mostly thanks to a little shadow grain during the early daylight opening scenes, this is truly a *Friday* like you've never seen. The mono soundtrack is noticeably cleaner than the laserdisc, with Harry Manfredini's classic repetitive score still sounding appropriately shrill and jarring. The DVD includes the long version of the theatrical "countdown" trailer, and while it's a shame Paramount obviously didn't pack this one with extras as well as the treatment of its most obvious counterparts, *Elm Street* and *Halloween*, horror fans should be pleased with its presentation here.

FRIDAY THE 13TH PART 2

Colour, 1981, 87m. / Produced and Directed by Steve Miner / Starring Amy Steel, John Furey / Paramount (US R1 NTSC, UK R2 PAL) / WS (1.85:1) (16:9)

 Usually dismissed as a lesser remake of the first film, *Friday the 13th Part II* has aged interestingly over the years and in many respects surpasses its predecessor. Like the original, the level of artistic craftsmanship (not to mention story and character depth) is practically nonexistent, but these films are drenched in that creepy, atmospheric, and strangely innocent early '80s slasher atmosphere that was sadly killed off by too many imitations and jokey sequels. Significantly, this film also marks the first extended appearance of the maniacal, deformed Jason Voorhees, a silent behemoth who stalks teenagers as retribution for his drowning experience as a child. However, in this film he sports a torn cloth bag over his head (a la *The Elephant Man*) and only donned his famous hockey mask beginning with *Part III*.

Beginning with a brief, arbitrary prologue in which Alice (Adrienne King) suffers from nightmares of her Camp Crystal Lake experience and winds up encountering Jason in the flesh, the film gets down to business as another group of counsellors coming to open a summer camp near "Camp Blood" five years after the bloody slaughter. After the obligatory warning from Crazy Ralph, the not terribly bright pack settles down and gets ready for an evening of adolescent abandon. Some of the teens go to town and mingle with the locals, while others stick around and find themselves winding up as fodder for Jason's implements of death. As the body count builds, two survivors remain to fight Jason on his own, brutal terms.

Unlike *Friday the 13th*, which suffered only subliminal trims to achieve an R rating, the sequel wound up on the chopping block as it were and lost most of its gory highlights along the way. Virtually every genre publication has noted this film's debt to Mario Bava's *Twitch of the Death Nerve* thanks to two murder sequences (a machete to the face and a double impaling during sex), but virtually no blood is actually spilled on camera during the entire film. Despite the series' reputation, most of the violence occurs through suggestion and shock cuts starting with this entry, and Steve Miner handles the directorial chores with enough verve to make this look like a masterpiece compared to *Halloween: H20*. Thanks to some moody cinematography and the usual nerve-grating music score, Miner manages to work up some effective chills; unfortunately, he still can't cover up the fact that the last two minutes - while undeniably jolting and haunting - make no sense whatsoever.

As with the original *Friday*, Paramount has delivered an impressive new anamorphic transfer that looks much cleaner and more colourful than most viewers know from ratty VHS and late night cable screenings. While it's regrettable that none of the legendary lost gore footage could be reinstated, the film makes a nice time capsule and should now enjoy an improved reputation. The US trailer, another countdown starting from the number 14 and working up(!), mistakenly implies that there were 13 counsellors in the first film; in any case, it's a fun reminder of how horror salesmanship used to operate.

FRIDAY THE 13TH PART 3

Colour, 1982, 96m. / Directed by Steve Miner / Starring Dana Kimmell, Paul Kratka / Paramount (US R1 NTSC, UK R2 PAL) / WS (2.35:1) (16:9)

 A group of teenage friends head out into the woods for a camping holiday at an old farm on the shores of Crystal Lake. There they encounter the marauding menace of Jason Voorhees and his arsenal of death-dealing weaponry. Released during the not particularly successful push to revive 3-D movies, this is one of the weaker *Friday*s of the bunch, populated by unappealing characters and - even this early on - a pervading sense of *déjà-vu*. Even the "shock" ending is pilfered wholesale, a clumsy replay of the climax to film number one, and returning director Steve Miner fails to imbue the proceedings with any originality whatsoever. The 3-D effects, however, are excellent, ranging from the prosaic (popping popcorn and juggling balls) to the creative (a spear hurtling across the water and a head squeezed until the eyes pop out). A sub-plot with some revenge-driven bikers - one of whom is miraculously resuscitated some considerable time after he's been taken down - smacks of padding and really only serves to provide some additional slaughter fodder for our Jase. Complete with its disco-derived theme music, this is the one that introduced the now eponymous hockey mask (retrieved from the face of one of the bozo victims).

In the wake of *Friday*s 1 and 2, Paramount's DVD of *Friday the 13th Part 3-D* will come as a real surprise, particularly to British viewers who have previously only seen the truncated CIC video cassette version. All the mayhem of the original release print has been left intact, including the brief but decidedly horrible bisection of actor Jeffrey Rogers whilst doing a handstand. Although regrettably (but predictably) the 3-D version has been forsaken in favour of a standard flat release, the 2.35:1 letterbox ratio has been preserved and the 14-chapter-stopped print is bright and colourful. A standard trailer is the sole extra feature. There are language options in English and French, plus subtitles in English. - TG

FRIDAY THE 13TH: THE FINAL CHAPTER

Colour, 1984, 90m. / Produced and Directed by Joseph Zito / Starring Kimberley Beck, Corey Feldman / Paramount (US R1 NTSC) / WS (1.85:1) (16:9)

 A new group of happy campers descends on Crystal Lake for a weekend of fun and frolics and end up falling prey to the wrath of maniac Jason Voorhees. Only this time the retarded killing machine appears to have met his match in the shape of young monster make-up buff Tommy Jarvis (Feldman).

A true story: When I *saw Part V: A New Beginning* at the cinema it was billed with a reissue of *The Final Chapter* and, as the latter ended, the dozen or so other patrons in the place got up and left. Myself excepted, the second half of the bill played to an empty auditorium. The poster outside the cinema was for *Part V* only with no mention of it being doubled with an earlier movie, thus everyone else sat through *The Final Chapter* thinking it was *Part V*, so when it ended they all went home. How ludicrous is that? Evidence, as if it were needed, of how unidentifiably interchangeable these films had become. Regardless, *The Final Chapter* is actually the best of the *Friday* sequels, director Joseph Zito breathing a little life into the formula after the turgidity of Steve Miner's *Part 3*. Though we're once again in overly familiar territory, he keeps the action moving along at a cracking pace and stirs in sufficient suspense and gore to keep the crowds smiling.

Tom Savini is back orchestrating the mayhem and the excessively unpleasant manner in which Jason finally gets his come-uppance is the dubious highlight of a glut of nastiness that includes deaths by scalpel, poker, hatchet, surgical hacksaw, spear and garden harrow. Of the largely unknown cast, only Crispin Glover (who gets a corkscrew through his hand and a cleaver in the face) went on to make a mark of any note, cropping up as recently as the *Charlie's Angels* big screen romp. So, was this *Friday* really the final instalment? Of course it wasn't!

As with the previous film in the series, Paramount used the DVD platform to release *Friday the 13th: The Final Chapter* in an unmolested version, with all the bloodthirstiness of the original release intact, including the aforementioned moment when Jason's head is turned into hamburger chuck (denied British viewers in CIC's appalling cassette version). The 1.85:1 matted print is broken into 14 chapters, with a choice of English or French dialogue and subtitles in English only. The original theatrical trailer represents the only bonus feature. - TG

FRIDAY THE 13TH PART V: A NEW BEGINNING

Colour, 1985, 92m. / Directed by Danny Steinmann / Starring Melanie Kinneman, John Shepard / Paramount (US R1 NTSC) / WS (1.85:1) (16:9) / DD 2.0

 Several years after he planted a machine in Jason Voorhees' skull, Tommy Jarvis (Shepard) is sent by the State to stay in a remote halfway house for problem kids. Troubled by visions of the deadly leviathan, no sooner has Tommy arrived than a new spate of barbaric murders begins. This is a *Friday the 13th* with a difference; the killer isn't Jason at all, rather a paramedic whose secret illegitimate son is hacked to bits by a crazed inmate at the halfway house - so he dons a hockey mask and goes on a killing spree of vengeance. It actually isn't a bad twist on the theme, though the final revelation alienated a lot of *Friday* fans who weren't happy to discover the killer wasn't really Jason. Who cares? His *modus operandi* is the same - we get all manner of bodily invasions via road flare, garden shears, machete, axe, hunting knife, etc. - and he clocks up a body count that ol' Jase himself would be proud to lay claim to. But there are only so many variations on attacks with pointy stabby things and writers Martin Kitrosser, David Cohen and Danny Steinmann (the latter also taking the helm as director) should be applauded for at least trying to do something different with the plot supporting the carnage, albeit not wholly successful. John Shepard

is the suitably paranoid, mean-fisted, grown-up version of *Part IV*'s Corey Feldman (who himself cameos in the pre-credits sequence). There's a great Pseudo Echo track entitled "His Eyes," as metaphorical of Jason Voorhees as Alice Cooper's "He's Back" in episode VI. The more extreme effects lost their punch via self-imposed editing- many of them unfortunately having been telegraphed via photos in *Fangoria* magazine, which set up expectations that the release print failed to meet.

Though it's no surprise that British viewers weren't getting the full enchilada with regard the violence, few were likely to have been aware the BBFC was short-changing them on something as harmless as a little nudity in the 18-rated cassette release of *Friday V*. Although Paramount's DVD is the R-rated version, even a cursory glance reveals further nakedness from actresses Juliette Cummins and aptly named Debisue Voorhees, plus a number of additional snippets of violence; these include a post eye-gouging shot of Voorhees, John Robert Dixon's tourniquet head mashing, protracted pre-slaughter throttling for Tiffany Helm, and additional shots of the stacked up mutilated corpses of Helm, Cummins and Jerry Pavlon. As for additional features, Paramount offer up only the theatrical trailer. The feature is a 14-chapter presentation with English or French sound and an English subtitling option. - TG

FRIDAY THE 13TH PART VI: JASON LIVES

Colour, 1986, 87m. / Directed by Tom McLoughlin / Starring Thom Matthews, Jennifer Cooke / Paramount (US R1 NTSC, UK R2 PAL) / WS (1.85:1) (16:9) / DD 2.0

 Tormented by hallucinations of Jason Voorhees, Tommy Jarvis (Matthews) decides to pay a late-night visit to the cemetery at Crystal Lake (now renamed Forest Green in a bid to allay the atrocities of its past) to make absolutely certain that the masked one is really dead. But when he unearths the body a bolt of lightning strikes the open casket and the maggot-ridden corpse of Jason rises and walks again.

The unstoppable executioner who finds it easier to smash his way through a door than simply open it is back for more mutilation and mayhem. Director Tom McLoughlin proves that there's no such thing as life after death, for despite the fact Jason Voorhees is resurrected, at the time of its release this was the weakest link in the *Friday* chain... though the true stain on the underpants of the series still lay ahead. While there was no doubt much rejoicing that the real Jason was back in the wake of *Part V*'s impostor, the whole circus was becoming far too predictable and tiresome.

Once again censorship reared its ugly head and timid film-makers, wary of MPAA restrictions, invoked the power of suggestion and kept much of the grisly stuff off camera; in a *Friday the 13th* movie that just doesn't hack it. So how did director McLoughlin make amends? He didn't. The plotting is even more risibly thin than usual and even the level of standard compensation sweetmeat - superfluous nudity - is zero. Thom Matthews (an insubstantial replacement for *Part V*'s John Shepard) leads as Tommy Jarvis, teaming up with Forest Green Sheriff's daughter Megan (Jennifer Cooke) to put Jason back in the grave he wouldn't have vacated in the first place if Jarvis hadn't dug him up. Opening with a spoof of the gun barrel sequence from the Bond movies, there's a more conscious injection of humour this time round, plus a crackerjack Alice Cooper theme song, "He's Back (The Man Behind the Mask)".

A short and rather uninspired teaser trailer is the sole bonus goodie on the DVD release from Paramount, who, among others, several years on from the birth of the DVD format, still have the audacity to assert that interactive menus and scene selection are "special features". The film itself gets a 16-chapter divide and is available with either an English or French soundtrack. English subtitles are also provided. - TG

FRIGHT

Colour, 1971, 87m. / Directed by Peter Collinson / Starring Susan George, Ian Bannen / Anchor Bay (US R1 NTSC) / WS (1.85:1) (16:9)

Time may have dulled the edge a bit off of *Fright*, an early entry in the babysitter-in-distress cycle that took off with 1978's *Halloween*, but fans of offbeat thrillers should find enough to enjoy in this erratic but well acted shocker. Perpetually abused sex kitten Susan George (who went through even more hell the same year in *Straw Dogs*) stars as Amanda, a blonde teen in a short skirt whose babysitting job for socialite Helen Lloyd (Honor Blackman) leaves her in charge of a young child, Tara (played, disturbingly enough, by the son of director Peter Collinson). A number of

vague, scary incidents set Amanda on edge, even after her less than appealing boyfriend shows up. Soon it's clear that a homicidal maniac is at work here, and his connection to the household may be closer than Amanda realizes.

An oddly melancholy and brutal film, *Fright* is never really explicit but captures that odd, distinctly English nastiness found in other Collinson films like *The Penthouse* and *Straight on Till Morning*. For once the '70s setting is largely kept to the background, rearing its head mainly when we're treated to the sight of Blackman frugging to some groovy lounge music at a cocktail party. Otherwise the film works as a decent precursor to the likes of *Black Christmas* and *When a Stranger Calls*, both of which may have taken a page or two from Collinson's book. (Note the swinging clock pendulum shots, for one.) As much style as the film has to burn, however, it's hard to conceal the fact that this film is sometimes creepy and disturbing but never really frightening. The scares are poorly timed and often ruined by clumsy zooms, while Bannen's leering psycho routine goes overboard near the end and nearly derails the entire film.

As expected, Anchor Bay's DVD looks much better than the previous VHS releases (the most widely available one as an EP-mode edition from Republic). The 1.85:1 framing crops off some peripheral information at the top and bottom of the screen compared to past transfers, but it doesn't seem detrimental to Collinson's compositions (which include some interesting, handheld shots). Since the film takes place at night and mostly in deep shadows, the conversion to a digital format could have been an riddled-riddled nightmare; fortunately these problems are kept in check with a relatively smooth, film-like appearance, with that beloved '70s film grain only rearing its head when it should. Mono audio is also acceptable and appropriately piercing whenever George lets out a good scream. Extras include the long, hilarious theatrical trailer ("Babysitter!") and a very informative Collinson biography sprinkled with quotes from his widow.

FRIGHT NIGHT

Colour, 1986, 106m. / Directed by Tom Holland / Starring Chris Sarandon, Roddy McDowall / Columbia (US R1 NTSC, UK R2 PAL) / WS (2.35:1) (16:9) / DD 2.0

When horror film buff Charlie Brewster (William Ragsdale) starts telling people a vampire has moved in next door, it's no surprise that no-one believes

him. In desperation Charlie turns to his favourite TV horror show host Peter Vincent (Roddy McDowall) for help. At first Vincent thinks he's dealing with a crank and duly turns him away. But when Amy (Amanda Bearse) and Ed (Stephen Geoffreys), fearful for Charlie's sanity, offer Vincent money to humour their friend, with his TV show facing cancellation, the actor agrees. What he doesn't realise is that Charlie's new neighbour, the suave but sly Jerry Dandrige (Chris Sarandon), really is a vampire.

Playing on the obvious premise that vampires can operate safely and undetected in normal modern society because no-one believes they exist anymore, writer/director Tom Holland's fertile script is one of the earliest examples I can recall enjoying of an intentional horror-comedy crossover. The blend is well measured in this case, however, and unlike so many later films that ploughed the same territory, the comic aspect is never taken to destructive excess. It's also one of the earliest horror films to employ a score rooted in rock, and includes superlative numbers from Sparks, Brad Fiedel and White Sister.

Chris Sarandon is perfect in the role of the charismatic, cucumber cool and cunning vampire, oozing charm and sex appeal in best screen bloodsucker tradition; there's a palpable lift to the proceedings whenever he appears on screen. Ragsdale and Bearse (who shortly after making this film began a long stint on TV's *Married… with Children*) are adequate and likeable enough leads, but Geoffreys is just plain annoying as Brewster's chortling buddy "Evil" Ed. Although Sarandon's Dandrige is unquestionably a lady's man (and gets to make out with some extremely attractive young fillies), there's an unusually refreshing twist in that the homo-erotic proclivities of the vampire are touched upon during the moments when he seduces Geoffreys into his sect. There are a few jolts and some nifty effects throughout, but the R-rating seems a little bit stiff by today's standards. Ragsdale and McDowall were reunited for the awful *Fright Night 2*.

The double-sided Columbia DVD offers a colourful 28-chaptered transfer in both 2.35:1 letterbox and fullscreen versions. Otherwise the disc is a slight disappointment with a solitary trailer being the only extra feature. Sound is in English Dolby, French Dolby and Portuguese, with subtitle choices in English, French, Spanish, Portuguese, Thai, Chinese and Korean. - TG

THE FRIGHTENED WOMAN

Colour, 1969, 84m. / Directed by Piero Schivazappa / Starring Philippe Leroy, Dagmar Lassander / First Run (US R1 NTSC) / WS (1.78:1)

Though Radley Metzger didn't actually direct *The Frightened Woman* (originally *Femina Ridens* or *The Laughing Woman*), you wouldn't know it by looking at the actual film. A kinkier stepsister to *Camille 2000* (with which it shares the amazing production designer Enrico Sabbatini), this eye-popping trip into a world of pop art S&M is one of the most sensually dazzling films of the late '60s; no wonder Metzger rushed it out immediately under the imprint of his Audubon Films.

Following a cryptic opening in which a frizzy-haired secretary and a mysterious accomplice have a deadly encounter with a man in an eye-patch, the story proper begins with the seemingly mild mannered Dr. Sayer (Philippe Leroy) convincing the sweet, innocent, and beautiful Maria (Dagmar Lassander) to join him at his home. Once there he initiates her into a series of exercises in bondage and discipline (though fairly mild considering the time period), which mostly consists of him spraying her down under a power hose, showing her a graphic slideshow while playing a tape of women screaming, and forcing her to cut her hair. Eventually Maria begins to become a more pliable partner in Sayer's game, and under her influence, he begins to fall in love. However, there's much more here than meets the eye.

Like most soft erotica from Europe during the period, *The Frightened Woman* is low on plot and only features a few teasing bits of nudity. What makes it so powerful and compulsively watchable (even on repeated viewings) is the impeccable command of both visuals and sound by the filmmakers, with each scene offering a new delight. Whether it's the famous "Sex" sculpture (into which Leroy enters through the memorable *vagina dentata* and returns as a skeleton during one memorable fantasy) or Lassander's scorching dance in the swanky pad while wearing an unravelling gauze dress, this film tweaks the viewer's imagination and continuously peels off one layer to reveal another surprise underneath. Along with *Forbidden Photos of a Lady Above Suspicion*, Lassander has never looked more stunning than she does here; take a look at her in Lucio Fulci's *The House by the Cemetery* to see what ten years of hard living in Italy can do to a girl. Special kudos goes out to composer Stelvio

Cipriani, who adds to the film's spell with his brilliant, infernally catchy lounge score. Someone really needs to release it commercially on CD one of these days.

Rarely seen after its initial release, *The Frightened Woman* turned up on VHS from Audubon in 1995 in a disappointing transfer which slapped a fake 2.00:1 matte over the opening credits and squeezed the rest of the image for the duration of the film. On top of that, image quality was chalky, hazy, and virtually unwatchable. The same transfer was rehashed for First Run's VHS release in early 1999, which coincided with a British PAL edition from Redemption. Beautifully colourful and letterboxed, the Redemption version would seem definitive except for one fatal flaw - both the slideshow and skeleton sequences were cut!

For its DVD debut of *The Frightened Woman*, First Run has at least gotten two out of three right - the print is uncut and correctly letterboxed. The framing is absolutely crucial to enjoying this film on every level, and it's nice to finally see it back the way it belongs. Unfortunately, while the image quality is definitely a couple of notches above the tape and looks crisp enough, the colour is still distractingly muted, almost sepia during several scenes, and the print displays a lot of wear (with some mysterious dropouts in evidence as well). The audio is adequate but very hissy in a few spots. Don't let these shortcomings prevent you from watching the film, though; it's definitely worth seeking out and a guaranteed delight for anyone in love with the surreal delights of European exploitation. The disc also includes Audubon's exceptional original trailer.

THE FRIGHTENERS

Colour, 1996, 110m. / Directed by Peter Jackson / Starring Michael J. Fox, Trini Alvaredo, Dee Wallace Stone / Universal / WS (2.35) (16:9) / DD5.1

 Peter Jackson's wacko blend of off the wall comedy and rollercoaster horror sank rapidly at the US box office, thanks mainly to lukewarm studio promotion and bad word of mouth from moviegoers unfamiliar with his pre-*Heavenly Creatures* genre hybrids like *Bad Taste* and *Meet the Feebles*. While this film is undeniably milder in tone, thanks most likely the participation of executive producer Robert Zemeckis, *The Frighteners* has amassed a steadily growing cult

following since its release and was issued onlaserdisc by Universal in what could very well be, for its time, the most exhaustive special edition released to the public.

In what could best be described as a collision of *The Ghost and Mr. Chicken* with *Silence of the Lambs* by way of Terry Gillian, psychic exterminator Michael J. Fox arranges for his three ghost pals (including an impressively prosthetic-drenched John Astin) to stage hauntings and allow Fox to reap the financial rewards of ridding them from suburbanites' homes. Meanwhile, a series of strange deaths by heart failure plague the same town, and Fox finds himself entangled with a beautiful, young, and recently widowed doctor (Trini Alvarado). As if that weren't enough, Dee Wallace Stone (a lot closer here to *The Howling* than *E.T.*), recently released from confinement in a mental institution after accompanying her lover on a murder spree at the age of 15, is tormented by a ghost burrowing under walls and floorboards.

The excellent image quality of Universal's multiple region DVD editions of *The Frighteners* (with the UK Region 2 one falling prey to the BBFC's objections to the massacre scene) can't begin to compensate for the loss compared to the lavish and now outrageously rare laserdisc box set. The laser contained extra footage (over 12 minutes) and bonus material copious enough to make any genre fan thankful for hanging on to their laserdisc player. The extra scenes in the film don't really enhance the plot, but they do help the pacing a great deal and include some fascinating character quirks (most notably a jaw-dropping monologue by FBI agent Jeffrey Combs about his undercover cult work). Two restored sequences with Stone and Jake Busey rank up there with Jackson at his most perverse (one of them involves a queasy morgue make-out session), and Astin gets a good deal more screen time as well.

Of course, this is just the beginning - the rest of the box set consists of a four and a half hour documentary directed by Jackson himself, *The Making of The Frighteners*, which remains surprisingly interesting and brisk throughout its running time. Interviews with all of the principals and exhaustive explorations of the special effects work are enhanced with additional deleted scenes (including one entire character missing from the final print), bloopers, and an interview with composer Danny Elfman about his quirky, *Dementia-13*-inspired music score. Other bonuses include running commentary during the feature with Jackson (which doesn't overlap noticeably with the material in the documentary) and the original trailer.

Apparently the prohibitive length of the extras wasn't enough to spur on a double disc DVD release, but hopefully Universal will see the light after Jackson's *Lord of the Rings* success.

FRIGHTMARE

Colour, 1974, 83m. / Directed by Pete Walker / Starring Sheila Keith, Rupert Davies / Image (US R0 NTSC), Metrodome (UK R0 PAL)

Arguably one of Pete Walker's best films, *Frightmare* turns the Anglo Saxon concept of the family unit upside down with a diabolical, unflinching narrative that follows its doom-laden train of thought all the way to the bitter end. Using cannibalism as a destructive force that cuts through generations both old and young, this is horror at its most dangerous and unsettling.

In a black and white prologue, Dorothy Yates (Sheila Keith) is sentenced to rehabilitation in a psychiatric ward after her uncontrollable taste for human flesh is uncovered by the local police. Her spineless husband, Edmund (Rupert Davies), is sentenced along with her, leaving their daughter, Debbie (Kim Butcher) in the care of Jackie (Deborah Fairfax), Edmund's child from a previous marriage. Years later, both Dorothy and Edmund have been released and live an isolated life out in the country, where Dorothy passes the time by reading tarot cards. Meanwhile in London, Debbie has become an embittered juvenile delinquent, much to the dismay of Jackie and her doctor boyfriend, Graham (Paul Greenwood). Jackie has kept the truth hidden from Debbie and makes occasional trips to the country, where she delivers oddly wet packages of meat to her parents. Unfortunately Dorothy's bloodlust continues unabated, with many customers falling prey to her crafty work with power drills, pokers, and sharp kitchen implements. Although Jackie begins to suspect that her family may be crumbling around her, there are even darker, more terrifying secrets ready to erupt.

While everyone involved in *Frightmare* seems to be giving their best, this is unquestionably Sheila Keith's show all the way. This rare leading role for the Walker regular allows her to run the gamut from a tremulous and confused aging woman to a crazed, bloodthirsty maniac in the span of a few seconds, and her attacks are shocking, explicit, and intense, even by today's standards. Walker cleverly subverts expectations by pointing out that corruption stems not from the "free" swinging lifestyle shown at the

beginning of the film, but rather from barbaric familial practices spread down from one generation to another and which fester right under the noses of polite society. From a technical standpoint this is also one of Walker's most accomplished features, with his usual knack for creating an oppressive atmosphere serving him well as he contrasts the bustling city life with the dark, damp, lonely country locations, all enhanced by a chilling Stanley Myers score. Just be warned that this is not a happy ride, and while one can almost always expect a downbeat ending for a Walker film, this one takes that expectation to new extremes.

Frightmare first appeared on US video under the title *Frightmare II*, to avoid confusion with a later unrelated American horror film. It was later reissued as *Once Upon a Frightmare*, and both transfers left quite a bit to be desired. The print used for the DVD is a marked improvement in every respect and actually looks quite colourful, a welcome change from the grey, bleary looking VHS editions. Note the beautiful saturation of the colours during the opening credits, which come as a visual shock after the lengthy monochromatic first few minutes. The open matte, full frame presentation reveals all of the visible film area, leaving a little more headroom than usual but aesthetic enough all the same. This being a '70s British film, grain and unstable blacks crop up here and there, along with some fleeting and minor instances of film scratches, but the pros far outweigh the cons here. The mono audio sounds fine, approximately the same as the earlier versions.

The Metrodome/Salvation edition looks even nicer and features some excellent publicity material, stills, video art, and the theatrical trailer, though one must negotiate the almost insultingly cursory menu screens to access them.

FRIVOLOUS LOLA

Colour, 1998, 105m. / Directed by Tinto Brass / Starring Anna Ammirati, Patrick Mower / Indies (Holland R2 PAL), Arrow (UK R2 PAL), CVC (Italy R2 PAL) / WS (1.85:1) / DD2.0

With *Frivolous Lola (Monella)*, Tinto Brass was back to more familiar territory with what amounts to a sillier '50s spin on Miranda. Cute young Lola (Anna Ammirati) speeds around the Italian countryside on her bicycle, often flashing her fanny for the passing clergy and attracting the attention of randy young men along the way. She entertains a group of soldiers to a jukebox dance (one of Brass' most memorable scenes), accompanied all the way by a jaunty, pop-flavoured Pino Donaggio score. Here Brass reels back a bit from the more hardcore direction of his past two films, focusing more on his heroine's public flashing and the sexual playfulness of the various characters. The provincial Italian setting is vividly rendered, with the community frequently gathering to celebrate life, love, and food, a spectacle that will leave viewers feeling more than a tad bloated.

The letterboxed transfer on this Dutch DVD (and its identical release in the UK) looks good despite the low budget origins, while the stereo soundtrack is more ambitious than usual, spreading out both Donaggio's score and ambient sound effects to the rear speakers. The English dubbing is much worse than usual, however, making the absence of the Italian track especially irritating. Unfortunately the Italian DVD in its native language includes no English subtitles.

FROGS

Colour, 1972, 91m. / Directed by George McCowan / Starring Ray Milland, Sam Elliott / MGM (US R1 NTSC) / WS (1.85:1) (16:9)

Ribbit! Though a more accurate title would be *Reptiles and Amphibians*, this latter day drive-in favourite from AIP fully exploits its ridiculous premise of nature running amok in a swampland, complete with hammy actors as fodder. Yes, it's basically stupid trash, but you won't be able to turn away before the typical "they must be warned" finale.

Following a very minor boating incident, good guy photographer Pickett Smith (a clean shaven Sam Elliott) is escorted to the isolated marshland home of the Crocketts, headed by their animal-hating patriarch and birthday boy Jason (Ray Milland). The Crocketts regularly douse their lands with insecticides and repellents, not to mention hauling out the occasional shotgun to dispatch with some of the larger pests. Meanwhile the family toils in a virtual hotbed of soap opera dramatics, with lovely Karen (*Knots Landing* regular Joan Van Ark) as just one of the many players in this complicated game. (Think of it as *Lisa and the Devil*, minus the poetic subtext.) The animals have apparently had enough of these shenanigans, so the huge frog population conspires a sort of revenge scheme whereby snakes, gators, and other green critters attack the humans and take over the property. Honest.

By playing its story almost completely straight, *Frogs* looks and feels like a real horror movie even during its most ridiculous moments. The setting is surprisingly atmospheric, with one swimming sequence that predates *Jaws* by several years. The environmentalist message is regularly hammered home right from the opening credits, which linger obsessively on the pollution piling up along the waterline. Regular AIP composer and loungemaster Les Baxter is credited with the music score, which more often than not is indistinguishable from the croaks and ambient swamp noises on the soundtrack.

In another bizarre move designed to confound any rational DVD fan, MGM has given *Frogs* the red carpet treatment on DVD with a brand new anamorphic widescreen transfer. The full frame version of the film opens the matte on the top and bottom but looks very dull, while the letterboxed version is better composed and considerably sharper. The cheapo film stock and erratic lighting produce some weird effects from time to time, but for its vintage the film looks great, almost unrecognizable compared to the muddy old Warner VHS tapes. The disc also includes an inexplicably squeezed theatrical trailer, which sells the film in high style. In the end, well, it's cheap and it's a blast. What more could you want?

FROM BEYOND

Colour, 1986, 85m. / Directed by Stuart Gordon / Starring Jeffrey Combs, Barbara Crampton / Ocean Shores (HK R0 NTSC) / WS (1.66:1)

Proving that his spectacular *Re-Animator* was no fluke, director Stuart Gordon returned to H.P. Lovecraft waters again with *From Beyond*, a lesser known but worthy successor which offers a more subdued (in relative terms) fusion of slimy beasties and perverse black humour. Featuring much of the same cast and crew, the film has been relegated mostly to late night cable screenings but does have a moderate and deserved horror following.

The prologue, essentially a rehash of *Re-Animator*, features an innocent neighbour and her pet dog stumbling in on the middle of an experiment by the feverish Dr. Pretorius (Ted Sorel). During a bizarre display of techno wizardry and colourful flashing lights, the good doctor loses his head and his assistant, Crawford Tillinghast (Jeffrey Combs), runs amok with an axe. Tillinghast winds up at a medical institution where he catches the attention of

F

Dr. Katherine McMichaels (Barbara Crampton), a specialist in mental illness. She comes to believe Tillinghast's claims that he and Pretorius had developed the "sonic resonator," a machine capable of stimulating the pineal gland, a largely dormant sensory organ in the brain. Ignoring pretty much every rule in the medical books, Katherine escorts Tillinghast back to the Pretorius house along with a comical security guard, Bubba (Ken Foree). The trio crank up the resonator and witness a completely new dimension existing all around us, filled with swimming monsters who can only see humans when the machine is turned on. Pretorius himself shows up, looking far less human, and makes slimy advances towards Katherine, averted only when the machine is shut off just in time. Once again displaying a lack of intellectual savvy, Katherine decides to repeat the experiment, resulting in a feast of monstrous goo, S&M experimentation, and organ munching.

Mining territory similar to the following year's *Brain Damage*, Gordon's squishy study of addiction and perception largely benefits from the enthusiastic performances of its cast. While Crampton has a wholly unbelievable role, she looks terrific and displays some real gusto during the finale. Combs makes a likeable nutcase as always, while the underused Foree (*Dawn of the Dead*) offers some welcome comic relief and drops out of the film far too early (perhaps due to his unappealing choice in underwear). As would be expected, the creature effects are overdone and gloriously self-indulgent, a reminder of the good old days before cheap CGI effects took over the monster genre.

Long unavailable in the UK or US in any format, *From Beyond* has surfaced on DVD from Hong Kong in a very attractive, mildly letterboxed transfer. The kitschy red and blue colour schemes look much better here than on the pasty, faded Vestron laserdisc, though it doesn't quite match the vibrancy of Elite's *Re-Animator* special edition. The print sports an Ultra-Stereo logo but is presented in mono; the original theatrical mix was indeed a very mild stereo mix almost entirely confined to Band's score, and for some reason the HK VCD edition retains it.

Rumours abounded that the film had to be toned down to achieve an R rating, but the grotesque beasties on display should satisfy most gorehounds. Only one brain-munching death during the hospital mayhem near the end of the film seems to be shortened in any way, though one can only wonder whether Crampton's memorable dominatrix act went any further in Gordon's original cut. However, if it doesn't even exist in Asia, chances are we'll never

see it. The Chinese subtitles, alas, are not optional and rather large. No extras are included (not even chapter stops!).

FROM DUSK TILL DAWN

Colour, 1996, 108m. / Directed by Robert Rodriguez / Starring George Clooney, Harvey Keitel / Buena Vista (US R1 NTSC, UK R2 PAL) / WS (1.85:1) / DD5.1

A pure popcorn movie if there ever was one, *From Dusk Till Dawn* is so eager to impress the audience by any means necessary that its numerous flaws can be overlooked, even long after the novelty of Quentin Tarantino's hipster schtick has passed into the ether. Part high octane hostage film and part rip-roaring horror, this is at least a more successful genre hybrid than director Robert Rodriguez's later misfire, *The Faculty*, and Dimension's long awaited special edition DVD proved to be well worth the wait.

Two hardened criminal brothers, Seth (George Clooney) and Richard Gecko (Quentin Tarantino), are embarking on a crime spree across the American Southwest after escaping from prison. Richard's psychotic tendencies prove to be the thorn in Seth's side, particularly when hostages wind up unnecessarily dead, and things take a turn for the bizarre when they decide to cross the border to Mexico by hijacking a camper driven by fallen preacher Jacob Fuller (Harvey Keitel) and his two children, Kate (Juliette Lewis) and Scott (Ernest Liu). Seth has arranged a rendezvous point at a stripper joint called the Titty Twister, where the two convicts and their captives stop to kick back and enjoy a few drinks. Unfortunately fate has a very nasty surprise in store for them, and soon the patrons are fighting for their lives in a gun-blazing, blood-splattering showdown.

The schizophrenic structure of *From Dusk Till Dawn* throws the story for such a loop than the film never quite regains its footing; as a very early script by Tarantino, this was apparently dusted off and shot as is. All of the actors do their best- even Tarantino himself, who's almost impossible to watch (or listen to) as an actor but at least proves convincing as a complete menace to society. Lewis has the most thankless job, simpering on the sidelines and engaging in the film's most serious misstep, a ludicrous and appallingly sexist final scene that could only have sprung from a woefully infantile imagination. The highly touted special effects pretty much save the second half of the film, with an avalanche of fluid and latex hurled at the screen enough to make one wonder how on earth this movie escaped with an R rating. Definitely put your brain in neutral for this one, and just enjoy it on a visceral level. And bonus points for Salma Hayek's short but intensely memorable role, featuring one of the sexiest non-nude stripteases ever committed to film.

For their Collector's Edition DVD, Dimension rehashed the same passable 1.85:1 transfer from the previous laserdisc and DVD editions. It looks fine if unspectacular, but home theatre owners won't be happy by the obviously dated levels of detail and colour saturation. The Dolby Digital 5.1 audio is more successful, with bullet blasts, shrieks, and pounding music swirling around the room non-stop during the second half. However, the real reason to grab this disc is *Full Tilt Boogie,* a feature length documentary shot behind the scenes. Sort of a careening plunge into the world of indie action filming, this features no jaw-dropping insights but instead paints a breezy, sometimes tense portrait of working off the cuff with a diverse cast and crew. (Note: the first pressing switches the labels on the two discs.) The laserdisc extras are also included here, such as running commentary with Tarantino and Rodriguez (alternately informative and extremely annoying), deleted scenes (including some splashy gore trimmed at the MPAA's "request"), the theatrical trailer, and a standard Dimension featurette produced for the theatrical release. The UK edition contains no noteworthy extras.

FROM RUSSIA WITH LOVE

Colour, 1963, 115m. / Directed by Terence Young / Starring Sean Connery, Daniela Bianchi / MGM (US R1 NTSC, UK R2 PAL) / WS (1.78:1) (16:9)

An opportunity to acquire a top secret decoding device takes James Bond (Connery) to Istanbul where, in order to get his hands on the goods, he must arrange a defection for Russian cipher clerk Tatiana Romanava (Bianchi). But SPECTRE agents are watching his every move, preparing to relieve him of both the device and his life. After the unprecedented success of *Dr. No,* director Terence Young brought Bond back with a bang for this gritty serving of espionage. This is easily one of the best, if only by virtue of the fact everything is credible. Even at this early stage the elements of villainy were at least as interesting as Mr. Bond himself, if not more so, and *From Russia*

with Love boasts two of the greats in the form of Lotte Lenya's toad-like harpy Rosa Klebb (with a taste in footwear that runs to hidden switchblades in the toes) and Robert Shaw's psychotic powerhouse Donald Grant. The setpieces include Bond taking on a flotilla of highly flammable speedboats, a fast-paced shoot-out in an Istanbul gypsy camp (preceded by a captivating catfight between Martine Beswick and Aliza Gur) and a brawl between 007 and Grant aboard the Orient Express, brutal even by today's standards. This is also the one that introduced Desmond Llewelyn as Q and one of the most famous of all the gadgets, the exploding briefcase. Former Miss Italy Daniela Bianchi is sexy double agent Tatiana Romanava, Pedro Armendariz (who took his own life shortly after completing the film) is amiable Istanbul operative Kerim Bey and Vladek Sheybal is SPECTRE's slimy man-with-the-plan Kronsteen. See it and savour.

MGM's 32-chapter encoded transfer of *From Russia with Love* is, in a word, glorious, though it's a shame that a couple of tiny snippets of polemical dialogue that have been missing since the film's original 1963 release could not have been located and restored. The movie aside, the disc contains the wealth of extras standard to their Special Edition releases. Beginning with a 35-minute documentary about the making of the film, there follows a second documentary about legendary co-producer Harry Saltzman, who broke away from the series after *The Man with the Golden Gun.* A commentary with observations from Terence Young and a number of the film's cast and technical crew accompanies the feature. There are some trailers (one solo, a second for a reissue billing with *Dr. No,* and a third teaming it with *Thunderball*), three TV and three radio spots (all for the re-release with *Thunderball*), a storyboard sequence depicting the boat chase and a sizeable stills gallery. Language choices are English or Spanish, subtitling is provided in Spanish and French. - TG

FRUITS OF PASSION

Colour, 1981, 82m. / Directed by Shuji Terayama / Starring Klaus Kinski, Isabelle Illiers / Anchor Bay / WS (1.66:1) (16:9)

During the late '70s and early '80s, countless filmmakers scrambled to cash in on the controversial firestorm ignited by director Just Jaeckin's *Story of O,* a stylish and popular S&M epic based on the scandalous novel by

"Pauline Réage." Hardcore and softcore imitations abounded, with one mediocre legitimate sequel, *Story of O Part 2*, rearing its head in 1984. A few years earlier, however, another sequel of sorts appeared with *Fruits of Passion*, based very loosely on Réage's follow up novel, *Return to Roissy*.

This kinky, surreal film was produced by Anatole Dauman, the soul also responsible for Nagisa Oshima's blend of art house pretension and hardcore sex, *In the Realm of the Senses*. The combination is even more delirious here as the film chucks aside conventional narrative, instead contenting itself with any bizarre path the actors feel like following.

Shortly following the events of the original story, the naive, beautiful and submissive O (Isabelle Illiers) accompanies her master and lover, Sir Stephen (Klaus Kinski), to 1920s Hong Kong where he enlists her to work in the House of Flowers, the most demanding brothel in town. The creepy Madame (played by cross-dressing actor Peter, also in Akira Kurosawa's *Ran* and the fifth *Guinea Pig* film) explains that refusing any client's demands will result in starvation, gang rape, or torture on a wheel. The despairing O submits to her fate and keeps a picture of Sir Stephen on her wall to sustain her through the ordeal. Meanwhile Sir Stephen makes deals with revolutionaries while dallying with local prostitutes and a scheming French blonde (Pauline at the Beach's Arielle Dombasle) who urges him to leave O for good. The other women at the House of Flowers include a failed actress who constantly hears a piano playing underwater, and participates in amateur porn films. O fails to establish a connection with the other women but does her job, observed often from the street below by a young man hoping one day to hire her services. Naturally, it all ends quite bizarrely and tragically.

Rarely seen outside of its initial theatrical run, *Fruits of Passion* bounced from one video label to another in a horribly butchered, 74 minute edition, which featured dreary image quality and few aspects of interest. Anchor Bay's DVD makes for an eye opening revelation; not only is it beautiful to behold and now far more significant as an aesthetic achievement, but this print contains eight minutes of extremely graphic, often hardcore footage. Not really lingering or exploitative, the added scenes are all the more jolting for their unexpected integration into the story, with even Klaus himself participating in a few scenes of blatantly unsimulated coupling. Since this marks Anchor Bay's first hardcore title, one can only wonder how much it will impact any of their future title choices. The direction by poet Shuji Terayama (who died shortly after this film's

completion) features a number of startling touches, with a particular and haunting emphasis on water (the submerged piano, a floating doll, the climactic door-bursting). The music score by "J.A. Seazer" is likewise a beautiful achievement, delicate and haunting with a memorable main theme. The film isn't perfect, with Illiers in particular given little to do besides mope around naked and occasionally suffer the abuse of her clients. Compared to the original O, Corinne Clery, she simply fades off into the woodwork. Otherwise, this compares favourably to the original and now earns its place as one of the best films from the final days of classy erotica.

The DVD also includes a graceful, striking animated menu design and two language options- one completely dubbed (poorly) into English, the other retaining the Tower of Babel audio mix of English, French, Cantonese, and Japanese with most of the actors' original voices. Only the latter really works in the context of the film, which thrives on intercultural confusion.

FULL METAL JACKET

Colour, 1987, 116m. / Directed by Stanley Kubrick / Starring Matthew Modine, Adam Baldwin / Warner / DD5.1

Just as every filmmaker in the '70s had to do a Hitchcock homage, the '80s found most major directors tackling the previously touchy subject of Vietnam. Most of the results were terrible handwringers (check out Coppola's *Gardens of Stone*), while the one that started it all, Oliver Stone's *Platoon*, has aged so badly it now plays like a weak TV movie. Arguably the best of this trend, Kubrick's *Full Metal Jacket*, has improved over the years, though its flaws remain undeniable. The biggest problem, of course, is that the first 45 minutes are so blistering, powerful, and simply perfect that there's no way the film can recover in its aftermath. After standing at what seems like the gateway to the inferno for the first act, the ultimate descent into Vietnam is well-crafted but ultimately a conventional return to territory Kubrick explored earlier in *Paths of Glory*. However, as a depiction of war, Kubrick's treatment is technically brilliant and obviously influenced the similar *Saving Private Ryan*.

The film begins at a Parris Island boot camp where men are brutalized into instinctive killing machines bent on destruction and their own survival. Private "Joker" (Matthew Modine), a wisecracking Jewish soldier, is nominally the audience identification figure, growing further into his designated role as the film progresses. "Gomer Pyle" (as christened by outrageously foul-mouthed drill sergeant R. Lee Ermey), unforgettably portrayed by Vincent D'Onofrio, seems to be the "runt" of the recruits, an overweight guy who seems destined for failure. However, the repeated physical and psychological battering builds to a conflict between sergeant and trainee that culminates in one of the most chilling, horrific sequences Kubrick ever filmed.

This riveting, brutal first movement allows the film to hit the ground running from the first frame, and when Joker finally ships out to Vietnam, the film radically shifts gears. Essentially following Joker's squad as it experiences the taboo pleasures of the native land and then moving into a death-trap presided over by a mysterious sniper, this two-act portion of the film drew a lot of critical fire but contains some haunting, memorable moments nonetheless, particularly the final two minutes and the footage involving the news crew. The wisecracking soldier routine does manage to increase tension here rather than simply being an annoying intrusion like most films, and as always, the photography and attention to physical detail are remarkable (hard to believe this was shot in England!).

As usual, Kubrick's use of patchwork pre-existing music provides some memorable moments, including terrific use of "Surfin' Bird" and, as a spooky requiem for the end credits, the Rolling Stones' "Paint It Black" (later copied in Warner's *The Devil's Advocate* and the dubious Vietnam TV series *Tour of Duty*). Warner's full frame transfer, the one preferred by Kubrick, has always looked pretty good, and the DVD looks fine - better than Warner's budget DVD line but not breathtaking by any means. Interestingly, the boot camp sequence bears a number of visual similarities to the photography of *The Shining*, particularly those eerie wide angle tracking shots, and the Vietnam cinematography does possess a ragged, unearthly quality obviously sprung from the work of Vittorio Storaro on *Apocalypse Now*. Warner's first DVD contains the original theatrical mono mix, while the reissue tweaks the audio elements into an active, generally satisfying 5.1 soundscape. The DVD also includes the original US trailer, a boring, oblique mess that indicates Warner must have been having a hard time deciding how to sell this film. It didn't work then, and it still doesn't.

FUNNY GAMES

Colour, 1997, 108m. / Directed by Michael Haneke / Starring Susanne Lothar, Ulrich Mühe / Wellspring (US R0 NTSC), Tartan (UK R0 PAL) / WS (1.85:1) / DD2.0

The first hour of this German horror art film is so close to greatness that it's disheartening when the whole thing goes off the rails and undercuts itself. Imagine *Last House on the Left* directed with the static psychological probing of Claude Chabrol, and that should give you some idea of what to expect from this bizarre, sometimes startling thrill-kill film festival hit, which kicks off with a roar but regrettably spirals downward into pretension and self-indulgent "winks" at the audience.

In the best backwoods terror tradition (*I Spit on Your Grave, House by the Lake*, or any other domestic siege movie from the '70s), a husband (Ulrich Muhe) and wife (Susanne Lothar), their young son (Stefan Clapczynski), and their dog go for a quiet stay at a lakehouse. Two young men wearing white gloves (a big warning sign to any family whose collective I.Q. breaks the double digits) show up at their door and begin to play an elaborate game involving borrowing some eggs for a neighbour. Soon things get out of hand, and the lads find sport in cracking the husband's shins open with a golf club, wrapping a pillowcase over the son's head, and clubbing the family pooch to death and stuffing it in the station wagon. Having fun yet? As you can tell, this is not the most uplifting movie in the world, but it's quite slickly done; the acting is consistently effective, with the two preppy snot psychos making a solid impression and each family member eliciting enough sympathy to make you care about their participation in the "funny games."

Unfortunately, the mounting suspense all comes to a screeching halt when the killers abruptly leave and the film indulges in a long, *long* 20 minute sequence in which two characters sit on the floor, cry, and walk around aimlessly. Apparently this is meant to invoke some sort of Ingmar Bergmanesque expression of emptiness and despair, but it only results in extreme audience boredom. The pace tries to pick back up with a rushed finale, but to no avail; by this point, the psychos have worn out their welcome, and the story limps along to an all-too-obvious "twist" ending. At various points during the film, the more "charming" of the villains (Arno Frisch) turns to the camera and offers knowing comments to the audience; these Brechtian distancing devices are fine at first, but Haneke apparently felt himself being painted into a corner and uses a lame *deus ex machina* narrative device in which Frisch actually takes control of the film via a VCR remote control to change the events happening onscreen. These cutesy "killer manipulating the movie" tactics were already tired in the French serial killer drama *Man Bites Dog*, and they're simply risible and insulting here. The pretentious music score consists entirely of classical standards alternating with John Zorn thrash metal, aiming for some sort of dislocatory effect that never takes hold.

Funny Games is one of Wellspring's better looking titles, with rich, sharp colour and details. Though the packaging makes no note of it, the film is in Dolby Surround, a very important and disorienting asset to the story. The clear, legible English subtitles are not optional, unfortunately. The disc also includes filmographies for the director and cast (who all apparently worked on the same films) and a very obtuse English trailer. Apparently this transfer was derived from a British source print, as the subtitles contain UK colloquialisms throughout. The hyperbolic liner notes warn consumers that this film contains scenes "some audiences may find shocking" and boasts, "See it if you dare!" Don't be misled, though; aside from one fleeting and very splashy gunshot death, there's no onscreen bloodshed and very little overt violence, with most of the brutality wisely contained to offscreen sound effects and facial reactions. If you're expecting a gorefest a la *Reservoir Dogs* (or, more to the point, *Straw Dogs*), this is going to be a letdown. The same transfer was later released on UK DVD from Tartan, with a bonus video interview with Haneke.

THE FURY

Colour, 1978, 118m. / Directed by Brian De Palma / Starring Kirk Douglas, John Cassavetes / Fox (US R1 NTSC) / WS (1.85:1) (16:9) / DD4.0

Following the surprise critical and popular success of *Carrie*, director Brian De Palma returned to the subject of telekinesis for a broader, more spectacular riff on the same subject, this time expanded into the realm of political intrigue and shadowy conspiracies. While *Carrie* confined its gruesome activities to the memorable double climax, its successor instead throws the audience headlong into the action and rarely pauses for breath for two hours, bombarding the screen with chases and bloody demises. As an

exercise in logic or restraint *The Fury* obviously comes up lacking, but as an early example of Hollywood junk food treated like a high art thrill machine, *The Fury* has few peers.

On a Middle Eastern beach, two friendly secret agents, Peter Sandza (Kirk Douglas) and Childress (John Cassavetes), clown around with Peter's teenage son, Robin (Andrew Stevens). A sudden machine gun attack by Arabs sends Peter scurrying into the water, only to see Childress spiriting Robin away with the aid of the attackers obviously recruited to stage a diversion. One year later in Chicago, Gillian (Amy Irving) discovers her immense psychic powers while undergoing a paranormal seminar at school. Queasy at her ability to make others bleed during moments of intense stress, Gillian agrees to become a study case at an institute under the care of Hester (Carrie Snodgress), who also has a relationship with Peter, now skulking the Chicago streets in search of clues leading to the whereabouts of his abducted son. Peter hopes to use Gillian's powers to track down Robin, who is now being manipulated by Childress (for reasons never really explained) with the sexual dominance of the alluring Susan (Fiona Lewis). A series of pursuits and nasty incidents ensue, the most memorable of which involves a Ferris wheel of Arabic tourists. And then of course there's the splatter packed ending, which is best left for new viewers to discover for themselves...

Devoid of the emotional core and thematic resonance that elevated *Carrie* above a typical teen horror romp, *The Fury* exists solely for the sake of experimenting with visual style and narrative intricacy. Surprisingly for a film told almost entirely in parallel action, De Palma avoids his usual penchant for split screen photography, and the expected Hitchcock homages have been dropped in favour of a more naturalistic visual style. The few visual gimmicks (glowing eyes, blood popping out of psychically traumatized victims, slow motion, and visions rendered by swirling rear projection) spring naturally from the subject matter, glossing over the fact that very little of it makes any sense.

The performances are professional but occasionally dip over into hamminess, particularly Cassavetes, who might as well be sprouting horns. Some of Douglas' comic moments in the first third sit a little uneasily with what essentially amounts to a tragic story, but he gradually slips into the tone of the film and enlists some sympathy for his quest.

One of the most overlooked stars of the film is composer John Williams, who provided one of his finest scores before succumbing to copying himself over and over for Spielberg films. Rich, evocative, and haunting, this is easily one of the most criminally neglected musical achievements of the '70s.

For a film so heavily dependent on its visuals, *The Fury* has ironically had a disastrous history on home video. Most viewers probably know it through butchered TV prints which omit most of the bloody highlights, while the open matte VHS and laserdiscs from Fox suffered from unwatchably orange skin tones, a murky and blurred visual texture, and awkward, unfocused framing that destroyed the point of several significant shots. Those problems are largely corrected in the DVD edition, which restores much of the film's impact in its original aspect ratio. (The spinning death of one female character late in the film benefits especially from the tighter framing.) Flesh tones are now accurate, and the image quality looks very sharp and appealing. That nasty bugaboo of '70s filmmaking, zoom lens photography, invests the film with some distracting graininess in several darker scenes that becomes even more distracting in 16:9 playback; check out the effective fingernail scratching scene for one obvious example.

Originally released in mono, *The Fury* has been given something of an audio overhaul for its DVD premiere. By combining what appear to be the music stereo tracks with a reconfigured music and effects track, Fox has produced a 4.0 surround track in which the rear channels are largely quiet, instead spreading sound effects and music mostly in stereo to the two front channels while dialogue remains centred. Occasionally the mix sounds strained and artificial, particularly when voices trail off to the front channels by mistake, but overall it's effective and establishes a grander aural sense than the film had before. Contrary to the packaging, the disc does not come with a 4.0 and 2.0 surround track; instead it contains the 4.0 track and the original English mono track, in addition to a much quieter French sub (also in mono). The disc also includes a bombastic three minute theatrical trailer and a small gallery of photos, including a funny, oft-printed outtake shot of the final scene.

GALAXINA

Colour, 1980, 85m. / Directed by William Sachs / Starring Dorothy Stratten, Stephen Macht / Rhino (US R1 NTSC) / DD5.1

If its star hadn't been murdered just in time to coincide with its premiere, the terminally limp sci-fi parody *Galaxina* would have dropped into obscurity so low it wouldn't pass muster for late nights on the

USA Network. Perhaps the apex of cheap, brainless spoofs churned out during the heyday of Mel Brooks, this film trots out facile jabs at *Star Wars* and *Alien* so low they make *The Ice Pirates* look like Orson Welles. And if you actually remember both of these movies, this DVD will obviously be worth a look for nostalgic reasons.

Aboard the spaceship Infinity, Captain Butt (Silent Scream's Avery Schreiber, slumming even lower than usual) and his motley crew rely on the mute android Galaxina (Stratten) to navigate their ship from one mission to the next. Heroic space dude Thor (Stephen Macht) falls in love with Galaxina, but her built-in force field (or something like that) prevents them from making contact. The crew's newest mission, to find something called the Blue Star, forces them into hypersleep, while Galaxina deprograms herself and gains the capacity for speech and other, err, human functions. On a weird planet that looks suspiciously like an abandoned Western town set in L.A., lots of monsters get in the way and cause even more mayhem. Galaxina then gets separated from the crew. Then the audience hurls objects at the screen.

Rhino's DVD is a prime example of how to build a nice glossy finish around a centre of pure junk; from the terrific video game-style menus to the outrageously weird and clunky 5.1 remix(!), it's obvious someone holds this movie dear to their heart. A rough-looking but watchable full screen trailer is included, along with some hard to read bios.

So what's the problem? Well, the movie itself looks terrible. One of the film's few assets, the skilful scope photography by Dean Cundey (*Halloween*), has been brutally sliced into a claustrophobic pan and scan transfer sure to induce a headache within minutes. If these are the best elements still surviving for such a relatively recent film, the future of our drive-in heritage is in great trouble indeed. The image quality itself is pale and smeary, a little better than the old Media VHS tapes (which were completely unwatchable) but not by much.

Still, for a pretty low price you can have the kick of seeing the title *Galaxina* lined up on your DVD shelf, so maybe that's worth the investment by itself. The packaging promises a "hilarious Easter Egg;" if anyone figures out what it is, please write in and let us know. As far as space spoofs go, this is one to pull out when you've gotten tired of *Space Truckers* and *Flesh Gordon*.

THE GAME

Colour, 1997, 128m. / Directed by David Fincher / Starring Michael Douglas, Sean Penn / Polygram (US R1 NTSC), 4 Front (UK R2 PAL) / WS (2.35:1) / DD5.1

While most directors seem to suffer early burnouts and sophomore slumps, occasionally moviegoers have the opportunity to watch a talent mature before their eyes as he grows and continues to refine his craft. One such example is David Fincher, who started out with the shaky *Alien 3*, progressed to the unsettling but flawed *Seven*, and finally hit his stride with *The Game*, a magnificently controlled exercise in narrative and visual manipulation.

Michael Douglas, as always the expert at depicting slow rot occurring under the facade of the successful middle-aged businessman WASP, has a field day as Benjamin Van Orton, a ruthless corporate shark whose years of building up emotional calluses have resulted in a complete alienation from his surroundings. He hovels himself up in his vast, empty house with only his housekeeper (a very welcome Carroll Baker) for company. Benjamin reluctantly shows up for a birthday lunch with his brother, Nicky (Sean Penn, in a role originally intended for Jodie Foster!), who gives Benjamin a most unusual birthday gift: a free membership in "the game," a vaguely defined diversion catered towards bored businessmen by a company called CRS (Consumer Recreation Services). Benjamin shows up for "the game" and is subjected to a full day of rigorous tests ranging from word association to violent visual stimuli a la *A Clockwork Orange*. Frustrated, Benjamin finally leaves only to receive a call soon afterwards that CRS has turned him down. That night, Benjamin drives home to find the deserted form of a clown doll lying in his driveway. He takes the doll inside, and soon afterwards, Benjamin begins to suspect that perhaps he is enrolled after all... and it's a very sinister game indeed.

To give away more of the plot would be criminal, as *The Game* derives much of its momentum from the constant doubt lingering about the motives behind the elaborate scenarios in which Douglas finds himself. Is the company ruled by fiendish pranksters having a laugh at pampering rich folks? Is it a scam designed to kill Douglas and cover up all of the tracks? Significantly, the script mines territory far richer than a simple Chinese box narrative, and this aspect becomes more apparent upon repeated viewings. Douglas' repeated flashbacks to his father's suicide (rendered in stark Super 8) provoke a sense of unease and dread within the viewer about Douglas' stability, but more importantly, it sets up the film's final, ultimately poignant few minutes. [WARNING: Mild spoilers ahead.] Fincher craftily inverts his reputation as a "depressing" director by toying with his now infamous finale from *Alien 3* and casting it into a completely different light. Furthermore, both the script and visual design richly evoke the English language tradition of morality tales, best described as a Gothic fusion *of A Christmas Carol* and *Alice in Wonderland*. In this case, Douglas' bitter Scrooge figure finds himself at the mercy of forces which might be supernatural but, more importantly, are ultimately trying to teach him a lesson; like Alice, his persistent questioning of those around him only leads to more confusion and deliberate dead ends which become a swirling mass of contradictions. Mind games like these can threaten to become pretentious bores on film, but here the audience is consistently left one step behind as Douglas is thrust from one perplexing situation to another.

Interestingly, *The Game* often enters the same tricky narrative waters previously explored in Richard Rush's *The Stunt Man*. In Rush's film, the flawed male protagonist is thrust against his will into the hands of a trickster whose motives may be moral or malicious; furthermore, Rush also incorporates numerous motifs from *Alice in Wonderland* and presents a mysterious, beautiful woman (Barbara Hershey's tantalizing actress in *The Stunt Man*, Deborah Kara Unger's waitress in *The Game*) whose recurring appearance continues to cloud the waters. The finales also bounce off each other nicely thanks to some similar visual motifs and twists, but watch them back to back for the full effect; strikingly, both films also force their protagonists to become trapped in submerged cars and fall through glass skylights from a seemingly deadly height. Like *The Stunt Man*, *The Game* continues to resonate well after the finale when analyzed closely. If the game is indeed as benign as we're led to think, the bullets being fired at Douglas and Unger were most definitely real and managed to splinter wooden beams apart... so perhaps the finish isn't as clear cut and unquestionably positive as we're led to believe. Furthermore, the amusing final shot is deliberately open-ended (though the Criterion laserdisc included a dull alternate choice that was thankfully rejected) and indicates that the film is indeed open to multiple interpretations.

The Polygram DVD of *The Game* (and its identical mirror release in the UK) should be more than sufficient for most viewers, offering a beautiful, dusky transfer similar in texture to the one prepared by Fincher for *Seven*. The DVD also contains the full frame edition of the Super 35 film, but this framing is quite disastrous in some scenes, opening up the tight facial and two character shots and dissipating much of the tension. Still, it's better than pan and scan. The disorienting Dolby Digital sound mix is generally subdued, with Howard Shore's melancholy score drifting from channel to channel punctuated by the occasional bursting pane of glass or gunshot, and the supplements are limited to the effective teaser and theatrical trailers.

The much more expensive Criterion laserdisc (sporting a softer transfer, oddly enough) is adequate for a rental but comes nowhere near their monumental job on *Seven*, which was worth every penny. Here the extras are confined to a running commentary track by Fincher and Douglas (fun for a single listen but primarily limited to production information), a full version of the CRS visual test, and some production design materials. Not bad, but not spectacular either. For anyone on a budget, the Polygram DVD looks better overall and is most likely the best way to go.

GANJA AND HESS

Colour, 1973, 109m. / Directed by Bill Gunn / Starring Duane Jones, Marlene Clark / AllDay (US R1 NTSC) / WS (1.85) (16:9)

Often cited as the thinking man's black horror film, this has become something of a legend to collectors who have often heard about it but never actually seen it (except in awful, blurry bootleg tapes). *Video Watchdog* devoted one of its earliest issues to the saga of Gunn's lost classic, and a heavily edited (by over 30 minutes) version called *Blood Couple* has been circulating on video and haunting the shelves of Blockbuster under a wide variety of titles (*Black Vampire*, etc.). Apart from unwatchable bootleg tapes, no one really had a chance to see the full length director's cut until this DVD release. Much closer to Dreyer's *Vampyr* than *Blacula* in its elliptical storytelling methods and deliberate pace, *Ganja and Hess* is bound to disappoint fans of fang-chomping and gore. Gunn's film is a challenging, rich, and invigorating effort, crammed with ruminations on the conflict between African and modern Christian American culture, the suppression of instinct through will, and blood as a lifeforce and sustainer of heritage. Duane Jones

(best known as Ben in the immortal *Night of the Living Dead*) makes for a great iconic hero (of sorts), and the gorgeous Marlene Clark matches him scene for scene.

The plot, such as it is, involves a noted anthropology professor (Gunn himself) who is stabbed with a knife from the mystical culture of Myrthia. He finds himself unable to age and addicted to blood, an affliction he passes on to Jones before killing himself. Gunn's wife, Ganja (Clark), arrives and becomes involved in a dark, passionate relationship with Jones, leading to unexpected consequences. Though the film is fairly strong (it contains a good deal of blood and what must be, at the time, a record amount of frontal male nudity, including the director himself), the overall tone is meditative and subdued, leaving a subliminal chill that lingers on the back of your neck long after the film is over.

AllDay has done a stunning job with the transfer, revealing astonishing detail and colour sensitivity, which immeasurably add to the impact of Gunn's achievement. The running feature commentary by Clark and several of the crew members affirms that this film was made with a great deal of energy, verve, and shoestring survival tactics. Also included are some promotional materials, including a number of really odd ultra-'70's cast photos. It's unfortunate that they couldn't have included the alternate, shorter *Blood Couple* print for comparison on the other side of the DVD, as this "butchered" version does contain some footage that was scrapped from the original cut and merits some side-by-side study. In any case, this is an essential purchase for film scholars and horror fans interested in seeing what the fuss is all about, as long as you're willing to set aside the slice and dice expectations ingrained by modern slasher films.

GARGOYLES

Colour, 1972, 74m. / Directed by Bill L. Norton / Starring Cornel Wilde, Jennifer Salt / VCI (US R1 NTSC)

Now here's a movie whose effectiveness depends almost entirely on viewers' ages when they saw it on television. Back when scary TV movies were *de rigeur*, *Gargoyles* made a strong impression on many young fantasy fans and even captivated some older ones with its weird desert atmosphere and striking Stan Winston gargoyle creations. Of course, modern audiences who cut their teeth on animatronics and wild CGI effects will wonder what all the fuss is about, but overall the film holds up pretty well. Devotees of Ridley Scott's *Legend* should be especially interested in the design for main gargoyle Bernie Casey, which obviously influenced the look of Tim Curry's sensual demon in that later fantasy epic.

Anthropologist Mercer Boley, played by Cornel Wilde (*The Naked Prey*), and his daughter, Diana (Jennifer Salt, just before Brian De Palma's *Sisters*) make a trek through the Southwest to perform research on some strange uncovered skeletal remains. After removing the skeleton from its burial location, Boley believes the species of the dead creature has yet to be discovered by human scientists. Of course, the prologue helpfully explains that gargoyles are real creatures who have become mythologized through the ages, so audiences should know what to expect next. Sure enough, the small Arizona town is crawling with scaly beasts bent on recovering the remains of their ancestors. Of course, they also have several hundred eggs located in their vast cave lair, which clues Boley in that maybe the monsters have grown tired of hiding out away from human eyes.

Strongly atmospheric and generally superior to most TV fare, *Gargoyles* has been brought to DVD in fine style. While the previous Roan laser looked pretty good, the DVD is a knockout, far better than any low budget '70s TV movie could ever be expected to look and easily on a par with Anchor Bay's excellent Dan Curtis releases. The packaging claims this is the longer European version, but any extra footage must be very minor as there isn't any violence or character development added here. The gargoyles themselves stand as unique and impressive creations; however, the slow motion shots of guys in monster suits lumbering through the desert wear out their welcome pretty quickly, at times looking like a horrific Sid and Marty Krofft program. Wilde, an interesting actor who never made it to the A-list, does a convincing job as the human voice of semi-reason, and Salt makes a stronger damsel in distress than usual. Worth a look, but if you haven't seen this in a long time, don't expect it to be as scary as you might remember it.

THE GATE

Colour, 1987, 86m. / Directed by Tibor Takács / Starring Stephen Dorff, Christa Denton / Digital Entertainment (UK R2 PAL) / DD2.0

To see what li'l Stephen Dorff looked like way before he turned into a snarling anti-establishment type in *Blade* and *Cecil B. Demented*, look no further

than his debut in *The Gate*, an '80s Canadian item which snuck into theatres during the last gasp of big screen horror obscurities and, most infamously, nearly beat out the megabudgeted flop *Ishtar* during its opening US weekend. Imperfect it may be, but at least *The Gate* is a whole lot more entertaining. An unusual change of pace for its time, this PG-13 film focuses on bizarre supernatural imagery rather than a mad slasher on the loose, and while the results are uneven to say the least, you could do a lot worse.

The opening half of *The Gate* gets off to a very shaky start, with a story that makes your average *Goosebumps* book look cutting edge in comparison. Schoolboy Glen (Dorff) begins to suspect something's not quite right with the huge, gaping hole in his backyard opened up by the removal of a tree. Glen's parents take off for the weekend, leaving him alone with his sister, Al (Christa Denton), and his best friend, Terry (Louis Tripp). In a timely move, it turns out the key to opening (and possibly closing) the mysterious backyard gateway to the underworld is contained in a heavy metal record, and soon the kids are fighting a sinister demonic force which unleashes hordes of tiny evil creatures onto the household.

Though clearly aimed at a younger horror crowd and not exactly blessed with the most skilful acting on the planet, *The Gate* is one example of how special effects can indeed carry and even redeem a film. The bizarre, often grotesque images of the second half often hark back to the delirious preteen angst of *Phantasm*, with the demon constantly splintering, shifting shapes, and even inflicting transformations on the kids' bodies. The fever dream pacing here may have been some kind of accident, since the same director, Tibor Takács, and Tripp returned for *Gate II: The Trespassers* and completely missed anything that worked in the first film. For a more worthy effort by Takács, look for the flawed but interesting *I, Madman*.

Until some company gives the same special edition to *The Gate* afforded to other marginal '80s horror titles, this DVD from Digital Entertainment is an acceptable but unremarkable viewing option. Virtually impossible to find now on VHS, the film's presentation on this disc is at least an improvement transfer-wise and features a passable if bland open matte transfer (contrary to the packaging, it's not letterboxed at 1.85:1 but should have been). The movie really didn't look too great in the theatre, so perhaps there wasn't much to work with. The surround audio is fairly limited, with the generic synth score and some occasional spooky sound effects offering some channel separation from time to time. Open this *Gate* with caution.

GEMINI

Colour, 1999, 83m. / Directed by Shinya Tsukamoto / Starring Masahiro Motoki, Ryo, Yasutaka Tsutsui / Warner (Japan R2 NTSC) / WS (1.85:1) (16:9), Golden Scene (HK R3 NTSC) / DD2.0

 Though not overtly supernatural, *Gemini* is a skin-crawling gothic horror film packed with enough colourful, nightmarish imagery to send most Western critics into fits. Adapted by maverick director Shinya Tsukamoto (*Tokyo Fist* and the *Tetsuo* films) from a novel by Edogawa Rampo, the simple narrative is broken apart into hallucinatory fragments peppered with flashbacks and horrific subliminal visuals; the results are more accessible and linear than *Tetsuo* but no less effective.

Financially secure doctor Yukio (Masahiro Motoki) is shaken when his family members begin dying one by one. After the mysterious and gruesome death of his father, Yukio's mother is literally frightened to death by a shadowy, razor-toothed intruder bearing a large, snake-like birthmark on one of his legs. Meanwhile a plague ravages the nearby slums, with Yukio reluctant to admit any of the impoverished residents into his home for treatment. His beautiful amnesiac wife, Rin (Ryo), tries to convince Yukio that the slum people are human, too, but he finds his views following those of his elitist father. One sunny afternoon Yukio is suddenly hurled down into the family well by the intruder, who boards up the top of the well and occasionally tosses in food scraps for Yukio to eat. The sinister man cleans himself up and turns out to be almost the identical double of Yukio, even to the extent that he takes the doctor's place in the marriage bed. Gradually Yukio's physical and mental abilities are affected by his confinement, and only after the avenging stranger reveals his true agenda does Yukio come to understand the horrific consequences of his family's actions.

A creepy little chamber piece, *Gemini* retains its tight grip on the viewer's imagination right from the opening moments which, in chilling flash-frame images, depict rats gnawing on the rotting, orange-lit remains of a dead animal. The soundtrack is no more comforting, with Tsukamoto offering one of the most manipulative and gut-wrenching aural landscapes since *The Texas Chainsaw Massacre*. Most of the performers remain confined to one-note roles, but Motoki, the prettyboy thug from *Gonin*, shines his dual lead roles and slips from one mental state to another with convincing ease. Tsukamoto also makes striking use of colour design, with the present day sequences usually drenched in grey and blue while the hyperactive slum flashbacks vibrate with eye-popping orange and red.

Warner's Japanese DVD of *Gemini* provides an eye-opening demonstration once and for all that, with the proper studio treatment, any country's films can be made to look as polished and impressive as any American product - or perhaps even better. There simply aren't enough superlatives to heap on this transfer, and the entire disc itself for that matter. The razor-sharp anamorphic transfer looks even fresher and sharper than a theatrical print, while the optional white English subtitles are easy to read and well written. The surround audio may not be 5.1, but the loss is only minor as this is one sound mix guaranteed to keep you on edge for an hour and a half. Sound constantly buzzes and swirls from each speaker, even in the quietest scenes; watching this film only through a television monitor cannot come close to approximating the power of its full soundtrack. That's just the beginning, though. The disc also includes one full Japanese trailer, two short teasers, cast and crew bios, and a series of making-of featurettes focusing on behind the scenes rehearsals, the make up and production design, and the film's presentation at the 1999 Venice Film Festival. A cheaper, bare bones Hong Kong release (Region 3) offers a drastically downgraded transfer but may be a preferable option for curious, budget conscious viewers.

GET CARTER

Colour, 1971, 112m. / Directed by Mike Hodges / Starring Michael Caine, Ian Hendry / Warner (US R1 NTSC, UK R2 PAL) / WS (1.85:1) (16:9)

 A cold, hard, and thoroughly gripping crime film, *Get Carter* languished for years as a minor cult item before its sudden popular and critical recognition during the late '90s, thanks primarily to the smash success of its spectacular, groove-laden soundtrack by the late Roy Budd and its placement as one of the BFI's Top British Films of All Time. Of course, the popularity of crime chic films in the wake of Quentin Tarantino probably didn't hurt, either, and Warner even tried to cash in with an ill-advised remake starring Sylvester Stallone. Stick with the original, for obvious reasons.

Hired heavy Jack Carter (Michael Caine) annoys his gangster bosses in London by leaving for a few days to attend the funeral of his brother, who died under suspicious circumstances in their hometown, Newcastle. Carter wades through the pubs, boarding houses, and upper crust manors, prodding the denizens of the local underworld for details. Virtually everyone he encounters has something to hide, and Carter uses his instinctual violent nature and diamond hard demeanour to shatter the web of crime and exploitation, which ultimately leads right to the doorstep of Carter's own family.

While most mainstream crime films either depict their protagonist as a decent guy corrupted by his surroundings or a corrupt hooligan trying to improve himself, *Get Carter* never even tries to romanticize its title character. Caine hits the bullseye throughout the film, underplaying his scenes and delivering laconic one liners that often sting more than his punches. His cause may be noble at heart, but the brutal lengths he resorts to are unsettling, to say the least. Granted, lucky viewers who have experienced the wild and morally unpredictable world of Euro crime thrillers will find this old territory, but it's still unsettling seeing an actor like Caine, the nominal "hero," being such a ruthless bastard. The supporting cast is tremendous fun to watch, with the late Ian Hendry (*Theatre of Blood*) at his best in that unforgettable racetrack scene. Look for *When a Stranger Calls'* psycho, the also deceased Tony Beckley, as one of the thugs, and Britt Ekland in what amounts to an extended humorous, erotic cameo as Carter's gangster moll mistress.

Thanks to its newfound popularity, Warner embarked on a restoration and reissue project with *Get Carter* in the UK (and to a much lesser extent in the US) after acquiring it from MGM. Their efforts were well worth it, as the DVD release truly looks smashing in every respect. Given that this is a deliberately drab looking early '70s film shot for less than a million dollars, the source material is flawless and extremely faithful to its theatrical appearance. (And yes, the opening night-time shot is supposed to look like that.) The same goes for the densely mixed mono soundtrack, which the studio thankfully left alone without any fancy new audio separation bells and whistles. The haunting soundtrack is also isolated on a separate track, though the stereo soundtrack release on CD is also highly recommended as much music wound up missing from the final cut.

Bonus material includes a very entertaining commentary track spliced together from separate sessions with director Mike Hodges, Caine (who reteamed with the director for the lesser known *Pulp*), and cinematographer Walter Suschitzky, father of Cronenberg lenser Peter Suschitzky. All of the men have amazing tidbits to offer about the film, such as quirky touches in the wallpaper to the alcoholism and personal problems of certain supporting actors. Though many of the remarks are scene specific, some of the chronology seems a little strange; for example, Caine introduces himself for the first time several minutes after he has already begun speaking. Hodges, who later went on to direct *Flash Gordon*, got fired from *Damien: Omen II*, and made a comeback with the critically lauded *Croupier*, has every reason to be proud of this film, and it's nice to see the other participants feel the same way. Also included are the violent British MGM theatrical trailer and a "music trailer," which is actually a piecemeal music video for the main title theme with great footage of Budd in the recording studio.

THE GHOST GOES GEAR

Colour, 1966, 79m. / Directed by Hugh Gladwish / Starring The Spencer Davis Group / Anchor Bay (US R1 NTSC) / WS (1.66:1) (16:9)

 This bizarre, meandering attempt to cash in on the success of The Beatles' *A Hard Day's Night* whips up a story that makes Scooby Doo look intellectual as an excuse to feature some of Britain's rising pop acts of the time. This may not be too rewarding as a movie-going experience, but as a time capsule, it's priceless.

While hanging out on a trawler and heading downstream through England, The Spencer Davis Group (featuring a young "Stevie" Winwood) is forced to abandon ship when their drum winds up tossed in the river. An elderly fisherman clumsily retrieves it for them and turns out to be the butler of the group's manager (Nicholas Parsons). Of course, since they evidently didn't have anything to do that day, the whole group packs off and decides to spend the night at the manager's ancestral home, which is also populated by his dotty mother and father. That night a benign ghost shows up to do a ballad for the boys, who are not especially frightened by its appearance. The mansion quickly earns a reputation for being haunted, allowing the family to exploit the media and grab some much needed cash from curious visitors. Of course, the only thing to do after that is... put on a show! The entire second half of the film consists of one band after another doing their own mini-music videos around the mansion until a sufficient running time has been achieved; then it all simply stops.

The Spencer Davis Group was at its peak with this film and performs some very appealing and catchy numbers (though not "Gimme Some Lovin'," alas). Davis himself is an adequate lead, while the rest of the musicians are pretty generic clowns running around the castle. The only major casting goof is Sheila White as the family maid, Polly; she's so homely and uncharismatic, it's impossible to imagine how she talked her way into this film as the love interest (more or less). The rest of the music acts consist of St. Louis Union, Acker Bilk, The M6, Dave Berry, The Lorne Gibson Trio, and The Three Bells; all are listenable, none are outstanding. The Three Bells in particular are really odd, sort of a white British attempt to copy The Supremes. Davis and "humorist" Martin Lewis contribute a commentary track, which seems to focus a lot more on Davis' career than on the movie (though how much could you really say about it?).

There's no trailer, but it's doubtful one ever existed since this was mostly shuffled to the bottom of Hammer horror double bills. Anchor Bay's DVD of *The Ghost Goes Gear* rescues this odd little curio from oblivion in an edition that would do any better known movies proud. The image is windowboxed during the opening credits (which recall William Castle's *13 Ghosts!*) and letterboxed at 1.66:1 afterwards. Flesh tones have that slightly dull '60s film stock look, but otherwise the picture quality is top notch. The sound is also remarkably good and dynamic, making the absence of stereo almost negligible.

GHOST STORY

Colour, 1981, 111m. / Directed by John Irvin / Starring Fred Astaire, John Houseman / Image (US R1 NTSC) / WS (1.85:1)

Four elderly gentlemen, self-dubbed The Chowder Society, meet weekly in the winter shrouded town of Milburn to exchange horror stories. Good natured entertainment takes a deadly turn when a dark secret from 50 years previous returns to haunt them. Finding themselves faced with an entity far more terrifying than anything conjured up in their yarns, one by one they are visited by the harbinger of death.

Fred Astaire made a horror movie? Yes indeedy. Discarding his top hat and tails, he joined up for this very average, though never less than involving, tale of retribution from beyond the grave. *Ghost Story* is of an ilk of Hollywood product we don't see so much of any more, setting out solely to raise chills, not chuckles. Although it never touches on outright scary, the film certainly has its share of edgy moments, its mediocre facets compensated for with sturdy and suitably earnest performances from all involved. Astaire, John Houseman, Douglas Fairbanks Jr. and Melvyn Douglas, if not exactly the most likely horror film combo, are of a stature that lends dramatic credibility to the fantastical goings-on. And it's testament to the time invested in establishing the characters of the four leads that they are immediately identifiable in their youthful incarnations (Tim Choate, Ken Olin, Kurt Johnson and Mark Chamberlin, respectively). Dick Smith's make-up effects are excellent and there's a performance that is provocative and unnerving in equal measure from (Borg Queen to be) Alice Krige.

Overlong by at least 15 minutes, the story verges on ponderous in the middle third (though it is essential to the plot), and the narrative is unquestionably at its most effective when laid out against the crisp New England snowscapes. In concluding, it should be noted that the most fearsome aspect of *Ghost Story* is Craig Wasson's full frontal nude scene. Shudder! Though hardly deserving of Special Edition treatment, *Ghost Story* certainly warrants better than Image's DVD presentation. It comes as a mild disappointment to discover that it is devoid of even the most basic of extras - there's no trailer, no production notes, nothing. The film itself, however, looks nice and clean, matted to 1.85:1 and divided by a substantial 28 chapter stops. - TG

G

GIANTS AND TOYS

Colour, 1958, 95 m. / Directed by Yasuzo Masumura / Starring Hiroshi Kawaguchi, Hitomi Nozoe / Fantoma (US R1 NTSC) / WS (2.35:1) (16:9)

"I just see them all as caramels," remarks one executive about the crowds swarming at the bottom of his skyscraper during an early scene in the corporate satire *Giants and Toys*, the third film by the delirious Yasuzo Masumura which plays like a frothy dry run for the fever pitch tone of his more mature works during the 1960s.

Though the subject of competitive advertising during the international business boom of the '50s might not sound like prime material for cinematic entertainment, Masumura somehow keeps all of the story's elements bouncing in the air thanks to some kind of fiendish juggling act, resulting in a striking film impossible to fully absorb in one viewing.

Distraught by the growing dominance of American candymakers in the international marketplace, three Japanese companies have stepped up their cutthroat promotional practices. At the offices of World Caramels, Nishi (Hiroshi Kawaguchi) keeps an eye on his competitors - Giant and Apollo - thanks to close friends planted inside the companies (including his girlfriend). However, the balance of World Caramels is upset by their newest spokesperson, Kyoko (Hitomi Nozoe), a dentally challenged ingénue who develops a crush on Nishi, who is less captivated by her charms than his boss, Goda (Hideo Takamatsu). Armed with plastic ray guns and a plastic astronaut helmet, Kyoko becomes a pop culture hit and proves to be more capable then Nishi could have imagined, as his entire world goes spinning out of control.

Like many Japanese filmmakers, Masumura displays an astonishing command of the scope frame quite unlike Western directors. The punchy opening credits, the head spinning montages, and the hilarious ad campaigns provide plenty of opportunities for snappy camerawork and editing, but never at the expense of the absurdist but strangely familiar characters. Though lensed in 1958, this already feels like a prime '60s Japanese title, perfectly in line with the aesthetic excess of that decade.

As with its release of *Blind Beast*, Fantoma has done its part to bring Masumura's cockeyed vision to a wider audience. The anamorphic widescreen framing looks perfect, and the punchy colours look quite good and make this a gaudier viewing experience than the comparatively subdued *Blind Beast*. The removable English subtitles appear to be literate and well paced, while the mono audio sounds fine. The bouncy theatrical trailer is included along with a Masumura biography and filmography. Incidentally, the cover art on the actual box is different from the triptych design used for the disc's announcement and press material, so look carefully for this one on the shelf.

THE GIFT

Colour, 2000, 111m. / Directed by Sam Raimi / Starring Cate Blanchett, Giovanni Ribisi / Warner (UK R2 PAL), Paramount (US R1 NTSC), Columbia (Australia R4 PAL) / WS (1.85:1) / DD5.1

Sam Raimi's poorly marketed *The Gift* continues the director's attempt to reconcile his low budget *Evil Dead* roots with the more grandiose demands of Hollywood cinema. With *A Simple Plan* he proved he could tell a story rich in characterization without directorial flashiness, but this film finds him merging the two with mostly successful results to craft what could best be described as a Southern fried tribute to Italian murder mysteries.

The story, which owes more than a nod to Lucio Fulci's *The Psychic*, concerns Georgia fortune-teller named Annie Wilson (Kate Blanchett, expertly trading in her Aussie accent for a convincing twang). Annie's clients include Valerie (Hilary Swank), a battered housewife whose reactionary husband, Donnie (a gut-wrenching Keanu Reeves), doesn't take too kindly to a "witch" tampering with his family's affairs. Living alone with her two children to bring up out in the middle of nowhere, Annie proves a vulnerable target to Donnie's threats, but that's nothing compared to the horrific, murderous visions she experiences involving Jessica (Katie Holmes), a sweet young debutante engaged to the local principal, Wayne (Greg Kinnear). Suddenly Annie disappears without a trace, and only Valerie's "gift" can solve what proves to be a dark, complex mystery.

The most obvious attributes of *The Gift* include its assured direction by Raimi, which proves he can still orchestrate a magnificent jolt or two without the aid of zombies, and the top rung cast obviously having a field day without resorting to hamminess or hambone, overdone accents. The potent atmosphere generated by skilful lighting and art design (which naturally includes lots of Spanish moss) creates a sense of foreboding from the opening credits, while Annie's visions (including a terrifying cameo by Danny Elfman as a fiddler) are among Raimi's best work to date. Unfortunately the script by Billy Bob Thornton, reportedly inspired by his own mother, proves to be too simplistic and ultimately clumsy to really carry the film over the top, with far too many nagging plot holes left wide open during the unconvincing feel-good fade out at the end. Blanchett does her best to cover up some of the story's more glaring inconsistencies, and by and large she succeeds; had Paramount done a more honest job of marketing the film as the next Sixth Sense rather than a dreary ensemble piece, she could have nabbed a bounty of award nominations for her fiery courtroom showdown with Michael Jeter alone.

Paramount's inability to come to grips with the film extends to the DVD's US packaging, perhaps the worst in the studio's history. Ignore the cut and paste, brown-tinted cover and focus instead on the film itself, which sports a magnificent anamorphic transfer rich with ominous blacks and only some faint dustings of grainy texture where it originally existed in the film elements. The subtle but effective 5.1 mix offers a wonderfully spacious aural environment, with natural sounds constantly wafting from all of the speakers with the big show moments offering more traditional show-off material for audiophiles. As with *A Simple Plan*, the US disc is sparse in the extras department, offering a shaky theatrical trailer and a ten minute promo piece. The subsequent UK and Australian discs contain an additional making-of featurette, while the former also tacks on a grab bag of TV and radio spots. Even so, the potential for a more extensive study of this film is mind boggling.

jazz constantly forces the viewer to wonder what kind of psychotic fever dream he's stepped into. By the time Mike decides to constructively use nails on one culprit, many viewers may have to pull their jaws up off the floor.

Considering this is from the director of the surreal Dr. Seuss head trip *The 5,000 Fingers of Dr. T*, the delirious results aren't that surprising. Long unavailable outside of late night TV screenings, *The Girl Hunters* has been brought to DVD in a marvellous scope edition that preserves the original queasy widescreen compositions. Some shots have a gauzy, faded look, most likely intentional, but the source materials are in good shape and deliver all the way thanks to the surprising anamorphic enhancement for this transfer. On the downside, regular TV sets will exhibit the weird two-tone letterbox bands found on such 16:9 discs as *Halloween* and *Bird with the Crystal Plumage*, but it's a minor distraction and easily overlooked.

G

THE GIRL HUNTERS

B&W, 1963, 103m. / Directed by Roy Rowland / Starring Mickey Spillane, Shirley Eaton / Image (US R1 NTSC) / WS (2.35:1) (16:9)

One of the strangest attempts to translate hard boiled detective fiction to the screen, *The Girl Hunters* takes the unique step of casting the author himself as his own hero. While Mickey Spillane novels had already been adapted to the screen, most notably with *Kiss Me Deadly*, Spillane apparently felt he could portray the tough-talking, hard-punching Mike Hammer just as well as anybody else. And he was right.

The bitter, strange, and convoluted story wrenches Hammer up from the depths of long alcoholic funk, brought on by the death of his secretary, Velda. Brought in on a new case, he tangles with the lovely and possibly lethal Laura Knapp (Shirley Eaton, the spray-painted girl from *Goldfinger*) and the memorable Art Rickerby (Lloyd Nolan). Sure enough, it turns out there's an insidious plot afoot to spread Communist agents throughout the United States, and it's up to Mike to take no prisoners regardless of the cost.

As brutal and twisted as censors would allow, *The Girl Hunters* is swaggering fun from start to finish and deserves more of a cult following than it already has. Spillane's lack of acting chops makes him a strange and oddly vulnerable Hammer, while the swinging off-kilter atmosphere of sadism and

GIRL ON A MOTORCYCLE

Colour, 1968, 91m. / Directed by Jack Cardiff / Starring Marianne Faithful / Anchor Bay (US R0 NTSC) / WS (1.66:1), Metrodome (UK R2 PAL) / WS (1.66:1) (16:9)

This dizzy example of '60s Eurotrash has been stunning late night viewers for decades now, and the wonders of DVD are now bringing to a new audience who will doubtless be left just as speechless (or extremely amused). Skilled cinematographer Jack Cardiff (who provides a very sparse commentary on the disc) helmed this fetishistic romantic fable about a young woman (chanteuse Marianne Faithfull) who leaves her newlywed husband and tears across the German countryside to see her ex-lover (Alain Delon) on the motorcycle he gave her.

Due to both Faithfull's black leather garb (and nothing else) and the numerous dreamy love scenes and fantasies, the film was also titled *Naked Under Leather* on its original release. Perhaps the most memorable sequence features the fetching Faithfull imagining herself riding horseback while Delon gradually whips away her leather garb, and lots of solarized landscape and sky shots make this prime material for acidheads. Unprepared audiences, however, may not respond so respectfully; this one has really dated, folks. Nevertheless, it's fun to see pros like Faithfull and Delon together, and the cinematography and editing are often breathtaking.

The startling ending is really the perfect capper - totally outrageous and beyond description. Of course, mention also must be made of the funky Les Reed score (recently reissued on CD), which should prove to be popular considering the recent resurgence of interest in lounge and funk music (Peter Thomas, et al).

The mildly letterboxed image (anamorphic on the UK version) looks fine if unremarkable; the film was obviously shot on less than ideal stock and features a number of image-altering and laboratory effects that increase the grain and darkness of a few shots. However, this is easily the best transfer this film has received. Unfortunately, the sound is shallow and scarcely an improvement over the old video editions (contrary to the liner notes, Monterey issued this uncut print - complete with full frontal Faithfull - in the mid-'80s). The music should come roaring out at the beginning; instead, it's a mild whimper. This is one movie in great need of a sonic overhaul to restore its psychedelic punch; the DVD features more extras than usual for Anchor Bay, including cast and director bios and the US trailer in addition to the aforementioned commentary.

THE GIRL WHO KNEW TOO MUCH

B&W, 1963, 83m. / Directed by Mario Bava / Starring Leticia Roman, John Saxon / Image (US R0 NTSC) / WS (1.85:1) (16:9)

The great granddaddy of the moody Italian slasher film, *The Girl Who Knew Too Much (La ragazza che sapeva troppo)* was a marked departure for director Mario Bava after his classic *Black Sunday*. Here for the first time he turned his camera to modern Rome, where naive American whodunit fan Nora Davis (Leticia Roman) flies in to visit her Aunt Adele. After unknowingly pocketing some hemp-laced cigarettes from a charming man on the plane, Nora reaches her aunt's apartment and meets the handsome Dr. Marcello Bassi (John Saxon), who informs Nora that her aunt is not in the best of health. That night Nora is horrified to witness Adele dying of a heart attack and flees out into the street, where a mugger leaves her unconscious. In a daze Nora awakens to hazily witness the stabbing death of a young woman in the street, then passes out again. At the hospital no one believes Nora's story, so she's left with only Marcello to help her uncover the truth. Nora quickly comes to believe that a killer known for a series of gruesome "Alphabet Murders" is still at large in the city and may have targeted our heroine as the next victim.

Widely regarded as the first feature film to lay down the ground rules of the Italian *giallo* (mysteries with horrific elements), *The Girl Who Knew Too Much* is a lightweight and enjoyable concoction despite its grim subject matter. The murderer's modus operandi, an obvious homage to Agatha Christie's *The ABC Murders*, is basically a mechanism to propel the film from one setpiece to the next, with the audience left in the dark as to the killer's identity until the very end.

Since the film was partially financed by American money (AIP), the studio mandated that Bava shoot some alternate comic scenes to make the film more palatable for general audiences; the result, *The Evil Eye*, plays like an entirely different film. The opening twenty minutes in particular are radically different, with Nora introduced after a series of voiceovers revealing the thoughts of each plane passenger. Nora also undergoes a head-butting incident with another visitor at the airport and spends her first night evading the watchful eyes of her uncle (a cameo by Bava himself) - in a portrait hanging on her bedroom wall. The original Italian cut, presented here with subtitles for the first time, is a much more streamlined and taut affair, not to mention a more appropriate instalment in Bava's progression as a filmmaker. The AIP version also substituted the jazzy, amusing score by Roberto Nicolosi with a more straightforward one by Les Baxter, a fate that befell quite a few Bava titles over the years.

Apart from the ragged looking opening credits, the DVD of *The Girl Who Knew Too Much* looks extremely good, with the anamorphically enhanced widescreen image accurately framed and pleasingly detailed. The moody black and white cinematography looks sharp as a tack, while the mono audio is clean if limited somewhat by its age. The optional yellow English subtitles are easy to read and seem to be accurately translated and timed. Also included is the engaging Italian trailer (without subtitles, alas), accompanied by the swinging main title song, and a plethora of Bava stills, poster art, and factual tidbits.

GLEN OR GLENDA?

B&W, 1953, 67m. / Directed by Ed Wood, Jr. / Starring Bela Lugosi, Dolores Fuller / Image (US R0 NTSC)

The most unlikely subject imaginable for an early 1950s feature, *Glen or Glenda?* began life under the title *I Changed My Sex* to capitalize on the

worldwide Christine Jorgensen scandal. This first film to really possess that certain magical "Ed Wood feel" earnestly pleads for tolerance of gender issues including transvestitism and sex changes. Of course, Ed's inability to assemble a rational motion picture from his various scraps of footage resulted in something much greater than the sum of its parts - a Grade-Z surreal experience that remains compelling after enough viewings to cause permanent brain damage.

The framework of the film features a police officer, Inspector Warren (Lyle Talbot), confused by recent gender crisis cases, and the helpful Dr. Alton (Timothy Farrell), who relates two case histories to explain the psychology underlying these incidents. In the first, Glen (Mr. Wood himself) is a good old macho, heterosexual American guy, except for one thing: he loves putting on women's clothing, right down to the undies. His particular fondness for angora sweaters causes some friction with his fiancée, Barbara (Dolores Fuller), who doesn't understand his erratic behaviour. Thanks to bizarre introspective visions, Glen finally decides to confront his alter ego, Glenda, and expose himself for all the world to see. In the second, the hapless Alan (Tommy Haynes) decides to undergo sex change surgery, with unexpected results. Meanwhile, Bela Lugosi (as "the scientist") sits in a chair and offers now-legendary narration ("Pull the string!") bearing no relationship to anything else in the film.

In *Glen or Glenda?*, Wood juggles narratives and stock footage of stampeding buffalo and scantily clad women in bondage for results that can only be described as stupefying. Unlike his notorious attempts at science fiction and horror, this particular effort makes little attempt at a commercial storyline, instead shambling from one hallucinatory sequence to the next simply on its creator's whims.

Considering its patchwork nature, the Image DVD from the Wade Williams Collection looks about as good as could be expected. The level of detail is impressive, extending to the obvious grain and scratchiness in the stock footage. Incidentally, this is the extended print with the soft cheesecake footage missing from most public domain tapes. The soundtrack, originally slapped together from a variety of sources, gets the job done and only displays moderate levels of hiss and distortion. Also included is the theatrical trailer, which features a jarringly different take in which Fuller flings her sweater at Wood rather than handing it to him.

GO, GO SECOND TIME VIRGIN

Colour/B&W, 1969, 65m. / Directed by Koji Wakamatsu / Starring Mimi Kozakura, Michio Akiyama / Image (US R0 NTSC) / WS (2.35:1) (16:9)

While cutting edge cinema has long been the terrain of art house cinemas, no country can lay a claim to stranger art films than Japan. Leading the experimental pack is director Koji Wakamatsu, whose bizarre career spans from the early '60s to the late '90s and threatens to make the work of contemporaries like Seijun Suzuki (*Branded to Kill*) look almost genteel in comparison.

In *Go, Go Second Time Virgin (Yuke yuke nidome no shojo)*, two psychologically battered teenagers meet on a desolate urban rooftop and bare their psychic scars to each other. The boy (Michio Akiyama) feels a mixture of arousal and anguish when he sees the unclothed girl (Mimi Kozakura) following a gang rape on the rooftop, in which he was a partial participant, but their relationship becomes far more devastating and perverse than a forced sexual encounter. He relates how his parents forced him to watch and participate in group sex, a trauma he eventually curtailed with the aid of a butcher knife. Eventually the boy takes a surprising action against his peers, leading to the inevitable tragic finale.

Though running barely over an hour, *Go, Go Second Time Virgin* packs a tremendous amount of artistry into every scene. The relentless, downbeat atmosphere will prove tough going for many viewers, as will such bizarre flourishes as alternating the predominantly black and white footage with startling colour inserts (usually for violent moments). Despite the casual, frequent displays of nudity, the film's depiction of sex could hardly be described as erotic; instead, physical contact is presented as a temporary balm to relieve the agony of day to day existence in the big city with families insensitive to the needs of their children. Teen rebellion has never looked so grim.

The elements used for this DVD, another in the impressive line of Japanese cult releases from Image and the American Cinematheque, appear to be in excellent shape and boast a nicely detailed, clean image. The scope photography is well preserved with anamorphic enhancement to wring every last detail out of the print, while the burned in subtitles are easy to read. The disc also includes a shot-on-video interview with Wakamatsu, introduced with some on-the-fly artsy tracking shots, in which he

G

discusses his career and offers some concise remarks about the state of Japanese cinema both past and present. Not for everyone, obviously, but this is a good place to start to learn more about a director who remains almost entirely unknown in the West.

GODMONSTER OF INDIAN FLATS

Colour, 1973, 83m. / Directed by Fredric Hobbs / Starring E. Kerrigan Prescott, Stuart Lancaster / Image (US R1 NTSC)

Just down the road apiece from Las Vegas is the small town of Indian Flats, a hot-bed of financial corruption, racism, shady property dealing... and genetically mutated sheep. The town, kept for tourist purposes in the style of a Wild West prospecting settlement, is home to a variety of crooks and reprobates, whilst decency of a sort is represented by a young farmer, a research scientist and his hippie-chick assistant. When the youth discovers a mutated lamb after sleeping rough one night in the sheep pen, the trio move the creature to the lab, away from the prying eyes of the town's scheming Mayor. However, their attempt to study the mutton mutation only creates more havoc, as the grotesque (and rather unlikely-looking) monster grows to enormous size and breaks free to terrorize the town.

Godmonster of Indian Flats is a bizarre effort, part monster movie, part small-town melodrama, part nihilistic political fable, and the sort of release that gives you hope for the future of DVD releasing. If a film as hard to categorize and (previously) hard to see as this one can make it onto disc, there's hope for anything! Its eccentricity must be obvious from the simplest of descriptions, but there's a strange, counter-cultural chill running through it too - watch out for a rather unsympathetic use of the monster, whose ungainly (dare I say sheepish) appearance generates the sort of affection one feels for *Robot Monster*'s Ro-Man, only to be cold-shouldered at the film's climax in favour of social criticism.

Picture quality looks generally clear, well balanced and free of artefacts, with daylight scenes especially well rendered. The transfer is perhaps slightly too dark, a factor which exacerbates some variable day-for-night photography, but the steadiness and clarity of the image, struck from a nice clean print, make this a handsome release for such a rarity. This is another of Something Weird's extremely generous double-feature discs, with a second full-length film, unmentioned on the front

cover and spine, tucked away among the short subjects and other ephemera. *Passion in the Sun* (aka *The Girl and the Geek*) is an extended riff on the old "Monster and the Girl" chase routine, with burlesque dancer Rosette Valague taking to the Hollywood Hills to escape the clutches of a fairground geek who lusts after her cellulitic charms. Mildly amusing, inconsequential, it's the sort of thing you'll watch drunk and then forget you ever saw: but at least it gives us another peek at the wonderfully tawdry '60s burlesque circuit, as explored by other luminaries of the period such as David Friedman and H.G. Lewis. Plus: "Rural Rat Control" (a sick educational short subject), "Community Fly Control Operations," "The Geek" (a naughtier short subject), and "You Cannot Fart Around With Love," a musical number from director Frederic Hobbs' 1970 opus, *Roseland*, which feels like an out-take from Frank Zappa's *200 Motels*. Oddball or awful, it's hard to tell without seeing the rest of this ultra-rarity. - ST

GODS AND MONSTERS

Colour, 1998, 100m. / Directed by Bill Condon / Starring Ian McKellan, Brendan Fraser / Universal (US R1 NTSC), MGM (UK R2 PAL) / WS (2.35:1) (16:9) / DD5.1

As far as early Hollywood directors go, James Whale fared better than most: he produced a number of horror classics and directed the definitive version of *Showboat* as well as a number of skilful intimate dramas. Amazingly, his openly gay status didn't sabotage his career; instead, he chose to gradually step out of the business and retire into Hollywood seclusion. *Gods and Monsters*, adapted by Bill Condon from the magnificent Christopher Bram biographical novel, *Father of Frankenstein,* eloquently paints a portrait of Whale as a man coming to terms with his own inner struggles near the end of his life as a neurological disorder causes memories of the past to "wash over" him, as he puts it. This chamber drama is brought to perfection by three wonderful performances by McKellan as Whale, Fraser as his yardman, Boone (a performance for which Fraser hasn't received nearly enough credit), and Redgrave as his doting housekeeper, Hanna.

The loose, semi-linear narrative follows Whale in his twilight days as he finds himself out of the hospital and longing to take up painting. He sees inspiration in the form of Boone, a rugged and somewhat simple man hired to tend the lawn. The two strike up a friendship, and the director regales his friend with tales of his World War I antics and the filming of his classic horror films. In Boone, Whale sees traces of the sympathetic monster that appeared in all of his films, and the two even attend a Hollywood garden party together. However, the psychological tensions seething between the two men threaten to prevent any kind of ultimate understanding between them... or do they?

Filmed in Super 35, *Gods and Monsters* is presented on DVD in its preferred framing of 2.35:1. The film actually looks much better than the theatrical prints distributed by Lions Gate, allowing this low budget effort to now look like a million bucks. Carter Burwell's restrained, melancholy score benefits greatly from the subtle 5.1 mix, which comes to life mostly during the stylized flashbacks and fantasy sequences (Condon cleverly plays with imagery from *Bride of Frankenstein* throughout the film).

The DVD also includes an excellent "Making of" documentary (absent on the UK release) in which all of the principals discuss their involvement with the film and their various philosophies about its ultimate message(s). No simple studio puff piece, this is an enlightening supplement, though whether it justifies the steep price tag is another story. The film itself, though, is an excellent addition to any movie library; less a horror film than a meditation on the impulses and subliminal images which haunt us throughout our lives and make us feel "different," *Gods and Monsters* bears repeat visits and attention far beyond the restraints of art house audiences.

GOHATTO

Colour, 1999, 100m. / Directed by Nagisa Oshima / Starring Takeshi Kitano, Ryuhei Matsuda / Columbia (Canada R1 NTSC), Shochiku (Japan) / WS (1.78:1) (16:9), Ocean Shores (Hong Kong) / WS (1.70:1) / DD5.1

 Promoted in its native country as the return of a cinematic master, *Gohatto* (known internationally as *Taboo*) never stirred up the same level of controversy as *In the Realm of the Senses* but is a far more accomplished feat of storytelling. Delicately sketched in muted colours and spare performances, this mixture of psychological tension, violence, homosexual desire, swordsmanship, and evocative period detail may have limited audience appeal but is worth seeking out for the adventurous.

In 1865 Kyoto, a group of Shinsen-gumi soldiers under the command of lieutenant Hijikata (renowned actor/director Takeshi Kitano) observes the latest recruits, including the young, ruthless, and attractive fencing master Sozaburo (Ryuhei Matsuda). Another new soldier, Tashiro (Tadanobu Asano), falls desperately in love with Sozaburo, who is also chosen to perform a particularly difficult execution, and gradually wins him over. However, Sozaburo's charms also catch the eyes of many other military men who vie for his attentions. Hijikata schemes with his right hand man, Soji (Shinji Takeda), to initiate Sozaburo into manhood thanks to a trip to a local brothel, but things do not go as planned. Soon a series of brutal killings erupt among the clan, who are bound by a strict code of honour whose violations demand immediate death. Is the murderer someone whose passions have been thwarted too long? Or could there be a darker reason?

Despite the proliferation of one-on-one combat scenes and sexual encounters, *Gohatto* will seem alarmingly restrained to anyone expecting a shockfest. Apart from the execution, the gruesomeness is kept to a minimum while most of the sexual interaction takes place through characters' gazes. Completely devoid of a female presence, the film disturbs the conventions of the military and samurai genres, culminating in an unsettling and oddly beautiful final sequence capped by a single perfect gesture. Though Takeshi Kitano provides much of the film's marquee value, Oshima is clearly the star here, his camera seeking out the darkest shadows and the subtlest of facial expressions to tell his tale. The eerie, minimalist score by Ryuichi Sakamoto (reunited with Oshima after *Merry Christmas, Mr. Lawrence*) perfectly underscores the stirring passions beneath the rigorous exterior of military life. While the film remains satisfying even on the most obvious surface level as a sensually charged murder mystery (with a *Basic Instinct*-style confrontation at the end to boot), Oshima continuously probes under the surface, using two of Ryotaro Shiba's novellas *(Maegami no Sozaburo* and *Sanjogawara Ranjiin)* as the springboard to paint a portrait of Japan teetering over an abyss between the ages of feudalism and modernization.

Though New Yorker Films gave *Gohatto* a cursory art house run in the US, two DVD editions have already appeared overseas. The first from Japan's Shochiku offers an anamorphically enhanced, perfectly clean transfer with a 5.1 Dolby Digital mix and sports extras devoted to Oshima, including a bounty of unsubtitled trailers from his New Wave-inspired films during the 1960s. For half the price, Ocean Shores issued their own DVD with a non-anamorphic transfer, with slightly milder letterboxing at 1.70:1 compared to the 1.85:1 framing of the Shochiku edition. The Ocean Shores version also features a 2.1 surround mix and no extras apart from some very sketchy bios. Image quality is duller, with noticeable waves passing through a couple of the darkest scenes, but it's a perfectly acceptable option compared to the other, much pricier alternative and will most likely be at least the equal of any edition New Yorker may see fit to release. Both discs contain optional English subtitles and appear to be the same, thankfully including translations for the often humorous intertitles used to remark on the passing of time or the psychological geometry of the characters.

G

GOLD OF THE AMAZON WOMEN

Colour, 1979, 89m. / Directed by Mark L. Lester / Starring Bo Svenson, Anita Ekberg / Image (US R0 NTSC)

Though you'd never guess it from that cast, *Gold of the Amazon Women* was intended as an all-star international television production in the late '70s, apparently in a bid to bring the scale and star power of big screen productions to the cathode tube. What viewers got instead was one of the most unintentionally hilarious chunks of Eurocheese imaginable, a companion piece to such jungle disasters as *Hundra* and *Mighty Peking Man*. Break out the hard booze for this one, folks.

We begin in a modern day city, apparently meant to be New York, where a couple of feisty Amazon women are running rampant across the rooftops and causing all sorts of mayhem. Eventually they wind up dead thanks to a handy crossbow, but there are more where they came from. Evidently a group of amazons guard the prized city of gold, El Dorado, and it's up to two intrepid explorers, Tom (Bo Svenson) and Luis (Robert Romanus), to cut through the miles of wilderness to reach it. Along the way they encounter various jungle adventures, mostly involving one or both of them getting tossed into bamboo cages and having encounters with scantily clad women, while another nefarious rival explorer, Clarence (Donald Pleasence), searches for the golden city with his two bubble-headed sidekicks. The Amazon queen, Winnina (Anita Ekberg), proves more receptive than expected to the great American hunters, and much tepid mayhem ensues.

You'd really be hard pressed to find a more peculiar mix of actors stranded in a weirder project.

Well past her prime, Ekberg looks less than flattering in her revealing, strapless dresses, while Romanus looks tired and cranky. Pleasence livens up his relatively brief screen time, bouncing around and cackling with glee, while Svenson... well, if you've seen a single movie with him, you know what to expect. Nothing terribly violent or sexy ever happens, this being a TV movie and all, but the kitsch piles on fast and furious. Directorial chores were handled by Mark Lester, who later hit his stride, relatively speaking, with '80s actioners like *Class of 1984, Commando*, and *Firestarter*. Obviously his heart wasn't really in this one, but can you blame him? At least everyone got to have a nice vacation in the jungle and seemed to be having a good time, which is nice.

Various video companies like Embassy have been trying to lure in rental patrons with this sucker under such titles as *Quest for the Seven Cities*, but the DVD preserves the original title and looks about as good as one could expect. It still has that flat, slightly cruddy look prevalent in '70s television films, particularly during the opening scenes, but the colours are strong enough and the compression appears flawless. The mono audio is about the same as it's always been, with the bombastic score by Gil Melle (best known for his work on *Night Gallery*) trying desperately to keep the action going. If you're a big fan of surreal, late night TV movies that seem to have wandered in from some alternate universe, this should be just your plate of cheese.

GOLDEN BALLS

Colour, 1993, 88m. / Directed by Bigas Luna / Starring Javier Bardem, Maria de Madeiros / Tartan (UK R0 PAL) / WS (2.35:1) / DD2.0

Evidently still intrigued by the inherent problems with Spanish machismo, Spanish director followed up his successful *Jamón Jamón* the next year with this equally absurd tale of a lothario's rise and fall in the construction business. Sort of a sexed-up European variation on Ayn Rand's *The Fountainhead, Golden Balls (Huevos de oro)* takes that novel's already blatant phallic symbolism and pushes it to ludicrous extremes that would make Harold Robbins and Sidney Sheldon blush.

We first meet enthusiastic young Benito Gonzalez (Javier Bardem) as a recently released soldier intent on making his fortune in the construction business. He decides to bring along his best friend, Mosca (Francesco Dominedò), and his faithful girlfriend, Ana (Raquel Bianca), to whom he promises her own lobster tank and a private bathroom with a bidet. "Don't ever lose that smell," he growls to her as they make love in the sand, a pretty clear indicator of where this film is heading. Benito's plans are shattered when his two companions fall in love and take off together, leaving him to erect his superstructure all alone. Despite a lack of finances, he proceeds with his plans and begins an affair with his sultry secretary, Claudia (Maribel Verdu), who is also a struggling model. Benito talks Claudia into bedding potential bankers and financiers, then turns around and marries beautiful but naive banker's daughter Marta (*Pulp Fiction*'s Maria de Madeiros). Eventually Marta and Claudia find out about each other, compare notes (and breast drawings - don't ask), and wind up engaging in a torrid *ménage a trois* with Benito. However, our overbearing antihero's plans don't really fall into place as we follow him over the next few years through wild parties, temporary paralysis (see *Live Flesh* for more of Bardem in a wheelchair), suburban hell, and an ill-advised trek to Miami, complete with a surprise appearance by a young Benicio del Toro (*Traffic*).

Despite his gritty visual style, Luna makes a few interesting attempts here at Almodóvar-style outrageousness thanks to giant lip-shaped couches, Douglas Sirk-inspired plot turns, and torrid soap opera style dialogue. However, this is still unmistakably a Luna film; just check out the surreal dream sequence (complete with flying eggs, crumbling towers, and a woman's genitalia swarming with ants!) or the proliferation of sweaty, overheated, fleshy sex scenes. Bardem is excellent as usual, making his essentially worthless character a whole lot more compelling than he has any right to be, while the women all look appropriately sexy even when it's impossible to comprehend why they would choose to stay with such a deadbeat.

Though *Golden Balls* never made it to American theatres, it did fairly well in Great Britain (where *Jamón Jamón* was a surprise hit) and made it to a widescreen presentation on videotape. Many bootleg outfitters have circulated it around ever since, which makes the overdue DVD release a welcome relief. The muted picture quality isn't much of an improvement over the tape, with some fairly harsh shimmering abundant in most of the landscape shots, but the film was shot in a dark, subdued fashion by Luna anyway. The scope framing looks just right and preserves the film's bizarre compositions, while the burned-in white subtitles are almost always legible but tend to smear slightly. More satisfying is the Dolby surround audio, which is surprisingly aggressive throughout even the more subdued scenes and does an effective jobs of rendering Nicola Piovani's elegant score from the front and rear speakers. However, for some reason the sound features a few fleeting audio dropouts; these only last for under a second at a time but are a little disorienting. The disc also includes a series of "director's notes" by Luna (which are quite rambling but essentially sum up the major themes of the film), cast and crew bios, and a text interview with Luna in which he discusses his views on gender roles and filmmaking.

G

THE GOLDEN VOYAGE OF SINBAD

Colour, 1974, 105m. / Directed by Gordon Hessler / Starring John Phillip Law, Caroline Munro / Columbia (US R1 NTSC) / WS (1.85:1) (16:9)

Customary movie wisdom has it that the epic Sinbad films, best known for their spectacular "Dynamation / Dynarama" stop motion monsters by Ray Harryhausen, deteriorated with each entry. *7th Voyage of Sinbad* is the best, *Golden Voyage* is adequate, and *Sinbad and the Eye of the Tiger* is the worst. Not surprisingly this view springs from the fact that the major critics and filmmakers of the past few decades came of age in the '50s popcorn era, and in some respects they may be right. However, *Golden Voyage* is a supremely enjoyable treat and a cracking good adventure film for all ages, and apart from some very minor quibbles, the generations who grew up with it will be pleased to see that time has been very kind to it indeed.

While embarking on one of their usual seafaring voyages, Sinbad (John Phillip Law) and his crew spy a flying homunculus up in the air. One of the men shoots at it, causing the creature to drop a golden amulet onto the ship. Sinbad places the trinket around his neck and goes about his business, only to experience a strange dream that night involving a sinister man in black and a beautiful woman with a large eye tattooed on her hand. On land Sinbad encounters the sinister Koura (*Dr. Who's* Tom Baker), who resembles the man in Sinbad's dream and demands that our hero return the amulet to him, "the rightful owner." Sinbad refuses and escapes from Koura's men. In town he then meets the Vizier (Douglas Wilmer), whose face has been covered with a gold mask since he was disfigured by Koura. The Vizier possesses a similar amulet which, combined with Sinbad, forms a map which leads to untold treasures including, according to legend, the fountain of youth. More of Sinbad's dream comes to pass when he meets Margiana (Caroline Munro), a beautiful slave girl with - yep - a tattooed eye on her hand. Soon the band is sailing off to discover this secret land of riches, with Koura throwing up obstacles all along the way. A masthead comes to life, the six-armed statue of the goddess Kali comes to life, and for the climax, a griffin and a centaur even join the battle.

Obviously this film's entire reason for being is the creatures, all of which are up to Harryhausen's usual high standards of quality. However, the story is more engrossing and interesting than usual, and in a rare leading role, Munro as usual is stunning to behold. Law makes for an adequate Sinbad, though oddly he lacks the twinkle he brought to *Danger: Diabolik* five years earlier. With the death of regular Harryhausen composer Bernard Herrmann, the filmmakers here chose Miklos Rozsa, one of the best decisions imaginable. The score is quite melodic and rousing (though unlike the laserdisc, it's not isolated on the DVD).

Though not quite as feature-packed as the first Sinbad film, Columbia's DVD is a noticeable improvement in one major area. While *7th Voyage* was only presented in an attractive but irritating overmatted transfer, this disc offers both an anamorphic widescreen edition and the original open matte presentation. As with most Harryhausen titles, the latter is preferable and gives the visuals far more breathing room. The vivid colours and sharp detail are essentially the same on either option, and a tremendous improvement over the previous laserdiscs. The mono soundtrack (wisely presented in two channel Dolby Digital) sounds fine considering the limitations of the time; don't expect any major bass activity. Extras include the rarely seen long version of the theatrical trailer, as well as three recent, shot on video featurettes concerning the making of *Earth vs. the Flying Saucers, Mysterious Island*, and *3 Worlds of Gulliver* (with a surprise appearance by Joe Dante, to boot).

GOLDENEYE

Colour, 1995, 130m. / Directed by Martin Campbell / Starring Pierce Brosnan, Sean Bean / MGM / WS (2.35:1) (16:9) / DD5.1

In the wake of the theft of a Russian GPS system code-named GoldenEye, James Bond (Brosnan) is sent to St. Petersburg to investigate. His enquiries lead him to the discovery that an old government

ally (Bean) - believed to be have been murdered, something for which Bond held himself indirectly responsible - is still very much alive and planning a sophisticated heist using satellite and computer technology.

Pierce Brosnan steps effortlessly into the shoes of the king of espionage in this caper which unashamedly pilfers elements from most of the 16 Bonds that preceded it; it's hard to ignore the sense of *déjà vu* engendered whilst watching the myriad of chases, punch-ups, outrageous stunts, and grand scale decimation. And yet rather than being detrimental to the whole, the reprise works in the film's favour, serving to re-establish and enforce the superiority of the series after an absence from the screen of more than six years, a period which had seen wannabe interlopers such as Stallone, Schwarzenegger and Willis taking a bite of the action-hero cherry. Brosnan exudes the best traits of Connery and Moore whilst mixing in a splash of his own secret sauce to formulate an admirable depiction of the superspy.

Sean Bean is a fairly unmemorable addition to the Bond rogues gallery, although his showdown with 007 atop the world's largest radio telescope makes for some pulse-racing moments. Fortunately his shortcomings are compensated for by Famke Janssen as a psychotic executioner with a penchant for squeezing her prey to death between her thighs. Introducing the first female 'M' was undoubtedly a risk but Judi Dench repays the gamble ten-fold with a faultless performance that ensured her return in three further Bonds.

Director Martin Campbell orchestrates the requisite action with aplomb, allowing the integrity of the piece to slip just once when a chaotic tank chase through St. Petersburg degrades into slapstick. The employ of Eric Serra - who provided outstanding scores for *Leon* and *The Fifth Element* - was a misstep, for though some of his motifs are as good as anything the legendary John Barry brought to past parties, much of his work here is injuriously misjudged. It would take Brosnan several more adventures before he truly adopted Bond as his own, but *Goldeneye* is a debut finer than anyone could have hoped for or anticipated.

The film is showcased on a special edition disc which offers far more than a spotless transfer of the film itself. However, Bond buffs should be wary that the Region 2 version suffers from BBFC intervention that led to the loss of several seconds of material, including the moment when Janssen headbutts Izabella Scorupco. The Region 1 platter on

G

the other hand delivers the movie intact with a generous 49 chapter marks, along with a number of extra features. Although a documentary akin to those boasted by most of the other Bond releases is conspicuous by its absence, there is some nice behind the scenes material presented under the banner "GoldenEye Video Journal". And the inclusion of the 50-minute US TV special "The World of 007" (hosted by Elizabeth Hurley) is certainly a welcome inclusion. The addition of a promotional featurette, a chummy commentary from director Campbell and producer Michael Wilson, a dozen (very similar) TV spots, a pair of trailers and the glitzy Tina Turner music video make this a disc you can't afford not to have in your collection. Language and subtitle options are provided in English and French. - TG

GOLDFINGER

Colour, 1964, 110m. / Directed by Guy Hamilton / Starring Sean Connery, Honour Blackman / MGM (US R1 NTSC) / WS (1.78:1) (16:9)

Assigned to check into the alleged smuggling activities of Auric Goldfinger (Frobe), James Bond (Connery) tails him to Switzerland and reconnoitres his private smelting plant. It transpires that Goldfinger is devising the ultimate heist - a raid on the impenetrable gold vaults of Fort Knox. The one that everyone's heard of. The movie betters its Ian Fleming source, substituting the author's implausible plot that has Goldfinger poised to steal the entire contents of Fort Knox with a (still implausible, but less so) scheme to detonate an atomic bomb in the vault, rendering it inaccessible and increasing the value of his private holdings tenfold.

Highlights include Bond's near emasculation beneath Goldfinger's laser beam (prompting a classic exchange of dialogue: Bond - "You expect me to talk?" Goldfinger - "No, Mr. Bond, I expect you to die!"), the golf match as the two men strive to out-cheat each other, the pre-credits sequence with Bond peeling off his wet-suit to reveal an impeccably pressed tuxedo beneath, every scene with legendary bad guy Oddjob (Harold Sakata) and his steel-rimmed headwear, and the chase in the Aston Martin DB5 (replete with magical optional extras).

It's hard to imagine a better choice than Gert Frobe to fill the title role; he chews up the scenery with every line of dialogue and facial twitch. Ex-

Avenger Honour Blackman brings to the screen Pussy Galore ("I must be dreaming", mumbles a dazed Bond), the most risqué among Fleming's panoply of character names and one that ignited the ire of our censorious moral guardians. Shirley Eaton is the girl who gets a make-over in gold paint for double-crossing Goldfinger, Tania Mallett is the sister whose quest for revenge is curtailed by a blow to the neck from the sharp rim of Oddjob's bowler hat. Robert Brownjohn's eminent titles (substituting Harrison Marks model Margaret Nolan for Shirley Eaton as the "golden girl") set the standard for future 007 titles sequences, many of which are almost as striking as anything in the movies. The John Barry/Shirley Bassey titles number is an unmitigated classic.

Goldfinger has never had more glitter than on MGM's special edition DVD; the gorgeous 1.78:1 widescreen transfer is divided by 32 chapters, with sound and subtitles in English and French. Bonus materials comprise two commentaries (one from director Guy Hamilton, the second from members of the cast and production team), a chunky stills gallery, two half hour documentaries that cover most aspects of the film's production and marketing, a trailer, three TV spots (one in black & white, the other two teaming the film with *Dr. No*), over 20 minutes worth of innovative and witty US radio spots and an audio interview with Connery. The highlight though is an original (if short and rather the worse for wear) 1964 black & white featurette spotlighting the participation of Harold Sakata and Honour Blackman, featuring plenty of off-camera footage. - TG

GONIN

Colour, 1995, 108m. / Written and Directed by Takashi Ishii / Starring Koichi Sato, Masahiro Motoki / Ocean Shores (HK R0 NTSC), Tai Seng (US R0 NTSC), MIA (UK R2 PAL) / WS (1.85:1) / DD2.0

A stylish and disturbing crime film, the Japanese production *Gonin (The Five)* fuses the darkest popular arthouse trends into one eye-catching, brutal package guaranteed to linger in viewers' memories long after the film is over. Director Takashi Ishii (*Black Angel*), an established manga artist, depicts Japan - and indeed, civilization as a whole, perhaps - as a rapidly degenerating social structure where outcasts and corrupters feed on each other, with tragic results.

A young disco owner, Bandai (Koichi Sato), suffers from surrealistic nightmares as he tries to cope with his debts to the Yakuza. Mitsuya (Masahiro Motoki), a young gender bender fresh out of jail, makes a living blackmailing rich gay men and thinks Bandai was involved in his conviction. The two men sort things out and cook up a foolproof scheme to come up with some fast cash: rob the mob! Hizu (Jinpachi Nezu), a former cop disgraced in the public eye for his gambling problems, joins the fold, as does a bleach-blond pimp, Jimmy (Kippei Shiina). Their plotting is overheard by a jittery businessman, Ogiwara (Naoto Takenaka, that dancing fool from *Shall We Dance?*), who has been recently shattered by his corporation's downsizing, and he manages to weasel his way in, too. Together, the five men manage to pull off the robbery, but the mob kingpin, Ogoshi (Toshiyuki Nagashima), immediately hires two hitmen to track down the five thieves and dispatch them... at any cost.

Unlike many gangster/heist films, which operate on a purely superficial level with plenty of gloss to distract unsuspecting viewers, *Gonin* has quite a few agendas tucked under its beautifully designed sleeves. The vicious social commentary attacks depersonalized corporations that allow crime to fester and grow while individuals wind up torn to shreds in the process, and the startling homoeroticism that crops up throughout the film comes as a slap in the face to the usual buddy/buddy action formula. The two hitmen, featuring legendary director and Jolt spokesman "Beat" Takeshi, happen to be an incredibly dysfunctional gay couple and provide the film's most shocking, memorable scene, but the other characters also contain submerged traits indicating that sexuality, just like morality, isn't simply a matter of black or white.

The opening half hour may seem jagged and difficult to follow on first viewing, but it skilfully sets up the atmosphere of disorientation which ultimately swerves from standard fare to full blooded visceral horror in the final hour. Thoroughly unpredictable, *Gonin* tosses in a number of creepy surprises to add some flavour to the usual gun battles, leading to a chilling final scene that would have made Edgar Allan Poe proud.

Released briefly to US specialty houses by Phaedra in 1998, *Gonin* was inexplicably unavailable to most home viewers outside of The Sundance Channel's handful of graveyard shift screenings in the US. Several years down the line, the variant DVD editions have been taken from an exceptionally clean and vibrant print. Like another homoerotic mob heist film by former comic artists, *Bound*, this film is drenched in darkness virtually from start to finish, with only a few brief (but highly effective) moments set in broad daylight. The dream opening and club scenes in particular are very murky looking, as originally intended, but look clear, well-defined, and similar to the theatrical appearance. Colours are vivid, solid, and appealing, often drenched in bright neon and stylish Argentoesque bursts of primary hues.

All of the DVD options look comparable, except the Ocean Shores (whose logo is emblazoned twice on the print) adds Chinese subtitles above the English ones. Though not entirely comprehensive and occasionally difficult to read against white backgrounds, the burned-in English subtitles are large and easily get the point across. While the Phaedra prints featured a dull, one-dimensional sound mix, the DVDs boast a spacious and effective, full-bodied surround mix. The imaginative score, which uses castanets as musical harbingers of death a la *The Leopard Man*, sounds fantastic and often looms up from the rear speakers, though sound effects outside of the usual directional gunfire are essentially limited to the centre and occasionally front speakers. Due to the proliferation of extra company logos in America, the US cut actually runs almost a minute longer, but the prints are identical in terms of the film's content. Shot hard-matted at 1.85:1, the framing looks perfect and appears to expose the entire available image. Don't miss the fantastic original Japanese trailer as well.

THE GOOD, THE BAD, AND THE UGLY

Colour, 1966, 162m. / Directed by Sergio Leone / Starring Clint Eastwood, Lee Van Cleef, Eli Wallach / MGM (US R1 NTSC, UK R2 PAL) / WS (2.35:1) (16:9)

The prototypical spaghetti western arrives to DVD in grand style, with a brand new transfer that perfectly showcases the incredible widescreen desert textures of Sergio Leone's violent, hyper-stylish masterpiece. Though it may not be his best film (*Once Upon a Time in the West* takes that honour), this is definitely his most famous, archetypal effort and perfectly wraps up the "Dollars" trilogy with Clint Eastwood.

A nameless stranger (Eastwood) - the "Good" - enters a twisted arrangement with the cranky Tucco (Eli Wallach), the "Ugly," to earn money by turning Tucco in for crimes, collecting the reward, and rescuing him just before he gets hanged as just punishment. The two learn of a stash of hidden gold

G

in the grave of a Civil War soldier and become instant rivals, only to find themselves in violent competition with a third party, the "Bad" Angel Eyes (Lee Van Cleef, in a complete reversal on his role in *For a Few Dollars More*).

While the widescreen aspect ratio here is about the same as MGM's laserdisc release, the colour and clarity far exceed the laser's chalky appearance. The Dolby Digital sound accentuates each quirky sound effect and shows off Ennio Morricone's classic, bizarre score to ravishing effect. Interestingly, this different print introduces the characters during the opening scenes by their English titles, while the laser version was in Italian. A few minor signs of wear appear at the reel changes, but it's not too distracting.

The extras include the US theatrical trailer, some skimpy production notes, and the highlight, 12 minutes of scenes deleted from the film after its original Italian release. Because the footage only exists (dubbed) in Italian, it's presented with English subtitles and looks as good as the accompanying feature. Though little really affects the plot one way or the other, the scenes reveal some great bits of character acting (the desert scene between Eastwood and Wallach in particular) and more elaboration on Cleef's shenanigans while Eastwood is held captive in the Civil War camp. Too bad these goodies couldn't have been reinstated back in the original film, though.

THE GORE GORE GIRLS

Colour, 1972, 81m. / Directed by Herschell Gordon Lewis / Starring Amy Farrell, Hedda Lubin / Image (US R0 NTSC), Tartan (UK R0 PAL)

 Here the Godfather of Gore, H.G. Lewis, takes his predilection for outrageously violent death scenes to the most absurd extremes ever captured on American film. As the title implies, the film splits its time down the middle between jiggling '70s go go acts (complete with tacky pasties) and brutal, very moist murder scenes that play like sick black comedy skits from some lost cable variety show.

At a sleazy nightclub (run by Henny Youngman!), the clientele is somewhat less than normal. An unstable Vietnam vet uses markers to draw faces on melons, then smashes them with his fist all over the bar. Women's lib activists carrying picket signs flood the stage. And a killer dressed up in full Italian slasher regalia (black gloves, black slicker, etc.) is picking off the club's talent one by one. In the opening scene, a young woman's face is repeatedly ground into a broken mirror; another has her bottom mushed by a meat tenderizer and sprinkled with salt; a girl with a big afro gets slam dunked into a bunch of french fries; and in the most notorious scene, the killer comes up with a whole new meaning for "Got milk?" The only hope for unmasking this deviant lies with an obnoxious police consultant (Frank Kress) and a plucky female reporter (Amy Farrell). Will they get to the truth before they fall under the knife as well?

A perfect companion piece to Lewis' earlier *The Wizard of Gore* (whose star, Ray Sager, pops up here as a bartender), *The Gore Gore Girls* definitely isn't the best film to show your parents on a slow evening, but horror fans with strong stomachs and a high tolerance for offensive black humour could do a lot worse. The dialogue is blatantly satiric, with characters even addressing the screen and making quips after the killings, and the final dialogue wrap up is one of the longest in slasher history. Incidentally, the killer's identity directly contradicts some visual information from earlier in the film, but you can discover that bit of wondrous non-continuity for yourself. Like all of Lewis' '70s work, *The Gore Gore Girls* is much darker and grimier than the vibrantly colourful days of *Blood Feast*.

The transfer here is acceptable and probably as good as it's going to get, much like *Wizard*, but don't expect visual fireworks. The dialogue is sometimes difficult to understand, but this is a flaw in the original sound recording. The stock jazz and grindhouse music is also quite amusing. As usual, Lewis contributes an animated and informative commentary track in which he explains his rationale for the film's more extreme moments, the circumstances for his final glory days behind the movie camera, and the stories behind certain actors. (He holds off his anecdote about the unforgettable Hedda Lubin right until the very end.) Of course, you also learn how the heck Henny Youngman wound up in this movie and how he was as an actor. The disc also includes a jolting clip from something called *Love Goddess of Blood Island*. We'll let you discover that sick little puppy all for yourself. The UK version from Tartan includes the trailer, stills, filmographies, Chris Campion liner notes, and an H.G. Lewis "Copy Class."

THE GOSPEL ACCORDING TO ST. MATTHEW

B&W, 1964, 137m. / Directed by Pier Paolo Pasolini / Image (US R0 NTSC) / WS (1.85:1)

G

273

After wading through years of grandiose, ultra-long religious epics like *King of Kings, The Ten Commandments,* and *The Greatest Story Ever Told,* this modern classic by the late Pier Paolo Pasolini must have come as a huge shock to viewers around the world. Commonly regarded as the high point of Pasolini's career, *The Gospel According to St. Matthew (Il Vangelo secondo Matteo)* renders the familiar story of Jesus Christ from birth to death in a style that can only be described as a fusion of neorealism, *cinéma vérité,* and Felliniesque strangeness. Using zooms, handheld shots, and stark black and white photography, Pasolini created a dusty, highly believable world and cast it largely with amateurs and people whose faces he found interesting to achieve a "true life" interpretation of the Biblical story and bring it home to even the lowest class viewers. The meditative pacing and sympathetic treatment of all of the characters (even Judas Iscariot) make this an uncommonly humane and, yes, reverent treatment, and it's interesting to note that Pasolini manages to accomplish in a little over two hours what took Franco Zeffirelli an entire week with his popular *Jesus of Nazareth.*

The majority of the film focuses on the progression of Christ (Enrique Irazoqui) as he gathers his disciple and discards his aspirations of self-glory to become a symbol of repressed people everywhere. His trial by suffering involves such familiar side trips as the Salome/John the Baptist encounter (a great sequence) and the Last Supper, which leads into his persecution and the hanging of Judas. The performances are all typical Pasolini - naturalistic almost to a fault. This is also the rare film in which Mary actually ages along with the narrative from a young girl to an older woman (played by Pasolini's mother; what's the message here?). While the decision to film this subject matter may seem strange for an avowed gay Catholic and Marxist, Pasolini adapts the story as an underdog tale for universal audiences, an everyman who could be walking among us in the streets right now.

While the transfer appears to be derived from the same print used for Water Bearer's tapes and Image's laserdisc a few years ago, the results here are noticeably improved. The opening credits are still in very rough shape, but the rest of the print (featuring legible, non-optional subtitles) is consistently sharp and detailed, with rich black scales and no noticeable pixilation or other artefacts. A few ragged points around the reel changes and the occasional scratch notwithstanding, this is easily the best this film has ever looked. The music, a surreal combination of excerpts from Mozart, Beethoven, and Prokofiev alternating with an original percussive score by Luis Bacalov, sounds as well as could be expected given the film's limited budget, and foreshadows Pasolini's use of patchwork music sources (with Ennio Morricone's consultation) for his "Trilogy of Life." If you're a Pasolini fan, looking to expand your foreign film collection, or simply want to see a good religious film without any pretensions or overacting, this is definitely a must-see.

GOSSIP

Colour, 2000, 90m. / Directed by Davis Guggenheim / Starring James Marsden, Lena Headey / Warner (US R1 NTSC, UK R2 PAL) / WS (2.35:1) (16:9) / DD5.1

Chalk up another one for the guilty pleasures list. Tossing elements of *Wild Things* and *Shallow Grave* into a sinfully glossy package, *Gossip* tries to undo the degradation of the youth thriller genre from the likes of trash like *Urban Legend* and *The Skulls* by reigning in the sex and gore quotient, focusing instead on plot-driven thrills and surprising character developments. Indeed, there's little reason for this film to be rated R (as compared to *The In Crowd*'s PG-13?), and by the end it even defies categorization by piling twist upon twist with a dash of moral posturing for good measure. No wonder the marketing folks at Warner had no idea what to do with this one, saddling it instead with another one of those uninspired face collage posters that need to be put out to pasture immediately. *Gossip* won't please everyone, but its alluring cheap thrills certainly offer their own rewards.

Trust fund kid Derrick (James Marsden) splits his swanky college loft with two friends, Cathy Jones (Lena Headey) and struggling artist Travis (Norman Reedus). They decide to collaborate on a paper for their sociology class with Professor Goodwin (Eric Bogosian) by starting a nasty rumour about repressed society girl Naomi (Kate Hudson) and charting its progress throughout the campus. The gossip chain transforms the story from a slightly kinky anecdote into an account of rape involving another blueblood, Beau (Joshua Jackson), who winds up interrogated by the police when a drunken Naomi can't really remember what happened at a party. However, Cathy begins to suspect that there may be other motivations lying beneath the rumour, particularly when Naomi reacts with horror upon hearing Derrick's name. By the end, truth and fiction become difficult to separate, and no one is quite whom they seem.

Most obviously, *Gossip* is designed as a sensual thrill ride, with each shot offering absurdly overstuffed visions of gaudy nightclubs, glittery multi-room parties decked out with slide projectors, and Travis' perverse wall-sized art installations involving Naomi's face. The soundtrack follows suit with a terrific, catchy Graeme Revell score and, for once, a well-chosen and thematically appropriate selection of pop songs. The actors all look great and wrap their tongues nicely around their tart, thoroughly implausible dialogue. The script throws in a nice little kicker of a twist ending (which some notable critics felt ruined the movie, but it does work), as well as enough shady motivations to keep you guessing.

Though it vanished quickly in theatres, Warner and Morgan Creek packaged *Gossip* as a special edition DVD without labelling it as one. In keeping with the studio's track record, the scope transfer looks fantastic, with a subtle but effective 5.1 audio mix that gradually picks up steam as the film progresses. The alternate full frame version opens up the Super 35 matte without losing much on the sides, but it just doesn't look as striking and well composed; stick with the widescreen option. The commentary track features TV vet director Davis Guggenheim and Marsden casually chatting about production of the film, including some details about production shooting. (It's often hilarious how this film, supposedly set somewhere between New York and Vermont, features so many supporting characters with pronounced Canadian accents.) An extended series of takes of Hudson and Jackson's party tryst is included, along with four deleted scenes, one of which features Marsden's finest moment in the entire film and should have been retained.

Also included is a widely excised longer version of the final scene, which offers a ridiculous new fate for one character, along a collage of Travis' video interviews and a "Grab Bag" featuring music videos by Poe and Tonic, plus longer raw footage of its gossip montage. Right down to the core of its Velveeta-scented heart, this is cinematic junk food all the way, but at least it's quite tasty all the same.

GOTHIC

Colour, 1986, 87m. / Directed by Ken Russell / Starring Natasha Richardson, Gabriel Byrne / Artisan (US R1 NTSC) / DD2.0

One of Ken Russell's more misunderstood and poorly marketed films, *Gothic* provoked almost universal disappointment from filmgoers expecting a wild, trashy horror film crammed with rampaging beasties. Instead, they got a surreal, melancholy, and eccentric study of four tortured souls locked together for one very long evening. What a difference a simple matter of perspective makes.

During a balmy summer evening in 1816, Percy Shelley (Julian Sands) and his mistress (and eventual wife), Mary (Natasha Richardson), arrive by boat at the lakeside estate of Lord Byron (Gabriel Byrne). Accompanying them is Mary's cousin, Claire (Miriam Cyr), who is secretly pregnant with Byron's illegitimate child. The night starts out harmlessly enough with some light drinking, psychological torture, and group sex, but the trouble really starts their substance abuse and an ill-advised séance around a skull provoke a series of group hallucinations. Mary is tortured by images of her miscarried child, Shelley indulges in his darkest fantasy of a woman with eyes in her breasts, and the creepy Dr. Polidori (Timothy Spall), a literary acquaintance of Byron, is torn apart by his repressed sexuality. Soon the unholy quintet comes to believe that their communal fear may be spawning a physical manifestation, something dark and unavoidable that they will have to confront before morning comes.

Almost impossible to appreciate on its first viewing, *Gothic* is definitely not one of Russell's major films but does offer its own modest giddy pleasures. Byrne and Richardson are both standouts in their first high profile leading roles, with the only weak link provided by Sands, even whinier than usual here. Synth pop maestro Thomas Dolby (yes, the guy who did "She Blinded Me with Science") provides a genuinely strange electronic score that ranges from kitschy to terrifying, and the costumes and scenery are consistently beautiful to behold. The sheer oddness and nastiness of the film's imagery makes it impossible to forget: the prodigiously endowed living suit of armour, Polidori's forced stigmatizing by a nail, and the screen's most grotesque (and stylish) abortion sequence, to name just a few.

Sadly, Artisan's DVD really isn't up to the demands of Russell's visually intricate film. While their transfers of *Salome's Last Dance* and especially *Lair of the White Worm* were tremendous improvements upon the old VHS and laser editions from Vestron, this DVD is simply a rehash of the very outdated and unsatisfying Vestron print. The opening ten minutes are especially disastrous, with distracting print damage and muddy colours completely undermining the lyrical main titles and lakeshore arrival. Things improve somewhat once the night-time activities begin, and the colours look more natural and accurate, but this movie truly screams out for a new transfer. The mono audio is also muddy and unsatisfying; to make matters worse, the film was originally recorded in stereo but is presented here in very flat mono.

On the positive side, the DVD does include the terrific original US trailer, which is almost worth the price by itself. If you can find this reasonably priced and don't already have the tape or LD, this disc is worth picking up for the movie itself; just don't expect anything special.

GRAND ILLUSION

B&W, 1937, 117m. / Directed by Jean Renoir / Starring Jean Gabin, Marcel Dalio / Criterion (US R1 NTSC)

The anti-war film to end all anti-war films, *Grand Illusion* opened just before World War II and suffered from drastic censorship and shoddy print duplication in virtually every country, yet by the 1950s, it had already become regarded as one of the crown jewels of world cinema. Its influence is certainly undeniable, including such diverse films as *The 49th Parallel*, *The Great Escape*, and *The Deer Hunter*, though the actual theme of a "gentleman's war" coming to an end has never been addressed as eloquently or powerfully as it is here.

During World War I, two disparate French soldiers are captured by the Germans and brought to a camp where they come in contact with men from all walks of life. The lower class but intelligent Lieutenant Maréchal (Jean Gabin) and former aristocrat Captain de Boieldieu (Pierre Fresnay) begin a rapport with the Jewish Lieutenant Rosenthal (Marcel Dalio), and after a temporary separation, the three wind up together again under the supervision of an imposing German officer, Captain von Rauffenstein (Erich von Stroheim). The Germans treat their prisoners with relative dignity and consideration; in fact, Rauffenstein and Maréchal respect each other on a basic human level and realize that war as a concept is completely unproductive and a hindrance to the progress of humanity. However, the French soldiers decide to escape, with a memorable sequence in which Maréchal finds love in the French countryside before the jarring, bullet-ridden climax.

Never afraid of delving into unfamiliar genres, director Jean Renoir (*Rules of the Game*) made his definitive celluloid statement with *Grand Illusion*, and not surprisingly, his subsequent films in the United States and then back in France could only offer echoes of his impassioned plea for human consideration among nations. The son of Pierre Auguste Renoir, the famous Impressionist painter, Jean Renoir opts for a flat, realist style as a filmmaker, though his sparing and effective fluid camerawork could sometimes give Max Ophuls a run for his money. Scripted and filmed with razor sharp precision, *Grand Illusion* avoids the flashy pyrotechnics associated with most war films, offering instead a delicate balance of psychology and art. In his unforgettable outfit, von Stroheim immediately steals every scene in which he appears and manages to wipe the skilled Gabin off the screen at several points; the rest of the men do their best with roles best described as familiar archetypes.

The Criterion DVD does this film justice by restoring the complete French cut with optional English subtitles, culled directly from a pristine negative that must be seen to be believed. Anyone who has had the misfortune of sitting through bad VHS copies or shoddy 16mm prints in film class won't believe their eyes after seeing this restoration, which also enjoyed a theatrical art house run from Rialto. The disc includes Renoir's much later four minute introduction/trailer to the film for its 1958 US reissue, a feature length audio essay on the film by historian Peter Cowie which focuses on its historical minutiae more than its thematic material, pressbook excerpts and essays (including notes on the negative's rescue), and the 1938 New York Film Critics Awards acceptance speech by Renoir and von Stroheim.

LA GRANDE BOUFFE

Colour, 1973, 129m. / Directed by Marco Ferreri / Starring Marcello Mastroianni, Michel Piccoli / Image (US R0 NTSC)

Long before Peter Greenaway combined sex, death, and cuisine in *The Cook, the Thief, His Wife and Her Lover*, controversial Italian auteur Marco Ferreri jolted arthouse and festival audiences with *La Grande Bouffe* (aka *Blow-Out*), a visually sumptuous study of modern excess. Not exactly a pleasant or traditional cinematic experience, this is bold but darkly funny territory where adventurous treasure seekers will find many rewards.

Four men of good means in '70s Paris decide to get away from the hustle and bustle of city life for an isolated retreat in a country chateau. A cook (Ugo Tognazzi), judge (Philippe Noiret), pilot (Marcello Mastroianni), and TV producer (Michel Piccoli), they seem to have plenty to live for, but the ennui of modern life has worn them down. They eat gluttonously from their table, gaze lazily at images of vintage pornography, and bring in prostitutes to satisfy their sexual appetites. Why all this indulgence? Simple! It's a lavish suicide scheme whereby the men will literally die from too much pleasure, their vulnerable bodies unable to cope with the avalanche of material intake. Marcello becomes taken with the presence of a lovely, full-bodied schoolteacher, Andrea (Andrea Ferreol), whose sweet demeanour conceals a feminine appetite easily the equal of her peers. How far will the madness go, and who will be left to tell the tale?

Though definitely not a film to pull out at dinner time, La Grande Bouffe has mellowed considerably with age and hardly seems to merit the NC-17 rating slapped on it by the MPAA in the late '90s. The opportunity to observe four of Europe's finest actors at the peak of their form is an opportunity to be cherished all by itself, and Ferreri relishes the opportunity to simply train his camera on his performers and let them go to work. The film obviously had a heavy influence on Greenaway, who provided a very similar leading role for Ferreol in his A Zed and Two Noughts and duplicated this film's gimmick of naming its protagonists after the actors portraying them in The Cook, the Thief... (though three of the original actors eventually dropped out of the latter project). Ferreri's semi-regular composer, Philippe Sarde, contributes another sparse, intelligent score, which will hopefully see the light of a commercial compilation release one of these days.

Long available on home video in Great Britain, La Grande Bouffe turned up on American VHS in the mid-'90s from Water Bearer in a slightly letterboxed, washed-out transfer from the same PAL source. The Image DVD is taken from cleaner, more colourful source materials and is far easier on the eyes, though inexplicably the transfer is full frame with some slivers of information missing from the right and left sides of the image. The richness of the quality itself compensates for the loss, and the optional yellow English subtitles are far more legible, to boot - except they leave some pertinent chunks of dialogue untranslated at the beginning.

THE GRAPES OF DEATH (PESTICIDE)

Colour, 1978, 84m. / Directed by Jean Rollin / Starring Marie-Georges Pascal, Brigitte Lahaie / Synapse (US R0 NTSC), Cine Club (Germany R2 PAL) / WS (1.66:1) (16:9)

Between his stylish vampire fantasies and less personal sex films, Jean Rollin pushed the French horror cinema in a new direction by introducing two new elements - zombies and explicit gore - to which he would return later with the vastly inferior Zombie Lake and the more poetic Living Dead Girl. The most traditional of his walking dead trilogy, The Grapes of Death (Les raisins de la mort) retains his slow, dreamlike pace while jolting viewers with unexpected bouts of bloodletting.

The episodic plot follows the misadventures of young Elizabeth (Marie-Georges Pascal) journeying through the French countryside by train. Her companion falls prey to a bloodthirsty zombie, while she barely escapes with her life and dodges an undead shambler with a penchant for bashing his head against car windshields. She finds shelter in a nearby farmhouse inhabited by a man and wife, but alas her safety is short-lived when the farmer takes a pitchfork to his spouse on the kitchen table. Apparently their consumption of wine for the local vineyards is to blame, and soon the countryside is filled with the anguished, half-conscious victims of the grapes contaminated by chemical exposure. With the aid of two die hard beer drinkers, Elizabeth fights back against the growing zombie population during a long night of unrelenting terror.

Along with the power of its individual sequences (particularly the memorable fate of a helpful blind girl), The Grapes of Death benefits from Rollin's increasing control of cinematic language within the horror medium. His skilful assembly of landscape shots and claustrophobic interiors creates an uneasy yet beautiful atmosphere, and he gains quite a bit of mileage in the furious third act from the presence of his most famous porn leading lady, Brigitte Lahaie, who steals the show with her two big scenes. The bizarre, pulsating electronic score is also a notable change of pace, creating a hypnotic if somewhat unorthodox mood in the style of Tangerine Dream.

Viewers used to awful VHS bootlegs of this film will be astonished by the quality of Synapse's DVD, transferred from the original negative, which looks absolutely spotless. Rollin's colour scheme is generally subdued throughout, but the occasional bursts of searing reds and blue which come through

G

occasionally look marvellous. The soundtrack is also considerably improved, with a much more dynamic range than any of his other titles on video to date. The optional English subtitles are large, easy to read, and appear to be appropriately translated.

Extras include the somewhat fragmented theatrical trailer, a Rollin bio, and video interviews with Rollin and Lahaie, both of whom offer some interesting insights into their horror careers, once one adjusts to their strong accents. (Those who got through Rollin's commentary on the briefly released *Living Dead Girl* laserdisc should have no problem at all.) Lahaie teamed up with Rollin again for two of her best lead roles in *Fascination* and *The Night of the Hunted*, making *The Grapes of Death* the start of another type of trilogy as well. A concurrent German release (as *Pesticide*) features a 35 minute documentary, "Bloody Lips & Iron Roses," with plenty of Rollin interview footage and film clips, as well as a 3 minute short, "La Griffe d'Horus." Language options are German or French, with German, English, or Dutch subtitles.

THE GREAT SILENCE

Colour, 1968, 105m. / Directed by Sergio Corbucci / Starring Jean-Louis Trintignant, Klaus Kinski / Fantoma (US R1 NTSC) / WS (1.66:1)

Never given a wide international release for reasons never made clear, *The Great Silence* is one of the more neglected top line spaghetti westerns. The constant snowfall and eccentric storyline immediately set it apart from its desert-bound ilk like the Sergio Leone classics, and the downbeat, gritty approach still makes it a potent, unforgettable experience.

In the snowswept wilds of Utah, the mysterious outlaw Silence (Jean-Louis Trintignant) coldly guns down armed bounty hunters who cross his path. The most nefarious of these legalized killers, Loco (Klaus Kinski), crosses paths with Silence in a remote and despairing mountainside town, where Pauline (Vonetta McGee) enlists Silence's services to avenge the death of her husband. The town's owner, Pollicut (Luigi Pistilli), allows the bounty hunters to commit legalized murder with impunity, but the genial new sheriff (*The Lickerish Quartet*'s Frank Wolff) has other ideas and crosses paths with Loco. Pauline and Silence also begin a tentative love affair, but greater, more sinister powers control their destiny.

One of the greatest international actors, Trintignant makes the most of his non-speaking part to convey a dense moral ambiguity lurking within a gun-slinging mute (his vocal chords have been slit), able to strike back only in self-defence. He's matched every step of the way by the Aryan Kinski, whose fascist behaviour gives the film a more disturbing political subtext than your average Euro oater. The film also marks the debut of McGee, an interesting actress who later returned to snowy climes for Clint Eastwood's *The Eiger Sanction*. Her interracial love scene here is something of an anomaly in westerns, Italian or otherwise, and her relationship with Silence gives the unexpected finale an even greater resonance. And as for that ending... well, let's just say it's one of a kind and will either make or break the film for most viewers.

Director Sergio Corbucci made a name for himself by directing *Django*, one of the most popular non-Leone spaghetti westerns, but *The Great Silence* is a more impressive work. As with *Django* he avoids the spacious scope framing one normally associates with the genre, choosing instead to evoke a tight, claustrophobic atmosphere through bizarre framing and cramped visual spaces. The oppressive snowstorms which punctuate the film provide some startling tableaux of men on horseback trudging through the hills; even more than the notorious *Cut-Throats Nine*, this is a western that seeps into your bones and makes you want to curl up in front of a fireplace for a few hours.

The rough technical nature of the film (some rough edits, a few shaky camera shots, visible imperfections in some of the film stock) in many ways enhances its curiosity value, distinguishing it from the slick Hollywood product of a director like John Ford. Naturally it also wouldn't be complete without an Ennio Morricone score, and the maestro doesn't disappoint. The main theme is one of his most haunting, and the rest of the music perfectly captures the violence and melancholy inherent in the story.

Most viewers first experienced *The Great Silence* in some video incarnation of the Japanese laserdisc, which was slightly overmatted but good for its time. The Fantoma DVD marks the extremely overdue US release of the film, and it's hard to imagine the film looking much better. The original negative with the English soundtrack was used for the transfer, and every blemish and imperfection in the original material has been left intact. The opening credits look a bit tight on the sides, but overall the framing seems balanced and complimments the sharp, colourful image quality.

The disc also includes a battered theatrical trailer, extensive liner notes, an appreciative introduction by director Alex Cox (who used McGee in *Repo Man*), and best of all, an unused "happy ending" (which, spoiler haters will note, gives away the fact that the movie's real ending is about as horrifically depressing as they come). This bizarre resolution (including a freakish twist involving Trintignant's hand) contains no existing audio, so Cox contributes his own analysis of this anomaly on an optional audio track. Obviously one of the key cult releases on DVD, this disc is a must see for western fans, exploitation buffs, and art house audiences alike.

THE GRUESOME TWOSOME

Colour, 1967, 71m. / Directed by Herschell Gordon Lewis / Starring Elizabeth Davis, Chris Martell / Image (US R1 NTSC), Tartan (UK R0 PAL)

An unofficial return to gory form for director H.G. Lewis, *The Gruesome Twosome* found him once again rolling around in the ultra-realistic fake blood he had earlier devised for such "classics" as *Blood Feast* and *Two Thousand Maniacs!* Here more than ever before, comedy takes centre stage as Lewis spins out what can only be described as a very low budget riff on *The Addams Family,* albeit with torrents of bodily fluid coursing across the screen.

After a completely bizarre six minute opener in which two Styrofoam mannequin heads with phoney Southern accents set up the storyline (concluding with one of them being knifed in the head), we meet our two tongue in cheek criminals, wig store owner Mrs. Pringle (Elizabeth Davis) and her mentally deficient son, Rodney (Chris Martell). As with all college towns, Mrs. Pringle has set up shop next to the campus to lure in all those young schoolgirls eager to sell their locks for a little handy spare cash. However, once inside the girls wind up on the wrong end of Rodney's electric knife, which he uses to remove their scalps (in loving detail, natch). Enter Nancy Drew wannabe Kathy (Gretchen Wells), who sniffs out the disappearance of a school friend to the door of Mrs. Pringle's wig shop and finds more than she bargained for inside.

After the groundbreaking explicitness of his Blood Trilogy, Lewis decided to tweak the genre a bit with *Gruesome Twosome* by subverting the carnage with goofy, *non sequitur* gags aimed at everything from sixties campus flicks to pretentious foreign films (at a drive-in, no less, in the film's oddest and most memorable bit). Probably not the best place to start if you're a Lewis newcomer, *The Gruesome Twosome* is so crazed and challenging to watch that it could be considered a final course in the H.G. Lewis School of Filmmaking.

Something Weird's DVD looks much better and more vividly colourful than the impossible to find VHS version released in the '80s (which even popped up on a few shelves at Blockbuster Video, believe it or not) and later resurfaced on VHS from Something Weird. The colours are quite as hallucinatory as *Blood Feast* but darn close. Once again Lewis and Mike Vraney chip in with a lively commentary track covering the location shooting, the vagaries of financing a gore film in '67, and the various cast members. Lewis affirms that this is indeed a comedy, and unlike some questionable items like *The Gore Gore Girls*, which dangerously tread the line, it's hard to disagree with him on this one, explicit bloodletting notwithstanding.

On the disc you also get the amusing theatrical trailer (in rough shape and recycling the warning from "Thomas Wood" used for the *Blood Feast* trailer) and a very unnerving '60s education short, "Wig-o-Rama," which... well, it's best to let adventurous viewers discover that one all for themselves. Minus the commentary track, the disc is also carried in the UK by Tartan, surprisingly free of BBFC edits.

GUMNAAM

Colour, 1965, 143m. / Directed by Raja Nawathe / Starring Manoj Kumar, Nanda / Eros International (India R0 NTSC) / DD4.0

Billed in its outlandish trailer as "India's First Horror Thriller," *Gumnaam* follows the common Bollywood tradition of adapting a familiar convention or story into a psychedelic feast of music and mind-warping genre collisions. Up on the chopping block this time is Agatha Christie's *Ten Little Indians*, first filmed as *And Then There Were None,* which is followed with surprising faithfulness despite the frequent detours along the way.

A planeload of random passengers is forced into an emergency landing on a very large island with only one spooky house offering refuge from the torrential rain. Representing a cross section of society, the bewildered guests include a doctor (Madan Puri), a perpetually happy dancer (Nanda), studly would-be heartthrob Anand ('60s singer and director Manoj Kumar), and most memorably, a drunken showgirl named Miss Kitty (Bollywood

G

favourite Helen). Inside the house they see a shrouded body, which turns out to be the prankster butler/cook (Mehmood, with an odd Hitler moustache), who indicates he has been expecting them all to arrive and shows them into the dining room. There they find a book indicating that each person has committed murder at some point in their lives but escaped conviction, so their mysterious host has now decided to dole out punishment. One by one the visitors die over the following two evenings, but that doesn't stop them from indulging in a little beach party, a drunken duet, and an elaborate MGM-style dance fantasia in between all of the screaming and dead bodies. Christie fans, of course, shouldn't be remotely surprised by the way it all turns out.

In the sprawling Indian cinematic tradition, *Gumnaam* is ridiculously long considering the threadbare story, but the madcap efforts to keep viewers entertained at all costs make the running time speed by faster than one might expect. The film really kicks off with a bang thanks to the go-go number "Jan Pahechan Ho," which looks like an outtake from *Black Tight Killers* and popped up most memorably during the opening credits of *Ghost World*. However, points for sheer spectacle go to the butler's lavish dance fantasy, a visual orgy of Bava-style colours and twirling showgirls that must be witnessed to be believed. Speaking of Bava, most of the violence occurs offscreen a la *Five Dolls for an August Moon* apart from one surprisingly brutal hanging; thus the interjections of music and humour aren't quite as jarring as they would be in a bona fide slasher film.

For a mid-'60s Indian title, *Gumnaam* looks fairly nice on DVD if not quite immaculate. The first reel in particular displays a lot of wear and tear, but colours are extremely vivid and strong and detail is satisfactory. The full frame compositions appear to be intact, so any possible cropping is extremely minimal. The disc also comes with chapter and song index pages, two very odd commercials, and the aforementioned theatrical trailer, which is almost worth the price of admission by itself.

GUNMAN IN THE STREETS

B&W, 1950, 88m. / Directed by Aleksandr Row / Starring Dane Clark, Simone Signoret / AllDay (US R1 NTSC)

A fascinating cross-pollination of cultures, *Gunman in the Streets* was made near the end of the traditional film noir era, just when the nihilist movie trend began to turn in on itself in films like *Kiss Me*

Deadly. A sort of tough guy twist on Hitchcock's *Notorious* with a few ripples of feminism (before such a thing even really existed), *Gunman* was shot in both English and French language versions; the former is represented on this DVD and was directed by noir veteran Frank Tuttle (*This Gun for Hire*). Never shown in the US until a repertory appearance last year, the film's enjoyment level will depend primarily on how familiar you are with both noir in America and its strong influence on European directors like Jean-Luc Godard, Jules Dassin, and François Truffaut.

Crime moll/high society dame Denise (*Diabolique*'s Simone Signoret) attempts to arrange for the escape of her lover, incarcerated bank robber Eddy Roback (*Destination Tokyo*'s Dane Clark), who has been sent up the river along with his gang of cohorts by the dogged Inspector Dufresne (Fernand Gravet). Denise uses her charms on naive reporter Frank Clinton (Robert Duke), whose role in Eddy's getaway proves to be far more complicated than Denise originally intended.

A perfectly respectable and accomplished crime film, *Gunman in the Streets* is more stylish and intriguing than the *Scarface*-style cover art might lead consumers to believe. The Parisian setting adds considerably to the novelty value, but the real trump card of course is the young Signoret, who was shortly to become an international star. Despite its lack of a US release, the film was evidently successful enough to merit a remake twenty-five years later by Serge Leroy, starring Mimsy Farmer and Michel Lonsdale under its original French title, *La Traque*.

Once again AllDay has given the royal treatment to a title most other studios would have probably shrugged off without a second glance. Their transfer of *Gunman* is a class act all the way, retaining all of the lustre in the original black and white photography while admirably capturing the grit of the street scenes. According to a 43 second supplement reel, the film was censored upon export to the UK but is presented intact here; the extra bits of brutality mostly involve some pulled punches and a protracted bullet removal sequence, mostly shown in apostrophe. The violence is low by today's standards, but it's easy to see how some of the queasier moments might have been a bit much at the time. Extras include the aforementioned censor reel, a photo gallery of (mostly awful) poster art and stills, production notes, and a nice booklet consisting of the original pressbook art.

HALLOWEEN

Colour, 1978, 93m. / Directed by John Carpenter / Starring Jamie Lee Curtis, Donald Pleasence / Anchor Bay (US R0 NTSC, UK R2 PAL) / WS (2.35:1) (16:9) / DD5.1

 The ultimate seasonal horror film, *Halloween* put a lot of names on the map, most notably director / writer / composer John Carpenter, star Jamie Lee Curtis, and amazing cinematographer Dean Cundey. At the time *Halloween* justifiably earned a reputation as the scary movie to see and influenced a slew of inferior imitations that continue to plague audiences in the post-modern '90s. And then, of course, there are the sequels.

Fifteen years ago (ah, love those timeless mad killer movies), little Michael Myers stabbed his sister to death on Halloween night and wound up in an asylum. In the present day, he escapes on October 30 when his doctor, Sam Loomis (Donald Pleasence), comes to visit. Loomis believes Michael is heading back to his hometown, Haddonfield, Illinois, for another night of carnage. Meanwhile, three likable teenage girls - Laurie Strode (Curtis), Lynda (P.J. Soles from *Carrie* and *Rock 'n' Roll High School*), and Annie (Nancy Loomis from The Fog) - are stalked by Michael as they prepare for a Halloween evening of babysitting, scary movies, and covertly making out with boyfriends. As Michael draws closer and the night grows darker, only one survivor remains to battle for her life against the masked, wordless killer.

Though the actual body count and gore content are refreshingly low, Carpenter keeps events moving at a fever pitch thanks to a very sharp script and some spectacularly manipulative mobile camerawork. Unlike many directors who simply use the horror genre as a calling card to "bigger and better" things, Carpenter and company obviously love the genre and honour its rules while creating a few new ones of their own. Amazingly, each setpiece builds perfectly upon the last and creates a cumulative effect of relentless terror during the final half hour, one of the grand tour de forces of '70s filmmaking. Not surprisingly, this remains one of the most profitable independent films ever made and, in the process, revolutionized the process of movie production and distribution.

Few films make better use of widescreen framing than *Halloween*, though home viewers were unable to see a good scope version until Criterion's special edition CAV laserdisc in 1995. During the shooting of *Halloween II*, Carpenter also filmed three sequences to insert into the original film for its network premiere on NBC, and Criterion included these fullscreen scenes as supplements on the disc. Anchor Bay subsequently issued a letterboxed version on DVD, containing only the trailer, and the result immediately earned the scorn of many viewers as the most riddled-riddled major film on the DVD market. Obviously anxious to make amends, Anchor Bay prepared a lavish special edition, two disc DVD set. So how does it stack up to previous editions? Most obviously, the transfer (approved by THX, which doesn't count for much these days but is still a nice gesture) blows away the previous DVD, and it's even anamorphically enhanced to provide an even more detailed and enveloping experience. The Criterion laser transfer looked great to begin with, but Anchor Bay's improves upon it even more by providing a smoother, darker, and richer visual texture. One minor quibble: when played non-anamorphic on a standard television, the black letter-boxing bars are actually two slightly different shades, with the area roughly inside the 1.85:1 matte area a slightly lighter and bluer hue. It's not a huge visual problem, but it is a strange one.

Much more obvious (in a good way) is the 5.1 remix, a startling audio overhaul that allows this film to even scare viewers who know the movie by heart. Carpenter's shameless musical "stings" burst from various speakers, and that unforgettable music has never sounded better. A standard surround and the original mono soundtracks are also included.

The disc also features a half hour documentary, "*Halloween* Unmasked 2000," including interviews with most of the principal players. Though sketchy at times, this featurette makes for a satisfying addition to Myers video memorabilia, and it's nice to see that everyone still holds nothing but fond memories for the film. (The *Touch of Evil* analogy is especially interesting.)

The real coup for Anchor Bay, however, lies on the second disc, available only in a limited pressing. Disc two contains the complete feature with the extra television footage reinstated back into the film. Though you'd never know it from earlier editions, the TV footage was actually filmed in scope and looks terrific, merging seamlessly into the rest of the film. The expanded version runs 101 minutes, and many a Myers fan will find this treat long overdue. Even this alternate version is 16:9 enhanced (though mono), so hats off for going that extra mile even on the extras. Other bonuses include the original and reissue trailers, TV and radio spots, a still gallery, and a small series of trivia tidbits. And watch out for those menu screens! To put it mildly, Anchor Bay has been doing the creepiest menus around (also see

H

Hell Night, Phenomena, and *Demons*), and this is no exception. The first disc will also be available separately at a lower price, but the expanded version is really worth the extra money for anyone who can afford it. However, anyone with the CAV laser would be wise to hold on to it for a number of reasons. Most obviously the laser contains a very entertaining running commentary with Carpenter, Hill, and Curtis, and it's too bad Anchor Bay couldn't license it for their edition. The laser also features a number of interesting extras, particularly a snippet from the notorious episode of *Sneak Previews* in which Siskel and Ebert praise *Halloween* to the skies while trashing a number of other films like *Friday the 13th* and *I Spit on Your Grave*. Obviously it's not worth spending a fortune on now, but the laser remains a valuable part of any completist's horror movie library.

HALLOWEEN 4: THE RETURN OF MICHAEL MYERS

Colour, 1988, 83m. / Directed by Dwight H. Little / Starring Donald Pleasence, Danielle Harris / Anchor Bay (US R1 NTSC, UK R2 PAL) / WS (1.85:1) (16:9) / DD5.1

 The strongest of the *Halloween* sequels, this film repairs much of the damage done by the sluggish and notoriously problematic *Halloween II* while obviously ignoring the unrelated *Halloween III: Season of the Witch*. While John Carpenter had nothing to do with this film, which was simply intended as a seasonal cash-in on the famous slasher franchise, most horror fans were pleasantly surprised by the level of craftsmanship on display here. Most of the credit probably belongs to director Dwight Little, who also helmed the flawed but extremely stylish 1989 version of *Phantom of the Opera* and two of the more visually interesting action films of the period, *Rapid Fire* and *Marked for Death*, before settling into a career doing TV series like *The Practice*. Little obviously knows his stuff, throwing in countless little touches that fans of the original film will appreciate and even pulling off a large number of genuinely effective scares along the way.

On a dark and stormy night (of course), Michael Myers escapes during his transportation from one asylum to another in Illinois. Followed as always by the dogged Dr. Loomis (Donald Pleasence, inexplicably burned only slightly from the final conflagration of the previous Myers entry), Michael heads back to Haddonfield where he stalks his niece, Jamie (Danielle Harris). Of course, everyone who stands in his way meets a grisly end, courtesy of John Carl Buechler's rubbery skull-puncturing latex effects (most of which were mercifully cut before the film's release to ensure an R rating).

Though nowhere near the original, *Halloween 4* stands quite nicely on its own and looks even better in the wake of the three substandard sequels that followed it. Alan Howarth's judicious use of the original musical theme works perfectly (seeing this in the theatre with a large crowd is a really special experience), and Harris and Cornell make sympathetic young heroines. Most interestingly, this is that rare horror film in which the police are called in early on to the scene, but even that doesn't stop Michael on his rampage. The twist ending, while hardly original to this film, caps things off nicely without resorting to the usual back from the dead killer routine.

Anchor Bay's presentation of *Halloween 4* improves on the previous Fox version in every respect. Originally filmed with a hard matte at 1.85:1 (not in scope, surprisingly enough for a *Halloween* title), the entire image is accurately transferred with much greater clarity and truer colours. While the Fox version had a vaguely gauzy, grainy texture, this version looks quite sharp and colourful, marred only by the limited resources of the film stock used for such a low budget. The Ultra-Stereo soundtrack sounds fine in its 5.1 incarnation, basically a straight surround-style presentation with music and ambient effects shunted to the exterior channels. The original theatrical trailer is included, while the more common special edition (packaged in an Amaray or tin) also includes "Final Cut," a retrospective featurette that covers the bases well enough. Avoid the earlier non-anamorphic Anchor Bay disc and the first UK DVD from Digital Entertainment, both of which feature less satisfying transfers.

HAMMER HOUSE OF HORROR

Colour, 1980, 672m. / Directed by Tom Clegg, Peter Sasdy, Alan Gibson, Don Leaver, Don Sharp, Robert Young, Francis Megahy / Starring Peter Cushing, Denholm Elliott, Jon Finch / A&E (US R1 NTSC)

 After taking their final theatrical bow in 1979 with a remake of *The Lady Vanishes*, Hammer Films attempted to break into the television market with a 13 episode series entitled *Hammer House of Horror* in 1980.

Featuring many notable British film and television actors and several familiar horror faces behind the camera as well, the series failed to make much of a splash despite its generally superior production levels for the time. Though not genuinely frightening, the series contains enough macabre flourishes and strong doses of nudity and violence to make it a fascinating anomaly in the horror anthology sweepstakes.

The four-disc DVD box set from A&E begins with "Witching Time," in which Jon Finch (*Frenzy*) becomes drawn into the realm of black magic by a seductive witch, Patricia Quinn *(Rocky Horror*'s Magenta), who turns up naked in his barn. A promising if uneven starter for the show, this feels much like mid-'70s Hammer with plentiful bare flesh and grue on display. More subdued is "The Thirteenth Reunion," a darkly comic conspiracy tale about a weight loss retreat in the country with a gruesome agenda buried among its members. The clever "Rude Awakening," a highlight of the first disc, offers a sort of nightmarish alternative to Groundhog Day as Denholm Elliott (in an excellent performance) finds himself trapped in a seemingly endless Chinese box scenario of recurring nightmares.

Disc two kicks off with "Growing Pains," in which a couple brings a new child into their home after their son accidentally chugs some chemicals in his father's lab. Naturally the new cuckoo in the nest turns out to be quite a bad seed indeed. Amazingly, "The House that Bled to Death" contains nary a drop of blood as it follows an unfortunate couple (Nicholas Ball and Rachel Davies) through the terrors of moving into a new, cursed home. Finally, "Charlie Boy" takes a British twist on the Zuni fetish doll episode from Trilogy of Terror, with an African doll (which alas doesn't run around the house) bringing all sorts of misfortune on its new owners.

In "The Silent Scream," the first episode on disc three, Hammer vet Peter Cushing stars as an unhinged pet store owner conducting elaborate behavioural control experiments in the massive basement beneath his store. Eventually he decides to broaden his scope to humans, namely a recently released parolee (a young Brian Cox) whose girlfriend becomes suspicious following his abrupt disappearance. Interestingly, Clive Barker must have seen this before writing his haunting *Books of Blood* short story, "Dread," with which this shares a few interesting similarities. "Children of the Full Moon" relies on that reliable chestnut, a couple stranded out in the middle of nowhere, to launch into a twisted, Angela Carter-style tale about preteen werewolves raised in an English manor under the supervision of former Euro sex kitten Diana Dors. Finally, "The Carpathian Eagle" concerns a murderess who slashes open her lovers in bed; is she a real person or the remnant of a horrible supernatural secret? Look for a small role for future 007 Pierce Brosnan in this, one of the most lurid and overstuffed episodes in the series.

In the style of A&E's Avengers DVD series, the fourth disc tacks on one extra episode to complete the series. "Guardian of the Abyss" finds a young woman tearing through the woods and escaping by car with an antique dealer (Ray Lonnen); both of them soon become involved in the machinations of a sinister cult. Though heavily indebted to Hammer's earlier classic, The Devil Rides Out, this is still one of the stronger and more atmospheric entries in the series and concludes on an appropriately baroque note. The more traditional "Visitor from the Grave" finds poor Penny (Kathryn Leigh Scott), recently released from an institution, shooting a man to death when he tries to attack her in her bedroom. Her husband (Simon MacCorkindale) covers up the crime when the police arrive, but soon she's seeing the deceased in the most unfortunate public places. The mechanical double twist ending is effective if not entirely successful. A family of three finds tragedy in "Two Faces of Evil" when a violent car wreck sends the father (Gary Raymond) into the hospital. He returns home in severely damaged condition but doesn't seem to be quite the same person... Is something diabolical afoot? Finally, the most berserk and perplexing episode of the bunch, "The Mark of Satan," features Peter McEnery as a morgue worker who believes he has been implanted with a disease engineered to bring about Satan's work on earth. Dream sequences, baby eating, and a rough-looking Georgina Hale are just a few of the ingredients in this helter skelter stew.

Two of Hammer's most underrated veteran directors, Peter Sasdy (*Countess Dracula*) and Don Sharp, do a fine job with their multiple turns on the series, and generally the actors acquit themselves well even when the stories are stretched out past the breaking point. The prevailing atmosphere resembles that of other British programs from the same era, particularly *The New Avengers*, in its misguided but striking attempts to reel in the youth audience while paying lip service to classic traditions from an earlier generation. Overall, it's a worthwhile experience bearing in mind the peculiar situation from which it sprang. Most interesting is the fact, while most Hammer Films opted for relatively happy and conventional endings after offering the audience its requisite amount of thrills and spills, this television incarnation usually features dark, pessimistic twists at the end, leaving the viewer feeling unsettled. No doubt inspired by the bleak vantage points of such hits as *The Omen* and *The Stepford Wives*, this move was to be later adopted by American TV horror on such series as *Tales from the Darkside* and the short-lived but memorable *Darkroom*.

Not surprisingly, the transfers here are a quantum leap above the blurry, unattractive video editions from the mid-'80s. Detail and colour are perfectly rendered and look surprisingly fresh, though the conversion from what appears to be a PAL source results in some obvious ghosting during fast motion scenes. Those familiar with the show from cable or VHS will be surprised at some of the nudity and bloodshed restored here; in fact, the very first episode kicks off with quite an eyeful. The problematic mono sound shares flaws inherent in the original program recording, namely muted and sometimes unintelligible dialogue bookended by loud, brash passages of music. "The Silent Scream" suffers from this in particular, given Cox's tendency to mumble right down his chin. Each disc also contains a Hammer filmography; amazingly, the boxes offer no plot synopses, opting instead for the same overview on each sleeve and a brief listing of the episode title, two or three stars, and the director. A little more effort bonus-wise to put the show in its historical context would have been helpful, but the simple availability of this program, flaws and all, offers a fascinating and welcome addition to any horror lover's library, Hammer or otherwise.

THE HARDER THEY COME

Colour, 1973, 98m. / Directed by Perry Henzell / Starring Jimmy Cliff, Janet Barkley / Criterion (US R1 NTSC) / WS (1.66:1)

Even after nearly three decades of widespread familiarity with Jamaican culture, the opening moments of *The Harder They Come* are still electric with the feeling of cinematic discovery. A bus slowly ambles through the streets of Kingston, where fruit sellers, young boys, and colourfully dressed women conduct their daily business despite the hardships around them. No glossed over travelogue, this film would be a landmark achievement for its setting alone, but there's much more. Underneath this scenery, Jimmy Cliff exuberantly sings the first song, "You Can Get It If You Really Want It," a damnably catchy little number, and thus a new kind of gangster film is

born. Country boy Ivan (Cliff), a struggling singer in Kingston, attempts to obtain a record contract and cut some demo tracks. However, the other hungry artists around him diminish his own hopes of success, and he resorts to menial handiwork at a local church to earn a little cash. The church's preacher has a female charge, Elsa, who snags Ivan's eye, and she becomes part of his inspiration to succeed. Eventually he records some tracks but is discouraged by the insulting offer of $20 per song. After a nasty scuffle at the church which leads to a bloody crime of passion, Ivan is incarcerated and released. However, fate conspires against him, turning him into a ganja dealer and a criminal on the lam as his music simultaneously becomes an anthem for the people, ironically earning him a national voice as he falls deeper into trouble with the law.

The mixture of crime drama, folk hero lore, and musical could easily have proven disastrous, but somehow the dynamic Cliff and director Henzell manage to pull it off. *The Harder They Come* moves very quickly, with enough elements for the various sectors of the audience to keep just about anyone happy. There's a love story, lots of shooting, drug elements, memorable music, and lush scenery, all perfectly balanced and edited. No wonder the record became a smash hit and put reggae music on the map. The only drawback is the extremely thick patois accents, which have been known to turn off viewers even with the presence of subtitles. (In some prints Cliff's character is referred to as "Juan" for some reason.) Even more confounding is the sound mix itself, which features only dialogue recorded on the spot during shooting. Therefore, if someone mumbles or a truck passes by, well, that's the way you hear it. Luckily Criterion's DVD features optional English subtitles (which still feature more than a few captions reading "[inaudible]") to help viewers adjust to the dialect; it's well worth the effort.

The Criterion DVD features a slightly sharper variation on the letterboxed print they released on laserdisc. For an early '70s low budget film it looks fairly good, with vivid colours and enough detail to compensate for the flaws in the film stock. It certainly beats the various VHS editions floating around from Xenon and other companies. The mono audio also sounds at least as good as it did in theatres, though inexplicably the sound has been relegated to the centre channel only and cannot be split to the front channels in Dolby Digital playback. Some good extras put the film in its historical context, such as a video interview with Island Records founder Chris Blackwell, who was instrumental in getting the film exposed to American audiences. Henzell and Cliff also appear for an audio commentary during the feature in which they elaborate on the social conditions at the time, the intentions they had while making the film, and the various ways music was recorded and manipulated for the final result. The disc also includes some solid liner notes and a discography/filmography guide to the primary musicians who appear in the film and on the soundtrack.

A HATCHET FOR THE HONEYMOON

Colour, 1969, 83m. / Directed by Mario Bava / Starring Stephen Forsyth, Laura Betti / Image (US R0 NTSC) / WS (1.66:1)

Lurid title aside, *A Hatchet for the Honeymoon* is one of Mario Bava's lightest and most playful thrillers, a demented black comedy that pokes fun at the murderous psychos which were littering the European cinema screens during the late '60s. This approach may be jarring for anyone expecting a standard stalk and slash marathon; instead, willing Euro film fans will be rewarded with a beautifully filmed drawing room murder tale which unexpectedly leaps midstream into a bizarre and wholly original ghost story.

Returning once again to the colourful fashion salon setting of his classic *Blood and Black Lace*, Bava introduces us in the opening to his handsome killer, John Harrington (Stephen Forsyth, who bears an eerie resemblance to John Phillip Law in Bava's previous film, Diabolik). John devotes most of his time to running the fashion business begun by his late mother, while his shrewish wife, Mildred (Laura Betti), sits around all day and berates him for not being a real man. John's fashion specialty is wedding dresses, and he becomes unnaturally attached to his female models - so much so that he hacks them up and disposes of their remains in the nearby hot house whenever they intend to get married and leave their jobs. The police naturally become suspicious after a few women disappear but are helpless without any solid evidence. Finally fed up with Mildred, he bumps her off with his cleaver and buries her body, but unfortunately, this particular victim has no intention of resting in piece.

Originally released in Italy as *The Red Sign of Madness (Il rosso sengo della folia), A Hatchet for the Honeymoon* is as visually impressive and technically accomplished as one would expect from a Bava thriller. The fractured narrative allows him to experiment with a number of different styles, such as

the hallucinatory flashbacks John experiences every time he kills; as the pieces involving his past fall into place, the flashbacks become less delirious. The fetishistic wedding imagery also makes for some striking set pieces, such as John's impressive murderous waltz among bridal mannequins with Italian starlet Femi Benussi. While Forsyth does fine as the charming lunatic (an interesting precursor to Christian Bale's *American Psycho*), the great Laura Betti walks off with the film as the vengeful Mildred. It's no wonder Bava was willing to bring her back two years later for *Twitch of the Death Nerve*. Other notable aspects include an early appearance by the gorgeous Dagmar Lassander, who had a thriving Italian film career through the '70s and '80s, and stunning music by Sante Maria Romitelli (his first and best score). Bava fans should be especially amused by a cameo clip from the "Wurdulak" segment of his *Black Sabbath*, which actually plays a role in the plot of this film! Since *Hatchet* largely avoids onscreen gore and violence in the first place, the film has experienced few censorship problems over the years. In fact, its US release received a PG rating (or GP as it was called at the time), with the MPAA card still present at the beginning of this DVD edition.

Various video labels have taken a crack at this title over the years, largely with unimpressive results, so the Image DVD is, relatively speaking, the best so far. The print's colours and detail are miles ahead of previous video transfers, and the letterboxed framing looks dead on. However, the source material is not pristine, with scratches and speckles evident at several points and some hefty soundtrack distortion evident whenever the music swells up for an emotional moment. Casual viewers probably won't be bothered, and bear in mind it's great to have this film in decent condition on DVD at all. The disc also includes some lengthy and very informative liner notes and the usual helping of Bava bio/filmography facts.

HÄXAN

Colour Tinted, 1922, 104m. / Directed by Benjamin Christensen / Starring Astrid Holm, Karen Winther / Criterion (US R1 NTSC) / DD5.0

Those who think horror films before the 1960s were stodgy, lightweight affairs should be quickly directed to Benjamin Christensen's jaw-dropping *Häxan*, later reissued as *Witchcraft through the Ages* in

H

1967 with William S. Burroughs narration and an experimental, jazz-influenced score. Like most silent films, this cheeky, horrific look at witchcraft as a form of mania has endured in various forms over the years, though fortunately no amount of tinkering can dilute its peculiar power.

Ostensibly beginning as a documentary, *Häxan* begins with woodcuts and period recreations to depict the rise of witchcraft in medieval times, where demons were said to roam the land and interfere with the lives of peasants. Through a series of vignettes we see the interaction of clergy and witches, with the priests either persecuting their satanic foes, suffering from the onslaught of demonic forces, or even complying with the supernatural agents. Witch hunting is depicted in an unflattering light not unlike Carl Dreyer's later *Day of Wrath*, and even Satan himself makes a cameo with the director made up in an elaborate, terrifying facsimile of a woodcut monster. Nocturnal witches' Sabbats, meals made of toads and children, and other unsavoury elements are depicted for the viewer's edification before a truly bizarre finale, which makes analogies between witchcraft and modern day technology.

A difficult film to describe, *Häxan* flows along like a waking dream. Alternating between hallucinatory nightmare, black humour, and straight faced documentation, the film is never less than visually stunning and contains more imaginative visuals than any ten Hollywood blockbusters combined. Christensen would later make a brief, unspectacular move to America where he directed the rare, highly sought after *Seven Footprints to Satan* before returning to Denmark to finish out his career. Incidentally, fragments of the film later made their way into Dwain Esper's 1934 exploitation legend, *Maniac*, which is just as amazing in an entirely different way. Commonly screened in its 76-minute incarnation with the Burroughs narration, *Häxan* has run as long as 125 minutes on home video in its slowed down VHS edition from Video Yesteryear.

The Criterion DVD is a quantum leap in visual quality over the ragged prints and dupey tapes collectors have had to endure; according to the liner notes, it was transferred from a restoration overseen by the Swedish Film Institute. As with their presentation of *The Passion of Joan of Arc*, the original foreign language intertitles have been left intact with optional subtitles in English placed at the bottom of the screen. This method takes some adjustment at first, but after a couple of minutes the eye can be trained to read the lower text, not the words in the middle of the screen. The tinting is surprisingly effective, with a hellish rosy red glow rendered over interior scenes and a chilly blue tint added to the exterior scenes, which mostly take place at night anyway. Image quality is very crisp and clean for a film of its vintage, and the expected speckling and tearing is nowhere to be found.

The Dolby 5.0 musical accompaniment (with explanatory text included from its organizer, Gillian Anderson) compiles numerous classical selections used in the film's premiere screening, and indeed the music enhances the off-kilter, mystical mood of the film quite well. The audio separation is beautifully rendered and keeps the film moving along even during some of the earlier historical scenes, which can be a tad dry. On a second audio track Casper Tybjerg explains the history behind the film, the production methods used by Denmark and Sweden at the time, and the various permutations of the film after its release. Generally interesting both as a look at this film and a portrait of Danish cinema at the time, this is a solid track well in keeping with the Criterion tradition.

Other extras include Christensen's onscreen intro to the film (tacked on for its unlikely 1941 reissue which probably didn't find much favour with audiences poised for war), a gallery of woodcuts, historical artwork, and texts which influenced the film's visual scheme, a smattering of outtake footage including shots of Christensen rehearsing a flying sequence, and another gallery of promotional and production stills. Of course, the biggest bonus is the alternate Burroughs version, with optional English subtitles to caption the narration. Obviously much speedier without intertitles and trimmed down a bit to focus on the "good stuff," this is the most widely seen version of the film in many countries and still holds up as a handy distillation. Image quality of this black and white edition is fine and certainly an improvement over the PD tapes, though it's in rougher condition than the Swedish edition. Overall, the original version of *Häxan* remains the strongest and contains the most immediacy for viewers who have grown accustomed to taking their horror with a solid dose of irony, wit, and visual flair.

HEAT

Colour, 1972, 100m. / Directed by Paul Morrissey / Starring Joe Dallesandro, Sylvia Miles / Image (US R1 NTSC)

Basically an acknowledged campy riff on Billy Wilder's *Sunset Boulevard*, *Heat* represents the transition in Morrissey's career from formless deadpan character sketches to traditional linear

storylines. This change is due in no small part to the presence of an established actress, Sylvia Miles (*Midnight Cowboy*), who stamps the celluloid with her persona in much the same way as Carroll Baker in *Andy Warhol's Bad*. Down on his luck actor Joe Dallesandro portrays another variation on his jaded yet childlike hustler persona, this time entangled in the web of faded hack actress Miles and an assortment of bizarre inhabitants at the florid hacienda hotel where most of the film was shot.

Morrissey floods every frame with sunlight, sweating flesh, and tropical colours, making this a quantum leap in artistic terms over his patented "nail down the camera and shoot whatever moves" technique in the early Warhol titles. Cult fanatics may be disappointed by a relative toning down of outrageous sequences (aside from a couple of amusing and lewd poolside encounters), at least in comparison to *Trash*, but the witty dialogue and improved acting more than make up for it. In particular, the final scene hilariously parodies its Hollywood origins and makes one wonder what on earth Morrissey could have done if Gloria Swanson had still been around...

HEAVEN

Colour, 1998, 103m. / Directed by Scott Reynolds / Starring Martin Donovan, Joanna Going / Miramax (US R1 NTSC) / WS (2.35:1) / DD2.0

The second feature film from New Zealand director Scott Reynolds (*The Ugly*), *Heaven* never got a chance to find its audience in theatres. Robert Marling (Martin Donovan), an architect, has moved out from his estranged wife, Jennifer (played by *Dark Shadows'* Joanna Going), to an isolated apartment where he spends most of his nights gambling at a local club with the brutish Stanner (Richard Schiff). Meanwhile, Jennifer is fighting for sole custody of her and Robert's child, Sean, and has begun an affair with the couple's slimy therapist (Patrick Malahide). One night after a hefty win, Robert stumbles into an alleyway and inadvertently stops two thugs from beating up Heaven (Danny Edwards), a psychic transvestite stripper (yes, you read that correctly) who works at Stanner's club. In return, Heaven strikes up a tender friendship with Robert and, using her powers of foresight, offers him some helpful advice on the card game the following evening. Unfortunately, Heaven's visions become increasingly violent and sinister, and as she explains, she can only see the future, not change it.

In many ways *Heaven* picks up where *The Ugly* left off, telling a similarly fragmented narrative related with scenes frequently cut into each other and out of sequence. While this approach could easily become a confusing stunt in lesser hands, the effect here is often devastating as the viewer begins to simulate Heaven's own precognitive abilities and piece together the various characters and events into an emotionally resonant whole. Also like *The Ugly*, Reynolds adopts notably skilful colour coding to provoke a separate response for each character and location: the unearthly blue walls crowned with flickering lights in the club, the suffused gold of a posh restaurant, the lime green decor of a apartment. Though impressive, the visual panache only serves the story instead of overwhelming it, a very welcome change from the "style for style's sake" method.

The performers are all well up to the demands of the intricate script, with Hal Hartley regular Donovan in particular delivering yet another in his run of outstanding performances. His sudden joyous outburst after his big win is worth the price of admission alone. In the tricky role of Heaven, Edwards mixes fear and defiance equally well, preventing the character from becoming an echo of Dil in *The Crying Game*. In fact, despite the strong violence throughout (and particularly during the climax), the cumulative effect of *Heaven* is a compassionate, unusually sensitive portrait of well-meaning, flawed people who deserve to have fate deal them a good hand.

Miramax's DVD is simply the only way to see *Heaven* outside of a theatre. Carefully filmed in scope, the compositions would be completely wrecked in a cropped VHS transfer but look nicely preserved here. The Dolby surround soundtrack features some nice if unspectacular directional effects, with Victoria Kelly's elegiac score contributing most of the rear channel activity. Though non-anamorphic, the image quality is consistently satisfying and film-like, with rich colours and detail and no over-reliance on digital enhancement in the transfer process.

Oddly, the trailer has not been included, though it was available as a download from Miramax's website at the time of the film's release. Unfortunately Reynolds failed to live up to the promise of this film with his next effort, the disheartening *When Strangers Appear*, available from Columbia on DVD.

HELL NIGHT

Colour, 1981, 101m. / Directed by Tom DeSimone / Starring Linda Blair, Vincent Van Patten / Anchor Bay (US R1 NTSC), Odyssey (UK R2 PAL) / WS (1.85:1) (16:9)

 Usually dismissed as yet another Halloween clone, in retrospect *Hell Night* plays more like a charming gothic throwback to those old teens in a castle/haunted house movies like *The Headless Ghost*, albeit laced with a little '80s gore and mild sexiness to spice things up. Furthermore, freed from the need to deliver a massive body count, the creative parties involved (both director DeSimone and cinematographer Ahlberg, who also lensed most of Stuart Gordon's films) delivered a visually beautiful film, crammed with elegant and sometimes startling touches that often defy logic (the constant armies of lit candles, for instance, and some of the plot developments in the final act). While not a classic by any means, *Hell Night* outranks the pedestrian slasher efforts of the period and has fortunately managed to withstand the test of time.

Any semblance of plot is quickly handled in the first fifteen minutes, which finds four college pledges forced to spend Hell Night in Garth mansion, where the owner killed his wife and three of his four children twelve years earlier. The disfigured youngest son, so the legend goes, continues to roam the house, which lacks such features as electricity and a telephone. Our virginal heroine, Marti (Linda Blair, doing a nice job), pairs up with the nice guy, Jeff (Peter Barton of *Friday the 13th: The Final Chapter* and TV's *The Powers of Matthew Starr*). Meanwhile, naughty boy Seth (*Rock 'n' Roll High School*'s Vincent Van Patten) chases after druggie slut Denise (Suki Goodwin), so the latter two spend most of the film in their skivvies. Meanwhile, some frat and sorority pranksters sneak around outside the house to play tricks on the four victims but wind up being dispatched themselves by a hulking killer. Will our resourceful quartet of pledges make it out alive before dawn?

In *Hell Night*, setting and atmosphere are everything. The tale of Garth at the beginning is delivered as a host of costumed teens wander through the nocturnal gardens of the estate, a nice sequence that gives an indication of the stylish events to come. Blair makes a better than average heroine; in one particularly nice touch, she reveals that she's an amateur mechanic, setting up a moment during the especially nice and refreshing moment during the

climax. The finale itself is especially rousing and well delivered without the requisite endless series of fake endings ("He's dead! Wait, he's not! Oh yeah, he is!").

The DVDs from Anchor Bay and Odyssey far surpass what anyone could have expected for this film. The previous VHS version from Media completely opened the upper and lower matte, exposing the boom mic and numerous other goofs that made viewing this an unintentional comedy. Fortunately, the hard matte improves the compositions tremendously, and the image quality is superb, especially considering how bad most early '80s low budget films look. Likewise, the mono soundtrack has been nicely presented; it won't blow anyone away, but it gets the job done.

A far too revealing theatrical trailer and TV spots have also been included, but the real treat is running commentary by Blair, producers Yablans and Curtis, and director DeSimone, who dabbled in everything from hardcore porn to women in prison films and TV shows. Quite a career, and he provides some good insights into the perils and pleasures of undertaking a maverick horror film for an indie producer. Blair also makes some insightful and positive comments about the project, indicating she probably has about as much affection for this as Jamie Lee does for *Halloween*. While this film did surprisingly well at the box office, the promised *Hell Night II* never materialized, which may be a good thing as it has allowed this underrated little film to continue standing on its own significant merits.

HELL OF THE LIVING DEAD

Colour, 1983, 103 m. / Directed by Bruno Mattei / Starring Margit Evelyn Newton, Frank Garfield / Anchor Bay (US R0 NTSC) / WS (1.85:1) (16:9), Vipco (UK R2 PAL) / WS (1.85:1)

 While the zombie films of Lucio Fulci were busy traumatizing audiences around the world, Bruno Mattei's insane *Hell of the Living Dead* managed to ride along on a wave of unrated ultra-violence. Its zero budget, patchwork construction desperate to ape the success of George Romero's *Dawn of the Dead* (right down to cribbing its Goblin score along with a handful of the band's other cues from *Contamination*), this film played unrated in the US as *Night of the Zombies* and in the UK as *Zombie Creeping Flesh*. Granted, the film does deliver gore in spades, but that's probably the least interesting thing about it.

A chemical lab in New Guinea is sent into an uproar when two of the co-workers accidentally unleash a contagion, thanks to interference of a pesky rat. Rampant flesh eating madness ensues as this company, designed to provide for its third world environment, instead unleashes zombies on the jungle dwelling populace. The International Criminal Police Organization sends a four member team into the fray, led by the intrepid Mike London (Frank Garfield); while not busy trading wisecracks, the men collide with female reporter Lia (Margit Evelyn Newton), an expert on local customs who goes undercover with the natives by painting her naked body and mingling with National Geographic stock footage. After fighting the zombies for an eternity, the gunmen eventually figure out that the zombies must be shot in the head, but that doesn't help much as they continue to pump bullets into the shuffling undeads' chests. A lively zombie kid keeps things brewing, too, until we return once again to the chemical plant for the not too shocking final revelation.

Apart from the aforementioned stock footage, Mattei throws just about everything against the wall here to see what might stick. A little mondo footage, some nudity, some city mayhem, jungle mayhem, and in the oddest bit during the climax, one character turned into a human puppet, years before Peter Jackson did the same bit with *Brain Dead*. The surreal use of Goblin's music proves once and for all that even a good score can be turned to mush in the wrong context, and the hilarious dubbing never comes close to matching the actors' lip movements. God knows what language they were all speaking, considering the Spanish writers and international hodgepodge of performers, but the English voice artists decided to just goof off and cram in as many off the wall lines as they could. The film might be more sombre in its Italian incarnation, but it will take a hardy soul to examine both back to back.

Whatever its considerable debits as a film might be, *Hell of the Living Dead* fares remarkably well on DVD under Anchor Bay's guidance. The transfer improves miraculously over the muddy, grainy theatrical prints that have circulated over the past twenty years, and the less said about the murky VHS editions from Vestron and the like, the better. Most fans will be shocked to see how colourful Mattei's film really is, and at least the gore scenes improve considerably from the bright shades of crimson on display. (The bare bones UK release is non-anamorphic widescreen.)

Also included is a nine minute interview, "Hell Rats of the Living Dead" (also on AB's *Rats: Nights of Terror* disc), in which Mattei discusses his status as a filmmaker at the time and points out his influences and intentions. The bio by Mark Wickum covers the many odd bases of his career, which ranges from sci-fi to hardcore porn. Add to that a very long European theatrical trailer (which blows far too many highlights), some irreverent and often funny liner notes transcribing a conversation between *Shatter Dead* director Scooter McCrae and *Fangoria* editor Mike Gingold, and a poster/still gallery, and you've got a sure-fire recipe for one can't-miss party disc guaranteed to be a conversation piece for years to come.

THE HITCHER

Colour, 1986, 97m. / Directed by Robert Harmon / Starring Rutger Hauer, C. Thomas Howell / HBO (US R1 NTSC) / WS (2.35:1) (16:9) / DD5.1

You'd be hard pressed to name a mainstream film more atypical for the mid-'80s than *The Hitcher*, which died a quick box-office death but gradually won a large cult of admirers thanks to endless late night screenings on HBO. Brutal and uncompromising, this film gets down and dirty with the audience and pulls no punches, though like such films as *The Texas Chainsaw Massacre*, most of the gore is created in the audience's imaginations. Much like people still swear they saw the knife actually tear Janet Leigh's body in *Psycho*, theatregoers continue to insist they saw various gory snippets during the infamous truck-pulling scene. What sets this apart from standard slasher films is its relentless narrative drive, sort of a cross between *Duel* and *Candyman*, and the compelling script by Eric Red (who also penned the cult favourite vampire road film, *Near Dark*, and directed the less successful *Blood Moon*, also with Hauer, and *Body Parts*).

Jim Halsey (Howell), a Chicago kid transporting a drive-away car to San Diego, decides to relieve his late night road fatigue by picking up a hitchhiker during a rainstorm. The hitchhiker, John Ryder (Hauer), explains to Jim that the last man who picked him up is lying dismembered in his car down the road and that Jim will be next. After narrowly escaping with his life and continuing cross country, Jim is stalked by Ryder as he tears a bloody swath across the desert and frames Jim for the crimes. With the state troopers in hot pursuit, Jim finds the only person he can trust is a kindly waitress, Nash (Leigh), who puts her own life on the line to keep Jim from being killed by either side.

Designed as a macabre rite of passage into manhood, *The Hitcher* presents its villain as an almost supernatural force anxious to transmit its evil force on to Jim. "There's something funny going on between the two of you," one character observes late in the film, and Hauer and Howell (doing some of their best work here) make the entire bizarre metaphysical conflict all too believable and chilling. Leigh's delicately etched performance elicits quite a bit of sympathy from viewers, but... let's not spoil it. Mark Isham's moody New Age score eerily drifts in and out of the scenic desert landscape shots like an icy breeze, and Harmon does a fine job handling all the road action (whatever happened to him?).

Previous transfers have been mostly hit and miss. The US release from HBO on laser and VHS was watchable but badly pan and scanned and definitely on the soft side; the British widescreen release from Warner in 1997 restored the entire scope image but was noticeably less colourful. The DVD from HBO is a substantial improvement on all counts, though unfortunately the image is so crisply transferred that it exposes too much grain during some of the darker scenes. This quibble aside, the long overdue scope release of *The Hitcher* finally presents one of the '80s' most significant horror releases in a version approximating the harrowing theatrical experience, and hopefully this release will allow its reputation to continue to soar.

HOLLYWOOD CHAINSAW HOOKERS

Colour, 1988, 75m. / Directed by Fred Olen Ray / Starring Gunnar Hansen, Linnea Quigley, Michelle Bauer / Ventura (US R0 NTSC), Midnite Video (UK R0 PAL) / WS (1.85:1)

Well, you've gotta give 'em points for truth in advertising with this one. The title sums it all up quite nicely, as hookers played by scream queens terrorize the seedy backstreets of Hollywood by carving up their clients with chainsaws. As with other films by drive-in favourite Fred Olen Ray, *Hollywood Chainsaw Hookers* is deliberate kitsch all the way, too ridiculous to take seriously but gory and sexy enough to please exploitation buffs.

Our story begins with L.A. private dick Jack Chandler (Jay Richardson) allowing blonde runaway Samantha (Linnea Quigley) to crash out on his couch. He slowly thinks back on the events leading to his meeting with this waif, who has become entangled with a bizarre religious cult whose female members pick up unsuspecting johns for an evening of unabashed sex and dismemberment. The queen killer, Samantha (Michelle McLellan, aka Bauer), steals the film with her giddy sawfest in which a client's rubber body parts go flying and spatter blood across her Elvis Presley black velvet painting, carefully shielded in plastic. As the body count climbs, Jack and Samantha are drawn to the mysterious Temple, where the leader (*The Texas Chainsaw Massacre*'s Leatherface himself, Gunnar Hansen) oversees a surreal ritual involving chainsaw dancing and sacrifices. You can probably guess where this is all heading, of course: a catfight/chainsaw duel between scream queens Bauer and Quigley, a sequence that has earned its place in sleaze movie history books.

Like Ray's other films of the period like *Sorority Babes in the Slimeball Bowl-a-Rama*, this one tries so hard to please that it gets by on sheer energy alone. The filmmaking on display is your basic nail down the camera approach, but it's fun to see trashy L.A. locales adorned with horror goddesses in their prime. Add to that a campy soundtrack of pop tunes and more neon than an Alan Rudolph film, and you've got a unique time capsule of low budget indie horror before the whole industry wound up going straight to video.

Released under the banner of "Fred Olen Ray's Nite Owl Theatre," this fun interactive package kicks off with an intro shot in Ray's "mansion," in which he and several lovelies introduce the film while a couple of naked starlets play Twister on the floor. (Really.) The film itself looks about the same as the out of print Roan laserdisc, with a matted presentation cropping off the excess TV safe area from the full frame VHS edition. The compositions look a little better with the more "aesthetic" framing, but this isn't exactly a work of visual art in the first place. The visual texture is pretty gritty but colourful, in keeping with its ultra low budget roots, and audio is intelligible and free of distortion. Ray then returns after the film for a wrap up, followed by a giveaway for an *Evil Toons* animation cel. Other extras include trailers for this film, *Angel Eyes*, and *Fatal Justice*, and a "Making of" featurette consisting of shot on video interviews with Ray, Quigley, and Bauer. Ray gets in most of the best moments, including a funny closing demonstration of the film's British promotional campaign, which legally had to remove the word "Chainsaw" from the title in a ludicrous BBFC policy decision that has recently been overturned. Unfortunately, the poorly authored British disc release features no noteworthy extras apart from the reinstatement of the film's original title.

HORROR EXPRESS

Colour, 1972, 88m. / Directed by Eugenio Martin / Starring Christopher Lee, Peter Cushing / Image (US R0 NTSC) / WS (1.66:1)

Definitely not your typical Peter Cushing/Christopher Lee monster fest, *Horror Express* has long been a personal, secret favourite of late night TV fans and devoted videophiles. The very definition of both a great popcorn movie and a "thinking man's" horror/sci-fi opus, this gem actually possesses the ability to cross over and appeal far beyond die hard fans of European horror.

This Spanish/British co-production, lensed under the title of *Panic on the Trans-Siberian Express*, kicks off with a pompous English professor, Alexander Saxton (Lee), discovering a weird, hairy creature preserved in ice during an excavation in Manchuria. Believing this may be the missing link, Saxton stashes the icy fossil into a wooden crate and boards it onto his train ride back to Europe. On the same train is one of his academic rivals, Dr. Wells (Cushing), whose nosiness gets him into trouble when he bribes one of the coachmen to drill a whole into the box and see what's inside. A sinister, Rasputin-style monk notices that ordinary chalk cannot mark the creature's wooden prison and deduces that Saxton is harbouring something evil aboard the train. Meanwhile, passengers begin turning up with their eyes turned completely white and their brains, err, "wiped clean" of their memory. During one of his examinations, Wells comes upon a startling discovery... one that carries implications stretching beyond the boundaries of Planet Earth.

Directed with a skilful and stylish hand by Eugenio Martin (*A Candle for the Devil*), this film is pure entertainment and paced as steadily as the title vehicle. Apart from the two leads (both in top form), the cast includes a third act appearance by Telly Savalas (as a Cossack!) and an all too brief role for Eurosleaze starlet Helga Line (*Black Candles*). While some of the special effects are obviously dated now, it's to Martin's credit that the ferocious, scary climax still packs a wallop as the surviving passengers have to fight off both a horde of possessed zombies and a very precipitous cliff. Special mention must also be more of John Cacavas' haunting music score; once heard, that whistling theme is never forgotten.

Thanks to a legal technicality, *Horror Express* fell into the public domain and has been available from a number of different labels in shoddy, scratchy editions. One of the worst of these offenders was Simitar's DVD edition, one of the first titles to hit the market and a complete disaster from start to finish. Image rectified the problem with their drastically improved letterboxed DVD, which is the best this has ever looked on home video. The opening credits are still a bit scratchy and murky, evidently a flaw in all of the source materials ever used for this film, but after that it's a visual oasis of vivid, punchy colours: the luminous indigo of Line's dress, the bloody crimson of the dining compartment curtains, the burnished ochre of the oil lamps. The 1.66:1 framing looks perfect, and the audio is likewise clear and free of noise. The disc also offers a few other tidbits: an alternate Spanish language track (with some overdone studio dubbing); a most welcome isolated music and effects track, all the better to savour the film's creepy sound design; and thorough, informative liner notes detailing the production's amusing history.

HORROR HOSPITAL

Colour, 1973, 91m. / Directed by Antony Balch / Starring Michael Gough, Robin Askwith / Elite Entertainment (US R1 NTSC) / WS (1.85:1)

An obvious, gory attempt to cash in on the success of the *Dr. Phibes* films, *Horror Hospital* (also known as *Computer Killers* and *Doctor Bloodbath*) never musters up that same level of wit or twisted violence, but it certainly does try. Besides, any film offering a hammy lead role to horror veteran Michael Gough (now best known as Alfred in the *Batman* movies) is always worth a look.

Two escapees from a local hospital stumble down a lonely country road. Their heads are bloodily bandaged, and their torn clothes show signs of a violent struggle. A sleek car pulls up behind them, and the passenger in the back seat intones, "Make a clean job of it; after all, we just washed the car." Lo and behold, a blade springs out from the side of the automobile and lops off the escapees' heads. Thanks to a handy basket, the wicked doctor manages to catch the heads and decides to hold on to them for safekeeping. Shift gears now to Jason (Robin Askwith), a stereotypical early '70s mod rocker who decides to go to the country for a little R&R. On the train he meets the lovely Judy (Vanessa Shaw), niece of the eccentric Aunt Harris (Ellen Pollock). Jason and Judy strike up an immediate rapport and wind up staying at the hospital owned by Aunt Harris' husband, Dr. Storm (Gough). Unfortunately, it seems

Dr. Storm has taken to brain noodling with his visitors, and the young couple may very well be next on the list.

Filled with mordant black humour and largely inconsequential killings, including an appearance from Dennis Price (*Venus in Furs, Kind Hearts and Coronets*) solely designed for a sick, gory laugh, *Horror Hospital* at least delivers as a party movie. In the tradition of *Psychomania*, the lucky viewer also gets some '70s motorbikers and lots of outrageous hairstyles. Not to be taken seriously for one second, this gory cult item definitely won't appeal to the mainstream but should find more acceptance among devotees of European black humour.

Long unavailable on video after a brief, mediocre release on VHS from MPI, *Horror Hospital* looks much better on DVD than anyone could have possibly expected. The 1.85:1 framing looks balanced, removing only a sliver of extraneous information from the top and bottom while adding much to the sides, and the colour and richness of detail are excellent for an early '70s British title. The disc also includes the original trailer, which contains only one quick snippet of actual movie footage and mostly consists of some amusing voiceover hyperbole.

HORRORS OF SPIDER ISLAND

Colour, 1960, 77m. / Directed by Jamie Nolan (Fritz Böttger) / Starring Alex D'Arcy, Barbara Valentin / Image (US R0 NTSC) / WS (1.66:1)

 More familiar as a nonsensical episode of *Mystery Science Theatre 3000* than an actual movie, *Horrors of Spider Island* is one of the odder fusions of monster mashing and cheesecake girlie ogling from the early days of Euro exploitation. The German/Yugoslavian co-production was filmed as *Ein toter hing im netz (A Corpse Hangs in the Web)* but christened with the more direct *Horrors of Spider Island* for its general US assault on movie houses from coast to coast. However, a spicier adult variant called *It's Hot in Paradise* also surfaced, and it's under that title that this oft-maligned little slice of lunacy makes its digital debut.

The usual corral of ditzy girlie models winds up on a plane with burly, neckerchief-wearing Gary (Alex D'Arcy), but unfortunately their trip to Singapore is waylaid when they crash onto a seemingly deserted island. The girls, including the unbelievably over-voluptuous Babs (Barbara Valentin), pass the time by dishing out inane dialogue, catfighting, dancing, and skinny-dipping. Unfortunately they also discover a dead professor's body hanging in a huge spiderweb, and then poor Gary is nipped by an eight-legged horror out in the woods. Soon he's transformed into a fanged beast, running rampant through the island and scaring the poor models out of their wits.

While watchable even in its shortest version, *Horrors of Spider Island* becomes a delirious experience with the added nude swimming footage. The atrocious dubbing contains some of the more quotable one-liners around, while D'Arcy's weird but decidedly non-threatening monster makes up for the decided lack of actual arachnids onscreen. (D'Arcy also claimed to have directed most of the film, an achievement not too many Hollywood actors would be proud of.)

Something Weird's affectionate, lavishly produced DVD features a crisp (albeit oddly squeezed) transfer which maximizes the sweaty atmosphere imbedded in the glossy black and white photography. It's also easier than ever to spot the inserts of D'Arcy with monster make up, apparently shot in a completely different location. The disc includes another variation of their ad slick/radio spot combos, complete with tinted stills for this film, as well as a trio of slinky, eight-legged treats. "The Stripper and the Spider Girl" and "The Spider Girl" are your average surreal bump and grind routines, but the real treat is "Web of Love," a splashy, funky number in which chanteuse Joi Lansing cavorts with a guy who could have stepped from the pages of *Diabolik*. Thanks to the magic of DVD, we can now watch this one in pristine shape without the distraction of Mike and the robots; this one's loony and funny enough to stand quite well on its own, thank you very much.

HOT SUMMER

Colour, 1967, 91m. / Directed by Joachim Hasler / Starring Frank Schöbel, Chris Doerk / First Run Features (US R1 NTSC) / WS (2.35:1)

 How can a movie be thoroughly innocuous and compellingly weird at the same time? Look no further than *Hot Summer (Heisser Sommer)*, an East German rendition of the Frankie and Annette beach musicals pouring out from AIP during the 1960s. Apparently the Cold War and the grip of Communism in East Berlin had little effect on the spirits of beach-going youths who, according to this film, have little to think about besides kissing members of the opposite sex and dancing around in the countryside.

There isn't much actual plot to go around, but here's the idea. A group of nineteen Berlin "teens" decide to take a break from the "long, hot summer" in the city and hit the Baltic sea for some sun, romance, and frolicking in the waves. Crop-haired Stupsi (German pop star Chris Doerk) is wary of the boys and mockingly sings with her female companions about the wiles of those naughty rascals, while the boys (including hip-twisting singer Frank Schöbel) bicker and fight about who gets to pair up with whom once they meet the girls again at the ocean. Along the way boy meets girl, boy loses girl, and various couples dance in front of windmills, hop around inside haystacks, and sing to a comical St. Bernard. It's all very energetic and, well, very strange indeed.

Viewers of the fascinating story of Communist "tractor musicals," 1997's *East Side Story*, will have an inkling of what to expect from *Hot Summer*, though the film really needs to be experienced from start to finish for the full effect. Though most of the bodies on display are barely dressed, there's nary a flicker of real sexual desire in the entire film; at least Frankie and Annette managed to slip in a few double entendres here and there. Instead everyone seems intent on putting out as much energy as possible during their numbers, all of which are fortunately bouncy, catchy, and visually interesting. Director Joachim Hasler makes inventive use of the scope frame, another nod to the AIP beach films, as the performers line up in odd configurations and do unexpected things like hanging from windmill blades.

The nifty visual compositions are rendered quite well by the First Run DVD, which is framed at 2.35:1 but appears to be mildly cropped on the right side, judging from the cartoony opening credits. The elements seem to be slightly faded over the years, resulting in flesh tones that look a little off during outdoor scenes, but overall the presentation is quite nice and boasts a warm colour palette. The burned-in subtitles largely succeed in translated the songs with rhymes intact for English speaking viewers; inexplicably the disc also contains an optional subtitle track that doesn't seem to serve any function at all. Considering the limited means available, First Run's DVD is a good introduction to both *Hot Summer* and its offbeat national genre.

A bizarre music video short featuring Doerk in pigtails and animated segues comes off like a cross between *Wonderwall* and Lene Lovich; a DEFA promo devotes 11 minutes to highlights from the major East German cinema; and "Hot Summer Is Cult: An Introduction" places the entire film in its historical and cultural context. Hopefully this will be just the first of an ongoing look at Cold War era escapism, where even the most generic of genre imitations takes on a fascinating, delicious life of its own thanks to its home country's unique point of view.

HOUSE
Colour, 1985, 92m. / Directed by Steve Miner / Starring William Katt, George Wendt
HOUSE II: THE SECOND STORY
Colour, 1987, 88m. / Directed by Ethan Wiley / Starring Arye Gross, Jonathan Stark
Anchor Bay (US R1 NTSC, UK R2 PAL) / WS (1.85:1) (16:9)

After making a fortune with the *Friday the 13th* franchise (not to mention an early profitable career in porn), producer/director Sean Cunningham kicked off another successful horror money making machine with *House*, a fondly remembered '80s mishmash of gothic horror, goofy comedy, and rubbery monsters. Though hardly remarkable, the film is endearing and off-kilter enough to grab one's attention, and while it doesn't quite scale the heights of its similar contemporaries like *Fright Night* or *Gremlins*, the film holds up well enough to justify another look.

Recovering from the trauma of a separation from his wife (Kay Lenz), struggling writer Roger Cobb *(The Greatest American Hero'*s William Katt) moves into the spooky house owned by his aunt, who recently hanged herself. Roger attempts to turn his disturbing memories of Vietnam into a gripping memoir, but his creative efforts are thwarted by an eager neighbour named Harold (*Cheers'* George Wendt), not to mention a slew of inconvenient monsters like the unforgettable SandyWitch and a decrepit old Army buddy, Big Ben (*Night Court'*s Richard Moll).

Considering the heavy roster of TV actors and the erratic pedigree of director Steve Miner, whose horror output ranges from the decent (*Friday the 13th Part 2*) to the worthless (*Halloween: H2O*), *House* should have been an unremarkable timewaster at best. The fact that it works as well as it does can be attributed to a happy union of elements ranging from a feisty, surprising screenplay to a playful, diverse score from Harry ("Ki-ki-kill ha-ha-how") Manfredini. Cinematographer Mac gives the low budget production a nice, glossy sheen, expertly capturing every little shiny, menacing wooden detail in the house itself. The film has dated fairly gracefully, and as a Reagan era meditation on the aftermath of Vietnam, it's at least a more sensitive, palatable, and complex meditation on the subject than *Rambo: First Blood II.*

A surprise money-maker (and box office champ in its opening weekend), *House* was naturally followed by a sequel, *House II: The Second Story.* Despite the title, the second film really had nothing to do with the first film, intended instead as more of a continuing house-oriented series of horror films in the same vein as John Carpenter's experiment with *Halloween III: Season of the Witch.* Often regarded as one of the worst sequels in history, *House II* really isn't by a long shot, but it certainly is disappointing. Virtually dropping any pretence at horror apart from a mildly atmospheric opening sequence, the film spins its loosely connected vignettes around a magical crystal skull, which has become the holy grail of Gramps (Royal Dano), who, unfortunately, is dead. His yuppie descendant, Jesse (Arye Gross), moves into the jinxed house with his record exec wife and, along with the rather snotty Charlie (Jonathan Stark), embarks on a journey through time and space. Neanderthals, Aztec warriors, oogy boogy creatures, and even a "caterpuppy" flit across the screen, which is also occupied by hamming from a young Bill Maher, along with *Cheers'* John Ratzenberger (as a comical electrician) stepping in after George Wendt from the first film. It's all harmless, nonsensical popcorn junk, but don't expect anything more.

For years *House* fans were long dismayed at the thought of ever getting the equivalent of the special edition released years ago on laserdisc by Lumivision. The Anchor Bay presentation is really an impressive job all around, and the first 20,000 US units come with both films contained in one of those double-snapper, single title size Amaray cases. The first *House* gets most of the attention, of course, kicking off with a genial feature length commentary by Miner, Cunningham, writer Ethan Wiley (who went on to direct the second film), and Katt. All of the men have fond memories about the film and go into detail about how they went about constructing the crowd pleaser. Wiley and Cunningham return for commentary on *House II*, and while they have to strain a lot more to fill the time, they still have a few good anecdotes to share about putting together an essentially unrelated sequel to an unexpected smash.

Both films feature sharp, well framed anamorphic transfers with colours about as solid as you could expect for '80s New World titles. The mono audio tracks are much better than the godawful old VHS editions, most of which have long passed on to the dropout-riddled video graveyard anyway.

Other extras include "The Making of *House*," basically a 12 minute promotional featurette used to promote the theatrical release. A combination of cast and crew interviews with footage of special effects creation, this is an interesting if superficial overview of the production. You also get two trailers for *House* (the second of which appears to be lifted off a very ragged, third generation VHS tape), one trailer for *House II*, and a surprisingly extensive, often hilarious gallery of production shots from the first film. The UK Anchor Bay version drops the second feature (which was instead issued separately) but does boast a remixed 5.1 track for the first film, so completists may just want to snap up all of them.

HOUSE BY THE CEMETERY

Colour, 1981, 86m. / Directed by Lucio Fulci / Starring Catriona MacColl, Paolo Malco / Anchor Bay (US R1 NTSC) / WS (2.35:1) (16:9) / DD2.0, Diamond (US R0 NTSC), EC Entertainment (Holland R0 NTSC), Vipco (UK PAL R2), Astro (Germany R2 PAL) / WS (2.35:1)

A film even Fulci haters tend to enjoy, *House by the Cemetery* contains the erratic director's typically strong emphasis on atmosphere and shocking visuals but also devotes more time than usual to character development and surprising plotting, allowing the graphic gore to serve as a function of the story rather than an end unto itself. The last of Fulci's gothic zombie excursions, *House* is also a strangely beautiful film, with Sergio Salvati's expert scope photography crafting a strange world of childhood fairy tales gone very bad and Walter Rizzati's poignant score providing much needed emotional support.

A middle class couple (Catriona MacColl and *New York Ripper*'s Paolo Malco) move to New Whitby, Boston, ignoring the protests of their young son, Bob (Giovanni Frezza), who experiences visions of a spooky freckled girl warning him about bloody events in their new house. While MacColl is a little miffed to find out the house is next door to a cemetery (irrelevant, but it does give the movie a cool title) and the tomb of a Dr. Freudstein is situated in the middle of their hallway, the couple decide to tough it out and make the best of the situation. Not surprisingly, nasty things begin to happen: Malco is attacked by a bat (and this is a Fulci bat attack, folks- he paints the walls red with this one), spooky-looking babysitter Ania Pieroni (*Tenebre*) inexplicably disappears, and real estate agent Dagmar Lassander (a long way from her sex starlet days) meets up with a poker-wielding assailant. In the last half hour, Fulci really shines and produces some of his finest work; the claustrophobic mixture of chills and supernatural poetry would do Mario Bava proud, with an unexpected but very satisfying supernatural resolution. He also wreaks havoc with audience expectations, which adds immensely to the air of childhood uneasiness in which the whole world feels like it can collapse from underneath you at any moment.

When *House* was released to US theatres and on Lightning Home Video, the gore remained intact but two of the reels were placed out of sequence and much of Rizzati's score was stupidly replaced. The Japanese Daie laserdisc, letterboxed and uncut, was a very welcome alternative, and EC's Holland-produced Region 2 DVD went one even better by removing those pesky subtitles. To make things even more confusing, EC then anamorphically remastered their DVD, supposedly from the original negative, while retaining the same extras: the European theatrical trailer (be warned, it contains a lot of spoilers), juicy trailers for *A Blade in the Dark* and *Mountain of the Cannibal God*, and a half hour 1994 Eurofest interview with Fulci (in Italian with a translator on hand).

Anchor Bay's *House* marks the first widescreen and correctly sequenced appearance in America, discounting an unauthorized bootleg disc from the notorious Diamond. The image quality is the best of all, with exceptionally rich colours, less grain than its counterparts, and a sharp overall appearance that mostly belies the film's age. Inexplicably, the disc does not contain the same jolting 5.1 remix treatment afforded to *The Beyond* or *City of the Living Dead*; instead the viewer is left to settle with a moderately effective two channel surround mix, which tosses in a few nice directional effects to the front speakers but leaves the rear channels largely silent apart from some very mild ambient support to Rizzati's score. The striking full motion menus (which take the viewer through the house, of course) lead to the hilariously lurid US trailer ("Be sure to read the fine print! You may have just mortgaged... your life!"), the European trailer, a handful of abbreviated TV spots, a gooey still gallery, and cast and crew bios. However, completists may not want to toss out those EC discs just yet, as that's still the only way to own both the Fulci interview and a version of the film with (optional but handy) English subtitles.

HOUSE OF GAMES

Colour, 1987, 102m. / Directed by David Mamet / Starring Lindsay Crouse, Joe Mantegna / MGM (US R1 NTSC) / WS (1.85:1)

 The reputation of David Mamet as one of America's finest living playwrights has gone hand in hand with criticism of his use of profanity and his stagy tendencies, neither of which really hold water the more one sees of his work as a director. His first cinematic mindbender, *House of Games*, is a densely layered, self-contained narrative in which mental trickery and deception take precedence over character development and the viewer becomes as active a participant as the people involved on the screen. When all is said and done, nobody comes out of this one without a few bruises for their trouble.

Despite her success with a recent book, psychiatrist Margaret Ford (Lindsay Crouse, Mrs. Mamet at the time) longs for something more to jolt her out of complacency. One of her patients, Billy Hahn (Steven Goldstein), threatens suicide because of an outstanding debt that he is unable to pay. Using his abandoned notebook as a guide, Margaret tracks down his debtors to the House of Games, where charming and not terribly trustworthy Mike (Joe Mantegna) agrees to write off Billy's debt if she helps him con his way through a game of poker. After that... well, the surprises of this plot rely a great deal on the viewer's willingness to play along without any warning, so let's just say that nothing is what it appears to be and the stakes go much, much higher.

At the time of its release, *House of Games* became a critical favourite and a modest art house success. Its mannered dialogue posed a difficulty for those used to naturalistic rhythms, while the jolting climax could be read as either wickedly conceived or arbitrary and sadistic, depending upon one's viewpoint. In any case, all of the actors do a tremendous job with their roles; even Crouse, who has proven to have quite a few limitations ever since, proves she did have at least one great performance in her, though this is really Mantegna's show all the way. Along with other Mamet stage regulars like Ricky Jay and a very young William H.

Macy, Mantegna reveals his consummate skill in rattling off the playwright's tricky, ambiguous dialogue, in which every word seems to sugarcoat a much more venomous intention underneath. Despite his stage roots, Mamet also reveals a singular visual style here, using the conventions of film noir imagery to construct his own paranoid universe in which daylight can become as menacing as nightfall and smoke constantly seems to drift at the corners of the screen.

First released on laserdisc in a very drab edition from Orion, *House of Games* has been given a much needed makeover on DVD. The lack of anamorphic enhancement is puzzling and frustrating, but the film still looks very good, with more solid colours than even its theatrical screenings. The theatrical trailer indicates a Dolby Stereo mix, but the credits on the print itself indicate nothing of the kind. In any case, the mono audio here sounds just fine, with Alaric Jans' terrifically moody jazz score represented with every creepy little nuance intact. The full frame version on the opposite side is completely open matte and loses nothing on the sides; as with the dual framing options for Mamet's other fiendish movie mind game, *The Spanish Prisoner*, the extra information on the DVD gives the characters some extra breathing room but also takes away from some of the oppressiveness of Mamet's visual compositions Either way should serve just fine for newcomers, and Mamet fans will enjoy comparing the dramatic effect of scenes both with and without those confining black bars at the top and bottom.

HOUSE OF WHIPCORD

Colour, 1974, 101m. / Directed by Pete Walker / Starring Ann Michelle, Penny Irving / Salvation (UK R2 PAL), Image (US R1 NTSC)

For a marvellous, regrettably brief period, director Pete Walker and his crew made some of the most striking, disturbing horror films to come out of 1970s British cinema. Titles like *House of Mortal Sin* and *Frightmare* used lurid exploitation devices to lure viewers in and then deal with the inherent hypocrisy of "civilized" foundations ranging from organized religion to the nuclear family unit. In *House of Whipcord*, Walker set his sights on the judicial and penal systems, delivering a scathing and frightening view of what happens when individuals decide to mete out justice in their own backyard.

Ann Michelle (*The Virgin Witch*), a very naive young French girl exploring the swinging scene in London, hooks up with a charming, slightly sinister young man named Mark E. DeSade. Even after Mark asks her to close her eyes, then tells her he's holding a knife to her face and swipes an ice cube across her cheek, she doesn't seem to grasp that he might not be such a wholesome character. Sure enough, Mark whisks her away to a remote estate where his mother is part of a band of concerned folks disillusioned with the British court system. Thanks to a makeshift prison ruled over by sadistic warden Sheila Keith (a wonderful Pete Walker regular), these bitter folks have managed to imprison those they deem impure or corrupt. A doddering old former judge presides over each victim, and the young girls are punished by whip for their indiscretions and escape attempts. However, our protagonist's disappearance is noticed, and her friends begin the difficult process of tracking her down.

According to filmmakers like Tobe Hooper and Wes Craven, one necessity for a horror director is convincing the audience that the filmmaker himself might actually be insane. Pete Walker understood this all too well, and in his films, anyone can die - any time, any place. *House of Whipcord* follows this pattern, and while the ending is slightly more uplifting and closed than his usual denouements, the overall mood of the film is one of despair and depravity reigning supreme. Even the requisite nudity is of *the Caged Heat* variety, deglamorized to the point of discomfort for even watching the film.

The American DVD *of House of Whipcord* from Image looks better than the awful VHS presentations over the years, usually from Monterey Video, but still comes up short. The transfer bears a disturbing brown and yellow colour scheme, and the problems of cheap shooting on substandard stock results in the magnification of film grain and some muddy day for night process shots (the opening, for example). The UK Salvation release looks much better, at least a couple of generations ahead in terms of clarity anyway, and also features a still gallery and the theatrical trailer. Sound quality on both, featuring an early, austere score by the late Stanley Myers, is fine considering the limitations of the original mono mix, and the packaging includes a reproduction of the original theatrical poster.

HOUSE OF YES

Colour, 1997, 85m. / Directed by Mark S. Waters / Starring Parker Posey, Freddie Prinze, Jr. / Miramax (US R1 NTSC) / WS (1.85:1) / DD2.0

Chock full of quotable dialogue, *The House of Yes* faithfully and skilfully adapts Wendy MacLeod's acerbic black comedy to celluloid without losing an ounce of its disturbing wit. Though the film was plainly designed primarily to be a showcase for Parker Posey (perhaps ironically this film does in fact feature her best role), the film improves with repeated viewings, though its appeal obviously will not extend to everyone.

On a dark and stormy Thanksgiving night, Marty (Josh Hamilton), a seemingly normal all-American guy, brings his fiancée, Lesly (Tori Spelling - yes, that Tori Spelling), to visit his family in New England. Marty's sister, Jackie-O (Parker Posey), has just been released from a stay in a mental institution, while her mother (Genevieve Bujold) and younger brother, Anthony (Freddie Prinze, Jr.) are hardly more stable than she. Over the course of the evening, the power goes out and various nasty family secrets rise to the surface. It transpires that Jackie-O has been obsessed with the Kennedy family ever since her father walked out on the day of JFK's assassination; thus, she has an unfortunate propensity for acting out the President's death in a strange incestuous game, which may or may not involve real bullets. And that's just the beginning...

The most obvious strength of *House of Yes* lies in its cast, which is uniformly excellent. It's very heartening to see Genevieve Bujold back on the screen again, and she gets some of the funniest lines. Even the normally woeful Tori Spelling, wisely cast here as a giggly blonde, pulls off her role with surprising skill and weaves through the tricky dialogue like a pro.

Though not cinematically audacious, the film looks and sounds terrific, with evocative gothic candlelight and Rolfe Kent's lyrical score creating a palpable, melancholy atmosphere that lingers long after the inevitable finale.

As usual, the Miramax DVD is a sparse and overpriced package, but the image and sound quality are acceptable given the film's low budget limitations. The shadows look rich and well-defined, while the basic surround mix gets the job done considering most of the dialogue remains well centred. The trailer, which in typical Miramax fashion tries to make this look much more frivolous than it really is, clocks in as the only extra. For fans of the film, though, this will be a welcome release all the same, and anyone with a taste for pitch black comedy should find plenty to enjoy here.

HOUSE ON HAUNTED HILL

B&W, 1958, 75m. / Directed by William Castle / Starring Vincent Price, Carol Ohmart / Warner (US R1 NTSC); The Roan Group (US R1 NTSC) / WS (1.78:1 / 1.66:1)

THE BAT

B&W, 1959, 80m. / Written and Directed by Crane Wilbur / Starring Vincent Price, Agnes Moorehead / The Roan Group (US R1 NTSC) / WS (1.66:1), Anchor Bay (US R0 NTSC)

The art of movie gimmicks really got its start with legendary showman/director William Castle, the man conjured up insurance policies against fright, the "Fright Break," and the "Ghost Viewer." While his virtues as an artist have been debated throughout the years, his growing cult attests to the fact that his films remained utterly entertaining and, in retrospect, have a nostalgic innocence for a time when theatres would allow skeletons to be wheeled out into the audience for the amusement of popcorn-munching kids. In fact, Castle employed this last device, "Emergo," on a little gem called *House on Haunted Hill*, made just before Price hit paydirt with his Roger Corman series of Poe adaptations. While *Haunted Hill* may not be quite as delirious and relentless as Castle's gimmick masterpiece, *The Tingler*, it is perhaps the director's slickest, most assured film, one that finds him perfectly balancing atmosphere and characterization with good, old-fashioned drive-in thrills.

Price stars as Frederick Loren, a man with too much time and money on his hands. He decides to throw a little party for six guests (including his scheming blonde wife) with pistols in tiny coffins handed out as party favours. The game: each guest who stays in the house all night and survives gets $10,000. The catch: seven bizarre murders have already been committed in the house... and there's always room for more. Featuring a game cast including the reliably wacko Elisha Cook, Jr., *Haunted Hill* spins out a series of delicious shocks and twists in an efficient, rollercoaster fashion that makes the 75 minutes fly by so fast you'll be reaching for another Castle film as soon as it's over. Price had already mastered the suave scoundrel routine for which he became famous, and the spooky noir-flavoured photography only adds to the film's countless pleasures. Von Dexter's fun-spooky music lends just the right touch, and watch out for that housekeeper. The film has been issued twice on DVD (not counting a handful of bleary bargain basement PD versions from Front Row, Slingshot, and Goodtimes). The first version arrived from The Roan Group, who opened the matte to approximately 1.66:1. The shadows are noticeably rich and deep in the Roan edition, though the print contains more than a few distracting washes of speckles and print damage. Subsequently Warner issued a spruced-up anamorphic transfer from a cleaner source; this version eliminates some vertical information present in the full frame version (available from Lorimar/CBS Fox on laserdisc as a double feature with *Attack of the 50-Foot Woman*). However, the framing is not detrimental, and some of the compositions look more balanced and intriguing this way. Best of all, the print is several generations above the flat, washed-out Fox version, without the overly hot glare whenever someone steps near a light source. The sound also contains far more presence, with each bump and creak presented in sparkling digital sound.

The Warner DVD also features an unmatted full frame side for those who want to see the extra headroom; in this respect, you really get the best of both worlds. Also, only the Warner DVD contains the delightful theatrical trailer, which features Price introducing the audience to Haunted Hill and its jittery guests.

The Roan DVD pairs up *Haunted Hill* with another Vincent Price old dark house favourite, *The Bat*, a lesser film in every respect but still fun if you're in an undemanding mood. Based on the Mary Roberts Rinehart yarn adapted as a play by Avery Hopwood, *The Bat* is a funhouse version of the familiar killer stalking a country household routine. Think *The Cat and the Canary* with a bat instead of a feline. Though previously filmed (better) in 1930 as *The Bat Whispers* (in 70mm!), this version does have the trump card of Vincent Price, who's always fun to watch even in minor material. As Dr. Malcolm Wells, Price lends a wry twist to every line, and of course the presence of Agnes Moorehead (post Orson Welles but pre-*Bewitched*) as Cordelia van Gorder doesn't hurt, either. Like *Haunted Hill*, the contrast scale of this transfer is quite impressive, with cavernous black shadows, which still yield an impressive amount of detail.

The film is also available as a stand-alone release from Anchor Bay in an unmatted transfer that looks quite good and also boasts the original theatrical trailer.

HOUSE ON HAUNTED HILL

Colour, 1999, 93m. / Directed by William Malone / Starring Geoffrey Rush, Famke Janssen, Taye Diggs / Warner / WS (1.85:1) (16:9) / DD5.1

An alternately reverent and grating twist on the old William Castle popcorn classic, *House on Haunted Hill* transports the 1958 storyline into the postmodern horror era with some success, at least for its first half. The film turned out to be an unexpected Halloween money-maker for the new horror-oriented Dark Castle (headed by Joel Silver and Robert Zemeckis), prompting a spate of new Castle remakes including the dismal *Thirteen Ghosts*.

In the astoundingly gory opening sequence which should have landed this movie an NC-17 rating in the US, a gothic asylum run by the sadistic Dr. Vannacutt (Jeffrey Combs) goes straight to hell when the patients revolt and decide to practice dissection on their medical care providers. Fast forward several decades later as the house's current owner, snide prankster/millionaire Steven Price (Geoffrey Rush), decides to use the creepy setting to host a birthday party for his bitchy wife, Evelyn (Famke Janssen). The party's gimmick, according to the invitation, is a reward of one million dollars to every person who manages to survive the night. However, apart from neurotic caretaker Watson Pritchett (Chris Kattan, providing some surprisingly good comic relief), none of the guests seem to be the ones Price invited. Pretty soon the house seems to have other ideas of how to throw a party, and even Price's dapper party gifts of loaded guns don't seem to be much use against a horde of irate ghosts.

On a visual level, this spookfest from *Tales from the Crypt* helmer William Malone is quite impressive, and unlike the disastrous remake of *The Haunting*, this house really is creepy. Technical credits are all impressive, with Don Davis (*The Matrix*) in particular delivering a fascinating experimental music score. The Brothers Quay-inspired opening credits are striking as well, and horror fans should get a big kick out of the sick little scene added after the end credits. On the other hand, too much of the film focuses on characters wandering up and down corridors... and up and down again... and so on. The level of profanity is also distracting, with expletives failing to cover up the total absence of wit. The biggest problem, however, is the avalanche of highly unconvincing and unfrightening special effects that bombard the viewer during the climax. However, the filmmakers at least had the relative restraint to save this display for the end rather than plastering it all over the entire film (again, think of *The Haunting*). As for the performers, Janssen is great fun to watch as always, though Rush is way too nasty and bitter for such an urbane role. Ali Larter

(*Final Destination*) and the ubiquitous Taye Diggs make a decent heroic couple, while Bridgette Wilson turns up all too briefly as a nosy reporter who uncovers the ghosts in the film's creepiest scene.

Not surprisingly, Warner's DVD is a powerhouse. From the startling animated menus to the perfect widescreen transfer, this is a class act all the way. As in the theatre, the thunderous surround mix often renders the whispered dialogue completely unintelligible, so consider using that English subtitle option on your DVD remote before disturbing the neighbours. The disc contains three outstanding deleted scenes (well, four, technically); for once, this isn't just useless filler, as it introduces an entirely new character played by Debbie Mazar. The best of these is a Fulciesque zombie attack in the basement, but the discarded epilogue also offers a nasty twist on the fate of the house itself.

A twenty minute featurette, *Tale of Two Houses*, focuses on the numerous comparisons between the Castle and Malone versions, with a few cursory interview bits thrown in to make it all seem official. More illuminating is the audio commentary by Malone, which expounds upon the difficulties of remaking a drive-in classic and the laborious special effects and production design required for the film. He's quite good company, really, and hopefully this won't be his last horror special edition on DVD. The '58 and '99 trailers are also included, with the latter very awkwardly reedited to remove references to a giveaway contest conducted during the film's theatrical run. To round it all of, you also get some DVD-ROM content (an essay and web links) and a very strange option called "The Chamber," which simulates a bizarre David Lynch-inspired sequence in the film.

THE HOUSE ON SORORITY ROW

Colour, 1983, 92m. / Directed by Mark Rosman / Starring Kate McNeill, Eileen Davidson / Elite (US R1 NTSC) / WS (1.85:1) (16·9)

Released during the seemingly endless stream of low budget slasher films during the early '80s, *The House on Sorority Row* is less a *Friday the 13th* copy than an arty, flawed, but fascinating blend of *Diabolique* and *Black Christmas*. (Really, it is.) Don't let the sorority setting fool you; this isn't quite your average slice and dicer.

After a puzzling blue-tinted prologue in which a distraught mother gives birth under traumatic circumstances, we meet the same woman, Mrs. Slater (Lois Kelso Hunt), several years later as the house mother of Theta Pi sorority. One of the girls, Katherine (*Monkey Shines'* Kate McNeill), refuses to move back home and decides to stay with her Greek sisters for a final graduation party. Unfortunately, a lack of funds has forced the girls to throw their party at the house instead of off campus as originally planned. Mrs. Slater always demands the house be closed down by June 19th, but since she'll be off at the mental institution for treatment, she won't mind... right? Unfortunately Mrs. Slater cancels her stay and shows up unannounced while the girls are planning during a binge of boozing and smoking. Even worse, she catches one of the girls fooling around with a college boy and takes a poker to their waterbed, with messy results. The girls decide to get back at the old tyrant by pulling a practical joke involving a partially loaded pistol and the house's swimming pool; naturally this little joke backfires, leaving Mrs. Slater dead and the girls conspiring to leave her body submerged in the water. However, the body later disappears, and the girls begin dying one by one. Even worse, Mrs. Slater's nasty secret reason for closing the house every year might have something to do with an ugly surprise lurking in the attic...

Though hardly groundbreaking, *House on Sorority Row* stands as a diverting time killer and contains enough stylish touches to lift it above the norm. The repeated use of clown imagery is undeniably creepy, particularly during one nicely executed moment during the lively attic climax. Some occasional surreal shock effects also work well, such as a creepy climactic discovery in the pool and a nasty throwaway gag involving a girl's severed head in a toilet. Bearing a striking resemblance here to a brunette Nicole Kidman, McNeill handles the main girl duties admirably and is more sympathetic and intelligent than your average screaming bimbo in these films, while the script gives her an opportunity to show off some genuine acting ability. Director Rosman, who started out under the wing of Brian DePalma but found his B-movie career cut short by getting kicked off of *Mutant*, displays a flair for suspenseful set pieces but not necessarily for pacing and logic. He's aided considerably by one of Richard Band's finest scores, a rich orchestral work well worth seeking out on CD.

Elite's DVD presentation is the best of numerous video incarnations over the years though not without problems of its own. The anamorphically enhanced, letterboxed image looks clean and detailed enough, with solid compositions trimming off some of the dead space from the open matte VHS versions while adding a little to the sides. On the other hand, flesh tones look a little drab (probably a problem with the original source material), while a handful of scenes are marred by repeated vertical scratches running along the left side of the frame. Overall, though, it's a solid and satisfying appearance given the film's history, and it probably couldn't look much better. The disc also includes the vague theatrical trailer, apparently lifted from a mediocre VHS source.

HOUSE ON THE EDGE OF THE PARK

Colour, 1980, 88m. / Directed by Ruggero Deodato / Starring David Hess, Giovanni Lombardo Radice / EC Entertainment (Holland R0 PAL) / WS (1.85:1)

An obvious European riff on Wes Craven's *Last House on the Left,* this graphic yet stagy shocker (known in Italy as *La casa sperduta nel parco*) ranks just behind director Ruggero Deodato's *Cannibal Holocaust* as his most familiar and notorious work. American actor David Hess, best known as *Last House*'s psychotic Krug, takes centre stage here as a scenery chewing brute hell-bent on making life rough for a bunch of bland yuppies, and while Deodato has dismissed the film in several interviews, the film is still an interesting contribution to early '80s shock filmmaking.

Alex (Hess), a lowlife mechanic, is preparing to head out in his best disco duck suit for a night of boogie action with his mentally deficient pal, Ricky (Giovanni Lombardo Radice, aka John Morghen). However, a couple of rich folks stop by the garage at the last minute and ask for help with their car. After Alex and Ricky reluctantly help out, the boring couple asks them to tag along for a little party out in the suburbs. The party proves to be pretty bland, mostly consisting of poker games and bad dancing, though the orchestrator, Tom (*Tenebre*'s Christian Borromeo), doesn't seem to mind Alex and Ricky taking advantage of a few female guests. Pretty soon Alex is spinning out of control, raping and tormenting his hosts in a self-destructive orgy like an uncontrolled animal.

While Hess' relentless performance ultimately drives the film, European sleaze fanatics will be more interested in the supporting players. Radice, the oft-abused star of *Cannibal Ferox* and Lucio Fulci's *The Gates of Hell*, walks his usual thin line between endearing and hammy, while fellow *Cannibal Ferox* alumnus Lorraine De Selle appears as the glowering Gloria. Considering the film's horrific reputation, it's surprising that the actual

body count including the rape/murder prologue only amounts to two. Most of the violence is psychological, though Hess does provide a gruelling and appallingly gratuitous straight razor torture scene on a visiting "virgin" just for kicks. This dubious scene aside, *House* is far less harrowing than Craven's model, not necessarily a bad thing.

Composer Riz Ortolani's contribution consists primarily of two trashy but insanely catchy songs, one of them a seemingly endless ABBA-styled disco anthem (with a diva repeatedly crooning, "Do it to me once more"), while regular Deodato cinematographer Sergio d'Offizi gives the sordid subject a suitably stylized, quasi-American visual gloss. Much of the attention directed towards this film focuses on the surprise ending, which rips open an alarming number of holes in the plot but does provide a memorable and strangely resonant final scene. Not a classic by any means, but they sure don't make 'em like this anymore.

House on the Edge of the Park has been most widely seen in the US thanks to Vestron's fuzzy but uncut VHS release in the early '80s. Not surprisingly, the DVD from EC Entertainment looks infinitely better, and the 1.85:1 letterboxing adds some much needed spatial depth to the talkier scenes. For some reason, the Italian opening and closing titles have been bluntly spliced into the print, but otherwise the source materials are in excellent shape. The soundtrack hasn't aged remotely as well, unfortunately; the English dialogue track is fine from a standard TV monitor but suffers from distracting scratching and background noise when amplified. The German audio track has also deteriorated rather badly but, oddly enough, features a much livelier audio mix, filled with ambient noise like crickets and passing traffic.

The disc also includes the lively and very sleazy Italian trailer, which features most of the film's copious frontal nudity (except for Hess, mercifully), the usual violent highlights, and spastic editing that would make Russ Meyer proud. An NTSC edition from Media Blasters is forthcoming at the time of this writing, as is a very heavily cut PAL version for the UK, issued by Vipco.

THE HUMAN TORNADO

Colour, 1976, 85m. / Directed by Cliff Roquemore / Starring Rudy Ray Moore, J.B. Baron / Xenon (US R1 NTSC)

Rudy Ray Moore's rude, crude *Dolemite* became a surprise smash hit around the country (though not surprisingly, it didn't go over too well in suburban hardtops). Naturally the next year saw a sequel, filmed under the title *Dolemite II* but shown almost everywhere as *The Human Tornado*. Determined to make the sequel more outrageous than the original, Moore really goes to town here, speaking virtually every single line in rap (his acting, relatively speaking, has improved by this point) and, in one memorable scene, even posing as a Chinese door-to-door salesman of erotic paintings (…honest!).

In the raucous opening, a redneck cop catches his wife in bed with Dolemite (hopefully the only time Rudy will ever feel compelled to bare it all on-camera), leading to Dolemite rolling naked down a hill and taking off on a high speed car chase. This time the story involves an evildoer named Cavalletti, an Italian gangster who busts up Queen Bee's place and holds the Queen Bee girls hostage so he can take over the club scene. You can tell these are really evil folks because they live in Pasadena and hold parties where boys in bikini briefs come out and do tricks with nunchukas. Dolemite seduces Cavalletti's wife (who has fantasies about bodybuilders popping out of a toybox) in a scene worthy of Russ Meyer, and soon Dolemite's gang (featuring a bald Ernie Hudson, way before *Ghostbusters*) decides to pay the mobsters a visit in person. It all culminates, oddly enough, with a gruesome act of dismemberment in a Gothic basement.

More polished and ambitious than its predecessor, *The Human Tornado* loses some scrappy charm in the process but should still please viewers with its outrageous setpieces and Moore's incomparable verbal talents; in many ways, this is the closest thing we've ever had to a black John Waters film.

Like *Dolemite*, the film is presented fullscreen and exposes a lot of extraneous image area at the top and bottom. Unlike *Dolemite*, however, the boom mike doesn't drop into frame every two minutes, and the compositions are more carefully arranged. Once again, the picture quality is excellent, which is especially surprising considering the tattered production history of these films.

HUMANOIDS FROM THE DEEP

Colour, 1980, 80m. / Directed by Barbara Peeters / Starring Doug McClure, Ann Turkel, Vic Morrow / New Concorde (US R1 NTSC)

Roger Corman's New World Pictures spawned a lot of drive-in hits during the late '70s and early '80s, and for many impressionable teens, *Humanoids from*

the Deep was a raunchy, gory thrill ride where slimy beasts and gratuitous T&A filled the screen from start to finish. Much of its shock value has since worn off in the ensuing twenty years (though the nasty sting in the tale finale still packs a punch), and anyone unfamiliar with this film's history will probably wonder what all the fuss is about.

In Noyo, a fishing village poised directly below an aquatic research centre, a series of strange and violent events are beginning to upset the sleepy townspeople. Most of the town dogs are mysteriously slain, a small fishing boat mysteriously explodes, and a few bikini-clad women have disappeared without a trace. Local scientist Ann Turkel's pleas for help after the release of a genetic experiment on salmon gone awry fall on deaf ears, and sure enough, it seems mutated beasties are responsible for the mayhem. Corrupt local developer Vic Morrow tries to prevent an investigation and blames the crimes on the local Indian population, but Turkel and hero Doug McClure know better. However, can they stop the monsters before the town holds its local fishing festival?

Basically a remake of New World's *Piranha* with monster suits and rape scenes, *Humanoids* certainly has sleazy fun value but also demonstrates just how much difference a talent like Joe Dante can make behind the camera. Director Peeters claimed that Roger Corman added some of the more explicit shots of slimy nudity at the last minute to give the film some extra kick, but frankly, the movie needed it. Though competently handled, the lack of visual style, occasionally slow pacing, and peculiar lack of (intentional) humour hinder this from becoming an all-out trash masterpiece, at least for the first hour. Thankfully the slam-bang climax really delivers, with apparently the entire town being trashed by marauding fishfolk.

The austere musical score by James Horner (back in the days when he was doing good work for stuff like *The Hand* and *Deadly Blessing*) manages to keep things marginally serious, and kudos for avoiding a predictable romantic subplot between Turkel and McClure. While it's hard to discern any particular gender basis in the filmmaker's viewpoint, the climactic scene with McClure's wife handling herself while under siege is a welcome relief from the usual hero to the rescue scenario.

New Concorde' presentation of *Humanoids* far outclasses the muddy print released by Warner Home Video ages ago. The fullscreen transfer removes the 1.85:1 matte from the theatrical version, though the film isn't framed with much artistry either way. Picture quality is generally excellent and colourful, though the sound has obviously deteriorated and sounds a little hissy when amplified through a sound system.

Check out the end credits for a few unexpected names like future *Terminator* producer Gale Ann Hurd (a production assistant here) and director Rowdy Herrington (serving as electrician). Also includes the original red-card US trailer and a brief interview with Corman by Leonard Maltin.

HYPNOSIS (THE HYPNOTIST)

Colour, 1999, 109m. / Starring Goro Inagaki, Miho Kanno / ERA/Carnival (Hong Kong R3 NTSC), ADV Films (US R1 NTSC) / WS (1.85:1) / DD5.1

 Hypnosis, a stylish fusion of hoary '40s thrillers like *The Amazing Dr. X* with the modern Japanese shocks of *Ring*, offers a decidedly different take on the use of hypnotism as a gimmicky movie device. Deliberately uneasy and burning far more on style than sense, the film hits the ground running with a serious of gruesome, imaginative murders and barely stops to catch its breath for the following two hours.

A series of bizarre suicides in Tokyo have left the police bewildered. A female sprinter runs until her legs fracture apart, a groom strangles himself with his tie during his own wedding ceremony, and a distraught elderly man hurls himself through a glass door. An experienced cop, Sakurai, teams up with a wet behind the ears psychoanalyst, Saga (Goro Inagaki), who theorizes that the misuse of hypnotism could be causing the inexplicable events. A local television program, in which a creepy host uses subliminal suggestion to cause guests to perform all kinds of outrageous and silly functions in front of the camera, could be behind the deaths, all of which share one factor - the victims spoke of a "green monkey" immediately before taking their lives. Saga believes an outside triggering device, like an image or sound, could be responsible, but he soon discovers that hypnosis may be even more prevalent and insidious than he had previously imagined. Yuka (Miho Kanno), a young girl from the program, goes to the police for help and believes her life is in danger from the "green monkey." Unfortunately, a hypnotic suggestion causes her to suddenly behave like an alien at the most inconvenient moments, and during one especially creepy scene an entire room of policemen is even rendered unconscious. As Saga

delves deeper into the mystery, which also involves a mysterious one-eyed club girl named Reiko, he finds that his life and the well-being of everyone around him could be in mortal danger.

Drawing inspiration from seemingly every genre available, from Italian *gialli* to a concert hall assassination straight out of Hitchcock's *The Man who Knew Too Much*, the film attempts to cover a tremendous amount of ground and often feels more like a patchwork of elements than a coherent narrative. The final swerve into possibly supernatural territory during the final twenty minutes offers some especially memorable, skin-crawling moments, though the filmmakers don't skimp on the gore, either. While the splatter ranges from effective (a cranial close encounter with a coat rack) to completely absurd (death by hard balls), the film derives most of its power through the force of suggestion, appropriate considering the subject matter. Several images of the hypnotically induced Yuka work particularly well (lovely pinup idol Miho Kanno is especially good in this), and the manipulative Dolby 5.1 soundtrack provides some gleefully manipulative shocks.

Disregard for logic and coherence aside, *Hypnosis* should satisfy even non-Asian film fans looking for a good chill, and the efficient DVD presentation makes for an ideal viewing showcase. The sharp image quality features rich colour reproduction and a smooth compression job, though some darker scenes curiously suffer from those pesky "glowing blue" shadows often found in older, poorly preserved films. Optional Chinese and English subtitles are included; the English translation, done with a heavy reliance on British spelling and slang, is more awkward than usual, with a number of presumably important plot points unfortunately garbled in the process. The disc also includes the rapid-fire Japanese trailer (only subtitled in Chinese) and a silly "photo gallery" that must be seen to be believed. The American disc (under the alternate title of *The Hypnotist*) features the same transfer but none of the endearing idiosyncrasies found on the Hong Kong DVD.

I, A WOMAN

B&W, 1965, 89m. / Directed by Mac Ahlberg / Starring Essy Persson, Jørgen Reenberg / Image (US R0 NTSC) / WS (1.66:1)

A few years before the notorious political skinfest *I Am Curious (Yellow)*, Swedish cinema had already become synonymous with naughtiness thanks to *I, a Woman*, the skilfully crafted import that put Radley

Metzger and his Audubon Films on the map. According to Metzger, he had to make a few alterations to the original film, namely shuffling the narrative structure a bit and making a few judicious trims to render the pace more palatable for American audiences. The result became a smash , thanks in no small part to the remarkable performance of Essy Persson in the lead role. Over thirty years later, the film may not seem explicit, but Persson, thanks to her wholesome and intelligent looks and subtle shifts in emotion conveyed through her eyes, still manages to smoulder all over the screen.

Based on the autobiographical novel by Agnethe Thomsen (writing as Siv Holm), the film immediately introduces us to a young woman named Siv (of course) who encounters a man in a restaurant and arranges to later meet him up in her room. As she looks in the mirror, she ponders, "I'm not that girl who used to sing in church," and away we go. Once upon a time, Siv was a wholesome girl who used to sit up in front of her evangelical congregation and strum the guitar while everyone sang Swedish revival songs (not an experience easily forgotten). Just to make the contrast clear, director Ahlberg frequently segues from this song to a mod pop version, indicating just how far Siv has gone. Siv strays from her sheltered environment when she takes up nursing duties, where a patient quips, "I'd like to see what you look like under all that. Can I take some Polaroids?" Naturally Siv complies and, after losing her virginity, is amazed upon looking in the mirror that she doesn't look any different. Her church-going best friend is appalled ("You talk like a whore!") and, just to show her the error of her ways, pounces on her in the middle of a field. Siv's tryst with a married man leads to heartbreak, not surprisingly, so she takes up with a doctor in the hopes that both her emotions and sexual urges will be satisfied. As the opening already indicated, though, Siv's journey will be far more complicated as long as she remains in a world that simply regards women as either Madonnas or sluts.

Surprisingly proto-feminist in its approach, *I, a Woman* has dated far better than many films of its ilk thanks to the sympathetic treatment and refusal to force a certain belief on audiences. Ahlberg simply presents the facts and allows the viewers to judge for themselves, a very wise move. The actual sexual content isn't a whole lot more graphic than the old Heddy Lamarr erotic '30s opus *Ecstasy*, but the light and sure touch of the filmmakers inspired a whole wave of European erotica personified by the

directorial efforts of Metzger himself. Interestingly, Ahlberg directed two marginally related sequels to this film before going to the US as a cinematographer for such films as *Re-Animator, Hell Night*, and *Space Truckers* (how's that for contrast?). On the other hand, Persson made another Audubon Swedish mod film, *Vibrations*, provided her best performance in Metzger's *Therese and Isabelle*, and then turned up in the Vincent Price shocker *Cry of the Banshee* before vanishing entirely from the cinematic landscape. Though she still looks an awful lot like a girl after passing into womanhood, Persson ranks up there with Brigitte Bardot for defining how a woman could etch her own persona into an erotic film.

The DVD from Image provides the same transfer from First Run's VHS edition, and the film has obviously seen some rough times over the years. Though greatly improved from the splicy public domain versions circulated through various companies over the years, the materials suffer from some regrettable wear and tear around the reel changes and the opening titles, while some of the brighter scenes suffer from some strobing and fluttering. None of these factors really ruin the film, given its tattered distribution history, and having it on DVD at all is something of a miracle; just don't expect it to look immaculate. The letterboxing is a welcome gesture not mentioned on the packaging and appears to be accurate, and the English-dubbed dialogue is rendered clearly (most of Audubon's dub jobs were far better than average). The original spicy US trailer is also included for good measure, making this a welcome tribute to a once popular film in danger of sinking into obscurity.

I KNOW WHERE I'M GOING!

B&W, 1945, 92m. / Directed by Michael Powell and Emeric Pressburger / Starring Wendy Hiller, Roger Livesey / Criterion (US R1 NTSC)

A cult film for the mystical romantic in everyone, *I Know Where I'm Going* has often been overlooked as one of the early masterpieces from the team of Michael Powell and Emeric Pressburger, coming hot on the heels of their previous gems, *A Canterbury Tale* and *The Life and Death of Colonel Blimp*. This time Powell brought his love for Scotland in front of the camera with this whimsical look at a post-war woman who knows exactly where she's going but might not end up exactly where she planned.

After a delightful opening credits montage which provides a thumbnail sketch of headstrong Joan Webster (Wendy Hiller), we meet our heroine as she prepares to head off to Kiloran, an island in the Hebrides. There she intends to marry the wealthy Sir Robert Bellinger, who runs the successful Consolidated Chemical Industries. Along the way she experiences a surreal dream involving tartan-covered hills and her betrothal ceremony to the large corporation itself, but her steely, neurotic edge is gradually whittled away upon reaching Scotland. Waylaid by a nasty fog and an even nastier storm, she spends the night in a room directly across from charming naval officer Torquil MacNiel (Roger Livesy), who takes an instant liking to her. As Joan and Torquil embark on a journey the next day across the Scottish Highlands, they come across the ruined Castle Mull, home of an ancient curse governing the Lairds of Kiloran. Unfortunately Torquil is the most recent descendant, and he rents space in the castle but tries to downplay his heritage. Despite her shaken sense of destiny, Joan confronts such perils as Torquil's possibly jealous friend Catriona (Pamela Brown) and the terrifying Corryvreckan whirlpool, ultimately emerging a far different person than when she first arrived.

Though essentially light on plot and quite frothy on the surface, *I Know Where I'm Going* is an inventive feast for the adventurous moviegoer. Hiller and Livesey are both in top form and make a wonderful couple, while the spectacular Scottish scenery allows Powell and Pressburger to craft some of the loveliest visuals in their entire body of work. The delicious twist ending just adds to the fun after the viewer has already been led through several satisfying vignettes mixing together comedy, suspense, romance, and mystery, while the little dashes of surrealism are well integrated and predate a similar approach in *The Red Shoes*. For maximum effect, curl up and watch this by the fireplace with someone you care about.

The DVD transfer of *I Know Where I'm Going* looks pretty much the same as Criterion's earlier laserdisc and the Home Vision videocassette. Despite some mild damage to the print (and a horribly ragged Rank Organization opening logo), the source material is in quite good condition for the most part and does justice to the delicate imagery. The mono soundtrack is rendered as well as possible, given the low budget nature of British sound recording at the time.

The DVD carries over the supplements from the laserdisc, starting with the audio commentary by film historian Ian Christie. While better than the atrocious *Peeping Tom* commentary, this probably

isn't something fans will return to very often, though it does contain some nice bits of trivia and offers some worthy historical notes about the time period and the location shooting. Mark Cousins' 1994 documentary, *I Know Where I'm Going Revisited*, offers an exhaustive look at the film and its fan base, with testimonials from the likes of Martin Scorsese mingling with loving observations about the film and colour footage of the breathtaking locales. This featurette has proven surprisingly influential over the years since its laserdisc appearance; in fact, it's remarkable how many DVD documentaries have come to resemble it in recent years.

Some smaller scale extras include snippets from *The Edge of the World* and *Return to the Edge of the World*, also demonstrating Powell's visual fascination with the Scottish landscape, along with Scottish home movies (with commentary by Thelma Schoonmaker Powell) and Nancy Franklin's photo essay, which elaborates even further on the locations and their history. All in all, the price tag may be a little steep for a DVD, but it's still a lot cheaper than the laserdisc and packs in quite a bit of value for both the film's fans and newcomers alike.

I SAW WHAT YOU DID

B&W, 1965, 82m. / Directed by William Castle / Starring Joan Crawford, John Ireland / Anchor Bay (US R1 NTSC) / WS (1.78:1)

An early example of the teen horror novel into film trend most recently personified by *I Know What You Did Last Summer*, this film has gained an almost legendary status as one of gimmicky director William Castle's finest achievements among horror buffs. Impossible to see outside of trimmed afternoon screenings on TV, *I Saw What You Did* lingered fondly in many baby boomers' memories and was even remade with surprising competence as a 1988 made for TV movie with Robert Carradine. The original is pretty mild stuff by Castle standards, coming off such outrageous horror fests as *The Tingler* and *Homicidal*, but the results are still great fun and unmistakably display the touch of the master.

Kit and Libby (Sarah Lane and Andi Garrett, in their only big screen roles) are two bored teens left alone at home to babysit. To pass the time, they begin making prank phone calls to names chosen randomly from the phone book. At first they pretend to be girlfriends and play harmless pranks, but things turn nasty when they call a man named Steve Marak and utter the line, "I saw what you did, and I know who you are." Unfortunately, Steve has just stabbed his wife to death in the shower, and the girls aren't too swift about covering their tracks.

Top-billed Joan Crawford, looking befuddled after her earlier axe-wielding turn in Castle's *Strait Jacket*, has little to do as Amy, a neighbour with a hopeless crush on the murderous Steve. This quibble aside, Castle handles the production slickly and suspensefully. The shower sequence is one of the more amusing Psycho imitations; in this case, the victim is fully dressed, outside the shower, and wielding the knife. Figure that one out! It also climaxes in a nice bit of pre-Argento glass-shattering that really seems strong for a 1965 film aimed at adolescents.

Anchor Bay's DVD indicates that Universal has been doing a nice job preserving this film despite their bizarre refusal to release it on video. The materials are in excellent shape, with a rich, crisp black and white transfer framed nicely at 1.78:1. The limited range of the audio presents no significant problems, with Van Alexander's puffball score and each piercing shriek coming through very clearly. This DVD is obviously a labour of love, with Anchor Bay also tossing in a "World Premiere Announcement" in which Castle offers to bring some lucky participants to Hollywood for a "real live premiere," as well as the lovable theatrical trailer. Cook up some popcorn, get your phone handy, and enjoy.

I SPIT ON YOUR GRAVE

Colour, 1978, 100m. / Directed by Meir Zarchi / Starring Camille Keaton / Elite Entertainment (US R1 NTSC), Screen Entertainment (UK R2 PAL) / WS (1.85:1)

 Some people react violently upon even hearing a mention of this film, so let's first examine it without lapsing into either a flat-out defence or condemnation of its treatment of the lead female character (Camille Keaton).

The plot is about as bare bones as you can get: New York writer Keaton rents a house in the boonies to work on her novel and winds up being raped (three times in succession) by four idiot yokels. When they make the stupid mistake of letting her live, Keaton tracks them down one by one and, to paraphrase the salacious poster blurb, cuts, breaks, and burns them beyond recognition. Actually there

isn't any burning (and the trailer claims it's five guys!), but yes, folks, this 100 minute print is the same uncut version that's been making the rounds since the golden days of Wizard Video in the USA. Incidentally Wizard also released this film in the early days of UK video, but this edition, along with the much more widely available release from Astra was duly banned in the video nasties heyday.

Originally titled *Day of the Woman*, this was reissued by Jerry "*I Drink Your Blood*" Gross under its current name (swiped from a 1960s racism drama imported by Radley Metzger) to great box-office and a controversial critical reception. Interestingly, the more critics denounced it (most vocally Roger Ebert), the more money it made. Given Ebert's warm appraisal of Wes Craven's *Last House on the Left*, you can probably gather that this film is definitely a matter of taste. The rape scenes are horrifically brutal and drawn-out, but it's impossible to see how one could ever sympathize with the assailants. Keaton is the only recognizably sympathetic human being in the film, and the camera squarely situates her as the centre of almost every scene. Interestingly, the film features no music whatsoever, a startling contrast to the bizarre pop and country crooning that served as a counterpoint in *Last House*. In fact, if you look closely, *I Spit*, while hardly a fun or upbeat film, is clearly a descendant of the Russ Meyer sex and brutality morality tales like *Mudhoney* and *Lorna*, though here the woman is actually more empowered (she never "asks for it" and is never punished for dishing out revenge). Here, as with Meyer, you have a backwoods setting where a woman's presence alone is enough to send men into a savage fury of conflicted sexual impulses, and the sexual tension winds up exploding into brutal, vigilante-style violence. At no point does Keaton ever enjoy the rape (which is a lot more than can be said of Lorna!), and her final boat ride is presented without comment or moralizing.

Unfortunately director Meir Zarchi does not drive all of his points home; by focusing so much on delivering the requisite exploitation elements (including way too much leering nudity during the seduction/murders of the second half), he fudges the issue, giving critics plenty of obvious ammunition. Criticism aside, Elite Entertainment has presented the film in a crystal-clear, ideally letterboxed edition (from the same master as its earlier laserdisc), including the original US trailer. It's really too bad Zarchi wasn't on hand to do audio commentary for the film's first DVD release, but a "Millenium Edition" with his participation is in the works as we go to press. Not surprisingly, the UK disc (*sans* extras) runs seven minutes shorter, so beware.

I STILL KNOW WHAT YOU DID LAST SUMMER

Colour, 1998, 100m. / Directed by Danny Cannon / Starring Jennifer Love Hewitt, Brandy / Columbia / WS (2.35:1) (16:9) / DD5.1

Of all the teen slasher retreads being churned out, *I Know What You Did Last Summer* deserved a sequel less than any of its colleagues but got one anyway. While no classic by a long shot, *I Still Know* is an improvement over its predecessor (thought it could hardly get worse). Most obviously, the self-absorbed high school jerks from Kevin Williamson's original hack-and-slash gloss on the Lois Duncan teen novel have mercifully been replaced by fairly likable, amiable college students. Further, the basic stalk and die premise has been nicely twisted here into a tense *Ten Little Indians* scenario that contains more than its fair share of surprises along the way. Like Paramount's embarrassed treatment of its *Friday the 13th* series, Columbia basically threw this one out into theatres and apparently regarded it with little more respect on home video.

Here is the complete, uncut summary of the film as they explain on the video jacket: "Remember Ben Willis? He's the fisherman who killed the boy who was driving the car when it went off the road in the fatal accident that killed his daughter Sara... he's the man in the slicker with a hook in his hand ready to exact bloody justice... well, he's back. It's hard to forget a man who refuses to die." Apparently nobody in the packaging department even bothered to watch the movie, but that's hardly new. So here's what it's really about: survivor Julie James (Jennifer Love Hewitt, doing a post-trauma routine *a la* Neve Campbell in *Scream 2*) is now in college and finds her relationship with high school sweetheart Ray (Freddie Prinze, Jr. in a glorified cameo) strained by his refusal to leave their hometown. Meanwhile, her best friend Karla (self-promoting teen ingénue Brandy, making a passable starring big screen debut here) and her boyfriend Tyrell (*Clockers'* Mekhi Pfifer) urge Julie to start dating love-struck college boy Will (Matthew Settle). When Karla wins a free trip for four to the Bahamas on a radio trivia contest, she brings along Julie, Will, and Tyrell for a carefree vacation. Unfortunately they arrive to see the tourists leaving in anticipation of the start of storm season. Besides, they should know something is wrong when their hotel is managed by *Re-Animator*'s Jeffrey Combs. Sure enough, the foursome quickly finds itself shut off from the outside world and fending for their lives on the tropical equivalent of a dark and stormy night.

The real star of this film is visually gifted director Cannon, who redeems himself from the studio butchery performed on *Judge Dredd* and displays a disarming familiarity with the ins and outs of the horror genre. From the evocative opening sequence to the beautifully sustained creepy atmosphere of the tropical murder trap, Cannon constantly to at least keep the action at a high level of eye candy even when the script fails to deliver. John Frizzell's eerie, nerve-jangling score (featuring a beautiful theme for Julie) is up to par with John Debney's work on the first film, and a number of suspense sequences, especially Brandy's jittery encounter on top of a greenhouse, set this a few notches above the standard screamer hokum. Unfortunately the filmmakers end things on an irritating note with yet another inane "back from the dead" ending that should have been cut, but overall it's a more sincere and substantial effort at a sequel than the cynical *Scream 2*.

The DVD is generally satisfying, though occasional mild artefacting crops up in a couple of the darkest shots (notably the shots of Julie's face in the confessional), and the anamorphically enhanced transfer is more colourful and detailed than the film looked in theatres. It's a shame Columbia didn't include commentary like the first film; extras include the standard theatrical trailer (but not the more interesting teaser, unfortunately), as well as the original *I Know* trailer (minus the notorious "From the creator of *Scream*" tag) and a video for Hewitt's "How Do I Deal?" (featuring so much hilarious digital overdubbing that one doubts whether Hewitt has ever stepped in front of a microphone).

I, ZOMBIE

Colour, 1998, 79m. / Directed by Andrew Parkinson / Starring Giles Aspen, Ellen Softley / MTI (US R1 NTSC)

Described by its newcomer director (*Dead Creatures'* Andrew Parkinson) as a "thirtysomething coming of age story," *I, Zombie* stands dramatically apart from some of the more half-baked stabs at British horror in the late 1990s. Though imperfect, its dead serious tone (often downright grim for the most part) and refusal to resort to nudging comedy guarantee a worthwhile look for adventurous horror fans looking for a nasty little treat. However, though this film was picked up and distributed on video by Fangoria, the bloodthirsty Full Moon crowd for whom this is clearly aimed will most likely be disappointed by the overwhelming sense of malaise and artistic flourishes which serve as a counterpoint to all the graphic bloodshed.

Basically a male remake of Jean Rollin's *The Living Dead Girl*, the film follows the sad path of Mark (Giles Aspen), a young man who finds his time consumed by the demands of his doctoral studies and daytime job to the point that his relations with Sarah (Ellen Softley) have become strained. While out collecting moss samples for a botany study, Mark comes across an seemingly abandoned house that contains a rotting corpse on a mattress and a young woman huddled in the corner. When he attempts to carry the woman out of the house to safety, she bites a chunk out of his neck and flees into the woods. Mark awakens much later and finds himself overcome by a compulsive hunger for flesh. Naturally, after consuming a hapless passer-by, he decides to rent an apartment and deal with his illness. However, the absence from Sarah proves to be too much, so he knocks her out with chloroform and takes her back to his place. Unfortunately, he realizes that their relationship was not meant to be, and he returns his beloved to her home. As Mark sinks deeper into depression and his hunger becomes all-consuming, he decides to seek another way out of his hellish condition.

Like most '90s horror films, *I, Zombie* can be easily read as a metaphor for AIDS and drug use, with Mark's bodily deterioration and his DT-inspired fits recalling some of the grimmer late night news features. The film contains more than its share of disturbing passages, particularly a gruesome (though cleverly filmed) bit in which Mark tries to set his broken rotting leg by screwing a metal plate into the bone. The perpetual shifts between reality and Mark's fantasies generally work well, with a nicely poignant payoff at the end, and Aspen does an efficient job of eliciting sympathy as he turns into a rotting eyesore. The odd narrative device of inserting on-camera interviews with Sarah and other related acquaintances talking about Mark doesn't make a whole lot of sense but does function within the irrational context of the film. Parkinson really shines during the fleeting hallucinations, particularly the striking Rollin-inspired image of Mark, his bodily rifts sealed with chunks of metal, affixed in silhouette with other afflicted souls on a stark, deserted junkheap littered with jagged steel poles. On the downside, even at such a brief running time, this often feels like a short film dragged kicking and screaming out to feature length, and Mark's long,

silent passages of walking around and moping (underscored a little too heavily by Parkinson himself with guitar, piano, and synth) tend to overstay their welcome. The droning music and weird air of alienation and despair, coupled with over the top gore, often recall the tone of *Nekromantik*, a similar example of downbeat, self-destructive modern Euro-horror.

MTI does an adequate job of preserving this film, considering it was shot over a period of four years for next to nothing on 16mm. Film grain tends to erupt in many of the darker shots, along with a few traces of faulty compression, but the transfer is generally watchable. The DVD contains a feature commentary by Parkinson and Aspen (though we're never sufficiently told why this film is subtitled *The Chronicles of Pain*), who reminisce about their long, life-altering experience making the film. Other extras include an intriguing ten minute behind the scenes featurette, three bland deleted scenes, a TV spot on *Fangoria* editor Tony Timpone, and a trailer for *Lady of the Lake*.

IDLE HANDS

Colour, 1999, 90m. / Directed by Rodman Flender / Starring Devon Sawa, Seth Green / Columbia / WS (1.85:1) (16:9) / DD5.1

 The horror comedy *Idle Hands* became smothered (in America at least) by the national hysteria surrounding the high school shootings. Of course, a terrible, misleading trailer and unappealing poster design didn't really help matters, and not surprisingly, the movie disappeared quickly from theatres. Its underperformance aside, Columbia has done a terrific job of showcasing this deranged little item as well as possible.

Sort of a pothead cross between the horror classics *Mad Love* and *The Beast with Five Fingers*, the wacko story begins when Anton Tobias (Devon Sawa), a lazy stoner content to spend his days in front of the TV, fails to notice that his parents have been brutally butchered by a serial killer prowling the town. Anton's two tokin' buddies, Mick (Seth Green) and Pnub (Elden Ratcliff), come by to visit just in time to discover that Anton's hand has been possessed by an evil spirit responsible for all the mayhem, and neither of them makes it back out the front door. However, Anton's pals return as dismembered zombies, which makes about as much sense as anything else in the movie but allows since nice riffs on the old *American Werewolf in London* dead buddy routine. Meanwhile the object of Anton's affections, Molly (future *Dark Angel* Jessica Alba), asks him to a Halloween dance, and a "Druidic priestess" named Debi (Viveca Fox, a nice bit of bizarre casting) tears across the country to expunge the evil spirit before it opens a gateway to hell. Unable to cope with his murderous extremity, Anton lops off his hand at the wrist, resulting in some *Evil Dead 2*-inspired schtick at the dance where The Offspring happen to be playing (and doing a pretty good cover of The Ramones' "I Wanna Be Sedated"). Will Anton stop his hand? Will Molly and Anton find true love? And how much blood can be crammed into a major studio film?

Misleadingly promoted as a "hot comedy," *Idle Hands* works best as an irreverent and very sick horror film laced with black humour. All of the killings, including a couple of cop murders, are surprisingly rough and creepy, while the film's unexpected message seems to be that laziness is bad and pot is good. Green does a great job as usual, Sawa does his best Bruce Campbell impression, and the rest of the cast seems to be having plenty of fun. Even the requisite topless sex scene is handled in a highly unorthodox fashion, with both participants wearing KISS makeup! Only the last two scenes which seem to have accidentally stumbled in from *The Frighteners* fail to satisfy, but a more unconventional ending would have most likely been out of the question considering how many risks were taken over the preceding 80 minutes. The film also displays a few other minor flaws, notably the umpteenth *Seven*-inspired credits sequence and that irritating '90s teen movie trait, a bad grunge soundtrack overstuffed with forgettable songs. On the other hand, Graeme Revell's puckish, weird score definitely satisfies and recalls his earlier work on *Bride of Chucky*, a similar rough and tumble splatter comedy. For even more fun, keep your eyes peeled for some amusing clips from *Glen or Glenda?* and *Dawn of the Dead*!

Though not labelled as a collector's edition, Columbia's DVD really pulls out all the stops. As usual, image quality and sound are first rate demo material, hardly surprising given the studio's track record so far. Director Flender (a Roger Corman alum) provides a laid-back feature length commentary with Green and Ratliff, then introduces an alternate, *Spawn*-inspired swimming pool ending for the film (it's not that great, either). Other extras include a studio puff piece featurette and the "second" theatrical trailer, which re-dubs the tag line that this film "gives scary movies the backhand" instead of "the finger." Interestingly, both the featurette and trailer feature some lines and footage trimmed from the film itself, including a few glimpses of the alternate ending.

IGUANA

Colour, 1988, 98m. / Directed by Monte Hellman / Starring Everett McGill, Michael Madsen / Anchor Bay (US R1 NTSC) / WS (1.85:1) (16:9) / DD2.0

Cited by cult director Monte Hellman as one of the most miserable shooting experiences of his career, *Iguana* was consigned to video oblivion in the US and received a half hearted theatrical run through Europe. Too bad, really, as this peculiar and often compelling cross between *The Tempest* and *The Phantom of the Opera* is one of Hellman's more satisfying and visually fascinating films. However, those of a politically correct nature may want to find entertainment elsewhere.

After enduring endless ridicule and torture at the hands of his fellow shipmates and their unsympathetic captain, Gamboa (Fabio Testi), facially disfigured sailor Oberlus (*Twin Peaks'* Everett McGill) dives into the ocean and washes onto a deserted Gallapagos island. Oberlus performs a private ritual in which he renounces God and declares a personal war against humanity, which he begins to exercise when ship's cook Sebastian (Michael Madsen) washes ashore soon after. Oberlus threatens to sever one of Sebastian's fingers for every unpleasant comment, a threat which produces Oberlus' first servant. Two more additions to Oberlus' domain, good friends Dominic (Joseph Culp) and George (Tim Ryan), find their bond tested by Oberlus' demands, culminating in an unforgettable execution ritual. Meanwhile unhappily married Spanish lady Carmen (*Lovers of the Arctic Circle's* Maru Valdivielso) goes for a romantic nocturnal trip to the island with her lover, a decision that sends her into sexual servitude for Oberlus. This strange community forms its own bizarre, unhealthy dynamic which begins to fray when Oberlus finally snatches Gamboa from his ship, a vengeful gesture which crosses with a bizarre twist of fate involving Carmen as well.

It's probably safe to say that there has never been another film quite like *Iguana*. Brutally horrific and sexually blunt (both verbally and physically), it mixes pirate movie conventions, horror, visual splendour, and twisted domestic drama into one unholy stew, capped off with a stunning final shot as poetic as anything you'll ever see. Like most Hellman films, this one isn't perfect and sports its own set of idiosyncrasies, such as McGill's bizarre half-English accent and the weird mix of American, Italian, and Spanish actors. However, this potpourri casting tactic also adds to the film's flavour, making it a worthwhile venture for fans of both Eurocult oddities and psychotronic cinema in general.

Iguana was partially funded with a US video deal to Media, who in turn handed it over to Imperial for a brief VHS release. The fullscreen transfer quickly vanished from the shelves and is now virtually impossible to find apart from the occasional mom and pop store. Anchor Bay's version looks quite attractive, with careful attention paid to the dusky lighting inside the ships and Oberlus' cave.

The moody look is vital to appreciating this film's eerie atmosphere, and the DVD gets it just right. The surround audio is generally restrained but comes to life during some Oceanside sequences, including one knife duel near the end, which sends the sounds of crashing waves exploding from all of the speakers. The only drawback is what appears to be the accidental omission of one sadly important dialogue sequence, following the newcomers' arrival on Oberlus' island in which we learn the fate of one crucial character. Anchor Bay has announced its intentions to reissue a corrected pressing, though to date none has surfaced. Since a trailer for this wouldn't exist, the only notable extra on the DVD is a running feature length commentary by Hellman, McGill, screenwriter Steven Gaydos, and the American Cinematheque's Dennis Bartok. The candid discussion explains the production difficulties (which Hellman refers to as abusive to both himself and his crew), the location and casting decisions, and the changes (often for the better, apparently) made to the original source novel by Albert Vasquez Figueroa. Interestingly, no one mentions the presence of two familiar Jess Franco actors, Jack Taylor and Luis Barboo (the butler from *Female Vampire*), during the opening ship sequences.

ILSA, SHE WOLF OF THE SS
Colour, 1973, 96m. / Directed by Don Edmonds / Starring Dyanne Thorne, Gregory Knoph
ILSA, HAREM KEEPER OF THE OIL SHEIKS
Colour, 1974, 93m. / Directed by Don Edmonds / Starring Dyanne Thorne, Victor Alexander
ILSA, THE WICKED WARDEN
Colour, 1977, 94m. / Directed by Jess Franco / Starring Dyanne Thorne, Lina Romay
Anchor Bay (US R1 NTSC) / WS (1.85:1) (16:9)

A rare exploitation film that actually surpasses the lurid promises of its title, *Ilsa, She Wolf of the SS* became one of the most notorious titles on videotape, due to both its rarity and the numerous different versions floating around. The sheer tastelessness of its concept had already earned it a reputation as a nasty puppy, even worse than the likes of *Love Camp 7* or *Salon Kitty*, primarily thanks to the unforgettable, hammy performance by Dyanne Thorne as everyone's favourite domineering commandant of the Third Reich.

Our tender story begins with a batch of new arrivals at Ilsa's medical camp (actually the sets of *Hogan's Heroes*, as most know by now), where Ilsa quickly gets to work. She's already castrated her latest bed partner, who failed to satisfy her ravenous sexual cravings, and now she's ticked off at the entire human race. Determined to prove that women can withstand more pain than men, she doles out countless atrocities on her victims to prove that the fairer sex should serve in Hitler's army. Ilsa's work routine is momentarily disrupted when she chooses an American prisoner, Wolfe (Gregory Knoph), from the latest batch of male prospects, and in his words, he "can hold it back all night, like a human machine - faster, slower, anything." Naturally Ilsa turns into a growling kitten in the sack with our studly Yank, and she even throws in a couple of extra women the following night to prove his stamina wasn't a one time fluke. Little does Ilsa know that Wolfe is also busy staging a revolt which will make the camp's grounds run red with Nazi blood!

Produced under a pseudonym by cinema's greatest huckster, David F. Friedman, *Ilsa, She Wolf of the SS* is made with enough skill to make the viewer very, very uncomfortable. Every campy line of dialogue and outrageous plot development is immediately deflated by a stomach churning image of bodily torture, courtesy of latex master Joe Blasco (*Shivers*). Thankfully the accents and sets are so ludicrous that one never believes the film is taking place anywhere near Nazi Germany, and Thorne is always worth watching in just about anything.

Anchor Bay's presentation of the initial Ilsa offering most obviously sports a brand new, crystal clear widescreen transfer that wipes the floor with those old chopped up VHS tapes. You simply won't believe a '70s exploitation film could ever look this good. (Not so for the trailer, lifted directly from a dupey videotape.)

Any drive-in fan with a perverse streak should have this film in their collection, but only the die hard will want to venture into the commentary track. Featuring Thorne, Friedman, and director Don Edmonds, this could have been a golden moment for sleaze fans, but unfortunately British "humorist" Martin Lewis (who had already stinted on Anchor Bay's *The Ghost Goes Gear* commentary) moderates with a snide sledgehammer approach that obviously irritates all of the participants, not to mention the listener. His jarring, unfunny cracks reference everything from Mel Brooks to the film's low budget without eliciting a single chuckle. This problem aside, the disc is nicely (and sleazily) packaged, complete with filmographies and nasty menu screens to get you in the right mood.

Following the sex-and-death-camp antics of *She Wolf,* busty Dyanne returned to the screen in some unspecified time period for a new job as the *Harem Keeper of the Oil Sheiks.* Well, it's only one sheik actually, but who's counting? Ilsa's boss, El Sharif ("Victor Alexander"), delights in her nasty antics, which include kidnapping and importing girls in crates to the palace along with the help of black sidekicks Velvet and Satin. (Honestly.) A diplomat from the US arrives at the palace along with CIA agent Adam Scott (Michael Thayer), the requisite All-American stud whose bed skills melt Ilsa into a demure love toy. Well, not quite; she still has time to torture a harem spy (Russ Meyer regular Haji) throughout most of the film by feeding her eyeball to the diplomat (who's married but likes young boys), covering her leg in fire ants, and ultimately doing something with an certain electric device which can't be described in words. Yep, it's revolution time again, so it looks like Ilsa just might get her comeuppance for a second time.

Less slick but more guilt-free compared to its predecessor, this film chugs along with plenty of nudity and gore along the way to keep the crowds cheering. The familiar cast of exploitation vets is a joy to watch, with busty Uschi Digard turning up as one recent kidnappee and the ubiquitous George "Buck" Flower as a beggar with syphilis who figures prominently in the climax. Thorne seems more relaxed and active in her role this time, though that beige outfit doesn't quite pack the same kinky wallop as her first uniform, for obvious reasons. And now is probably as good a time as any to address one rampant legend concerning this film. Many sources claim the actor who plays El Sharif is actually actor and monologist Spalding Gray underneath the fake hair, eyeliner, and heavy beard. While the facial resemblance is striking, Spalding had just performed in a hardcore porn film (*The Farmer's Daughters*) under his real name. Let's just say he must have sprouted a whole lot of body hair before doing Ilsa... if that's really him. And why would he bother using a pseudonym for this film but not for a XXX title? The commentary track here is no help, since no one on the set knew the actor's real name(!) and he was supposedly a jerk who got his just desserts when someone ran over his foot. Ah, the foibles of '70s exploitation filmmaking. In any case, this same guy also popped up doing hardcore in some '70s loops, but his real name may never be known.

Thanks to its deliberately gritty visual texture, *Harem Keeper* doesn't look as dazzling as the first film on DVD but is miles ahead of any of the (often censored) videotape editions. That's California's sunny San Fernando Valley standing in for the Middle East throughout the film, and now you can fully bask in all the glorious... uh, scenery. The trailer here is in much better shape than the first one, and the commentary track is more easygoing than *She Wolf*'s. Apparently someone must have slapped moderator Martin Lewis around a couple of times so everyone else could finally get a word in.

So after *Harem Keeper,* you thought the Ilsa movies couldn't get any sicker? Well, just wait until you see what happened when Spain's notorious sex and violence maverick Jess Franco got his hands on the franchise. Actually this isn't technically an *Ilsa* film, but it might as well be. Originally titled *Greta the Mad Butcher,* then *Wanda the Wicked Warden* (the version on this disc's trailer), this twisted puppy ultimately wound up with its most famous title thanks to drive-in revivals and video reissues.

A more cheesecake-oriented film than its predecessors, *Wicked Warden* features Dyanne once again (this time with a redhead perm) as the sadistic warden of a jungle prison for women. One escaped inmate, Rosa, flees to the nearby home of Dr. Arcos (Jess Franco), who believes something is rotten inside the jail walls. Ilsa/Greta/Wanda shows up to reclaim her property, provoking Arcos to send Rosa's sister inside as a prisoner to discover the truth. In between numerous hosings, catfights, and other rampant displays of Franco's favourite pubic areas, Ilsa indulges in fleshy delights with the twisted Juana (Franco's wife, Lina Romay), who doesn't seem to mind when Ilsa uses her as a human pincushion in the sack. It all ends violently, as these things must, when the inmates revolt with a most unusual and depraved method of revenge.

Throughout its long, looong history on home video, *Wicked Warden* has never looked this good.

Colourful and crisp, this is sleaze at its finest and most well preserved. The film's European producers are promising to launch a separate DVD edition with different extras, but they've got their work cut out for them to make this look any better. Thorne and her husband, Howard Maurer, return for the commentary track, this time with the annoying Mr. Lewis back to provide "comic" relief when absolutely none is really necessary. Just listen to Thorne and cover your ears for the rest. The menus and trailer are a real hoot, with a female voice on both repeatedly cooing, "wicked... warden...." It's a shame this marked the end of Ilsa's reign of drive-in cinema, but thankfully her heritage has been left in very capable hands at Anchor Bay. Come on in... Ilsa's waiting for you.

IMMORAL TALES

Colour, 1974, 103m. / Directed by Walerian Borowczyk / Starring Paloma Picasso, Lise Danvers / Anchor Bay (US R1 NTSC) / WS (1.66:1)

 Ah, the European anthology film. This long lost art of the '60s and '70s allowed notable directors of all stripes and nationalities to experiment with any number of running times and story genres, with a wide range of actors at their disposal. Polish director and former animator Walerian Borowczyk found his greatest international success with an artsy, ultra-erotic variation on this formula, *Immoral Tales*, for which he somehow managed to rope in Pablo Picasso's fashion-savvy daughter, Paloma, to portray the real life, bloodthirsty Erzebeth Bathory. Needless to say, the results are unlike anything else ever committed to celluloid.

The lustful nature of mankind reveals itself in a quartet of tales ranging from medieval Italy to the present day. In the first, a rakish twenty year old escorts his naive young sixteen year old cousin to the seaside, where he talks her into performing sexual favours as the tide rolls in. Then in "Therese the Philosopher," a young Victorian-era girl undergoes a rapturous sexual awakening with the aid of a few handy household props and vegetables. But that's nothing compared to Countess Bathory, who rides into a local village, rounds up dozens of nubile young virgins, and escorts them back to her castle. There the girls strip, engage in harmless horseplay, and then... Well, if you don't know the legend, there's no point in spoiling the grisly surprise. Finally Lucrezia Borgia sexually cavorts with two men in her private chambers while a heretic burns

outside; afterwards the true identity of her partners is revealed.

Straddling uneasily somewhere between '70s art house pretension and softcore sleaze, *Immoral Tales* is beautiful to look at but so slowly paced that much of its target audience may give up by the time the second story is over. Borowczyk's following film, *The Beast*, started life as a segment of this film but expanded into an entire, unforgettable perverse feature on its own. His best work was yet to come with such delirious gems as *Dr. Jekyll and His Women*, but this naughty collection still makes for a decent introduction and, sluggish pacing aside, contains what must be a record amount of nudity for a non-hardcore title. Though *Immoral Tales* played US theatres with an X rating, a small amount of footage was lost from most prints compared to the stronger European cut. One bit in particular of a girl "stuffing" herself with pearls is a bit more graphic on Anchor Bay's DVD, though it still lacks an alternate, live action prologue setting up the theme of the stories which appeared in the first French and Polish editions.

Very briefly released on US home video during the format's infancy and later on UK VHS, *Immoral Tales* looks good if not pristine on DVD. The original film has always looked a bit soft and grainy, with muted colours. The disc features burned-in English subtitles (alas), with the original French and English-dubbed tracks included. The mono sound is fine, again limited by its age and the quiet nature of the film. The lurid US trailer, complete with critical blurbs, is also included. Contrary to the packaging, the film is not enhanced for 16:9 playback and looks no different, transfer-wise, from its PAL VHS cousin.

IMMORTAL BELOVED

Colour, 1994, 120m. / Written and Directed by Bernard Rose / Starring Gary Oldman, Isabella Rossellini / Columbia (US R1 NTSC) / WS (2.35:1) / DD5.1

 Along with David Fincher, British director Bernard Rose is one of the few genuinely gifted visionaries to enter feature films after dabbling in the world of music videos. Rather than simply using fancy stylistics to gloss over a shaky grasp of narrative (as is so often the case), Rose used his visual and editing skills to produce two striking horror films, *Candyman* and *Paperhouse*. For his next project, the logical choice was... the story of

Ludwig van Beethoven. *Immortal Beloved* combines the dramatic formalism of *Amadeus* with the sensory avalanche of Ken Russell's composer biopics (*The Music Lovers, Mahler, Lisztomania,* etc.) to produce an extremely engrossing and ultimately wrenching historical fantasy, crammed to the corners with visual delights and astonishing directorial flourishes.

At the beginning of the film, Ludwig van Beethoven is dead. Following his funeral, Beethoven's friend, Anton Schindler (the excellent Jeroen Krabbe), uncovers the composer's final will and testament, scrawled on his deathbed, in which he leaves all of his property to "my immortal beloved." Enclosed is a note from years earlier in which he pleads to his anonymous love to wait for him at their rendezvous point. Who was this mysterious woman? Schindler begins questioning Beethoven's acquaintances and uncovers a number of women in the maestro's life, including the mature and dedicated Anna (Isabella Rossellini), the sensualist Giulietta (Valeria Golino), and Beethoven's ultimate nemesis, his sister-in-law, Johanna (Johanna ter Steege). Along the way Schlinder also learns of Beethoven's stormy relationship with his nephew, Karl (*Europa Europa*'s Marco Hofschneider), and the gradual process by which the composer's escalating deafness became known to the public.

As Beethoven, there could not have been a better choice than Gary Oldman. A genuine actor's showcase, the role requires tenderness, anguish, fury, and even insanity, all of which find Oldman well up to the task. The three beautiful female leads all make a vivid impression, with Rossellini and ter Steege especially gripping with difficult, multi-layered portrayals. And then, of course, there is the music itself; conducted by Georg Solti and featuring such modern masters as Yo-Yo Ma and Emanuel Ax, this soundtrack makes Beethoven sound better than ever. However, the imagery is no less impressive; from the breathtaking beauty of the funeral opening to the powerhouse "Ode to Joy" sequence (one of the unsung high points of 1990s cinema), *Immortal Beloved* constantly pulls one ornate surprise after another from its seemingly endless pockets.

For some reason, Beethoven scholars took issue with the film's resolution, forgetting the fact that (a) this is not a strictly realistic film, and (b) no one will ever know the identity and the entire circumstances of Beethoven's "immortal beloved." The woman in question may or may not have been in prison depending upon when the original letter was written; however, attacking this film for making conjectures based on a romantic notion is as valid as tearing into *Amadeus* because no one really knows what Mozart and Salieri talked about on the former's deathbed.

Unfortunately, the scholars' jibes were enough to prevent this film from quite achieving the wide release and acclaim it deserved, not to mention several well-deserved Oscar nominations that sadly were not meant to be.

While no home viewing can fully recapture the experience of this film on the big screen, Columbia's DVD comes much closer than their earlier laserdisc. The laser presentation was marred by Sony's irritating "video improvement" process, which simply slapped a bright yellow tint over the entire movie (see *Wolf* for another glaring example). The new anamorphic transfer looks much closer to the theatrical prints, with an exquisite level of detail and no visible artefacts.

Surprisingly, Columbia has actually decked out this DVD as a full blown special edition and is one of their most lavish efforts to date. Rose provides a full running feature commentary, in which he covers everything from historical minutiae to the creation of the decor. Also included is the original ten minute "making of" featurette, basically a standard studio promo piece with cast members talking about their roles - though it does contain the odd experience of Gary Oldman speaking in his normal thick British accent while in his Beethoven costumes. More interestingly, the DVD contains a new half hour documentary, "Beloved Beethoven," featuring on camera interviews with Oldman, ter Steege, Golino, producer Bruce Davey, and Rose. The director seems to have been humbled quite a bit in the last five years, perhaps due to the failure of his sumptuous but flawed adaptation of *Anna Karenina*, but hopefully he will return to form behind the camera in the near future. Rossellini's absence here is regrettable, but everyone else offers some intriguing reflections on the experience of making the film and its reception in years since. The original US trailer rounds out this satisfying package.

IMMORTALITY (THE WISDOM OF CROCODILES)

Colour, 1998, 99m. / Directed by Po Chih Leong / Starring Jude Law, Elina Löwensohn / Buena Vista (US R1 NTSC) / WS (1.85:1) (16:9) / DD5.1

Following closely in the footsteps of *The Hunger*, here's a modern day vampire tale (known everywhere except on DVD as *The Wisdom of Crocodiles*) in which the main bloodsucker can move about in daylight, touch crosses, and weep, while no one ever utters the word "vampire" even while someone's chomping on their neck. Rather than a straight up horror film, this sombre meditation on human duality uses its basic monstrous conceit to explore such heady topics as conflicting gender roles, man's will to live versus the right to die, and that old Cronenbergian standby, the body's ability to physically manifest its emotions.

As we open, lonely and upwardly mobile Steven Grlscz (Jude Law) stands beneath a tree where the smashed car carrying his now deceased girlfriend has been lodged after a tragic accident. After the police finally extricate the wreckage, Steven returns home and scribbles a cryptic note in one of his diaries. He then becomes involved with the emotionally fragile Maria (Kerry Fox), whom he drains of blood by biting her throat open during a lovemaking session. Apart from being a sensitive strain of vampire, Steven can externalize the emotions of his victims by expelling a tough, dagger-like shard from his throat after feeding. Two policemen, Inspector Healey (*Gothic*'s Timothy Spall) and Sergeant Roche (Jack Davenport, who reunited with Law for *The Talented Mr. Ripley*) suspect that Steven may be criminally responsible for the deaths of his last two girlfriends, but they have nothing more than circumstantial evidence. Steven begins yet another romance when he saves Anna (*Nadja*'s Elina Löwensohn) from hurling herself in front of a subway car. At first she rejects his advances, but the two tentatively establish a connection in which it becomes clear that Anna may be the woman Steven has been looking for.

If it weren't for the solid performances by all of the leads, *The Wisdom of Crocodiles* - er, *Immortality* - could have been a disaster. Law brings some much needed sympathetic layers to his portrayal, and his solid chemistry with Löwensohn compensates for the fact that very little actually happens until the last ten minutes of the film. Much of the thematic material is interesting, such as the basis for the original title (referring to the conflict between the predatory "reptilian" side of the human psyche versus the warmer "mammalian" one) and the symbiotic relationship between man and woman, good and evil.

While director Po Chih Leong (who previously specialized in stylish Chinese dramas) piles on the visual flair and keeps a tight grip on the basic emotional core of the story, he hedges his bets in several frustrating instances. Obviously not confident with the methodical pacing, he occasionally interjects flashes of gore (including a thematically relevant but very squishy tracheotomy), nudity, and an incongruous sword/stickfight sequence involving a street gang.

Apart from a clumsy computer generated title card, the Miramax DVD of this film is pretty close to perfect. The image quality looks terrific, a vast improvement over the bland, cropped UK VHS version, and the 5.1 audio mix is active and manipulative for most of the running time. Some of the rear ambient effects are especially strange, while the orchestral music score is well rendered and atmospheric. Amazingly, the packaging gives no indication whatsoever that this is a vampire film, describing it instead as "a dark, mysterious crime thriller in the tradition of *The Talented Mr. Ripley* and *Double Jeopardy!*" Now doesn't that sound exciting? As far as supplements go, the disc contains the US theatrical trailer (for all six screens where it actually played) and an insubstantial making-of featurette, both of which retain the film's original title. The latter contains videotaped interview footage with both the star and director, as well as some behind the scenes footage. The disc also includes a dubbed French language track in standard surround.

IMPULSE

Colour, 1984, 91m. / Directed by Graham Baker / Starring Tim Matheson, Meg Tilly / Anchor Bay (US R0 NTSC)

Some films simply defy classification, and *Impulse* is a perfect example. Is it a horror film? Not really, though it is capable of giving viewers a serious case of the creeps. Is it science fiction? There's nothing drastically beyond the scope of feasible scientific accomplishments already, but it does mine the same vein of paranoid small town fear as *Invasion of the Body Snatchers*. Is it drama? Yes, but anyone looking for a straightforward tale of human conflict will be very shaken. This refusal to conform to genre standards was most likely responsible for Impulse's relative oblivion today, though Anchor Bay's new incarnation may go some way to correcting this oversight. While hardly a classic, *Impulse* is something of an anomaly in the slasher-happy mid-'80s.

A young unmarried couple, Stuart (Tim Matheson in one of his last really good roles) and Jennifer (Meg Tilly, fresh off of *Psycho II*), travel to their small hometown after Jennifer's mother shoots herself over the phone. The local doctor, Hume Cronyn, is tending to the comatose mother, and the couple attempts to uncover the cause of her drastic action while staying with Jennifer's father (John

Karlen) and brother (a scrawny-looking Bill Paxton). Meanwhile the local townsfolk are behaving very strangely: urinating on car bumpers, swiping cash from bank tills, setting things on fire, and so on. The entire town seems afflicted, and events begin to spiral violently and tragically out of control.

Boasting strong performances all around and a slow, gradually mounting atmosphere of unavoidable doom, *Impulse* will be a pleasant surprise for those who overlooked it during its theatrical run. The film's original VHS release from Vestron, long out of print, was a fuzzy eyesore; the new Anchor Bay DVD is greatly improved, with detail and colour invisible on cable and video versions. The fullscreen transfer contains more information at the top and bottom of the image and slightly less on the sides than theatrical screenings, most likely cropped from a 1.66:1 master. While the DVD contains no extras, this presentation is acceptable and mostly likely the best this will look for a very long time. Don't be misled by the cover art, which tries to pass this off as a sexy sci-fi thriller; this is a sombre, effective look at society going to hell, with a most haunting and nihilistic ending.

THE IN CROWD

Colour, 2000, 105m. / Directed by Mary Lambert / Starring Susan Ward, Lori Heuring / Warner (US R1 NTSC, UK R2 PAL) / WS (1.85:1) (16:9) / DD5.1

To pick the most influential teen movie of the past decade, most fingers would point to *Scream*. Of course they would be correct, but few could have predicted another copycat strain, the *Wild Things* rip-off (which usually throws in heavy dashes of *Melrose Place* and *Dawson's Creek*). Instead of a marauding postmodern slasher, these films focus on twisty plots involving coming of age teens trapped in social conspiracies, with a little homoeroticism often thrown in for good measure. These films can range from slick diversions (*Gossip*) to worthless dreck (*The Skulls*), but sometimes they can be truly deranged. Just look at the acidic black comedy *Jawbreaker* or its closest cinematic relative, *The In Crowd*, directed by the long absent Mary Lambert (*Pet Sematary*) with all the panache of a Mentos commercial.

After being released from a mental institution, nervous young Adrien (Lori Huering) gets a job as a cabana girl at a posh country club populated by uncommonly stupid rich kids. Chief among these are head teen queen Brittany (Susan Ward), squeaky clean Matt (Matthew Settle), and butch good girl Kelly (Laurie Fortier). Brittany takes Adrien under her wing after being saved from drowning, and the two become like sisters. Odd, really, considering Brittany's bitchy sister, Sondra, looked exactly like Adrien and has been missing for several years, sending only oblique postcards to Matt - who shows an undue amount of interest in Adrien. Quicker than you can say "giallo," a mysterious evildoer is causing mayhem around the country club, tampering with people's motorcycles and spying on folks in the shower. Has Adrien's mind snapped? Is Brittany less mentally balanced than she appears? The answer isn't terribly shocking, but it does lead to catfights, lesbian liplocks, and a hilarious shovel-slinging finale in evening gowns.

The concept of an outsider encountering evil beneath the glossy veneer of the comfortably rich isn't really anything new, but the theme could still have produced dozens of premises more interesting than the one on display here. The storyline really doesn't offer any surprises, giving away the identity of its villain halfway into the film and going through the motions by telegraphing all of its shocks. The film is also clumsily plastered with an instrumental techno score that should have this film nice and dated in about six more months or so, and the first half is paced so slowly most viewers will wonder whether this is even supposed to be a thriller or another teen soap opera. So why bother watching it? Two reasons: Susan Ward and terrific camp value. The bitchy and hopelessly deluded Brittany manages to provide some spark even in her mildest scenes and chomps the scenery with wild abandon, while the script offers some exchanges so purple they almost punish the ear. (Just check out the "pointer" discussion between the two lead girls.) It's also astonishing to watch how Lambert constantly veers her film right to the edge of PG-13 territory, with bare breasts (but no nipples!) and see-through bras on frequent display and characters engaging in lusty but skin-free gropings. Toss in some violence, sexual dementia, a mouldy corpse, and a final scene cribbed from Roger Vadim's *The Game is Over*(!), and you've got a prime piece of trash for your next cinematic drinking party.

As usual, Morgan Creek has gone the extra mile and created a loaded special edition for an amazingly low price. Ward and Huering appear for a very loose and breezy commentary track, in which they chatter about everything from the location shooting to their fellow actors to... well, you name it, it's in there somewhere. You also get an isolated music track, three deleted scenes, including an extraneous secondary ending, as well as two theatrical trailers, a slew of TV spots, cast and crew bios, a photo gallery, and some pretty swanky animated menus. The DVD-Rom features include a gallery of preliminary and final poster art, as well as production notes and various related links. The transfer itself is very good, though the film itself has some problems worth noting. The lighting is colourful but often low key to the point of turning to mud, while an early beach party scene has the most eye-punishing day for night processing in recent memory. For some reason, Adrien's flashbacks are rendered in washed out black and white (very similar to *The Rage: Carrie 2*), but they're supposed to look that grainy. The 5.1 audio is another story, with each speaker awash with clearly separated channels. The three-way club scene in particular sounds great and should have home theatre owners chuckling with glee.

IN DREAMS

Colour, 1998, 100m. / Directed by Neil Jordan / Starring Annette Bening, Aidan Quinn / DreamWorks (US R1 NTSC, UK R2 PAL) / WS (1.85:1) (16:9) / DD5.1

Though he finally gained mainstream recognition with *The Crying Game* and *Interview with the Vampire*, Irish director and novelist Neil Jordan caught the eyes of several horror and arthouse devotees back in 1984 with his stylish *The Company of Wolves*, an erotic, unsettling collaboration with writer Angela Carter which pried open the seamy psychosexual underbelly of the Little Red Riding Hood tale. Thirteen years later, Jordan returned to the fairy tale milieu with *In Dreams*, a widely misunderstood horrific fantasy in which the Snow White story is interwoven into a modern tale of loss and psychic torment.

Claire Cooper (Annette Bening in her strongest performance since *The Grifters*), an illustrator of children's novels, finds her marital happiness and sanity being tested by a series of recurring dreams involving a young girl being led by a dark, long-haired stranger through a moonlit apple orchard. Her husband, Paul (Quinn), goes along with her claims, even to the point of going to police when Claire (as in "clairvoyant," get it?) believes her visions involve an actual serial killer prone to dumping his young victims into a reservoir filled with the remains of a town flooded in 1965. Strangely, Claire also begins

to have visions of a young boy chained to a bed inside an underwater town, and after an unexpected tragedy hits close to home, she finds the line between dreams and reality becoming increasingly blurry... which doesn't help when she winds up face to face with the killer.

Critical and mass response to *In Dreams* largely dismissed it as "weird" and "stupid," and for anyone expecting a linear, traditional horror film, these terms are understandable. Though this is technically an American film, *In Dreams* (originally shot under the puzzling title *Blue Vision*) has "European" stamped all over it. The plot intentionally defies traditional lines of logic and often unexpectedly shifts gears without warning; furthermore, its surreal, startling imagery is some of the strongest the US horror genre has seen since *Candyman* (with which this shares more than a few narrative similarities). This film works best if experienced on an almost entirely sensory level, thanks in no small part to Darius Khondji's dazzling cinematography (the varied dream sequences are all knockouts), Jordan's skilful use of camera movement and cross cutting throughout the major suspense scenes, and best of all, the jittery, experimental score by Elliot Goldenthal, which often uses wispy female vocals and shuddering electric guitars to dazzling effect.

For an interesting experience, compare this film with Dario Argento's *The Stendhal Syndrome*, which also concerns a woman whose shared visions with a serial killer cause him to stalk and torment her, eventually leading to her complete mental breakdown (signified by a change in hairstyle) and her imprisonment in his remote countryside lair. Oddly enough, both films also share a peculiar fascination with bloody lip-biting... However, *In Dreams'* hypnotic flow is disrupted by a few unfortunate flaws. After such a powerful, malefic build-up, Robert Downey, Jr.'s on-camera performance as the killer in the final quarter of the film is bound to be a letdown, though he tries mightily (perhaps too hard). Also, as Claire's psychiatrist, Stephen Rea sports an inexplicable Dan Hedaya accent that renders some of his lines unintentionally comic. These glitches aside, *In Dreams* is far more fascinating and rewarding than the recent teen slasher swill, proving that edgy adult horror is still possible (though perhaps not encouraged, judging by the disappointing box office returns).

While this is much more daring than most DreamWorks projects, the DVD has been treated with the same care as their more high profile releases. The beautiful anamorphically enhanced transfer shimmers with the bizarre autumnal colour schemes which made this such a haunting experience in the theatre, and the highly manipulative, often jarring Dolby Digital soundtrack is just as terrifying at home. The only extras are cast and crew bios and the US theatrical trailer.

IN SEARCH OF DRACULA

Colour, 1975, 81m. / Directed by Calvin Floyd / Starring Christopher Lee / Image (US R0 NTSC)

Back in the late '60s and early '70s, literary studies experienced an explosion of interest that popularized such concepts as psychological and historical criticism. Basically what these approaches do is treat the characters in books like real people and use shreds of historical fact and established psychological theories to gain more insight into fictitious people. Sound flaky? It usually is. While a handful of good works came out of this (Jean Rhys' *Wide Sargasso Sea* being the most obvious example), most of the time the results were just downright silly. In one of the most famous examples, Romanian scholars Radu Florescu and Raymond McNally stumbled onto a cash cow with *In Search of Dracula*, their novelized explanation of how author Bram Stoker derived his legendary Dracula from the real-life bloodthirsty exploits of Vlad Tepes, aka Vlad the Impaler. While this connection has been assumed as historical fact over the years (even forming the basis for Francis Ford Coppola's wildly off the rails adaptation), the constant assertions that Dracula was "a real person" seem pretty implausible now.

So where does this film come in? While Florescu and McNally were working on their book, they also served as consultants on this Swedish-financed film, originally intended for television, which features Christopher Lee's narration attempting to tie the film's numerous trains of thought together into a coherent whole. The film veers madly from travelogue footage of Transylvanian peasants to staged bits with Lee in a bad wig playing Vlad himself. Along the way we also get a lot of clips from *Scars of Dracula* and Jess Franco's *Count Dracula*, both of which also feature Lee, as well as bizarre scientific footage of a vampire bat feeding from a guinea pig. Half an hour in, the film really becomes crazed by introducing a real life vampire, basically a poor pathetic Swedish schmuck who, in staged scenes, cuts himself open and drinks his own blood, mopes around in the park, and dreams of feeding on little kids. But wait! We also get coverage

of the Bloody Countess herself, Elizabeth Bathory, some incongruous footage of a naked girl on horseback, and a look at the Vampire of Dusseldorf and an unrelated bit on lycanthropy. Then Lee expounds at great length on the history of Mary Shelley's famous stay at the Villa Deodati, which inspired *Frankenstein* (barely connected by virtue of the fact that Polidori's *The Vampire* may have been inspired during the same stay). The quasi-documentary then comes to a close with movie vampires, including some clips of the "vamp" Theda Bara (talk about stretching your point!) and brief mentions of *Nosferatu*, Bela Lugosi (shown in clips from another unrelated film), and the Hammer classics.

This patchwork ode to vampirism may not be good cinema, but horror fans should find plenty of amusement here. Obviously anything with Lee for an hour and a half is worth watching, and the mixture of historical tidbits and far-flung analysis makes for compellingly odd viewing at times. Randomly scrapped together from a number of sources (mostly 16mm, apparently), the source quality obviously must shift every few minutes between clean new footage and old archival material. That said, the DVD looks as good as could be expected, with stable colours and a surprisingly low amount of grain considering that '70s Swedish films weren't exactly shot on the finest film stock and under the greatest conditions.

IN THE MOOD FOR LOVE

Colour, 2000, 97 m. / Written and Directed by Wong Kar-wai / Starring Tony Leung, Maggie Cheung / Criterion (US R1 NTSC) / WS (1.85:1) (16:9) / DD5.0, Mei Ah (HK R3 NTSC) / WS (1.85:1) / DD5.1, Tartan (UK R2 PAL) / WS (1.85:1) (16:9) / DD2.0

Originally planned under the title *Summer in Beijing,* this evocative drama continues the string of Wong Kar-wai masterpieces named after pop standards (e.g., *Happy Together*). Though the director already enjoyed a solid arthouse and cult reputation, *In the Mood for Love* garnered his widest mainstream acclaim thanks to its dizzying atmosphere and the star power of its two leads, a period dressed pairing made in movie heaven.

In 1962 Hong Kong, newspaper man Chow (Tony Leung) and his wife move into an apartment where another couple by chance is also settling in down the hall. Left alone to unpack due to his wife's perpetual absence, Chow strikes up a silent rapport with the other couple's female half, Li-zhen (Maggie Cheung), a secretary whose husband also leaves her constantly in solitude. They pass each other on the stairs and in the hall, but significant clues lead to an encounter in a noodle shop where they realizes their respective spouses are having an affair. The tentative friendship that blossoms between them, indicating a potential for passion which may never erupt.

The succulent, dreamy air of *In the Mood for Love* would make it a memorable film on its own, but the perfectly timed physical and emotional steps performed by the two leads elevate to the status of a classic. The marriage of camerawork, colour, and thespian nuance create a hermetic world in which love and sex rarely collide. Furthermore, the suppressed and ultimately doomed battle between the heart and social morality recalls Edith Wharton, though Kar-wai's approach far surpasses the similarly themed *Ethan Frome* and *The Age of Innocence*, the latter of which was filmed in a visually lush but ultimately botched attempt by Martin Scorsese. Here the Wharton principle is carried through perfectly thanks to the film's understatement and deliberately hypnotic pace, which may be off-putting to some viewers. As with the director's previous efforts, the refusal to conform to standards of genre and plotting results in some fascinating new experimental effects. He leaves open gaps in his story for viewers to fill in their own details, an approach which pays off here with breathtaking results. The haunting coda in particular has a peculiar resonance, which lingers in the air far longer than the smoke from the characters' omnipresent cigarettes.

The widely imported Mei Ah DVD of *In the Mood for Love* from Hong Kong hit most shores well before its theatrical release in most English speaking territories, though its flawed non-anamorphic presentation and erratic English subtitles (which don't translate any of the written onscreen intertitles or text) made it only a passable temporary option. In the UK, Tartan issued a single disc version with minimal extras, followed several months later by a two disc set loaded with supplemental features. These bonuses have been carried over in the U.S. to the Criterion two-disc set, which boasts the trump card of a new, fully restored anamorphic transfer that outclasses its predecessors by a wide margin. The print looks flawless and richly detailed, with colours that appear luminous without becoming oversaturated. English subtitles are optional, and the audio options include a 5.0 mix

(which sounds nice and spacious) and the theatrical 2.0 mix. (For some reason the Mei Ah disc contained a quasi-5.1 track that never really used the subwoofer and sounds much less textured than the Criterion one.)

Extras include deleted scenes (including an alternate ending and a fascinating '70s sequence jettisoned from the final assembly), a 22-minute interview reel with Wong Kar-wai, a terrific 53-minute documentary involving the director's painstaking creative process (which reportedly drove the actors nearly mad), an assortment of teasers, TV spots, and trailers from Hong Kong, France, and the U.S. (the last scored with Bryan Ferry's rendition of the title tune), a 15-minute press conference interview with Kar-wai, cast and crew bios, a delectable gallery of preliminary poster art and the final promotional artwork from around the world (with the Japanese one a particular standout),the 18-minute international press kit reel, a text essay about the director's work entitled "The Searcher," a written study of 1960s Hong Kong by Gina Marchetti, a 43-minute Tokyo International Film Festival conference with Cheung and Leung from 2000, a study of the source music and score used in the film, and finally, "Hua yang ne nian hau," a lyrical montage of archival nitrate material from Hong Kong cinema assembled by Kar-wai. Easily one of Criterion's finest forays into a current film already being acknowledged by many as a classic, this elegant set provides hours of engrossing entertainment and should help bolster the already stellar reputation of this remarkable film.

IN THE MOUTH OF MADNESS

Colour, 1995, 95m. / Directed by John Carpenter / Starring Sam Neill, Julie Carmen / New Line (US R1 NTSC) / WS (2.35:1) (16:9) / DD5.1

Apparently inspired by the growing cult following for his neglected, masterful *Prince of Darkness*, John Carpenter decided to explore similar waters again in the Lovecraftian *In the Mouth of Madness*, a jittery study of reality going straight to hell. Though this material proved to be a little too heady for the multiplex crowd, Carpenter's film has, not surprisingly, enjoyed a solid reputation in the horror crowd thanks to home video and cable.

Called in to investigate the disappearance of popular horror writer Sutter Cane (Jurgen Prochnow), insurance investigator John Trent (Sam

Neill) decides the whole thing is a huge publicity stunt. Meanwhile the release of Cane's latest novel is provoking outbreaks of violence and maniacal behaviour among readers who treat Cane's fiction like an addictive drug. Accompanied by book editor Linda Styles (Julie Carmen, also seen in *Fright Night II*), Trent decides to take an investigative road trip after discovering a hidden map in the covers of Cane's novels. The pair stumble into what appears to be a real life version of Hobbs' End, a cursed town depicted in Cane's novels, and soon the line between reality and nightmare begins to horribly blur.

Though equipped with the usual number of Carpenter cheap shocks (including a reprise of the *Prince of Darkness* double whammy dream sequence), *In the Mouth of Madness* works best as a creepy, subversive "what if?" scenario in which the viewer's perspective is constantly called into question. The first half in particular delivers some skin-crawling chills that rank with the director's most accomplished cinematic tricks, such as the nocturnal drive to Hobbs' End (love the boy on the bicycle) and Styles' initial realization that the town may be just as dangerous and supernaturally afflicted as its fictional counterpart. The underrated Neill makes for an engaging Doubting Thomas protagonist, though one can only wonder how the fervently left wing Carpenter managed to talk NRA spokesman Charlton Heston into making an appearance as Carmen's boss.

New Line's DVD edition looks better than their good but flawed widescreen laserdisc, and viewers now have the option of also checking the fullscreen version for comparison. Though visually butchered, the pan and scan option allows for further appreciation of the quirky, creepy details in the production design and a few crafty subliminal background touches along the way. Colours and shadow depth are quite strong, but the real showcase of this disc is the 5.1 soundtrack, guaranteed to have the hairs on the back of your neck standing on end from the very beginning.

The disc also includes the theatrical trailer (but no TV spots or featurette from the laserdisc - not much of a loss, though), a hidden trailer for *Twin Peaks: Fire Walk with Me*, and the now infamous commentary track by Carpenter and cinematographer Gary M. Kibbe. While the advent of DVD has provided some even more tedious and pointless rambling feature discussions, this one is still pretty tough going, with the technical details of lighting and camera focus filling up virtually all of the 90 minute running time. Fortunately, Carpenter's other commentary tracks are much better.

IN THE REALM OF THE SENSES

Colour, 1976, 100m. / Directed by Nagisa Oshima / Starring Tatsuya Fuji, Eiko Matsuda, Aoi Nakajima / Wellspring (US R1 NTSC), Nouveaux (UK R2 PAL) / WS (1.66:1)

The old cinematic debate of "Is it art or porn?" went into overdrive with *L'empire des sens (The Realm of the Senses)*. An art film with hardcore sex was previously unheard of; while Jean Genet, John Waters, and Andy Warhol had tiptoed around this area for a few years, the gifted Nagisa Oshima (*Max Mon Amour*) plunged in headfirst and paved the way for such other art films with on-camera sex as Marco Bellochio's *Devil in the Flesh* and Lars Von Trier's *The Idiots*. Thankfully, the film itself is excellent; don't let Madonna's oft-quoted blurb, "It turns me on because it's real," turn you off.

Sada (Eiko Martsuda), a young geisha, begins an affair with a handsome, married master of the house (Tatsuya Fuji, also in Oshima's *In the Realm of Passion*). The intensity of their affair escalates until Sada informs her lover that she will kill him if he makes love to his wife or anyone else again. He agrees, and in defiance of social barriers, they run off together. However, their romantic abandon continues fuelling itself until they find there is only one very disturbing way for it all to end... Aside from the explicit sex, most of the film's attention centred on the shocking finale, which was known to send audience members fleeing in horror. Be warned, if you're the least bit squeamish, this is probably not the movie for you.

Originally released by Image Entertainment on laserdisc as part of its CinemaDisc Collection, the film was issued on DVD from Wellspring (formerly Fox Lorber) in the US no less than three times! Strangely, the packaging contains no warning about the rough content of the unrated film, which sits comfortably in many family-friendly retailers. Unfortunately, the presentation was botched in every case. The laserdisc was marginally letterboxed at approximately 1.55:1; despite some mild wear on the source print, it looked fine and boasted rich, attractive colours, and featured the alternate English-dubbed track on the analogue channels.

The DVD is a bit sharper than the laserdisc and features optional English subtitles, but regrettably it's full frame and features even less information on the top and bottom of the image, too! Colours are noticeably washed out in comparison to the laser, with an ugly brownish cast over many scenes.

Infuriatingly, Wellspring also issued a poorly dubbed English version in a vastly superior letter-boxed transfer and repackaged the subtitled edition with a new cover and opening logo, leaving these separate versions floating around on the market. Unfortunately the British DVD from Nouveaux is equally compromised; despite the "uncut" packaging claims, it optically crops and zooms an "offensive" image involving underage genitalia. At least it's letterboxed and subtitled, though. Perhaps someday they'll get it right on DVD, somewhere in the world.

IN THE WOODS

Colour, 1999, 80m. / Directed by Lynn Drzick / Starring DJ Perry, Stuart MacDonald, Aimee Tenalia / Dead Alive (US R1 NTSC), Film 2000 (UK R2 PAL) / DD2.0

"Creepier than *Blair Witch*!" exclaims the box art for *In the Woods*, which is about as useful as saying a film is "Smarter than *Glitter*!" Actually, this entertaining indie project is more of a cross between *The Evil Dead* and *Razorback*, with a little *Backdraft* tossed in for good measure.

Struggling alcoholic fire-fighter Alex (DJ Perry) and one of his co-worker buddies are out shooting in the woods one afternoon when they come across a large handmade cross over a burial mound. Thinking their discovery might be related to an outbreak of strange disappearances in town, the men dig into the grave only to find large, unidentifiable animal bones. Soon a large, mysterious force chases them out of the woods, forcing them back into town where they swear to never tell anyone of their discovery. Meanwhile Alex's wife, Helen, threatens to leave him if he takes another drink, so naturally he disappoints her. Left alone in the house, Alex is distressed to find dismembered body parts left on his property as sort of a bloody offering. A local pathol-ogist helpfully explains that the victims have been gnawed to death by a carnivore unknown to modern science, so it's up to Alex to track down the marauding beast and put it out of the town's misery.

Obviously made with a great deal of love and reverence for the horror genre, *In the Woods* (no relation to the Sondheim musical, *Into the Woods*) is obviously very low budget and feels very rough around the edges. However, for undemanding monster fun, it does deliver the goods and features at least two very good scares. Though the opening scenes are a little shaky, leading man Perry makes for a good, flawed protagonist, strangely reminiscent of Ron Livingston in *Office Space* (go figure!). Many of the other actors don't fare as well, delivering many awkward stage pauses that simply don't work on film. The monster effects are fine, considering, and mostly amusing once the story takes a third act twist into Toho territory. On the downside, the script leaves way too many plot threads dangling in the last scene, and the screen's most superfluous serial killer since *Malice* is thrown in just to muddle the story. Construction problems aside, though, the film still packs in some nice twists and, for once, involves actual human beings who are all over 18.

Though fairly difficult to find, the Dead Alive DVD does an admirable job of presenting *In the Woods*. The image quality is understandably compromised by the budget, with some heavy graininess popping up in a few shots, but overall the presentation is stable and satisfying. More impressive is the stereo sound mix, which offers some surprising aural jolts and directional effects. Considering only about fifteen minutes of the film actually takes place in the woods, the filmmakers utilize the natural ambience as much as possible. The score alternates between effective symphonic and choir arrangements to some jarring fuzz guitar metal riffs, but it also sounds just fine. A far too revealing trailer is included, along with some production photos. A nice package, though the steep price tag is ludicrous. Rent it or look for a steep discount online, though, and your efforts will not go unrewarded.

INCUBUS

B&W, 1966, 76m. / Directed by Leslie Stevens / Starring William Shatner, Allyson Ames / Wellspring (US R1 NTSC)

While the idea of William Shatner acting in the unsuccessful, fabricated "international" language of Esperanto sounds like the makings of a camp classic, *Incubus* is really anything but. This pet project of *Outer Limits* producer Leslie Stevens was rarely seen during its release and appeared to vanish entirely, existing more as a whispered about curio than a genuine film. The result, a sort of mythological mishmash of *Horror Hotel* and *The Seventh Seal*, is a strange and compelling experience that demands both imagination and patience from its viewers.

The pared down storyline, set in a vaguely identified pastoral netherworld known as Nomen Tuum, follows the spiritual battle for the soul of Marc (William Shatner), a former soldier who has settled down into a quiet domestic life with his innocent sister, Arndis (Ann Atman). An alluring blonde succubus named Kia (Allyson Ames) appears and proceeds to seduce the inherently virtuous Marc, but when she falls in love with him, a diabolical incubus (the ill-fated Milos Milos) arrives to even the score.

Though less than satisfying as a horror film per se, *Incubus* works as an attempt to create an art film out of purely California bred film talent. The Big Sur locations are magically transformed into a dreamy, disorienting alternate universe, while the supernatural is firmly grounded in poetic visuals based in nature. Shatner is restrained and sympathetic for once, with his usual scenery chewing inclinations held firmly in check here. *Outer Limits* fans in particular will enjoy contributions from the usual behind the scenes crew, including a score from Dominic Frontiere. From the woodcut opening credits to the bizarre, demonic final scene, *Incubus* stands alone from any of its contemporaries and certainly deserved to be rescued from oblivion.

Considering we're lucky to be able to view this film at all, the video presentation is more than satisfying. The only existing source material, a print with permanent French subtitles, was unearthed by the French Cinematheque after the original negative was either lost or destroyed, depending on who tells the story. Image quality looks fine - nearly pristine in most cases, actually - and is marred only by the English subtitles superimposed over large black bars to conceal the French subtitles. The unaltered version with simply the small French subs is worth checking out for a second viewing, when one can focus more on the visuals without worrying about the dialogue.

Extras include a camcorder interview by David Schow with cinematographer Conrad Hall (*American Beauty*), Bill Fraker, and producer Taylor; the men also provide a running commentary track in which they discuss the threadbare production, with Shatner providing his own separate commentary to discuss everything from the rigors of acting in an unfamiliar language to the challenges of evoking the supernatural onscreen. Less valuable are "Curse of the Incubus," an *Exorcist*-style catalogue of tragic events which befell the cast and crew, and a "trailer" which is actually a new, surprisingly condescending commercial hawking the VHS release.

INFERNO

Colour, 1980, 107m. / Directed by Dario Argento / Starring Leigh McCloskey, Irene Miracle / Anchor Bay (US R1 NTSC) / WS (1.85:1) (16:9) / DD5.1

When naysayers claim that Dario Argento movies are loaded with style but have no coherent storyline, *Inferno* is usually cited as the worst offender along with its immediate predecessor, *Suspiria*. However, its champions claim that *Inferno* is a deliberately nonsensical nightmare from which the viewer is never allowed to awaken. Given the difficult circumstances of its production (and the fact that very few have actually seen the film all the way through), the truth probably lies somewhere in between, but for Italian horror fans, *Inferno* is a dazzling, stylish feast loaded with some of Argento's strongest visual strokes of genius.

Rose Elliott (Irene Miracle), a young poetess in New York, acquires a rare book, The Three Mothers, written by an alchemist named Varelli. The book chronicles three houses of the damned inhabited by a trio of malefic sisters: the Mother of Tears, the Mother of Sighs, and the Mother of Shadows. Rose believes that her own ancient apartment building is one of these cursed locations, and she tries to pass the information on to her musicologist brother, Mark (Leigh McCloskey), who resides in Rome. After a gruesome incident in his apartment, Mark rushes to New York only to find that Rose is now missing. The bookseller Kazanian (Sacha Pitoeff) seems to offer a few clues to Rose's disappearance, but ultimately Mark himself must unravel the hellish mystery lurking within the bowels of this strange building.

Designed more or less as a sequel to *Suspiria* (which focused on Mater Suspiriorum, or the Mother of Sighs), *Inferno* is a more challenging and languid affair that tosses out even the shreds of a Nancy Drew storyline found in the first film. Early on the film announces its refusal to adhere to reality when Rose drops her keys into a puddle of water and finds herself submerged in a flooded ballroom littered with decrepit floating corpses. Only on subsequent viewings do some of the film's odder elements really come together, such as the recurring animal imagery; just stop and think for a moment about the chopped up meat Alida Valli feeds those cats. All of the actors seem to be completely in a daze, with the lovely Daria Nicolodi turning up again as a rich hypochondriac who meets one of the film's more absurd violent fates. Also, look fast in the Rome sequence for a cameo by the Mother of Tears, played by the striking Ania Pieroni (also in Argento's *Tenebre* but best known as the ill-fated babysitter in Lucio Fulci's *House by the Cemetery*). Keith Emerson, formerly of Emerson Lake & Palmer, contributes an audacious and often brilliant piano-heavy music score, the first of many to come during his Italian film music career.

Thanks to a typo on the sleeve for Key Video's first VHS release claiming an erroneous 83 minute running time, rumours have persisted for years that Argento's film has been subjected to massive cuts outside of Italy. In fact, the US version has always been complete, running a full 107 minutes like Anchor Bay's current DVD. The only major censorship hassles turned up in Britain, where Fox's VHS release was trimmed by a few seconds to omit some "animal cruelty" (the mouse chomping and kitty bashing). In any case, the DVD is by far the best way to experience *Inferno* thanks to its lustrous picture quality, which brings out all of Argento's heavily saturated colour lighting. The 1.85:1 Technovision aspect ratio is accurately duplicated here, with a significant amount of extra information added in comparison to the fullscreen videotapes. The original Dolby Stereo soundtrack has been tweaked very slightly to modern 5.1 specifications, resulting in a subtle but often creepy directional mix that does what it can with the material's limitations.

While Argento was unwilling to provide a full commentary for this release, he does appear during an informative and endearing video interview segment, which should satisfy the curious. His outlook on the film seems to have improved somewhat over the years, considering all of the painful associations he had (the studio held it up after its completion in 1978, Argento was plagued with hepatitis during filming, and so on). The disc also includes a spectacular but spoiler-filled European trailer, and an attractive but relatively skimpy still gallery and talent bio section round out this deliciously nasty package, obviously a must for Euro horror fans.

INSEMINOID

Colour, 1980, 91m. / Directed by Norman J. Warren / Elite Entertainment (US R1 NTSC), Stonevision (UK R0 PAL) / WS (2.35:1)

Of all the *Alien* rip-offs churned out in the early '80s, *Inseminoid* gained the most notoriety thanks to its graphic gore, which had to be drastically trimmed for its US release (primarily to drive-ins, under the title *Horror Planet*).

Looking at Elite's uncut release of the British film on DVD (don't be fooled by the "Rated R" designation on the back!), whatever shock value the film may have ever possessed has disappeared completely over the years. Anyone who chuckled through this back in their formative adolescence will find plenty of cheesy enjoyment here, but sadly, the film itself won't please anyone else.

A not very intrepid space crew has established a cavernous station below the surface of an icy planet. During an exploration, two members stumble on some glowing crystals which cause one of them to die. The other humans, including Jennifer Ashley and former soap opera trash queen Stephanie Beacham, naturally act as if nothing out of the usual is happening, even when Judy Geeson (a long way from *To Sir, with Love*) starts acting strangely and disembowels a young Victoria Tennant (the former Mrs. Steve Martin) with a pair of scissors. It seems Geeson has been impregnated by malicious alien hand puppets who control her behaviour and provoke homicidal rampages. Eventually Geeson gives birth to a couple of smaller puppets just in time for the budget-deprived finale.

Director Norman J. Warren tries valiantly to cover up the film's deficiencies with colourful lighting and mobile camera work when people run up and down halls, but the endless, static dialogue scenes produce little besides viewer apathy. The notorious gore scenes are little more than splattery paint jobs, while the actual alien rape sequence pales in comparison to the slimy beastie breeding in the similar (and much more enjoyable) *Galaxy of Terror*.

The irritating synthesizer score grates on the ear and dissipates whatever suspense could have ever been achieved, and the bland underground sets (foreshadowing George Romero's *Day of the Dead*) fail to ever convince the eyes that any of this is actually happening in space. In fact, the space angle has so little to do with the story that it could have been removed without much damage being done at all; an alien impregnation within a group of miners would run about the same course.

Drawbacks aside, the widescreen transfer on both DVD editions is a huge improvement over the old Nelson/Embassy video release and even the previous widescreen, uncut Japanese laserdisc. The colours are consistently stable, and the scope framing looks perfect. The film isn't lensed with any particular flair, but at least interested viewers can see it on its best behaviour.

The UK disc also includes a workmanlike half hour documentary on Norman J. Warren along with the theatrical trailer.

INTRUDER

Colour, 1987, 84m. / Directed by Scott Spiegel / Starring Elizabeth Cox, Danny Hicks / Dragon (Germany R0 PAL)

With a cloud of impending unemployment hanging over them, the night staff at the Walnut Lake grocery store gloomily set about the task of sale-pricing the stock. But in the shadows lurks a maniac intent on relieving them of more than their jobs... If you thought the surfeit of films preceding *Intruder* had ravaged the stalk'n'slash subgenre to the point that there was no inventive slaying left unplundered, Scott Spiegel's tasty slice of terror theatre has a grisly surprise or two up its sleeve. The first-time director spruced up the relatively uninteresting backdrop of an open-all-hours supermarket with a profusion of creative camera tricks that give us POV shots from (among others) beneath a broom, the surface of a turning doorknob and, most memorably of all, behind a telephone dial.

The cast are less irritating than the usual teens-in-peril assemblies, among them Elizabeth Cox as the spunky heroine for whom it doesn't all come good in the end, *Evil Dead / Spiderman* director Sam Raimi as a butcher who ends up dangling from one of his own meathooks, and Ted "Joxer" Raimi as a nerdy produce worker who's cranium is breached with a cleaver. The real joy of *Intruder* though is its resident loony-tune, Danny Hicks, the identification of whom isn't all that unsporting since it's not only patently obvious from the outset that he's the killer but his guilt is underscored in the film's trailer and most of its promotional materials too. Hicks' incredulous expression as the cornered Cox unexpectedly retaliates and stabs him in the gut - "Where'd you get the knife?" he grins as he keels over - brings to a close a satisfying confection of black humour and carnage, which (as an example of the former) includes a beating to death with a severed head and (of the latter) a hard-to-watch face bisection with the aid of a bandsaw!

Released by Dragon Entertainment of Germany, the 9-chapter full screen transfer on this Region 0 PAL DVD is only a marginal step up in quality from VHS, with conspicuous grain and stretches of intrusive hiss on the soundtrack. It is, however, uncut, which is a bonus to UK viewers who have only ever seen the Colourbox cassette release of some years back, which was devoid of most of the graphic killing. Much as does this review, the trailer (the only additional feature on the platter) leaves one in no doubt as to the killer's identity and it also includes a couple of shots of Sam Raimi's demise that didn't make the final cut, presumably being discarded due to their less than convincing look. Shot under the title *Night Crew: The Final Checkout*, Dragon have released the film *as Night of the Intruder*, although the title on the film itself is simply *Intruder*. - TG

THE INTRUDER

B&W, 1961, 83m. / Directed by Roger Corman / Starring William Shatner, Frank Maxwell / New Concorde (US R1 NTSC) / WS (1.85:1)

Though technically not a horror film, Roger Corman's *The Intruder* is as unsettling a film as you're likely to see from America during the early '60s. The topic of desegregation was still a very hot topic in 1961, and aided by a blistering performance from William Shatner and a pitch perfect script by noted *Twilight Zone* scribe Charles Beaumont, Corman delivered a wrenching portrayal of racial hatred and social manipulation that was understandably too hot for many viewers to touch at the time.

In a small Missouri town, charismatic Adam Cramer (Shatner) arrives by bus and gradually insinuates himself into the local populace, spewing messages of hatred and gradually turning opinion against the recent legally enforced segregation. Cramer also sparks up an affair with a married woman (Jeanne Cooper) and finds a flawed nemesis in the form of Tom McDaniel (Frank Maxwell), a newspaper reporter whose family can't quite grasp his tentative acceptance of blacks and whites coexisting on equal terms. Tensions escalate, leading to the arrival of the KKK and the formation of a lynch mob whose terrifying scale exceeds even Cramer's diseased imagination.

An uncomfortable viewing experience in the best possible way, *The Intruder* has never really received its due, probably because the major white protagonist is both terrifyingly real and villainous instead of a comfortable identification figure for the audience. Corman constantly undercuts viewer expectations, delivering a portrait of the South unlike anything seen from a major studio; in fact, the stark realism of the location shooting resulted in more than its share of problems, as this DVD reveals in its limited but revealing extras. Shatner's barnstorming theatrical approach is used to excellent effect here as he makes an all too believable demon in human form, one who uses words rather than physical violence to achieve his ends. Be warned that the film contains unflinching language to depict the period and rarely pulls any punches, so approach with caution if you're PC-inclined.

Rarely shown apart from occasional late night TV broadcasts, dupey VHS copies, and shredded 16mm prints, *The Intruder* looks comparatively spectacular on DVD, despite some unavoidable blemishes brought on by its advancing age. Contrast is sturdy and looks dead on, while the sound is far more clean and legible than ever before. Not a demo disc by a long shot, this is nevertheless a welcome opportunity to reassess a film too often overlooked. Press materials before its release indicated a commentary track with Corman and Shatner, though what actually materializes is a videotaped discussion with both men in which they discuss the challenging, uncomfortable, and borderline dangerous circumstances surrounding the filming. A worn looking trailer is also included, indicating there's only so much one can do with a great little film that, by and large, speaks just fine for itself.

INVASION OF THE BLOOD FARMERS

Colour, 1972, 84m. / Directed by Ed Adlum / Starring Bruce Detrick, Norman Kelley / Ventura (US R0 NTSC) / WS (1.85:1)

Shot on the ultra-cheap in upstate New York, *Invasion of the Blood Farmers* belongs comfortably with the efforts of 16mm sleaze wizards like Andy Milligan, William Girdler, and Michael Findlay, who not so coincidentally edited this one (along with director Ed Adlum's more widely seen follow up, *Shriek of the Mutilated*). Barely coherent but rarely dull, this madcap tour through a backwoods region populated by scientists, mad cults, and bloody mayhem became something of a drive-in staple during its day, and now the DVD can astonish and mentally damage a whole new generation on DVD.

During the fiery, crimson-tinted intro, we learn about the history of Druids who continue to thrive to this day across the globe. Why, they've even shacked up in the great American Northeast, where locals are falling prey to a pair of farmers who bleed their victims in a wooden shack. A nasty incident at a local bar in which a man collapses dead from means unknown triggers a local investigation, which touches on the bizarre experiments of one Dr. Anderson (Norman Kelley). The scientist's tinkering

with human blood triggers the interest of our modern Druids, led by the not terribly imposing Creton (Paul Craig Jennings). It seems their bloody actions (which include ambushing a woman in the shower) can all be justified because they intend to revive their dead queen, a beautiful blonde preserved in a glass coffin.

The memorable poster art for *Blood Farmers* depicted a hillbilly farmer preparing to gouge a top-heavy woman with a pitchfork, but the film is a little stranger than your average exploitation effort. Like the thematically similar *Motel Hell*, the film uses its rural setting and farmland locations to interesting effect, a far cry from the gothic castles and bubbling laboratories that had populated horror films in the previous decade. Some sequences in particular, such as an extended bloodletting ritual by masked farmers in a barn, foreshadow the later (and obviously far superior) *The Texas Chainsaw Massacre*; while the intensity level is kept at bay by numerous unintentional chuckles (check out the shoe polish hairdos) and gaping plot inconsistencies, the film has enough going on to keep fans of Z-grade trash busy munching on their popcorn.

Briefly released on VHS in the format's infancy, *Blood Farmers* has been difficult to track down for the past fifteen years or so. Thankfully its DVD incarnation is vastly superior to the muddy, cropped tape edition; in fact, it's unlikely this no budget 35mm effort could look much better. Some problems caused by shoddy lighting and obviously clumsy lab work show up in the source material, so don't expect this to look like a big budget Hollywood feature. That said, the letterboxing at least offers some semblance of formal composition (something it always seemed to lack before), and the colours and detail level are fine. As part of Fred Olen Ray's Nite Owl Theatre, this release features the director camping it up with his wife and a bevy of semi-nude starlets; the release is also augmented with the original theatrical trailer and spots for Ray's films both available and forthcoming on disc.

THE INVISIBLE MAN

B&W, 1933, 71m. / Directed by James Whale / Starring Claude Rains, Gloria Stuart / Universal (US R1 NTSC)

Out of the thick of a blizzard comes a stranger, his face swathed in bandages, his eyes hidden beneath blacked-out goggles. This is scientist Dr. Jack Griffin (Rains). Taking a room at The Lion's Head inn, he curtly demands that he be left in peace. But the mysterious guest piques the inquisitive nature of the locals, whose persistent prying culminates in Griffin tearing off the gauze to reveal... nothing! The man beneath is completely invisible! His condition the result of a drug experiment gone awry, the now half-crazed Griffin goes on the rampage, an unseen force hell-bent on destruction.

Not so much scary nowadays (if ever it really was) as darkly comic, this is a solid classic that holds its own alongside Whale's *Frankenstein* and *Bride of Frankenstein* as one of Universal's finest. Like *Frankenstein*, this is a cautionary tale of scientific meddling gone wrong. Whale infuses his film with plenty of creepy fun, much of it arising from the quirky villagers, and there's a masterful performance by Rains, whose gravely laughter and intimidatingly silky voice imbue every scene with a tinge of menace. Ironically it was to be his finest performance, even though his face remains unseen until the very end, and it is without question the role that earned him his place in movie history. The rest of the cast is adequate - though Una O'Connor (later the comic relief in *Bride of Frankenstein*) goes exasperatingly over the top as the screeching landlady - but the pace lags whenever Rains isn't on screen and thus, even at a modest 71 minutes, the film feels too long.

Although John Fulton's trick photography looks dated by today's standards (look to *Hollow Man* for the bee's knees in state of the art invisibility f/x), it still has the ability to impress. With a fabulously evocative W. Franke Harling score (some of which was recycled by Universal for their wonderful 1936 *Flash Gordon* serial) this is must-see entertainment from the true Golden Age of cinema.

Universal's DVD, part of the "Classic Monster Collection", continues in the tradition of their earlier releases by coupling the film (punctuated by 18 chapter points) with a fascinating documentary. The 35-minute "Now You See Him: The Invisible Man Revealed!" was written and directed by aficionado David J. Skal and is hosted by film historian Rudy Behlmer who also provides the feature-length commentary. There is an entertaining gallery of old artwork, stills and lobby cards, plus production notes and cast and crew biographies, yet curiously no trailer. The print of the film itself shows no sign of any attempted restoration; the picture is often speckly (with several obtrusive spots of damage) and the sound crackles away like a log fire. Yet overall it's respectable enough when one considers that the source materials are now almost 70 years old.

Purists take note: It has been reported that this DVD release has been modified slightly from all previous VHS and laserdisc versions of the film. In the scene when Kemp (William Harrigan) is listening to the radio, what's playing in the cassette and laserdisc versions (and, one assumes, in the original 1933 release print) is a vintage jazz tune typical of the era. For the DVD release it would appear that the rights to this piece must have unattainable, because an alternative track has been drafted in as substitute. - TG

THE IRREFUTABLE TRUTH ABOUT DEMONS

Colour, 2000, 86m. / Directed by Glenn Standring / Starring Karl Urban, Katie Wolfe / City Heat, Ventura (US R1 NTSC), High Fliers (UK R2 PAL) / DD2.0

A slick but awkward post-punk updating of occult shockers like *Curse of the Demon* and *The Devil Rides Out*, this New Zealand production drops the hipster posturing of most recent horror in favour of an ominous study of one man's very long single night journey from doubting sceptic to... well, something else entirely. Sporting one of the more unwieldy titles in recent memory (shortened to *The Truth about Demons* only on the video art), this film became a mild horror community sensation a la *The Blair Witch Project* when it ignited a distributor buying frenzy, only to largely fade into video shelf oblivion. However, horror fans will find it well worth seeking out, to study its flaws as well as its achievements.

A haughty anthropology professor named Harry Ballard (Karl Urban) receives a sinister videotape showing a cult called the Black Lodge ranting about some kind of demonic plot. As it turns out, Harry's brother, Robert, killed himself a few months earlier under mysterious circumstances, possibly related to this cult; in any event, the loss has been preying on Harry's mind, sending his relationship with his girlfriend (Sally Stockwell) into a tailspin. Meanwhile a seemingly schizophrenic young woman named Bennie (Katie Wolfe), who has a penchant for lighting sparklers in alleyways for no good reason, follows Harry around and snatches him from the jaws of doom after he falls into the cult's hands. The devilish leader, Le Valliant (Jonathan Hendry), apparently has big plans in store for Harry, and soon our protagonist's grip on reality slips as the cult targets him for an upcoming ritual.

In many respects, *Demons* is a frustrating experience as it counters every misstep with an unexpected artistic flourish. The cult itself is an irritating conception, relying on prosaic Goth clichés, which are ultimately about as frightening as the Backstreet Boys, but the film's incidentals provide some real shocks. Harry's nocturnal bathtub encounter early in the film is a real showstopper, as is a cringe-inducing sequence in which Harry (poor Mr. Urban) is splashed across the face with real cockroaches. The film looks great and manages to stay on its feet most of the time, but ultimately its premise is too half-baked to carry it over all the way as a genuinely satisfying experience. The third act revelation of Harry's possession of some vaguely defined power seems thrown in more for plot convenience than anything else, leading to a frustrating epilogue that tries to pull a reality-spinning horror twist on the story straight out of a Jonathan Carroll novel, but not nearly as effective. More obviously confounding is director Glenn Standring's urge to defuse some of his best moments by having characters suddenly awake from a dream and gasp, "Jesus Christ!" (This happens more often than you can imagine.)

It's somehow ironic that Blockbuster, the most staunchly conservative and pro-censorship entertainment corporation in existence, would bother to obtain exclusive DVD rights to an unrated horror title that pours on the gore so heavily. This title wound up as part of the City Heat deal, which means you either had to rent it from BB or buy a used copy somewhere else. Apart from this film and *The Misadventures of Margaret*, the titles from this batch aren't worth mentioning and make one wonder what on earth the familiar video store empire was planning to do with them.

In any case, the disc is a few notches above its companion releases, with a solid if not outstanding transfer. The compositions look open matte but may be slightly cropped from 1.66:1; either way, the framing appears just fine. The manipulative surround audio is well rendered and benefits from very loud playback on your home theatre system. The disc also includes the flashy theatrical trailer and some rather bland press kit style interviews with Standring and four cast members. For some reason these talking head bits are referred to on the packaging as a "director's commentary," but don't be fooled. A more elaborate special edition was released by Ventura, featuring a director's commentary, but unfortunately the transfer is a shoddy job all around; it looks worse than an EP-speed VHS tape, is almost entirely devoid of colour, and suffers from one of the worst compression jobs imaginable. The UK DVD at the time of this writing is only available as a rental title.

J.D.'S REVENGE

Colour, 1976, 95m. / Directed by Arthur Marks / Starring Glynn Turman, Louis Gossett, Jr. / MGM (US R1 NTSC) / WS (1.85:1) (16:9)

The "revenge" of this odd genre hybrid's title applies to J.D. Walker, a vicious gangster gunned down in the opening soft focus prologue. Cut to a 1970s college campus where sweet, innocent law student Ike (*Cooley High*'s Glynn Turman) passes his time by playing football in the quad and earning some extra cash by driving a cab. His stress might be relieved by a little hypnosis therapy at a strip club(!), but unfortunately this procedure causes J.D's spirit to possess Ike and send him on a devilish spree through town. When he's not too busy hitting on the honeys at local New Orleans dives or causing mayhem with his handy straight razor, Ike/J.D. decides to exact a little vengeance on the holier than thou preacher, Reverend Bliss (Louis Gossett, Jr.), who has some guilty ties to J.D.'s past.

Though released at the height of the blaxploitation trend, *J.D.'s Revenge* is surprisingly low on exploitative elements and makes along at a nice clip thanks to director Arthur Marks (*Detroit 9000*). The premise was obviously designed to cash in on the string of possession films initiated by *The Exorcist*, but Marks (almost) always takes the high road and avoids the overt bodily horror and campy profanity usually found in its ilk. Instead this is more of a traditional ghost story, tweaked a bit for '70s audiences and carried off by a surprisingly sincere cast. Unfortunately *J.D.* may disappoint much of its target audience in this respect, as the horror elements are very weak tea indeed. From this standpoint, Curtis Harrington pulled off the same possession by gangster idea with a lot more panache the following year with *Ruby*, which also shares a nearly identical opening and a similar nostalgia-washed visual texture. Oddly, the T&A actually outnumbers the violence by far, perhaps the justify the odd feel good ending. At least blaxploitation fans are sure to get a charge out of J.D.'s antics, which include some come on lines perfectly designed for answering machines or computer sound bites. And what would an AIP black film be without a groovy theme song, in this case Robert Prince's "I Will Never Let You Go."

Originally released on VHS by Orion (and briefly on laserdisc through Image), *J.D.'s Revenge* has long accompanied its better known AIP ilk like *Foxy Brown* and Marks' *Friday Foster* on the home video market. MGM has continued the trend by issuing the DVD as part of its "Soul Cinema" collection, complete with artwork completely devoid of any horror elements. At least the presentation of the film itself is as good as one could expect, finally offering the option of viewing the film in its unmatted, full frame aspect ratio or a sharper 16:9 enhanced, 1.85:1 matted alternative. The former makes for more comfortable viewing compositionally, while the latter boasts more pleasing visuals and detail. Either way, you can't really lose. The mono sound is just fine, with substantially more bass than the flat Orion transfer. The only extra is the ghoulish theatrical trailer, but considering the low price tag, it's still a pretty sweet deal.

JACK BE NIMBLE

Colour, 1993, 95m. / Directed by Garth Maxwell / Starring Alexis Arquette, Sarah Smuts Kennedy / Image (US R0 NTSC) / DD2.0

A rare horror export from New Zealand that has nothing to do with Peter Jackson, *Jack Be Nimble* never really caught on with the midnight movie crowd but, thanks to video, has gained a small but loyal following. Its release was trumpeted in many of the horror trades as a new terror classic, a claim easy to believe based on the truly chilling trailer, but in fact the film is more of a bittersweet fable which happens to contain a few effective horrific elements along the way. Director Maxwell, who has since worked on the popular *Hercules* and *Xena* TV series, displays a keen eye for colour and detail here despite the impoverished budget, and the performers all do an effective job of pulling off a potentially silly storyline and pushing the material into surreal and often fascinating territory.

As children, Jack and Dora are separated after the deaths of their parents. Dora (Sarah Smuts Kennedy) winds up in a decent home and grows up to be a stable young adult who happens to possess a psychic link to her brother (Alexis Arquette, doing a good faux-Zealand accent). Unfortunately, Jack's adopted family leaves a lot to be desired; in fact, the poor boy often winds up on the wrong end of a belt and receives nothing but scorn from his three evil stepsisters. Jack devises a unique machine capable of hypnotizing an observer, so naturally he turns his invention on his adopted parents and commands them to go kill themselves. Dora senses Jack's predicament, and the two embark on an unnerving odyssey reminiscent of *Night of the Hunter*, aided by Dora's older lover, Teddy (*The Quiet Earth*'s

Bruno Lawrence) and pursued by the wicked stepsisters.

Most horror fans may be stymied by the weird mixture of Lynchian surrealism and unexpected moments of pathos, but *Jack* merits a look for adventurous viewers willing to go along with its quirky mindset. Gay/drag icon Arquette may seem an odd casting choice for a battered, vengeful New Zealand lad, but his subdued and sometimes creepy work here proves his abilities as an actor have yet to be fully explored in America. Lawrence, one of New Zealand's finest actors, really has little to do but nevertheless comes off as capable and assured in his limited role, while Kennedy artfully balances hysteria and sisterly affection. The film loses its grip somewhat in the final third, which ultimately winds down to a strangely anticlimactic semi-happy ending. Otherwise, the striking imagery and unusual plot twists make this a refreshing change of pace from standard slasher and pretentious arthouse fare.

The DVD edition from Image improves on the prior VHS release from Triboro, though this film will never really look pristine due to the cheap film stock, dark lighting, and oversaturated colour schemes. Some lab tampering has resulted in a strange, "blotted" appearance through most of the film, which could easily be misread as a faulty transfer, but the film has always looked this way, even on cable. The standard surround audio track renders the film's powerful score quite effectively, and the heavily accented dialogue remains clear and intelligible throughout. Too bad the disc doesn't include the original trailer, which is much scarier than the movie itself. An offbeat little creature, this film's reputation should steadily increase as more people discover it, and DVD is easily the best way to do so.

JACK THE RIPPER

Colour, 1976, 98m. / Directed by Jess Franco / Starring Klaus Kinski, Josephine Chaplin / VIP (Switzerland R0 NTSC) / WS (1.78:1) (16:9), Diamond (US R1 NTSC), Platinum (US R1 NTSC)

One of the rare post-'60s Jess Franco films to receive a significant theatrical stateside release, *Jack the Ripper* offers the promising collaboration of Spain's wildest director and Germany's most unhinged actor, Klaus Kinski. The results are actually more sedate than one might expect, especially given that Franco's script tosses out any similarity to the actual crimes committed by Saucy Jack apart from the Victorian English setting and the concept of a serial murderer preying on prostitutes.

The story begins well into the Ripper's reign of terror, as another prostitute falls victim to his blade on a foggy evening. With only the aural testimony of a blind man to go on, Scotland Yard has nary a clue to track down the psychopath, who actually turns out to be semi-respectable Dr. Dennis Orloff (Kinski). While fishermen are busy fishing lady's body parts out of the local river (which looks suspiciously more like an outlet from the Danube than the Thames), the good doctor endures horrible flashbacks to his childhood (involving his hooker mother) and goes out on killing sprees, aided by his complicit housekeeper. Eventually Scotland Yard gets wise to the doc's nocturnal activities, and in a plot turn swiped from Mario Bava's *Hatchet for the Honeymoon*, the chief inspector's girlfriend (Josephine Chaplin, fresh off Pasolini's *The Canterbury Tales*) is pressed into service to pose as a potential victim.

Though laced with occasional bursts of nudity and gory bits partially created with ceramics, *Jack the Ripper* is a relatively upscale and classy affair for Franco. His usual sedate pacing is functional given the attractive setting for his camera to probe, though it's strange to see Kinski tackling such a meaty role with so little interest. His eerie eyes and expressions are put to good use, but even when he's ravishing the freshly expired bodies of his victims, the actor's expected hysteria never surfaces. Franco regular and future wife Lina Romay (still at the height of her beauty) turns up for the film's most memorable (and gruesome) extended setpiece, as a dancehall girl who winds up taking a fatal moonlight stroll with Kinski.

The Swiss disc supervised by the film's producer, Edwin C. Dietrich, marks an auspicious beginning for his proposed line of Franco DVDs. The meticulously restored image quality is nothing short of remarkable, with detail and colours so vivid the film could have been shot this year. A couple of bootleg DVD companies (e.g., Diamond) have passed off their own sorry looking renditions of the shorter US print of this film on DVD, but accept no substitutes; this one really delivers. Dietrich also offers a reasonably interesting commentary track focusing on the technical and production angles, though the absence of Franco (reportedly not his best buddy in the world) is a shame. Extras include the theatrical trailer for both *Jack* and Franco's excellent *Love Letters of a Portuguese Nun* (both in German) as well as a restoration featurette, a documentary featuring Dietrich discussing the film and his

relationship with Franco, and a 16mm excerpt of the oft-published deleted shot of Romay's mutilated body. Language options include German, French, Italian, and the clumsy English dub track, which ranks up there with *The Stendhal Syndrome* as one of the most awkward in the Eurocult annals. Unfortunately subtitles are only present in Dutch, Finnish, and Greek, with English translations for Dietrich's commentary. The set is rounded out by a host of production and location shots.

JACOB'S LADDER

Colour, 1990, 111m. / Directed by Adrian Lyne / Starring Tim Robbins, Elizabeth Pena / Artisan / WS (1.85:1) / DD5.1

New York postal worker Jacob Singer (Robbins) is tormented by nightmares and backflashes to a terrible incident that occurred whilst he was serving in Vietnam. Shadowy demons haunt his every turn and as his apparent paranoia becomes ever more pronounced, his relationship with girlfriend Jezzie (Pena) comes under a great deal of strain. Then Jacob ascertains that the other surviving members of his Nam unit are being plagued by similar visions and furthermore learns of an apparent conspiracy to cover up experiments in a drug-induced combat technique... a technique that had unexpected effects when put to the test on Jacob's platoon.

Provided you don't try too hard to figure out what's going on, or attempt to rationalise the dreams-within-dreams structure of the narrative, then the climb up *Jacob's Ladder* (and the not entirely unexpected, but nonetheless poignant, denouement awaiting you on the top rung) is an immensely rewarding one. The story taps into man's deepest fears and serves up a tableau brimming with the stuff of sweat-sodden nightmares, most notably a hallucinatory lobotomy in one of the most unpleasant asylums ever put on screen and flashes of demons with their faces vibrating maniacally.

Robbins, Aiello and Pena are all tremendous, and there are brief appearances by Ving Rhames and Eriq La Salle. Damn it, though I'm pained to say it, even Macaulay Culkin turns in a moving performance and his final scenes with Robbins will bring a lump to the throat of all but the most stonehearted. Aiello claims the best line in the script: "If you're frightened of death and you're holding on, you'll see devils tearing your life away. If you've made your peace then the devils are really angels freeing you from the Earth." Not only the best line, it also explains the entire premise of this cinematic enigma in a beautifully delivered 32 words.

Although available uncut in various VHS and Laserdisc versions, it's Artisan Entertainment's' Special Edition DVD which provides *Ladder* buffs with the superior option. As well as the pristine print of the movie itself (broken into a generous 36 chapters), there's a 25-minute documentary, "Building Jacob's Ladder", which comprises interviews with all the leads, as well as director Lyne and writer Bruce Joel Rubin, plus some invaluable behind the scenes footage. There is also a trailer, a TV spot, production notes and a commentary from Lyne. The real bonus comes in the form of three scenes that were excised from the film prior to its release (totalling an additional 13+ minutes of footage). These are a sequence set in a train station, the originally conceived (and, it has to be said, inferior) ending for the film, and a gut-wrenching scenario in which Jacob takes an antidote to relieve the hallucinogenic nightmares but instead suffers an adverse reaction and has the spawn of hell unleashed upon him. Presented with 5.1 Dolby digital sound, subtitling is provided in Spanish only. - TG

JAIL BAIT

Colour, 1954, 72m. / Directed by Ed Wood, Jr. / Starring Lyle Talbot, Dolores Fuller / Image (US R0 NTSC)

Sort of an Ed Wood take on the classic noir thriller *Gun Crazy* minus the sexual tension and storytelling finesse, *Jail Bait* tosses a number of wacko elements into its mix ranging from plastic surgery to high melodrama. The results, as might be expected, are unforgettable.

Marilyn (Dolores Fuller), a sweet young thing, is distressed at the descent of her brother, Don (Clancy Malone), into a life of crime. Fuelled by his attraction to firearms, Don falls under the sway of the evil Vic Brady (Timothy Farrell), who conspires a bizarre plot involving Don and Marilyn's surgeon father. Can the intrepid police inspector (Lyle Talbot) get to the bottom of things before it's too late?

Featuring the first appearance of Steve Reeves (Hercules himself) as a police officer, *Jail Bait* isn't as riotously awful as some other Wood films but should still entertain fans of celluloid camp. The usual continuity glitches, over-baked drama and clumsy acting abound, though the obvious personal urge to entertain the audience despite a lack of resources is subservient here to a fairly linear and sometimes surprising narrative, including a head-spinning twist ending.

The DVD features a good transfer of the film, which will always look like a staged black and white TV production but still looks miles better than the old PD prints available to collectors over the years. The soundtrack is limited by its age and the lack of resources to begin with, but dialogue remains clear and intelligible throughout and doesn't suffer from distracting background noise. Don't miss the hilarious "flavourful" music, which also turned up in *Mesa of Lost Women*. The original trailer is also included.

JAMÓN JAMÓN

Colour, 1992, 94m. / Directed by Bigas Luna / Starring Penélope Cruz, Javier Bardem / Manga (Spain PAL R0), Tartan (UK R2 PAL) / WS (1.85:1) / DD2.0

This overwrought and often very funny soap opera provided Bigas Luna with a good shot at the same critical and popular following afforded his fellow countryman Pedro Almodóvar, at least in Europe where this became an unexpected hit. Unfortunately it was all but ignored in America, where its mixture of provincial satire and luscious sex scenes proved bewildering. Fortunately Luna still continued unabated with films like *Golden Balls* and *The Tit and the Moon*, and it's about time English speaking audiences caught up with him.

A dusty Spanish town is the setting for our saga of lovelorn families, where the biggest local industry is an underwear manufacturer whose slogan reads: "Inside every man's trousers is a Samson." Naturally the town landmark is a huge cut-out of a ridiculously over-endowed bull. The underwear tycoons, led by matriarch Carmen (Anna Galiena), are appalled when the heir to their fortune, Jose Luis (Jordi Mollà), sets his sights on the beautiful Silvia (Penélope Cruz), daughter of the village brothel owner, Conchita (Stefania Sandrelli). Got all that? Things get complicated when one of the prime underwear stud models, Raul (Javier Bardem), takes a liking to Silvia (after bullfighting in the nude at midnight with his best friend - err, don't ask), and Carmen recruits Raul to lure Silvia away. Of course Carmen samples the hardware first, and Jose Luis has no intention of giving up his beloved without a fight, regardless of her feelings. Even worse, Jose Luis is more than a little familiar with Silvia's mother, setting off a whole chain of jealousy and passion that culminates in two men whacking each other senseless with giant hambones.

The title of this film translates as *Ham Ham*, which could account for all the strange pig imagery running through it. Flesh is the controlling theme here, whether it's animal or human, and the actors engage in lots of sweaty, revealing, and goofy sex scenes, with the gorgeous Sandrelli (*The Hairdresser's Husband*) performing one truly bizarre bit involving a parrot. Up and comer Cruz makes a lovely heroine and, for you celebrity skin watchers, takes the time to appear naked about every ten minutes or so. The film's real force of nature is Bardem, who has since gone on to impressive lead roles in *Live Flesh* and *Perdita Durango*, among others. Keep an eye on this guy. The film is exceptionally well photographed, with some nice twilight landscape shots bracketing the story at key moments, and Nicola Piovani (*Life Is Beautiful*) provides a subdued, haunting music score.

The previous laserdisc edition of *Jamón Jamón* from Academy was a terribly washed out, grainy transfer with vital image area missing on all four sides. The PAL Manga DVD is a tremendous improvement, with perfect 1.66:1 framing and much more robust colours. The original film has always looked rather grainy and gritty, at least during the exteriors, but the disc looks quite good considering the source material. The stereo sound is also very strong, with clear channel separation and some nifty effects between the channels. The optional English subtitles are the same as the US edition but much easier to read. The disc also includes talent bios, the Spanish trailer, and something called "Mas Jamón," which amounts to snippets from the film edited to a love ballad.

JASON GOES TO HELL: THE FINAL FRIDAY

Colour, 1993, 87m. / Directed by Adam Marcus / Starring John D. LeMay, Kari Keegan / Pathé (UK R2 PAL) / DD2.0

An FBI sting operation draws maniac killer Jason Voorhees (Kane Hodder) into an ambush where he's blown to smithereens. When the coroner conducting the post mortem finds himself compelled to chow down on the still-pulsing black heart, Jason's soul penetrates him and goes on the rampage, swapping bodies at will, questing for rebirth via the sole surviving member of the Voorhees dynasty.

With the *Friday the 13th* series having been in steady decline for some time, *Jason Goes to Hell* proved a long overdue fillip. Fans of the hockey masked slayer may be disappointed by his limited screen time, but the fact remains that this one - more supernaturally rooted than any episode preceding it - is more fertile than the previous three stitched together. Director/co-writer Adam Marcus keeps the adrenaline pumping with more grisly a barrage of violence than ever before. This includes a copulating couple (who've evidently never seen a *Friday the 13th* movie) slaughtered in their tent - the girl is sliced in half lengthways - a face shoved into a deep fat fryer, a pulverised head, a hideous wrist-fracture, a liquefying corpse that challenges *The Incredible Melting Man* for gloop superiority, and more stabbings, gunshot hits and impalings than it's possible to keep tally of.

John LeMay, fresh from *Friday the 13th: The TV Series*, makes for a dreary hero, upstaged at every turn by spunky Kari Keegan as Jason's niece, the intended conduit to his resurrection. Steven Williams' bounty hunter, Creighton Duke, is a nice addition to the saga, poaching and adapting one of the best lines from *Jaws* ("For that you get the mask, the machete, the whole damned thing."). Erin (*Buck Rogers in the 25th Century*) Grey is ripe for execution as Jason's sanity-blessed sibling. The body-swapping premise may be filched from *The Hidden*, but it adds to the proceedings an edge sorely lacking in recent years. Harry Manfredini's score meanwhile maintains a nice thread of continuity. The final shot of Freddy Krueger's clawed glove grabbing the hockey mask kindled anticipation of a *Freddy vs. Jason* movie; though several scripts were devised, eight years on the project has yet to be filmed.

Unexpectedly the British Region 2 DVD of *Jason Goes to Hell* from Pathé reinstates the extreme carnage excised from its earlier UK cassette release. The fullscreen feature is clean, if a fraction too saturated, and divided by 17 chapters. Additionally there's a short theatrical trailer and a brief textual history of the series. Sound and subtitling for the hard of hearing are in English only. - TG

JAWBREAKER

Colour, 1999, 87m. / Directed by Darren Stein / Starring Rose McGowan, Rebecca Gayheart / Columbia (US R1 NTSC, UK R2 PAL) / WS (1.85:1) (16:9) / DD5.1

Liz Purr, a beautiful high school senior, seems to have it all - looks, charm, and power - until she wakes up on the morning of her seventeenth birthday to find herself bound and gagged in her bed with a jawbreaker stuffed into her mouth. Her three friends - Courtney (Rose McGowan, aka Mrs. Marilyn Manson), Julie (Rebecca Gayheart), and Foxy (Julie Benz) - stuff her into Courtney's trunk and plan a nasty bit of birthday morning humiliation, but it all goes awry when Liz gags on the jawbreaker and suffocates to death. Stuck with a body on a school day, the girls decide to return Liz back to bed and arrange the scene to look like a sexual assault. Unfortunately, they're witnessed by mousy nerd Fern Mayo (Judy Greer, a mini-Anne Heche); to buy Fern's silence, Courtney gives Fern a makeover, makes her popular, and christens her with a new name, Vylette. Of course, like all good American morality tales, everything spirals out of control when the girls' rival power trips force them to do unspeakable things to each other, egged on by the police investigation of Detective Vera Cruz (Pam Grier, excellent and looking great but terribly underused). Like all good high school tales, the sordid saga ends at the prom where everybody gets exactly what's coming to them.

Jawbreaker gets most of its mileage from superb casting, from McGowan's showstopping bitch goddess turn to amusing bit parts (*Carrie*'s William Katt and P.J. Soles reteaming for a don't-blink cameo, *Grease*'s Jeff Conaway as Julie's dad, *When a Stranger Calls'* Carol Kane as the principal, an unrecognizable Marilyn Manson, and so on). Director Stein's gaudy eye captures every inch of the gaudy, ultra-vibrant decor and fashion design so perfectly this winds up playing like a nasty Valley version of *The Umbrellas of Cherbourg*, and his acidic, often hilarious dialogue fires off one rapid clip after another. *Jawbreaker* doesn't work completely: it's far too indebted to *Heathers*, the final act feels thrown together at the last minute, and there's the simple, inescapable fact that films specifically designed to be cult movies always trip over their own self-aware "hipness." The real strong suit is McGowan, who finally gets to strut her stuff full force and at last has the acting ability to pull off the snippy diva routine she first attempted in *The Doom Generation* and *Scream*.

As usual, Columbia's DVD of *Jawbreaker* is first rate, from the eye-popping anamorphic transfer to the deliriously expansive Dolby Digital sound mix. The soundtrack is overstuffed with pop songs from beginning to end, but at least for once the tunes are well chosen and comment humorously on the action. Stephen Endelman's quirky score (which seems to be a deliberate homage to David Newman's *Heathers*) enhances the frothy, zippy scenario with a macabre humorous tone, and Stein provides a feature-length commentary ranging from humorous anecdotes to unfortunate film school student self-indulgence. A satisfying disc overall, this sweet and sour confection isn't quite perfect but richly deserves to find its intended audience on the small screen where its modest, vinegar-laced charms can perhaps be better appreciated.

JEWEL OF THE NILE

Colour, 1985, 106m. / Directed by Lewis Teague / Starring Michael Douglas, Kathleen Turner / Fox (US NTSC R1) / WS (1.85:1) (16:9) / DD2.0

Six months after their adventures in Colombia, Jack Colton (Douglas) and Joan Wilder (Turner) are living the high-life, touring the world on their yacht. When a wealthy potentate invites Joan to accompany him to North Africa to write his biography, Jack declines to go along, intent instead on a trip round the Greek islands. No sooner has Joan departed than he learns that she may be in danger and so, with the added incentive of locating the fabled Jewel of the Nile, he heads off after her.

Despite a succession of (admittedly well staged) action-packed setpieces, Lewis (*Alligator*) Teague's sequel doesn't have nearly as much energy or finesse as *Romancing the Stone*. Basically a series of furiously-paced chases, one following rapidly on the heels of another, what was entertainment of the highest order first time round feels laboured here and consequently gives rise to mild tedium. A severe handicap is the bad guy, Omar (Spiros Focas), who's simply not odious enough to be threatening and is played as a bit of an oaf - he certainly doesn't have any of the seething malignancy of the original's Zolo. The story also loses momentum mid-way with a daft interlude at a native camp when Douglas plays fisticuffs with the chief's gargantuan son in a duel for Joan's honour. In spite of the fact it's less polished that its predecessor, Douglas and Turner continue to bounce well off each other (even though their fluctuant romance stretches one's patience at times), and DeVito returns as the comic relief, providing a few genuine chuckles along the way.

The film's biggest boon is Avner Eisenberg, who turns in an endearing performance as the titular "Jewel"; yes, poor old Jack thinks he's searching for a precious stone, when in actual fact the Jewel turns out to be a revered holy man... one can empathize with his disenchantment.

A trailer akin to the one created for *Romancing the Stone*, hosted by DeVito in specially shot footage, is a welcome additional feature on Fox's disc, though sadly it's the only one. As with its sibling, the opportunity to include the catchy tie-in music video - this time the No. 1 chart hit "When the Going Gets Tough" by Billy Ocean (featuring Douglas, Turner and DeVito in his backing band) has been overlooked. The 22-chapter movie can be viewed with English Dolby or French Dolby sound, and there are subtitles available in English or Spanish. - TG

THE JOHNSONS

Colour, 1992, 98m. / Directed by Rudolf Van Den Berg / Starring Monique Van De Ven / Anchor Bay (US R1 NTSC) / WS (1.85:1) / DD2.0

The Johnsons, a Dutch horror film obviously targeted for an English language release, strangely failed to receive an American release in any format until its long overdue presentation on video by Anchor Bay. Fortunately, the wait has not been in vain as the film looks and sounds far better than the bootlegs and import prints floating around for years; also, the running commentary by Van Den Berg, Simonelli, and Frumkes (*Document of the Dead, Street Trash*) provides even more of an appreciation for this odd, strangely effective tale of cultural displacement and familial horror.

Monique Van De Ven, best known for her sexy early appearances in Paul Verhoeven dramas and the underrated thriller *Amsterdamned*, portrays Victoria, a single mom whose 13 year old daughter, Emalee (Bretoniere), begins to experience visions of seven brothers using blood to etch strange symbols into a wall and, in older form, joining up to sexually assault her. Victoria's assignment to photograph a rare bird in the marshy outlands of Holland provokes more extreme visions within Emalee's fragile psyche. According to the legend of the dangerous Mahxitu Indians, Xangadix, an evil god resembling a big, malevolent foetus, will instigate the creation of seven brothers who, by impregnating their sister, will unleash a powerful, destructive force over all creation.

While *The Johnsons* (which derives its title from the professor whose work unleashes the menace in the opening sequence) contains its fair share of gory thrills, particularly in the rousing final half hour, the overall mood is one of subliminal menace lurking beneath the delicate sheen of reality, in the best tradition of Val Lewton. The most powerful images are driven home more by suggestion than explicit gore, particularly the startling image of the brothers escaping their asylum and shambling onto the roof. Van De Ven makes a compelling maternal heroine, a welcome change from the usual teens in peril, though the abrupt resolution (the film's only major shortcoming) doesn't make much sense and seems like an easy way out for a writer painted into a corner. Van Den Berg's sociological film background serves him well as he uses environment to mirror the characters' evolving, disintegrating personas and reflect the bizarre cultural clashes occurring within Europe. The brothers, silent and menacing with their faces encrusted with pale dried mud, are villains not easily forgotten and make this a spooky little gem that makes one long for the golden days of European horror.

Anchor Bay's DVD is one of the more surprising of their recent special editions, with the film available either in Dutch with optional English subtitles or (ick) English dubbed. The DVD also includes filmographies and the original European trailer.

JOSIE AND THE PUSSYCATS

Colour, 2001, 98m. / Directed by Deborah Kaplan and Harry Elfont / Starring Rachel Leigh Cook, Tara Reid / Universal (US R1 NTSC, UK R2 PAL) / WS (1.85:1) (16:9) / DD5.1

Struggling small town girl band The Pussycats - Josie (Cook), Melody (Reid) and Valerie (Rosario Dawson) - become an overnight success when they sign a deal with Mega Records. However, stardom loses its sparkle as the trio discover that their bosses Wyatt (Alan Cumming) and Fiona (Parker Posey) have devised a hi-tech scheme to control youth culture by planting subliminal messages in their songs.

Pre-empting the all-girl band phenomenon by some 25 years, the Hanna-Barbera show *Josie and the Pussycats* was a Scooby-Doo-ish confection about a mystery solving trio who were also a pop group. Anyone who recalls the cartoon (or its sequel series *Josie and the Pussycats in Outer Space*) won't

J

find much nostalgic value in this high-camp 21st century live action version. Pipping the live rendering of *Scooby Doo* to the post by a year, this is like one of those barrels of multiplex popcorn; toothsome and moreish, but ultimately not very filling. And considering that the crux of the plot is the manipulation of trends through subliminal advertising, the movie employs abundant product placement with all the subtlety of a sledgehammer. Intentional irony, or blatant hypocrisy? Roasted by most critics upon its initial release, their venom was somewhat perplexing. What did they expect? High art? Insightful cultural comment? Gripping drama? *Josie and the Pussycats* is over the top fluff of the fluffiest variety, and if accepted on that level then it's quite a bit of fun.

Cook is the stand-out as Josie, endearingly naive, doe-eyed and attractive, whilst Reid generates most of the wittier moments as ditzy blonde Melody. Dawson completes the trio as Valerie, the only one with half a brain and thus the anchor-point of sanity amidst all the absurdity. The message that friendship is more important than fame is a touch saccharine, but the veracity with which the trio interact is such that you can really believe they're bosom pals. Cumming is fabulous as the double-dealing Wyatt Frame, with a tasty sideline in acerbic put-downs. The gags are mostly silly, but still raise a chuckle, and the music is surprisingly catchy; several tracks - in particular "3 Small Words" and "Pretend to be Nice" - could well have been valid chart-climbers had someone had the foresight to push them out. The (generally mild) profanity, however, jars a little in a film essentially aimed at a younger audience. And how on earth did they get away with those lyrics in the double-entendre-laden "Backdoor Lover"? Meeowch!

A purrfect selection of goodies embroiders Universal's DVD release of *Josie and the Pussycats*. Along with feature-length commentary from the two directors (missing on the UK release), there's a 25-minute "making of" documentary (which reveals that the actresses actually learned to play their instruments for the film, whilst neglecting to mention that Cook is lip-synching Kay Hanley of Letters To Cleo), 3 music videos (including the aforementioned "3 Small Words" and "Backdoor Lover"), a trailer, cast biographies and 3 deleted scenes, 2 of which are just extensions of material in the film anyway, the other a funny sequence which should definitely have been retained. The transfer of the 18-chapter feature is, as you would expect from a recent film, flawless. Languages are in English Dolby, English Digital DTS Surround or French Dolby, with subtitling in English only. - TG

JOY HOUSE

Colour, 1964, 91m. / Directed by René Clément / Starring Alain Delon, Jane Fonda, Lola Albright / Image (US R1 NTSC) / WS (2.35:1) (16:9)

 An often overlooked follow up collaboration between director René Clément and star Alain Delon after their sultry *Purple Noon* (later remade as *The Talented Mr. Ripley*), this eerie, visually striking thriller is an equally impressive achievement, albeit in very terms. Back in the 1960s, European co-productions with multinational casts were all the rage, and *Joy House* (or as it's titled on the print, *Les félins*) is one rare example of how the formula could work with the right participants.

Poor Marc (Alain Delon) isn't exactly the brightest guy in the world. His carefree playboy lifestyle on the Riviera comes to an abrupt halt when the American gangster husband of his mistress finds out about the relationship and puts out a bounty on the young man's head. Marc hides out in a homeless shelter where he draws the attention of Barbara Hill (*A Cold Wind in August*'s Lola Albright), a wealthy widow, and her sexy, coquettish niece, Melinda (Jane Fonda in her Roger Vadim phase). The two ladies invite Marc to their remote villa where they take him on as their chauffeur and make not terribly subtle sexual overtures toward him. Unfortunately there's a macabre undercurrent to this idyllic lifestyle, as Marc begins to suspect that he's not the only one taking refuge in the house.

Aiming for the widest international release possible, Clement shot this film in English, allowing all of the cast members to use their original voices. This decision proved to be a smart one, as Joy House flows more smoothly than many contemporary thrillers and light erotica films from the period. Clement and cinematographer Henri Decae show an impeccable eye for scope compositions, filling the frame with eye-catching little bits of detail and making superb use of mirrors as both recurring visual and thematic devices. Delon's shadowy explorations of the villa recall similar passages in both *Dementia 13* and *Deep Red*, though one can't help sensing a little *Jane Eyre* hovering over the proceedings as well. Great Argentinean composer Lalo Schifrin contributes another one of his catchy, slinky, jazz-laced scores, which were quite in vogue at the time. Chic, fast paced, and wonderfully European, this film is company well worth keeping.

The Image DVD of *Joy House* is obviously a huge improvement over the terribly cropped VHS edition from USA, which has been out of print for ages. An alternate French language track is also included, but the English one is really the only way to go. Despite the opening MGM logo, the French title indicates this print is European in origin. The anamorphically enhanced image quality looks very good, with a crystalline sleekness undiluted by any major print defects or compression flaws. As with a handful of other anamorphic transfers like *Halloween*, playback on 4:3 monitors yields an odd two-tone effect in the letterbox areas. No extras to speak of, but the film itself is the prime attraction here and worth seeking out.

JOY RIDE

Colour, 2001, 96m. / Directed by John Dahl / Starring Steve Zahn, Paul Walker / Fox (US R1 NTSC) / WS (2.35:1) (16:9) / DD5.1

 College guy Lewis (Paul Walker) decides to cash in his plane ticket for a new set of wheels after the chaste object of his affections, Venna (Leelee Sobieski), breaks up with her boyfriend and asks for a ride home from Colorado. Along the way he stops by a prison to pick up his no good brother, Fuller (Steve Zahn), and the two pass the time on their road trip by playing pranks on their CB radio. Unfortunately their victim, Rusty Nail, doesn't take too kindly to being led by Lewis' female voice impersonation for a one nighter at a local motel, and soon the boys find themselves on the wrong end of the angry trucker's seemingly endless thirst for revenge.

Tautly paced and thankfully free of the irritating mannerisms which plague most modern "youth" horror films, *Joy Ride* marks a thankful return to form for director John Dahl (*The Last Seduction, Red Rock West*) after a temporary break from thrillers with the underperforming *Rounders*. Originally filmed as *Squelch*, the film maintains a solid balance of chills and humour without lapsing into either sadism or hipness; even more remarkably, the characters are well drawn and acted with believable flaws and behaviour patterns. The hotel room prank sequence is a small masterpiece of mood and creative imagery, with the brilliant flourish of lightning shimmering off a painting of a boat at sea providing an elegant taste of the scares to come. Even the finale, which incorporates all the requisite elements like a relentless madman and a damsel in distress, ratchets up the tension without lapsing into overt gore or unbelievable stretches of credulity. For

some reason *Joy Ride* was largely overlooked in theatres (unlike the similar chilling but ultimately less effective *Jeepers Creepers*), but it should have no problem finding an appreciative audience on video and, most likely, late night television where it can jolt unsuspecting viewers.

Fox's DVD provides a fascinating model of how to present a film from its initial filming to the final release cut. While it went through several titles, the film was shelved long after completion while Dahl and company tackled the film's troublesome final act. The original half hour finale, which picks up from the well publicized naked diner scene, is a fairly lacklustre affair (apart from one nice jolt), focusing too much on brotherly bonding and carelessly lifting a scene from *The Hitcher* for no good reason. Thankfully this entire story direction was scrapped in favour of a more inventive climax, which also went through no less than four permutations.

Included on the DVD are the original finale and the subsequent variations, though ultimately the best resolution wound up in the release prints. Even more information can be found in the supplements, which include three voice tests for Rusty Nail (Eric Roberts, Stephen Shellen, and the final choice, *The Silence of the Lambs'* Ted Levine), a thankfully discarded bit of extended kissing business between Zahn and Sobieski, and no less than three commentary tracks featuring input from Dahl, writers Clay Tarver and J.J. Abrams, Zahn, and Sobieski. All of them offer wildly different observations about the film thanks to their relative perspectives on the production; the first three are the most insightful, but the two actors also do a solid job of bringing their own stories up to bat.

The supplements also include a typical puff piece featurette and the theatrical trailer, which includes several fleeting glimpses of the original finale. The picture quality of Fox's anamorphic transfer admirably replicates the theatrical viewing experience, with colourful washes of red neon bathing several scenes and the numerous night scenes illuminated by tricky headlight beams. It could have been a compression nightmare, but the disc looks just fine. Not surprisingly the 5.1 audio track remains active throughout, with the loud suspense scenes bristling with nifty split surround effects.

JURASSIC PARK III

Colour, 2001, 92m. / Directed by Joe Johnston / Starring Sam Neill, William H. Macy / Universal (US R1 NTSC, UK R2 PAL) / WS (1.85:1) (16:9) / DD5.1

Enticed by substantial funding for his excavation, palaeontologist Alan Grant (Neill) accepts an invite to host a flight over the island site of genetic experiments with dinosaurs. In fact it is a ruse by Paul and Amanda Kirby (Macy and Leoni) to circumvent official red tape and get on to the island to find their son, who went missing in a boating accident several months beforehand. Grant reluctantly finds himself heading up a survival party as their plane is trashed and they become potential hors d'oeuvres for a host of savage predators.

Few will deny that *Jurassic Park* was a groundbreaking film and an immense amount of fun, or that its director Steven Spielberg is one of the kings of blockbuster screen entertainment. So why his sequel, *The Lost World,* was as disappointingly hollow as it turned out to be is a puzzler. With the second sequel, however, Joe Johnston takes up the reins and betters the previous two films combined by feeding audiences precisely what they came for in the first place - dinosaurs, dinosaurs and more dinosaurs. In an age when movies - blockbusters in particular - outstay their welcome with needlessly expansive running times, *Jurassic Park III*'s pithy and punchy 92-minutes works considerably in its favour. Johnston dispenses with Spielberg's style of protracted preliminaries and after a brief passage of character establishment lurches headlong into the jaw-dropping action.

With the exception of a credibility-stretcher concerning the unheard approach of a several ton dinosaur, and the risibly OTT rescue finale, the non-stop theme park ride is kept relatively feasible with Neill and his troupe fleeing from a ravenous Spinosaurus, acrimonious Velociraptors and a flock of rancorous Pteranodons in a cliffside aviary. There's a touch more humour this time out, including a running gag with a mobile phone, but it's never taken to extremes and marries well with the breathless pace of the adventure. Stir in Don Davis' score (which blends new material with John Williams' original spellbinding themes) and you have the recipe for high excitement par excellence.

Universal do their usual tip-top job with *Jurassic Park III,* delivering a nicely framed 1.85:1 widescreen transfer with 20 chapter breaks and loading the disc with a host of bonus features. Along with a behind the scenes documentary and a similar segment that focuses on the dinosaurs chosen to populate the film, there's additional material on the creation of the full-size models and their computer generated cousins. There is also behind the scenes footage from three key sequences in the film and storyboard to film comparisons for a trio of scenes. "Dinosaur Turntables" comprises physiological data on the reptilian stars of the film and we also get a peek at a genuine dino-excavation in the States. An attractive slideshow presentation of colour photos from the film is included, along with the trailer and those for the first two JP movies. Rounding out the disc is a commentary provided by the effects team, plus production notes and cast & crew biographies, as well as DVD-ROM materials. Sound is provided in English 5.1 Dolby Digital, English 5.1 DTS and French 5.1 Dolby Digital, and subtitle choices are English or Spanish. - TG

JUST FOR THE HELL OF IT
Colour, 1968, 81m. / Directed by Herschell Gordon Lewis / Starring Rodney Bedell, Ray Sager
BLAST-OFF GIRLS
Colour, 1967, 82m. / Directed by Herschell Gordon Lewis / Starring Dan Conway, Ray Sager
Image (US R0 NTSC) /WS (1.66:1)

After his partnership with producer David F. Friedman dissolved, H.G. Lewis found his exploitation career spinning in a number of different directions. Two of the more compelling "unclassifiable" efforts from his wild late '60s period can be found in this 100% H.G. double feature from Something Weird, complete with the onslaught of nostalgic goodies that have made their drive-in collections one of a kind.

Our first walk on the wild side is the aptly named *Just for the Hell of It*, a study of juvenile delinquency that makes *Rebel without a Cause* look like a model for civilized teen behaviour. A group of youths partying in an apartment turn to rampant destruction after one member gets a fishbowl of water over the head, with even the smallest piece of furniture winding up splintered and smashed underneath their feet. There's no reason for this, of course; they're just out of control and looking for kicks... just for the hell of it! Then they're off to trash a bar, terrorize innocent bystanders along the road, and pick fights at a coffee shop where the owner winds up with his hands sizzled to a crisp. The police are helpless to stop these hooligans, who even have the nerve to beat up a poor cripple with his crutches and toss a baby in the garbage can! Things get even more out of hand when the group is torn apart by that old dramatic standby, vigilante justice, when the hoods rape an innocent girl.

One year earlier Lewis took a very different look at modern youth with *Blast-Off Girls*, a sort of low budget attempt to emulate the success of The Monkees and The Beatles. This time we're taken backstage to witness the rise and fall of The Faded Blue, a real life aspiring band rechristened as The Big Blast by manipulative manager Boogie Baker (Dan Conway). Thanks to the temptations of fast living and wild women (the titular Blast-Off Girls, who are hired to rip at the boys' clothes during their act), the Big Blast only gradually comes to resent their boss, who slips aside all of their hard earned cash for his own benefit. In one of Boogie's more amusing schemes, he pockets some money from the boys when they agree to sing for none other than Mr. Kentucky Fried Chicken himself, Col. Harland Sanders. When Boogie tries to lock them into a three year contract, however, things turn seriously nasty.

Though neither of these films really qualifies as horror, both display the characteristics that have endeared Lewis to generations of sleaze hounds. The nailed down camerawork, bizarre humour, DIY opticals and editing, and unpredictable pacing are all in abundance. Fans of *The Wizard of Gore* will be especially interested to see two sides of Ray Sager (aka Montag the Magnificent) in both films, smoking pot and raising hell well before his Lewis swan song in *The Gore Gore Girls*. Both films have been available for a few years as part of Something Weird's H.G. Lewis collection on VHS, and the transfers look similar albeit sharper and more colourful. *Just for the Hell of It* is presented in fullscreen with extra headroom where matting would have appeared in theatres, while *Blast-Off Girls* is slightly matted at 1.66:1. The latter features some clumsy camerawork and film processing which causes a horizontal jittery in some scenes, but for low budget films which could have easily been lost altogether, they look just fine. The mono sound is serviceable and free of any undue distortion; the theme song for the first film ("Destruction, Inc.") and the numerous pop tunes in the second come through clearly enough to reveal their, um, musical limitations.

Of course the extras here threaten to steal away much of the thunder from the films themselves. The usual reels of Something Weird drive-in promos hawk everything from hot dogs to mosquito repellent, but you also get another taste of Lewis '60s madness ("Hot Night at the Go Go Lounge"), a facts of life book pitch, the usual lurid posters and radio come-ons, and a host of Lewis trailers. Feast your eyes on the original promos for *This Stuff'll Kill Ya, The Psychic, Alley Tramp, Suburban Roulette, Something Weird, The Gore Gore Girls,*

and that long lost country music/political rarity, *Year of the Yahoo*. The trailer menu also contains an Easter Egg for a trailer to the most terrifying, unspeakable project Lewis ever tackled, but only the hardiest of souls need venture there.

KENTUCKY FRIED MOVIE

Colour, 1977, 83m. / Directed by John Landis / Anchor Bay (US R1 NTSC), Arrow (UK R2 PAL) / WS (1.85:1) (16:9)

A collection of some fairly amusing - and quite a number not at all amusing - sketches, strung together to feature length. As the silver anniversary of *Kentucky Fried Movie* approaches, the combined talents of John Landis, Jim Abrahams, David and Jerry Zucker and Robert Weiss have not survived the years well. Material that was (possibly) astutely witty back in 1977 has been superseded many times over by the even more daring and the infinitely more funny. Parts of the 23 sketch show still raise a snigger or two; the 'Feel-A-Round' movie presentation, the mock commercial for neutralising embarrassing household odours, the hysterically naughty trailer for *Catholic High School Girls in Trouble*, the newsreader distracted by the couple making love in front of their TV set, and - this reviewer's favourite - the silly but beautifully played "High Adventure" talk show. However, much of the remaining material falls flat nowadays (some of it did 25 years ago!), and that includes the over-praised 30-minute middle third *Enter the Dragon* spoof, "A Fistful of Yen". Despite a spot-on Bruce Lee impression from Evan Kim, much of the humour is obvious and rather lame. Whether or not the oases of funnies in a desert of lacklustre fare warrant adding this title to your collection or not is purely down to individual taste. I admit to purchasing it for the aforementioned "High Adventure" (with Joe Medalis and a riotously deadpan Barry Dennen) alone. Other skits deliver lukewarm cameos by the likes of Henry Gibson, George (ex-007) Lazenby, Donald Sutherland, Felix (Twiki) Silla, Uschi Digard, Forrest J. Ackerman, Donald Sutherland and Bill Bixby.

Anchor Bay have delivered a disc that far exceeds the value of the material on offer. The picture quality is variable throughout, but then it always was. Each of the 23 sketches has its own chapter stop, beneficial for skipping past the detritus. Additionally for your pennies you get a spirited audio commentary from the five principals behind the film (though not on the UK DVD for some reason), a trailer and a stills gallery. There is also the rather unique inclusion of some 8mm home movie footage, shot on set by the Zuckers to prove to their mother that they'd made it to Hollywood! - TG

KILL, BABY KILL!

Colour, 1966, 85m. / Directed by Mario Bava / Starring Giacomo Rossi Stuart, Erika Blanc / VCI, Diamond (US R0 NTSC),

This oppressive and visually overwhelming exercise in atmosphere allowed Mario Bava to crank the gothic stylistic tendencies of *Black Sunday* into full gear, finally permitting him to churn out scene after scene of hallucinatory intensity with only the barest threads of a plot to hold it all together. The avenging demonic forces of his past films have been distilled here into the single, chilling image of a ghostly young girl, rolling a sinister pale ball down hallways and street corners as she drives those around her to certain death. Rarely has a more haunting or unforgettable spectre graced the horror cinema, and even had he never made another film after this, Bava would have already proven himself as a master filmmaker.

A young coroner named Dr. Eswai (or Eswe, depending on your source) (Giacomo Rossi-Stuart) arrives at a desolate Eastern European village and makes the acquaintance of the beautiful Monica (Erika Blanc), a medically trained native who has recently returned to her home. Together they perform an autopsy on a young maid who died under mysterious circumstances while employed at the eerie Villa Graps on the edge of town. The autopsy turns up a gold coin imbedded into the girl's heart, a local superstition carried out by the local witch, Ruth (Fabienne Dali), who uses home remedies to aid her townspeople. Eswai goes to the Villa Graps where the reclusive Baroness (Gianna Vivaldi) proves to be less than forthcoming. Apparently the villagers' callous irresponsibility led to the death of her young daughter, Melissa, who now haunts the town at night and strikes down those who even dare to mention her name...

Years before he exploded the conventions of spatial reality in *Lisa and the Devil*, Bava was already tampering quite daringly with cinematic storytelling in this film. The final half hour contains some magnificent sequences bound to disorient the hardiest viewer, including effective use of a seemingly endless spiralling staircase and a brilliant, *Avengers*-like conceit which finds the doctor trapped in endless circle within the same cluster of room. Fans of Euro starlets will also enjoy the presence of Blanc, who later steamed up drive-in screens as the star of *The Devil's Nightmare*. Regular Bava composer Carlo Rustichelli provides the score once again (supplemented by some Roman Vlad passages), including a few quotes from his previous *Blood and Black Lace* score, some apparently augmented by the US distributor.

Though picked up by MGM for one of its many theatrical runs, *Kill, Baby... Kill!* (original title: *Operazione Paura*, or *Operation Fear*) has remained one of the more difficult Bava horror titles to see in a form even close to its creator's intentions. A heavily truncated version entitled *Curse of the Living Dead* made the rounds as part of a notorious "Living Dead" triple bill in the late '60s, while the original version occasionally turned up on late night television and various public domain video labels. Relatively speaking, VCI's disc is the most watchable of the available options, thanks to the restoration of Bava's vibrant colour schemes in which unnatural bursts of green, red, and blue accompany the characters' gradual descent into supernatural madness. Flesh tones look pale and dull, however, and the heavy graininess resulting from the 16mm makes the film look rougher and cheaper than it probably should. Also, the mild cropping from the original compositions (somewhere between 1.66:1 and 1.78:1) results in actors' faces scraping perilously close to the edge of frame. These debits aside, however, it's a leap over the familiar public domain versions, for example.

A 16:9 enhanced widescreen version is forthcoming from Image, and a German DVD (under the odd title of *Die toten Augen des Dr. Dracula!*) features a 20 minute Erica Blanc interview.

KILLER KLOWNS FROM OUTER SPACE

Colour, 1988, 81m. / Directed by Stephen Chiodo / Starring Grant Cramer, Suzanne Snyder / MGM (US R1 NTSC) / WS (1.85:1) (16:9) / DD2.0

One of the earlier horror cult favourites generated entirely by home video, *Killer Klowns from Outer Space* recounts the *Blob*-like story of an alien invasion engineered by malicious, alien clowns whose practical jokes have a habit of turning nasty. An obvious influence on Tim Burton's *Mars Attacks!* (which owes as much to this film as the true comic book source), *Killer Klowns* is a dark, goofy diversion and a cheerful reminder of how much more fun movies could be without overloading the viewer with tacky CGI effects.

Drawing more than a tad of its storyline from *The Blob*, our interstellar saga begins with two randy quasi-teens, Mike (*Hardbodies'* Grant Cramer) and Debbie (Suzanne Snyder), find their petting session in a van interrupted by a falling object from space that turns into a big top circus tent. Disguised as clowns outfitted with deadly devices like lethal popcorn and balloon hunting dogs, the alien force first attacks a local old farmer (Royal Dano) and then gradually lays siege to the town, all to the ignorance of the local sheriff (John Vernon). Mike and Debbie try to warn their peers about the encroaching clown menace, which traps its human captives in cotton candy and stores them aboard its Day-Glo-coloured spaceship.

It's not much of a secret that many people are actually creeped out by clowns, whose leering faces are often the exact opposite of the happy, kid-friendly appearance they intend to convey. Therefore *Killer Klowns* will seem extremely goofy and funny or simply unbearably creepy, depending on your mood (or perhaps a little of both). The clown designs are extremely effective, ranging from a baby dwarf clown to snapping, fanged clown heads attached to snakes; likewise, the ingenious use of typical clown props like cream pies to mouths lifts this film well above your average B-movie quickie. Then of course there's the classic biker scene, a showstopper in its own right, and a playful score highlighted by the Dickies' insanely catchy theme song. Apart from Vernon's scenery chewing which perhaps even exceeds his performance in *Animal House*, the performers generally play second bananas to the marauding clowns, which is just as it should be.

The riotously colourful appearance of *Killer Klowns* is perfectly rendered on this sharp-looking DVD, which easily outclasses the earlier videotape and laserdisc. Adding about as much to the sides as it loses from the top and bottom compared to the full frame version, the letterboxed transfer overall looks more balanced and serves as a better showcase for the bizarre visuals. The punchy surround soundtrack is also expertly crafted and a lot of fun. The disc is also jammed with enough krafty extras to keep klown fans busy for hours, starting with the rapid fire, informative commentary track from the Chiodo Brothers. Though their expertise lies in special effects, their solo feature filmmaking venture indicates the potential for greater results outside of their chosen area. Obviously the FX talk dominates

much of the track, but they also have a few funny stories about the production as well. The circus goodies hardly stop there, however. A new 21-minute "Making of Killer Klowns" featurette combines new interviews of the Chiodo Brothers with extensive behind the scenes camcorder footage, focusing mostly on the clowns effects footage. The basic conception behind each clown creation is further explored in the 12-minute "Kreating Klowns," while "Komposing Klowns" devotes 13 minutes to an interview with composer John Massari, whose enthusiasm for the film is quite infectious. "Visual Effects with Gene Warren, Jr." focuses more on the non-clown effects, including the creation of the circus tent and the various visual sleights of hand required to bring the film to life. "Chiodo Brothers' Earliest Films" assembles four minutes of stop motion footage created by the young filmmakers, including a miniature Satan and a Harryhausen-style beast on the loose. Two deleted scenes, "Bad Experience" and "Tight Rope," are included from the extended television cut; the former focuses on the heroine's personal, *Gremlins*-like phobia of clowns. Add onto that the original theatrical trailer, a huge gallery of photos and artwork, a storyboard gallery, and three minutes of bloopers (also camcorder footage, apparently). There are also some krafty Easter Eggs tucked away: over three minutes of funny raw footage from the klown auditions, and a quick comment from John Vernon. Oddly enough, the Dickies music video (which contains some additional excised footage) included on the VHS tape is conspicuously absent but may very well be tucked away in another Easter Egg somewhere.

KING KONG

Colour, 1976, 134m. / Directed by John Guillermin / Starring Jeff Bridges, Jessica Lange / Paramount (US R1 NTSC) / WS (2.35:1) (16:9) / DD5.1

First of all, yes, it's simply embarrassing that this film made it out to DVD before the original 1933 version. And yes, it's flawed, often stupid, and represents Hollywood commercialism at its most blatant. (It's also easy to hate a movie that launched the film careers of Joe Piscopo and Corbin Bernsen.) That said, *King Kong* belongs to that group of films that imbedded themselves in an entire generation who grew up on stuff like *Battlestar Galactica, The Black Hole, Moonraker...* you get the idea. Divorced from its cinematic origins, this *Kong* is still brainless fun. In fact the first half, which follows the original fairly closely aside from the regrettable switch from documentary filmmakers to an oil expedition, still looks pretty good. The island atmosphere is beautifully captured, the actors do a capable job with their roles (including Jessica Lange, often unfairly maligned in her debut role). Unfortunately Kong himself is somewhat less impressive, a mixture of Rick Baker's monkey man suit (helped by an uncredited Rob Bottin) and a brief, cheesy Carlo Rambaldi animatronic thingy that should have been left in the trash. Still, it's better than many of the Japanese stabs at the Kong myth and definitely miles ahead of the laughable US sequel, King Kong Lives. Incidentally, the dead ape used here also turned up in Marco Ferreri's bizarre art film, *Bye Bye Monkey*.

An oil expedition ship for the Petrox company, led by the slimy Fred Wilson (Grodin in a rare villainous role), comes across a shipwreck survivor, the beautiful blonde Dwan (Lange - and no, that's not a typo). She strikes up a rapport with the resident anti-establishment guy, Jack Prescott (Bridges), but their relationship is cut short when the group arrives at a mysterious tropical island where Dwan is swept up and offered as a sacrifice to the mysterious god Kong. Of course, Kong turns out to be a giant ape who takes quite a liking to Dwan, but the big guy is ultimately captured and spirited off to New York for a public exhibition that goes disastrously awry. They rest, as they say, is history - or, as Dino says, "When monkey die, people cry."

Paramount has continued its schizophrenic DVD release pattern by giving *King Kong* a solid anamorphic transfer. Anybody used to seeing this on television (where it contained more padded footage) will be amazed by the shadowy, finely composed photography and crisp colour schemes on display here, while the surprisingly rich 5.1 mix does full justice to John Barry's marvellous score.

KISS ME DEADLY

B&W, 1955, 106m. / Directed by Robert Aldrich / Starring Ralph Meeker, Albert Dekker / MGM (US R1 NTSC) / WS (1.66:1)

Film noir cynicism and atomic panic collide in *Kiss Me Deadly*, one of the oddest and most important mainstream films from the 1950s. Though based on a Mickey Spillane novel, the film apparently did not please the hardboiled author who later took a turn himself

playing his impulsive private eye, Mike Hammer, in *The Girl Hunters*. However, time has been very kind to this Robert Aldrich classic and ultimately allowed it to stand as the best Spillane adaptations, and one of the best crime movies in general, to date.

While driving back at night to L.A., Mike Hammer (Ralph Meeker) is stopped along a dark road by a panic stricken woman (Cloris Leachman), clad only in a trenchcoat, running down the asphalt. He picks her up and listens to her sobbing hysteria, accompanied all the while by eerie Nat "King" Cole music, as she explains that her name is Christina and that she has been forcibly imprisoned in an asylum. Suddenly a car runs them off the road, and Christina is brutally tortured to death while a drugged Hammer languishes on a dirty mattress. Mike survives the assault and, after refusing to cooperate with the police, does a little investigating of his own with his faithful, sexy secretary, Velda (Maxine Cooper). A trail of clues leads him to Christina's former roommate, Lily (Gaby Rogers), and a series of bizarre encounters at a boxing hall, a swimming pool party, and a sinister scientist named Dr. Soberin (ill-fated *Dr. Cyclops* himself, Albert Dekker), all of them related to a mysterious case containing something dark, dangerous... and glowing.

Though the plotline seems terribly complicated, *Kiss Me Deadly* sweeps the viewer up in its dazzling rhythmic patterns, created through unbalanced, enigmatic dialogue and sharp editing which creates the illusion of wandering through the film in a drug-induced haze. The overall tone is more like that of a horror film, with the various genre elements (gumshoes, atomic terrors, stark lighting) combining in a way never successfully imitated. Frank DeVol contributes an effectively jarring aural atmosphere with his clashing symphonic riffs and jazz compositions, an indication of the equally fine work he would do on later Aldrich projects like *What Ever Happened to Baby Jane?* and *The Dirty Dozen*.

For many years after its release, *Kiss Me Deadly* ended with an abrupt, apocalyptic conclusion that trimmed off the last few shots of the film as Aldrich originally planned. A restored version surfaced on television in the late 1990s, followed by repertory screenings and a widescreen laserdisc release (replacing an earlier, full frame edition of the shorter cut). The MGM DVD looks about the same as the laserdisc, which isn't a bad thing considering how terrific it looked in the first place. Contrast is excellent, and the whites are strong and subtly rendered without any blooming. The DVD also follows the laserdisc by including the original shortened ending as an extra, along with the jittery theatrical trailer. The only missing extra is the isolated music and effects score, but the DVD compensates by finally offering closed captions, which are quite helpful in discerning a few rushed plot points.

KISS ME, KILL ME (BABA YAGA)

Colour, 1973, 89m. / Directed by Corrado Farina / Starring Carroll Baker, Isabelle de Funès / Diamond (US R0 NTSC)

An especially odd entry in the line of Eurocult comic book adaptations (also including the likes of *Diabolik* and *Satanik*), the sex/horror madness of *Baba Yaga* (retitled *Kiss Me, Kill Me* for home video) must have been an impossible sell in the '70s. Still at the height of her Continental exploitation career, actress and Hollywood expatriate Carroll Baker serves as the nominal marquee name for what amounts to an extended groovy mood piece, mixing together gothic horror and glossy S&M for an experience unlike any other.

Sexy, bob-haired fashion photographer Valentina (Isabelle de Funès) leaves a lifestyle of excess and delight with her latest colleague and sex partner, Arno (George Eastman, the *Anthropophagus* monster himself). One night in a scene reminiscent of *Daughters of Darkness*, she bumps into the chic and mysterious Baba Yaga (Baker), a blonde society woman in a limo. Later Baba shows up at Valentina's apartment during an erotic photo shoot and puts a strange curse on her camera. Faster than you can say *Eyes of Laura Mars*, Valentina is plagued by strange visions involving leather dolls and finds herself drawn to the house of this bewitching woman, who harbours more than a few kinky supernatural secrets.

A film seemingly made on its own little planet (probably very close to the one in *Spermula*), this peculiar international production doesn't offer its actors much of opportunity to be more than moving mannequins. That said, Baker - made up to look older than she really was at the time - is a compelling presence as always and even dubs in her own voice. Also effective are the film's pop art editing techniques; the credits themselves are interspersed between jagged shots of a swinging party and comic book frames, while Valentina's visions are related by graphic art interpretations of images from the film. The ultimately aimless and nonlinear nature of the storyline is eventually consumed by the film's style, where the visual alignments of the actors' bodies and faces become more important than any kind of

rational plotting. *Valentina*, a more traditional, softcore version of the comic book, was later made in 1988 for Italian television and briefly appeared on US home video.

As usual, this presumably unauthorized DVD from Diamond is a riot of misinformation. The packaging promotes this as an Umberto Lenzi production, perhaps confusing this with *Paranoia or A Quiet Place to Kill* (which teamed him up with Baker). For some reason Jean-Louis Trintignant's name also appears on the box. In any case, the disc is a wholesale rip of the long discontinued American VHS release from Paragon, right down to the tape dropouts and the sloppy computer generated title card. The image is soft and often distractingly cropped from its original 1.85:1 aspect ratio, with additional information trimmed from the top and bottom as well. It's a disheartening option for anyone interested in the film; hopefully a passable version will turn up from the film's actual owners one of these days. In the meantime fans with the proper resources may want to seek out the letterboxed Italian VHS, which beats this DVD hands down.

KISS ME MONSTER

Colour, 1966, 78m. / Directed by Jess Franco / Starring Janine Reynaud, Rosanna Yanni / Anchor Bay (US R1 NTSC) / WS (1.66:1)

Compared to *Succubus, Kiss Me Monster* (*Besame mostruo*) seems almost insignificant, but Franco's peculiar obsessions still manifest themselves in this seemingly fluffy tribute to those swinging '60's spy films. Reynaud appears again, this time as half of the sexy female Red Lips detective team. The threadbare plot, involving a strange cult and murders connected to a piece of music, are basically an excuse to get the private eyes in a string of situations where they can shimmy, shake, and shoot at the drop of a hat. As with *Succubus*, the sex and nudity quotient is fairly mild compared to modern erotic thrillers, but the dizzy atmosphere of carefree sexuality that spins through both films makes them incredibly entertaining and delightful if you're in the right frame of mind.

Aside from the ragged opening titles, the print is in nice shape, with punchy colours and nice, rich shadows. Basically it's a little better than the Redemption print released in the UK and a huge improvement over the very old US video from the early '80s. The letterboxing looks just right, and the

K

score, mostly by Jerry Van Rooyen (a Franco regular), sounds just dandy. Both DVDs also feature the original trailers (the *Succubus* one is a riot, and for some reason the *Kiss Me Monster* trailer has a digital number "13" in the corner of the image).

KNIGHTRIDERS

Colour, 1981, 142m. / Directed by George A. Romero / Starring Ed Harris, Tom Savini / Anchor Bay (US R1 NTSC) / WS (1.85:1) (16:9) / Mono

Taking a break from the gory social commentary of *Dawn of the Dead*, director George Romero turned his eye to the crumbling status of '60s idealism and independent filmmaking with *Knightriders*, a personal statement cloaked in the story of performing knights on bikes whose ideals ultimately prove to be their undoing.

In a loose riff on the classic Arthurian legend, Billy (Ed Harris) serves as the ruler over a roaming band of jousting bikers who put on shows for money in various towns. The band relishes its freedom from the constraints of society, enjoying an equal balance of races, sexual orientations, personality types, and social backgrounds. The promise of commercial success proves to be too tempting for some members, particularly the easily corrupted Mordred figure, Morgan (FX master Tom Savini), who has already wounded Billy and begun a damaging cycle of self-doubt among the group. Some of the other characters' roles within this modern Arthurian legend don't become clear until well into the story, but as Billy soon learns, history has a nasty habit of repeating itself.

As with many Romero films, *Knightriders* can feel rough around the edges to those unfamiliar with his work and, as his longest film to date, seems to go on forever. However, the high level of action and the many interweaving subplots demand a dense, lengthy structure for Romero to create what amounts to a modern day tapestry demonstrating the moral questions troubling its creator. The performers all tackle their roles with gusto, including such familiar faces as *Dawn*'s Ken Foree and Scott H. Reiniger, Savini's future *Night of the Living Dead* leading lady Patricia Tallmann (as a bobbysoxer recruit), and as usual, Romero's wife Christine. Look fast in the crowd scenes near the beginning for Stephen King and his wife Tabitha as redneck spectators; of course, Romero and King officially joined forces soon afterwards for the much more commercial *Creepshow*. Obviously a deeply felt family project at

its heart, *Knightriders* may not appease those who only like Romero for his violent gore operas but is definitely one of the most rigorous, fascinating attempts by a filmmaker to express his views through an action film.

Anchor Bay's special edition of *Knightriders* obviously lays waste to all previous home video editions from Media and Republic, both in terms of presentation and extras. Rarely seen during its initial run and just barely a notable cult item, the film has had a surprisingly lucky history on video and looks about as good now as one could possibly hope. The fleshtones have always looked a little strange for some reason, and they still do, but otherwise the print used here is top notch and blemish-free. The commentary track pretty much reunites the crew from Elite's *Dawn of the Dead*, but this time they're much better organized and seem to be at ease with the whole commentary process. Everyone from Romero to Savini to lesser known players like John Amplas joins in here, with Chris Stavrakis moderating. Some of the tidbits about the film's stunt work are especially revealing, while Romero still obviously has quite a bit of affection for this unusual pet project.

The disc also contains a so-so theatrical trailer (which probably didn't help its box office fate), two TV teasers, 15 minutes of silent home video footage which most viewers will only sit through once at best, and a truly scary colour insert photo.

KNOCKING ON DEATH'S DOOR

Colour, 1998, 83m. / Directed by Mitch Marcus / Starring Brian Bloom, Kimberly Rowe / New Concorde (US R1 NTSC) / DD2.0

Hard to believe, but New Concorde has actually made a pretty good little horror film. While Roger Corman's latest film company has generated a few interesting horror titles in the past ranging from not bad (*Blood Song*, aka *Haunted Symphony*) to laughably campy (*Burial of the Rats*), the ghostly *Knocking on Death's Door* is by far the best of the batch so far.

Brad Gallagher (soap heartthrob Brian Bloom) and his newlywed wife, Danielle (fledgling scream queen Kimberly Rowe) are recruited by Professor Paul Ballard (John Doe), who had a fling with Danielle during her college days, to investigate paranormal happenings at the legendary Sunset House (not Hillside House as the packaging states). Aside from the stereotypical hick neighbours, the couple are tormented by constant intrusions on their lovemaking (falling grandfather clocks, flying red-hot pokers, etc.). Soon Brad's hitting the bottle hard and becoming jealous about Danielle's relationship with their boss. Meanwhile, Danielle, who gained psychic abilities after a bizarre skating accident in her childhood, comes in contact with several ghostly presence within the house. The major ghost identifies himself as "Samuel," possibly the husband of the house's previous owner, a woman named Elizabeth who died under mysterious circumstances.

Aside from a gruesome axe murder during the prologue, *Knocking on Death's Door* is a welcome return to horror films which rely on atmosphere, character development, plot, and genuine chills to tell a good story. Even the requisite nudity is erotic, tasteful, and integrated into the story, and all of the performers do solid jobs. Carradine, whose career has suffered as of late even to the point of appearing in Fred Olen Ray films, does better work here than we've seen in a while, and Bloom looks almost unrecognizable as a man being torn apart by both inner and outer demons. Director Marcus does an efficient job of manipulating the viewer through stylish camerawork (and boy does this look good for a recent Corman film!), unsettling imagery, and a beautifully manipulative sound mix with some startling directional effects. The only major flaw is Protis' serviceable but derivative music score, which blatantly apes Wendy Carlos' *The Shining* (probably because the opening credits also show a couple driving through the countryside).

The DVD presentation is a genuine special edition by New Concorde standards, with the video trailer and four chunks of additional footage included as supplements. The extra scenes (integrated into the entire scenes in which they belong) don't really add a whole lot aside from an extra vision during Brad's fall into the grave near the end, but it's a nice gesture all the same. Most of the trims were apparently made to extraneous dialogue in the usual Corman fashion to keep the film well under a 90 minute running time. While there isn't much here that hasn't already been explored in films like *The Changeling, The Haunting, Legend of Hell House*, or *Poltergeist, Knocking on Death's Door* is nevertheless a solid ghost story and a welcome throwback to good campfire-style creepy fun.

KOLOBOS

Colour, 1999, 87m. / Directed by Daniel Liatowitsch and David Todd Ocvirk / Starring Amy Weber, Donny Terranova / York (US R1 NTSC) / WS (1.85:1) / DD5.1, Metrodome (UK R2 PAL)

Until Italian directors go back to making old-fashioned gory slasher mysteries, audiences will have to content themselves with American imitations - of which *Kolobos* is one of many examples. Though apparently shot on a very low budget, the film sports visual style to burn, some extraordinarily graphic murder sequences, earnest performances, and a crackerjack premise.

The films begins with a lengthy subjective sequence in which a badly mutilated girl is brought out of a rainstorm into a hospital, where her wounds are treated and she begins to recover in a hospital room. Thanks to the interrogations of her bedridden neighbour and an attending nurse, the girl begins experiencing flashbacks to the previous day. Five young people respond to a classified ad seeking adventurous, open-minded people for a *Real World*-style experimental film. The various participants include a low budget soft porn/horror actress, a struggling stand-up comedian, a smartass fast food worker, and a clean cut college guy. The fifth guinea pig, Kyra (soap actress Amy Weber, sort of a less perky Jennifer Love Hewitt), is an anxiety-ridden young psychiatric patient prone to doodling gruesome images. The "actors" convene in an isolated house where video cameras monitor their every move, though the director stops by to offer them some pizza and offer some general guidelines about the project. Unfortunately, after he leaves, the windows and doors are all sealed with unbreakable metal plating, and lethal booby traps begin decimating the young hopefuls at the most unexpected moments.

Though structurally a generic slasher film and little more (if you've seen *Curtains*, you know the routine), *Kolobos* generates a surprising amount of mileage out of its creepy, unsettling framing and recurring images, including one doozy of a scare exactly one hour into the film. The filmmakers are obvious lovers of the horror genre, with some welcome nods to author Poppy Z. Brite and particularly Argento, whose *Deep Red* tooth-bashing is reprised during one especially splashy scene. The effective but irritatingly derivative score by William Kidd manages to swipe from *Suspiria, Inferno*, and *Phenomena* in the first five minutes alone, but it still works wonders and enhances the garish, candy-coloured lighting schemes. Washed up scream queen Linnea Quigley turns up briefly at the beginning, an amusing touch considering the tribute to her antler murder in *Silent Night, Deadly Night* performed later in the film. None of the characters are especially appealing, but the actors all do a passable job and conquer the sometimes scrappy dialogue recording, which suffers from that familiar, hollow "made for video" sound.

Unfortunately, like most horror films in the past couple of years, *Kolobos* proves to be too clever for its own good and paints itself into a corner. Just when the film works up to a creepy, tense climax, the film stops dead in its tracks, refuses to explain itself, and lumbers along for a deadening ten minute epilogue that defiantly goes against everything that preceded it. As with *The Last Broadcast* and especially *The Blair Witch Project*, it's really a shame to see a potentially classic premise flushed away by filmmakers unable to resolve their own narrative and resorting to a "figure it out for yourself" technique that only worked for *Cube*.

Apart from the wretched cover design which makes this look like some kind of kinky werewolf movie (?!), York has done a surprisingly top drawer job of bringing *Kolobos* to US DVD, and the British release from Metrodome features a similar transfer with far more suggestive promotional art. The image quality is very clear and stable; every hue in the palette drenches the shadowy hallways, making this a very satisfying piece of eye candy. The highly manipulative 5.1 audio features some jolting directional sound effects (love those flying buzzsaws!), despite the aforementioned "canned" dialogue problems. A pretty good trailer is also included, though oddly, it neglects to give the film's title. Other extras include Spanish subtitles and a "behind the scenes" which just amounts to a two page bio of Ms. Weber.

KWAIDAN

Colour, 1964, 161m. / Directed by Masaki Kobayashi / Starring Rentaro Mikuni, Tatsuya Nakadai / Criterion (US R1 NTSC) / WS (2.35:1) (16:9)

 One of the most internationally revered Japanese films, *Kwaidan* is that rare creature, a horror film capable of impressing even the staunchest critics and capable of functioning as a work of art regardless of genre. Based on the oft-translated stories of Greek-born writer Lafcadio Hearn, this quartet of ghost stories caused a sensation when released, racking up awards at Cannes and, along with *Onibaba* and *Ugetsu*, introducing English-speaking viewers to an entirely different kind of cinematic terror.

Our first story, "Black Hair," concerns an impoverished samurai (Rentaro Mikuni) who abandons his wife (Michiyo Aratama) and rides off to richer pastures. He marries a richer woman but ultimately finds his marriage in ruins. Dejected, he returns to his first wife years later, only to find her exactly the same as he left her. However, the evening spent in her arms takes a decidedly chilling turn.

In "The Woman in the Snow," which was trimmed from the initial US prints and later remade (poorly) in *Tales from the Darkside: The Movie*, two woodcutters trudging through a snowy forest come across a ghostly woman who kills one them and decides to leave the other alive, only on the condition that he never tell a living soul about their encounter. Years pass, and the woodcutter has established a family with a beautiful wife; however, his loose tongue proves to have tragic consequences.

In the opulent and unforgettable "Hoichi the Earless," a young blind singer/storyteller named Hoichi (Katsuo Nakamura) skilfully delivers the saga of warring clans during a sea battle. The ghosts of one clan are so impressed with his skill that they repeatedly summon him to perform for them, a demand which takes a heavy toll on Hoichi's own spirit. The local priests learn of his plight and cover him with holy symbols to render him invisible to the ghosts. Unfortunately the priests make a slight mistake, which yields a gruesome penalty.

Finally, "In a Cup of Tea" a writer (Noboru Nakaya) looks into a cup of tea and finds a completely different, younger man's reflection staring back at him. That evening the strange apparition appears, causing the frightened writer to attack him. Later three more ghosts appear with a sinister command from their master, resulting in one final, bizarre twist.

From the opening images of web-like strands of brightly coloured paint slowly twisting through water, *Kwaidan* is a sensually amazing experience. Every frame of the film is perfectly composed and a wondrous feat of colour lighting; you could literally freeze frame at any point and have a painting on your television screen. Director Masaki Kobayashi (*The Human Condition*) displays a remarkable command of the medium here, a huge departure from his gritty earlier work, and the vibrant, unnatural backdrops have influenced several generations of filmmakers both in the East and West. Imagine *The Twilight Zone* with the scope of Akira Kurosawa and the visual flair of Dario Argento, and that might convey some of the tone of this unique masterpiece. Though the pace is extremely deliberate and may prove difficult for some viewers, the effort is well worth it.

Someone at Criterion must really love *Kwaidan*, for they have always had excellent source materials even from their first impressive laserdisc and tape releases. The scope framing is vital to appreciating this film, and the DVD is an even more satisfying presentation thanks to additional restoration work and a colour palette that can only be described as hallucinatory. Apart from some very minor scratches near the reel changes, the print is in wonderful condition and looks as close to immaculate as any '60s title from Japan. The mono audio sounds fine, with the excellent, experimental score by Toku Takemitsu (*Ran*) filled with bizarre, atonal rumblings of bass and high treble shrieking. The English subtitles have reportedly been retranslated and improved, but the variations appear to be minor. The disc also includes the original Japanese trailer (with optional subtitles) but, strangely, no background information on the film or its participants to put it in any historical context, with only a brief liner notes essay covering the very basics.

LABYRINTH

Colour, 1986, 101m. / Directed by Jim Henson / Starring David Bowie, Jennifer Connelly / Columbia (US R1 NTSC, UK R2 PAL) / WS (2.35:1) (16:9) / DD2.0

 Following the less than joyous reception for *The Dark Crystal*, Jim Henson decided to lighten things up and return to charted Muppet territory. Thanks to a collaboration with George Lucas (and ILM), as well as the acting and musical input of David Bowie, Henson came up with *Labyrinth*, a fable reminiscent of such children's quest tales as *Alice's Adventures in Wonderland* and *The Wonderful Wizard of Oz*.

Sarah (Jennifer Connelly), a young preteen, is left for the evening in charge of her baby brother, Toby, who won't stop crying. Driven to her wit's end, Sarah wishes aloud that the Goblin King would come and take him away. Sure enough, the Goblin King (Bowie) appears and spirits the baby away. Sarah immediately regrets her words and makes a dangerous pact: if she can manoeuvre through the Goblin King's maze and get to his castle before midnight, she can have her brother back. Along the way, Sarah encounters numerous bizarre characters, including the diminutive Hoggle and the twisted Junk Lady. Of course, the Goblin King also appears at regular intervals to follow Sarah's progress and provide the occasional toe-tapping song.

Penned by Monty Python's Terry Jones, the sketchy script of *Labyrinth* mostly serves as a framework allowing Henson and company to make up events as they go along. This aimless approach has caused many critics to label the film as juvenile, and while it certainly doesn't approach *Dark Crystal* in terms of formal approach or technical virtuosity, *Labyrinth* offers plenty of modest charms of its own. Accompanied by a playful Trevor Jones electronic score, Bowie's songs keep things bubbling along, particularly during the catchy "Magic Dance" and the ethereal "As the World Falls Down." Connelly, following up on her memorable turn in *Phenomena*, makes a beautiful heroine, and her scenes with Bowie (sporting a legendary bad wig) remain emotionally charged and tastefully sensual. Incidentally, this was perhaps the first film to feature one of those "Hey, the movie's over now so let's hop around and party!" endings, later used *ad nauseum* in almost every early '90s Buena Vista film (e.g., *Dangerous Minds*).

Previously issued as a soft-looking but acceptable widescreen laserdisc from Orion, Labyrinth has been given an anamorphic visual makeover from Columbia, looking about as good as it did in theatres. Impossible to appreciate in cropped form, the scope framing makes ingenious use of the inventive art direction (especially the labyrinth itself) and the elaborate ILM effects. The original stereo surround audio is fine but obviously hasn't been given quite as much attention; in what may be an irritant for many, the opening reel is a frame or two out of synch! Casual viewers probably won't notice the discrepancy, especially since most of the film doesn't involve on camera human dialogue, but it's amazing that a studio would let this casually slip through while paying so much attention to everything else. This glitch aside, the film's fans should find this edition worth the wait, particularly considering the inclusion of "Inside the Labyrinth," a one hour television special containing behind the scenes footage of Bowie, conceptual artist Brian Froud (who also designed *The Dark Crystal*), and the ILM folks hard at work.

LADY CHATTERLEY

Colour, 1992, 206m. / Directed by Ken Russell / Starring Joely Richardson, Sean Bean / Metrodome (UK R2 PAL) / DD2.0

For more than a century, the name "Lady Chatterley" has become synonymous with softcore naughtiness. The scandal surrounding D.H. Lawrence's oft-censored novel (and two subsequent, tangentially

related works) was just the beginning, really, as various attempts to film the book also ran into trouble around the world. From the relatively tame 1955 French version to Just Jaeckin's soft focus 1981 adaptation with Sylvia Kristel (and a host of cruddy cable knockoffs), Ms. Chatterley has gone through quite a bit and yet continues to come out unscathed. In 1992, Ken Russell decided to take a crack at the *Lady Chatterley* story, a logical decision following his successful films of Lawrence's *Women in Love* and its literary prequel, *The Rainbow*. Russell decided to make a miniseries instead of a feature film, thus allowing him to adapt nearly every single word from Lawrence's text. Like *The Rainbow*, this adaptation finds the outrageous filmmaker more subdued than usual, with delicate pastoral photography and some great period costumes providing all of the visual flair.

The story is pretty familiar by now: Lady Connie Chatterley (Joely Richardson) is saddled with an intelligent but embittered, wheelchair bound husband, Clifford (James Wilby). Emotionally and physically frustrated, she finds herself drawn to the feral, simple gamekeeper, Mellors (Sean Bean). The lovers are soon faced with a number of obstacles, primarily their differences in class and education. Is it just a matter of animal passion, or could it be true love?

While literature and Russell devotees will find plenty to enjoy here, there's no denying that the running time (over three hours) will prove daunting to the average viewer. Metrodome's DVD breaks down each of the four episodes, allowing for periodic viewing (the best option) and, since we all know the selling point of this disc anyway, a menu option to skip to all the sex scenes. Actually, the "very erotic sex" promised on the packaging looks like pretty weak tea, but for TV this is spicier than usual. Fans of Ms. Richardson will be happy to know that she disrobes often and still manages to turn in a solid performance, while the underrated Bean is great as always. The image quality is very good, with crisp detail and solid colour rendering, and the sparse surround track focuses mainly on ambient woodland noises and the restrained, neoclassical music score.

LADY IN WHITE

Colour, 1988, 117m. / Directed by Frank La Loggia / Starring Lukas Haas, Katherine Helmond / Elite Entertainment (US R1 NTSC) / WS (1.85) / DD5.1

Elite Entertainment's *Lady in White* showcases this cult effort from La Loggia (*Fear No Evil*) about as well as possible. The very good picture quality and spectacular five-channel sound makes this a fine sensory experience if you're willing to overlook some serious flaws in the film itself.

While locked overnight in the school coat closet due to a practical joke, Frankie Scarlatti (Lukas Haas) witnesses a ghostly re-enacting of a young girl's murder. After the real killer actually bursts into the closet to look for a lost ring and nearly kills Frankie, the boy is continuously haunted by the girl's ghost as she looks for the spirit of her dead mother, the spectral "lady in white." Meanwhile, Katherine Helmond (dressed in white) lurks nearby... is the real ghost, or is it someone else? And who is the real killer? (If you can't guess the second one 30 minutes into the movie, you need serious help.)

A film whose intentions obviously exceed its grasp, *Lady in White* is one of those films you enjoy watching and recommending to friends while apologizing for the more glaring goofs in the technique and story. Most obviously there's a really heavy reliance on special effects, which would be fine if the effects were any good, but... In particular, you'll have to look hard to find phonier-looking blue screen work. The ending looks especially unconvincing, sapping a lot of tension from the climax. Also, so many subplots clutter the storyline that you'll often find yourself saying "huh?" For example, a black school janitor is accused of the child murders, leading to a whole sub-*To Kill a Mockingbird* race relations study that looks like it wandered in from a different movie.

Despite these shortcomings, this really is an enjoyable film to watch, and the astounding bonus material Elite has bestowed upon it makes this a good bet for any horror collection . This "director's cut" contains about six minutes of nice if inconsequential extra scenes, and La Loggia's commentary, while occasionally self-absorbed, provides some useful insight into the blood, sweat and tears he poured into the film. Other goodies include the theatrical trailer, TV and radio spots, jillions of production photos, and an amateur behind-the-scenes peek via camcorder. The outstanding bonus, though, is a seven-minute promotional version of *Lady in White* shot before the actual film, featuring Helmond and condensing most of the story into a thrilling Reader's Digest form. The main child actor here is very different from Haas, though most of the shots and locations are identical to those in the final product, and ironically, the visual effects are actually more convincing and exciting than those in the actual movie. The only bonus on the DVD not present on the laserdisc is the complete three-suite music score, identical to the Southeast Records version but missing the two bonus cues. Be forewarned: some DVD owners have complained about problems accessing certain features of the supplementary menu.

LADY OF THE LAKE

Colour, 1998, 82m. / Directed by Maurice Devereaux / Starring Erik Rutherford, Tennyson Loeh / MTI (US R1 NTSC) WS (1.66:1) / DD2.0

 Another independent horror title that would have probably vanished into oblivion had it not been picked up by Fangoria, *Lady of the Lake* will surprise many viewers expecting a monstrous gorefest. More of a soulful erotic fairy tale, the film is obviously a heartfelt production from French Canadian director Maurice Devereaux (*$LASHER$*) and his crew, as they spent over six years working on it from initial preproduction (as a short film) until completion.

David (Erik Rutherford), a young painter, experiences a strange dream in which, while standing over his uncle's casket, a demonic man taunts him. When David awakes, he receives a phone call informing him that his uncle has indeed just passed away, leaving David - the last living relative - his uncle's lakeside cabin for whatever use he sees fit. David drives out to investigate the property and spend some time relaxing away from the city; soon after, a local neighbour informs David that his uncle drowned under mysterious circumstances, just like many of the men living in the area. Quicker than you can say *Phantasm*, David rummages through the cabin and, thanks to some photographs, discovers that his uncle was involved with a mysterious woman who may have been involved in his death. That night, David is awakened by strange noises, and lo and behold, the end of his hallway has turned into a glassy underwater lake with a floating woman (Tennyson Loeh) beckoning to be welcoming inside. David pulls the woman into the hallway, and they make love (the punchline for this scene is a riot). Over the next few days, the woman continues to return and finally makes David an offer: she will stay with him unconditionally for a week and offer him unlimited happiness, but after that she must leave and never see him again. David accepts, and after much pleading, the woman, Viviane, allows him to step into the past and discover the truth behind her ghostly torment.

Aside from some medieval sequences, *Lady of the Lake* largely ignores the Arthurian implications of its title and instead focuses on a supernatural romance along the lines of *Girl in a Swing*. Homages to other films abound, ranging from Jean Cocteau's *Orpheus* to Roger Vadim's *Blood and Roses* and John Boorman's *Excalibur*. The fantasy and dramatic elements work well, with a large amount of tastefully handled nudity, and the gory horror sequences look tacked on to increase the film's commercial potential. Viviane's briefly glimpsed monster makeup, her bile-spewing attacks on unsuspecting males, and the zombie-hacking finale might draw in some gorehounds who would have ignored the film otherwise, but frankly the story could work just as well (and maybe better) without them.

Approaching this film with the same criteria as a big budget Hollywood effort is obviously not the best approach; the low budget and occasionally stilted acting are obvious, and the hero's age seems to change dramatically throughout the film due to the shooting schedule. The obviously talented Devereaux displays a sure hand in dealing with his material, and the purity of his vision on film is something to be commended. One can only hope viewers will see what he's capable of with a more reasonable budget in the future.

The MTI/Fangoria DVD special edition contains the same presentation afforded to their earlier *I, Zombie*. Presented in a matted 1.66:1 transfer, the film (apparently shot on hi-def video and transferred to film) looks fine for the most part, though turning down the brightness on the TV monitor produced the best results. The basic stereo soundtrack adequately showcases producer Martin Gauthier's eloquent electronic score, one of the film's greatest assets, and features a few token directional effects, particularly during the climax. Devereaux provides a very cheerful commentary track in which he focuses on the technical aspects of the film; it's a welcome and entertaining bonus, but it would have been nice if he had delved deeper into some of the thematic and literary influences on the film as well. The excellent Canadian trailer and a half hour collage of behind the scenes camcorder footage round out the package.

LAIR OF THE WHITE WORM

Colour, 1988, 93m. / Directed by Ken Russell / Starring Amanda Donohoe, Hugh Grant / Artisan (US R1 NTSC) / WS (1.85:1) (16:9) / DD4.0

L

Perhaps an acquired taste, *Lair of the White Worm* is in many ways the ultimate Ken Russell film. All of his filmmaking strengths really hit their stride here: a twisty, insane narrative; outlandish sexual imagery and hallucinatory visuals; and pithy, literate banter focusing on class conflicts. Of course, it's also fortunately a ripping good horror film, packed with jolts and sick giggles. Though still relegated to minor cult status for some reason, *Lair* deserves far more acclaim and, aside from being a key film for anyone interested in Russell, also happens to be a pivotal entry in late 1980s terror cinema.

Eve (Catherine Oxenberg) and Mary (Sammi Davis) Trent, two sisters, run their family farm after the mysterious deaths of their parents. A visiting Scottish archaeology student, Angus (Peter Capaldi), digs around their property and comes across a strange, dragon-like skull and a bizarre mosaic. Soon bizarre events begin to engulf the countryside, including weird visions and an attack on the local aristocrat, Lord James D'Ampton (Hugh Grant), whose distant relative made history by slaying a medieval wyrm (dragon). Could it all have something to do with the seasonal residence of the slinky, sexy Lady Sylvia Marsh (Amanda Donohoe)? And why do the locals keep disappearing?

To reveal any more would be heresy, but Russell manages to use Bram Stoker's seldom read, radically different novel as a springboard for a dizzying array of recurring motifs contrasting paganism with Christianity, sensuality with purity, and earth with fire. All of the actors bite into their roles with pure gusto, though Donohoe easily takes top honours for her intensely erotic and amusing Lady Sylvia, tormenting policemen and Boy Scouts alike with her beautiful allure. Davis, a sadly underused actress best known for *Hope and Glory*, makes a fine, vulnerable heroine, as does Royal Family relative Oxenberg in her stylish designer underwear. Hugh Grant fans may be a little startled by his flawed "heroic" portrayal (he ultimately has little to do with the outcome), but he proves here that he can be subdued and avoid most of his familiar mannerisms when the job calls for it.

Russell fans should have a ball picking out some subtle touches, including a cameo appearance by regular Christopher Gable as the late Mr. Trent during one dream sequence. Russell's penchant for theatrical, campy special effects really shines here, from the drive-in style worm to the outrageous images of impaled nuns! As with *Crimes of Passion*, Russell also manages to pack in enough phallic imagery to make a Freudian's head swim, drawing some obvious parallels between the white snake and... well, figure it out. And finally, don't forget that theme song!

Originally released in a very disappointing, murky transfer from Vestron on laserdisc and VHS, *Lair of the White Worm* has never even remotely resembled its theatrical incarnation on home video until now. Thanks to a new visual facelift from Artisan and Pioneer, Russell's film looks better than it has in years, with the hellish orange flames of the Trent girls' snaky hallucinations now thoughtfully intact. It still can't quite compare to the eye-popping colours of the theatrical experience (Lady Sylvia's lime green windows under the stairwell, for instance, still look a dull grey on the small screen), but this is a highly satisfying presentation. The letterboxed, anamorphic transfer shaves a tiny sliver from the full frame presentation while adding considerably to the left and right sides. The Ultra-Stereo sound mix pales compared to standard Dolby, but the DVD sounds fine and features crisp channel separation.

Like *Salome's Last Dance*, this title has been outfitted with a running Ken Russell commentary; as usual, he provides some witty, precise insight into his rationale behind the film and his experiences while making it, particularly the odd local customs and cultural quirks which fuelled his writing of the script. The DVD also includes some solid production notes, including effects studies and a cursory comparison to the novel, as well as the frisky US theatrical trailer (which spoils the last scene's punchline) and a 30 second TV spot apparently lifted from a very old videotape.

LARA CROFT: TOMB RAIDER

Colour, 2001, 100m. / Directed by Simon West / Starring Angelina Jolie, Iain Glen / Paramount (US R1 NTSC, UK R2 PAL) / WS (2.35:1) (16:9) / DD5.1

Aristocratic fortune hunter Lara Croft (Jolie) learns of the existence of The Triangle of Light, an ancient artefact that can alter the course of time. Legendarily broken in half to debilitate its power, she sets off to find the pieces. But danger lurks in the form of The Illuminati, a secret society who want the Triangle for their own perfidious reasons. *Lara Croft: Tomb Raider* took a lot of flack when it first opened, most of the unrest coming from those comparing the film to its mega-successful computer game origins. The plot isn't going to put a strain on anyone's little grey cells, but those less familiar with the joystick operated Croft, or with a passion for the excesses of Indiana Jones and Ray Harryhausen movies, are sure to get a buzz out of the gelignite-fuelled action, top notch effects and sweat-sheened Angelina Jolie dashing around in slow-mo with optimum jiggle factor in operation. On the down side the editing of some of the action sequences is so frenetic it's difficult to digest everything, and combined with the screeching (and, at the risk of seeming parochial, inappropriate) rock soundtrack it all becomes an assault on the senses too far. Regardless, Brit director Simon West orchestrates the hijinks with a sure hand and peppers his story with familiar faces from TV and film that include Daniel Craig, Chris Barrie and Leslie Phillips. Ian Glen's villainous Powell is the archetypal rotten apple. There's even an appearance from Jolie's real life dad, Jon Voight, as - who else? - Lara Croft's dad. It's all fairly forgettable stuff, but if you've a hankering for crackerjack thrills'n'spills this ably fits the bill.

As one would expect from such a recent release, the transfer on Paramount's DVD is practically criticism-free (unless one counts the oddly slender 12 chapter stops). Beyond this, the disc is embellished with more trinkets than you'll find on most Paramount releases. "Digging into Tomb Raider" is a 25-minute behind the scenes look at the making of the film in which most of the key movers and shakers have their say, with two extra featurettes totalling 15 minutes but repeating segments from the main documentary. There are four deleted / extended sequences, one in which Leslie Phillips gets his head lopped off. Among the series of 8 special effects vignettes is an additional deleted scene in which Iain Glen meets an alternate (superior) fate. Also included is a classy unused title sequence. U2's "Elevation" promo music video and a short history of the game that started it all rounds out the package. Clicking on the pulsing water symbol at the foot of the special features menu accesses some "hidden" co-interview footage with Jolie and Voight. The feature is accompanied by a commentary from director West. The sound is in English 5.1 Surround, English Dolby Surround and French. Subtitling is in English only. - TG

THE LAST BROADCAST

Colour, 1998, 86m. / Directed by Stefan Avalos and Lance Weiler / Starring David Beard, Jim Seward / Ventura (US R1 NTSC), Metrodome (UK R2 PAL) / DD2.0

Another instalment in the "reality or not?" school of horror filmmaking, *The Last Broadcast* follows in the footsteps of *Cannibal Holocaust, Man Bites Dog*, etc., as it presents a fictitious investigation into the deaths of two public access TV producers in the middle of the New Jersey Pine Barrens. Deriving most of its notoriety from supposed similarities to the later *The Blair Witch Project*, this film (to use the term loosely - it was shot mostly on video equipment) only resembles that brilliantly marketed cash cow in terms of its basic setting and premise. While *Blair Witch* aspires to be little more than an imaginary (and not all that compelling) campfire tale, *The Last Broadcast* attacks its subject as a satire of modern "homemade" journalism and the public's fascination with reality TV shows that turn out to be anything but. Few seem to agree which film is better, but at heart, both are essentially ambitious, low budget experiments crippled by deeply flawed executions.

Structured as a television documentary, *The Last Broadcast* presents a reporter/filmmaker (David Beard) deconstructing the mystery behind the deaths of Stefan Avalos and Lance Weiler, the hosts of *Fact or Fiction?*, a basement TV production devoted to local urban legends. The murders were pinned on Jim Seward, a mentally unstable young man who monitored the Internet Relay Chat during what was supposed to be a live broadcast concerning the mythical Jersey Devil. Compiling interview footage intercut with the actual "last broadcast," the story coils tighter as the horrific truth begins to emerge, and nothing is what it seems.

First of all, is *The Last Broadcast* frightening? Well, yes, in a way. There's a devious, sneaky imagination at work here, and a sequence near the end detailing the reconstruction of a damaged videotape generates some deep, palpable chills. More often, though, it's fascinating as a face-slapping answer to the *Hard Copy* mentality of the '90s and strikes pretty deeply at the modern standards of journalism. Unfortunately the creators throw most of their good work out the window during the last five minutes; frankly, it's hard to imagine a worse possible ending. The concept behind the ending is fine (though filled with plot holes), but its execution is so clumsy, jarring, and ineptly handled that most viewers will either be shaking their heads or laughing in confusion. This major flaw aside, the other 80 minutes provides some worthy food for thought and at least merits a rental.

Projected digitally rather than screened as a piece of celluloid, *The Last Broadcast* obviously makes for a somewhat unorthodox DVD experience. The video quality ranges from deliberately fuzzy and pixellized (the *Fact or Fiction?* excerpts) to clear and vivid (the interview footage). Despite the potential for added clarity, the disc looks about the same as the VHS tape, which was first issued as a limited edition through Amazon. In the end, it's really no better or worse than watching a television broadcast.

Considering the low price, the DVD packs in an admirable number of extras, including director's commentary (almost entirely technical, but interesting), some "trailers" (for lack of a better term), behind the scenes footage showing how the project was composed and edited, and a mini-documentary on the Jersey Devil, which is never really defined in the actual film. (A first season episode of *The X-Files* was devoted to this mythical creature as well.) While *Blair Witch* may have drawn inspiration (ahem) from *The Last Broadcast*, the reverse is apparently true for the DVD, which closely resembles Artisan's presentation. Far more money probably went into the DVD than into the actual film, which really says something about filmmaking in the '90s. In any case, *The Last Broadcast* offers a solid, well-chosen package of extras, and an occasionally creepy little movie to boot.

THE LAST STARFIGHTER

Colour, 1984, 101m. / Directed by Nick Castle / Starring Lance Guest, Robert Preston / Universal (US R1 NTSC) / WS (2.35:1) (16:9) / DD5.1

The rise of video games over the past twenty years has inspired quite a few movies - and most of them are really, really bad. The few happy exceptions, like this film and *WarGames*, understand that special effects alone cannot carry a film, and while movies like *Streetfighter* may have money to burn, there's not much underneath to hold them up. *The Last Starfighter* was largely overlooked as a Spielberg wannabe on its original theatrical release but quickly amassed a devoted following through home video and frequent screenings on HBO. However, fans who have never seen it in scope will be amazed at how different it looks now on DVD.

A typical all-American teenage dreamer, Alex Rogan (Lance Guest of *Halloween II*), lives in a trailer park managed by his mother. While he enjoys the company of his friends and neighbours, including girlfriend Catherine Mary Stuart (*Night of the Comet*), he longs for something more (and if this were a Disney film he'd have one of those "I gotta be free so I'll run through a field and sing" numbers). In one day Alex experiences a double whammy: he's turned down for a college scholarship and manages to beat the seemingly invincible Starfighter video game. That night, a mysterious man, Centauri (Robert Preston, doing a terrific alien spin on his Harold Hill persona), drives up and offers to escort Alex to his destiny. Much to Alex's surprise, they immediately zoom into the air and off to his distant planet. Centauri explains that the Starfighter game is an elaborate test to find a human starfighter who can help the them defeat the evil Xur, an upstart who's starting a rebellion and planning on wiping out numerous planets throughout the galaxy, including Earth. Meanwhile an alien lookalike substitute for Alex is placed on Earth, and Xur sends assassins to wipe out our hero. The conflict mounts as Alex is torn between his life at home and the possibility of becoming a hero... or losing his life.

While being far from a masterpiece of pioneering science-fiction, *The Last Starfighter* has fortunately held up well over the years. Its sweet-natured spin on the hoary sci-war premise is a welcome change from the usual ear-splitting hardware clashes in space, and the interesting, well-drawn characters go a long way towards endearing the film to its audience.

The computer effects (which were pretty advanced for its time, a fact noted repeatedly on the packaging and in the half hour documentary included on the DVD) look much better when presented in scope (though occasionally seem a little reminiscent of one of those Mind's Eye videos), and Craig Safan's rousing score (his best to date) sweeps the action along and effectively builds tension along the way.

The DVD also features a fun half hour documentary hosted by Guest, which details some of the FX production work and features interviews with primary cast and crew, including director Castle and composer Safan. Though the film was issued in a less accurately letterboxed CAV edition in Japan back in the early days of laserdisc, this new rendition easily blows away every previous transfer. While audiences who can't remember Galaga may not experience a dizzy nostalgic smile while watching *The Last Starfighter*, this remains a solid and refreshingly upbeat film that viewers of all ages can enjoy.

LAST TANGO IN PARIS

Colour, 1972, 129m. / Directed by Bernardo Bertolucci / Starring Marlon Brando, Maria Schneider / MGM (US R1 NTSC, UK R2 PAL) / WS (1.85) (16:9)

After being numbed over the years by such in-your-face erotica as *91/2 Weeks* and *Basic Instinct*, American audiences now may find it hard to believe what a stir *Last Tango in Paris* caused when it was first released. In essence, this movie brought the "is it art or porn?" argument into the average living room, and so far no one has come to a definite answer. Not surprisingly, the film's sexual content looks pretty mild by now (though the butter scene still raises a few eyebrows), but master Italian director Bernardo Bertolucci wisely decided to make a great movie that just happens to have a lot of bare flesh in it. The real centrepiece of *Last Tango* is undoubtedly the lead performance by Marlon Brando, who has rarely been better. His portrait of a middle aged American man falling to pieces in Paris after the suicide of his wife is a stunning tour de force of cinematic acting. In comparison, Maria Schneider (who pretty much disappeared from the international scene after Michelangelo Antonioni's *The Passenger*) is adequate enough as the frequently naked nymphet with whom Brando enters a strange, childish love affair. They agree to meet in a jointly rented apartment for sex and never reveal each other's names; unfortunately, emotions eventually get in the way.

Last Tango may not be Bertolucci's best film (that would probably have to be *1900* or *The Conformist*), but it is his most accessible and popular. It's rare for what is essentially a European art film (and a slow paced one at that) to strike a nerve with the public, but this is that happy exception. The film has a number of pleasures to savour beyond the naughty parts, including the tongue in cheek casting of François Truffaut doppelganger Jean-Pierre Leaud as Schneider's film director fiancé.

There have been numerous video versions of *Last Tango*: Fox/Magnetic Video's mediocre VHS, MGM's R-rated cut taken from the film's mid-'70s R-rated theatrical reissue (in which one offending shot is obscured by what looks like a lamp), and Criterion and MGM's laserdiscs, letterboxed at approximately 1.85:1 with the image at the top of the frame and the subtitles relegated to the black bar at the bottom. The remastered DVD features a 16:9 transfer and is more colourful and detailed, with Vittorio Storaro's cinematography revealing previously unseen layers of lighting and gold and brown textures within the frame. The optional subtitles adapt between standard and anamorphic playback, and the disc also includes the vague theatrical trailer. The Dolby Digital mono soundtrack is fine if unspectacular, with Gato Barbieri's sultry jazz soundtrack simmering as always and heating up the audience as much as the characters onscreen.

THE LAST WAVE

Colour, 1977, 106m. / Directed by Peter Weir / Starring Richard Chamberlain, Olivia Hammett / Criterion (US R1 NTSC) / WS (1.78:1) (16:9) / DD5.1

You'll never hear a rain shower in quite the same way after experiencing Peter Weir's *The Last Wave*, his third genre-bending "horror" film in a row after *The Cars that Ate Paris* and the sublime *Picnic at Hanging Rock*. His usual fascination with the collision between natural and constructed cultures remains prominent here, but the intrusion of the supernatural and uncanny becomes even more pronounced than *Picnic*. The result is an odd, mystical, and unsettling film which, given the current social climate, is now even more capable of inducing chills.

After a quiet opening sequence in which an Aborigine paints colourful symbols inside a cave, the film presents the first of its many inexplicable incidents when a violent hailstorm pulverizes an outback schoolhouse in the middle of the afternoon... with nary a cloud in the sky. Meanwhile in Sydney, which has been pelted with an abnormal amount of strange rainfall, happily married tax lawyer David Burton (Richard Chamberlain) agrees to take on a side *pro bono* case defending a group of Aborigines implicated in the mysterious death of one of their own outside a bar. The accused turn out to be less than forthcoming, and soon David's dreams are invaded by visions of one of the Aborigines holding up a sacred stone. Even worse, David begins to suspect that his clients may be tuned in to a different plane of consciousness (including a mysterious law of dreams), which foretells of an apocalypse by water.

Deliberately paced and filled with an almost suffocating atmosphere, *The Last Wave* requires some adjustment for viewers expecting a literal, cut and dry story that connects all of its dots. The exact

L

roles of Aborigines (who thrive in tribes despite the imposition of major cities) and the more "civilized" European descendants appear to be constantly in flux, with each new revelation opening a new set of possibilities for our hapless protagonist.

The introduction of uncanny elements (hordes of frogs, darkened rain, eerie rumblings) works because the film establishes an off kilter atmosphere from the beginning, and so the viewer can gradually accept the existence of supernatural (or technically preternatural) elements beneath the fabric of everyday reality. In a sense Weir has crafted one of the better examples of dark magic realism on film, a genre that normally works better on the page than a movie screen. Chamberlain is also very good and subdued, proving again his status as a solid leading man before he eventually became bogged down in soppy TV projects.

Like *Picnic, The Last Wave* had an elusive history on home video from the beginning. Warner issued the first, extremely scarce tape back in the mid-'80s, and it suffered from a muddy, hazy appearance, which often left the film drenched in total blackness. After years on moratorium, Rhino eventually revived it on tape with a slightly improved transfer, though the film had still seen far better days.

A promised laserdisc at the same time never materialized and the tape quickly disappeared, but Criterion's excellent DVD has proven to be worth the wait. While the low budget '70s film stock is still inevitably evident in a few gritty looking night shots, the amount of detail visible here looks positively astounding compared to past tapes. The appearance is also faithful to the new restored prints Criterion struck for revival house screenings, and the transfer itself appears to be impeccable. Particularly interesting is the audio mix for the film, which is technically Dolby Digital 5.1 but not presented as newly retooled multi-channel mix. Instead, the film remains largely monaural, with the LFE channel activated for some of the louder rain and thunder passages. Hearing the subwoofer suddenly kick in provides a solid shudder at strategic points, and the now famous final scene packs a terrific, gut wrenching punch from an audio standpoint alone.

Extras on the disc are unfortunately limited, but were dictated by Weir's involvement in the project, which means we get the appropriately creepy theatrical trailer (featuring that great, Tangerine Dream style music) and an elliptical but interesting video interview with Weir, who discusses the film's production and its significance at a relatively early point in his career.

LAST YEAR AT MARIENBAD

B&W, 1961, 89m. / Directed by Alain Resnais / Starring Delphine Seyrig, Giorgio Albertazzi / Wellspring (US R1 NTSC) / WS (2.35:1)

Art cinema in the 1960s was a strange, wonderful quirk of film history. While directors like Truffaut and Godard regularly flourished with a stream of challenging masterpieces, other gems also managed to slip through into the American consciousness in ways unimaginable to modern audiences weaned on Miramax's flavour of the month. Alain Resnais' elliptic *Last Year at Marienbad*, arguably the quintessential plotless art film, caused an icy shock wave on its original release, though its reputation has suffered mostly due to a chequered history on video beginning with awful pan and scan transfers from companies like Video Yesteryear (which sliced the elegant Dyaliscope compositions into senseless visual squares). Connoisseur issued a widescreen release on VHS in the early '90s, but this grainy, green-tinged transfer failed to convey the sensuous, glittering surfaces that drift through every shot. Wellspring has now issued what could very well be the definitive *Marienbad* in a lustrous new DVD transfer whose virtues as eye candy should even please viewers who dismiss the film itself as pretentious game-playing boredom. This is simply one of the most beautiful black and white DVDs to date, and the delicate Dolby Digital soundtrack delivers the music and sound effects far more clearly than ever before. The English subtitles (positioned at bottom of the image, alas, unlike the Connoisseur subtitles in the lower band of the letterboxing) are optional, allowing the viewer to remove the words and savour the film for its visual power alone.

Most importantly, *Marienbad* marks the union of three major French talents: French writer/director Alain Robbe-Grillet, whose script here remains his mostly widely familiar contribution to world cinema despite his direction of such kinky art house gems like *Trans-Europe Express* and *La belle captive*; director Alain Resnais, fresh off his success with the international favourite, *Hiroshima Mon Amour*; and brilliant cinematographer Sacha Vierny, whose work on *Hiroshima* explodes here into a riot of stunning widescreen tracking shots and deep focus compositions which continually engage the eye and the mind, not to be outdone until he teamed decades later with Peter Greenaway.

Any attempt at a narrative summary of this film is inadequate, as Robbe-Grillet intended it as an intellectual puzzle open to each viewer's interpretation. At a chic spa for the well to do, Giorgio Albertazzi approaches the beautiful, detached Delphine Seyrig (*Daughters of Darkness*) and informs her that they had an affair a year ago, "at Frederiksbad or perhaps Marienbad." She claims not to know him, and as the games at the resort accumulate (ranging from cards to rifle target practice), so do Albertazzi's attempts to convince the object of his desire that they have met before. Meanwhile, fellow player Sacha Pitoeff (who later wound up drowning cats in Dario Argento's *Inferno*) intercepts as Albertazzi vies for Seyrig's attentions... or does he? Events grow increasingly dazed, becoming alternately romantic and nightmarish, as Vierny's camera continues to rove and prowl over each luscious piece of furniture, the marble steps, and the glittering chandeliers.

A haunting, truly unique work of cinema, certainly not for all tastes but definitely worth a try for the adventurous. Fans may also want to seek out the video greatest hits compilation by Blur, which features an elaborate *Marienbad* homage for the song "Until the End."

THE LATHE OF HEAVEN

Colour, 1980, 105m. / Directed by Fred Barzyk and David R. Loxton / Starring Bruce Davison, Kevin Conway / New Video (US R1 NTSC)

 What would you do if your dreams could shape reality? Furthermore, what if you could control someone with this ability? These questions form the basis of *The Lathe of Heaven*, a PBS adaptation of Ursula K. LeGuin's multilayered science fiction novel. One of public television's earlier attempts at a genuine feature length film, *Lathe* impressed many viewers with its haunting imagery, engaging concept, and earnest performances, but thanks to a legal issue, it sank into limbo for two decades. After an escalating demand to save the film, its eventual return to the public has allowed for a long overdue appraisal.

In the future, a young man named George Orr (Bruce Davison) resorts to chemical dependency to suppress his dreams, which he believes are capable of affecting his surrounding reality. He explains his ability to "dream effectively" to Dr. William Haber (Kevin Conway), who gradually comes to believe his patient's claims. George is more interesting in achieving some semblance of a stable, normal life and begins an intimate relationship with Heather

LeLache (Margaret Avery), but the good intentions of Dr. Haber lead them down a very different path. Haber deduces that George could be used to solve the world's problems, including racial strife and warfare, so with the aid of a brainwave machine called the Augmentor, he offers hypnotic suggestions to the sleeping George... with unexpected and often painful consequences.

Hardly a special effects extravaganza along the lines of its contemporaries like *Battlestar Galactic*, this production is more a study of provocative ideas within the conventions of science fiction, and for this reason it has lingered in the consciousness of fans over the years. The gradual cry for its return picked up steam when magazines brought it to the attention of generations too young to catch it on television or unable to snag bootleg copies on video. The main reason for its obscurity lies with the Beatles song "A Little Help from My Friends," which has now been replaced with a different vocal performance. It's a very small price to pay to salvage the film, which threatened to be lost forever. In particular it's gratifying to see Davison and Conway, two excellent character and supporting actors over the years, take centre stage and prove how deep they could go as actors with such fertile territory to explore. Hopefully the film's soaring reputation won't overwhelm it, as this is after all a fairly primitive looking public TV production; the frayed edges still show, and it must be watched with an understanding of the time it was made and the limitations of its budget. With an open mind, however, its possibilities are limitless, and the power of its imagery has not dissipated over the years.

Judging the video quality of *The Lathe of Heaven* on DVD is extremely problematic. An opening crawl explains that the original materials have been lost, so this was mastered from the best surviving version, a 2" videotape from the vaults. While obviously better than a blurry VHS, the image is extremely grainy and plagued by heavy ghosting, which causes colour streaking and lingering object imprints during any kind of motion. Contrast and black levels are also noticeably flat and have a dupey, "late '70s TV" appearance. Therefore it's hard to judge the DVD compression, which displays some blocky digital artefacting during dark scenes. By DVD standards this won't come close to cutting it for technophiles, so pick it up for the quality of the movie itself. The disc also includes a recent 22 minute Bill Moyers interview with the reclusive LeGuin, who discusses the themes of the story as well as her own positive reactions to the film. This supplement makes a welcome addition to the film, but don't make the mistake of watching it first.

L

L'AVVENTURA

B&W, 1960, 145m. / Directed by Michelangelo Antonioni / Starring Gabriele Ferzetti, Monica Vitti / Criterion (US R1 NTSC) / WS (1.78:1) (16:9)

Those who claim Michelangelo Antonioni directs pompous films with no purpose like *Blow-Up* and *The Passenger* probably have few kind words for *L'avventura* (or, essentially translated, *The Adventure*), a deliberately paced and hypnotic look at the effect of one disappearance on the rich and idle in Italy. Sort of like *Picnic at Hanging Rock* without the bloom of innocence, the film is more about mood and psychological tension rendered through visuals rather than gripping plotting or naturalistic acting. Challenging to be sure and not for all viewers, but *L'avventura* is a rich and rewarding journey for those who are game.

A yacht containing a handful of wealthy passengers heading for a remote Mediterranean island proves to be the last trip for Anna (Lea Massari), who vanishes without a trace. Her two companions during shore leave include her boyfriend, Sanro (Gabriele Ferzetti), and her best friend, Claudia (Monica Vitti), both of whom engage in a search for the missing girl but find their quest derailed when they begin an affair. Numbed by the confusing events surrounding them and their own day to day ennui, Sandro and Claudia find themselves incapable of generating any true emotion, even when they're later accompanied by Gloria (Dorothy De Poliolo), another companion and an expert tease for no good reason. Eventually the entire situation disintegrates over the course of one fateful night.

Almost unbearable in its starkness and the unflinching manner in which it studies its damaged characters like specimens under a microscope, *L'avventura* is never an easy or immediately gratifying experience; as with other Antonioni films, expectations of a grand dramatic payoff or a revelatory plot twist should be set aside to focus instead on the relationship of the characters to such larger factors as fate and nature. Everyone drifts through the film as if each character could also vanish at any second, so there's no point in putting down roots in a passive, stony landscape bereft of warmth.

Criterion first released *L'avventura* in its restored, 146 minute European length on laserdisc years ago, and their DVD edition marks just how much technology has advanced in just a few years. The image quality is razor sharp, exhibiting a great

deal of care into restoring a potentially tricky film composed of subtle gradations of grey and fluctuating contrasts. The optional English subtitles are much clearer and more coherent than before, and now the subtle textures ranging from Vitti's silken hair to the sun-dappled waves of the ocean can be studied with a crystalline intensity which exceeds what you could ever hope to see in a revival house screening. The disc also includes cursory but interesting liner notes by the University of London's Geoffrey Nowell-Smith and a more in depth critical audio commentary by film historian Gene Youngblood (previously on the laser as well), who focuses on Antonioni's recurring visual and thematic schemes and the social conditions of the time in which the film was made. A second disc of supplementary material includes an hour long documentary, "Antonioni: Documents and Testimonials," directed by Gianfranco Mingozzi. A fine companion piece to the Antonioni-at-work documentary included on Image's *Beyond the Clouds* DVD, this comprehensive look at Antonioni's career covers both this milestone film and his other symbolic forays into the human psyche, both his European (*La Notte*) and his more misunderstood American work (*Zabriskie Point*).

Other extras include the international theatrical trailer (which sells the film the only way possible, as a multi-layered art film) and a selection of Antonioni's written work and reminiscences, read by Jack Nicholson (who starred in Antonioni's sadly underrated masterpiece, *The Passenger*). Finally and most amusingly, the fold out insert also contains Antonioni's written statement to accompany the film's controversial exhibition at the Cannes Film Festival (where it took home the Grand Jury Prize despite a chorus of boos), followed by a signed list of judges who supported the award.

THE LEGEND OF HELL HOUSE

Colour, 1973, 81m. / Directed by John Hough / Starring Pamela Franklin, Roddy McDowall / Fox (US R1 NTSC) / WS (1.85:1) (16:9) / DD4.0

Adapted by the legendary Richard Matheson from his novel *Hell House*, this unnerving combination of old-fashioned haunted house tricks with modern scientific jargon and (comparatively mild) sex and violence makes for a memorable, atmospheric experience. The set up will be nothing new to viewers of *The Haunting*, but Matheson's story weaves in some unusual directions and certainly layers on the chills, culminating in a memorably odd finale.

Four brave souls enter the foreboding, windowless Belasco house, nicknamed "Hell House," to conduct an experiment determining the existence of life after death. The lone survivor from the disastrous previous investigation, a physical medium named Ben Fisher (Roddy McDowall), reluctantly agrees to spend a few days in the house along with mental medium Florence Tanner (Pamela Franklin) and physicist Lionel Barrett (Clive Revill) and his wife, Ann (Gayle Hunnicutt). Their first two psychic sitting sessions prove to be hostile and violent, leading Lionel to suspect that Florence may be either causing the manifestations or is being used by some force in the house - perhaps its debauched owner, Belasco, who vanished under mysterious circumstances years ago. Florence claims to receive nightly visits from Belasco's previously unknown son, who had died in the house, and the mystery gradually deepens as each day becomes more perilous to the investigator's lives.

While films like *The Innocents* (also with Franklin) contained a perverse subtext if one was looking for it, *The Legend of Hell House* was the first ghost film to inject overt sexuality as a necessary part of its storyline. Significantly, even after the film is over the audience is not certain that Ann's memorable "sleepwalking" episode and Florence's seduction were in fact caused by the supernatural. Furthermore, both men are depicted as stodgy and repressed, which could explain why both women respond in such a carnal fashion to the influence of ghosts. Apart from one misstep involving a cat attack (almost as goofy as the one in Dario Argento's *Inferno*), the manifestations are well handled and often frightening, such as the ectoplasm appearance. Though all four performances are excellent, Franklin and McDowall (who gets some of the choicest, most quotable dialogue) stand out with two of the best performances of their careers, delivering an avalanche of potentially difficult lingo with committed gusto.

A continuous staple on VHS and two time laserdisc release from Fox, *The Legend of Hell House* has never looked better than this widescreen DVD release. The 1.85:1 matting looks a bit odd at first after years of open matte framing, but ultimately it's better judged and more suggestive of the oppressive nature of Hell House than the previous square appearance. The colours are also far more vivid and richly saturated than before, apart from a few exterior shots in the opening third that still look pretty awful thanks to the original film materials. Just check out the crimson art direction in Franklin's bedroom or the ethereal stained glass in the chapel for a demonstration of how poorly this film was served on television and video before now. The new 4.0 stereo mix is often subtle but does a nice job of spreading out that creepy, haunting electronic score (if indeed it can technically be termed a score), and the dinner attack offers some nice surround action. Don't expect an audio experience on the level of *Poltergeist*, but this gets the job done just fine. The original mono track is also included for comparison, along with a nicely done French dub track.

The only extra is the original theatrical trailer, which effectively captures the dark, sinister nature of the film without spoiling too many surprises; alas, the same can't be said for the cover art, which follows the tradition of the VHS sleeves by blowing a key surprise late in the film.

L'ENFER

Colour, 1995, 92m. / Directed by Claude Chabrol
Wellspring (US R0 NTSC) / WS (1.66:1)

 Claude Chabrol, the reigning master of French suspense films with miniature classics like *Le Boucher* and *La Ceremonie*, directed this emotionally probing look at a marriage torn about by suspicion and jealousy. Lovely Emanuelle Beart (*Mission: Impossible*) makes a strong impression as a victimized wife, and the long-unfilmed script by Henri-Georges Clouzot (*Diabolique*) seethes with menace and tragedy. The pace may be too slow and the ending too elliptical for some viewers, but the film certainly deserves better than the treatment it receives here.

The print itself is crawling with grain, the colours are distorted and smeary, and the DVD is poorly authored, with blotchy artefacts marring every night scene (of which there are many). The film was shot in Dolby Stereo, but this version is in very flat mono. The brief US trailer is included, and the subtitles cannot be removed from the image. Chalk this up as a wonderful film sadly mistreated.

LET SLEEPING CORPSES LIE (THE LIVING DEAD AT THE MANCHESTER MORGUE)

Colour, 1974, 96m. / Directed by Jorge Grau / Starring Ray Lovelock, Cristina Galbo, Arthur Kennedy / Anchor Bay (US R1 NTSC, UK R2 PAL) / WS (1.85:1) (16:9) / DD5.1

The English countryside isn't usually regarded as a hotbed of terror, but the early '70s tried to change all that. Sam Peckinpah exposed the gruesome underbelly of the British provinces in *Straw Dogs*, and then the Continental neighbours had their turn with *Let Sleeping Corpses Lie* (*Fin de semana para los muertos*), the first European imitation of *Night of the Living Dead*. Sort of like an Agatha Christie whodunit gone horribly wrong, this moody, haunting little gem in turn influenced an entire decade of undead gut-munchers from the likes of Lucio Fulci and Umberto Lenzi, but thanks to clever plotting and a creepy, blood-soaked atmosphere, time has done little to dilute its impact.

Motorcycle riding antique owner George (*Autopsy*'s Ray Lovelock) heads off to the countryside for a little break from noisy, polluted city life. During a stop at a gas station, his bike is accidentally run over by Edna (Cristina Galbo), a young woman journeying to see her sister. George leaves his bike for repairs and bullies Edna into taking him to Windermere, where he can spend the weekend in peace. Edna insists she go to her sister first, but a stop along the way results in a riverside attack from a creepy, water-covered vagrant. The attacker's description matches that of Guthrie, a tramp who drowned a week earlier. That night Edna's neurotic sister, Katie (Jeannine Mestre), flees from her abusive husband, who is killed by a zombie. Katie is accused of the crime by the belligerent, bigoted police inspector (Arthur Kennedy), who in turn lashes out at George and Edna as decadent, drug-addled youths. The inspector orders them to stay in town at a local inn, so George and Edna decide to do some snooping of their own. Thanks to a handy roll of film and a jaunt through the countryside, George discovers a group of scientists and agricultural workers testing out a new device using sonic waves as a kind of pesticide. Unfortunately, this process has the nasty habit of over-stimulating the nervous systems of newborn babies and, more devastatingly, the corpses of the recently deceased. Soon the countryside runs red with blood, as George and Edna are forced to elude both the police and the shambling corpses emerging from the earth...

A skilful production in every respect, *Let Sleeping Corpses Lie* is a rare zombie film even traditional horror fans tend to enjoy. The gore is mostly contained in the final act, though it's not much more explicit than George Romero's original film. The deliberate pacing allows the viewer to spend some time with the characters and develop some sympathy, with Galbo making an especially winning and fragile heroine. Lovelock is great fun to watch, despite his grating and overdone dubbed accent, but Kennedy really steals the film as the hateful inspector with a personal grudge. (As Grau reveals, the character wasn't too far removed from the embittered actor himself.) Unlike most cut and dried zombie films, this one layers its narrative with some interesting shadings, such as the concurrent police investigation (revolving around the Hitchcockian wrong man conceit) and the bizarre notion of the corpses creating more of their kind by applying blood to the eyelids of the dead. The satisfying twist ending still manages to provoke a sick chuckle; it's amazing more genre films haven't ripped it off in the following decades.

Let Sleeping Corpses Lie has undergone many title changes, and just as many alternate versions seem to exist. In America it played as *Don't Open the Window,* a fairly useless slasher-type moniker, while overseas it played as *The Living Dead at Manchester Morgue, Breakfast at Manchester Morgue*, and even *Zombi 3* during a later Italian reissue. The US prints were obviously cut, removing two brief but moist scenes of gut-pulling and a few other snippets. Most horror fans from the video age have seen the Japanese laserdisc edition (as *Let Sleeping Corpses Lie*), the Venezuelan video release, or the uncut PAL release in the UK which was banned as a video nasty back in the 1980s!

The complete print from Anchor Bay differs significantly from the Japanese disc, which featured swirling opticals and a superimposed Guthrie face over the opening credits, dropped a significant amount of footage from the opening urban blight montage (and optically censored the female streaker), and removed the ambient music from the closing credits. Though colourful, the print was also in rough shape and, though letterboxed, featured open matte inserts for the pesticide scenes. Therefore the Anchor Bay DVD can truly be considered the first pristine, complete, and correctly letterboxed edition ever available. The quality looks terrific under the circumstances; the film will always look a little on the grainy side, especially during the night scenes (which display a few minor compression anomalies), but the colours are exceptionally well rendered and the level of detail is impressive. The 5.1 audio mix tweaks the original stereo tracks a little bit, with some minor separation effects in the rear speakers; it sounds fine and faithfully captures the ambience of the film's subdued, intricately mixed soundtrack. The disc also includes a brief intro and a twenty minute interview with director

Jorge Grau, who filmed this as a follow up to his fascinating, underrated *Ceremonia sangrienta (The Female Butcher)*, which deserves a DVD release as well. Grau is likeable and candid throughout, offering an amusing anecdote about the film's producer which openly acknowledges this film's debt to Romero's classic. He also discusses most of the actors, with the bit on Kennedy obviously containing the juiciest details. The disc also includes the US TV spot, a familiar staple from public domain horror trailer tapes, and similar radio spots, along with a reproduction of the German theatrical poster. Anchor Bay's uncut UK disc (as *The Living Dead at the Manchester Morgue*) adds on the aforementioned alternate opening and features a thick insert booklet comparable to the material in the US limited tin edition.

THE LIBERTINE

Colour, 1969, 91m. / Directed by Pasquale Festa-Campanile / Starring Catherine Spaak, Jean-Louis Trintignant / First Run (US R0 NTSC) / WS (1.85:1)

Many European sex comedies are about as much fun as having a root canal, but here's a welcome exception. Produced at the height of groovy op art mania, *The Libertine (La matriarca)* is a bubbly, enchanting meditation on the foibles of the human libido as seen through the eyes of Mimi (Catherine Spaak at her loveliest), an unlikely and wealthy young widow who - thanks to the advice of her lecherous attorney - discovers her husband kept a swanky sex pad on the other side of town where he indulged in all manner of perverse sexplay. Jealous and more than a little intrigued, Mimi picks up a copy of *Psychopathia Sexualis* and decides to dabble a bit in alternative lifestyles. After being mistaken for a hooker by a randy stranger (Black Emanuelle star Gabriele Tinti), tangling with an oddball dentist (Frank Wolff), and discovering the sexual side of living beetle necklaces, Mimi finally sets her sights on a sweet natured X-ray specialist (Jean-Louis Trintignant). Along the way she also learns the real cause of her random sneezing fits and discovers her own oddball perversion, which resolves itself in a most unusual and charming fashion.

Those expecting an orgy of bare flesh and dirty jokes may be confused by *The Libertine*, which lures the viewer in with the promise of a walk on the wild side and winds up delivering something far more interesting and profound. By far the most extreme visuals belong to the late husband's stag film reels, which seem jarringly out of place with the rest of the film. In fact, almost all of Spaak's relatively restrained nudity was performed by a body double, though she does remain scantily clad enough to make one wonder why she bothered. Trintignant seems oddly cast at first, as he doesn't even enter the film until the third act and seems way too buttoned down, but fortunately he and Spaak prove to be able sparring partners for the delicious final scenes, worthy of a classic screwball comedy. Their expressions during the film's post-credits fadeout are simply priceless.

The Libertine first appeared on VHS from Audubon and then First Run in a drab, cropped, nearly colourless edition, derived from the U.S. print which trimmed down some early exposition from the Italian cut and added some extra S&M and frontal nudity to the aforementioned stag reels. Meanwhile a Japanese DVD of the Italian version (with optional Japanese subtitles) appeared as part of a Catherine Spaak box set(!). The First Run DVD conflates the best of both versions with a composite print containing a lovely, colourful widescreen transfer of the Italian cut (with the English soundtrack) and the alternate U.S. footage inserted to make the most complete version to date. The mono soundtrack is fine if somewhat limited; at least the bouncy and infernally hummable score by lounge master Armando Trovajoli comes through with clarity.

Extras include an interesting outtake reel (which contains the alternate Italian shots with some fascinating trimmed bits from the raw takes), the strangely edited but appealing U.S. trailer, step-frame liner notes (which can't be commented on here for reasons which will become obvious), and a couple of nice photo and poster galleries, not to mention the usual round of trailers for other Audubon titles. See it with someone you plan to seduce.

LICENCE TO KILL

Colour, 1989, 133m. / Directed by John Glen / Starring Timothy Dalton, Robert Davi / MGM / WS (2.35:1) (16:9) / DD5.1

South American drug baron Franz Sanchez (Davi), exacting revenge for his incarceration, maims DEA agent Felix Leiter (David Hedison) and murders his new wife. Leiter's best friend, James Bond (Dalton), defies orders from his superiors and, licence to kill revoked, sets out on a personal vendetta. After Tim Dalton's fine debut in *The Living Daylights*, which pulled Bond back to his Fleming-esque roots, events took an even darker turn for his second and last bite of the cherry; the renegade agent immediately ran into censorship problems - not only in Britain, but almost everywhere - over the level of violence which, though not excessive by comparison with many films, was transgressive for Bond. Even with cuts the film landed a higher rating than any before it. Exploding heads, human fireballs, and minced-up henchmen notwithstanding, it was Bond himself - who hadn't really been roughed up since *Dr. No* - who drew media dismay, never having looked as bloody and beaten as he does at *Licence to Kill*'s climax. The language too is fruitier than usual.

There's lots of good stuff going on here, the highlights being Bond barefoot water-skiing behind a seaplane, a bar-room brawl (something no-one ever expected to see in a JB flick) and the finale in which 007 wrecks a convoy of tankers. Robert Davi is quietly menacing as Sanchez, whilst Anthony Zerbe is lower than a rattlesnake's gonads as craven sleazebag Milton Krest. In Carey Lowell and Talisa Soto we get a pleasant contrast; Lowell is the gutsy one who doesn't need Bond to survive (yet still melts into his arms before the closing credits, precisely as audiences would have it), Soto is the airhead gangster's moll who falls for our man but is fickle enough to have transferred her affections to a more affluent quarry by film's end. Nice to see David Hedison back as Felix Leiter, the only actor of six to play the part more than once. Other ties to the early days are implanted with the casting of Pedro (*From Russia with Love*) Armendariz's son in a minor role. The last of John Glen's five 007 directorial stints, the film was lensed as *Licence Revoked*, its title altered prior to release when it became apparent many Americans didn't know what 'revoked' meant.

MGM missed a golden opportunity to issue the unexpurgated version of *Licence to Kill* on DVD, something which would have made this Special Edition release truly special. Though more intact than the only version available in the UK for over a decade, Leiter's maiming by sharks, Krest's explosive fate and Sanchez's fiery demise are among several sequences that remain abridged. This disappointment aside, the disc is among the more generously laden releases in the series. The 56-chapter movie is accompanied by the requisite behind-the-scenes documentary and an original 1989 featurette. There's an additional short focusing on the action with the Kenworth tankers, a nice collection of still images, and two trailers (including

the superb teaser, which utilises specially shot footage of an exceptionally mean-looking Dalton wearing a digital watch that counts down to '007'). A lively but slightly washy-looking promo video of the Gladys Knight titles song is also in attendance, along with the rather more sober one for Patti LaBelle's closing credits number. Rounding out the deal are two commentaries, one from director John Glen and his cast, the second by co-producer/co-writer Michael G. Wilson and various crew members. Language and subtitles choices are in English and French. - TG

THE LICKERISH QUARTET

Colour, 1970, 87m. / Directed by Radley Metzger / Starring Silvana Venturelli, Frank Wolff / Image (US R0 NTSC) / WS (1.85:1)

 Radley Metzger would be a crucial director had he only made *The Lickerish Quartet*. On its own terms as cinema and outside the boundaries of European erotica, this remarkable film operates on levels of narrative gamesmanship, visual architecture, and technical virtuosity that put most modern films to shame.

Many illusion versus reality films tend to fall flat on their own pretension, but this, along with *8½*, *The Stunt Man*, and *Last Year at Marienbad*, is one of the few exceptions. Unfortunately, the film's sorry presentation on video for the past twenty years has done nothing to enhance its reputation; while virtually all prints have remained uncut, the majority of video transfers (often from public domain companies and sporting title changes like *Erotic Illusion*) have been washed out and poorly cropped. Metzger's short-lived Audubon Video label briefly issued a striking new transfer of the film a few years ago; this presentation mixed a mostly letterboxed presentation with full frame during the stag film footage and the motorcycle daredevil sequence. First Run's edition, also supervised by Metzger, performs some additional colour correction and looks even better, with the entire film uniformly matted at 1.85:1 to prevent those jarring shifts in aspect ratio (a la most Stanley Kubrick titles).

Frank Wolff (a late Eurosleaze veteran of such titles as *Cold Eyes of Fear*) and the austere Erika Remberg (the bitchy big top diva from *Circus of Horrors*) are an unhappily married couple spending their time in a vast, deserted castle with Remberg's petulant son, Paolo Turco. One evening the three sit around watching a scratchy B&W porno reel on Wolf's 16mm projector and are taken with a blonde beauty (Silvana Venturelli, coming off her memorable cuffs and cages stint in *Camille 2000*) in the film. Afterwards they embark on a carnival where a young woman performs a gravity-defying motorcycle stunt. When she removes her helmet, she looks just like the woman in the film... but with brown hair. Wolff conspires to lure the woman back to the castle and surprise her with the film, but upon doing so, they find that the film has inexplicably changed so that the actress' face is no longer visible. Venturelli stays the night, and the following day, she takes turns seducing the family members one by one and freeing them from their sexual shackles.

While *The Lickerish Quartet* contains a great deal of sex, the love scenes are ingeniously presented as moody vignettes which reflect the nature and transformation of the characters. The film's celebrated highlight, in which Venturelli and Wolff ferociously roll around in a library whose floor is decorated with blow ups of dictionary definitions of sexual terms, is only one of the many pleasures to be found in savouring and gradually taking apart this elaborate puzzle. All of the actors are well up to the task here, and the twangy, vibrant score by Stelvio Cipriani (or Stephen Cipriani, as the film credits him) adds to the twisted, playful ambience. Beautifully shot and enhanced with razor sharp editing (including many disorienting cross cuts between time and space), *The Lickerish Quartet* is that rare film that not only benefits from repeated viewings but actually requires them.

LIFE OF BRIAN

Colour, 1979, 94m. / Directed by Terry Jones / Starring Graham Chapman, John Cleese, Eric Idle / Criterion (US R1 NTSC) / WS (1.85:1) (16:9), Anchor Bay (US R1 NTSC) / WS (1.85:1), Paramount (UK R2 PAL) / DD2.0

 One of the first major films to send the modern religious right into public fits, Monty Python's *Life of Brian* marked the British comedy troupe's follow up to their spectacular *Monty Python and the Holy Grail*. While *Holy Grail* was shot for virtually nothing out in the middle of the woods, their satire on religious convention uses a much broader canvas. Crowd scenes, sweeping desert landscapes, and inventive set design provide a constantly surprising arena for this comedic circus, which remains their only attempt to use a completely linear, sequential narrative for a full length movie. And it's also very, very funny, too.

Brian, a baby born on the same night as Jesus Christ, grows up in the same area and finds his life running a comically parallel course. In adulthood (as Graham Chapman), he experiences a number of mishaps ranging from encounters with the Romans to aliens to a troupe of followers who believe him to be the true Messiah.

Less an attack on the Bible itself than a Swiftian portrayal of people who follow religion blindly, the film has been surprisingly influential over the years, most recently in Kevin Smith's ham-fisted *Dogma*. Though it lacks the outrageous setpieces of the Pythons' more famous work (no killer bunnies here, folks), Brian focuses more on the characters and verbal wit with an occasional dash of slapstick thrown in. There are highlights, to be sure, particularly the riotous stoning sequence ("Jehovah!") and the funniest nude scene in movie history, but these all serve to push the story forward rather than exist in their own vacuums. It's useless to try to determine which Python film is the best; this one, *Holy Grail*, and *Meaning of Life* are really so different that each can be considered a masterpiece in its own right. Brian earns its place thanks to the vivid historical setting (far more convincing than most serious biblical epics, oddly enough) and the fierce, enthusiastic conviction it displays for its unorthodox central concept.

Filmed hard matted at 1.85:1, *Life of Brian* must be experienced in a theatre or letterboxed for the full effect. Criterion first issued a widescreen special edition on laserdisc with a bounty of extras which have been duplicated on the DVD. Anchor Bay's DVD featured only the film and the trailer (and Paramount's 4:3 edition for the UK had no extras at all), so Criterion sweetened the deal even more by making a fresh, anamorphically enhanced transfer. Thankfully their trouble was well worth the effort, as *Brian* has never looked better. Rich, undiluted golds and browns flood the screen, and the grain which has plagued every past version looks far less noticeable here. However, Terry Gilliam's eye-popping credits are still illegible and most likely will be anywhere except on the big screen. The early Dolby Stereo soundtrack has been left in its original theatrical mix and sounds just fine.

Extras include commentary from Terry Jones, who offers his usual rapier-sharp observations about the film and religious humour in general, along with Terry Gilliam and Eric Idle, who chip in but remain more in the background for obvious reasons. Co-writer John Cleese and Michael Palin appear on a separate commentary track, which is a little jauntier and tends to wander off in some fairly bizarre directions. Other goodies include radio spots and a handful of deleted scenes (one of which absolutely should have been left in the film). The theatrical trailer and radio spot round out the package along with *The Pythons*, a sprawling 50 minute documentary covering the location shooting of the film. Here you can see the boys cutting up behind the camera and getting into character, oblivious of the religious furore they were about to stir up.

LIPS OF BLOOD

Colour, 1975, 87m. / Directed by Jean Rollin / Starring Jean-Lou Philippe, Annie Belle / Image (US R0 NTSC) / WS (1.66:1)

The most restrained and eloquent of Rollin's '70s vampire saga, *Lèvres de sang (Lips of Blood)* drags his familiar beautiful bloodsuckers into a modern day context, focusing more on the psychological underpinnings of the vampire mythos than the simple images of naked women chomping on victims' throats. Perhaps for these reasons, *Lips of Blood* has become one of the most difficult of Rollin's horror titles to see, a situation now corrected on DVD.

In the opening sequence, a middle aged woman supervises the ceremonial placement of a still breathing girl into a coffin, which is then sealed and left in a subterranean room. Flash forward to the present day, in which Pierre (co-writer Jean-Lou Philippe) is plagued by visions of a childhood in which he encounters a beautiful girl in white. He spends the night under her care in a decaying castle, and she releases him in the morning, only to find the gate slammed in her face. He believes these visions are actually memories from his boyhood, but his mother dismisses such thoughts, claiming he should go see a doctor. At a reception for a new brand of perfume, he stumbles upon a promotional shot of a castle which strongly resembles the one in his visions. The photographer responsible for the shot arranges to meet him at midnight; when he waits for her in a local cinema (showing *Shiver of the Vampires*), he spies the same girl in white and pursues her to a basement, where he unintentionally unleashes a quartet of scantily clad vampires on the city. As the quest for the girl and her strange castle continues, he finds himself constantly thwarted by his family and the nubile vampires, who for some strange reason refuse to kill him. The truth, alas, is much stranger than he could have possibly imagined.

Aside from a few passages, *Lips of Blood* contains very little dialogue and maintains a surreal, dreamlike stance throughout its running time. The final half hour is Rollin at his best, with an unbearably poignant beachside finale that perfectly sums up his themes as a director. The bizarre locations, ranging from modern day offices to an abandoned nocturnal aquarium, mark the film as a transition piece from his dislocated vampire fantasies to his more realistic later horrors like *The Grapes of Death*. The familiar Castel twins make another appearance but have little to do besides licking blood off their lips in striking surgical outfits and transparent gowns, and most of the actors perform in a deliberately somnambulist fashion reminiscent of Werner Herzog. A difficult, often enchanting film, *Lips of Blood* will most likely reward viewers already well versed in Rollin's powerful alternate universe.

The transfer from Redemption and presented on DVD by Image is derived from the original negative and, naturally, looks fantastic. The dark opening scene offers little opportunity to judge the disc's quality, but afterwards, the visuals are clear and rank up there with *Demoniacs* as one of the most attractive presentations in the series. Of course, it still looks like a '70s film, but after years of suffering through bad SECAM bootlegs, this DVD is truly a revelation. The optional English subtitles appear to be accurate, as does the mild 1.66:1 framing (listed as 1.85:1 on the packaging). No trailer is included (and apparently never existed), but the disc does include a number of production and publicity photos.

LIQUID SKY

Colour, 1982, 114m. / Directed by Slava Tsukerman / Starring Anne Carlisle, Paula E. Sheppard / MTI (US R1 NTSC)

A film that couldn't have possibly been made here on Planet Earth, *Liquid Sky* is a midnight movie taken to radical, sensibility-shattering extremes that make *Eraserhead* look like a Julia Roberts vehicle.

The omnisexual drug culture of early '80s Greenwich Village is transformed when a UFO arrives and converts one of the locals, Margaret (Anne Carlisle), whose cohorts include a German performance artist (the scowling Paula Sheppard from *Alice, Sweet Alice*) and Margaret's gay brother, Jimmy (also Carlisle). Margaret's bisexual

L

encounters produce a chemical which feeds the aliens, but these clandestine activities can only go on for so long without being noticed, even in this subculture.

The sole American film by Russian avant garde specialist Slava Tsukerman (who also co-wrote the jarring synth score), *Liquid Sky* garnered positive reviews upon its release and became a natural for the midnight movie crowd. Seen today, it feels almost quaint in its skewed sensibilities, pretty Day-Glo colours, and pre-AIDS occupations with the interactions of human bodies. The sci-fi element is largely downplayed, with the tiny alien saucers scarcely presented more credibly than in *Plan 9 from Outer Space*, and most of the dialogue simply boggles the mind. Carlisle and Sheppard easily swipe the film from their co-stars, with the former's androgynous beauty serving both of her roles very effectively.

For a fringe title, this oddity has received the major red carpet treatment on DVD. The transfer itself is an improvement upon the old VHS edition from Media, with the blinding saturations of red, pink, and blue now carefully in their place and not bleeding back and forth all over the screen. Unaccountably, the first half hour is noticeably paler than the rest of the film, though adjusting the brightness control on the player or TV reduces the problem (though some compression artefacts do remain noticeable, alas). The mono sound is just fine, with the often piercing soundtrack thankfully free of distortion even in its highest registers.

The disc also includes three trailers (of varying lengths and all very odd), several minutes of salvaged rehearsal footage recorded on Betacam (the Sheppard bits are the best), and a tremendously expanded alternate version of the opening title sequence, with many chunks of footage removed from the final film. Definitely not recommended for everyone, but if you know what you're getting into, this is quite a wild ride.

LISA AND THE DEVIL

Colour, 1972, 98m. / Directed by Mario Bava / Starring Elke Sommer, Telly Savalas / Image (US R0 NTSC) / WS (1.85:1)

In 1972, director Mario Bava was still riding a successful wave in Italy as the director of profitable and beautifully filmed exploitation films like *Twitch of the Death Nerve*. After the international success of *Baron Blood* for producer Alfredo Leone, Bava was allowed to shoot any personal project of his choice. The result was *Lisa and the Devil*, a heartfelt and defiantly anti-commercial story of death, erotic frustration, and spiritual longing in which the living and the dead merge to the point of being indistinguishable. However, despite a warm reception at Cannes, the film languished without a distributor. Desperate to recoup some of the costs, Leone arranged for Bava to shoot several new framing scenes in which the star, Elke Sommer, would be possessed by... well, something nasty, though it doesn't seem to be Satan. Robert Alda appeared in the new footage as a bewildered priest, calmly surveying the obligatory possession antics involving green vomit and slimy toads. Naturally, only an hour of *Lisa* remained in this new version entitled *House of Exorcism*, which is ultimately a completely different movie.

The original version of *Lisa and the Devil* follows the experiences of a beautiful young tourist, Lisa Reiner (Sommer). After viewing a fresco of the devil in a local village, she loses her way and catches a ride with the wealthy Lehar couple (Sylva Koscina and Eduardo Fajardo) and their chauffeur, George (Black Emanuelle regular Gabriele Tinti). The car breaks down, forcing the troupe to spend the night in a decaying villa inhabited by a blind Contessa (Alida Valli), her bizarre son Max (Alessio Orano), and sardonic butler Leandro (Telly Savalas), whom Lisa had seen earlier in the village. As the night wears on, Lisa realizes that she bears a striking resemblance to Elena, a woman loved both by Max and his dead father, Carlo. Unfortunately, a series of murders begins to decimate the guest list, and the truth is actually far stranger than Lisa could have ever imagined.

Beautifully filmed and exquisitely scored by Carlo Savina, who executes several tasteful variations on Rodrigo's "Concierto per Aranjuez," *Lisa and the Devil* is as much a dreamy art film as it is a European horror opus. Many of the images rank among Bava's best: Lisa's doe-like eyes staring through a macabre music box, the shimmering of spilled wine on the dining room floor, the gothic and satirical mock up of "The Last Supper" during the climax, and so much more. The elliptical narrative raises more questions than it answers, with a strange and haunting finale that offers several levels of interpretation. On the other hand, *House of Exorcism* is a completely disjointed and incoherent mess, endearing only through its sheer lunacy and willingness to go sailing far past the barriers of good taste. Sommer's profane tirades are among the silliest ever put on film and offer more quotable lines than *The Exorcist*, while the footage from *Lisa* is

L

intercut so randomly that drive-in viewers must have been clutching their heads in agony. A fun curio of its time, to be sure, but it should never be confused with the Bava original.

For over a decade after its release, the original cut of *Lisa and the Devil* remained one of the great "lost films" of European cinema, at least until it turned up without fanfare in TV syndication and on the bootleg video market. However, *House of Exorcism* has always been very, very easy to find. *Lisa* finally surfaced on legitimate video, first from Redemption in the UK and then on laserdisc and VHS from Elite in America. The same transfer has been used for the Image DVD; it's quite good for what it is, though the graininess and somewhat pallid flesh tones date the source material a bit. In an ironic twist of fate, *House of Exorcism* actually looks quite stunning; apart from the battered opening credits, the image quality is stunningly rich and colourful throughout. The Elite disc contained two longer, alternate scenes from *Lisa* that were included in *House*, namely a necrophilic love scene and a brutal murder by poker. However, these scenes are not included separately on the DVD, for obvious reasons. The disc instead segregates the one bit of footage which appears in neither version, a hilariously explicit and inappropriate series of shots of Koscina (or more likely her body double) ravaging Tinti in bed. Other extras include the unfinished European trailer for *Lisa* (with more nudity than anything in the actual film) and two slightly different trailers for *House of Exorcism*. The latter film also includes a revealing and enjoyable audio commentary which edits together comments by Leone and Sommer; time may have eroded their memory of some pertinent details, but the whole story is basically here. How much did Bava really shoot? What was it like working on the set? Listen to the commentary and find out!

A LITTLE BIT OF SOUL

Colour, 1998, 87m. / Directed by Peter Duncan / Starring Geoffrey Rush, Frances O'Connor / Vanguard (US R1 NTSC) / WS (1.85:1) / DD2.0

Nobody does comedies quite like Australia, and *A Little Bit of Soul* proves to be another flawed but intriguing step in their apparent goal to produce the most insane roster of films under the planet. Even more wild and woolly than its director's previous effort, *Children of the Revolution*, this horror-tinged bit of social

commentary will either leave viewers chuckling nastily or scratching their heads in utter confusion.

A nerdy scientist, Richard Shorkinghorn (David Wenham), is on the verge of discovering progeria, a degenerative aging disease, thanks to his experiments with chickens. To seek additional funding, he accepts an invitation from the wealthy Grace Michael (Heather Mitchell) to spend the weekend at her estate. However, Richard is miffed to learn that his former assistant and girlfriend, Kate (Frances O'Connor), has been invited along as well. Grace's husband turns out to be Godfrey Usher (Geoffrey Rush), the possibly deranged finance minister of Australia. Both Godfrey and Grace take turns making passes at their houseguests, but things get very odd when another visiting guest slashes her throat in the bathroom, leaving a very bloody mess for Godfrey to tidy up. As the film reveals halfway through (but the packaging gives away right from the beginning), the affluent couple turns out to be practicing a very dark and twisted lifestyle choice which may put Richard and Kate in mortal danger.

Deliberately eccentric from its opening scene (which blasts "Ain't Nobody Here But Us Chickens" during a thunderstorm), *A Little Bit of Soul* (shame about the title) doesn't work all the way through but does manage to hit the occasional bullseye. Veering from political comedy to gothic horror to a courtroom drama(!), director Duncan fearlessly hops around wherever he pleases and takes his willing cast right along with him. Rush obviously has a field day, clearly warming up for his later role in *House on Haunted Hill,* and Jessica Harper lookalike O'Connor wrings a hefty amount of comedy from her thinly written role. Add to that the quasi-classical score by Nigel Westlake (*Babe*), and you've really got a film like no other.

Vanguard's transfer is a tremendous step up from their previous releases, with a vivid and sharp picture and a constantly active surround track that throws jolting effects around the room every minute. The letterboxing looks dead on, and some of the tutti frutti colour schemes (with red taking precedence, not surprisingly) come off just fine without any noticeable smearing or compression problems.

LITTLE MOTHER

Colour, 1973, 90m. / Directed by Radley Metzger / Starring Christiane Kruger, Mark Damon / Image (US R0 NTSC) / WS (1.85:1)

A far cry from Andrew Lloyd Weber's musical *Evita*, Metzger's political saga adapts the famous real life rise to power of Eva Peron (here called Marina

Pinares) as a sexy, violent narrative filled with backstabbing and power plays. Though the film does feature two memorable sex scenes, one involving a shower door and the other an orgy that pushes the R rating about as far as it will go, most of the running time focuses on Marina's vicious rise to power and the parallel story of Annette (Elga Sorbas), whose revolutionary romance directly leads to the assassination finale. While the story more or less follows the familiar Evita framework (Pinares has learned of her terminal cancer at the beginning of the film and engages in Machiavellian tangos with the Cardinal, aptly played by Anton Diffring), the gritty tone and strange, ultra-European ambiance yield completely different results. Christiane Kruger easily owns the film, murdering and seducing her way into viewers' hearts; the bizarre clash of accents and intricate story require more attention than usual from viewers, but Metzger fans should find it worth the effort.

The DVD from Image and First Run is derived from the same source used for the film's video release in Holland as *Blood Queen*. Inappropriate moniker aside (the original *Little Mother* title refers to the people's nickname for Marina), the print is good if not quite pristine. The image is free of any noticeable damage, while the colour looks about as good as one could expect from a '70s European film. Not a demo piece, but at least the sound has been cleaned up dramatically from the warbly, distorted PAL version. A true anomaly in Metzger's career, *Little Mother* will surprise fans but provides some juicy food for thought and a few good cheap thrills along the way for good measure.

LIVE AND LET DIE

Colour, 1973, 121m. / Directed by Guy Hamilton / Starring Roger Moore, Jane Seymour / MGM / WS (1.85:1) (16:9)

When three British agents are murdered, Agent 007 (Moore) is sent to New York where he links their deaths to a drug-pushing operation masterminded by covert gangster Mr. Big (Kotto). Flying on to the Caribbean he finds himself in dangerous territory ruled by voodoo ritual and the superstitious power of Tarot. Although Roger Moore's seven-film tarriance with the Bond series had its highs and lows, his first shindig is a fast-paced, colourful fantasy with its tongue forced

further into its cheek than any 007 adventure preceding it. *Goldfinger* director Guy Hamilton orchestrates the proceedings astutely, and the cast - which includes Yaphet Kotto as the ruthless drugs baron, a youthful Jane Seymour as beautiful sibyl Solitaire and Clifton James as crowd-pleaser redneck cop J. W. Pepper - is a joy. Julius Harris's metal-clawed killer Tee Hee is a classic slice of Bond villainy. David (*The Fly*) Hedison takes up the reins as Bond's CIA buddy Felix Leiter.

Moore's interracial smooch with *Playboy* model Gloria Hendry caused minor controversy upon the film's initial release and in some territories the sequence was edited out. This is the one where Bond decapitates a double-decker bus, jumps a speedboat over a car, hang-glides up to a cliff-top retreat, employs an aerosol canister as a makeshift flame-thrower, wreaks havoc in a hangar full of light aircraft, and escapes a lake full of hungry crocodiles by leaping across their backs like stepping stones. There's some nifty Bond gadgetry on display too, notably a rotating buzz-saw watch and a gun that fires gas pellets. Rousing entertainment.

Matted to 1.85:1, MGM's pristine special edition presentation of *Live and Let Die* is accompanied by plenty of additional Bondy treats. First and foremost there's a behind the scenes documentary, the highlight of which is a series of outtakes revealing just how dangerous attempting to use crocodiles as stepping stones can be. There's also a respectable stills gallery, two trailers, two TV spots, two radio spots and a couple of short, slightly fuzzy-looking 1973 featurettes that show the shooting of the jazz funeral in New Orleans and Moore being taught the finer points of hang-gliding. For the truly esoteric look no further than the inclusion of an old cinema commercial made by the Milk Marketing Board that features Moore quaffing a pinta on the set! The feature (divided into a healthy 48 chapters) is accompanied by an optional commentary featuring, among others, director Hamilton and screenwriter Tom Mankiewicz. Languages and subtitles are available in English and French. - TG

LIVE FLESH

Colour, 1997, 103m. / Directed by Pedro Almodóvar / Starring Javier Bardem, Francesca Neri / MGM (US R1 NTSC) WS (2.35:1) (16:9), Pathé (UK PAL 2) WS (2.35:1) / DD5.1, Filmax (Spain R2 PAL)

Returning to the murder mystery format he explored so lovingly in *Matador* and *High Heels*, Spain's most popular '90s director, Pedro Almodóvar, paints on an even broader canvas than usual here and treats

his outrageous tale with a generally straight face. Victor (Liberto Rabal), a young and naive pizza delivery boy who made Spanish news by being born on a public bus(!), pays a visit to Helena (Francesca Neri), an insecure and bitter woman with whom he had a (sort of) quick sexual encounter. Helena turns him away, but he refuses to leave. Two policemen arrive, and one of the them is shot in the ensuing scuffle. Years later, Victor is released from prison to find that his home is gone and the world has gone by without him. David (Javier Bardem), the policeman who was shot, has married Helena and become a celebrated wheelchair basketball star. At first David and Helena are unnerved by the thought of Victor at large in the public again, but as it turns out, there is far more to his story than meets the eye.

While this film certainly delivers the expected number of outrageous coincidences and steamy sexual encounters, *Live Flesh* (aka *Carne Tremula*) also marks a more serious and personalized turning point in Almodóvar's career. After stumbling somewhat with *The Flower of My Secret*, he proves here that his gift for melodrama has become sharper with his growing maturity, a trait he explored even further in *All About My Mother*. Bardem is excellent as usual, proving that his chameleon-like roles for Bigas Luna and Alex de la Iglesia were no fluke. Also, look for up and coming Spanish starlet Penelope Cruz as Victor's mother.

Released in the US in a letterboxed but very smudgy-looking laserdisc edition by MGM (following its acquisition of the Orion library), *Live Flesh* fared slightly better in its British DVD rendition. Even better is the later MGM DVD, which finally drops the murky gold and brown colour schemes in favour of a more pleasant visual palette. The director's first scope film, this looks quite nice in widescreen - and even better with anamorphic enhancement. The 5.1 audio mix focuses mostly on the melancholy music score, though some sound effects like gunshots and blowing wind offer a few sonic surprises along the way. Though optional, the English subtitles remain at the bottom of the film image instead of the lower letterbox band. The stylish trailer is also included on both versions.

THE LIVING DAYLIGHTS

Colour, 1987, 131m. / Directed by John Glen / Starring Timothy Dalton, Jeroen Krabbe / MGM (US R1 NTSC), (UK R2 PAL) / WS (2.35:1) (16:9) / DD5.1

James Bond (Dalton) orchestrates the defection of General Koskov (Krabbe), but when the Russian is snatched back 007 smells a rat. He follows a trail of clues, beginning with Koskov's ex-girlfriend Kara (d'Abo) in Bratislava, which eventually lead him into Afghanistan and the midst of a plot to exchange hi-tech weapons for millions of dollars worth of drugs. After Roger Moore's disappointing swan song as 007, a chameleonic change into Timothy Dalton gave a life-saving transfusion to a series edging dangerously towards implosion. Dalton reinvents the Bond character, planting him in more grounded a reality than audiences had seen in years, the results being a superior blend of thrills, fast-paced action and suspense. Aspirations of global domination are discarded in favour of a more feasible (if overly complex) plot by a seedy arms dealer and a renegade Russian to line their pockets via a deal with rebel factions to swap guns for dope.

A spectacular pre-credits brawl on Gibraltar kicks off a series of globe-trotting antics that take in a car chase across a frozen Czechoslovakian lake, assassination in a Viennese amusement park, pursuit across the rooftops in Morocco, and an explosive assault on a Russian military base in Afghanistan. Old hand John Barry serves up his best score since 1969's *OHMSS*. Maryam d'Abo brings an endearing fragility to heroine Kara, Jeroen Krabbe as the duplicitous Koskov is a nice mix of devious, suave, craven and callous, and Andreas Wisniewski is all muscle and menace as hit-man Necros. Dalton was to return only one more time as 007 before the series was plunged into legal problems, eventually resurfacing with Pierce Brosnan in the lead. *The Living Daylights*, however, is without doubt the better half of Dalton's two-movie tenure. Director John Glen lives up to the promise he showed with his debut *For Your Eyes Only* (Moore's best) - yet failed to follow through with on the intervening *Octopussy and A View to a Kill* - by delivering what is arguably the finest Bond of the 1980s.

First the bad news where purists are concerned: The burnt-in captions that appear on theatrical, video and laser prints of *The Living Daylights* (for example, the translation of Julie T. Wallace's line in Russian) were erroneously omitted on MGM's Special Edition DVD release, though a mail-out replacement to US buyers was briefly offered. This minor *faux pas* aside, it's as slick a Bondian package as you could hope for. Along with the requisite behind-the-scenes documentary, there's an additional documentary about the life of Ian

Fleming, the A-Ha music video (splashy back in '87 but rather hokey-looking nowadays), a short featurette on the making of said video, and three trailers. The highlight is the inclusion of a deleted scene, not so much because it's any good - it isn't - but because it illustrates how the producers endeavoured to pare down the frivolity that had become part and parcel of the formula to forge a grittier framework for the new era. Legendary in Bond circles, the "Flying Carpet" sequence features 007 sliding down telegraph wires in Tangiers on a rug, much to the amazement of pot-smoking locals. The 2.35:1 matted 36-chapter feature is accompanied by a commentary from director John Glen and others. Language options are English and Spanish. Subs are in Spanish and French. - TG

THE LIVING DEAD GIRL

Colour, 1982, 89m. / Directed by Jean Rollin / Starring Françoise Blanchard, Marina Pierro / Image (US R0 NTSC) / WS (1.66:1)

 For anyone daunted by the prospect of diving into the films of Jean Rollin, *La morte vivante (The Living Dead Girl)* is an excellent place to start. Boasting a stronger and more linear narrative than usual, not to mention solid performances from most of the cast, this film confirms Rollin's firm grasp of cinematic technique regardless of budgetary constraints.

A minor earthquake causes a chemical spill in a cave/mausoleum; as a result, a deceased young woman, Catherine (Françoise Blanchard), suddenly rises from her coffin, bloodily dispatches two men, and returns to her ancestral home. Equipped with only vague memories of her existence among the living, she mournfully devours flesh and blood to survive, including two teenagers who happen to wander into the house for a little privacy. Catherine telephones her childhood friend, Helene (Marina Pierro), with whom she had made a devotional blood pact as a little girl. Helene immediately comes to Catherine's aid and, in an act of extreme friendship, procures girls from the local village to satisfy her soulmate's bloodlust.

Rollin is simply at his lyrical and haunting best with *The Living Dead Girl*. Aside from the unconvincing opening sequence, the film never releases its grasp on the viewer's imagination, conjuring up a strange fairy tale ambience in which nudity and violence are presented as natural, integral elements of life. Blanchard makes for a gorgeous,

morose flesh-eater, and Pierro, most famous for her roles in Walerian Borowczyk's cinematic erotica, turns in a splendid, compelling performance. Regular Rollin composer Philippe d'Aram contributes one of his best scores, a nostalgic and often sad chamber work tinged with a simple music box melody. The only storytelling quibble is a lengthy, barely relevant *Demons*-like subplot about two American tourists whose paths eventually lead straight to the deadly girls.

The first subtitled prints of *Living Dead Girl* appeared courtesy of Redemption in the UK Sadly, this edition lost several minutes of gory footage (most notably during the climax and a lengthy torture sequence). The same transfer, albeit uncut, appeared on Dutch laserdisc from Copper Sky, complete with Rollin commentary, the French trailer, an alternate German track with different music, and the trailer for Rollin's *Rose de fer (The Crystal Rose)*. For its DVD premiere, Image and Redemption have supplied the best-looking version to date, several generations in quality above the others. The slight letterboxing appears accurate, and the muted colours and shadowy lighting appear undiluted and distortion-free (apart from an occasional flicker of grain in the original film negative). The optional yellow subtitles also improve dramatically over the stripped-stripped subs on the other versions, and once again the French trailer is included. Completists may still want the laserdisc for the extras, but as far as the film itself is concerned, the DVD is really the only way to go.

LOLITA

B&W, 1961, 153m. / Directed by Stanley Kubrick / Starring James Mason, Peter Sellers, Shelley Winters / MGM / Warner / WS (1.66:1)

 The first big studio project that Kubrick truly called his own, *Lolita* reinvents Nabokov's scandalous novel into a blackly comic hymn to thwarted love and skewed social conventions. Kubrick distilled Nabokov's original screenplay (which would have clocked in at over three hours) into a more commercially viable format which unfortunately also sacrificed some of its shock value due to censorship restrictions of the time. However, considering Adrian Lyne's regrettable attempt to translate his 1998 *Lolita* into a blood-soaked orgy of sweaty flesh, that may not be such a bad thing.

Humbert Humbert (James Mason), a clever and cultured middle-aged man drifting without a destiny, becomes infatuated with the teenage nymphet Lolita (Sue Lyon) while renting a room in the house owned by her oblivious mother, Charlotte Haze (Shelley Winters). Initially Humbert attempts to keep his lustful thoughts hidden, but after fate deals him a pleasant wild card, Humbert takes it upon himself to become Lolita's guardian and escorts her on a debauched road trip. Unfortunately, Lolita also catches the eye of Quilty (Peter Sellers), a man who uses various disguises and voice tricks to win the eye of the young maiden. Everything ends tragically, as all American morality tales must.

From the startling opening scene, which veers abruptly from drunken comedy to (offscreen) violence, Kubrick keeps the tricky layers of narrative and subtext under admirable control. In fact, *Lolita* has aged marvellously well, brimming with wit and surprises thanks to the excellent performances by everyone involved. Nelson Riddle's champagne-flavoured score (not to mention that catchy "yi-yi" song!) keeps the events flowing along despite the sordid undercurrents, and Kubrick's precise, elegant visual style aptly reflects Nabokov's evocation of a society rapidly going the way of Ancient Rome. As an adaptation of the novel, the film isn't completely successful, often swerving away from the venomous interior monologues offered by Humbert throughout the book (oddly enough, Kubrick later felt confident enough to tackle this narrative aspect successfully in *A Clockwork Orange*).

The Criterion laser presentation of *Lolita* supervised by Kubrick alternated between fullscreen and soft-matted (1.66:1) framing which seemed to cause more problems than it solved. Though fairly clean, the transfer was too soft and often broke the seductive flow of the film thanks to the jarring shifts in aspect ratio. The MGM laserdisc presented a more consistent hard matte of 1.66:1, which Warner has reproduced on its DVD incarnation. The DVD looks even crisper with darker blacks, though this also brings out a few more flaws in the source material (occasionally grain and dirt) which were not so readily apparent before. Still, it's a satisfying presentation and the best we'll see unless some unlikely soul down the road decides to perform a costly digital restoration job on the film. Also includes the US trailer from the laser versions.

LORD OF ILLUSIONS

Colour, 1996, 120m. / Directed by Clive Barker / Starring Scott Bakula, Famke Jenssen / MGM (US R1 NTSC, UK R2 PAL) / WS (1.85:1) (16:9) / DD5.1

Clive Barker's most ambitious project sank like a stone at the box office but has earned a moderate cult following, and this extended Director's Cut shows him off at the prime of his chill-inducing powers. Scott Bakula stars as private eye Harry D'Amour, whose proclivity for attracting evil leads to some highly unorthodox cases. His latest involves a long vanished cult, a celebrity magician (Kevin J. O'Connor) and his glamorous wife (Famke Janssen), and a rampaging maniac in bondage gear with a talent for torture.

Don't get too excited by the claim on the back of the DVD box that this "contains footage not seen in theatres or as part of the Director's Cut!" Actually, it's just the same deleted scene reel that was tacked onto the MGM laserdisc. The DVD is missing many of the supplements from the laser (the documentary, the stills, promo art, etc.) but at least retains the trailer and commentary. The anamorphically enhanced transfer is noticeably crisper than the laser but lacks that previous transfer's vivid, pumped-up colour design; it's a toss up really as to which is better. The real reason to pick up the DVD (for score fans anyway) is the isolated Simon Boswell music track, which contains a number of cues missing from the soundtrack album.

LORD OF THE FLIES

B&W, 1963, 92m. / Directed by Peter Brook / Starring James Aubrey, Tom Chapin / Criterion (US R1 NTSC)

Best known for his confrontational stage productions and films like *Marat/Sade*, director Peter Brook in many ways seemed the ideal choice for an adaptation of William Golding's staple novel of teenage English courses, *Lord of the Flies*. Cast with amateurs and shot in stark black and white, the film deliberately avoids the pitfalls of a Hollywood production (big special effects, phoney sets, etc.), thus largely capturing the flavour and nuances of its literary source.

Stranded on a deserted island after a plane crash, a group of English boys form a microcosm of society as they struggle for survival. What begins as a long summertime frolic degenerates with time as their barbaric instincts take hold, and fewer of them manage to retain a semblance of "civilization." The evil Jack and the morally centred Ralph become the major forces of the story, while the rational and often mocked Piggy vainly cries for a return to order.

While time has somewhat dulled the impact of Golding's central message that everyone, including children, is capable of savagery, the primal horrific drive of its narrative still manages to unsettle. Brook's naturalistic approach is heightened by some unexpected injections of nightmarish imagery: the pig killing and the boys' subsequent ritual, the elegiac climactic shot of a boy's body gently wafting in the tide, and one genuinely horrifying murder. The rough, spontaneous quality of the actors generally pays off, with Hugh Edwards in particular capturing the good-hearted but irritating Piggy exactly as he appeared in the novel. For anyone who doubts the merits of Brook's film, take a look at the misguided 1990 American version for a study in contrast.

Criterion's restored transfer of *Lord of the Flies* mercifully undoes the damage done by years of public domain tapes and crummy 16mm prints. Long thought to be a borderline lost film, *Lord of the Flies* looks even sharper and cleaner on DVD than on the previous laserdisc, and it even includes more extras to boot. The commentary track features Brook, producer Lewis Allen, and cinematographers Tom Hollyman and Gerald Feil discussing their experiences on the film, ranging from technical difficulties to their methods of dealing with the young actors. On a separate track, portions of the audio version of Golding's novel are included, and extras include the original trailer (with a funny anecdote on the alternate audio track), outtake footage (containing a lot of underage nudity wisely trimmed down in the film) with commentary, a minor deleted scene, some ragged home movie footage showing the production behind the scenes, and a brief snippet from *The Empty Space*, Feils' 1972 documentary on Brooks' stage training methods. Interestingly, the disc never deeply confronts how much Brook altered from the source; for example, the title itself won't make as much sense for anyone who hasn't read the book.

THE LOST CONTINENT

Colour, 1968, 96m. / Directed by Michael Carreras / Starring Eric Porter, Charles Houston / Anchor Bay (US R1 NTSC) / WS (1.78:1) (16:9)

An incredibly weird hodgepodge of genres, *The Lost Continent* certainly isn't good filmmaking but makes for oddly compelling viewing from start to finish. Starting off like a trashy Sidney Sheldon story about a tramp steamer filled with international types screwing over each other, the story veers constantly from one popular drive-in style to the next, leaving

the impression of a particularly disjointed comic book designed by 14 year olds on acid. En route to Caracas, the aforementioned passengers all decide to keep going despite the threat of an oncoming hurricane. The usual suspects are all here, including a mysterious foreign movie star (Hildegard Knef) and an insatiable, back-talking blonde (Suzanna Leigh) under the thumb of her hypocritical father. Obviously these less than brilliant folks get what they deserve and run smack into the storm, which leaves them stranded on an island populated by the forgotten descendants of Spanish conquistadors. The boat is carried along by self-propelling, living seaweed to the high court, where a strange boy king oversees his crazy hordes. Lots of action ensues, little of which makes any sense, before a number of rubbery giant crustaceans show up. Giant crabs! Giant lobsters! Big hot air balloons! And some gratuitous sex scenes! How on earth will it all end?

Helmed with all the sensitivity and intelligence that marked Carreras' *Prehistoric Women*, this film has been enhanced with an additional six minutes of footage never before seen in the US. Considering that the first of these restored scenes features Leigh being called a "hellcat" and almost punched during sex, viewers should have a pretty good idea of what to expect. This delirious experience is enhanced by a terrific anamorphic widescreen transfer, though the source material was obviously crafted from at least three different prints. The bulk of the film looks fantastic, while the restored footage displays somewhat duller fleshtones and less clearly defined backgrounds. The yellow, orange, and brown colour schemes don't really make for very good eye candy, but fans will be happy to know that this is about as good as it's going to get. The audio is clean and sharp, though plagued by an occasional tinniness inherent in many late '60s Hammer productions... and don't forget that campy, swooning theme song. The disc also includes the long theatrical trailer and the same "Lands Before Time" special included on the "Hammer glamour" Anchor Bay titles.

LOST HORIZON

B&W, 1937, 132m. / Directed by Frank Capra / Starring Ronald Colman, Jane Wyatt / Columbia (US R1 NTSC, UK R2 PAL)

The first film adaptation of James Hilton's classic novel (originally published as Shangri-La), this elegant fantasy from director Frank Capra remains

extremely popular and critically revered over sixty years later but seems somehow out of step with the rest of his filmography. Set for the most part in an idyllic mountainous utopia, *Lost Horizon* contains numerous multinational and philosophical issues which question the concepts of true "happiness" and gung ho patriotism. However, the true meaning of many of these implications is left up to the viewer's interpretation, particularly in the original 1937 (more on that in a moment).

A planeload of Westerners crashes in the Himalayas and are spirited away to Shangri-La, a happy place where everyone is equal and such petty things as war and strife have ceased to exist. Could such a place be supernatural? You bet. The hero of the tale, Robert Conway (Colman), falls in love with one of the residents, Sondra (Jane Wyatt), while his brother, George (John Howard), is not quite so eager to stay. Ultimately each Westerner must make his choice: stay in Shangri-La for an eternity of (awfully monotonous) happiness, or leave and face the perils of World War II brewing just over the mountains.

Along with George Cukor's *A Star Is Born, Lost Horizon* was one of the first butchered Hollywood classics to receive the deluxe restoration treatment in the early 1980s. The 138 minute film had been hacked down to as little as 118 minutes for most showings since its initial release, and Sony and UCLA managed to reinstate the previously lost footage in highly variable quality back into the print. Only audio remained for a few snippets, so this was played over stills to provide as complete an experience as possible.

Simply put, if you're looking for a demo piece DVD to show off a black and white film, this is not the title to buy. Most of the film looks quite good, marred only by an occasional blemish, while the restored footage ranges from passable to extremely rough. However, as a piece of film history and a presentation of Capra's classic, reallistically this is as good as it's going to get. The commentary indicates that the original rough cut ran even longer, with some of Jaffe's interminable speeches as the High Lama going on for as long as twenty minutes! Even in its final form, the film drags a bit in its midsection and may be a bit daunting for first time viewers. Flaws aside, this is an important film which, despite its dated elements, fully deserves this special treatment. Colman and Wyatt make a fine, convincing couple, and horror fans should get a kick out of seeing Margo and Isabel Jewell years before they appeared in Val Lewton's *The Leopard Man.*

Columbia's supplements for *Lost Horizon* easily justify purchasing this edition even for those who already have the laserdisc. Aside from the excellent commentary, the disc offers a revealing comparison of the original '37 opening with the reissue prints which include a jab at the Japanese. A more blatant alternate ending is also included, as well as a brief teaser trailer that contains no actual footage from the film. The liner notes provide a thorough and surprisingly frank account of how the big budget film brought the studio to the brink of bankruptcy but ultimately established Columbia as a major studio in the long run. Note: *Lost Horizon* was later remade less successfully by Ross Hunter as a 1973 musical with Peter Finch and Michael York; though widely maligned, that version is not without its points of interest and, judging from Pioneer's special edition laserdisc, would probably make for a pretty fascinating DVD, too, and given Columbia's recent and startling track record, that might not be such a crazy idea. Also, for a science fiction take on the same plot, check out *Star Trek: Insurrection*, which basically transfers Shangri-La into space.

LOST IN SPACE

Colour, 1998, 130m. / Directed by Stephen Hopkins / Starring William Hurt, Mimi Rogers / New Line (US R1 NTSC), EIV (UK R2 PAL) / WS (2.35:1) (16:9) / DD5.1

It's the year 2058 and the Earth's resources are almost depleted. John Robinson (Hurt) and his family are launched into space to begin colonisation of the planet Alpha Prime, the only hope for the future of mankind. But a saboteur is aboard and the Robinsons are hurled through a time vortex into uncharted deep space. "Danger, Will Robinson, danger! Duff movie experience imminent..." Taking one of US TV's more juvenile sci-fi shows of the 1960s and upgrading it to 1990s big screen extravaganza status is one of those projects it's hard to imagine ever "seemed like a good idea at the time". That the task was handed to Steven Hopkins (director of a disastrous sequel in the *Nightmare on Elm Street* saga) and *Batman* franchise co-assassin Akiva Goldsman (who proves unequivocally that he hasn't an ounce of talent for screenwriting) is simply mind-boggling. Together they take a large bite out of the cult TV show, have a good old masticate and spit out the profligate mess for our edification. The cast struggle manfully on in an attempt to make something of the flimsy and muddled script, but even Gary Oldman is strained to be as convincingly insidious as we know so well he can be. Adding wall to wall special (and some not at all special) effects is not the recipe for a good movie fellas. To be fair the plot does start to get interesting about half an hour from the finish line, but by then a reprieve is beyond consent. When a film's only discernible value is giving male viewers the opportunity to muse over how long it took Mimi Rogers and Heather Graham to wiggle into those body-hugging "cryo-suits", and its smashing update of the TV show's theme tune, it has serious problems.

Endeavouring to disguise this sow's ear, New Line gilded their DVD with a silky assortment of supplemental treats, yet still failed to hide the inherent problem that the movie is lousy. It may be a beautifully mastered 24-chapter presentation, but bilge is still bilge no matter how you perfume it. Said extras are two commentaries (one from the indefensible team of Hopkins and Goldman, the other from various other members of the crew), three featurettes, a section providing a complete episode guide to the TV series as well as interviews with members of the original cast, the energetic Apollo Four Forty music video, a large number of deleted scenes minus their finished effects (they should have deleted a few more!), the trailer, and cast/crew bios. Finally there's an interactive quiz - answering 16 questions correctly grants you access to a "Lost in Space Joke Reel", a substandard quality selection of bloopers and blunders. There are also a number of oddments available to PC viewers only. Sound and subtitling is (unusually) in English alone. - TG

LUST FOR A VAMPIRE

Colour, 1971, 94m. / Directed by Jimmy Sangster / Starring Ralph Bates, Yutte Stensgaard / Anchor Bay (US R1 NTSC) / WS (1.78:1) (16:9)

Easily the dippiest of Hammer's three vampire films based on J. Sheridan LeFanu's *Carmilla*, this extended *Playboy* spread masquerading as a horror film was closely sandwiched between the classier *The Vampire Lovers* and *Twins of Evil*. However, this mongrel entry has earned a reputation as a Hammer fan's guilty pleasure thanks to its unabashed celebration of all the erotic vampire clichés, from women in flowing gowns wandering through mist to extended love scenes replete with bared fangs. Thirty years later it still isn't really all that good, but at least now the film's visual lustre has been restored and its cheesecake quotient remains undiminished.

Picking up the role from Ingrid Pitt, lovely Danish actress Yutte Stensgaard stars as Mircalla, the conflicted vampiress who preys upon the countryside. Here she's joined by the less important Count Karnstein (Mike Raven), seemingly afflicted with the same case of redeye as Christopher Lee's Dracula, and together they arrange rampant (but decidedly cut rate) sacrifices and orgies in their remote castle. Their latest target is a nearby girl's school, where jittery teacher Giles (Ralph Bates) takes the girls on educational strolls through the woods. Mircalla gradually insinuates herself into this distaff community, dabbling in moonlight skinny-dipping and light lesbian foreplay. However, her plans are disrupted when she runs into superstud Richard LeStrange (Michael Johnson), who tries to make her an honest woman despite her need to ravage people's throats. Not surprisingly, it all ends badly... and bloodily.

Released by MGM-EMI back in the early '70s, *Lust for a Vampire* met the same fate of its predecessor - namely, an attack of the censor's scissors. The truncated US version (usually shown as *To Love a Vampire*) turned up most often on television and even more inexplicably was released on VHS by Republic, following an uncut presentation by HBO on videotape and, coupled with *Die Monster Die*, on laserdisc from Image.

Production values are still admirable for a later period Hammer title, and the decision to retain the period gothic setting is admirable; however, the ramping up of sex and violence results in some unintentional guffaws, the most infamous being Mircalla's cross-eyed rapture accompanied by the film's theme song, "Strange Love." (Actually the music by Harry Robinson is excellent as always, but the film never fails to misuse it.) Bates is mostly wasted in a role that basically serves no function at all, but Stensgaard is passable considering the fact that she's dubbed and usually unclothed. When people trash Hammer films for focusing entirely on women's cleavage and melodramatics at the expense of substance, this is usually the title they have in mind - but really, is there anything wrong with that?

The aforementioned video versions of *Lust for a Vampire* have been abysmal, in keeping with HBO's early treatment of its other catalogue titles. The difference here is night and day as the film now erupts with riotous colours of every scheme; the blood (of which there is plenty) looks a blinding red, and the night schemes are now appropriately drenched in those blue day for night lighting gels. Most importantly this is the full, uncut version back in circulation at last. The mono soundtrack is more full bodied than the laserdisc by several yards, and the music is no longer shrill and distorted. Only the overly tight 1.85:1 framing mars what is otherwise an immaculate presentation.

The disc also includes the British theatrical trailer, as well as a photo and poster gallery, but the big plus here is a commentary track with Sangster and actress Suzanna Leigh. They spend most of the time going over production details (clothing, sets, etc.) but offer some good yarns, including a detailed account of Terence Fisher's slated involvement.

LUST FOR FRANKENSTEIN

Colour, 1998, 79m. / Directed by Jess Franco / Starring Lina Romay, Michelle Bauer / Shock-o-Rama Cinema (US R1 NTSC) / WS (1.50:1) / DD2.0

Moira Frankenstein (Romay) is bedevilled by visions of her dead father (Carlos Subterfuge). Finding the body of his hermaph-rodite creation Godess (Bauer) hidden in stasis, she revives her and they embark upon an intense affair of the flesh. But when Moira succumbs to the advances of her nymphomaniac stepmother (Ivers), the enraged Godess moves in for the kill... Widely acknowledged as being among the more interesting products of the 1980s "Scream Queen" phenomenon, Michelle Bauer enjoyed a diverse career, spinning out of hard core pornography through the world of bizarre fetish videos and on to a slew of B-movie features. In spite of all this, playing the Frankenstein monster opposite Spanish cult princess Lina Romay in a Jess Franco movie wasn't the most predictable next step, but it assuredly proved a unique one. She's certainly one of the few boons to this sour Franconian tidbit.

An over-reliance on MTV-style video effects sequences, a less than euphonious rock score and dialogue delivery impeded by thick accents amalgamate to form a rather pedestrian exercise in sleaze; yes, as one would expect from the director there's sleaze aplenty, but a profusion of (not always attractive) naked bodies fails to compensate for a flimsy plot and although whenever Bauer is on screen the proceedings crank up a notch or two, when she isn't it's frequently fast-forward fare. Analia Ivers doesn't have to contend with anything as memorably outrageous as in *Tender Flesh*, although the sequence in which she's so deeply engrossed in *soixante-neuf* with Romay that she doesn't notice her boyfriend (Pedro Temboury), just

three feet away, getting his neck snapped by Bauer is unintentionally hilarious. Romay serves up her usual dedicated performance, Amber Newman is back for her third and final appearance in a Franco flick, and Raquel Cabra (who served as DoP on several of his latter-day projects) proves both capable and attractive in front of the cameras. Watchable enough but some distance from being essential Franco.

Average film, below average disc. The lesser quality of the source material is reflected in a slightly unsatisfactory transfer to DVD on Shock-O-Rama's release. The inclusion of two versions of the film itself (the American cut which runs 79 minutes with 18-chapters and the extended European version which runs 87 minutes with 23 chapters) is sure to delight Franco completists and genre historians, but since the longer cut was procurable the inclusion of the edited one is rather pointless; those keen enough to purchase the disc in the first place will be unlikely to want to watch the movie with 8 minutes of the juicier stuff chopped out! The sound is intrusively hissy in several places throughout. The bonus material is made up of a little over 20 minutes of shot-on-video footage which looks as if its been duped from a 3rd or 4th generation bootleg tape. There's also a light-hearted interview with Michelle Bauer (which was probably intended for cable TV or an in-house project), shot at a 1994 convention in the States. Trailers for other films in the company's catalogue conclude the package. - TG

M

B&W, 1931, 110m. / Directed by Fritz Lang / Starring Peter Lorre / Criterion (US R1 NTSC)

Thanks to DVD, Fritz Lang's cinema classic has finally been released in a version that, while not exactly "immaculate," shows this chilling classic off as well as we're likely to see it in this lifetime. Peter Lorre gives the performance of a lifetime as a pathetic child killer who finds himself stalked by the police and the criminal underworld, leading to an unforgettable "courtroom" climax.

Lang's amazing visual touches have rarely been surpassed here; while *Metropolis* may be more dazzling for sheer scale, *M* remains his greatest storytelling feat. The film is also amazingly rich for an early talkie, most notably in its haunting use of Grieg's "In the Hall of the Mountain King" as Lorre's *leitmotif* (and supposedly performed by Lang himself). Considering the film's age, the materials have been restored amazingly well. A few hairline scratches here and there (especially during the first few minutes) don't detract too badly, and more importantly, this is the original, 110 minute cut that was released in Germany, not the 99 minute version most English speakers have seen. The quality is amazing, all things considered, and the DVD features optional English subtitles.

MABOROSI

Colour, 1995, 110m. / Directed by Hirokazu Kore-eda / Starring Makiko Esumi, Takashi Naitô, Tadanobu Asano / New Yorker (US R1 NTSC) / WS (2.00:1)

Apart from the lack of an insane or twisted main character, *Maborosi* would make perfect companion viewing with any Werner Herzog film. This hypnotic and visually stunning widescreen treasure marked the feature directorial debut of Hirokazu Kore-eda (*After Life*), whose artful control of the medium was already well in evidence. Here he tackles the many difficult concepts involving spirituality, mortality, and man's relationship with nature, all set to a throbbing, haunting soundtrack reminiscent of Popol Vuh and other progressive European bands.

Maborosi (full title: *Maboroshi no hikari*) follows the journey of Yumiko (Makiko Esumi), an urban woman who is forced to raise her child alone after the apparent suicide of her husband. Even after remarrying to Tamio (Takashi Naitoh) and relocating to the seaside, she finds herself unsatisfied and searches for a sense of meaning underneath all the mess of her day to day life.

The storyline may be nothing terribly groundbreaking (see Kieslowski's *Three Colours: Blue* for another variation), but the same certainly can't be said for the images concocted by the director and cinematographer, who unveil a seemingly endless series of tableaux from the most basic elements. Bridges, silhouettes, and even the play of sunlight off the surfaces of wood and clothing turn the film into a dramatic tour de force, quiet yet devastating in its impact. A funeral sequence provides one unforgettable highlight, in which the distant procession is viewed at length from above in a snow-speckled forest and in silhouette across a vast expanse of beach. Fashion model Esumi looks perfect for the role, and her static, wooden quality actually brings an effective passive tranquillity to the film, which could have been destructive in another project.

New Yorker's DVD is visually pleasing, offering a widescreen presentation at approximately 2.00:1 with burned-in English subtitles for the Japanese dialogue. The mono sound is clear and intelligible enough, though with such a tranquil film the presence of pure, unadulterated silence is the most important thing. The disc also includes both the US and Japanese trailers, which appropriately make this look like a cross between Ingmar Bergman and Yasujiro Ozu, as well as a variety of factual profiles on the director (who made his auspicious debut with this film) and the entire production process.

MACABRE

Colour, 1980, 90m. / Directed by Lamberto Bava / Starring Bernice Stegers, Stanko Molnar / Anchor Bay (US R1 NTSC) / WS (1.85:1) (16:9)

After years of working as an assistant director on his father Mario's films, Lamberto Bava finally went solo in 1980 with *Macabre*, an atmospheric psychological study which joins *The Beyond* and *Cannibal Apocalypse* for the largest number of Italian actors impersonating American Southerners. The central gimmick of the film has been spoiled by everything from reviewers to the US video box cover, but for the uninitiated, we'll leave it to the mysterious basics here.

Jane (*City of Women*'s Bernice Stegers), a wife and mother of two, relieves the tedium of her New Orleans social life by dallying on the side with her passionate lover, Fred, in a boarding house inhabited by the blind and unfortunately named Robert Duval (Stanko Molnar) and his mother. One day Jane's erotic idyll is interrupted when her psychotic daughter, Lucy (Veronica Zinny, sister of horror actor Urbano Barberini), calls up her mom and then drowns her little brother in a jealous snit. Jane and Fred leap into the car and tear across town when they hear the news, only to ram straight into a construction site which leaves Fred mangled beyond repair. One year later, Jane is released from a mental institution and takes a room at Robert's house. Lucy now lives only with her father but maintains contact with her mother; however, Jane may not be quite all there. Every night Robert hears his newest tenant engaging in hot and heavy sessions in her bedroom, always following the sound of something being unlocked from the refrigerator...

Based very loosely on a newspaper story discovered by co-producer Pupi Avati, *Macabre* was

M

originally written as a kind of joke but quickly developed into a serious gothic chamber piece. Apart from the occasional New Orleans exterior shot, this is unmistakably the work of Bava blood, steeped in the same overripe visual decay which earmarked such masterpieces as *Lisa and the Devil* (another European meditation on necrophilia, by the way). The badly dubbed Southern accents become grating rather quickly, but Bava's steady visual sense carries the film over its rough spots and really crackles to life for the finale, in which Stegers' unnerving, fragile beauty finally tips over the cliff into full blown psychotic mania.

The influence of Avati is evident as well, mainly in the deliberate, restrained pacing and the emphasis on psychological rifts forming beneath the surface of normality; unfortunately, this is the only Lamberto film that could ever really be termed "subtle," as it plays for the most part like a particularly skewed episode of *Night Gallery* instead of the splatter-heavy contemporaries of its time. Apart from the aforementioned accents, the film's only major misstep is a terribly conceived shock ending which ends the film on a ridiculous illogical note and renders its origin as a "true story" dubious at best.

First released on VHS by Lightning Video as *Frozen Terror* and in Canada (by CIC) and the UK (by Vipco) under its original title, this sick little gem has suffered from some awfully bland transfers over the years which sapped away much of its visual allure. Anchor Bay's DVD corrects much of the damage and restores the intricate, colourful production design to its proper overripe splendour. The screen is frequently oversaturated with acres of red velvet, gold décor trim, and shimmering silk sheets, all of which add considerably to the film's potent atmosphere. The disc also includes a nice 8 minute interview with Lamberto (entitled "A Head for Horror"), in which he discusses the genesis of the story, his father's reaction after the premiere, and more. Other goodies include the European theatrical trailer (which blows the entire ending, so be careful!), some solid (and unfortunately well hidden) liner notes by Travis Crawford, and a Lamberto bio.

THE MAD BUTCHER

Colour, 1971, 83m. / Directed by Guido Zurli / Starring Victor Buono, Brad Harris, Karin Field / Image (US R0 NTSC) / WS (1.85:1) / Mono

Though not your traditional leading man, the rotund and compellingly odd Victor Buono had earned enough of a reputation for his grotesque turns as the mama's boy songwriter in *What Ever Happened to*

Baby Jane? and the patriarch in *Hush... Hush, Sweet Charlotte* to ensure a long career in Hollywood as a character actor. However, he got to take the centre spotlight in *Lo strangolatore di Vienna (The Strangler of Vienna)*, a bizarre Italian/German black comedy retitled *Meat Is Meat* for the English market. Sex and violence maven Harry Novak picked it up for Box Office International and changed the title to *The Mad Butcher*, its most famous incarnation, though the print for this widescreen DVD edition still bears the onscreen title of *Meat Is Meat*. By any name, it's one of the oddest Eurosleaze items you'll ever see.

After spending three years in a mental institution, Otto Lehmann (Victor Buono) returns to his home and business accompanied by his blonde, shrewish wife (Franca Polcelli). When he's not busy spying on his sexy neighbour (Karin Field), who enjoys undressing in front of the window, Otto peddles his yummy sausages around town and tries to rebuild his reputation as one of Vienna's finest butchers. Unfortunately his temper gets the better of him when he strangles his wife, then grinds her up into sausage meat for public consumption. Mike (Brad Harris), a nosy newspaper reporter, swiftly begins to suspect that Otto might be responsible for the growing number of disappearing acquaintances, but his cries to the police fall on deaf ears. Meanwhile Otto's business begins to boom, and people just can't get enough of those plump, juicy, meaty treats.

Despite the sick subject matter and the obvious parallels to the grim tale of Sweeney Todd, *The Mad Butcher* contains nary a drop of a blood during its entire running time. All of the murders are restricted to strangulation, while the grinding scenes are limited to darkly humorous shots of linked sausages pouring out of Otto's machinery. Instead the film earns its R rating thanks to heavy injections of cheesecake topless nudity, thanks to Otto's voyeurism, but any genuine sexuality is used only for comic effect. Buono is actually quite good in the leading role, wearing a variety of wacko Austrian outfits and bantering with the police and customers.

The tone is very similar to another contemporary European black comedy, *Bluebeard* (with Richard Burton), which combined skin and sick laughs with a similar candy coloured visual palette. The eccentric score by spaghetti western legend Alessandro Alessandroni (credited as Alex Alexander) features a catchy Bertolt Brecht style motif; in fact, you'll half expect Otto to start singing

"Mack the Knife" as he strolls his human meat cart around town.

The image quality of Something Weird's DVD is quite nice, from Novak's well preserved negative preserved in the US The letterboxing adds some much needed breathing room compared to past VHS editions, while the mono sound comes through just fine. All of the dialogue has been dubbed (as it is in every version due to the multinational cast), though Buono and Harris loop their own voices.

Of course, this wouldn't be an SW disc without those crazy extras, and you certainly get them here. Apart from the US trailer (which contains some major spoilers), you also get a ton of other Novak trailers including the astounding *Mother* (which teams Buono with Julie Newmar - how about a DVD of that one?!), *Caged Virgins* (the Americanized *Requiem for a Vampire*), *Rattlers*, *Frankenstein's Castle of Freaks*, and a hidden trailer of *Kiss Me Quick*. Don't forget to try out that "Maim" option on the navigation menu, either. Other morsels include "Cannibal Island," a B&W mondo look at native flesh-eaters partially culled from silent era footage, and the more memorable "Cannibal Massage," a gritty 20 minute film (sans credits) in which a New York businessman keeps going back for nude backrubs from a burly black masseuse before relenting to a most bizarre and perversely executed fate. The last five minutes will leave most viewers, particularly the devout, numb with disbelief.

MAHLER

Colour, 1974, 110m. / Directed by Ken Russell / Starring Robert Powell, Georgina Hale / Image (US R0 NTSC) / DD2.0

 Arguably the high point of controversial British director Ken Russell's forays into musical biographies (which include *Clouds of Glory* and the outrageous *Lisztomania*), the 1974 biopic *Mahler* remains lesser known most likely due to the absence of any really big stars.

Robert Powell (a veteran of horror and art films who later went on to star in the title role of *Jesus of Nazareth*) plays the legendary Gustav Mahler, whose duties as a conductor supplemented his less profitable efforts as a composer. En route by train from a prematurely cancelled concert tour and accompanied by his wife (the marvellous Georgina Hale), Mahler flashes back on his life and indulges in some alternately disturbing and amusing fantasy

sequences. Along the way Russell tips his hat with a number of cinematic references including *Vampyr, Siegfried*, his own Tchaikovsky biopic, *The Music Lovers*, and an amusing riff on Visconti's *Death in Venice*.

While the typical Russell extravagant touches and outrageous humour are in abundant evidence here (witness the nude funeral sequence and bizarre Nazi-Chaplin fantasia), he's backed up by a solid cast and some exquisite photography and production values that should make this enjoyable even for non-Russell film fans. Interestingly, this film makes an odd companion piece with *Lisztomania*, which was filmed four years later but is set just a few years before this film and contains many of the same characters and themes. It's amazing what a difference (for better or worse) a bigger budget and a pounding rock score can do!

This new DVD edition of *Mahler* is a tremendous improvement over the old Thorn/EMI VHS video released back in the mid-'80s, with smooth, beautiful visuals and a spacious two-channel stereo soundtrack that brings the music vividly to life. It may not be quite the visceral sonic experience of, say, *Tommy*, but the presentation here delivers the best *Mahler* we're likely to see.

THE MAN WITH THE GOLDEN GUN

Colour, 1974, 125m. / Directed by Guy Hamilton / Starring Roger Moore, Christopher Lee / MGM (US R1 NTSC) / WS (1.85:1) (16:9) / DD2.0

 James Bond (Moore) is sent a golden bullet engraved with his double-O prefix, a warning that he is on the hit list of million dollar assassin Francisco Scaramanga (Lee). He decides to head off any attempt on his life by travelling to Beirut to find the killer first.

The presence of Christopher Lee elevates this Bond from being the weakest in the series, though it still languishes down there near the bottom of the heap. The former Dracula actor's cultured hatchet man is one of the few good aspects of this lackadaisical escapade, which rides in on the coat-tails of the kung fu craze of the period. That said, he meets the most prosaic fate ever to befall a Bond baddie; 007 shoots him, he falls down, he's dead. In his second outing as the superspy, Moore was still finding his feet and although the Thailand, Hong Kong and Macau locations are fabulous - particularly the exotic setting of Scaramanga's hideout, one of a vast scattering of small islands in the South

China Sea - the business played out against them lacks oomph. And when Bond is upstaged in a punch-up by two teenage schoolgirls he really ought to consider calling it a day!

Fresh out of *The Wicker Man,* Britt Ekland is irritatingly poor as Bond's Hong Kong liaison Mary Goodnight, though Maud Adams (who returned to the series in *Octopussy*) makes for eye-catching recompense. It's hard to take Herve (*Seizure*) Villechaize's diminutive killer Nick-Nack as a serious threat and as if to acknowledge the fact, the makers employ him primarily for laughs. Bringing back Clifton James's Louisiana Sheriff - popular with audiences in *Live and Let Die* - backfires too, and he graduates from likeable oaf to complete goon. It's not all bad news though. There's some inventive production design (at it's best in the covert Secret Service HQ inside the wreck of the Queen Elizabeth), Maurice Binder's stimulating titles (with Lulu belting out a grand John Barry/Don Black theme song) are cheekily phallic, and there's some excellent integrated model work; you'd honestly think they really blew up that beautiful island. Hardly Bond at his best, but well worth a look-see.

Irrespective of the inferior nature of the film itself, MGM's disc of *The Man with the Golden Gun* boasts a nice assortment of goodies. Along with a documentary that looks back on the production of the film, there's a second documentary surveying the stunts that embellish the movies, a reasonably generous photo gallery, two TV spots, three radio spots and two trailers; the teaser is the most interesting of the pair, comprising some footage from the final 007/Scaramanga shoot-out that was cut from the finished movie. The 1.85:1 feature is divided by 32 chapter-stops and has an optional commentary track from director Guy Hamilton and some of the cast and crew. Stereo sound is in English only, with subtitling in French and Spanish. - TG

THE MAN WITH TWO BRAINS

Colour, 1983, 90m. / Directed by Carl Reiner / Starring Steve Martin, Kathleen Turner / Warner (US R1 NTSC)

Eminent brain surgeon Dr. Michael Hfuhruhurr (Martin) almost kills Dolores Benedict (Turner) in a motoring accident. Saving her life on the operating table, he falls in love with and marries her, unaware that she's the most heartless god-digger on the face of the earth. Hfuhruhurr's life subsequently becomes purgatory

until he meets fellow surgeon Dr. Alfred Necessiter (Warner) and falls in love with the disembodied brain of Ann Uumellmahaye (voiced by Sissy Spacek), kept in a jar in Necessiter's lab.

The third and best of Carl Reiner and Steve Martin's collaborative projects to date (the others being *The Jerk, Dead Men Don't Wear Plaid* and *All of Me*), *The Man with Two Brains* is a tour de force in absurdity. The gags may sometimes be incongruous, but the chemistry between the always reliable Martin and Turner's "cheap vulgar slut" makes even the moments of bad taste appetising. David Warner is a laugh riot as the crazed scientist with a castle built into his condominium, but Turner gets the best dialogue, from the whimsically deadpan "Were you out on the lake today kissing your brain?" to the preposterous exclamation (as Martin knees her in the crotch) "Owww, my balls!" Watch out for *Re-Animator's* Jeffery Combs in a bit part as a hospital orderly who, despite the fact he's preparing Turner for a brain operation, shaves her pubic hair into the shape of a heart; "Since it's Valentine's day," he says defensively, to which an enraged Martin responds, "I suppose if it were Christmas you'd hang ornaments on it!" As you might have gathered, subtlety isn't in these guys' vocabulary.

A 28-chapter divide may be more generous a break-down than on many DVD releases, but when you're talking about a fullscreen (though admittedly above average quality) transfer on a disc that has precisely nothing extra to offer, can it really be recommended over its VHS counterparts? - TG

MANHATTAN BABY

Colour, 1982, 87m. / Directed by Lucio Fulci / Starring Christopher Connelly, Martha Taylor / Anchor Bay (US R1 NTSC) / WS (2.35:1) (16:9)

Essentially the last film in Lucio Fulci's amazing streak of supernatural '80s horror films, *Manhattan Baby* is perhaps the most problematic and should be approached by those who have already developed a tolerance for Fulci's cinematic flights of fancy. The film's reputation has suffered over the years due to poorly framed pan and scan transfers and only one showstopping gore scene, but the maestro's ability to render poetic visuals from the most mundane settings turns this patchwork homage to the horror genre into a quirky, challenging visual feast.

While archaeologist George Hacker (Christopher Connelly) and his assistant explore a dark Egyptian tomb, his daughter, Susie (Brigitta Boccoli), is approached outside by a white-eyed blind local woman who utters "Tombs are for the dead" and hands the girl a jewelled amulet. Shortly thereafter, George is struck blind by a supernatural blue light within the tomb, and the entire family returns to New York. Mysterious apparitions involving scorpions, desert sands, and interdimensional passageways plague the family as Susie and her annoying little brother (*House by the Cemetery*'s blond anti-moppet, Giovanni Frezza) appear to become the pawns of an ancient Egyptian evil. George's eyesight returns, but Susie's mental and physical condition rapidly deteriorate thanks to a case of apparent possession. With the aid of a wise antiquarian named Adrian Marcato (Laurence Welles) - can you identify that character name, genre buffs? - George races against time to turn back the curse which is slowly consuming his family.

The spectres of past Fulci films hang heavily over *Manhattan Baby*, thanks in no small part to a driving music score comprised of original Fabio Frizzi compositions (excellent as usual) and disorienting passages lifted from *The Beyond* and *City of the Living Dead*. Fulci's love for marauding animals is once again present, as actors are menaced by cobras, scuttling scorpions lurking in office furniture, and most memorably, a stuffed bird which comes to life during the squishy, downbeat climax. The opening sequence of the film is arguably its strongest, with minimal dialogue and Frizzi's theme accompanying a striking succession of interlaced visuals depicting Connelly's tomb defiling and his daughter's own corruption. Unlike Fulci's gore epics, the horror here seems to exist on the periphery: a wall splits open to disgorge a pair of monstrous hands, a man is trapped in an elevator which splits open into a bottomless abyss, a room's ceiling transforms into a blue lit desert landscape, and a splash of blood on a wall spreads across the screen with a life of its own. Very little of this makes much sense, but Italian horror regulars should already expect that.

Manhattan Baby (whose title means nothing really) was the last Fulci film to receive a notable theatrical release, under the title of *Eye of the Evil Dead* (complete with a poster depicting a blonde lass in a bikini standing in front of some pyramids!). Lighting Video issued an eyesore VHS release, and overseas versions were little better, turning the lyrical scope photography into a senseless jumble of eyeballs and out of focus location shots. Not that it had much competition, but Anchor Bay's DVD looks as good as one could expect and completely restores the correct framing. Fulci's use of the zoom lens

produces some unsightly excessive grain in a few shots, but otherwise the colours and detail are stable and pleasing to the eye. The disc also includes the European theatrical trailer (which has already appeared on numerous Japanese releases) and a nice video interview with screenwriter Dardano Sacchetti, who collaborated with Fulci for the last time on this film after a number of smash international hits. He has some interesting things to say about the film, which was plagued with difficulties but remains an oddly compelling entry in the last golden age of Italian horror.

MANIAC

B&W, 1934, 51m. / Directed by Dwain Esper /
Starring Bill Woods, Phyllis Diller, Theo Ramscy
NARCOTIC
B&W, 1933, 57m.
Directed by Dwain Esper and Vival Sodar't /
Starring Harry Cording, Joan Dix
Kino (US R1 NTSC)

There are bad movies, and then there are Dwain Esper movies. Now regarded as the Ed Wood, Jr. of his day, Esper and his wife, Hildegarde Stadie, churned out a host of ludicrous, zero budget "educational" films during the '30s and '40s, often exhibited like a sideshow in tents and makeshift theatres. Esper's cutthroat distribution tactics and hilariously misleading advertising eventually caught up with him as the drive-in took hold, but for anyone lucky enough to witness the weird magic of his films, the experience will never be forgotten. Esper's most famous opus, *Maniac*, opens as a treatise on the dangers of mental illness but quickly swerves off in directions no sane person could ever predict.

Dr. Meirschultz (Horace B. Carpenter), a prototypical mad scientist, recruits a vaudeville performer, Don (Bill Woods), who happens to possess uncanny impersonation skills. The two swipe a female corpse and revive her by rubbing her arms. After another bodysnatching expedition goes awry, Meirschultz comes up with a great idea - he hands Don a gun and asks him to shoot himself so the doctor can bring him back. Don decides to shoot Meirschultz instead and impersonates the doctor when a pair of strangers arrive. A young woman claims that her husband believes he is the gorilla from Poe's "Murders in the Rue Morgue," so Don grabs a needle at random and injects him. The poor guy immediately bursts into a spastic transformation routine that defies description, then grabs the reanimated female corpse and, after conveniently tearing open her dress (yes, there's nudity), ravages her in the woods. But wait! There's much more, as the narrative suddenly turns into a reprise of Poe's "The Black Cat." The fake Dr. Meirschultz pops out a kitty's eyeball and eats it, the walled up corpse of the doctor proves to be more trouble than it's worth, and two women have a catfight with hypodermic needles. In the meantime, Esper treats his audience with title cards explaining various forms of mental disease which have relation whatsoever to the onscreen action.

The earlier *Narcotic* isn't as consistently depraved as *Maniac* but offers many goofy charms all its own. Dr. Davis (Harry Cording), a promising medical talent, winds up experiencing the forbidden pleasures of smoking opium, thanks to the influence of that old '30s standby, the wise but decadent Asian. Actually, it's a terrible American actor with bad make up and a riotous sub-Charlie Chan accent, but you get the idea. Davis' wife doesn't think too highly of her hubby's new habit, especially when he decides to peddle opium as a new medical wonder to Americans. Eventually she talks him into going into rehab, where the doctors treat the poor soul by giving him... heroin! Yep, it's a real slippery slope from there, as Davis plunges into the depths of a real "dope party" at which participants dress up in evening wear, shoot up, smoke pot, and tell awful jokes. Oh, the horror! Anyone could predict where the good doctor winds up next - the carnival sideshow, of course. When that venue doesn't work out, it's time for Davis to go huddle up in a cheap hotel room with heroin and a pistol. You can figure out the rest.

Designed to violate every censorship code in the book, Esper's films wallow in wretched acting, *non sequitur* editing, and gleeful exploitation. Just a few minutes into *Narcotic*, for example, the audience is treated to a Caesarean birth sequence, just for shock value. Likewise, *Maniac* trots out so much sleaze it plays like a catalogue of everything the legendary Hays Code opposed. Not surprisingly, both of the films are in rough shape on this DVD, but their survival in any form is something to behold. *Maniac* looks better in its Kino incarnation than rotten public domain copies floating around, most of which look projected through a fishbowl. Scratches and splices abound, especially in the opening credits, but the actual clarity of the image is impressive and satisfying. *Narcotic* appears to be edited with Scotch tape to begin with, so the presentation obviously isn't much better. Dialogue is often clipped off (deliberately?), and many frames appear to be missing. As with most Esper titles, the bizarre insert footage (cats fighting, snakes eating each other, the Caesarean birth, etc.) have been spliced in without sound and stick out jarringly against the surrounding footage. The sound quality is fine, considering it was always muddled anyway.

The DVD includes a side-splitting trailer for *Maniac* ("It will make thy blood to freeze and thy hair to stand!"), excerpts from the *Maniac* screenplay (yes, it did have one), some amusing correspondence between Esper's office and the New York Film Censor Board, and a running commentary by the co-author of *Forbidden Fruit*, Bret Wood. Almost Criterion-like in its exhaustiveness, this presentation benefits greatly from Wood's laconic treatment of the two films, which obviously still inspire him beyond words during a few scenes. As long as viewers know what they're getting, this double feature really delivers the goods and makes one wonder about the future of fringe DVD.

MANJI

Colour, 1964, 92m. / Directed by Yasuzo Masumura / Starring Ayako Wakao, Kyôko Kishida / Fantoma (US R1 NTSC) / WS (2.35:1) (16:9)

"You're so beautiful I could kill you!" "Kill me! Kill me!" Such purple prose positively percolates in this florid melodrama, a hyperventilating Douglas Sirk style yarn about a love rectangle gone horribly wrong.

Our story begins when married, middle class Sonoko Kakiuci (*Woman in the Dunes'* Kyôko Kishida) develops a fixation on beautiful Mitsuko (*Floating Weeds'* Ayako Wakao), a fellow student in her art class. Rumours erupt that the two women are involved, and soon gossip turns to fact when Sonoko frantically pushes herself onto Mitsuko - who proves to be more than willing. Sonoko is more than forthcoming with her husband, Kotaro (*Blind Beast's* Eiji Funakoshi), but becomes distraught upon learning that Mitsuko is engaged to the shifty Eijiro (Yusuke Kawazu). Even more strangely, Eijiro knows of the women's involvement and insists they continue their relationship through Mitsuko's marriage. A literal blood oath, double crosses, infidelities galore, and two group suicide pacts ensue before the appropriately morose conclusion.

Based upon a novel of the same name by Junichirô Tanizaki (who also wrote *Kagi*, the source for Tinto Brass' *The Key*), *Manji* speeds along so quickly one can only wonder how it will possibly manage to keep up its pace for a feature length running time. Somehow director Yasuzo Masumura pulls it off, from the haunting opening credits through the story itself (told in flashback by Sonoko to a police inspector - thus ensuring the proper tragic air). All of the actors operate at a fever pitch, but the gorgeous Ayako Wakao takes top honours as the central love object, a manipulative, pouting, tender, and perplexing woman whose motives may seem different from one viewer to the next.

Italian director Liliana Cavani (*The Night Porter*) adapted the same novel in 1985 as *The Berlin Affair*, transposing the tangled story to Nazi Germany with supremely eccentric results. Interestingly, Pino Donaggio's string-laden score for that version strongly recalls *Manji*'s eerie quasi-classical chamber music, which wafts in and out of the story at just the right moments.

As with their other Masumura titles, Fantoma has done a thorough job of presenting a rarely seen gem to international audiences. The transfer appears once again to originate from a Japanese production house, as the brightness levels are a bit higher than usual and conform more closely to Japanese standards. Adjust your TV set or DVD player accordingly, but the image quality is top notch in terms of colour and detail. The mono soundtrack is also stronger than usual, with even the most ear-splitting dialogue free of distortion. The disc comes with a panting theatrical trailer, the usual filmographies and promotional stills, and extremely useful liner notes by Earl Jackson, Jr. which, among many other things, explain the odd, reversed swastika symbol - "manji" - whose presence on the cover and during the main credits may cause viewers to erroneously expect some sort of oddball statement on lesbian chic fascism.

MANTIS IN LACE

Colour, 1968, 84m. / Directed by William Rotsler / Starring Susan Stewart, Stuart Lancaster / Image (US R0 NTSC)

One of the key films bridging sexploitation and gory horror, *Mantis in Lace* belongs with such sordid company as Michael and Roberta Findley's *Flesh* series and the kitschy *Olga* torture films. However, *Mantis* is a considerably more enjoyable film, at least on a surface level, thanks to its heavy helpings of psychedelia and go go dance numbers, aided in no small amount by imaginative, colourful cinematography by Laszlo Kovacs, who went on to fame next year for his hit and run photography on *Easy Rider* (and which also includes a memorable LSD trip scene, by the way).

The plot, such as it is, concerns a troubled topless dancer named Lila (skin flick veteran Susan Stewart), whose mind is being eaten away by bad acid trips. After she gets off work, Lila takes her gentleman of the evening to a spooky warehouse, where they make passionate love capped off by a handy screwdriver in the back and a round with Lila's meat cleaver. During this drug induced butchery, Lila can only shout "Leave me alone!" over and over, followed by a period of amnesia. Led by Sergeant Collins (Steve Vincent), the police begin to close in on our murderous stripper, particularly after she offs prying shrink Stuart Lancaster (a familiar face to Russ Meyer fans).

As far as sleazy quickies go, you could certainly do a lot worse than this trippy little ghoulie. The treatment of Lila's character is actually rather interesting for the time period, culminating in an oddly humane finale that foreshadows Dario Argento's *The Stendhal Syndrome,* while the murders are executed with enough visual panache to keep horror fans happy. The film was originally released as a straight softcore film called *Lila*, but after its immediate box office failure, producer Harry Novak ushered it back into theatres in a slimmed down version, *Mantis in Lace*, with a more horrific variation of the first meat cleaver murder. Naturally the mixture of splashing blood with T&A proved irresistible to crowds tired of benign monster mashes like *House on Bare Mountain*, and a new grindhouse genre was born.

Something Weird's DVD contains the original, longer *Lila* cut in an edition which can only be described as hallucinatory in its appearance. The gaudy colours have never looked more eye popping, and the negative used to creative this transfer is close to immaculate. The disc also includes a variety of nasty nuggets like the alternate *Mantis* murder sequence (containing added acid effects like a masked guy holding a bunch of bananas, some gory footage of blood spattering on Stewart, and a nasty cannibalistic punchline), the *Lila* theatrical trailer, a fun 20 minute educational short called "LSD: Trip or Trap" ("Maybe the world sure is all fouled up, but we don't have to do our bit to make it worse!"), the climactic colour trip scene from *Alice in Acidland*, a campy tropical go go loop called "Lady in a Cage," and a gallery of Novak exploitation posters accompanied by lurid radio spots. The real jewel, though, is no less than one hour and forty minutes of *Mantis* outtakes, including more gore, more trip footage, more nudity and sex, and anything else you could imagine. You can also see undoctored footage of such hilarious LSD visuals as a smashing piñata and the aforementioned banana man. Since these were also lifted from the original camera negative, the quality of the outtakes is also quite stunning and equal to the film itself (while actually surpassing it in running time as well!). The package is rounded out with a "Something Weird Trailer Park" containing previews for *The Mad Butcher, The Curious Dr. Humpp*, and *Frankenstein's Castle of Freaks*.

MARIHUANA

B&W, 1936, 56m. / Directed by Dwain Esper / Starring Harley Wood, Hugh McArthur

ASSASSIN OF YOUTH

B&W, 1937, 73m. / Directed by Elmer Clifton / Starring Luana Walters, Arthur Gardner

REEFER MADNESS (DOPED YOUTH)

B&W, 1936, 65m. / Directed by Louis J. Gasnier / Starring Dorothy Short, Kenneth Craig
Image (US R0 NTSC)

 Anyone who went to high school in the past few decades can recall sitting through "scare films," those graphic educational shorts shown on cheap videotape or scratchy 16mm prints in which impressionable youths are taught the horrific consequences of indulging in drinking, drugs, loose sex, and other forms of moral turpitude. This peculiar art form is really nothing new; in the early days of the Hayes Code in Hollywood, exploitation producers made a killing by churning out feature length moral lessons which also provided a quick and easy way to include nudity, violence, and trashiness, all coated with a family-friendly message. (For a great spoof, check out Joe Dante's twist on this subgenre in the final skit from *Amazon Women on the Moon*.) Something Weird has now paid tribute to these huckster classics with a triple header of pothead wonders: *Marihuana (The Weed with Roots in Hell), Assassin of Youth,* and the immortal *Reefer Madness*.

In *Marihuana*, the handiwork of mind-bending director Dwain Esper (*Maniac, Narcotic*), a batch of homely and suspiciously old-looking teens are turned on to the joys of those odd little cigarettes with a funny smell. Naturally the local pot dealers want their youthful customers to be instantly hooked, so pot parties thus transform into debauched orgies of giggling, skinny-dipping (yes, there is nudity), and Lord knows what else. Can the madness

be stopped? Can the snooping local reporter warn parents before it's too late? What do you think?

For a very similar treatment of the same subject, *Assassin of Youth* (also known as *Marihuana* - how's that for confusing?) begins when high school girl Joan (Luana Walters) winds up making friends with some dope fiends at school, leading her to antisocial behaviour, apathy, and criminal delinquency. Naturally it's up to intrepid reporter Art Brighton (Arthur Gardner) to save the day by getting the scope on this menace to morality.

Finally, *Reefer Madness* became a sensation under its most famous title after circulating as *Tell Your Children, The Burning Question*, and *Doped Youth*, the title featured on Something Weird's print. By far the most familiar of the drug scare films, this insane little number was recently transformed into an Off-Broadway musical and has become a stock footage staple on comedy shows and late night TV. The sordid story, related by a principal to concerned members of a PTA meeting, follows poor high school girl Mary (Dorothy Short)'s increasing alarm when her brother (Carleton Young) and boyfriend Bill (Kenneth Craig) fall into the clutches of demonic dope peddlers Dave O'Brien and his adult sponsors, who throw trashy parties filled with rampant pot smoke, drinking, and loose sex. Naturally there's only one way this can all end: murder, insanity, and hysteria.

Though Madacy previously issued a wretched public domain disc of *Reefer Madness*, the other two titles are new to DVD and deserve to become at least as popular as their companion film. All three look about as good as possible given their vintage; some scratches and speckles crop up regularly, and *Reefer Madness* still looks pretty rough but much sharper than any previous video edition. Each film is allocated its own menu with animated puffs of smoke designating each chapter option, with some hilarious, judiciously placed snippets popping up before each film (including *Reefer*'s celebrated piano playing scene).

In typical SW fashion, the disc is packed (or should we say rolled?) with plenty of goodies tucked away in every little crevice. Walking sleaze film encyclopedia David F. Friedman contributes a great, off the cuff commentary during *Marihuana* discussing Dwain Esper's influence on the carnival barkers of the cinematic grindhouse and explains exactly how you got butts in the theatre seats back in those days. You also get trailers for *Marihuana, Assassin of Youth*, and *The Devil's Harvest*, along with a collage of pot-related poster art and hyperbolic radio spots. Three archival snippets include Esper's giddy short form treatise "The

Sinister Menace," a brief glimpse from the silent 1924 cowboy tokin' yarn "High on the Range" (God knows what its original title was), and a brief bit of herbal refreshment from "Wages of Sin." You could get a contact high just watching this thing!

MARNIE

Colour, 1964, 130m. / Directed by Alfred Hitchcock / Starring Tippi Hedren, Sean Connery, Diane Baker / Universal (US R1 NTSC) / WS (1.85:1) (16:9), Universal (UK R2 PAL)

 Possibly the most difficult Hitchcock film one could watch as an introduction to the Master of Suspense's style, *Marnie* is in many ways the final exam after an overview of his other Hollywood efforts. The last American film in which he seemed to be at the peak of his craft, *Marnie* left many critics and viewers cold during its initial release but steadily gained a cult following through repertory and TV screenings - and with very good reason. The circumstances behind the film's creation have become at least as famous as the film itself, and pulling the two apart can be quite tricky indeed.

Unlike most working girls, Marnie Edgar (Tippi Hedren) makes her money the old fashioned way: she steals it. Thanks to a simply name change and some handy hair colouring, she can flit from one office to another and use her looks to land a position near the company safe, where she promptly takes off with the corporate cash and leaves no traces behind. Unfortunately for Marnie, the rich, young Mark Rutland (Sean Connery) recognizes her from a past job and offers a most unusual arrangement. If she marries him, Mark will not turn her in to the police; instead, he intends to study her like an animal and discover what makes her tick. Marnie's unhappy home life stems from a dysfunctional relationship with her mother (Louise Latham), and her hatred of men drives her to seek escape by riding her beloved horse, Forio. Meanwhile Mark's sister, Lil (Diane Baker), smells a rat in her brother's marriage and uncovers a few nasty facts about Marnie which could prove to be the less than happy couple's undoing.

While Hedren had already undergone an excessive amount of physical and psychological anguish during the shooting of Hitchcock's *The Birds*, nothing could prepare her for the experience of *Marnie*. Hitch's legendary fetish for ice cold blondes resulted in his attempting to mould her according to his wishes, with miserable consequences for nearly everyone concerned. However, this situation actually served to help the film, which constantly seems to be in the grip of a psychosexual fever dream. Marnie's aversion to the colour red recalls Gregory Peck's similar affliction in *Spellbound*, but here the Freudian analysis has been dropped in favour of a probing look at two deeply twisted individuals whose only hope is to heal each other. Connery, who was about to hit the big time as James Bond, manages to evoke some sympathy for Mark, even considering what transpires on their wedding night, while Hedren is effective in a nearly impossible role. Sadly, this was the last Hitchcock film to be scored by the great Bernard Herrmann; the two parted ways during *Torn Curtain*.

Universal's presentation of *Marnie* on VHS was considered an excellent transfer at the time, but the DVD easily puts it to shame. Gone are the pastel, powdery textures we've seen for so many years; instead the image is now razor sharp and full bodied, though somewhat grainy on theatre sized televisions. Unlike the fake 1.85:1 framing imposed on *Psycho*, the widescreen presentation here is essential and reveals critical information on every side of the frame. The extras are welcome and about as extensive as possible, with an excellent documentary, "The Trouble with *Marnie*," leading the pack. Featuring input from participants like Hedren and Joseph Stefano (who was originally approached with *Marnie* as a follow up to *Psycho*), this covers all of the important ground but skirts a few of the production's more tawdry backstage episodes. Also included is the hilarious theatrical trailer and a pleasingly large, interesting gallery of stills and poster art. As with *The Birds*, Universal's UK special edition offers a flat, full frame version only with the same extras.

MARTIN

Colour, 1978, 94m. / Directed by George A. Romero / Starring John Amplas, Lincoln Maazel, Christine Forrest / Anchor Bay (US R1 NTSC)

 "Don't worry, I'm always careful with the needles," advises troubled teenager Martin to his female victim as he injects her with a sedative. In a dimly lit train compartment, he embraces her unconscious body and uses a handy razor blade to open her veins and drink her blood, modern vampire style. With this unforgettable opening, director George A. Romero reveals the same precision found in his previous studies of

M

zombies (*Night of the Living Dead*) and witchcraft (*Jack's Wife*), though *Martin* finds him taking vampire lore into dangerously personal and devastating waters.

Here the bloodsucker is an 18 year old en route to stay with his sternly traditional uncle, Cuda (Lincoln Maazel), and his more progressive cousin, Christina (Romero's wife, Christine Forrest). Cuda claims that Martin is actually over one hundred years old and is a traditional vampire who stalks the streets at night. First he will save Martin's soul, and then he will kill him. Martin doesn't take the old man's claims seriously and continues about business, wandering the streets of Pittsburgh and occasionally finding a hapless victim for nourishment. He even begins calling in to a radio talk show as "The Count" to discuss the problems of the modern day blood drinker. When Martin becomes sexually involved with a lonely housewife, however, his perspective on life begins to change.

The kind of film that horror buffs seem to adore and the general public completely shuns, *Martin* is a perfect example of Romero's personal expression as a filmmaker. The viewer is never completely sure about the true nature of Martin's identity, with eerie gothic flashbacks (in grainy black and white) serving as flashbacks or fantasies to reinforce the uneasy coexistence between past and present in his family. Romero's dark but undeniably effective sense of humour pops up when least expected, such as Martin's amusing nose-thumbing at his uncle's rabid claims and a nifty cameo by Romero himself as a priest who enjoys talking about *The Exorcist*. The violence is tastefully handled, with startling bursts of blood suddenly pooling out of characters who seem all too human. (The nastiest fate- involving a twig- is reserved for actor Al Levitsky, aka hardcore porn actor Roger Caine, during the film's most impressive suspense sequence.) The film's resonance is even stronger now, with some high profile confused teens and college students adopting quasi-vampiric lifestyles to fit into the goth lifestyle. It's clearly a dead end street, and anyone who thinks being a vampire is cool and trendy might want to take a good hard look at this film.

Die hard Romero fans will be especially pleased to see his usual compatriots working on this film, including FX master Tom Savini also appearing as Christina's boyfriend and Donald Rubinstein providing one of his finest, eeriest music scores. (Note: the Italian version, *Wampyr*, was completely reedited into chronological order and featured an alternate score by Goblin, who also were also busy rescoring the Australian shocker *Patrick* around the same time.)

Anchor Bay's DVD looks very close to the old Thorn/EMI fullscreen transfer, which was lifted from the original 16mm source materials. Colours are a little less saturated here, which causes less noise and bleeding in the picture, but the extra resolution of DVD makes it look even grainier and shows off the film's age and low budget origins to a sometimes disconcerting degree. It's not a bad presentation, but be aware that this film will never look too impressive. The limited range of the original audio recording is faithfully reproduced here, and like all other versions, it gets the job done.

The commentary track with Romero, Savini, and Amplas is just as casual and affectionate as their other collaborations, and they offer plenty of anecdotes encountered during filming. Amplas obviously gets to participate in this track much more than his other appearances, and he makes for good company. Of course, the infamous original three hour cut of *Martin* which was mysteriously stolen from Romero comes up in the conversation, making one wonder exactly where it might have strayed off to for the past twenty-plus years. The DVD also includes the terrific original US trailer, which features some exclusive footage of Amplas explaining his plight directly to the camera.

MAY MORNING

Colour, 1970, 95m. / Directed by Ugo Liberatore / Starring Jane Birkin, Alessio Orano, John Steiner / VCI (US R0 NTSC) / WS (2.35:1) (16:9)

Or, *Oxford Blues Goes to Hell*. The opening of this oh so mod depiction of Oxford college life circa 1970 offers a word of thanks to the university and its students for their participation in this film, leading one to wonder whether anyone considered just how scathingly the school is depicted here. This Italian production is something of an oddity in that it was filmed on location, and the majority of the cast members retain their original voices. However, anyone seeking a "kinky, sexy, violent thriller," as the packaging describes it, will be quite disappointed.

The presence of Italian student *Valerio (Lisa and the Devil*'s Alessio Orano) disrupts the social structure at Oxford, particularly when he establishes a love/hate relationship with Flora (pop chanteuse Jane Birkin), daughter of one of the head professors. Flora's solemn mother (Rossella Falk) has a few sexual peculiarities of her own and leaves her daughter to do what she pleases, a situation which doesn't bother Flora's snobby boyfriend (Italian sleaze vet John Steiner, who does snooty better than anyone). Valerio winds up almost bedding Flora, resulting in his being subjected to "sconcing"- a horrible, sadistic punishment in which the victim is publicly forced to, uh, drink a pitcher of beer. The film constantly counts down the plot towards May Morning, a traditional annual ritual in which Oxford students put on fancy clothes, dance to groovy music, and make out on the floor until dawn. However, as our two main characters soon learn, tradition also has some painful and violent consequences.

Like most early '70s Italian films, *May Morning* is primarily a feast for the eyes and ears. The scope photography, mod fashions, and peculiar decor (including a huge dorm room poster of Ewa Aulin in *Candy*) lift this one out of the rut of average TV movies, and as usual Birkin doesn't shy away from doing a long topless scene for no good reason. Unfortunately, there isn't a single character in the film worth caring about or identifying with, so their sorry fates leave the viewer with little more than an indifferent - shrug. The vicious, spiteful sexual assault at the end - not to mention its victim's subsequent reaction - leaves a very foul and dirty feeling over the entire film, and the grating pop score by The Tremclocs (?) even over the ugliest scenes fails to work as effective counterpoint.

Director Ugo Liberatore had previously distinguished himself as a screenwriter on such films as *Mill of the Stone Women* and later directed the much better *Damned in Venice*; here, however, he seems lost at sea trying to depict British vs. Italian class struggles and ultimately making both sides look like petty, self-absorbed jerks. For a more controlled and effective treatment of the same thematic material, check out *The Wicker Man* or *The Draughtsman's Contract* instead.

Not exactly a likely candidate for a US DVD release, *May Morning* has been rescued from oblivion by VCI. The anamorphic transfer looks very good, with the film's age only evident in some film grain and a few odd yellowish colour schemes that may or may not have been part of the original photography. The disc also includes the original American trailer for the film's brief US run (it was also known as *Murder at Oxford* and *Alba Pagana*), as well as a transcript of the UMC pressbook. The entry for Jane Birkin in particular is priceless.

THE MEDUSA TOUCH

Colour, 1978, 105m. / Directed by Jack Gold / Starring Richard Burton, Lee Remick / Carlton (UK R0 PAL)

Completely forgotten now, *The Medusa Touch* was a British attempt to combine the sensationalist horror and disaster movie genres that were littering the nation's movie screens at the time. This movie really has it all: Richard Burton at the height of his booze-induced *Exorcist II* hamminess, Lee Remick (circa *The Omen*) at her loveliest, lots of explosions, baffled policemen, a marvellous blood and thunder music score by the great Michael J. Lewis, and a truly creepy, downbeat twist ending.

The film begins with John Morlar (Richard Burton) being bashed over the head as he watches television at home. While Morlar languishes unconscious in the hospital, the police try to investigate what led to this attack and how Morlar might be connected to a disastrous plane crash. Thanks to the help of Morlar's psychiatrist (Remick), the story begins to come together. Thanks to a hefty case of telekinesis, Morlar believed he had the ability to create catastrophe wherever he went. Anyone who opposed him met a horrible death, and no institution is safe from his destructive impulses. Morlar should have died from the blow to his head, but he remains alive... which may have something to do with a large royal ceremony about to take place at Westminster Abbey.

Like something Nigel Kneale might have written on a particularly feverish day, *The Medusa Touch* may not be a "good" movie in the traditional sense, but there's something creepy and compelling about it from start to finish. Burton's subtlety-be-damned acting actually works in his favour here, and a fine roster of British actors (including Jeremy Brett, the future Sherlock Holmes) adds credibility even when events are at their silliest. The disaster scenes range from mediocre to genuinely impressive, particularly the aforementioned finale, and there's enough violence and trauma to make one wonder how on earth it got a PG rating in the US.

Only available in the US as a muddy, cheapo EP edition on videotape, *The Medusa Touch* has been released on DVD in Britain, amazingly enough. The disc is part of Carlton's budget line, The Silver Collection, so a first rate transfer wouldn't seem to be likely. Well, surprise! The film looks fantastic on DVD, taken from an immaculate print with gorgeously saturated colours. The full frame transfer exposes all of the image and looks just fine, with the tiniest details in the antiquated set design clearly visible throughout. The mono audio is likewise crystal clear and features healthy bass, a necessity for appreciating the score and all those

M

thunderous sound effects. On the other hand, the "trailer" included here is a just a promo for other Carlton titles.

MEET THE FEEBLES

Colour, 1989, 92m. / Directed by Peter Jackson / Substance (Canada R0 NTSC), Arrow (UK R2 PAL)

In the wake of his monster-budget version of *Lord of the Rings*, many forgot how New Zealand's most famous cult director, Peter Jackson, got his start. After helming the hysterical, zero budget alien gorefest *Bad Taste*, Jackson turned his satirical eye to cosy family puppet variety shows with *Meet the Feebles*, a shocking and often uproarious film performed entirely by puppets.

Heidi, the star of the *Feebles Variety Hour*, has problems: she's overweight, and her bloated walrus husband, Bletch, is a drug-dealing porno producer who's cheating on her with a Siamese cat ingénue. Meanwhile a newcomer to the show, Robert (or "Wobert") the hedgehog, falls in love with Lucy, a poodle who's drugged and seduced by a rat porno director known for filming underground S&M videos with a cow and a cockroach. And let's not forget the panty-sniffing elephant who has a love child with a chicken, the VD-infested bunny, a gay fox director, and a muckraking fly reporter who hangs out in toilets.

And that's just for starters! Sporting outrageous musical numbers from the quirky Peter Dasent and some eye-popping production design and puppet characters, this is truly a film unlike any ever made. A lot of viewers will have problems sticking with it, but for those willing to look underneath the layers of bodily fluids and gore, there's a pretty devious and clever mind at work here.

While no one could seriously expect the *Feebles* DVD (currently available only in Canada and Great Britain) to rise up to the level of, say, Universal's *The Frighteners* special edition, most will be disappointed by the bare bones presentation. The transfer is culled from the same materials used for the US VHS release, definitely an improvement from the overly dark Japanese laserdisc - but it could still look better. Like *Bad Taste*, this was never really a glossy-looking film to begin with, so some inherent softness and murkiness will likely be inherent within the film for quite a while. The gaudy colour design shines through just fine, and the daylight scenes are crystal clear. The "enhanced

audio" (as the packaging claims) sounds about the same as it always has: fine, but naturally limited by its budget.

MEMENTO

Colour, 2000, 109m. / Directed by Christopher Nolan / Starring Guy Pearce, Joe Pantoliano / Columbia (US R1 NTSC), Pathé (UK R2 PAL, France R2 PAL) / WS (2.35:1) (16:9) / DD5.1

Leonard Shelby (Pearce) is an ex-insurance investigator hunting for the man who raped and murdered his wife. The incident that left her dead also resulted in Shelby receiving a blow to the head, the upshot of which is that he has lost his ability to make new memories. Everything up until his wife's murder is clear, everything that has occurred since is forgotten within minutes of it happening. The only way Shelby is able to retain anything that may be vital to his search for the elusive killer is to make notes, take photographs and even tattoo information on his body... he's smothered with them. With the help of an apparent ally, Edward Gammell (Pantoliano), it appears as if, at last, the end of the trail is in sight.

Combine charismatic Guy Pearce (brilliant in *Ravenous*) with sleazy Joe Pantoliano (equally brilliant in *Bound*) and sultry Carrie-Anne Moss (the only salient reason for enduring the dull *Matrix*) and you get a gold-plated casting combo in a cunning and intricate thriller which you'll yearn to see at least two or three times just to comprehend its enormity. It's pretty garrulous stuff, made no easier to follow by virtue of the fact it begins at the end of the story, then proceeds to jump backwards in 5-10 minute segments. The edge of your seat suspense is derived not from seeing what happens (technically you see the conclusion of the story in the first thirty seconds), but rather in learning why it happens. As the tale retrogresses, you discover how Shelby has reached the jaw-droppingly erroneous point of violence at which we first meet him and discover more about the characters he has encountered on the way, not all of whom are who or what they first seem. And don't even think about entering the fray without your concentration in peak condition, or you may blink and miss the stealthily planted subliminal clues scattered throughout, all of which become pertinent during the final devastating revelations.

Pearce is perfection as Shelby, conveying a genuine sense of tragedy at his dual loss (wife and memory) yet still able to invoke wry humour from his debilitating condition. Pantoliano and Moss lend excellent support. Quite possibly the best movie to come out of 2000, this one will haunt you long after you've ejected the little silver disc.

In Britain, *Memento* first fell victim to the reprehensible "rental only" window, languishing there for some months with no sign of a sell-through release in sight (while the film was playing concurrently in US theatres). Meanwhile it became available to purchase only on Region 2 PAL format in France and Spain, although a nearly no-frills Region 1 release in the USA was eventually released in Autumn 2001. The Pathé and original Columbia releases offer trailers (one in French and the same thing over again in English with burnt-in French subtitles on the French version, obviously), a Nolan interview, the short story "Memento Mori," a tattoo gallery, and DVD-Rom material. The film itself is naturally enough a flawless presentation, divided by 18 chapters (with sound options in English and French, plus subtitling in French only on the French edition). Rather uniquely this disc also offers one the opportunity to watch the film backwards (or, in terms of time-line narrative, forwards), but it's ultimately a rather superfluous option and not nearly as rewarding an experience as viewing it in the manner intended. The US Columbia two-disc special edition, which arrived much later, includes a dizzying amount of video and text extras accessible from some "mind game" menus, in addition to commentaries and hidden treats which should keep fans busy for hours on end. - TG

MESA OF LOST WOMEN

B&W, 1953, 70m. / Directed by Ron Ormond and Herbert Tevos / Starring Jackie Coogan, Mary Hill / Image (US R0 NTSC)

Given all the ink devoted to Ed Wood in recent years, it's time now to take a quick look at the career of one of his contemporaries, the equally skewed filmmaker Ron Ormond. He and his wife, June, made a living churning out dozens of "educational" short films, exploitation quickies, and westerns before finally discovering the wonders of Christianity. Their greatest (and sadly, mostly unseen) contribution to modern civilization is undoubtedly *If Footmen Tire You, What Will Horses Do?*, a lunatic fundamentalist depiction of America's invasion by Jesus-hating, drawling Russkies who perform bloodthirsty acts that would make H.G. Lewis squirm. Until someone gets around to salvaging this nasty little number, at least we have a DVD edition of *Mesa of Lost Women*, a close contender behind *Footmen* in the wacko film sweepstakes, written by Hungarian one hit wonder Herbert Tevos and directed by Ormond, who reportedly took over for Tevos behind the camera.

The rambling, often incoherent storyline takes place out in the Muerto Desert (which the jabbering narrator helpfully translates), where the nefarious, one-eyed Dr. Araña (Jackie Coogan - yep, Uncle Fester from *The Addams Family*) manipulates human glands to produce horrific spider women destined to prey on humans. He also keeps some dwarves handy, too, because they make the best lab assistants. A recent asylum escapee, he and his undying creations find their latest prey when a planeload of idiot tourists (including a jaw-droppingly stereotyped Asian valet named Wu) go wandering off into the woods, exchange awkward dedications of love (and cigarettes), and dodge the clutches of the spider women, one of whom, Tarantella, had earlier put in a showstopping dance number at the local cantina. Before that we're treated to the irrelevant story of another poor guy who goes wandering into the desert, intercut with scenes of Coogan explaining his plans to conquer the world. Meanwhile the soundtrack thrums constantly with pseudo-Mexican guitar and piano music guaranteed to drive your fingernails down into your seat. Sensing a winner, Ed Wood naturally seized it and used the same music again in *Jail Bait*. Fans of Coogan may be disappointed that he doesn't particularly humiliate himself here, but bad movie fans will be more than content with Mesa's assemblage of dropped plot threads, wooden acting, gaping hurdles of logic, and a physically impaired giant spider.

Though barely over an hour in length, this is one of those films able to transcend the limits of time, stretching out indefinitely until you're convinced there's no way it will ever end. Largely a staple of blurry late night TV showings and the unwatchable public domain tape circuit, the film looks sharper on DVD but still bears those telltale scratches, speckles, and blips that tell you this is one obscure, battered up piece of celluloid offal. These could very well be the finest elements in existence, given the patchwork nature of the film and a total absence of technical polish; just don't expect anything close to the razor-sharp clarity and blemish-free standards of other releases in the Wade Williams collection. Just enjoy the fact that this one is out on DVD at all and in watchable condition. The disc also includes the theatrical trailer, which offers a much closer look at Tarantella's killer fingernails which remain noticeably absent in this cut of the film itself.

M

THE MIGHTY PEKING MAN

Colour, 1977, 90m. / Directed by Homer Gaugh (Ho Meng-Hwa) / Starring Li Hsiu-Hsien (Danny Lee), Evelyne Kraft / Buena Vista (US R1 NTSC) / WS (2.35:1) (16:9)

An utterly berserk attempt to ride the very short coattails of Dino De Laurentiis' 1976 version of *King Kong*, this Hong Kong production (originally titled *Hsing Hsing Wang*) first amazed drive-in viewers under the name *Goliathon* throughout the late '70s before disappearing to the wilderness of late night television. Ever the cinematic archaeologist, Quentin Tarantino's Rolling Thunder Pictures salvaged this oddity from oblivion to greet a new, appalled public, and the results have been lovingly preserved on DVD.

Legend has it that a remote jungle area in India is the stomping ground for a huge, ape-like creature known as the *Mighty Peking Man*. An expedition controlled by the greedy Norman Chu (*We Are Going to Eat You*) recruits the aid of young adventurer Johnnie Fang (a young, shaggy-haired Danny Lee, who is recovering from the heartbreak of discovering his girl in bed with his best friend. Out in the wilderness he encounters a beautiful blonde woman (Russian actress Evelyne Kraft), who swings Tarzan-like from vines and somehow barely conceals her body with a sticky piece of fabric. In fact she became a soulmate to the Mighty Peking Man after her parents died in a plane crash when she was a child; she then introduces our hero to the giant ape, who is a bit uncomfortable when he spies his little blonde woman making the beast with two backs with Lee. Pretty soon it's back to Kong territory as the ape is packed up for the big city, where he doesn't take very well to all the big buildings and loud noises.

A thoroughly loony movie, *The Mighty Peking Man* is nowhere near being good in any cinematic category at all. However, it still piles on the entertainment value thanks to its howlingly awful dubbing and wacko plot tangents, such as a kitschy romantic montage (complete with pop music) that should leave the most stone-faced viewer howling for mercy. Somehow Roger Ebert, not exactly a model of critical consistency, gave this a thumbs up and proclaimed it "Genius!" (according to the cover box) while trashing Lucio Fulci's *The Beyond*. Can anyone offer an explanation? Buena Vista's DVD looks remarkably good for a zero budget Hong Kong movie from the '70s. Some awkward splices in the

source material still crop up, but the print itself is exceptionally clean and colourful, certainly the best this film has looked in ages. The dubbed audio (English only, of course) sounds fine for mono, with no distracting hiss or crackling.

The DVD also includes the original English-language trailer (with the Rolling Thunder logos tacked on) as well as the trailer for *Switchblade Sisters*, a radically different cult item also presented by Rolling Thunder.

MIRANDA

Colour, 1985, 94m. / Directed by Tinto Brass / Starring Serena Grandi, Andrea Occhipinti / Arrow (UK R0 PAL)

In 1983, Tinto Brass returned to low budget Italian films with *The Key*, a visually refined softcore opus briefly released on British videotape. More widely available is its 1985 follow-up, *Miranda*, which pushed the boundaries just up to the verge of hardcore without losing any of the director's trademark compositions.

Top-heavy Serena Grandi (*The Grim Reaper, Delirium*) stars in the title role as a lusty tavern owner carrying on an affair with the local village stud (horror regular Andrea Occhipinti), all the while scouting around for a suitable lifetime mate. Among her conquests are a middle aged politician, Norman (Andy J. Forrest), and a visiting American soldier with peculiar outdoor bathroom habits. Meanwhile she uses her wiles to torment her sexually frustrated head waiter, Carlo (Franco Interlinghi), before fate finally steps in and she winds up choosing the man of her dreams.

One of Brass' wittiest films, *Miranda* benefits from a sharp, pun-laden script lifted from a farcical Carlo Collodi play. Meanwhile, Grandi lets loose with a completely uninhibited performance, her look changing from one sequence to the next in an amazing succession of glamorous, sexy set pieces.

Bootleg videotapes of this title have been floating around for ages, so the Arrow DVD can't help but look better in comparison. However, while the compositions (intended for 1.66:1 projection) aren't unduly harmed by the full frame transfer, the image is plagued by distracting compression artefacts and pale contrast; however, the film is completely intact (including some shots that must have flickered by when the BBFC wasn't looking) and represents the most acceptable overall presentation to date.

The disc also includes a ribald European theatrical trailer (letterboxed, natch) and a subtitled interview with Brass on the set of his *Trasgredire* (which also appears on the discs of *All Ladies Do It* and, without subtitles, *Trasgredire* itself).

THE MIRROR CRACK'D

Colour, 1980, 106m. / Directed by Guy Hamilton / Starring Angela Lansbury, Elizabeth Taylor, Rock Hudson, Kim Novak / Anchor Bay (US R1 NTSC) / WS (1.85:1) (16:9)

 Since all-star murder mysteries and disaster films were all the rage during the late '70s, it was inevitable that someone would turn to Agatha Christie's Miss Marple mysteries. After all, *Murder on the Orient Express* and *Death on the Nile* had been big hits for Christie's other major sleuth, Hercule Poirot, and Margaret Rutherford had previously pulled off a quartet of decidedly unfaithful but enjoyable Marple mysteries in the '50s. This time a disturbingly young Angela Lansbury was caked up in old lady makeup as the frail but brilliant amateur detective, but she definitely takes a back seat to the high voltage star power on display in the line up of suspects.

The tranquil village of St. Mary Mead is sent into a tizzy when American director Jason Rudd (Rock Hudson) and his wife, Marina (Elizabeth Taylor), arrive to shoot a film about Mary, Queen of Scots. A welcome dinner party turns into a catty bitchfest when Marina's new co-star and rival, Lola Brewster (Kim Novak), shows up unexpectedly with her husband, producer Marty Fenn (Tony Curtis). As the fur flies, murder strikes unexpectedly when poor star struck Heather Babcock (Maureen Bennett) drops dead from a poisoned daiquiri during the soiree. Evidence soon mounts indicating that someone could have an axe to grind with Marina, and it's up to Miss Marple to put the pieces together and dig up some nasty secrets from the past to unmask the murderer.

Though wildly uneven, *The Mirror Crack'd* (which takes its title from Tennyson's "The Lady of Shallott") offers some nice treats for mystery fans, particularly the delicious opening sequence, an homage to old dark house whodunits called Murder by Moonlight (featuring an appearance by *Story of O*'s Sir Stephen himself, Anthony Steel!). Naturally the film breaks just before the murderer is revealed, leaving audience member Miss Marple to fill in the blanks. From a mystery angle the plot is somewhat lacking, as it dispenses with much of Christie's more complex narrative and whittles down the number of suspects to virtually nothing. However, Taylor and Novak notch the camp value up through the roof, and you'll probably never see a cast like this assembled for such a "little" picture again. Director Guy Hamilton, better known for his work on several James Bond films, is obviously cruising on autopilot here but does a good job of keeping the pace going while the stars chomp hunks out of the scenery. The late, great Charles Gray also turns up as a butler, and the always reliable Edward Fox puts in a good if underused turn as Miss Marple's nephew and fellow sleuth, Inspector Craddock. Keep your expectations low and enjoy.

Like most other EMI films, *The Mirror Crack'd* has passed through several hands over the years, beginning with a fuzzy full frame VHS transfer from Thorn/EMI. The same master was later used for a briefly available HBO/Image laserdisc, and the film since passed out of public hands for quite a while before returning to Republic via Canal Plus. Anchor Bay's version is by far the best looking of the bunch; while some of the photography has a deliberately misty veneer, the detail is much crisper than before. Colours also look just fine, and the 1.85:1 framing adds a bit to the sides while lopping off some excess headroom compared to the old transfer. The disc also contains a fun theatrical trailer, two TV spots ("You may not have liked her last film, but that's no reason to kill her!"), bios and filmographies for the major cast members, and a fold out booklet with an Agatha Christie primer.

MISSISSIPPI MERMAID

Colour, 1969, 122m. / Directed by François Truffaut / Starring Jean-Paul Belmondo, Catherine Deneuve / MGM (US R1 NTSC) / WS (2.35:1)

 After a brief addition to the world of his alter ego Antoine Doinel with *Stolen Kisses*, François Truffaut returned to Hitchcock country with *Mississippi Mermaid (La sirène du Mississippi)*. Like *The Bride Wore Black*, the film was adapted from a Cornell Woolrich novel, *Waltz into Darkness* (remade in 2001 as *Original Sin* with Angelina Jolie and Antonio Banderas). Despite the title, there are no mermaids, Mississippian or otherwise; instead it's back to the familiar territory of *amour fou* with the usual deadly consequences.

On the isolated island of Reunion, tobacco plantation owner Louis Mahe (Jean-Paul Belmondo)

M

eagerly greets his new bride, Julie Roussel (Catherine Deneuve), with whom he has been corresponding by mail. Though she doesn't really look like the girl in the photographs he has received, Louis carries on with their prompt wedding and finds her a very receptive bride. Unfortunately, their connubial bliss is shattered when Julie vanishes, taking all of Louis' money along with her. Armed with a pistol and recovering from a nervous breakdown, Louis hunts her down and discovers the woman he loves is actually someone else entirely. Louis re-establishes his relationship with the beautiful siren, but his willingness to go along with her dangerous impulses proves to have an unnaturally high price.

As with his previous Woolrich adaptation, Truffaut altered the book's more fatalistic ending in favour of a more complicated, enigmatic resolution which forces the audience to fill in the story's blanks. Critics at the time were lukewarm at best towards this film, no doubt in part thanks to United Artists' decision to hack away 13 vital minutes (including an exceptional fireside discussion between Deneuve and Belmondo). Time has been kind, however, and *Mermaid* (whose incongruous name comes from Belmondo's boat) stands as a work as emotionally rich and satisfying as the director's other 1960s films.

While Belmondo is excellent as always, Deneuve fans in particular will enjoy seeing one of the world's most beautiful women going through a wide variety of physical transformations, from demure and innocent bride to a gaudy showgirl to a cold-hearted predator. Regardless of her demeanour from scene to scene, she's always a pleasure to watch and makes a most alluring femme fatale. *Mississippi Mermaid* was Truffaut's first (and final) film in scope after 1961's Jules and Jim, and his use of the wide framing is essential to understanding the psychological interactions of the characters.

Like the previous laserdisc edition, MGM's DVD retains the original aspect ratio and does an adequate job of capturing the difficult colour schemes, consisting primarily of brown, orange, and gold. The location shooting and strangely lit interiors result in more film grain than most home viewers would probably prefer, but this film will never look too slick and polished. The source material (from the uncut European prints struck for a limited reissue in the early '90s) contains some distracting nicks and scratches during the first reel, but overall the presentation is acceptable if not outstanding.

The optional white subtitles in English, Spanish, or French appear in the lower letterbox band and are

much larger than the laserdisc subs. The DVD also contains the excellent UA theatrical trailer, narrated by none other than Rod Serling.

MODERN VAMPIRES

Colour, 1998, 96m. / Directed by Richard Elfman / Starring Casper Van Dien, Natasha Gregson Wagner, Kim Cattrall, Rod Steiger, Udo Kier / Sterling (US R1 NTSC) / DD2.0

One of the more unlikely straight to video titles in recent years, *Modern Vampires* (known as *Revenant* in Europe) sports a surprisingly high profile cast and enough clever twists and turns to make one regret that gutsy horror projects like this usually don't wind up on the big screen anymore. Cleverly helmed by the delirious Richard Elfman (*Forbidden Zone, Shrunken Heads*), this isn't a perfect film by a long shot but should develop a sizable cult following, if enough people actually get the opportunity to see it.

Dallas (*Starship Troopers'* Casper Van Dien), a world weary vampire, returns to Los Angeles after twenty years in exile. The Count (Robert Pastorelli) receives his presence with less than open arms; even worse, Dr. Van Helsing (Rod Steiger, sporting a funny accent akin to Dr. Evil) has arrived from Germany to kill Dallas, who was responsible for turning Van Helsing's son. Van Helsing recruits a funny gangsta crew of vampire killers, including *Fallen*'s Gabriel Casseus, while Dallas busies himself transforming a trashy wannabe indie vampire, Nico (Natasha Gregson Wagner), into a sleekly elegant bloodsucker. When the two foes finally face each other down, much fang-baring and staking ensues.

Modern Vampires' greatest strength lies in its supporting characters, with Kim Cattrall doing a hysterical, heavily accented routine as the uptown Ulrike (imagine Teri Garr in *Young Frankenstein*, but with fangs). Craig Ferguson, familiar as the British overlord boss on *The Drew Carrey Show*, also has an amusing turn as an overzealous bisexual predator (with the best throwaway lines), and Pastorelli makes an unlikely but funny Count. Van Dien and Wagner essentially carry the film as the two "straight" leads, with most of the comic bits relegated to everyone else, but they make a great looking couple and seem to be giving their all. Udo Kier (*Blood for Dracula*) does yet another maniacal variation on his signature role in a funny extended cameo. Finally, rising teen star Natasha Lyonne once again rises above an underwritten part to provide some sass as Wagner's low class lesbian protégée (and what's with all the Natashas in this movie, anyway?). However, the film itself is far from perfect. Had Elfman been given a reasonable budget and more resources, *Modern Vampires* could have been one of the year's most noteworthy genre films, but it's ultimately hampered in the end by its chintzy budget (the flat TV look doesn't help), as well as a few terribly strained lines and too much artsy editing in several of the attack and sex scenes. Still, for adventurous horror fans, this is guaranteed to grab your attention and is definitely miles ahead *of Dracula: Dead and Loving It.*

The DVD from Sterling features a good if unspectacular fullscreen transfer. No significant information seems to be missing from the image, though it doesn't really look open matte either. The red on black opening credits look awful, but the quality improves dramatically during the film itself. The standard surround audio gets the job done, with a few flashy panning effects and a nicely separated music score (filled with those typical Danny Elfman choral voices, as well as homages to everything from Handel to the theme from *Lolita*). The DVD contains the unrated director's cut, and they really do mean it; some surprisingly rough gore and full frontal nudity (not to mention a general air of kinkiness) definitely qualify this as non-MPAA friendly material. The disc also features trailers for this and *Progeny,* as well as a sincere but bland 12 minute "making of" featurette in which everyone involved takes turns praising their co-workers.

Elfman and Van Dien also provide an audio commentary in which they enthusiastically recount the various low budget difficulties encountered in getting the film off the ground. While Elfman's biting and eccentric comments come as no surprise, Van Dien manages to keep up with him throughout and makes some fine, insightful observations along the way, proving he really is more than your average coverboy. Where both men go from here should be very interesting to observe indeed; let's just hope they manage to keep their sense of humour. In the end, Elfman must be simply credited for managing to pull off something seemingly impossible: a film with no sympathetic characters, gender bending sex, and extreme gore that also happens to be a good natured comedy.

MON ONCLE D'AMERIQUE

Colour, 1980, 87m. / Directed by Alain Resnais / Starring Gérard Depardieu, Nicole Garcia / New Yorker (US R1 NTSC)

Back in the 1960s, director Alain Resnais was all the rage with his brain-teasing visual puzzles like *Hiroshima Mon Amour* and *Last Year at Marienbad.* However, his style transformed over the years, as he took increasingly tremendous amounts of time to work on each project before finally settling into apparent retirement. With *Mon Oncle d'Amerique (or My American Uncle),* Resnais collaborates with renowned psychologist Henri Laborit (who also appears in the film) to produce a discerning, often hilarious study of human behaviour and its consequences.

The delicate chain of cause and effect concerns three people and their struggles to achieve happiness and equilibrium: Rene (Gérard Depardieu), a businessman faced with the impending threat of being laid off; Janine (Nicole Garcia), an actress who must decide on the proper moral choice when her lover's wife becomes terminally ill; and Jean Le Gall (Roger Pierre), an ambitious, politically motivated executive and writer slammed with an early midlife crisis. All of these stories revolve around the concept of a (fictitious?) American uncle, a symbol of the idealism by which a benevolent force will arrive and solve everyone's problems.

More recognizably human and witty than some of Resnais' past films, this fragile little treat replaces his trademark visual flashiness with a wry look at the depths of man's soul, which isn't quite the perilous trip one might imagine. Resnais' usual cinematographer, the amazing Sacha Vierny, works his usual alchemy here, transforming hallways, kitchen, and offices into striking visual tableaux, while incorporating organic depictions of nature to mirror the film's themes in a manner similar to his later work for director Peter Greenaway, particularly *A Zed and Two Noughts.*

New Yorker's DVD of *Mon Oncle d'Amerique* is derived from the same master as their previous videotape version. The full frame image looks well composed but may be marginally cropped from a 1.66:1 aspect ratio. The burned-in yellow subtitles are easy to read but sometimes smear onto the image. The film itself is a rather chalky, grainy affair, so any defects of the DVD itself are hard to judge. Detail levels are acceptable, and colour levels look fine if unspectacular.

The rather overpriced disc also includes a Resnais filmography and print interview, as well as a well chosen reproduction of the original poster art on the front of the packaging.

M

MONA LISA

Colour, 1986, 104m. / Directed by Neil Jordan / Starring Bob Hoskins, Cathy Tyson, Michael Caine / Criterion (US R1 NTSC) / WS (1.66:1), Anchor Bay (UK R2 PAL) / WS (1.85:1) (16.9) / DD 5.1

One of the crucial films in the art house revolution of the '80s, Neil Jordan's *Mona Lisa* was a dramatic change of pace from the director's previous critical success, the delirious 1984 fairytale meditation, *The Company of Wolves*. In many respects *Mona Lisa* could be seen as a transitional piece towards the crime drama subversion which Jordan pushed to extremes with *The Crying Game*, while Bob Hoskins turns in yet another magnificent performance after his memorable hardboiled turn in *The Long Good Friday*. Drawing on the iconography of both film noir and rough and tumble British gangster sagas, this one of a kind film has lost none of its power to astonish.

In the haunting and wry opening sequence, flower carrying ex-convict George (Hoskins) returns from prison to his warm and comfy home only to receive a slammed door in the face. Mortwell (Michael Caine), a mobster with a heart of ice, takes on George as the chauffeur to high priced call girl Simone (Cathy Tyson). The driver and the hooker are initially resentful of each other but gradually come to a deeper understanding, particularly when she tries to polish George up and pass him off as an upper crust member of society. He even attempts to rescue one of Simone's less fortunate colleagues, May (a young Sammi Davis), from life on the streets, but this proves to be the first of several unexpected and emotionally loaded reversals.

Though it could have been little more than a glorified TV movie in lesser hands, *Mona Lisa* succeeds thanks to its razor sharp performances. Hoskins and Tyson create some genuinely compelling chemistry, while Caine is terrifying in what could best be described as his character from *Get Carter* many years down the road and devoid of any conscience.

As usual Jordan's visual style is gripping, from the rain-washed Soho streets dappled with neon to the dimly lit motel rooms which seem to hide a secret behind every mirror. Both the visual and narrative aspects would impact much of Jordan's future work, such as the thwarted romances in the aforementioned *The Crying Game* (particularly its relationship between Jaye Davidson and Stephen Rea), *The End of the Affair*, and *Interview with the Vampire*. Even had Jordan stopped with this film, however, that would have been enough.

Criterion's DVD directly transposes their transfer and extras prepared for the laserdisc release. While the image quality is a tad sharper, it looks about the same and unfortunately is not anamorphically enhanced. Black levels are also a bit lighter and more washed out than normal, but a little adjustment to your TV or DVD player settings can tweak it back into shape. Otherwise the colours and detail are just fine. The mono audio sounds identical to previous releases, with the melancholy Nat "King" Cole tune kicking off the elegant soundtrack punctuated with dialogue rendered in numerous British dialects. (Viewers outside the UK might benefit from the optional English subtitles!)

Extras include the US theatrical trailer (which shows what a hard sell this thing was back in '86) and a commentary track with Jordan and Hoskins. Obviously at ease with each other, both men have plenty to say about the characters' motivations, the conscious attempts to deal with established genres, and the methods of creating a new look out of locations used in numerous other British productions. The UK disc contains two soundtrack options (mono and a 5.1 remix), the commentary track, the trailer, and video interviews with Jordan and Hoskins.

MONKEY SHINES

Colour, 1988, 114m. / Directed by George A. Romero / Starring Jason Beghe, John Pankow, Stanley Tucci / MGM (US R1 NTSC) / WS (1.85:1) (16:9) / DD4.0

A restrained psychological horror effort from Pittsburgh's greatest filmmaker, *Monkey Shines* vanished almost immediately upon its theatrical release and has remained strangely neglected ever since. While not Romero's greatest work by a long shot, the film does display many of his savvy filmmaking gifts for suspense and characterization while spinning an entertaining and sometimes frightening yarn.

Allan (Jason Beghe), an athletic young man, is injured in a car accident which leaves him paralyzed from the neck down. Miserable with his confined existence, he finds his internal rage building as he is saddled with an unsympathetic nurse (Christine Forrest, aka Mrs. Romero) and an irritating bird. His girlfriend, Linda (Janine Turner), tries to help him, but the real aid seems to come from his shady friend

M

Geoffrey (*Mad about You*'s John Pankow), who supplies Allan with a cute little monkey as a kind of helper around the house. The monkey, Ella, belongs to a test group of monkeys being scientifically manipulated to become abnormally intelligent and responsive to human commands. Unfortunately, Ella and Allan begin to bond a little too closely, as the recipients of Allan's mounting rage start to turn up dead... and it seems little Ella may be the one responsible.

Nicely acted and visually slick, *Monkey Shines* perhaps remains most significant as the first real example of how Romero could manipulate his own style within the confines of a studio system (in this case, Orion). While *Creepshow* was distributed by Warner, he largely had carte blanche on that film; here he was forced to answer to higher powers, who nixed his original ending (which finds researchers packing up trucks with dozens of little Ellas in training in favour of a more streamlined, upbeat finale laced with a phoney, *Carrie*-style shock ending. The tampering really doesn't hurt, though one's mind can certainly play around with the idea of a sequel - something like a monkey version of *The Crazies*. Oddly, the studio had no problem with the film's rather protracted two hour running time, which could have used just a little trimming to speed up the pace.

After a few intermittent appearances on home video, the film has finally been treated to a decent transfer thanks to its acquisition by MGM. Amazingly, they even lavished upon it a new 16:9 transfer that arguably makes the film look better than it did in theatres. The fullscreen version, which is open matte and loses nothing on the sides, looks excellent as well, and while neither version may be quite as visually ravishing as a film shot this year, the results are nevertheless quite impressive. Like most Romero films, the framing doesn't matter much one way or the other, as he generally frames everything important dead in the middle of the scene. The Dolby surround soundtrack is cleaner and punchier than the earlier Orion master, with David Shire's serviceable score creeping nicely from all four channels. Also includes the original US trailer.

MONSTERS CRASH THE PAJAMA PARTY

B&W/Colour, 2001, 214m. / Image (US R0 NTSC)

This is a hugely enjoyable presentation, especially if you put aside cynicism and allow yourself to watch some of the corniest horror-vaudeville on celluloid.

What makes it work is an ingenious redesign of the DVD experience. The standard menu format is dispensed with altogether: instead, Something Weird's Mike Vraney has taken the Easter-egg principle into orbit, with the access points for more than three and a half hours of spook-show ephemera hidden within ghostly cartoon landscapes - there are no written headings, no chapters or lists, simply use the cursor of your DVD remote to explore and see what you find!

Part of the pleasure of this package is the sheer wealth of oddball clips and short featurettes included. Some are perfect at just a few minutes in length whilst others are best observed with a gathering of friends, in the mood to lob good-natured abuse at the lamer items. For instance, short film *Monsters Crash the Pajama Party* may have given the package its excellently lurid title but it's actually a pretty inane piece of work, and on its own would scarcely be worth mentioning. More substantial is the surprise inclusion of Bert I. Gordon's black-and-white ghost feature *Tormented!* from 1960. It's this unpredictable shuffling of contents, where a feature film is merely another "extra" among hordes of shorts, trailers and assorted off-cuts that makes the whole thing work.

The contents are listed on the back cover, but there's so much to take in you soon lose track and surrender to the DVD's layout concept. Something Weird are to be commended for coming up with an entirely new style of home-viewing pleasure, and should also be admired for their canny way of marketing some creakier-than-a-tomb-door archive material.

For the record, the features to be discovered here include a special "Hypnoscope" Introduction, the 45-minute *Monsters Crash the Pajama Party* (1965), the 72-minute *Tormented!*, "Asylum of the Insane" 3D short subject (two pairs of glasses included), 45-minute Spooks-a-Poppin' Trailer Show, Spooky Musical Soundies, Horror Home Productions, the educational short "Don't Be Afraid," a short subject spook house ride, "Drive-In Werewolf" (a family friendly clip from *Dracula the Dirty Old Man*), "Chased By Monsters" short subject, a gallery of spook show stills and exploitation art with radio spot rarities, "How To Put On Your Own Spook Show" illustrated essay, audio commentaries by ghostmasters Philip "Dr. Evil" Morris and Harry "Dr. Jekyl" Wise, and an illustrated spook show history booklet by Jim Ridenour. - ST

MOONRAKER

Colour, 1979, 126m. / Directed by Lewis Gilbert / Starring Roger Moore, Lois Chiles / MGM / WS (2.35:1) (16:9) / DD5.1

Following the hijacking of a Moonraker space shuttle, James Bond (Moore) is assigned to investigate. His enquiries take him from California to Venice, where it appears that the industrialist owner of the shuttle manufacturing plant, Hugo Drax (Lonsdale), was involved in its disappearance. Travelling on to Rio and then the jungles of Brazil, Bond blasts off into space for a rendezvous aboard Drax's celestial satellite outpost orbiting the Earth, where the true enormity of his plans for global annihilation are revealed.

The comfortable blend of action and humour established in *The Spy Who Loved Me* as best fitted to Roger Moore's interpretation of 007 misfires in *Moonraker*, which ladles out the funnies with all the subtlety of a second rate variety act. The screenplay by Christopher Wood (who authored the "Confessions" books under the nom de plume Timothy Lea) is laden with misjudged slapstick. After the embarrassment of Bond's trip through Venice in a gondola-cum-hovercraft the film never quite regains its dignity. Michael Lonsdale is one of the better facets, a suitably urbane baddie whose one-liners often upstage Bond's ("At least I shall have the pleasure of putting you out of my misery"). Richard Kiel - 7ft 2ins. of razor-toothed bulk, whose reluctance to lay down and die was a novel and amusing ingredient of *Spy* - returns as a gurning idiot. Lois Chiles is barely adequate as love interest Holly Goodhead (and fails to appear in the skimpy costume she's wearing on the poster art!); Corinne (*Story of O*) Clery is far better but exits too early, mauled by ravenous Dobermans.

Yet irrespective of its shortcomings, the film bears some standout moments as good as, if not better than, any in Bond's history. His escape from death in the astronaut trainer is Moore's finest moment ever as 007 (no daft quip here; he's hurt and he doesn't want to talk about it). The eye-popping pre-credits in which the agent is pushed out of a plane without a parachute, commandeering one from the opposition on the way down, has yet to be surpassed.

There have certainly been worse Bonds (*A View to a Kill*) and the sheer spectacle of *Moonraker* still sets it head and shoulders above most of the wannabees, but coming from the usually reliable Lewis Gilbert it's a bitter pill to swallow.

Fortunately Bond returned to Earth - and top form - for his next adventure, *For Your Eyes Only*.

Rather slim pickings by most MGM 007 Special Edition DVD standards. The film itself is admittedly a superb quality 32-chapter divided presentation, with optional commentary supplied by director Gilbert, executive producer Michael G. Wilson, associate producer William P. Cartlidge, and scripter Wood. The "Inside *Moonraker*" documentary is lengthy and fascinating, worth watching for the stunning freefall footage alone, and concludes with some rare outtake footage interspersed through the end credits. A second, shorter documentary looks at the wizards behind some of the effects that have graced the series over the years. Finally there's a trailer and a gallery of stills and poster art. The sound is in English and French, with subtitling in French and Spanish. - TG

THE MOST DANGEROUS GAME

B&W, 1932, 63m. / Directed by Irving Pichel & Ernest B. Schoedsack / Starring Leslie Banks, Fay Wray / Criterion (US R1 NTSC)

If you ever read the short story "The Most Dangerous Game," you'll already be familiar with this film's basic premise: a wealthy madman who owns a remote island uses shipwreck survivors who wash up on his shores as prey in an elaborate human hunt for his own amusement. However, while this brief O. Henry-style sketch left the gruesome details of the action to the readers' imaginations, the film necessarily embellishes this sinister premise with new characters and a long, memorable hunt sequence in which the deranged Count Zaroff stalks his prey with bow and arrow.

Long remembered primarily as a precursor to RKO's *King Kong* (which featured most of the same cast, sets, and crew, not to mention very similar camera setups), *The Most Dangerous Game* has increasingly come into its own as a landmark horror and action title which holds up today as an exciting piece of entertainment. Originally released at a running time approximated by most scholars around 76 minutes, this film was pared down to a speedy 63 minutes and moves like a bullet. The infamous shots of mounted severed heads and bloody shark attacks were trimmed or altered from many reissue versions and most video editions but remain intact here. While the extra footage will probably never be found, what remains is quite powerful as Joel McCrea and a dark-haired Fay Wray are sent into the jungle by Zaroff (Leslie Banks, a very effective classic villain) with a few hours' head start to make his game interesting. Packed with startling images (hard to believe this was done on a set!) and some truly kinky touches along the way, this film has been imitated countless times over the years, most recently in its unofficial remake as John Woo's *Hard Target*. Max Steiner does an interesting dry run for his King Kong score here, mostly playing around with atmospheric tribal sounds and swirling action cues, and Wray still makes for a fetching heroine.

The Roan Group issued a fine restored edition of *The Most Dangerous Game* in 1995, but the DVD version from Criterion is, amazingly, even better. The source materials are far closer to mint than have ever been seen before; the detail throughout is extraordinary, and the source materials are much cleaner (even the shark attack footage looks good!). Devoid of the visual and sonic damage which has harmed it over the years, this *Game* packs a punch now more than ever and, at a surprisingly low price for Criterion, is quite a steal. While the packaging is disappointingly bland (the Roan version easily beats it in this respect), the disc does boast an interesting running commentary covering the historical bases of the film. The LD also included a different commentary track, snippets from Willis O'Brien's *Creation*, and trailers for *King Kong and Mighty Joe Young,* extras which are noticeably absent here - but the movie's the thing, and the DVD is clearly the winner.

MOTHER'S DAY

Colour, 1980, 98m. / Directed by Charles Kaufman / Starring Rose Ross, Holden McGuire / Troma (US R1 NTSC)

 Blistering social satire or misogynist trash? Twenty years later, *Mother's Day* really doesn't feel much like either anymore. Countless other Troma films ranging from *The Toxic Avenger* to *Terror Firmer* have established the quasi-studio's desire to become an equal opportunity offender, and if seen as sort of a shaky precursor to the films of Peter Jackson and the Farrelly Brothers, *Mother's Day* serves as an above average example of how to serve up extreme exploitation with a little more wit than usual. In the unforgettable pre-credit sequence, a female hitchhiker catches a ride out in the woods and winds up the victim of Ike (Holden McGuire) and Addley (Billy Ray McQuade), two leering yokels who kidnap, rape, and murder at the behest of their grotesque, domineering mother (Rose Ross). Brought up on a diet of junk food and television, they have become the embodiment of pop culture at its most destructive. Meanwhile, a trio of female college friends - Abbey (Nancy Hendrickson), Jackie (Deborah Luce), and Trina (Tiana Pierce) - meet up in the woods for a reunion. They spend the evening camping out, smoking pot, and reminiscing about the payback they dished out to the campus ladies' man; unfortunately, their idyll is disrupted when one of the girls is dragged off in her sleeping bag by the brothers, who take her back to their isolated cabin for another round of ultraviolence. After much woodland pursuit, the other two girls wind up in the clutches of mother and her boys as well, but things do go quite as planned this time.

Significantly, *Mother's Day* opened the same year as the much more serious *Friday the 13th,* another backwoods slasher yarn. In this case, the violence is exaggerated to a cartoonish degree, from the syrup-spouting head severing in the beginning to the hyperbolic table-turning final act in which Drano, a television set, an inflatable toy, and a hatchet come into play with gory consequences. From a technical standpoint, the film really isn't very good; the pace drags, the acting is uneven at best, and any attempts at characterization are negligible at best. However, many scenes are genuinely funny, including one featuring the world's ultimate New Yawk slacker boyfriend, and like it or not, this is one experience you never forget. One of the last releases during Troma's short-lived foray into laserdiscs, *Mother's Day* took a very long time to reach DVD.

The disc basically contains the same extras as the laser, with re-filmed intros by a typically rambling Lloyd Kaufman to omit use of the word "laserdisc." The transfer is noticeably improved, with strong colours and a smooth compression job, two qualities virtually unheard of in a Troma disc. The open matte presentation looks balanced enough, while the mono audio sounds the same as it always has. Of course, this is the full unrated version. The disc includes a running feature length commentary by Charles Kaufman, which could best be described as loose and breezy. Like his brother (and the rest of the Kaufman family members who have populated the Troma payroll), he definitely has a gift for gab and manages to kill off 90 minutes without much effort. The disc also includes the usual Troma filler for extras, including a grab bag of trailers (but no trailer for *Mother's Day*, alas), the usual trivia test and studio profiles, and a featurette on "growing up with Lloyd." Pretty much what you'd expect, of course.

M

MOUNTAIN OF THE CANNIBAL GOD

Colour, 1978, 91m. / Directed by Sergio Martino / Starring Ursula Andress, Stacy Keach / Anchor Bay (US, US R1 NTSC) / WS (2.35:1) (16:9), EC Entertainment (Holland R0 NTSC), Astro (Germany R2 PAL) / WS (2.35:1)

The closest thing to a reputable Italian cannibal film, *Mountain of the Cannibal God* sports a much higher pedigree than expected. Director Sergio Martino brought a certain amount of professionalism and a brisk pace to this pulpy adventure, which straddles the line somewhere between the mundane cynicism of *Eaten Alive!* and the mind-shattering depravity of *Cannibal Holocaust.*

Wealthy explorer's wife and clotheshorse Susan Stevenson (Ursula Andress) decides to do something about her husband's mysterious disappearance in the jungles of New Guinea. Along with her petulant brother, Arthur (*Keoma's* Antonio Marsina), she decides to follow her spouse's expedition path into the green inferno with the aid of anthropological guide Dr. Edward Foster (Stacy Keach), who knows a lot more than he's telling. Along the way Susan nearly falls prey to a tarantula, whose death inspires their native companions to skin and eat an iguana in penance to the gods. Another native then falls prey to a clever body-piercing tree trap, but still they press on, determined to reach a mysterious, uncharted mountain populated by a tribe known as the Pooka. (Yes, the Pooka, as in James Stewart's companion in *Harvey.*) Along the way they also tackle treacherous rapids, ambush-happy boa constrictors, and torn Gucci safari clothing before reaching the mountain, where Susan is promptly tied up, stripped, painted, dressed up in a She-like costume, and trotted out as a sacrificial goddess.

From a historical standpoint, *Mountain* established many of the conventions later copied in leering gorefests like *Cannibal Ferox.* Natives are castrated, reptiles suffer agonizing deaths, and in the most unwatchable scene, a monkey is slowly eaten by a snake. Fortunately these stomach churning scenes are few and far between, with most of the running time devoted to more traditional jungle fare involving Keach's great white explorer and Andress' glamorous jungle girl poses. Sure, it's basically racist and idiotic, but as far as Italian cannibal movies go, this isn't a bad place to start and may not make you run for a shower after the end credits. Released in the US minus five minutes of gore footage as *Slave of the Cannibal God*, this film

became a familiar title among Italian exploitation fans, usually more often discussed than seen.

An uncut print first surfaced on video thanks to the Venezuelan market, but the full scope photography was impossible to appreciate until EC's European DVD. Anchor Bay's disc surpasses the EC disc with a richer and more film-like transfer, with surprisingly natural colours which translate well to 16:9 enhancement. *Mountain* looks much better here than anyone had a right to expect, and apart from some softness inherent in the original print, there isn't any room to complain. The perfect widescreen framing adds immensely to the film's visual sweep as well. The effective, percussive score by the De Angelis brothers sounds just fine in mono (how about a soundtrack, somebody?), and the discs also include the original (and very funny) theatrical trailer; the EC disc has a gallery of international poster and video arts, stills, and trailers for *House on the Edge of the Park* and *A Blade in the Dark*, while the Anchor Bay disc has a different still gallery and the trailer.

The real ace in the hole for the AB disc is the inclusion of some four-plus minutes of sexual depravity, including a simulated bit of native bestiality and a not-so-simulated depiction of a cannibal girl pleasuring herself. (Portions of this footage, *sans* pig, turned up on the German DVD as well.) Martino discusses the film in a 12-minute featurette which puts his claims into serious question by juxtaposing his tale of the monkey's death by snake with slow mo analysis of matting trickery to cover up crewhands shoving the poor animal to its death. It would be interesting to get more of Martino's side of the story, as the editing makes him look a bit more foolish than most directors would probably like. In any case, one can only wonder what Keach and Andress might have to say about this project now...

MR. SARDONICUS

B&W, 1961, 89m. / Directed by William Castle / Starring Guy Rolfe, Ronald Lewis / Columbia (US R1 NTSC) / WS (1.85:1) (16:9)

After his outrageous modern day spookfests, it only seemed natural for gimmick guru William Castle to make a gothic period yarn in the Hammer vein. Relatively speaking, *Mr. Sardonicus* is one of his more restrained works, taking its time to spin out a complex storyline with intricate characters. Of course, Castle fans should have no fear as he also makes time for bloodsucking leeches, grave robbing, disfigurement, revenge, and other sundry nastiness.

Gifted surgeon Sir Robert (*Scream of Fear*'s Ronald Lewis) is summoned to the home of Mr. Sardonicus (Guy Rolfe), a retiring nobleman who wears a featureless mask to conceal his horribly disfigured face. At first the good doctor refuses to treat Sardonicus' affliction, citing in part his former involvement with Sardonicus' beautiful wife (Audrey Dalton), but through various persuasive and sadistic means (some involving put upon manservant Oskar Homolka), Sir Robert falls under Sardonicus' control. As we learn in flashback, Sardonicus was once a decent guy who felt compelled to raid his father's grave to retrieve a winning lottery ticket buried in the dead man's jacket. Unfortunately the sight of his father's decayed face sent Sardonicus into a state of grotesque facial paralysis, a condition which has begun to infect his soul as well...

Combining the lottery ticket narrative from Cornell Woolrich's short story "Post Mortem" with Victor Hugo's more famous *The Man Who Laughs*, this Castle concoction is by far the most elegant of his films. Its slow pace and reliance on psychological horror may be off-putting at first, but the film has developed a steadfast cult following over the years and remains effective for more patient viewers. Most of its notoriety centres on Castle's sole gimmick here, the "Punishment Poll." Castle appears twice: at the beginning of the film to introduce the dictionary meaning of a "ghoul" (only used in the film in a metaphorical sense), and then again before the finale to administer a poll in the audience to determine Sardonicus' fate. All ticket holders were given a card featuring a thumbs up or thumbs down option, and after tabulation, the villain (who isn't that evil, really) is given his due. Of course, Castle only attached one real ending to his prints; never underestimate the bloodlust of the general public. (And can anyone with lip-reading abilities decipher what Castle was originally saying before he clumsily re-looped his line, "And I hope your nightmares are nice ones"?).

Though *Mr. Sardonicus* popped up on television occasionally over the years, it remained curiously unavailable on home video for decades. Columbia's DVD is obviously welcome as it marks the first wide release of the film since its theatrical run, though the years have apparently not been kind. The image quality (especially during the prologue) is surprisingly ragged and worn for a Columbia transfer, and the gritty, high contrast appearance of the rest of the print creates the least impressive of their Castle transfers to date. It's about the same as the repertory prints still in circulation, however, and fans should still pick this up as it will no doubt be the only buying option for a very long time. From most companies this would still be passable, perhaps even impressive, but one has to hope that a better element is lying in Columbia's vaults somewhere. More inexplicably, the music goes several seconds out of sync during Chapter 15 (immediately before the grave digging), cutting into the previous dialogue sequence and remaining slightly out of whack throughout the reel.

Extras include a new historical featurette, "Taking the Punishment Poll," which offers an affectionate scholarly look at Castle's promotional approach to the film, and trailers for this film along with *13 Ghosts*.

MR. VAMPIRE

Colour, 1985, 94m. / Directed by Ricky Lau / Starring Lam Ching Ying, Chin Siu Ho, Ricky Hui / Media Asia / Tai Seng (HK R0 NTSC) / WS (1.78:1) / DD5.1

Many Hong Kong devotees have strong feelings about hopping vampires. Some love the springy bloodsuckers, while others find the depiction hackneyed and stupid. That said, the film that started it all, *Mr. Vampire*, is by far the best of the lot (though its two immediate sequels aren't bad). Sort of an Eastern response to *Ghostbusters* (which spawned many imitations and parodies), *Mr. Vampire* uses Oriental culture as the springboard for a unique, creepily amusing vampire mythos. Here, the vampires can be controlled by Taoist incantations, administered on an enchanted written parchment affixed to the creature's forehead. Unfortunately, if the spell falls off, the vampire immediately begins to hop and search for blood. In a clever twist reminiscent of the Spanish Blind Dead series, the vampires can also be thwarted from detecting a human's presence if the potential victims hold their breath. Kou (Lam Ching Ying), a priest and expert vampire wrangler with the most memorable case of unibrow in cinema history, tries to teach his two bumbling apprentices, Chou (Chin Siu-Ho) and Man-Chor (Ricky Hui), the ins and outs of vampire control, but several comedic (and horrific) mishaps along the way to derail their education.

The bulk of the story concerns an elder, now converted to vampirism, whose son recruits the trio for help; however, the narrative also tosses in a variety of marginally related supernatural hijinks, including a bewitching female ghost whose flying head participates in a memorable acrobatic attack scene.

Like most of the imported Media Asia titles, *Mr. Vampire* benefits greatly from its DVD remastering. Anyone used to those old faded VHS eyesores will be thankful for this release and should be clamouring for parts II and III as well. That said, the image isn't really demo material; the moderate letterboxing is a nice gesture, but the film still looks like a mid-'80s product, with some harsh over-lighting here and there and some colour smearing that causes blue-lit shadowy scenes to melt into mud. Still, it's by far the best presentation out there, and the limited 5.1 remix does the best it can with a thrifty, low budget soundtrack. The usual wide assortment of subtitles are offered; the English translation is identical to the prior theatrical and video releases, which means plenty of skipping, broken paraphrasing, and humorous typos, but it gets the job done all the same.

The jokey theatrical trailer is included, as well as the usual Media Asia promo reel. Thankfully, the company seems to have finally embraced workable, animated menu screens (not to mention time encoding), which makes navigation smoother and more entertaining. In the end, *Mr. Vampire* is a long overdue and welcome release, particularly for fans of vampires and knockabout kung fu action; Hong Kong fans should eat it up, and newcomers should find that this, along with the more serious and ambitious

MS. 45 (ANGEL OF VENGEANCE)

Colour, 1981, 84m. / Directed by Abel Ferrara / Starring Zoë Tamerlis, Albert Sinkys / Image (US R0 NTSC) / WS (1.78:1)

By far the best of the drive-in vigilante films kicked off by *Death Wish* back in the '70s, *Ms. 45* puts a novel spin on the premise by turning its avenging gun-packer into a beautiful young mute woman cleaning up the streets of New York. Director Abel Ferrara, who went on to indie glory with *Bad Lieutenant*, displays an amazing command of the film medium in this, only his second legitimate film after the similarly themed *Driller Killer*.

Thana (the late Zoë Tamerlis), a lovely and diligent worker in New York's garment district, has the ultimate bad day. On the way home, she's brutally raped in an alleyway by a masked assailant

(Ferrara himself). When she returns back to her apartment, a burglar is waiting for her... and she's raped again. This time she kills her attacker with an iron, then packages up his dismembered body parts and drops them off at discreet locations across the city. (Seriously.) While she does her best to keep a normal appearance in public, Thana's nights are consumed by her seductive prowls through the city streets which often result in male pigs winding up on the wrong end of a bullet.

As much a horror film as an action yarn, *Ms. 45* rises far above the standard B-move fare of its era. Ferrara perfectly captures the glossy yet scuzzy ambience of the Big Apple, with broad daylight only thinly veiling the danger lurking around every corner. The beautiful Tamerlis offers a compelling, almost silent performance that eerily echoes Catherine Deneuve in *Repulsion*, while the supporting actors are all appropriately cast. However, the film's real trump card is its vivid climax at a Halloween office party, which once seen is never forgotten.

The Image DVD improves upon their colourful but grainy laserdisc edition, with even snazzier, electric hues popping forth in every scene. The letterboxing adds to the sides and slices some dead space off the top, restoring compositional balance to many scenes (e.g., the sequence in the photographer's studio). The audio bears some of the flaws of the original source material (that relentless sax music will always sound shrill), but this is about as good as it will get. Only debits: the DVD doesn't include the memorable theatrical trailer, which was present on the laserdisc, and also lacks some of the extra rape footage and a single shot (showing a man being shot in the thigh) from the climactic massacre, both present on its laser counterpart. The same uncut version also briefly appeared on VHS in the UK from Warner, though the tapes were quickly withdrawn.

THE MUMMY

B&W, 1932, 74m. / Directed by Karl Freund / Starring Boris Karloff, Zita Johann / Universal (US R1 NTSC)

A solid entry in the Universal monster movie sweepstakes, *The Mummy* fell victim over the years to countless misconceptions from the wave of fake sequels and remakes. While Boris Karloff does indeed make his initial appearance in the film in Im-Ho-Tep mummy garb (a fantastic sequence and one of horrordom's finest), the majority of the tale finds him resuscitated in human form (albeit a little strange looking) as Ardath Bey. Not really a traditional monster film, *The Mummy* is more of a dark supernatural romance in which one of the characters happens to be a few thousand years old.

A group of not terribly bright archaeologists, including the "hero," Frank (David Manners), uncover an Egyptian burial structure and, ignoring the warnings plastered all over the coffin, open up the tomb of Im-Ho-Tep, who promptly comes to life and "goes for a little walk." Ten years later, Ardath Bey arrives and establishes a hypnotic rapport with Helen (Zita Johann), the reincarnation of his lost Egyptian love.

While Universal usually had some kind of source material from which to draw its monstrous visions, *The Mummy* had to be fabricated from scratch following the national craze for all things Egyptian (King Tut's tomb in particular). Interestingly, though few seem to notice, it is also one of the most sexually suggestive and perverse films of its era, with Manners' bizarre seduction of Helen prefiguring an even more open-ended flashback in which viewers are allowed to see why high priest Karloff was punished for doing "unspeakable" things in his love's tomb. Fortunately, taste and tact prevail, unlike the studio's *Murders in the Rue Morgue*, which gleefully showed almost everything but failed to establish the overwhelming sense of morbid passion exhibited here.

Karloff makes an excellent "romantic" figure, while Edward Van Sloan appears in yet another variation on his Van Helsing character. The two "straight" romantic leads fare less successfully, though Johann looks great in her quasi-Egyptian garb. The real star is unquestionably the director, Karl Freund, an exceptional cinematographer for such directors as F.W. Murnau and Fritz Lang who went on to do one more horror film, the stunning *Mad Love*, before revolutionizing the sitcom three-camera setup on *I Love Lucy*. Freud's poetic eye, previously seen in Tod Browning's *Dracula*, brings an austere sense of beauty to the most mundane scenes and carries along a film that could have easily become a dull talkfest.

Numerous other films made the mistake of keeping the mummy under wraps for the entire running time, with only Terence Fisher's 1958 version for Hammer managing to pull off this trick with any degree of success. Fortunately Stephen Sommers' 1999 remake for Universal focused on the mummy as a supernatural, love-struck entity perfectly willing to shed its bandages in his quest for eternal romance and vengeance (an aspect completely lost in its worthless sequel).

Universal fans who complained about the sterility of their digitally restored soundtrack for *Frankenstein* should have no cause for complaint here, as this *Mummy* sounds pretty much like it always has. While the soundtrack is always intelligible and usually fairly crisp, it still possesses that faint, familiar background rumble prevalent in most '30s titles. The image quality fares better; though not as immaculately restored as some other recent efforts, the depth of the shadows and precision of detail are noticeably improved over Universal's outdated VHS and laser editions. The transfer is generally impressive and, for the most part, quite clean; only a few bumpy real changes and a couple of jagged scene edits betray that this has been taken from a print.

As befits a classic, Universal has decked this out with a host of supplementary features, including David J. Skal's half hour "Mummy Dearest" documentary, hosted by Rudy Behlmer, and Paul M. Jensen's informative commentary track. Both historical tours provide some fascinating behind the scenes tidbits including details on Karloff's make up by the legendary Jack Pierce (Rick Baker appears to make a few comments) and the origins of *Cagliostro*, the unfilmed Karloff project which this replaced.

M

THE MUMMY'S SHROUD

Colour, 1967, 90m. / Directed by John Gilling / Starring Andre Morrell, John Phillips / Anchor Bay (US R1 NTSC) / WS (1.85:1) (16:9)

More or less a remake of Hammer's own *Mummy* adaptation in 1959, this third go at the cloth-wrapped terror is generally regarded as the least of the series, primarily because the actors spend much more time standing around chit-chatting than they do running from the mummy himself. Indeed, compared to its contemporaries, something is definitely lacking from *The Mummy's Shroud*, but that endearing Hammer atmosphere still drenches every frame and makes it more notable than most of the horror product being churned out today.

In 1920s Egypt, the British explorer Basil Walden (Andre Morrell) leads his men into the uncharted desert and becomes lost in a sandstorm. Miraculously they discover their holy grail, the tomb of Pharoah's son Kah-to-bey, where they are warned by an eccentric and creepy crypt keeper Hasmid to leave the grave's contents alone. Of course they don't, removing the body of Kah-to-bey, his mummified servant Prem, and his sacred shroud in the process. Back in England, Hasmid avenges the defiling of the tomb by reviving the mummy, which promptly goes about destroying those who dared to enter his resting place.

Though directed by the often impressive John Gilling (*The Plague of the Zombies, Mania*), this is obviously not a film in which he invested a great deal of passion. Still, it looks and sounds great, with the mummy causing enough mayhem to keep popcorn munchers happy. Morrell and Hammer vets like Michael Ripper add credibility to the threadbare (oops) plotline, which recaps its predecessors without adding much of significance along the way. The lovely Maggie Kimberley fills the role of the requisite buxom Hammer screamer this time, and while doesn't have much to do, at least she offers some cheesecake eye candy while the mummy's offscreen.

Despite any shortcomings in the film itself, Anchor Bay has given it a first class treatment on DVD with a tremendously colourful and razor sharp presentation. If only the 1959 original could look this good! The score by Don Banks does a good job of filling in for James Bernard's absence, with plenty of dramatic percussion to keep viewers awake. The disc also includes the usual trailer and TV spots (coupled with *Frankenstein Created Woman*), the "Mummies, Werewolves, and the Living Dead" episode of *World of Hammer*, and the usual witty animated menus.

MUTANT

Colour, 1984, 99m. / Directed by John "Bud" Cardos / Starring Wings Hauser, Bo Hopkins / Elite (US R1 NTSC) / WS (1.85:1) (16:9), Diamond (US R0 NTSC)

An odd little film from the waning final days of grassroots horror before the big studios stomped all over their competition, *Mutant* comes across much better than it really should. The film was shot around Norcross, Georgia and first distributed in drive-ins and shopping mall theatres around the South and Midwest under the title *Night Shadows*. When that strategy failed, it was reissued to theatres and video as *Mutant*, a laughably misleading title since this is, in fact, a good old-fashioned zombie flick.

Josh (Wings Hauser) and his younger brother, Mike (Lee Montgomery), find their road trip vacation waylaid when a truckfull of rednecks pushes them off the road and into a creek. The brothers stumble into a nearby town and begin a bar fight with their assailants. Luckily the alcoholic sheriff, Will (Bo Hopkins), steps in to break it up. Josh and Mike find a boarding house for the night, but Mike is suddenly attacked by something under his bed. The next morning Josh searches for his brother and enlists the aid of a doctor, Myra (Jennifer Warren), and the perky schoolteacher, Holly (*Chained Heat*'s Jody Medford, one of the worst actresses on the planet). Mike stumbles across the gaunt, creepy looking corpse of a young girl, which Myra hauls off to her office. Meanwhile Holly falls for Mike after he calls her a redneck (don't ask) and develops her own theories about what might be happening in this small, quiet town. A local fledgling corporation has set up a toxic waste site, and since then people have been disappearing right and left. Sure enough, the townsfolk are being zombified, leaving them with weird pus-spewing slits in their hands capable of transforming others by touch and burning through glass. Luckily the zombies are also sensitive to light, but how can the survivors hold out until morning?

Most obviously, the first half of *Mutant* is pretty drab stuff, with far too much talking and an over-reliance on unpleasant Southern stereotypes that really should have been put out to pasture decades earlier. However, the patient will be rewarded when the second half kicks into gear, providing some solid and scary zombie attacks in such confined settings as a basement and an elementary school bathroom. With a cast headed by Hauser (who never outdid *Vice Squad*) and Hopkins, this film really shouldn't be any good at all; however, it does have its charm and definitely delivers the goods, particularly during the rousing climax which oddly recalls *Children Shouldn't Play with Dead Things*. Add to that a superlative orchestral score by Richard Band which effectively becomes more lyrical and haunting as the film progresses, and you've got a rough, interesting little find for you movie treasure hunters out there.

Credit is also due to director John "Bud" Cardos, who turned dross into gold with underrated '70s drive-in favourites like *Kingdom of the Spiders* and *The Dark*. Say what you will, but the guy definitely knows how to milk a scary environment for all it's worth. (Incidentally this film was begun by Mark Rosman as a follow up to *House on Sorority Row*, but he got canned by producer Dick Clark- yes, that Dick Clark.)

God knows *Mutant* couldn't have been a title thrown around too much for a prospective DVD release, but that hasn't stopped Elite from giving it the first class treatment. The transfer from the original negative looks spotless, a radical departure from the washed out theatrical prints, many of which were inexplicably tinted blue (as were some video editions). Apparently the prevalence of blue shirts gave some lab technician a boneheaded burst of inspiration one day. Diamond Entertainment also promoted its own DVD release, a budget line pan-and-scan issue; avoid that one at all costs. The DVD also includes a dupey looking theatrical trailer under the *Mutant* title, totally failing to convey even a basic impression of the film's storyline. Not an elaborate or overwhelming presentation by any means, but the film itself looks terrific and it's nice to have it back on the video market again.

MY BEST FIEND

Colour, 1999, 95m. / Directed by Werner Herzog / Anchor Bay (US R1 NTSC) / WS (1.78:1) (16:9) / DD2.0

Many famous directors have that one special actor with whom they become associated forever. John Ford had John Wayne. Federico Fellini had Marcello Mastroianni. John Waters had Divine. And Werner Herzog had Klaus Kinski. Of course, at least as far as we know, John Wayne and John Ford never conspired to kill each other during a shoot, nor did they haul a steamship over a mountain in a rainforest. *My Best Fiend (Mein liebster feind)* is Herzog's oddly tranquil attempt to make sense of his relationship with Kinski, a sort of cathartic, nostalgic piece of therapy on film. It's entirely subjective and possibly unreliable, but this documentary offers the most fascinating and piercing look into the infamous lunacy of this partnership to date.

My Best Fiend begins with a creepy excerpt of Kinski's early "Jesus Tour" in which he spastically insults his audience. Apparently believing himself to be a genius, a modern day Christ, and Paganini at different points in his life, Kinski was notoriously difficult to manage during filming but displayed a softer side as well to his female co-stars, at least according to recent interviews with the likes of Claudia Cardinale (*Fitzcarraldo*).

The bulk of the film consists of Herzog popping in at historically significant places in Germany and revisiting the locations of their films, particularly *Aguirre, the Wrath of God*. Along the way he offers jaw-dropping anecdotes about their five films together, during which both men were quite clearly

insane. From sleeping in huts stuffed with guinea pigs being bred for food to dealing with natives who hated Kinski so much they offered to conveniently kill him during a film, Herzog covers all the bases and, in the process, discourages any glamorous concepts about international filmmaking. As reprehensible as he may have been as a human being, Kinski doesn't come off as all bad; Herzog relates their tender moments of friendship together, and the film closes with a beautiful, haunting sequence involving a butterfly that lingers in the mind long after the end credits. Naturally Kinski is no longer with us to offer his side of the story, but for the benefit of mankind, perhaps that's just as well.

Anchor Bay's DVD of *My Best Fiend* looks sharp and impressive throughout, not surprising for such a recent production. In a unique language option, the film can be played in the original German throughout with optional English subtitles or with an alternate audio track in which Herzog overdubs himself in English, leaving only the film and interview clips to be subtitles for those who don't feel like reading. The disc also includes the intriguing trailer prepared for the film's domestic release.

MYLENE FARMER: MUSIC VIDEOS / MUSIC VIDEOS II & III

Colour, 1985-1992, 150 / 130m. / Directed by Laurent Boutonnat, Ching Siu Tung, Luc Besson, Abel Ferrara, and more / Universal/Polygram (France) / WS (Variable) (16:9) / DD2.0

Though still fairly unknown in the United States, singer/songwriter Mylene Farmer has earned a name for herself as one of France's finest pop musicians. Her albums since the mid-'80s have built up a solid fan base and led to a series of successful concerts, but perhaps her most enduring achievement is her body of music videos. These are not simply music promotional clips; instead, each song becomes the centrepiece of a lavish mini-movie, produced with immaculate care on a healthy budget and packed with violence, nudity, and stunning visuals. All of Mylene's videos have been collected onto two DVDs, appropriately titled *Music Videos* and *Music Videos II & III*.

The first disc focuses on her films directed by Laurent Boutonnat, her long-time partner, producer, and co-writer. First up is "Plus Grandir," in which a young Mylene languishes in a lonely gothic castle before a brutal rape attempt by an intruder produces tragic consequences. In "Libertine," still arguably her most famous video, she's a free-spirited 18th Century woman who kills a man in a duel, engages in a catfight with the deceased's lover, and enjoys a passionate candlelit affair before the unexpected, bloody climax. "Pourvu Qu'Elles Soient Douces" picks up exactly where "Libertine" left off, as Mylene becomes entangled in the middle of a spectacular, violent battle between the French and English armies. "Tristana" offers a macabre Russian twist on the familiar tale of Snow White, in which our peach skinned heroine becomes the target of a malicious witch and seeks the aid of seven very small men. "Sans Contrefacon" plays with another children's story, Pinocchio, as a wooden doll of Mylene becomes all too real. After the plotless, beautifully shot black and white mood piece of "Ainsi Soit Je," Mylene acts out a gruesome *mano a mujere* bullfighting match for one of her best songs, "Sans Logique." The characters we've met so far appear together for a kind of curtain call in "A Quoi Je Sers," followed by the visually astounding Dickensian epic "Desenchantee," in which Mylene is an orphan who leads an impoverished children's refuge in battle against their elders. Narrative takes a break from the moody duet of "Regrets" and the choreographed boxing of "Je T'Aime Melancholy," leaving the finale for "Beyond My Control," which mixes witch burning, gory werewolf sex, and dialogue samples of John Malkovich from *Dangerous Liaisons* into one heady brew.

All of the videos are presented in anamorphic widescreen, a very welcome gesture when one considers that the majority were filmed in scope and even exhibited in French theatres. The PCM audio sounds terrific and less pinched than a Dolby Digital transition might rendered it, and the quality overall outclasses the previous commercial VHS releases. (Incidentally, bootleg videotapes with computerized English subtitles have been available on the video grey market; collectors may want to hang on to these for the lyric translations, but these discs are infinitely more watchable.) Disc extras include Mylene's first "video," "Maman a Tort," a quick paste job which was left out of the regular line up for obvious reasons, as well as the live video versions of "Allan" and "Plus Grandir" (partially lifted from her Live in Concert video). Two documentaries are included: the making of "Pourvu Qu'Elles Soient Douces" (23m.) and the making of "Desenchantee" (14m.), both of which offer extensive behind-the-scenes footage illustrating the massive effort devoted to each of these films.

With disc two (*Music Videos II & III*) we move to a new batch of directors, starting with none other than Luc Besson for "Que Mon Coeur Lache," whose (loose) English translation was used as both the title and theme song for the Japanese horror film, *My Soul Is Slashed*. Here Mylene plays an angel sent by a bureaucratic God to discover the true nature of love on Earth. Among the bizarre sights she encounters is a Michael Jackson imitator being crushed by a huge cross; clearly not to be missed. Then the videos move to her two most recent albums with "XXL," a mind-boggling piece which finds Mylene lashed to the front of a speeding locomotive (for real), and "L'Instant X," which can only be described as a moodier version of Larry Cohen's *The Stuff*. Abel Ferrara in his *King of New York* mode directed "California," in which high society woman Mylene spots her exact double, a hooker, while driving through the mean streets of Los Angeles (with Giancarlo Esposito, to boot). Filled with saturated colours and erotic visuals, this makes one wonder what she and Ferrara could have accomplished with another collaboration. The creepy "Comme J'ai Mal" depicts Mylene's bizarre woodland transformation into a winged, clawed insect creature, followed by the arguable high point of the disc, "L'Ame-Stram-Gram." This beautiful homage to Hong Kong cinema was helmed by Ching Siu Tung, who also directed the three *Chinese Ghost Story* films, *Swordsman II*, *Witch from Nepal*, *The Heroic Trio*, and many others. Shot in Hong Kong with the best technicians around, this is a dazzling crash course in pre-*Crouching Tiger* Asian fantasy as Mylene plays identical twin sisters with supernatural powers (including super strong monster tongues) separated by an invading Mongol horde, only to be reunited for a battle royale against their enemies. "Je Te Rends Ton Amour," sort of a supernatural horror/religious piece, climaxes with the memorable image of Mylene crawling naked across a church floor drenched in blood, while the equally dramatic "Souviens-Toi du Jour" posits her in the middle of a burning chateau. "Optimistique-Moi" takes Mylene to a Felliniesque circus as she does numerous balancing acts to get across the stage to her boyfriend, distracted all the way by knife throwers, tigers, and naked female stagehands. The dullest video of the bunch (but one of the best songs), "Innamoramento," closes with some pastoral footage intercut with Mylene's most recent concert performance.

Since most of the videos are full frame, disc two is presented in standard 4x3 but looks very good all the same. The extra clips this time are less interesting, comprised of three excerpts from her *Live at Bercy* concert (also on DVD): "Ainsi Soit Je," "La Poupee Qui Fait Non," and "Rever." The real treat here is two behind-the-scenes documentaries for "California" (27m.) and "L'Am-Stram-Gram" (18m.), detailing Mylene's working relationship with these two very different directors. The package is rounded out with "M.F. Confidential," an 11 minute featurette detailing Mylene's experience in Los Angeles while recording her album *Anamorphosee.* In short, even if you can't speak French or aren't a pop music fan, these discs offer a wealth of unforgettable visuals far beyond anything you'll ever see on MTV. Fortunately the music happens to be terrific as well, and even if you can't understand what she's saying, chances are you'll be a Mylene fanatic long before the final video ends. (Note: Universal has also released Mylene's *Mylenium Tour* on DVD as well in a nice 16:9 transfer with a 5.1 Dolby Digital mix, coupled with numerous documentaries and other extra goodies. Highly recommended.)

NADIE CONOCE A NADIE

Colour, 1999, 104m. / Directed by Mateo Gil / Starring Eduardo Noriega, Jordi Mollà / Sogepaq (Spain R2 PAL) / WS (2.35:1) / DD5.1

"I feel as if I'm observing my life without really living it," ponders young crossword designer and frustrated novelist Simón (Eduardo Noriega). Stuck in a dead end job for a newspaper in Seville and content with the innocuous presence of his roommate, Sapo ("Toad") (Jordi Mollà), he soon finds his dissatisfaction changing dramatically when an eerie voice leaves a message on his answering machine to place the word "Adversary" in his Sunday crossword puzzle. A series of messages and notes begins to accumulate, all tying in with the current Holy Week in Seville, a Catholic ritual involving parades and celebrations at all of the major churches. Unfortunately a diabolical force seems to be at work, releasing nerve gas from a statue of Christ and leaving Simón's friend, Father Andre (Pedro Alvarez-Ossorio), dead from a hallucinogenic overdose in a grotesque parody of the pieta. Simón consults Maria (Natalia Verbeke), a reporter at his paper, concerning possible links to an international group of religious terrorists known as the Sacred Truth. Even worse, Simón recognizes a symbol from the nerve gas attack as the same logo his roommate left on his computer. Sapo denies any

involvement, but Simón's suspicions mount when he uncovers an ancient drawing featuring the same symbol, accompanied by a representation of Satan himself as a toad...

While American thrillers like *Arlington Road* and *Single White Female* routinely explore those nagging suspicions that those close to you might actually be your worst enemy, *Nadie Conoce a Nadie* ("Nobody Knows Anyone") manages a fresh spin on the material by placing its story against the picturesque and gothic backdrop of Seville's Holy Week. The use of religious iconography and the entire city as a huge game board provides some unique visual chills, and the story takes some very unpredictable turns in the second half which raise the stakes considerably. Writer/director Mateo Gil, a long-time collaborator of Alejandro Amenábar, has obviously been studying his Hitchcock and Val Lewton, particularly a rousing sequence in which a convocation of black hooded figures in the streets turns into a sinister game of laser tag! Amenábar also co-wrote the script and provided the excellent music score, while the group's regular leading man, Noriega, does an excellent job as usual.

Sogepaq's DVD is just as outstanding as their previous job on *Open Your Eyes.* The scope transfer looks colourful and razor sharp without any blemishes, while the optional English or Spanish subtitles are well written and placed in the lower letterbox band. The 5.1 audio is mostly confined to the music score (also isolated in 5.1 on a separate audio track) and a few well placed explosions. Extras include the theatrical trailer, an 18 minute short film by Gil entitled "Allanamiento de Morada" (also starring Noriega and co-written and scored by Amenábar), and a 17 minute behind the scenes featurette which takes the novel step of also covering the creation of the film's website! These features are in Spanish only, but English speaking viewers can probably get through them without much trouble.

THE NAMELESS (LOS SIN NOMBRE)

Colour, 1999, 102m. / Directed by Jaume Balagueró / Starring Emma Vilarasau, Karra Elejalde / Filmax (Spain R2 PAL), Universe (HK R3 NTSC) / WS (1.85:1) / DD5.1

It took three decades for someone to attempt a feature film based on the work of horror novelist Ramsey Campbell, and if *The Nameless (Los sin nombre)* is any indication, many more filmmakers should give it a try. This promising

N

debut for director Jaume Balagueró transplants the story to modern day Spain, where the police discover the grotesquely burned and mutilated body of a young girl. Despite the absence of teeth, the corpse's uneven hip structure alerts them to its true identity: Angela, the daughter of Claudia (Emma Vilarasau). Needless to say the mother doesn't take the news very well. Flash forward five years later. Abandoned by her husband, grief-stricken Claudia works like a drone in the big city but is shaken from her malaise by a telephone call. "Mummy, it's me. Come and get me," says Angela's voice. "They'll be coming back soon." Claudia follows Angela's directions to an abandoned motel where she discovers a plastic bag containing one of Angela's lost boots, so she immediately seeks help from Massera (Karra Elejalde), the recently resigned cop who was in charge of the case. Together they begin to piece together the mystery and link it to The Nameless, an evil sect derived from the Nazis which rose to prominence in the '60s. The group's leader, Santini (Carlos Lasarte), currently resides in a criminal asylum where he may still be masterminding their activities, and Claudia is followed along the way by a parallel investigation by tabloid reporter Quiroga (Tristán Ulloa), who uncovers a few sinister secrets of his own.

Though heavily indebted both in visual style and tone to the films of David Fincher, *The Nameless* displays a solid diabolical imagination behind the camera and delivers more than a few good shudders along the way. Apart from two relatively brief sequences, Balagueró uses lighting and menacing background figures and objects for scare value rather than explicit gore, and the film's emotional core is kept intact by Vilarasau's fragile performance and a sparse, effective piano score. The film isn't perfect; the subliminal cutaways become unnecessary and almost humorously overstated at times, as when one character proclaims "It was like building a spider's web!" as the film randomly cuts back and forth to, yes, a spider building a web.

Like *Seven*, the film also works up such a powerful sense of dread from its opening scenes that there's no way the ending can possibly live up to its promise of "the ultimate evil." While the final scene is effective enough in its own right, the resolution is so abrupt and puzzling at first that it leaves the viewer with a whole lot to sift through as the end credits roll. These debits aside, *The Nameless* is an impressive and often refreshing attempt to translate a difficult author to the big screen.

As proof that European DVDs can rank right up there with the best of 'em, this Spanish release from Filmax is one of the most impressive horror releases on the silver disc to date. The widescreen transfer looks impeccable, with the difficult, shadowy cinematography perfectly rendered without any distracting compression flaws. The 5.1 audio is restrained for the most part but bursts to life during a few well-timed scares, while the score receives broad separation from all of the speakers. The disc also includes the theatrical trailer, two more effective TV spots, and an 18 minute featurette which offers interviews with the director and cast, interspersed with behind the scenes footage. An eerie, fascinating music video for the haunting end titles song (which sounds a lot like Siouxsie and the Banshees) is also included. The film itself is presented with both Spanish and English-dubbed 5.1 tracks, as well as optional Spanish or English subtitles. (Obviously the Spanish version with subtitles is far more effective.)

Even if a British or US company decides to release a DVD of *The Nameless* for the English-speaking market, this one will be hard to top. A bare bones disc is also available from Hong Kong with the same technical specs, as well as optional Chinese or English subtitles.

NATIONAL LAMPOON'S VACATION

Colour, 1983, 94m. / Directed by Harold Ramis / Starring Chevy Chase, Beverly D'Angelo / Warner (US R1 NTSC), Warner (UK R2 PAL) / WS (1.85:1) (16:9)

For Clark W. Griswold (Chase), half the fun of a family holiday away is gleaned from the getting there. So why, he postulates, hop on a flight that gets one to the Walley World theme park in a few hours when they can make the 2500-mile trip by car in a week? Setting out in the brand new "family truckster" with wife Ellen (D'Angelo) and kids Rusty (Anthony Michael Hall) and Audrey (Dana Barron) in tow, Clark's finely laid out schedule goes awry almost immediately when they take the wrong exit from the interstate and cruise into the ghetto...

Anyone who has ever been on a family holiday will identify with *Vacation*, though pity the poor souls who ever suffered the succession of pratfalls that befall the Griswolds; they're ripped off at every turn, they get mugged, they get lost in the desert, the car breaks down, the dog dies, their aunt dies... and to top it all, when they finally reach their destination the place is closed for refurbishment. Harold Ramis directs from a zany John Hughes script, spooning out material that's highbrow, lowbrow and everything in between. The situations the family find themselves in are often ludicrous, but they're also just grounded enough to remain feasible.

Vacation is consistently funny throughout, due mainly to endearing performances from Chase, D'Angelo, Hall, Barron, Imogene Coca as acid-tongued harridan Aunt Edna, Eddie Bracken (in a wicked Walt Disney send-up) as Roy Walley, John Candy as a Walley World security guard and not least of all Randy Quaid (in a role he reprised in the third and fourth instalments of the series) as the inimitable Cousin Eddie, with a metal plate in his head and a heart way bigger than his brain. The moment when Chase finally loses his cool and turns on his family is a comedic milestone: "This is no longer a vacation. It's a quest! It's a quest for fun. I'm gonna have fun and you're gonna have fun. We're all gonna have so much fucking fun we'll need plastic surgery to remove our Goddamn smiles. You'll be whistling Zipa-Dee-Doo-Dah out of your assholes!" The toe-tapper of a theme song ("Holiday Road") is performed by Lindsey Buckingham, formerly of Fleetwood Mac.

The Region 2 Warner Brothers DVD has the slight edge over its Region 1 counterpart in that it's presented (across 33 chapters) as a 1.85:1 widescreen transfer, where the US disc is fullscreen. It doesn't, however, have the trailer that's present on its American cousin, so it's swings and roundabouts when deliberating over which one to plunk down your cash for. In fact, the absence of even a simple trailer on the UK disc means it's completely devoid of extras. The picture quality is an improvement on the VHS release however, so if you love the movie the upgrade from cassette to disc is worthwhile considering. - TG

NATIONAL LAMPOON'S CHRISTMAS VACATION

Colour, 1989, 97m. / Directed by Jeremiah Checkik / Starring Chevy Chase, Beverly D'Angelo / Warner (US R1 NTSC)

Clark Griswold (Chase) tries his hardest to host a "fun-filled family Christmas" only to be plagued by every disaster imaginable. His long-suffering wife Ellen (D'Angelo) and kids - Audrey (Juliette Lewis) and Rusty (Johnny Galecki) - can only look on helplessly as one misfortune after another strikes them. Clark's continual bad luck is worsened by a house full of obnoxious family guests, but he manages to keep smiling in the face of adversity, knowing that his Christmas bonus is due to arrive any day. But then rancid Cousin Eddie (Quaid) and his family arrive unannounced...

If you ever think your Christmas is going badly, take a look at *Christmas Vacation* and you'll realise just how good you've actually got it. A little more slapstick laden that the earlier films, this is nonetheless a sack full of laughs. There's an exploding turkey, a squirrel takes up residence in the Christmas tree (which later catches fire), Eddie's dog Snot (so named for his unfortunate sinus infection) tears up the household, and Clark's yuppie neighbours constantly belittle him. Directed by Jeremiah Chechik from yet another esprit-driven John Hughes script, Randy Quaid - missing from *European Vacation* but making a welcome return here - would have stolen the show as sponging deadbeat Cousin Eddie, but for John Randolph as Clark's laid-back father, who pinches it by a whisker. His conciliatory monologue to a brow-beaten Chase about the real secret to the perfect family Christmas is a gem. Once again, however, the highlight comes when poor, beleaguered Chase can take no more of his festive failings and sounds off about his miserly employer: "I wanna look him straight in the eye and I wanna tell him what a cheap, lying, no-good, rotten, low-life, snake-licking, dirt-eating, inbred, over-stuffed, ignorant, blood-sucking, dog-kissing, brainless, dickless, hopeless, heartless, fat-assed, bug-eyed, stiff-legged, spotty-lipped, worm-headed sack of monkey shit he is!". With a choice score by Angelo Badalamenti, intercut with some Seasonal favourites, and a chucklesome animated opening credits sequence (backed up with a toe-tapping titles song by Mavis Staples), this is a guaranteed tonic when you're suffering those post-Christmas blues. The undisputed jewel in the crown of the *Vacation* series, and mandatory festive viewing.

The only advantage to owning this one on DVD is its durability factor; you'll have worn out a VHS copy by New Year for sure! Seriously however, it's a shame that a matted transfer has been forsaken in favour of one which, in Warner's phraseology, has been "modified from it's original version" and "formatted to fit your screen". The fullscreen picture quality of the 29-chaptered feature isn't particularly strong and this being a Warner release it'll come as no surprise that the disc contains few extras. What little there is comprises some illustrated production notes, cast and crew biographies and trailers for all four of the *Vacation* flicks to date (though the second in the series, *European Vacation*, remains the only one as yet unreleased to disc). - TG

NATURAL BORN KILLERS

Colour, 1994, 121m. / Directed by Oliver Stone / Starring Woody Harrelson, Juliette Lewis, Robert Downey, Jr. / Trimark (US R1 NTSC) / WS (1.85:1) / DD5.1, Warner (US R1 NTSC, UK R2 PAL) / WS (1.85:1) (16:9) / DD5.1

After trying to inject experimental film techniques into a straight movie biography in his loopy *The Doors*, Oliver Stone decided three years later to just ignore any attempts at commercial filmmaking with *Natural Born Killers*, a shrieking descent into the director's own view of modern media-driven Hell. Slapping together virtually every kind of film format (Super 8, 16mm, B&W, video) and avant garde technique known to man, his jittery collage of operatic gore and black humour wound up on the MPAA chopping block and split audiences down the middle. Even today after its full restoration and lavish special edition treatment, the film continues to win praise for its daredevil visuals and damnation (most notably in courtrooms and from John Grisham) for its relentless onslaught of violence.

Mickey and Mallory Knox (Woody Harrelson and Juliette Lewis) like to kill people. Celebrated in the media as a kind of psychopathic, modern day Bonnie and Clyde, the couple always leaves a witness at their crime scenes to ensure their future folk legend status, while an equally deranged cop (Tom Sizemore) tries to track them down. Breaking with standard road movie tradition, the couple is captured about halfway into the film, leading to a second act which focuses on the exploitation of violence by the media (represented by Robert Downey, Jr.'s Aussie reporter) and the pure weirdness of the modern penal system (Tommy Lee Jones' hilariously over the top warden).

The most obvious appeal of *Natural Born Killers* lies in its breakneck pacing and visual style, accompanied by a hellish soundtrack alternating between perversely chosen golden oldies and Trent Reznor's brash song-score. All of the actors toss subtlety out the window from the opening moments, with Harrelson and Lewis barrelling across the screen in performances that seem possessed by some unholy fusion of mind-altering substances and pure mental dementia. Thus, as a purely sensory joyride, the film's popularity as a catalogue of resources available to the modern filmmaker is beyond reproach. Furthermore, this may be the most extreme example of that bizarre '90s trend, the hyper-violent romantic road movie, which also includes such

seemingly disparate entries as *Wild at Heart*, *The Doom Generation*, and *Kiss or Kill*, among many others. *Natural Born Killers* also tries to be both a social commentary and a scathing satire, which is where it stumbles. Hard. Blissfully unaware of his own status as a self-manufactured media object, Stone directs his venom at an America which celebrates suffering and sucks the life force out of its human beings. Unfortunately, this message looks more trite with each passing year, resembling a clumsy junior high essay more than a finely crafting critique of modern society. Stone's final summation, which awkwardly fuses clips of Tonya Harding, O.J. Simpson, and the giant killer bunnies from *Night of the Lepus*, is ridiculous in all the wrong ways, and his attempts to be hip through absurdity ultimately wind up saying very little once the smoke clears. For every sequence that effectively hits a nerve, such as the *I Love Mallory* sitcom parody, another five flounder by to continue bashing home a point that was already made within the first ten minutes of the film. In essence, all of the unfair criticisms hurled at George Romero's similarly themed *Dawn of the Dead* hold water far more here: the violence becomes dull and repetitious long before the end, and the jabs at modern consumerist mentalities are far too obvious to sustain an entire narrative. A compelling experience it may be, but *Natural Born Killers* winds up saying more about its creator than the decade which spawned it.

One of the most widely overanalyzed titles in recent memory, Stone's film almost immediately spawned a special edition laserdisc which restored the unrated director's cut (purportedly with 150 shots trimmed from the abortive R-rated edition in theatres). Critics have picked apart virtually every aspect of the film, with producer Jane Hamsher even contributing a bitter, scathing behind-the-scenes book, *Killer Instinct* (following *The Devil's Candy* as the second literary pulverizing of a Warner Brothers production during the 1990s).

Despite the basic lack of depth, the technical aspects alone make for fascinating study material, borne out in Trimark's DVD edition. Duplicating most of the Pioneer laserdisc supplements, the DVD omits the Nine Inch Nails song "Burn" from the film itself (and the accompanying video) for legal reasons but otherwise makes for an ideal showcase. The image quality is comparable to the Pioneer laser and Trimark VHS edition: colourful, sharp, and kind of grainy at times, due to the vagaries of mixing and matching formats. The extra footage mostly helps the film, particularly Jones' ultimate fate during the prison riot, but the real showstopper is almost an hour of deleted scenes. From Ashley Judd's notorious courtroom scene to Denis Leary's hilarious excised rant, this is good stuff all around and easily merits viewing as much as the final film itself. Best of all is Stone's alternate ending, which offers a much more appropriate finale to Mickey and Mallory's nightmarish journey. In a rare audio commentary, Stone delivers a personable and illuminating account of the film, focusing more on the highlights than its infamous trouble spots. Also included are a half hour documentary on the making of the film (mostly cast and crew interviews summarizing the action and character motivations), as well as a useless DVD promo passed off as a "trailer" (the real thing is nowhere to be found, presumably still in Warner's possession).

Speaking of Warner, the studio reportedly shunted the director's cut of this film off to Trimark because they didn't want to handle unrated product (see the *Eyes Wide Shut* controversy as well), but they experienced no problems whatsoever with the graphic, unrated cut of *True Romance* (another Tarantino-penned road movie!) on laser and DVD. How's that for logic? In any case, Warner later brought out its own DVD of the R-rated cut for an Oliver Stone box set. The improved 16:9 transfer is a marvel, but otherwise it falls short compared to the Trimark disc.

NEKROMANTIK

Colour, 1987, 71m. / Directed by Jörg Buttgereit / Starring Daktari Lorenz, Beatrice M. / Barrel (US R1 NTSC) / DD2.0

Less a traditional movie experience than a slimy slap in the face, *Nekromantik* was an instrumental title in the '80s gore renaissance and quickly passed in bootleg form from one eager collector to another, long before its official and short-lived VHS debut through *Film Threat* magazine. Unlike many German horror films which fail to distinguish themselves apart from the sheer level of bodily fluid spilled in front of the camera (e.g., *The German Chainsaw Massacre* and *Violent Shit*), *Nekromantik* at least demonstrates some level of talent behind the camera and led director Jörg Buttgereit on a strange career which is hopefully far from over. How enjoyable this film will be, however, depends entirely on each viewer's individual sensitivities.

Quiet little Rob (Daktari Lorenz) seems like such a happy guy. Every day he goes to work for Joe's Streetcleaning Agency, where he and his co-workers clean up the gory remains of car accidents, and he goes home at night to his girlfriend, Betty (Beatrice Manowski, who later turned up in Wim Wenders' *Wings of Desire* the same year!). The young lovers display an unhealthy fascination with all things dead, so Rob decides to spice up their sex life by bringing home - yup - a corpse. With the aid of a few household implements, they engage in a sticky *ménage a trois*, which should cause most sane viewers to flee for the nearest exit. When Rob loses his job, Betty takes off with the corpse and leaves him a farewell note. Unfortunately he's unable to cope with single life and experiments with various ways of recapturing that old magic, with one unforgettable bit involving a handy prostitute. If this all sounds too warped, well, just wait until the last five minutes...

A film whose reputation rests mostly on its lurid title, *Nekromantik* is at least not as realistic as one might fear. The special effects by and large are competent but exaggerated to the point of black comedy, such as a partial shovel decapitation that seems to have strayed in from a Peter Jackson film. The potential for black humour isn't squandered, either, with the funniest bit involving Rob's reaction when he stumbles into a theatre showing a slasher film (with the soundtrack of Lucio Fulci's *Zombie*!). All of this would be far more unbearable without the excellent music score, partially composed by Lorenz himself, one of the finest and most memorable to grace an '80s horror film.

Shot on 8mm and blown up to 16mm for theatrical and video screenings, *Nekromantik* has always looked quite rough. The DVD doesn't seem too promising at first, with that notorious opening scene (at night, natch) still grainy and muddy as always. After that, however, this is a *Nekromantik* you've never seen before. The image is extraordinarily good for 8mm (a first for a DVD feature?), and even on the big screen it could probably never look this good. Contrary to the packaging, the soundtrack is presented in a modest stereo mix which makes this film feel a lot more slick than it probably should. The channel separation during the music is very satisfying, with some hilarious directional effects tossed into the mix as well. The stereo is also more prominent and balanced when played in simple two channel stereo rather than simulated Dolby Digital surround; a very impressive job all around.

Even those who hate the movie (and they probably outnumber the film's fans) should be impressed by the wealth of extras, including much participation by Buttgereit himself. Gorehounds in the late '80s speculated that he must be one of those creepy guys you'd never want to meet in person, but in fact he's a clean cut, charming guy with an obvious love for horror films and a quirky sense of humour. As anyone who heard his commentary on *Combat Shock* and *Killer Condom* can attest, he's good company for an entire film and really needs to make another feature after *Schramm*. He even offers some semblance of a defence for the film's most objectionable and repulsive sequence(s), the actual killing and skinning of a rabbit: "Just because we show it doesn't mean we like it." Apparently this activity was filmed during the day-to-day activity on a rabbit farm, but that doesn't make it any easier to watch. Co-writer Franz Rodenkirchen also chimes in on the commentary track and proves to be just as personable as the director, who also hosts a short making-of featurette packed with behind the scenes photos and anecdotes.

Another brief feature, *The Making of Nekromantik*, covers similar ground in a more documentary style fashion, with a series of outtakes and clips. An incredibly lavish still gallery is accompanied by what appears to be the film's entire score, isolated in perfect stereo sound. Not enough, you say? Buttgereit's early short film, *Horror Heaven*, also turns up and sports loving homages to the Mummy, Frankenstein, cannibal girl flicks, and most amusingly Godzilla, all hosted in quasi-Hitchcock style by the director himself. His other work is represented by two(!) *Nekromantik* trailers as well as previews for *Der Tödesking*, *Nekromantik 2*, and *Schramm*. And for you Easter Egg hunters out there, be sure to check his filmography under *Corpse Fucking Art*.

NEVER SAY NEVER AGAIN

Colour, 1983, 134m. / Directed by Irvin Kerschner / Starring Sean Connery, Kim Basinger / MGM / WS (2.35:1) (16:9) / DD2.0

 Sent by M (Edward Fox) to undertake a health and fitness regimen at a countryside spa, James Bond (Connery) stumbles upon the beginnings of a SPECTRE plot to hijack two nuclear missiles with which they will blackmail the world's governments. Sean Connery was the ultimate James Bond but even he struggles to keep this sorry 007 adventure afloat.

Due to lengthy legal wrangles with the Bond copyright holders the plot is largely anchored on material already mined by 1965's *Thunderball* and in spite of Connery's presence the results lack the panache of the "official" Bonds. In fact, once one gets over the natural elation of seeing Connery back in the role after an absence of 12 years, *Never Say Never Again* is the most painfully hollow experience. Rather than playing Bond in the manner he had done back in the 60s, our man adopts the light-hearted approach of Roger Moore and comes off wanting. The pacing is funereal, the action sequences lack polish - the best they could devise is motorbike chase which goes on for far too long- the gadgets are uninspired, the one-liners are lazily written (and delivered), Kim Basinger is a bland leading lady, the climax feels flat, and a woefully inappropriate score from Michel Legrand damages the proceedings immeasurably. That this could have come from the director of *The Empire Strikes Back* (arguably the best entry in the original *Star Wars* trilogy) beggars belief. It's not *all* bad news of course. The sets, particularly the underground "Tears of Allah" temple, are pretty impressive and we get suitably unhinged baddies in the shape of Klaus Maria Brandauer and Barbara Carrera. Nice performances too from Max Von Sydow as SPECTRE main man Blofeld and Bernie Casey as Bond's CIA pal Felix Leiter. But at the end of it all you can't help thinking it might have been better if, when *Diamonds Are Forever* wrapped back in 1971, Connery *had* said "never again"... and meant it.

Beware early pressings of the Region 1 *Never Say Never Again* platter - an error during manufacture resulted in the loss of over four minutes of footage at the layer change, during which Bond introduces himself to Domino in the casino and then meets Largo at the bar. Beyond an excellent 32-chapter print of the film (which includes a short segment excised "for humane reasons" from all UK prints by the BBFC, in which Connery and Basinger on horseback plunge from the battlements of Palmyra into the sea), the only additional material is a short teaser trailer. If ever a disc cried out for a retrospective documentary, *Never Say Never Again* is it; a warts'n'all chronicle of just how, in the face of much legal muscle, the project ever got off the starting blocks would have made for fascinating viewing and on such a sparsely decorated disc its exclusion is sorely highlighted. Languages and subtitling are provided in English and Spanish. - TG

NEW ROSE HOTEL

Colour, 1998, 95m. / Directed by Abel Ferrara / Starring Christopher Walken, Willem Dafoe, Asia Argento / Sterling (US R1 NTSC) / WS (1.85:1) / DD5.1

Never a director to go along with the mainstream, Abel Ferrara has directed films ranging from the sublime (*Ms. 45*) to the unwatchable (*Dangerous Game*), with very few falling anywhere in between. *New Rose Hotel* may be his most frustrating effort: an hour of a potentially interesting film grafted onto a complete mess for its final third.

In the near future, the scheming Fox (Christopher Walken) teams up with X (Willem Dafoe) for a plot to lure a leading scientist, Hiroshi, away to a rival corporation. As bait, the men recruit lovely Italian prostitute Sandii (Asia Argento), whose mission is to seduce Hiroshi away from his wife and plant ideas in his head. However, during her "training," Sandii and X fall in love... or so it seems.

Freely adapted from the introspective short story by William Gibson (*Johnny Mnemonic*), Ferrara's film takes several chances which promise to pay off. Hiroshi is never viewed directly, only as a flickering image on cameras; Sandii's actual seduction of Hiroshi is relayed only through dialogue and inference; and some kind of vaguely defined corporate conspiracy from the other side appears to be brewing on the sidelines. The actors generally do what they can with the material, with Asia taking top honours both for her sincere portrayal and her startling, unabashed nude scenes. Unfortunately, anything the film accomplished goes skidding downhill for the resolution, which consists entirely of Dafoe sitting in a dark room having flashbacks to the rest of the film. Period.

A difficult film to assess in terms of visual quality, *New Rose Hotel* features grainy digitized images, 16mm, 8mm... you name it. Many scenes are deliberately drenched so deeply in shadows that the actors are almost impossible to see, while others are startlingly clear and beautiful to behold. The opening credits in particular are a knockout, and the throbbing techno score manages to eke tension seemingly out of nothing.

That said, Sterling's DVD is about as good as could be expected. The 5.1 sound mix is extremely rich, with strong bass and evocative separation effects throughout. The transfer represents the film well enough, though the matting appears to trim a little too much from the top and bottom of the image. The disc also includes a commentary track by co-writer Christ Zois, who largely addresses the issues of adapting the Gibson story and is polite enough to sidestep some of Ferrara's more notorious working habits. An overzealous trailer,

the film's script, and a bizarre trivia game (which, when completed, simply leads to a message congratulating the player, and telling them that $100 million has been credited to their bank account. Alas, it's a lie...) complete this strange package for a very, very strange film.

THE NEW YORK RIPPER

Colour, 1982, 91m. / Directed by Lucio Fulci / Starring Jack Hedley, Almanta Keller / Anchor Bay (US R0 NTSC), Donut (Holland R2 PAL) / WS (2.35:1) (16:9), Creative Axa (Japan R2 NTSC) / WS (2.35:1)

In *Zombie Flesh-Eaters*, Lucio Fulci turned a tropical island into a desolate wasteland of the walking dead. In *The Beyond*, he transformed Louisiana into a nightmarish doorway to the underworld. However, none of Fulci's elegiac, haunting visions can compare to what he inflicts on the landscape in *New York Ripper (Lo squartatore di New York)*, his most controversial film. Rough, unsettling, and surprisingly well crafted, *New York Ripper* bore the brunt of countless charges of misogyny and other cinematic hate crimes, particularly after being banned in the UK as a video nasty. Like most entries in the European cinema of the extreme, this will outrage many and provoke more than a little laughter (probably intentional), but for any viewer, *New York Ripper* is a difficult film to forget.

N

Lieutenant Williams (Jack Hedley), a hooker-loving police detective, finds himself pursuing a brutal serial killer who, according to one eyewitness, quacks like a duck as he slashes his victims. Yes, indeed, every time a broken bottle or razor blade is wielded in malice, the soundtrack explodes with a deafening "quack quack quack!" Each murder becomes more unsavoury than the last, with women from all walks of life falling victim to the madman. Dr. Davis, a gay professor (Paolo Malco), offers his services to the police, and a young potential victim, Faye (Almanta Keller), escapes the killer's clutches (a splendidly weird half-dream sequence) and begins to unravel the mystery herself. When the killer cuts a little too close to home for Williams, the stakes increase and uncover a startling revelation lurking behind the madman's psychosis.

Tossing in every convention of the Italian giallo formula, Fulci emerges with an unholy response to such slick urban thrillers as *Tenebre* and *Dressed to Kill*. Like *Tenebre*, with which this film shares more than a few interesting structural similarities, the earlier scenes of brutality focus mainly on women, but the director turns this malefic gaze back on the viewer by ultimately offing virtually every cast member in a spectacularly nihilistic display of misanthropy.

While the gore scenes here are alarming and convincingly executed (for the most part), the killings also elicit a great deal of agony from the viewer and ultimately implicate any observer for participating in a society where "you have to be the best." Granted, most of Fulci's social observations may be complete hooey when you consider they're being delivered by a homicidal duck (a weird tribute to his earlier *Don't Torture a Duckling*, perhaps?), but the eerie final ten minutes provide enough food for thought to at least indicate Fulci had more on his mind than simply trading in hardcore sexist gore.

Even many Fulci fans find this film repugnant, an understandable reaction given the treatment and subject matter, but a few elements are noteworthy even with these misgivings. Francesco De Masi's marvellous big city crime score gives the proceedings an appropriately jazzy and sleazy bent, while cinematographer Luigi Kuveiller (*Deep Red*) magnificently uses the scope frame to capture an atmosphere of rotting claustrophobia completely lost on previous transfers. Though only a small portion of the film was actually shot on location in New York, the setting is all too convincing and bizarre. The actors generally do a good job despite the chaotic and frequently hilarious dubbing job, with Hedley making an interesting social hypocrite and genre stalwart Andrea Occhipinti (*A Blade in the Dark*) expanding his range somewhat as Faye's boyfriend. And finally, if you ever wanted to know where Dario Argento got the idea for the cheek-piercing bullet in *The Stendhal Syndrome*, look no further than this film's showstopping finale.

Most viewers first encountered *New York Ripper* through Vidmark's atrocious US VHS release in the mid-'80s. Unwatchable panning and scanning, coupled with an ugly faded and brown transfer, immediately earned the film a bad reputation which was only slightly improved when Cult Epics issued a much needed widescreen laserdisc several years later. Though smudgy and over-bright, the laserdisc at least provided some indication of the visual artistry inherent in the film and restored several brief bits of sex deleted from the US cut. Surprisingly, the most notorious restored scene involves no gore but involves a toe job in a local Puerto Rican dive, and for better or worse, Anchor Bay has retained all of this legendary footage in their DVD release. The transfer looks terrific, much better than any other

release in the US or Europe, with some delicious candy-coloured lighting designs that should have gothic Italian buffs gasping with delight. (Just check out that green light in the stripper's dressing room.) A couple of scenes will always look a little cruddy, such as the opening doggie hand-fetching, but overall the materials are in excellent shape. Strangely, the last shot of Malco standing on the sidewalk froze and faded into a wild psychedelic pattern on the laserdisc, while the DVD simply fades to black - a much more rational choice. Unlike *Zombie*, we'll probably never get a remixed 5.1 soundtrack for this one. However, the mono track sounds fine and renders De Masi's score with plenty of gritty punch. The explicit European trailer is included, as well as a handy Fulci filmography.

The film is also available in an anamorphic transfer (with different framing, oddly enough) in Holland and a non-anamorphic, optically censored disc from Japan.

NIGHT CALLER FROM OUTER SPACE

B&W, 1965, 85m. / Directed by John Gilling / Starring John Saxon, Alfred Burke, Patricia Haines / Image (US R0 NTSC)

One of the stronger British sci-fi films during the avalanche of sinister alien movies begun in the mid-'50s, this film was originally exported to US drive-ins under a far less subtle title, *Blood Beast from Outer Space*. While the DVD sports the film's original British title, the print simply identifies itself in the credits as *The Night Caller*, the original shooting title.

Judging from the pristine and often breathtaking quality on display here, it appears the film was mastered directly from the negative- particularly astonishing considering this film has been only available in ragged PD and cut TV prints for many years. Also, bonus points for the extremely amusing and well-done menu screen.

A trio of scientists are astonished when something that appears to be a meteorite enters the Earth's atmosphere and changes its course directly before landing. After investigating the site, Dr. Jack Costain (John Saxon) takes the remnants, a strange globe-like object, back to the lab for tests. The lone female scientist, Ann Barlow (Patricia Haines), is later terrorized while alone in the lab by something with a strange claw-like hand, but the creature vanishes before anyone else can arrive. Soon girls all over London are missing, with only one thing in common: they answered an ad in *Bikini Girl* magazine! It seems an alien is lurking in disguise somewhere in London and auditioning young nymphets for jobs as models (he comes by to visit at night, hence the title), at which point he abducts them for insidious uses back at home on Ganymede, the third moon of Jupiter. Naturally, Ann decides to go undercover to get to the bottom of this alien plot, but things don't turn out quite as smoothly as expected.

Strongly reminiscent of the Hammer *Quatermass* films, *Night Caller* obviously isn't up to that level but offers plenty of fun nonetheless. Saxon does an efficient job as always, but the real star of the film is director John Gilling, making a rare sci-fi monster outing in between such gothic gems as *Flesh and the Fiends, Plague of the Zombies*, and *The Reptile*. While the film begins like a standard, flatly shot scientist procedural, the photography becomes increasingly surreal and noirish as the film progresses, leading to a grim and stylishly bizarre final twenty minutes that crackles with some unexpected and shocking plot twists. The bizarre finale would never have been acceptable to a US studio, but then again, predictable happy endings were never absolutely mandated in Britain. Best of all, though, is the theme song, a real howler of a lounge piece that tries to shoehorn the style of "Goldfinger" into an evocative ditty about an alien. Overall, tons of fun for '60s drive-in fans.

NIGHT OF THE BLOODY APES

Colour, 1968, 83m. / Directed by Rene Cardona / Starring Armando Silvestre, Norma Lazareno / Beverly Wilshire (US R0 NTSC)

If you can stand the gore, this is probably the funniest of the many sleaze epics generated over the years by Rene Cardona, the man behind such delicious anti-classics as *Doctor of Doom* and *Santa Claus*. Apparently determined to take advantage of the increasing lenience of the censors during the late '60s, he piles on the exploitation here with unbridled glee, tossing in topless women, gory real life open heart surgery footage, a mad doctor, wrestling women, and a shirtless muscleman with an ape mask running around attacking innocent women. What's not to love?

The plot is more or less a retread of *Doctor of Doom* with the silliness notched up even higher. We begin with an extended she-wrestling match between

Lucy (Norma Lazareno, in a red satin kitty-demon suit) and a Santo look-alike, which culminates in a violent move that sends Lucy scurrying for a more appropriate day job. Her boyfriend (Carlos Lopez Moctezuma), a policeman, is soon occupied by a string of gory murders committed by a strange ape-man. This monstrosity has resulted from the efforts of Dr. Krallman (Jose Elias Moreno), a well-meaning physician who tries to reverse the effects of his son's leukaemia by giving him the heart of an ape (in graphic detail). Naturally the son quickly turns simian, and the local women walking alone at night have much to fear...

While *Night of the Bloody Apes (La horripilante bestia humana)* would be compelling enough based on the sheer lunacy of its premise, Cardona apparently decided to spice it up with some extra gore footage to go along with the cheesecake nudity. Apart from the aforementioned heart transplant, the killings all contain gruesome close ups of characters being dismembered, skinned, or otherwise abused, all rendered in loving colour. If H.G. Lewis had made a wrestling/killer monkey man movie, it would have probably looked a lot like this. The crazy dubbing just adds to the fun, as characters spout nonsensical observations right and left, turning the story into a maddening jumble.

The Beverly Wilshire DVD of *Night of the Bloody Apes* looks about the same as MPI/Gorgon's long unavailable VHS version - on other words, awful - with which it shares the same memorable, trashy cover art. The mono audio is clear if unexceptional, capturing every nuance of that giddy canned dialogue. A DVD mastered from the original negative, courtesy of Something Weird Video, will soon supplant this now discontinued edition, and a British release is in preparation too as we go to press.

(right margin: N)

NIGHT OF THE HUNTED

Colour, 1980, 93m. / Directed by Jean Rollin / Starring Brigitte Lahaie, Alain Duclos / Image (US R0 NTSC) / WS (1.66:1)

A far cry from his familiar universe of luscious yet melancholy vampires, the vaguely futuristic thriller *Night of the Hunted (La nuit des traquees)* seemed an odd choice to kick off a series of Rollin titles on DVD in the format's infancy. However, many of his most familiar elements are well in place: poignant and doomed romanticism, vibrant comic book colours, and startling, graphic violence. The film was long regarded as a lesser work, thanks in no small part to its availability only via unwatchable and edited bootleg tapes, but with this sparkling transfer, Rollin's much maligned low budget effort is much easier to appreciate.

Driving along a desolate road at night, Vincent Gardnere is startled to see a disoriented young woman (Rollin regular and former adult film actress Brigitte Lahaie) running through the woods. Another woman (Dominique Journet), nude and bordering on catatonia, watches in despair. Lahaie collapses in front of the car, and Gardnere takes her home where she reveals that she is suffering from amnesia. The two feel an immediate attraction and make love (for a long time); unfortunately, their momentary bliss is shattered when Lahaie is abducted and returned to an austere, postmodern asylum (actually a block of office buildings in which Rollin shot after hours). Gardnere plays detective and follows her back to the institute, where Journet has also been captured and returned. A series of bizarre events ensue: a nude woman is found with her eyes pierced by scissors (a memorably surreal image), two sexual encounters turn very nasty, and doctors apparently don't seem to care that the people around them are gradually deteriorating into lunatics or walking corpses.

Much in the spirit of David Cronenberg, Rollin makes expert use of the stark office complex to mirror the characters' emptiness, with its vast windows opening up on chilly expanses of night and unexpected bursts of red neon appearing around corridors. The film moves very deliberately, a Rollin trademark and retains a dark fairy tale quality despite the sci-fi trappings (exposure to a radiation leak is blamed for the outbreak). While the acting is mostly touch and go, not surprising considering the largely amateur cast and rushed production schedule, Lahaie does quite a fine job as the tragic heroine, and the central romance leads to an outstanding payoff during the haunting finale, set in a deserted train station.

A difficult, somewhat challenging film, *The Night of the Hunted* is well worth checking out, particularly considering the fine presentation. While some grain is evident during the night scenes (mostly the opening credits), the film looks far better than could ever be expected; the bright colours and razor-sharp resolution lend this a dignity completely missing from all other versions. The optional English subtitles are generally accurate, and the DVD also includes the original, perplexing French trailer (which mostly contains shots of people wielding guns and walking down hallways).

NIGHT OF THE HUNTER

Colour, 1955, 93m. / Directed by Charles Laughton / Starring Robert Mitchum, Shelley Winters, Lillian Gish / MGM (US R1 NTSC, UK R2 PAL)

Though it enjoys a reputation as one of the most frightening films ever made, *The Night of the Hunter* offers so many layers of enjoyment even after countless viewings that critics' refusal to categorize it as a horror film almost seems understandable. The sole directorial effort of actor Charles Laughton, the film offers a terrifying view of evil from a young perspective and, along with *Curse of the Cat People* and *The Sixth Sense*, remains one of the few successful portrayals of childhood terror.

A malevolent preacher, Harry Powell (Robert Mitchum), travels the back roads of America, killing off innocent widows and living off of their stolen money. He winds up in prison on a petty charge and shares a cell with Ben Harper (Peter Graves), who shot two men while robbing a bank. Harry tries to learn the hiding place of Ben's money but fails when Ben is finally hanged. Released from prison, Harry charms his way into the home of Ben's widow, Willa (Shelley Winters). Willa's daughter, Pearl (Sally Jane Bruce), takes a shine to the preacher, who entertains the masses by performing an unforgettable wrestling match with his hands, tattooed "LOVE" on one set of fingers and "HATE" on the other. However, Willia's older son, John (Billy Chapin), is the only one in town who senses the preacher's true motives, even after Harry marries Willa and converts her into a fiery religious zealot. The two children wind up on the run from Harry, who pursues them on horseback until they wind up in the home of the kindly Rachel Cooper (Lillian Gish), a mother hen who finally may prove to be a match for the false man of God.

As visually remarkable as any film ever made, *Night of the Hunter* uses rich black and white imagery to stir up primal, haunting imagery that must have made Jean Cocteau jealous. The chilling tableau of one character chained underwater to a submerged car is just one highlight; other unforgettable touches include Harry's shadow consuming John as he tells Pearl a bedtime story and the suspenseful basement sequence, in which Harry first corners the two children. Laughton wisely follows Davis Grubb's fairytale-influenced novel almost to the letter, while Walter Schumann contributes a forceful yet lyrical score which perfectly supports the film at every turn. Mitchum and Winters give perhaps the best performances of their careers, while Gish proves she could still perform on the same level found in her best work for D.W. Griffith.

Previously released on laserdisc in similar transfers from both Criterion and MGM, this film has always looked very good on home video. However, MGM's DVD outclasses them all with an astonishingly crisp transfer sporting amazing clarity of detail and rich, black shadows which add considerably to the ominous tone of the film. Apart from the same washed out theatrical trailer, the disc also includes some adequate production notes, but the film itself is the real showpiece.

NIGHT OF THE LIVING DEAD

B&W, 1968, 96m. / Directed by George A. Romero / Starring Duane Jones, Judith O'Dea, Karl Hardman, Marilyn Eastman / Elite (US R0 NTSC, UK R0 PAL), Anchor Bay (US R0 NTSC), Moonstone (UK R2 PAL), Stax Entertainment (UK R2 PAL), Third Millennium (UK R2 PAL), Madacy, Master Tone, United American (US R0 NTSC)

 George Romero's groundbreaking black and white zombie classic, *Night of the Living Dead*, has gone through a lot over the years. It's been sequelized (by both Romero and writer John Russo), remade, ripped off, spoofed, and even colourized. But could it survive the horrific debacle of Russo's "30th Anniversary" edition? Probably, but the sheer greed and pointlessness of this venture under the Anchor Bay banner make it an awfully bitter experience for horror fans expecting a special edition and instead getting a soulless (and late) attempt to jump on the zombie bandwagon. Elite's immaculate edition of the film prepared back for its 25th anniversary already covered the bases, so anyone with a sense of respect for the original would be well advised to stick to that earlier DVD edition instead or Elite's tombstone cover "Millennium Edition," which adds on a 5.1 remix and all of the extras from the two platter laserdisc.

The familiar storyline operates like an irrational nightmare from which one never manages to awake. Barbara (Judith O'Dea) visits a graveyard with her brother, Johnny (producer Streiner) and winds up fleeing for her life from a shambling, wordless zombie (Bill Hinzman). She hides in an abandoned farmhouse and slides into complete catatonia, though she's joined by several others. Ben (Duane Jones of Ganja and Hess) - horror's first black hero! - locks horns with the obstinate Harry Cooper (Karl

Hardman), whose wife, Helen (Marilyn Eastman) is more concerned about the welfare of their ailing daughter in the basement. Armies of the undead begin to congregate outside, forcing the survivors to barricade the windows and hope that somehow they will make it through the night.

Writer Russo, a talented novelist and screenwriter, claims in the Anchor Bay version that he originally had several other concepts which were never filmed because of budgetary reasons. According to the interview contained with the DVD, these scenes "were discussed back in 1967 during our first story sessions, but were not carried out due to lack of time and money." If that's the case, the discussion may have gone something like this:

> JOHN. *Hey, George, why don't we tack on a really boring opening scene with a redneck preacher where the cemetery zombie comes to life and a lot of bad actors who look like they're reading cue cards run around screaming? Then we could throw in this stupid female reporter and a corny epilogue that makes no sense just to make sure viewers don't get too scared or involved in what they're watching?*
>
> GEORGE: *No, John, that's stupid.*

Of course, if these concepts were so important to Russo, he could have introduced them into his worthy 1970s novelization of the film, but no, he had to actually shoot these scenes and attempt to work them into the film. But wait! We also get a wall to wall new synth score by Scott Vladimir Licina, who also plays the aforementioned preacher (badly). The score itself, contained on a separate soundtrack CD with the DVD box, isn't bad in and of itself, but within the film the results are laughable. Ironically, Romero's original library cues worked far better and worked as an integral part of the film's sensory fabric. The new footage looks awful; reportedly shot on black and white film stock, it comes off more like your average shot on video quickie job, and for some reason (read: money) Hinzman felt the need to return as the cemetery zombie. Even with pounds of makeup, the difference in thirty years is jarring and ruins whatever effect was intended. Other "new" footage includes an additional, earlier sequence with zombies munching car victims, though it adds nothing besides unconvincing effects and grinds the story even further to a complete halt. As Romero knew all too well, more is definitely less. Just for the record, image and sound quality are excellent, but the same superb quality can also be found on the Elite DVD, which presents the original film and a wealth of extras (commentary, stills, prop photographs, a short film parody, and a clip from Romero's *There's Always Vanilla*). The Anchor Bay version also includes the original cut of the film, which was diced down by several minutes to make room for Russo's new footage. However, the original cut is still slathered with the new music score - hardly an improvement. The Russo version is also available in the UK from Third Millennium, for what it's worth. The extras for Russo's cut are limited entirely to self-promoting behind the scenes pieces with little attention given to the original film or its historical significance. The film (which is still presumed to be public domain, though it really isn't) has also been released in several cheapjack editions. In short: if the disc has an Elite logo, pick it up. If it doesn't, skip it.

NIGHT OF THE LIVING DEAD

Colour, 1990, 88m. / Directed by Tom Savini / Starring Tony Todd, Patricia Tallman / Columbia (US R1 NTSC, UK R2 PAL) / WS (1.85:1) (16:9) / DD4.0

Remakes by their very definition are a very tricky business, and when it comes to remaking a classic horror film, the stakes can go even higher. *Night of the Hunter*, *Invasion of the Body Snatchers*, *The Haunting*, *Black Sunday*, and even *Psycho* have all come under the axe with varying results. So why would George Romero and the crew from the original 1968 *Night of the Living Dead* want to remake the undisputed daddy of all modern zombie films? Money, obviously; since the original was thought to be public domain, no one involved in the '68 production received their cut of the profits the film generated, so a colour remake seemed like a good way to give everyone their share. Fortunately, the resulting film turned out much better than anyone had a right to expect. While there simply isn't a way to duplicate the horrific drive of the black and white original, the 1990 edition, capably helmed by effects master Tom Savini, stands as a respectable addition to Romero's "Dead" series and features enough new wrinkles of its own to merit attention from horror fans.

After a wayward zombie kills her brother, the withdrawn Barbara (Patricia Tallman, a familiar face to *Babylon 5* fans) flees through the countryside and winds up at an abandoned farmhouse. Other human survivors gather at the house to avoid the onslaught of flesh-hungry,

walking dead: Ben (*Candyman* himself, Tony Todd), Harry Cooper (Tom Towles, aka Otis from *Henry: Portrait of a Serial Killer*), his wife Helen, and a young redneck couple including *Leatherface's* William Butler.

If this scenario sounds familiar, it should... at least until the last twenty minutes. While Savini includes some nice twists bound to surprise fans of the original throughout the film, starting with a nice jolt in the graveyard opener, he and writer Romero begin throwing some severe curveballs for the finale. Many critics felt betrayed by what seemed to be a radical departure from the jaded '60s nihilism of the original conclusion, but in an E.C. Comics-cum-*Dawn of the Dead* fashion, the new ending is very satisfying and perfectly in keeping with Romero's vision. Compare this to the "new" finale tacked on by John Russo for his 30th Anniversary edition of the '68 film, and there's no question who best captured the insight and attitude of Romero's classic.

Continuing its surprising dedication to the horror titles in its vaults, Columbia has presented *Night of the Living Dead* with some nice special features indicating more studio respect than one could have possibly guessed. Tom Savini provides a jam packed audio commentary filled with the usual Pittsburgh trivia and anecdotes about the difficulties of zombie wrangling. "The Dead Walk," a very well-edited half hour featurette, also contains interviews with some of the principals, including Savini again, and includes some brief but juicy snippets of gory gunshots trimmed from the final cut to avoid an X rating. The film itself is surprisingly "sterile," to use Savini's term, with regards to graphic bloodshed, and this surprising approach also makes his film a worthwhile and unorthodox addition to American zombie cinema. Rounded off with the original trailer as well as one for William Castle's *The Tingler*, this one should leave horror fans drooling for more.

The film itself looks better than ever, with the original orange tints (black and white on the laserdisc) restored to their hellish glory over the end credits. The full frame edition of the film itself (included only on the US disc) looks fine but, with the squarish compositions imposed by removing the mattes, the result suffers from a bland, made-for-video appearance that does the movie itself no favours. The anamorphic 1.85:1 presentation, on the other hand, restores a great deal of atmosphere and intensity to the proceedings, with a much tighter focus revealed during both the action scenes and dialogue interactions. Either one should suffice and deserves a look, but the comparisons back to back are quite surprising.

THE NIGHT PORTER

Colour, 1974, 117m. / Directed by Liliana Cavani / Starring Dirk Bogarde, Charlotte Rampling / Criterion (US R1 NTSC) / WS (1.85:1)

A stylish and astoundingly seamy fusion of erotica and stark concentration camp trauma. While many subsequent films, mostly Italian, took the Nazi sexploitation route to unbelievably tasteless levels, Liliana Cavani's treatment in *The Night Porter* remains more problematic. More concerned with mood and characterization than cheap thrills, the film is nevertheless extremely kinky and shocking enough to prove that its R rating is the product of a ratings system far different than the one we have now.

At a swanky Vienna hotel in 1957, the head porter, Maximilian (Dirk Bogarde), is startled when he recognizes a female guest, Lucia (Charlotte Rampling). Max is generally regarded as a noble and professional man, but as it turns out, he was once a Nazi official and engaged in an anguished, tormenting sexual relationship with Lucia during her hellish tenure as a concentration camp prisoner. Even more startling is her willing submission to Max when they meet again, and the two become so consumed by their fatalistic passion that they barricade themselves into a room where they can plunge into the darkness of their own souls. Unfortunately, Max's former Nazi colleagues have noticed his activities and conspire to keep him from revealing any of the dark secrets of his past.

Regardless of how one reacts to *The Night Porter*, few can argue that Cavani was a director of convictions in her heyday. Before plunging into mediocre TV fare, she managed to shock the Italian bourgeois critics with films like this and her rarely seen *Beyond Good and Evil*. Of course, the excellent cast helps; Bogarde has never received enough credit for his performance here, which is complex and fascinating enough to rank with the best work of his often stunning career, while Rampling's icy beauty makes her a fascinating enigma, oscillating between pleasure and pain. The fact that the two had previously appeared in Luciano Visconti's notorious Nazi epic, *The Damned*, adds further dimensions to the actors' presence, while sleaze/art regular Philippe Leroy (*The Wild Eye, The Frightened Woman*) once again mines his effortless ability to weave charm and menace into one suave characterization.

Criterion's DVD, mastered from the same elements used for the laserdisc and Home Vision VHS editions, is a veritable feast for the eyes. The burnished, opulent hues of the hotel sequences contrast effectively with the chilly greys and blues of the World War II flashbacks, and the letterboxed framing (which removes some extraneous information from the top and bottom of the image while adding to the sides) improves the focus of the many strangely composed dialogue scenes. Unfortunately, no bonus materials were available for the DVD (not even a trailer!), but the film itself still makes for a noteworthy release and deserves at least a rental for adventurous viewers.

NIGHT TIDE

B&W, 1963, 84m. / Directed by Curtis Harrington / Starring Dennis Hopper, Linda Lawson, Luana Anders / Image (US R0 NTSC) / WS (1.85:1)

The first feature film by cult horror director Curtis Harrington (*Games*), this bizarre little tribute to both experimental cinema and Val Lewton's methods of "suggestive terror" is one of the more memorable independent films of the 1960s. Rarely seen in any form other than choppy TV screenings or blurry public domain titles, *Night Tide* was finally remastered for its laserdisc debut from the Roan Group and has now been given the same red carpet treatment for DVD.

Johnny (a very young Dennis Hopper), a sailor on shore leave, roams along the California coastal boardwalks and encounters many of the local residents. He meets and immediately falls in love with Mora (Linda Lawson), who poses as a mermaid in a local sideshow. Their romance takes a sinister turn when Johnny begins to suspect that Mora may in fact be a cursed sea creature who murders a hapless man during every lunar cycle.

Barely a horror film in the traditional sense, *Night Tide* is soaked in atmosphere from the opening frames. Harrington's skilful use of the desolate seaside locations (mostly shot around the Venice and Santa Monica Beaches) yields some terrific results, but the stately pacing and deliberately low key acting may put off drive-in monster buffs. Dennis Hopper fans in particular will be jarred to see the familiar stoner in what may be his most restrained performance ever, while the supporting cast manages to find quirky little shadings in what could have been thankless roles. Lawson makes a fetching mermaid of the deadliest kind, while the great, perpetually underused Luana Anders (*Dementia 13, The Killing Kind*) turns up as a more wholesome boardwalk girl. Most surprisingly, established

Hollywood composer David Raksin (*Laura*) turns in a subtle, jazz-laced score perfectly in keeping with Harrington's dreamy imagery.

Night Tide's DVD presentation is attractively matted and looks better than its fans could have ever expected. A few nicks and tears in the print aside, the black and white imagery remains clean and powerfully rendered. Extras include the theatrical trailer (talk about a tough film to sell!) and an informative, affectionate, and laid back commentary track with Harrington and Hopper reminiscing fondly about their youthful days shooting along the beach. Many of this film's themes were later explored in a worthwhile 2001 cable feature, *She Creature*, available on DVD from Columbia.

A NIGHT TO DISMEMBER

Colour, 1983, 72m. / Directed by Doris Wishman / Starring Samantha Fox, Diane Cummins / Elite (US R1 NTSC) / WS (1.78:1) (16:9)

Even among the deranged wilds of Doris Wishman cinema, *A Night to Dismember* holds a special place as the single most incoherent, lunatic chunk of random footage to ever bear her name. (Or any of her pseudonyms, for that matter.) Wishman shot the film in 1979, only to lose the footage for her final cut due to a lab mishap. Using trims and alternate takes, she then assembled an entirely new narrative to appease her backers, though the result no doubt left a few jaws scraping the floor. This is no mere bad movie, afflicted by some minor inconveniences as wooden acting and hapless direction; here we have something almost breathtaking in its inability to assemble two coherent shots together.

As the babbling opener informs us during a random string of unlikely deaths: "What makes this story so strange is that all of the murders and deaths happened on October 15th. What makes this story even stranger is that most of the murders and deaths happened to the Kent brothers and their families." Told in fractured narration by a police detective who sits at a table answering the telephone, the rough sketch of a plot concerns these ill-fated Kents whose most publicly loony member, Mary (porn actress Samantha Fox), has been released into the care of her oblivious parents and her two scheming siblings, Mary (Diane Cummins) and Billy (William Szarka). Both of them conspire to drive Mary back into the nuthouse - or frame her for murders - or something... Meanwhile a series of gory murders send the local

population into the morgue, leaving our narrator to investigate by watching Mary do an impromptu striptease at her window. Endless fantasy/nightmare sequences, random chases, and a schizophrenic soundtrack consisting of looped dialogue, warbling Muzak, and random animal noises(!) pad out the proceedings until the whole nightmarish experience limps to a close.

Those who love the idiosyncratic touches of Wishman will find her fetishes pushed into overdrive here. Furniture, feet, and badly lit close ups often pop into view, while the use of senseless narration to comment on every single banal action produces levels of hilarity that can only be achieved by accident. It's impossible to evaluate Fox's performance since she never utters a word of dialogue, but she does seem to run and look around nervously well enough. Another porn veteran, Henry Paris regular Levi Richards, also turns up uncredited during the opening montage only to hang himself for no apparent reason. (He also appeared in *Come with Me, My Love*, aka *The Haunted Pussy*, reputedly one of Wishman's rare ventures into hardcore.) Gorehounds in search of some mindless bloodletting will find plenty of the red stuff on display here as Wishman apparently tries to outdo her buddy H.G. Lewis; though poorly shot and entirely unmotivated, most of the effects are actually pretty impressive for the time, including one needle through the neck gag that almost looks real. Just don't say you weren't warned!

Very briefly released on video (possibly bootlegged), *A Night to Dismember* has been nearly impossible to see, remaining an odd footnote in Wishman filmographies and interviews. Now this patchwork atrocity has been released on DVD courtesy of Elite, who have probably done the best they could with a film made up of scraps. The visual quality varies from shot to shot depending on the inconsistent lighting and film stock, and it all has a grainy and washed out appearance. That said, it's still miles ahead of any videocassette versions, which were too murky and blurry to watch. The 1.85:1 framing sometimes looks tighter than what Wishman may have intended, but considering her inability to compose a formal shot, the real aspect ratio is anyone's guess.

The disc contains an inane promotional trailer apparently shot before the movie was even made, but the real extra of note here is a commentary track with Wishman and her long-time cinematographer, C. Davis Smith (who decided to go the XXX route after Wishman bowed out). The cover boasts that this is one of the most "entertaining" commentaries ever recorded, and, well, who are we to argue? For the entire running time Wishman verbally berates her associate ("Stop interrupting me!" is a frequent order) and gushes about the results she achieved under the circumstances. Somehow it's comforting to hear that her commentaries can be as delusional and head-spinningly weird as her movies themselves.

NIGHTMARE CITY

Colour, 1980, 88m. / Directed by Umberto Lenzi / Starring Hugo Stiglitz, Laura Trotter, Mel Ferrer / Laser Paradise (Germany R0 NTSC), EC (Holland R0 NTSC), Creative Axa (Japan R2 NTSC), Italian Shock (Holland R0 PAL) / WS (2.35:1)

 One of the first Italian zombie films to follow in the wake of Lucio Fulci's *Zombie*, this delirious, campy gorefest was the only subgenre contribution by crime/cannibal specialist Umberto Lenzi (*Cannibal Ferox*) and once again betrays his preference for focusing on action sequences. Most Americans encountered this one through drive-ins and many, many video editions as *City of the Walking Dead*, though for once the zombies do more than just walk. Heck, in this one they can run, stab, fire machine guns, and apparently even operate a plane.

Resourceful reporter Dean Miller (*Tintorera*'s Hugo Stiglitz) arrives at an airport in an unnamed American city (which looks suspiciously like Madrid) to meet a noted atomic scientist. Along with a group of military men and police, he watches in anticipation as the plane lands on the runway... and zombies begin to pour out, slashing and hacking through the waiting crowd. Pretty soon the whole city is under siege, with Lenzi cutting back and forth between bad *Solid Gold* dancing and military leader Mel Ferrer explaining that radiation has created these undead bloodsuckers. Dean's doctor wife, Ann (Laura Trotter), is forced to contend with the growing legions of zombies at work, so the couple tries to leave town and contain the madness. Meanwhile the blood continues to flow as the citizens succumb one by one to the atomic terror.

A "bad" movie by any conventional standards, *Nightmare City* (or as it's known in Italian, *Incubo sulla citta contaminata*) is loads of fun for anyone in a silly mood. The unforgettable zombies sport exceptionally poor make-up jobs and have distinctive, amusing personalities in their brief screen time, while each scene drips with staples of early '80s exploitation. The underrated Stelvio Cipriani

pitches in with one of his best scores, a feisty, pop-driven musical pastiche that even tosses in a Grace Jones tune for good measure. Never one of the more visually gifted Italian directors, Lenzi instead points his camera at the action and lets it roll, so don't expect much from the grainy scope photography.

Laser Paradise's DVD instantly became one of their more high profile items when the German title was discontinued due to an unauthorized English language track. The disc itself was apparently mastered from the long unavailable Japanese laserdisc, which is at least completely uncut, properly letterboxed, and has all of the scenes in their original order (as opposed to the jumbled mess shown in the US). The visual quality is obviously quite a mess, with colour timing wildly fluctuating from scene to scene, artefacts popping up in every dark scene, and Japanese subtitles occasionally popping up over the lower matte. The subsequent German and Dutch editions look somewhat better and are similarly letterboxed, while the priciest option from Japan contains a digital port of the old widescreen version. Most valuable is the Italian Shock version, which includes a rollicking Lenzi commentary. A US edition from Anchor Bay is also forthcoming at the time of this writing, making this *five* DVD releases to date. It's a sick world, isn't it?

NIGHTMARES

Colour, 1983, 100m. / Directed by Joseph Sargent / Starring Cristina Raines, Emilio Estevez, Veronica Cartwright / Anchor Bay (US R1 NTSC)

Neither the best nor the worst of the '80s horror anthology boom, *Nightmares* began as a television project of four horror stories helmed by TV specialist Joseph Sargent, whose only previous horrific experience was the underrated *Colossus: The Forbin Project*. Surprisingly, the results were deemed too strong for the small screen, so a gory and pointless opening scene was tacked on and the project was instead shipped into theatres by Universal. The results fit in squarely with the horror TV series of the period; the excellent *Darkroom* (also from Universal and sporting similar music by Craig Safan) and George Romero's *Tales from the Darkside* immediately spring to mind. Veering away from the ghoulish moral tales of the '60s (*Thriller, Night Gallery*) and '70s (those great Amicus anthologies), '80s horror compendiums focus more on special effects and surreal atmosphere, a trend really kick-started by

Creepshow. Unfortunately, fans of the period who didn't grow up with *Nightmares* will be baffled by the fact that the film isn't especially scary or gory, but kids of the '80s should find their hunger for this little cult item well served here.

In the opening story, "Terror in Topanga," Cristina Raines (*The Sentinel*) portrays a chain-smoking woman whose night drive to fetch some smokes may be quickly cut short by a serial killer prowling the countryside. This segment was later recreated - badly - in *Urban Legend*, which attempted to pass off both this and the opening of When a Stranger Calls as modern folklore.

In the second and most amusingly dated story, "The Bishop of Battle," Emilio Estevez plays a video game junkie whose hours in the arcade begin to take their toll on both his life and his sanity.

"Benediction," another sub-Duel evil vehicle tale, features a black pick up truck terrorizing a priest (Lance Henrikson, pre-Aliens) who has recently lost his faith.

In the last and most critically popular story, "Night of the Rat," married couple Veronica Cartwright and Richard Masur are alarmed to discover that the rodent problem inhabiting their house has gone really, really out of control.

While none of the "twist" endings really pack much of a punch, *Nightmares* kills an hour and a half nicely and at least deserves a rental now that Anchor Bay's DVD managed to bring the film back to the public after years of moratorium hell from MCA. The fullscreen transfer, which features a lot of spare headroom, looks fine - about as good as the film has ever been, considering it's drenched in that murky early '80s TV look. Apparently some post-production work on the film was deemed unnecessary, as many of the effects still look unfinished (notably the disappointing giant rat). However, the video game effects look... well, like *Tron*, for what that's worth. Overall, while the rat episode may be the only genuine monster entry in the film, all four are adequate little macabre sketches designed to be shown late on a Friday night, when their flaws might not seem quite so obvious. Also includes the memorable theatrical trailer.

NIGHTS OF CABIRIA

B&W, 1957, 118m. / Directed by Federico Fellini / Starring Giulietta Masina, François Périer / Criterion (US R1 NTSC)

While America was celebrating its insulated world of the nuclear family and flag-waving in the 1950s, foreign cinema gradually slipped into public

consciousness and exposed viewers to some visions that wouldn't be seen coming out of Hollywood until the late '60s at best. One of the pioneers in this field, Federico Fellini, took the post-World War II concept of neorealism and gave it his own unique twist, and of all of his films, perhaps *Nights of Cabiria* (*Le notti di Cabiria*) was the most ahead of its time. Here is a film with an individualistic female protagonist in a world where - gasp! - most of the men are jerks, she doesn't experience a magical rescue a la *Pretty Woman*, and the only salvation comes through her own steadfast positive attitude. Rather than flinging one misery after another at his characters like such other neorealist films as *Umberto D.*, Fellini displays admiration and concern for his heroine, most likely due in part to the fact that the role is played by his wife, Giulietta Masina. While Masina sometimes seemed hammy and miscast in her other films for her husband, here she's absolutely perfect and offers many startling non-verbal moments in which her gorgeous, soulful eyes communicate everything the audience needs to know. And what a glorious final shot!

The story of *Cabiria* should be familiar to anyone has seen its American musical stage version, *Sweet Charity*, which was later filmed (very well) with Shirley MacLaine. Most of the vignettes in the film lead to the perky prostitute Cabiria being tossed aside or attacked in some way, but Fellini counters this potentially downbeat material by introducing moments of quirky humour (Cabiria runs into a door, goes to an odd and utterly Fellini vaudeville show, etc.) and surprising pathos, thanks in no small part to Nino Rota's beautiful score. The DVD reinstates a seven minute sequence in which Cabiria encounters an impoverished former fellow hooker out in the country and returns to Rome with a nameless man carrying a sack. The scene is nicely acted and more than a little sad; according to the interview with producer De Laurentiis, he sliced the sequence from the film and stole it from Fellini, only to return it to the director several years later.

The quality of the presentation here is immaculate, and any film students who have suffered through horrendous, washed-out, scratchy prints or public domain tapes will find this a completely new experience. While the sound still remains undeniably of its era, with a few shrill moments of dialogue, the audio is a radical improvement. Dialogue plays an especially important role here, as Fellini had up and coming filmmaker Pier Paolo Pasolini adapt the script into common street dialect. While Fellini usually shot without sound and dubbed the dialogue in later (see *Satyricon* for a particularly obvious example), *Cabiria* remains that rarity, an Italian film that really is in Italian. The new optional subtitles are consistently clear and accurate, while the new English dub track is surprisingly well done, with most of the characters sporting appropriate Italian accents. Criterion's satisfying package also includes an early Masina/Cabiria appearance from Fellini's *The White Sheik* (in noticeably rougher condition) and the original and US reissue trailers. The price tag may seem a little steep, but anyone with a genuine love for cinema and Fellini in particular should find this well worth it.

NIGHTWATCH

Colour, 1994, 107m. / Directed by Ole Bornedal / Starring Nikolaj Coster Waldau, Sofie Gråbøl / Anchor Bay (US R1 NTSC) / WS (1.85:1) (16:9) / DD5.1, Ocean Shores (HK R0 NTSC) / WS (1.85:1) / DD2.0

 Though Denmark isn't generally known for turning out horror films, director Ole Bornedal created a minor splash throughout Europe with *Nightwatch*, an efficient, atmospheric, and occasionally striking mixture of whodunit and Grand Guignol. Unfortunately American audiences were deprived of the opportunity to see it when Miramax picked up US distribution rights, only to promptly lock the film away while director Ole Bornedal helmed a remake starring Ewan McGregor, Nick Nolte, and Patricia Arquette. After sitting on the shelf for over a year, the remake was drastically watered down, barely released, and tanked. Now years later, viewers can finally see what all the shouting was about.

Martin (Nikolaj Coster Waldau), a young law student, takes on a job as the overnight watchman at a local morgue, while his girlfriend, Kalinka (Sofie Gråbøl), studies to be an actress. Martin's repetitive nocturnal routine sitting at his desk is interrupted by occasional visits from the police, mainly an inspector named Peter Wormer (Ulf Pilgaard), thanks to the activities of a psychopath out slicing the scalps off young prostitutes. Meanwhile Martin's personal life is tested when he and his hellraising, potentially insane best friend, Jens (Kim Bodnia), embark on a test whereby they challenge each other to an escalating series of audacious stunts. Naturally, the first one to back down must

marry his respective girlfriend. One challenge involves a teenage prostitute named Joyce (Rikke Louise Andersson), who may know more about the killer than she realizes.

At least for its first half, *Nightwatch* is a powerful exercise in suspense which skilfully plays off anyone's inherent fear of being left alone in a vast, dark building for extended periods of time, not to mention the chilling experience of wandering down empty hallways lined with doors behind which lie unimaginable terrors. The script also wrings some surprising tension and emotional resonance from the challenge scheme, in which two essentially overgrown boys try to fight off the encroaching threat of manhood. Along the way they thumb their noses at convention by tossing beer bottles onto a statue of Hans Christian Anderson, destroying communion during a church service, and engaging in sexual horseplay in the middle of a fancy restaurant. However, following one marvellous, shiver-inducing sequence in which Kalinka comes to visit Joyce's apartment, the film lapses into standard, Hollywood-safe conventions as the villain menaces the protagonists with a variety of sadistic plots involving bonesaws and, most memorably, a pair of handcuffs. For all its perverse subject matter and dead bodies on display, Bornedal reigns in any overtly graphic material in favour of suggestion, even during two sequences in which most directors would have drenched the walls in blood.

Surprisingly, Anchor Bay's DVD retains the Miramax tag at the beginning of the film. The print looks excellent for a low budget European production - certainly better than the UK videotape and the lacklustre Ocean Shores DVD and VCD from Hong Kong - with even the potentially troublesome (and frequent) night scenes coming through with rich blacks and solid contrast. The 5.1 audio mix is used sparingly but very, very effectively at times, particularly when Martin's quiet job is shattered by an unexpected noise. Also, the optional and large English subtitles are a huge improvement over the hard to read sloppily printed on previous editions.

Bornedal also contributes a very soft-spoken audio commentary in which he generally points out various details in the lighting, music, and dialogue to create a macabre mood; however, he never really goes much deeper than that and avoids going into the tortuous studio politics which nearly demolished his breakthrough film and its ill-fated American counterpart. The disc also contains the original, evocative Danish trailer, which thankfully avoids spoiling any of the film's surprises.

THE NINTH GATE

Colour, 1999, 133m. / Directed by Roman Polanski / Starring Johnny Depp, Frank Langella, Lena Olin, Emmanuelle Seigner / Artisan (US R1 NTSC), Vision (UK R2 PAL) / WS (2.35:1) (16:9) / DD5.1

Roman Polanski's misleadingly marketed *The Ninth Gate* was sold as a fiery, action-filled demonic epic for the goth crowd, and audiences and critics both reacted with confusion. The hostility which greeted the film, particularly its final shot which - horror of horrors - actually requires the viewer to think, is especially disheartening considering the indifferent shrugs which greeted the wretched *End of Days* and *Stigmata*. Hopefully as time passes, expectations surrounding this film have changed somewhat and viewers can finally appreciate *The Ninth Gate* for what it actually is, an eccentric and intelligent black comedy laced with hearty gothic horror.

Adapted from Arturo Perez-Reverte's *El Club Dumas*, the plot feels on the surface like a glossy literary twist on Alan Parker's *Angel Heart*. Likeable but unscrupulous "book detective" Dean Corso (Johnny Depp) is hired by the elegant, slimy Boris Balkan (Frank Langella) to track down two of the three existing copies of The Nine Gates of the Kingdom of the Shadows, a text co-written by Lucifer himself in 1666. Balkan possesses the third copy and believes that only one of the three is genuine. Hopping from New York (or at least a CGI replica of it) to Portugal to Paris, Corso encounters a number of eccentric personalities including a wine-sipping book collector (warmly played by Jess Franco regular Jack Taylor!) and a beguiling, obviously supernatural nymphet (Polanski's wife, Emmanuelle Seigner), who's prone to popping up in odd places with some very funny reading material.

Filled with the disorienting malaise which characterized such films as *The Tenant* and *Frantic,* this elliptical tale is crammed with intriguing symbols (count the use of "9" throughout) and characters whose motivations only become clear as the layers of the story begin to peel off during the final half hour. The horrific set pieces are as grimly amusing as they are creepy, with the fate of wheelchair-bound baroness Barbara Jefford a particular standout. The flawless, breathtaking cinematography by current wunderkind Darius Khondji and Depp's amusing, compelling lead performance, a noticeable step up from *Sleepy Hollow* and *The Astronaut's Wife,* are all strong assets, but the real coup is easily Wojciech Kilar's beautiful score, one of the finest composed for a horror film in this or any other decade. Fans of European horror in particular will have fun comparing this film to some of its similar cinematic predecessors. Dario Argento's *Inferno*, also concerned with unholy texts, houses of the damned, and creepy young girls popping up out of nowhere, makes for a good point of comparison, as does the Polish masterpiece *The Saragossa Manuscript*. The latter film revolves around a series of interlocking narratives sprung from a demonic manuscript, and Polanski amusingly quotes directly from it during the effective, beautiful, and thankfully ambiguous final scene. Oddly enough, all three films are based on literary sources, some more loosely than others...

Artisan and Vision's fully loaded DVDs make for quite a bewitching experience even apart from the film, with beautiful menu designs replicating the woodcut illustrations and passing smoothly from one feature to the next. The discs include the standard first theatrical trailer as well as the more widely seen, ineffectual heavy metal promos which turned up after the release date was pushed back several months. An interesting storyboard comparison and a much less interesting promotional featurette are also included, but the highlight is undeniably the feature length commentary by Polanski himself, his first for DVD. While newcomers may find his accent difficult at first, he offers some nice observations about the casting, special effects, and adaptation process without going very deeply into the secrets of the film itself. He makes for a good tour guide, and his apologies at the end ("I hope I haven't been too boring") are quite unnecessary. Despite his unfortunate legal troubles with Artisan over this film's financing, he will hopefully continue to be with us for decades to come and create even more cinematic gems, as underrated as they may often be.

NOSFERATU THE VAMPYRE

Colour, 1979, 107m. / Directed by Werner Herzog / Starring Klaus Kinski, Isabelle Adjani, Bruno Ganz / Anchor Bay (US R1 NTSC) / WS (1.85:1), Anchor Bay (UK R2 PAL) WS (1.85:1) (16:9) / DD5.1

After twenty long years, German director Werner Herzog's most famous film, *Nosferatu the Vampyre*, was released on international video in its full, uncut German version. For reasons which remain unclear (many say the insistence of studio 20th Century Fox, while Herzog himself cites the variant languages of the onset actors), *Nosferatu* was shot in two versions, English and German. The English version still had to be partially redubbed because of many of the thick accents and has remained the most commonly seen print on TV. However, both can be compared thanks to the various buying options from Anchor Bay. The picture quality of both is absolutely stunning, with more colours and shadows than you could ever guess from the washed-out TV prints, and the soundtrack on the German version has been tastefully remixed into 5.1 (limited primarily to ambient sound effects and Popol Vuh's eerie music score, though a few moments - such as Adjani's opening scream - have been strangely pulled back in the sound mix). To round things out, the DVD also includes trailers for the English language and subtitled versions, as well as a nifty little Spanish trailer (zooming in and out of movie stills, in the same vein as *Suspiria*), plus a fun 12-minute "making of" featurette in which Herzog speaks during shooting and we can see the crew at work. Subtitles for the German version are optional, a nice plus.

Klaus Kinski has one of his best roles ever as Count Dracula, who vampirizes the naive Jonathan (Bruno Ganz) and proceeds to travel by ship to Hamburg, where he brings the plague along in his quest for Jonathan's beautiful wife, Lucy (Isabelle Adjani, who has never looked better). Many critics were frustrated by Herzog's attempts to duplicate certain shots from the original silent version directed by F.W. Murnau, not to mention Kinski's uncanny duplication of Max Schreck's rodent-like vampire appearance. However, in an age where people throw fits over the thought of an arty filmmaker trying to do a shot-for-shot remake of *Psycho*, this is that rarest of creatures, an outstanding remake of an already classic film. In fact, Herzog's film has taken on a life of its own outside of the original.

For every person who criticizes this version as slow or derivative, it's just as easy to find another who finds it breathtaking and haunting. The photography is stunning, with lingering images that will stay in your mind long after the film over, and the revisionist finale manages to preserve the tragic tone of the original while throwing a few new twists into the plot.

The audio commentary by Herzog enhances the film even more and definitely indicates that this notorious, temperamental genius has mellowed a lot with age, definitely not the same guy who allegedly pulled a gun on Klaus Kinski during the shooting of *Aguirre, the Wrath of God*. He brushes off the legendary stories of his fights with Kinski and provides a number of interesting anecdotes about the location shooting and actors. Anchor Bay also slated

two separate US DVD releases with upgraded 16:9 transfers, splitting the English and German editions apart (perhaps to take up more shelf space), though 16:9 transfers of both are available on the same disc in the UK.

NOT OF THIS EARTH

Colour, 1988, 81m. / Directed by Jim Wynorski / Starring Traci Lords, Arthur Roberts / New Concorde (US R1 NTSC)

The mysterious Mr. Johnson (Roberts) hires nurse Nadine Story (Lords) as his private physician, claiming that he needs regular blood transfusions to forestall an impending death. Nadine's suspicions about her employer are aroused when she notices that visitors to his house are never seen leaving. Buddying up with Johnson's chauffeur Jeremy (Juliano), she uncovers a nefarious alien plot to supply human blood to the inhabitants of a dying world.

A minor classic of its time, Roger Corman's 1957 sci-fi opus *Not of This Earth* has remarkably been remade twice, most recently in 1995 starring Michael York and Elizabeth Barondes. That was a straight and surprisingly well executed affair. Although Jim Wynorski's 1988 version adheres relatively closely to the plot of Corman's original, it also deigns to peddle us a heap of tongue in cheek humour and a liberal smattering of bared breasts.

The real coup was securing Traci Lords - fresh from her underage adult film-making scandal - for her first mainstream role and, some embarrassing overacting (in keeping with the tone) aside, she carries it off rather well. Lenny Juliano basically strolls through the action as himself, Wynorski acolyte Ace Mask plays the ludicrous material given him so deadly straight that he's funnier than anyone else in the picture, and Arthur Roberts imbues his alien life form with the requisite degree of solemnity. A peppering of glam cameos from Rebecca Perle and Ava Cadell - not forgetting Wynorski babes Kelli (*Chopping Mall*) Marony, Becky (*Dinosaur Island*) LeBeau and an unrecognisable Monique (*Deathstalker II*) Gabrielle - help to keep things bubbling along nicely. The f/x are surprisingly good given the minuscule budget and tight production schedule. The titles sequence cheekily comprises a bunch of gory clips which have nothing whatsoever to do with *Not of This Earth* - they were (rather pointlessly) culled from a host of other movies. With a cracking theme tune from regular Wynorski collaborator Chuck Cirino, this is a goodly measure of fun and is certainly one of the best titles on the director's prodigious CV. Which, depending on your opinion of his stuff, may or may not be considered a recommendation.

With its wallet-friendly price tag, the New Concorde DVD, released under the "Roger Corman Classics" banner, is as good a value package as one could hope for given the cheap and cheerful nature of the production. Notably conspicuous by its absence, however, is the sleeve-listed theatrical trailer, with the trio of ho-hum trailers for other Concorde titles hardly compensating for its omission. The movie itself is a fullscreen presentation with a more than adequate 24 chapter breaks. The phrase "digitally remastered" is noticeably becoming the subject of abuse and if *Not of This Earth* was subjected to it (as the sleeve claims) I'd hate to have seen what sort of shape it was in beforehand; the colour isn't as vivid as it should be and there's a nasty splice repair in evidence, which Wynorski remarks upon in his commentary, noting that it probably won't be fixed for the disc as "They're too cheap to remaster these things." Wynorski 1, Sleeve Notes 0. Regardless, I imagine this is still the best looking print we're likely to see on DVD.

The real bonus here is the amiable feature length commentary by the director and actor Juliano. Wynorski's memory is razor sharp and he is quick to point out the many errors in his film - re-used props, crew reflections in car doors, continuity glitches etc. Both the director and star, the latter in particular, are wont to having fits of drooling whenever Traci Lords is on screen (in fact, Wynorski even urges viewers to post images of her brief nude scenes on the Internet!); it's just a shame that Miss Lords herself couldn't (or wouldn't) participate in the banter. - TG

NOTORIOUS

B&W, 1946, 101m. / Directed by Alfred Hitchcock / Starring Cary Grant, Ingrid Bergman, Claude Rains / Criterion (US R1 NTSC), Anchor Bay (US R1 NTSC), PT Video (UK R2 PAL)

The most commercially and critically successful of Hitchcock's conspiracy films centring around World War II, *Notorious* picks up in the aftermath of that "Great War" when America was struggling to put together the pieces after a devastating global conflict. A sleek and fascinating Hollywood product, the film is now immediately relevant again as a study of human emotions sometimes running irrationally along with or counter to patriotic duty; most heartening to film fans is the fact that Hitchcock's taut entertainment has lost none of its suspenseful impact or romantic allure over the decades.

After her Nazi sympathizer father is sentenced to prison for treason, troubled party girl and closet US patriot Alicia Huberman (Ingrid Bergman) finds her self-destructive downward spiral in Miami halted by the presence of Devlin (Cary Grant), a CIA agent who crashes one of her bungalow parties and persuades her to do a little undercover work for her country. The two also begin a tentative affair, though her chequered past and his lack of personal initiative make for uneasy bedfellows. Things become more complicated when Alicia and Devlin learn of her assignment, to work her way into the heart of Alex Sebastian (Claude Rains), an old friend of her father who may now be brewing a plot with his cronies in South America. Another nasty situation awaits when Alex asks Alicia to marry him, a situation which would force her to live perilously within a nest of serpents.

An expertly paced film, *Notorious* begins with a languorous first half which delicately establishes the characters and lays out the groundwork for the battle of wills over a nation's future and an insecure woman's life. Almost imperceptibly, the story then begins to weave amazing suspense sequences into its fabric, most notably the long and justifiably celebrated sequence involving a purloined key and an all too short supply of champagne. However, these scenes do not exist as style for its own sake; the three recognizably human characters remain front and centre, as each heartbreaking turn of the plot tightens the screws on their precarious situation. By the end, a simple climb up and down a flight of stairs becomes a minefield of emotions, where the timing of even a few seconds or the sight of someone approaching in the background could be enough to alter an entire espionage plan.

The romantic angle was hot stuff during the film's original release, when the simple sight of a man and woman interlocked and sharing kisses while they plan dinner was enough to send temperatures through the roof. Combined with a globally relevant plot which foreshadows the atomic scares of the 1950s, *Notorious* proved to be remarkably ahead of its time as it used then-recent news items involving the end of WWII to spin out a compelling drama in which even the most superficially evil people harbour confused, all too human emotions.

Released in several different incarnations over the years, *Notorious* has generally fared well if not perfectly on home video. After years of VHS editions, the film was released on laserdisc by Criterion in both a two-disc special edition and a CAV one-discer. Despite some noticeable print damage throughout, the image had a silky, smooth quality that suited the film perfectly.

Anchor Bay's no-frills DVD was somewhat cleaner but also less glossy, making for an acceptable if unremarkable presentation. The Criterion DVD is markedly different in many respects; the opening credits are now severely windowboxed (almost to the point where they appear to be shot through a camcorder viewfinder), and the film elements (presumably from the restoration project funded by Disney) look free of wear and tear. However, the increase in resolution also pumps up the amount of grain in the image, creating a grittier visual texture than the Criterion laserdisc. Which version is closer to Hitchcock's intention is anyone's guess, but laser friendly fans may want to hold on to their older platters for comparison. The mono audio is fine and free of distortion, and the DVD also marks the first availability of this title with closed captions (as optional English subtitles).

The extras from the laserdisc edition have been ported over with a few new bonuses thrown into the mix. Best of the new goodies is an isolated music track for the score by Val Lewton veteran Roy Webb, while other audio options include commentaries by classic movie host Rudy Behlmer (who offers an interesting analysis of Alicia's decidedly tame swinging lifestyle) and Hitchcock analyst Marian Keane, who also narrates a quick video description of Ingrid Bergman's unexpected and poignant gesture for Hitch at his 1976 AFI tribute. Also included are the lurid theatrical trailer ("She was a notorious woman of affairs!"), the 1948 Lux Radio Theatre dramatization with Bergman and Joseph Cotten (originally included as an analogue track on the laser), an extensive gallery of production and promotional photos and artwork, excerpts of shortened and deleted scenes, snippets from "The Song of the Dragon" (a short story which indirectly served as the basis for this film), newsreel clips of Hitch and Bergman, and the usual fold-out liner notes, this time by *Murderous Gaze* author William Rothman.

UK viewers can also pick up the PT Video edition, which features a number of extras in addition to the remastered presentation: "A Conversation with Hitchcock" (available separately from Image Entertainment), an interview with Kim Newman, extracts from Truffaut's "Hitchcock/Truffaut" book, and an assortment of trivia, quote, and bio-related goodies.

NUDE FOR SATAN

Colour, 1974, 82m. / Directed by Paolo Solvay (Luigi Batzella) / Starring Rita Calderoni, James Harris / Image (US R0 NTSC) / WS (2.35:1)

Another astonishing rescue by Redemption from the jaws of oblivion, *Nude for Satan (Nuda per Satana)* has remained largely unseen over the years and would make a fitting double feature with the even loonier *Reincarnation of Isabel* (also featuring frequently nude Italian starlet Rita Calderoni, who gets billing above the title here!). Like Redemption bedfellow *Night of the Hunted*, this opens with a man (James Harris) stumbling upon an unconscious young woman in the middle of the woods at night. Here the similarities end, however; he takes her to a spooky estate where they find themselves confronted by their identical evil doubles (flip sides of the same coin, as the evil Harris helpfully explains), and it seems the whole crazy plot is a satanic concoction designed to lure our virtuous pair into complete debauchery. In the biggest howler, Calderoni is very slowly assaulted by a big *papier mache* spider, and it all culminates in the usual naked ooga-booga demonic ritual, complete with flaming skulls. These silly moments aside, Batzella (best known for *The Devil's Wedding Night*) generally sustains an eerie Gothic mood directly in keeping with the well established conventions of '60s horror cinema, and unlike Isabel, the story flows in a fairly linear (albeit wild) fashion with each spooky setpiece building upon the last.

Considering the fact that no one ever expected to see *Nude for Satan* turn up at all, the source materials (from the only surviving print) are in very good shape. The Techniscope framing is accurately presented at 2.35:1, and the print looks close to pristine. The film can be played either in Italian with optional English subtitles below the frame (the better choice since this was actually shot in Italian, not dubbed after the fact), or English dubbed, which is competent but less effective (and often pulls the evocative music score so far into the background it can barely be heard). The DVD also includes the film's rare European trailer in both its Italian and English incarnations. A version with hardcore inserts also made the rounds in '70s Europe, but this disc represents the director's original "soft" edition.

OASIS OF THE ZOMBIES

Colour, 1983, 82m. / Directed by Jess Franco (as A.M. Frank) / Starring Manuel Gelin, France Jordan / Image (US R1 NTSC) / WS (1.76:1) (16:9), KultDVD (Germany R2 PAL) / WS (1.66:1)

As most Jess Franco fans know, his work took a decidedly weird turn in the late '70s and throughout the '80s. His combinations of outrageous gore and explicit sex on the tiniest of budgets are a far cry from the opulent (if equally idiosyncratic) films of the Harry Allan Towers era, but those willing to persist with the director's odd flights of fancy can very occasionally find some odd bits of gold here and there. While *Oasis of the Zombies* is basically a work for hire Franco assignment filled with an outrageous amount of padding, it does offer a revealing glimpse of the manner in which Spain's most troublesome cinematic talent approaches a cut and dry genre film.

In the typical vague prologue, a pair of nymphets strolling hand in hand through a jungle (while showing off their early '80s bun hugger shorts, of course) pass by a hidden Nazi crate filled with gold. Unfortunately their idyllic afternoon is shattered when a pair of rotting hands burst from the earth, presumably dragging both of them to a slow, horrific death. The source of this mysterious, guarded gold is soon revealed when young student Robert (Manuel Gelin) is summoned to the African desert following the death of his father. Along with some airhead friends, Robert goes through the effects of the deceased and uncovers a strange story (told in very long flashback) involving millions in Nazi gold buried in the sand, protected by hordes of undead soldiers from the Third Reich, and Robert's late mother, a sheik's daughter who died during childbirth. Naturally Robert decides to fulfil his father's quest and sets out to find this hazardous oasis, with a gang of fellow explorers in tow. Naturally the zombies are none too pleased when the infidels arrive.

A long way from the classy, intelligent zombie antics of *Dawn of the Dead* or *Let Sleeping Corpses Lie*, this film is more along the dumb but endearing lines of such disreputable gut-munchers as Bruno Mattei's *Hell of the Living Dead*. The Nazi zombie gimmick was evidently a popular one at Eurociné, who also used it in the more skin heavy *Zombie Lake*. In fact, Franco's original assignment to direct that film fell through, resulting in his helming of this one instead.

The film was purportedly shot in both French and Spanish versions, though the former (usually dubbed in English) has been the easiest to find on video around the globe. International viewers have seen this under a wide variety of titles, such as *Treasure of the Living Dead, Bloodsucking Nazi Zombies, Grave of the Living Dead*, and *Oasis of the Living Dead*; the last of these was the version used for Wizard's out of print VHS edition. Likewise, cuts of this film have ranged wildly in content and running time, with one particularly guilty offender dropping all of the zombie footage!

This DVD, presented under the more marketable title of *Oasis of the Zombies*, comes closer to the original blend of *Raiders*-style exploration and gory horror envisioned by Franco, though that doesn't necessarily make it a "good" film. The finale is the real reason to wade through the slow stuff, as an army of zombies marches over the dunes through an oil fire at dusk and rips the encampment apart. Sure, the make up is still the same old half hearted latex and cereal mixture found in most '80s walking dead films (Lucio Fulci excepted, naturally), but there's a certain eerie power to Franco's gritty, gory visuals during this climax. Image quality is about as good as this film could look, considering the limitations of the source. The colours are solid, and the letterboxing makes the film far less claustrophobic than the out of print Wizard VHS edition, which was an unwatchable eyesore. Some rough splices and scratches show up here and there, but most Franco fans will be delighted to see this frequently maligned black sheep getting the deluxe digital treatment. The English and French audio tracks are included in glorious mono. The back of the box indicates an alternate English opening credit sequence, but this is the one actually included within the print.

OCTOPUSSY

Colour, 1983, 130m. / Directed by John Glen / Starring Roger Moore, Maud Adams / MGM (US R1 NTSC, UK R2 PAL) / WS (2.35:1) / DD2.0

When agent 009 turns up dead in Berlin, James Bond (Moore) is plunged into a plot to detonate a bomb on a US airbase in East Germany, which will lead to a lateral European disarmament directive that in turn will enable unchallenged Russian invasion and dominion. One of a couple of Bonds to suffer from the unnecessary complexity of its script, *Octopussy* also bears intrusive continuity defects. The first act is by far the best, set in India and pitching our man against a smuggling operation presided over by the capricious Miss Octopussy (Maud Adams) and her affiliate Prince Kamal Khan (a surprisingly effective Louis Jourdan). When the action moves to East Germany the story becomes bogged down in hum-drum double and treble crosses involving stolen jewellery and a bomb hidden in a circus cannon.

Having retrieved a modicum of sobriety with the previous film, the temptation to reintroduce the sillies proved just too great, and so we get a jungle-bound Bond doing a (then trendy, now arcane) Barbara Woodhouse impression and commanding a marauding tiger to "Siiiii-t!," warning a snake to "Hiss off," and, in a moment that represents the nadir of the entire series, swinging through the trees on a vine whilst hollering like Tarzan. After this the prospect of seeing him in full clown's regalia seems rather appropriate, yet extraordinarily that is not as stupid as one expects.

It's not all grim though. There's some good stuff too, including a punch-up when Octopussy's palace is invaded by thugs (one of whom is armed with a lethal yo-yo buzz-saw), the pre-titles sequence as Bond is chased across the skies by a heat-seeking missile, fisticuffs on the fuselage of a plane in flight, and the climactic siege on Khan's Monsoon Palace with eye candy aplenty courtesy of the chic black leather bikinis sported by Octopussy's all-female army. Kabir Bedi's Gobinda is a clichéd disciple straight out of the "Bond Guide to Hired Henchmen", but still makes for a formidable enough opponent. Statuesque Kristina Wayborn is the gorgeous Magda and performs most of her own stunts (which is more than can be said for good old Roger, who steps shamelessly in for the close-ups after the latest in a line of stuntmen has risked life and limb in the name of rollicking entertainment). There have certainly been worse Bonds than Octopussy but most are better, and coming in the wake of the magnificent For Your Eyes Only this one has to be dubbed mildly disappointing.

MGM's Octopussy special edition DVD is certainly on a par with the quality of the other Bonds but sadly suffers from the same anomaly tarnishing their release of The Living Daylights; the burnt-in subtitles have been erroneously omitted (though oddly the post-titles caption informing us that we're in East Berlin is still present). The silver lining to this cloud is that we lose a lame subtitle gag that follows Bond depositing an assailant on a bed of nails. Its owner flies into a rage and the caption "Get off my bed" appears; the scene works far better without it. The feature itself has 36 chapter-stops, and the supporting package is as strong as usual,

with a 35-minute "Inside Octopussy" documentary, a profile of Art Director Peter Lamont, a commentary from director John Glen, four trailers (several of which open with some specially shot introductory lines from Maud Adams and close with a Moore/Wayborn outtake), two slideshow format storyboard presentations set to the film's soundtrack, and the promo video for Rita Coolidge's smoochy titles song "All Time High". Languages are accessible in English and Spanish with subtitling in Spanish and French. - TG

THE OLD DARK HOUSE

B&W, 1932, 71m. / Directed by James Whale / Starring Boris Karloff, Melvyn Douglas, Charles Laughton / Image (US R1 NTSC)

The spooky old dark house genre made famous in The Cat and the Canary had already become a timeworn cliché by the time director James Whale decided to fling a few satiric barbs in its direction with a film called, appropriately enough, The Old Dark House. Based on the J.B. Priestly novel Benighted (also the basis for William Castle's 1963 colour version), Whale's film was lost for decades, a fate that has been attributed to everything from Priestly's dissatisfaction with the film to Columbia's attempts to suppress it to favour their remake. In any case, thanks to the efforts of director Curtis Harrington, the film was rescued from oblivion in 1968 but remained largely unseen by the general public aside from muddy bootleg copies until it was screened on American Movies Classics in conjunction with its first video release through Kino Home Video.

On a dark, stormy night in Wales, several weary travellers find their way to a foreboding old house run by the prissy Horace Femm (Ernest Thesiger, doing a dry run for Bride of Frankenstein) and his religious fanatic sister, Rebecca (Eva Moore). Their mute butler, Morgan (Boris Karloff), shambles around and gets drunker as the night progresses; when the power goes out, strange things begin to happen, mostly involving two other members of the household mysteriously kept behind closed doors.

Light on plot but heavy on atmosphere and witty dialogue, this Charles Addams-style black comedy no doubt confounded many horror fans expecting a traditional monster show. At first glance the film feels like a slightly elaborate stage play, though Whale's evocative use of shadows and sound effects manages to transcend any possibility of a stagebound presentation. While Karloff looks great and has a fun climactic fight, he has surprisingly little screen time through the rest of the film, thus leaving most of the work to the speaking cast members. Most of the cast does a fine job, particularly Thesiger's hilarious portrayal featuring the infamous "have a potato" dinner scene; surprisingly, only Laughton disappoints with a grating fake-Welsh comic boy performance that wears out its welcome very quickly. Gloria Stuart (best known as the narrator of *Titanic*) brings some welcome glamour as the nominal heroine of the piece, while Lilian Bond adds a quirky and vaguely kinky twist to her role of a showgirl anxious to find a husband and extricate herself from platonic sugar daddy Laughton. Of course, the film is almost stolen entirely by the final act appearance of Cousin Saul (Brember Wills), a cackling pyromaniac whose few minutes of screen time are arguably the creepiest Whale ever committed to film.

The print originally released by Kino on VHS and shown on AMC was something of a muddy mess, but thankfully the Image version (still licensed through Kino) was struck from far superior source materials reportedly discovered in a private collection. Though a few imperfections exist (the conversation with Elspeth Dudgeon in old man drag as the 102 year old Roderick Fenn suffers from constant frame shifting), this version looks extremely clean and crisp considering the tattered distribution history. Of course, the commentary by Stuart (the only surviving cast member) will be of particular interest since it inspired James Cameron to cast her in that famous big boat movie. The packaging, which features extensive historical liner notes and two nice poster reproductions, makes this a nice deal all unto itself for horror fans and film historians; fortunately, the film itself has held up and should provide more than a couple of laughs and shivers on a dark and stormy night.

THE OMEN
Colour, 1976, 111m. / Directed by Richard Donner / Starring Gregory Peck, Lee Remick, David Warner
DAMIEN: OMEN II
Colour, 1978, 107m. / Directed by Don Taylor / Starring William Holden, Lee Grant
THE FINAL CONFLICT
Colour, 1981, 108m. / Directed by Graham Baker / Starring Sam Neill, Rossano Brazzi
OMEN IV: THE AWAKENING
Colour, 1991, 97m. / Directed by Jorge Montesi and Dominique Othenin-Gerard / Starring Faye Grant
Fox / WS (16:9) / DD2.0

Riding the wave of modern demonic horror begun with *Rosemary's Baby* and *The Exorcist*, hysterical religious horror cinema hit an all-time high with the *Omen* series, which charted the rise of the Antichrist in the world of British-American politics by way of some outrageously contrived death schemes. Proving the law of diminishing returns, the series started with a bang with *The Omen*, a finely crafted yarn which kept its absurdity in check thanks to an earnest cast and some unforgettable set pieces. Financially speaking it was all downhill from there, with the series closing its initial trilogy in 1981 before a belated and unnecessary fourth instalment - on TV, no less - in 1991.

Our story begins with *The Omen*, in which American ambassador Robert Thorn (Gregory Peck) is informed at the hospital that his son died shortly after childbirth. Robert agrees to allow a newly orphaned baby take his child's place without the knowledge of his fragile wife, Katherine (Lee Remick). Shortly thereafter Robert is appointed the ambassador to Great Britain, where he settles into a roomy home to raise his son, Damien (Harvey Stephens). However, the boy's fifth birthday is disrupted when the nanny hangs herself in full view of their birthday party, a trip to church for a wedding turns disastrous, animals attack during a zoo trip, and the new nanny, Mrs. Baylock (Billie Whitelaw), seems to have a few sinister secrets of her own. Shortly before his own freakish death, a fanatical priest named Father Brennan (Patrick Troughton) warns Robert that Damien is the son of Satan and must be killed. Robert scoffs at first, but the piling on of tragic incidents forces him to confront the horrible truth.

Picking up several years after the original, *Damien: Omen II* finds little devil Damien (Jonathan Scott-Taylor) entering military school with the blessing of his uncle Richard (William Holden) and his aunt Ann (Lee Grant). As usual, those who suspect Damien's true origins wind up on the bad side of ol' Scratch, such as a nosy reporter (*Tomb of Ligeia*'s Elizabeth Shepherd) and the great Sylvia Sydney, who pops in for an extended cameo. It all has something to do with this big corporate plan to feed third world nations through chemical experimentation, so we also get some hi-tech death scenes involving toxic fumes and, in the film's crowd-pleasing high point, a malfunctioning elevator.

And finally in *The Final Conflict* (rechristened *Omen III* on DVD for no good reason), Damien's all grown up to the age of 33, handling the chores of running a huge worldwide corporation bearing his family name and, thanks to a convenient suicide, serving as the new ambassador to England. Meanwhile a hit squad of seven Italian monks led by Rossano Brazzi plans to dispatch the Antichrist using seven holy daggers, the only means to send the evil one back to Hell. Damien strikes up a romance with English TV reporter Lisa Harrow (who also had a son by Neill in real life - yikes!), whose son idolizes Damien. When an astronomical phenomenon announces the birth of the new Messiah on Earth, Damien orders his legions of followers to dispatch all of the babies born on that fateful evening, resulting in one of the more tasteless montages of '80s cinema. Will good prevail in the face of such monstrous evil?

Oh, but wait, there's more. *Omen IV: The Awakening* is basically a retread of the original *Omen*, this time with a young girl named Delia (Asia Vieira) adopted by lawyer parents who suspect their daughter isn't all sugar and spice, especially when she does satanic things like forcing school bullies to pee their pants. Other TV-safe murders crop up as Delia plots to pick up where Damien left off, though by the end few viewers will feel distressed that we were never blessed with *Delia: Omen V.*

Originally released on laserdisc by Fox, these films all look markedly better on DVD thanks to corrected widescreen presentations and stronger sound mixes. *The Final Conflict* in particular is a huge leap over the awful original pressing, one of the worst lasers ever manufactured. The first film looks exceptionally clean for its age, and the difficult hazy photography has been captured as well as possible for television. All of the films feature basic surround mixes, with Jerry Goldsmith's outstanding music for the first three films sounding just as chilling and powerful as it does on CD. (For the record, the third film has the most impressive score; just check out the fox hunt scene.) The fourth film suffers from a terrible synth score peppered with distracting snippets of Goldsmith's work, and the 1.85:1 framing wipes out the dead space at the top and bottom of the frame. Unfortunately even a more cinematic presentation can't help that one, though collectors may want to just pick up the box set anyway for sheer thoroughness. (Oddly, the fourth film is missing from the UK edition of the box set.)

The first *Omen* receives the full special edition treatment, with a terrific behind-the-scenes documentary featuring interviews with director Richard Donner (who got his break here before going on to *Superman* and the *Lethal Weapon* series) and writer David Seltzer, among others. The genesis of the story and the process of shooting are covered in often humorous detail, with one highlight concerning the casting of little Damien himself. Donner and editor Stuart Baird also appear on the commentary track, which goes into even more depth on the various technical aspects and weird anecdotes concerning the cast and crew. Finally you get trailers for the first three films along with "Curse or Coincidence," an *Exorcist*-style featurette on all the "strange" and "spooky" incidents which befell the production.

Damien: Omen II features a more bare bones commentary by producer Harvey Bernard, who mostly focuses on the various locations and the production difficulties which resulted in the original writer/director being tossed from the project.

Finally *The Final Conflict*, a flawed but extremely interesting film, is accompanied by commentary from director Graham Baker, who goes into detail about this globe-hopping film, the attempts to make a star out of Neill (the only screen Damien who's gone on to future film projects), and the attempts by writer Andrew Birkin (Jane's brother and director of *The Cement Garden*) to fashion an understated finale to this inherently ridiculous series.

When all's said and done, *Omen* fans should be very happy with this set, either separately or as a box, and while the films themselves are uneven to say the least, they mark a bizarre and unforgettable age in which Hollywood could churn out unabashedly exploitative horror films as efficiently as any low budget shock studio.

ON HER MAJESTY'S SECRET SERVICE
Colour, 1969, 140m. / Directed by Peter Hunt / Starring George Lazenby, Diana Rigg / MGM / WS (2.35:1) (16:9)

James Bond (Lazenby) uncovers evidence that his arch enemy Ernst Blofeld (Savalas) is holed up in Switzerland, using an allergy research clinic named Piz Gloria as a front for a plot to blackmail the world. Posing as a genealogist whom Blofeld has commissioned to establish his right to titled nobility, Bond infiltrates the stronghold and discovers that Blofeld plans to use female allergy patients as unwitting agents in bacteriological warfare.

Often derided by Connery advocates, the first film made after his (temporary) departure from the series is actually one of the best of them all, faithfully adhering to Ian Fleming's novel, right down to the uncharacteristically downbeat ending which finds Bond cradling the body of his bride who has just been shot through the head. Despite his inexperience, new boy George Lazenby equips himself well, especially so considering that Connery was a nigh on impossible act to follow. Former editor Peter Hunt graduates to the helm and handles both the top notch action and the realistic character development with a sure hand. Savalas is the best of several actors to play SPECTRE head honcho Blofeld, and Diana Rigg brings a greater degree of emancipated confidence to the Bond girl mould than audiences had witnessed to that point.

The supporting players include George Baker, Joanna Lumley, Jenny Hanley, Anouska Hempel, Yuri Borienko, Julie Ege and Gabriele Ferzetti. Although in keeping with its source material there's a more serious approach to the story - Q Department gadgetry is redundant - there are still plenty of witty one-liners scattered through the script, the best of which has Bond observing the remains of a baddie who's just been minced up in the blades of a snowplough: "He had lots of guts". The breathtaking ski-chase escape from Piz Gloria, coupled with John Barry's pulse-pounding score, is a pointed highlight. Pure 007 magic.

Although MGM have loaded their special edition DVD of the sixth Bond escapade with a trove of extras, the film itself is liable to disappoint eagle-eyed aficionados, for it's devoid of several small bits and pieces including parts of the stockcar rally smash-up. Beyond this the 2.35:1 ratio print, divided into 32 chapters, is a beautiful transfer with fabulously vibrant colours. A lengthy documentary tells you everything you could possibly want to know about the making of the movie and the film has a commentary track from director Hunt and various members of the cast and crew. An additional featurette focuses on the part played by Q's gadgets throughout the series. There's also a trailer, five TV spots, seven radio spots, cast interview soundbites, a stills gallery and a rather scratchy 1969 featurette entitled "Above It All" which reveals the daredevil activities that went into shooting the Alpine action sequences. English or Spanish language tracks are accessible, with subtitles provided in English, Spanish and French. - TG

100 DAYS

Colour, 1991, 160m. / Directed by Partho Ghosh / Starring Madhuri Dixit, Jackie Shroff / Indura (India R0 NTSC) / WS (1.85:1)

Now here's just what the world needs: a musical Hindi remake of Lucio Fulci's *The Psychic*! That's right, the classic Italian horror mystery with Jennifer

O'Neill (also known as *Murder to the Tune of Seven Black Notes*) was remade scene for scene in India as a sprawling song and dance slasher film, and Euro film fans will be left grasping at the fragile remnants of their sanity by the time it's all over. It may be a while before we get *City of the Dancing Dead* or *New York Ripper on the Roof*, but this will do just fine in the meantime.

The film opens with lovely Devi (Madhuri Dixit) experiencing a series of psychic visions while playing tennis. A killer clad in black gloves and a trenchcoat (what else?) murders a young woman, drags her body to a remote house over the credits (a fun homage to *Blood and Black Lace* here), and entombs her behind a wall of bricks and mortar. For no apparent reason, the film's prankster cop hero shows up with a bunch of guys in Michael Jackson "Beat It" outfits. Soon they're all doing a full fledged dance number in which they spit water in women's faces, cover themselves with shaving cream, and thrash around on a table. Um... then the story kicks back in. Our heroine marries a nice older man and provokes another series of musical interludes, including one amazingly kitschy stint on a TV variety show. Eventually Devi winds up at the house from her vision and, thanks to a handy pickaxe, knocks down the wall to discover the woman' skeleton inside. However, the visions continue, and she is inundated with psychic clues involving a horse on a magazine cover, a cigarette smouldering in an ashtray, a plate mounted on a wall, a woman drowning in a swimming pool, and a printed label which reads "100 Days." It appears a nasty bald crime boss may have been responsible for the murder, and he soon decides to put our intrepid psychic out of commission. But is there more here than meets the eye?

An amusing pastiche of Euro clichés and Bollywood musical excess, *100 Days* really must be seen to be believed. Actually this is even more of a straightforward giallo than Fulci's film thanks to the prevalent black gloved slasher and an increase in the amount of bloodshed, though the Indian setting gives the proceedings a distinctly off kilter ambience. The finale follows the Fulci original almost to the letter, with the protagonist meeting a Poe-like fate by misinterpreting her visions and relying on a handy watch chime when the police come a-calling. However, this version tweaks the killer's identity and lunges overboard to include an elaborate fistfight/kickboxing finale that probably never occurred to Master Lucio.

The DVD of *100 Days* isn't up to the hi-tech 5.1 standards of more recent Bollywood efforts, but curious viewers should still make an effort to seek it out. A few shots are framed at 2.35:1 (and indeed the opening censor notification card lists this as Cinemascope); however, the bulk of the transfer is 1.85:1 but doesn't look terribly compromised. The print quality ranges from attractive to scratchy, and unfortunately no English subtitle option is included. However, the amount of dialogue is very low and seems to follow the Italian version verbatim.

OPEN YOUR EYES (ABRE LOS OJOS)

Colour, 1997, 120m. / Directed by Alejandro Amenábar / Starring Eduardo Noriega, Penelope Cruz / Artisan (US R1 NTSC) / WS (1.85:1) (16:9), Sogepaq (Spain R2 PAL) / WS (1.85:1), Momentum (UK R2 PAL) / WS (1.78:1) / DD5.1

The old movie chestnut of dreams versus reality has been pounded into the ground for the past few decades, but every now and then a filmmaker finds an ingenious new spin on this hoary concept. Such is the case with *Open Your Eyes* (*Abre los ojos*), the second feature from Alejandro Amenábar and the one which earned him well-deserved international attention. Utilizing many of the same cast and crew members from his first film, *Thesis*, he crafted a challenging and constantly surprising work which now places him as one of the most significant current voices in fantastic cinema.

To discuss the plot of *Open Your Eyes* in depth would give away many of its surprises, but here's a brief idea. Ladies' man and rich boy César (Eduardo Noriega) enjoys an indulgent lifestyle as one of the city's best caterers. Rarely seen with the same woman twice, he even takes time out from his own birthday party to chase the potential girlfriend, Sofia (Penelope Cruz), of his best friend, Pelayo (Fele Martínez). Unfortunately one of César's past conquests, Nuria (Najwa Nimri), refuses to let him go and displays more than a little mental instability. One day she takes drastic measures which result in the destruction of César's face. Hidden behind an immobile mask, he finds his life falling apart and descending to the level of an uncontrollable nightmare. But that's just the beginning. The entire story is related by the masked César to a psychiatrist, Antonio (Chete Lara), who asks him vague questions about a murder.

The narrative swerves back and forth, containing dreams within dreams, but never losing its grip on the viewer's imagination. Amenábar and co-writer Mateo Gil wisely devote their attention to building the characters as believable human beings, which makes each revelation a wrenching experience free of gimmickry or manipulation. Carefully selecting elements from cyberpunk novels and Victor Hugo's *The Man Who Laughs*, the film escalates in complexity until it finally reaches an unforgettable final sequence (very reminiscent of a certain big budget 1999 blockbuster) which manages to be both poignant and devastating at the same time. The excellent Noriega offers a startling reversal of his performance in *Thesis*, covering every emotional base with consummate skill, while beautiful rising star Cruz (who does a lengthy but tasteful nude scene) makes an indelible impression as César's true love. Incidentally, one of the associate producers was Andrea Occhipinti, the Italian actor from such films as *New York Ripper* and *A Blade in the Dark*.

Artisan's US DVD offers the best available transfer, enhanced for widescreen TVs with few discernable flaws. Otherwise it's strictly a bare bones affair, rushed out to cash in on the American remake, *Vanilla Sky*. The UK Momentum disc features more cramped widescreen framing and no extras. The PAL disc from Sogepaq is non-anamorphic but looks impressive and smooth, with dead on framing and optional English subtitles (identical to those on the American prints). The 5.1 audio mix on all discs sounds terrific, using the rear and front speakers more for ambient creepiness than jolting split effects. The Spanish disc is packed with extras, including a feature length audio commentary track by Amenábar (in Spanish only) and his elegant music score isolated on a separate track in 5.1. A 23 minute making-of featurette (without subtitles) includes interviews with all of the principal cast and crew, with on location footage offering a peek at some of the more memorable moments in the film. Other bonuses include the original Spanish theatrical trailer, the earlier trailer for *Thesis*, and a 17 minute black and white short film by Amenábar, "Luna," which features Noriega as a hapless hitchhiker who catches a ride with a mysterious woman and faces dire consequences. Letterboxed at approximately 1.66:1, this early film is a little rough around the edges (not to mention grainy looking), but it's an intriguing look at these talents in their earliest stages.

THE OPENING OF MISTY BEETHOVEN

Colour, 1976, 84m. / Directed by Henry Paris (Radley Metzger) / Starring Constance Money, Jamie Gillis / VCA (US R1 NTSC)

While all of adult film auteur Radley Metzger's soft and hardcore films bear his unmistakable stamp of elegance, only *The Opening of Misty Beethoven* broke the XXX mould and earned respect as a well made film which happened to contain actual sex. Thanks to a witty script, deft performances (yes, everyone here can act), striking sets, and continental locales, this is one for the time capsule.

While cruising the red light district of Paris, best-selling author and sex expert Seymour Love (Jamie Gillis) finds his adult film viewing (at a theatre advertising the French classic, *Pussy Talk!*) interrupted by a crass hooker, Misty Beethoven (Constance Money), who offers to take him out for a quick, good time for fifty dollars. Seymour agrees and begins to quiz the enterprising but unappealing Misty about her lack of experience. Striking up a bet with his partner Geraldine (terrific one shot wonder Jacqueline Beaudant), Seymour wagers he can turn Misty into the toast of the town as the revered Golden Rod Girl at the next high society party thrown by vain magazine publisher Lawrence Layman (Ras Kean) and his wife (Gloria Leonard). Seymour, Geraldine, and Misty jet off to New York, where he instructs his pupil in the arts of pleasure and sends her out to build her reputation with a variety of men, including a mostly gay dealer played by *Score*'s Calvin Culver. As Misty's fame spreads, Seymour's arrogance conceals a growing attraction to his ugly duckling.. but can he still have her?

As most lit. students will recognize from the above description, *Opening* is actually a thinly disguised retelling of George Bernard Shaw's *Pygmalion*, also musicalised as *My Fair Lady*. Metzger had already experimented with sexy literary twists on Carmen and Camille, but this proved to be his most radical and critically successful attempt yet. The impeccable soundtrack of Euro lounge and pop music (culled from library tracks) and tastefully chosen locations (art galleries, opera theatres) establish just the right touch of playfulness, though the sex itself remains graphic and raunchy enough to satisfy the raincoat crowd. In fact, the satirical tone allows Metzger to get away with slipping in an amazing number of taboo images involving senior citizens, strap-ons, and cross dressing, among others.

The box art for this DVD announces it contains previously censored material and never before seen footage, though this isn't exactly true. The large oversize VHS edition from VCA contained the entire *ménage a trois* between Money, Leonard, and Kean,

one of the most memorable kinky set pieces in the annals of '70s porn, which was later heavily censored for the regular sell-through edition. The DVD reinstates the footage (whose penetration close ups were performed by Culver, better known as gay porn actor Casey Donovan) and, VCA's restoration claims notwithstanding, appears to be taken from the same video master they've been going back to for years. The colours are punchier than usual, but given the fact that the film was originally shot in 16mm and blown up to 35mm before being slightly cropped for video, this is about as good as one could expect. Metzger himself owns the original materials for *Misty*, so hopefully a sharper, more carefully framed edition will turn up someday. The cropping isn't as damaging or claustrophobic when the DVD is viewed without overscan on a DVD-Rom drive, allowing more peripheral information on the sides to creep through.

The disc includes some nifty extras, the most notable being a running feature commentary by Gillis and Leonard. Obviously old pals, the two dish out an amazing number of anecdotes about the film, many of them involving the notoriously uncooperative Money. Leonard also drops a couple of bombshells, including the revelation that she slept with Metzger (once) and a reference to the actual name of this film's cinematographer, who won an Oscar a few months later. A couple of factual goofs aside (Leonard insists Calvin Culver and Casey Donovan weren't the same person, and Gillis erroneously refers to this as his first film for Metzger), the commentary makes for an enlightening and joyous experience. Other goodies include a gallery of promotional stills for this film and *Barbara Broadcast*, a three minute reflection by Jim Holliday, and some promotional filler for VCA products. Sadly, the softcore version of *Misty Beethoven* has long been out of circulation and isn't included here - a shame, really, as it includes numerous additional dialogue scenes and alternate takes which would have made for a fascinating comparison.

OPERA

Colour, 1988, 105m. / Directed by Dario Argento / Starring Cristina Marsillach, Ian Charleson / Anchor Bay (US R0 NTSC) / WS (2.35:1) (16:9) / DD-EX/DTS-ES, Cecchi Gori (Italy R0 PAL) / WS (1.85:1) (16:9) / DD2.0

In many respects the last full throttle Dario Argento film to date, *Opera* pushes his stylistic tendencies into overdrive right from the opening Steadicam shots through an opera house. Both melancholy and vibrant as a fond farewell to the '80s should be, the storyline encapsulates many of the successful elements from Argento's previous films while packaging them in a disturbing, sexually twisted package laced with some unforgettable murder sequences.

After an unfortunate car accident makes a career casualty of opera diva Mara Cecova, young understudy Betty (Cristina Marsillach) is pressed into service as the new lead by her director, Marc (Ian Charleson), a horror movie pro trying to move upscale. Betty's agent, Myra (Daria Nicolodi), feels nothing but enthusiasm for her young star in the making, and indeed Betty's debut turns into a smash success. Unfortunately, an usher is murdered in one of the theatre boxes during the performance, indicating that one of Betty's new fans may have homicidal tendencies. Inspector Santini (Urbano Barberini) investigates the mysterious goings on, while Betty's celebratory but unsuccessful opening night tryst with the stage manager (William McNamara) turns nasty when the killer arrives and performs gruesome acts while pinning Betty's eyes open with taped needles. Terrified and confused, Betty plunges into a disoriented state in which she acts as the pawn of a devious mind with violent ties to Betty's past.

Many of *Opera*'s highlights have already passed into gorehound legend, including a jaw-dropping slow motion bullet sequence that cannot be adequately described in words. As with most of Argento's other films, this is also a treat to watch as his camera performs ungodly acrobatics: swirling up staircases, thumping along with the killer's palpitating heartbeat, and swooping through the opera house itself from the point of view of a raven. Most complaints about the film centre on its bizarre, appropriately operatic ending, which begins with a tongue in cheek homage to *Phenomena* and winds up on a disturbingly ambiguous note. The preceding climax is actually more difficult to justify, as it features more logic loopholes than the rest of Argento's oeuvre combined. The soundtrack is equally daring and likely to turn off inexperienced viewers as it weaves back and forth from Claudio Simonetti's haunting, Goblin-style music to lashings of heavy metal and classical opera. Beautiful, shocking, frustrating, and thoroughly entertaining, *Opera* has only become more fascinating with time and easily deserves a spot as one of Argento's most revealing and accomplished efforts.

Its video history is one of the most tangled and confusing in the director's career so far. Some necessary spoilers from the film have been included here for clarification, so anyone who has not seen the film would be well advised to skip down to the next paragraph. And now, let's proceed. The Italian language VHS release eliminated several violent sequences (most of McNamara's death, the scissors tracheotomy performed on *Demons 2*'s Coralina Cataldi Tassoni, and the raven eyeball swallowing). The film's original English dub was greeted with laughter by exhibitors, so Barberini's original fey dubbed voice was re-looped, though alas this left much of his climactic monologue difficult to decipher. Orion picked up international distribution of the film and changed the title to *Terror at the Opera*, allowing frustrated Argento fans to finally see the forbidden gore courtesy of RCA/Columbia's gorgeous full frame laserdisc. Alas, this version was also heavily compromised as Orion removed several expository passages (the perfume pouring into the sink, several linking bits of footage and dialogue, the scene between Charleson and his girlfriend, and the entire "happy/crazy" epilogue with Betty shuffling through the grass, to name but a few). Contrary to the DVD packaging, a full, uncut version of *Opera* (under the revised title) was released on VHS in an unrated edition from Southgate; in fact, apart from those unlucky few who checked out the slightly edited R-rated cut at Blockbuster, the Anchor Bay version will be nothing new, content wise.

Now here's where things get complicated. *Opera* was filmed in Super 35, so the aspect ratio has varied wildly on both the big and small screens. Orion's theatrical edition (intended for US release but never fulfilled) was struck in the 1.85:1 aspect ratio, which exposed a huge amount of dead space and distracting details at the top and bottom of the frame, such as Marsillach's underwear throughout her bed scene with McNamara. The same version was used for the mildly cropped Japanese laserdisc, and the recent Italian DVD release (with no English subtitles, alas) is also from this "opened up" 1.85:1 edition. However, a bootleg tape of the first English dub has circulated for years in Argento's preferred 2.35:1 aspect ratio, and the director himself has exhibited the film this way at several public appearances. The "scope" version is a markedly different experience and really feels more like an Argento film. The opera sequences in particular benefit from the tighter framing; just check out the shrouded figures immediately before the "raven attack" sequence, or the rectangular stage framing during Betty's first stage appearance. Anchor Bay's DVD edition contains the second, revised English dub, letterboxed at 2.35:1 version. Despite the THX certification, the image is too bright during normal playback. However, viewers with a "black enhance" control on their DVD player or a good grasp of the contrast and brightness controls on their TV can tweak the image until it looks just as vibrant and rich as the Japanese laser. The DD and DTS-ES audio mixes actually sound pretty much the same as the theatrical surround version; rear channel activity is surprisingly sparse given the aggressive nature of the film, offering mostly ambient support and some musical carryover during the louder passages, along with the expected squawk or two from the ravens.

Those who sprang for the Italian DVD should hang on to their discs, as the Anchor Bay DVD contains only the English track. While this might not seem like such a big issue, the Italian track is superior in many respects, particularly the music mix. Several passages of music in the Italian version are nonexistent in the English one; for example, during Ian Charleson's bedroom conversation with his girlfriend in which they read the early newspaper reviews, Simonetti's "Crows" can be heard playing on the radio in the background, and Betty's stroll through several hallways of red curtains after the air duct sequence and Ian Charleson's *Hamlet* reverie are accompanied quite audibly by Simonetti's "Confusion." In the English version, both scenes play without any notable music at all or are severely muted down. Also in the Italian version, an ironic song gurgles on the radio during Betty's first needle experience, though here the only music during the scene is a barely audible Brian Eno piece.

Despite the minor reservations about the image brightness and soundtrack, the Anchor Bay disc is easily the best way to experience the film both for first time viewers and seasoned Argentophiles. The imaginatively designed menus lead to some eye-popping (ahem) extras, beginning with the mediocre European trailer (in 2.35:1) and Orion's excellent, striking trailer for the scrapped US release (at 1.85:1). Oddly, Southgate's marvellously well-edited video trailer is not included. The disc also contains a very good 36-minute documentary, "Conducting *Opera*," featuring on-camera interviews with Argento, Nicolodi, cinematographer Ronnie Taylor, Simonetti, and a particularly good Barberini, whose appealing English-speaking voice would have been much better suited for his role than either of the dubbed options. All of the participants have notable things to say about the production and offer candid observations about the difficulties behind the scenes, including the tempestuous behaviour of a noticeably absent Marsillach. Interestingly, no one mentions another actress

problem; according to Argento expert Alan Jones, Vanessa Redgrave reportedly backed out of playing Cecova at the last minute, leaving a voiceover and subjective camera to play her role instead. The documentary also includes the Argento/Taylor car commercial filmed prior to *Opera*, which had previously been available only on PAL VHS video.

A limited edition of 30,000 units offers a double-disc set of *Opera* with the CD soundtrack. The second disc incorporates the complete Simonetti score (previously available only on vinyl from Cinevox) as well as the two heavy metal songs by Steel Grave. However, the opera selections from the original album have been dropped in favour of the Daemonia "Opera" theme remix (also featured as a music video on the first disc), accompanied by the *Rollerball* Daemonia cue from their earlier albums and Simonetti's overused "I'll Take the Night" song from *The Versace Murders*. The score proper is really the best reason to spring for the set; even without a cue listing, it now completes the entire music availability from *Opera* on CD when paired up with Cinevox's official CD release (containing the Brian Eno cues and other musical odds and ends).

ORCA THE KILLER WHALE

Colour, 1977, 89m. / Directed by Michael Anderson / Starring Richard Harris, Charlotte Rampling / Bridge Pictures Classics (Holland R2 PAL) / WS (2.35:1)

Having witnessed an Orca - a killer whale - effortlessly slaughtering a shark, fisherman Captain Nolan (Harris) smells money and sets about hooking one, in spite of advice to the contrary from oceanographer Rachel Bedford (Rampling). Things go awry when he accidentally maims a pregnant female. A highly intelligent mammal, its enraged mate trails Nolan back to port hell-bent on retribution.

Swimming in on the tail fin of Spielberg's *Jaws*, Michael Anderson's compelling cetaceous tragedy, though not entirely credible, is actually better than it probably had any right to be. This is thanks in the main to a committed central performance from Richard Harris as the not so much malicious as misguided Nolan; by picture's end the audience feels sympathy for both him and the justifiably vengeful whale. At under an hour and a half, there's always been a feel of pre-release truncation about the film, but its succinct running time works in its favour, culminating in a downbeat, tundra-wreathed conclusion that's just different and unpredictable enough to tickle the most jaded palate. Charlotte Rampling is rather insipid, but there's enjoyably hammy support from Will Sampson, Keenan Wynn and a pre-*10* Bo Derek getting her leg bitten off.

The scene in which the dying female Orca aborts her under-developed foetus on the deck is more than enough to put you off your cod'n'chips. And yet the most haunting image in the movie is also one of the most matter of fact - a shot of an ashen-faced Nolan leaving port, standing hooded and hunch-shouldered on the bow of his boat, staring gravely ahead, his fate unavoidable; coupled with Ennio Morricone's rousing theme, it's a moment of pure movie magic. Morricone's score (arguably his best ever) accentuates the imperial majesty of the Orcas to perfection, the only misstep being the cringingly awful addition of vocals to the closing theme, the artiste in question sounding as if she's wrestling with a stubborn bowel movement the size of the titular beastie!

The Dutch DVD release from Bridge Pictures is a sadly unenhanced affair, containing the film alone in a clean, albeit occasionally too dark, letterboxed transfer. Sound options are in Dutch or English (with removable Dutch subtitles). There are a woefully meagre 8 chapter marks. - TG

ORGAN

Colour, 1996, 105m. / Directed by Kei Fujiwara / Starring Kimihiko Hasegawa, Kei Fujiwara / Synapse (US R1 NTSC) / DD2.0

Anyone who grew up after the '70s may remember those tasteless jokes that always began, "What's grosser than gross?" Well, the members of a Japanese theatrical troupe called Vital Organ decided to carry that philosophy over into a movie, *Organ*, which functions more as a series of dreamlike, nauseating images instead of a coherent story. One of the few hard splatter movies to be directed by a woman, Kei Fujiwara (who acted in the equally surreal *Tetsuo: The Iron Man*), this sick little film is flooded with bodily fluids of every conceivable substance and colour; however, the cold avant garde approach ensures that it never becomes as unwatchable or sickening as terminal cases like *Man Behind the Sun*.

The plot, to use the term very loosely, begins with two cops, Tosaka and Numata, preparing to crack down on a black market human organ

syndicate connected to the Yakuza. The operation goes terribly wrong, however, and Tosaka falls into the hands of the two depraved organ dealing leaders, one-eyed banshee Yoko (played by Fujiwara herself) and her biologist teacher brother, Seaki. Numata is kicked off the force but decides to track down the nefarious organ stealers, who have a nasty habit of leaving their victims still barely alive without their livers. Morbid curiosity presumably causes Seaki to keep the limbless Tosaka alive in a hothouse, where the mutilated body is sustained with the fluids of Seaki's young female students. And from here it just gets nastier.

Though unmistakably Japanese in its emphasis on the warped factions of urban society, *Organ* also springs from the darker side of Western filmmaking. The influences of David Lynch and particularly the bodily horrors of David Cronenberg are strongly felt, while the excellent, dreamy electronic score could have wandered in from a Michael Mann film. Despite the high level of gore, the film remains chillingly distant and deliberately paced throughout, while the eye-catching effects are more colourful than repellent. Just think of *Street Trash* without the comic relief.

Synapse's DVD of *Organ* is, like *Deadbeat at Dawn*, a matter of making the best from the available materials. The film uses grainy stock, harsh lighting, and zoomed in camera set ups, all in glorious 16mm, so don't expect it to look like a sweeping epic. On its own terms, the image quality is fine, as is the creepy and subtle stereo soundtrack. The optional English subtitles are very easy to read and well paced. The disc also includes a twenty minute "behind the scenes" of *Organ 2*, which consists mainly of Fujiwara talking about the film over a random series of clips. This sequel looks much more stylized and theatrical than the original, which may be a good thing.

ORLOFF AND THE INVISIBLE MAN

Colour, 1971, 76m. / Directed by Pierre Chevalier / Starring Howard Vernon, Brigitte Carva / Image (US R1 NTSC) / WS (1.76:1) (16:9)

It looks and feels for all the world like a Jess Franco film, but this outrageous cheapjack European mixture of Gothic ambience and Ed Wood insanity was actually the handiwork of director Pierre Chevalier. Chock full of the usual Eurociné staples like nudity, insane plotting, even crazier dubbing, and a very limited cast of characters, this potentially hazardous brew haunted video stores for years as *The Invisible Dead* before turning up on DVD with its Orloff origins intact.

Our story begins in tried and true fashion with a stalwart, naive hero, Doctor Garondet, welcomed into the decaying castle of Doctor Orloff (Franco regular Howard Vernon). Apparently the doc's experiments have taken their toll on the local peasants and even Orloff's own nubile daughter, Cecile (Brigitte Carva), who is convinced that an invisible maniac has sprung from her father's work. As it turns out, Orloff has been experimenting with the creation of a "superior" race of homo sapiens, though the punchline is not at all what most viewers will expect. In the meantime a peasant girl is ravished by an invisible man (conveyed by having the girl roll around naked in the hay while flailing her arms around), and the only way to expose the transparent fiend involves our protagonists walking around the castle hurling talcum powder in the air.

There really isn't much else that can be said about this film without spoiling the ending, which ranks up there with *Night of the Lepus* for insane monster concepts. At 76 minutes, the film moves along from one heavy breathing incident to another with lots of moody sets and lighting to set the scene. As usual Vernon is fun to watch, trying his best to get through the material with a straight face, while the screenplay throws in every convention you can think of: terrified villagers, dank dungeons, damsels in peril, long walks through dark hallways... but it's all rendered in such a deliberately skewed fashion that even die hard Eurofanatics will be glued to their televisions in disbelief.

Apart from its most famous incarnation as *The Invisible Dead* (complete with a misleading but terrific cover depicting zombies bursting from the earth in front of a castle), this film has also been known as *Orloff Against the Invisible Man, Love Life of an Invisible Man*, and *Dr. Orloff's Invisible Monster*. The Image DVD retains the *Against* title on the print and menu but bills the film on the cover under the more accurate *Orloff and the Invisible Man*, since the two entities are technically not against each other.

The source material is in wonderful shape, apart from the weird splices and erratic film stock conditions which have plagued this film since its inception. Colours are dynamic and striking, while grain is kept to a surprising minimum even in the darkest scenes. The disc contains the dialogue tracks in English, French, and German mono, all of which are at least partially dubbed. As with many Eurociné titles, there is no truly definitive edition; however, this is probably as close as we'll ever come. The disc

also contains a French trailer (with most of the sleazy highlights), as well as alternate sequences shot with clothed actresses. The "rape" sequence is especially surreal in this variant form and makes for a welcome albeit highly bizarre addition.

THE ORPHIC TRILOGY:
THE BLOOD OF A POET
B&W, 1930, 55m. / Directed by Jean Cocteau / Starring Enrique Rivero, Lee Miller
ORPHEUS
B&W, 1949, 95m. / Directed by Jean Cocteau / Starring Jean Marais, François Perier, Maria Casares
THE TESTAMENT OF ORPHEUS
B&W, 1960, 83m. / Directed by Jean Cocteau / Starring Jean Cocteau, Edouard Dermithe, Jean Marais
Criterion (US R1 NTSC)

One of the great voices of the avant garde cinema, Jean Cocteau is that rare director who could make experimental cinema appealing even for the masses. Though best remembered for his innovative and simply perfect version of *Beauty and the Beast (La belle et la bête)*, he directed seven other feature films and also made a name for himself as a liberal arts renaissance man: painter, writer, visual designer, and actor, among others.

Cocteau's first film, *The Blood of a Poet (Le sang d'un poète)*, serves as a kind of Rosetta stone both for the European avant garde and for the controlling images of Cocteau's cinema in general. The dreamlike series of images revolves around a young poet (Enrique Rivero) whose drawings instigate a string of bizarre incidents: a statue comes to life, a mirror leads through to a corridor (a common Cocteau situation), a ritualistic suicide results in reincarnation. The film swerves into "normalcy" when the poet, now transported to a ritzy gambling hall, finds himself subjected to the whims of the social elite, while outside a group of boys have a most unusual snowball fight. Cocteau frames this device with the image of a crumbling chimney, a famous image whose meaning has been the subject of numerous interpretations. Is it a symbol for the inevitability of fate? The potential destruction of the artist's will? A symbol for the images which can flicker through a human mind in the blink of an eye? Cocteau provides no clear answers, and much of the film's enjoyment derives from trying to sort through the fragmented pieces.

Criterion designates *The Blood of a Poet* as the first instalment in Cocteau's "Orphic trilogy," a loose interpretation supported mostly by his choice of a young poet as his hero and the fixation with images that would occur in his subsequent films.

Cocteau's *Orpheus (Orphée)*, released nineteen years later, is a far more accessible work and is one of his best loved. Derived very loosely from the famous Greek myth, this film begins in contemporary France where the poet Orphée (Cocteau regular Jean Marais) resides with his wife, Eurydice (Marie Déa), in an existence filled with post-war cafes and sleek automobiles. Our hero becomes enchanted with a mysterious and beautiful Princess (Maria Casarès), the personification of Death, who lures him into the underworld through a mirror (what else?). Though Orphée believes himself to be in love with the Princess, he finds his will tested when Eurydice falls prey to the Princess' servants.

Eleven years later, Cocteau took self-reflexive cinema a step further with *The Testament of Orpheus (Le testament d'Orphée)*, the least seen film of the "trilogy." Here Cocteau himself appears as... well, himself, a poet. He wanders through a completely fantastic world populated by his own previous creations (including characters/actors from *Orpheus*), with Cocteau's close friends and artistic compatriots popping by for surreal cameos. Look fast for appearances by director Roger Vadim, Charles Aznavour, Pablo Picasso, and Yul Brynner, with young future Truffaut star Jean-Pierre Leaud turning up in an homage to *Blood of a Poet*. More of an internal exploration than a narrative film, *Testament* has only recently begun to receive acclaim on a level comparable to Cocteau's masterworks thanks to its exposure on cable television and home video.

Criterion's lovingly produced box set treats these films as both a thematic triptych of films and a kind of visual continuum of Cocteau's life and career. The iconoclastic youth of *Blood of a Poet* makes for fascinating viewing compared to its more refined and contemplative follow up films, which delve more philosophically into the nature of being an artist in a world far different from what one might wish. The transfer quality of the three films is remarkable given the age of these titles; however, the print used for *Blood of a Poet*, while most likely the best available, has still succumbed to the ravages of time as evident from a number of running scratches and tears which plague the entire running time. However, the other two films look virtually pristine; *Orpheus* in particular is a revelation compared to the old out of print video editions. The first disc pairs up *Blood of a Poet* with an inform-ative, carefully designed one hour documentary, *Jean Cocteau: Autobiography of an Unknown (Autoportrait d'un inconnu)*, which covers the artist's seemingly endless capacity for imagination in every artistic field. While the equally sterling *South Bank Show* episode devoted to Cocteau would have made an ideal companion piece (and shares some of the same footage), this is more than enough for academics and casual viewers alike. As with the other two discs, a number of essays and lecture transcripts reveal both the keen intellect and warm humanity that informed Cocteau's thought processes. The third disc appends a 16mm colour film, *Villa Santo Sospir*, sort of a dreamy travelogue filmed on the same striking European locations used for *Testament of Orpheus*.

THE PASSENGER

Colour, 1975, 126m. / Directed by Michelangelo Antonioni / Starring Jack Nicholson, Maria Schneider / Imagica (Japan R2 NTSC) / WS (1.85:1)

Despite losing a sinful amount of money on Michelangelo Antonioni's *Zabriskie Point* in 1970, MGM decided to take a gamble on the admired Italian director again when he managed to secure Jack Nicholson for a long delayed follow up film, *Profession: Reporter*, or *The Passenger* as it's more widely known. Devoid of the kinky mind games of *Blow Up* or *Chinatown*, the film was not a financial hit and has remained difficult to see ever since. However, patient admirers of European cinema and Nicholson fans who want to see him in an atypical subdued role will be more willing to go along for this deliberately paced, beautiful ride.

Reporter and documentarian David Locke (Nicholson) has wandered into a remote area of Africa hoping to interview political extremists about whom he knows little and cares even less. Another man staying at his hotel, the mysterious Mr. Robertson, has no ties to any friends or family, only a book of appointments that he must keep. Locke discovers Robertson dead from a heart attack in his hotel room and, in a fit of midlife crisis soul searching, decides to swap their identities, including a passport photo switch. Locke then embarks on a journey from Africa to Europe, focusing only on keeping the dead man's appointments. Along the way he discovers the true nature of his alternate identity and becomes entangled with a beautiful girl (Maria Schneider) who encourages him on his mission. Meanwhile Locke's estranged wife (Jenny Runacre) and the police attempt to track him down before a band of counter-revolutionaries puts a fatal end to his quest for identity.

A eloquent summation of the themes throughout Antonioni's films to date, *The Passenger* is equal parts character study, thriller, and travelogue. The methodical pace is difficult to accept at first, but once Antonioni begins to weave his spell, the film pays off with a series of beautiful, unforgettable images, such as Schneider standing up in a convertible while riding through lanes of trees or the stunning uninterrupted six minute shot which forms the climax of the film. Cinematographer Luciano Tovoli (*Tenebre*) deserves a huge amount of the credit here; his gift for conjuring up visual magic from the barest elements reaches its peak here. In her first international role since *Last Tango in Paris*, Schneider looks great but, to the consternation of male viewers everywhere, remains fully clothed. Nicholson is excellent as always, acting more with his facial expressions than dialogue this time around. In fact, maybe twenty words are spoken during the entire first half hour of the film, with most of the story forcing viewers to pay attention and put together the various details they have witnessed.

Though released in the early days of home video by Warner, *The Passenger* has been maddeningly neglected, thanks mainly to dull, grainy, and brutally cropped transfers which sap away much of its magic. The Japanese DVD release is therefore a welcome and highly overdue antidote, bearing the title of *Profession: Reporter* and restoring much of its original lustre. The opening few minutes of African exteriors are shot in a deliberately faded style with brownish shadows, but the rest of the film looks excellent, with vivid colours and perfect framing. Some of the reel changes are a little ragged, but this only lasts for a few seconds. The film is in English (mono) with removable Japanese subtitles, and most notably, this is the complete European print, with seven extra minutes deleted from the US edition. The disc also includes the US theatrical trailer, which focuses on the film's few moments of action and probably led to some very unsatisfied audiences.

THE PASSION OF JOAN OF ARC

B&W, 1928, 82m. / Directed by Carl Theodore Dreyer / Starring Maria Falconetti / Criterion (US R1 NTSC) / DD5.1

Anyone who doubts the transformative powers of cinema should immediately take a look at Carl Dreyer's *La passion de Jeanne d'Arc (Passion of*

 Joan of Arc), one of the indisputable high points of world cinema. An alternately lacerating, moving, and transcendent experience, the film has long been unavailable in a watchable print thanks to years of bad distribution and censorship. Ironically, both of the negatives cut by Dreyer himself perished in mysterious fires, but a complete, clean version was discovered in the mid-'80s in a Norwegian mental institution.

Criterion's DVD presents this restored, original edition (complete with French intertitles, subtitled optionally in English) in a presentation long overdue and bound to win the film a legion of new followers. Even if you don't like silent films, give this one a try; you will not be sorry. Most of the Western world knows the story of young Jeanne, the French peasant girl who heard divine voices (including St. Michael) and led an army against the British hordes. Dreyer's film focuses on the actual transcripts of her trial for heresy (conducted covertly by the British under the guise of a religious investigation); in fact, most of the film takes place in the courtroom, with the shots focusing almost entirely on Jeanne and her accusers. Drama doesn't get much higher than this, and Dreyer refuses to moralize or use the narrative as a vehicle for some hidden political agenda. By the time the infamous burning at the stake arrives, the viewer is completely battered and exhilarated, both emotionally and intellectually.

Along with the stylish *Vampyr*, *Passion* remains Dreyer's signature film in the history books, and rightfully so. Maria Falconetti, a comedic stage actress in her only film appearance, renders Jeanne so eloquently and perfectly (those marvellous eyes!) that every acting student should be forced to study her every move in front of the camera. Dreyer reportedly pushed her to physical and spiritual extremes to get the desired result, but whatever the means, he certainly succeeded. In aesthetic terms, *Passion* hasn't been as influential as other landmark works like *Citizen Kane*, perhaps because many of the editing and compositional techniques simply can't be duplicated. (Interestingly, Ken Russell did try to duplicate the effect in some sequences of *The Devils*, a blistering flipside to Dreyer's film.)

The DVD doesn't simply include the film, however. Rather than tossing in some random organ score, Criterion has included Richard Einhorn's *Visions of Light*, a fusion of oratorio and opera written specifically to be played with the film (as it has been performed live on several occasions). The music is spectacular on its own terms, but married to

Dreyer's visuals, the result is 82 minutes guaranteed to provoke goosebumps. The fiery climax, filled with voices bursting from every channel (including the group Anonymous 4), will rigorously test out anyone's home sound system, and Einhorn's use of voice (in Latin, but a translated libretto is included) always manages to complement the film's shifts in mood from start to finish. The film itself looks remarkably good - one of the best silent film restorations to date, in fact.

PECKER

Colour, 1998, 87m. / Directed by John Waters / Starring Edward Furlong, Christina Ricci, Mary Kay Place / New Line (US R1 NTSC) / WS (1.85:1) (16:9) / DD5.1

You've got to credit John Waters with doing his best to cheerfully corrupt his viewing public. After introducing underground movie audiences to bizarre sexual practices like "rosary jobs" and "shrimping," here he turns to "teabagging." If you want to find out what that is, you'll just have to see *Pecker*, his latest bad taste opus. While the title itself is pure Waters, it refers to the name of the film's hero (the underwhelming Edward Furlong), who has a practice of "pecking" at his food. Or at least that's how Waters explains it to get it past the ratings board. Ever since *Polyester*, critics more often than not take pot-shots at his films as "selling out." While this may be true in the instance of *Crybaby*, the rest of his work has remained true to his own skewed vision of reality (including the PG-rated *Hairspray*). While *Pecker* may not have as many huge belly laugh moments as *Serial Mom* (or most of his other movies, for that matter), it's still a pretty good time if you're in an undemanding mood.

Pecker, a young man living in Baltimore with his family, goes around the city and snaps pictures of everyday life with a second hand camera he found at a thrift store owned by his mother (Mary Kay Place, who's become quite the indie film queen lately). His inspiration comes from his girlfriend (Christina Ricci), who works in a laundromat, and his kleptomaniac best friend (*Welcome to the Dollhouse*'s Brendan Sexton III). His bizarre family includes his older sister (a scene-stealing Martha Plimpton, easily the best thing in the film), a bartender at a gay strip joint, his compulsive, sugar-addicted little sister, and his grandmother, who believes her ventriloquist figurine of the Virgin Mary is a miracle on

earth. Pecker has a local exhibition of his imperfect photographs, which catch the eye of New York art gallery owner Lili Taylor. Soon he's caught in a whirlwind of fame and exploitation that threatens to destroy his family and his neighbourhood, and Pecker comes up with an unlikely solution to reconcile his art with his life.

During the film's finale, a character proclaims an end to "irony," and this pretty well sums up Waters' disposition in this film. The attitude throughout is sunny, sincere, and cheerfully twisted, which can be off-putting to viewers expecting the intricate humiliation gags of *There's Something about Mary* (a very different breed of comedy). *Pecker* feels more like a transition film for Waters than a fully formed masterpiece, which may explain the lack of uproarious setpieces. However, his fans will find plenty to enjoy, including cameos by regulars like Mink Stole (as a fanatical voting booth monitor) and an unrecognizable Mary Vivian Pearce.

While the film was a resounding failure at the box office, New Line has given it the usual red carpet treatment. The colourful transfer is a beauty to behold, with all of the tacky clothes and set design shining through in all their "culturally deprived" glory. One of the best commentators around (check out Criterion's *Polyester* and *Pink Flamingos*), Waters once again provides a rollicking commentary that's easily as entertaining as the movie itself; his anecdote about the opening credits' "rat" scene is almost worth the price tag alone. The DVD also includes the original trailer and an interesting 9-minute interview and gallery with Chuck Shacochis, the Baltimore photographer who shot all of the photos for the film. Also available as Volume 1 in New Line's John Waters series, paired up with his marvellous PG-rated look at racial tension in 1960s Baltimore, *Hairspray*.

PEEPING TOM

Colour, 1960, 101m. / Directed by Michael Powell / Starring Carl Boehm, Moira Shearer, Anna Massey / Criterion (US R1 NTSC), Warner (UK R2 PAL) / WS (1.66:1) (16:9)

The basic conceit of *Peeping Tom* is quite simple: a seemingly normal but unbalanced photographer, Mark Lewis (Carl Boehm), kills beautiful women with a spiked camera tripod while filming their horrified reactions at the moment of death. However, he also shows the victims something off camera as they die, and only in the last five minutes does the viewer learn what it is. Like most of Hitchcock's films, *Peeping Tom* pries into the viewer's voyeuristic impulse and turns it back on the audience, though in this case, British critics revolted and drove the film from theatres, effectively ruining the career of its once esteemed director.

Set in modern day London, an environment that encourages the pornography industry inside quaint looking buildings, the film follows Mark as he does his day to day work photographing women for girlie photo spreads. At night, Carl kills the occasional model or prostitute, then films the police investigations the next day. To his neighbours, he seems like a nice, quiet chap, and a young girl, Helen (*Frenzy's* Anna Massey), develops a crush on him. Helen's blind aunt (Maxine Audley) knows better, of course, but can't put her finger on what makes Mark such an unusual guy. He provides a clue to Helen when he reveals that his own father (played by Powell - talk about disturbing casting!) would perform sadistic psychological experiments with film on his young son, and the results have left the poor photographer quite psychologically damaged.

Though condemned as a sadistic piece of trash by British critics at the time, *Peeping Tom* developed a steady cult following over the years before a US theatrical reissue thanks to Powell devotee Martin Scorsese. The running time of *Peeping Tom* has been the object of some dispute over the years, with the original press materials reporting it as 109 minutes. The original US release prints were reportedly trimmed down to 86 minutes, though this variant is impossible to locate now, and the 101 minutes at which it actually runs now appears to be the true complete edition. Criterion's DVD presents the British cut in an even more gorgeous rendition than their earlier laserdisc, anamorphically enhanced and featuring some astoundingly rich colour photography. The opening scene, a precursor of *Marnie*, features a deliberately artificial street set bathed in pools of unnatural coloured lighting, and the effect on DVD is eye-popping. A few of the exterior daylight scenes betray the film's age thanks to a muddy skin tone here or there, but it's safe to say that outside of a theatre, this film simply won't look better.

Considering its reputation, *Peeping Tom* is a surprisingly restrained and contemplative film, with no gore or sex actually depicted on camera. Horror fans may be frustrated by the lack of visceral thrills, and like *Psycho*, the deliberate pacing may take some adjustments for anyone expecting a terrorfest. The film's sympathetic depiction of the killer provoked outrage in the '60s but has become far more common now (for better or worse), and Boehm (who later worked for Rainer Werner Fassbinder!) makes an effectively vulnerable, complex cinephilic figure.

The DVD goes some way towards shedding some light on the creation of this peculiar and fascinating film, thanks largely to the inclusion of "A Very British Psycho," a superlative 1997 documentary (50m.) commissioned by Britain's Channel Four. Devoted to the creation of *Peeping Tom* and the life of its screenwriter, Leo Marks, this is brisk, fascinating viewing, crammed with odd and unusual details about the various themes and life experiences which led a one time World War II codebreaker to write such a challenging, unorthodox screenplay. Boehm, Massey, and Marks all appear for new interview segments, and the film even includes some modern day looks at the areas in which the film was shot. In comparison, the commentary by feminist scholar and "gaze" expert Laura Mulley (also present on the laserdisc) simply pales to nothing; her readings of the film require no summary here; simply put, it's probably the weakest track Criterion produced (and she sounds distractingly like Eileen Daly at times). Too bad Scorsese wasn't on hand to provide some genuine factual and critical insight into the project. The DVD also includes the lengthy original British theatrical trailer (not to mention a depressingly lacklustre package design), while the UK release from Warner contains only the trailer and a photo gallery.

THE PEOPLE THAT TIME FORGOT

Colour, 1977, 91m. / Directed by Kevin Connor / Starring Patrick Wayne, Sarah Douglas / MGM (US R1 NTSC) / WS (1.85:1) (16:9)

 Ben McBride (Wayne) leads an expedition into an uncharted world beyond the Arctic wastes to try and locate his missing friend Bowan Tyler (Doug McClure). Immediately the party is set upon by primitive tribes and species of prehistoric creature believed long extinct. Good old American International - they might have made 'em cheap but they always made sure they were cheerful. *The People that Time Forgot* is one of several similar escapades from director/producer team Kevin Connor and John Dark. Their monsters were notoriously awful, but the papier-mâché and Plasticine look here plunders new dimensions of budgetary frugality. In spite of this, and the fact that the whole premise is dreadfully formulaic, the sense of adventure is so potent that the shortcomings fail to detract from the fun, in fact they add to it.

Then-resident king of the monster B's Doug McClure - who headed up Connor/Dark *productions* *At the Earth's Core, Warlords of Atlantis* and the one which *People* is a direct sequel to, *The Land that Time Forgot* - merely cameos here, handing over the main chores to Patrick Wayne (son of John and one-time Sinbad). Wayne aside, the team comprises mostly British players, among them Sarah *Superman II* Douglas as the newspaper photographer, Thorley *Vampire Circus* Walters as the eccentric palaeontologist and blues singer Dana Gillespie as the generously endowed native whose perspiration-sprinkled assets constantly threaten to decamp their gloriously insubstantial chamois-leather dwellings. Also with Dave Prowse, Tony Britton, Shane Rimmer and Milton Reid (as the suitably demonic king of the Naga tribe). Very much a product of its time, this sort of stuff has long been obsolete from our screens, supplanted by far better crafted but often rather soulless affairs.

Consistent with all MGM's spiffy "Midnite Movies" candidates, this Region 1 DVD is as short on frills as one has come to expect (a solitary trailer sums it up) but as usual excels in the transfer department, delivering a gloriously colourful 1.85:1 matted, 16-chapter print that has probably never looked as good before. Language options are English and French, subtitling is in French and Spanish. - TG

PERCY

Colour, 1971, 103m. / Directed by Ralph Thomas / Starring Hywel Bennett, Denholm Elliott, Elke Sommer, Britt Ekland / Anchor Bay (US R1 NTSC) / WS (1.66:1) (16:9)

Billed as the world's first penis transplant movie, *Percy* was (unbelievably) beaten to the punch by one year thanks to Doris Wishman's 1970 grindhouse shocker, *The Amazing Transplant*. However, *Percy* can lay claim as the first comedy about the subject (and thanks to *Sex and Zen* it wasn't the last, either). Apart from its saucy subject matter, this is really a standard British sex comedy with the usual double entendres, coy starlets, and featherweight storytelling.

The title character is technically just a piece of anatomy whose owner actually lasts a few minutes into the film as he plunges from the window of bedmate Helga (Elke Sommer), whose husband arrives home unexpectedly. Unfortunately the airborne stud lands on top of poor young Edwin (the usually sinister Hywel Bennett), who somehow winds up damaging his manhood beyond repair in the process thanks to a strategically placed chandelier. Luckily Dr. Whitbread (Denholm Elliott) is on hand to test out his recently perfected organ transplant process, which moves "Percy" to Edwin, a procedure likened by one character to trading in a malfunctioning old car for a Rolls Royce. The hospital staff even tests out the new "Percy" by sending a stripper nurse into Edwin's room, with spectacular results. However, Edwin finds his latest addition affecting his personality; in short, apart from coping with the departure of his wife with his best friend, he's traumatized by the thought of walking around with used goods and decides to research Percy's past to uncover the truth behind this mysterious "gift." Thanks to a helpful nurse who arms him with a list of deceased patients from that fateful day, Edwin sets off to meet his destiny.

Firmly in line with the *Carry On* films and the more racy line of Brit comedies like *Here We Go 'Round the Mulberry Bush*, *Percy* offers enough titillation to keep mainstream audiences happy without pushing any nasty buttons that could really offend anybody. The women all look nice and wholesome, with established pin up goddesses Sommer and Britt Ekland (who takes a bath of course) making the most vivid impressions during Edwin and Percy's voyage of self-discovery. Most of the one-liners fall flat, but the film is so casual and upbeat that it's hard to really dislike. Part of this credit must go to the sterling music by the Kinks(!), again in keeping with the use of bands like Traffic to add some hip value to jittery sex comedies. The most curious thing about *Percy* is trying to figure out exactly who its target audience was; music aside, there's really no one young enough in the film to make it all that appealing for the youth market, but the approach is too simplistic to make it solid adult viewing fare. What we're left with is an odd little curio, enjoyed best as a time capsule of Britain during a turbulent period of cultural change. Harmless, disposable, and a quirky little entry in post-mod cinema.

Anchor Bay has added yet another long unavailable swinging classic to the home video roster, following its miraculous salvaging of such other seemingly lost causes as *Candy* and *I'll Never Forget What's 'Is Name*. This really isn't a pretty film to look at, so despite the latest advances in transfer technology, this still looks like a cheap, washed out early '70s British film shot on questionable film stock. The elements themselves appear to be in good shape, and it's hard to imagine how the film could have been improved. The 1.66:1 framing appears to be accurate and perfectly captures the few split screen sequences. Extras are limited to the jokey theatrical trailer (complete with fig leaf) and solid liner notes by Matt Kiernan, who puts the film and its entire genre into cultural context.

PERDITA DURANGO

Colour, 1997, 121m. / Directed by Alex de la Iglesia / Starring Rosie Perez, Javier Bardem, James Gandolfini / A-Pix (US R1 NTSC) / WS (2.35:1) / DD5.1, EMS (Germany R2 PAL) / WS (2.35:1) (16:9) / DD5.1, DTS

In the nearly three years it took to reach America, *Perdita Durango*, a ferocious adaptation of the novel/comic *59 Degrees and Raining: The Story of Perdita Durango* by Barry Gifford (*Wild at Heart*), went through countless distribution and legal transformations. Amazingly, the surviving film has been brought to DVD with a great deal of care and respect by A-Pix, though unfortunately some technicalities prevent this from being the genuine "unrated director's cut" as promised on the packaging. Near the US/Mexican border, trashy hellcat Perdita (Rosie Perez in her best performance) hooks up with Romeo Dolorosa (Javier Bardem). A mystical, demonic criminal and cult practitioner, he talks her into a sacrificial road trip involving a young American couple as hostages and blood offerings. Simultaneously carrying out orders by crime boss Santos (Don Stroud) to smuggle foetuses for the black market cosmetics industry, Romeo is also pursued by dogged DEA agent Dumas (*The Sopranos'* James Gandolfini) all the way to that hotbed of perdition, Las Vegas.

As jittery and confrontational as its director's previous two films, *Accion Mutante* and *Day of the Beast*, this film finds its creator honing his craft thanks to a sharp script partially written by Gifford himself. The excellent ensemble cast relies on Perez for its star power but really provides a showcase for Bardem, making a head-spinning switch from his stud boy roles in *Jamón Jamón* and *Live Flesh*. Aimee Graham (yes, Heather's sister) plays one of the hostages and gets to show off her, uh, talents, while supporting roles feature '70s drive-in staple Don Stroud and gritty British director Alex Cox. Incidentally, the characters of Perdita and Santos also appeared in both the novel and film of *Wild at Heart*.

Retitled *Dance with the Devil* and sporting a video generated title card for its US release from A-Pix, *Perdita Durango* is complete on DVD in terms of violence but lost some other footage along the way. Apart from a purported glimpse of potentially underage nudity, the film has also been shorn of a climactic sequence in which Romeo finds himself literally interacting with the film *Vera Cruz*, his heroic ideal. While this loss due to the film's legal restrictions doesn't really harm the narrative flow, it does remove the emotional punchline for his character and sacrifices one of Iglesia's more interesting stylistic innovations in the film.

The German DVD (packaged with a nice Milan CD of Simon Boswell's score) is absolutely complete and sports a beautiful anamorphic transfer; the only debit is the English subtitles must be manually switched on and off during the Spanish language scenes or left on for the film's entirety. The Dolby Digital mix for either version is a real room shaker, with the thunderous Latin-flavoured score simmering from every speaker throughout the film. The US disc features optional English subtitles, which turn on by default for the Spanish language sequences, as well as a Spanish subtitle option. The original excellent European and Mexican trailers are included, as well as the less impressive video trailer (which "introduces" Bardem for some reason). The German disc also includes optional German subs, a photo gallery, cast bios, and the German and English language trailers, as well as a striking cover.

PET SEMATARY

Colour, 1989, 103m. / Directed by Mary Lambert / Starring Dale Midkiff, Fred Gwynne, Denise Crosby / Paramount (US R1 NTSC) / WS (1.85:1) (16:9) / DD5.1

When Stephen King first hit paydirt as the world's leading horror writer in the early '80s, he often referred to the unpublished *Pet Sematary* as the scariest thing he'd ever written, something so disturbing that it might never even reach the general public. As we all know, King's gruesome twist on that old chestnut "The Monkey's Paw" finally did see the light of day, and while it's one of his most morbid creations, the hype far outweighed the final product. Still holding this tale close to his heart, King insisted on writing the screenplay for *Pet Sematary* and controlling many aspects of the production, which was helmed by music video director Mary Lambert.

Dr. Louis Creed (Dale Midkiff) and his wife, Rachel (Denise Crosby), relocate to the Maine countryside along with their two children. Their house lies along a treacherous road for speeding semis, while their eccentric neighbour, Jud Crandall (the late Fred Gwynne), points out another sinister location: a pet cemetery located deep within the woods. Louis takes his place as the head college physician, where he soon loses one young man, Victor Pascow (Brad Greenquist), during a grisly operating room procedure. Rachel and the kids take off for one weekend to visit family members, leaving Louis to tend to the beloved family cat, Church. Naturally the kitty wanders into the road and falls under the speeding wheels of a truck. Jud reluctantly offers a solution to Louis' problem: the pet cemetery can restore life to dead animals, but at a high price. As Jud cautions, "Sometimes dead is better." Louis decides to do it anyway, but the zombified Church which returns doesn't seem quite the same. After tragedy strikes again, Louis is confronted with an even more horrific possibility... what would happen if you buried a person in the pet cemetery?

During its release *Pet Sematary* became one of the highest grossing King adaptations and, despite the jeers of critics, went over well with audiences looking for pure, stripped down scares. It's not a good movie by a long shot, but for a cheap and nasty party movie, this does the trick well enough. The final third is particularly unsettling, with some gruesome latex and mutilation effects that can still provoke a decent shudder or two, despite the occasionally exploitative and pandering approach of Lambert's direction. (Amazingly, she returned to direct the worthless *Pet Sematary 2*, starring a pre-*ER* Anthony Edwards.)

The acting here ranges from atrocious (namely Crosby, whose brittle and flat delivery may account for her stalling career since *Star Trek: The Next Generation*) to the amusing hambone antics of Gwynne, best known to the world as Herman Munster. TV actor Midkiff is actually quite good in a difficult role, and he manages to wring some emotion from some potentially silly scenes. Had King's screenplay pared the story down simply to the Creed's plight, this could have been a devastating and haunting film; unfortunately he carried over some hoary devices from his book, such as having Pascow's ghost constantly pop up at inane moments to warn the family about impending danger. This recurring irritation offers some easy laughs and nasty gooey brain-spilling effects, but nothing else. On the other hand King made a good call by carrying out his final scene beyond the cryptic fade-out of his novel, which wouldn't have translated to film at all. Elliot Goldenthal turns in one of his earliest mainstream music scores, which manages to provoke chills despite a few jarring quotations from Lalo Schifrin's *The Amityville Horror*. In short, be in a lenient mood when you see this one, or you could be very disappointed.

Paramount's DVD amazingly offers no extra material of any kind, but at least the transfer blows away those pale laserdiscs, most of which have apparently rotted by now anyway. This marks its first availability in a letterboxed presentation, and the quality mirrors the theatrical appearance very well. Lambert's flat, static visual style doesn't offer many punchy visuals, with a drab colour scheme that translates here about as well as possible. The 5.1 remix fares better, with those deafening trucks offering plenty of jolting opportunities to pan very loud sounds from left to right in the rear speakers. And hey, you get to hear that great Ramones theme song in roaring 5.1, so that's almost worth the price tag alone.

PETEY WHEATSTRAW: THE DEVIL'S SON-IN-LAW

Colour, 1978, 95m. / Directed by Cliff Roquemore / Starring Rudy Ray Moore, Jimmy Lynch / Xenon (US R1 NTSC)

Apparently deciding to expand his routine beyond the Dolemite persona, Rudy Ray Moore went for all out comedy with *Petey Wheatstraw: The Devil's Son-in-Law*, a surreal mixture of sass and Satanism.

Born as a full grown boy out in the boonies, little Petey is tormented by his friends but learns martial arts from a kindly old man (G. Tito Shaw) as a means of revenge. When he grows up, Petey becomes - what else? - a stand up comedian and uses his kung fu prowess to keep order in the neighbourhood. Unfortunately, his plans to open a new club conflicts with the money-grubbing interests of wicked rival comedians Leroy and Skillet (a real comedy team from the '70s), who rub out Petey and virtually all of his friends and family during a funeral. In Hell, Petey learns that Shaw was actually Lucifer himself, and the two strike a deal: Petey can return to life and use the powers of evil to seek revenge, in exchange for which he will marry the Devil's butt ugly daughter. Thanks to the Devil's magical cane, Petey walks around turning no good husbands into little dogs, making fat women thin, and so on, while he comes up with a plan to get out of his unholy marriage plans. The scheme he comes up with will leave viewers speechless.

The print used for this DVD looks more worn than the other Rudy Ray Moore titles. However, the heavy saturations of red during the Hell scenes look better than might be expected, and the funky disco score sounds just fine. Moore himself provides a commentary track, which would normally make this a great collector's item. Unfortunately, this ranks with *Driller Killer, Resurrection*, and *In the Mouth of Madness* as one of the most useless commentaries ever recorded. Moore explains that the film is one of his favourites, then vanishes completely for 99% of the film. He occasionally pops in to offer a completely irrelevant comment or point out stock footage, only to vanish again into silence. A real disappointment. Extras include the same trailers on the other Xenon titles.

PHANTASM

Colour, 1979, 88m. / Directed by Don Coscarelli / Starring Michael Baldwin, Bill Thornbury / MGM (US R1 NTSC), Digital (UK R2 PAL) / WS (1.85:1) / DD5.1

 If someone found a way to transfer the grief-ridden fever dream of a preadolescent horror fan directly onto film, the result would look a lot like *Phantasm*, a rare entry in the late '70s horror sweepstakes that doesn't involve mad slashers or demonic children. Filmed on a ridiculously low budget and extremely popular upon its theatrical release and subsequent incarnations on video, *Phantasm* in many ways prefigures the "irrational" horrors of the '80s (*A Nightmare on Elm Street* in particular) and, despite a few dated but lovable trappings of its period, has managed to retain its scare value over the past twenty years.

Jodie (Bill Thornbury) and his younger brother, Mike (Michael Baldwin), relocate to a small town where they attend the funeral of one of Jodie's old buddies. Mike begins noticing strange events in the local cemetery, Morningside, which usually involve the sinister caretaker (Angus Scrimm), whom Mike dubs "the Tall Man." Mike already suffers from anxiety over the death of his parents, and he harbours fears that Jodie will take off and desert him. After dealing with rampaging robed dwarfs and other odd occurrences, Mike finally decides he's had enough and sneaks into Morningside after hours, where he has a very close encounter with the Tall Man. Mike manages to sever and hold on to one of the Tall Man's fingers, which continues to ooze and spew yellow glop. Mike shows the finger to Jodie, who, along with plucky ice cream man Reggie (Reggie Bannister), decides to help Mike get to the bottom of this bizarre mystery.

Deftly mixing elements of gothic horror, sci-fi, and surrealism, director Don Coscarelli performed most of the major production functions on this film, an amazing feat considering his young age and the impressive results. In fact, *Phantasm* proved to become such a surprise cult hit that it spawned no less than three sequels, though only the third, *Lord of the Dead*, came close to recapturing the same terrifying delirium on display here. Wisely, Coscarelli chose to place a great deal of emphasis on the human characters, all of whom are sympathetic and quirky. Oddly enough, Reggie, basically a supporting character here, became the protagonist in the other films, and Bannister wound up becoming an impressive comic and action presence in the process. As the audience identifier, Baldwin's lack of acting experience is countered by his sheer believability as a real kid - neurotic, foul mouthed, and imaginative. Though Thornbury was relegated to bit parts afterwards for reasons best not discussed here, he also does a fine job and even does a little singing (included as a separate audio track here as well). Of course, the most memorable presence, Scrimm, has few lines but quickly became a horror icon, thanks in no small part to his creepy agents of death: flying metal spheres that burrow into victims' heads and expunge their blood. The ideal *Phantasm* seemed to arrive from New Line thanks to their deluxe laserdisc box set, which included a widescreen transfer and an avalanche of extras including outtakes, TV appearances, trailers, deleted scenes, and commentary from Coscarelli, Baldwin, Thornbury, and Scrimm.

MGM's nicely packaged DVD edition offers the same extras at a fraction of the price, as well as even more deleted scenes (including a splattery encounter between the Tall Man and a fire extinguisher). The transfer actually looks even better, with richer shadows and duskier colours that very closely resemble how this looked back on drive-in screens in '79. The re-channelled 5.1 mix obviously isn't as smooth and elegant as a recent film, but the startling sound effects bursting from every channel are guaranteed to send viewers flying out of their seats. Of course, the eerie, elegant electronic score (second to *Halloween* as one of the decade's finest) also sounds greatly improved.

MGM's animated menus remain perfectly in keeping with the film's imagery, featuring characters' faces and film stills morphing into spheres from one screen to another. The scaled down UK release includes the Fangoria spot, a Scrimm interview, photos, and the trailer and TV spots.

PHANTOM OF THE OPERA

Colour, 1943, 92m. / Directed by Arthur Lubin / Starring Nelson Eddy, Susanna Foster, Claude Rains / Universal (US R1 NTSC)

Hollywood's second stab at the venerable Gaston Leroux novel took its cue from the Lon Chaney original by tossing huge amounts of money at the screen, creating a visual spectacle barely rooted in the gothic tale of a disfigured madman lurking in the Paris sewers and pining for the love of an operatic ingénue. It's to the credit of everyone involved that this *Phantom* turned out as well as it did, for even with its flaws, the film has become a regular favourite even outside the circle of monster movie fanatics.

Shy, middle aged violinist Enrique Claudin (Claude Rains) harbours a secret love for the Paris Opera's newest vocal discovery, Christine DuBois (Susanna Foster), but finds his dreams torn asunder when he loses his job and, in a fit of rage, murders a devious music publisher and receives a faceful of acid for his trouble. The scarred Enrique retires below the opera house, where he observes Christine's progress and the amorous advances of both dashing singer Anatole Garron (Nelson Eddy) and police inspector Raoul de Chagny (Edgar Barrier). (Exactly why there had to be two romantic heroes in this piece is anyone's guess.) Enrique becomes the dreaded phantom, who lurks in the shadows and uses his craftiness to dispose of those who stand in the way of Christine's happiness. Ultimately he whisks the young diva down to his lair, where she discovers the horrifying truth about her benefactor.

Though far removed from the original novel and the silent film in terms of plot, this *Phantom* retains enough horror elements to overcome the long passages in which Foster and Eddy sing... and sing and sing and sing. The chandelier cutting is a particular highlight, and Rains' excellent performance indicates his potential as a leading man, which was never quite fully realized. The lavish sets and Technicolor photography are among the best ever captured on film, while Foster proves capable as both an actress and singer, something no other Christines have managed to pull of on film. As far as all of the *Phantom*s go, this isn't as thrilling as the

1925 version or as poetic as the 1963 variation from Hammer, but this film occupies its own justified spot as a respectable twist on a well worn tale.

Fans of this film have long bemoaned the miserable video and TV presentations, with the pastel-looking laserdisc the best of a truly lousy bunch. The Universal DVD goes a huge distance towards correcting this oversight with an eye-popping transfer that finally resembles genuine Technicolor. The print is a little too spotty and scratchy to be called pristine, but the robust restoration of the original colour schemes and the astonishing depth of detail make this a welcome sight indeed.

As with their other Universal monster classics, the studio has decked out this DVD with a lavish series of extras, including a feature length commentary track by Scott MacQueen in which he methodically lays out every shred of detail you could possibly want to know about the production. You also get "The Opera Ghost: The Phantom Unmasked," a 50 minute documentary from David J. Skal covering the various incarnations of the Phantom from his literary inception through the '60s. (Not surprisingly, the four filmed versions since the early '80s are brushed off entirely.) The original trailer is included and, like the other Universal trailers, is in noticeably rough shape. Chalk up another victory for the Universal monster series, and pray for more titles to come.

PHANTOM OF THE OPERA

Colour, 1990, 185m. / Directed by Tony Richardson / Starring Burt Lancaster, Charles Dance, Teri Polo / Image (US R1 NTSC)

This second television version of Gaston Leroux's classic novel plays up the romantic, theatrical, and humorous aspects inherent in the story while ignoring the cliff-hanger and horrific elements of the famous Lon Chaney version.

Adapted by Arthur Kopit from his stage play (which preceded Andrew Lloyd Webber's version and, unlike Webber, gave credit to the original author!), this two night production was helmed by the unlikely choice of Tony Richardson, best known for his British studies of nonconformity like *Tom Jones* and *The Loneliness of the Long Distance Runner*. Partially shot in the real Paris Opera House (a filmic first), this version of the familiar story may not really be strictly faithful to its source but does make for entertaining and elegant viewing.

Young ingénue Christine (Teri Polo) toils away as an underling at the esteemed Paris Opera House where Carriere (Burt Lancaster) oversees the mammoth productions. Coached by a mysterious phantom teacher (Charles Dance, excellent as always), Christine steps in and becomes the star of the evening when misfortune befalls the reigning diva, Carlotta (art film regular Andrea Ferreol from *A Zed and Two Noughts* and *La Grande Bouffe*). It turns out that Carriere is the phantom's father; his masked son resides beneath the opera house where he attempts to deal with his deep-rooted psychological torment and pines for a normal existence.

Though shot for television, this production looks relatively opulent and could often pass for feature work. While Lancaster seems a bit out of place with the rest of the proceedings in a role mostly created from scratch, everyone else performs convincingly, with tongue suitably but not distractingly placed in cheek. Kolpit's script makes a relatively smooth transition to the small screen, even with the removal of a few musical numbers present in his stage version. This full frame DVD presentation looks much cleaner and glossier than the television broadcast, which aired most recently on A&E. Even better, the full stereo soundtrack has been restored, and it's a knockout. Astonishingly clear channel separation and rich, robust bass make this a true sonic delight, despite the fact that some of Christine's solo bits were rather sloppily dubbed. The score by the late John Addison (Sleuth) particularly benefits from the audio upgrade, as the music often subtly plays around the romantic and comic angles without resorting to traditional shrieking horror motifs.

The DVD (whose chapters are split between the two separate halves of the program) also includes a "trailer," i.e., the four minute recap aired before the second night. While this may be skewed more for the Beauty and the Beast crowd than die-hard monster fans (after all, you never get to see the phantom's face, only Christine's reaction), this *Phantom* should make for a breezy, hokum-filled three hours with few complaints.

PHANTOM OF THE OPERA

Colour, 1998, 100m. / Directed by Dario Argento / Starring Julian Sands, Asia Argento / A-Pix (US R1 NTSC), Medusa (Italy R2 PAL), TFI (France R2 PAL) / WS (1.85:1) (16:9) / DD5.1

The first Italian adaptation of the familiar Gaston Leroux story, *The Phantom of the Opera* marked a deliberately calculated attempt to break into the

international horror market with what seemed to be a "sure thing." Unfortunately a chilly critical reception overseas prevented it from finding an audience, leaving director Dario Argento to turn back to his familiar *giallo* formula. While the film's less than stellar reception is understandable, it does offer mild rewards for seasoned Italian cinema fans and isn't quite the shambling debacle one might be led to fear.

After a brief prologue in which a rejected infant is dumped into a Parisian river and saved inside the sewers by hordes of rats (shades of *Batman Returns*), the film begins in 1877 at the Paris Opera House, where young Christine (Asia Argento) works as a chorus girl in the latest production. When he's not busy killing nosy construction workers and treasure seeking interlopers, the mysterious phantom (Julian Sands), infatuated with Christine's voice, uses his telepathic powers to seduce the willing ingénue and allow her to supplant the tempestuous diva, Carlotta (Nadia Rinaldi). Meanwhile the exotic Count Raoul de Chagney (Andrea di Stefano) reveals his own designs on Christine and takes it up himself to free her from the romantic but irretrievably psychopathic phantom.

Like most of Argento's films, *Phantom* is first and foremost a feast for the eyes. Packed with luscious scenery and ominous caverns, the film is primarily a work of scenic stylization, though the bland cinematography by Ronnie Taylor (*Tommy* and Argento's *Opera*) avoids the expected Argento camera gymnastics. Ennio Morricone provides an elegant, subdued score, and Sergio Stivaletti's gore effects by and large get the job done, including a nasty stalagmite impaling and a Fulciesque tongue-ripping.

In many respects *Phantom* marks a progression of ideas Argento introduced with *The Stendhal Syndrome*; most obviously, his murderer is unmasked right from the beginning and is far more sexualized than the usual black-gloved serial killer. Once again he utilizes odd bursts of CGI, represented here by a floating Christine in the clouds(?) and the bizarre image of naked childish bodies transfixed in a giant rat trap. Unlike *Stendhal*, this film benefits greatly from the presence of the actors' original voices, making it far more accessible and easy on the ears. Roman Polanski's favourite screenwriter, Gérard Brach, collaborated with Argento on the screenplay, imbuing it with the same delirious, overripe exchanges that characterized *Bitter Moon*. The unusual locales are generally interesting and well handled, making this a more successful and interesting foray into Parisian period horror than Argento's last effort, the unbearable *Wax Mask* (which he mercifully only produced).

The trouble with *Phantom* lies mostly with its context in the entire Argento canon. While Argento has often cited the Claude Rains version of *Phantom* as one of his earliest and most influential movie memories, he already covered most of this ground quite thoroughly in the excellent 1989 film *Opera*, essentially a modern day updating of the Leroux story. From an artistic standpoint, there was really no reason for this film to be made in the first place. However, a poll with the Italian movie-going public decreed that they wanted him to do a straight version of the familiar story, and he complied.

In essence, the film is a commercial enterprise at heart rather than the anguished, stylish exorcism of internal demons Argento followers have come to expect. Saddled with such familiar material, he apparently decided to have fun and injected the film with far more humour than one expects. The Leroux novel is indeed surprisingly witty, but horror fans are understandably confused by this approach. With its emphasis of bizarre gimmickry (the rat-catching machine), grotesque faces, and weird *non sequitur* humour, *Phantom* more often resembles a Jeunet and Caro film, sort of a gory *City of Lost Children*. The film abounds with bizarre, potentially laughable moments: an unexpected visit by Raoul to an Eastern bathhouse (complete with unpleasant frontal nudity), in which he envisions Christine as a wine-dribbling whore; the phantom obtaining sexual communion with the rats whom he regards as his family; and the graphic chandelier dropping, a scene reminiscent of the *Opera* raven attack.

The actors themselves are largely ineffectual, with Sands in his moping *Boxing Helena* mode and lovely Asia serving more as window dressing through most of the running time. (Also, look for Coralina Cataldi Tassoni, the ill-fated wardrobe mistress from *Opera*, reprising her role here.)

Acting quibbles aside, the romantic and sexualized elements provide some points of interest, with Christine experiencing a similar personality dualism as *Stendhal*'s Anna, represented here by the temptations of two very different men ("I may have fallen in love with them both"). Once again Argento provides a wistful, sad, but ultimately merciful coda for his daughter, complete with her literally running towards the light. Ultimately, this is the most positive and heartfelt rendition of the tale since Terence Fisher's underrated Hammer version back in 1962.

A-Pix's DVD release of *Phantom* is one of the more successful presentations of a recent Argento film in the United States. Attractively letterboxed at 1.85:1 and anamorphically enhanced, the image quality is velvety and looks colourful and finely detailed throughout. Nothing notable appears to be missing from this "unrated director's cut," though it has reportedly been time-compressed down from 103 minutes with few detrimental effects on the film. The 5.1 sound mix suffers somewhat from some artificial post-production canned sound and ambient effects (typical of recent Italian productions for some reason) but at least isn't a wretched padded-down mono mix like *Trauma*; unfortunately the music of the 5.1 track slips out of synch several times, while the 2.0 track remains consistent. The disc includes both the original theatrical trailer and the far less impressive video preview, as well as a "making of" featurette consisting of camcorder footage during the shooting of several sequences such as the finale. A brief Julian Sands interview and a reprint of the first Fangoria article on the film round out the package.

The Italian DVD features a darker, even richer transfer, with both the English track and the more elegant Italian track with optional English or Italian subtitles, while also porting over most of the extras from the US disc as well. On the other hand, the censored French disc omits the bathhouse footage and, despite an attractive transfer, is best avoided.

PHANTOM OF THE PARADISE

Colour, 1974, 92m. / Directed by Brian De Palma / Starring Paul Williams, William Finely, Jessica Harper / Fox (US R1 NTSC) / WS (1.85:1) (16:9) / DD2.0

One of the most challenging films from Brian De Palma, *Phantom of the Paradise* marks the turning point between his edgy early films (such as *Greetings* and *Sisters*) and more commercially accessible but no less worthy fare like *Carrie* and *The Fury*. While both of these phases contain the quirky humour and film buff in-jokes which grabbed critics' attention, *Phantom* feels in many ways like the work of a director determined to go for broke with his one shot at directing. Every idea no matter how insane appears to have been thrown in the blender, producing a collage of music, horror, and satire unlike any other.

Recording mogul Swan (Paul Williams) - "He has no other name," according to the Rod Serling intro - makes a new enemy in the form of Winslow Leach (William Finley), an aspiring songwriter whose Faust cantata is stolen to be the opening performance of Swan's rock dream palace, the Paradise. In a fit of rage Winslow attempts to exact revenge on Swan, only to wind up with his face disfigured in a vinyl pressing plant mishap. The misshapen Swan dons a bird-like metal mask and becomes the Phantom, a thorn in Swan's side determined to see Faust performed by Winslow's own choice for the lead role, upcoming ingénue Phoenix (Jessica Harper). Swan instead betrays Winslow and opts to give the plum role to Beef (Gerrit Graham), a comical glam queen; naturally this double cross sets off an inevitable, supernatural chain of events culminating in a wild finale during the Paradise curtain raiser.

With its barrage of classic horror references, its simultaneous embrace and critique of the glam rock lifestyle, and its pansexual playfulness, *Phantom* has often drawn comparisons to its more famous contemporary, *The Rocky Horror Picture Show*, with which it also shares an inability to keep the storyline under control during a frenzied climax. Fortunately its flaws are glossed over by the sheer energy involved, from De Palma's creative and resourceful staging to the fine performances (both in terms of acting and singing). Williams may be an acquired taste, but his witty score kicks along nicely from '50s be bop to surfer parody to KISS-style rock without missing a beat.

As usual Harper steals all of her scenes, making one wish she had become a much bigger star in an age when both musical and acting talent were appreciated. (Ironically, she later appeared as Janet and acquitted herself quite well in the ill-fated but not uninteresting *Rocky Horror* sequel, *Shock Treatment*.) De Palma fans will have fun looking for early examples of his directorial quirks, such as his trademark use of split screen during the Beach Bums number. It doesn't outdo *Sisters*, but at least he tried. Of course there's also a Hitchcock nod this time around, thanks to one of the first and greatest *Psycho* parodies on record.

Owners of the godawful laserdisc and VHS editions of *Phantom of the Paradise* will be relieved to know that Fox has done wonders for the film's reputation with this DVD transfer. The earlier "stereo" sound simply presented the mono channel with slightly different volumes from left to right, but the DVD contains the original full, vibrant stereo mix, with dialogue located in the centre channel and music nicely spread out to the left and right. Don't expect any surround activity - an optional 5.1 mix would have been nice, if not necessary - but this is the best the film has sounded by far since it played in theatres. The image quality is also a vast improvement; the fuzzy, muddy video of the past can now be forgotten. The cropping of the 1.85:1 original image didn't really harm the film (and the split screen bit was always letterboxed), but the extra breathing room on the left and right makes some of the more chaotic camera set ups easier to take.

The disc also includes a "theatrical trailer," which lacks even a basic title card and actually looks more like a random assortment of scenes slapped together by someone on a video deck. It's too bad a film with a relatively respectable cult pedigree couldn't earn even a minimal special edition treatment (especially when *Rocky Horror* merits two fully stuffed discs), but considering Fox's spotty track record with genre films, *Phantom* phans should be pleased indeed to finally have a respectable video edition in their hands.

PHENOMENA

Colour, 1984, 110m. / Directed by Dario Argento / Starring Jennifer Connelly, Donald Pleasence, Daria Nicolodi / Anchor Bay (US R1 NTSC) / WS (1.66:1) / DD5.1, Divid 2000 (UK R2 PAL) / WS (1.78:1) / DD2.0, Dragon (Germany R0 PAL) / WS (1.66):1) / DD2.0

Argento's wildest and woolliest shocker, *Phenomena* is usually regarded by critics as his worst film (including writer Maitland McDonough, who wrote the liner notes for the laserdisc!). However, a number of his followers look very fondly upon it, and these diverse responses are due to how willing the viewer is to enjoy a film with complete disregard for standard cinematic laws of narrative logic and linear plotting. Part of the film's sorry reputation may be due to the fact that most countries only have access to the butchered 82 minutes print, *Creepers*, which amazingly enough actually played in US theatres in 1985 under the auspices of New Line. While this longer edition may not clarify much in the way of storyline, it does greatly aid the film's pacing and overall effect as the eye and mind are given more time to absorb the bizarre, shocking collision of images and storylines.

On the surface, *Phenomena* is a return to *Suspiria* territory, with a virginal American girl, Jennifer (Jennifer Connelly), arriving at a boarding school for girls in Switzerland. Her awkward habit of sleepwalking gets her into trouble on her first night when she wanders out of her room and witnesses the murder of a schoolmate, and on top of that, it appears she has a telepathic connection to insects. A local Scottish entomologist, John McGregor (Donald Pleasence) tells Jennifer about a string of bizarre serial killings in the area, and with the aid of Jennifer's uncanny powers, they set out to find the murderer.

In many ways this film is the perfect stepping stone between the crystal-clear, razor-edged photography of *Tenebre* and the baroque wackiness of *Opera*, delivering essentially two split narratives that finally converge in the amazing, excruciatingly violent final half hour. The eclectic supporting cast includes Argento regular and ex-partner Daria Nicolodi, the icy Dalila Di Lazzaro (*Andy Warhol's Frankenstein*), and Patrick Bauchau (*A View to a Kill*) as a nosy police inspector. Add to that top notch make-up effects by Sergio Stivaletti (*Demons*) and an unsettling score featuring Goblin, Claudio Simonetti, and Simon Boswell, and the result is an undeniably unique and haunting experience.

The film boasts a few strange quirks, such as a voiceover narrator inexplicably appearing 15 minutes into the film and an irritating tendency to rely on heavy metal tunes to get the viewers' blood pumping. In many ways, though, these "flaws" can be almost as endearing as the film's good qualities; its sheer daffiness is almost beyond criticism. The off-kilter, dreamlike performances have also drawn critical fire, and again it's a matter of taste. Most unfairly, though, *Phenomena* has been termed a work of style over substance with no internal schematics to hold it up. On closer analysis, this simply isn't true. With ruthless precision, Argento dissects the notions of how families can fragment and become distorted- Jennifer's father has abandoned her for a year's shooting on a film, her mother left without so much as a goodbye, and the bizarre genetic quirks that explain the identity of the killer(s) reflect Argento's own disintegrating domestic state at the time. Significantly, the film takes place at Passover, with Jennifer attaining a kind of virginal Zen state at the finale after her trial by blood and killing off the firstborn of her nemesis. The clash of languages and dialects (German, French, American) and the placement of the action at the "Richard Wagner School" also indicate that Argento was comparing the idealized notions of what a family should be and how easily it can crumble and destroy its children; Jennifer's early declaration, "Screw the past," quickly comes back to haunt her as the sins of the fathers (and mothers) stalk across the countryside. On a more visceral level, though, the film is also quite entertaining and boasts some of Argento's most delicious shocks

(particularly the final scene). Either way, this is a film seriously in need of re-evaluation.

Likewise, Anchor Bay has presented *Phenomena* in its best condition to date. While a 116 minute print also exists in Italian, Argento dismisses that as the equivalent of a rough cut. This pristine print is a tremendous improvement over the Columbia laserdisc from Japan, which featured good clarity and colour but suffered from an horrendous sound mix, with the music blasting out ten times louder than the dialogue and drowning out entire scenes (such as Bauchau's asylum visit). This problem has thankfully been corrected with a new, extremely disorienting and surprising Dolby Digital sound mix that presents all of the sound elements as they should be. However, this edition also has its share of idiosyncrasies; for example, early on when Pleasence unveils a maggot-covered severed head in a glass cage, the moment unfolds with a deafening blast of music on the Japanese disc but contains no music at all here. The image quality is somewhat sleeker and more pleasing than the Japanese version, though the letterboxing (which adds a bit to the left side and shears some information from the bottom of the image) doesn't particularly affect the film and seems more of a respectful gesture than anything else. The commentary by Argento, Stivaletti, and Simonetti is enthusiastic and occasionally helpful but also has a tendency to become completely quiet for long stretches of the film. The feature is followed by a bizarre European trailer and, finally, the music video for the cue "Phenomena" (incorrectly identified onscreen as "Jennifer" and credited onscreen to Argento himself, though some sources actually cite Michele Soavi as the director). This odd little treat, also letterboxed, mostly features Connelly running down hallways while Simonetti jams away on his keyboard. The DVD also contains Soavi's trailer for "The Valley" and the infamous appearance by Argento on New York's *The Joe Franklin Show*.

The longer Italian cut is available on laserdisc as the "Integral Hard" edition, coupled with Luigi Cozzi's hit and miss *Dario Argento's World of Horror 3*, while DVD buyers can pick up the Dragon two-disc set, which packs most of the Anchor Bay extras with the longer cut in English (with Italian footage inserted) or, better, the full Italian dialogue track with optional English subtitles. Though not the original studio track, the Italian dialogue is much classier and easier on the ears than the English one and makes for a significantly different experience. On the other hand, the UK disc features an outstanding transfer but maddeningly only includes a mono track and some very skimpy interviews.

PICNIC AT HANGING ROCK

Colour, 1975, 107m. / Directed by Peter Weir / Starring Rachel Roberts, Vivean Gray / Criterion (US R1 NTSC) / WS (1.66:1) / DD5.1

After a seeming eternity on video moratorium, Peter Weir's delirious Australian arthouse favourite received the Criterion treatment in a digitally restored transfer that will simply knock your socks off. The remixed Dolby Digital 5.1 soundtrack subtly enhances the palpable, sweaty environment of the film, allowing the ethereal New Age score and natural sound effects to swirl around you and add immeasurably to the intoxicating atmosphere. Unprepared viewers may be puzzled at the fact that the film presents a mystery which it refuses to solve. Based on the 1967 Joan Linday novel, Weir's ode to female adolescence concerns a repressive girl's school led by Rachel Roberts. On Valentine's Day in 1900, the girls go out for an expedition to a wondrous natural volcanic formation called Hanging Rock Three girls and a teacher vanish without a trace, sending the other students into a state of near hysteria.

Criterion's edition also includes the original (very long) trailer and optional subtitles for the hearing and Aussie-speaking impaired. Here's the strange thing, though - the packaging refers to this as "the long awaited director's cut of the film." Well, it looks like the same edited US print, but apparently Weir oversaw the entire transfer and remixing process, so it's obviously this shorter edition that he prefers. However, the Japanese laserdisc edition (which looks much worse) runs nine minutes longer; this 116 minute version is the standard for the rest of the world. While Weir may not like the extended cut, it would have been nice to have some of the scissored bits included as an option for viewers who want to see what was cut. So basically, if you shelled out already for the Japanese LD, hold on to it! However, Criterion has obviously invested a great deal of care into this fragile miniature masterpiece, and this is easily the best way to see it.

PIECES

Colour, 1981, 89m. / Directed by Juan Piquer Simon / Starring Christopher George Ian Sera, Lynda Day George / Diamond Entertainment (US R1 NTSC)

Poor J.P. Simon. While directors like Jess Franco and Joe D'Amato certainly had their moments of hackwork, nobody else has managed to hit the

bottom of the barrel as consistently as this guy, who punished audiences with the likes of *Cthulu Mansion* and the *MST3K* favourite, *The Pod People*. Thankfully two of his anti-masterworks qualify for the "so bad it's good" camp: the tasteless and giddy *Slugs* and his most famous international release, *Pieces*.

In the obligatory slasher prologue, set here in 1942, a young boy works on a jigsaw puzzle of a nude woman. His mother bursts in and angrily chastises him, to which he responds by taking an axe to her head. The neighbours arrive with the police to find the house splattered with blood and the little boy hiding in the closet. Flash forward forty years later, as an idyllic Boston campus is being terrorized by a chainsaw killer who removes different body parts from his victims. The officer in charge, Lieutenant Bracken (*City of the Living Dead*'s Christopher George), enlists the aid of tennis player Mary (Lynda Day George) and unbelievably dippy college student Kendall (Ian Sera) to sniff around for clues on campus. Meanwhile young girls continue to fall prey to the killer, in settings ranging from a swimming pool to a waterbed(!), all executed in graphic detail. Can our undercover sleuths discover the killer before he realizes their plan? And can anyone explain the ridiculous final scene?

Though made in Spain, *Pieces* feels for all the world like a desperate attempt to ape the Italian *giallo* formula. Plentiful suspects (including a chainsaw wielding groundsman!), endless police procedurals, a mysterious killer in black, and often naked women being terrorized in dark settings - yep, it's all right here. Even the catchy, pulsating CAM library soundtrack copies everything from Stelvio Cipriani's *The Bloodstained Shadow* to John Carpenter's *Halloween*. The best way to enjoy *Pieces* is probably as an unintentional comedy, thanks to Sera's hysterically overwrought and wholly unsympathetic performance, while the endless parade of female nudity is too ludicrous to take seriously. Sleaze fans should also watch for Franco regular Jack Taylor as a know it all professor, who has some of the best lines when he stumbles onto one gory crime scene.

Thanks to its profitable grassroots theatrical run (with the taglines "It's exactly what you think it is!" and "You don't have to go to Texas for a chainsaw massacre!") and wide video distribution, *Pieces* became one of the more notorious splatter titles during the '80s. The gore content is fairly high but never convincing, with rubber torsos and latex mouths getting shredding by various sharp implements.

Vestron released it unrated on video, and the same lacklustre full frame master was used for a Japanese laserdisc release. Meanwhile a very mildly WS (1.55:1) edition turned up on Venezuelan video under its Spanish title, *Mil gritos tiene la noche* (or *One Thousand Cries Has the Night*). Diamond's bargain priced, probably unlicensed DVD duplicates the Vestron transfer; as expected it's nothing to shout about, with shallow contrast, careless compression, and inconsistent colours, but somehow the treatment seems suitable for this scrappy little movie. The mono audio also isn't any better than your average budget line VHS tape. But would it really be as much fun if Anchor Bay issued a pristine 16:9 edition with a piercing 5.1 remix? Wait, don't answer that...

PIG

B&W, 1998, 23m. / Directed by Nico B and Rozz Williams / Starring Rozz Williams, James Hollan / Cult Epics (US R0 NTSC)

 Underground cinema has always thrived on producing shocking, unshakable imagery that could never appear in front of a Hollywood camera. In the tradition of Richard Kern, Nick Zedd, Jörg Buttgereit, et al, the 16mm black and white film *Pig* is largely an exercise in shock value packaged as an art film, and quite an effective one at that. However, if you're even the slightest bit squeamish, approach with caution.

Co-directed by and starring indie artist and rock performer Rozz Williams (who headlined Christian Death and died in the same year that this film was shot), this skull-rattling 23 minute helltrain uses a barely linear narrative to explore the nature of evil and the limits of man's moral transgressions. Even more strangely, it doesn't feature a single actor's visible face or a word of dialogue (in English, anyway). A faceless maniac (Williams), whose pig mask in the vein of *Motel Hell* justifies the literal meaning of the film's title (seen carved on a victim's chest), abducts a young man (James Hollan) in the desert who is then subjected to a variety of ordeals. And that's about it, really, as far as the story goes; much of the running time consists of abstract collages illustrating madness, a diabolical text, sign language, an out of body experience, and so on, all accompanied by a jarring, musique concrete soundtrack. Hardly enjoyable in the traditional

sense, this is a good way to drive some humility into those who claim they've seen it all.

This first instalment in Cult Epic's promising Underground Cinema series comes in a limited 1,500 piece edition DVD packed with a surprising amount of extras for such a marginalized title. Dutch director Nico B, who co-directed the film and also served as producer, writer, editor, and cinematographer, provides a commentary for both the film and a string of outtakes; despite his thick accent, he has some useful insights into the making of the film and his collaborative relationship with Williams. Other extras include an audio interview with Williams by John E. Ellenberger, behind the scenes image and photo gallery accompanied by previously unreleased R.W. music, a Super-8 test reel in black and white featuring the aforementioned pig gear, a tribute video by Nico B, and a very heavy, lavish booklet, "Why God Permits Evil," modelled after the text seen in the film. There's also an odd little Easter Egg showing Williams' apartment prior to filming, accessible from the unsettling menu design. Image quality is about what you'd expect for a zero budget, ragged black and white film, though the compression appears to be fine. The heavily layered soundtrack is also rendered with deeply disturbing clarity.

THE PILLOW BOOK

Colour, 1995, 120m. / Directed by Peter Greenaway / Starring Vivian Wu, Ewan McGregor / Columbia (US R1 NTSC) / DD2.0

 After a brief tenure as Miramax's arthouse golden boy, Peter Greenaway stumbled badly in the public eye. Following a falling out with composer Michael Nyman (an unfortunate end to one of the most fruitful modern cinematic relationships in European cinema), Greenaway was forced to adapt his all-song morality tale, *The Baby of Macon*, into a more straightforward play within a play format that simply left most viewers completely baffled.

Despite the undraped presences of Julia Ormand and Ralph Fiennes, the film remains unreleased in several major countries including the US. Fortunately Greenaway's follow up film, *The Pillow Book*, opened widely, albeit years after its completion. Greenaway still flings viewers into a stunning mixture of visual technology, classical aesthetic style, plentiful artistic nudity, and jarring moments of graphic violence. While this certainly may not be everyone's cup of tea, adventurous viewers willing to delve into this modern artist's uncompromising, ravishing feast for the eyes will find themselves amply rewarded.

The intricately structured narrative revolves around Nagiko (*The Joy Luck Club*'s Vivian Wu), whose favourite childhood ritual is having calligraphy drawn on her face by her father on the event of each of her birthdays. After witnessing a sexually traumatic event involving her father, she grows up to find herself completely absorbed in a sexual fetish for having calligraphy drawn upon her body. She takes a young Scottish man, Jerome (an exhibitionistic Ewan McGregor), as her lover but is dismayed to find his penmanship lacking. Instead she finds herself becoming "the pen as well as the paper," drawing pleasure from inking upon willing flesh. She sends Jerome's inscribed body to her father's publisher, and several erotic and grisly complications ensue.

Deriving his inspiration from Sei Shonagon's literary "pillow book," Greenaway has fashioned an elusive series of vignettes combining text, flesh, and eroticism into an uneasy but ultimately transcendent whole.

Fortunately the DVD edition preserves the nuances and colourful schemes of his compositions very well. Letterboxing purists will balk at the claim on the packaging that the film, "while filmed in multi-aspect ratios, has been re-formatted to fit your TV." In fact, this is the same fullscreen transfer supervised by Greenaway himself, which first debuted on British video some time ago. Like much of his television work, *The Pillow Book* was created with digital Japanese technology and involves layer upon layer of images interacting in various aspect ratios (ranging from anamorphic Cinemascope to 1.33:1). This version looks far more satisfying than the film's theatrical showings at 1.85:1, which constantly lopped images and subtitles off at the top and bottom of the screen. Occasional shots framed at an even slighter aspect ratio than 1.66:1 seem slightly clipped on the left side of the screen (notably the end titles and an occasional title card), but this in no way affects the compositions. This is a marked contrast to Greenaway's other digital Paintbox epic, *Prospero's Books*, which was shot hard-matted at 1.66:1 and completely collapsed when subjected to Fox's careless pan and scan video transfer.

The Dolby Surround track is effective and shows off the eclectic soundtrack (ranging from Buddhist chants to techno) with plenty of directional presence. The DVD also includes the fairly explicit US theatrical trailer.

PINK FLOYD: THE WALL

Colour, 1982, 99m. / Directed by Alan Parker / Starring Bob Geldof, Bob Hoskins / Sony (US R1 NTSC, UK R0 PAL) / WS (2.35:1) (16:9) / DD5.1

The rare major director who still cranks out an occasional musical, Alan Parker has done everything from melodramatic Broadway hits (*Evita*) to genre-bending feasts of modern rock and soul (*Fame*, *The Commitments*), and even downright bizarre concoctions that defy description (*Bugsy Malone*). However, nothing in his career could have prepared viewers for *Pink Floyd The Wall*, in which he collaborated with the legendary former Pink Floyd front man, Roger Waters, on a visualization of the group's popular double album. Drawing (perhaps too much) inspiration from Ken Russell's version of The Who's *Tommy*, Parker and Waters utilized everything from harsh animation by political cartoonist Gerald Scarfe to grotesque, Buñuel-style surrealism. While many critics dismissed the film as a long, rambling music video, a fervent cult following immediately formed, first at midnight screenings and then on video. Apart from the obvious appeal to drug-addled perceptions, viewers still relish picking apart the seemingly endless layers of symbolism and potential meanings within the music and film, and Sony's long awaited special edition DVD should provide answers to more than a few of those nagging questions.

Told almost entirely through music rather than dialogue, the film begins in a Los Angeles hotel room where Pink (Bob Geldof), a popular rock singer addled by the ravages of fame and substance abuse, wastes away in front of the television and feels his entire life rushing back over him. His father was killed in the war, his mother felt isolated from him, and his wife and agent controlled and manipulated him as a cash cow. Unable to break the wall that separates him from sanity and contact with his fellow human beings, Pink slides further and further into an abyss where he imagines himself as a fascist ruler ordering the destruction of civilization.

Though compelling and often visually dazzling, *The Wall* definitely isn't a film for every taste. Deliberately downbeat and aggressive, the film constantly hurls confrontational images in the viewer's face ranging from grotesque (maggots, chest shaving, bloody riots) to brilliantly twisted (kids being ground up into beef). Unlike *Tommy*, which charts a similar personal course from a single man's exploitation to an ultimate realization of himself, *The Wall* offers little actual redemption in the end, only the basic message that "the wall" must be torn down. Several of the song setpieces work beautifully ("Another Brick in the Wall Part II," most obviously, along with "Comfortably Numb"), while others go on far too long and wear out their welcome.

While many of the film's cultists cite this as the ultimate fusion of film and music, Parker's style was obviously still in its early stages. Future efforts like *Birdy* and *Angel Heart* also managed to bury numerous layers of meaning within a simple storyline far more effectively, and he managed to develop a firmer grasp of how to modulate viewers' emotions without bashing them over the head. For this reason *The Wall* functions best as a sort of musical rough draft for what was to come - not a masterpiece, but a crucial instalment in early '80s cinema all the same. Geldof (former lead singer of the Boomtown Rats - remember them?) does an excellent job with a very difficult part, singing himself in several numbers and communicating 90% of his role through his dynamic, expressive eyes. The other actors function more as archetypes than flesh and blood human beings, though horror fans should look for an early, very naked appearance by the willowy Jenny Wright, who went on to bloodsucking fame in *Near Dark*.

Sony's ambitious DVD represents a great deal of hard work, and happily it all paid off. The anamorphic transfer instantly wipes the previous letterboxed laserdiscs from MGM out of one's memory, while the refurbished Dolby Digital soundtrack offers a spacious soundscape, devoted as much to ambient effects and Michael Kamen's sensitive orchestrations as to the songs themselves. Parker, Waters, and Scarfe contribute on numerous levels throughout the disc, from their engaging feature-length commentary (surprisingly witty and playful, considering the morbid nature of the film) to the excellent new two part (of course) documentary, "Retrospective: A Look Back at The Wall." All three offer insights ranging from the philosophical to the technical, including their own theories of how to analyze the film's avalanche of symbols. Also included is a less impressive half hour "behind the scenes" piece made back in 1982; it's better than the average studio featurette but nothing terribly profound or revealing. One intriguing bonus is the excised "Hey You" number, presented in black and white rough cut form; it's easy to see why the song was cut out, as it would have quickly dragged the film to a halt. Other bonus materials range from the theatrical trailer (the same one from the laserdisc) to a music video for "Another Brick" aired back in the infancy of MTV.

PIONEERS IN INGOLSTADT

Colour, 1971, 84m. / Directed by Rainer Werner Fassbinder / Starring Hanna Schygulla, Harry Baer / Fantoma (US R1 NTSC)

Though best known for his visually florid, emotionally overwrought warscapes like *The Bitter Tears of Petra von Kant* and *The Marriage of Maria Braun*, the prolific and self-destructive Rainer Werner Fassbinder began his career with low key, downbeat portraits in kitchen sink realism like *Why Does Herr R. Run Amok?* and *The Gods of the Plague*, whose titles give a fairly clear idea of their emotional timbre. In this respect, *Pioneers in Ingolstadt* is a pivotal work, sandwiched in between these two periods and offering a sort of backward glance at the style he was soon to leave behind.

Over the credits we witness the processional arrival of a group of military engineers and labourers into the small town of Ingolstadt, where the citizens await the construction of bridge that will unite it more directly with the rest of the country. The women in particular take a liking to the new male arrivals, with young Berta (Hanna Schygulla) taking a particular liking to the handsome Karl (Harry Baer). Meanwhile the sole black soldier, Max (Günther Kaufmann), becomes the object of desire for more than a few women. Soon simple evenings spent at the local taverns become fraught with sexual interplay and suspicion, leaving the town marked forever in the name of progress.

An emotionally subdued work by Fassbinder standards, Pioneers could almost pass for a small scale, early Werner Herzog film instead. Most of the sex takes place offscreen and remains confined to longing looks and erotically charged discussions on benches; the joy, of course, comes instead from watching the director's regular stable of performers at their height. As usual Schygulla steals the show and proves her worth as one of international cinema's greatest performers; she could simply file her nails for 90 minutes and make the experience fascinating.

Considering it has almost been completely forgotten in light of Fassbinder's later films, *Pioneers* seems to have been given a second lease on life via the magic of DVD. No one will be likely to peg the film a masterpiece, but it's exceptionally direct and finely tuned from start to finish, making it a fascinating experience for those with an adventurous taste for movie-going. As with most of Fassbinder's early, low budget efforts, the image quality varies wildly depending on the film stock and lighting at hand, made all the more erratic by the fact this was evidently lensed in 16mm and intended for German television. DVD fanatics may bristle during the opening credits, in which the optical processing necessary to layer the titles has rendered the image with a strong blanket of haze and grain. However, things improve about five minutes in once we switch indoors, and from there onward the material is pleasantly colourful and clean. The optional yellow English subtitles move at a good speed and are well articulated throughout. The rest of the extras are understandably limited, consisting of a Fassbinder filmography and excellent, thorough liner notes by Chuck Stephens.

For an interesting comparison at just how much Fassbinder's available means increased within the span of less than one year, take a look at *Whity* (1971), a glossy, Cinemascope riot of boisterous colours and artificial sets. Even for those who dislike Fassbinder's work, there's no denying that his versatility as an artist could be astonishing.

PIRANHA

Colour, 1978, 92m. / Directed by Joe Dante / Starring Bradford Dillman, Heather Menzies, Kevin McCarthy / New Concorde (US R1 NTSC)

Long before he became famous for directing quirky, monster-friendly studio films, director Joe Dante cut his teeth (so to speak) on two standout horror cult films, *Piranha* and *The Howling*. When *Piranha* first opened, many critics didn't quite know how to take the offbeat mixture of movie buff humour and brutal violence, but audiences ate it up. By the time Dante got around to doing the same thing for werewolves, reviewers finally started catching on, and in retrospect *Piranha* was quickly hailed as more than a simple *Jaws* imitation. While Dante's first film, *Hollywood Boulevard*, was a comedy with violent flourishes, his two early monster films have also been categorized by many as spoofs. Certainly *Piranha* and *The Howling* have their share of great one liners and sly nods to horror movie history, but at heart, both are bare knuckle scarefests, filled with unexpected violence in which anyone, no matter how sympathetic, can die anywhere, anytime. Mercifully, even in the wake of James Cameron's lacklustre sequel (*Piranha II: The Spawning*) and a dismal 1995 Roger Corman remake, the original still holds up as a solid mixture of chills and chuckles, and the

shoestring piranha attacks (with those great sound effects!) are still as much fun as ever.

The deft screenplay by John Sayles (who also penned *The Howling*) begins with two amusing references to Spielberg's big shark hit: a skinny-dipping couple winds up getting chomped while trespassing in a swimming pool, and the heroine, Maggie (Heather Menzies), is introduced playing one of those old Jaws video games. Sent by Richard Deacon (*The Dick Van Dyke Show*) to find the missing kids, Maggie soon makes the acquaintance of Paul (TV pro Bradford Dillman), an alcoholic recluse who agrees to help her quest. The two stumble upon a seemingly abandoned military testing site; a curious Maggie empties out the site's pool into the nearby stream but fails to uncover any evidence. Dr. Hoak (Kevin McCarthy) surprises the two and begins a mad rant in which he explains that the duo has unleashed the product of "Operation Razorteeth," a scientific military project designed to breed mutant piranhas for destroying the North Vietnamese rivers. Of course, the piranhas are now rapidly making their way downstream... towards the local summer camp and lakeside real estate development. The predators snack on a few hapless residents, including Paul's buddy, Keenan Wynn, and Paul, Maggie, and Hoak hurriedly raft down the river to reach the camp where Paul's daughter is staying. Meanwhile, Dr. Mengers (scream queen Barbara Steele) and company arrive for damage control, and the real estate mavens hurriedly try to cover up the panic in order to avoid scaring off their potential buyers. Can the fish be stopped in time?

Piranha has enjoyed a growing cult reputation and earned its special edition DVD treatment. The film is presented in unmatted full frame with all of the image exposed; however, the main titles (done by Dante himself) were filmed soft matted at 1.66:1 and are presented as such on the disc. The film itself looks like a million bucks (about $340,000 more than it cost to make!), with vivid, beautifully defined colours and no noticeable compression defects. The murky opening scene still looks pretty dull, but it always has, even in theatres. The audio hasn't aged quite as well, with a dull hiss evident on the soundtrack throughout the picture; however, those with adequate surround processors or better can filter this out. The diverse, lyrical Pino Donaggio score sounds fine, and dialogue is consistently clear and intelligible.

Dante and producer Jon Davison provide a very interesting, brisk audio commentary in which they discuss the budget wrangling and goofy incidents during production, then point out the various familiar actors and stock footage popping up throughout the movie. The disc also includes the original theatrical trailer, a very funny outtake reel (Barbara Steele's blooper is the highlight), and nine minutes of silent "home movie" style footage behind the scenes (accompanied by Dante and Davison's commentary), including a peek at a clean shaven, 17 year old Rob Bottin working on the fishies. As if that weren't enough, the disc is also packaged with a reproduction of the theatrical sales marketing guide, and the fun animated menus feature piranha fish darting around the screen and chomping on various menu items.

PIRATES OF CAPRI

B&W, 1949, 95m. / Directed by Edgar G. Ulmer / Starring Louis Hayward, Mariella Lotti / AllDay (US R1 NTSC)

 To the Italian aristocracy, he's known as Count di Amalfi. However, to the common people and voyagers of the sea, he's Captain Sirocco, avenger of the downtrodden who roams the sea with his band of pirates. Into this swashbuckling twist on chestnuts like *The Scarlet Pimpernel* and *The Mask of Zorro* we also find the villainous Baron von Holstein (Rudolph Serato), who encourages the ignorance of Queen Carolina (Binnie Barnes), the sister of the recently beheaded Marie Antoinette, about the suffering of her people. For love interest we also have Count di Amalfi's betrothed, the beautiful Countess Mercedes de Lopez (Mariella Lotti), who undergoes several rounds of identity confusion and winds up tortured at the villain's hands. Does she escape? Well, what do you think?

Though it sounds like your average sword-clanging costumer, *The Pirates of Capri* is unusual primarily because of its director. Here Edgar G. Ulmer cranks up the expressionist touches found in *Bluebeard*, for example, and benefits from some of the finest cinematography in his career. The opening pirate duel in particular is a stunner, from the surreal costumes worn by the theatrical "players" to the razor sharp editing as men scurry up masts and traverse planks over the ocean.

While colour would have seemed a natural choice for this film, the use of black and white is impeccable, with light and shadow manipulated to produce a series of beautiful, painterly images. A full scale theatrical production at the end, with puppet-like masks and nooses adorning the stage, is also a brilliant extension of the expressionist and marionette motifs found in *Bluebeard*, and the opulence of the Italian location shooting, the massive sets built at Cinecittà, and the rousing score by future Fellini collaborator Nino Rota ably demonstrate what Ulmer could have accomplished had he been given larger budgets on a regular basis. The actors also perform ably under their lavish costumes, with leading man Louis Hayward (*Son of Dr. Jekyll*) making an interesting dual personality hero serving both the crown and the people.

As usual, AllDay has pulled out all the stops for a film few others would have even acknowledged as a possibility for home video. The Ulmer family continued to participate with this disc, including his late wife, Shirley, and his daughter, Arianne, both of whom appear in a 16 minute featurette, "In Search of the Pirates of Capri." This breezy documentary recounts the history of the film's shooting and includes some interesting artefacts, such as the first page of the film's score inscribed from Rota to Ulmer. The quality of the print itself is quite magnificent, with excellent contrast. Some very minor scuffs and scratches are visible from time to time, and a couple of shots of men standing against a bright sky cause some of the blooming you often see in lower budget films, but overall there's no room to complain at all.

The extensive, interesting liner notes provide some additional information about the film, interestingly placing it in context both in terms of Ulmer's career and the political slant of post WWII filmmaking. The disc also includes an odd little extra: the half hour 1957 pilot episode of *Swiss Family Robinson*, a proposed 13 part series Ulmer planned to shoot in Mexico with Hayward. Apparently this episode is all that survives, and it has been restored about as much as possible for this DVD. The colour elements still look a little separated, but it's quite watchable and makes for interesting viewing in comparison with Ulmer's earlier, more lavish seafaring epic. Strangely AllDay has fingerprinted this feature alone with their logo in the bottom right corner; it's distracting but probably a necessity considering the proliferation of a modern, very different form of piracy.

PIT AND THE PENDULUM

Colour, 1961, 80m. / Directed by Roger Corman / Starring Vincent Price, John Kerr, Barbara Steele / MGM (US R1 NTSC) / WS (2.35:1)

If *House of Usher* is a delicate work of grotesque art, *Pit and the Pendulum* is its gleefully brash sibling, a delicious popcorn muncher of the highest order.

Vincent Price has a field day alternating from gibbering terror to teeth-gnashing insanity (sometimes in the same scene), nicely guided along by a spectacular, twist-filled screenplay by the great Richard Matheson (*The Incredible Shrinking Man*). No other Corman/Poe film is this much sheer fun, and the last ten minutes still pack a tremendous kick with an unforgettable, terrifying final image.

Our sullen hero, Francis Barnard (John Kerr), travels to the creepy Medina castle by the seaside to uncover the truth behind the mysterious death of his sister, Elizabeth (Barbara Steele). Her husband, Nicholas Medina (Vincent Price), expresses grief but offers few details, while the sister, Catherine (*Dementia 13*'s Luana Anders), offers a few jittery clues that Elizabeth's demise may not have been completely natural. As we learn in flashback, she was obsessed with the Medina family history, a saga filled with adultery, murder, and madness. Meanwhile a ghost seems to haunt the castle halls, driving Nicholas to the brink of madness while Francis, Elizabeth, and the family doctor (Antony Carbone) come to grips with the fact that something evil indeed is going on within the thick stone walls.

More than any other Corman film, *Pit* features amazing pacing as it piles incident upon incident to create an incipient air of madness seemingly trapped within the very frames of the film. During the famous climax which finds one unfortunate victim suffering beneath the title device, Corman goes berserk with distorted lenses, psychedelic colours, and rapid editing, all accompanied by Les Baxter's unnerving, experimental score. While Kerr makes a less than sympathetic hero, Price and his fellow performers compensate for this flaw by tearing the scenery to bits, with Europe's favourite scream queen, Barbara Steele, making a vivid impression in her relatively brief screen time.

The bad news first: due to a reported lack of decent source material, the transfer for the DVD is non-anamorphic. Superficially similar to the previous widescreen master for the Image/Orion laserdisc, which was great for the time, this does look a bit smoother than the laserdisc, with more delineated blacks and more stable colours. At least it's letterboxed, though, and the print used at the time is in excellent condition. Corman returns for another commentary track, in which he discusses the tactics used to follow up their hit first film so quickly and how an entirely new narrative was generated out of a story that lasts all of about three pages. The disc

also includes the original theatrical trailer and, in an unexpected coup, the video premiere of a four minute prologue shot for the original TV broadcast, which finds Luana Anders suffering inside an asylum following the events of the film. The prologue is in perfect condition, and it's a fascinating bonus from a time when such additional scenes were par for the course in drive-in film making.

THE PIT AND THE PENDULUM

Colour, 1990, 97m. / Directed by Stuart Gordon / Starring Lance Henrikson, Rona De Ricci, Jonathan Fuller / Full Moon (US R1 NTSC)

Apart from the torture device of the title, this outlandish shocker from director Stuart Gordon (*Re-Animator*) bears no resemblance to Roger Corman's beloved 1961 Vincent Price vehicle or the brief Edgar Allan Poe story. Injecting his usual blend of black comedy and startling violence, Gordon managed to produce a seemingly impossible miracle: a great straight-to-video feature and, even more amazingly, the best release to date from the highly erratic Full Moon studio.

During the Spanish Inquisition, naive baker's wife Maria (Rona De Ricci) protests the religious persecution committed during a public ceremony. Maria is seized as a witch, much to the distress of her husband, Antonio (*Castle Freak*'s Jonathan Fuller). The grand inquisitor, Torquemada (Lance Henrikson), becomes smitten with Maria but channels his emotions into violence and hatred, with the poor girl suffering a heinous array of tortures. Maria's cellmate, a helpful witch named Esmeralda (Frances Bay), teaches her some magic secrets to deal with her persecutors and even doles out a little poetic justice herself, but it's up to Antonio to infiltrate the castle and allow Maria the chance to face down Torquemada face to face.

Unabashedly theatrical and sporting a cast picked to please the fans, *Pit* simply deserves more than the obscurity guaranteed by its direct to video fate. Though all video versions have claimed an R rating for the film, the gore and nudity level goes way past what the MPAA would even remotely deem acceptable, particularly the suspenseful and blood-soaked climax which borrows amusingly from Jan Svankmajer's short film, "The Pit, the Pendulum and Hope." Henrikson chews the scenery from his first moments onscreen, while genre vets like Jeffrey Combs (the *Re-Animator* himself),

Oliver Reed, and Tom Towles (Otis in *Henry: Portrait of a Serial Killer*) add amusing shadings to their supporting roles. Gordon's wife, Carolyn Purdy-Gordon, even turns up at the beginning as the wife of a man whose skeleton is whipped(!) for heresy. The production values are also substantially better than your average Full Moon production, with that photogenic Italian castle (recycled in *Meridian*, among many others) and some elaborate art design making this a feast for the eyes. Finally, Richard Band contributes one of his best scores, a rich mixture of choir and electronics.

The Amazing Fantasy/Full Moon DVD is basically the same in every respect as the earlier Paramount laserdisc, though the open matte transfer is a bit crisper and more colourful. The Videozone segment is easily Full Moon's best, with some great behind the scenes interviews and one of the funniest blooper reels you'll ever see. The basic surround audio mostly relies on Band's score and a few judicious sound effects like explosions for directional effects. One nice extra bonus is the film's trailer, presumably created for a nonexistent theatrical release.

PIT STOP

B&W, 1967, 91m. / Directed by Jack Hill / Starring Brian Donlevy, Dick Davalos, Ellen Burstyn, Sid Haig / Anchor Bay (US R1 NTSC) / WS (1.78:1) (16:9)

Something of an oddity in the career of director Jack Hill, *Pit Stop* features no cannibals, jailed women, or girl gang members. What he delivers instead is a lean, entertaining morality play set in the fast lane of American racetrack driving, as far from the expected follow up to *Spider Baby* as one could imagine.

Racecar promoter Grant Willard (Brian Donlevy) watches one night as a gang of drag racers tears through the streets, sending one member careening straight into a house. He offers to sponsor the best driver, Rick Bowman (Dick Davalos), as a professional racer in a new kind of racetrack called the "Figure 8." This two-loop track with an intersection in the middle is basically designed to cause as many crashes as possible, but Rick takes the offer. The reigning champ, Hawk Sidney (Sid Haig - with hair!), doesn't take too kindly to the newcomer, especially when the local gumsmacking racing groupie, Jolene (*Spider Baby's* Beverly Washburn), turns her doey eyes towards Richard.

Grant skilfully plays both sides against each other, particularly when Richard wins a race and trashes Hawk's brand new car in the process. Hawk retaliates with an axe in the film's most memorable scene, but Richard persists in his climb up the ladder to become the back up driver for bigshot racer Ed McLeod (George Washburn). Richard also sets his sights on Ed's auto-wise wife, Ellen (a young Ellen McRae, aka Ellen Burstyn).

Giving one of his best late career performances, Donlevy leads one of the best casts in his career and injects fire into what could have been an average B-movie programmer. Haig is also a joy to watch and in some respects the most interesting, sympathetic character of the film, all manic energy and fiery vinegar. The racetrack footage is both exciting and alarming to watch, with one vehicle after another wiping out in a heap of smashed metal. Toss in a catchy theme by "The Daily Flash," and this is a great drive-in movie to savour with a big bowl of popcorn.

Not exactly a major studio release, *Pit Stop* was virtually unavailable for public viewing at all until Johnny Legend and Jack Hill had it privately released onto VHS in mid-'90s. The camcorder interview (in which Hill hilariously discusses his brief stint on John Lamb nudist camp films) and the dual B&W/colourized theatrical trailers have been duplicated for this refurbished widescreen transfer, which is quite good under the circumstances. Some vertical scratches and other printing anomalies pop up here and there, especially during the racing footage, but the materials overall are in fine shape and quite watchable. Hill and Legend also return once again for another loose, affectionate commentary track, in which they deftly cover all of the production background behind the film, the financing, and various distribution tactics (as evidenced by the Anchor Bay print itself which bears the onscreen title of *The Winner*).

PITCH BLACK

Colour, 2000, 109m. / Directed by David N. Twohy / Starring Vin Diesel, Radha Mitchell, Cole Hauser / Universal (US R1 NTSC, UK R2 PAL) / WS (2.35:1) (16:9) / DD5.1

Proving there's still life yet in the old monsters in space formula, *Pitch Black* seemingly came out of nowhere and proved that a modern thrill ride can be crafted without resorting to tired MTV camera tricks and seizure-inducing editing. Though it doesn't possess a single original (or logical) bone in its body, this is crackerjack filmmaking and thoroughly satisfying as a visceral and artistic experience. Put your brain in neutral, grab some popcorn, and have fun.

A sudden meteor storm forces a manned spaceship to crash land on a nearby planet. The death of the captain along with most of the other passengers leaves tremulous Fry (Radha Mitchell) in charge of the remaining crew and cargo, including a fearsome convict, Riddick (Vin Diesel), who possesses immense strength and the ability to see in the dark. The marooned humans, including an amoral bounty hunter (Cole Hauser) intent on keeping Riddick under his thumb, investigate their strange terrain, which bears telltale signs of previous human habitation. However, no one appears to have survived in this world where the sun apparently never sets. However, a telltale model of the solar system reveals that an imminent eclipse is due any minute, and when nightfall does indeed come, they are quite far from alone.

"It's hip, sexy, and scary as hell!" screams the DVD box for this film, and thankfully they're only one third right. Diesel cuts a formidable villain and hero, using his brutish skills to defeat alien predators and even pulling off the occasional Schwarzenegger-style one liner without inducing groans. The rest of the cast can't hope to compete with him, and fortunately the filmmakers rely on the clever use of manipulated sounds, film stocks, and trick photography to create a genuinely unique and unnerving atmosphere in which the darkness literally does hold a nasty surprise in every corner. For once the mixture of models and CGI works marvellously well, as the devilish critters are rarely seen in their entirety and instead serve as a sort of multipurpose nightmare come to life, tearing through the air and bursting up from behind your back. Sure, *Alien* already covered this territory, but the sheer energy and style-to-burn presentation here makes it more vital and fascinating than most of the other imitations we've had to endure over the past twenty years. A leap over director Twohy's previous film, the moderately entertaining but slight *The Arrival*, this is one thrill ride that actually delivers.

Universal's DVD of *Pitch Black* continues their laudable policy of offering both R and unrated cuts of major releases in the US. As with *American Psycho*, the differences here are negligible at best, surprisingly consisting almost entirely of dramatic exposition. Image and sound quality are all superlative, and the barrage of aggressive split surrounds (in both Dolby Digital 5.1 and DTS) makes this ideal demo material for your home theatre, or a nice way to scare the pants off of unprepared guests. The disc includes both the green and red band theatrical trailers, a puff piece featurette, a Raveworld.com spotlight (which has little to do with the film and looks like an attempt to tie this in the with trance/goth crowd), and two commentaries: one sporadically silent chat between Twohy, Diesel, and Hauser, and another denser, more technically oriented discussion with Twohy, FX supervisor Peter Chang, and producer Tom Engelman.

PLAGUE OF THE ZOMBIES

Colour, 1966, 90m. / Directed by John Gilling / Starring Andre Morell, Diane Clare / Anchor Bay (US R1 NTSC) / WS (1.85:1) (16:9)

Though not usually mentioned as one of Hammer's landmark horror films (e.g., most of the Terence Fisher titles), *Plague of the Zombies* may well be the scariest. Skilfully shot and paced, *Plague* maximizes its dark, desolate Cornwall setting for maximum effect and delivers a surprising number of jolts (gory and otherwise) for a mid-'60s British title.

A strange, deadly curse has swept over a small Cornish village, causing several labourers to die mysteriously only to turn up shambling through the night near a mine several days later. Sir James Forbes (Hammer regular Andre Morell) offers his assistance to the desperate Dr. Tompson (Brook Williams), who cannot fathom the presumably supernatural cause of this epidemic. Any horror fan will naturally know the answer, thanks to the voodoo ritual opening sequence - someone is killing off the residents and turning them into zombies.

Leaping off from the same basic story conceit used in the '30s horror favourite *White Zombie*, this Hammer version turns the concept on its head by presenting the zombies as horrifying, menacing creatures freshly risen from the earth, particularly in the legendary dream sequence which shows a zombie clawing out of the ground. Several equally potent moments are worth mentioning, however, particularly the first real zombie appearance on a nocturnal hillside, one of the most horrifying moments in the Hammer canon. The cast manages to wring a high amount of tension and believability out of this material, turning it into more than a visceral series of shock mechanisms, and a typically excellent score by James Bernard works up a heavy sense of dread right from the first scene. The fiery mine finale disappoints slightly due to some clumsy flaming zombie costumes, but otherwise, *Plague of the Zombies* has held up remarkably well over the years and deserves even more than the cult reputation it has already achieved.

Interestingly, apart from the occasional oddity like *Sugar Hill*, this was really the last major horror film to utilize the voodoo master concept in relation to zombies, serving as an efficient bridge between the classic-style walking dead and the terrifying, independently animated zombies of George Romero and Lucio Fulci.

Anchor Bay's DVD looks essentially the same as Elite's laserdisc, albeit with more textured shadows and the added bonus of anamorphic enhancement. The mono soundtrack is clear and impressive throughout, and while the dull brown and green colour schemes don't really make for dazzling eye candy, the image is very satisfying nonetheless. The disc also includes the theatrical trailer and double bill TV spot (with *Dracula, Prince of Darkness*), plus another instalment in the *World of Hammer* British TV retrospective hosted by Oliver Reed. This edition, focusing on mummies, werewolves, and zombies, features the usual potpourri of clips from films ranging from this one to *The Mummy's Shroud* and *Curse of the Werewolf*. Not terribly deep, this treat is still great fun and offers some rare film snippets in nice DVD quality. The non-animated menu features a mono version of James Bernard's theme music.

PLAN 9 FROM OUTER SPACE

Colour, 1958, 74m. / Directed by Ed Wood, Jr. / Starring Bela Lugosi (more or less), Gregory Walcott, Tor Johnson / Image (US R0 NTSC), MPIC (UK R0 PAL), Steeplechase (US R0 NTSC)

The *Citizen Kane* of bad movies hardly needs an introduction here; however, it's impossible to believe that anything this entertaining could be "the worst film ever made." Basically a traditional UFO movie completely turned on its head, this utterly deranged and loveable puppy is impossible to dislike and more often draws admiration for how much Wood's ambitions went careening past anything in his grasp.

As part of their insidious string of plans to conquer the simple minds of Earth, a group of aliens (led by the unforgettably named Dudley Manlove) plots to resurrect the dead in a California cemetery as the start of a worldwide zombie army. The first revived corpses are "the old man" (first Bela Lugosi, then a chiropractor in a cape), his wife (Vampira), and a Swedish cop (Tor Johnson). Airline pilot Jeff Trent (Gregory Walcott) lives near the cemetery and suspects these events might be related to all those flying saucer sightings around Hollywood. Could it be?

Few films can live up to their legendary status, but *Plan 9* has no such problems. The paper plate saucers on strings, bad graveyard sets, and cardboard airplane cockpits are all well in abundance, all designed for your maximum viewing pleasure. Wood's stilted dialogue reaches new heights of lunacy, as even the basic laws of reality like night and day go flying out the window. Nowhere is this madness better enjoyed than in the Image/Wade Williams DVD, which presents *Plan 9* on its best behaviour. Image and sound quality are excellent, even better than the previous Lumivision laserdisc release, and the disc is even decked out with the original trailer and a great documentary, *Flying Saucers over Hollywood: The Plan 9 Companion,* which features loving interviews ranging from cast members (Walcott, Vampira) to familiar faces like Forry Ackerman and Joe Dante. Essential viewing.

The UK disc also includes a "Saucer Vision" feature, in which a UFO logo appears during the film and allows the view to hop to a relevant portion of the documentary.

PLANET OF THE APES

Colour, 2001, 120m. / Directed by Tim Burton / Starring Mark Wahlberg, Tim Roth / Fox / WS (2.35:1) (16:9) / DD5.1

Hurled through a time warp into the 25th century, astronaut Leo Davidson (Wahlberg) crash lands on a primeval planet where the rulers are apes and humans are their slaves. Tim Burton has made some extraordinary films, but this "reimagining" of *Planet of the Apes* isn't one of them. When Tim Roth peers into Mark Wahlberg's mouth and muses "Is there a soul in there?" he might just be talking about the movie he's starring in. It may be a visual extravaganza, but looking good isn't enough. Compared to Franklin J. Schaffner's original (comparison, of course, being unavoidable) it's a disappointingly shallow vessel. Unlike the primal world of simian barbarism depicted back in '68, this society is relatively civilised, albeit taxed with the diverse morals and ethics found in any culture.

Wahlberg was excellent in *Boogie Nights*, but whatever the X ingredient of an action hero is he just doesn't have it and it's hard to take him seriously in that capacity. Model Estella Warren as Daena - Burton's decorative replacement for Linda Harrison's rough-hewn mute in the original - is sex on legs, but fails to convince as a subjugated primitive... and just where on Ape planet does she get her hair permed?! Performance honours go to Tim Roth's conniving General Thade, a Josef Mengele wannabe in a chimp suit. Charlton Heston and Linda Harrison cameo as orang-utan and human slave respectively. Other players are Kris Kristofferson, Michael Clarke Duncan, Helena Bonham Carter, Cary-Hiroyuki Tagawa and Lisa Marie, most of them hidden beneath latex applications. Actually, Rick Baker's make-ups - with the exception of Carter and Marie's peculiar ape/human hybrids - are the true stars of the film.

The '68 finale with the Statue of Liberty is a classic and was going to take some beating and the conclusion here doesn't begin to approximate its impact. Burton's denouement is at first laughable, then, on reflection, inexplicably contrived and likely to leave baffled viewers scratching their heads like... well, like monkeys. One of so many blockbusters that held great promise but fell short on delivery day, if this had been made by anyone other than Burton, it might have been deemed a success. But coming from the eccentric master of the esoteric, it lacks his usual magical touch to the point of distraction.

Not just content to "Rule the Planet" with the movie, for the DVD of *Planet of the Apes* Fox produced one of their most elaborately laden discs yet. But if it's possible to have too much of a good thing then it's definitely possible to have too much of a mediocre thing. Their 2-platter Region 1 release smacks of an attempt to disguise an ape's ear as a silk purse, and no matter how much additional material they throw at you the movie itself remains a decidedly middling experience.

Disc #1 contains a 32-chapter transfer of the film (which can be watched with commentary from either director Tim Burton or composer Danny Elfman). One can also watch the film in "Enhanced Viewing Mode" which places picture-in-picture behind the scenes segments throughout the film. This disc also includes features accessible only by those with DVD-Rom and Nuon facilities.

Disc #2 encompasses a whole host of extra material. There are seven featurettes - covering make-up, costumes, stunts, location shooting, music, etc. - which run a little under 2 hours in total, parts of which would definitely have benefited from judicious pruning. A series of multi-angle featurettes show the construction of various sequences (with additional access to them in script, artwork and completed form), 5 extended scenes (each time-coded and of marginally lesser quality), a 25-minute HBO puff piece about the making of the film, the Paul Oakenfold promo music video, 2 theatrical trailers, 6 TV spots, a commercial for the soundtrack album, some poster artwork, lengthy production notes and extensive galleries of production art and storyboards. There are extra DVD-Rom features too. As if all this weren't sufficient to sate your simian sensibilities, there are a couple of hidden extras lurking on Disc #1. Under Special Features choose Commentaries, select "Back", then press up to highlight an ape symbol; press enter and you access a short segment of the film presented as if a monkey had command of the remote control... you need to see it to realise just how pointlessly stupid it is. Under the cast biographies, if you highlight the small arrows on the photos for the Estella Warren, Erick Avari and Luke Eberl entries, you can see their first audition tapes for the film; based on the evidence here, it's unclear why Warren was ever invited back! Language options are English 5.1 DTS, English 5.1 Surround and Spanish Dolby Surround, whilst subtitling is in English only. - TG

PLANET OF THE VAMPIRES

Colour, 1965, 88m. / Directed by Mario Bava / Starring Barry Sullivan, Norma Bengel / MGM (US R1 NTSC) / WS (1.85:1)

After altering the face of gothic horror and establishing the slasher film, Mario Bava returned to American International Pictures for a low budget science fiction project entitled *Terrore nello spazio*. Known by various titles over the years but most widely available on video as *Planet of the Vampires*, the film posed a formidable challenge through the demand for extensive special effects and the creation of an otherworldly atmosphere created with limited means. Once again Bava's ingenuity and crafty visual sense produced an effective genre classic whose influence still lingers today.

An S.O.S. signal in space draws two ships to a seemingly uninhabited, mist enshrouded planet. For no apparent reason the crew members of one ship kill each other in a violent frenzy, while the second ship, the Argos, is saved by the will of the steadfast Captain Markary (Barry Sullivan). While the bodies of the dead are buried in transparent bags (and a few of the deceased vanish without a trace), the astronauts explore their new terrain and discover traces of past alien voyagers left to die on the planet. Furthermore, the dead crew members seem to be still roaming the dark, misty landscape, and the lines separating the living and the dead begin to blur. The invisible force which destroyed one ship now seems to be wreaking havoc across the planet, and Markary and his crew have only a limited amount of time to repair their damaged ship and escape this terrain of the dead.

Though consigned to the matinee crowd during its release, *Planet of the Vampires* (which really doesn't have any literal vampires at all) has enjoyed a steadily growing reputation both through the increased appreciation of its director and the frequently noted story parallels to 1979's *Alien*. However, the film also functions perfectly well on its own terms; the slow pacing allows each creepy visual to seemingly pop out of nowhere, and the images of resuscitated astronauts tearing the plastic away as they rise of the earth are not easily forgotten. As usual Bava floods the screen with unnatural, saturated colours, and the sincerity of its construction allows the viewer to easily overlook the typical '60s conventions of its sci-fi trappings. While Antonio Margheriti's space sagas like *Wild, Wild Planet* offer delightful, eye-catching fun, Bava's film is really the only legitimate Italian science fiction film capable of being appreciated as a genuine work of art. Though the actors (Sullivan included) are workmanlike at best, the story (penned by AIP regular Ib Melchior, from Renato Pestriniero's short story, "One Night of 21 Hours") grips through its sheer oddness and the power of its memorable, *Twilight Zone*-style twist denouement.

First available on video from HBO and Thorn/EMI, *Planet of the Vampires* featured a decent but cropped transfer with a passable new Kendall Schmidt electronic score. The same edition appeared on laserdisc through Orion and Image, doubled up with Curtis Harrington's endearingly bizarre *Queen of Blood* (which shares two similar alternate titles, *Planet of Blood* and *Planet of Vampires*, with those given to Bava's film). After vanishing for a few years, *Planet* went through the restoration process at MGM, where it has surfaced in a dramatically improved widescreen (but non-anamorphic) transfer. The ads claimed the film was shot in "Colorscope," though this seems to be just standard hard matting (around 1.78:1 to 1.85:1) like Bava's other titles from the same period. The original, more subdued theatrical score has been reinstated (though to be honest, it won't make a tremendous difference to casual viewers), but more importantly, the image now glows with a hellish luminous quality sorely missing from previous editions. The film runs about two minutes longer than the 86 minute HBO print, presumably confined to some more character exposition or footage of actors wandering through the mist. Hopefully some Bava fanatics out there can more accurately pinpoint where the restored footage has been placed, as it doesn't immediately stand out.

The disc also includes the amusing US theatrical trailer, which makes the film look like a particularly unhinged episode of *Star Trek*. While Bava fanatics would have probably appreciated a few more extras, there's no arguing with the low price for a disc that unquestionably delivers. A French DVD from Studio Canal containing a separate restoration (in 16:9 widescreen) was briefly released but withdrawn over a rights issue.

THE PLAYGIRLS AND THE VAMPIRE

B&W, 1960, 80m. / Directed by Piero Regnoli / Starring Walter Brandi, Lila Rocco / Image (US R0 NTSC)

The first instalment in Image's promising EuroShock Collection, *The Playgirls and the Vampire* is actually a rare example of truth in advertising in the annals of cinematic exploitation. The plot involves, not surprisingly, a quintet of curvaceous nightclub performers and two male companions who take refuge in a dark, mysterious castle after being caught in a violent storm. Though penniless, the group is perfectly willing to accommodate their host, Count Gabor Kernassy (vampire movie staple Walter Brandi/Brandt), with plenty of sleazy stripteases to pass the night away. Kernassy notices a striking resemblance between one of the ingénues, Vera (Lila Rocco), and Margherita, the great love of Kernassy's 200 year ancestor... who, unfortunately, has gone vampire and still stalks the premises. After much wandering through corridors and surprisingly sleazy fang activity, Kernassy faces down his ancestor, resulting in a peculiar dual confrontation which, as virtually every viewer has noticed, owes more than a nod to 1958's *Horror of Dracula*.

Originally released in Italy as *L'ultima preda del vampiro (The Last Prey of the Vampire* or *The Vampire's Last Victim*, depending on your source), this film isn't great art but definitely delivers the drive-in goods. Amazingly, this opened the same year as Mario Bava's *Black Sunday* and *Mill of the Stone Women*, which just goes to show that the dichotomy in Italian horror cinema between art and sleaze was already well in place right from the beginning. The previous year had already seen Renato Polselli's eccentric *Vampire and the Ballerina*, and while Polselli later blew his private little fetishes into full-blown exhibitionism during the '70s, *Playgirls'* Regnoli only churned out five minor period films as a director before settling into a career as a screenwriter on zombie films like *City of the Walking Dead* and *Burial Ground*. He does a competent job here and probably could have been a notable player in the spooky-sexy European sweepstakes of the '60s and '70s had he chosen to pursue it. Anybody who could deliver naked girls with big fangs *con gusto* like this definitely deserved to have a longer career.

The Image DVD, taken from the archive print held by US distributor Richard Gordon, looks better than the numerous bootleg and quasi-PD copies floating around for years, though a few flaws still exist in the source. While the DVD itself is fine with no noticeable compression flaws, some mild scratching and other signs of wear mar a few shots. One problem with the film in every US version (and presumably in the Italian original as well) is the photography of some long shots, which has a tendency to blur and resembles ragged shooting with a zoom lens (but before that device really came into vogue). For example, the well-lit castle interiors look fine and razor sharp, as do the dancers' skimpy attire, but some of the darker hallway two-shots resemble an on-the-fly documentary. Regardless, the film itself doesn't really suffer, and this is probably as good as it's going to get.

No noticeable image appears to be cropped from the full frame transfer, indicating this is either open matte or very slightly altered from a 1.66:1 master. The Dolby Digital mono soundtrack does a perfectly good job of rendering the throwaway grindhouse music and thunderous rumblings in the background; surprisingly, the audio elements seem to have held up better with time than the visuals.

Running times for *Playgirls and the Vampire* range wildly from 66 minutes (the US reissue which removed most of the stripteases and nudity) to 85 minutes. Clocking in somewhere between, this print doesn't seem to be missing anything noteworthy, though the Italian original may have contained some dialogue or "exploring the castle" footage that wouldn't be missed. Tim Lucas does an informative job with the liner notes, though he strangely implies that Regnoli actually directed 1980's *Burial Ground*, which was helmed by Andrea Bianchi. The DVD also includes the amusing first run US trailer, and the menu screen should provoke a nice chuckle.

P.O. BOX TINTO BRASS

Colour, 1997, 88m. / Directed by Tinto Brass / Starring Cinzia Roccaforte, Cristina Rinaldi / CVC (Italy R2 PAL) / WS (1.85:1), Dutch Filmworks (Holland R2 PAL), Nouveaux (UK R2 PAL) / DD2.0

Spurred on by the success of *The Voyeur*, Tinto Brass churned out his next epic, *P.O. Box Tinto Brass*, a random collection of vignettes strung together by the framing device of Brass himself reading letters detailing the erotic tales sent in by avid viewers. A jealous housewife, a woman's fascination with her new bidet, and various other situations round out an amusing but generally slapdash concoction which aims more for shock value than cinematic craftsmanship.

Ortolani's *Voyeur* score is clumsily recycled here, and while some of the visuals are typically erotic, the overall impression is that of a man biding time while he decides on his next real script. The censored Dutch DVD release (and its identical port over to UK DVD) is full frame, just like the Italian prerecord version. The compositions may be slightly sheared off at the sides, but the camerawork is so arbitrary here the damage is relatively minor. The stereo soundtrack is mostly confined to the music, while the disc also includes a still gallery and the Italian theatrical trailer. The Holland disc also contains Dutch subtitles, which are removable. The Italian DVD (which contains explicit footage missing from all English language variants) is letterboxed but features no alternate language options.

POISON

Colour, 1991, 85m. / Directed by Todd Haynes / Starring Scott Renderer, Millie White / Wellspring (US R0 NTSC)

A fascinating, narratively perverse triptych of stories, *Poison* ignited a firestorm of controversy when its postproduction funding by the National Endowment for the Arts became a target of the religious right. Par for the course, none of the accusers bothered to watch the film or even do their homework, but the damage was still inflicted, evaporating many government-sponsored arts programs for future generations. Designed as a feature follow up to the celebrated (and sadly unavailable) *Superstar: The Karen Carpenter Story*, this film quickly put Todd Haynes on the map outside of the standard "gay filmmaker" status, though none of his subsequent efforts have garnered the notoriety of this acidic debut. Sprinkled with quotes and situations from the literature of renowned French writer/thief/convict Jean Genet, the film posits three stories relentlessly intercut within each other to produce an escalating sense of unease.

In "Hero," a pseudo-documentary, various family members and acquaintances discuss Richie Beacon, a very different young boy who, according to his mother, killed his father and flew out the window.

In "Horror," Dr. Graves (Larry Maxwell) manages to chemically isolate the human sex drive but, in a moment of carelessness, becomes infected by his own serum and experiences a bodily degeneration akin to leprosy. His beautiful colleague, Nancy (Susan Norman), attempts to deal with her simultaneous feelings of pity, attraction, and revulsion as the city revolts against what it perceives as a diseased menace.

In "Homo," the most Genet-inspired segment, an inveterate thief, John Broom (Scott Renderer), finds his prison life disrupted with the arrival of Bolton (James Lyons), the object of his affection from their old reformatory days. However, Bolton does not return Broom's affections... or does he? A graphic and unsettling flashback to their youth unveils the traumas that bind the two men and ultimately lead to one man's tragic fate.

Elegantly assembled and often disturbing, *Poison* operates primarily through subliminal suggestions, which only take hold in the viewer's mind long after the closing credits have rolled. The three stories contrast wildly in terms of style and acting methods, linked only by their vaguely overlapping themes of social ostracism and sexual anxiety in the tradition of David Cronenberg. The intercutting of the stories is alternately compelling and frustrating as it constantly tweaks expectations to the breaking point; in particular, "Horror" (which plays like a depraved, AIDS-inspired variation on Joe Dante's "Mant!" from *Matinee*) could just as easily flow as a single narrative without the interruptions. Considering the lack of budget and experience, the performers all do well, with Renderer standing out in particular thanks to his marvellously expressive facial reactions.

Shot on 16mm and blown up to 35 for theatrical distribution, *Poison* has always suffered from graininess and a somewhat muddy image during the darker scenes, problems that are still present on the uncensored DVD. Under the circumstances, Wellspring has probably done about as well as could

be expected, and the daylight sequences look better and cleaner than they ever have before. Unfortunately, the darker scenes (i.e., the opening credits and virtually all of the prison interiors) suffer from what looks like a substandard compression job, littered with jittering and rolling digital patterns in the background and shadows. Turning down the monitor's brightness control helps solve most of the problem, but not all of them. Otherwise this is an adequate DVD release, complete with the trailer (and yes, in a Wellspring rarity, it really is the theatrical trailer), and- a commentary by Haynes, Lyons, and producer Christine Vachon (who went on to *Happiness* and *Boys Don't Cry*). Haynes frequently expresses his surprise at how linear the film is considering its experimental roots, and he often throws in a humorous aside to keep things bouncing along. Vachon and Lyons focus more on the production end of the film, relating the various difficulties in getting it financed and filmed. In particular Vachon offers the real paydirt of the commentary one hour into the film with a lengthy, fascinating account of her dealings with Genet's estate (a surprising revelation).

POISON IVY

Colour, 1992, 93m. / Directed by Katt Shea / Starring Drew Barrymore, Sara Gilbert, Tom Skerritt / New Line (US R1 NTSC) / WS (1.85:1) (16:9) / DD2.0

The movie that truly kicked off the home video "erotic thriller" trend, *Poison Ivy* was virtually overlooked in theatres but became a smash hit thanks to video stores and TV, spawning two very generic sequels and a host of imitators. Unlike its closest contemporaries with starlets like Shannon Tweed, the more *giallo*-influenced *Poison Ivy* is more intimate and deliberately paced, though not without its share of exploitative elements and moments of hilarious lunacy (it didn't wind up in the pages of *Bad Movies We Love* for nothing!).

Homely young Sylvie Cooper (*Roseanne*'s Sara Gilbert) becomes fascinated by one of her classmates, the tattooed, bleach-blonde Ivy (Drew Barrymore). Sylvie can barely communicate with her gruff father, Darryl (Tom Skerritt) and her ailing mother, Georgie (Cheryl Ladd). Pretty soon Ivy's worked her way into the family unit and gotten Darryl twisted around her little finger. Sylvie becomes alarmed at the amount of power Ivy seems to be exerting over everyone, including her dog (the most unintentionally hilarious scene), and things take a particularly nasty turn after one family member dies under mysterious circumstances.

A slick mixture of cheap thrills and sincere drama, *Poison Ivy* may be trash at heart but distinguishes itself for its peers thanks to much better performances than the material really deserves. Gilbert, whose voiceovers frame the film, is a particular standout and manages to ground the story every time it threatens to wander off into heavy-panting late night cable territory. Barrymore obviously makes a great Ivy, still one of her most entertaining roles despite the distracting use of a body double (Barrymore was barely underage at the time). David Michael Franke's lyrical score and some extremely stylish cinematography also help director Ruben *(The Rage: Carrie II)* pull of this tricky genre bender, which at least deserves an evening's rental.

New Line's presentation of *Poison Ivy* is essentially the same as their other unrated/rated hybrid titles like *Crash* and *Damage*. The full version, which contains more footage of Drew's double heaving and huffing, is obviously preferable but doesn't make a huge difference in the movie itself. The anamorphic widescreen transfer looks extremely good, with excellent saturations of green and red in particular; the full frame (open matte) option reveals far too much headroom and looks too "TV safe" for comfort, but its quality is excellent as well. The standard surround mix won't blow anyone away but conveys the score and ambient effects just fine. The two sequels have been given the same deluxe presentation but are hardly worth the effort.

POLA X

Colour, 1999, 127m. / Directed by Leos Carax / Starring Guillaume Depardieu, Yekaterina Golubyova, Catherine Deneuve / Wellspring (US R1 NTSC) / WS (1.75:1) (16:9) / DD5.1

 There isn't much that hasn't already been said about grandstanding French director Leos Carax, whose work remains largely unknown in the US apart from the lacklustre released given by Miramax to his stylistically dazzling but dramatically shaky *Lovers on the Bridge* (*Les amants du Pont-Neuf*). Dropping many of the blatant visual fireworks that became his trademark, Carax turned his attention to the obscure, often censored Herman Melville novel from 1852,

Pierre, ou les Ambiguites. An acronym from the book's title plus the Roman numeral "X" (for the tenth draft of the film's script) form the unusual moniker for this bizarre sojourn into passion, insanity, incest, and violence, which could easily strike a viewer as unbearably pretentious or deeply profound, depending upon one's mood.

Pierre (Guillaume Depardieu, son of Gérard), a pampered aristocratic brat, lives in the country with his mother, Marie (Catherine Deneuve), with whom he shares an obviously unnatural physical relationship. The two refer to each other as brother and sister, and she doesn't seem to mind a bit that Pierre's engaged to his sweet blonde cousin, Lucie (Delphine Chuillot). Another cousin, Thibault (Laurent Lucas), arrives to shake things up a bit and may have a bit of interest in Lucie himself, but that's nothing compared to the dark woman who haunts Pierre's dreams and seems to be lurking always just out of the edge of his vision. One night on his motorcycle Pierre startles the feral woman, who turns out to be his secret half sister, Isabelle (Yekaterina Golubyova). After she explains her plight, the two run off together, sending Marie spiralling into despair. Pierre and Isabelle shack up in a warehouse doubling as a terrorist base and, their genetic connection aside, become lovers. An aspiring novelist with one anonymous bestseller to his credit, Pierre returns to the typewriter but finds his creativity stifled by his surroundings. Things get even worse when Lucie comes to stay with the unhealthy pair, and destructive emotions begin to surface.

Apart from the jarring opening credits, *Pola X* feels far more sedate than Carax's other films, at least for the first half hour or so. Gradually he introduces different film stocks (including some bizarre day for night exposures), eccentric surround sound effects in which simple background sounds come to dominate the soundtrack, and hallucinatory fantasies including one brief but unforgettable moment which finds an embracing Pierre and Isabelle floating down and being consumed by an outdoor river of blood. Most jarring is the inclusion of a very heated, hardcore sex scene halfway into the film, performed by Depardieu himself along with a female contortionist body double (and, according to the commentary track, aided by Depardieu's girlfriend). Naturally it's mostly intended for shock value, but it still works and packs more of a punch than the similar explicit imagery in another recent French film, *Romance*.

On the surface, Wellspring's DVD of *Pola X* seems like one of their best efforts thanks to such snazzy whistles and bells as a 16:9 transfer and a 5.1

remix. However, there are a few flaws worth noting. While the image quality is crisp and quite impressive, it was obviously derived from a PAL source and betrays some streaking and overlapping frames during a few bits of fast onscreen motion. The running time also wound up compressed in the process from 134 minutes to 127. The 5.1 mix is also misleading, as it simply channels the 2.0 mix into a 5.1 matrix and leaves out the centre channel, so the dialogue instead comes from the front speakers. The alternate 2.0 surround mix is less powerful but far more accurate, while the dialogue remains firmly front and centre. The optional white English subtitles are well written and always easy to read, while the surround activity is usually strong and nicely separated.

Extras on the disc include two "outtakes," which actually consist of a montage from the film's scoring session (and the lyrical music is indeed impressive) along with a brief collection of behind the scenes shots from Deneuve's motorcycle scene. Other extras include the US theatrical trailer and a commentary track from Depardieu, whose comments are sparse and rather shyly delivered at first but become more insightful and endearing as the film progresses. In a strange juxtaposition, which could only have come from a European actor, he blushes at his brief nude scene early in the film but seems rather nonchalant about his graphic copulation later on. Well, c'est la vie.

PORTRAIT OF JENNIE

B&W, 1948, 86m. / Directed by William Dieterle / Starring Jennifer Jones, Joseph Cotten, Ethel Barrymore / Anchor Bay (US R0 NTSC)

An eerie, romantic oddity from producer David O. Selznick, *Portrait of Jennie* is much closer in spirit to his cycle of Hitchcock films like Rebecca than his famous grandiose epics like *Gone with the Wind* or *Duel in the Sun,* the latter starring his lover and eventual wife, Jennifer Jones. Selznick and Jones reteamed more successfully with this film, a delicate New York ghost story produced under conditions which would have defeated a film in lesser hands. Fortunately, director William Dieterle (*The Devil and Daniel Webster*) never loses his grip on the story's poetic edge, bringing it close to an American equivalent to the unearthly surrealism of Jean Cocteau.

Struggling artist Eben Adams (Joseph Cotten) passes his days in post-war New York by trying to sell his landscape paintings to anyone in sight. A local art dealer and curator, Miss Spinney (Ethel Barrymore), takes an interest in him, noting that his technically perfect work lacks passion but shows some promise for development. One day in the park Eben meets a strange young girl, Jennie Appleton (Jones), who prattles on about long past events and locations as if they were recent. Claiming to be the daughter of acrobats, she captures his imagination and sings a ghostly song about being alone before vanishing off into the woods. Adams goes about his routine and gets a job painting a mural of Michael Collins for a pub owner but finds himself distracted when he meets Jennie again while ice skating, though now she appears several years older. The two begin to fall in love, and Eben sketches out a possible portrait of the young woman. However, Eben investigates her story and learns that Jennie's story really happened many years earlier, with a few tragic surprises in store. In fact, the object of his love and artistic passion may not be entirely of this world. Nevertheless, Eben continues to meet Jennie, inspired at last to create a work of art worthy of his talents. However, his relationship with the elusive Jennie is far from over.

Though the storyline doesn't hold up at all under scrutiny (for example, can anyone explain exactly why that tidal wave happens to show up at the end?), *Portrait of Jennie* is an unusually effective, memorable ghost story, with Cotten's melancholy and intelligent presence anchoring material that could have been trite. The film went through many different rewrites and edits, and the cloying opening sequence (which features pretentious quotes from both Archimedes and Keats) shows just how much trouble studio execs had in trying to hammer this film into some kind of genre. Fortunately the breathtaking cinematography by Joseph August (who died immediately after filming) ties together the film's various moods, from romantic to menacing to spiritual, and glosses over some technical problems like Jones' awkward impersonation of a preteen girl and some sloppily looped dialogue (see Jennie's song and her dialogue with Eben during the climax, in which no one's lips actually move). Bernard Herrmann originally began the film, but due to scheduling problems (and a reported clashing of wills) he stepped aside to allow Dimitri Tiomkin to complete the music, with some judicious use of Debussy for good measure. The musical tapestry works very well, creating a subtle and wistful atmosphere without ever becoming sugary or obvious. (Herrmann still receives a brief nod in the end credits, however.) The film also features some novel cinematic devices, such as superimposing a canvas-like texture over establishing shots of the city and some of Jones' close-ups to recreate the "portrait" effect on film.

Originally announced on laserdisc by Fox but never released, *Portrait of Jennie* has been surprisingly difficult to see over the years, with only a few brief VHS releases and cable screenings keeping it from obscurity. Anchor Bay's DVD is a great improvement over prior versions, with crisp definition and only some moderate print damage and scratching visible during the last reel. Some TV and video prints concluded with a final Technicolor shot of the portrait (shades of *The Picture of Dorian Gray*), but the DVD goes one step better by restoring the original tinting: green during the climax, and a reddish sepia during the aftermath. The mono audio is very strong and clear for a film of this vintage, and the disc also includes the original theatrical trailer, which tries to sell the film as something far more sprawling and socially important than it actually is.

POSSESSION

Colour, 1981, 127m. / Directed by Andrzej Zulawski / Starring Isabelle Adjani, Sam Neill, Heinz Bennett / Anchor Bay (US R0 NTSC) / WS (1.85:1) (16:9)

The best known and most widely distributed film from idiosyncratic Polish director Andrzej Zulawski, *Possession* combines his familiar themes of thwarted love and psychological torment with a completely insane parable about monsters and murder in Berlin, a combination one doesn't see on the screen very often. Many viewers have been known to run screaming from this film, which is deliberately abrasive and queasy from the opening scenes and never stops to let the audience breathe. However, those who know what they're getting into should be receptive to Zulawski's challenging, fascinating layering of interlocking symbols and storylines, which forces one to connect the dots and fill in plot threads more than any American film would ever dare.

Returning home from a vaguely defined government mission, Marc (Sam Neill) is alarmed to discover that his relationship with his wife, Anna (Isabelle Adjani), has disintegrated into complete disgust and hostility. Completely oblivious to the needs of their young son, Marc and Anna viciously rip into themselves and each other, both literally and metaphorically. Marc hires private detectives to follow Anna and learns that she has a lover, Heinrich (Heinz Bennett). However, Heinrich believes that Anna has yet another lover she meets in a grungy apartment; unfortunately, intruders quickly learn that Anna's secret companion is not exactly human.

A technically astounding film, *Possession's* camera wavers and swerves constantly under the steady hand of master cinematographer/director Bruno Nuytten (Adjani's lover at the time), while Zulawski obviously relishes the opportunity to vent his own personal demons on such a broad canvas.

Neill and Adjani truly seem to be possessed in this film as they scream almost every line, their dilating eyes always transfixed by some force beyond the viewer's perception. Adjani's award-winning performance defies any rational description as she alternates between the character of Anna and her peaceful doppelganger, the schoolteacher Helen, who becomes Marc's bed partner. Anna's showstopping miscarriage in a Berlin subway has become known as the film's outrageous high point, but frankly, it's hard to find a peak in a film constantly on the verge of a total breakdown.

Most people acquainted with European cinema have already heard the stories of the butchery performed on *Possession* when it hit American theatres in 1982. Not only did it lose 50 minutes, but also the distributors randomly reshuffled entire sequences from the middle of the film to the beginning, wiped over the music score with a droning batch of generic horror cues, and bathed the edited climax in garish solarized effects for no discernible reason. The result was a hobbled, gibbering mess that did nothing for the reputations of anyone involved. The longer cut became available in a nicely transferred letterboxed Japanese laserdisc from Daeie (and a subsequent DVD with non-removable Japanese subtitles), though the prohibitive price tag caused many horror fans to resort to bootleg tapes instead. UK viewers could also find two VHS editions of the complete print, first in the early '80s from VTC and then in the late '90s from Visual. Not surprisingly, Anchor Bay's DVD lays waste to all previous versions with a beautiful uncut, widescreen transfer that perfectly captures the film's unearthly blue and green colour schemes. Much of the film was shot on varying types of stock footage, resulting in deliberate film flaws and grain in some sequences, so this edition of *Possession* is, relatively speaking, quite pristine. The audio is noticeably cleaner than the Japanese disc, with many lines of dialogue now easier to understand.

Zulawski also appears for a fascinating, invaluable commentary track, which thankfully leaves many of the film's tantalizing questions still unanswered. Instead he discusses the circumstances under which the film was produced, why it takes place in Berlin, how his World War II upbringing influenced his psyche (check out the last scene), and how he addresses the issues that run throughout his body of work. Other extras include the US (1.85:1) and European (2.00:1) trailers; for once the US one is a lot more entertaining and tantalizing, a much finer piece of work than anything in the American cut of the film itself.

PRACTICAL MAGIC

Colour, 1998, 104m. / Directed by Griffin Dunne / Starring Sandra Bullock, Nicole Kidman, Aidan Quinn / Warner / WS (2.35:1) (16:9) / DD5.1

 Following the charming and underrated *Addicted to Love,* actor-turned-director Dunne made the odd choice of bringing Alice Hoffman's feminist witchcraft novel *Practical Magic* to the screen. However, he thankfully avoids the sophomore jinx by delivering another delicate, visually sumptuous romance here, this time elevated by a pro-supernatural message that should have had the Moral Majority screaming for blood. The film received a mixed critical response, and while it may not be much more than a sweeter, New Age twist on *Witches of Eastwick* without the Mephisto angle, *Practical Magic* delivers its fair share of entertainment and confirms that Dunne is an artist to watch.

Two sisters, Sally (Sandra Bullock) and Gillian (Nicole Kidman) Owens, are raised by their dotty witch aunts, Stockard Channing and Dianne Weist (excellent as usual but tragically underused). Gillian goes wild and runs away from home to sample a life filled with men and winds up being abused and abducted by creepy Romanian cowboy(?) Goran Visnjic. Sally comes to the rescue, and the sisters use their spells to bump off the guy twice, then dump his body in their garden. Soon an Arizona policeman (Aidan Quinn) comes sniffing around, and Sally finds herself attracted to him and feels he may be the soulmate she's always been looking for...

Practical Magic tries to pull off a trick witches' brew of humour, romance, drama, and horror; if you're willing to go along with its dizzy mood swings, the rewards to be had are plenty. The film stumbles during the sappy pro-sisterhood finale, which is so feel-good it just had to be studio-imposed, and it suffers from that aggravating bugaboo of '90s filmmaking, an overbearing rock soundtrack. Taking a cue from *Hope Floats,* the film swells up with forgettable alterna-tunes every time

Bullock walks down a street; cramming songs at random into a movie hardly justifies selling a few more soundtrack albums. Too bad this one already sounds completely dated; with a more sensitive music supervisor, the songs could have worked (though the choice of witchy Stevie Nicks is *apropos*).

The DVD features commentary by Bullock, Dunne, producer Denise Di Novi, and composer Alan Silvestri, who stepped in at the last minute to replace a score by Michael Nyman (too bad; Nyman's lilting melodies would have been perfect). Typically for Warner, the DVD is also brimming with extra goodies, including two making-of documentaries which can be accessed on Side B with a lot of hassle by going through a "Cauldron" game (check out the cast bios to get the ingredients' correct order), as well as the theatrical trailers and, hidden in the "Reel Recommendations," a whopping 10 other trailers.

PREHISTORIC WOMEN

Colour, 1967, 95m. / Directed by Michael Carreras / Starring Martine Beswick, Edina Ronay / Anchor Bay (US R1 NTSC) / WS (2.35:1)

 Following the unexpected and resounding success of *One Million Years B.C.* (boosted most obviously by Raquel Welch in her fur bikini), the prolific Hammer Films began churning out a number of historical period pieces which became known as "Hammer Glamour" thanks to their blend of fetching starlets and visual opulence on a stretched budget. One of the first and most amusing of these entries, *Prehistoric Women,* is more or less a remake of the goofy 1950s American film of the same title and was most widely seen in a heavily truncated 77 minute version, sometimes under the title *Slave Girls.*

David (Michael Latimer), your standard young great white hunter, finds his African hunting expedition stalled when he winds up in a cave devoted to the mysterious white rhino god. Suddenly he's magically transported back in time (or maybe he's dreaming, we never really know for sure) back to the early days of man - or, more precisely, woman. David finds himself in a land ruled by, uh, brunettes, who are using blonde women as their slaves. The wicked brunette ruler, Kari (Martine Beswick), tries to use David for her own ends, unhappy with the fact that he may be falling for the perky and vacuous Saria (Edina Ronay). After much catfighting and hairstyle changes, everything sorts itself out, but not after the cast has delivered reams of campy, quotable dialogue in the process.

Nicely shot and rarely dull, *Prehistoric Women* comes nowhere near *One Million Years B.C.* (no cool Harryhausen dinosaurs, for one thing) but does work as a comical sexy cave fantasy. The film remains worth watching primarily for Beswick, a compelling actress in the Barbara Steele mould who had a few moments in the sun with *Dr. Jekyll and Sister Hyde, Seizure,* and a couple of James Bond films. Although she previously appeared as Nupondi in *One Million Years,* Beswick rarely got juicy lead roles, a shame considered what she was capable of when given the chance.

Anchor Bay's lavish DVD treatment seems almost surreal, consisting of a poster reproduction card, trailers, and another one of those *World of Hammer* television programs, "Lands Before Time," hosted by Oliver Reed. The scope framing looks just right and the colour and clarity are sensational, so toss out those old pan and scan tapes. Hammer didn't film in scope all that often, but when they did, look out!

PRETTY AS A PICTURE: THE ART OF DAVID LYNCH

Colour, 1998, 80m. / Directed by Toby Keeler / Image (US R1 NTSC)

Not many avant garde directors manage to cross over into the mainstream, but David Lynch has come as close as anyone can. From *Eraserhead* to *Dune* to the controversial *Lost Highway*, his career has been consistently fascinating and surprising, arguably reaching its apex with the landmark television series *Twin Peaks*.

Obviously this documentary's target audience already knows who they are, so if you like David Lynch's films (and other tangent projects), this DVD is an essential purchase. While *Pretty as a Picture* has been available on video for quite a while, the new DVD edition is not only much sharper but also contains an additional 15 minutes of footage (tacked on after the end, making the full running time 95 minutes) and a one-minute photo montage of Lynch family pictures. The shooting of *Lost Highway* forms the structural backbone of the film, which dissects Lynch's creative process and reveals the financial ins and outs of independent filmmaking. Along the way we get interviews with Mel Brooks (who released

The Elephant Man), Jennifer Lynch (no further comments necessary there), Dean Stockwell, the recently deceased Jack Nance, and the primary cast of *Lost Highway* (Bill Pullman, Robert Blake, Patricia Arquette, Balthazar Getty, etc.).

The documentary also offers a welcome glimpse of the composing process of Lynch's long-time musical collaborator, Angelo Badalamenti, and even presents a reunion of the *Eraserhead* cast at that film's shooting location. As if that weren't enough, Lynch also leads the viewer on a tour of gallery showings of his photographs and paintings (one of which adorns the DVD cover - once you've seen his painting process, you'll never forget it) and speaks candidly about his domestic life as a child and what he views as the strongest influence on his craft. While anyone unfamiliar with Lynch's work will be crawling the walls after the first 10 minutes, well-versed midnight movie addicts should find plenty to savour here.

Though shot professionally on video, *Pretty as a Picture* looks very good here; the arid desert locations are consistently colourful and provide some surprising atmosphere for the interview sequences. The film clips range from excellent (letterboxed snippets from *Eraserhead*, for example) to dismal (*Blue Velvet* panned and scanned will induce shudders). No visible artefacts or distortion are evident, and the mono audio, while obviously not demo material due to the source, is well recorded and clearly presented. Bracing, illuminating, and occasionally unsettling stuff.

PRINCE OF DARKNESS

Colour, 1987, 101m. / Directed by John Carpenter / Starring Jameson Parker, Donald Pleasence / Image / WS (2.35:1) (16:9)

Even today, people can't seem to agree on *Prince of Darkness*: is it a neglected masterpiece or glorified B-movie trash? A group of theology, physics, and mathematics doctoral students are shut in for the weekend in a dilapidated inner city church to study a newly discovered lava lamp-style structure containing what appears to be the essence of Satan.

Sound weird? Well, yeah, and the acting is a little stilted here and there, but Carpenter's astonishing visual sense and uncanny knack for maintaining separate, suspenseful storylines is enough to make this serious nightmare material. The script by "Martin Quatermass" (a cutesy pen name for Carpenter himself, as Hammer Film fans will recognize) has gotten flack for being alternately too cerebral and too pandering. On the contrary, the ambitious and lofty notions contained in the seemingly basic premise are quite provocative, especially after repeated viewings, and make this one of those rare films that actually becomes scarier the more you think about it. The throbbing synthesizer score and eerie wide-angle scope compositions have never been presented remotely as well as they are here.

As with *They Live*, Image has done an admirable job of presenting the film as its fans have longed to see it. Previous editions included a watchable but distracting pan and scan transfer in the US and a widescreen Japanese laserdisc that only presented the image at a compromised 1.90:1 aspect ratio and drained most of the colour out of the picture (not to mention those pesky subtitles). Here the film is presented in its exact anamorphic ratio and once again glows with the eerie shades of ochre, brown, and green that give the images an uneasy, quasi-baroque atmosphere. Detail is a bit wanting but still sharper than previous editions.

In short, no horror fan should pass this one up. While the lack of any bonus materials is a little disappointing (the original trailer was quite effective, and the TV version contained a small amount of alternate and additional material), the presentation of the film itself easily justifies the price tag. "I live... I live..."

THE PRINCESS AND THE CALL GIRL

Colour, 1983, 90m. / Directed by Radley Metzger / Starring Carol Levy, Victor Bevine / Image (US R0 NTSC) / WS (1.66:1)

Radley Metzger's last film to date, *The Princess and the Call Girl* originally debuted in the US on The Playboy Channel but, as demonstrated by this release, was clearly designed to be shown in a theatre. Like most of Metzger's films, the plot jumps off from a popular literary source (in this case, Mark Twain's *The Prince and the Pauper*, though credited to a French story entitled "Frontispiece"), using glamorous locales and sophisticated characters to give its eroticism that unique Metzger atmosphere.

The globe-hopping story concerns two identical former college friends (both played by Carol Levy) - one a naive rich girl engaged to a virginal preppy guy, the other a high priced prostitute skilled in the methods of manipulating the passions of a variety of men. The prostitute, Lucy Darling (!), accidentally overbooks herself and resorts to asking her friend to swap places for the weekend, a situation which rapidly spins out of control and leads to numerous comic consequences. Of course, the climactic engagement party finds various attendees, including the identical women, hopping bedrooms and guests in an attempt to sort out the confused identities.

Cheerfully fluffy and consistently erotic without pandering to its audience, Princess sports a likable performance from Levy, best known for the terrifying knife in the mattress sequence in Jack Sholder's *Alone in the Dark*. She handles both roles quite well, though her wry, doe-eyed mannerisms take some getting used to, and she fits perfectly in with the tradition of classy Metzger heroines who smoulder even when fully dressed. The rest of the cast does well, too, delivering Metzger's wordplay-packed dialogue with plenty of zest and wit. In the most typical scene, Levy exchanges cinematic *bon mots* with a movie buff client and nearly brings him to climax by naming several classic movie stars in rapid succession.

The incessant disco score gets a little tiresome after a while but definitely adds some nostalgia value to the proceedings, while Loubeau's skilful camerawork nicely contrasts the visual textures of Park Avenue and the Riviera.

The Image DVD presents the same transfer from First Run's VHS edition, albeit in a crisper and more colourful rendition. Prior VHS versions back in the '80s looked awful, and while this was intended primarily for cable exhibition, the 1.66:1 framing here looks far more satisfying and balanced, lending the film a visual glossiness lost of previous versions. The actual print is still in less than pristine condition, with the opening sequence displaying some negative dirt and a small but pesky recurring tear, which appears for a few minutes. However, this is still by far the most pleasing edition of the film, a sweet little valentine that, outside of his Henry Paris titles, stands as Metzger's funniest achievement. In fact, *Princess* in many ways is a fitting epilogue for the age of sexual freedom; they may not make 'em like this anymore, but as long as these films continue to be appreciated, viewers can relive the experience and have quite a few good, hearty laughs along the way.

THE PRISONER

Colour, 1967, 51m. per episode / Starring Patrick McGoohan / A&E (US R1 NTSC), Carlton (UK R2 PAL)

The television show most often cited as an example of intellectually challenging science fiction, *The Prisoner* actually defies any kind of classification. A heady mixture of espionage drama, existential philosophizing, pop art collage, and unabashed surrealism, this is truly a one of a kind creation well deserving of its fervent cult following.

The 17 episode saga concerns an unnamed government agent (Patrick McGoohan) who angrily resigns his position and is immediately abducted after being gassed in his home. He awakens in the Village, a seemingly tranquil but oppressive society run by Number Two (whose identity changes with each episode). Christened Number Six, our protagonist is subjected to a variety of clever and insidious plots to learn the reasons for his resignation. Is this dominating power his own employer or some evil competing nation? Is his refusal to explain his rationale for leaving an adherence to his own moral principles or part of a larger gambit? Ultimately a reading of the show varies from viewer to viewer, but few who watch it can remain untouched.

The series kicks off with "Arrival," in which Number Six feels his way around the Village after being unable to buy a useful map. He meets Number Two (*Thunderball*'s Guy Doleman), who tries to coax information from him. Number Six attempts to escape by sea but is brought back by the Village sentinels- huge floating white orbs which drag off their prey. In "Free for All," a satire of the electoral process, Number Six agrees to run for "public" office under the condition that, if victorious, he will learn the identity of the mysterious Number One. Naturally, all does not go as planned. Hammer regular Eric Portman turns up as Number Two in this episode, which was ghost written by McGoohan himself. In one of the more surreal high points of the series, "Dance of the Dead," Number Six discovers a mysterious, murderous conspiracy on the beach and becomes entangled in a strange Village carnival, complete with an elaborate fancy dress ball. Other highlights include "Checkmate," an especially nifty episode featuring Peter Wyngarde (*Burn, Witch, Burn*) as Number Two, overseeing a menacing game of human chess, which conceals a rebellious plan by one of the participants. In "The Chimes of Big Ben," Number Six's new neighbour gives him an idea for an elaborate escape plan, right under the nose of the new Number Two (Leo McKern). Our hero seemingly escapes... but as usual, you can't always believe what you see. In "A, B & C," an especially druggy time out for Number Six, a dream projection system is used with the aid of injected drugs to peer into the former agent's unconscious. Three candidates who may have been responsible for his resignation, nicknamed A, B and C, are brought forth in his dreams to dig around for secrets. In "The General," an experiment conducted by a mysterious entity known as The General sends subliminal educational lessons into the minds of Village residents via television; naturally Number Six is less than pleased with the implications of this method and decides to undermine this potential brainwashing technique. "The Girl Who Was Death" and the notorious "Fallout" offer the darkest moments in which the series went truly over the edge, cramming in enough head-spinning symbolism and philosophy to make the average television set explode.

The US and UK DVD sets include the legendary "alternate" version of "The Chimes of Big Ben," which contains numerous variations from its broadcast version as well as some rationale behind the recurring bicycle. All of the episodes look quite good for their age and a bit more crisp than the previous laserdisc editions, though the alternate "Chimes" is taken from the only existing, rather washed out print *Prisoner* fans have seen for years.

Obviously die hard *Prisoner* fans and newcomers will be pleased to have the series neatly lined up in matching DVD cases, and the transfers do the series justice. One can only wonder why A&E chose to offer only two episodes per disc when dual layering could have provided twice the value; presumably the intention is to stretch out the limited series as far as possible; the British DVDs from Carlton feature more episodes per disc and are obviously a cheaper deal. The US DVDs also feature some nifty extras thanks to the involvement of the Prisoner Appreciation Society, Six of One, including bios and trivia tidbits, alternate opening and closing sequences, and a rarely seen television interview with the antisocial McGoohan, who makes a rare exception to his policy and discusses the series in a moderate amount of depth.

PROPHECY

Colour, 1979, 102m. / Directed by John Frankenheimer / Starring Talia Shire, Robert Foxworth, Armand Assante / Paramount (US R1 NTSC) / WS (2.35:1) (16:9) / DD2.0

Released during the peak of the new horror revival which also saw such entries as *The Omen*, *Dawn of the Dead*, and *Alien*, John Frankenheimer's shaggy dog - err, bear - of a monster movie, *Prophecy*,

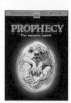

became the object of immediate ridicule for its big budget squandered in the service of a pandering, sermonistic diatribe about the environment. Over twenty years later, *Prophecy* still suffers from a bum rep but has gained something of a cult following for its unintentional comic highlights, including the nasty fate of one helicopter pilot and an unbelievable vignette involving a sleeping bag. So, is it really that bad? Well, yes, it is, but for all its problems, *Prophecy* certainly isn't boring.

The wilds of Maine have become a breeding ground for hatred when the local Indian tribes clash with industrial paper mill developers running roughshod over Mother Nature. For some reason Dr. Robert Verne (Robert Foxworth) and his wife, Maggie (*Rocky*'s Talia Shire), head up to deal with the problem, which also involves the mysterious disappearances of several locals. The discovery of some mutated bear cubs tip off the doctor that a mutated grizzly bear, caused by the rampant mercury poisoning in the water, is responsible for all of the mayhem, so he packs up the cubs and heads back to home base. Naturally, mama bear (referred to as Kataden) is none too pleased and, quicker than you can say Gorgo, stomps through the woods hell-bent on revenge.

Considering the relative competence of most of the actors (including a young Armand Assante as an intrepid Indian activist) and Frankenheimer's good track record with popcorn fare, *Prophecy* stood a chance of at least turning out as a good, dumb monster movie. Despite some lashings of gore and the obviously surreal make up effects (both of which are strong enough to make one really question the PG rating), the film is undone by its awkward dialogue and the attempt to wedge some kind of moral into the proceedings. Horror movies should never, ever try to preach, but that hasn't stopped people from continuing to try. Frankenheimer has publicly stated he was brought on as a director for hire and was never too keen on the whole environmental angle, so apparently a bulk of the blame must be shifted to screenwriter David Seltzer, whose preaching in *The Omen* at least fit the subject matter and scared the bejeezus out of God-fearing viewers everywhere. However, as far as horror movies involving Indians and nature running amok go, *Prophecy* is more entertaining and compulsively watchable than the sleep-inducing *Nightwing* from the same year.

Whatever its debits, *Prophecy* is at least a visually pleasing film thanks to its sprawling British Columbia scenery and professional widescreen lensing. The Panavision compositions have been brutalized for years by Paramount's blurry, badly cropped TV and video transfers, so it's gratifying (and not a little bit startling) that they chose to release it on DVD in its original aspect ratio. The transfer is about what you'd expect for a late '70s title - a little on the drab side, colour and detail-wise, but it's a sharp rendering of the original elements and thankfully doesn't heap on any digital cleaning effects to wipe out the natural grain of several shots (including clumsy zoomed-in close ups). The early Dolby Stereo track verges on mono most of the time, with some mild separation in the music tracks and a few directional foley effects making up most of the front channel soundscape.

As for extras, well, there are "scene selections" and "interactive menus," so those of you expecting the solemn theatrical trailer will be sorely disappointed.

PSYCHIC KILLER

Colour, 1975, 87m. / Directed by Ray Danton / Starring Paul Burke, Jim Hutton, Julie Adams / Elite Entertainment (US R1 NTSC) / WS (1.85:1), Vipco (UK R2 PAL)

For those uninitiated into the fold of 1960s comedies, Jim Hutton (Timothy's dad) was an actor best known for playing nice, aw-shucks guys in froth like *Where the Boys Are, Walk Don't Run*, and *Who's Minding the Mint?*. However, when the 1970s arrived and cinema took a darker turn, Hutton shifted gears and tried to change his image. Perhaps the most startling case is *Psychic Killer*, originally filmed as *The Kirlian Effect* (hence the replaced title card), a low budget horror outing directed by Ray Danton, a former actor also known for directing such drive-in favourites as *Deathmaster* and *Crypt of the Living Dead* until he turned to TV fare like *The Incredible Hulk*.

The movie begins with Hutton running and screaming full force towards the camera, and it really never settles down for the next hour and a half. As Paul Masters, an innocent man unjustly convicted for murder and committed to a mental institution, Hutton really pulls out all the stops here as a basically sympathetic guy who finds himself consumed by the darkness of revenge after he acquires the ability to "project" himself out of his body and kill those responsible for his own incarceration and the death of his mother. Thanks to the aid of his doctor, Laura

(Julie Adams, best known for *Creature from the Black Lagoon*), Masters is released after the real culprit is found, and he immediately causes the judge responsible for his case to shoot himself with a rifle during a tryst with a married blonde bimbo. In the most sordid sequence, the nurse who neglected Masters' mother and let her die meets her end in a hot shower stall, and pretty soon local cop Paul Burke (one of the unflattering depictions of a supposedly heroic law enforcer ever committed to film) starts putting two and two together. After Burke sleeps with the doctor during a romantic interlude (an especially weird scene), Masters really finds himself going over the edge.

It's amazing that this film was ever considered eligible for its PG rating in the US. Sleazy, sordid, and filled with nudity and violence, this surreal oddity leaps from one bizarre setpiece to the next with little regard for logic. At least one sequence in which an opera-singing teamster is crushed by a concrete block indicates that the film was partially intended to be funny, which might explain some of the other goofy moments along the way (the nurse's go go dance, a butcher's hand getting ground into burger meat, and so on). Even *Touched by an Angel*'s Della Reese pops by for an abrasive cameo appearance that must be seen to be believed, and it all ends with a surprisingly grim and sadistic finale (given away in the trailer, alas) that leaves the viewer with no one to root for.

Not really all that good, *Psychic Killer* is at least never boring and should please any discriminating sleazy drive-in moviehound. Furthermore, Elite's transfer is astonishingly good. The 1.85:1 framing shaves a little off the fullscreen transfer but looks far better composed, and the colour and clarity are amazing considering the movie's budget and vintage.

PSYCHO

B&W, 1960, 108m. / Directed by Alfred Hitchcock / Starring Anthony Perkins, Vera Miles, John Gavin, Janet Leigh / Universal (US R1 NTSC), Columbia (UK R2 PAL) / WS (1.85:1)

A film completely steeped in its own iconography, *Psycho* forever changed the face of American horror and has become such a familiar part of our cinematic language that it rarely scares anyone now. The radical techniques on display here from the first frame to the last (Hitch often insisted it was a comedy!) actually

seem quaint, but even without the shriek value it once possessed, *Psycho* remains a crucial film - not as personal as *Vertigo* by any means nor as gloriously entertaining as *Rear Window*, but an icy, perfect jewel nonetheless.

Universal's transfer of *Psycho* is generally first rate, marred only by overmatting (according to the hard matte always visible in the shower scene, it should be around 1.66:1). This glitch aside, *Psycho* looks quite sharp and clean, while Herrmann's "black and white" string score sounds robust and absolutely chilling. Anthony Perkins' portrayal of Norman Bates, the mother's boy motel owner who encounters fleeing embezzler Marion Crane (Janet Leigh), remains one of the cinema's definitive performances (just check out Gus Van Sant's disastrous colour remake to see how difficult this role is to pull off). So many scenes have become classic: the parlour talk between Marion and Norman, the shower sequences, the ascent (and descent) of Detective Arbogast (Martin Balsam) on the Bates stairs, and of course, the utterly creepy subliminal final shot.

The US DVD also sports a number of extras including an exhaustive one hour documentary (though the "censored scene" bonus is a bit misleading), trailers, and assorted production notes and tidbits; for some reason the documentary is missing from Columbia's UK release.

PSYCHO III

Colour, 1986, 93m. / Directed by Anthony Perkins / Starring Anthony Perkins, Diana Scarwid, Jeff Fahey / Goodtimes (US R1 NTSC) / WS (1.85:1) / DD2.0

Following the surprise box office and critical success of *Psycho II*, a film no one thought could be done, Universal set the wheels in motion for a third instalment. While Hitchcock disciple Richard Franklin had done an efficient job helming the sequel, Anthony Perkins, a man who knew the ins and outs of Norman Bates better than anyone else, took charge of the next film. For a number of reasons, audiences and critics were puzzled and underwhelmed by the results, but in retrospect, *Psycho III* is by far the most audacious and striking follow up to the classic 1960 film.

"There is no God!" howls the anguished voice of Maureen Coyle, a young nun, in the moody pre-credits sequence. Poised at the top of a mission bell tower, she plans to commit suicide by leaping to her death. Meanwhile, a group of nuns gather behind her and plead for her to reconsider. One of the sisters accosts Maureen and winds up falling through the wooden railing, several stories down to her death (a nice homage to *Vertigo*). Banished into the desert with only a suitcase in hand, Maureen catches a ride with Duane (Jeff Fahey, in a good sleazy role for once), a lowlife driving to California with dreams of becoming a musician. When Duane gets a little too friendly, Maureen bolts off into the night. Duane arrives at the Bates Motel, where Norman (Perkins) takes him on as a cashier and assistant. Meanwhile, Norman goes to the local diner at which he worked in the previous film and has an impromptu chat with Tracy Venable (Roberta Maxwell), a reporter investigating the repercussions of Norman's release from the sanitarium. During their interview, Norman notices Maureen walking into the diner - and she bears a striking resemblance to someone from the first film whose initials were also M.C. Norman allows Maureen to stay in Cabin No. 1 for free; however, when his old instincts kick in and he bursts in on Maureen in the bathtub, he gets a nasty surprise.

To reveal more of the plot would be unthinkable, but *Psycho III* offers a number of startling twists and turns which remain consistent with the Norman Bates persona established in the prior films while introducing a number of intriguing, damaged new characters. Norman's pitiful attempts at establishing a romance with Maureen are extremely well handled, right down to the unexpected use of that Cupid statue in Mother's house. While the studio insisted on adding some gory violence to a couple of sideline murder sequences as well as a more open ending, Perkins handled the demands with bravura, even including an unexpected homage to Dario Argento's *Tenebre* in the phone booth scene. Sensitively acted and laced with a fine dose of black humour, the film really deserves a much better reputation than it currently enjoys, though a small cult following has justifiably been building over the years. While the relentlessly dark, uncompromising aspects of this film certainly won't appeal to everyone, the utter critical dismissal of this film is bewildering; for example, Leonard Maltin claims it plays Norman "strictly for laughs," as drastic a misreading of the film as one could imagine.

Technical aspects of the film are remarkable, especially considering Perkins' lack of previous experience as a director; the dark, beautiful chiaroscuro photography punctuated with colourful flashes of saturated neon lighting is a complete departure from the hard edged look of the other *Psycho* films. Best of all, Carter Burwell's magnif-

icent, terrifying, and haunting score (written right after his work on *Blood Simple*) adds immensely to the skewed atmosphere of putrefaction and tortured love; MCA sorely needs to give it an overdue release on CD. On the downside viewers must have seen the other two films in order to make sense of several major story points, and even so, Maxwell's frantic climactic explanation (sort of like Simon Oakland's psychiatric speech in the first film, only faster) remains a little hard to follow.

Goodtimes' DVD finally presents *Psycho III* in its intended 1.85:1 aspect ratio. Filmed with a hard matte, the film has looked terrible on every other home video version, with only the opening credits letterboxed. In contrast to the dull laserdisc, the DVD looks much more colourful and detailed, while the improved composition restores several intriguing camera setups missing since its brief theatrical release. The standard Dolby Surround soundtrack has also been greatly improved, with clearer separation and deeper bass. Image quality is just a tad on the dark side, not really a bad thing considering the look of the film. The compression job looks fine, much more than can be said for Goodtimes' edition of *Psycho II*. Also includes the original US trailer.

PSYCHOMANIA
Colour, 1972, 95m. / Directed by Don Sharp / Starring Nicky Henson, George Sanders, Beryl Reid / Image (US R0 NTSC) / WS (1.66:1)

This loopy British biker/zombie film has been haunting the shelves of countless video stores through various public domain labels over the years, sneakily lurking in wait for unsuspecting viewers destined to be left speechless by its hallucinatory fusion of rebellious mod youths, spooky zombie mayhem, loud motorcycle chases, and... uh, supernatural frogs.

A hellraising biker gang called The Living Dead finds its course of destiny changing dramatically when shaggy-haired leader Tom (Nicky Henson) decides to try out a theory of his occult-loving mother (Beryl Reid) that a strong-willed person can return from the dead. After offing himself following a particularly frisky chase sequence, Tom is buried while still straddling his chopper and left with a strange amulet from the spooky family butler, Shadwell (George Sanders). Sure enough, Tom has soon risen from the dead and begun a reign of terror across the countryside. He talks his small cult of followers into following his example, with good girl Abby (Mary Larkin) backing out and incurring the wrath of her undead compatriots.

Though it contains all the elements of a perfect drive-in film, *Psychomania* plays out as anything but a run of the mill B-movie. The strange mingling of old pros like Sanders and Reid with the game young cast makes for an odd clash of youth movement and classic horror, with some froggy cult worship thrown in to make the plot even odder. Director Don Sharp, best known for the Hammer masterpiece *Kiss of the Vampire*, keeps things percolating along even when they don't make a bit of sense, and the suicide/resurrection sequences are undeniably fascinating to behold. The strange, creepy quasi-pop score puts just the right '70s polish on the action, making this a unique artefact for any horror collection.

Image's DVD of *Psychomania* starts off with a bumpy opening ten minutes which, like all previous transfers, is murky, grainy, and difficult to watch. After that, however, the quality improves tremendously and represents by far the best presentation this has ever received on the small screen. Colours are faithfully reproduced and amazingly vivid for an early '70s film, while print damage is minimal and never distracting. No extras to speak of, apart from a fun Spanish language track and the cartoon frog on the back of the box.

PUPPET MASTER
Colour, 1989, 95m. / Directed by David Schmoeller / Starring Paul LeMat, Irene Miracle
PUPPET MASTER II
Colour, 1990, 88m. / Directed by Dave Allen / Starring Collin Bersen, Elizabeth Maclellan
PUPPET MASTER III: TOULON'S REVENGE
Colour, 1991, 86m. / Directed by David DeCoteau / Starring Guy Rolfe, Richard Lynch
PUPPET MASTER 4
Colour, 1993, 79m. / Directed by Jeff Burr / Starring Gordon Currie, Chandra West
PUPPET MASTER 5
Colour, 1994, 82m. / Directed by Jeff Burr / Starring Gordon Currie, Ian Ogilvy
CURSE OF THE PUPPET MASTER
Colour, 1998, 77m. / Directed by David DeCoteau / Starring George Peck, Emily Harrison
RETRO PUPPET MASTER
Colour, 1999, 95m. / Directed by David DeCoteau and Joseph Tennent / Starring Greg Sestero, Brigitta Dau
Full Moon (US R1 NTSC) / DD2.0

Over the past thirty years, most studios have managed to scare up at least one decent horror franchise. Paramount had Jason, New Line had Freddy, and Universal had Chucky, among others. Full Moon carved its own little niche with the Puppet Master films, a ridiculously extended series based upon studio head Charles Band's obvious fondness for sinister living puppets. No less than seven instalments so far have chronicled the adventures of puppeteer Andre Toulon and his horde of scuttling, murderous puppets whose forces are used either for evil or good, depending on the whims of the storyline.

In the first and most high profile *Puppet Master*, a cadre of psychics convenes at the isolated Bodega Bay Hotel (get it?) where their colleague, Neil Gallagher (Jimmie F. Skaggs), has been performing mysterious experiments in the occult. Apparently he has been following in the footsteps of Andre Toulon (William Hickey), a "puppet master" whose power to control a band of superintelligent homicidal puppets could have now fallen into the wrong hands. As the hotel's population quickly dwindles, the survivors race against time to uncover Toulon's dark secrets. Sporting a better than average cast, including Paul LeMat and Irene Miracle, *Puppet Master* is more intriguing, amusing, and disgusting than it is frightening; the puppets themselves make an auspicious debut, though their members will change dramatically over the course of the series. For the record, the initial puppets here are the memorable Blade (a knife-wielding guy in black), Ms. Leech (aka Leech Woman - see it for yourself), Tunneler, Jester, and Pinhead. The film features some effective ground-level tracking shots throughout the hotel (by Lucio Fulci's former cinematographer, Sergio Salvati) and a memorable, whimsical music score by Richard Band, all of which give it a slick veneer beyond the standard Full Moon production. Director David Schmoeller once again mines the eerie use of "inanimate" figures found in his earlier favourite, *Tourist Trap*, and it still works ten years later.

Basically a gorier, more outrageous remake of the previous film, *Puppet Master II* trots out another hapless group of victims to Bodega Bay where the still living Andre Toulon's lifeforce is dwindling away to nothing. Desperate to replenish their creator's energy, the puppets go about their usual mayhem and lose one of their members in the process. A new puppet, Torch, enters the fray along with his master, now decked out like Claude Rains in

The Invisible Man. Faster paced and more complex than the original, this film is in many ways the cleanest and most efficient of the series, a good old fashioned body count epic whose only intention is to entertain the sick at heart.

Striving for a change of pace, Full Moon decided to do a prequel with *Puppet Master III: Toulon's Revenge.* In World War II, Toulon (Guy Rolfe) and his wife aggravate the growing Nazi powers that be, although the tyrants soon learn the hard way that one shouldn't mess with the forces of darkness. Considerably more ambitious and designed on a larger scale than its predecessors, *Puppet Master III* makes few attempts at all out horror, instead functioning as a blackly comic period piece with puppets giving the Nazis their just desserts. Another puppet, Six-Shooter, makes his appearance here and would quickly become a fan favourite.

Puppet Master 4 introduces yet another new puppet, Decapitron (purportedly left over from an unrealized Charles Band project) and marks the series debut of director Jeff Burr, who had earlier helmed *The Offspring* and *Leatherface: Texas Chainsaw Massacre III.* The story returns to the same territory of Parts I and II, but with a bizarre twist: the puppets are now fighting for the forces of good. Here the puppets help a young scientist battle a race of evil creatures terrorizing his laboratory, and... well, that's about it. Guy Rolfe returns as Toulon in a considerably reduced role, but it's nice to see the William Castle pro still at work.

Shot back to back with *Part 4*, *Puppet Master 5* is one of the weakest of the bunch and should be for die hard fans only. This entry picks up where the last one left off, with a new evil puppet being popping up and battling the puppets for a while. The cast completely goes through the motions here as the puppets are once again fighting for good and displaying no menace whatsoever.

A change in directors to David DeCoteau (who earlier helmed *Part III*) should have marked a step back up in the series... but *Curse of the Puppet Master* belongs with Part 4 as a low point for the series. Here a young scientist becomes embroiled in a plot to transfer human souls in and out of puppets, with cosmically weird results. The film never really builds to a finale and feels like the screenwriters stopped when they ran out of money; a shame, but the effective (albeit sparse) effects may keep the faithful engaged enough to make this worth a view.

Luckily DeCoteau fared better with *Retro Puppet Master*, another prequel in which a very young Toulon learns highly protected Egyptian secrets of life and death, which allow him to commence his infamous puppet experiments. The

Paris settings consist of a few sparsely decorated rooms (Ed Wood, eat your heart out) and the film runs an insanely short amount of time, but at least it marks a return to the basic territory mined in the first three films.

Full Moon's DVD box set compiles all of these films with all of the extras included on the previous VHS and laserdisc editions. This basically means a slew of trailers and making-of "Videozone" sequences slapped onto the same full frame, old matte transfers fans have grown to know and love. While the image and sound quality won't be much of an improvement, it's quite handy to have the entire set of films packaged together where the series can be better evaluated for its strengths and weaknesses. Overall the Puppet Master films are a peculiar side road in horror filmmaking, which fans either enjoy or detest; for those who belong in the former camp, this box set should be more than satisfying. The image quality varies from title to title and generally improves as the films become more current. However, the audio track for *Retro Puppet Master* splits the audio into two shallow channels which make for a very awkward listening experience; watch it through a TV monitor or not at all.

QUATERMASS AND THE PIT
B&W, 1958, 180m. / Directed by Rudolph Carter / Starring André Morell, Cec Linder / Revelation (UK R2 PAL)

QUATERMASS AND THE PIT
Colour, 1967, 98m. / Directed by Roy Ward Baker / Starring Andrew Keir, Barbara Shelley, Julian Glover / Anchor Bay (US R1 NTSC) / WS (1.78:1) / DD5.1

One of the key series of dramatic science fiction during the Cold War era, Nigel Kneale's Quatermass stories integrated touchy issues of environment, evolution, and basic scientific ethics into what had could have been brainless pulp yarns involving aliens and rampaging beasties. Arguably the high water mark of the cycle is *Quatermass and the Pit*, a challenging saga that began life as a 1957 production shown in six episodes on live British television. Nine years later, Hammer Films had already established itself as a strong voice in science fiction with films like *Quatermass 2* and *X the Unknown*, so a big screen remake was in order. The result appeared in US theatres as *Five Million Years to Earth* and captured an entire generation of stunned kiddie matinee audiences. While the latter has come to be regarded as a classic, the previous version is no less effective and deserves to be appreciated on its own terms.

During an excavation beneath the concrete surfaces of Knightsbridge, a group of construction workers uncover a strange, unidentifiable skull, which may actually be the missing link. Professor Bernard Quatermass is called in when further investigation uncovers a metallic structure, seemingly missile-like in appearance but actually containing a huge, locust-like creature's corpse. The resemblance of this alien being to man's conception of the devil poses a series of tantalizing questions, indicating that perhaps man did not originate as he had always believed. The ship and its contents begin to exert a powerful, dangerous psychic influence over London, where natural disasters begin to rip the city and its populace apart.

The more widely known theatrical version of *Quatermass and the Pit* made its debut on DVD from Anchor Bay in an excellent widescreen edition with a rich palette of colours and a dynamic 5.1 remix (which unfortunately splits most of the voices into the right and left front speakers - quite distracting at times). The disc also includes the *World of Hammer* sci-fi episode, an informative and elegant commentary track with Kneale and director Roy Ward Baker (*Asylum*), and a host of American and UK promotional spots and trailers.

The UK DVD release of the original *Quatermass and the Pit* from Revelation is indeed quite that - a bold and clean presentation of what had previously been available only in blurry, almost unwatchable grey market rental VHS dupes. Bear in mind that this is still taken from a kinescope and the technical limitations are many, but Quatermass fans should be overjoyed to see it looking this good. The three hour running time obviously offers more room for expansion with the supporting characters, while the cataclysmic finale is stretched out much longer here to encompass a deeper look at its effects on everyone involved. Future Hammer vet Andre Morrell makes for an interesting and convincing Professor Quatermass, equal in every way to the later turn provided by Andrew Keir.

The only notable drawback with the Revelation edition is its packaging, which is about as unappealing and cheap-looking as can be. This is bracing, scary, thought-provoking stuff; no matter which version you choose to watch, you really can't lose.

QUATERMASS II

B&W, 1956, 85m. / Directed by Val Guest / Starring Brian Donlevy, John Longden / Anchor Bay (US R1 NTSC)

A chilling example of '50s science fiction at its best, *Quatermass II* (released in the US as *Enemy from Space*) often turns up on people's "hidden treasures" list as a scary childhood favourite no one else has ever seen. The middle instalment in Hammer Films' Quatermass trilogy (also including *The Quatermass Experiment* and *Quatermass and the Pit*), this film was often lost in the shuffle until the past decade or so in which it has finally received the critical attention it richly deserves.

Disgruntled by the British government's refusal to back his plans for moon colonization, Professor Bernard Quatermass (film noir regular Brian Donlevy) is nearly hit while driving along a country road. The other driver was apparently wounded by a meteorite-like object from the sky. Upon returning to his lab, Quatermass is informed of a series of strange formations falling from the sky towards the nearby Winnerden Flats. Accompanied by one of his assistants, Quatermass drives out to the site and discovers a facility similar to his own moon colony designs. However, Quatermass is apprehended by mysterious security guards and escorted to a government created housing project. Upon further study, however, the tenacious scientist discovers that perhaps the eerie dome structure houses alien forces whose intentions are quite sinister indeed.

A lean and intelligent thriller along the same lines as such novels as Jack Finney's *The Body Snatchers* and Robert A. Heinlein's *The Puppet Masters*, this film also concerns itself with the concept of human identity as the ideal facade for alien invaders. The moral ambiguities of this premise are not lost on writer Nigel Kneale, who provides yet another literate and engaging screenplay which ventures far past the standard film conventions of science fiction. Looking at this film decades after the fact, it's a shame Hammer largely abandoned projects like this and focused almost entirely on gothic monsters during its heyday. Both could have coexisted together quite nicely. James Bernard also supplies an effective, deliberately grating music score, which anticipates his later masterworks like the Dracula films.

Anchor Bay's DVD of *Quatermass II* contains an insert explaining that the edition restored from the original British negative did not include the original two minute prologue, which is grafted on here from a different, grainier source. This hiccup aside, the image quality is exceptionally clear and looks like it was filmed a week ago - a far cry indeed from the hazy, battered print used for the old domestic Corinth laserdisc. Also included is a commentary track prepared for the Roan laserdisc reissue, featuring Guest and Kneale discussing the various locations and actors used for the film and how the story evolved through Kneale's various drafts. The audio quality on the commentary is distractingly hollow and hissy sounding, but the quality of the chatting makes it worth the effort. Also included is the US theatrical trailer and another *World of Hammer* episode, "Sci-Fi," which covers everything from classics like the *Quatermass* films to, uh, not-so-classics like *Moon Zero Two*.

QUERELLE

Colour, 1982, 108m. / Directed by Rainer Werner Fassbinder / Starring Brad Davis, Franco Nero / Columbia (US R1 NTSC), Second Sight (UK R2 PAL) / WS (2.35:1) (16:9)

Four years after escaping from both a Turkish prison and a potential change of sexual orientation in the shower room in *Midnight Express*, late actor Brad Davis went over the edge in *Querelle*, the last film by Rainer Werner Fassbinder, who died of a drug overdose before the film's US premiere. The director's most blatantly homoerotic work (to put it mildly), *Querelle* throws aside the touchy gay politics of realistic studies like *Fox and His Friends* in favour of what can only be described as a hellish, horny mixture of Hieronymus Bosch and *Kwaidan*.

Derived more or less from a novel by revered thief/poet/novelist Jean Genet (who also inspired *Poison* and *The Balcony*), the fractured story follows the misadventures of Querelle (Davis), a sexually undecided sailor who winds up at a port in Brest and encounters a variety of colourful characters, including his brother, Robert (Hanno Pöschl), who is having an affair with saloon owner and singer Lysiane (Jeanne Moreau). Meanwhile her burly black husband, Nono (Günther Kaufmann), sets his sights on Querelle, whose lust is temporarily distracted when he impulsively knifes a fellow sailor to death and diverts the blame to Gil (Pöschl with different facial hair), a murderous criminal with whom Querelle begins to fall in love. Meanwhile Querelle's commanding officer, Seblon

(Franco Nero), lusts from afar and begins devising his own agenda.

Upon its release, *Querelle* was critically scorned (especially in the US) for its jolting and deliberately artificial storytelling technique, which regularly punctuates the action with rambling voiceovers and onscreen quotations from Genet and other seemingly random sources. Davis' performance deliberately turns Querelle into a blank slate upon which the other characters project their desires; the crafty, intense charm which made him famous is transformed here into a casually voracious presence, whether engaging in choreographed knife and fist fights or lolling around in a different character's bed every night. While Nero has virtually nothing to do but gaze intensely from afar, Moreau fares better (in her second Genet adaptation after the underrated and startling *Mademoiselle*) thanks to her ability to give poignancy to even the silliest lines and lyrics. The studio sets used to represent Brest are a visual feast of blazing oranges, reds, and yellows, which can make the whole experience queasy after a while but certainly give the film a distinctive, unforgettable look. From the phallic statue formations to the corruptively ripe saloon interiors, this is Fassbinder in full throttle, choking the screen with as much overstuffed excess as he can possibly muster.

For those unfortunate enough to suffer through Columbia's old pan and scan VHS transfer, *Querelle* on DVD will look like a different film entirely. Fassbinder uses the entire scope frame to experiment with bizarre angles, distorting lenses, and deeply layered compositions and tableaux, while the saturated colours which bleed all over the screen on videotape look more refined and tolerable here. The anamorphic transfer provided by Gaumont most likely comes from a PAL source, and for some reason in 16:9 playback the image looked a bit coarse and noisy (as if suffering from excessive digital noise reduction), while on another widescreen monitor it looked perfectly smooth and glossy. If it looks a little odd on your television, you might want to try another.

The end titles sport a Dolby Stereo tag, though the film is presented in mono in both English and French. Davis, Moreau, and Nero provide their own voices, while virtually all of the other actors are very artificially dubbed in a manner that may cause even diehard Italian horror fans to bristle with annoyance. The alternate French track (which can be played with optional English, Spanish, or French subtitles) is a little easier on the ears, but it also suppresses or eliminates altogether most of the sound effects and music. (The UK disc from Second Sight is letter-boxed but only retains the English dubbed option.)

This unrated edition also runs about two minutes longer than the US edition; while there's still virtually no nudity in the film per se, a few sequences (such as Davis' forced manual stimulation of another sailor at knifepoint) are more explicit and may not have been faked. Inexplicably, the US disc's only supplements are trailers for *The Opposite of Sex* and *sex, lies and videotape*, which might give you an idea of where the marketing people are coming from.

QUILLS

Colour, 2000, 124m. / Directed by Philip Kaufman / Starring Geoffrey Rush, Kate Winslet / Fox (US R1 NTSC, UK R2 PAL) / WS (1.85:1) (16:9) / DD5.1

Paris. 1794. Due to his libertine habits and immoral literary works, the Marquis de Sade (Rush) is incarcerated in Charenton lunatic asylum. Yet he continues to write, the results smuggled out for him by laundry maid Madeleine (Winslet). When "Justine" is published it incites outrage and scandal in decent society, so the Government assigns Dr. Royer-Collard (Michael Caine) to "cure" the Marquis of his mental depravities. At first deprived of ink, quill pens and parchment, he must resort to ever more desperate schemes to continue his writing.

"This has all the makings of a farce!", scoffs Geoffrey Rush as the Marquis de Sade in Phil Kaufman's *Quills*. How very apt. This spurious and tainted account of the latter years in the eventful life of the infamous writer undermines its own integrity by supplanting historical veracity with theatrical histrionics; *Carry On Marquis* might have been more appropriate a moniker. Yet if one accepts it as nothing more than a piece of fiction (and can forgive some of the more heavy handed passages) then lines like "Don't tell me... you've come to read my trousers" give rise to genuine chuckles.

Rush's wickedly funny portrayal is an animated triumph, though he delivers the often frenetic dialogue by Doug Wright (who adapted this from his own play) as if he's performing in local rep. Outrageously flamboyant, he minces about the screen spewing reams of glib and pithy rhetoric, though admittedly the proceedings do sizzle whenever he's on screen. Caine's amoral doctor and Phoenix's naive priest are accomplished characterizations and there's distinctly guilty pleasure to be derived from hearing winsome Winslet verbalizing some of the Marquis' saucy prose (and yes, she doffs her clothing - again!). The film would certainly have

benefited from a little judicious pruning; two hours plus feels about twenty minutes too long. But the ensemble cast (which also includes worthy turns from Patrick Malahide, Billie Whitelaw and even Ed Tudor Pole!) holds court well enough that *Quills* - its irksome factual misdemeanours aside - is a relatively painless way to pass an evening.

Fox's DVD delivers a number of bonus features, including three featurettes (which, though entertaining, when strung together barely amount to a standard length behind-the-scenes promo piece), a slender gallery of production designs and prop artefacts, a commentary from scripter Wright (Rush's input would have been nice, but alas...), a trailer (presented twice, the second time with the addition of Spanish subs) and a TV spot. The film itself is a 1.85:1 matte divided by twenty chapter stops. The picture has a vaguely greenish hue, which may or may not represent the original theatrical look, I can't say for sure. Sound is provided in English 5.1 Surround, English Dolby Surround and French Dolby Surround. Subtitling is in English and Spanish. - TG

RABID

Colour, 1976, 91m. / Directed by David Cronenberg / Starring Marilyn Chambers, Frank Moore / Metrodome (UK R2 PAL) / WS (1.85:1) (16:9) / New Concorde (US R1 NTSC)

Following the success and controversy ignited by *Shivers*, David Cronenberg expanded his view of clinical, sexualized horror with *Rabid*, a chilly account of venereal disease gone absolutely haywire through Montreal. Most notable in the history books as the first attempt by hardcore actress Marilyn Chambers (*Behind the Green Door*) to go straight, the film has gained considerably in both meaning and chilling effectiveness in context with Cronenberg's later films.

A devastating motorcycle accident in the countryside leaves beautiful young Rose (Chambers) seriously burned and mutilated while her boyfriend, Hart (Frank Moore), is thrown clear. Luckily employees at the nearby Keloid Clinic witness the accident and, using innovative new techniques in plastic surgery and tissue regeneration, manage to save Rose from certain death (or at least horrible disfigurement). Dr Keloid (Howard Ryshpan) and his partner, Murray Cypher (Joe Silver), feel their procedure has been successful, so Rose is left alone to recover. A month later she regains consciousness in a state of utter hysteria, causing one of her fellow patients to come to her aid. She embraces him tightly, an act which causes him to react with horror. Later the patient, bloody and dazed, staggers down the hospital hallways, but no one is able to treat him. One by one Rose seduces and attacks others in the hospital, draining them of just enough blood to satisfy her hunger. Keloid discovers a strange, vaginal growth in her armpit which hosts a horrendous side effect of her skin graft, one that is also capable of leaving its victims in a dangerous, rabid condition capable of spreading through the population like wildfire.

Though undeniably rough around the edges, *Rabid* is a strangely potent and haunting film. Chambers is surprisingly good in the role, which doesn't require much range but definitely exploits the mixture of pleasure and dangerous hunger lurking beneath her attractive features. As usual Cronenberg maximizes the chilly potential out of his sterile, angular settings and barren countrysides, while the city locales are cleverly manipulated to expose the dangerous underbelly of urban life. Chambers' visit to a porn theatre in particular and subsequent response to a horny fellow patron is a disturbing, multilayered example of Cronenberg at his finest. The uncredited stock music is also eerily spare and well chosen, though it wasn't until Cronenberg's next horror film, *The Brood*, that music finally took centre stage thanks to Howard Shore. As usual the director also relishes throwing in some iconoclastic and often downright rude imagery, such as a shopping mall Santa Claus riddled with bullets and the grim, marvellously ironic coda, which relays most of its horror through the telephone rather than explicit gore.

Long unavailable on home video after an early, substandard appearance from Warner Home Video, *Rabid* has been remastered by Roger Corman's New Concorde. Like their other '70s restorations, this film has never looked so good outside of first run theatres. However, bear in mind that some sequences were shot in a deliberately desaturated and grainy style, while the opening credits were printed with dirt and specks imbedded in the script overlays, so the visual flaws are actually supposed to be there. Like all of Cronenberg's early films, *Rabid* was shot full frame and soft matted in theatres; the US DVD contains the entire exposed image with (clumsily transitioned) 1.66:1 closing credits, though letterbox purists with 16:9 sets can matte it off if they so desire. The UK disc features an improved and colourful anamorphic transfer which mattes off some information from the top; the increase in resolution is noticeable and quite welcome. The

mono audio is adequate given the source materials and is free from distracting background noise or distortion. The US disc also includes the gleefully dramatic US theatrical trailer, while the UK disc instead contains a Cronenberg intro, notes by Kim Newman, and an image gallery.

RABID DOGS

Colour, 1974, 96m. / Directed by Mario Bava / Starring Lea Lander, George Eastman / Lucertola Media (Germany R0 NTSC), Astro (Germany R2 PAL) / WS (1.66:1)

More than any other title, this one got horror and Italian cinema fans out to the stores to buy DVD players during the format's early days. This long-lost crime film from director Mario Bava, best known for the films *Black Sunday* and *Black Sabbath*, restores an important part of Italian cinema and sheds some amazing light on this neglected master of macabre cinema. Described in the liner notes as what would happen if Quentin Tarantino remade *Last House on the Left* in a speeding car, *Rabid Dogs (Cani arrabbiati)* is even grimmer and more nihilistic than such a description would suggest.

After pulling a minor heist, three robbers abduct a young woman (Lea Lander) and take her hostage along with a middle-aged man (Riccardo Cucciolla), who is attempting to drive his sedated son to the hospital. Most of this uncomfortable, gritty film takes place within the car itself, allowing Bava to explore some seriously twisted character dynamics and deliver more than a couple of disturbing plot twists. The downbeat ending would have probably been a lot more shocking in 1974 than it is now, but it still packs a nasty punch.

If *Rabid Dogs* can be likened to any other Bava film, it would have to be *Twitch of the Death Nerve*, historically the first real body count movie and the only other film in the maestro's canon to display the same level of pessimism for human nature. However, *Twitch*'s sick, playful undertones are discarded here for an unflinchingly bleak gaze at the underbelly of man's killer instinct for money. Despite the less-than-groundbreaking storyline, Bava milks the situation for all it's worth and draws on the same eerie, desolate European countryside atmosphere later depicted unforgettably in George Sluizer's *The Vanishing*. Stylistically, *Rabid Dogs* bears little resemblance to the candy-coloured fantasias of his other films; here, he indulges in

R

some truly odd touches, such as the intercutting of a pinball game to symbolize a character's conflicted mental state during a crucial violent moment. It would have been interesting to see this with an audience, and whether it would have received any distribution outside of Italy at the time will regrettably never be known.

The acting is almost too good for comfort, with George Eastman (Luigi Montefiori), best known for his roles in Joe D'Amato exploiters such as *The Grim Reaper* and *Absurd*, actually delivering an effective performance as the pathetic, stupid, and pathological "32," while Lander (who was primarily responsible for the film's restoration) makes a very convincing woman in peril. Mention must also be made of Stelvio Cipriani's terrific, jittery '70's crime score; it's one of his finest efforts.

Lucertola Media, best known for their incredible releases of classic European horror and sleaze scores on CD, has done a first-rate job of presenting the film, with abundant extras including the 1997 release trailer and biographies and filmographies for the major cast and crew. The numerous beautiful Bava posters are worth it alone. The nicely letterboxed transfer shows off the stark cinematography to good effect, though the notes explain the colour had to be toned down due to the various source materials cobbled together to create a complete release print. While some minor signs of wear are evident now and then, it's nothing too distracting. The very clear sound adds to the increasing claustrophobia.

The film is subtitled in English (German subtitles are included as well), though the font type, while legible, is almost too small for comfort. A later version from Astro omits many of the supplements but features a somewhat more stable transfer, colour-wise.

RABID GRANNIES

Colour, 1989, 89m. / Directed by Emmanuel Kervyn / Starring Florine Elslande, Danielle Daven / Troma (US R1 NTSC), Laser Paradise (Germany R2 PAL), Japan Shock (Holland R2 PAL)

If Peter Jackson and Walerian Borowczyk decided to drop acid and do a bottom of the barrel zombie film with wretched dubbing, the end result would look a lot like *Rabid Grannies*, a trashy, gory epic that starts off like gangbusters but degenerates into a repetitive, plotless series of gory dismemberment gags. Of

course, this should be enough to pass the time quite nicely for undiscriminating gorehounds.

Here's the entire plot: a bunch of relatives convene for a party at the home of two sweet old aunties. An evil old woman arrives at the gate and delivers a mysterious box, which the aunties promptly open. Aunties turn into bald, clawed demons, running around and tearing everyone to pieces. The end.

Though hardly a great stylist, Belgian director Emmanuel Kervyn does a decent job of keeping things moving at a nice and bloody clip. Too bad the headache inducing, haphazard dubbing ruins most of the admittedly eye-catching visual atmosphere; turn down the volume, however, and at least the avalanche of special effects makes for a decent party film.

Unfortunately, Troma's DVD is something of a mixed bag. The film itself looks better than it ever has, not counting a few nicks and speckles inherent to the (cheaply done) negative. Unfortunately, the only existing materials in prime condition, at least in Troma's vaults, are severely edited from the original Belgian running time, deleting much of the juicy splatter in the process. The Troma VHS release was almost bloodless, and while the DVD reinstates a little of the gore, it's still far less complete than the edition on Danish video, which actually clocks in at 81 minutes thanks to the vagaries of SECAM conversion. Don't despair, though; most of the gore is included on the DVD - as a separate reel of gory outtakes. This long, long sampler of limb-tearing mayhem includes most of the deleted footage, though for some reason the last shot of the film is still trimmed down to omit the sound of an arm being torn off.

Other DVD extras include an almost incomprehensible commentary by Kervyn (though it does contain some nice nuggets of trivia if you pay attention), as well as a funny outtake reel of flubs and gags. To round things off, you get the usual Troma tour and T.I.T. test, as well as a dippy interview spoof with a "real rabid granny." It's really a shame that Troma couldn't present this film as it was originally intended, but the full version can be located in Germany as part of the "Red Edition" series- alas, without an English language option - and in Dutch with English subtitles as part of the Japan Shock series.

THE RAGE: CARRIE II

Colour, 1999, 104m. / Directed by Katt Shea / Starring Emily Bergl, Jason London / MGM (US R1 NTSC, UK R2 PAL) / WS (1.85:1) / DD5.1

Pillaging the horror classics of the '60s and '70s became a popular sport in the late '90s, thanks to the mudballs volleyed at *Psycho* and *The Haunting*, among others. Horror sequels have become big business, too, thanks to postmodern teen slashers and the recent reappearances of Chucky and company. So the next logical step would be... a sequel to *Carrie*? Well, that may not be exactly what the world needed, but that's what viewers got. Judging from the lukewarm box office reception (and icy critical response), another sequel probably won't be coming around the corner anytime soon, but all things considered, *The Rage: Carrie 2* could have been a lot worse and, on its own terms, offers some decent thrills along the way.

Rachel Lang (Emily Bergl), a standard goth girl who finds herself isolated from the popular kids at school, has a secret. Like the infamous Carrie White, she can move objects with her mind, but luckily self-control has kept this little talent well hidden. Her mother wound up in an asylum after finding this out, so Rachel's extreme denial keeps her shuttered away, kept under the thumb of her foster parents. When her best friend, Lisa (*American Beauty*'s Mena Suvari), commits suicide after being used by a heartless jock in a sexual "points" contest, Rachel realizes the truth about her cold-hearted predatory surroundings and decides to do something about it. She strikes up an unlikely romance with Jesse (*Dazed and Confused*'s Jason London), who tells his football buddies to back off and leave Rachel alone. Unfortunately, Jesse's jilted girlfriend, Tracy (Charlotte Lopez), cooks up a scheme with the diabolical jocks to teach Rachel a lesson. Of course, they never counted on Rachel's secret power...

A strange mixture of the powerful and the mundane, *The Rage* starts off uneasily with a gag-inducing retread of the usual idiotic high school clichés (all but one of the jocks are evil, cool girls are the devil incarnate, outsiders are all trendy and really better than everyone else, etc., etc.). Fortunately, the film pulls itself up thanks to the unexpected romantic element, which could have carried the film completely had it been developed even further. Bergl and London are both excellent in their roles and alone make this worth seeing; without this much-needed core of human warmth in the centre of the film, the rest would simply collapse into a trivial heap. Director Shea (a Roger Corman alumnus who picked up shooting after Robert Mandel) exhibits her usual traits as a director, with haunting, surprising scenes alternating with dull,

television-style ones. (See *Poison Ivy* for a textbook example.) She handles all of the actors very well and pulls off the gory climax with enough panache to make one wonder how on earth it managed to get an R rating. The interesting last minute shock is also skilfully delivered, and the use of black and white footage to represent Rachel's telekinetic moments is used with taste and restraint.

While *The Rage* could have functioned perfectly well on its own terms, the script unfortunately trivializes itself at too many turns by trying to deliberately link back to the first film. Flashbacks (both visual and aural) abound, and thanks to the laughably superfluous use of Amy Irving as Sue Snell (the original's lone survivor, now a high school counsellor), the plot even tosses in an unnecessary twist linking Rachel directly to Carrie. These debits aside, the film is at least worth a rental and may be worth owning for the teen-horror crowd.

Not surprisingly, MGM's DVD is an immaculate showcase for the film, with a delicately rendered anamorphic transfer and a spacious 5.1 sound mix. The plentiful extras include commentary by Shea and a handful of deleted scenes, also introduced by the director. Most of these scenes are basically filler, though at least one does explain Rachel's current relationship with her mother. An alternate last scene is also included and was thankfully jettisoned from the final cut. Strangely, the theatrical trailer is conspicuously absent.

RAINBOW BRIDGE

Colour, 1968, 127m. / Directed by Chuck Wein / Starring Jimi Hendrix / Rhino (US R1 NTSC), International Licensing (UK R2 PAL)

You'd have to look far and wide to find a more excessive piece of trippy cinema than this delirious ode to everyone's favourite booze and drugs guitar god, Jimi Hendrix. Of course, personal taste will dictate your reaction to this free-form exploration of Hendrix's music performed live in Hawaii (including the standards "Purple Haze," "Foxy Lady," and a lot of improvised sessions), which is embellished with tons of psychedelic visuals and marginally related fantasy sequences. However, the Hendrix performance footage comes after what seems like hours of not too deep philosophizing about our alien heritage, governmental conspiracies, and other pre-*X-Files* ramblings. It's all pretty funny, though, if you're in the right mood. Fans of late-'60s bizarre cinema *a la*

Something Weird Video should prove to be the most appreciative audience for this unintentionally knee-slapping flower power exploitation. *Rainbow Bridge* has never enjoyed much praise from critics; you could say this is to Hendrix what *Magical Mystery Tour* is to the Beatles: fans will love it (at least the last third, anyway), while the uninitiated need not apply.

The film has been long unavailable on home video and even was released in various edited, almost unwatchable editions. Rhino's vivid restoration contains the full 127 minutes version, plus an additional 10 minutes of alternate trailers for the film. Considering the extreme low budget and the less than optimal source materials, this DVD goes a long way towards making the film more enjoyable not to watch, if not necessarily more coherent. The mono sound quality is the best available, but it's a shame a stereo master doesn't exist somewhere to show off Jimi's scorching guitar gymnastics at their finest; the mind boggles to think of what a Dolby Digital 5.1 remix would sound like. For the impatient, the UK disc also offers the option of skipping over the "story" and going straight to the songs.

RASPUTIN THE MAD MONK

Colour, 1966, 91m. / Directed by Don Sharp / Starring Christopher Lee, Barbara Shelley / Anchor Bay (US R1 NTSC) / WS (2.10:1) (16:9)

Stretching out a bit in its quest to cover all of the major historical monsters, Hammer Films turned to the unlikely subject of Rasputin, the mesmeric monk whose exploits inspired a number of book and film treatments. Obviously the only choice to play the lead was Christopher Lee, whose imposing stature and dynamic classical persona could forcefully bring the evildoer to the screen. While the film is rarely noted as one of Hammer's best, horror devotees should find enough to keep them entertained, particularly by counting all of the crossover elements from *Dracula, Prince of Darkness*, which was shot back to back with this production.

Rasputin (Christopher Lee), a monk living in Czarist Russia, leads an outward life of religious devotion which masks his true nature: a bestial, murdering lout who uses his mysterious powers of hypnotism and his gift for healing as tools of manipulation. In St. Petersburg, he uses the lovely Sonia (Barbara Shelley) to infiltrate the royal family

of Nicholas II and exercise his wicked control over Russia itself. However, political forces begin to brew and conspire to bring an end to the monk's subversive reign.

Conveying all the blood and thunder one would expect from a "golden age" Hammer Film, *Rasputin* barely qualifies as a horror film *per se* but includes a number of grisly elements, such as a hand amputation and acid in the face (a very popular '60s act of cinematic violence). Lee is at his best here, and the lovely redheaded Barbara Shelley (*The Gorgon*) always makes a watchable female lead. Director Don Sharp does his usual efficient job, though the results aren't quite up to the lyrical savagery of, say, *Kiss of the Vampire*.

Anchor Bay's DVD looks similar to the Elite laserdisc; as noted in many other sources, the Cinemascope image was trimmed at the sides per Bill Lustig's request to 2.10:1 to avoid some distracting curvature at the edges. The framing still looks fine, with only some marginal cropping in a few scenes. The transfer is colourful though a bit over-bright; turning down the brightness control gives the film a much more robust and effective appearance. The mono audio is clean and clear throughout, though not particularly overwhelming. Extras include a running audio commentary track with Lee (in fine witty form), Shelley, Francis Matthews, and Suzan Farmer, all of whom take the listener on a thorough journey through the making of a Hammer title during its heyday. The theatrical trailer and two TV spots (coupled with *The Reptile*) are also thrown in, along with another fun *World of Hammer* episode, this time focusing on Christopher Lee in all his heroic and villainous guises.

RAVENOUS

Colour, 1999, 100m. / Directed by Antonia Bird / Starring Guy Pearce, Robert Carlyle, Jeremy Davies / Fox (US R1 NTSC, UK R2 PAL) / WS (2.35:1) / DD5.1

In the mountains of California, Captain John Boyd (Guy Pearce), a decorated soldier from the Mexican-American War, is sent by his superior officers to a wintry outpost called Fort Spencer. There he finds himself surrounded by a host of misfits, including a drunken former veterinarian for a doctor (Stephen Spinella), an ice cold demoted officer named Reich (Neal McDonough), and a recreational pot smoker, Cleaves (David Arquette). When some of the men leave to fetch provisions their Indian guide, Martha (Sheila Tousey), Boyd and the company buckle down for a long, cold night. Excitement arrives in the form of a shambling, near-dead stranger who appears at the window. The men take him inside, tend to his wounds, and finally revive him. The new arrival, Colquhoun (Robert Carlyle), explains that he is a man of God on a wagon trail who found himself and his fellow passengers stranded in the wilderness. Unable to escape, the party turned to their cattle and horses for food; when the humans began dying off, the survivors came up with a grisly source for nourishment. The leader, a diabolical colonel named Ives, showed every sign of turning on both his wife and Colquhoun, who took to the hills in an effort to save his life. A local Indian informs Boyd that anyone who consumes the flesh of another man becomes a Weendigo - a demon who gains strength from human flesh and whose hunger cannot be satiated until he is destroyed. Not surprisingly, Boyd - who already had a brief encounter with accidental cannibalism during his harrowing "heroic" war experience - does not take this news very well. Boyd and the others pack up and, with Colquhoun in tow, head into the mountains to save the remaining members of the ill-fated trip, but fate has quite a few surprises in store for them.

At first glance, the chilling and blood-drenched *Ravenous* seems a bizarre choice for British director Antonia Bird, best known to US audiences for her controversial clergy drama, *Priest* (also with Carlyle, and cut to shreds in the US by Miramax, like most of their other films). However, the troubled production (on which she was the third director) benefited greatly from her talents, as she skilfully builds the story to a nerve-wracking degree of intensity by the end of the first third. The unappealing trailers and poster art tried to pass this off as an arty gore comedy, but the laughs here are dark and sardonic at best, eliciting more sick chuckles than hearty guffaws.

Pearce, doing another impressive American accent after *L.A. Confidential*, and *The Full Monty*'s Carlyle make a dynamic pair of foes and serve up a fascinating study in contrasting acting styles. Carlyle's psychopathic performance works especially well and builds up a solid sense of dread even when the man himself is offscreen. The solid supporting cast, including fine bits by Jeremy Davies ("He was licking me!") and Arquette in a glorified cameo, integrate believably into the off-kilter atmosphere without drawing attention to themselves.

The beautiful scenery, filmed mostly in Czechoslovakia, doubles nicely for the US wilds, lending a genuine sense of isolation and untamed savagery while perfectly driving home the film's message: European colonialism, most obviously in America, drew its strength entirely from callously feeding off of other human beings. To top it off, Michael Nyman and Blur's Damon Albarn provide a dazzling experimental score that could easily drive mainstream audiences nuts. If this all sounds too heady, have no fear; *Ravenous* is also a terrific little horror film, packed with shocking violence (especially remarkable considering its R rating) and a number of suspenseful, creepy set pieces. How a film like this managed to get financed and produced by a major US studio remains one of those bizarre little miracles that one should probably accept without any questions.

Originally announced as a feature-only DVD by Fox, the disc was thankfully upgraded to special edition status after protests by the filmmakers and the small but hopefully growing cult of loyal viewers. The DVD is one of their more satisfying efforts, a particularly welcome gesture considering this is a "small" film that very few actually saw during its brief run through the multiplexes. The scope transfer (non-anamorphic, alas, but still beautiful) accurately captures the landscape shots and bizarre character framing (note the "manifest destiny" scene!), while the 5.1 mix packs quite a punch, particularly during a key slaughter sequence early in the film. Extras include the US trailer and TV spot, production design and costume drawings, a nine minute reel of deleted scenes (mostly dialogue involving Jeffrey Jones, aka Ed Rooney, and McDonough), and a fun little Easter Egg.

The real coup, though, is no less than three audio commentary tracks, all of which provide various bits of insight into the film. Interestingly, these tracks were obviously designed to play off each other, as the participants frequently refer to the other tracks being recorded. On the first, Bird and Albarn go through the elaborate production history of the film and dash off a few nice anecdotes, such as how Carlyle got Pearce sloppy drunk for a pivotal scene near the end. Bird also relates some of the petty minor changes dictated to avoid an NC-17 rating and how the studio altered the film's final shot, which still stands just fine the way it is. Robert Carlyle goes solo for the second track, in which his appealing Scottish brogue spins his own experiences and interpretations regarding the film. In the third and loosest of the bunch, Jones and writer Ted Griffin explain how the story drifted through the Hollywood machinery and, like everyone else, emphasize the difficult but rewarding process of shooting the actual film.

R

The efforts of all involved were clearly worth it, and all of the participants' enthusiasm and affection for the film add immeasurably to appreciating the final work. While the movie itself may not quite be to everyone's taste (sorry, had to throw a food pun in there somewhere), *Ravenous* should entertain horror fans and arthouse crowds with strong stomachs who don't mind some intelligence, surrealism, and diabolical wit mixed in with their cheap thrills. And you'll never look at stew quite the same way again.

RAZOR BLADE SMILE

Colour, 1998, 101m. / Directed by Jake West / Starring Eileen Daly, David Warbeck / A-Pix (US R1 NTSC) / WS (1.85:1) / DD4.0

An amusing little time killer, *Razor Blade Smile* marks the big(ish) screen debut of Eileen Daly, the Redemption poster girl with a voice that would sedate Quentin Tarantino. While no classic by any means, the film is at least a few cuts above the tedious lesbian-gore chic promos for which Daly remains best known, though she displays all the acting finesse of Pamela Anderson Lee on a particularly bad day.

Lilith Silver (Daly), a leather-clad vampire hitwoman, got her fang-chomping start when she tried to save her boyfriend in a duel and wound up on the wrong end of a pistol. A vampire "saved" her by transforming her into one of the undead, and now she passes the centuries by offing humans for money. Apparently being assigned targets takes the nasty decision-making process out of planning for dinner, and she covers up her feeding rituals by firing a few bullets into her victims' throats. In her off time, she hangs out at the local goth club where vamp wannabes lecture about what they think vampires are like, much to Lilith's amusement. However, things get complicated when a nasty sect called the Illuminati (signified by their cultists' gumball machine eyeball rings) get ticked off at Lilith for bumping off a few members, and she finds herself in deep trouble. To make matters worse, one of the cultists, Officer Price, keeps arresting her and chasing her around with a stake. Lilith manages to deal with the stress by engaging in a couple of hilariously gratuitous sex scenes and baring her fangs at the camera a lot.

Most obviously, *Razor Blade Smile* lacks a single original bone in its body; after the opening sequence, which owes more than a tad to Roger Vadim's *Blood and Roses*, the plot proceeds to lift

entire chunks from *Blade, The Hunger*, and most obviously, John Landis' *Innocent Blood*. This quibble aside (along with Daly's aforementioned lack of thespian skills), director West has fashioned a great looking film for next to no money. The pace is fast, the visuals lush, the soundtrack involving, and there's even a nifty (if highly illogical) surprise ending, which, now that you know, may not come as much of a surprise. Italian horror and Brit sex film regular David Warbeck pops in for one of his last appearances as "the horror film man" and explains what PCP is to our not very bright detective. The kitschy James Bond-inspired opening credits are a blast, too, not to mention the hysterically foul-mouthed end titles song.

A-Pix has done a surprisingly lavish DVD presentation for such an obscure horror film. Aside from the (useless) video trailer and a few other A-Pix samplers (for *Bleeders*, etc.), the disc presents the film in what appears to be an overmatted 1.85:1 transfer. The quasi-artsy framing makes it impossible to gauge what this was supposed to look like originally, but some vital information (like a close-up of a tarot card) appears to be missing. The basic surround mix is well handled, considering, and the techno score should keep goth fans tapping their feet contentedly. Inexplicably, the transfer itself runs at the incorrect speed (24 frames per second rather than the 25 fps at which it was shot).

REBECCA

B&W, 1940, 133m. / Directed by Alfred Hitchcock / Starring Joan Fontaine, Laurence Olivier / Criterion, Anchor Bay (US R1 NTSC), PT Video (UK R2 PAL)

Following his less than warmly received 1939 adaptation of Daphne Du Maurier's *Jamaica Inn*, Alfred Hitchcock surprisingly chose another of the esteemed mystery writer's novels for his first American project under the supervision of David O. Selznick. The result, of course, became one of the Master of Suspense's most enduring and popular creations, though it's rarely cited as a good representative of his style. Perhaps the "woman's picture" stigma associated with this genre has prevented this film from the historical recognition of *Psycho* or *Rear Window*, but in terms of both storytelling and technical craftsmanship, *Rebecca* can scarcely be faulted and has aged as magnificently as any Hollywood product.

A young woman (Joan Fontaine), whose name is never given, meets the brooding, attractive, and wealthy Maxim De Winter (Laurence Olivier) while serving as a paid companion on the Riviera. Much to her employer's disapproval, our heroine takes off with Maxim and becomes his second wife; apparently, the first Mrs. De Winter, Rebecca, died in a mysterious boating accident. Upon her arrival at Manderley, the De Winter home, the second Mrs. De Winter receives a cool reception from the main housekeeper, Mrs. Danvers (Judith Anderson, walking off with the film in her pocket). Apparently Mrs. Danvers had more than a slight obsession with Rebecca and takes every opportunity to remind the new wife of her inferiority in every possible respect. However, a few less than pleasant skeletons in the closet begin to emerge, and the newlyweds find their happiness and even their lives in jeopardy as the ghosts of the past begin to return with a vengeance.

Fontaine's performance, beginning as nervous and submissive but gaining confidence as the dark events begin to unfurl, provides the emotional anchor for what could have been a routine Gothic potboiler. Everyone involved lifts this tale to the highest notch of slick professionalism, ranging from Franz Waxman's beautiful, eerie score to Hitchcock's subtle manipulation of spatial relationships and décor details (note Rebecca's embroidering). Though Rebecca is naturally deceased before the film even begins, her presence consumes the entire film and channels through the unforgettable Mrs. Danvers, leading to the memorable and often imitated fiery climax. While Olivier does a fine job doing a rich twist on his tragic hero persona from *Wuthering Heights* and George Sanders provides his usual sardonic and nasty wit, the women both seen and unseen definitely carry this film, establishing most of the central conflicts along the way.

Criteron's transfer of *Rebecca* corrects most of the damage done to this gem over the years, with most of the image meticulously restored and featuring a more robust contrast scale than even the lovely Anchor Bay DVD. The sound has also been noticeably cleaned up, with the opening musical strains freed from background noise and hiss. The two-disc Criterion version (which features overly severe windowboxed credits) retains all of the laserdisc extras, including hosts of auditions, interviews, costume drawings, test footage, and voluminous text studies. The UK disc features the restored transfer with the same Hitchcock-related extras as their release of *Notorious*. Note: *Rebecca* was Hitchcock's only Best Picture Academy Award winner, though at the time only the producer received the award. Thus, Hitch would have to wait until his honorary Irving G. Thalberg award before he could have a statuette of his own.

THE RED SHOES

Colour, 1948, 134m. / Directed and Produced by Michael Powell & Emeric Pressburger / Starring Anton Wallbrook, Marius Goring, Moira Shearer / Criterion (US R1 NTSC), Carlton (UK R2 PAL)

Long regarded as one of the finest British films and a watershed in the art of Technicolor cinematography, *The Red Shoes* inspired countless female viewers to take up ballet but, more significantly, also inspired generations of moviegoers to accept art as an integral part of one's life. Of the numerous masterpieces by Powell and Pressburger, *The Red Shoes* remains the best-loved and continues to enjoy a growing critical reputation.

The opening scenes of the film quickly establish the central theme: people will do anything for the sake of art. Impassioned theatregoers quickly flood into their seats for the debut of a new ballet; comically, they all claim to be there for different reasons - to hear the music, to fawn over the dancers, etc. As the show begins, we are introduced to Boris Lermontov (Wallbrook), a talented but controlling impresario who enjoys full control over his protégées' lives. After the show, he arranges for his next show to present a gentry girl, Victoria Page (stunning redheaded Shearer, making her debut), whose desire to dance overwhelms all social obstacles. Julian Craster, a talented young composer, writes the score for the next ballet, an adaptation of Hans Christian Andersen's "The Red Shoes," about a woman whose acquisition of a pair of a magical red shoes carries a heavy price: she dances herself to death. Julian and Victoria fall in love, much to Boris' consternation, but their happiness is tortured by her longing desire to return to the stage. Art and reality tragically merge together as Victoria finds herself unable to reconcile the two greatest loves in her life.

In a few fortunate films, all of the necessary elements come together perfectly, and this is one of those occasions - acting, music, writing, and imagery all fuse into a cohesive, magical whole. While the grimmer aspects of the story (Victoria really does suffer!) have turned off some critics, this film's ever-growing cult following focuses on the positive, cathartic aspects of the story, particularly the nobility of sacrifice for one's ideals. The central "Red Shoes Ballet" is a marvel of cinematic craftsmanship and has understandably influenced countless other directors over the years (Martin Scorsese, who participates in the lively commentary here with Shearer and Jack Cardiff, counts it as a personal favourite and even presents his collection

R

of memorabilia for one of the supplementary features). Cardiff's brilliant use of colour ranks with his equally amazing accomplishment on Powell and Pressburger's *Black Narcissus*, and Shearer simply looks radiant in every frame (unfortunately her career, like Powell's, came to a screeching halt after *Peeping Tom*).

The Red Shoes has generally fared well on video and TV over the years, but the Criterion edition mastered from the original negative is a stunner. The amazing clarity and vividness of colour don't really burst forth until a few minutes into film (the first scenes are deliberately shot with a sort of gauzy overcast), and the results rank up there with the best of the MGM Technicolor musical restorations. A few very mild print blemishes aside, this is very close to a pristine presentation.

The DVD includes the same extras as the laserdisc special edition (but at a much lower price), with a few new surprises thrown in as well. The theatrical trailer (amusingly cropped from 1.85:1 so that Shearer is described onscreen as possessing a "bewitching loveline" instead of "loveliness") and Jeremy Irons reading excerpts from the film novelization are nice little bonuses, but the real point of fascination is the Powell/Pressburger filmography, which includes brief snippets from all of their films together. Seeing crisp DVD excerpts from *Tales of Hoffman* and *A Matter of Life and Death* is enough to make a film buff's mouth water, but even more compelling are the clips from films currently unavailable; a letterboxed fragment from the sadly unavailable *Oh Rosalinda!* looks especially appealing. More bare bones is the Carlton UK DVD, which features the trailer and a 25-minute featurette in which surviving crew and relatives discuss making the film.

THE RED VIOLIN

Colour, 1999, 132m. / Directed by François Girard / Starring Greta Scacchi, Samuel L. Jackson, Jason Flemyng / Universal (US R1 NTSC) / WS (1.85:1) (16:9) / DD5.1/DTS, FilmFour (UK R2 PAL) / WS (1.78:1) (16:9), Alliance (Canada R1 NTSC) / DD2.0

An intricate, elegantly mounted puzzle laced with macabre surprises, *The Red Violin* marks one of the few occasions in film history in which the central character is an object, not a living human being. Both entertaining and drenched in historical and artistic details, the film ambitiously traces the titular musical instrument across the globe and through the centuries in a bizarre, head-spinning chronicle of chance and human frailty.

In Cremona, Italy during the late 1600s, a master craftsman, Nicolo Bussotti (Carlo Cecchi), prepares a violin as a gift for the unborn son of his beautiful expectant wife, Anna (Irene Grazioli). Their housekeeper provides a tarot reading for Anna, which actually applies to the violin itself, foretelling a rich and dangerous life filled with trials and a wide array of people. Possibly cursed, the crimson violin passes into the hands of an orphaned music prodigy at an Austrian monastery. Renowned French composing legend Georges Poussin (Jean-Luc Bideau) brings the boy to Vienna; however, the ailing boy shows an unnatural, almost supernatural attachment to the instrument - to such a degree that he even sleeps with the violin in his bed. The next owner, Frederick Pope (Jason Flemyng), is a passionate and perhaps demonic virtuoso who rises to fame and carries on a torrid affair with Victoria Byrd (Greta Scacchi), a beautiful novelist. However, she becomes resentful of the violin's presence, resorting to extreme behaviour in a mixture of jealousy and revenge. In the 20th Century, the violin passes to Xiang Pei (Sylvia Chang), a Communist party official in Shanghai who cannot reconcile herself to the demands of her comrades to destroy all symbols of useless Western culture. Finally, in the present day (and the film's entire framing device), the Red Violin turns up in a prestigious Montreal auction where its authenticity is being determined by Charles Morritz (Samuel L. Jackson), a brusque man whose lifelong quest for Bussotti's last masterpiece uncovers a strange, disturbing secret.

Like a rich collection of short stories, *The Red Violin* succeeds by offering a wide palette of textures and characterizations which still manage to coalesce into a satisfying whole. The auction structuring device allows the film to deftly slip between time periods without disrupting its dreamlike flow, pausing along the way for some wry commentary on modern society's materialistic fixations with status and possession (often overlooking true value in the process). Though a somewhat foregone conclusion, the tantalizing finale really poses more questions than it answers. As with the entire film, the ending suggests that morality and fate are entirely subjective, with people often projecting their destinies onto objects as a means of propelling themselves through life.

Director Girard (*32 Short Films about Glenn Gould*) and writer/actor Don McKellar (*Exotica, eXistenZ*) admirably capture the atmosphere and period detail of each story along the way, with Jackson and Scacchi (who will apparently keep doing nude scenes for eternity) offering some of their best work to date. However, the Shanghai segment really steals the film thanks to some beautiful visual storytelling and Chang's expressive face, which speaks volumes where dialogue cannot. John Corigliano (*Altered States*) contributes his first film score in over fifteen years, and thankfully the wait was worth it; coupled with musician Joshua Bell's remarkable performances in each story, this *Violin* truly sings. Fans of less highbrow elements should also find plenty to enjoy, including the unexpected supernatural elements, fairly heated love scenes, and some startling, gruesome twists.

Universal's DVD of *The Red Violin* made history as one of the first discs to incorporate both a Dolby Digital 5.1 and a DTS track, which makes it an ideal showcase for audiophiles. As would be expected, the soundtrack offers a non-stop barrage of panning effects, though the video looks impressive as well. Deliberately shot in a range of colour schemes, the film no doubt proved to be a technical nightmare to transfer (and failed mightily on the full frame Canadian DVD). However, the image quality on the Universal disc is consistently strong if not the kind of demo material found on some major studio titles. Interestingly, the title colour only appears moderately throughout the film, with a much heavier emphasis on grey and blue occupying the visuals. Extras include the usual cursory production notes and bios, as well as the US theatrical trailer.

REPO MAN

Colour, 1984, 92m. / Directed by Alex Cox / Starring Emilio Estevez, Harry Dean Stanton, Tracey Walter / Anchor Bay (US R1 NTSC) / WS (1.85:1) (16:9) / DD5.1

"So what's it all about?" This question commonly pops up from first time viewers of *Repo Man*, one of the Reagan era's great anti-establishment cult films which, along with oddities like *Liquid Sky*, dragged early '80s underground sensibilities into mainstream acceptance. It's also a whole lot of fun and, unlike many of its contemporaries, has aged quite gracefully.

While a plot summary is only marginally related to this film's charm, here we go... Aimless slacker teen Otto (Emilio Estevez) walks out on his menial job at a grocery store and, through a twist of fate, hooks up with Bud (Harry Dean Stanton), a "repo man" who repossesses cars for a living. At first Otto recoils at the thought of joining this oddball lifestyle (in which, according to the speed-snorting Bud, the goal is to intentionally get into tense situations). Otto comes to know his fellow repo men, such as rambling Zen-freak Miller (Tracey Walter) and Lite (Sy Richardson). Things take a turn for the weird when the office gets a report for a high repo reward on a Chevy Malibu, which contains a Kiss Me Deadly style piece of mysterious glowing cargo in its trunk. Otto learns more about the target from UFO fanatic Leila (Olivia Barash), who shows him a photograph of four alien bodies connected not indirectly to the maverick car now being driven by an unhinged scientist (Fox Harris). It all spirals downhill from there, with a mind-bending finale not to be believed.

While director Alex Cox went on to acclaim with *Sid and Nancy* before alienating many fans with *Walker*, *Straight to Hell*, and *Highway Patrolman*, he will always be best remembered for this film. Financed by The Monkees' Michael Nesmith, this is as much a sonic experience as a visual one, with a delirious punk soundtrack kicked off by Iggy Pop's catch main title theme. While Estevez has his best role ever as Otto, this is really Stanton's film all the way. His laconic delivery of the Repo Man creed and his droopy-eyed, world weary demeanour couldn't be better, and this is a rare cult film with young viewers that provides unique, interesting roles for actors of all ages and races. (And look out for the repo secretary, played by the great Vonetta McGee from *Blacula* and *The Eiger Sanction*, and a fleeting appearance by legit and hardcore porn actress Angelique Pettyjohn, star of *Mad Doctor of Blood Island*). The next time you feel the '80s were just a cinematic wasteland, pop this one in for a nice antidote. And you'll never look at John Wayne quite the same way again.

Anchor Bay's DVD of *Repo Man* looks excellent as expected, with appropriately bleary white tones approximating the look of a Los Angeles sliding fast into decay. All of the quirky visual details are vividly rendered, from the hilarious food and drink labels to the odd touches in the background designs and outfits. The 5.1 remix is only as good as the original sound material, which is limited but effective enough when the music kicks in. As for extras, you get the original theatrical and video trailers (it was released almost simultaneously in both formats, as well as shown on cable), a bouncy commentary track with Cox, Nesmith, Richardson, actors Del Zamora and Zander Schloss, and casting director Victoria Thomas, along with the usual talent bios. The film is also available in a deluxe collector's tin, packaged in a jewel case along with a booklet, poster reproduction, and soundtrack CD, with an amusing license plate design for the outer case. The only debit, and it's a minor one, is the absence of the notorious alternate TV version which, much like *Fast Times at Ridgemont High*, adds several unused scenes and concocts some hilarious new terms to replace the strongest profanity.

THE REPTILE

Colour, 1966, 90m. / Directed by John Gilling / Starring Noel Willman, Jennifer Daniel / Anchor Bay (US R1 NTSC) / WS (1.85:1) (16:9)

Featuring the same director and much of the same cast and crew from *Plague of the Zombies, The Reptile* was originally intended to belong with that film as a kind of "Cornwall terror" double feature that sadly was never meant to be. Interestingly, many of the new cast members are carryovers from *Kiss of the Vampire*, making *The Reptile* a kind of visual fusion between Hammer's different styles of monster movies.

A series of mysterious murders in a small village leads a victim's brother, Harry Spalding (Ray Barrett), to arrive and investigate along with his wife, Valerie (Jennifer Daniel). After snooping around and listening to local gossip, the couple makes the acquaintance of the secretive Dr. Franklyn (Noel Willman), who resides in a lonely estate with his young daughter, Anna (Jacqueline Pearce). Legend has it that the creature prowling the countryside is actually a strange reptile woman who sheds her skin, transforming from a seemingly human appearance into a venomous, deadly monster. Who could it possibly be?

Though powered by John Gilling's usual strong visual and narrative skills, *The Reptile* only occasionally manages the full throttle force of such other Gilling titles as *Plague* and *Mania*. That said, the film does manage to conjure up a sinister, magical atmosphere unlike any other, and Pearce makes for a fascinating, sympathetic character despite her clumsy (but oddly endearing) monster makeup. The actual horror content is fairly low, confined to a few brief and subdued attack sequences, but the overall effect of the film was strong enough that Ken Russell even used it as a partial inspiration for *Lair of the White Worm*, notably the sensual snake charming sequence.

Like *Plague, The Reptile* resembles its previous Elite laserdisc version but in this case suffers somewhat from the added clarity of DVD. The opening in particular swarms with grain, not helped by the inaccurate day for night tinting, but the image improves dramatically during the daylight sequences and those haunting, dusky fireside shots. It's a perfectly acceptable presentation, but don't expect to be astonished by any major revelations in the image quality. The disc includes the usual supplementary goodies: the theatrical and 30 second spots (with *Rasputin the Mad Monk*), as well as a juicy episode of *World of Hammer*, entitled "Vamps" (focusing on female bloodsuckers, naturally).

REQUIEM FOR A VAMPIRE

Colour, 1971, 88m. / Directed by Jean Rollin / Starring Marie-Pierre Castel, Mireille Dargent / Image (US R0 NTSC) / WS (1.66:1)

Jean Rollin's most mainstream effort at the time of its release, *Requiem for a Vampire* nevertheless displays his obsessions as clearly as his most experimental work. Devoid of any spoken dialogue for most of its running time, *Requiem* introduces for the first time the beguiling twin girl characters who would later appear in such films as *Les Demoniaques* and, most blatantly, *Two Orphan Vampires*. Originally conceived and occasionally screened under the title of *Vierges et vampires (Virgins and Vampires)*, the film has remained most strongly associated with the *Requiem* title due most likely to its slow, sombre pace and palpable sense of enchanted, erotic dread. Unfortunately, this impression was pretty much blasted to pieces when Harry Novak trimmed it down for a US grindhouse release as *Caged Virgins*, though it did sport a fairly nifty poster. Now audiences can toss out those old SECAM transfers and cruddy bootlegs to finally savour what is by far the most complete and ravishing presentation of this film to date.

Two blonde, pigtailed girls (Castel and Dargent), escaping from a robbery they have just committed, are forced to flee through the countryside after their car breaks down. Decked in clown costumes (?), the girls wind up at a desolate castle presided over by a cult of vampires. Though essentially a reprise of the plot from *Shiver of the Vampires*, this film further removes the tethers of standard narrative as the girls undergo a serious of sensual, hallucinatory encounters, the most notorious of which features a vampire bat dining on menstrual blood. The free form pacing eventually disintegrates into a nocturnal horrific montage as the girls find themselves succumbing completely to the will of the bloodsuckers.

Steadily paced and obviously personal, this "naive" film (to use Rollin's term) resembles an elegant jazz session played out in a twilight dreamworld, perhaps inspired to some degree by the Serge Gainsbourg song, "Requiem pour un Con," which was popular at the time. All of the actors function as visual elements, not recognizable human characters, though the girls make a fetching pair (Castel went on to do hardcore porn films with her twin sister.) While horror fans unaccustomed to Rollin's recurring visual images and bizarre symbolism may find the entire brew off-putting, followers of European film will be rejoicing at yet another fragile little masterpiece from Monsieur Rollin.

The image is accurately letterboxed and razor sharp; the transfer from the negative reveals countless layers of colour and visual texture completely invisible on all other editions. The craggy edges of stones in the castle walls, the delicate sheen of fabric and cloaks sliding over bare skin, and the warm glow of sunlight over a country field look beguiling and realistic. The DVD includes the original French soundtrack with optional English subtitles, as well as the US dubbed track (it frankly doesn't matter, given the rarity of spoken words in the film). The European trailer (English and French language versions) is included as well, though alas, no *Caged Virgins* trailer... [Note: Some have experienced compatibility problems between their systems and this disc, e.g., overly sensitive comb filter settings that cause extreme moiré patterns and colour distortion. Some recalibration may be necessary, including adjustment of your sharpness controls.]

RESURRECTION

Colour, 1999, 107m. / Directed by Russell Mulcahy / Starring Christopher Lambert, Barbara Tyson / Columbia (US R1 NTSC) / WS (1.85:1) (16:9) / DD5.1

Just as overwrought, awkward, and guiltily entertaining as you'd expect from the director and star of *Highlander*, the gruesome serial killer opus *Resurrection* (no relation to the Ellen Burstyn film) went straight to HBO in the United States without even a cursory appearance in

theatres. Though virtually the entire story structure and numerous individual scenes are hilariously plagiarized from *Seven*, *Resurrection* at least boasts a few novel twists and qualifies as one of the more outrageous recent entries in the over-stylish serial murder sweepstakes (*Kiss the Girls*, *The Bone Collector*, and so on).

While investigating a grisly murder in which a conscious victim's arm was removed, Detective John Prudhomme (Lambert) becomes intrigued by a number of oddities at the crime scene, such as numbers carved into the back of the corpse. Along with his joke-cracking partner, Andrew (good character actor Leland Orser), Prudhomme is then called in each subsequent Friday to investigate another similar murder in which a vital portion of the victim's body has been amputated. Prudhomme's wife, Sara (Barbara Tyson), is understandably not too happy with her husband's growing obsession with the case, particularly when he pieces together the killer's riddles and deduces that our humble maniac is trying to assemble his own Body of Christ in time for Easter Sunday.

More explicitly gory than its cinematic model, *Resurrection* lingers in morbid detail on the bodily havoc performed by its villain with a somnolent, *NYPD Blue*-style *vérité* approach - hardly original, but still effective. In fact, by the time the "shocking" revelation of the killer's goal has been revealed in all its decomposed glory, the effect is completely muffed by all the graphic carnage preceding it. Mulcahy's vertigo-inducing mobile camerawork still reveals his music video origins, though he makes atmospheric use of some dark, claustrophobic settings throughout. The religious killer's identity is revealed fairly early on, leaving most of the film to focus on the police procedural and pursuit aspects until the incredibly unlikely rooftop finale, which opens up more plot holes than you can count. Orser takes top acting honours for his relatively small amount of screen time, and Lambert is... well, Lambert. Since the film was mostly shot in Toronto, David Cronenberg pops up in a couple of brief scenes as a priest(!), ironic considering the serial killer's garb strongly resembles Cronenberg's zipperhead in *Nightbreed* crossed with the maniac from Sergio Martino's *Torso*. The Euro horror connection is quite obvious throughout, with the plot also lifting a few devices from *Pieces* and *Body Puzzle* and a few visuals plucked from *Cat o' Nine Tails* for good measure.

Columbia's DVD treats this "small" title with a surprising amount of respect. Creepy animated menus, a trailer, and TV spots, not to mention full frame or anamorphic widescreen editions, prove

R

their commitment to even the most unlikely releases. The image quality is fine if unspectacular, given the dark and smudgy nature of the film itself, but the 5.1 sound mix (much louder than the 2.0 one for some reason) features some startling rear effects ranging from splashing rain to weird ambient humming and rumbling. Mulcahy contributes a commentary track so dull it makes *In the Mouth of Madness* look high voltage in comparison; he often lets fifteen minutes or so drift by without making a comment. On the other hand, he does point out that a horrific leg cutting sequence was trimmed down to get an R rating, but the extreme bloodshed that remains will still satisfy demanding gorehounds.

All told, *Resurrection* may not be close to a classic but still merits an evening's rental for horror fans looking for a quick, grisly fix.

RETURN OF THE 5 DEADLY VENOMS
Colour, 1979, 106m. / Directed by Chang Cheh / Starring Chen Kuan Tai, Philip Kwok / Crash Cinema (US R1 NTSC) / WS (2.35:1)

A re-titling of *Can Que*, better known to Saturday afternoon viewers as *Crippled Avengers, Crippled Heroes,* and *Mortal Combat*, this above average and occasionally outrageous marital arts extravaganza has nothing to do with *The Five Deadly Venoms*. However, it does feature the same director and much of the same cast, so fans should be quite happy all the same, and the bizarre storyline which has been captivating chop socky fans for years continues to amaze even now.

Chen Kuan Tai (*Shaolin Executioner*) and marital arts stalwart Lo Meng (also in the astonishing *Super Ninjas* and the original *Venoms*) head the cast as two members of a four team squad of martial arts masters. Sound familiar? Well, not quite; all of the men bear some kind of physical handicap that they have managed to parlay into a unique fighting skill. The standard revenge plot aside (Chen got his hands cut off as a child, natch), *Return* delivers some high voltage action and the usual "flaws," e.g., laughable dubbing and a hyperactive use of the zoom lens. Some of the gore and close contact battering is surprisingly rough, indicating that Crash's designation of this as the uncut print is most likely true.

The DVD presentation of *Return of the 5 Deadly Venoms*, packaged and distributed by Crash Cinema, looks better than the earlier VHS release from the same company but will obviously never be demo

material. The opening credits have been replaced by a simple title card for some reason, and some scratches and scuffs appear throughout but never enough to mar enjoyment of the film. The scope framing looks too tight but is far more watchable than the blurry full frame versions familiar from TV showings, and the dubbed audio is, well, passable, given the source. The outrageous fight scenes really carry this film, and this DVD renders them about as well as could be expected. How can you not love a film with black metal hands that pop out and shoot deadly darts at their opponents? Not for all tastes, obviously, but if you want to venture beyond Bruce Lee, this is a good place to start.

RETURN OF THE LIVING DEAD 3
Colour, 1993, 93m. / Directed by Brian Yuzna / Starring Mindy Clarke, J. Trevor Edmond / High Fliers (UK R2 PAL), Trimark (US R1 NTSC)

For adolescent kicks, Curt (Edmond) and his girlfriend Julie (Clarke) borrow his father's security pass and break into the military bio-weapons research facility where he works. Witnessing an astounding test in the reanimation of a corpse, they beat a hasty retreat, failing to see the violent conclusion to the immoral experiment. When a motorcycle accident results in Julie's death, the grief-stricken Curt realises that the potential to resurrect her is only a security pass away.

A fast and furious zombie-fest that does away with the chuckles of Dan O'Bannon's original and the slapstick of Ken Wiederhorn's sequel and stakes its claim in straight horror territory. As such you need have no knowledge whatsoever of the first two films to appreciate *Re-Animator* producer Brian Yuzna's dark, original and exciting (if, in conclusion, vaguely depressing) opus.

Despite the presence of a number of nightmarish monstrosities throughout, Yuzna's focus is firmly on Clarke's back-from-the-dead character and her inability to control a burgeoning hunger for human brains, despite initially successful - but later futile - attempts to stave off the craving via self-mutilation. The make-up when she becomes a fully-fledged S&M-pierced zombie babe is breathtaking. She may be somewhat removed from the gut-munching strolling cadavers of Fulci and Romero, but the make-up effects (by Screaming Mad George) are every bit as quease-inducing and the story is engrossing right through to its downbeat climax.

Sarah Douglas, erstwhile Ursa in a couple of *Superman* movies, cameos as a blinkered scientist who can't see the error of her ways till it jumps up and chows down on her. Nasty.

High Fliers' Region 2 PAL disc presents the film complete with all its grisly excesses in a fullscreen transfer with 13 chapter points. The picture seems a little dark at times, but no more so than on the film's previous PAL VHS incarnation. The only additional feature is a trailer. - TG

[*Unfortunately the US DVD inexplicably contains the edited R-rated version, though Trimark released the uncut version on laserdisc. - ed.*]

RETURN TO OZ

Colour, 1985, 109m. / Directed by Walter Murch / Starring Nicol Williamson, Jean Marsh, Fairuza Balk / Anchor Bay (US R1 NTSC) / WS (1.85:1) / DD5.1

Not really a sequel to the popular MGM musical, this strangely neglected adaptation of L. Frank Baum's *Ozma of Oz* and *The Land of Oz* marked the sole directorial outing for esteemed editor Walter Murch (making him perhaps the '80s equivalent of Charles Laughton and *Night of the Hunter*). Fairuza Balk, now best known for her memorable turns in films like *The Craft* and *American History X,* made a terrific debut as Dorothy, giving a remarkably insightful and convincing performance for an eleven year old actress. Visually, the film is unlike any other and faithfully evokes the off-kilter and sometimes frightening look of Baum's illustrated stories, while Murch also makes excellent use of music (David Shire's score is among the finest of the decade) and visual motifs like mirrors and metal vs. flesh. Perhaps not suitable for all children due to some frightening imagery, *Return to Oz* should prove extremely satisfying to fans of fantastic cinema and iconoclastic filmmaking in general.

Six months after her trip to Oz, little Dorothy Gayle finds herself plagued by distress and insomnia. No one believes her stories, and Aunt Em (Piper Laurie) takes her to visit Dr. Worley (Nicol Williamson), a man who proclaims that his use of shock therapy will revolutionize medical treatment in the 20th Century. Dorothy escapes the doctor's clutches thanks to the aid of a mysterious young girl in the asylum, and Dorothy leaps into a river during a thunderstorm to escape. Upon waking, Dorothy finds herself back in Oz along with her chicken,

Bellina, who now talks. Unfortunately, the yellow brick road has crumbled and the inhabitants of the Emerald City have been turned to stone. Strange sentinels called Wheelers (men strangely contorted onto huge wheel limbs) trap Dorothy and eventually force her into the clutches of the petulant Princess Mombi (Jean Marsh), who keeps a gallery of severed female heads that she changes for her own on a regular basis. With the aid of a robotic Emerald City guard, Tik-Tok, and the Gump (a reanimated creature consisting of a couch and a moose head - don't ask), Dorothy escapes Mombi's castle and tries to find the Nome King, who is apparently responsible for the troubles plaguing the once-happy Land of Oz.

Anchor Bay's DVD of *Return to Oz* looks simply stunning. Though non-anamorphic, the detail and colour fidelity are remarkable. Some very minor signs of wear are evident in the first reel, but otherwise the print is in excellent condition and easily blows away the old Disney VHS edition and even the letterboxed but murky Japanese LD. The film was shot hard-matted at 1.85:1, so the alternate full frame version on the DVD is actually pan and scan. The widescreen version satisfies far more in every respect, and the 5.1 remix delivers the beautiful score and occasional sound effects well if unspectacularly (this is a pretty quiet film overall aside from the finale). The elaborate Claymation effects and Jim Henson animatronics still look quite good, and on a supplementary interview, Fairuza goes into detail describing how some of the effects were achieved. Surprisingly, her anecdote about the operation of Tik-Tok is one of the most painful concepts imaginable! It doesn't have Judy Garland and it doesn't have musical numbers, but if approached on its own terms, *Return to Oz* easily belongs in any self-respecting fantasy film lover's library.

R

RICHARD KERN: THE HARDCORE COLLECTION

Colour, 1984-1993, 180m. / Directed by Richard Kern / Starring Richard Kern, Lydia Lunch, Nick Zedd, Henry Rollins, Karen Finley / Music Video (US R1 NTSC)

The pioneering voice in New York's "cinema of transgression," photographer/director Richard Kern churns out short films which are, to put it mildly, not for everyone. Grungy, grainy, and crass, these volatile little nuggets

of celluloid deliberately cram their fingers down your throat and never let go. By the time you've waded through just a fraction of this disc, the early works of John Waters start to look genteel by comparison. Though it shares its title with the original two tape *Hardcore* set of Kern films released on VHS by Film Threat back in the '80s, this DVD is a somewhat different animal. Assembling the entirety of the two "remastered" Hardcore videotapes currently being sold by Kern along with three films left off the new set (but on the previous Film Threat versions), this disc operates like a crash course in Kern and his eccentric cinematic cohorts.

The two most famous films, "Fingered" and "The Right Side of My Brain," feature his abrasive muse, performance artist Lydia Lunch, verbally assaulting her co-actors, delivering spacey voiceover monologues, and performing various sexual acts that would pass for hardcore porn if they were clearly shot in and colour. The former film is the more accessible of the two, with Lydia embarking on a crime spree with her phone sex partner.

Kern himself appears in several films, as a suburban father married to performance artist Karen Finley ("You Killed Me First") or, more often, a photographer ("The Evil Cameraman" and the more recent "My Nightmare") indulging in literally masturbatory fantasies. Amazingly, the likes of Skinny Puppy, the Butthole Surfers, and Henry Rollins pop up on his soundtracks, with a few films like "Submit to Me" and "Submit to Me Now" playing like music videos gone horribly wrong.

One of Kern's frequent partners in filmic crime, Nick Zedd (*They Eat Scum*), pops up now and then as well, most memorably in "Thrust in Me" which finds him essaying a truly perverse dual role. This film actually belongs to a weird half hour collection entitled "Manhattan Love Suicides," which also includes the bizarre monster romp "I Hate You Now" and "Woman at the Wheel" (none of which are listed on the packaging or the chapter index).

Though Kern has mostly retired from filmmaking to pursue his photography of unclothed New York ladies, some of his rarely seen '90s work pops up here, such as the nearly unwatchable "The Sewing Circle" (don't even ask) and the jaw-dropping "The Bitches," the most traditionally pornographic film of the bunch. Pretty scary stuff, but you might have a hard time turning away.

The first pressing of this DVD from Music Video turned out to be a defective disaster, with an inaccessible second layer and constant player problems. The repressing (which features a sticker over the bar code on the back) features identical packaging but divides the films into separate sides of the disc. The films boast a "remastered" tag but look exactly as they did back in the '80s: rough, grainy, and cheap. Of course, this is probably the best way to see them. The audio is surprisingly good and most likely received all of the restoration attention.

The disc also includes a gallery of photos, mostly focusing on Kern's various female discoveries. While an interview or some kind of commentary would have been welcome to put the films in perspective, the works speak well enough by themselves. Approach at your own risk, but fans will most likely be satisfied with this long, unflinching look at the dark underbelly of maverick filmmaking.

RING

Colour, 1998, 91m. / Directed by Hideo Nakata / Starring Matsushima Nanako, Sanada Hiroyuki / Tartan (UK PAL R0) / WS (1.85:1) (16:9) / DD2.0

 Imagine you woke up one morning and were told you had exactly one week to live... and you even know the exact minute you would die. This eerie feeling permeates the entire running time of *Ring*, the most internationally successful horror export from Japan. While US distributors fumbled their chance to get in on the action (though a remake was greenlighted at DreamWorks), *Ring* became something of a legend in the horror community for its solid blend of psychological depth, a startling storyline, and enough chills to maintain a freezer through summertime. Completely devoid of blood, the film instead draws the viewer in slowly until the chilling, unforgettable finale.

A series of strange deaths have been cropping up around Japan. The latest victim, Tomoko, was a young teenage girl who was found dead while spending the evening with her best friend, who went insane after finding the body. No signs of violence can be found, but a reporter named Reiko (Matsushima Nanako) learns that the girl and two other friends, now dead as well, had watched a strange videotape at a remote cabin. After viewing the tape, a phone call told them they would all die in exactly one week. A little detective work leads Reiko to the mysterious tape at the cabin. Curiosity gets the better of her, so she views the tape in one of the guest rooms. The TV displays a series of grainy, surreal images and words: a group of people clawing through an erupting volcano, a hooded figure pointing offscreen, a woman brushing her hair in the mirror. Then the phone rings... and Reiko's terrifying journey begins.

To give away any more of *Ring*'s plot would be heresy, but anyone who enjoys well-crafted ghost stories should get a solid shudder out of the believable, understated manner in which the tale unfolds. The source novel, *Ringu*, has been adapted and sequelized many times in Japan with varying degrees of success, such as *Ring 0* and the worthy *Ring 2;* however, this is the one to seek out.

The cast does an excellent job of gradually building hysteria without resorting to running or screaming; in particular, Sanada Hiroyuki is quietly effective as Reiko's ex-husband, a university professor with psychic abilities who aids her quest to beat the clock before her own death. The people behind the camera also perform outstanding jobs, with the subtly manipulative cinematography, jolting editing, and spooky ambient music score gradually building tension to the breaking point.

Video collectors have long been looking for a decent subtitled version of *Ring*, which has appeared on VCD and DVD in various unsubtitled forms for the past two years. The British DVD from Tartan marks the first legitimate English subtitled version to the general public; lifted from a festival print with visibly battered reel changes and burned-in subs, the transfer is generally satisfying. The anamorphic image quality is richly colourful and contains deep blacks, essential to appreciating the film, while the manipulative surround audio is boisterous, often filled with ringing telephones, exploding camera flashes, and creepy, unidentifiable noises designed to give you the feeling of someone lurking just behind your shoulder. The menu design is especially crafty, with the chilling images on the videotape manipulated to identify the various disc functions.

Extra goodies include a UK theatrical trailer, a teaser for the British release of *Ring 2,* a trailer for the creepy *Audition* (better than the trailer included on that film's Hong Kong DVD release), a gallery of stills and talent bios, and an enthusiastic appraisal by critic Mark Kermode.

While a more pristine transfer with optional subs will no doubt surface someday, this DVD is more than satisfying in the meantime and presents a perfectly chilling way of making this future classic's acquaintance.

THE ROCKY HORROR PICTURE SHOW
Colour, 1975, 100m. / Directed by Jim Sharman / Starring Tim Curry, Susan Sarandon, Barry Bostwick / Fox (US R1 NTSC, UK R2 PAL) / WS (1.66:1) (16:9) / DD5.1

The trials and tribulations of *The Rocky Horror Picture Show* have been well documented over the years, from its initial neglect in 1975 from Fox and its resurrection as the original mass midnight movie to the various video incarnations over the years which, at least temporarily, took a chunk out of its theatregoing audience. However, rest assured that even with all the bells and whistles of DVD, there's no substitute for seeing *Rocky Horror* in a theatre, and hopefully it will continue to play loud and proud - even if that means actually having to leave your house to experience it.

The storyline, a giddy pastiche of horror, sci-fi, and exploitation elements from the '30s to the '50s, follows strait-laced couple Brad Majors (Barry Bostwick) and Janet Weiss (Susan Sarandon), an engaged couple from Denton, Ohio who get stranded during a thunderstorm. They seek shelter in the castle of Dr. Frank-N-Furter (Tim Curry), an omnisexual transvestite/mad scientist throwing a party for a convention from Transsexual, Transylvania. The doctor's incestuous servants, Riff Raff (Richard O'Brien) and Magenta (Patricia Quinn), assist in the unveiling of a new creation, Rocky Horror (Peter Hinwood), a blond and muscular man created for the doctor's pleasure. Frank's ex, a biker named Eddie (Meat Loaf) who supplied Rocky's brain matter, crashes the party and gets a very hostile reception, after which the characters embark on an evening of sexual experimentation, identity crises, and startling revelations from Eddie's uncle, the wheelchair-bound Dr. Scott (Jonathan Adams). Everything comes to a head during the cosmic musical finale, all related by our laconic narrator, The Criminologist (the late Charles Gray).

While the storyline of the film pretty much degenerates into a glitter rock orgy long before the end, the primary appeal of *Rocky Horror* lies in the hilarious responses from its cult audience, whose script seems to change every week to incorporate new pop culture references, raunchy jokes, and musical routines.

The use of props like newspapers, rice, toast, and so on creates the perfect party atmosphere, though you might want to be careful in a theatre when you see water spritzers and hot dogs coming out of people's pockets. Drive-in movie fans can always have fun picking out the avalanche of movie references; the opening "Science Fiction Double Feature" song alone refers to everything from *The Day of the Triffids* to *Curse of the Demon.*

485

When *Rocky Horror* was released in US theatres, the final musical number, "Super Heroes," wound up on the cutting room floor but later resurfaced in some alternate prints and on Japanese laserdisc. The first US video and laser releases were still trimmed, but the song did turn up as part of the 20th Anniversary box set along with the excised "Once in a While," a nice, slight little number by Bostwick that would have stopped the film cold. However, this DVD marks the first wide release of the entire UK cut of *Rocky Horror* from beginning to end, with a retooled stereo soundtrack now pumped up to 5.1 proportions. Don't expect much surround activity, but the music sounds great and, though lifted from the soundtrack recordings, has been tweaked to better match the performers' lip movements. A mono mix has also been included, with some tweaks made to the original mix *a la* the Japanese disc. The image quality is razor sharp and beautifully showcases the colourful cinematography by Peter Suschitzky, who went on to shoot most of David Cronenberg's films. The framing has been mildly windowboxed, with more information visible than the overmatted laserdisc to more closely approximate its European theatrical appearance.

The astounding extras from the laser box have been duplicated here along with some excellent new surprises. Apart from the US and UK cuts, there's also a hidden third version which, conforming roughly to the original screenplay, plays out in black and white (*a la* The *Wizard of Oz*) until midway through "The Time Warp." O'Brien (who also wrote the original stage version, *The Rocky Horror Show*) and Quinn are reunited for a surprisingly dense commentary track, in which the two old friends banter about the production and offer some nifty bits of trivia. What's the connection between this film and *The Innocents*? What famous starlet was Charles Gray's next door neighbour until her death? These answers and many more can be found within.

The DVD also contains a stereo mix of the laser's audience participation track, which still sounds like total gibberish and doesn't convey any of the enthusiasm found in a real theatre. Good luck understanding more than a dozen words or so during the entire movie. More handy is a subtitle option directing viewers when to use appropriate props, using a written list found in the packaging, and an optional audience viewer in which a pair of red lips alert you to watch a separate window of cultists in action. Apart from the aforementioned deleted numbers, you also get alternate takes of Brad and Janet's stripping scene, some karaoke versions of two songs, two alternate end credit sequences, a photo gallery, two slightly different theatrical

trailers, and cast and crew bios (also found on the DVD-Rom section along with The Masochistic Trivia Challenge, Riff Raff's Story Lab, a timeline, and weblinks). One terrific new bonus is Rocky on VH-1, a collection of interview footage compiled into a "Whatever Happened To..." special with all profanity and ribald remarks intact. Bostwick, Sarandon, O'Brien, Quinn, and Meatloaf share their thoughts on the phenomenon, with most making some valid and surprisingly insightful points about the film's place in history. You also get a tour of the castle used in the film courtesy of O'Brien as well as the Pop Up Video version of Meat Loaf's "Hot Patootie, Bless My Soul." And don't forget the terrific menu design, which features a pair of lips offering commentary on your menu choices, which are carried out by, naturally, a pair of legs in fishnet stockings. Good Lordy.

While one can only wonder why on earth Sharman, "Little Nell," and Curry weren't around to participate in any of this, the DVD should be enough to keep even the most ardent Frank-o-phile busy. Just don't forget to pop into a theatre from time to time and see *Rocky* on its best behaviour.

ROLLERBALL

Colour, 1975, 124m. / Directed by Norman Jewison / Starring James Caan, Maude Adams / MGM (US R1 NTSC, UK R2 PAL) / WS (1.85:1)

Someone at MGM must really love this movie, since this is no less than the third time it's been released by them in a digital format. While the gushing liner notes would have you believe this is a deeply philosophical, underrated classic of the '70's, it's actually more of a guilty pleasure. A cross between *North Dallas 40, Slap Shot,* and *Death Race 2000*, Jewison's heavy-handed treatment makes such efforts to convey the importance of its profound meaning (people are inherently violent, and violence is bad) that it has no idea how silly it all is.

James Caan does his method acting best as a champion in the 21st century sport called "Rollerball." Sort of a gruesome motocross/hockey/football hybrid, the game elicits the most violent, bloodthirsty responses from its fans because violence is otherwise outlawed in this futuristic, utopian society (oh, yeah, there's some *Logan's Run* in here, too). John Houseman, the head of the corporation sponsoring Rollerball, demands that Caan be more brutal and life-threatening in his

R

tactics, so the film also slides in some nasty messages about how evil and corrupt corporate America is (never mind that millions were blown by corporate executives on this movie). Of course, Caan is also kept away from his true love, two-time Bond girl Maud Adams, so we are also told that big money and fame are no substitute for real romance.

Relatively speaking, *Rollerball* looks better here than it ever has before. Though filmed on pretty bad Eastmancolor stock (like a lot of '70's films, unfortunately) in London and Munich, the image's clarity and sharpness carry it along most of the way. The souped-up Dolby Digital surround remix adds immensely to the Rollerball sequences, with plenty of thunderous crashing and whooshing wheels to keep you awake. The electronic "Hooked on Classics" score sounds vibrant and very dimensional as well. The deluxe edition (later issued in the UK as well after a discontinued bare bones edition) also contains commentary by director Jewison (who points out all of the major themes for you, in case you missed them the first time) and a cool ten-minute behind the scenes documentary. By the way, the main menu featuring a digital scoreboard embossed over Rollerball clips is a really nice touch. It hasn't aged all that well, but this is plenty of fun if you're in an undemanding mood. Besides, it beats that awful remake…

ROMANCE

Colour, 1999, 90m. / Directed by Catherine Breillat / Starring Caroline Trousselard, Sagamore Stévenin / Trimark (US R1 NTSC) / WS (1.85:1), Bluelight (UK R2 PAL) / WS (1.66:1) / DD2.0

 A difficult and often unsettling film, *Romance* was promoted as a sexy foreign import, though in reality it is anything but. The film surveys human sexuality from a female perspective, to be sure, but anyone expecting lascivious thrills is going to be in for a rude awakening.

Marie (Caroline Trousselard), a young schoolteacher, is unsatisfied with her live-in relationship with handsome but icy Paul (Sagamore Stévenin). Compelled to test her own mental and physical limits when Paul admits he's no longer interested in sex, Marie pushes herself through a series of increasingly anonymous, taboo-breaking encounters, including a lengthy bondage session with her weirdly compassionate headmaster. Eventually Marie's explorations bring her back to Paul, but, to put it mildly, life will never be the same again.

Relentlessly self-indulgent and designed to test viewers' sensibilities (with a number of images existing solely to startle or repulse), *Romance* is completely a matter of taste. While the film seems to have a sense of humour, it's difficult to discern how much of Trousselard's long, rambling monologues about her sexual needs were meant to be taken seriously. However, all of the actors have to be commended at the very least for the fearless chutzpah they invest in their roles, even if the final product may not be worth it. Italian porn legend Rocco Siffredi turns up as one of Marie's lovers and, oddly enough, provides the most believable and least pretentious performance in the film!

The last five minutes provide an interesting twist, with a final ambiguous and resonant image that seems to have strayed in from a completely different film. Incidentally, director Catherine Breillat *(36 Fillette)* started out as an actress in another controversial foreign film, Bernardo Bertolucci's *Last Tango in Paris*.

Trimark's DVD of *Romance* offers about as good a presentation as one could expect. The letterboxed image looks clean and nicely colourful throughout, though most of this film has that "European soft" look accentuated by the colour schemes that emphasize white, grey, and beige. The audio is almost entirely dead centre dialogue, though some of the generic background music seeps to the exterior channels from time to time. The English subtitles are quite easy to read and seem to be accurate. The original US trailer is included, though you may have to hunt a bit to find it. The British disc contains the French trailer instead and is missing precisely one second - specifically, the infamous "money shot" near the end.

ROMANCING THE STONE

Colour, 1984, 106m. / Directed by Robert Zemeckis / Starring Michael Douglas, Kathleen Turner / Fox (US R1 NTSC, UK R2 PAL) / WS (2.35:1) / DD2.0

 Timid romance novelist Joan Wilder (Turner) comes into possession of an ancient treasure map. When her sister is held to ransom by crooks who want it for themselves, Wilder travels to Colombia to hand it over. During an unplanned detour when she gets on the wrong bus, she meets free-wheeling fortune hunter Jack Colton (Douglas), who convinces her that they should quietly locate the treasure themselves and then hand over the map.

Breakneck adventure in the Indiana Jones mould. The pace is relentless and the dialogue pithy as the action thunders along through the rain-sodden Colombian jungles where Jack and Joan grapple with collapsing rope bridges, turbulent waterfalls, deadly underground caverns, a backwoods town brimming with gun-happy drugs dealers, and a hoard of man-eating crocodiles. Bob Zemeckis wouldn't know how to make a bad movie if you paid him to and, laden with panache, *Romancing the Stone* is among his best. The only small mis-step is a bloody dismemberment towards the end of the film that betrays its otherwise light-hearted nature.

Douglas is pretty good as the egocentric hero, but this is really Turner's film; watching her blossom from introverted, mousy and prim to self-confident and dazzlingly sexy is a delight. She and Douglas play the simmering love-hate relationship between Wilder and Colton to perfection. Two sets of villains round out the protagonists; bungling and inept kidnappers Ira (Zack Norman) and Ralph (Danny DeVito), and a more serious threat in the shape of corrupt law enforcement officer and all round nasty piece of work Colonel Zolo (Manuel Ojeda). Although the formula loses some of its zest on repeat viewing, it still possesses just as much durability as the Spielberg films it set out to emulate.

Where former British releases of *Romancing the Stone* have suffered at the hands of the censor's shears, this fine quality Region 1 disc presents the movie in all its uncut glory, with 28 chapter breaks. It's an extras-light release, however, offering only the trailer (a collection of clips intercut with some amusing, specially shot footage of DeVito), and it's a shame that no-one saw fit to include the stylish music video, "Romancing the Stone" by Eddy Grant. Sound is available in English Dolby and French Dolby. Subtitling is in English and Spanish. - TG

ROSEMARY'S BABY

Colour, 1968, 136m. / Directed by Roman Polanski / Starring Mia Farrow, John Cassavetes, Ruth Gordon / Paramount (US R1 NTSC, UK R2 PAL) / WS (1.85:1) (16:9)

Nobody would ever say that pregnancy is all fun and games, but few expectant mothers have ever gone through anything as horrific as poor Rosemary Woodhouse, the protagonist of Ira Levin's novel, *Rosemary's Baby*. This tale of occult terror lurking beneath the tranquil brownstones of New York became a nationwide bestseller during the theological turmoil of the '60s, and amazingly enough, Hollywood managed to bring it to the screen without a hitch. For his first American film, Roman Polanski wisely stuck closely to the book, only tweaking the ending to make it even more effective. The result is an eerie and deeply upsetting film, all the more remarkable for its restraint (one dream sequence notwithstanding), a particularly remarkable achievement considering it was produced by the king of cinematic sideshows, William "*The Tingler*" Castle. They just don't come any better than this.

Rosemary (Mia Farrow) and her struggling actor husband, Guy (John Cassavetes), settle comfortably into their new apartment and become friends with an elderly couple, Roman and Minnie Castevet (Sidney Blackmer and Ruth Gordon). A drug-addled young woman named Terry (Hammer starlet Victoria Vetri, using the pseudonym Angela Dorian) turns up dead shortly after meeting Rosemary in the laundry room, and Minnie gives Rosemary a strange smelling locket which had belong to the deceased. Rosemary becomes pregnant after a hallucinatory, alcohol-induced evening of marital rape, and the Castevets insist she go to renowned obstetrician Dr. Abe Saperstein (Ralph Bellamy). However, the herbal medications don't seem to agree with Rosemary, who experiences constant, tortuous pain and begins to doubt those around her. Rosemary's friend, Hutch (Maurice Evans), falls into a coma after making an alarming discovery and leaves Rosemary a book called *All of Them Witches*. Using her Scrabble game, Rosemary makes a sinister discovery about her neighbours and suspects that the devil's work may be responsible. Or is it all in her mind?

The various spooky coincidences sprang up around *Rosemary's Baby* as much as other renowned horror hits like *The Exorcist* and *The Omen*, from the notorious murder of Polanski's wife, Sharon Tate (who makes a fleeting cameo here), at the hands of Charles Manson's followers, to the assassination of John Lennon outside the Dakota building where this was filmed. The founder of The Church of Satan, Anton LaVey, began his bizarre Hollywood association here (see also *The Devil's Rain* and *The Car*) by providing input and turning in a brief, memorable appearance as Old Scratch himself.

Farrow's porcelain-thin portrayal is pitch perfect throughout, and it's no wonder she became an immediate star; however, the supporting cast is equally praiseworthy, with Gordon's Oscar-winning performance leading a pack of veteran actors clearly having the time of their lives. Polanski's regular composer, the late Krzysztof Komeda, excels with a chilling, unforgettable score highlighted by Farrow's famous lullaby theme, while producer Castle (watch for him stepping into a phone booth) had the wisdom to stand back and let Roman work his magic. For a real mindbender, watch this back to back with Polanski's later European variation on the same theme, *The Tenant*.

For many years the video transfers of *Rosemary's Baby* were a hideous bunch, brutally cropped and almost completely faded. A glossy restored version finally turned up on laserdisc from Paramount in the late '90s, and the DVD looks very similar, albeit with a little more sharpness from anamorphic resolution. The colours are very natural and vibrant, from the pastel pink of the opening titles to the dizzying colours during the mod party scene. The extra detail also uncovers some quirky little discoveries, such as the visible face of Farrow's nude body double during the impregnation scene. The sound is the original glorious mono audio track, with excellent range and fidelity to the theatrical source.

For some reason a trailer for this film has failed to surface, but the disc does include two featurettes. The first, "Mia and Roman," is a fascinating little 1968 film which goes behind the scenes for an educational look at the novel-to-film process. The footage of Polanski directing his cast is practically worth the price tag alone. Also included is a newly produced featurette containing on-camera interviews with Polanski, Paramount exec Robert Evans, and production designer Richard Sylbert, all of whom have fond memories of this high point from their careers. They cover all of the bases, from the occult incidents behind the camera to Castle's involvement to the initial casting doubts regarding Farrow and her own personal tragedy during filming. A basic part of any horror film library.

ROUGE

Colour, 1987, 93m. / Directed by Stanley Kwan / Media Asia (HK R0 NTSC) / WS (1.85:1) / DD5.1

Even people who don't care for Hong Kong fantasy films have been known to fall under the spell of this bewitching little treasure, which has sadly been ignored in the wake of bigger international hits *like A Chinese Ghost Story* and the John Woo canon. Best described as a wistful precursor to Kenneth Branagh's *Dead Again*, the intricate storyline revolves around Fleur (Anita Mui), a melancholy courtesan who falls in love with the number two son (Leslie Cheung) of a wealthy

family. When their double suicide pact by opium overdose goes awry and only she goes to the underworld, she returns years later as a ghost and enlists the aid of two married journalists to help her find her lost love. Boosted by a haunting music score and fine, subtly shaded performances, this is a rare ghost story that focuses on character and mood more than flying, sword-swiping spectres (which provides a nice in-joke at the film's finale).

Though expensive, this import DVD is worth the investment. While the graininess of some night scenes apparently couldn't be avoided, the film on the whole looks very good, certainly a huge improvement over the old pan-and-scan Tai Seng videotapes. The film is subtitled optionally in nine languages, including English, and features Mandarin and the superior Cantonese audio tracks. Unfortunately, the songs are only partially subtitled, which is a shame as some of lyrics provide a nice commentary on the story itself.

THE RULING CLASS

Colour, 1972, 154m. / Directed by Peter Medak / Starring Peter O'Toole, Alastair Sim / Criterion (US R1 NTSC) / WS (1.77:1) (16:9)

You know you're in for a strange film when the opening sequence carefully lays out the daily routines of the British aristocracy, only to finish with the prim, aging head of the household, the 13th Earl of Gurney, casually accepting his butler's help while he plops his neck into a noose, slips on a ballet tutu, and prepares for an evening of kinky fun only to wind up hanging dead from the ceiling. The entire family is thrown into an uproar when the family attorney reveals everything now goes directly to the most insane Gurney, Jack (Peter O'Toole), who happens to think he's God and Jesus at the same time. The solution? Simple, of course; they marry him off to gold digging Grace Shelly (Carolyn Seymour) to produce a more acceptable heir. While Grace is busy pretending to be Jack's own personal Camille, the scheming Lady Claire (Coral Browne) consults and beds Dr. Herder (Michael Bryant) in order to bring about a more immediate solution: to cure Jack with the aid of the unforgettable Electric Messiah. This shock tactic seems to work at first, but another iconic personality begins to emerge, this one not quite so kindly as the first.

Not exactly the most consistent director around, Peter Medak has dabbled in everything from top

R

notch suggestive horror (*The Changeling*) to anonymous garbage (*Species 2*). In keeping with this track record, *The Ruling Class* is basically as good as the talent Medak has in front of and behind his camera; fortunately, said ensemble is quite formidable in this case. Peter O'Toole turns in one of his best performances (or maybe two performances, technically) with a belated entrance to die for, and while the tonal shifts from rollicking comedy to eccentric musical numbers to bitter horror are sometimes more than the film can comfortably bear, Medak and company generally keep things bizarre enough to maintain interest. If you don't like a scene, have no fear; something completely different lies just around the corner.

As with most Monty Python skits, the potentially blasphemous bits are handled in such a ludicrous, unrealistic fashion that it never becomes uncomfortably offensive; the object of attack here is more the institution of the Church of England rather than the concept of divinity itself. While Browne does a great job as usual doing her viper tongued routine and Sim does his expert doddering bit, the usually underused Seymour actually impresses most now among the supporting cast in perhaps the second most difficult role. Whether addressing the camera, switching from strumpet to virgin in the blink of an eye, or doing an athletic wedding night striptease, she's always an interesting presence and even offers the most affecting, memorable moment of the film's oddball climax.

Probably not a sure-fire bet for everyone, but recommended viewing and quite a welcome entry on DVD from Criterion. To say that this transfer obliterates its predecessors doesn't say much considering this Avco Embassy title has been out of circulation for many years, and its previous video transfers were hideous to behold and brutally cut by at least 13 minutes. This complete edition looks as good as the original film ever could; mostly it's clean and colourful, though some of the darker footage during Jack's turn to the nasty side looks more grainy and unstable than one might expect.

The mono sound is fine, but some of the dialogue was noticeably looped in later and, aside from sounded occasionally canned, slips in and out of synch with the actors' lip movements. (Just check out "Dem Bones" for one egregious example.) Apparently becoming more amenable to the idea of commentaries, O'Toole joins Medak on the commentary track for a fairly thorough look at the making of the film. Much time is spent discussing the actors and the differences between the stage and screen presentations; having spent time behind the mic already for the aforementioned *Species 2* (how's

that for contrast?), Medak seems more comfortable and chatty. Both men obviously still feel a great deal of affection for the film, and while it's questionable how much immediacy it will have for new viewers without a cultural frame of reference in which to place it, there's no question that *The Ruling Class* deserves the royal treatment it receives here. Other extras include the understandably vague British trailer (talk about a hard sell!) and over thirty minutes of silent home movie excerpts showing the cast and crew at work and play during filming. Choose your own musical accompaniment for this particular supplement, which will seem pretty dry if your ears don't have anything to do.

RUN LOLA RUN

Colour, 1998, 81m. / Directed by Tom Tykwer / Starring Franka Potente, Moritz Bleibtreu / Columbia (US R1 NTSC, UK R2 PAL) / WS (1.85:1) (16:9) / DD5.1

Not many films can make time itself the central antagonist of a story, but the breakout German film *Run Lola Run (Lola Rennt)* executes this tricky idea along with a barrage of creative cinematic devices bound to leave viewers' heads spinning. A rare foreign film capable of crossing over to virtually any other culture, the film has understandably managed to strike a global chord and makes for a high velocity, entertaining sensory experience, too.

The storyline boils down very simply. Lola (Franka Potente), a crimson-haired young woman, receives a phone call from her boyfriend, Manni (Moritz Bleibtreu). In twenty minutes, he must provide one hundred thousand deutschmarks to drug dealers for whom he had agreed to run an errand. Unfortunately, he lost the money and now finds his life in danger. In this short time span, Lola must run across town, formulate a plan to save Manni, and avert countless obstacles along the way.

How this concept manages to comprise an 80 minute film is one of the many unexpected surprises bursting forth from director Tykwer's whirling dervish of an imagination. Though *Lola* could be considered more a work of flash and style than substance, it easily bests most other time/space manipulating films (such as *Sliding Doors*) and offers some interesting shadings which reward repeated viewings. (How much information does Lola actually gain throughout the film? Which characters are actually aware of what is happening?)

The propulsive music score (co-composed by Tykwer and featuring vocals by the talented Potente) drives the film as much as Lola's sprinting feet, and even the most tangential supporting characters are fleshed out with a few deft, perfectly rendered brushstrokes. On the most basic level, the film's greatest accomplishment is featuring a storyline in which the main character literally runs for almost the entire time, but the ultimate effect is invigorating rather than exhausting. The flashy music video stylistics never overwhelm the story but serve to advance the ideas which could arise in a universe which can actually be controlled by the human will. Simply put, it's an apt and somehow positive affirmation of life heading into a new century.

Not surprisingly, Columbia's DVD excels in all departments. The eye-popping colours of the film come through with vibrant clarity, and the option of playing either subtitled or dubbed versions of the film (in Dolby Digital 5.1 or 2.0) should increase the film's potentially broad appeal even more. For some reason the subtitles are out of synch with the dialogue for the opening scene but straighten up after the main titles. The enveloping soundtrack works in any of the versions, with the relentless score constantly flooding from the speakers and enhancing the numerous panning sound effects. Extras include an affectionate, lively English commentary track by the director and star, filled with amusing little anecdotes about the production and the difficulty of maintaining the continuity and pace throughout the preproduction and editing process. Also included are the theatrical trailer and a surprisingly bland, uncredited music video.

RUNNING TIME

B&W, 1997, 70m. / Directed by Josh Becker / Starring Bruce Campbell, Jeremy Roberts / Anchor Bay (US R1 NTSC)

 A notable twist on that old movie chestnut, the heist gone bad, *Running Time* takes its inspiration from Alfred Hitchcock's *Rope* (designing the movie as one continuous shot in real time without cuts) and fuses it to a small scale story in the tradition of Stanley Kubrick's *The Killing*. While the very low budget hampers a few of the film's more ambitious attempts, the overall result is extremely impressive and, most importantly, very entertaining.

Immediately after being released from a five year stint in prison, the conceited Carl (Bruce Campbell) hooks up with his old partner in crime, Patrick (Jeremy Roberts), who has brought along a driver and a safecracker to help steal a quarter of a million dollars stashed through the prison's corrupt laundry fund. After a brief tryst with a hooker (Anita Barone) who turns out to be an old flame from high school, Carl leads the men from one botched detail to the next until they finally commit the robbery itself, which naturally goes awry and leads to bloodshed. Panicked, the men go on the run through L.A. and try to figure out how to extricate themselves from a seemingly no-win situation.

A veteran of the Sam Raimi guerrilla school of filmmaking, Becker has shown considerable improvement with each of his films (also including *Thou Shalt Not Kill... Except* and *Lunatics: A Love Story*), and *Running Time* is his most impressive to date. Boosted by a typically strong lead performance by Campbell, who really would be a huge star by now if there were any justice at all, the simple story barrels along quickly through the film's brief length and deftly fills in some endearing character details right to the end. While the subject matter could have lapsed into familiar sub-Tarantino pretension, the unexpected, emotional final act between Carl and Janie is what really distinguishes this film from the rest of the pack. Refreshingly devoid of hip dialogue and flashy cutting, *Running Time* simply focuses on the people and the events and tells the story, and is all the better for it. The single take technique results in some awkwardly forced moments (let's watch everyone synchronize their watches again...), but these flaws are few and far between.

Shot in black and white 16mm and blown up to 35mm for some festival engagements, *Running Time* looks better than could be expected on Anchor Bay's DVD. The full frame image looks well composed and clear throughout, though some unavoidable grain in the source material shows through, particularly during the first reel. The mono audio track sounds fine under the circumstances, with Raimi's semi-regular composer Joseph LoDuca contributing a sparse score (which he composed for free!). Since virtually all of the dialogue was recorded live, a couple of lines are muffled in the process but not enough to damage the film. Becker and Campbell contribute an affectionate commentary track which, as might be expected, offers a very good time. Campbell provides some hilarious observations and anecdotes as usual, while Becker rigorously accounts the trials of making an experimental indie film in Los Angeles. A mostly useless "theatrical trailer" is included, which simply consists of the first two minutes of the film and probably wouldn't convince anyone to see the final product.

SACRED FLESH

Colour, 1999, 72m. / Directed by Nigel Wingrove / Starring Sally Tremaine, Moyna Cope / Salvation (UK R0 PAL) / WS (1.66:1)

A Mediaeval nun wrestles with personal demons as her fidelity is challenged by lusty sexual fantasies. Disregard the gossamer veneer of arthouse pretension, this is sexploitation pure and simple, beautifully shot and heaving with eroticism. Director Nigel Wingrove is no stranger to the genre and has a keen eye for visual detail; there's no denying that everything looks the business, including a surfeit of cheap but functional special effects. Story telling, however, is not his strong point and plot is all but inconsequential to the parade of copulating bodies - most of them far too catwalk-style-drop-dead-gorgeous to be believable as nuns, but who cares? - wheeled out in a series of vignettes that paddle the middle waters between softcore and hardcore.

The lack of plot does prove counterproductive in so much as, even at just over 70 minutes, exposure to the entire film in a single sitting is a trial of endurance. But while naughty nuns continue to fuel the ardour of the initiated there will always be a place for films such as *Sacred Flesh* and for those with a penchant for nunsploitation this is probably tantamount to manna from heaven. For everyone else, however, it has to be consigned to the closet of passing curiosities, suitable for partaking of once but offering little to etch it into the long-term memory. Kinky? Probably. Sacrilegious? Certainly. Entertaining? You bet your sweet wimple!

The all region PAL disc from Salvation offers up more supplemental treasures than a Mother Superior has vestments. Along with a pair of trailers there's a commentary from director Nigel Wingrove and his Salvation cohort Mick Southworth, a gallery of publicity materials, images designed to adorn the CD soundtrack packaging, a selection of storyboards and an impressively large collection of off-set and on still photographs.

The film itself bears the look of a shot-on-video-for-TV movie, particularly during exterior scenes, and the pristine 1.66:1 22-chapter encoded transfer emulates it. - TG

SALEM'S LOT

Colour, 1979, 183m. / Directed by Tobe Hooper / Starring David Soul, James Mason / Warner (US R1 NTSC)

While *The Shining* may be Stephen King's finest novel, his second, *'Salem's Lot*, could easily be the scariest. Following the theatrical success of *Carrie*, King's sprawling book was ushered into the two night, four hour miniseries format for television and subsequently issued in a 112-minute cut for European theatres. This shorter variant, which omitted numerous subplots, turned up on pay cable and home video where it found an accepting audience eager to see the full length version again. Warner finally issued the miniseries edition on VHS and laserdisc a few years ago, but now fans can finally savour the entire thing uninterrupted on DVD. It's been a long time coming.

Ben Mears (David Soul), one of King's usual tortured novelists, returns to his home of *Salem's Lot* (where did the apostrophe go, one wonders). While striking up a romance with the lovely Susan Norton (*Die Hard*'s Bonnie Bedelia), he begins to suspect that something may be amiss in the town. Residents are turning up dead, drained of blood, while others are listless and stay indoors all day. A young monster movie fan, Mark Petrie (Lance Kerwin), even spies one of his dead friends floating outside his bedroom window and scratching on the glass (a great image). Ben deduces that this macabre transformation may have something to do with the arrival of Mr. Barlow, a mysterious antique dealer living in the spooky old Marsden house? And what about Straker (James Mason), his suave but menacing right hand man? Ben, Mark, and a handful of the others decide to infiltrate the old house, only to uncover a very nasty surprise.

Director Tobe Hooper (*The Texas Chainsaw Massacre*) may not seem like the ideal choice for a suggestive, epic length saga about small town vampirism, but here he pulled off a rare successful King adaptation for television. Unlike such subsequent missteps as *The Tommyknockers* and *The Langoliers*, *Salem's Lot* keeps a tight grip on the characters and the viewer's emotions by delivering a hefty number of scares and adhering faithfully to the novel. From Soul's restrained heroism to Mason's seething menace, all of the actors are well up to the task of King's tricky narrative. Horror regular Reggie Nalder (*Mark of the Devil*) turns up intermittently in *Nosferatu* drag as Mr. Barlow, and while some fans of the novel found this visual choice questionable, there's no denying that Nalder is scary in the role. The climax really packs a wallop thanks to brilliant atmosphere, lighting, and editing; the image of Mark crouching up against the door during the basement climax is not one easily forgotten. While the running time would suggest a simple presentation of the miniseries, Warner's home video version is actually a third version of *Salem's Lot*. The shorter European cut contained some mild differences, most notably a gory shot of one character impaled against a wall of antlers near the end. That shot has been reinstated into this version, though completists may want to hang on to their old videotapes anyway. In the TV and DVD versions, the sequence in which George Dzundza catches his wife in bed with Fred Willard climaxes with Dzundza forcing Willard to hold a loaded shotgun up to his face. In the rougher European cut, Dzundza (following King's novel) actually forces Willard to slide the rifle barrels down into his throat before pulling the trigger. Otherwise, the DVD is the definitive presentation of *Salem's Lot* and should make fans quite happy.

The transfer is similar to the earlier laserdisc, with surprisingly vibrant colours for a late '70s miniseries. A few scuffs and scratches pop up in the source material, most noticeably prior to the commercial break points, but it doesn't really detract from the film at all. Simply put, if you've only seen *Salem's Lot* as a TV broadcast, you haven't really seen it at all. The laserdisc included the original teaser and wrap up from the two night screening, which the DVD omits in favour of the international theatrical trailer - a fair trade off. Incidentally, unlike the theatrical cut, the miniseries leaves the door way open at the end for a prospective television series which ultimately never materialized.

SALOME'S LAST DANCE

Colour, 1988, 89m. / Directed by Ken Russell / Starring Glenda Jackson, Stratford Johns / Pioneer (US R1 NTSC)

 A relatively obscure entry in the Ken Russell canon, *Salome's Last Dance* fell during the director's creative outpouring for Vestron Pictures during the 1980s (*Lair of the White Worm, The Rainbow, Gothic*). The film presents a straightforward adaptation of the notorious Oscar Wilde play, a fetishistic retelling of the John the Baptist and Salome story from the Old Testament, mixed with more than a few of Russell's expected dotty touches. The results divided viewers sharply down the middle, with the literate and often claustrophobic approach faring better on the small screen than in the theatre.

At a plush brothel catering to the kinky and well-to-do, Oscar Wilde (Nickolas Grace) arrives to observe a production of Salome performed by the locals. While the performers go about their stylized business, Wilde comments on the action and takes time out for an occasional liaison; however, the play itself consumes the bulk of the running time. The production, a gaudy and colourful concoction in the style of *Café Flesh*, presents Salome (Imogen Millais-Scott) as a petulant brat whose mother, Herodias (a marvellous Glenda Jackson), constantly bickers with the flatulent King Herod (Stratford Johns). Salome's infatuation with John the Baptist (Douglas Hodge) remains unconsummated thanks to his conversion to Christianity, and after he refuses to even offer her a kiss, she strikes a bargain with the Herod - in return for the head of John the Baptist on a plate, Salome will dance for the king. The results, of course, are extremely outlandish and visually startling, with a few dollops of sexually perverse imagery thrown in for good measure.

As with the other Vestron titles passed over to Artisan and Pioneer (e.g., *Parents*), this DVD has been transferred from the same full frame master used for the Vestron/Image laserdisc. The results are significantly better, with much improved colour and some eye-popping detail obscured in the old edition; however, a fresh new transfer could have probably been even better, as that old '80s video mist still lingers in a few shots, notably over the opening credits. The Ultra-Stereo sound is nothing special but serviceable, offering some nice musical directional effects. Ken Russell himself provides his second commentary track to date, offering some amusing literary and cinematic insights into this quirky little chamber piece. A scholarly wit, Russell makes for good company and will hopefully continue to perform this service on future DVD releases. The DVD also includes the original trailer, as well as a trailer for *Lair of the White Worm*.

SANJURO

B&W, 1962, 96m. / Directed by Akira Kurosawa / Starring Toshiro Mifune, Tatsuya Nakadai / Criterion (US R1 NTSC) / WS (2.35:1)

 Following the success of *Yojimbo*, Kurosawa reworked his next script into another vehicle for Mifune's wily swordsman. The result, *Sanjuro*, features a protagonist with the same name but otherwise feels like quite a different film. Nine young samurai neophytes determine that their town has become overrun with corruption following the abduction of their Chamberlain (Yunosuke Ito). They enlist the aid of Sanjuro and are immediately underwhelmed by his uncouth behaviour and lack of respect for authority. However, as most viewers could easily figure out, Sanjuro still clings to the moral foundations of the "honourable" Japan and hides these qualities beneath his shaggy exterior.

While *Yojimbo* had more than its share of humorous and ironic moments, *Sanjuro* revels in them; the Chamberlain's pacifist wife and daughter constantly urge the ragtag army to avoid unnecessary violence and spare as many lives as possible, leading to some humorous complications during the battle scenes. Of course, Sanjuro eventually realizes that the women are correct, a nice little jab at the standard notions in Japanese society. From this perspective, *Sanjuro* would have been a fascinating viewing experience with a progressive 1960s audience. In particular, the social commentary which usually runs throughout Kurosawa's work takes a skewed and particularly delightful front seat here, with the idealistic youths constantly trying to come to grips with an elder who sometimes appears to be out of his mind. Though comical and handled with an astonishing degree of filmmaking skill, the swordplay and bloodshed become surprisingly graphic at times, with a finale that wouldn't be out of place in one of the '70s Lone Wolf and Cub epics.

Criterion's DVD looks very similar to the *Yojimbo* presentation and shares its mild flaws: a nice but less than pristine print, US opening credits, marginally inaccurate framing, and lousy packaging. However, like its predecessor, this is probably as good as US audiences are going to see it, and any Kurosawa films coming to American DVD letter-boxed and with optional subtitles are definitely a cause for celebration. The subtitled Japanese trailer is just as amusing as the one for *Yojimbo*. Often overlooked in the shadow of sprawling masterpieces like *Seven Samurai* and *Ran*, both of these films are essential parts of any world cinema collection and make a fine, entertaining introduction for those unfamiliar with one of the cinema's great visionary masters.

SCARS OF DRACULA

Colour, 1970, 95m. / Directed by Roy Ward Baker / Starring Christopher Lee, Dennis Waterman / Anchor Bay (US R1 NTSC) / WS (1.85:1) (16:9)

On the run after false accusations of rape by the Burgomeister's daughter, lothario Paul Carlson (Christopher Matthews) seeks refuge for the night at

Castle Dracula. When days pass by with no word from Paul, his worried brother Simon (Waterman) and girlfriend Sarah Framsen (Jenny Hanley) follow the trail to the castle where they encounter terrors beyond belief.

For some unfathomable reason the fifth Christopher Lee Dracula entry is glared at by most Hammer fans and genre critics with equal disdain. Would they really have been happier had it been yet another retread of already mined-to-death territory? As a lone voice in the crowd I would proffer that *Scars of Dracula* is actually one of the best and most original - albeit violent to excess - of all the Draculas. As the last of the Count's Gothic features it's certainly superior to the two "modern day" adventures that followed, but it's primarily down to Lee's mesmerizing presence (in which he is afforded more screen time and dialogue than before or after) that the film is as good as it is. Of the other leads, admittedly Waterman makes for an ineffectual hero and Hanley, though attractive, is pretty vapid as our heroine. More noteworthy turns come from the supporting cast, specifically Patrick Troughton (who transforms Dracula's formerly urbane butler Klove into a ramshackle gofer), Anouska Hempel as vulpine vampire apostle Tania, Michael Gwynn as the craven priest and bug-eyed Michael Ripper as - what else? - a surly innkeeper.

That Lee himself doesn't care for the film is of little consequence, for an acute disinterest in the role didn't harm his professional integrity one iota. Anthony Hinds (scripting as John Elder) was astute enough to realise that after several very similar episodes (the previous one, *Taste the Blood of Dracula*, being dreadfully short of vitality) the series was in need of a fillip. Thus, in tandem with the standard neck-nibbling activities, we get an interpolation of brutality that includes bat-mauled faces, a frenetic stabbing, a dismembered corpse deposited in a tub of acid, a grotesque impaling and a vicious branding with the heated blade of a sword. Audiences may have been taken aback by the unexpectedly sadistic menu, but the results were Grade-A exploitation. Which, considering that's precisely what it set out to be, in context renders *Scars of Dracula* worthy of far more even-handed a level of regard than to date it's been granted.

I've seen *Scars* more times than I'd care to admit, but it's never looked as good as it does on Anchor Bay's Region 1 DVD. The 1.85:1 matted, 25-chapter-encoded print is so clean and eye-scorchingly colourful - the vivid blue of Sarah's cloak, the searing red of the Kensington Gore! - that it barely looks a couple of years old! Additional features are a commentary from Baker and Lee, brief biographies, two trailers (the UK version and the US combo that paired it with *Horror of Frankenstein*) and a nicely substantial slideshow format gallery of poster art, stills and lobby cards which plays out against James Bernard's charming score. Upon its initial issue Anchor Bay included a bonus disc comprising a 57-minute, 15-chapter documentary entitled "The Many Faces of Christopher Lee" - in which the actor lectures on some of his favourite film roles - and two recent music videos, a rousing rendition of "It's Now Or Never" and the jaw-droppingly awful "She'll Fall For Me". - TG

SCHIZO

Colour, 1976, 109m. / Directed by Pete Walker / Starring Lynne Frederick, Stephanie Beacham / Image (US R0 NTSC) / WS (1.85:1) (16:9)

 Ice skating champion Samantha (Frederick) is to be married but she's being terrorized by Haskin (Jack Watson) a man from her distant past, fresh out of prison where he has been serving a sentence for murdering her mother. No-one believes Samantha when she professes that Haskin is out to kill her, and her worst fears seem to be confirmed when people around her begin to die horribly. You don't have to be the sharpest tool in a maniac's collection to figure out the ending of this leisurely paced Pete Walker flimflam.

Written by David McGillivray (who does a "Hitchcock" during a séance) this has all the trademark schlock one expects from Walker, yet in spite of its sizeable quota of slashed psychiatrists, mutilated mediums and hacked-up housekeepers, there's really not much going on here to keep you on the edge of your seat. In fact the biggest shock in the picture is the price of coffee in the supermarket where Samantha goes shopping! The late Lynne Frederick makes for a comely focal point. Good old Jack Watson is suitably shifty as the reddest red herring this side of Red Herring City, suffering everything Walker can throw at him, from being forced to wear an embarrassingly ineffectual "age reducing" wig during a flashback sequence through to feeling the sharp end of an eye-watering impaling. John Leyton, Stephanie Beacham (also in Walker's *House of Mortal Sin*) and John Fraser fill in the supporting roles. Walker certainly gave us better in his time, but if plenty of blood, a sprinkling of nudity, a host of familiar faces and a plot that doesn't command too great an attention span is your cup of tea then *Schizo* is the film for you. And if the title alone doesn't give away the twist ending then you clearly need to find a dictionary and look up schizophrenia!

The print utilised on Image Entertainment's DVD shows minor signs of degradation in comparison to earlier VHS incarnations (only specks of dirt and occasional missing frames, but all nonetheless noticeable). However, where purchases will benefit British Walker aficionados is in the completeness of the 14-chapter print, which includes the bloody demises of housekeeper Mrs. Wallace (Queenie Watts) and her clairvoyant daughter Joy (Tricia Mortimer), both truncated to the point of virtual non-existence in the deleted Warner video cassette of some years back. The inclusion of at least a trailer would have been nice, but as it stands additional offerings total none. - TG

SCHRAMM

Colour, 1993, 65m. / Directed by Jörg Buttgereit / Starring Florian Koerner, Monika M. / Barrel (US R1 NTSC) / DD2.0

 Hardly your average splatter director, Jörg Buttgereit confounded critics by mixing high art aesthetics with painfully explicit bloodletting and sexual depravity, resulting in peculiar, downbeat hybrids like *Nekromantik 2* and *Der Tödesking*. Nowhere is this dichotomy more troubling than in *Schramm*, the director's concession to the serial killer craze which dominated horror during the 1990s. However, this is truly unlike any other psycho movie ever made.

The nonlinear story begins with taxi driver and troubled murderer Lothar Schramm (former porn actor Florian Koerner) plunging from a ladder while painting his walls. One of his apparently artificial legs pops off, and he crashes to the wooden floor, evidently in his death throes. The film then switches into partial reverse, introducing a pair of door to door religious converters who wind up on the wrong end of Schramm's knife. Gradually the layers are peeled away as we see Schramm living a tormented existence as the "Lipstick Killer," who drugs and photographs his female victims, adorns their lips with rouge, and then sometimes kills them. He also develops a crush on svelte hooker Marianna (Monika M.) and suffers through terrifying, blackly comic fantasies involving eyeball-plucking dentists, furry vagina monsters with teeth, and much more. Of course, that's nothing compared to the self-mutilation ritual he performs on his most sensitive bodily area with a hammer and some nails, so the squeamish would be well advised to steer clear. Eventually the whole story comes full circle as we come to experience the numbing day to day experience which can turn even the quietest guy next door into a potential menace.

As most readers can probably guess from the synopsis, *Schramm* is not a film for everybody and won't be a good choice to convert the uninitiated into the realm of European horror. However, adventurous souls will be more receptive to Buttgereit's quirky vision, which has become more refined and impressive with each film. (Unfortunately, this remains his last directorial effort to date.) As usual, some of his camera angles and his use of music are extremely impressive considering the limited financial means, and some of the special effects are a little too realistic for comfort.

For a 16mm title, *Schramm* looks very impressive on DVD. The image displays virtually no grain or instability at all (apart from some visually distorted dream sequences), while colours are smooth and often vibrant. The newly remixed stereo soundtrack is focused primarily on the music, which benefits greatly from the extra sonic field, though the original mono soundtrack is also included for purists. The sharp optional subtitles are also a huge relief after years of blurry, unwatchable bootleg videotapes. As with Barrel's *Nekromantik* release, the disc is stuffed with a staggering array of extras (both advertised and hidden), starting with a commentary track by Buttgereit himself alongside co-writer Franz Rodenkirchen (also in the film as a dentist); the film maker remains as self-deprecating and insightful as always. An alternate commentary track by Koerner and Monika M. proves to be somewhat juicier, including some frank revelations about the various simulated sexual scenes scattered throughout the movie. Other extras both big and small: "The Making of *Schramm*," a frank half hour documentary built around Koerner interview material and exhibitionistic behind the scenes footage; a Buttgereit music video clip for the group Mutter entitled "Die Neue Zeit;" a huge number of candid shots from the film's shooting; trailers for *Schramm, Nekromantik* (two versions), *Der Tödesking*, and *Nekromantik 2;* two subtitled short films, "Mein Papi" and "Captain Berlin," which show off the director's emotional and goofy sides, respectively; and an Easter Egg feature which leads to a banned four minute profile of Buttgereit prepared for Britain's Channel Four but never aired.

SCORE

Colour, 1973, 83m. / Directed by Radley Metzger / Starring Lynn Lowry, Gerald Grant / Image (US R0 NTSC) / WS (1.85:1)

Of all of Metzger's films, *Score* has had the strangest history on both the big screen and on home video. Conceived as an adaptation of a sexy off-Broadway play about bisexual couple-swapping, Metzger's film transplants the action to a fictitious European riverside town (actually in Luxembourg, though it looks for all the world like the Riviera) where everyone has a cushy, fulfilling job and submits to any sexual whim that strikes their fancy. While the play was fairly coy about the actual sexual interaction between the characters, Metzger's film holds back nothing and treads into waters which have never really been explored since.

Elvira (Clare Wilbur, a veteran of the play) and Jack (Gerald Grant, who later appeared in Metzger's *Naked Came the Stranger* and the Italian gore favourite *Eaten Alive*), a happily married swinging couple, play a game with each other in which they earn points by seducing unwitting members of the same sex. In the midst of exchanging savvy film history *bon mots*, they agree that they have become bored with the lack of challenge in picking up folks from magazine ads and set their sights on a young new couple: Betsy (Lynn Lowry, a great B-movie actress in the similarly themed *Shivers* as well as *Sugar Cookies, I Drink Your Blood*, and *Cat People*) and Eddie (Calvin Culver, aka gay porn actor Casey Donovan, who gained notoriety for dating late novelist/actor Tom Tryon and going straight, sort of, in Metzger's *The Opening of Misty Beethoven*). Elvira's plan entails her inviting Betsy over while Jack's away. In front of Betsy, Elvira seduces the studly phone repairman (Carl Parker, also in Metzger's remarkable *The Punishment of Anne / The Image*), a part originally played onstage by Sylvester Stallone(!), by dumping scalding coffee on his lap (there's a new one). Betsy and Eddie return for a little dinner and costume party in which they don outfits as reflections of their personalities, allowing the experienced couple to close in and make their move.

While *Score* could easily have become yet another stagnant play on film, the good performances, sharp and very funny writing, eye-catching locations, and inventive camerawork manage to keep things moving at a rapid clip. Once again, Metzger's sense of rhythm during both the dialogue and seduction sequences is impeccable, with the film's centrepiece (crosscutting between Elvira/Betsy and Jack/Eddie) churning up tremendous momentum thanks to the delirious quasi-Morricone score and inventive lighting and camera movements.

Most obviously, the DVD is by far the best this film has ever looked, even more richly colourful and sharp than the First Run VHS release. The Magnum video edition from the late '80s looks extremely sick in comparison as it brutally chops the careful compositions into mincemeat, and for some reason, the Magnum print was also cut to remove virtually every trace of frontal nudity from the film (and that's quite a bit).

Metzger's Audubon Films video label very briefly allowed a complete print of *Score* onto the market; this print, seen only in a few theatres originally, contains about two minutes' worth of mild hardcore male footage and some steamy lesbian groping. Not surprisingly, the hardcore material is missing from the First Run print, reportedly Metzger's preference, but it's strange that alternate takes weren't done to cover what surely would have been responded to with outrage by most audiences. While the frontal nudity is intact through most of the film, the big finale has been very heavily trimmed (at least over 20 brief cuts by a simple side-by-side comparison); the loss of the footage itself isn't that painful (in many ways, the film benefits overall from it), but the haphazard dicing destroys the flow of editing for what remains; the music consistently jumps with each cut, causing a nasty case of aural whiplash. This problem aside, the DVD is overall the best way to see *Score* and definitely looks better than the earlier uncut but fuzzy-looking, fullscreen Audubon release.

Unprepared audiences may greet it with disgust or extreme discomfort, but for open-minded viewers, this is a fun, light-hearted, and almost sinfully entertaining treat, not to mention a nostalgic (and for many, fantastic and alien) depiction of a time when sex could be enjoyed without guilt or fear.

SCREAM

Colour, 1996, 111m. / Directed by Wes Craven / Starring Neve Campbell, Courtney Cox
SCREAM 2
Colour, 1997, 116m. / Directed by Wes Craven / Starring Neve Campbell, David Arquette
SCREAM 3
Colour, 2000, 117m. / Directed by Wes Craven / Starring Neve Campbell, Courtney Cox
Buena Vista / WS (2.35:1) / DD5.1

Love him or hate him, Wes Craven has accomplished something no other filmmaker has managed to pull off. For three successive decades he completely redefined the horror genre and set a pace many have tried (and often failed) to follow. In the '70s he jolted audiences with the ultra-realistic revenge pageants of *Last House on the Left* and *The Hills Have Eyes*. In the '80s he dragged the slasher genre - and mainstream cinema, for that matter - into the realm of surrealism with *A Nightmare on Elm Street*. And in the '90s he brought the seemingly moribund slasher film back again by turning it on its ear with a reflexive "postmodern" approach which has since become as familiar and clichéd as its predecessors. One can only imagine what the next decade will bring.

For those completely oblivious to pop culture, the first *Scream* condenses the primary shock of *Psycho* into its unforgettable ten minute opener, which features Drew Barrymore in a whirling and scary homage to everything from *When a Stranger Calls* to *Friday the 13th*. Our story proper introduces Sidney Prescott (Neve Campbell), a teenager still recovering one year later from the brutal stabbing death of her mother. Her high school in the tranquil town of Woodsboro is shaken by news of a brutal double murder which cuts a little too close to home when the killer, dressed in black and wearing a ghostface mask, attacks Sidney that night. At first Sidney pinpoints her boyfriend, Billy (Skeet Ulrich), as the attacker, but evidence suggests otherwise. Meanwhile muckraking TV reporter Gale Weathers (Courtney Cox) follows Sidney's trail and keeps an eye on a boozing teen party, where Sidney's classmates party down and watch *Halloween*. Gale also takes an interest in the bumbling Deputy Dewey Riley (David Arquette), who has taken to sniffing out clues on his own. As the body count rises, Sidney must fight for her life and hope she manages to survive until morning.

In *Scream 2*, Sidney's off to college. A movie called *Stab* based on Gale's successful book, *The Woodsboro Murders*, sparks a controversy when two audience members are knifed during a sneak preview. Sidney's fratboy sweetheart, Derek (Jerry O'Connell), offers some semblance of normalcy, at least until Gale and Dewey show up (for different reasons) in the aftermath of the killings. The recently released Cotton Weary (Liev Schreiber) shows up hoping for a national TV interview with Sidney, but to no avail. Following a traumatic attack after a sorority party, Sidney finds her life eerily repeating

S

itself, causing numerous disruptions despite her intention to play Cassandra in a college theatre production. Is the killer a copycat, or someone with a deeper motive connected to Sidney's past?

In what Craven announced as the conclusion to an intended trilogy, *Scream 3* skips ahead several years and finds Sidney living a reclusive life under an assumed name, taking calls for a women's crisis centre. In Hollywood the third *Stab* sequel is in production, with Gale visiting the set and encountering her bitchy actress alter ego (Parker Posey). Dewey is also back, serving as a consultant on the film, and Sidney finds herself drawn to L.A. to confront her fears following the death of one *Scream* alumnus. The new killer leaves pictures of Sidney's mother at the death scenes, indicating yet another dark secret from her past ready to erupt. Reality and illusion collide in the finale, which shakily resolves several story threads for a sense of closure to the entire trilogy.

One of the most popular aspects of the *Scream* series is its "rules," which are delivered by film geek Randy (Jamie Kennedy). In the first film we're told the familiar basics of surviving a slasher film, such as avoiding sex and alcohol. In the second film the necessary requirements for sequels are skewered, such as more blood and wilder plot twists. The third film stretches the formula to the breaking point with nonexistent rules about trilogies, blithely ignoring the fact that there really aren't any horror trilogies *per se*, and even if there were, nobody's ever come up with the rules spouted off in *Scream 3* (which the film doesn't even bother to follow later on anyway). This disintegration is mirrored in the series itself, which kicks off with its strongest instalment. As easy as it may be to resent its offspring, the first *Scream* remains a lean and entertaining jaunt through the horror cinema funhouse, though its knowing attitude and relentless desire to maintain a rollercoaster pace has rubbed more than a viewers the wrong way. The film abounds in wry in-jokes, such as Linda Blair's fleeting cameo to Craven's own appearance as "Fred" the janitor, wearing a very suspicious looking sweater. *Scream* was also the director's first film in scope, a decision that results in more artful framing than one usually expects from his films. Though the self-referential trick had already been tried before in *Wes Craven's New Nightmare*, here he perfects the hall of mirrors approach to fine, chilling perfection. In *Scream 2*, a witty but strangely depressing film, the circumstances which torpedoed rushed sequels like *The Texas Chainsaw Massacre 2* are repeated here. Don't studios ever learn? The film constantly feels like new script pages are being tossed in actors' faces minutes before filming, a stark contrast to the rigorous structure of Kevin Williamson's original screenplay (a fluke, perhaps, based on his subsequent work). The identity of the murderer(s) is astoundingly arbitrary, a flaw repeated to equally grating effect in *Scream 3*. What's the point of making a mystery when the killer might as well be drawn out of a hat? Though deeply flawed, at least the third film strives for a more positive and productive result than the second film, with Sidney and her friends looking for some sense of healing and resolution to their lives. Like the second film, which contained at least two masterful sequences (the cop car and the film school editing lab), the third boasts at least one brilliant setpiece in which Sidney stumbles onto the Hollywood reproduction of her own former house and finds the experience both disorienting and terrifying. The continuity of the actors through the series also provides an amazing display of how much four years can alter a performer, with Cox and Arquette's morphing physical appearances mirroring the more subtle hardening of Campbell's face and demeanour.

Though Miramax expressed intentions to create a fourth *Scream* film (no, God, no!), their tribute to the series with *The Scream Trilogy* is mostly satisfying and should keep fans happy. Amazingly enough, they've managed to screw up their DVD of the original *Scream* for the third time, an amazing bungle considering the format's brief history. Rather than providing a new updated 16:9 transfer of the film in its director's cut as presented on laserdisc, we get the same "Collector's Edition" with a handful of extras. Oddly enough this is not the R-rated version shown in theatres, contrary to the packaging, and some of the added footage referenced by Craven and Williamson in their commentary has actually been restored, notably some gory intestine spilling in the opening scene and a shot of a crushed face during the automatic garage door sequence. Still missing, alas, are several crucial stabs during the climax, resulting in both a visual and sonic rupture in continuity. Since the extra materials are unrated anyway, why couldn't the sequence have been included there? At least the DVD looks much better than the laserdisc, and the 5.1 audio mix (as with the sequels) is real powerhouse material. *Scream 2* is the newest disc of the bunch, with a new improved transfer and a bounty of extra material. Craven's commentary track is the same, but the disc now includes outtakes, deleted scenes (including a fascinating alternate version of the "sequels suck" discussion), and music videos, along with a very creepy menu design. *Scream 3* sports a commentary track with Craven (and the noticeable absence of writer Ehren Kruger, who took over for the absent

Williamson and has so far churned out three mediocre-to-awful filmed screenplays), deleted scenes (including two superior alternate openings), a music video from Creed with Arquette doing his Dewey thing, and outtakes. The funniest bloopers, however, can be found on the fourth disc, included only with the *Scream* box set. Other extras on the fourth disc include a host of fake trailers for Sunrise Studios (the location for much of *Scream 3*), DVD-Rom material pertaining to the series and its characters, and a nifty new documentary on the production of the three films featuring interviews with the cast and crew. A nice package overall, and apart from the flaws with the films themselves and the needless repetition of the first film's previous release, you'll get your money's worth.

SECOND SKIN (SEGUNDA PIEL)

Colour, 1999, 110m. / Directed by Gerardo Vera / Starring Javier Bardem, Jordi Molla / Manga (Spain R0 PAL) / WS (2.35:1) (16:9) / DD5.1

 You would think that movies had exhausted all the possibilities of that reliable standby, the romantic triangle, and as *Second Skin* proves, you'd be right. This time the catalyst is Alberto Garcia (Jordi Molla), an aerodynamics engineer whose marriage to beautiful graphic artist Elena (Ariadna Gil) is slowly crumbling. While she struggles to hold their house and marriage together, not to mention the day to day maintenance of their young son, he's becoming more distant by the day. Things get worse when she picks up her husband's dry cleaning and finds a mysterious hotel bill, indicating he's most likely having an affair. When she confronts him, Alberto brusquely confesses to a one night stand with a female acquaintance from school, which couldn't be farther from the truth. In fact the third party is Diego (Javier Bardem), a good natured surgeon who has no idea his beloved is leading a double life, despite the fact that Alberto never bothers to stick around to eat dinner or spend the night. When Alberto and Diego finally take off together for a medical conference, Diego's best friend and colleague, Eva (*All About My Mother*'s Cecilia Roth), smells a rat. How long can the two parallel relationships hold out before everything goes straight to hell?

The glossy bisexual tragedy has been a movie staple dating back at least to John Schlesinger's 1971 depressfest, *Sunday Bloody Sunday*, though American cinema has generally veered away from

anything this controversial aside from the justifiably forgotten *Making Love*. What sets *Second Skin* apart from run of the mill soap opera junk is the pedigree of talent involved; frankly, without this talented quartet of actors involved (though Roth is basically a glorified cameo), the film would collapse under the weight of its own sense of melodrama. It's especially infuriating how two intelligent characters can become so enamoured of Alberto, who's such a drab, sullen jerk that he doesn't deserve either of them. Director Gerardo Vera, better known as a production designer on numerous Spanish productions, gives every scene a glossy, colourful look, sort of a cross between Almodóvar and *Maxim*, aided by intelligent use of scope framing. It's also odd to see Bardem and Molla, last seen together as the two macho stars of *Jamón Jamón* bashing each other over the head with giant hambones, going at it between the sheets here instead. Of course, this being a European film, the sex scenes of various persuasions are graphic enough to merit an NC-17 rating in the United States, but it's all kept tasteful and sensitive enough. Watch this on a double bill with *Happy Together*, which paired up two of Hong Kong's biggest male stars under similar circumstances, for an unforgettable international double feature.

The Manga DVD of *Second Skin* looks pretty good overall, with a colourful 16:9 transfer. The compression job slips up a few times, notably during a smoky nightclub sequence early on that turns into a series of dancing cubist blocks in the background. At least the disc's quality accurately captures the strong visuals of the film, particularly the stunning opening credits sequence, a Maurice Binder style series of azure X-rays which blossom into various tableaux like motorcycles and flowers (watch the film to find out why). The 5.1 sound mix mostly emphasizes the beautiful score by Roque Baños (in definite John Barry mode), an up and comer who also worked on several Alex de la Iglesia films. The disc includes optional English or Spanish subtitles, a couple of minor deleted scenes containing unsubtitled dialogue, a teaser and theatrical trailer (neither terribly good), and a short behind the scenes featurette.

THE SENTINEL

Colour, 1976, 92m. / Directed by Michael Winner / Starring Cristina Raines, Chris Sarandon / Goodtimes (US R1 NTSC)

Boasting a jaw-dropping cast and a plot that combines almost every successful '70s horror trend into one tight little package, *The Sentinel* is one of

those films that either makes viewers ill or scares the bejeezus out of them. Thanks to director Michael Winner (*Death Wish, The Nightcomers*), the exploitation angle is pumped up to an uncomfortable degree, particularly in the use of real life freaks mixed in with Dick Smith's unsettling make up effects for the jittery finale. Sort of like a Sidney Sheldon novel gone straight to hell, *The Sentinel* definitely isn't great cinema, but it can do quite a number on you just the same. Besides, any movie with Beverly D'Angelo and Sylvia Miles as topless cannibal lesbians in leotards can't be all bad.

After a lengthy, oh so mysterious opening in Italy which finds Catholic defenders of the faith Arthur Kennedy and Mel Ferrer muttering about something evil brewing over in America (*a la The Exorcist*), the film introduces our heroine, Alison Parker (Cristina Raines), a glamorous young fashion model. Faster than you can say *Eyes of Laura Mars*, the credits unspool over a pointless but stylish montage covering her fashion shoots and exploits throughout the Big Apple. Alison decides to settle into a brownstone apartment (*a la Rosemary's Baby*) thanks to landlady Ava Gardner, who informs her that a blind old priest (John Carradine) is her neighbour but never does anything but sit at his window all day and night. Seeing nothing odd in this, Alison moves in and becomes perturbed by the unsettling behavioural patterns of her neighbours. Creepy old Burgess Meredith prowls around, D'Angelo and Miles make out on the couch in full view of their neighbour, and someone in the apartment above Alison keeps pacing loudly back and forth all night. Alison goes to complain to her landlady, who blithely informs her that no one has lived in the building for the past three years besides Carradine. Even worse, Alison's sort-of-boyfriend, Michael (Chris Sarandon), informs her that Carradine is the latest in a long line of suicide attempts who wound up sitting in that room guarding the gateway to hell.

Goodtimes' DVD of this Universal title looks markedly better than the outdated VHS version and is presented fullscreen with an open matte, which doesn't seem to affect the composition one way or another. Picture quality is generally sharp and very good, particularly for a mid-'70s title, and while this was never a very colourful film to begin with, the Technicolor transfer looks fine; only a few minor flickering compression flaws are visible upon close inspection but shouldn't distract any casual viewers. The sound, on the other hand, has not fared as well; the quiet moments have a faint but discernable hiss that becomes more obvious when turned up loud. The kitschy score by Gil Melle, who did much better work on *Night Gallery*, sounds a little pinched but was never really all that powerful to begin with. The scare scenes still hold up well and look great here; a *Repulsion*-inspired sequence in which Raines finds herself lost in her own apartment building at night and comes upon the reanimated body of her dead father is genuinely frightening stuff and should prevent anyone from trying to watch this alone in the dark. Not a horror classic, but the chills are definitely here for anyone willing to overlook some of the tackier elements.

In a nice gesture, Goodtimes has also included the original trailer, which is in rough shape but still a lot of fun ("Look behind you, Alison!").

7 FACES OF DR. LAO

Colour, 1964, 100m. / Directed by George Pal / Starring Tony Randall, Barbara Eden / Warner (US R1 NTSC) / WS (1.85:1) (16:9)

The last film officially directed by the legendary George Pal, *The 7 Faces of Dr. Lao* remains something of a celebrated cult item, a title film buffs regularly cite as a buried treasure no one else seems to know about. Based on Charles Finney's excellent novel *The Circus of Dr. Lao* (which is actually even better), this beguiling fantasy operates on several different levels depending on the viewer's age and succeeds admirably in every respect. Gather up the family and enjoy.

At the turn of the 20th century, the western town of Abalone is shaken up by the magical arrival of Dr. Lao's circus, a series of attractions highlighting exotic creatures from around the world. Dr. Lao himself (Tony Randall) is a quirky, energetic type prone to dispensing nuggets of cockeyed wisdom to all of his patrons, though few take his words to heart. Meanwhile the people are debating whether they should sacrifice their property to the rich, scheming Clint Stark (Arthur O'Connell), who knows of plans to build a railroad in their direction and intends to cash in. Good guy newspaper editor Ed Cunningham (John Ericson) opposes the plan and spends his spare time wooing lovely librarian Angela (Barbara Eden). The townspeople keep returning to Dr. Lao's circus, where attractions like Merlin the Magician, the abominable snowman, Medusa, Pan, Apollonius, and a giant codger snake (all played by Randall as well) hold up mirrors to the faults and foibles of each person's inner nature. Ultimately everyone is changed by their encounter with Dr. Lao - some for the better, and some worse.

In many respects *Dr. Lao* can be seen as a wistful ode to the golden age of cinematic fantasy that preceded it. The entire production is bathed in a nostalgic glow and a sense of warmth and respect for humanity's innocence, which would soon become trampled during the turmoil of the late '60s. From the beautifully nuanced screenplay by veteran Twilight Zone writer Charles Beaumont to the lyrical Leigh Harline score, all of the elements here come perfectly into alignment. Randall gives an outstanding performance (or is that performances?), always unpredictable and charming even at his most monstrous in appearance. (Note: many of the impressive stop motion effects during the climax were provided by animation pro Jim Danforth, who had just cut his teeth earlier on *Jack the Giant Killer*.) Perhaps this film remains neglected because it doesn't take place on the same lavish scale of Pal's *War of the Worlds* or *The Time Machine*, so viewers will just have to discover this treasure on their own terms.

Fortunately, there's no better place to make Dr. Lao's acquaintance outside of a movie theatre than Warner's DVD special edition, which offers a beautifully textured transfer bursting with saturated layers of gold and brown, contrasting nicely with the psychedelic colour schemes inside Dr. Lao's wagons. Apart from a slightly damaged and noticeably gritty-looking opening scene, the print is in excellent condition and looks appreciably sharper than the previous MGM laserdisc. The disc also includes the theatrical trailer (which gives away far too much) and an eight minute archival featurette devoted to makeup maestro William Tuttle, who worked on almost every '50s MGM musical and really had his work cut out for him this time.

THE 7TH VOYAGE OF SINBAD

Colour, 1958, 88m. / Directed by Nathan Juran / Starring Kerwin Matthews, Kathryn Grant / Columbia (US R1 NTSC, UK R2 PAL) / WS (1.85:1) (16:9)

The definitive Saturday matinee movie, *The 7th Voyage of Sinbad* inspired waves of impressionable little kids to go into the special effects business and made Ray Harryhausen a cinematic god for fantasy fans. A pioneer in the art of stop motion animation, Harryhausen had already made an impression with his black and white sci-fi spectacles like *20 Million Miles to Earth* and *It Came from Beneath the Sea*. However, *Sinbad* offered the first time his effects could be seen in vivid colour, and even better, Harryhausen provided a whole slew of imaginative creatures, rather than one simple octopus or alien. *Sinbad* proved so popular that Harryhausen remained busy doing other fantastic literary adaptations and even two more fun Sinbad adventures.

Arriving with his crew at the mysterious island of Colossa, Sinbad encounters a shifty bald magician, Sokurah (Torin Thatcher), who uses his magical powers (including a child-like genie, Baronni) to help the men escape from a beastly Cyclops. However, the magician loses his magic lamp on the way back to Baghdad, and he insists that they return to Colossa. To get his way, Sokurah shrinks the Princess Parisa (Kathryn Grant) down to miniature size and abducts her. The only potion which can restore the princess to normal size requires a fragment from the egg of a Roc, a mythical giant two-headed bird. Sinbad and his men embark on an adventure to retrieve the Roc egg, save the princess, defeat the magician, and deal with any monsters they may encounter on the way.

While Harryhausen is obviously the major creative force behind his films, some credit should really be given to his directors, too. Doing his best work here, director Juran had already proven himself on *20 Million Miles to Earth* and showed an expert hand with turning junk into fun drive-in fodder (*The Brain from Planet Arous, The Deadly Mantis, Attack of the 50 Foot Woman*, etc.). While *Sinbad* isn't as beautifully paced and lyrically executed as Harryhausen's crowning masterpiece, *Jason and the Argonauts*, it really was the first of its kind and still delivers everything it promises. Kerwin Matthews is the first of Harryhausen's unorthodox, non-muscular heroes who use their wits and personalities to deal with obstacles, though they manage to come through with sword-swinging in a crisis. The famed skeleton battle is still the highlight of the film (repeated even more effectively in *Jason*), but all of the creatures are memorable and ingeniously executed. Thatcher makes a terrific villain, and Grant's fetching princess makes Sinbad's quest all the more believable. Of course, the rich, roaring score by Bernard Herrmann doesn't exactly hurt, either.

Columbia's DVD of *Sinbad* is generally satisfying but displays a few oddities in the presentation of the film itself. The anamorphic video looks excellent for a film of this vintage, with especially strong and stable colours (after the noisy opening credits), but the image has been severely matted at 1.85:1. Previous video incarnations were completely unmatted at 1.33:1 and allowed plenty of breathing room, but this edition looks very tight. No crucial information appears to be missing, but the creatures and actors often scrape perilously close to the upper matte, making the film more claustrophobic than it was probably intended.

The mono audio is fine and clear throughout (oddly, the alternate Portuguese track contains a completely different main title cue) but unfortunatelly it sounds extremely flat in comparison to the rich stereo track prepared for the Pioneer Special Edition on laserdisc and Columbia's subsequent Sinbad box set. The stereo track consisted of the original mix for Herrmann's music, and it's odd that Columbia wouldn't at least include it as one listening option.

In the extras department, however, the disc cannot be faulted. "This Is Dynamation," a three minute featurette produced to plug the release of *Sinbad*, examines some of the more basic effects in the film, while an 11 minute television interview with Harryhausen and the John Landis interview from the *Jason and the Argonauts* disc are included for more recent examinations of Harryhausen's craft. "The Ray Harryhausen Chronicles," a treasure trove of creature feature tidbits, examines all of Harryhausen's big screen work and includes some peeks at the various time-consuming technical processes used to bring his models to life. A large helping of trailers ranging from *3 Worlds of Gulliver* to *The Golden Voyage of Sinbad* rounds out this appetizing package.

SEXTETTE

Colour, 1978, 91m. / Directed by Ken Hughes / Starring Mae West, Timothy Dalton / Rhino (US R1 NTSC)

In 1970, legendary comedienne Mae West came out of a nearly thirty year retirement to appear in the notorious all-star X-rated spectacle, *Myra Breckinridge*. One highlight of this compelling Hollywood train wreck featured West doing a glittery stage show revue including the catchy ditty, "You Gotta Taste All the Fruit." Well, eight years later someone had the bright idea of dragging this sequence out for an entire movie, with a barrage of guest stars swirling around a script based on West's puffball play, *Sex*. To say the least, the results were not pretty.

Fabulously popular movie goddess Marlo Manners (West, of course) steps out of the church where she has just married her sixth husband, Sir Michael Barrington (Timothy Dalton, post-*Lion in Winter* and pre-007). Among the hundreds of screaming fans, the reporter covering the wedding is none other than Regis Philbin (as himself), which should give you an idea of where this is heading. In their honeymoon suite, Marlo and Michael make goo goo eyes at each other and sing a duet of "Love Will Keep Us Together" (yep, the Captain and Tenille song). Before they can finally consummate their marriage (shudder), the happy couple are interrupted by a steady stream of interlopers, fans, reporters, and former husbands. For starters, there's brash movie director Laslo (Ringo Starr), who orders his ex-wife around while shooting a love scene for his movie, and "Sexy Alexei" (Tony Curtis), a Russian diplomat still pining for Marlo and begging for her help with some kind of international conference in progress upstairs. Meanwhile the new groom gives a series of embarrassing TV interviews in which his British naiveté confounds his dirty minded hosts ("Did you say oars or whores?"). Then another ex-husband, Vance (George Hamilton), turns up to proclaim he's still legally married to Marlo, who scurries off to do perform "Happy Birthday (Twenty-One)" at a gymnasium populated by bodybuilders. (If you think this movie inspired the Village People's *Can't Stop the Music*, you'd probably be right.) Then it's back to the hotel, where Marlo sings a disco version of "Baby Face" to the diplomats and a nearly unrecognizable Alice Cooper turns up as a room service waiter, doing another disco routine on the piano.

It's hard to fathom exactly what the target audience was for *Sextette*, but devotees of camp cinema will have a blast. Many of Mae's lines are blatantly recycled from her earlier films, but a few of the zingers are still quite funny if you can overlook her unsettling appearance. After what appear to be far too many facelifts, she could evidently form only one expression on her face and didn't bother to inspect any of her tacky costumes, which change every three minutes or so. As far as star vehicles go, at least this isn't as humiliating as, say, *Wicked Stepmother*, *Trog*, or, God help us, *Body of Evidence*.

Not surprisingly, Rhino's budget priced DVD looks exactly the same as the long out of print VHS version released in the early '80s; pasty, pale, and ragged, it delivers about what you'd expect and somehow seems in keeping with the chintzy tone of the film itself. Besides, the fuzzy transfer also manages to cover up those blatant soft focus close ups of Mae's face. The sound is also very low and strident, but a little manipulation through a receiver can fix that without much effort. Throw it on at your next party and watch the guests' jaws sink to the floor in disbelief.

SHE FREAK

Colour, 1967, 83m. / Directed by Byron Mabe / Starring Claire Brennan, Lee Raymond / Image (US R0 NTSC)

Something of an odd man out in the run of '60s exploitation films, *She Freak* is an obvious labour of love for producer David Friedman, a lifelong fan of the carnival and huckster scene. While the premise and ads promise grotesque thrills and perverse shocks, what the viewer actually gets is something much more peculiar, sort of Tod Browning's *Freaks* redux with a tangy Southern slant.

A group of customers at a local carnival shuffle into a tent, lured in by the come-ons of the local barker (played by Friedman himself). Inside they see something monstrous, something terrifying... and in flashback, we learn the story of how this freak came to be. Jade Cochran (the appealing Claire Brennen - whatever happened to her?), a waitress at a greasy spoon, walks out on her job to work at a local carnival. However, she soon learns the hard way that a life among human oddities is not for her. She uses her home grown charms to catch and marry the carny owner, Steven St. John (Bill McKinney), but on the side she carries on an affair with the piggish Blackie (Lee Raymond). The local freaks notice Jade and Blackie's scheming ways, and after the illicit couple takes things a bit too far, it's time for revenge.

Unlike the original *Freaks*, Friedman's version paints the female lead in a somewhat more sympathetic light, thanks in no small part to Brennan. Unfortunately, there also weren't as many freaks at Friedman's disposal for this film, with most of them making a sudden first appearance during the creepy finale. While the lack of any overt gore or sex might put off some horror fans, *She Freak* is really more of a mood piece, a candy-coloured ode to the carny life. Several minutes on end are devoted to the camera swirling inside Ferris wheels, following men setting up tents, skirting along the sideshows, and prowling into the trailers. You can almost smell the cotton candy and peanuts from the opening minutes, and the quirky, off-kilter jazz score twists the atmosphere even more out of the ordinary.

While *She Freak* has been issued on video in several variants from Magnum and Something Weird, the DVD is truly an entirely new experience. The eye-popping colour on display here simply defies description; even Brennen's dresses, ranging from saturated sherbet to luminous crimson, are perfectly defined and seem to glow like neon. If only all movies of this vintage could look so good!

The disc also includes a commentary track with Friedman, conducted by Something Weird's Mike Vraney, in which he elaborates on his own carny experiences and the process of adapting Browning's classic for the '60s grindhouse crowd. Other goodies include a theatrical trailer (whose muddy quality emphasizes just how good the feature itself really looks) and a jaw-dropping reel of actual black and white film footage of a carnival sideshow during the '30s, along with interview footage of the Hilton Sisters (from *Freaks*) and the Gibb Sisters, two sets of Siamese twins. Definitely not for the politically correct.

SHE KILLED IN ECSTASY

Colour, 1970, 77m. / Directed by Jess Franco / Starring Soledad Miranda, Paul Müller / Synapse (US R1 NTSC) / WS (1.66:1), Second Sight (UK R2 PAL) / WS (1.66:1) (16:9)

Returning once again for inspiration to the plotline of Cornell Woolrich's *The Bride Wore Black*, which had already at least partially inspired his *Venus in Furs* and *The Diabolical Dr. Z*, Jess Franco spins his most erotic take on a beautiful woman avenging a death by picking off the guilty parties one by one. The late slinky screen siren Soledad Miranda (*Vampyros Lesbos*) returned for the third of five collaborations with Franco before her untimely death, and her presence ignites what could have been another routine revenge potboiler.

A beautiful woman (Miranda) lives in bliss with her lover, Dr. Johnson (Fred Williams), who conducts unorthodox experiments with human embryos kept in jars around the lab. When a medical committee rejects his findings and orders him to discontinue his work, the unstable doctor does the only sensible thing: he slashes his wrists in the bathroom. The devastated Miranda then takes it upon herself to seduce and kill the three men and one woman "responsible" for the suicide. Two of the potential victims include Dr. Orloff himself, Howard Vernon, and Franco in one of his largest roles.

S

As dreamlike and Eurotrashy as *Vampyros Lesbos*, this film, also known as *Mrs. Hyde*, differs mainly in its adherence to a non-supernatural plotline. Miranda's erotic presence once again drives the film along even when the plot doesn't seem to be going anywhere, and her systematic seduction/murders are all memorable set pieces complete with plentiful nudity. (Unfortunately this also requires Vernon to get naked, so viewer beware.) German musicians Manfred Hubler and Siegfried Schwab (*Vampyros Lesbos*) return for another mind-bending assemblage of funky grooves on the soundtrack, while the Mediterranean locales and pop art set design make this early '70s eye candy of the first order. Not a film for everyone, of course, but then Franco fans already know that.

Synapse's DVD of *She Killed in Ecstasy* (or *Sie tötete in extase*) is essentially a cleaner, sharper rendition of the same print used for Redemption's UK video release. Apparently this was the best surviving material that could be found at the time, though the image often contains hairline scratches and other telltale signs of age. It's a thousand times better than those old bootleg tapes, though, and has good, removable yellow English subtitles. The disc also includes the delirious original German trailer and some surprisingly explicit artwork of Ms. Miranda, though some US sleeves feature a toned down version.

The best of the bunch, though, is the UK disc from Second Sight, which sports a glossier anamorphic transfer, with vastly improved colour and image quality. Not too shabby for a film nobody could even see a few years ago except in blurry, incomplete German dupes.

SHE-DEVILS ON WHEELS

Colour, 1968, 82m. / Directed by Herschell Gordon Lewis / Starring Betty Conell, Pat Poston / Image (US R0 NTSC), Tartan (UK R2 PAL)

There's nothing worse than a good girl gone bad, and it doesn't get much worse than a girl biker gang. Meet The Maneaters, a hellraising pack of distaff rebels whose newest member, sweet little Karen (Christie Wagner), has just turned on to the feel of hot metal tearing down the highway. The Maneaters, led by the ruthless Queen (Betty Conell), hold races and pick their sexual conquests from a stud line of willing male participants. When Karen picks the wrong guy, Queen forces her to drag the poor sap behind her chopper and render him bloody and battered. The Maneaters then lock horns with a rival male gang led by the rough, tough Joe Boy and terrorize the local town without fear of reprisals from the citizens or the police. Can these wanton hooligan girls ever be stopped? Will the gang warfare leave anyone alive? See the movie and find out!

This surprisingly extreme biker film marked Lewis' attempt to further reinvent the splatter genre after *The Gruesome Twosome*. Here the storyline controls the carnage, and the characters and performances are realized well enough to keep the viewer engaged even in the stretches without beatings and dismemberments.

While it doesn't quite hit the delirious heights of Russ Meyer's *Faster, Pussycat! Kill! Kill!*, Lewis' opus comes in a close second and unquestionably delivers the exploitation goods. The snappy, often uproarious dialogue wouldn't look out of place in a John Waters movie, and it's no wonder the legendary Baltimore director holds a special place for Lewis in his heart.

Kudos go out as well to the theme song, "Get Off the Road," which gives *Two Thousand Maniacs'* "The South's Gonna Rise Again" a run for its money. And believe it or not, this played many drive-ins as a double bill with the first Billy Jack film, *Born Losers*, and proved to be one of H.G.'s biggest money-makers ever. Perhaps the generous flow of fake blood proved to be more acceptable at the hands of biker women instead of knife-wielding maniacs.

Something Weird's DVD of *She-Devils on Wheels* obviously outclasses previous VHS editions of this video store staple, and considering the film's touch and go theatrical heritage, the disc presentation is miraculous. Those vivid '60s colours Lewis had already demonstrated in *Blood Feast* are back again, this time punched up with some trippy colour schemes that make the proceedings all the more surreal. Once again Lewis provides a commentary track in which he extols the virtues of low budget filmmaking and resourcefulness, prodded on by informative contributions from Mike Vraney and Jimmy Maslon.

Extras accessible from the amusing menu design include the gut-busting theatrical trailer and a bizarre short christened here as "Biker Beach Party." Scary, scary stuff.

SHEBA, BABY

Colour, 1975, 90m. / Directed by William Girdler / Starring Pam Grier, Austin Stoker / MGM (US R1 NTSC) / WS (1.85:1) (16:9)

The same year as *Friday Foster*, Grier returned in her flimsiest action vehicle, *Sheba, Baby*, a disappointing, PG-rated attempt to bring her magic to a wider audience. Amazingly, very little comes from the combination of Grier with the eccentric sleaze director William Girdler (*The Manitou, Abby*), who died three years later at the age of 31. Here his lovable tendency to go overboard at all costs is kept firmly in check, resulting in a toothless detective yarn that would have been instantly forgotten had it featured any other leading lady.

After her father's loan office is trashed by hoodlums, sexy private eye Sheba Shayne (Grier) returns home to Louisville to find out who's responsible for the local terrorism. She begins an affair with the handsome Brick (*Assault on Precinct 13*'s Austin Stoker) and pokes around in the criminal underworld. Naturally there's an evil white guy behind it all, so Sheba hunts him down in the film's only notable action scene, an extended boat chase with Sheba clad in a skin-tight diving suit. Obviously, the decision to go with a cleaner, sweet image for Pam Grier backfired tremendously with this film, which was allegedly written in less than a day - and it shows. The Louisville setting, Girdler's original stomping grounds, is also less interesting than the gritty urban locales of Grier's prior films.

Oddly, this version from the Orion vaults contains a little more skin than the US PG version, though it still falls way short of Pam's other appearances. At least those into '70s culture can enjoy her flamboyant outfits and the typically funky score, which is best served during the memorable opening credits (including great close ups of Pam's designer jeans).

Sheba, Baby sports a terrific anamorphic transfer from a spotless, razor sharp print. The 1.85:1 framing looks a bit tight now and then, but it's more visually pleasing than the distracting amount of headroom visible on the open matte VHS versions. The theatrical trailer appears to be a rough cut in which the film's title is nowhere to be seen.

THE SHINING

Colour, 1980, 144m. / Directed by Stanley Kubrick / Starring Jack Nicholson, Shelley Duvall / Warner (US R1 NTSC), (UK R2 PAL) / DD5.1

More than any other Kubrick film, *The Shining* fell victim to the *2001* syndrome when originally released. After a massive promotional build-up,

audiences expecting the ultimate philosophical experience in elegant horror were startled to be confronted with a steadily building descent into hell courtesy of Jack Nicholson's on-camera mental breakdown. Furthermore, inevitable comparisons to Stephen King's source novel often led to the film suffering in comparison - even according to King himself. In retrospect, *The Shining* is a key horror film of the '80s, a pivotal work whose influence continues to be felt today and whose impact on the so-called Generation-X age group (if such a thing really exists) has yet to dissipate.

The plot is simple enough: Jack Torrance (Jack Nicholson), his wife Wendy (Shelley Duvall), and their son, Danny (Danny Lloyd), move into a sprawling Colorado hotel after Jack accepts a position there as the winter caretaker. After being shown the ropes by the cook, Halloran (Scatman Crothers), the family is left to their own devices for a long, snowy winter. Danny's possession of a strange psychic gift, dubbed "the shining" by the similarly-gifted Halloran, causes the boy to believe the hotel is haunted by ghosts, including those of the twin daughters murdered with an axe by the previous caretaker. A recovering alcoholic and struggling writer, Jack finds his tenuous grip on reality slipping away as the hotel begins to exert its evil spectral influence.

The Shining contains some of the most indelible images of the horror genre: the blood-spilling elevator, the two girl ghosts, Nicholson's axe-wielding chase through the snowy maze. However, the film is unsettling for other, more intangible reasons as well, particularly through its manipulation of time and space. The film is broken up by title cards ("Closing Day," "4 A.M.," etc.) which become increasingly meaningless as the story progresses and the present and past begin to merge into a horrific jumble of images and sounds. The collision of the spiritual and physical planes becomes complete when first Jack and then Wendy begin to physically witness the apparitions, and the ghosts even intrude on the physical level by unlocking a door. While a number of horror films achieve their power through psychological suggestion (*The Haunting* being the most obvious example), *The Shining* takes an entirely different approach of horror through sensory accumulation. Rather than being presented with showstopping moments of terror, the film's progression of chills operates like a near-death experience - the full impact doesn't register until hours later when the

S

viewer thinks back on the film and suddenly begins to shiver at how it all locks together. Wendy's discovery of Jack's manuscript in essence sums up the whole approach of the film - just one page is a little creepy and strange, but in context with the whole work, it's simply terrifying.

More than perhaps any other Kubrick film, this also relies heavily upon its actors to carry the film, and while Nicholson is indeed a wonder to behold in his bulldozer psycho performance, Duvall is his equal on every level, conveying a normal woman brought to the threshold of hysteria. Significantly, in 1998 King took a shot at literally translating his novel into a TV miniseries and, while fairly successful overall, the more recent version proved that many of Kubrick's choices (such as omitting the haunted topiary animals) were sound indeed. The film's final image, the harshest object of criticism back in 1980, makes sound narrative sense in retrospect and works far better than the soppy feel-good ending King himself tacked onto the miniseries.

Kubrick preferred this film to be presented completely open matte (even in theatres, though few projectionists complied), and that's how it has existed on video since its first release in the early '80s apart from a matted Japanese release. Warner's first DVD was a disaster; the increased clarity of DVD increased the grain in a number of shots, and worse, the colour on the DVD was pulled back too far. The studio's second DVD version from a new hi-def transfer improves things considerably and looks astonishingly colourful and dimensional. Furthermore, the 5.1 remix tastefully mixes the music to the exterior channels with surprising effectiveness and fidelity to the original presentation.

Both discs contain the creepy US trailer and Vivian Kubrick's notorious half hour documentary, "Making The Shining." This astonishing chamber piece features interviews with the principal cast and shows Kubrick at work, several times cursing Shelley Duvall presumably in an attempt to shake her into character. Duvall comes off as something of a flake here, while Jack comes off as... well, Jack. Great stuff, and almost worth the price tag by itself. Unfortunately, there's one supplement we'll probably never see: a two minute epilogue present in some first run theatrical prints which finds the film's survivors in the hospital. Since Kubrick had the film recalled and reedited, his estate will probably never release it; too bad.

Incidentally, most European release cuts of this film (both theatrical and video) run a relatively scant 118 minutes; avoid this version at all costs.

SHIVER OF THE VAMPIRES

Colour, 1970, 95m. / Directed by Jean Rollin / Starring Sandra Julien, Michel Delahaye / Image (US R0 NTSC) / WS (1.66:1)

While Jean Rollin directed two experimental vampire films before this one, *Shiver of the Vampires (Le frisson des vampires)* fully established the visual motifs and overall stylistic approach to which he would return for most of his subsequent horror efforts. A blatant homage to the erotic/horrific comics and serials of which Rollin is so fond, *Shiver* played more widely than prior Rollin titles in various countries under so many alternate versions that trying to assemble a genuine, complete cut has become virtually impossible. However, this edition from Image and Redemption is purportedly Rollin's personal preferred cut, and at 95 minutes, it remains the longest and most purely "Rollin-esque" edition available.

The plot, to use the term loosely, finds a newlywed couple arriving at a castle populated by mysterious lovely women and two hippie hosts. Their odd but uneventful stay is interrupted when a strange, Amazonian vampire (Dominique) steps out of a tall grandfather clock at midnight and exerts her bloodthirsty influence on the other vampiric inhabitants. Like most Rollin films, this winds up on a beach for one of his traditional visually striking, melancholy finales that linger in the mind long after the film is over.

Drenched in bizarre, candy-coloured lighting, which predates Dario Argento's *Suspiria* by at least six years, *Frisson* is still one of its creator's most visually intoxicating works. The extremely thin storyline only has the slightest relationship to the actions onscreen, which tend to involve various performers falling into sexual and vampiric poses. Extremely long, non-dialogue passages provide some beautifully poetic moments seething with gothic malaise and decay, a treatment that would reach its zenith in *Requiem for a Vampire*.

Though not his most polished effort by a long shot, *Shiver* is really where it all started and remains an important contribution to European vampire cinema. In an attempt to make this film as commercially viable as possible, distributors have inserted new scenes, thrown in outtakes, and hacked away entire sequences to create a number of wildly different variations. One English-language version, *Sex and the Vampire*, runs as short as 75 minutes, while a longer English cut, *Thrill of the Vampires*, contains some additional S&M footage thrown in for extra salacious value. Most European video collectors first became acquainted with this film on the grey market thanks to a Spanish-language release, which features some alternate dialogue and sex scene takes as well as a different (and quite good) music score. The original French score by the amateur group Acanthus is wild and consistently amusing progressive rock, as garish and outré as the irrational lighting schemes.

The DVD contains the original French language version with optional English subtitles. The film is slightly letterboxed, revealing the maximum amount of image available, and easily outclasses any other version available. The eye-popping colours look as good as the ridiculously cheap shooting conditions will allow, and the level of detail and sharpness is impressive.

SHIVERS

Colour, 1975, 87m. / Directed by David Cronenberg / Starring Paul Hampton, Lynn Lowry / Metrodome (UK R2 PAL) / WS (1.85:1) (16:9), Image (US R0 NTSC)

David Cronenberg's first film, better known to US viewers as *They Came from Within*, is one of those little gems in which a director's first feature already displays his major themes and concerns, similar in many ways to Romero's *Night of the Living Dead*. A similarly revisionist look at society pulled inside out by modern technology, Cronenberg ups the ante by throwing the era's cavalier attitude towards sexuality into the mix. Thus, in this film, the residents of a technologically advanced hi-rise are transformed into decadent, violent mirrors of their former selves by fecalesque parasites that invade the body through sexual (mostly oral) contact.

Not exactly pleasant stuff, but Cronenberg's chilly, piercing style makes this impossible to turn away from, regardless of how you may feel about it. Cult film fans will also enjoy the presence of Italian horror diva Barbara Steele in one of her most perverse roles, as well as a memorable part by underrated exploitation starlet Lynn Lowry (*Score, I Drink Your Blood, Sugar Cookies*).

This new "director's cut" really isn't anything new; most of the nasty footage which was previously censored from the US prints has been available to horror fans in various editions, including the CIC Canada videotape, an uncut release from Vestron video, various uncut British VHS releases and a Japanese laserdisc (released with *Rabid* and *The Brood*). However, the big news is the picture quality, which is a quantum leap over any previous edition. While the opening titles still look pretty washed out (and must have been filmed that way), the rest looks very clear and sharp, with startling bursts of colour throughout. The film is presented full frame in a transfer that is either unmatted or very slightly cropped from 1.66:1; either way, it looks just fine. DVD-philes may be put off by the visual limitations of the low budget (a little grain here, an overdone exposure there), but horror buffs will be more than pleased.

As a bonus, the DVD includes the original (and very creepy) Canadian trailer and an informative 20-minute interview with Cronenberg about his tax shelter days in Canada and the birth of his first feature film. The interesting liner notes (including a surprise tidbit about Jonathan Demme) make this package even more desirable. Note: the 110-minute running time on the box refers to the film and all of the supplements combined. The UK edition from Metrodome was released later and mattes off the image to 1.85:1, with anamorphic enhancement; it looks a bit tight overall and magnifies the grain in the image, but fans may find the increase in resolution worth it.

SHOCK

Colour, 1977, 94m. / Directed by Mario Bava / Starring Daria Nicolodi, John Steiner / Anchor Bay (US R1 NTSC) / WS (1.85:1) (16:9)

Twitch of the Death Nerve may be gorier, *Black Sunday* may be more influential, and *Blood and Black Lace* may be more beautiful, but Mario Bava never made a more purely frightening film than *Shock*. A claustrophobic gut punch that drags the viewer straight down into the mind of a woman going mad, the film features a few bloody concessions to the '70s horror market but also remains a beautifully crafted, psychologically devastating little chamber piece, not to mention a strangely appropriate final feature for the maestro.

Dora (Daria Nicolodi) and her new husband, Bruno (John Steiner), move into a new house along with Marco (David Colin, Jr.), Dora's son from a previous marriage. Strange events immediately plague the household, with cute little Marco prone to such homilies as "I'm going to have to kill you, mommy." Bruno's job as an airline pilot forces him

S

to stay away from home for extended periods, leaving Dora to cope with either her own onset of insanity or the realization that her son might be possessed by the ghost of husband number one, a sleazy drug addict. Soon Marco's slicing up his mother's underwear and doing nasty tricks with razor blades, while Dora experiences horrific visions of clutching hands from beyond the grave.

Originally released to US theatres and home video as *Beyond the Door II,* this film has nothing to do with *Beyond the Door* apart from the vague possession theme and the presence of Colin, Jr. Argento's former muse, Nicolodi delivers the best performance of her career, beginning as a sweet and maternal figure but gradually shattering into a completely hysterical wreck. Interestingly, she would later reteam with Steiner for Argento's equally nihilistic *Tenebre.*

hock is rarely cited as a prime example of Bava's style, but he pulls off so many magnificent little flourishes that the most demanding Eurofanatics should be quite happy. This film also marked an increased collaboration with his son, Lamberto (*Demons*), who was allowed to take over the reins in several scenes. Together they orchestrated some of the most effective jolts in either director's career, particularly a brilliant sequence near the end (the hallway bit) that has scarred more than a few late night TV viewers. The free form prog rock score by I Libra (consisting of two Goblin members but, contrary to Anchor Bay's liner notes, not Goblin themselves) strikes just the right balance between lyricism and oppression; the *Deep Red*-style main theme alone is a musical *tour de force.*

The previous American video release of *Shock* from the Media label bore the *Beyond the Door II* title and was missing a few minor bits of footage, mostly involving child psychologist Ivan Rassimov. Anchor Bay's presentation is the full European print, though most viewers probably won't notice anything different. The film was originally lensed with a soft, brownish visual texture, which emphasizes the film's atmosphere of decay and delirium, and this presentation captures that appearance quite well. It's also a considerable improvement compared to the letterboxed but over-bright edition on Japanese video that floated through the bootleg market over the years.

The disc also includes an 8 minute interview with Lamberto Bava, who discusses the extent of his own involvement in the film's shooting and his collaboration with screenwriter Dardano Sacchetti; not surprisingly, with this film they were aiming for an approach similar to Stephen King novels. Two US TV spots (one paired up with *The Dark*) pale in comparison to the long, surreal Italian trailer; be warned now that all of these extras blow some crucial moments in the story, so be sure to watch the film first.

SHOCK WAVES

Colour, 1977, 85m. / Directed by Ken Wiederhorn / Starring Peter Cushing, Brooke Adams / Vipco (UK R0 PAL) / WS (1.85:1) (16:9)

 Virtually forgotten today, this atmospheric zombie gem from the late '70s became a minor cult hit on the drive-in circuit and spawned the brief directorial career of Ken Wiederhorn, who went on to 1981's flawed but interesting *Eyes of a Stranger* before lapsing into mediocrity with *Return of the Living Dead II.* Here we have a fine genre cast, including relatively brief appearances by legends Peter Cushing and John Carradine, placed in a restrained, memorable mood piece which comes out short on blood but long on chills.

A lifeboat carrying a visibly traumatized survivor, Rose (a pre-*Invasion of the Body Snatchers* Brooke Adams), proves to be the only remnant of an ill-fated vacation cruise in the tropics. In flashback, Rose recalls the damage done to her companions' ship (captained by Carradine) by the submerged hull of a mysterious vessel, leaving them stranded on a remote island seemingly untouched by human hands. However, one resident, a former SS officer (Cushing), calls the island his home and uses his hidden facility to breed zombies from the bodies of his deceased Aryan soldiers. The blond, goggle-wearing members of Cushing's self-appointed Death Corps now lurk beneath the lake and ocean surfaces dotting the island, ready to drag the new visitors to a watery death.

Despite its lack of technical polish and obvious low budget, *Shock Waves* is one of those buried treasures horror fans love to discover and recommend to their friends. The surreal, dreamlike setting plays like a cross between Lucio Fulci's *Zombie* and the haunted wastelands of Val Lewton, and the detached, somnambulist performances, coupled with a skin-crawling electronic score, make for a unique and unsettling experience. The images of soldiers rising from the water are the most memorable, but the film contains several other worthy sequences like Adams' tranquil swim across a lake and a tense showdown in a darkened laboratory. The dark little twist in the final scene isn't easy to overlook, either. Incidentally, the make-up chores were handled by director/producer Alan Ormsby, whose *Children Shouldn't Play with Dead Things* would make a perfect double feature with this one.

First released on US videotape by Prism in a soft but watchable transfer, *Shock Waves* has been difficult to locate for years. While one might expect it to be a sure-fire entry in the American DVD renaissance of obscure horror releases, Britain has instead given the film its DVD inauguration. Sadly the transfer isn't much of an improvement over the videotape; the print is colourful enough but it is unfortunately extremely battered, particularly during the opening reel. The opening sequence in particular looks the worse for wear, and while the rest is watchable, detail fluctuates from acceptable to slightly smudgy. This title certainly deserves better treatment from more pristine elements, hopefully in the near future, but those who have tried to hunt it down should find this a passable but deeply compromised edition. The mono audio sounds muddy, but the music and dialogue are at least coherent and don't suffer from scratchiness or other distracting defects.

The disc carries an "18" rating, which is most likely attributable to the presence of graphic trailers for *Cannibal Holocaust*, *Mountain of the Cannibal God*, and *Psychic Killer*. The film itself actually garnered a PG rating in the US and a "15" in Britain, though the nightmarish ambience makes it less than ideal viewing for sensitive children. A special edition in the U.S. is slated at the time of this writing from Blue Underground.

SHOGUN ASSASSIN

Colour, 1980, 86m. / Directed by Kenji Misumi / Robert Houston / Starring Tomisaburo Wakayama / Vipco (UK R0 PAL) / WS (2.35:1)

"The greatest team in the history of mass slaughter!" proclaimed the ads, and indeed, the merits of this incredible film have not been exaggerated. One of the most sublimely bloody films ever made, *Shogun Assassin* pushes samurai cinema to the most surreal extremes of violence ever presented in commercial cinema, but it also happens to be a rip roaring good time.

Derived from *Lone Wolf and Cub*, a popular comic book series by the amazing Kazuo Koike, this film begins with a ten minute tour through the events of *Sword of Vengeance*, the first (or third, depending on your country) film in the popular Lone Wolf films in Japan. Most of *Shogun Assassin* consists of *Baby Cart at the River Styx (Kozure Ôkami: Sanzu no kawa no ubaguruma)*, the hyperbolic second entry in the series, albeit with Americanized dubbing and a compelling electronic score engineered by Mark Lindsay (of Paul Revere and the Raiders). Got all that?

In feudal Japan, the shogun becomes afraid of his top assassin, Ogami Itto (Tomisaburo Wakayama), and sends men to kill him. Unfortunately, only Ogami's wife dies during the attack, and Ogami offers his son Daigoro a choice: instant death or a life on the road to Hell. Daigoro chooses the road, and so the two embark on a gory trek through the Japanese countryside, with Daigoro holstered in a lethally booby trapped baby carriage. A group of female ninjas from the deadly Yagyu clan track down Ogami as he cuts a bloody swath through the shogun's agents, and many unlucky people lose bodily appendages along the way.

While some purists may balk at the "blasphemous" concept of packaging this poetic film with such commercial trappings as a new score and dubbed voices, the fact remains that this version was responsible for converting many international viewers to the wonders of the Lone Wolf series, and indeed extreme Japanese cinema in general. (Trivia note: humourists Sandra Bernhard and Marshall Efron are among the American voices.) While the film was immediately successful in Japan and spawned a strong series of films (most notably *Lightning Swords of Death*) and a watered down television series, Americans remained oblivious until this repackaged edition appeared eight years later. Roger Corman's New World released this cut in the US, and urban theatres and drive-ins were never the same.

Although the original versions of the Lone Wolf and Cub films are readily available on VHS and laserdisc from AnimEigo, *Shogun Assassin* remained out of circulation after its early appearance on home video from Universal. Long banned in the UK for its extreme violence, this film surprisingly has turned up uncut and beautifully letterboxed on DVD. The print shows its age, not surprisingly, but the quality is better than the tape. While a full scale restoration is in order to recapture the luminous colours of the theatrical prints, this version is a welcome relief after years of enduring awful pan and scan transfers. The full widescreen ratio is crucial for an appreciation of the epic visual choreography, particularly the unforgettable finale in which Ogami takes on a series of attackers on a desolate stretch of desert. The disc also includes the feisty, memorable US trailer.

SHREK

Colour, 2001, 90m. / Directed by Andrew Adamson and Vicky Jenson / DreamWorks / WS (1.77:1) (16:9) / DD5.1, DTS

Lord Farquaad banishes all the fairytale characters from his kingdom whereupon they take refuge in the swamp. But this is the domain of reclusive ogre Shrek. When he complains to Farquaad, a deal is set whereby the unwelcome guests will be ousted if Shrek rescues Princess Fiona from the Dragon's castle so that Farquaad may take her for his bride.

The best kiddies film for grown-ups this side of a digitized swamp, out-Disneying Disney and every other pretender to the throne, this film is festooned with one-liners that go straight over the heads of most youngsters yet find a gleeful target with adults. The ogre himself, as voiced by Mike Myers, is not only the backbone of the movie, he's also the perfect straight man for Eddie Murphy's Donkey, who gets the crispiest dialogue and the cream of the (often slightly vulgar) funnies: "Pheeuw, Shrek, did you do that? Man, you gotta warn somebody before you just crack one off, my mouth was open and everything!" Other principal character voices are supplied by Cameron Diaz (Fiona) and John Lithgow (Farquaad).

There are more wonderful moments of creative genius than it's possible to assimilate, not to mention subtle sight gags on the periphery of the action; you need to see the film at least three times just to take everything on board. Distinct highlights are Farquaad torturing the Gingerbread Man (with some hilarious dialogue derived from that old chestnut "The Muffin Man"), Princess Fiona warbling to a bird which attempts to duplicate her timbre and explodes leaving a smoking pair of feet, and numerous scenes that affectionately parody archaic fairytale characters such as the Three Little Pigs, the Big Bad Wolf, the Three Blind Mice, Pinocchio, Snow White and the Seven Dwarfs and many more. An age old morality fable of accepting yourself and others for who and what they are, there's more than a passing piquancy of Beauty and the Beast about Shrek. But directors Andrew Adamson and Vicky Jenson, along with their team of CGI virtuosi, have conjured up a searingly colourful 3-D never-never land and a timeless classic that will have audiences laughing their larynxes sore for years to come. Really, really.

Forget the cheapskate Region 2 single disc of Shrek. The one to own is the two-platter Region 1 set, loaded with more extras than you can shake a Shrek at. Disc #1 contains the crystal clear, 20-chapter encoded fullscreen version of the film, a 25-minute "HBO First Look: The Making of Shrek" documentary, two music videos (Baha Men's "Best Years of Our Lives" - plus a short about its making - and Smash Mouth's "I'm A Believer"), the brilliantly conceived "Shrek's Karaoke Dance Party" music video, a collection of scene highlights (superfluous, since they can be easily accessed via the chapter menu), a batch of interactive games (mostly silly, though the "Magic Mirror" one is so daft as to be hilarious), some mock interview segments comprising newly generated footage that allows the characters themselves to do the talking, text biographies of the main voice artists, extensive crew biographies, production notes and loads of DVD-ROM fun for the little'uns (including a dubbing facility that enables you to record and apply your own voice to a character).

Disc #2 houses a 1.77:1 widescreen transfer of the movie (again with 20 chapter breaks), a 22-minute "Tech of Shrek" documentary (portions of which appear in the HBO special on Disc #1), multi-angle deleted scenes in narrated storyboard form, some weird technical goofs, text biographies, concept character artwork, a trailer, a short featurette on the film's re-dubbing round the world and a reprise of the karaoke video. This disc also includes a feature commentary, provided in English, Spanish and French. Language choices on Disc #1 are English 5.1 Dolby Digital and English, French or Spanish 2.0 Dolby Surround. On Disc #2 they are English DTS Digital Surround, English 2.0 Dolby Surround and English, French and Spanish 5.1 Dolby Digital. Subtitling on both discs is in English, French and Spanish. - TG

SILENT NIGHT, BLOODY NIGHT

Colour, 1973, 81m. / Directed by Theodore Gershuny / Starring Patrick O'Neal, Mary Woronov / Diamond (US R0 NTSC)

The first of many horror films to derive their titles from that most sombre of Christmas hymns, Silent Night, Bloody Night is one of those low budget horror quickies lucky enough to grow far more interesting with the passing of time. A long-time staple of late night TV (including regular showings in the US on Elvira's Movie Macabre which surprisingly left most of the shocking gore intact), this oddity has the power to haunt viewers willing to overlook its lack of technical polish.

In the creepy opener, an offscreen female narrator introduces the bizarre history behind East Willard, a dying snowy hamlet where the Butler estate, formerly a mental institution, became the springboard for an inexplicable burning death. This Christmas, a variety of people have descended upon the Butler estate, including middle-aged lawyer John Carter (Patrick O'Neal) and his mistress (Astrid Heeren). The pair decide to spend the night in the Butler house after a meeting with the town locals, including John Carradine in a quirky extended cameo. An escapee from nearby asylum infiltrates the Butler house and begins a spate of unnerving phone calls, punctuated by the occasional gory axe murder. The Butler heir, Jeffrey (James Patterson), enlists the aid of the touchy Diane (Mary Woronov), the mayor's daughter, to uncover the horrifying history behind the desolate house, culminating in an extended monochromatic, blood spattered flashback sequence.

Directed shortly before Bob Clark's classic *Black Christmas*, which was also given the similar alternate title of *Silent Night, Evil Night*, this rare directorial venture for New Yorker Theodore Gershuny (*Sugar Cookies*, also with Woronov) shares some odd parallels with its Canadian cousin, including wide-angle POV shots of a manic killer storming through an empty house, menacing whispered phone calls, the snowy setting, and a jarring willingness to off sympathetic characters at any moment. Though not as accomplished, this film is interesting enough on its own terms and contains several moments capable of producing a genuine chill ("Take my hand..."). Exploitation fans will especially get a kick out of that cast, which mixes pros like O'Neal and Carradine with members of Andy Warhol's Factory players sprinkled in the asylum scene (including a brief appearance by platinum-haired Candy Darling). Underground icon Jack Smith (*Flaming Creatures*) pops in there briefly, too.

Virtually impossible to see with all of its violence intact outside of Paragon's long out-of-print, cruddy looking VHS edition, the Diamond DVD is a slight step up but still makes one hunger for a pristine edition. The print is in battered condition during several scenes, but these flaws are obscured by the typically careless Diamond compression job, which leaves static wall shadows dancing around from one frame to another. Image quality is soft but reasonably colourful, while the open matte framing leaves plenty of headroom throughout. Audio is soft but passable, leaving only

a few lines of dialogue difficult to decipher. The disc also includes cursory bios for Carradine and O'Neal, while the print also contains some interesting anomalies compared to the Paragon version.

A SIMPLE PLAN

Colour, 1998, 121m. / Directed by Sam Raimi / Starring Bill Paxton, Billy Bob Thornton / Paramount (US R1 NTSC) / WS (1.85:1) (16:9) / DD5.1

Best known for his kinetic mixtures of slapstick and comic book horror, director Sam Raimi here makes a cinematic gearshift even more radical than his feminist western *The Quick and the Dead*, by tackling - gasp! - a subtle, psychological morality tale. Fortunately he succeeded beyond expectations and delivered a mature, insightful work. While long-time fans may regret the absence of those trademark whooshing "Sam cam" shots (and Bruce Campbell isn't anywhere in sight!), *A Simple Plan* nevertheless stands as one of his strongest efforts to date.

Hank Mitchell (Bill Paxton) and his wife, Sarah (Bridget Fonda), lead a humble but relatively content existence. During a snowy hunting day through the forest, Hank, his socially challenged brother, Jacob (Billy Bob Thornton), and Jacob's redneck friend, Lou (Brent Briscoe), stumble upon a small crashed airplane containing a dead pilot and a gym bag filled with money - $4.4 million, to be precise. After much deliberation, the men decide to stash the money until the snow melts, and if no one has come to claim it, they'll keep the cash and split it among themselves. Despite their pact of silence, Hank reveals the secret to Sarah, who immediately conjures up various schemes to keep their self-interests protected. Not surprisingly, the "simple" plan begins to spiral horribly out of control, leading to chilling and morally anguished consequences.

While the entire cast is at their solid best here, with Fonda playing amusingly against type as a pregnant Lady Macbeth, the film's real centre is Billy Bob Thornton's remarkable performance. Essentially an inversion of his role in *Sling Blade*, here Thornton portrays a simple man whose often surprising intelligence has never been used due to his gawky appearance and lacking social skills. The warmest and most human element of the film, Thornton imbues the character - and thus, the rest of the film - with a complexity and sense of a life trapped in futility, which allows the narrative to

S

transcend its familiar plot, setup and rise to level of bitter tragedy. While comparisons have been drawn between this film and other grim moral tales like *Shallow Grave* and *Fargo*, this basic storyline has been around with us since *The Canterbury Tales*. Thus, the magic lies in the reinvention of the tale, and thanks to Scott B. Smith's icily precise distillation of his novel, Raimi and company have conjured up their own shuddery, emotionally wrenching vision of the American dream gone horribly wrong.

Paramount's presentation *of A Simple Plan* on DVD is nothing less than remarkable and one of the crispest-looking titles released so far. The astonishing detail provided in the anamorphically enhanced image captures every snowflake and tree branch in razor-sharp detail, and the colours look astonishingly pure and "film-like." Though this isn't much of a audio showcase, Danny Elfman's marvellous, underrated score (which includes some unexpected homages to Mancini's *Wait Until Dark*!) sounds even better than it did in theatres. The only extra is the theatrical trailer.

SINBAD AND THE EYE OF THE TIGER
Colour, 1977, 114m. / Directed by Sam Wanamaker / Starring Patrick Wayne, Jane Seymour / Columbia (US R1 NTSC) / WS (1.85:1) (16:9)

The flimsiest of the Sinbad outings, *Sinbad and the Eye of the Tiger* is teeming with the usual dazzling array of Ray Harryhausen creatures and makes for a decent evening's viewing - but don't expect much more. Patrick Wayne (son of The Duke himself) is at the helm this time, filling in while John Phillip Law was off making thrillers in Europe. Sinbad's duty this time requires him to transport a monkey - actually a transformed prince - to distant Ademaspai so that he may be restored to his human form in time to ascend to the throne. Meanwhile the evil witch Zenobia (Margaret Whiting) and her spawn throw numerous obstacles in his way, with heroic support provided by two lovely ladies, the prince's sister Farah (Jane Seymour) and Dione (Taryn Power, Tyrone's daughter - what's with all the celebrity kids in this movie?). The big showdown occurs "at the top of the world" in the Arctic, where a sabre tooth tiger, a giant walrus, and a Cyclops join the battle.

Though mounted with the same care and exotic visuals afforded to the other Sinbad films, *Eye of the Tiger* proved to be the last cinematic voyage for Harryhausen's hero. The film gained a moderate cult following thanks to its continuous screenings on television, and *Seymour* in particular has never looked better. The late Roy Budd, a composer only now receiving any critical attention, provides an intriguing and melodic score that compares well with those of his predecessors, while Wayne is a passable if bland Sinbad. The main problem with the film is the final third of the story, which drags the action out far past the breaking point and could cause the younger target audience to start squirming before it's all over. On the other hand, Seymour and Power have a nude bathing scene - nothing too tawdry, but enough to make the G rating look awfully suspect.

Columbia's DVD backtracks after the great presentation of *The Golden Voyage of Sinbad* and offers only a widescreen, anamorphically enhanced transfer which blocks off a significant amount of information compared to the fullscreen laserdisc and VHS editions. However, by 1977 Harryhausen and company had apparently come to realize that 1.85:1 framing was going to be the norm, so the compositions don't suffer as much as the other two Sinbad films. Image quality is excellent and as close to pristine as this is probably going to get, while the mono audio is strong and vibrant. The same extras from the *Golden Voyage* disc are reproduced here, except the *Eye of the Tiger* trailer is substituted for the *Golden Voyage* one.

SIRENS
Colour, 1994, 90m. / Directed by John Duigan / Starring Sam Neill, Hugh Grant / Buena Vista (US R1 NTSC) / WS (1.85:1), Scanbox (Denmark R2 PAL)

1920s Australia. Concerned about the immoral aspects of some of the paintings in an exhibition by artist Norman Lindsay (Neill), church elders send an emissary in the form of clergyman Anthony Campion (Grant) to try and talk the man into withdrawing the more offensive works. At Lindsay's Bohemian retreat, nestled deep in the Outback, Campion and his wife Estella (Fitzgerald) are made welcome guests, but soon find their fusty values challenged by the lifestyle of the artist, his family, and his three beautiful models (Elle MacPherson, Kate Fischer and Portia de Rossi).

If the promise of copious nudity is what it takes to reel viewers in, then it's a worthy lure indeed. However, those drawn in solely by the prospect of seeing succulent Elle MacPherson naked will find more than the opportunity to peek at her short'n'curlies awaiting them. True, she looks phenomenal in her birthday suit (and, remarkably, gained weight specifically for the role), but it's pleasant to discover that she can act her socks off too. Intoxicatingly mellow and steeped in eroticism, John Duigan's film is a joy, naturally on a fundamental level but also in the exquisite cinematography which employs the wondrously photogenic Australian locale to its fullest.

Off camera, Rachel Portman's frisky score hits the mark perfectly, whilst on-screen the performances are all faultless. Grant is marvellous as the straight-laced pastor, as stuttering and tongue-tied as only Grant could play him. Fitzgerald is equally good as the timid wife who allows curiosity to consume her and by story's end has shaken off the shackles of sexual propriety. Neill's libertine artist takes something of a back seat, but there's delight to be found in his orchestration of the uptight couple's discomfort. Embroidered with Biblical nuances (such as the serpent, the embodiment of temptation, slithering unseen around the compound), the plot meanders along, never really going anywhere of import. Yet the gentle ambience compels you to drift with it. Writer/director Duigan keeps things ticking along nicely and builds up a fine head of steam for the sequence in which Fitzgerald dreams of submitting herself to the caresses of the naked sirens. Aside from the tasteful abundance of exposed feminine flesh, there's male frontal nudity too, though thankfully Grant retains his clothing! A sensual and light-hearted allegory of the avant-garde art world versus zealous religious censorship and the sexual repression born thereof, you should seek this out now and savour its rewards.

Seriously under-chaptered with just 15 breaks, unless you deem subtitle options to be a special feature, you'll find the Danish Region 2 disc from Scanbox offers little to sing about, although the fullscreen transfer is bright with lush colours. The sound is in English with default subtitles (in four different languages) which are, fortuitously, removable.

Buyers beware: Both the American and Canadian Region 1 discs are almost equally devoid of extras, and the latter's tape source suffers from some minor (but still intrusive) distortion during the sequence when the Campion's first arrive at the station, and then again during the end credits. Conspicuously absent bonus goodies aside, you'll still want to invest in this one for the perfect freeze-frame capabilities on all those mouth-watering naughty bits! - TG

SISTERS

Colour, 1973, 92m. / Directed by Brian De Palma / Starring Margot Kidder, Jennifer Salt / Criterion (US R1 NTSC) / WS (1.85:1) (16:9)

Already a minor cult figure with independent films like *Greetings* and *Hi, Mom!*, director Brian De Palma found his first mainstream success with *Sisters*, one of the best AIP studio offerings from the '70s. In a pattern which soon continued through his other thrillers and horror films, De Palma blatantly adopted many Hitchcock trademarks into his own style, which often involves quirky location details, split screen sequences, and startling flourishes of sex and violence. Along with the marvellous *Carrie, Obsession*, and *Dressed to Kill*, this is De Palma at his most exciting.

During a leering New York game show called "Peeping Toms," sweet Danielle Breton (a pre-*Superman* Margot Kidder), a relocated French Canadian, hooks up for dinner with nice guy Philip (Lisle Wilson). Their date is disrupted by Danielle's seemingly obsessive ex-husband, Emil (De Palma regular William Finley), who urges her to return with him. Danielle refuses and goes home with Philip, where they share a night of passion during which he fails to notice a huge scar along her abdomen. The next morning Philip overhears Danielle arguing with an angry woman in the apartment; Danielle explains that her twin, Dominique, has come to visit from a mental institution for their birthday. Later Danielle's neighbour, a pushy columnist named Grace Collier (Jennifer Salt), sees something nasty through the window and calls in the police to investigate a possible murder. Dominique is nowhere to be found, but Grace is infuriated by the police's lack of cooperation. With the help of a private eye (Charles Durning) and her own journalistic training, Grace decides to uncover the truth behind these two twins, who harbour a truly chilling past history.

De Palma's efficient and often dazzling visual style was already in full bloom with *Sisters*, which features a number of memorable set pieces and climaxes in full-blown horror with a justifiably famous hallucination sequence, shot in black and white through distorted lenses. The palpable atmosphere of urban insanity is aided immensely by Bernard Herrmann's jolting, electronic-flavoured score, which makes even the opening shots of Siamese twin foetuses creepy and ominous. While the actors are ultimately just pawns in De Palma's devious cinematic game, Kidder and particularly

S

Salt shine with some endearing bits of character acting. Salt's arrival at Emil's house is an especially creepy bit of viewer manipulation, in which a seemingly normal conversation with one of the residents suddenly takes an unexpected turn. While the film feels intense and extraordinarily violent, it's actually quite impressive how very little (paint-like) blood is truly spilled onscreen.

Criterion's *Sisters* obviously improves in every way on both the claustrophobic Warner videotape (which only letterboxed two crucial sequences) and the widescreen but muddy looking Japanese laserdisc. Colours are much stronger than ever before, and the now quite amusing '70s interiors look razor sharp and offer some delectable little details in the production design. Bear in mind that this is (a) a very low budget film, packed with (b) processed lab shots and (c) plenty of artificial zooms, so the picture does get very grainy from time to time. Thankfully Criterion decided to keep the grain and preserve the detail; this is one film that doesn't need to look glossy and over-polished. Apart from being slapped into one centre channel, the mono audio is very strong and dynamic, with Herrmann's score sounding punchier than the earlier video versions.

The extras are actually more paltry than you might think from the packaging; you just get De Palma's 1973 article on working with Herrmann, which has been quoted and referenced endlessly over the years, and an interview with De Palma which recites much of the same information. The film's effective theatrical trailer, which has appeared on numerous compilation tapes over the years, is inexplicably absent.

SIX DAYS IN ROSWELL

Colour, 1998, 81m./ Directed by Timothy B. Johnson / Starring Richard Kronfeld / Synapse (US R1 NTSC) / DD2.0

Another look at the quirky underbelly of America's heartland (well, a few states to the southwest of it anyway), *Six Days in Roswell* offers a novel spin on the sardonic lunacy of *True Stories, Gates of Heaven*, and *Trekkies*, the last of which happened to come from the same filmmakers. This time the documentary quest is led by *Trekkies* alum Richard Kronfeld, who's so dejected by the departure and success of all his friends that he decides live out his dream of taking off from Minnesota to Roswell, New Mexico, in hopes of being abducted by aliens. The film spends an unusual amount of time setting up Rich's motivation and personal circumstances, which makes the payoffs much more amusing and complex.

As viewers we desperately want to identify with Rich as our normal centre of gravity in a swirling storm of crazies, but by the halfway point it's impossible to deny that he's just as far gone as everybody else.

Though most of the film's humour comes from the UFO-crazy fanatics who either claim they've had an encounter with the visitors or are simply in the game to make a fast buck, the real pleasure in *Roswell* lies in the incidentals. Rich's camper rental arrangement with an elderly resident and his attempts to adjust to the climate are among the best anecdotes, while the filmmakers seek out the quirky little details like UFO pancakes and pizza, Rich's multicoloured UFO haircut, and gun-toting locals who critique our guide's preparation for an alien invasion. Along the way we also get dozens of interviews, including a surprise appearance by *Communion's* Whitley Streiber, who offers an astonishing amount of non-information which Rich nevertheless regards as one of the highlights of his life. However, the comedic climax is obviously reached during a production of *Roswell: The Musical*, a surreal spectacle that must be witnessed to be believed.

Along with a nice and crisp transfer from the original 16mm elements, Synapse's disc of *Six Days in Roswell* provides a treasure trove of goodies which are bound to amuse fans of the film and UFO lovers alike. Richard Kronfeld, producer Roger Nygard, and director Timothy B. Johnson all appear for a commentary track which is just as rollicking as the film itself, albeit a little more relaxed and down to earth. The video extras include a homemade 20 minute documentary ("Six Days in the Desert") that chronicles the filmmakers' attempts to bring their second cinematic effort to life, along with a hefty half hour of prime footage which had to be scrapped from the film's final cut. Each filmmakers' bio comes complete with snippets of their previous work, including a truly bizarre and hilarious montage of Richian highlights filled with deadpan quips.

The well designed menus provide plenty of room for exploring, with nooks and crannies leading you to various production photos, trivia tidbits, two theatrical trailers (plus one for *Trekkies*) and UFO ephemera, while clicking on map icons leads you to some nifty Easter Eggs (three in total), which include the strangest vacuum cleaner demonstration you'll ever see.

THE SIXTH SENSE

Colour, 1999, 106m. / Directed by M. Night Shyamalan / Starring Bruce Willis, Haley Joel Osment / Buena Vista (US R1 NTSC) / WS (2.35:1) (16:9) / DD5.1

First things first: *The Sixth Sense* is a horror film. It is not a "psychological thriller." And contrary to popular belief, horror films can be intelligent and emotionally resonant. A skilful throwback to the days of delicate child psychology ghost stories like *Curse of the Cat People* and the Christmas sequence from 1945's *Dead of Night*, this film breaks almost all of the established rules for supernatural films established over the past thirty years. Pyrotechnics, ear-splitting sound mixes, and CGI ectoplasm are all absent, replaced instead by a creeping sense of dread and memorable, interesting characters who develop over the course of the story. Much of the film's reputation rests on the highly touted twist ending, which is undeniably powerful but shouldn't overshadow the film's other equally laudable high points.

One night while staying at home with his wife, Anna (*Rushmore*'s Olivia Williams), child psychologist Malcolm Crowe (Bruce Willis) is startled when an intruder turns out to be one of his former patients, now grown up into a highly disturbed young man (Donnie Wahlberg). Malcolm is wounded when he tries to help his ex-patient, and his life afterwards takes a downward spiral. Months later, isolated from his wife and consumed by self-doubt, he is taken by the plight of Cole (Haley Joel Osment), a young boy exhibiting many of the same symptoms as his other patient. The boy is withdrawn and insecure, and even worse, he mysteriously exhibits strange scratches and bites on his body, Cole's mother (Toni Collette) attempts to break through his emotional barrier, but to no avail. After a traumatic incident at a birthday party, Cole finally breaks down and tells his eerie secret to Malcolm...

Following the neglect of his first mainstream film, *Wide Awake*, director M. Night Shyamalan apparently decided to inject a more commercially viable ghost story into his continuing study of children's psyches, and the result proved to be successful far beyond anyone's expectations. *The Sixth Sense* evokes a powerful mood from the very first shot, thanks also to pitch perfect cinematography by Jonathan Demme's favourite cinematographer, Tak Fujimoto, and a subdued, prickly score by James Newton Howard. While Osment walks off with almost all of the most memorable lines (he's supposed to be more intelligent than normal for his age), all of the actors are up to the task. Willis manages to keep his trademark smirk hidden for the entire running time, and Collette amazingly replaces her familiar Aussie accent with a Philly vocal lilt. Viewers expecting a cinematic powerhouse or a high dramatic *tour de force* may be disappointed by this chilly little gem, but those with a reasonable attention span and a willingness to go along with a challenging, atmospheric ghost story will find ample rewards long before the final transcendent fade-out.

When *The Sixth Sense* was released in theatres, Disney was in the middle of its refusal to provide anamorphic transfers to even its biggest titles. Fortunately, the studio did an about face just in time for its DVD presentation. The tricky, shadowy photography looks appropriately glitch-free, with the rich colour schemes (browns and reds in particular) often seeming to pop right off the screen. The 5.1 mix is enveloping and subtle, spreading the sound smoothly through all the speakers without many sharp isolated effects. It may not be demo material, but this is quite a fine job. The only real quibble with the DVD itself is the barrage of promo trailers at the beginning of the disc (now an irritating common Disney practice). The extras for the "Collector's Edition" are mostly introduced by the director, who obviously feels a great deal of fondness for the film. A study of the sound design, a look at the tricks of setting up the story, storyboard comparisons, promo interviews, and a handful of interesting but superfluous deleted scenes are the high points here, and fans will be intrigued by the extended "alternate ending" which was wisely trimmed down in the final cut. Add to that the theatrical trailer, TV spots, and a very funny early camcorder ghost story by Shyamalan (hidden in the jewel box), and you've got quite a package. A two-disc Vista Series version was later released, tacking on some useless padding involving investigations of the supernatural and, more usefully, a DTS track.

S

SKINNER

Colour, 1993, 91m. / Directed by Ivan Nagy / Starring Ted Raimi, Traci Lords / Simitar / A-Pix (US R0 NTSC)

Any horror movie starring Traci Lords, talk show princess Ricki Lake, and Ted Raimi (of TV's *Xena*, and brother of Sam) demands at least a look for curiosity value, and *Skinner* is... well, different. Yet another instalment in the endless retellings of Ed Gein, the Wisconsin serial killer who inspired *Psycho*, *The Texas Chainsaw Massacre*, *Deranged*, and *Three on a Meat hook*, this one adds a dollop of postmodern *Silence of the Lambs* humour into the brew for a truly weird mixture of hardcore gore and pitch black comedy. Unfortunately, the film is severely hampered by a low budget and a pace that could charitably be described as deliberate.

Dennis Skinner (Raimi) moves into a room rented out by married innocent Lake and occasionally wanders out into the streets to find victims. In several graphic and unsettling scenes, he skins his victims and wears their pelts, with one black victim meeting a particularly tasteless fate. Meanwhile, the disfigured Heidi (Lords), an escaped victim, attempts to hunt Skinner down and stop him as the body count continues to rise. While hardly a great movie, *Skinner* at least earns points for effort, with director Nagy attempting to inject some visual style with candy-coloured Argento lighting, and Lords cuts an impressive, memorable figure with her long bleached hair and trenchcoat. Some of the jokes do work, with Raimi delivering his lines *con gusto* and injecting life into the film when it threatens to drag to a halt.

Unfortunately most of the effectiveness is sapped away by A-Pix's ugly transfer, which doesn't benefit much from Simitar's transfer to DVD. Blotchy artefacts run rampant during the night scenes (about 80% of the movie!), and the sound exhibits some irritating distortion during loud moments (again, most of the movie). At least it beats the unwatchable VHS transfers; if you're in a forgiving mood, buy it for the film, not the quality of the DVD.

SLAVE GIRLS FROM BEYOND INFINITY

Colour, 1987, 74m. / Directed by Ken Dixon / Starring: Elizabeth Cayton, Brinke Stevens / Full Moon (US R1 NTSC)

In the distant future two beautiful slave girls, Daria and Tisa (Cayton and Beal, respectively) escape their starship imprisonment and crash-land on a desolate planet. Here they meet Zed (Don Scribner) whose gracious hospitality is but a cover for his true motives. When the moment is right he will set his unwitting guests loose into the jungle and hunt them down for sport.

When the opening sequence of a film presents the viewer with a scantily clad blonde, her magnif-

icent breasts bouncing hypnotically as she runs through the jungle with a homicidal android in hot pursuit, you just know that no matter how bad it gets from that point on, it's certainly going to excel in the eye candy department. Thus *Slave Girls from Beyond Infinity* succeeds admirably on both counts; it is bad, but it's embroidered with enough eye candy to rot your optic nerve.

A futuristic take on *The Most Dangerous Game* played for laughs, Ken Dixon's debut feature is entertaining enough for what it is. We've certainly been subjected to worse. Overlooking the lame stabs at raillery - which aren't remotely funny and would have been far more effective (on a different level) if played dead straight a la *Flash Gordon* - what you end up with is cheap and cheerful (but reasonably good-looking) f/x, inane dialogue, pretty girls showing plenty of skin and a pleasantly bright and breezy running time. The perfect Z-grade combo!

Punctuated by a ridiculously generous 30 chapter points, the fullscreen transfer on Surrender Cinema's DVD is the best looking print of the film to date. There are a small number of biographies thrown in, along with a trailer for *Slave Girls* and half a dozen other low grade Full Moon stocking fillers (amusingly summarized on the box as a "Cult Movie Trailer Reel"). - TG

SLEEPY HOLLOW

Colour, 1999, 87m. / Directed by Tim Burton / Starring Johnny Depp, Christina Ricci / Paramount (US R1 NTSC), Pathé (UK R2 PAL) / WS (1.85:1) (16:9) / DD5.1

Rarely one to go along with the mainstream, director Tim Burton has managed to usher in one personal project after another through the Hollywood system. The twilight gothic atmosphere of Washington Irving's classic American short story, "The Legend of Sleepy Hollow," seems tailor made for Burton's quirky sensibilities, so it was only a matter of time before the man behind such films as *Beetlejuice* and *Edward Scissorhands* took a crack at the Headless Horseman.

Lifting only its setting and a few characters and situations from the original story, Burton's edition concerns a New York constable, Ichabod Crane (Johnny Depp), who is summoned north to Sleepy Hollow, a region terrorized by a series of decapitation slayings. He is taken into the home of Baltus Van Tassel (Michael Gambon), his wife (Miranda

Richardson), and their bewitching daughter, Katrina (a refreshingly full-bodied Christina Ricci). Ichabod becomes smitten with Katrina, though his competition lies in the form of Brom Van Brunt (Casper Van Dien, whose part was whittled down to virtually nothing in the editing room). One night Ichabod himself witnesses a headless horseman prowling the countryside and lopping off one unfortunate's head; thus, our constable must deduce whether these killings are the work of an undead fiend or perhaps a human motive might be behind all of the carnage.

In terms of sight and sound, *Sleepy Hollow* is a completely intoxicating experience from the moody opening sequence (featuring a cameo by *Ed Wood*'s Martin Landau). Burton obviously has a field day trotting out a stream of bizarre images, including his beloved pumpkins and, in perhaps the film's best scene, an unforgettable tree. References abound in 1960s horror cinema, ranging from an early appearance by Hammer favourite Christopher Lee to flashback sequences drawn straight out of Mario Bava's *Black Sunday* and Antonio Margheriti's *The Virgin of Nuremberg*.

Burton's semi-regular composer, Danny Elfman, contributes a challenging but rewarding score, which grows on one with repeated listenings, while the cinematography and Oscar-winning art design are beyond reproach. Where the film unfortunately stumbles a bit is the screenplay and acting, both of which seem cobbled together from unrelated sources and crushed into an uneasy brew onscreen. The script by Kevin Yagher and Andrew Kevin Walker (*Seven*) bends over backwards to keep viewers mystified and intrigued, but most of the story's elements are irrelevant at best, incoherent at worst (e.g., the witch in the woods). Oddly enough - and be warned, this may be a bit of a spoiler - the entire main storyline is lifted in amazing detail from Dario Argento's *Trauma*, though with a less interesting motive. As a result the viewer is left with little invested in the breakneck finale, which winds up being much less frightening than even the animated Walt Disney version of the same story. Likewise, Depp's performance swerves wildly from scene to scene, with cowardly comic schtick alternating with heroic derring do and back again with no rhyme or reason. These structural flaws aside, however, *Sleepy Hollow* is undeniably successful as a piece of entertaining eye candy, and Burtonphiles will find much to savour in its dark little heart.

Widely promoted as Paramount's first full blown DVD special edition, *Sleepy Hollow* more than lives up to its promise on the small screen. The beautiful image quality is actually a dramatic improvement over the dim, poorly contrasted theatrical prints, while the 5.1 sound mix is subtle but bursts to life when it's needed. Burton appears solo on a commentary track that offers some valuable information tidbits but isn't as consistently engaging as, say, *Pee Wee's Big Adventure*, in which he could bounce off another commentator. Extras include the teaser and standard theatrical trailer, a bevy of stills, an engaging half hour documentary that explores the special effects and unorthodox location shooting, and the usual PR-oriented interviews. The UK disc from Pathé ports over the same extras and transfer.

THE SLIPPER AND THE ROSE

Colour, 1976, 146m. / Directed by Bryan Forbes / Starring Richard Chamberlain, Gemma Craven / Image (US R1 NTSC) / WS (2.35:1) (16:9) / DD5.1

 A criminally neglected musical, *The Slipper and the Rose* is one of those gems people enjoy discovering and showing to their friends just to prove what they've been missing. This stylish and imaginative British retelling of the "Cinderella" fairy tale puts a few novel twists on the familiar story, but the musical window dressing threatens to steal the entire film. Richard M. and Robert B. Sherman, the duo behind the songs for *Mary Poppins and Chitty Chitty Bang Bang,* deliver one of their catchiest and most emotionally rich combinations of music and lyrics, enough to engage both children and adults. Besides, how can you possibly turn down a fantasy featuring two cast members from Ken Russell's *The Music Lovers* and directed by the guy who brought you *The Stepford Wives* and *Deadfall*?

Rather than following the traditional fairy tale structure, *Slipper* first introduces us to the Prince of Euphrania, Edward (Richard Chamberlain), who's less than happy about his father's plans to marry him off for political convenience. Meanwhile Cinderella (Gemma Craven) is heartbroken when her wicked stepmother (Margaret Lockwood) and two snide stepsisters assume control of her late father's estate and force her into a life waiting on them hand and foot. When the royal family announces a bride-finding ball to match the Prince off to an eligible maiden, Cinderella wishes she could go... and of course, a helpful Fairy Godmother (Annette Crosbie) shows up to help her dreams come true. If you think you know the story from here, though, don't be so sure...

S

The most appealing aspect of *The Slipper and the Rose* is its sincere performances, particularly the charming couple of Craven and Chamberlain. While the film may lack powerhouse vocals and furious dance numbers *a la* Andrew Lloyd Webber, it more than compensates with artistic skill and gentle humour. The songs alternate between buoyant wordplay ("Protocoligorically Correct") and heartbreaking poignancy ("Tell Him Anything (But Not That I Love Him)"), an asset increased by the restoration of this complete British edition on DVD. (The US prints distributed by Universal and shown on cable chopped out several musical interludes for a total loss of almost 20 minutes.) Special mention should also be made of Crosbie, one of the screen's best Fairy Godmothers (up there with Delphine Seyrig in *Donkey Skin*), and the always reliable Christopher Gable as Edward's right hand man.

Image's DVD represents a long overdue relief for film buffs who have suffered through shortened and nearly unwatchable pan and scan prints over the years. The full scope framing has now been lovingly restored (all the better to savour that Austrian scenery!), but the beautiful colour schemes and elegant attention to detail have also been adjusted back to their original glory. Apart from a few print flaws due to the ravages of time (mostly the end credits), this presentation (enhanced for widescreen TVs) is very near immaculate. For anyone who's been holding on to those ancient and notorious Discovision laserdiscs from the early '80s, it's time to throw them in the trash. The sound is also very good for a film of this vintage, with both a standard two-channel stereo track and a newly tweaked 5.1 mix. Be warned, the music in this film is very powerful and constantly floods from all of the speakers, so don't turn it up too loud just to hear the dialogue!

This special edition disc also includes a running commentary by director Bryan Forbes, who offers some insight into how the project came about and how he decided to tackle it (after doing a run of thrillers). He also covers the manner in which the songs were approached and integrated into the story, which tackles its characters as real human beings rather than one dimensional storybook stick figures. The disc also includes a lovingly produced documentary, "Cinderella Story: The Making of *The Slipper and the Rose*," which includes interviews with The Sherman Brothers and a wealth of detail about this unusual production, correctly identified as one of the last genuinely great movie musicals. Oddly enough, no one really takes note of just how much this film must have influenced another humanized Cinderella film, 1998's *Ever After*. All in all, an amazing release and one that should proudly earn its place in the DVD collection for viewers of all ages.

SLUGS

Colour, 1987, 90m. / Directed by Juan Piquer Simon / Starring Michael Garfield, Santiago Alvarez / Anchor Bay (US R0 NTSC) / WS (1.85:1) (16:9)

 Talk about truth in advertising. *Slugs* (or as it's credited on film, *Slugs: The Movie* - as opposed to *Slugs: The Musical*) exists solely to provoke the viewer's gag reflex and, much like the director's other hilariously fumbled features, piles on unintentional laughs from a clueless, partially dubbed cast. They don't make 'em like this anymore, and while that might be a good thing, *Slugs* is rarely boring and never tasteful.

The "plot," adapted from a supermarket novel by Shaun Hutson(!), follows the ever so slowly paced attempt by slugs to take over a small town. You see, pollution has gifted the slimy creatures with teeth and a taste for meat, rather than the usual garden greens. In the opening sequence they chomp down on a hapless boater; then they slide into garden gloves, get chopped up into poisonous bits for a suburban husband's salad, and even attack a hamster. Enter our not terribly intrepid hero, health inspector Mike Brady (Michael Garfield), who suspects something slimy's going on when he's not busy fumbling around with his negligee-clad wife. Gradually the town escalates into a panic, so it's down into the sewers we go for an explosive finale.

Honestly, who ever thought this movie would wind up on DVD? The laserdisc back in the '80s seemed to be stretching it, but sure enough, *Slugs* has been dressed up in a sparkling new widescreen transfer and looks much better than it probably should. Colours are nice and splashy, especially when fake blood is spewing across the screen, and now you can really appreciate the artistic integrity in such showstoppers as a guy's head bursting into a mass of baby slugs right in the middle of a chic restaurant. The DVD also looks markedly different from the laserdisc and videotape versions, which were completely open matte and had a squarish, sitcom appearance that somehow added to the cheapness. Here it looks more like a real movie, with deeper blacks and more formal compositions, while also cropping out some hysterically accidental, goofy frontal nudity during the "teen" sexy-slug attack scene. The mono audio sounds fine and milks every bit of tension from that ridiculous stock music score, which wouldn't sound out of place in a Russ Meyer film.

The disc also includes the lurid theatrical trailer, which wouldn't get shown on a single screen today, and a nifty replica of the theatrical poster, a variation on the original book cover sleeve.

THE SLUMBER PARTY MASSACRE

Colour, 1982, 77m. / Directed by Amy Jones / Starring Michelle Michaels, Robin Stille / New Concorde (US R1 NTSC) / WS (1.85:1) / DD2.0

Thanks to its lurid title, a not terribly subtle poster showing a menacing power drill poised over four scantily clad girls, and the fact that it was written and directed by women, *The Slumber Party Massacre* became one of the more notorious surprise horror hits of the early '80s. Amid the glut of slasher films pouring into theatres after *Friday the 13th*, this zero budget effort struck a nerve with moviegoers and was heavily cut in the UK at the time of the video nasties debate. Seen in retrospect, it's quite astounding to note that, audiences' responses aside, none of the critics seemed to pick up on the fact that this is really a comedy.

High school senior Trish (Michelle Michaels) is left alone by her parents for the weekend, so she naturally invites the fellow members of her basketball team for a slumber party. However, new girl and fellow neighbour Valerie (the late Robin Stille) is left out of the fun, forced to spend the evening at home with her Playgirl-obsessed younger sister. Naturally an insane killer (Michael Villella) has just escaped and already killed off one team member (scream queen Brinke Stevens) at school. How many of the girls will survive until morning?

Long before *Scream*, this film already displayed a knowing sense of stalk 'n' slash conventions and made no hesitations about turning them on their head. Oddly enough, the film's two prolonged on-camera gore sequences are suffered by ineffectual male characters, while the women are all given strong, humanistic traits. The acting by several participants isn't strong enough to really drive this point home, but it's obvious screenwriter Rita Mae Browne (better known as the feminist author of novels like *Rubyfruit Jungle*) did not intend to play by the rules. Director Amy Jones (*Love Letters*) keeps the pace fast and furious, without a single moment of cinematic fat during the compact 77

minute running time. Sure, it's basically junk when all is said and done, but at least it's entertaining junk.

Amazingly enough, New Concorde has seen fit to bring *Slumber Party Massacre* to DVD with a brand spanking new transfer, correctly letterboxed at 1.85:1. The annoying open matte information from the Embassy videotape version is now gone, replaced with a sleeker and more balanced presentation and much brighter colours to boot. Bear in mind that an ultra-cheap early '80s horror flick will always look a little gritty, but this disc doesn't disappoint. The stereo soundtrack is also much stronger, with some nifty directional effects offered by the music and occasional bits of thunder and, naturally, whirring power equipment. Considering the ridiculously low price tag, this is a welcome surprise. The disc also comes with the original theatrical trailer, as well as trailers for the risible *Slumber Party Massacre II* and *Sorority House Massacre II*.

SMALL SOLDIERS

Colour, 1998, 110m. / Directed by Joe Dante / Starring Gregory Smith, Kirstin Dunst / DreamWorks (US R1 NTSC) / WS (2.35:1) (16:9) / DD5.1

Or, *Gremlins* go to war. Joe Dante's long awaited return to the screen following his underrated *Matinee* turned out to be another step for the high-aiming DreamWorks Studio in its bid for Hollywood success. While *Small Soldiers* failed to live up to its box office expectations (no doubt due to the problems of marketing a movie in which the title toys are purely evil and more than a little disturbing), film buffs may find enough in-jokes and surprises to compensate for the bizarre, sometimes upsetting shifts in tone.

A young boy (Gregory Smith) prone to getting into trouble finds himself in over his head when a new line of toys powered by super-military microchips go on the loose and wreak havoc in his town. The soldier toys (voiced by Tommy Lee Jones and cast members of the original *Dirty Dozen*) have made it their mission to obliterate the peace-loving Gorgonite toys (voiced by Frank Langella and the members of Spinal Tap). Other odd surprises along the way include literal killer Barbies (chirped by Christina Ricci and Sarah Michelle Geller), while the rest of the human cast consists of Kirsten Dunst, Phil Hartman (supposedly his last role, which is quite unnerving when you consider how many times

S

he's shot at during the film), Jay Mohr, and Denis Leary. On a technical level, the film is marvellous to look at, filled with candy colours and lots of action filling the frame (Dante's first scope film, incidentally). Furthermore, Jerry Goldsmith provides a punchy, exciting score, in fact one of the year's best.

Regardless of how you feel about the film - and parents have plenty of cause to be perturbed - DreamWorks has packaged it in a dandy DVD package, stuffed with amusing extras. While the lack of a Joe Dante commentary is unfortunate, you do get behind-the-scenes footage (highlighted by a funny "interview" with Chip Hazard), deleted scenes (mostly superfluous, but nice to have), a preview of the Small Soldiers game, and trailers. The transfer quality is fine if not overwhelming; some of the colour and shadow details look a little soft and muted, but this was also a problem with theatrical prints as well. The Dolby Digital 5.1 sound, on the other hand, is a stunner, with helicopters and firepower often raging back and forth in every speaker. If you're looking for a good demo piece for your sound system, step right up!

THE SMUGGLER

Colour, 1980, 91m. / Directed by Lucio Fulci / Starring Fabio Testi, Ivana Monti / Italian Shock (Holland PAL Region 0) / WS (1.85:1)

Taking a break after kick starting the Italian walking dead craze with *Zombie* in 1979, Lucio Fulci turned his blood-spattered camera to the popular spaghetti crime genre with *The Smuggler (Luca il contrabbandiere / The Naples Connection)*, a particularly nasty piece of work that pumps up the violence found in mob films by Umberto Lenzi and his ilk to ludicrous, operatic proportions. Though often confusing and strangely paced, this film coasts by on the sheer viciousness of its imagery and the effective use of various Naples locales, all sprinkled with a fine cast of exploitation veterans.

After a covert job on the ocean goes bad, cigarette smuggler Luca Di Angelo (Fabio Testi) realizes the nature of his job is rapidly changing. Drugs are taking over the business, new blood is pushing out the old Mafiosi, and hard times lie ahead. His wife Adele (Ivana Monti) feels uncomfortable in Naples and expresses concern for their child, but he decides to weather the storm even after his brother Mickey winds up dead. Hungry for revenge, Luca refuses to side with the younger drug

dealing mobsters and finds his crime family wiped out one by one, leaving him with nowhere to turn. Along the way Fulci piles on the sleaze, including swearing nuns, a face scorched off with a Bunsen burner, vaginal cocaine smuggling, rape, exploding bullet hits to the throat, and other miscellaneous nasty business before the inevitable gang war splashes the streets with blood.

Though technically not a horror film, *The Smuggler* should be of more than passing interest to fans of Fulci's gothic horrors like *The Beyond* and *House by the Cemetery*. Composer Fabio Frizzi and cinematographer Sergio Salvati are both present and contribute their usual professional jobs, though the sloppy sound editing wrecks the continuity of several scenes. Testi, a veteran of Fulci's brutal western opus *Four of the Apocalypse*, turns in a typically credible and sympathetic lead performance, while Fulci himself pops up for an unusually active cameo as a gun-blazing assassin during the climax. Sleaze fans should also look for a small role by the late transsexual Jess Franco regular Ajita Wilson as a pouting bar whore.

A long-time perennial on the bootleg market, *The Smuggler* has drifted around in various versions for years. An awful US commercial release on VHS under the title *Contraband* went out of print almost immediately in the early '80s, so fans have had to deal with smudgy (but letterboxed) European dupes and substandard laserdisc transfers. The Italian Shock DVD is the best of the bunch and could be the nicest this film will ever look considering the drab, desaturated visual scheme on display. Apart from the ragged opening credits, the print is in excellent condition with solid detail and dead on 1.85:1 framing. Unfortunately some fleeting trims have been made to the print, excising some bullet wounds and a fragment of the rape scene. The disc features the dubbed English audio track with optional Dutch subtitles, as well as a trailer for *Nightmare City* (but no trailer for *The Smuggler,* alas).

SOLARIS

Colour, 1972, 169m. / Directed by Andrei Tarkovsky / Starring Donatas Banionis / Ruscico (Russia R0 NTSC) / WS (2.35:1) (16:9) / DD5.1

Arguably the most successful attempt to create an art house science fiction film, *Solaris* remains the best known effort by controversial Russian director Andrei Tarkovsky. Overlapping memories, fantasies, and sparingly used fantastic visuals, Tarkovsky subverts expectations by delivering a space film more concerned with the inner workings of the human soul and psyche than the mechanics of flying ships.

Loosely based on the well-known novel by Stanislaw Lem (reportedly soon to be re-filmed by Steven Soderbergh), the film begins with the countryside reverie of scientist Chris Kelvin (Donatas Banionis), a scientist sent to investigate the strange occurrences plaguing the Solaris mission. Aboard a space station hovering over an oceanic planet, one scientist has already died, and the other two survivors are less than forthcoming with the details of their experience. A former cosmonaut had already told Kelvin about the strange influence of the Solaris waters on the human consciousness, but only when he witnesses firsthand the physical manifestation of his memories and desires does Kelvin begin to believe the claims that these are no ordinary waters below. Adding further confusion to his discovery is the appearance of Hari (Natalya Bondarchuk), who may be his wife reincarnate... or something else entirely.

As with other Tarkovsky films, *Solaris* is deliberately paced from start to finish, driven more by its heady atmosphere and delicate visuals than the demands of a typical linear plot. The framework of Lem's novel allows a flowing series of meditations on man's emotional nature and his often dangerous ties to the past, while the actors perform their often challenging roles with exquisite restraint and intensity. The startling interjections of surrealistic images (the swirling multi-coloured, cloud-like waters, the sun glistening off damp trees, the slick transition from black and white footage to colour as a car speeds through a tunnel) are accompanied by a haunting recurring Bach motif and a potent score by Eduard Artemiev; in fact, you'd be hard pressed to even guess this was a science fiction film based on the first half hour. Hypnotic and challenging, this is certainly not a film for all viewers (those who find *2001* slow will be crawling the walls), but the rewards for the faithful will be plenty.

Long unavailable on video, *Solaris* received a long overdue US theatrical reissue in its complete form during the 1980s and was issued on VHS and (in a more accurately letterboxed rendition) on laserdisc by Fox Lorber. However, those versions can be ignored in light of the Ruscico two-disc set, which is a marvel in every respect. The anamorphically enhanced scope image looks flawless (apart from a few limitations inherent in the original source material, such as the occasional fleck of dust or a brief scratch), and the 5.1 remix is so powerful the film is impossible to imagine without it. In fact, the gripping audio track pumps new life into scenes which previously felt like static filler, making this a much more engrossing experience from the beginning. Menu options are available in English, Russian, or French, while the film is viewable in 5.1 mixes of all three languages (the original Russian with English subtitles works best, but the dubs are also very well done). The disc also contains trailers for Tarkovsky's *Andrei Rublev* and *The Mirror* and the excellent Russian "western," *At Home with Strangers - A Stranger Among His Own*, as well as *Investigation of Pilot Pirx* (a snippet of another Lem adaptation), video interviews with Bondarchuk and Tarkovsky's family, and a featurette dedicated to Banionis with some interesting ties to the film itself. A forthcoming DVD edition from Criterion is also in the works.

SOMEONE TO WATCH OVER ME

Colour, 1987, 112m. / Directed by Ridley Scott / Starring Tom Berenger, Mimi Rogers / Columbia (US R1 NTSC) / WS (1.85:1) (16:9) / DD2.0

The word "glossy" could have easily been invented for Ridley Scott's *Someone to Watch over Me*, an often overlooked thriller which marked a radical departure from the director's usual science fiction and fantasy epics and, unlike his subsequent earthbound efforts as *White Squall* and *1492*, keeps a firm grasp on human emotions and naturalistic plotting.

Seasoned cop Mike Keegan (Tom Berenger) and his wife, Ellie (Lorraine Bracco), enjoy a typical domestic married existence in Queens. When Mike is called in to protect a Manhattan socialite, Claire (Mimi Rogers), who witnessed the knifing death of an acquaintance at a party, he finds his time and attention with his family severely strained. Claire is called in to identify the murderer, whom she recognizes, and Mike finds himself irresistibly attracted to the glamorous beauty. The two helplessly begin an affair, and as Mike's home life begins to fall apart, the killer decides to pay Claire a visit...

Ostensibly a tribute to slick 1940s thrillers like *Laura* and *The Glass Key*, this film captures the visually pleasing but chilly atmosphere of the idle rich and contrasts it nicely with the humble environs of our protagonist and his wife. As usual Scott creates a ravishing visual feast, and his typical colour coding bears more than a little significance: icy blues and greys for Manhattan, warm golds and umbers for Queens. He also displays a few flickers of the Italian thriller tradition, particularly during the pivotal stabbing in front of a reflective swimming pool (a terrific scene) and a lengthy, dark stalking sequence in Rogers' apartment that precedes Dario Argento's similar *Opera* by one year. Berenger and Rogers make for extremely appealing leads, and it's a shame no one uses them as well anymore. Bracco does what she can with a difficult part: a foul-mouthed, possessive mom who sticks up for her family. Unfortunately, the role isn't especially appealing; while the ending is a fairly foregone conclusion, the film actually paints itself into a corner so that the last scene, as one critic aptly noted, is strikingly similar to post-coital depression.

Long overdue for a decent remastering, the film has been given a sparkling new anamorphic transfer from Columbia. A rare non-scope film for Scott, this nevertheless relies heavily on precise visual framing for the best effect, and outside of a theatre, it simply won't look better. The existing Dolby Surround mix isn't labelled as 5.1 but sounds extremely good, with clean channel separation and strong, mobile bass during many key sequences. Furthermore, the diverse soundtrack, ranging from Vangelis to Michael Kamen's orchestral score to Sting's crooning of the title track, sounds better than ever. The DVD also includes the mediocre US trailer, which opens up with a discussion of Bracco's sagging derriere and could account for why this film didn't set the box office on fire.

SOMETHING WEIRD

Colour, 1967, 80m. / Directed by Herschell Gordon Lewis / Starring Tony McCabe, Elizabeth Lee / Image (US R0 NTSC) / WS (1.85:1)

While strong plotting has never been director H.G. Lewis' strongest point, in *Something Weird* he easily lives up to the title by spinning out a mad, drug-hazed string of events which will drive any rational viewer to contemplating some chemical relief before the 80 minutes are over. Of course, this is evidently what the film was designed to do, and at this it succeeds quite admirably.

After receiving a live power line in the face during his attempted rescue of a construction worker, Cronin Mitchell (Tony McCabe) winds up in the hospital with a permanently disfigured face and a peculiar gift of ESP. The local nurses don't take too kindly to his newly found talents, which he uses to exploit those around him and vent his frustration at the loss of his "beautiful face." In disguise he sets up a low rent fortune telling operation and is visited one day by a creepy old witch (Mudite Arums) who offers to restore his face if he agrees to marry her. She carries out her end of the bargain, and Cronin ditches her for better pastures. Unfortunately his next one night stand (Elizabeth Lee) turns out to be the witch in disguise; everyone but Cronin will see her as a beautiful woman. Meanwhile resourceful government agent Alex Jordan (William Brooker) snoops into Cronin's activities and falls for the "lovely" sorceress, with predictably disastrous results.

If this description sounds like your average linear drive-in movie, well, forget it. *Something Weird* tosses a number of wild and woolly surprises into the mix, ranging from an LSD freak-out showstopper to an unforgettable, truly deranged sequence in which Brooker is menaced by... well, you've just got to see it to believe it. With its weird metaphysical concerns and trippy plotting, *Something Weird* in many ways foreshadows Lewis' whacked-out Zen masterpiece, *The Wizard of Gore*, which would make an ideal viewing companion for this film.

One of the earliest Lewis films released on home video, this was never a huge box office hit but has become a highly familiar title, thanks in no small part to its application to Mike Vraney's formidable video company. Therefore it's only appropriate that Something Weird Video presents *Something Weird*, looking as good as possible. The first VHS versions were letterboxed at 1.85:1 (with the LSD scene featuring tinted widescreen bars, of course!), and the DVD replicates that framing, with mixed results. Lewis apparently wanted this to be his first "widescreen" film, but some scenes (especially the opening credits) lose some information from the top and bottom of the screen in the process. An open matte version has also circulated on tape, and the framing is at least partially more satisfying. With a Lewis film, though, visual composition is not exactly the main concern. Many scenes on the DVD look ideally framed, and the colours are amazingly punchy throughout.

The avalanche of extras, though, confirms this DVD's status as the definitive presentation of this film. Producer David F. Friedman and Vraney provide the bulk of the commentary track, with Lewis popping in at the beginning but ducking out for the bulk of the running time. The comments become increasingly surreal as the film progresses, with some technical glitches and bizarre audio dropout only adding to the disorienting experience.

By the end of the film, your confusion will be completely reflected by the commentary's participants as well, which is probably as it should be.

Extras include some nice drug-addled treats, such as a freakish excerpt from *Psyched by the 4-D Witch* (available from Something Weird on VHS in its entirety), an LSD casualty from *The Weird World of LSD* (called "Monsterama Nightmare!"), "LSD Psychedelic Freakout," and the usual thorough gallery of H.G. Lewis posters and ad art.

SORORITY HOUSE MASSACRE

Colour, 1986, 74m. / Directed by Carol Frank / Starring Angela O'Neill, Wendy Martel / New Concorde (US R1 NTSC)

Beth (O'Neill) arrives at Theta Omega Theta planning to join the sorority. Immediately she begins to suffer from nightmares in which she is haunted by a knife-wielding figure. When most of the other inhabitants depart for the weekend, Beth remains behind with three girls who are planning a private party with their boyfriends. One of them, a student in psychology, ascertains through hypnosis that Beth's dreams are the result of a childhood trauma that took place on these very premises, though Beth herself has no conscious recollection of it. She is also the only surviving member of a family massacred by her older brother, notorious killer Robert Henkel (Russell). What Beth doesn't realise is that Henkel, now locked away in an asylum, is experiencing similar dreams. As the preparations get underway for the party, driven by his own nightmares Henkel escapes. Armed and dangerous he sets out for Theta Omega Theta.

Something of a *Halloween* clone, 1986's *Sorority House Massacre* is a cut above many of its contemporaries. It may not be a great brain-strain to figure out where the plot is going fairly early on in the proceedings, and it also has to be noted that towards the end the film deteriorates into the trap of having characters do exactly the sort of thing you'd never do in a similar predicament. But writer/director Carol Frank (who worked as a production assistant on *Slumber Party Massacre*) maintains the suspense meritoriously throughout and for the first half at least imbues the story with a splash of style not always found in slasher territory. Beth's dream sequences, for example, are particularly creepy and filled with unnerving imagery. The players too are, for the most part, competent and likeable. Foremost Angela O'Neill, who not only

brings a degree of talent to the aid of the party, but also displays an endearing vulnerability that swiftly garners her audience empathy. John Russell is an adequate enough killer, although his escape from the State mental facility is laughably simple; unchallenged, he literally runs out of the door and scales the perimeter fence!

Any British-based readers interested in seeing *Sorority House Massacre* are strongly recommended to try and locate a copy of the deleted 1987 VHS cassette from Medusa. The New Concorde "Massacre Collection" DVD release should be avoided at all costs, for it's devoid of at least seven sequences of varying length that total almost 10 minutes of missing footage, consequently rendering it worthless. The feature itself is divided into 24 chapters. A trailer for the film (with burnt-in Spanish subtitles!) constitutes the only bonus item, unless you count the trio of previews of other movies. - TG

SORORITY HOUSE MASSACRE II

Colour, 1991, 77m. / Directed by Jim Wynorski / Starring Robyn Harris, Melissa Moore / New Concorde (US R1 NTSC)

The girls of Sigma Pi - that's Linda (Harris), Jessica (Moore), Kimberley (Stacia Zhivago), Suzanne (Michelle Verran) and Janey (Dana Bentley) - move into a dilapidated old residence which they plan to renovate into a sorority house. Learning that it was the site of a multiple slaying by a deranged psychopath, they decide to have a slumber party cum séance to see if they can summon up his spirit. Before you can say "Ouija board", a crazed killer with a meat hook begins picking off the lingerie-clad co-eds.

Diminutive Brit model Gail Robyn Harris (credited here minus the Gail) heads up a quintet of twenty-somethings trying to pass themselves off for teenagers in this serving of blood'n'boobs trash from Roger Corman protégé Jim Wynorski. It's actually a bare-faced rehash by Wynorski of his own *Hard to Die*, shot the previous year utilizing some of the same cast, only transposing the high-rise tower block setting of that film into a sorority house for the purposes of this one. Wynorski's tongue-firmly-in-cheek style of film-making has never been highbrow, but his output is rarely anything less than entertaining. This one's played strictly for laughs by a bunch of silicone enhanced girls with little or no clothing and even less acting ability. Okay, so no-one watches this sort of thing for revelatory

Thespian talent (and, as such, the chosen cast look very nice indeed both in and out of their lacy skimpies) but a smidgen of ability to convince certainly helps. Peter Spellos (who graduated to the sublime *Bound*) has fun as the sleazy next-door neighbour/red-herring character with a penchant for scoffing down chunks of raw meat like most people pig out on popcorn.

For some reason, despite the title, Wynorski integrated flashback footage from *Slumber Party Massacre* (rather than the first *Sorority House Massacre*) into the proceedings - maybe he got confused?? - adapting by way of voice-over narration the characters and situations in that film into something that suits the premise of his own.

New Concorde's DVD, one of several titles of a similar ilk in their "Massacre Collection", presents the film as an unmatted 24-chapter show. There are also some flimsy biographies (i.e., the one for Harris fails to mention her full name or that she's British) and trailers for this film plus *Slumber Party Massacre* Parts II and III. - TG

SOUTHERN COMFORT

Colour, 1981, 99m. / Directed by Walter Hill / Starring Keith Carradine, Powers Boothe / MGM (US R1 NTSC) / WS (1.85:1) (16:9), Universal (UK R2 PAL)

"Not since *Deliverance*," proclaimed the poster for *Southern Comfort*, director Walter Hill's underrated follow up to his solid western, *The Long Riders*. While the central concept of the film - a group of men stranded in the wilderness fighting the elements and unseen human foes - bears some resemblance to Boorman's 1973 film, the agenda here is quite different and much closer to horror film territory, resulting in an underrated, memorable film deserving of a much more sizeable cult following.

In the opening prologue, a group of weekend warriors for the National Guard are dispatched for a training mission into the bayous of Louisiana. The ostensible leader of the group, Poole (Peter Coyote), is unable to contain some of the more reckless recruits, who suggest swiping some of the locals' canoes for a little sunny rafting. When the Cajuns appear and begin shouting protest, one of the men fires back in jest, igniting an impromptu war that finds the amateur soldiers scurrying for their lives through dark, unfamiliar territory besieged with booby traps. Along the way they pick up a hostage,

a one-armed Cajun trapper (the late Brion James), but their captive only serves to further muddy the waters. As their numbers dwindle, the men must resort to increasingly extreme methods of survival to make it back to civilization alive.

Southern Comfort could be read on many levels: an indictment of blind macho posturing, a critique of myopic American military strategies in Vietnam and the ensuing trauma suffering by soldiers, and most obviously, a primal nightmare in which the viewer is trapped in a strange, menacing land, stalked by invisible assailants out for blood. Keith Carradine and the unfairly overlooked Powers Boothe provide excellent performances as the most sympathetic of the Guardsmen, and regular Hill composer Ry Cooder turns in his finest score ever, a chilling concoction of Cajun musical tradition and atonal suspense riffs. The supporting cast is also typically strong for Hill, including T.K. Carter (one year before Carpenter's *The Thing*), Fred Ward, and many others. (Look closely at one of the hunter Cajuns to spot Radley Metzger hardcore porn actor Sonny Landham, also a Hill regular.) However, the real star here is Hill, who perfectly evokes the soggy, treacherous environment with insidious skill, pulling one surprise after another as the men dodge falling trees, man traps, and much, much worse.

Hill's real moment to shine comes in the horrific final 20 minutes, which provides a devastating twist on the "return to civilization" coda from *Deliverance*, instead notching up the terror tenfold. Be warned, this sequence also contains a genuine (if extremely common) animal slaughter that may put you off bacon for the rest of your life. However, this element is responsibly handled and integrates smoothly as a powerful, extremely bloody metaphor for the survivors' plight.

Southern Comfort has suffered from notoriously bad video transfers, which drowned the shadowy cinematography in a blanket of grain and muddy colours. The MGM DVD undoes most of the damage with a sharp anamorphic transfer (which, like most other Hill titles, mattes off information from the top and bottom compared to the full frame VHS masters). The film will never look like a glossy big budget production, but this is by far the best edition ever available, in many respects outclassing the carelessly produced theatrical prints. For some reason a mild jitter is evident in highly detailed areas during anamorphic playback on some monitors (watch Coyote's mouth during the prologue) but is completely absent on others. The mono audio is fine, duplicating the original mono track with good fidelity and no fancy whistles and bells. The sole extra is an excellent, gripping theatrical trailer, which should be enough for the ridiculously low price tag. The only major gripe lies with the DVD cover art, which slaps a confederate flag behind the title and makes this look like a trashy, Z-grade '80s war film. Don't be fooled; this is an impressive, nerve-shredding film, recommended without reservations.

SPACEWAYS

B&W, 1953, 76m. / Directed by Terence Fisher / Starring Howard Duff, Eva Bartok / Image (US R0 NTSC)

Filmed the same year as *Four Sided Triangle*, this peculiar mixture of melodramatic Sidney Sheldon thriller and space drama finds director Terence Fisher mostly working as a filmmaker for hire adapting a radio play by Charles Eric Maine. The story's origins should come as no surprise given the low amount of onscreen action and the fact that no one really goes into outer space until the last ten minutes; in fact, taken at face value, *Spaceways* will seem extremely quaint and dull given the title and engaging premise. However, as an early Hammer attempt at science fiction and a rough draft of Fisher's later explorations into such themes as female duality and personal sacrifice, the film has enough to offer viewers willing to bear with its methodical pacing.

Cloistered in a top secret facility, a band of intrepid British scientists scramble against the clock to complete their latest rocket mission and inch closer to their goal of being the first major national power to conquer space. Dr. Stephen Mitchell (*While the City Sleep*'s Howard Duff) finds his job strained by an unhappy marriage to Vanessa (Cecile Chevreau), who can't stand having every detail of her life run by bureaucrats. Meanwhile Stephen becomes more intimate with one of his doctor colleagues, Lisa Frank (*Blood and Black Lace*'s Eva Bartok). Things take a nasty turn when Vanessa and her illicit lover, a German scientist, turn up missing, and suspicious fingers point to Stephen after their latest rocket launch reveals the mysterious emptying of a great deal of fuel. Could Stephen have dumped the fuel and tucked the two dead bodies into the rocket now circling the Earth? According to his supervisor, Dr. Crenshaw (Andrew Osborn), the only way to find out is to send Stephen and Lisa into space to investigate.

Alternately intriguing and thoroughly formulaic, *Spaceways* suffers from its budgetary limitations (which apparently dictated the use of folding chairs aboard British spacecraft!) but works more successfully as a mystery, including a third act surprise (which, now that you know, won't be much of one) that could have stepped from an episode of *As the World Turns*. However, Fisher keeps things glossy and attractive, and the lovely Bartok is always fun to watch in one of her rare English language film appearances. Duff is less interesting and makes for a rather glum leading man, so viewers would be better advised to watch all the nifty '50s space contraptions and look for some awkwardly inserted clips from *Rocketship X-M*.

For a rarely seen title never even officially released on videotape, *Spaceways* looks exceptionally good on DVD. The first two thirds in particular are nearly immaculate with superb contrast and detail. Some print damage rears its ugly head near the end with some telltale scratches and grit, but it's mostly fleeting and not a major distraction. The disc also includes the original theatrical trailer, which makes this look like more of a space exploration flick (as does the cover art) than it really is. A fun little curio for Hammer and Fisher completists, this isn't essential viewing but a decent way to kill time. Hopefully some more of Fisher's pre-horror work (*Mantrap*, anyone?) will turn up on video as well to provide a more complete portrait of this unheralded visual maestro.

SPELLBOUND

B&W, 1945, 111m. / Directed by Alfred Hitchcock / Starring Ingrid Bergman, Gregory Peck / Anchor Bay (US R1 NTSC), PT Video (UK R2 PAL)

Even more than most Alfred Hitchcock films, the 1945 psychological thriller *Spellbound* seems like pure glossy entertainment on the surface but becomes increasingly weird under closer scrutiny. Loosely derived from Francis Beeding's novel *The House of Doctor Edwardes*, the film assumes (rather implausibly now) that all of Sigmund Freud's theories of psychoanalysis were absolutely correct and could unlock any key to the human mind. Hitchcock's treatment adopts these Freudian techniques to a twisty murder plot, but more intriguingly for film buffs, he also throws in some nifty visual gimmicks indicative of what he would later achieve in his more extreme work beginning with *Vertigo*.

Dr. Constance Peterson (Ingrid Bergman, looking quite lovely but studious) has earned the respect of her peers despite her status as a woman in a profession dominated by males. To paraphrase one of her colleagues, women generally make the best psychoanalysts until they get married, at which point they make the best patients. Her life carries on normally at an institute in Vermont until she encounters John Ballantine (a boyish Gregory Peck), a disturbed young man suffering from amnesia. Constance is intrigued by his case, particularly when he reveals an aversion to parallel lines on white surfaces. Evidence begins to surface that Ballantine may have been involved with the mysterious ski slope death of Dr. Edwardes, the former head of the institute, but Constance believes that John is innocent and possesses the key to the mystery inside his tortured mind. The two become lovers and go on the run, though Constance realizes her new beau might not be too trustworthy, especially when he's prone to walking around at night with a straight razor in his hand. Of course, nothing is as it seems, and after much tortuous mental probing, Constance finally discovers the true sequence of events that led to the doctor's violent death.

Of all the Hitchcock films, *Spellbound* contains perhaps the greatest potential to make a truly spectacular special edition on home video. Aside from the obvious sociological and psychological aspects that could be explored, the film also boasts a memorable dream sequence designed by none other than the master of surrealist art, Salvador Dali. Though striking in its current form, this sequence originally ran about twenty minutes and, according to Bergman, features a sequence in which she turns to stone, is cracked open, and finds herself covered in swarming ants. Whether any of this footage still exists is anyone's guess, but a visual study of this sequence would be very welcome. Furthermore, the film contains the genesis for numerous ideas explored in other Hitchcock films, particularly the concept of past traumas burying themselves in someone's subconscious and emerging in radically different forms (see *Marnie* for a fuller extension of this idea). Sadly, we'll just have to keep on waiting, as Anchor Bay's DVD presents the film with no extras at all, as with the other ABC-licensed titles. The transfer by and large is excellent and improves tremendously on the soft, washed-out laserdisc released by Fox several years ago. Much of the film uses rich, pitch black shadows for a nice chiaroscuro texturing effect which becomes much more prominent here. Unfortunately, Anchor Bay dropped the ball on one nifty Hitchcockian touch which has remained intact in all other recent prints, including the laser and the versions screened on FXMovies and AMC. Not to give too much away, but during the

climax when the gun is pointed at the screen and fires, the black and white film contains two red-tinted frames at the moment of the bullet's explosion. Though subliminal, it's a nice effect; too bad the folks who prepared this DVD didn't do their homework (ditto for the Anchor Bay DVD of *The Paradine Case*).

The PT Video edition in the UK contains a number of Hitchcockian extras which also appear on their discs of *Rebecca* and *Notorious*. A forthcoming edition from Criterion is also planned at the time of this writing and will hopefully pick up the copious slack remaining from this release. Strangely underrated even now, *Spellbound* holds up very well aside from Bergman's occasional silly lines evoking Freud as her personal gospel. Even aside from the dream sequence, numerous eccentric and gimmicky moments provide a grand entertainment with some dubious psychosexual subtext thrown in for good measure.

SPIDER BABY

B&W, 1964, 81m. / Written and Directed by Jack Hill / Starring Lon Chaney, Jr., Carol Ohmart / Image (US R0 NTSC) / WS (1.66:1)

Ah, if only all directors could begin their careers this way! Boasting one of Lon Chaney, Jr.'s best performances (for which he reportedly stayed on the wagon for most of the filming) and a diabolical sense of humour, Jack Hill's debut film, *Spider Baby*, was virtually ignored upon its initial release but has acquired a rabid cult following thanks to television and video. The theatrical reissue and laserdisc special edition a few years ago continued to whet the public's interest in this depraved gem, and the new DVD should continue to improve its standing in the offbeat film community. Though superficially similar to some of Charles Addams' drawings, *Spider Baby* truly resembles nothing else in film.

Chaney stars as Bruno, the family chauffeur for the Merrye clan. It seems the Merryes have been plagued for generations by "the Merrye syndrome," a degenerative condition of the mind and body that causes physical deformity and homicidal mania. The eldest son, Ralph (a hilarious Sid Haig), teeters on the brink of being locked away with his older relatives who now reside out of sight in the family basement, while the younger daughters, Elizabeth (Beverly Washburn) and Virginia (Jill Banner), a great comedy horror pair if there ever was one, take amusement in torturing and murdering the occasional visitor. Two distant relatives, Peter (Quinn Redeker) and Emily Howe (Carol Ohmart), come to pay a visit with their family lawyer, Mr. Schlocker (Karl Schanzer), and his secretary, Ann (*Dementia 13* heroine Mary Mitchel). When the visitors decide to stay for dinner, Ralph obliges by catching and preparing a cat for the main course, and while we wouldn't dream of giving away the title, let's just say the girls aren't too happy when Schlocker squashes a spider at the dinner table.

Filmed for virtually no money in atmospheric black and white over a period of twelve days, *Spider Baby* (also known as *The Liver Eaters* and *Cannibal Orgy, or the Maddest Story Ever Told*) continuously surprises thanks to its sharp script and enthusiastic performances. Ohmart does a funny turn on her blonde bitch routine from House on Haunted Hill, albeit with less clothing here, and Chaney's emotional post-dinner scene with the two girls proves once and for all that he was a fine actor in and out of makeup. The script includes a number of marvellous in-jokes for fans, particularly some funny riffs on *The Wolf Man*, and really isn't as depraved as a simple plot description might sound.

Image's DVD looks very close to their earlier laser version but with an improved contrast scale. The elements are in very good shape; after countless years of watching bootlegs and dicey TV prints, it's refreshing to see a commercially marginal title being treated like this. The 1.66.1 framing looks balanced and well chosen, and the level of detail is consistently impressive with little distortion or visual noise. The occasional scratch or scuff aside, this is the best this film has ever looked.

The DVD includes the same extras from the laser, namely footage of the film's recent screening at the Nuart in L.A. attended by many of the cast and crew, as well as laid back and affectionate commentary by Hill himself. However, there's one nice new bonus; Hill recently discovered a longer answer print of the film containing a longer second reel in a warehouse, and the extra footage has been included as a supplement on the disc. Presented fullscreen, the extended reel (eight minutes total, some of it also present in the final cut) contains several bits of footage snipped out to speed up the film. Some extra comedy between Bruno and Schlocker in the car, an earlier introduction to Ann's character, and some chit chat on the front porch in which Emily spies Ralph for a second time make up most of the extra running time, and while none of these bits add anything of narrative significance to the film, it's nice to see them rescued from oblivion. Thirty five years later, *Spider Baby* can easily be

seen as a film ahead of its time; the morbid yet affectionate tone may have been too much for audiences at the time, but fortunately, pitch black twisted humour has come into vogue since then. For anyone predisposed to offbeat midnight movies, this is one title you can't afford to miss.

THE SPIRAL STAIRCASE

B&W, 1946, 83m. / Directed by Robert Siodmak / Starring Dorothy McGuire, George Brent / Anchor Bay (US R1 NTSC)

This crackerjack gothic yarn was one of Hollywood's first attempts at a pure horror film after the trauma of World War II, and despite the turn of the century setting, it seems remarkably contemporary in its effective scares and narrative devices which influenced decades of psycho on the loose movies.

Dorothy McGuire stars as Helen, a mute servant girl in the home of ailing Mrs. Warren (Ethel Barrymore). Several town girls have fallen prey to a serial killer who targets females with "afflictions" of some kind. Helen has already caught the eye of young Dr. Parry (Val Lewton regular Kent Smith), who is implored by Mrs. Warren to take her away before the killer claims her next. Unfortunately a nasty storm traps the residents of the Warren home inside for the evening, and a death inside reveals that the killer is indeed among the family. Could it be one of the Warren sons, Steven (Gordon Oliver) or Albert (George Brent)? Or the voluptuous Blanche (Rhonda Fleming)? Or perhaps the soused cook, Mrs. Oates (Elsa Lanchester)? Before long Helen finds herself alone in the dark old house, using only her wits to do battle with the faceless maniac.

For a glossy David O. Selznick production, *The Spiral Staircase* is remarkably potent stuff and deserves to be remembered apart from the Hitchcock thrillers Selznick was pushing more aggressively at the time. The opening sequence alone is a real chiller, with a blind girl murdered above a movie theatre while the camera focuses in on the killer's eyes (a trick later repeated by Dario Argento with equal finesse). Director Robert Siodmak (*Criss Cross*) builds tension throughout the brief running time and allows all of the actors to have a field day, with McGuire and Barrymore the obvious standouts. (Incidentally, the screenplay was based on the novel *Some Must Watch* by Ethel Lina White, whose work was also the basis for Hitchcock's *The Lady Vanishes*).) Another familiar Val Lewton collaborator, composer Roy Webb, raises gooseflesh from the opening credits with his eerie, perfectly modulated score, while the often striking and mobile cinematography by Nicholas Musuraca perfectly captures each shadowy corner and lightning flash with vivid clarity. In short, this is a rare horror film which fans can show to the unconverted to show just how good the genre can be. (This doesn't apply to the inferior 1975 colour remake by Peter Collinson, starring Jacqueline Bisset.)

Though briefly released on video and laserdisc by Fox several years ago, *The Spiral Staircase* has been surprisingly difficult to see and has earned its reputation primarily through word of mouth. Anchor Bay's DVD is the finest presentation of the film to date, with a very detailed and nicely balanced transfer as good as any around for titles of this vintage. The opening credits still look a little hazy as usual, but after that it's a top notch job all the way. The disc also includes the rather bland theatrical trailer, which makes this look like an average gothic potboiler.

SPIRITISM

B&W, 1961, 85m. / Directed by Benito Alazraki / Starring Carmelita Gonzalez / Beverly Wilshire (US R0 NTSC)

Thanks to television syndication from the '60s through the '80s, Mexican horror films have become recognized as the domain of wrestlers, campy monsters, and half-dressed women, often together within the same scene. *Spiritism* is an exception to that rule, instead providing riffs on the Val Lewton formula of atmospheric horror with a few nods to Jacques Tourneur's then-recent *Curse of the Demon*. Because the lurid thrills are confined mostly to the last half hour, this oddly effective little number has been largely forgotten but deserves a look.

A middle class Mexican couple finds their dinner party conversation going downhill when a psychic woman advises them that difficult times lie ahead for them. Upon returning home, the couple's son informs them that he needs to borrow the family's savings to kick off his private crop dusting business(!), at the suggestion of the son's manipulative fiancée. Naturally the venture quickly crashes and burns, leaving the mother (Carmelita Gonzalez) desperate to revive the family's sorry economic state. Her spiritual faith begins to dwindle when she turns to a psychic society for assistance and

witnesses a bizarre display of ghostly visitations. Afterwards she is visited by a dark stranger, perhaps Satan himself, who offers a wooden box capable of granting a wish each time it is opened. After she makes a wish for money and opens the box to release a cloud of smoke, however, things go from bad to worse... and anyone who ever read "The Monkey's Paw" can probably guess what happens next.

While the plotline is a standard bit of domestic hand-wringing, the fun of *Spiritism* lies in the incidentals. The psychic sequences, a lively episode involving a disembodied hand scuttling around the house, and the nightmarish finale goose up the film, essentially a patchwork of other horror efforts delivered with more gusto than expected. The moody black and white photography is a major asset, particularly after the overly talky opening half hour, and director Benito Alazraki (*Curse of the Doll People*) makes effective use of dark rooms and spatial relationships to generate tension where none should really exist.

As with most Mexican '60s titles, *Spiritism* was picked up by K. Gordon Murray, who dubbed and released it straight to American television courtesy of Trans-International Films. This domestic edition provides the source for Beverly Wilshire's DVD, which looks pretty rough but at least brings this obscure film to disc. Considering *Spiritism* has been nearly impossible to see for at least twenty years, a lacklustre disc is still better than none at all. The video quality is messy, with distorted colours rippling through ever scene. (Turn off your TV's colour control if possible.) The print displays some scratches and tears but remains watchable, though the contrasts are weak and washed out. As with several other Beverly Wilshire titles, the copy of the box was obviously written by someone who had no information about the film at all, and it makes for hilarious reading.

SPIRITS OF THE DEAD

Colour, 1968, 117m. / Directed by Roger Vadim, Louis Malle, and Federico Fellini / Starring Jane Fonda, Alain Delon, Brigitte Bardot / Home Vision (US R1 NTSC) / WS (1.78:1) (16:9), Image (US R0 NTSC) / WS (1.78:1)

This trilogy of Edgar Allan Poe stories by renowned European directors was long a frustrating grail for home video collectors in the US until Water Bearer somehow managed to finally get the AIP-released title on VHS and laserdisc through Image in a welcome but unsatisfying, washed-out print that spoils some of the wilder colour schemes. The original English soundtrack (more in synch than the French one for two of the episodes) is provided as an alternate audio track to the French one, but the English subtitles are stuck on the screen either way. Meanwhile superior VHS editions of both the English and French language editions appeared in the UK, providing a new opportunity to assess this difficult compendium. The most satisfying presentation of the English language version anywhere, the UK tape preserved the original English soundtrack as opposed to the DVD's Australian dub track. A vivid presentation of the European French edition later arrived courtesy of Home Vision, whose colourful transfer resembles that of the long discontinued Japanese laserdisc. The removable English subtitles for the French soundtrack are a plus, but the absence of the actual English track is not. Neither DVD sports extras, but for newcomers, the latter may suffice.

Vadim's 'Metzengerstein" segment stars a pre-*Barbarella* Jane Fonda swishing around in outrageous, revealing costumes as a cruel noblewoman whose orgiastic lifestyle comes to an end when she becomes fixated on the reincarnation of her unrequited love (Peter Fonda) in the form of... a horse. This oddity is pure Vadim, packed with opulent visual delights and kinky surprises. Incidentally, judging from a few oddly cropped shots and forced pans, it appears that Vadim actually shot this episode in scope, then had it cropped to the standard ratio of the other segments.

Malle's "William Wilson" is a cryptic, sadistic, and chilly account of a soldier (Alain Delon) constantly thwarted in his attempts to do evil by his identical double. Brigitte Bardot makes a bizarre cameo as Delon's cigar-chomping, card-playing adversary who submits to a public whipping, and a number of sequences (a child dropped into a pail of rats, a gruesome live dissection, etc.) mark this as one of Malle's most decadent films (which may not be saying much for him, but...).

The real *piece de resistance*, though, is Fellini's "Toby Dammit," about which so much has already said that, well, anyone who hasn't seen it should rush out and grab this immediately. Terence Stamp is amazing as a feverishly drunk actor flown in to Rome to shoot a spaghetti western; the outrageous media circus, involving the usual Fellini characters (fashion models, eccentric old men, etc.), is a literal feast for the eyes. Meanwhile, Stamp is haunted by images of the devil - a young, white-clad girl relentlessly bouncing a large ball - who is closing in on

him as he descends into a drunken stupor and tries to take advantage of the new Ferrari given to him by the filmmakers. A classic.

SPLENDOR

Colour, 1999, 93m. / Directed by Gregg Araki / Starring Kathleen Robertson, Jonathan Schaech / Columbia (US R1 NTSC) / WS (1.85:1) (16:9) / DD5.1

Like all of the films directed by Gregg Araki, the alternative Valley Boy poster child, *Splendor* may be an acquired taste but offers a much safer introduction than his teen angst dramas like *Nowhere* and *The Doom Generation*. Here he paints a sweeter, candy-coloured three way romance purportedly derived from the '30s and '40s screwball comedies he admired in film school, though the results obviously wander far afield when set in the more sexually ambiguous '90s.

After a year-long dating dry spell, Veronica (Kathleen Robertson) finds herself involved with two men at the same time: Abel (Jonathan Schaech), an artsy writer type, and Zed (Matt Keeslar), a buffed, bleach blond drummer. The two men agree to let Veronica date them both, but after a drunken round of Truth or Dare, the three eventually wind up in bed together and decide to keep things that way. The financially irresponsible Abel and Zed move into Veronica's place, where they set up a cosy Three's Company arrangement that makes more sense emotionally than intellectually. However, when Veronica goes through a little biological crisis and takes off to Maui with a young TV director (Eric Mabius), the boys begin to realize their party for three may be coming to an end.

Much more tender and easygoing than the usual Araki film, *Splendor* still relies on hip, trendy young people in Almodóvar-style colour coordinated settings, but the arch dialogue has thankfully been replaced by genuine acting and character development. Robertson easily steals the film from her deliberately bland male cohorts; potentially dangerous character traits ranging from her on-camera monologues to her rapid shifts in mood manage to work thanks almost entirely to her winning performance. Familiar indie faces Schaech, Keeslar (*Last Days of Disco*), and Mabius (*Welcome to the Dollhouse*) have little do besides serving as Robertson's objects of pleasure, but they make admirable comic foils all the same. For a screwball

S

comedy, though, there isn't much obvious humour; the deception, identity confusion, and rapid dialogue which mark the best of the genre (e.g., Howard Hawks and Preston Sturges) are completely absent here. Instead, *Splendor* plays more like a dreamy rewrite of Truffaut's Jules and Jim with a couple of very soft love scenes tossed in for good measure. Araki's usual reliance on graphic, acidic dialogue takes a back seat here, and he even deftly sidesteps the issue of exactly what Abel and Zed do with each other when Veronica's not in bed. Compared to the seemingly endless, profane *ménages a trois* in *Doom Generation* (also featuring Schaech), *Splendor* could almost pass for the work of an entirely different director.

Like *Nowhere*, this film was shot with a hard matte at 1.85:1 and requires the entire breadth of the frame to really work. Unlike the horrendous pan and scan VHS version, the DVD looks spacious and offers a wide, delicious palette of colours throughout. While the bright splashes of pink, green and blue could have been a technical nightmare during the transfer, they manage to come out just fine in this anamorphically enhanced presentation. The 5.1 sound mix is unspectacular but manages to showcase the tastefully chosen pop soundtrack, with a strong emphasis on light electronica. The red label US trailer is also included with the usual talent profiles and trailers for two other Schaech titles, *Hush* and *Finding Graceland*.

THE SPY WHO LOVED ME

Colour, 1977, 125m. / Directed by Lewis Gilbert / Starring Roger Moore, Barbara Bach / MGM / WS (2.35:1) (16:9) / DD5.1

When two nuclear submarines - one British and one Russian - are hijacked, the respective governments assign their top operatives, James Bond (Roger Moore) and Anya Amasova (Barbara Bach), to investigate the generally well-respected millionaire altruist Karl Stromberg (Curt Jurgens), who has come to be suspected of being behind the felony.

With this, his third 007 escapade, Roger Moore finally shook off the Connery shackles and (though he'd never replace his predecessor in the eyes of the purists) at last made the role his own. This is the one that opens with a spectacular stunt in which Bond skis off the top of a mountain and parachutes to safety. Cubby Broccoli, having parted company with co-producer Harry Saltzman for the first time

since the series began, called back *You Only Live Twice* helmsman Lewis Gilbert and together with Christopher Wood at the typewriter they managed to reactivate some of the fantastical sparkle that had been largely absent from the Bonds since the late '60s. One of the most memorable moments occurs when the sporty Lotus Esprit transforms into a weapons-laden submersible and takes on an legion of enemy frogmen.

The cinematography (particularly on the Egyptian locations) is stunning and the climactic battle in a submarine pen hidden inside the belly of a supertanker is action cinema at its best.

Curt Jurgens might not be one of the better Bond baddies, but it's not entirely his fault as he's dwarfed quite literally by the 7ft. 2ins. bulk of razor-toothed hitman Jaws played by Richard Kiel (*The Humanoid*), who brings to the character a perfect blend of menace and idiosyncrasy. The movie also serves up a wealth of Bondian glamour in the form of Barbara Bach (*The Unseen*) as the most breathtaking Russian spy in cinema history, Caroline Munro (*Maniac*) as a slinky chopper pilot with a mission to eliminate 007, and Valerie Leon (*Blood from the Mummy's Tomb*) as a promiscuous hotel receptionist. Considered by many to be Moore's finest - though I would argue that *For Your Eyes Only* is marginally superior - *The Spy Who Loved Me* is up there among the cream of the Bond blockbusters.

An excellent film commands an excellent disc release and MGM have certainly delivered the goods with their special edition release of *The Spy Who Loved Me*. The 32-chapter encoded film itself is matted to a pleasing 2.35:1 ratio and, except for the fact that the picture looks a shade too dark to these eyes, it is a glorious presentation.

The disc also excels in the extras department, primarily with a 41-minute documentary detailing the film's progress from script to screen, but also in an extensive collection of trailers and TV spots (some of which include specially shot footage of Moore), no less than 12 radio spots and a presentable step-by-step gallery of stills. An additional documentary examines the work of production designer Ken Adam (who, along with the supertanker set for *Spy*, was the man who created Fort Knox for *Goldfinger* and the magnificent volcano crater for *You Only Live Twice*).

A commentary track from Ken Adam, director Lewis Gilbert, writer Christopher Wood and current Bond producer Michael G. Wilson caps the package. There are English and French language options and captioning is also in English and French. - TG

STAGEFRIGHT

Colour, 1986, 87m. / Directed by Michele Soavi / Starring Barbara Cupisti, David Brandon / Anchor Bay (US NTSC R1) / WS (1.85:1) (16:9) / DD5.1, EC Entertainment (Holland R0 NTSC) / DD2.0

Whilst rehearsing for a theatrical show, "The Night Owl", dancer Alicia (Cupisti) twists her ankle and slips away to seek attention. The nearest medical facility also happens to be an asylum and when she returns to work she is the unwitting escort of escaped mental patient Irving Wallace (Clain Parker). When the frustrated director, Peter (Brandon), locks the door and hides the key in an effort to get some intensive toil from what he deigns to be his lazy cast, Wallace is locked in with them. Hidden beneath the mask of a giant owl, the maniac unleashes his rage upon the unsuspecting troupe.

I was first drawn to seek out *Stagefright* after reading a rave review by everyone's favourite genre journalist Alan Jones. It's a rare occasion that a movie affects me, but despite the fact I was watching a cut version it crawled under my skin and took up residence there like few other films I can recall. It actually kept me awake that night. Subsequent viewings lessened its impact dramatically, but the picture holds up extremely well as an above average giallo with barrels of hi-octane tension and an excess of blood and guts. Rarely have there been such ball-tightening moments as when, during rehearsals and believing the masked Wallace to be his leading man Brett (John Morghen), Peter hollers directions that he go through the motions of killing actress Corinne (Lori Parrel). Wallace obliges and, to the horror of everyone watching, draws a knife and proceeds to repeatedly stab the poor girl to within inches of her life.

Kathleen Stratton's rapid fire editing coupled with composer Stefano Mainetti's "Ballad for Corinne" fashions an unforgettable moment in the annals of horror cinema. Having Wallace (whose face isn't properly revealed until the final reel) hidden beneath an owl mask works remarkably well, the blank face and glass eyes conveying to perfection the soullessness of the unstoppable maniac lurking beneath. Soavi mines genuine terror out of the moments when victims-to-be plead with the killer - I mean, how does one even begin to bargain with someone whose actions have no reason or motive? There's more pulse-pounding suspense in the final 20 minutes of *Stagefright* than you'll find in a dozen *Friday the 13ths*. To the uninitiated I say run out and buy this post-haste. As for the initiated, what are you reading this for? Go and watch the film again... immediately!

Previously available as a Japanese laserdisc and a Red Edition DVD from Germany (in German language only), EC Entertainment's Deluxe Collector's Edition release brings *Stagefright* to a wider audience in a Region free 14-chapter disc that does the film proud. The spotless, uncut print makes up for various trimmed VHS releases of days past, and can be viewed fullscreen or with an added 1.66:1 theatrical matte. To be honest the matted option is rather worthless as all it does is crop the image top and tail, and renders the final shot of Wallace turning to face the camera useless. Bonus features comprise a trailer and an extensive gallery of stills, artwork and video sleeves from around the world. Most unusual of all there is a catchy music video entitled "Mystery Rouge". It's in pretty poor shape though, looking as if it has been transferred from a second generation VHS tape, decidedly murky and complete with flecks of dropout. The song doesn't feature in the movie but originally headlined a Japanese soundtrack album release, which wasn't the music of Simon Boswell. - TG

[*The US anamorphic Anchor Bay disc is matted at 1.85:1, the same ratio used for the film's theatrical exhibition. - ed.]*

STARMAN

Colour, 1985, 112m. / Directed by John Carpenter / Starring Jeff Bridges, Karen Allen / Columbia (US R1 NTSC) / WS (2.35:1) (16:9) / DD4.0

After two botched widescreen laser releases (one from Pioneer), John Carpenter's heartfelt science fiction favourite was fully letterboxed on DVD and looks even better here than it did in theatres.

As *Video Watchdog* noted, the two laser editions were "zoomboxed" (all of the edges of the widescreen image were zoomed in and cropped off to make the image larger, a practice repeated on the laser of *Big Trouble in Little China*). The DVD presents the entire widescreen image and more importantly, looks infinitely more crisp, with accurate flesh tones and remarkable background detail. Some of the landscape shots now look so startling, you could freeze frame them as works of art on your TV screen.

The film itself still holds up well, with Jeff Bridges shining in his Oscar-nominated performance as an alien who takes on the guise of a dead

S

housepainter and takes the man's widow (Karen Allen) on a cross-country odyssey. Characterization and romance take precedence over the effects (which are still good), and Jack Nitzsche's eerie, touching score sounds better than ever in Dolby Digital. Bonuses include the original trailer as well as, oddly enough, the trailer for Jeff Bridges' *The Mirror Has Two Faces*.

THE STENDHAL SYNDROME

Colour, 1996, 113m. / Directed by Dario Argento / Starring Asia Argento, Thomas Kretschmann / Troma (US R1 NTSC) / WS (1.66:1), Dutch Filmworks (Holland R2 PAL) / WS (1.66:1) (16:9), Pioneer (France R2 PAL) / WS (1.85:1) (16:9), Marquee (UK R0 PAL) / WS (1.66:1) / DD2.0

 Dario Argento shocked fans by delivering one of his most gruelling, difficult films, *The Stendhal Syndrome*, after a two film stint in America. This jittery study of psychosis hinges on the familiar Hitchcockian theme of transmission of guilt, here filtered through disturbing psychosexual imagery that contrasts harshly with the dreamy, asexual nightmares of *Suspiria* and *Phenomena*.

Argento's daughter, Asia, takes the lead once again as Anna Manni, a police detective whose pursuit of a serial killer leads her to the Uffizi Gallery in Florence. While gazing at the paintings among the stifling crowd, Anna is overcome, collapses to the floor, and experiences a bizarre underwater vision. The psychopath, Alfredo (Thomas Kretschmann), makes contact with Anna and continues to observe her, even dragging the young woman into the middle of a horrific gunshot killing. Gradually Alfredo closes in and plays sadistic mind games that ultimately distort Anna's entire perception of reality.

A rare Argento work to actually receive a theatrical run in America, *The Stendhal Syndrome* is definitely not a film for Italian horror beginners. Unprepared midnight movie audiences greeted the film with giggles and confusion, a problem exacerbated by its weird pacing. The film seems to reach its violent climax halfway into the story, only to abruptly switch gears and become an entirely different narrative for the following hour. On top of that, the dialogue was spoken phonetically in English but clumsily dubbed in both the English and Italian versions in a studio by different actors. As a result, some lines come off as unforgivably clunky

("I can let you ride my French scooter") and detract from what is otherwise a sombre, brutal, and nightmarish film that begs to be considered as a serious work of art. Asia's performance improves with repeated viewings as she is subjected to a variety of physical and psychological tortures; mercifully her father relents and shows some mercy in the final sequence. Along the way he also indulges in skewed references to both his own films (*Phenomena* in particular) and some unexpected riffs on other horror titles like *When a Stranger Calls*. Of historical note, the film also marked the reteaming of Argento with composer Ennio Morricone, who had scored Argento's first three landmark thrillers in the early '70s.

Troma's long awaited DVD was originally announced with a commentary track by Argento, which ultimately had to be pulled due to the director's discomfort with speaking English for long periods of time. The absence is regrettable, but the film transfer is above average for Troma if not exemplary. The letterboxing (slightly more than 1.66:1) looks dead on, with a more satisfying visual texture and framing than the previous, overly contrasted presentation on Japanese laserdisc and the overmatted theatrical screenings. Likewise the surround audio is quite powerful, with the rear speakers in particular constantly buzzing with activity. The dialogue still sounds canned and disjointed, but alas this flaw will apparently never be removed from the film.

The usual bizarre, unrelated Troma extras round out the package, including a frankly wretched US theatrical trailer, "coming distractions" for titles like *Killer Condom* and *Cannibal: The Musical*, a video interview with Argento and Lloyd Kaufman (also included on other Troma DVDs), some comments from FX maestro Sergio Stivaletti about the mixture of latex gore and CGI manipulation, a bizarre video interview with director Ruggero Deodato, some camcorder footage of Argento at a horror convention in Sweden, and the usual "Tromabilia."

The Dutch and (overmatted) French DVDs offer anamorphically enhanced transfers which are superior to Troma's, though the surround tracks are weaker. Both have optional subtitles and the usual Argento bio-related extras. The Dutch version also tacks on *Dario Argento's World of Horror* as a generous extra. The UK release from Marquee Pictures was pre-cut by the distributors before even being submitted to the BBFC (who let through what they had received unscathed). The cuts amounted to 2 minutes and 47 seconds. Muddying the waters somewhat was the initial batch of UK DVDs which were accidentally released uncut.

STOP MAKING SENSE

Colour, 1984, 88m. / Directed by Jonathan Demme / Starring Talking Heads / Palm (US R1 NTSC) / WS (1.85:1) (16:9) / DD5.1

The concert film against which all others should be judged, Jonathan Demme's buoyant *Stop Making Sense* presents the group Talking Heads at their creative and physical peak, right after the release of their remarkable *Speaking in Tongues* album. However, this is more than just a filmed concert; by eschewing the conventional audience reaction shots, flashy cutting, and trendy process effects shots, Demme managed to craft a sleek, powerful, and invigorating work of cinema which, along with *The Song Remains the Same*, *Home of the Brave*, and *The Cure in Orange*, has justifiably gone on to become a bona fide cult item in its own right.

Frontman David Byrne (who conceived the show) opens up performing the jittery "Psycho Killer" in front of a boom box on an empty stage; with each song, he's successively joined by other band members Tina Weymouth, Chris Frantz, and Jerry Harrison, with backing by vocalists Lynn Mabry and Ednah Holt and instrumental performances by Bernie Worrell, Alex Weir, and Steve Scales. Each song becomes its own unique visual/sonic experience: the eerie slideshow and lamp dance of "Naive Melody (This Must Be the Place)," Byrne's wobbling oversized suit during "Girlfriend Is Better," and the head-slapping intensity of "Once in a Lifetime" are just a few of the highlights. Even when Byrne leaves the stage for the remaining members (Tom Tom Club) to do "Genius of Love," the conceptual strands of the film and live performance amazingly remain intact. By the final two numbers, even the most repressed viewers should be tapping their feet along with the audience.

Shot over a period of three days in Hollywood, this film looks like no other and should have been more influential than it has been. While MTV continues to stick to those annoying overhead swooping crane shots and tiresome, whiplash editing, Demme and company show how it should be done. Interestingly, Demme pared down this formula even more for his Robyn Hitchcock concert film, *Storefront Hitchcock*.

Long unavailable outside of RCA/Columbia's, smudgy VHS release and a pricey Japanese laserdisc, *Stop Making Sense* looks its best on DVD. The three extra songs included on the VHS version ("Cities," "Big Business," and "I Zimbra") are added as a bonus feature, along with the reissue trailer and a hilarious, homemade video interview with Byrne interviewing himself in various wacko disguises. The anamorphic image quality is very good, especially considering the shooting conditions, with rich shadows and gorgeous colours (love those reds!). The sound has been remixed into a standard 5.1 version, a "studio" 5.1 remix (tighter and a little louder, thus more intimate), and the original surround mix. There isn't a huge difference between the three, and audiophiles will probably find the basic 5.1 mix to be the most preferable. Demme and all of the band members provide commentary, which had to be recorded separately at different studios (most likely due to extreme friction between Byrne and the rest of the group in the past few years). The commentary is generally well edited if a little choppy and cold, obviously, due to the circumstances.

STORY OF O

Colour, 1975, 92m. / Directed by Just Jaeckin / Starring Corinne Clery, Udo Kier / Heatwave (Hong Kong R0 NTSC) / WS (1.66:1), Arrow (UK R2 PAL) / WS (1.66:1) (16:9), GCTHV (France R2 PAL) / WS (1.66:1), Force (Australia R4 PAL) / WS (1.66:1)

The first and most successful adaptation of the scandalous S&M novel by the pseudonymous Pauline Réage, *Story of O* (*Histoire d'O*) is that rarest of birds, a soft erotic film that actually works. While the elements of bondage and submission in the story have earned its legendary reputation among the home video crowd, the film also ranks as perhaps the most successful attempt outside of Radley Metzger to lend elegance to bare flesh, far outclassing director Just Jaeckin's previous money-maker, *Emmanuelle*.

O (Corinne Clery), a beautiful young fashion photographer, is escorted by her lover, Rene (Udo Kier), to the gothic Chateau Roissy where she endures a succession of humiliations and erotic experiments designed to test her physical and emotional limitations. Desiring only to please Rene, she willingly submits to each new demand without question. Back in Paris, O resumes her romantic relationship with Rene, who strangely hands her over into the care of the older Sir Stephen (Anthony Steel). A primary member of the Roissy coterie, he performs a serious of mind games with O, who begins to feel unease about her status as a pawn in what appears to be a world of scheming men, focused on their own pleasure solely at her expense.

In design and execution, *Story of O* is essentially the erotic mirror to Dario Argento's *Suspiria*, an orgy of visual style in which the story takes a back seat to the relentless succession of powerful images and stunning music (composer Pierre Bachelet never topped himself after this one). Like Argento's film (which also features horror icon Kier, coincidentally), the curtain raising sequence is so magnificent in every respect that there's no way the rest of the film can compare- but it's still a very enjoyable ride. Clery, who later appeared in *Moonraker*, the brutal *Hitch-hike*, and Lucio Fulci's *The Devil's Honey*, looks ravishing in every shot and makes for a compelling heroine, though the men do little besides lounging around in their chic designer suits. The film itself takes some liberties with the source novel, including an additional scene at the end which makes for a far more satisfying resolution; in 1996, a very long Spanish-produced miniseries for European television attempted to reproduce every word of the text but couldn't approach its big screen predecessor.

A regular video favourite since the early '80s, *Story of O* has enjoyed numerous VHS incarnations but only two laserdisc releases, one from MGM in the US (a cropped but colourful transfer which stupidly omits Bachelet's main title theme) and one in Japan (also full frame, in French with Japanese subtitles). The original French cut of the film (also issued on VHS in Australia, of all places) runs about 10 minutes longer, consisting mainly of a scene in which Rene calls O from work to tell her to disrobe and remain naked until he comes home (which she does) and a sequence with O and her model protégé, Jacqueline, including a brief retreat to the beach. The Japanese version was subsequently issued on DVD (again, no English subtitles), while the English print received the DVD treatment in Hong Kong from Heatwave, an adult video label with an outrageously smutty promo opener on their discs. The absence of the extra French sequences is mildly regrettable (they don't add much to the film, but a special edition someday would be nice). However, apart from one brief video dropout at the beginning, the Hong Kong disc looks better than the MGM laser, sporting levels of detail during the Roissy sequences which were completely blurred in all other versions. (Much of the movie is soft focus, but not that soft.) Incidentally, even the French version was dubbed later in the studio by other actors, so the language isn't much of a factor either way. In fact, Kier, Clery, and Steel clearly spoke most of their lines in English

on the set, so the American dub is just as valid. The image is completely unmatted, exposing a filmed hard matte slightly under 1.66:1 for most of the film but full frame during certain shots. The sound quality is acceptable, though some slight warbling can be heard during the opening credits. For some reason, the back of the packaging only includes promo shots from the vastly inferior *Story of O 2*, a British-French co-production which avoided almost everything that made the original work.

An Australian release from Force is comparable in terms of both content and quality. The British disc from Arrow features a nice but mildly battered 16:9 transfer of the standard English cut, with the additional scenes tacked on as a supplement (with no audio!). Most respectable is the French DVD, which offers the English language edition with optional French, Spanish, or English subtitles, or the longer French cut with the same subtitle options, as well as a host of extras relating to softcore French erotica.

THE STRAIGHT STORY

Colour, 1999, 111m. / Directed by David Lynch / Starring Richard Farnsworth, Sissy Spacek / US (Buena Vista R1 NTSC), FilmFour (UK R2 PAL) / WS (2.35:1) (16:9) / DD5.1

When a virtual invalid, 73-year-old Alvin Straight (Farnsworth), learns that his estranged brother Lyle (Harry Dean Stanton) has suffered a heart attack, against his daughter's wishes he resolves to visit him and patch up their differences. With poor health denying him a driver's licence, he sets out on the 500-mile journey from Laurens, Iowa to Mount Zion, Wisconsin astride a ride-on lawnmower.

Justifiably hailed as David Lynch's best film to date - for indeed, it is - *The Straight Story* is probably the least typical example of his many achievements that you will encounter. If it weren't for the fistful of typically quirky Lynchian characters that Straight meets on his journey, the film would be scarcely unidentifiable as the great man's work at all. Based on the true story of Alvin Straight (who passed away in 1996), former stuntman Richard Farnsworth - who, stricken with terminal cancer, took his own life shortly after completing the film - gives a career best performance as the grizzled old buzzard with a twinkle in his eye and a forte for dishing out pearls of wisdom to all he encounters. Although, in making his point, these pearls occasionally veer towards the saccharine sweet -

most notably when draws an analogy between a bunch of tied twigs and family bonds in order to convince a runaway teenager to return home - John Roach and Mary Sweeney's superlative screenplay makes Straight so well meaning and loveable that you can't help but forgive them such little indulgences. It's the simplest dialogue that is the most profound and, in Farnsworth's hands, suitably dramatic impact. "What's the worst part of being old, Alvin?" asks one of the youths sat beside a campfire with Straight. "Rememberin' when you was young," the old fella replies. The expression on Straight's face during the silence that follows is among many emotionally stirring and magical moments that Farnsworth treats us to. A highlight comes in a remarkable scene between Straight and Verlyn Heller (Wiley Harker) as they sit at a bar discussing the war, and dark and disturbing secrets are revealed. Although he was nominated, the fact that Farnsworth wasn't presented with an Academy Award is, in retrospect, unbelievable. Mention too for Sissy Spacek's touching portrayal of Straight's daughter, Rose, speech impaired and with her own tragic burdens to bear.

Benefiting immeasurably from the tranquillity of cinematographer Freddie Francis's numerous, beautifully composed vistas - all complemented by a premium Angelo Badalamenti score - *The Straight Story* is quite possibly the unequalled feel good movie of all time.

Lamentably lacking in bonus features (beyond a standard trailer), FilmFour's Region 2 DVD nevertheless gets top marks, for the picture and sound quality are faultless. The Region 1 release, with equally few extras, is devoid of chaptering (with an explanatory note as to why from director Lynch), making the Region 2 disc with its 17 stops the preferred option. - TG

STRANGLER OF THE SWAMP

B&W, 1945, 59m. / Directed by Frank Wisbar / Starring Rosemary La Planche, Robert Barrat / Image (US R0 NTSC)

A perfect example of how a few critics can alter the fate of a film, *Strangler of the Swamp* languished in complete obscurity until the rise of formal film criticism in the '70s. Along with a handful of other films like *Mad Love, Strangler* was acknowledged as an example of auteurism flourishing in the world of zero budget schlock moviemaking. In particular, William K.

Everson's championing of the film led to repeated TV screenings and mentions in countless other horror books. Though hardly a classic on the level of some of the Universal monster films, *Strangler* does etch itself into one's memory and benefits greatly from the assured direction of Frank Wisbar, adapting his 1936 German fantasy *Fährmann Maria (Ferryman Maria)* into the US horror milieu. Because the film was made for PRC, the most notorious cut rate studio of its era, Wisbar had to make do with a heavily confined amount of shooting space on the set and virtually no budget. However, thanks to clever photography and editing, he managed to create a palpable sense of atmosphere to boost this subtle supernatural tale.

After the mob lynching of Ferryman Douglas (Charles Middleton, best known as *Flash Gordon*'s Ming the Merciless) for a murder he didn't commit, townspeople are terrified of a wraith haunting the swamp surrounding their humble little hamlet. Even suggestions of draining the swamp provoke little response ("That isn't gonna stop him!"), but no one seems to have a solution. When the real murderer and a several of the lynchers turn up choked from some swamp vines, the heroine, Maria (Rosemary La Plance), becomes convinced that, as a descendant of the bloodline that Douglas is avenging, she is the only person who can stop him. Her beau, Christian (Blake Edwards - yes, that Blake Edwards), expresses a noticeable lack of enthusiasm over her Nosferatu-like plan for self-sacrifice, but he cannot prevent Maria and the ferryman from meeting their fates out in the desolate mists of the swamp.

Like most smart horror directors, Wisbar leaves many terrifying aspects of the film completely to the viewers' imaginations. Middleton barely appears on camera, and even then he's mostly a distant, smoky apparition drifting in and out of shadows. Similar to the Val Lewton efforts of the day, or perhaps Curtis Harrington's Night Tide, this film relies primarily upon atmosphere and a gradually escalating sense of doom (relieved by an unlikely happy ending). Clocking in at less than an hour, the plot moves quickly and displays an admirable economy of plotting and editing.

As with all PRC films, the impoverished production values resulted in a less than slick final product, and the ravages of time have resulted in unwatchable, blurry, scratchy prints with muddy sound. Relatively speaking, Image's DVD is as good as it's going to get; though still ragged in spots, the contrast has been greatly improved, with some nice background detail now visible for the first time. The opening credits in particular are the worse for wear, but overall, the elements are cleaner and more sonically intelligible than those awful public domain tapes and late night TV screenings. The visual problems are obviously inherent to the original source, as scenes range from sharp and clear (most of the "daylight" footage) to relatively blurry. Anyone looking for a black and white demo piece is going to be sorely disappointed when comparing this to some of the elaborate digital restorations in recent years; instead, horror aficionados should simply seize the opportunity to finally have a watchable print of this intriguing little gem.

STREET TRASH

Colour, 1987, 101m. / Directed by James Muro / Starring Mike Lackey, Bill Chepil / Dragon (Germany R0 NTSC)

Hey, kids, here's the greatest movie ever made about exploding bums! Yes, indeed, the underground gorehound favourite *Street Trash* finally got the uncensored NTSC treatment thanks to some folks in Germany, who saw fit to issue this sick puppy in its full 101 minute version - over 12 minutes longer than the US Lightning Video edition back in the late '80s. While many horror fans will be scratching their heads at this one, a peculiar niche of viewers who came of age during this wild and woolly period (which also spawned *Re-Animator* and the first two *Evil Dead* films) should have a wide, nostalgic grin whenever it's mentioned. Is it a "good" movie? Not by a long shot, at least in the traditional sense, but for jittery energy and reckless gross-out attitude, you'd have to look far and wide to find a guiltier pleasure than this.

The, uh, story, for lack of a better term (sort of derived from Kurosawa's *Dodes-ka-den*), kicks in when a liquor store owner uncovers a long lost crate of booze called Viper. He sells the stuff off to homeless people for a dollar per bottle; unfortunately, Viper also causes the consumer to bubble, burst, and melt in a kitschy mess of pastel colours. Our hero, Freddie (Mike Lackey), goes on a desperate crusade to save his fellow bums and outmanoeuvre his nemesis, a crazed junkyard Vietnam vet... but this summary only scratches the surface. Director Muro (a great Steadicam operator whose affection for that device plays an integral part here) and writer Frumkes (*The Johnsons*, *Document of the Dead*) spin around so many subplots and weird characters that first time viewers could easily get a migraine trying to take it all in at once. The funniest subplot involves a two bit gangster and his

continuing antagonism with disgruntled doorman James Lorinz (*Frankenhooker*), but others involve a shoplifting wino, a fascist cop, and even an incident of rape and necrophilia. Sound tasteless? Yep - and that isn't even including a 2001 parody involving a severed portion of male anatomy. Absolutely not for all tastes, to be sure, but you'll never forget it.

The region free NTSC format DVD from Dragon looks good, but not great. Most of the daylight shots look extremely clear and vivid, while the night scenes have a tendency to become murky and dull. This flaw with the source material will always exist, but Synapse's announced special edition should be better. The disc also includes a new German trailer for the film, which pretty much spoils all of the highlights. While it's too bad we can't have a Frumkes/Muro commentary, the disc does feature the original English and German soundtracks with accompanying optional subtitles. For modern horror and cult movie fans, this should be just your cup of Viper.

THE STUFF

Colour, 1985, 93m. / Directed by Larry Cohen / Starring Michael Moriarty, Andrea Marcovicci / Anchor Bay (US R1 NTSC) / WS (1.85:1) (16:9)

If you've been looking for a good reason to skip dessert, *The Stuff* should do the trick. After satirizing urban cynicism and ennui in *Q*, director Larry Cohen turned his camera towards consumerism with this batty little film, which features another delicious hambone performance from Michael Moriarty and enough scattershot laughs to make it more of a black comedy than a horror film. The interplay between the characters is far more interesting than the monster itself, so as long as you're expecting a Cohen film instead of something genuinely scary, there's plenty of *Stuff* here to like.

An elderly, hungry oil refinery worker in Alaska notices some white goo bubbling up out of the ground. Curious, he decides to taste it and mentions to a co-worker that people might actually enjoy using it as a food source. Then voila, this white substance becomes a nationally popular dessert known as The Stuff. Low calorie and utterly yummy, it earns a place in every home and sends other food manufacturers into a financial tailspin. Enter industrial spy "Mo" (Moriarty), a smooth talking Southern boy hired to uncover the secret ingredient of The Stuff, which has already caused ruin to the likes of cookie guru "Chocolate" Charlie (*Saturday Night Live*'s Garrett Morris). Meanwhile little Jason (Scott Bloom) notices The Stuff moving of its own free will in the refrigerator late one night and refuses to touch it. His family loves it, however, though they begin to resemble zombies more than human beings. The two plot threads eventually collide, with Mo resorting to the military aid of extremist Colonel Spears (Paul Sorvino) to combat the national menace.

As with any Cohen film, *The Stuff* runs mainly on wit and sheer energy rather than logic or coherence. The editing is a mess, arguably even more than *God Told Me To*, but the film is so endearing in its own shaggy dog way that it's hard to quibble. The ad campaign dreamed up for *The Stuff* is hilarious, with personalities ranging from Brooke Adams to Clara "Where's the Beef?" Peller gushing about their favourite foodstuff.

Cohen's commentary track on the DVD increases one's appreciation of the film immensely, as he rattles off anecdotes involving everything from Teamsters to Moriarty's hairpieces. He also points out a number of actors from his other films, including a supermarket cameo from *Special Effects'* Eric Bogosian. Though he tends to repeat himself quite a bit, he keeps things making at a fast clip and proves to be just as witty as his infamous off-kilter dialogue. He also reveals that Morris was not quite, um, himself when they shot the film and reveals the original actor he wanted for the role. Incidentally, Jason's brother is played by the actor's real life sibling, Brian Bloom, who went on to become a TV heartthrob on *Bandit* and starred in *Knocking on Death's Door*. It's very odd and slightly creepy seeing him as a preteen.

As with most Cohen films, *The Stuff* was shot open matte and presented at 1.85:1 in theatres - that is, all thirty or so theatres that actually showed it. The film did much better on video, where its unforgettably gross (and misleading) cover art lured in plenty of '80s splatter fans. Anchor Bay's DVD contains the original poster artwork, which also erroneously implies that the stuff eats up its victims from the inside. The matted transfer here looks much better than the old VHS tapes, obviously, and the mono audio is stronger and punchier than ever before. The animated menus designed like a commercial for *The Stuff* are terrific, as is the phoney public service announcement trailer.

SUBCONSCIOUS CRUELTY
Colour, 1999, 80m. / Directed by Karim Hussein / Starring Brea Asher, Ivaylo Founev / PAND (Japan R2 NTSC) / DD2.0

A loosely constructed, visually rich and highly graphic meditation on man's relation to himself and the world around him, *Subconscious Cruelty* further blurs that already shaky line between art house pretension and unrepentant sleaze. Though the framework revolves around three (or arguably four) stories, this Canadian timebomb concealed in celluloid is definitely way beyond the land of Amicus and EC Comics.

Best known to the film festival crowd for their involvement in the annual FantAsia event in Montreal, director Karim Hussein and producer Mitch Davis (who previously collaborated on Davis' half hour directorial debut, *Divided into Zero*) had to endure an obscenity bust and the near loss of the film's negative due to legal entanglements, finally completing this opus after years of work. The final result is so odd, aggressive, and perpetually vicious, one has to admire the spirit of the piece even if it can't be termed "enjoyable" in the traditional sense.

The opening urges viewers to reject the left, "rational" side of the human brain and instead indulge in a world of free association, bestial instinct, and irrational hallucination. To back this up, viewers are treated to "Ovarian Eyeball," a quick, gruesome study about the primitive nature of childbirth.

The first full segment, "Human Larvae," establishes an unhealthy relationship between a young man and his pregnant sister; his obsessive, sexualized need to control her leads to a particularly nasty birthing scene that no doubt sent unprepared viewers scrambling for the exits.

Things take a turn for the lighter in the nonlinear second act, "Rebirth," a sort of nature worship bacchanal in which naked free spirits form a bloody communion with the earth, trees, and each other. It's quite upbeat and funny in a particularly bent way; pagans in particular should find this one enjoyable.

The harshest of the bunch, "Right Brain / Martyrdom," is saved for last; a man indulging in some mechanical self-gratification is suddenly transported into a nightmarish landscape of genital mutilation, clawed female demons, and a mock crucifixion tableau with a particularly nasty punchline. Don't say you weren't warned!

Currently the only legitimate DVD release in the world comes courtesy of Japan, whose gradually relaxing censorship standards have allowed the film's plentiful frontal nudity to pass without visual blurring or digitizing. Some glimpses of hardcore porn on a television screen remain understandably blurred, but more perplexing is the visual fogging during the aforementioned weenie torture scene. It's all done with prosthetics and fake blood, so one has to wonder exactly what the problem is when material like *Men Behind the Sun* gets through unscathed.

The film is transferred in its original 4:3 aspect ratio and looks quite detailed and colourful; grain inherent in the picture is due to the original materials. Though light on dialogue, the film can be played either dubbed in Japanese or in its original English with non-removable Japanese subtitles. The audio is more immediately impressive; a great deal of work went into the disturbing, heavily layered soundtrack, and the oppressive surround mix featuring Teruhiko Suzuki's score often equals or even overwhelms the already extreme visuals.

SUCCUBUS

Colour, 1967, 76m. / Directed by Jess Franco / Starring Janine Reynaud, Jack Taylor / Anchor Bay (US R0 NTSC)

In many ways, *Succubus* (released in Europe as *Necronomicon*) is the quintessential '60's Franco film. Sex, sadism, and a trippy disregard for logic are the order of the day as European starlet Janine Reynaud portrays Lorna, a nightclub performer whose S&M-inspired stage act inspires a series of hallucinatory encounters (flashbacks?) that tantalize the viewer more than they offer explanations. Reynaud's strong, sensual presence really powers the film, much as Soledad Miranda's does in *Vampyros Lesbos*, and her sultry series of dances and costume changes (supplied by Karl Lagerfeld!) make this a real treat for the eye.

Anchor Bay's DVD is apparently derived from the same materials used for Redemption Video's release in the UK (this is the English language version, and some foreign prints contain alternate sequences we'll most likely never see); the image is overall pleasant to look at, and quibbling aside, this is probably the best version we'll see in the near future. The colours are stable if a little too subdued (this is supposed to be one gaudy looking film), and more importantly, it's been cropped to full frame from the original 1:1.75 aspect ratio. This may not sound too crucial, but considering that this is one of Franco's most formally composed films, the image loss is noticeable in some of his three-character frame setups.

SURRENDER DOROTHY

B&W, 1998, 94m. / Directed by Kevin DiNovis / Starring Peter Pryor, Kevin DiNovis / First Run (US R1 NTSC) / WS (1.85:1) (16:9) / DD2.0

Nothing earmarks an art film like a sick captivity drama. Actors have been re-enacting the Stockholm syndrome as black comedy romantic fodder for a couple of decades, with typically touchy results for most viewers. However, *Surrender Dorothy*, sort of a *Singapore Sling* for the gay festival set, belongs in its own depraved little realm. Both well made and intensely unsettling, this study in gender manipulation and personality suppression is not for the easily offended but makes for a great walk on the cinematic wild side.

Antisocial waiter Trevor (Peter Pryor) lives an unfulfilled life in which he can't get a decent date and gratifies himself with the aid of silverware used by female patrons. His friend, a shady drug dealer named Denis (Jason Centeno), keeps Trevor hooked up and remains one of his few solid contacts to humanity, however squalid that may be. Denis' roommate, Lahn (played by the obviously fearless director, Kevin DiNovis), shows up on Trevor's doorstep after robbing Denis and asks for shelter. Though both men claim to be straight, they're soon acting out a twisted domestic melodrama of abuse and sexual gratification, with Trevor insisting that Lahn perform the role of his dream girl, "Dorothy" (who, judging from Trevor's preferred fetish attire, stems from a severe *Wizard of Oz* complex). Before you know it, female hormones, drag, bitch slapping, and other niceties enter the picture, leading to the grand oblique finale in which... well, you'll just have to see it for yourself, but it's not pretty.

Many directors have taken the leads in their own films, with Rainer Werner Fassbinder (*Fox and His Friends)* and Bruce LaBruce (*Super 8 1/2*, etc.) often taking top honours for the most daring examples. DiNovis easily enters this select company with his unorthodox character study, which defies genre classification; it's not really a comedy, a horror film, a drama, or an "alternative lifestyles" film, though it has elements of all these. Instead the grimy black and white cinematography coupled with some surprisingly fluid, mobile camerawork creates a chilling atmosphere all its own, where nervous laughter and gasps of horror usually alternate from the disbelieving viewer. The performers are all excellent, and DiNovis is obviously a smart, savvy storyteller who knows how to operate his narrative on several levels. His commentary track on the DVD backs up this impression, as he reasons out the jolting final shot by explaining his goal to build the film on an intellectual and theoretical level rather than allowing the audience a kind of physical release. This pent up tension really simmers throughout the entire film, with its European sense of accumulating angst and a wry fatalism that finds the characters either living out their idealized fantasies or descending into pure hell, depending on your point of view.

Given the limitations of the cinematography, the DVD of *Surrender Dorothy* (whose title is either a direct lift from *Wizard* or a skewed reference to Rosanna Arquette's wedding night recollection in Scorsese's *After Hours*) looks quite good for a scrappy indie project. The anamorphic enhancement probably doesn't add much in the way of detail, but the enhanced grain of the presentation actually works in the film's favour as it gives more of an organic texture to the monochromatic sets and stylized lighting schemes.

DiNovis is joined on the commentary track by producer Richard Goldberg, and the two have a lot to say about giving birth to this difficult project and seem justifiably proud of what they accomplished. Extras include some truly bizarre behind the scenes footage (in which DiNovis directs his film in a manner not unlike Ed Wood, Jr.), the nicely edited theatrical trailer, bios for DiNovis and Pryor, and some production notes essentially summarizing what was covered in the commentary. It's a solid package for a startling title worthy of discovery, though it may not make the best date movie...

SUSPIRIA

Colour, 1977, 98m. / Directed by Dario Argento / Starring Jessica Harper, Joan Bennett / Anchor Bay (US R1 NTSC) / WS (2.35:1) (16:9) / DD-EX/DTS-ES, CDE (Italy R2 PAL) / WS (2.35:1) (16:9) / DD5.1, TFI (France R2 PAL) / WS (2.35:1) (16:9) / DD2.0, Nouveaux (UK R2 PAL) / WS (2.35:1) / DD2.0

Whether seen as a glorious celebration of cinematic style as an instrument to terrorize or a shallow exercise in flashy visuals at the expense of content, *Suspiria* is a difficult experience to forget. Apart from its secured status as one of the most visually ravishing horror films, it stops at nothing to keep the audience in its grip and marks a radical departure from the rigorous narrative manipulation of *Deep Red*. Here the story offers few genuine surprises; instead, the pleasure lies in the bizarre little side roads it takes along the way, offering up a seemingly boundless array of nasty delights at 24 frames per second. Here the random, illogical plotting and mannered acting which would normally cripple a film instead become assets, creating the disorienting air of a nightmare that must simply be accepted in order to enjoy the ride.

As the opening narration helpfully informs us, American ballet student Suzy Banyon (Jessica Harper) arrives in Freiberg, Germany to continue her studies at the celebrated Tanz Akademie. Unfortunately she emerges from the airport several hours late during a violent thunderstorm and is turned away at the school door. Meanwhile another student rushes past her into the darkness and meets a sinister fate, the first sign of many indicating that this seemingly classical school of dance may not be all that it appears. Led by a mysteriously absent directress, the haughty Madame Blanc (Dark Shadows' Joan Bennett), and the perpetually grinning Miss Tanner (Alida Valli), the academy proves to be a challenging experience for Suzy right from the beginning. She's forced to room on the grounds after suffering an embarrassing collapse during class, her entire floor must vacate to the gym for a sleepover after a particularly nasty infestation, and anyone who crosses the powers that be seems to meet wind up missing or dead. Along with her only friend, Sara (Stefania Casini), Suzy pieces together the puzzle that leads to a dramatic supernatural finale.

Anchored by Harper's wonderfully sensitive lead performance, *Suspiria* is Argento's most female-oriented film. The five minor male characters in the film only have one or two scenes each and serve as nothing more than plot functions, while both sides of the moral coin here are controlled by either innocent or corrupt women. Though the students don't seem to be fully aware of the school's true occult nature, the evil influence nevertheless manifests itself even in the early scenes, which become more significant later on. For example, Harper's discovery that witches thrive on the gaining of personal wealth adds a sinister tone to the early comic relief scenes in which the girlish students snip about bilking money from their classmates, and that red wine Harper sips throughout the film doesn't look so harmless at all when she finally pours it into the sink. The intensity of its violence - most notably the vicious, unforgettable opening act - is filmed with the same visual care as the rest of the film. Never gratuitous, the killings instead function as a kind of brutal, ritualized occult practice carried over into modern times. The German setting and subtle allusions to its culture scarred by ritualized violence (note the Naziesque soldiers in the Munich square and the use of razor wire, for starters) add to the air of refined, decadent unease, creating a setting in which every well-appointed door and curtain leads to something dark and unspeakable behind it.

One of Argento's rare US commercial successes, *Suspiria* was released by 20th Century-Fox (under the International Classics banner) in an R-rated edition that toned down some of its more baroque bloodletting. Fortunately audiences never forget the experience, and for years the film became something of a holy grail for those who couldn't get their hands on the scarce Japanese pan and scan laserdisc or the halfway letterboxed Venezuelan VHS tapes. Relief finally arrived when Magnum Entertainment released a widescreen, uncensored VHS edition which later made it to laserdisc courtesy of Image, with the US and European trailers tacked on for good measure. Supervised by Bill Lustig, the transfer was very good for its time despite the deliberate desaturation of some colours to avoid video noise; even better, the stereo soundtrack was enough to inspire leagues of Euro horror fanatics to dump more money into their home video sound systems. The same transfer was later rehashed for a dupey UK DVD, about which the less said the better, and Wellspring's briefly released VHS edition was even more unsatisfying thanks to (blasphemy!) its mono soundtrack. Only the Italian DVD offered a reasonable balance of solid image quality and the correct surround soundtrack.

Anchor Bay announced its plans to release *Suspiria* a year in advance, with public details released about the efforts made to create the finest version possible from the original negative. The results certainly do meet expectations, as the splashy colours on display here outrank even those on the already heavily saturated Japanese laserdisc versions. The snoring directress scene in which Harper and Casini are bathed in solid red lighting benefits especially from the added resolution, as Harper's nicely modulated facial reactions can now be appreciated without any ruinous smearing or smudging. The horizontally squished appearance of the earlier widescreen version has now been corrected, and the scope framing looks perfect. Superficially the soundtrack appears to be a dynamic, thunderous presentation of the film, with the spectacular Goblin score beautifully separated between each channel and dialogue still creatively spread out between the front and centre channels (with the DTS track offering the most forceful option, closest to the previous laserdisc). However,

it's worth noting that this is not a tweaked DD/DTS presentation of the familiar stereo surround version we've all grown to know and love. On this DVD, many of the sound effects are completely different, and several odd vagaries pop up compared to earlier English language versions. Among the most notable differences (with some spoilers, so beware): Pat's shouted statement at the front door during the rainstorm is now partially silent, making it impossible to make out her words even when one knows what she is saying; after Pat says "I'd like to dry off" at the beginning, the door slam behind her is now a soft thud instead of the earlier split-channel slam; the eyes glaring at Pat through the window are accompanied by a shorter, more muted sound effect stinger; the cries of "Help me" during the first murder have been reduced and are much softer; Pat is now heard screaming "No! No!" as she begins to collapse through the stained glass ceiling; the growling heard inside the school hallway when Albert is attacked by the seeing eye dog is different and much more subdued; the whispering voices emanating during the beginning of Sarah's nocturnal pursuit through the building are not the same, and the sounds heard during the close up of the razor being removed are edited differently. Most blatantly, when Suzy observes Madame Blanc and company undergoing their witch ritual, Miss Tanner now has a line of dialogue when she leans forward: "She wouldn't eat or drink anything this evening." The thunder effects which occur in the same scene to coincide with the red flashes of light (as Blanc utters "Sickness! Sickness!") are now missing, though the scene works about as well without them. Also oddly enough, the screaming voices heard over the end credits music are gone, leaving instead Goblin's frenzied middle movement of the main title theme.

This release also marks the first availability of *Suspiria* with captions, and while this addition helps clarify a few lines of dialogue, it also contains quite a few errors and makes for hilarious reading when the captioner tries (and fails) to translate the Goblin music ("La la la la la la la - Wait!"). Available in both a single disc and three-disc special edition, *Suspiria* has been brought to DVD with the full red carpet treatment. The movie disc includes the two aforementioned theatrical trailers, a brief TV spot (condensed from the US trailer), radio spots, a gallery of international stills and poster art, talent bios, a very odd Daemonia music video (directed by Simonetti) for the main theme, and a funny Easter Egg involving Udo Kier.

The second disc contains a 52 minute documentary, "*Suspiria* 25th Anniversary," in which the main surviving participants offer their thoughts on the film's production and influence. Argento, Nicolodi, the members of Goblin, and cinematographer Luciano Tovoli offer elaborated versions of the familiar stories about the film's lensing on discontinued Technicolor stock, Nicolodi's inspiration from a relative's occult school experience, and the unorthodox process of the music composition. Argento offers a few nice new tidbits of information, such as his explanation behind the placement of all the school's doorknobs. Harper, Casini, and Kier all make very welcome appearances to offer an actor's perspective, and all of them seem to recall the production with great affection and seem even prouder of the film now. Harper and Casini's recollections of Bennett are a particular highlight, and Casini scores the biggest laughs with her vivacious impersonations of everyone involved on the set. Finally, Tovoli's anecdote about *Single White Female* is nearly worth the price of admission by itself.

Disc three offers the *Suspiria* soundtrack but isn't quite a direct carryover of the official Cinevox CD release. It contains the full album tracks and some of the bonus cues from the earlier expanded CD edition, along with the new Daemonia contributions to round out the CD on a more modern, rock-style note. Those who already have the CD probably won't notice much of a difference, so the expanded (and much heavier) three-disc version is mainly recommended for the excellent documentary and its hefty printed materials: nine colour lobby card and poster reproductions, and an extensive, colour booklet with well written, informative liner notes by Travis Crawford and a printed interview with Harper which expands a bit on her comments in the documentary.

SWAMP THING

Colour, 1982, 92m. / Directed by Wes Craven / Starring Louis Jourdan, Adrienne Barbeau / MGM (US R1 NTSC) / WS (1.85:1)

Years before he pandered to mainstream audiences with the "family"-oriented *Music of the Heart*, Wes Craven actually made a decent PG-rated film with *Swamp Thing*, a respectable but flawed adaptation of the D.C. Comics yarn about a most unusual superhero who fights evil in, yes, a swamp. Of course, the film's reputation rests primarily on the presence of Adrienne Barbeau, who fulfilled more than a few adolescents' fantasies by spending the whole film in a tight (often soggy) T-shirt and even indulging in her only bona fide topless scene to date. Okay, it ain't art, but if you belong to this film's target audience, *Swamp Thing* has finally arrived on home video in its first worthwhile edition.

Brought to the edge of an uncharted swampland to work on a scientific research project, intrepid Alice Cable (Barbeau) is amazing by the accomplishments of Dr. Alec Holland (Ray Wise, aka *Twin Peaks'* Leland Palmer). With the help of his sister, Linda (Nanette Brown), Holland has manipulated the cell structure of plants to make them more aggressive, with animal tendencies. Unfortunately his formula is the Holy Grail for the evil Dr. Arcane (Louis Jourdan), who attacks Holland's lab with the help of his henchmen (including sleaze/Craven vets David Hess and Nicholas Worth). In the ensuring scuffle, Holland winds up drenched in his own explosive creation and stumbles off, presumably dying, into the swamp waters. Cable escapes from the clutches of Arcane's men and tries to survive in the swamp, where she encounters a towering green man whose voice sounds a little bit familiar...

To get the bad out of the way first, *Swamp Thing* suffers from its attempts to perfectly replicate the appearance of a comic book without a decent budget. The rubber suits can be distracting, and the fancy wipes (a la *Creepshow*) come across as affected rather than creative. On the other hand, Barbeau is a joy to watch, blasting bad guys, modelling skimpy outfits, cracking one-liners, and even having a few romantic interludes with Swampy. Jourdan also makes a wonderfully slimy bad guy (circa *Octopussy*), despite his silly appearance during the last reel. *Friday the 13th* composer Harry Manfredini even pops up for the score, which features his usual abrasive violins and a pretty good love theme which complements the visual beauty of the swamplands (filmed in oh-so-scenic South Carolina).

One of the earliest titles released on videotape (from Embassy), *Swamp Thing* has been a cable TV and laserdisc staple for years. The fuzzy open matte transfer didn't do it any favours, though, and MGM's DVD looks infinitely better - in fact, more colourful and attractive than it did in theatres. The curious lack of 16:9 enhancement for a new transfer is a noticeable flaw, but seeing *Swamp Thing* look this good gives one hope for future drive-in titles. Incidentally, the film's original theatrical run under a PG rating contained Barbeau's nude scene, but many (if not all?) prints were missing a later sequence in which Arcane's men are entertained by a group of strippers who display much more nudity and breast-fondling than the family friendly rating has ever allowed. Needless to say, it's all intact on the DVD, with the PG rating still left on the box. While Wes Craven has often griped about the MPAA's irrational decisions, here's one example where he got off very easy. The disc also includes an open matte transfer with comparable image quality, as well as the dull US theatrical trailer.

THE SWINGING CHEERLEADERS

Colour, 1974, 91m. / Directed by Jack Hill / Starring Jo Johnston, Rainbeaux Smith / Anchor Bay (US R1 NTSC) / WS (1.66:1)

Not as exploitative as its title would suggest but neither quite as groundbreakingly feminist as its champions claim, *Swinging Cheerleaders* is director Jack Hill's above average entry in the '70s cycle of liberated girls who use their jobs (well, okay, cheerleading isn't exactly a job) as a means of obtaining personal fulfilment and sexual pleasure. After successfully tackling the horror and women in prison genres, Hill brings his usual directorial strengths to this one: fast pacing, bizarre supporting characters, ridiculous action, and funky dialogue. Drive-in fans should be plenty amused.

Kate (Johnston), a reporter for an underground student newspaper at Mesa University, joins the cheerleading squad to expose... well, something about exploitation of women, though she never really makes her goals all that clear. Her radical editor boyfriend disapproves when she moves into the dorm to get closer to her story, and he really gets ticked when she winds up sleeping with Buck (Hajek), the star quarterback. Unfortunately, he reveals some nasty traits of his own when he humiliates fellow cheerleader Andrea (*Caged Heat*'s Smith, playing a naive virgin - 'scuse me while I collapse with laughter for a moment). Buck's fiancé, rich blonde cheerleader Mary Ann (Camp, who has way too little screen time and, oddly enough, does no nudity), doesn't believe Kate's claims that the coach, a local store owner, and a math teacher are rigging all of the football games in the season to make themselves rich. Kate decides to expose the story, even though the married math teacher is sleeping with yet another cheerleader, Lisa (Katon, one of the first black Playmates). Got all that? After many double crosses and over-the-top dramatic moments, it all ends with a big nonsensical brawl in a warehouse before the strangely abrupt final scene.

Anchor Bay's transfer once again is far better than you would ever expect from a low budget drive-in teen flick; in fact, the print is so clean and sharp that the stock footage inserted during the football sequences is even more obvious now. The vivid '70s colours look rich and distortion-free, while the audio is... well, as clear as it will ever sound. Incidentally, composer Loose also wrote the music for most of Russ Meyer's late '60s and '70s films. If you ever caught some of those cheesy cheerleader movies on Cinemax late at night and wondered whether anyone ever bothered to make a good one, check this out. Incidentally, one earlier video version of this film was released under the title *H.O.T.S. 2*, though the original *H.O.T.S.* came out several years later. The DVD also includes two TV spots and running commentary with Hill and "film historian" Johnny Legend in which Hill warmly recalls his guerrilla filmmaking techniques from the period.

SWITCHBLADE SISTERS

Colour, 1975, 89m. / Directed by Jack Hill / Starring Robbie Lee, Joanne Nail / Buena Vista (US R1 NTSC) / WS (1.85:1)

An absurdist entry in the '70s cycle of gang drive-in movies, *Switchblade Sisters* began life under the title of *The Jezebels*, a reference to its quasi-feminist girl gang heroines. Quentin Tarantino's Rolling Thunder Pictures rescued it from oblivion over twenty years later under its reissue title, where it actually played multiplex theatres and stunned patrons expecting another *Pulp Fiction*. It looks like fame really is good for something after all.

A tough high school gang, the Dagger Debs, keep a tight grip on their turf under the leadership of the disturbingly childlike Lace (Robbie Lee). During a small rumble at a hot dog joint the girls meet loner Maggie (Joanne Nail), who winds up going into the juvenile slammer with them for a few days. The Dagger Debs save Maggie from the lesbian clutches of the evil warden and decide to make her their newest member. Maggie is released first and delivers a note from Lace to her boyfriend, Dominic (Asher Brauner), who runs the Silver Daggers. He repays Maggie by reading Lace's letter aloud to his boys, following her home, and raping her. When Lace gets out, her trusty sidekick, Patch (Monica Gayle), convinces her that Maggie has been sleeping with Dominic, and before long the fur begins to fly.

A veritable feast for drive-in fans, *Switchblade Sisters* moves so fast that most viewers won't care how little actual nudity or bloodshed there is in the movie. Hill's trademark off-kilter dialogue works especially well in this bizarre alternate universe, where the pre-*Grease* high school students are pushing 30 and a friendly roller rink can turn into a gun-blazing battlefield. Exploitation vets in particular should watch for an appearance by *Ganja and Hess* star Marlene Clark as "Muff," the leader of an all-female Black Panther type squad, and Lenny Bruce's daughter, Kitty, even turns up as the memorable Donut. The attempts at social commentary and feminist treatise fall a little short due to some narrative inconsistencies, particularly concerning Maggie (who seems to conveniently forget her rape the day after it happens). The action scenes are all a blast, with the final knife-wielding showdown (in expressionistic wall shadows, no less!) a particular standout; special kudos as well to Robbie Lee, whose Lace is one of Hill's most engaging characters. Later the actress reformed and provided cartoon voices for Rainbow Brite and Q-Bert, which just shows you how weird Hollywood can be.

Miramax's laserdisc special edition of *Switchblade Sisters* was something of a mixed bag, with a colourful but fuzzy letterboxed transfer and, wealth of extras aside, the noticeable absence of the film's trailer. Luckily the DVD incarnation fixes all of these glitches, with the trailer now reinstated along with a gorgeous, razor sharp image that makes the absence of 16:9 enhancement negligible. Tarantino provides an intro and closing statement, which have thankfully been relegated to the extras menu; he makes some interesting points, but his spastic delivery and the herky-jerky camerawork render them almost unwatchable. Better is the audio commentary track in which he and Hill pick apart every bit of minutiae involving the film from its inception to release.

Also included is a batch of Hill-related extras including his early short film, *The Host* (featuring regular Sid Haig), and trailers for *Coffy, Foxy Brown, Pit Stop, Sorceress, The Big Doll House, The Big Bird Cage,* and *The Swinging Cheerleaders,* some of which feature distracting new voiceovers. The *Spider Baby* section has been expanded to include a newly generated "trailer" along with a film clip and collection of review excerpts.

TALES OF ORDINARY MADNESS

Colour, 1981, 102m. / Directed by Marco Ferreri / Starring Ben Gazzara, Ornella Muti / Image (US R0 NTSC) / WS (1.75:1)

Years before the writings of boozing philosopher Charles Bukowski reached mainstream cinema (sort of) with *Barfly*, maverick Italian director Marco Ferreri tackled the same subject with *Tales of Ordinary Madness*, an Italian-French co-production that was apparently Ferreri's bid for mainstream acceptance. However, even streamlined Ferreri is still pretty bizarre; though set mostly in Los Angeles, the interiors were shot at Cinecittà and have a weird, colour coordinated, sleazy splendour. When most European directors do their exterior shooting in America, they have a way of making everything look really off-kilter (e.g., Antonioni's *Zabriskie Point*), and this is no exception. Ferreri visually transforms the California streets into a sun-drenched, decaying series of asphalt tombs, and the people who pass on them are all basically trying to inflict any emotional shocks upon themselves to remind them of what it feels like to be alive. Chief among them is our protagonist, Charles Serking (Ben Gazzara), a thinly disguised Bukowski stand-in, who drifts along between various bars and women as he spouts cynical poetry.

After delivering a booze-ridden speech at the opening, Serking escorts the viewer on a little tour of L.A., which first involves him spying a punk-blond woman (Susan Tyrrell) on the beach, and, noting "she had an ass like a wild animal," he follows her back to her apartment and rapes her (with her consent, oddly enough). Tyrrell's roles tend to be bizarre, and this is no exception. She calls the cops on Serking while he's taking a bath, causing him to intone, "She chewed me up like an enchilada and spit me into a police car." Undeterred, Serking winds up catching the eye of masochistic, beautiful barfly Ornella Muti (also in Ferreri's startling *The Last Woman* and most familiar to US viewers as Princess Aura in 1980's *Flash Gordon*). After she performs an impromptu cheek-piercing at a bar, Serking decides he'd better go home with this woman, and they sort of fall in love. It all ends badly, however, so Serking goes back and falls into the arms of Tyrrell's obese landlady (don't ask). Ah, but there's more! Eventually he and Muti get back together and go off to a beachhouse where there share a few idyllic moments; Muti falls apart, however, and performs a very nasty act of sexual self-mutilation (a recurring Ferreri motif) that sends him fleeing in dismay.

Obviously this is not a film for everybody, but if you're curious about Ferreri, this is as good a place to start as any. While it lacks the consistent outrageousness of his masterpiece *La Grande*

Bouffe, *Tales* is firmly anchored by Gazzara's authoritative and often devastating performance. His years of cutting teeth on Cassavetes films definitely served him well, and he has some truly great moments. The most memorable bit involves Serking's half-hearted attempt at getting a desk job at an office. where he can't resist the urge to start pelting his fellow co-workers in their cubicles with beer cans. As Ferreri's female icon of choice in this film, Muti looks fantastic as always and manages some nice dramatic moments; it's also nice to hear her speaking with her own voice for a change instead of the usual post-synch dubbing. Ferreri keeps a surprising grip on the material (he adapted it himself along with Sergio Amidei and Anthony Foutz), aided by Tonino Delli Colli's evocative photography and a delicate, restrained score by Philippe Sarde, obviously written around the same time as *Tess*.

Image's transfer is quite attractive, with vivid, clean colours that far surpass the mediocre VHS releases this received in the early '80s. While the print appears to be complete, it clocks in at 101 minutes, a fair bit shorter than the reference time of 107 minutes, indicating that the commonly quoted running time may be wrong (or is possibly based on an Italian screening that included an intermission).

The DVD is a nice presentation of a title you'd never expect to receive such a pristine transfer, and the outstanding packaging design, including an elegant (and erotic) cover design and concise, well-written liner notes, is the icing on the cake.

TALES OF TERROR

Colour, 1962, 89m. / Directed by Roger Corman / Starring Vincent Price, Peter Lorre / MGM (US R1 NTSC) / WS (2.35:1) (16:9)

After striking gold with his Edgar Allan Poe adaptations starring Vincent Price, *House of Usher* and *Pit and the Pendulum*, Roger Corman tweaked the formula a bit by presenting Poe's short stories as three vignettes, rather than dragging a ten page narrative kicking and screaming to an 80 minute running time. As with all horror anthologies, *Tales of Terror* has its highs and lows but makes for compelling viewing even during its weakest links.

In the first and most traditional story, "Morella," Vincent Price portrays an embittered, alcoholic recluse who finally receives a visitor in the form of his estranged daughter, Lenora (Maggie Price), whom he blames for the death of his beautiful, egocentric wife, Morella. Lenora reveals that she only has a short time left to live, and she wanted to see her father before shuffling off into the void. Gradually the father and daughter show signs of forgiveness, but the malefic spirit of Morella intervenes with tragic, fiery results.

In "The Black Cat," a very loose spin on Poe's most graphic tale crossed with "The Cask of Amontillado," Peter Lorre is Montresor Herringbone, a drunken lout who spends his evenings at the tavern and ignores his wife, Annabel (Joyce Jameson, who later reprised the same basic role in *Comedy of Terrors*). One night Montresor engages in a humorous wine tasting contest with snobby connoisseur Fortunato (Price), which indirectly ignites an affair between Fortunato and Annabel. Naturally our sloshed antihero loses his mind and plots the perfect murder, but the family pet, a black cat, has other plans...

Finally, "The Facts in the Case of Mr. Valdemar" pairs up Price as a dying aristocrat with Basil Rathbone as Carmichael, an unscrupulous mesmerist who uses hypnotism to alleviate his patient's pain. Unfortunately Carmichael abuses his position and manipulates a promise from Valdemar that his wife, Helene (Debra Paget), will wed Carmichael after her husband's demise. Things take a turn for the worse when Valdemar's body dies during a hypnotic state, resulting in horrific consequences for everyone involved.

Despite the title, there isn't a whole lot to be terrified about with *Tales of Terror*. Rather, it's a fascinating study in three different moods, with "The Black Cat" operating most successfully as a study in ghoulish humour. The silly tone would later dominate Corman's *The Raven*, but it really works best as an extended sketch. Lorre in particular dominates his every moment on film and proves to be a fine comedian, while his wine tasting scene with Price has justifiably become a fan favourite. (Note: for an amusing disorienting effect, try running Lorre's obligatory distorted nightmare sequence in 16:9 mode on a standard 4:3 television set.)

"Morella" is beautifully filmed and highly atmospheric, but it's too brief and indifferently acted to rank up there with its obvious inspiration, *House of Usher*. "Valdemar" is basically a comic book treatment of a more serious story and, while somewhat strangely paced, benefits from a memorable gruesome finale, which left a strong impression on more than a few matinee audiences. It all looks great as usual, with Floyd Crosby's adroit camerawork and Daniel Haller's inventive production design wringing every little visual detail out of the stories despite the low budget. Famed fantasy novelist Richard Matheson wrote the screenplay, which is literate enough but hard to separate from the other Corman scripts of the period.

MGM's DVD marks the second widescreen presentation of this film, which uses every inch of the Panavision frame and simply doesn't work at all in pan and scan. From the terrific animated segues with Price offering macabre bits of narration ("This is the heartbeat of a dying man...") to the simple payoff shot of "The Black Cat," you need to see the entire image just to understand what's happening before your eyes. The DVD is much brighter than the previous Orion/Image laserdisc (which was paired with the underrated *The Premature Burial*); this new presentation reveals many new details in the sets and costumes but also removes a great deal of the shadowy textures in the process. Overall the colours are well defined, and the clarity of a nice, mostly clean print in 16:9 is obviously the preferable choice in the long run. Apart from a couple of fleeting blemishes and some odd graininess during the second story, the elements seem to be in fine shape. The disc also includes the terrific theatrical trailer, also finally in scope. In short, this film makes for a handy intro to the Corman/Price/Poe cycle, which will hopefully be represented in its entirety on DVD someday.

A TASTE OF BLOOD

Colour, 1967, 120m. / Directed by Herschell Gordon Lewis / Starring Bill Rogers, Elizabeth Wilkinson / Image (US R0 NTSC)

Often discussed but rarely seen, *A Taste of Blood* remains memorable in cult horror circles both for its catchy title and its sprawling running time, a virtual miniseries by gore film standards. What lies within is perhaps the most ambitious project for director Herschell Gordon Lewis, who was trying to expand the parameters of the genre he kicked into mainstream awareness with *Blood Feast*. As uneven as the results may be, it's a fascinating artefact of its time and is perhaps the closest thing to a "real movie" in its creator's career.

Devised as a cloaked sequel to Bram Stoker's *Dracula*, the plot follows the corruption of one John Stone (Bill Rogers), who receives a rare bottle of wine from England. However, the fluid inside produces some unexpected changes in John; for example, he feels an aversion to daylight and normal food. Naturally he traipses off to England, which puts an unbearable strain on his already shaky marriage to Helene (Elizabeth Wilkinson). From one shore to the other, John avenges the fate of Dracula by tracking down his killer's descendants and plunging sharp objects into their hearts. Back in the America, the police try to save his latest potential victim, Sherri Morris (Dolores Carlos), the descendant of the novel's Quincey Morris, but the crafty vampire convert proves to be quite a challenge. Will the officers have to use Helene as bait to lure in her bloodsucking husband? What do you think?

Considering its reputation, there isn't much graphic gore in *A Taste of Blood*. Sure, the red stuff flows readily and looks just as realistic as ever, but for some reason in this context it isn't much more shocking than your average mid-period Hammer vampire film. The real fun lies in those unmistakable Lewis touches, ranging from the searing colours of those interiors to a jaw-dropping cameo by H.G. himself as a salty seaman. Considering the huge amount of dialogue and plot contained in this film, it wouldn't be surprising to learn that Staten Island horror hack Andy Milligan got more than a little inspiration after seeing this.

Something Weird's DVD line has done a spectacular job of preserving Lewis' filmic legacy so far, and *A Taste of Blood* is no exception. Most of the transfer is nothing short of amazing, making those older VHS versions completely obsolete. Even the most vivid hues of red are perfectly rendered, and the transfer boasts a pleasing film-like texture absent from many overly digitized recent films; the only drawback is a few passages in the middle marred by some print damage and jagged green spotting, with some visible streaking also near the end. Lewis and SW's Mike Vraney return again for a commentary track, this time featuring more detail than usual thanks to the longer running time of the film. Lewis offers a thorough history of this difficult period, during which he sampled different exploitation genres and tried to find his footing in one of the most volatile periods of American filmmaking. Along the way the guys also crack more than a few jokes to keep things lively, and you can learn all about the actors who, apart from Rogers and a supporting bit by the ubiquitous "Thomas Wood," seem to have vanished into the ether.

The disc also includes the original theatrical trailer (which gives a good indication of how bad earlier transfers looked) and an unrelated nudie-monster short, "Nightmare at Elm Manor," best described as a short-winded cousin to *House on Bare Mountain*.

TEENAGE MONSTER

B&W, 1957, 65m. / Directed by Jacques R. Marquette / Starring Anne Gwynne, Gloria Castillo / Image (US R0 NTSC)

God only knows what real teenagers during the '50s must have thought while watching (or at least listening) to this one at the drive-in. As an attempt to fuse the monster and western genres, this sole directorial effort for ace cinematographer Jacques Marquette falls way short of *The Valley of Gwangi* territory, coming a whole lot closer to *Jesse James Meets Frankenstein's Daughter*. That said, trash-loving monster maniacs will no doubt eat it up.

During the late 1800s, a family of miners named the Cannons is torn asunder when a crashing meteor leaves the father dead and renders the son, Charles, severely injured and exposed to some kind of bizarre radiation. The mother, Ruth (Anne Gwynne), spends the next few years bargaining with the local powers that be to maintain control of a nearby mine where the meteor crashed. Of course, the mine also makes a dandy hiding place for her now adolescent son (Gil Perkins), who has sprouted a very unnatural amount of facial and body hair and passes the time by killing the occasional passer-by in the woods. The town sheriff (Stuart Wade) and his officers are stumped by the murders, which become more conspicuous when Ruth comes across a gold streak and finds herself the centre of town scrutiny. How long can she conceal the horrible secret of her son... the teenage monster?

Despite the subject matter, *Teenage Monster* is a surprisingly restrained affair, with the setting resembling an unhinged episode of *Gunsmoke* rather than a member of the standard teen-horror cycle including more stupidly enjoyable entries like *Teenage Caveman* and *Blood of Dracula*. Instead this film is 90% dialogue, which wouldn't be a bad thing if the chit chat were interesting, but... At least the hairy monster shows up regularly to whimper, mope, rip up some poor innocents, and carry off a damsel in distress.

Thankfully the running time of just over one hour won't strain your endurance too far, and the obligatory romantic scenes are mercifully short and to the point. Incidentally, the appearance of the transformed Charles was created by legendary make-up maestro Jack Pierce (who had much more significant financial means when he turned Boris Karloff into Frankenstein), and screenwriter Ray Buffum churned this out the same year as his much better known *The Brain from Planet Arous*.

Despite its obscurity and dubious cultural value, *Teenage Monster* has been brought to DVD in excellent condition. The source material is close to spotless, with exceptionally rich, black shadows and crisp detail to bring out every bit of polish in those suspiciously clean-looking western backlot sets. Oddly, the western setting is completely ignored by the catchy, colourful, but wholly misleading cover art. The disc also includes the hyperbolic theatrical trailer, which tries to squeeze as much action as possible out of the proceedings.

THE TEMPEST

Colour, 1979, 94m. / Directed by Derek Jarman / Starring Heathcote Williams, Toyah Wilcox / Kino (US R1 NTSC)

Though his death at the age of 52 passed with little fanfare, director Derek Jarman forever changed the way filmgoers look at the relationship between sound and image on film. A talented art director (*The Devils*), he began making short avant garde films and progressed to art house features like *Sebastiane* and *The Last of England* before achieving his one bona fide international hit, *Edward II*. In the meantime he also directed music videos and concert films for such bands as The Smiths and Pet Shop Boys, usually integrating his beloved Super 8 home movies for both visual texture and a personal statement of his longing for a simpler time. Amazingly, Jarman was the first director to tackle a film version of William Shakespeare's last play, *The Tempest*.

This challenging fantasy concerns Prospero (Heathcote Williams), a reclusive magician stranded on an island with his sheltered daughter, Miranda (Toyah Wilcox), and a monster, Caliban (Jack Birkett). A sea storm washes ashore Prospero's brother, Alonso (Peter Bull), who had stolen the title of Duke of Milan from Prospero, and Alonso's son, Ferdinand (David Meyer). Of course, Ferdinand and Miranda are immediately smitten, and Prospero must decide at what cost he intends to pursue his revenge against those he perceives as his enemies.

Carefully cast with stage performers, singers, and dancers, *The Tempest* is a graceful tribute to the human gifts of creation and imagination. Surprisingly, Jarman allows his own style and obsessions to serve the story, rather than the other way around. His usual penchant for gay imagery mainly surfaces during the film's most famous sequence, the masque finale in which dancing sailors accompany a performance of "Stormy Weather" by Elisabeth Welch (the nightclub singer from 1945's *Dead of Night*). Pop star Toyah Wilcox, also in Jarman's *Jubilee*, provides an especially unorthodox interpretation of Miranda as a girl whose worldliness may actually extend beyond the boundaries of the island and her father's will. Another experimental filmmaker, Peter Greenaway, tackled the same play over ten years later with *Prospero's Books*, a visual spectacle which sometimes recalls the images first contained in Jarman's film: Ferdinand's unclothed rise from the sea, Prospero's lightning-streaked opening nightmare, and the riotous gold and red wedding ceremony.

Kino's DVD of *The Tempest* presents an unmatted transfer and looks much better than their previous VHS edition. The vibrant colours and burnished, dimensional lighting look very attractive throughout, and the source materials are in immaculate shape apart from some stock footage used during the storm sequence. Likewise, the mono soundtrack is free of flaws or distortion. The disc also includes a transcript of the original British pressbook, a still gallery, and three early '70s short films by Jarman. Never completed and presented without sound, these snippets range from five to ten minutes in length, with the striking "Art of Mirrors" providing the clearest indications of the striking visuals he would later achieve in his feature work.

TENDER FLESH

Colour, 1997, 93m. / Directed by Jess Franco / Starring Amber Newman, Monique Parent, Lina Romay / Seduction Cinema (US R1 NTSC) / WS (1.78:1) / DD2.0

As most European exploitation fans now acknowledge, the films of director Jess Franco divide into clean, separate categories, with his first two periods during the '60s usually cited as the best. His output since the early '90s has been much slower and more erratic than usual, with hardcore porn and shot-on-video projects consuming most of his time until very recently. Following a hiatus after the (relatively) big budget international production *Faceless*, Franco made another comeback of sorts with *Tender Flesh*, a campy summation of the obsessions that ran through his outrageous '70s cult epics.

After watching a kinky stage show audition performed by coke-snorting nymphet Paula (Amber Newman), decadent French chef Paul Radeck (Alain

Petit) and his scary wife (Lina Romay with a buzz cut) decide to invite her along for a mysterious, erotic island vacation. Paula and her boyfriend (who wears an array of T-shirts for Fangoria and the Killer Barbys) hop on board along with a successful businessman, Kallman (Aldo Sambrell) and his bossy spouse (Monique Parent). Nestled among palm trees and wild forests, the Radeck mansion at first promises erotic delights as Amber releases her inhibitions in front of the guests. Even a simple dinner turns into a kinkfest with the aid of the Radeck's slave girl, Furia (Analia Ivars). The Radecks offer Paula the chance to engage in a treasure hunt on the island which quickly turns into a nightmarish twist on *The Most Dangerous Game*, as the predatory couple stalks their prey with bow and arrow in hand to satisfy their cannibalistic urges.

Those who dismiss Franco as an untalented hack will find most of their arguments confirmed here, as *Tender Flesh* wildly ignores such niceties as logic and polished camerawork. The dialogue (recorded on the set in English) is unintelligible for much of the running time, the acting is atrocious (apart from the always fascinating Ms. Romay of course), no two characters have the same accent, and the story is virtually nonexistent. On the other hand, as with many Franco films, half the fun lies in tracing the evolution of his favourite characters and storylines. The second half is basically an updated remake of Franco's excellent *The Perverse Countess* (which really needs to be released on DVD, pronto), while the tropical island fun and games are pulled straight from *Macumba Sexual* and *Eugenie* (the '81 version). And of course, the nightclub opener is a direct descendent of *Succubus* and *Vampyros Lesbos*.

Silicone doll Newman doesn't make for a very compelling leading lady on a par with Franco's past starlets, at least until one considers that she isn't really supposed to be an admirable or even interesting character in the first place. *Tender Flesh* can be tough going for the uninitiated, but Franco-philes will no doubt eat it up.

Seduction Cinema's DVD looks only a slight step up from the previous VHS release, and for the record, yes, the infamous kitchen urination scene is back in all its uncut glory. The mild letterboxing looks about right, and apart from the muddy, noise-ridden opening five minutes, colours and detail levels are satisfying. The surround audio shows off Franco's catchy jazz score quite well and uses the rear channels fairly often, creating a sultry listening environment spoiled only by the aforementioned poorly recorded dialogue.

Side B of the DVD contains several extras, the most notable being the 51 minute "Making of *Tender*

Flesh" documentary. This shot on video peek behind the scenes contains random footage of Franco running amok with his camera, interspersed with interview footage (primarily Petit). The surprisingly poor image quality of the occasional film clips used here will make any viewer grateful for the DVD presentation. Also included is a six minute look at Amber Newman's photo shoot for the film's (very Redemption-like) promotional artwork, as well as a slew of trailers for Seduction Cinema's DVD releases. This may not be the best Franco film by a long shot, but the presentation and extras should find favour with any unrepentant Eurosleaze collector.

TENDERNESS OF THE WOLVES

Colour, 1974, 82m. / Directed by Ulli Lommel / Starring Kurt Raab, Rainer Werner Fassbinder / Anchor Bay (US R1 NTSC) / WS (1.66:1)

German director Ulli Lommel, a contemporary and semi-protégé of the famous Rainer Werner Fassbinder, seemed destined for an odd movie career beginning with the German cult classic, *Tenderness of the Wolves* (*Zärtlichkeit der Wölfe*). Using most of the cast and crew from Fassbinder's stylized angst-fests, Lommel crafted a deliberately paced, often explicit study of madness, boosted by a creepy and memorable performance by Kurt Raab (who also wrote and produced the film) in the lead.

Raab portrays Fritz Haarman, a charming early 20th Century serial killer known as "The Vampire of Hanover." An inveterate small time criminal, Haarman used a local hustler to round up young boys whom Haarman would take to his apartment. He then bit their throats open, drank their blood, and disposed of the bodies as black market meat. His neighbours thought of him as a nice, unassuming guy and didn't even question the strange hacking sounds that went on all night, so Haarman managed to scarf down several dozen young men before he was finally caught and publicly beheaded.

For its time, Lommel's film pulls few punches, though gore fans lured by the graphic violence warning on the back of the box will probably be disappointed. Aside from two graphic but brief gurgling throat wounds, most of the horror here remains left to the imagination; in fact, viewers may be more startled by the graphic gay content, which includes several molestation scenes and the heaviest non-hardcore frontal nudity this side of a Paul Morrissey film. Raab, almost unrecognizable with

extra weight and a bald head, makes an unforgettable psycho, gazing passively at his future victims and charming his neighbours with mysterious beef wares; his eager pursuit of his final victim down the stairs at the end is a moment that would make Peter Lorre proud (no coincidence, as Fritz Lang's *M* was partially derived from the same true story). Lommel relocates the action to post-World War II Germany for some reason, though as he clearly states, the time and place could really be anywhere. As if that weren't enough, Fassbinder himself even turns up in a memorable glorified cameo as a womanizing gangster!

Although the clear yellow subtitles are regrettably burned into the image, the quality of Anchor Bay's DVD is otherwise excellent and should definitely please anyone longing for a decent version. The DVD also includes the surprisingly explicit German theatrical trailer, and Bill Lustig and Lommel contribute an interesting, laid back commentary track in which the director fondly relates tales of working with all of the performers and analyzing why this film would never be made today.

TENEBRE

Colour, 1982, 101m. / Directed by Dario Argento / Starring Anthony Franciosa, Daria Nicolodi / Anchor Bay (US R1 NTSC), Sazuma (Austria R0 NTSC), Nouveaux (UK R2 PAL), TFI (France R2 PAL) / WS (1.85:1) / DD5.1

Among Dario Argento fans, *Tenebre* is usually mentioned as one of his most neglected films, a masterpiece lurking in the shadows of *Deep Red*. Perhaps the combination of extreme violence and sexual anxiety makes it too strong for many viewers (it was retitled *Unsane* and heavily chopped down for a sparse US release), but fortunately the longer version resurfaced and has become the easiest to find.

American writer Peter Neal (Anthony Franciosa) arrives in Rome to promote his new best-selling mystery novel, *Tenebre*, only to be informed by the police that a copycat killer is bumping off Italian citizens with a straight razor in the same manner portrayed in the book. Along with his secretary, Anne (Daria Nicolodi, dubbed by Teresa Russell), Neal attempts to uncover the killer's identity as the bodies begin to pile up.

The actual running time of *Tenebre* has been the cause of much speculation and debate, beginning with reports of its uncut length running anywhere from 101 to 110 minutes. The Japanese laserdisc, widely regarded as uncut, is the 101 minute version, though a few strange edits remain in the film (note the jarring jump cut in the middle of John Saxon's conversation with Giuliano Gemma at the TV studio). Essentially, the immaculate DVD version, perfectly letterboxed and more attractive than the Japanese disc, is "uncut" in terms of violence and dialogue, but purists have objected over the omission of a few fleeting seconds of footage (a quick glimpse of shoplifter Pieroni backing against the wall before her death, a brief shot of Saxon walking across a room, etc.). Since this is an alternate print from the Japanese one (note the different title cards, a different take of Lara Wendel rummaging through the killer's photos and clippings, etc.), as well as Argento's seal of approval on this print, this edition is satisfactory enough.

The commentary by Argento along with composer Claudio Simonetti just adds to the entertainment and collectable value (thick accents aside) and, as if that weren't enough, you also get the excellent European release trailer and the alternate pop song US end titles. The Dolby Digital remix is tastefully handled, confined mainly to the danceable music score and a few startling sound effects.

The Anchor Bay DVD also includes two brief "making of" snippets actually excerpted from Luigi Cozzi's *Dario Argento: Master of Horror*. The Sazuma disc boasts optional English subtitles for its Italian track and also cobbles together the missing fragments of footage as a supplement, while the French disc offers the full cut (with non-removable subs) and the lacklustre Nouveaux disc has been censored for violence.

THE 10TH VICTIM

Colour, 1965, 92m. / Directed by Elio Petri / Starring Marcello Mastroianni, Ursula Andress / Anchor Bay (US R1 NTSC) / WS (1.85:1) (16:9)

 An unhinged chunk of satirical sci-fi kitsch that could have only been made in the 1960s, *The 10th Victim* is a film far more often discussed than actually seen. Fans of Ursula Andress prize it for the unforgettable opening in which the Euro starlet guns down her prey with a bullet-firing bra in New York's Masoch Club (later duped in *Austin Powers*); however, that's just the first of many delirious moments scattered throughout this very mad film.

In the future, society entertains the violent impulses of the masses by arranging the Hunt (or, depending on the translation, the Big Game), an elaborate international game made up of alternating Victims and Hunters who must engage in ten rounds before winning the grand prize. Advertisers pay top dollar to have the victors spout slogans over their dead conquests, while the authorities frown upon murder unless it's all in the name of good sportsmanship. The latest standoff between celebrated huntress Caroline Meredith (Andress) and Marcello (a bleached Marcello Mastroianni) becomes complicated when Marcello, who's fretting over a separation from his wife, finds his attention more drawn to affairs of the heart than the demands of the pistol. Apart from dealing with the demands of his chic mistress Olga (*Blood and Roses'* Elsa Martinelli), Marcello also becomes increasingly fascinated by his media-dictated arch enemy, with whom he may actually be falling in love.

This premise will seem familiar even to those who have never heard of the film, thanks to decades of lip service paid by the likes of *Series 7, RoboCop, The Running Man,* and many others. As a satire, the story generally works and includes some hilarious concepts, beginning with Andress' early striptease in which she teasingly slaps her patrons before taking one out altogether. Though it never hits the rapturous heights of pop art perfection achieved by *Camille 2000, Danger Diabolik,* or *The Frightened Woman,* the film is nevertheless extremely appealing for its good natured eye candy tricks and hilarious retro/future shock fashions. Director Elio Petri was a little too off centre to really become a celebrated auteur outside Italy; after bending the sci-fi genre here, he later applied the same technique to the ghost story format (his disorienting *A Quiet Place in the Country*) and the crime procedural (his most critically respected effort, *Investigation of a Citizen above Suspicion*). Then there's the trippy, experimental score by Piero Piccioni, which can only be described as, well, insane. The opening theme song, "The Spiral Waltz," is infernally catchy and insinuates itself in various guises throughout the film, sprinkled here and there with some jazzy riffs for good measure.

Anyone who ever had to suffer through Embassy's dubbed, cropped videotape edition of *The 10th Victim* will be especially grateful for the Anchor Bay DVD, which restores Petri's quirky 1.85:1 framing. Unlike many Italian directors, Petri never showed a particular affinity for scope but still possessed a careful eye for composition, rendering pan and scan versions of his titles completely incoherent. The flesh tones throughout are maddeningly inconsistent, due more to the wacko lighting and apparent use of different film stocks; just watch in amazement as Andress' face goes from burnished brown to baby pink from one scene to the next. The technical limitations also produce a strong amount of grain throughout the film, which may drive technophiles up the wall, but alas, that's just how the movie is. Colours are less vivid than one might expect given the time period, but what's there is rendered well enough and, as noted before, looks positively ravishing compared to the earlier tape versions. Even more significantly, this edition reinstates the original Italian soundtrack and much of the film's dignity in the process. No longer do we have to hear those tin eared Americanized voices; while the Italian track doesn't seem to match anyone's lip movement either, at least it suits the characters and comes off as puckish and graceful rather than flat footed and obvious. The disc also contains the original Carlo Ponti theatrical trailer and some delicious animated menus.

TERROR IS A MAN

B&W, 1959, 89m. / Directed by Gerardo de Leon / Starring Francis Lederer, Greta Thyssen / Image (US R0 NTSC)

The Philippines aren't exactly known for their booming horror film industry, but for a brief period through the 1960s (and, to a small extent, 1970s), producer Eddie Romero made a tidy profit in America's drive-ins by shooting exotic low budget gore epics in the politically charged country and releasing them under campy titles guaranteed to have parents dragging their kids to church services for penance. Romero's career got off to a roaring start with *Terror Is a Man*, later a hit in drive-ins under the title *Blood Creature*, and he continued the string of creature features with the infamous *Mad Doctor of Blood Island, The Twilight People*, and the surreal *Brides of Blood*. Unfortunately, as the quantities of gore and skin increased, the films suffered overall; in this case, the first was by far the best.

Almost everyone familiar with *Terror Is a Man* has noted its extreme similarity to H.G. Wells' *Island of Dr. Moreau* (or more likely, its first film adaptation, *Island of Lost Souls*).

Poor William Fitzgerald (Derr) finds himself on the island of Dr. Charles Girard (Lederer) and his wife, Frances (Thyssen). It seems the doctor is convinced he can develop human beings through the

genetic components of animals - and of course, he's trying it out on a leopard, with disastrous results. The leopard creature (basically a bandaged man with pointy ears) is quite a sight - not one of the screen's greatest monsters, but definitely one of the oddest.

The opening credits warn that a warning bell (actually the sound of a telephone) will sound and alert the audience of a particularly horrifying sequence, which basically consists of a few seconds of Lederer slicing along a patch of skin with a scalpel. Pretty nasty for 1959, but the face-grafting in the same year's *Eyes without a Face* leaves it in the dust. Generally this is much better than your average drive-in beastie fare and deserves the attention it has garnered from dedicated late night TV viewers. The beginning is a bit talky, but once things get in gear, this is a lot of fun.

Fortunately, Image's newly transferred DVD is a revelation (and nifty cover art, too); the years of scratchy public domain prints and dupey TV screenings completely failed to capture the moody noirish photography and the richly textured jungle scenery. The fact that elements so clean and sharp could still exist for this film is frankly astonishing, and apart from a few dodgy compression moments during the night scenes (a by product of early DVD authoring), this is a fine presentation.

TERROR OF FRANKENSTEIN

Colour, 1977, 91m. / Directed by Calvin Floyd / Starring Per Oscarsson, Nicholas Clay / Image (US R0 NTSC)

Following the success of his *In Search of Dracula* documentary, Calvin Floyd decided to take a stab at Mary Shelley's horror classic, *Frankenstein*. Since he already exhausted the story's meagre historical precedents in his previous film, Floyd decided to simply present a straight adaptation of the tale itself. Not a bad move, really, considering nobody had ever tackled a faithful version; as great as the Boris Karloff and Hammer versions are, they wander very far afield from the source. While Floyd's adaptation (originally shown as *Victor Frankenstein*) may not be the best, it certainly is the closest. Interestingly, the only other English-language film version to depict the Arctic opening and closing sequences was Kenneth Branagh's film twenty years later, which unfortunately succumbed to story tampering despite its alleged fidelity to the novel.

Everybody knows the story by now, but here goes anyway. An Arctic expedition finds a man struggling in the middle of the icy wilderness. They take him aboard their ship, where he relates the strange story of how he, Victor Frankenstein, became a scientist fascinated with bringing life to dead biological matter. After many experiments, and unbeknownst to his fiancée, Elizabeth, Victor reanimates a stitched-together corpse which then escapes and embarks on a strange, violent journey through the countryside, eventually leading the monster back to Victor where tragedy befalls everyone involved.

In contrast to standard monster fare, this "European slow" treatment focuses on the emotional and psychological aspects of the narrative, which is also pretty much how Shelley's novel actually reads. Unfortunately, what can be provocative and compelling on the page doesn't translate quite as kinetically to the big screen. As a result, some passages of the film are too static and talky for their own good, but it's nice to see a film that tries to tell the story without the standard thunder and lightning effects. The fact that most of the actors remain completely unknown actually helps the film, though Brit film fans may recognize Victor's pal, Henry Clerval, played by Nicholas Clay (*Excalibur*). Better suited for the small screen thanks to its intimate approach and static setting, this isn't a half bad movie, really, and should provide some interesting food for thought.

The Image DVD far surpasses the cruddy 16mm transfers floating around late night TV for years, with the exterior scenes looking especially healthy, sharp and colourful.

TESS

Colour, 1979, 170m. / Directed by Roman Polanski / Starring Nastassja Kinski, Peter Firth / Culture (Japan R2 NTSC) / WS (2.35:1) / DD2.0

A radical change of pace following the psychological holocausts of *The Tenant* and *Macbeth*, this film was Roman Polanski's surprising first project after his flight from the United States due to statutory rape charges. On the surface, this pastoral Thomas Hardy novel seems a bizarre choice, but its themes of sexual power struggles and manipulation eventually consumed such later Polanski films as *Bitter Moon* and *Death and the Maiden*.

Informed that he is descended from a noble family line called the D'Urbervilles, a simple farmer named Durbeyfield (John Collins) decides to investigate his roots with the aid of his good hearted daughter, Tess (Nastassja Kinski), who pays a visit to a nearby family bearing that name. The handsome D'Urberville son, Alec (Leigh Lawson), seduces Tess and leaves her abandoned with child. As it turns out, Alec and his family had bought the D'Urberville title and are no relation at all. Tess returns home and marries Angel Clare (Peter Firth), a seemingly gentle man who finds himself unable to cope with Tess' less than illustrious past. In typical Hardy fashion, tragedy and surprising twists of fate soon follow.

Despite its protracted running time, *Tess* amazingly contains no narrative fat and represents an impassioned labour of love from everyone involved. In her star-making role, Kinski is magnificent to behold, thanks in no small part to the ravishing Oscar-winning cinematography. The English countryside has never looked more astonishing, with each scene as perfectly composed as a Corot painting and filled with fascinating visual details. Also noteworthy is Philippe Sarde's delicate score, which made him an internationally recognized name and benefits from the skilled conducting of Carlo Savina (*Lisa and the Devil*).

Though *Tess* was enthusiastically received upon its theatrical release in the US, it has become surprisingly obscure during its tenure on cable and home video. However, it has been held in much higher esteem overseas, where full frame laserdiscs have remained constantly in circulation in Japan. A welcome letterboxed release finally appeared on Region 2 Japanese DVD and finally preserves the necessary original scope dimensions of the film; outside of a theatre, there is simply no better way to see this film. The surround audio tracks are fairly subdued, with a few ambient sound effects and Sarde's music providing most of the activity. The widescreen image is slightly raised above centre to make room for the Japanese subtitles, which can be turned off.

T

THE TEXAS CHAINSAW MASSACRE

Colour, 1974, 84m. / Directed by Tobe Hooper / Starring Marilyn Burns, Gunnar Hansen / Pioneer/MPI (US R1 NTSC) / WS (1.85:1) / DD2.0

Tobe Hooper's ultra-realistic, gritty look at down home cannibalism in the outskirts of Texas became an instant drive-in legend and has already appeared in so many different video and cable variants it's impossible to count them. This film (narrated by future sitcom star John Larroquette) isn't exactly based on a true story as the ads purport (it's very loosely derived from Wisconsin serial killer Ed Gein), but you could easily believe every second after watching this.

The plot is your standard five young folks (led by impressive screamer Marilyn Burns) get stranded out in the middle of nowhere and attacked by local crazies routine, but the execution is completely unique. Using horrific bits of scenic detail - skeletal sculptures, dead animals, etc. - Hooper creates an atmosphere of pure hell on earth, like the actual celluloid has been soaking in the air of a slaughterhouse for far too long. As virtually every critic has already noted, the film contains a very small amount of actual gore; instead, the deaths are marvels of shell-shock editing technique to make you believe you've seen more than you really have.

The transfer for this DVD edition is the same used for Elite Entertainment's deluxe laserdisc last year, though some of the colour corrections look different in this digital counterpart. Like such other low-budget full frame movies as *Pink Flamingos*, this has been matted off at the top and bottom of the frame, so anyone familiar with the other video versions will notice a dramatic shift in the compositions of many shots. However, the image quality is magnificent (featuring some digitally sweetened colour schemes) and was supervised by Hooper himself; you may want to hang to the old laser or VHS versions, though, just for comparison purposes. The remixed stereo surround track is truly unnerving, and the other audio tracks contain the original mono soundtrack and commentary by Hooper, Gunnar "Leatherface" Hansen, and the film's DP, Daniel Pearl. The other extra materials are identical to Elite's version, including outtakes, trailers, bloopers, and tons of stills and photos.

THE TEXAS CHAINSAW MASSACRE 2

Colour, 1986, 100m. / Directed by Tobe Hooper / Starring Dennis Hopper, Caroline Williams / MGM (US R1 NTSC, UK R2 PAL) / WS (1.85:1) / DD2.0

 A project filled with high expectations unrealistic enough to almost guarantee its failure, *The Texas Chainsaw Massacre 2* hit theatres as a crushing disappointment to horror fans expecting the same visceral gut punch of the 1974 original. Instead director Tobe Hooper opted for a goofy, gory satire more akin to a homefried Peter Jackson (only not as effective). The implied violence

of the original here turns into a flesh-tearing cascade thanks to Tom Savini's squishy effects, one of the undeniable highlights of what is otherwise a hit-and-miss journey.

Though the Texas authorities have refused to acknowledge the rampage of Leatherface and his family, the ensuing years have been filled with strange incidents of people vanishing in the more remote areas of Texas. The crisis hits a fever pitch when two obnoxious yuppies are attacked by a marauding truck (the film's scariest scene), and the entire ordeal is heard through a cell phone by radio DJ "Stretch" Block (the vocally impressive Caroline Williams). Meanwhile Lieutenant "Lefty" Enright (Dennis Hopper) has had enough with the law's incompetence and decides to hunt down the cannibalistic clan himself. Leatherface makes an appearance at Stretch's radio station, along with his manic Vietnam Vet accomplice, Chop Top (Bill Moseley). However, thanks to a crafty bit of manipulation by Stretch, Leatherface realizes his chainsaw might have other uses than carving flesh... The whole twisted scenario winds up at a massive underground, bone-laden hideout where the family, led by the old Cook (Jim Siedow), has constructed a profitable chilli business selling fresh, peculiar meat products.

Shot on one of the most notorious rushed schedules in history thanks to the brilliant folks at now-defunct Cannon, *The Texas Chainsaw Massacre 2* (or *TCM2* for short) suffered from literally having script pages stuffed under doors every night during shooting. Under the circumstances, Hooper and screenwriter L.M. Kit Carson (*Paris, Texas*) pull out a few showstopping sequences and some hilarious one liners (mostly from Chop Top). The film's third act can't help but suffer from its repetitive scenes of people (one of them noticeably lacking skin) sulking around underground before Hooper finally paints himself into a corner for the final, unsatisfying finale which attempts a pale imitation of the original.

TCM2 has never looked too great either on theatre screens or home video; the special edition from Elite at least offered a letterboxed (but incorrectly matted) transfer with weak contrast and heavy levels of grain, a version used for subsequent VHS special editions. MGM's DVD surprisingly features a new, greatly improved transfer that punches up the colour schemes and increases the contrast levels dramatically. The rough nature of the original source is still evident at times, thanks to those gritty looking Texas landscapes and murky shadowy underground sequences, but this is - relatively speaking - the best it's ever looked on the small screen. The surround audio is quite punchy, with some nice directional effects and rear-channel music through most of the film.

The disc also includes the original trailer (in mediocre condition) and some terrific animated menus. However, it glaringly omits the bonus deleted material from the Elite laserdisc, consisting mainly of the football massacre sequence and Joe Bob Briggs' cameo. An even longer cut exists on pirated videotape, with scenes that have never been made commercially available. Hopefully these trims will be restored at some point when a studio feels the film is worth the expense.

THAT OBSCURE OBJECT OF DESIRE

Colour, 1977, 98m. / Directed by Luis Buñuel / Starring Fernando Rey, Carole Bouquet / Criterion (US R1 NTSC) / WS (1.66:1) (16:9)

The last film from surrealist master Luis Buñuel offers his own eccentric take on frustrated love and passion: *Cet obscur objet du désir (That Obscure Object of Desire)*. Most obviously that object would seem to be Conchita, played randomly by two different actresses, Carole Bouquet and Angela Molina. On the other side of the coin is the eternally frustrated Mathieu (Fernando Rey), a bachelor well past his prime who finds himself relentlessly confounded by this beauty. First seen boarding a train only to excuse himself in order to dump a pail of water on Conchita's head at the station, he then settles down to tell his fellow passengers (including a little girl and a midget professor of psychology) about the circumstances leading to such extreme behaviour. His story begins when he first meets Conchita, a maid living under great financial strain with her mother. At first she seems receptive to his charms, but despite his increasing romantic feelings, she refuses to sleep with him. Meanwhile the city continuously erupts in explosions from senseless terrorist attacks, a seeming parallel to the romantic events which continually keep these two sexes at war. From one scene to the next, Conchita's personality changes: a cunning vixen one moment, a doe eyed innocent the next. Which one, if either, is the real woman... and can Mathieu ever come to terms with her slippery personality?

As with many of Buñuel's other films, *Obscure Object* relies heavily on a narrative told by someone completely unreliable - a self-confessed chauvinist who admits to slapping Conchita so hard she bleeds.

The reasons for this action, of course, are the real subject in question here, and no doubt a film from her point of view would be radically different. The opening scene alone casts serious doubt in the viewer's mind, as Mathieu orders a butler to destroy various objects in a room related to Conchita and casually dismisses the man's alarm at seeing a splash of blood on a pillow. The ambiguity is carried even further in aural terms; Rey's voice was dubbed (for health reasons?) by Michel Piccoli (who appeared with Rey in other Buñuel projects), while both actresses were dubbed by a single other vocal performer. The layering here is more subtle than the onion-skin structure of *The Discreet Charm of the Bourgeoisie*, but the straightforward plotline is simply another trick at Buñuel's disposal to confound viewer expectations. The justifiably famous ending, a perfect closer for the master's film career, both resolves everything and still leaves the issues tumbling in the air, capping off his filmography both with nods to his other films (the mysterious bag here echoing the buzzing box in *Belle de Jour*) and a new reservoir of imagination to fuel one final, puckish study of the ultimately unknowable human heart.

That Obscure Object of Desire has always looked quite good on home video, dating back to the days of its VHS premiere from Samuel Goldwyn and an early laserdisc from Criterion. This refurbished print from Rialto therefore looks great, but the differences are minor. Colours are bit more pronounced and less ruddy than the laser, and some minor element damage around the reel changes is now thankfully absent. The blocky, bright red opening titles are still a bit more than NTSC resolution can comfortably handle, however. The optional subtitles are also larger and easier to follow than the earlier translation, and those interested in the director's visual techniques can now finally turn them off.

Buñuel fanatics will also appreciate the disc's history of the source novel, Pierre Louÿs' *La femme et le pantin*, represented here by snippets of the silent 1928 film adaptation by Jacques de Baroncelli. Obviously an influence on its '77 remake, this adaptation looks remarkably similar in certain shots and even includes some daring (but tasteful) frontal nudity during Conchita's dance which Buñuel was only too happy to replicate in his version. Incidentally, the novel was also adapted by Josef von Sternberg in 1935 for the Marlene Dietrich vehicle, *The Devil is a Woman*. Other extras include the lively US theatrical trailer and a printed booklet containing liner notes by *The Murderous Gaze*'s William Rothman and an informative interview with

Buñuel by journalists Jose de la Colina and Tomas Perez Turrent. Apart from debunking some of the critical myths surrounding the film, the interview also offers a nice portrait of the great director enjoying his autumn years in high style.

THEATRE OF BLOOD

Colour, 1973, 104m. / Directed by Douglas Hickox / Starring Vincent Price, Diana Rigg / MGM (US R1 NTSC) / WS (1.66:1)

 After reinventing himself once again as a horror icon for the '70s with *The Abominable Dr. Phibes*, Vincent Price returned to the theme of systematic literary revenge with one of his finest films, *Theatre of Blood*. A rare horror effort cherished even by those who normally turn their noses up at the genre, this mixture of Shakespeare, riotous gore, and biting comedy still stands up as an ideal showcase for Price's wonderfully melodramatic horror persona.

On the Ides of March, newspaper theatre critic George Maxwell is summoned to a piece of decrepit property he owns in London, only to be brutally beaten to death by a band of tramps. The assault is led by Edward Lionheart (Price), a Shakespearean actor presumed dead after flinging himself into the Thames, who now resides in an abandoned theatre where he plots revenge against his critic with the aid of a pack of indigents. Meanwhile Lionheart's daughter, Edwina (Diana Rigg), becomes both a likely suspect in the murders and the confidant of Devlin (Ian Hendry), the primary critic responsible for denying Lionheart the coveted Critics' Circle Award which led to the actor's dramatic "suicide." One by one the members of the circle are dispatched in scenarios derived from the Bard's plays, and the police find themselves unable to outwit a mad actor intent on bringing his gruesome onstage antics into the real world.

Resolutely British in tone, *Theatre of Blood* brings together a once in a lifetime cast of veteran thespians, including Coral Browne (Price's real life wife), Milo O'Shea as a perplexed inspector, Euro starlet Diana Dors in a funny twist on Othello, beloved Miss Marple actress Joan Hickson, and most memorably, Robert Morley as a poodle lover dragged into a berserk modern version of *Titus Andronicus*.

The lavish production design and razor sharp script allow Price and Rigg to storm through the proceedings in a delicious array of disguises, such as a '70s-styled hairdresser, a television host, a

masseuse, and a wine-tasting expert, to name but a few. Special notice should also go to the lyrical, poignant score by Michael J. Lewis, which kicks off with a poetic credits sequence cut together from Shakespeare silents but eventually becomes hysterically ironic, as in the *Cymbeline*/medical operation scene.

Released twice on laserdisc by Image/MGM, the MGM DVD uses the same transfer used for the second, widescreen release. The moderate 1.66:1 letterboxing looks correct, matting out a bit of excess vertical information compared to the first, open matte disc. While a new anamorphic transfer would have no doubt added some sparkle to the image, visual quality is satisfying and colourful considering the '70s origin of the original source material. The DVD omits the isolated music and effects track present on the laserdisc, though this loss is not so severe since Lewis' score has since been issued in stereo on CD. The disc also includes the long theatrical trailer, which admirably sums up the basics of the plot without spoiling too much of the fun apart from a few too many shots from the fiery climax.

THEATRE OF DEATH

Colour, 1966, 89 m. / Directed by Samuel Gallu / Starring Christopher Lee, Julian Glover / Anchor Bay (US R1 NTSC), Carlton (UK R2 PAL) / WS (2.35:1) (16:9)

 A cinematic tug of war between the entrenched blood and boobs gothic approach of Hammer and the approaching tide of more stylized, continental filmmaking which would characterize the films of Michael Reeves and most of the U.K.'s 1970s output, *Theatre of Death* is an odd, fascinating curio for horror fans. The presence of Christopher Lee in a sort-of leading role raises expectations for a catalogue of kitschy murders, but the film actually delivers something a little different.

The theatre crowds of Paris are flocking to the gruesome displays at the Theatre du Mort, a theatre based on the Grand Guignol where tyrannical director Philippe Darvas (Lee) arranges the persecutions and murders of his female actresses for the public's delight. Roommates Nicole (Jenny Till) and Dani (Leila Goldini) are employed as part of Darvas' troupe, but their harmonious lives are disrupted by the arrival of police inspector Charles Marquis (Julian Glover), whose investigation into a series of grisly "vampire" murders have led him to the theatre. Meanwhile Darvas shows an increasing interest in young Nicole, whom he hypnotizes into a dangerous trance which has a habit of resurfacing at awkward moments onstage. Could the brutish Darvas be linked to the killings, or is there an even more sinister force at work?

Though not overtly frightening, *Theatre of Death* operates like a mad funhouse ride through established horror techniques throughout the world. The theatrical setting and many of its themes echo Karl Freund's *Mad Love*, the expressionist primary colour design and witch persecution play draw upon the influence of Mario Bava, and the jagged whodunit structure owes more than a shade to the German krimi films derived from Edgar Wallace. Likewise, director Samuel Gallu tosses around a bizarre range of visual techniques ranging from elegant tableaux to dizzying hand held camera shots, making this a feast for the eyes even when the experiments don't quite pay off.

Even for the time period the level of violence is surprisingly restrained, with the nearly nude dancers during the finale offering more of a jolt than any of the mostly offscreen murders; however, the film still maintains its grip on the viewer thanks to the sheer oddness of it all, with each new scene promising another swerve into the unexpected.

The several virtues present in *Theatre of Death* have been completely smothered in years of faded, badly cropped TV and video prints (some under the U.S. title of *Blood Fiend*); thankfully those can all be set aside in the wake of Anchor Bay's DVD, which follows on the heels of a similar U.K. disc release.

The transfer is nothing short of a knockout, with vivid colours capable of drawing gasps from viewers. The scope framing is absolutely essential to following the story, which is elliptical enough anyway; one crucial moment at the end has never made any sense at all in the pan and scan variants. For what is widely considering a lower tier European horror title, *Theatre of Death* has been treated with a surprisingly lavish package (apart from the innocuous cover design, which in no way conveys the baroque visuals of the film itself). An 11-minute interview with Christopher Lee offers a quick sketch of his experience on the film, which he largely places in context with his Hammer work. Also included are the European trailer, radio spots, and a nice, extensive gallery of stills and posters from both sides of the Atlantic, as well as a Lee bio.

THERESE AND ISABELLE

B&W, 1968, 117m. / Directed by Radley Metzger / Starring Essy Persson, Anna Gael / Image (US R0 NTSC) / WS (2.35:1)

Metzger's highest profile effort at the time, *Therese and Isabelle* marks perhaps the most successful attempt to fuse eroticism with popular arthouse cinema. Utilizing an atmosphere best described as a randier François Truffaut, the film conjures up a melancholy girls' school at which the suppression of emotional attachments leads our two heroines to form a healthy, productive lesbian relationship, a rare development at the time.

Therese (*I, a Woman*'s Essy Persson), a middle aged woman, returns to the boarding school of her youth where her mother shunted her off to go frolic with Therese's new stepfather. Lonely and perplexed, Therese forges a friendship with the sultry Isabelle (Anna Gael), much to the chagrin of those around them. The girls' progression into a self-absorbed world to escape their surroundings (this would make a great double bill with *Heavenly Creatures*) eventually leads to sexual curiosity as well, though more obstacles continue to lie in their way.

Boasting a first rate cast headlined by Anne Vernon (Catherine Deneuve's mother in *The Umbrellas of Cherbourg*) as the headmistress, *Therese and Isabelle* is classy entertainment on all fronts and a haunting work of visual art as well, boosted by a shimmering Georges Auric score. The actual skin quotient is surprisingly low considering the film's reputation (about the equivalent of a soft "R" rating now), with Therese's voiceover recollections often becoming far more explicit than anything onscreen and increasing the heat tenfold as it stimulates viewers' imaginations.

Previously available in a fuzzy, brutally pan and scanned print from Monterey on VHS, the uncut First Run/Image transfer is a tremendous improvement in every respect. The full Franscope framing is vitally important to the majority of shots in the film, particularly the memorable images of the girls on bicycles (shades of "Les Mistons"), and the deeper contrast of the black and white photography increases its neoclassical visual depth. The image is a bit soft compared to some of the razor-sharp restoration work being done now, but this is most likely the best the film will ever look and is more than satisfying.

As for the qualities of the film itself, while Gael's role is fairly limited, Persson delivers a terrific, highly convincing performance both as the confused young Therese and as her older self. The film itself was shot in English and dubbed post-synch, which is how it is presented here, though a French-dubbed version with subtitles also circulated in some quarters. Reportedly, Metzger also shot an alternate "safer" ending in which Therese is joined at the end by her husband, then both walk away to apparently turn their backs on her little youthful indiscretion. While it would have been interesting to include this ending as a supplement, the one here is far more appropriate and poignant. While much of the puckish Metzger humour present in his later films had not really developed yet here, this justifiably remains one of his best-known and most popular titles.

THESIS (TESIS)

Colour, 1995, 121m. / Directed by Alejandro Amenábar / Starring Ana Torrent, Eduardo Noriega / Vanguard (US R1 NTSC) / WS (1.66:1), Tartan (UK R0 PAL) / WS (1.85:1), Universal (Spain R2 PAL) / DD2.0

 Some urban legends just refuse to die. Snuff movies, in which people are actually killed on camera (often during a sexual situation), have been the modern day bogeyman of urban streets since the 1970s. Of course, exploitation movies have been quick to hop on the bandwagon, ranging from Michael and Roberta Findlay's horrendous *Snuff* to glossy but inherently ludicrous mainstream product like *8MM* and *Mute Witness*. Though it took four years to get over to America, Alejandro Amenábar's *Thesis (Tesis)* is, relatively speaking, the best of the snuff thriller subgenre, and this self-advertised "American style thriller" at least manages to make its subject genuinely terrifying if not even remotely credible.

Angela (Ana Torrent), a young grad student doing her thesis on audiovisual violence, employs the services of a porn and gore mongering fellow student, Chema (Fele Martínez), to show her the dark and ugly corners of the video industry. Meanwhile her supervising professor happens to die from a heart attack while watching a videotape he pilfered from the school library. Angela swipes the tape, a snuff video involving a young student, Vanessa, who vanished two years ago. Chema identifies the camera used for the tape, and the pair do some investigating which leads to the charming Bosco (Eduardo Noriega), an acquaintance of Vanessa who may know more than he's telling. Angela finds herself attracted to Bosco, much to Chema's irritation. However, a nightmarish encounter in the college basement proves that there's much more to this mystery than meets the eye.

Obviously a talent to watch, Amenábar does an expert job of building characterization and suspense throughout. Credit must certainly be given when he can make a thriller running over two hours fly by in what seems like minutes, and his Polanski-inspired eye for unusual human behaviour gives a lot of mileage to the hoary storyline. His follow up film, *Open Your Eyes*, garnered notices as the biggest Spanish export since Almodóvar, and the attention is definitely justified compared to the anaemic thrillers generated recently in America. Actually, Amenábar in many ways seems to be the heir apparent to the Agustin Villaronga, the gloriously depraved soul who gave the world *In a Glass Cage* and the more recent *99.9*, a marvellous and underrated film that mirrors many of the same themes in *Thesis*. The gore level here is admirably restrained apart from a few blurry, nasty glimpses of the snuff tape, but European horror fans should find this approach a refreshing change of pace.

Where *Thesis* stumbles slightly is its attempt to appeal to the international market, apparently adopting the storytelling techniques of Joe Eszterhas (*Basic Instinct*) in the process. Since there are only two real possible suspects in the film, the final hour basically flip flops back and forth between them, pretty much eliminating any chance for a surprise ending. Also, the final scene is extremely unlikely, even for the most tasteless tabloid shows on television. On a cinematic and visceral level, though, *Thesis* is a knockout, particularly during one masterful sequence, an homage to *The Bird with the Crystal Plumage*, in which Angela and Chema use flickering matches to navigate through a series of dark tunnels beneath the college. The performers (Amenábar regulars, as it now appears) all do an excellent job of bringing their characters to life, with Noriega in particular walking a fine line between charisma and menace.

Vanguard's DVD appears to be lifted from a British PAL source, complete with a couple of video dropouts and a nasty ruffle in the audio for a few seconds one hour into the film. The quality is acceptable but looks much closer to a videotape than a DVD; the stereo soundtrack is mostly limited to the score (effectively composed by the director) and a few ambient effects like rain and video static. The marginally letterboxed transfer includes non-removable English subtitles, usually printed in the lower widescreen band, and illegible chapter selection options. The UK disc offers a more stable picture with optional English subtitles, as well as a making-of featurette, trailer, filmographies, and a poster/artwork gallery. The Spanish DVD features a solid transfer but no English subtitles.

THEY LIVE

Colour, 1988, 94m. / Directed by John Carpenter / Starring Roddy Piper, Meg Foster / Image (US R1 NTSC) / WS (2.35) (16:9) / DD2.0

Roddy Piper (yes, the wrestler) stars as Nada (as in "nothing," get it?), a homeless drifter who goes from job to job and winds up in a construction position in an unnamed large city. A group of radicals keep breaking in on the TV signals and warning of an evil conspiracy that's been brainwashing the general public, but everyone tends to ignore it. After a series of government attacks on one faction holing out in a local church, Nada uncovers a pair of sunglasses that reveal that the world is not quite as he thought. All advertising and written material contains subliminal messages, such as "Marry and Reproduce," "No Individual Thought," and "This Is Your God" (printed on money). Even worse, it appears all the wealthy people are - surprise! - ugly skeletal-faced aliens in disguise. Pretty soon Nada is suiting up for battle, and the fun begins.

Generally dismissed as one of Carpenter's goofier films (along with *Big Trouble in Little China*), *They Live* has some serious things to say about right-wing suppression and the growing apathy near the end of the millennium. Piper's role seems tailor-made for Carpenter buddy in crime Kurt Russell (including such lines as the immortal "I've come here to chew bubble gum and kick ass... and I'm all out of bubble gum"), but Piper fills the action hero shoes pretty well. He got a lot of bad press at the time, but after we've endured such action wannabes as Steven Seagal and Jean-Claude Van Damme, he looks like Laurence Olivier in comparison. In fact, it's surprising how well this film has aged over the past decade, though it does suffer from a few flaws. Piper's idiotic fight scene with Keith David seems thrown in for no good reason at all and drags on way past the breaking point; it seems including solely for the purpose of pleasing wrestling fans. Also, the final sequence is a serious let-down, a knee-jerk jokey finish that wraps the film up on an abrupt, unfinished note. Interestingly, *They Live* now feels like a dry run for Carpenter's subsequent *In the Mouth of Madness*, an even more extreme look at the world's seemingly normal sheen being slowly removed to expose a completely different, malicious force lurking underneath (and which also features an unsatisfying ending). As Carpenter has explained, all of his films in one way or another revolve around normal people who become heroes when thrust into situations beyond their control; here, the hero deals with corruption in the aliens and the human beings around him who have sold out for wealth from the invaders. It's one of the most interesting sci-fi conceits of the past few years, and while the execution doesn't always do it justice, there's plenty of food for thought here for the open-minded viewer.

The previous Japanese laserdisc version of *They Live* was incompletely letterboxed (about 1.90:1) and had a colourless, washed-out appearance that failed to do much justice to this satiric sci-fi political actioner. No director takes advantage of the full scope widescreen image more than Carpenter; and this DVD presents the full 2.35 image and features incredibly rich, vibrant colour and deep shadows, along with a fabulous Dolby Digital surround remix. Though it has no extras (the Japanese laser did have a pretty nifty behind-the-scenes featurette, so don't chuck it if you have it), this one was definitely worth the wait.

THEY SAVED HITLER'S BRAIN

B&W, 1963, 92m. / Directed by David Bradley / Starring Walter Stocker, Audrey Caire / Rhino (US R0 NTSC)

Now here's a level of cinematic pain that few will be able to sit through without giggling uncontrollably. The remnants of a disastrous 1963 B-movie entitled *Madmen of Mandoras* were haphazardly spliced into newer, late '60s footage (crafted at UCLA, according to the liner notes, but who really knows?) vaguely related to the story of Hitler's animated head plotting a takeover from South America. Needless to say, the opening newer sequences (which feel for all the world like a Doris Wishman grindhouse quickie) completely fail to cohere with the original film, which was surprisingly well photographed by the great Stanley Cortez (*Night of the Hunter, The Magnificent Ambersons*). Approach at your own risk.

The hallucinatory tale begins with a professor falling victim to a car bomb while apparently carrying the antidote to a nerve gas being developed by a rising Fourth Reich. A government agent named Vick is called in and ordered to follow up on the assassination, despite the fact that another professor actually developed the formula and is still among the living. Vick teams up with feminist agent Toni, and they track down the evildoers to an old house where carnage ensues. Shorn of our two leading characters,

T

we then hop over to Mandoras for another story about a kidnapped diplomat's daughter named Suzanne who now grinds away at a local bar. She tips off her would-be rescuers about some nefarious nouveau Nazis, who apparently have preserved the Fuhrer's severed head in a glass jar. Needless to say, Hitler's in a very foul mood and twitches spastically towards his minions. Chases follow. People die. None of it makes a lick of sense.

Somehow it's just tragic that one of the few examples of Cortez's photography on DVD lies within this film, which has been salvaged from public domain hell by the folks at Rhino. While most prints run 74 minutes, the Rhino disc contains every shred of alternate and additional footage ever shot, tallying up to a mind-boggling 92 minutes. More is not necessarily better, but it certainly is funnier. The image quality ranges wildly, from the ragged opening credits to the surprisingly crisp (if slightly damaged) 16mm inserts to the 35mm original. For some reason the sound goes all to hell for a few minutes one hour into the movie, with some odd fluttering noises in the background. The packaging claims to be mastered from the original 35mm film elements, which could very well be true; while no demo piece by any means, the film looks decent for the most part. Just keep your expectations low and enjoy. Special points for the animated menu, which features an animated Hitler head yammering away in quasi-German; however, it would have been even better to have him simply yelp repeatedly, "Mach schnell! Mach schnell!"

THE THING

Colour, 1982, 109m. / Directed by John Carpenter / Starring Kurt Russell / Universal / WS (2.35:1) / DD2.0

Upon its release *The Thing* was snubbed for daring to take Howard Hawks' rapid fire sci-fi classic and present it as a dark, deadly serious, and horrifically gory vision of mankind stripped down to its most primal elements in the Antarctic. Dispensing with the carrot monster, the female love interest, and the wisecracking newsman of the original, Carpenter instead returned to the original short story, John W. Campbell, Jr.'s "Who Goes There?," to fashion an alien story in which the shapeless menace can inhabit any living form. Thus, the male protagonists, trapped in a remote Army station, must fend off each other in an attempt to determine who is human... and who isn't.

Kurt Russell makes a solid, stoic leading man, a far cry from his other collaborations with Carpenter, and Rob Bottin's eye-popping special effects have become the stuff of legend.

Universal now treats their fledgling cult favourite to the deluxe treatment with what is easily one of the best special editions on DVD to date, starting off with a lustrous new THX-approved transfer. Believe it or not, they also finally shelled out the bucks to restore Stevie Wonder's "Superstition" back into an early scene, too! As per their welcome practice, Universal has included a fascinating 84-minute documentary, "Terror Takes Shape," which includes interviews with many of the principal players and some behind-the-scenes footage. It's not as lively or dramatic as their similar documentaries for *Psycho* or *To Kill a Mockingbird*, for example, but this is a good example of how to treat a film on DVD.

And the extras just keep on coming, including full feature commentary by Carpenter and Russell, an isolated music track for Ennio Morricone's score (access it by going to the documentary's language features button), Bottin's developmental effects footage and drawings, countless photos, drawings, and storyboards, and, most surprisingly, the extra snippets of unused footage which were stuck into the film's airings on CBS and the Sci-Fi Channel. The only complaint is that the alternate happy ending for the film, discussed at length in the documentary, isn't included.

THINGS TO COME

B&W, 1936, 93m. / Directed by William Cameron Menzies / Starring Raymond Massey, Ralph Richardson / Image (US R0 NTSC)

Time has been mostly kind to *Things to Come*, H.G. Wells' speculative study of progress and conflict from 1936 to 2036. Compressing his novel *The Shape of Things to Come* into a screenplay (which was later published), Wells begins his saga on Christmas Eve in "Everytown," which looks an awful lot like WWII London.

The country braces for war, which soon arrives full force, destroying entire city blocks, ripping the current political system to shreds, and leaving the citizens ravaged by plague. One of Everytown's citizens, a pilot named John Cabal (Raymond Massey), arrives a sadder and wiser man to confront the petulant Boss (Ralph Richardson), a dictator

T

intent on conquering surrounding territories littered with post-war rubble. A revolution ensues to restore Everytown to the growing order of unified nations, but more conflict is yet to come as scientists and artists (represented by charismatic Cedric Hardwicke) feud over the possibility of sending man into space.

From a technical standpoint, *Things to Come* is assembled as masterfully as any science fiction film of its time. While other 1930s films viewed the future as a puffball creation filled with flying cars and worldwide peace (check out the justifiably ignored *Just Imagine* for contrast), Wells' vision focuses on both the darkness and light. The gothic wreckage of the middle act bears an uncanny resemblance to the works of much later visionaries like Ridley Scott (*Blade Runner* in particular) and Terry Gilliam (almost everything), though the industrial deco approach of the space age conclusion has yet to be duplicated.

More difficult to warm up to is the film's reliance on preaching to the audience about the need for progress, though Wells readers will be more able to go along with these didactic passages. Massey in particular is saddled with some unwieldy dialogue, leaving Richardson to take top acting honours for his fascinating, complex, and frightening portrayal of a leader all too similar to the real ones that came to pass. Special mention must also be made of the score by Arthur Bliss, which manages to swerve from grandiose marches to quivering menace in the blink of an eye.

While *Things to Come* has never been a "lost" film per se, decent versions have been hard to come by. Video collectors have been forced to make do with horrendous public domain prints over the years, including a certain unmentionable DVD release during the format's infancy.

Relatively speaking, the Wade Williams release from Image is a feast for the eyes, offering nice contrast (at last!) and crisp detail. Some print damage and fluttering is evident from time to time, not to mention a few nasty instances of warping during the last reel, but the presentation is still a revelation all the same. Even more welcome is the cleaned up soundtrack, which is smooth and always intelligible in marked contrast to the muffled noise of all prior video versions.

While nothing has been trimmed out, the running time curiously clocks in at 93 minutes rather than the standard 97, indicating this may have originally been mastered in PAL. The disc also includes the original 1936 US theatrical trailer, which is in watchable but decidedly unspectacular condition.

THE THIRD MAN

B&W, 1949, 104m. / Directed by Carol Reed / Starring Joseph Cotten, Alida Valli, Orson Welles / Criterion (US R1 NTSC)

Aptly described by Peter Bogdanovich in his intro as perhaps the finest non-auteur film ever made, a "happy accident," *The Third Man* has remained steadily popular and critically revered since its release but has proven curiously impossible to imitate. Steeped in rich black and white cinematography, gorgeous shots of post-war Vienna, and a diverse cast operating at the top of its game, the film makes countless cinematic gambles along the way, all of which pay off in spades. Unfortunately *The Third Man* fell into quasi-public domain status around the dawn of home video and has been smeared by numerous awful bootleg transfers, usually cut, which put quite a severe damper on a viewer's enjoyment of the film. However, Criterion's impressive DVD following a successful theatrical reissue should quickly take its place as the definitive presentation of this stark, unforgettable noir classic.

Holly Martins (Joseph Cotten), an American novelist earning his keep with cheap western novels, travels to post-war Vienna to accept a job offer through his friend, Harry Lime (Orson Welles). Upon arriving, however, Martins is informed that Lime has just been killed in a car accident, where his body was carted off by three men. Unsatisfied with the police's declaration of accidental death, Martins smells a rat and begins investigating what appear to be conflicting stories from witnesses and friends. Holly tracks down two of the three men and also becomes entangled with Lime's girlfriend, Anna Schmidt (Alida Valli). Apparently Lime was involved in the flourishing black market gradually overtaking Vienna, though the products Lime was dealing proved to be far more deadly than Holly had imagined.

Though directed by the often overlooked Carol Reed, *The Third Man* has often been mistaken for an Orson Welles film thanks to the legendary actor/director's ten minute appearance as Lime. While the Welles influence can certainly be traced to the use of skewed angles and that old film school bugaboo, "deep focus," the film also falls squarely in line with Reed's elegant but cynical portraits of humanity like The Fallen Idol. In fact, it's remarkable how much people tend to overlook the uncompromising bitterness and borderline nihilism of this film, thanks to its glossy European sheen and snappy, often amusing dialogue, easily Graham Greene at his best. In typical Greene fashion, moral absolutes are turned upside down, with betrayal often substituting for friendship and grey dominating as the moral colour of choice. As far as surface pleasures, the catchy zither score by Anton Karas has become an institution in its own right; in fact, nowhere else has a single instrument become so completely identified with a film.

Aside from the impish yet menacing turn by Welles, the cast also features a terrific role for Cotten as the deeply flawed Holly, a gorgeous Valli (also in *Suspiria* and *The Paradine Case*) as the possible femme fatale, and a number of current and future British actors like Trevor Howard, Bernard Lee (the first "M" in the James Bond series), and the great Wilfrid Hyde-White.

Criterion's DVD presents the complete European cut of *The Third Man*, featuring an opening voiceover by Reed as an unidentified black marketer and a number of extra scenes which portray Holly in a less flattering light. The transfer simply looks spectacular; while a few unavoidable signs of age crop up here and there, mostly in the soundtrack, the presentation is by far the best this has looked since '49. The fragmented compositions and velvety chiaroscuro lighting seem to jump off the screen throughout, particularly during one pivotal scene an hour into the film; no distortion, grain, or noticeable damage is anywhere to be found.

A number of extras make this package even more tempting; rather than the usual commentary analysis track, the DVD features a radio presentation of the story with Cotten, Green's original treatment read by Richard Clarke, and an alternate radio drama with Welles reprising his character, far less effectively. Also included are the original (and utterly ridiculous) US trailer, the 1999 reissue trailer, the US opening sequence, documentary footage of Karas playing a number of standards on his zither, archival Vienna sewer footage, and production notes. Per Criterion's usual practice, the price may be a little steep, but no film fanatic should be able to pass this one up.

13 GHOSTS

B&W/Colour, 1960, 84m. / Directed by William Castle / Starring Donald Woods, Rosemary DeCamp / Columbia (US R1 NTSC) / WS (1.85:1) (16:9)

After at least three stabs on home video, Columbia perfected William Castle's family-friendly spook legend, *13 Ghosts*, on DVD. After Castle and co-scenarist Robb White devised the go for broke,

surrealist spectacle of *The Tingler*, they retreated somewhat with a more linear, restrained haunted house yarn - but this being a Castle film, it's still far more outlandish than what his contemporaries were cranking out at the time.

Strapped for cash, the Zorba family headed by father Cyrus (Donald Woods) and mother Hilda (Rosemary DeCamp) prepares for eviction by celebrating the birthday of their youngest son, Buck (Charles Herbert), who wishes for a real house with furniture. That wish is answered sooner than expected when a telegram arrives announcing their inheritance of a nearby Los Angeles estate owned by Cyrus' eccentric uncle, Plato Zorba, who was believed dead ten years earlier. The dead man's attorney and friend, Ben (*Route 66*'s Martin Milner), explains that the furnished house comes with a spooky maid (Margaret Hamilton) and a collection of ghosts amassed by Zorba during his trips around the world. The older daughter, Medea (Jo Morrow), finds her flirting with Ben interrupted when a Ouija board experiment points her out as the ghosts' next victim, and Buck develops a rapport with the spectres who can only be viewed with a special experimental viewer. Things get even more complicated when the Zobras learn that a large cache of money may be secreted somewhere in the house... and they must try to find the location of the treasure before the ghosts decide once and for all to get rid of the new residents.

Though the playful but macabre storyline sounds much like your average Don Knotts programmer (or Castle's later, goofier *The Spirit is Willing*), *13 Ghosts* is far weirder than one might expect. Apart from the highly unlikely character names, the film moves in a series of bizarre, unexpected directions in which every plot device feels like a whimsical tangent from out of nowhere. The Ouija board scene, the housekeeper, the glasses, the treasure, and even the ghosts themselves are all gimmicky elements that just barely add up but still don't make a tremendous amount of sense afterwards. Instead Castle gleefully ignores any logic loopholes and trots out his usual grab bag of tricks, best exemplified by the film's famous promotional gimmick, "Illusion-O." Each ghost appearance (regardless of whether it's seen through the ghost viewer in the film) in the black and white film is tinted blue, with the ghost opticals printed in red. Essentially a simpler variation on 3-D, this process allows the ghosts to be seen clearly when viewed through the red lens on the viewer, while they vanish altogether when seen through the blue one. Without the viewer, the ghosts are barely visible but look murky, a condition duplicated when the film was reissued in straight black and white. Though not as dramatic as the *House on Haunted Hill* method of barrelling skeletons out over the audience, it's a nice gesture and represents Castle at his most eager to please. Otherwise the film is a lot of fun, and its less than brilliant acting actually gives the ridiculous proceedings a more offbeat, tongue in cheek sense of flair, right down to the cheeky casting of *The Wizard of Oz*'s Wicked Witch, Hamilton, as the "witch" medium/housekeeper who provides the film with its nifty final wink at the viewer.

The early VHS release of *13 Ghosts* from Columbia and all widespread TV airings presented the standard, straight black and white version in a soft, dupey presentation. This same source was used for the Goodtimes VHS and Columbia laserdiscs, all of which omitted Castle's opening introduction (in which he explains the Illusion-O process at a desk accompanied by a skeleton secretary). However, Columbia eventually went back and struck new prints of *13 Ghosts* that reverted back to Castle's original vision, and this excellent source was used for the dramatically improved DVD edition. Castle's introduction is now back in place along with the visual cues for viewers to hold up and remove their ghost viewers. Most importantly, the red and blue tints are back and look magnificent; even the splashy colours of the opening titles are far more enjoyable with their original hues. The 1.85:1 letterboxing duplicates the theatrical presentation and looks nicely framed; the same framing is used for the shorter, non-Illusion-O version included on Side B of the DVD. (For some reason the respective sides have reversed labels, so if you pop in the disc in and see black and white credits, flip it over.)

The disc, timed to coincide with the FX-laden and much gorier remake, continues the respectful wave of Castle digital releases by including the punchy theatrical trailer, a nice but brief insert sheet, one ghost viewer, and a short but thorough featurette, "The Magic of Illusion-O," in which a variety of fans and showmen (including Fred Olen Ray!) explain how Castle's gimmick was executed in theatres and scared the daylights out of young popcorn munchers.

THE 39 STEPS

B&W, 1935, 86m. / Directed by Alfred Hitchcock / Starring Robert Donat, Madeleine Carroll / Criterion (US R1 NTSC), Delta (US R0 NTSC), Carlton (UK R2 PAL)

The richest film from Hitchcock's British filmmaking period, *The 39 Steps* loosely adapts John Buchan's classic novel into a prototypical "wrong man" scenario with an innocent hero chased across the English countryside by police and villains alike. Though recently neglected (especially by film schools) in favour of Hitch's productive Hollywood period, *The 39 Steps* represents the first developed version of "the Hitchcock formula" at work and, along with *North by Northwest*, remains one of his best mainstream thrillers.

Richard Hannay (Robert Donat), a Canadian staying in England, escorts a frantic, mysterious woman (Lucie Mannheim) back to his flat. She tells him that she is a spy being pursued by an organization called The 39 Steps, led by a man missing a finger from one of his hands. That night, the woman turns up in his bedroom with a knife in her back, and Hannay goes on the run to avoid arrest for her murder. Thanks to a number of tense and sometimes amusing complications, he winds up manacled to a beautiful, icy blonde (Madeleine Carroll) and runs through the Scottish countryside as he attempts to find the villains and clear his own name.

An excellent example of how to pace a film, *The 39 Steps* contains no dull moments along the way and packs a number of surprises into its brief running time. While some Hitch fans prefer *The Lady Vanishes* from the director's British output, this film offers far more substance and technical innovation (such as the now legendary shock cut from a screaming landlady to a rushing train). While Hitchcock may not have had much regard for his actors ("cattle"), Donat and Carroll make one of the most fetching couples in film history and give the film much of its necessary weight. Their witty, banter-filled dialogue perfectly mirrors their flight across the countryside, making this one of the earliest and best "road" movies.

Anyone unfortunate enough to sit through Criterion's laserdisc edition of *The 39 Steps* (or even worse, the countless wretched public domain editions over the years) will be in for a very pleasant shock upon seeing their restored DVD transfer. To say that this is like watching an entirely new film is an understatement, and in its own way, this is as revolutionary as Universal's DVD overhaul on the 1931 *Frankenstein*. Every existing video edition of *The 39 Steps* until now has been blurry, flat, and plagued by audio drowned in hissing and crackling. Thanks to what appears to be a lot of effort, the film now looks virtually as good as new. Countless levels of clothing detail, facial nuances, and landscape features are now plainly visible, as if a thick fog has suddenly been swept away from the camera. The sound now unfolds with amazing clarity, and the quiet portions are actually quiet. A few of the exterior shots during the Scotland section look a bit rough around the edges, apparently a flaw in the original source materials that could not be avoided, but otherwise, Criterion has for once completely justified its hefty price tag on this one.

The plentiful extras on the DVD include the 1937 Lux Radio Theatre broadcast (with Robert Montgomery and Ida Lupino), which owes far more to Hitchcock's film than the Buchan novel, and a 1970's educational film produced by Janus, "The Art of Film: Vintage Hitchcock," a study of his British suspense period. A good introduction for the uninitiated, the half hour film contains nothing groundbreaking but gives a nice thumbnail sketch of his filmmaking techniques, with *Young and Innocent* receiving most of the screen time. For some reason, the films are also covered out of sequence with *The 39 Steps* appearing last. The only disappointment is academian Marian Keane's audio commentary, which comes off as a recited lecture, recapping the onscreen action with some not terribly gripping observations about Hitchcock's visual placement of characters and dropping of clues. Otherwise, a job well done.

A host of public domain companies have attempted to cash in with substandard transfers, but for the budget conscious, the better options out there are the US Delta disc (which appears to be taken from the master used for Criterion's laserdisc and includes a very odd Tony Curtis intro) and the UK Carlton disc, packaged in a set with the original *The Man Who Knew Too Much.*

THIS NIGHT I'LL POSSESS YOUR CORPSE

B&W/Colour, 1966, 107m. / Directed by José Mojica Marins / Fantoma (US R1 NTSC) / WS (1.66:1)

Picking up shortly after *At Midnight I'll Take Your Soul* left off, Coffin Joe returns in *This Night I'll Possess Your Corpse.* After recuperating in the hospital from massive eye trauma (which looked significantly worse at the end of *At Midnight*, to say the least), he's back to

business as usual trying to scout out a future mother for his evil, "perfect" spawn.

After auditioning six beauties with his trusty tarantulas and subjecting another young woman to the suffocating clutch of a boa constrictor, all with the aid of his new, trusty hunchback assistant, Bruno (Nivaldo de Lima), Coffin Joe finally settles on the perfect mate and even wipes out his male competitor with the aid of a heavy rock to the cranium. Alas, a brutal twist of fate induces him to hallucinate a horrifying journey to hell (in full, bleeding colour), where the damned are cursed to an eternity locked into the walls of an icy cavern presided over by pitchfork-wielding minions of the devil, also played by Marins. Shaken to his senses, Coffin Joe embarks on one final, savage attempt to fulfil his destiny...

Encouraged by the popular reception *of At Midnight,* Marins pulls out all the stops for his second foray into horror territory. The vestiges of a storyline present in the first film are largely discarded for what instead resembles a collision between the aesthetic perversion of the Marquis De Sade and the violent, orgiastic visuals of the '60s S&M *Olga* films. This is no quick cut and paste sickie, however; Marins' craft had obviously been honed to allow him freer expression of his dark, comic book style fantasies. The sets are more elaborate, the photography is slicker, the acting is better, and the hell sequence is arguably the most striking set piece in Marins' entire canon. Newcomers may be startled by the film's excessiveness, so it's probably best to start with the first film to get one's feet wet; however, anyone curious about world horror cinema should make *This Night* required viewing.

The technical improvements evident in this film extend to the quality of the negative itself. The opening montage summarizing the highlights from the previous film still looks the worse for wear, but once the new footage begins, the resolution and print quality are wonderful. The colour footage in particular is so vivid it nearly leaps off the screen, laying waste to the earlier VHS edition, and the English subtitles are well written and easily accessible.

As with the other titles in the Fantoma DVD trilogy, the disc includes all three Coffin Joe trailers, as well as a fascinating interview in which Marins discusses the sudden celebrity he encountered while making this film, the ordeals suffered voluntarily by his cast members, and much, much more. Also, be sure to read the liner notes for an interesting bit of trivia about the film's frenetic closing line.

THE THOUSAND EYES OF DR. MABUSE

B&W, 1960, 105m. / Directed by Fritz Lang / Starring Dawn Addams, Gert Fröbe / AllDay (US R1 NTSC) / WS (1.78:1) (16:9)

THE TESTAMENT OF DR. MABUSE

B&W, 1962, 88m. / Directed by Werner Klinger / Starring Gert Fröbe, Senta Berger / AllDay (US R1 NTSC) / WS (1.78:1) (16:9)

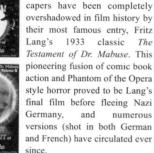

One of the great unknown film series, the Dr. Mabuse crime capers have been completely overshadowed in film history by their most famous entry, Fritz Lang's 1933 classic *The Testament of Dr. Mabuse*. This pioneering fusion of comic book action and Phantom of the Opera style horror proved to be Lang's final film before fleeing Nazi Germany, and numerous versions (shot in both German and French) have circulated ever since.

The series was revived in 1960 when Lang was offered the chance to remake his classic and instead chose to direct a highly unorthodox sequel, *The Thousand Eyes of Dr. Mabuse*. In what eventually proved to be his directorial swan song Lang produced one of his most underrated films, a fast-paced and invigorating pop art masterpiece of paranoia and Cold War era panic.

In the memorable opener, a reporter driving along a busy city street is murdered by a passing assassin (Howard Vernon) who fires a needle-thin bullet directly into the man's head. A blind medium named Cornelius (*Mill of the Stone Women*'s Wolfgang Preiss) informs Commissioner Kras (*Goldfinger* himself, Gert Fröbe) that he witnessed the murder in a vision but cannot determine the identity of the killer. Kras believes that this latest crime stems from a mysterious evil brewing at the Hotel Luxor, a magnet for peculiar events that resemble the handiwork of the late archcriminal Dr. Mabuse. Meanwhile a visiting American tourist, Henry Travers (Peter van Eyck), rescues beautiful young Marion (Dawn Addams) when she attempts to fling herself from the hotel's rooftop. What could have terrified her enough to take her own life? Could the evil doctor be back in business... or perhaps his successor, operating right under the police's noses?

A stylish and often dizzying ride through '60s art house and spy territory (two years before James Bond!), *The Thousand Eyes of Dr. Mabuse* never received the recognition it deserved in the US thanks to its drive-in oriented release in a dubbed version which has since become a public domain mainstay. The videos circulating from companies like Sinister Cinema are only a pale shadow of the DVD from AllDay, which boasts a magnificent, razor-sharp transfer. Lang's film relies on the nightmarish implications of technology, such as the thousands of cameras (Mabuse's "eyes") imbedded in the Luxor to monitor the guests, and this glossy restoration fully restores a much-needed clarity to convey a palpable atmosphere of doom-laden unease.

The DVD also restores the superior German soundtrack with optional English subtitles; again the audio is a quantum leap over the scratchy dub tracks we've been hearing for ages. The alternate English version is also included for those who don't want to read, and it's surprisingly good for a '60s German title. The disc also includes a 35 minute featurette, "The Thousand Eyes of Fritz Lang," which includes interviews with Lang fans like Forrest J. Ackerman and Richard Gordon tracing Lang's history and his influence from pre-WWII Germany to the '60s, as well as more extras discussed below.

Although it didn't break through around the world as much as its predecessor, Lang's film was successful enough in Europe to initiate a slew of further Mabuse films by other directors (with the last one by Jess Franco!), some of them better than others. One of the more unusual was a sequel-cum-remake of *The Testament of Dr. Mabuse*, an updated revamp of Lang's classic that transports the basic concept into a more hi-tech arena of '60s crime epics.

Since there's no way to top a classic, this film is best approached as a continuation of the series with several familiar returning faces from the earlier '60s films (*The Return of Dr. Mabuse* and *The Invisible Dr. Mabuse* were released in the interim). Commissioner Lohmann (Gert Fröbe again) is more than a little perturbed when Berlin is rocked by crimes that betray the involvement of the nefarious Dr. Mabuse (Wolfgang Preiss), who now resides within the walls of an insane asylum. A major gold heist from an armoured truck is the most recent criminal feat, with the perpetrators even having the wit to hand over some bus fare to their victims before taking off with the loot. The gang of evildoers receives its instructions from a shadowy figure behind a screen who keeps his latest secret hidden behind a deadly electrified wall, but no one knows the full evil plot or can see the mastermind's face. Could Mabuse be engineering the whole thing from his cell?

Once again this *Mabuse* features a strong international cast, with Helmut Schmid (*The Head*) and a turn by lovely Senta Berger as good girl Nelly. Also be sure to look for Günter Meisner, better known as Mr. Slugworth from *Willy Wonka and the Chocolate Factory* and the iron lung Nazi from *In a Glass Cage*, as one of Mabuse's cronies. The film itself holds up very well on its own terms and delivers plenty of twists and thrills along the way; the catchy jazz/lounge score is also a major asset.

AllDay's DVD once again looks magnificent, though the source materials have obviously weathered rougher storms than Lang's film. The opening twenty minutes in particular feature a few traces of irreparable damage, but the image quality itself is first rate and particularly remarkable when you consider that this film is lucky to exist now at all. Only fleetingly released in the US by Thunder Pictures in dubbed form as *The Terror of the Mad Doctor* and *The Terror of Dr. Mabuse* (this version's onscreen title), this film has been lovingly presented with its original German soundtrack intact (with optional subtitles) along with the serviceable English dub. The disc also includes *The Crimes of Dr. Mabuse,* the 75 minute '50s variant of Lang's original classic with an English dubbed soundtrack. It isn't a replacement for the two hour original, which will hopefully see the light of DVD one of these days, but this is a nice extra and features image quality comparable to an above average public domain tape.

Both Mabuse DVDs feature an amusing, stylish opener editing together the various cinematic incarnations of Mabuse (complete with the doctor's name repeated several dozen times in astonishment). The comic-style menus lead to a gallery of poster art from all of the Mabuse films, ranging from Lang's silent 1922 original (*Dr. Mabuse the Gambler*) to the rarely seen Franco instalment. Where available, English language trailers have also been included for each film, most of them apparently lifted from videotape but watchable nonetheless.

AllDay's David Kalat, a passionate devotee of Mabuse cinema, provides in-depth commentaries for both films which interlock together and are best experienced back to back. He provides a seemingly endless wealth of information, covering all of the participants in the transition of Mabuse from page to screen, the creation of the 1922 and 1933 version, the variant existing versions of the first Testament, the studio process that led to the Mabuse resurgence in 1960, and much, much more. Along the way he even debunks a few myths surrounding Lang and *Testament*, making one long to see even more Mabuse films turn up on DVD for further comparison.

THUNDERBALL

Colour, 1965, 130m. / Directed by Guy Hamilton / Starring Sean Connery, Claudine Auger / MGM / WS (2.35:1) (16:9) / DD5.1

James Bond (Connery) is recalled from the health clinic where he's recuperating from injuries incurred on a recent mission to probe the theft of two nuclear missiles by criminal organization SPECTRE. Following the trail to Nassau in the Bahamas, Bond crosses swords with wealthy playboy Emilio Largo (Celi), who he immediately suspects could be the man behind the crime.

By 1965 the Bond movies were in full swing; the previous year's *Goldfinger* had been a runaway success and the pressure was on to feed 007-hungry audiences with a bigger, brasher, even more fantastical adventure than any they had seen to date. Terence Young, who previously helmed *Dr. No* and *From Russia with Love*, was called back into service and Sean Connery, now slightly reluctantly, returned as Bond, donning the toupee for the fourth time. Connery was the ultimate 007 and here he's at his debonair best, striding confidently through the mayhem, bedding babes and bagging baddies with that inimitable ease unique to the James Bond universe.

Adolfo Celi is suitably nefarious as piratical Sicilian nasty Largo, whom Bond relieves of a pile of cash at the baccarat tables, the allegiance of his mistress *Domino (Twitch of the Death Nerve*'s Claudine Auger), the lives of most of his co-conspirators and, ultimately, his prized motorlaunch-cum-hydrofoil. Luciana Paluzzi is stunning as titian-haired assassin Fiona. Worth seeing for the climax alone - a beautifully lit and exquisitely staged underwater battle between brightly-wetsuited NATO troops and black-clad SPECTRE frogmen - *Thunderball* is quintessential Bond and remains one of the best in the 19-film Eon canon. Half-heartedly remade in 1983 (with Connery back for one last gasp) as the rogue *Never Say Never Again*.

Previously available as a deluxe boxed laserdisc set, most of the peripheral treasures included on that release have been included on MGM's Special Edition DVD. Except, that is, the hugely entertaining 1965 TV special "The Incredible World of James Bond," sadly omitted due to space. However, there's more than enough other material to make amends, including two commentaries (with input from director Young, editor Peter Hunt and screenwriter John Hopkins), a chunky gallery of

T

photographs, two half-hour documentaries narrated by Patrick Macnee, "Inside Thunderball" (a featurette comparing curious dialogue and musical cue variations between alternate versions of the film), three trailers, five TV spots and ten radio spots. The last time *Thunderball* itself looked this good was the first time I ever saw it, on a double bill with *Dr. No* back in 1972, when the film was a splice-free seven years old and I was only a little older. The 2.35:1 matted print is spectacularly flawless and divided into a ridiculously generous 52 chapters. Languages and subtitle options are available in English and French. - TG

TIE ME UP! TIE ME DOWN!

Colour, 1990, 111m. / Directed by Pedro Almodóvar / Starring Victoria Abril, Antonio Banderas / Anchor Bay (US R1 NTSC) / WS (1.85:1) (16:9)

Most notorious as one of the key films in establishing the ineffectual NC-17 rating in the US, Pedro Almodóvar's quirky romantic twist on *The Collector* didn't exactly win over too many feminist fans, though it looks positively politically correct compared to subsequent, similar efforts like *Boxing Helena* and *Buffalo 66*.

The film's highly promoted sexual content, which is mostly limited to a bit of self-gratification with a toy scuba diver and one sweaty sex scene, probably won't raise too many eyebrows among those who have ever watched cable TV, but Almodóvar fans will find this a poignant little comedy made just before the filmmaker took the plunge into full throttle melodrama with films like *Live Flesh* and *The Flower of My Secret*.

Upon his release from a mental institution, the handsome and superficially sweet Ricky (Antonio Banderas) seeks out neurotic junkie Marina (Victoria Abril), a former porn star and struggling legit actress with whom he had a one night stand. Naturally, he decides to propose to her by breaking into her apartment, smacking her around, and tying her up in her bed to prove what a worthy mate he can be. Meanwhile Marina's sister, Lola (Loles Leon), fears the fragile starlet has succumbed once again to her addictions and has retired from professional life. Mayhem ensues involving Marina's horny elderly director, a tough drug-dealing biker chick (played by Almodóvar's unforgettable beak-nosed muse, Rossy de Palma), musical numbers, and much more.

Had it been made by a straight American filmmaker, *Tie Me Up! Tie Me Down!* would seem irredeemably sexist and macho in its depiction of captive and captor becoming sympathetic to each other. However, Almodóvar typically has another agenda entirely hidden beneath the surface, gradually dissecting the relationship between two deeply battered souls unable to find their place in society. Ricky's use of physical abuse in one scene is difficult to swallow in this regard and throws in an unnecessary false note, but otherwise the film handles the material as delicately as possible and allows the two performers to shine. Their chemistry really carries the film, and Almodóvar's standard candy-coloured production design leaves a cheerful impression which negates some of the more bitter moments.

Stranded for the first time without his long-time composer, Bernardo Bonezzi, the director made the unusual choice of selecting the legendary Ennio Morricone to supply the tender and haunting music score, which happens to be one of his best during that decade. And make sure you don't miss that song at the end!

Back in the days when Miramax was free from the family-friendly control of Disney, they made a minor fortune with controversial items like this in art houses. The video rights originally went to Columbia/TriStar, who issued the film uncut in a very attractive, widescreen laserdisc edition. However, Miramax's switch to the Mickey Mouse Empire resulted in the sad unavailability of their more controversial material.

Fortunately a licensing deal allowed Anchor Bay to present the film intact on DVD in a striking new widescreen edition; even the theatrical prints didn't look this sharp and pristine. The optional yellow English subtitles are easy to read and identical to past editions, and the disc also includes the amusing Spanish trailer (with optional subs), which would never be shown in US movie houses and differs significantly from the bland trailer Miramax later supplied.

Alas, Anchor Bay has made one unfortunate goof: the DVD is in mono, while every other theatrical and home video incarnation has retained the original Dolby Stereo soundtrack. While the two channel mono sound here is perfectly clear and dynamic, the loss of surround support to Morricone's score is regrettable, and the oversight is especially irritating for a company that prides itself on providing the finest soundtracks possible. (Oddly, their press materials originally announced this film with a 5.1 remix, so one can only guess what happened.)

T

TIERRA

Colour, 1996, 117m. / Directed by Julio Medem / Starring Carmelo Gómez, Emma Suárez / Vanguard (US R1 NTSC) / WS (2.35:1) / DD2.0

One of the many new mavericks of the new wave of Spanish filmmakers, Julio Medem earned his name overseas first with his witty erotic thriller, *The Red Squirrel*, and on a more widespread front with his *Lovers of the Arctic Circle*. Between these films lies *Tierra*, a stunningly filmed and thoughtful psychological fantasy. Located entirely in the rugged outskirts of Spain, where the people rely upon the earth in more ways than one, this difficult but rewarding effort clearly establishes its creator as a voice worth hearing in the future.

Called in to lead a fumigation effort to rid a village of pesky woodlice that are causing an earthy taste in the local wine, Angel (Carmelo Gómez) arrives and immediately encounters (or sets off?) a series of mystical events. Believing he is half angel (and thus "half dead," in his words), Angel seems to offer far more answers than the average human being. On his way to town, he first encounters a shepherd who has been struck by lightning. As he dies, the shepherd bequeaths to Angel the sheep that were also killed by lightning, so Angel brings one of them to a local family. This household contains more than its fair share of problems, including a suicidal patriarch unable to cope with his wife's death and a sweet-natured daughter, Angela (Emma Suárez), saddled with a louse of a husband. The uninhibited Mari (Silke), who also happens to be the occasional mistress of Angela's husband, also makes a play for Angel, who relies upon his heavenly alter ego to guide him along and make the right decisions in his life.

Often surprising and certainly original, *Tierra* is one of the more intriguing foreign films of the past few years. Though overlong, its slow pacing and mystical imagery still make for compelling viewing, with the viewer often left in the dark as to what is real and what is fantasy, what is terrestrial and what is supernatural. The enveloping score by Almodóvar's current composer of choice, Alberto Iglesias, often lends poignancy and a sense of solidarity every time the film threatens to wander off into the cosmos, and the actors all do well with roles of varying degrees of difficulty.

Vanguard's acceptable if unspectacular presentation of *Tierra* looks crisp and preserves the full scope framing, with the surround audio track always rich and clear. The appropriately earth colour schemes pose a few problems during daylight scenes, with some grain and colour distortion occasionally evident, and a nasty transfer glitch (some jittery blue bars) inexplicably appears for a couple of frames near the 90 minute mark. These flaws aside, though, the DVD makes for the best way to see this outside a theatre, and the burned-in English subtitles are almost always legible and appropriately paced. The intriguing European trailer is also included.

TIGER BAY

B&W, 1959, 102m. / Directed by J. Lee Thompson / Starring Hayley Mills, Horst Buchholz / Image (US R1 NTSC)

Before she became America's favourite little import in a string of hit Disney films, Hayley Mills made a splash as a young tomboy who finds herself entangled with a murderer in this underrated, strangely effective thriller that manages to avoid almost every convention established by Hitchcock. If you thought Hayley never made a movie much more intense than *The Moonspinners*, take a look at this one.

In what could be seen as a kinder, gentler dry run for his later *Cape Fear*, director Thompson deftly weaves a simple, surprising tale about young Gillie (Mills), a neglected child who turns to dishonesty and pranks to get attention. One day in her apartment building she witnesses a young Polish sailor (Horst Buchholz, an underused actor best known for Billy Wilder's *One, Two, Three*) shoot his girlfriend during a heated argument. Gillie swipes the sailor's gun and takes it to church where she shows it off to her best friend. Unfortunately, the sailor tracks her down, and the two decide to go on the run with the police, led by inspector John Mills (Hayley's father) determined to uncover the truth.

While most TV and video prints of *Tiger Bay* have been pitiful (washed out, no grey scale, and so on), the Janus print presented by Image is extremely crisp and satisfying, with the only noticeable signs of wear appearing during the opening and closing titles. The image appears to have been opened up to expose the full frame, as a minor black matte briefly appears twice at the top of the screen during the film. The elegant film noir-style photography is enhanced greatly by this transfer, which features deep and smooth blacks with no noticeable artefacts and only occasional, mild film grain.

Unlike most American films of the period, *Tiger Bay* features an intriguing clash of cultures and races - black, Polish, Russian, Cockney, and Pakistani coexist in a sort of uneasy alliance against the forces of oppression (represented by the police), and this complete British print even includes some surprising profanity that would never have made it past US censors of the day. The actual violence level is very mild; suspense mounts because the filmmakers continually invert traditional stereotypes - the killer is sympathetic, the child is anything but sweet and innocent, and the man who is wrongly accused (Anthony Dawson, who excelled at playing slimeballs in *Dial M for Murder* and *Dr. No*) is the most unpleasant man in the film. The viewer's sympathies become more and more resistant to the efforts of the inspector to the point where loyalties are completely turned against him by the finale-you'll find yourself rooting for Hayley to lie to protect her guilt-ridden friend. The unexpected final scene is haunting and strangely satisfying for a narrative that seems to have no way out and manages to be sad, uplifting, and totally appropriate at the same time.

THE TIGER OF ESCHNAPUR
Colour, 1959, 101m.
THE INDIAN TOMB
Colour, 1959, 102m. / Directed by Fritz Lang / Starring Debra Paget, Paul Hubschmid, Walter Reyer
Fantoma (US R1 NTSC)

The films of legendary director Fritz Lang became increasingly difficult to see after his return to Germany, following a successful and varied career in Hollywood. In a sense this period found him reworking motifs and characters from his early days in pre-Nazi Germany, where he crafted such influential masterworks as *Metropolis* and *The Testament of Dr. Mabuse*. In his twilight years Lang turned out the fascinating *1,000 Eyes of Dr. Mabuse* and, most surprisingly, a vividly colourful quasi-serial, the conjoined *Tiger of Eschnapur* and *The Indian Tomb* (which here bears the onscreen title *Tomb of Love*). Dubbed and hacked down into one rushed and ineffective feature by AIP (who chose the name of *Journey to the Lost City* to christen the bastardized results), these films have

long remained a tantalizing footnote in most Lang scholarly studies, where few have actually seen these films and rumours of the unexpurgated versions remained a holy grail for many English-speaking viewers.

Fortunately Lang's original works have survived intact and made their way to DVD in editions that would have made their creator proud. Works of intense narrative and visual skill, these films chart the adventures of good guy Harald Berger (Paul Hubschmid), an architect whose arrival in the mystical Indian province of Eschnapur opens his eyes to a wide new array of customs and personalities. Chief among these is the Maharaja (Walter Reyer), whose beautiful handmaiden and sacred dancer, half-white Seetha (an amusingly dubbed Debra Paget at her most ravishing), steals Harald's heart. Their romantic idylls trigger a chain reaction of political deceit, with the Maharahaja's scheming brother (Rene Deltgen) conspiring to steal the throne by hunting down the lovers and using them as evidence of the ruling power's corruption. Throw into this mix a series of elaborate religious ceremonies, a horde of scary and malnourished quasi-zombie denizens beneath the holy palace, a showdown in a pit with a hungry tiger, and a cliff-hanger finale for Tiger which finds Harald and Seetha hounded into a desert storm, where they lie unconscious (but most likely not dead!). Tiger promises to tell of their further adventures in *The Indian Tomb*, which finds Harald's associate (Claus Holm) and sister Irene (Sabine Bethmann) drawn into the treacherous plot and roaming the vast, deadly caves of the holy city while Seetha is forced to perform one of the most eye-popping and sexually provocative dances filmed during the 1950s. Meanwhile armies clash, peasants revolt, and enough double crosses take place to... well, fuel an entire serial.

Lang contributed the screenplay to a silent 1921 version of *The Indian Tomb* (based upon the novel by his then-wife, Thea von Harbou, and directed by Joe May), which starred Conrad Veidt as the nefarious villain and featured a slightly different, more traditional structure. (This sprawling version is also available on DVD in a restored edition from Image courtesy of David Shepherd.) Now given the reigns as director, Lang indulges in a sumptuous array of locations shot in vivid colour, with each camera set up providing a treat for the eyes.

The cast also performs quite well once one gets over the shock of hearing German actors voicing all of the roles, regardless of the actors' nationalities. Paget - usually cast in prim and proper costume roles - really takes centre stage here, making a vivid

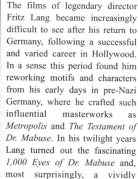

T

impression which takes hold even during the long stretches in the second film when she disappears. Even the potentially racist tactic of greasepainting German actors to portray Indian peasantry and royalty comes off better than expected, thanks to the sincere and convincing portrayals of everyone involved and the dynamic nature of Lang's location shooting. Whether filling the screen with marching elephants or billowing sandstorms, Lang's framing seems to soak in the atmosphere of a magical land about which most viewers can only dream.

Though VHS editions of the shortened US version have circulated among the PD and grey market venues, Fantoma's DVDs are a marvel, derived from the original unmatted negatives without any damage or visual compromises in sight (apart from some questionable technical glitches during the actual filming). The image is so razor sharp you can even see the wires holding up a tiger outfit during one crucial shot in the first film, and the colours have a deep, saturated quality which lifts this up with the best transfers of MGM musicals. Though not really known as a colour visual stylist, Lang proves himself quite comfortable here with the possibilities of a wide chromatic palette at his disposal.

Elegant and attractive menus offer the option of watching the films in dubbed English or the original German with optional English subtitles; while the latter still dubs Paget's voice, the dialogue is more often in sync with the actors and appears to be much truer to Lang's intent. The subtitles appear to be freshly translated, as they don't always quite match the dialogue of the dubbed track. The discs also contain fold-out liner notes by Tom Gunning, who offers a good thumbnail sketch of their production history and the status of Lang's career at the time.

THE TIME MACHINE

Colour, 1960, 103m. / Directed by George Pal / Starring Rod Taylor, Alan Young, Yvette Mimieux / Warner (US R1 NTSC) / WS (1.85:1) (16:9) / DD5.1

You'd be hard pressed to find a more satisfying matinee sci-fi movie than *The Time Machine*, George Pal's stupendously enjoyable look at time hopping from the Victorian era to the vast, unimaginable future. Based more or less on the novel by H.G. Wells, this film deftly avoids the fatal flaw of most modern science fiction yarns - namely, it never allows the special effects to supplant good, basic storytelling with believable, solid performances.

At the turn of the century, a dinner party of gentlemen arrives at the home of George (Rod Taylor), an inventor who seems to be running late after retiring to his basement for a few days. Suddenly George bursts into the room, looking exhausted and dirty, breathlessly exclaiming strange remarks about his recent experiences. "Go on," urges his friend, David Filby (Alan Young), "You have all the time in the world." Our bemused inventor agrees and tells his tale. Several days earlier he demonstrates to his friends a miniature device capable of time travel; however, he has also devised a larger mechanism capable of propelling himself through time. He tests the machine out, at first just a few hours and days at a time while watching a store mannequin outside his window change along with the seasons. He stops and wanders outside to meet Filby's grown son, who explains his father had died in "the war." An alarmed George returns to his machine and skips along past World War II. However, the advent of a nuclear attack in 1966 sends him outside again to witness the impending destruction, which sends lava(!) pouring through the streets of London. George returns to his machine again, where he is encased by a stone mountain and must skip forward thousands of years for the process of erosion to free him again. Sure enough, by the time he emerges, George observes a wholly different planet, populated by gentle, peace-loving, and thoroughly lazy blond people called the Eloi, who serve as the food source for a monstrous underground race called the Morlocks. George takes a particular liking to Weena (Yvette Mimieux), the prettiest of the Eloi. When the time machine is dragged off by the Morlocks, George must lead the Eloi in a struggle to earn their freedom and retrieve his means of going back to his own time.

Though it could have been an average afternoon programmer, *The Time Machine* epitomizes everything that set George Pal's films apart from their peers. The time machine itself is a fascinating conception, and it's no wonder this film sparked an entire generation of filmmakers obsessed with the concept (particularly *Time After Time* and the *Back to the Future* series). Aussie-born Taylor adapts reasonably well to his British character, while *Mr. Ed*'s Young is, well, passable doing a Scottish brogue. The special effects still hold up well, with the climactic battle in the Morlocks' cavern still a rousing achievement today. Though it may not seem like much now, the bittersweet ending is also very effective and an usually subtle gesture on the part of the filmmakers; it's nice to see a film that doesn't pander down to even its youngest audiences and instead allows them to use their imaginations.

Like their restoration of *North by Northwest*, Warner's DVD of *The Time Machine* is a stunner in every respect and easily obliterates every previous video edition. The source material looks fantastic, with perfect flesh tones and an astonishing depth of detail without any noticeable blemishes. It's so clear you can even spot which of the burning Morlocks are actually sporting padded T-shirts. The 5.1 audio mix remains faithful to the original stereo tracks while fleshing out some of the more dynamic music passages and loud sound effects, particularly during the nuclear destruction scene. A few subtle split surrounds creep in as well; just check out the exterior Victorian street shots.

The disc also includes the engaging theatrical trailer and "*The Time Machine*: The Journey Back," a nostalgic 47 minute documentary. Taylor serves as host and, as with his appearance on the special edition of *The Birds*, he still seems like a very nice, knowledgeable guy and makes for good company on this little voyage. The film covers all of the basics, from the source novel to the bizarre history behind the time machine itself. (You really won't believe what it went through over the years.) Mercifully this was completed before the ill-advised DreamWorks remake. Young and Whit Bissel also pop by to share their own experiences with the film, and the overwhelming impression is a sense of complete admiration and love for George Pal, who obviously put everything he had into this terrific movie.

THE TINGLER

B&W/Colour, 1959, 81m. / Directed by William Castle / Starring Vincent Price, Judith Evelyn / Columbia (US R1 NTSC) / WS (1.78:1) (16:9) / DD2.0

Fondly remembered by drive-in buffs and revered by cult movie addicts, William Castle's *The Tingler* features enough surprises and twists to confound any first-time viewer, not to mention a dynamic performance by Vincent Price as a doctor determined to uncover the physical results of human fear. Of course, it's also a pretty spiffy monster movie, too.

Dr. Warren Chapin (Price) has made an unusual discovery; his autopsies on executed prisoners reveal that humans who die in situations of extreme stress or panic have their spines torn and snapped. How could this be? Warren dubs this force "The Tingler" - that strange sensation people experience in situations of mounting fear. His gold-digging wife, Isabel (Patricia Cutts, doing a funny impersonation of Grace Kelly gone bad), scoffs at his notions and occasionally plans to murder him, just for the hell of it. However, Warren's assistant, David (Darryl Hickman from *The Many Loves of Dobie Gillis*), takes these studies more seriously as the good doctor uses any means at his disposal to further his studies. Warren pretends to kill his wife, causing her to faint, and the subsequent X-rays reveal that the Tingler is actually a strange, lobster-shaped creature that feeds on terror and grows at the base of the spine. The doc shoots up with LSD (apparently a screen first) to create a mindset of unrestrained hysteria, but he expresses his anguish with a scream, presumably the release that paralyzes this beast. Martha (Judith Evelyn), a deaf mute movie theatre owner who only shows silent films, provides an important find in the research process, but when our heroes find a real live extracted Tingler on their hands, matters veer wildly out of control... and the fun really begins.

Rapidly paced, luridly plotted, and enthusiastically executed, *The Tingler* shows off all of Castle's strengths as a master showman and filmmaker. While Hitchcock was crafting elegant Hollywood entertainment, Castle simply tried to grab his patrons by the throat and give them a rollicking good time, which he delivers here in spades. The original theatrical run was presented in "Percepto," whereby patrons during the "Tingler in a movie theatre" sequence were given little shocks of electricity to simulate the monster's attack. The result, of course, was giddy insanity as Price's voice urges patrons to "scream for your lives!" In another gimmick, the black and white image suddenly turns to blood red tinted colour for one scare sequence involving a sanguinary bathroom sink and tub, and some theatres even slammed on the house lights when Price informed patrons that someone in the audience had fainted and was being carried out - duplicated in the actual theatre by a planted viewer.

While Percepto would be impossible to duplicate in a home theatre environment (unless you're a very craft electrician), the other two gimmicks are more or less present and accounted for on the DVD. The colour sequence looks rich and startling, much better than the muddy brown "blood" on the laser (though grainy as always, a flaw inherent in the only decent existing material), and Columbia has actually uncovered a variation on the "Scream!" sequence amusingly designed for drive-ins. The anamorphic transfer (who woulda thought?) looks beautiful and well balanced, with Von Dexter's kitschy *Vertigo*-inspired score sounding clear and punchy. Though mono, the opening screams alone should give your sound system a real workout - and for those of you set up for surround, there's one very nice, well timed surprise. The DVD also includes a nifty featurette with Hickman talking about the making of the film, plus footage of Castle and reminiscences of the film's splashy opening in San Antonio. Also includes the original theatrical trailer.

TOKYO DECADENCE

Colour, 1992, 112m. / Directed by Ryu Murakami / Starring Miho Nikaido, Mashiko Shimada / Image (US R1 NTSC)

 The only film by noted Japanese novelist/filmmaker Ryu Murakami to genuinely gain international arthouse acceptance, *Tokyo Decadence (Topâzu)* gained notoriety for its sexual frankness and the obvious MPAA ratings controversy that ensued. Of course, as with most foreign imports, the erotic hype left a lot of viewers confused by the actual product itself, which focuses on the emotional and spiritual devastation wrought by the intense bureaucratizing of Japan.

More reliant on ambience than plot, the film follows the day to day routine of Ai (Miho Nikaido), a young prostitute specializing in bondage, sadomasochism, and any other sexual bent that might appeal to buttoned-down Japanese businessmen. Though she finds herself emotionally numbed by her work, she feels that she has no real worth or special talents that might allow her to make a decent contribution to society. When not fending off the impending dangers of the Yakuza or the pain-obsessed fetishes of some of her clients, she finds her time empty, capable of being filled only with the temporary void of her work.

Originally released in Japan at 135 minutes, *Tokyo Decadence* was trimmed down to a more workable running time (under two hours) for international distribution. This same cut is presented on DVD, in Japanese with English subtitles. Various sources have debated how much substance was actually cut out of the film, as it isn't close to hardcore but is quite explicit even in its current state here. (The Internet Movie Database features an exhaustive list of the purported trims from the Japanese print but incorrectly asserts that these cuts were done to achieve an R rating.) The film easily lives up to its title in a number of scenes, particularly one involving a twist on water sports, but the level of eroticism will depend primarily on the

viewer's individual tastes. As with all Japanese titles up to that time, the prohibition of pubic hair allows the filmmakers to channel the explicit thrills to the screen in some wildly unorthodox fashions, usually through the aid of suggestion and bizarre methods of body concealment (usually leather in this case). In one particularly strange and harrowing sequence, Ai is trussed up (in a fashion best not described here) and paraded around on the floor by a married man whose wife joins in on the phone, then in person. Certainly not for all tastes, but along with Just Jaeckin's *Story of O* and Radley Metzger's *The Image*, this remains one of the few successful attempts to present undiluted S&M designed for mainstream consumption.

The DVD of *Tokyo Decadence* replicates the same transfer used for the VHS and laserdisc releases but features the added bonus of the alternate English dubbed track in addition to the usual mono Japanese (with yellow, burned-in English subtitles). Compared to the natural Japanese, the English dubbing sounds rather harsh and stilted most of the time, but it's interesting to watch the film this way for a few minutes. The image appears to be mildly cropped from 1.66:1; while no significant information appears to be missing, it's a little on the claustrophobic side at times. Some of the darker blacks in the film have turned blue, a quality not present in the theatrical prints. Turning down the brightness control on the TV monitor corrects most of this problem and actually improves the image significantly, though the aforementioned floor crawling scene (mostly set in shadows) still presents some "glowing blue" flaws with the source material.

For anyone interested in Japanese arthouse erotica in the wake of Nagisa Oshima's *In the Realm of the Senses,* this film is highly recommended viewing for open-minded viewers willing to overlook some of the flaws.

TOKYO DRIFTER

Colour, 1966, 83m. / Directed by Seijun Suzuki / Starring Eiji Go, Chieko Matsubara, Tetsuya Watari / Criterion (US R1 NTSC) / WS (2.0:1)

 In its rapturous liner notes, Criterion describes *Tokyo Drifter (Tokyo Nagaremono)* as equal parts Russ Meyer, Samuel Fuller, and Nagisa Oshima, with packaging clearly designed to target the growing American audience primed for Japanese and Hong Kong cinema thanks to the efforts of John Woo, Quentin Tarantino, et al. However, viewers expecting a slam bang visceral ballet of non-stop gunplay and sex are bound to be disappointed; while Suzuki's film does contain these elements in fits and starts, it's generally a static visual study of alienation in a candy-coloured Tokyo gone mad, much closer to deliberately paced '60s Japanese camp like *Black Lizard* than *Hard Boiled*.

"Phoenix" Tetsu (Tetsuya Watari), a killer for hire, decides to go straight and follow the example set by his seemingly conscience-stricken boss. Unfortunately, he soon finds himself drifting around the deserted areas of Tokyo, both eluding and awaiting a certain death at the hands of the villainous Viper (Tamio Kawaji) but returning for the company of his nightclub singer girlfriend (Chieko Matsubara).

The gunfights are staged with detached elegance and precise editing that foreshadows many of the ironic showdowns popularized in modern action cinema, in much the same manner as Jean-Pierre Melville's similar output in France during the same period. For the impatient, though, the film can be a trial. The first half hour is extremely static and almost unbearably vague at times, but it does pick up and clarify itself once the story kicks into gear. Mostly, though, this is a work of sublime artifice, from Watari's wounded dog and sunglasses demeanour to Matsubara's pastel-coloured musical setpieces.

Simply having access to a film like this on DVD at all is something of a miracle, which makes the flaws in Criterion's presentation that much more forgivable. While the film was shot in full 2.35:1 scope, this transfer is squeezed out enough to give the characters' heads an irritating oblong appearance. Also, it doesn't quite live up to the box's hyperbolic claims of "a lush colour transfer from the original, glorious Nikkatsu-scope master." The colours are actually pretty dull and washed out most of the time, with far too much contrast in the skin tones (similar to the harsh transfer given to *Pulp Fiction*), but adjusting your TV (or your DVD player if you can) to boost up the colour allows the film to return to some semblance of its original eye-popping hues.

The English subtitles are optional, allowing you to gawk at some of the more outlandish camera setups without the impediment of words plastered across the screen.

Strangely, Manohla Dargis' generally inform-ative liner notes refer to the opening sequence (presented in black and white in this print) as being "tinted a bilious green," indicating either a faulty memory or a slip up during the film's transfer process.

The DVD also includes an endearing interview with Suzuki in which he describes his maverick filmmaking decisions, which eventually led to his banishment from the Japanese movie studio system. Overall, this is a nice, attractively packaged disc, but you may want to try to find a rental copy before buying it.

TOMB OF TORTURE

B&W, 1963, 88m. / Directed by William Grace (Antonio Boccaci) / Starring Annie Alberti, Adriano Micantoni / Image (US R0 NTSC) / WS (1.77:1)

This theatrical companion piece to *Cave of the Living Dead* is an ultra-gothic Italian affair originally known as *Metempsyco*. Sort of a second rung entry in the creepy castle shockers being turned out by Bava and Antonio Margheriti, this film stands out thanks to the sumptuous nature of its imagery and the viciousness of its horror elements.

A grotesquely deformed creature stalks the hallways of the castle of Countess Irene, a vanished and presumably dead aristocrat who may be inhabiting the body of beautiful young Anna (Annie Alberti). Tormented by nightmares, Anna goes to the castle with her father, Dr. Darnell (Adriano Micantoni), in hopes of uncovering the dark secrets of her psyche and possibly discovering the true fate of the countess. Anna's appearance strikes a number of dramatic responses from the locals, including the Countess' former paramour, an Indian inexplicably wearing brownface and a turban. Meanwhile a local reporter investigating two recent deaths at the castle meets Anna, and sparks fly - but soon after she's spirited off, perhaps to relive the violent fate of her predecessor...

Despite apparently being cobbled together from at least two different prints, this disc presentation of *Tomb of Torture* looks superb for most of its running time. Don't let the dog-eared opening shots fool you! The photography and set design provide most of the film's effectiveness, and the DVD is a perfect showcase to savour every carefully plotted frame. Incidentally, both films were tinted in some territories and subsequently released that way for some of their video incarnations. While *Cave of the Living Dead* indicates a sepia tone presentation, both titles are actually in original, lustrous black and white.

TOMBS OF THE BLIND DEAD
Colour, 1972, 102m. / Directed by Amando De Ossorio / Starring Lone Fleming, Cesar Burner
RETURN OF THE BLIND DEAD
Colour, 1973, 90m. / Directed by Amando De Ossorio / Starring Tony Kendall, Esther Roy
Anchor Bay (US R1 NTSC) / WS (1.66:1)

The early '70s Spanish shocker *Tombs of the Blind Dead* used to scare the daylights out of viewers when it regularly turned up in a cut version on late night TV (simply under the title *The Blind Dead*). The start of a successful four film series, this film introduces the Templar Knights, horseback-riding skeletal zombies who hunt their victims by sound (including their heartbeat) because the Knights' eyes were torn out by crows after they were tortured and left for dead by villagers. (The mythology is altered somewhat in the sequel, where their eyes are burned out by torches instead.) In the best horror tradition, De Ossorio allows a slow, steady build-up to the horror, stopping amusingly along the way for a totally gratuitous lesbian schoolgirl flashback (scissored from most prints). However, when a group of young men and women (obviously not Rhodes scholars) decide to camp out near the old stomping grounds of the Templars, the fun begins. This print features quite a bit of over the top gore that will startle anyone used to the US version (released on video in the early '80s by Paragon), and the choice to present it in Spanish with English subtitles (non-optional, alas) restores quite a bit of the film's dignity. The final train massacre is particularly shocking, with one image involving a small child that will make your jaw drop.

The Templars returned in *Ataque de los muertos sin ojos*, released to US drive-ins as *Return of the Evil Dead*. The film (retitled on the packaging to continue its Blind Dead heritage) is much more fast-moving than its predecessors and far more ferocious in its scares and violence. The story is basically a variation on the first, with a town gathering to celebrate the annual commemoration of the vanquishing of the Templars. Naturally, the boys crawl out of their graves and decide to crash the party. The blood flies fast and furious, with a nudity-filled flashback sequence thrown in to remind you of a similar bit in the first film. Though dubbed in English, this is really every bit as fun as the original; here's hoping the other films in the series, *Horror of the Zombies (The Ghost Galleon)* and the excellent *Night of the Seagulls* receive the same treatment in the near future.

The Elite laserdiscs and Anchor Bay DVD are quite similar in their presentations, though the Anchor Bay version is obviously a better bargain. The colour on the Elite laserdisc of *Tombs* is a little punchier, but the DVD looks crisper and can be boosted in colour to look the same with a capable DVD player. *Return* looks comparable in both editions. The packaging of Elite's *Tombs* is attractive, though, with appreciative essay liner notes. Amusingly, both versions of *Tombs* are dedicated at the beginning to the "late" De Ossorio, who at the time of the disc's release was still among the living after all. Incidentally, *Return of the Blind Dead* is the longest English language version available and more complete than the earlier Bingo VHS edition, though some footage is apparently still missing compared to the rarely seen Spanish original thanks to the scissor-happy folks at Atlas.

TOMMY
Colour, 1975, 111m. / Directed by Ken Russell / Starring Oliver Reed, Ann-Margret, Roger Daltrey / Columbia (US R1 NTSC, UK R2 PAL) / WS (1.85:1) (16:9) / DD5.0

Ken Russell's manic film of The Who's rock opera, *Tommy*, adapted that best-selling double album into a visual feast with a host of familiar names delivering one song after another without any dialogue to impede the flow of music. For such a purely sensory experience, the film has fared quite badly on the small screen. Originally shown in a pre-Dolby sound process dubbed "Quintophonic" (five separate discrete channels of sound were pumped into the theatre), the film first debuted on home video from Columbia in an ugly, orange-hued transfer with a pallid basic stereo mix in which one channel simply echoed off the other with no discernable separation effects at all. The remastered widescreen laserdisc a few years ago was only a marginal improvement, with the surround mix basically matrixing out two stereo channels from the original mix. To make matters worse, the image quality was too pale and bright, and the overzealous letterboxing matted off a crucial amount of information on the top and bottom of the screen. Now on its third go-round, Columbia has gone back and painstakingly restored the original five-channel sound mix, and the results are, to say the least, breathtaking.

The story follows the narrative threads of the original album but tosses in a couple of extra songs

("Champagne," "Bernie's Holiday Camp") as showcases for Ann-Margret and Oliver Reed, respectively. In World War II, a newlywed, Nora Walker (Ann-Margret) loses her pilot husband (*Mahler*'s Robert Powell) in an aerial attack. She bears a son, Tommy, and eventually remarries the sleazy, conniving Frank (Reed). However, Captain Walker, badly scarred, is still alive and catches Nora and Frank in bed. In the heat of the moment, Frank kills the Captain, and little Tommy witnesses the entire sordid event. The guilty pair scream, "You didn't see it! You didn't hear it! You won't say nothing to no one ever in your life." Unfortunately, Tommy takes them literally and becomes deaf, dumb, and blind. When he grows up to become Roger Daltrey, Tommy is subjected to a number of attempted cures, including a trip to a Marilyn Monroe cult and an acid-dispensing diva (Tina Turner), while his various relatives including Cousin Kevin (*Lisztomania*'s Paul Nicholas) and Uncle Ernie (Keith Moon) molest and torment the poor guy. Tommy inexplicably becomes a famous pinball champion, playing only judging from the vibrations of the machine. He defeats the reigning Pinball Wizard (Elton John in some really great shoes) and becomes a pop culture messiah to thousands of teens. The bizarre events continue to unfold as Tommy finds himself exploited and commercialized until he eventually decides he must try to go back and find his true self.

Russell's treatment of *Tommy* is open to many interpretations, though his jabs at the insanity of the constructs of most organized religions stand virtually at face value. On first viewing this can seem overwhelming and bombastic, but a closer look reveals that Russell constructed the film carefully down to the last detail - note the repeated pinball and spherical imagery, right down to the silver ball cane Tommy carries, which mirrors the circular nature of the narrative itself. Rather than providing a firm beginning and end that spoon-feed the entire message on a first pass, the film operates on a number of levels ranging from intellectual to pure visual and aural texture. All of the performers seem to be putting in their all, with Ann-Margret giving a particularly impressive and uninhibited performance for which she justifiably received an Oscar nomination.

The care that was obviously lavished on the film becomes even more apparent on the DVD, which represents the first fully successful presentation of this film outside a movie theatre. The fullscreen side presents most of the available image, and the picture quality is absolutely stunning. *Tommy* has simply never looked like this before on video. The widescreen version is somewhat better judged than the previous laser and, best of all, is anamorphically enhanced. The colour purity is startling on both editions; the heavily saturated orange-red hues that suffuse the film at regular intervals right from the opening titles have appeared distorted and noisy before but look pure and vivid now. The audio reveals countless new pleasures to savour, with numerous sound effects and musical touches now present. Most noticeably, the "Go to the Mirror, Son" sequence, which features a singing Jack Nicholson as a doctor, has been fully restored. (Most damagingly, the widescreen laserdisc flipped the image of this scene halfway through for no discernable reason.) On the DVD, the scene plays out correctly, and at last, Ann-Margret can be heard clearly singing along with all of Oliver Reed's lines. The DVD packaging also includes an exhaustive explanation of the efforts Columbia went through to present the Quintophonic soundtrack in Dolby Digital; their labours were absolutely worth it and paid off for everyone who loves this film. No notable extras besides some skimpy bios, but considering the quality of the presentation, there's really no room at all to complain.

TOMORROW NEVER COMES

Colour, 1978, 102m. / Directed by Peter Collinson / Starring Oliver Reed, Susan George / Carlton (UK R2 PAL)

On a sweltering afternoon in the dead of summer, police lieutenant Jim Wilson (Oliver Reed) says goodbye to his colleagues and prepares for his last day on the job before returning to his hometown away from the depressing grind of the city beat. Meanwhile, the volatile Frank (Stephen McHattie) has just returned to town and plans to reunite with his girl, Janie (Susan George). While having a drink at a bar, he learns that Janie now has a new man in her life, "one who can afford her." Frank loses his temper and winds up losing in a bloody brawl. Bruised and battered, he staggers to Janie's small house and berates her for being unfaithful to him. A passing police officer hears the squabble and comes inside; Frank orders the officer outside and begins a scuffle, during which the officer is accidentally shot with his own gun. Faster than you can say *Dog Day Afternoon*, more police swarm outside and soon the entire city comes to a halt, as Jim and his fellow officers try to avoid further bloodshed.

One of the later films by British cult director Peter Collinson (*The Italian Job, The Penthouse*), this uneasy crime drama bends over backwards trying to convince viewers that they're watching American actors in an American film. Flat, awkward accents and bizarre fabricated slang abound, with Reed and George in particular seeming far too focused on their enunciation to be believable. Had the film stuck to a gritty British setting and aimed for a *Get Carter* style atmosphere, it could have been a real gem. Instead what we get is something quite odd, an inert police standoff that drags on for over an hour as McHattie (fresh off his disastrous leading turn in *Look What's Happened to Rosemary's Baby*) and George patch up their relationship inside. Raymond Burr even pops up occasionally for no good reason as Reed's supervisor, and Donald Pleasence has a glorified cameo as a doctor.

The film isn't a complete washout, however; Collinson's direction offers some ingenious visual moments, particularly when he focuses on the plot's impact on the tourist population. Prolific '70s composer Roy Budd also pitches in with a catchy, diverse funk and jazz score that keeps the film percolating even when nothing is happening onscreen. Former James Bond crooner Matt Monro is even on hand to warble the overwrought theme song, "Alone Am I."

Completely ignored and impossible to find in America, *Tomorrow Never Comes* has been released as an instalment in Carlton's budget DVD line of Rank Organization titles. The open matte transfer is extremely clean and vividly colourful, with the typical '70s softness and graininess kept at a surprising minimum. The barely stereo soundtrack is clean and strong, with some channel separation evident in the background music. A real oddity for crime film fanatics and devotees of bizarre film casting, this is worth the low price tag despite the film's often crippling flaws.

TOMORROW NEVER DIES

Colour, 1997, 119m. / Directed by Roger Spottiswoode / Starring Pierce Brosnan, Michelle Yeoh / MGM / WS (2.35:1) (16:9) / DD5.1

Insane press baron Elliott Carver (Pryce) sets about instigating a war between Britain and China to boost the ratings for the new television branch of his media empire. James Bond (Brosnan) follows him from Germany to Vietnam and on to a showdown aboard his hi-tech stealth boat in the South China Sea. Having risen like a phoenix from the flames of a legal wrangle that kept the series on hold for six years, *Goldeneye* was a relatively impressive dais on which Pierce Brosnan pitched his 007 debut. With *Tomorrow Never Dies* things went slightly awry. Certainly the requisite trimmings are all present and correct - gadgets, girls, guns and spectacular action by the bucketful. But the character of Bond himself has parted from his roots, adopting far too cavalier an attitude to danger; witness the finale as he strolls through the mayhem, firearms in both hands blazing, seemingly impervious to bullets, grenades and everything else his foes can throw at him. Sure, we know Bond will win the day, but without some sense of vulnerability one might just as well be watching any of a handful of indistinguishable Willis, Schwarzenegger or Stallone romps. Fortunately this facet was righted for Brosnan's third entry *The World Is Not Enough*.

In any event, director Roger Spottiswoode stages some jaunty bouts of excitement including an above average pre-titles breath-taker, pursuit through a multi-storey car park in Hamburg (with Bond steering his BMW from the back seat via a remote control facility in his mobile phone!), and a chase on a motorcycle through the backstreets of Saigon. Drafting in Michelle Yeoh had potential but beyond a single martial arts scuffle her talents are wasted. Jonathan Pryce isn't particularly nasty or, because of that, memorable, whilst his sidekick (Gotz Otto) is almost a caricature, all muscle, grimace and little else. And the less said about Teri Hatcher the better. Unquestionable entertainment on a grand scale, but in summation not among the most striking of the Bonds.

The film itself (encoded with 28 chapter breaks) may be one of the lesser entries in the Bond series, but the standard of MGM's special edition DVD is exceptionally high. Ensure you purchase the Region 1 version, however, since the Region 2 disc issued on British shores has been subjected to some small cuts for violence. Regardless, one can watch the feature with picture-in-picture storyboard presentations during selected sequences, or with either of two commentary tracks, one provided by Producer Michael G. Wilson and 2nd Unit Director Vic Armstrong, the other from Director Roger Spottiswoode. You can even sit through the movie listening to composer David Arnold's exemplary score unhindered by dialogue and other sound effects.

Extras include an engaging 45-minute documentary entitled "The Secrets of 007", the promo music video of Sheryl Crow's title song, a short interview with David Arnold, a 4-minute "f/x reel", two trailers and some narrated technical data on one or two of the film's gadgets. Language choices are English and French, subtitles are provided in English, French and Spanish. -TG

TOO MUCH FLESH

Colour, 2000, 109 m. / Directed by Jean-Marc Barr and Pascal Arnold / Starring Élodie Bouchez, Jean-Marc Barr, Rosanna Arquette / Paramount (France R2 PAL) / WS (1.78:1) (16:9) / DD2.0

Sooner or later the Dogma trend initiated by Lars von Trier and cohorts will wear itself out, but until then we'll have to contend with films like *Too Much Flesh*. For the uninitiated, Dogma (or Dogme in its native country) is a set of naturalistic rules imposed on a film involving the use of natural light, no genre conventions, no tripods, and so on. Sometimes the approach works, most notably in the Danish masterpiece *Festen / The Celebration*, but more often it simply induces headaches. Jean-Marc Barr, a talented actor who has worked with von Trier on several occasions, decided to turn director by collaborating with his friend Pascal Arnold for the fifth official Dogme film, *Lovers*. They joined up again, with Barr directing and acting, for *Too Much Flesh*, a wacky indictment of American puritan values that must be seen to be believed.

We first see thirtysomething Illinois farmer Lyle (Barr) strolling naked through a cornfield, apparently having some kind of sexual communion with nature. You see, poor Lyle is still a virgin, unable to consummate his marriage with brittle Amy (Barr's *Big Blue* co-star, Rosanna Arquette) thanks his traumatic high school years during which he was taunted because of his oversized manhood. Really. Enter French coquette Juliette (Élodie Bouchez), who shakes up the conservative community when she begins a very public affair with Lyle. Amy doesn't take too kindly to the idea, and things quickly slide downhill after Lyle and Brigitte initiate a young farm boy into their sensual shenanigans.

While it seems Barr and Arnold intended this to be a scathing look at hypocrisy and sexual persecution, *Too Much Flesh* is undermined by its insistence on portraying the ridiculous events with a straight face. Attempts at small town Americana come off extremely cockeyed, as do most attempts by French and Italian directors to zero in on U.S. culture. In the grand tradition of *Romance, Intimacy,*

et al, the film also throws in lots of sex, much of it possibly unsimulated. Of course, the difference here is that the camera never really actually shows much; the normally uninhibited Bouchez (*The Dreamlife of Angels*) and Barr (who worked together before on *Lovers* and *Don't Let Me Die on a Sunday*) mostly do a lot of rubbing underneath clothing, and even the few nude scenes are oddly coy. The camera constantly contorts and swerves to avoid showing the main character's oft-discussed deformity, turning the sex scenes into unintentional comedy pieces. However, the most delirious high point must be the finale, an attempt at *Scarlet Letter* tragedy that pushes any semblance of credulity right out the window. At least the acting is fairly good, considering, and the always interesting Arquette - still proudly showing off her body well past forty - makes the most of her psychotic supporting role.

Though it's unlikely to play too widely outside of France, *Too Much Flesh* is worth checking out on DVD as an example of Dogma cinema gone haywire. Paramount's DVD looks fine considering the digital video origins, and the anamorphic widescreen framing doesn't seem to crop out anything vital. A standard Dolby 2.0 surround track mostly consists of ambient noise flooding to the rear speakers, while the dialogue (recorded in English) is usually clear despite the primitive sound recording. The film can also be played with a peculiar French dub track or in English with optional French subtitles. The disc also includes the theatrical trailer (with a few shots not in the film itself), a trailer for *Lovers*, and an audio commentary by Barr and Arnold, in French.

TORSO

Colour, 1973, 92m. / Directed by Sergio Martino / Starring Suzy Kendall, Tina Aumont / Anchor Bay (US R1 NTSC) / WS (1.85:1) (16:9)

The last real mystery directed by the underrated Sergio Martino, *Torso* was originally shown in Europe under the title *The Bodies Bear Traces of Carnal Violence (I corpi presentano tracce di violanza carnale)*. However, its American title (concocted by distributor Joseph Brenner) ensured its popularity on the drive-in and grindhouse circuit, where it played for years hooked up with films like *The Texas Chainsaw Massacre*. Not surprisingly, the film lost over three minutes of gore and dialogue outside of Europe, and Anchor Bay's DVD represents a feat of *giallo* restoration.

T

The tranquil University of Perugia is rocked by a series of brutal murders in which the female victims have been stripped and mutilated. Daniela (Tina Aumont), a pretty art student, recognizes a scarf found on one of the victims... but where did she see it? Meanwhile, a sidewalk peddler believes he knows the killer's identity but is mowed down when he attempts a round of blackmail. Afraid for her life, Daniela retreats to a remote country villa with three of her friends including an English girl, Jane (Suzy Kendall). Of course, the savvy killer follows them, ensuring that their little vacation turns into a nightmarish bloodbath.

A perfect example of the necessary elements for Italian horror, *Torso* throws in every convention of the *giallo* (mystery) films perfected by Martino (*Gently Before She Dies, All the Colours of the Dark*) and mixes them with the more recent slasher and sexploitation trends. Kendall, a veteran of Dario Argento's *The Bird with the Crystal Plumage*, once again makes a terrific scream queen; her cat and mouse showdown with the killer, which comprises the entire final third of the film(!), is not easily forgotten. However, the most noteworthy element of *Torso* is its stunning musical score by Guido and Maurizio De Angelis. One of the best musical contributions from Italy in the '70s, this astounding soundtrack mixes sultry jazz, chilling percussive suspense music, and funky folk rock without faltering once. The US version omitted the entire, nudity-filled credits sequence and the original music theme, but fortunately this European cut preserves this film in its original sleaze-soaked glory.

Simply put, the DVD of *Torso* is a revelation. The colours are crisp and vibrant, and the level of detail visible in the anamorphic transfer is remarkable. However, it's worth noting that this print bears a few discrepancies compared to the original Italian prints. The opening credits feature a replaced title card that turns the screen black for a moment, and the soundtrack submerges the opening music to a faint muffle while including an Italian-language lecture on art history. The general release Euro prints only contained the music before a retracting camera shutter introduced an alternate, close up shot of John Richardson concluding his lecture. The Italian dialogue is presented with optional English subtitles (but no subs for the rest of the film, despite the alternate all-Italian audio track), which also includes an extended offscreen dialogue during the last scene. European tapes of *Torso* in Italian and Spanish have included all of the relatively tame gore, which mainly consists of brief stabbings, eye gouging, and blurry hacksaw mayhem, but Anchor Bay's print also reinstates some previously unseen non-gore footage missing even from Euro tapes, such as police interrogating a crusty local after the first murder. The disc's menus are accompanied by the film's soundtrack music (in stereo), and the lengthy US trailer and a psychedelic European promo (under the shortened title of *Carnal Violence*) are included for your enjoyment. (Amusingly, the American trailer kicks off by promoting this as being from the makers of *Doctor Zhivago* and *War and Peace*!)

TOUCH OF EVIL

B&W, 1958, 111m. / Directed by Orson Welles / Starring Charlton Heston, Orson Welles, Janet Leigh / Universal (US R1 NTSC) / WS (1.85:1) (16:9)

Orson Welles' final attempt at a major American studio film became the template for turning sleaze into art, the ultimate example that content does not dictate artistic value. The storyline, lifted marginally from Whit Masterson's *Badge of Evil*, is virtually indistinguishable from any '50s late noir potboiler, but Welles' determination to push his stylistic gifts into overdrive while juggling overlapping narratives makes this a surreal, exhilarating experience worthy of its reputation.

In the legendary opening shot, an American millionaire and his wife drive across the border from Mexico to the United States, only to die from a car bomb planted on the other side. The disaster is witnessed by Mexican detective Mike Vargas (Charlton Heston) and his newlywed American wife, Susan (Janet Leigh); naturally, their honeymoon plans must be put on hold while Vargas investigates. Susan is holed up at a motel run by Uncle Joe Grandi (Akim Tamiroff), a drug dealing associate of corrupt detective Hank Quinlan (Orson Welles), who has a nasty habit of planting evidence to incriminate his suspects. Vargas' snooping provokes Quinlan to framing his adversary and subjecting Susan to a hellish fate in her motel room, while Vargas races against time to dig up enough dirt on Quinlan's past to halt the escalating, deadly chain of events.

Perfectly filmed and so atmospheric you can almost feel the oppressive heat seeping off the screen, *Touch of Evil* somehow feels just right despite its inherent absurdity. Heston delivers a riveting performance despite being cast as one of the least convincing Mexicans of all time, while Leigh looks terrific even in a high-necked nightgown. And check out that supporting cast: Marlene Dietrich in a crackerjack cameo as a gypsy with moral ties to Quinlan; Mercedes McCambridge as the sinister leader of a gang of J.D. thugs; Joseph Calleia as Quinlan's idolizing, fatally flawed right hand man; Dennis Weaver as the twitchy, sexually infantile motel desk jockey; and even Welles regular Joseph Cotten in a very brief bit (look fast!). Welles really steals the film, though, as a tantalizing, thoroughly repulsive villain, a deeply flawed man with his own misguided sense of morality. (Check out his Falstaff in *Chimes at Midnight* for a fascinating progression of Welles' acting persona.)

When *Touch of Evil* was released at 95 minutes in 1958, it was regarded as a flawed masterpiece, compromised by studio interference and Welles' waning abilities to maintain control behind the camera. The latter turned out to be false, of course, particularly when a longer, 105 minute cut was assembled for release on Universal videotape and laserdisc. However, this edition was still compromised by studio-imposed alterations to the film's editing scheme and opening shot, not to mention the integration of scenes filmed later without Welles' participation. In 1998, a second, more legitimate restoration was undertaken with editor Walter Murch basically re-cutting the film from scratch according to a 58 page memo by Welles to the studio heads in which he found himself admittedly calling upon deaf ears to retain the basic thematic thrust of the film. The resulting release became an art house favourite, though for long-time fans of the film, watching the restored cut now unfolds without opening credits, instead tacking all titles to the end of the film. Also, Henry Mancini's primary music has been jettisoned from the shot, focusing instead on an elaborate fluctuation of dialogue, sound effects, and ambient music pouring from Mexican nightclubs and restaurants. It does play more effectively this way, allowing the viewer to absorb each detail packed into the frame without the distraction of printed words, but be prepared for an entirely different experience. Many scenes have been reshuffled, extended, or otherwise tweaked according to Welles' specifications, making the film tighter and more powerful, though not as dramatically different as one might think.

Universal's DVD of *Touch of Evil* is something of a mixed bag. Obviously having the new cut of the film is the main attraction here, and the transfer overall is satisfying. While contrast levels are good and the elements are in pristine condition, the image quality is softer than most black and white films; even in anamorphic playback, the lack of detail is troubling in some of the more densely layered shots.

Still, it's miles ahead of the laserdisc. The 1.85:1 framing adds some information to the sides but also loses a bit off the top and bottom; as with Universal's overmatted *Psycho*, a less severe matte might have been welcome. Originally Universal announced a full fledged documentary on the film for inclusion here, but unfortunately this feature was yanked at the last minute due to vaguely defined legal reasons. Instead we get the theatrical trailer (in very poor condition) and Welles' original memo, along with cast and crew bios accessible through some nicely designed, poster-style menus. While the disc could have been a little more, this is evidently the best it's going to get. Considering the film located at the heart of this package, that should be more than enough.

TOURIST TRAP

Colour, 1979, 90m. / Directed by David Schmoeller / Starring Chuck Connors, Tanya Roberts / Cult Video (US R1 NTSC) / WS (1.85:1) (16:9) / DD2.0

One of the great archetypal drive-in horror movies, *Tourist Trap* isn't really "good" in the traditional sense but has been haunting countless viewers over the past twenty years. Senseless as an experimental film and as graphic as a PG rating will allow, it really began to develop a fan base thanks to the enthusiastic gushing of Stephen King in his non-fiction horror study, *Danse Macabre*, and always used to traumatize unwitting preteens during its regular television screenings.

In the classic horror tradition, a quartet of hapless youths journeying through some back roads winds up at a desolate tourist trap run by the suspiciously hospitable Mr. Slausen (Chuck Connors). In between episodes of skinny-dipping and exploring the creepy series of cheap resort attractions, the victims-to-be encounter Mr. Slausen's mannequins, which have a nasty habit of coming to life and killing people. Meanwhile another resident in a strange mask swipes the occasional innocent visitor for bizarre experiments in which humans are turned into mannequins. Pretty soon it's down to the standard sole survivor who must fight for her life against a host of bizarre, plasticized terrors.

Thanks to its bizarre, startling music score by Pino Donaggio and efficient direction by David Schmoeller (*Crawlspace*), this little oddity seemingly evokes many of the successful elements of *The Texas Chainsaw Massacre*, including a chilling rural setting and a reliance on suggestion rather than explicit gore. Connors' truly crazed performance makes him one of the more memorable grassroots psychopaths, even if the exact nature of his villainy is never made clear. (Is he telekinetic? Is he under the control of the mannequins or vice versa? Is he a genuine split personality?) The final half hour in particular lifts *Tourist Trap* out of the mould, combining a weird lyrical romance with the obviously creepy images of jittering, animated mannequins on the prowl.

A long time in the making, the DVD release of *Tourist Trap* boasts a treatment far more respectful than anyone could have hoped. The anamorphic widescreen transfer looks terrific under the circumstances, far better than the dull, grainy full frame editions in the past from Media and Paramount/Full Moon. The darkly lit scenes feature rich, distortion-free shadows and startling splashes of colour (usually red or violet), though some signs of wear (mostly tiny singe-frame scratches) pop up around a few reel changes. Obviously this will never look as polished as a major studio effort, but this lovingly restored transfer is quite a treat, with the letterboxing adding great compositional flair to most of the interior scenes. Schmoeller also contributes a feature length commentary track and a six minute on-camera interview in which he affectionately discusses the film's shooting, his relationship with the various actors, his inspiration for the story (J.C. Penney!), and the techniques used to create terror without a budget. The disc also includes the fun '79 theatrical trailer (which gives away a lot) and a handful of Full Moon trailers (*Parasite, Cannibal Women in the Avocado Jungle of Death,* etc.); lots of fun, but obviously much less than the 40(!) trailers promised on the back of the box. (Maybe they're tucked away as an Easter egg somewhere.) The box also indicates an R rating and a "DX Stereo" soundtrack, neither of which are accurate.

TOWER OF EVIL

Colour, 1972, 89m. / Directed by Jim O'Connolly / Starring Bryant Haliday, Jill Haworth / Elite (US R1 NTSC) / WS (1.85:1)

This odd entry in British horror cinema was better known in the US as *Horror of Snape Island* and later rode the short coattails of John Carpenter's 1979 film under the title *Beyond the Fog*. Thanks to the diminishing censorship of the early '70s, *Tower of Evil* managed to inject heavy doses of gore and nudity into a standard '60s "teens in a dark house" plot, and the result, while hardly a classic, is not without interest.

On the desolate, foggy Snape Island, a young nude girl is found after she murders one of her would-be rescuers out of fright. Mutilated bodies litter the craggy surface of the island. What could be responsible? Well, thanks to a band of intrepid, horny teenagers, an ancient evil has been stirring and bumping off everyone in sight with a valuable Phoenician axe. When a private investigator and some treasure-hunting museum folk arrive at the island to get to the bottom of the mystery, the blood really begins to fly.

More successful as a mood piece than a standard slasher film, *Tower of Evil* offers some haunting moments of atmospheric terror discreetly tucked in during all of the usual horror clichés, gratuitous sex, and teen slang. The eerie opening credits (a model, but still effective) and jittery opening sequence show off the film's greatest strengths, and a cast of British horror pros helps give some class to the proceedings. In particular, look for Robin Askwith and Dennis Price (both also in *Horror Hospital*), top-billed Bryant Halliday (*Curse of the Voodoo*), and Jill Haworth (*The Mutations*). The film also makes effective use of sound, with rushing wind, scuttling crabs, and eerie whistling creating a memorable horror soundscape, while the effective night-time seaside locations may remind some viewers of Jean Rollin's similar poetic fondness for aquatic locales.

Released in the early '80s under the same title, *Tower of Evil* has rarely looked as good as it does here. As with its other films from producer Richard Gordon, Elite appears to have struck this directly from the negative, as the film is completely free from any blemishes or distortion. Though not really a visual powerhouse, with most of the visual colour schemes relying on grey, blue, and brown, the film looks quite impressive given its low budget, and anyone accustomed to the muddy old VHS versions will be amazed at the improvement. Likewise, the mono soundtrack is generally subdued and quiet but displays no particular flaws. While the liner notes tend to play up the film more than it really deserves, *Tower of Evil* will most likely never receive any other treatment remotely as respectful as this. A lengthy trailer is also included.

TRADER HORNEE

Colour, 1970, 84m. / Directed by Tsanusdi (Jonathan Lucas) / Starring Buddy Pantasari, Elisabeth Monica / Image (US R0 NTSC) / WS (1.66:1)

A surprisingly benevolent and playful "adult" film from producer David F. Friedman, *Trader Hornee* represents an effort to break out of the grindhouse circuit thanks to more lavish visuals and silly humour. Decades after its production, the film is quite an odd curio, a mixture of *Carol Burnett Show* lampooning and harmless cheesecake nudity - a combination we will most likely not see again.

In order to satisfy the technicalities of the will in a large family's estate, intrepid private eye Hamilton Hornee (that's pronounced "Horn!") is hired to venture into the jungles of Africa to ascertain whether a long lost heiress is actually dead. He's joined along the way by his luscious assistant, Jane (Elisabeth Monica), as well as a pair of scheming heirs to the fortune, dedicated scientist Stanley Livingston (who's searching for Africa's mysterious "white gorilla," Nabucco), and the frisky Tender Lee (Lisa Grant). When Hornee learns of the local African white goddess, Algona, he believes he may have stumbled upon the lost heiress after all.

Though hilariously filmed in the Hollywood Hills instead of Africa (except for stock footage), *Trader Hornee* is nevertheless a sprawling epic by Friedman's standards. Real elephants, colourful and varied costumes, and a surprising number of subplots and cross cutting give the film a patina of respectability, aided by the fact that the generous amounts of female nudity rarely lead to anything resembling a true sex scene. For anyone yearning to try out the sexploitation genre without the nasty intrusion of "roughie" footage, this is the perfect place to start.

While no one could have ever pegged *Trader Hornee* as a candidate for special edition treatment on DVD, well, here it is! The film unfortunately suffers a little bit from its late '60s film stock, which produces duller colours compared to some of the earlier erotic films, but the transfer quality is top notch for what it is. The mild letterboxing looks fine, trimming off some dead space from the top and bottom while revealing a bit on the sides when compared to Something Weird's older VHS edition (and the first VHS edition, *Legend of the Blonde Goddess*).

The disc also includes the funny original trailer (in rougher shape) and, as usual, a bouncy commentary by Friedman and SW's Mike Vraney, which dishes out the usual head-spinning amount of detail about financing and shooting a naughty epic back in the golden days of sleaze.

THE TRIAL

B&W, 1963, 119m. / Directed by Orson Welles / Starring Anthony Perkins, Orson Welles / Image (US R1 NTSC) / WS (1.66:1)

A logical extension of the paranoid and corrupt worlds found in *Touch of Evil* and *Macbeth*, *The Trial* found director Orson Welles tackling the social horrors of Franz Kafka.

An archetypal wrong man scenario, this spare and frightening narrative allowed Welles to run wild with visual decor, sound manipulation, and experimental compositions, resulting in one of his most difficult but rewarding creations.

After being awakened by the arrival of police in his room, Joseph K. (Anthony Perkins) is escorted away and accused of a crime. Unfortunately he has no idea what the crime is, what the penalty will be, or how to defend himself. Alternately terrified by and indignant towards his situation, Joseph appeals to all of those around him, with even perfect strangers invariably turning out to be untrustworthy or at least suspicious.

Featuring a stellar European cast headlined by French icon Jeanne Moreau, lovely Elsa Martinelli (*Blood and Roses*), and '70s starlet Romy Schneider, *The Trial* is one of Welles' most hauntingly realized concoctions. As usual, Welles himself appears in a sterling role as the Advocate, whose attitude towards Joseph remains impossible to truly gauge throughout most of the film. Perkins makes a fine identification figure, even as his grip on sanity begins to slip during his treatment by the judicial process, and the surreal mania of his final scene is either absurdly over the top or purely brilliant... or both. Arguably the most Hitchcockian of Welles' films, this would also make an effective double bill with *The Wrong Man* or perhaps *Frenzy*.

Available for years only through muddy, scratched prints and unwatchable public domain videos, *The Trial* was given a much needed facelift for its laserdisc debut in 1998. The DVD presents the same transfer, albeit with a digitally sharpened image that looks even better. The fine detail and vivid contrasts between light and shadow so crucial to Welles' work are in full abundance here, and only a few unavoidable glitches in the negative itself betray the film's age. The DVD also contains the alternate, heavy handed opening narration tacked on by Desilu for its television broadcast, as well as a "theatrical teaser" that runs much longer than most trailers.

T

TRILOGY OF TERROR

Colour, 1975, 72m. / Directed by Dan Curtis / Starring Karen Black, Robert Burton / Anchor Bay (US R1 NTSC)

Yikes! Here it is, folks - the scariest movie ever made for TV. Well, more accurately, the scariest twenty minutes ever made for TV. While Dan Curtis, the man behind *Dark Shadows* and *The Night Stalker*, and legendary fantasy writer Richard Matheson deserve the lion's share of the credit for this seat-jumping little gem, Karen Black also earns kudos for delivering convincing performances in the first two stories and a flat out tour de force in the last one.

The first story, "Julie," features Black as a college professor whose affair with a young student winds up taking a nasty and supernatural turn. Featuring an early appearance by Gregory Harrison, it's little more than a slightly more perverse episode of Alfred Hitchcock Presents but passes the time well enough.

The second, "Therese and Millicent," offers a mild spin on Robert Bloch's "Lucy Came to Stay" from the British horror anthology *Asylum*. Black portrays the two title characters, feuding sisters whose lust for a man leads to violent consequences.

After this, however, the film really pulls out all the stops for "Amelia," based on Matheson's short story "Prey." Amelia, a single woman living alone in an apartment, finds her love life stymied by the interference of her mother. Our heroine comes into possession of a Zuni fetish doll, a creepy African warrior figure wielding a spear and wearing an amulet. When Amelia removes the amulet, the doll disappears... and begins hunting her inside the apartment. What follows is definitely not for the weak of heart. Imitated countless times (most amusingly in Lamberto Bava's *Demons 2*) and even remade by Curtis himself for the inferior cable TV film, *Trilogy of Terror II,* this remains the first and best of its kind.

Trilogy of Terror made brief appearances on video countless times through MPI, but Anchor Bay's DVD looks substantially better than any other version. While this is still a '70s television movie, the colour and detail look consistently sharp and stable, with some lustrous, rich hues of gold and brown often overtaking the visual schemes. For most viewers this movie was just designed for DVD; all you have to do is skip forward to the third segment and not worry about fast-forwarding the tape. The nerve-jangling score by Bob Cobert (*Dark Shadows*)

sounds fine, though much of the dialogue has a pinched TV sound that cannot be avoided. No extras aside from a printed interview with Black (too bad the original TV promo spots aren't around!), but fans should be more than pleased with this presentation.

TURKISH DELIGHT

Colour, 1973, 112m. / Directed by Paul Verhoeven / Starring Rutger Hauer, Monique van de Ven / Anchor Bay (US R1 NTSC), Tartan (UK R2 PAL) / WS (1.85:1) (16:9)

This international breakthrough film for director Paul Verhoeven and actor Rutger Hauer joined a number of its European contemporaries by drawing in both the art house and sexploitation crowds. Of course, its wide availability mostly in dubbed, edited prints didn't help its reputation over the years, its Best Foreign Film Oscar nomination notwithstanding, but the damage done by countless public domain editions over the years has finally been kept at bay by a disc that allows one to appreciate just how extreme and affecting the film remains to this day.

The fractured opening sequence introduces us to Eric (Hauer), a petulant sculptor suffering a breakdown apparently related to a young woman, Olga (Monique van de Ven), whose photograph he keeps handy for a variety of purposes. After wallowing in a series of violent fantasies, he eventually recovers from his slump and engages on a wild round of purgative sex. In flashback we learn the full story about how he and Olga met and began a passionate, extremely physical affair, with highlights both comic (an encounter between Eric's manhood and a jeans zipper) and tragic (a car accident), as the two come to grips with family interference, living together, and other obstacles posed by day to day life. Fate intervenes with a nasty twist, leading to a series of jolting and eventually poignant revelations, which bring the couple to their predestined end.

Verhoeven fans will be the most receptive audience to this anarchic blend of emotions, bodily functions, and seemingly non-stop sex scenes; though it doesn't go completely over the edge like the later *Spetters* (sadly still missing in action on DVD), this is still taboo stretching material today, even by European standards. The full throttle, exhibitionist performances from both leads ground what could have been a sappy, incoherent jumble of a story, and Hauer fans in particular will be astonished to see how the familiar laconic matinee idol got his start. His other borderline softcore films (like *Dandelions* or Verhoeven's *Keetje Tippel*, more of a showcase for van de Ven) aren't humiliating by any means, but this is by far the best of the bunch.

The most obvious attribute of these DVD releases is the presence of the original Dutch language track with optional English subtitles. For anyone who ever had to suffer through the dubbed VHS releases, this is a welcome relief for the ears. Several shots which were either shortened or deleted entirely from many US prints are now back in their proper place, including a relatively innocuous bit of doggie relief that predates John Waters' *Pink Flamingos*. The image quality is about as fine and detailed as one could expect given the source; it's certainly the best this film has ever looked, and the tricky colour schemes (lots of brown and orange) come through just fine.

As with most of his other films, Verhoeven chips in directly with a commentary track (sadly missing from the Tartan release) in which he recalls in fine detail the making of the film and describes the social conditions under which it was made. As usual he doesn't pull many punches and displays a mordant sense of humour; it's a shame his dangerous talent has been largely kept in check in recent years with filler like *Hollow Man*. The Dutch trailer is included on both releases, though an American one would have been an amusing bonus, too, if one still exists.

THE TWILIGHT PEOPLE

Colour, 1972, 84m. / Directed by Eddie Romero / Starring John Ashley, Pam Grier / VCI (US R1 NTSC)

Yet another Filipino retread of *The Island of Dr. Moreau*, this trashy drive-in favourite is most memorable now for the sight of Pam Grier with a fake nose, letting loose dubbed growls as "the Panther Woman." Otherwise this is pretty much par for the course, not much better or worse than Eddie Romero's other '70s stabs at the mad scientist on a tropical island subgenre. This time our hapless hero is intrepid diver Matt Farrell (John Ashley), who is picked up by the eccentric Dr. Gordon (Charles Macauley), a former SS doctor, and taken to a remote island populated with strange human mutations. These man/animal creations are the offspring of Dr. Gordon's attempts to craft a super race of beings who will populate and improve the earth, with Farrell playing a more than

minor role in these nefarious plans. The creatures, including the savage Ayesa (Pam Grier), are less than happy with their fate, as is the doctor's rebellious daughter, Neva (Pat Woodell).

While Eddie Romero first produced a competent and sometimes striking variation on this story with *Terror Is a Man*, this PG-rated '70s drive-in variation stumbles noticeably with its inept make-up jobs and stilted dialogue. As a campy comedy, though, this is quite priceless, and few lovers of trash cinema will be bored.

VCI's DVD looks as good as this film ever possibly could and appears to be taken from a source very close to the original negative. No scratches or dirt are evident, and colours are strong and very well reproduced. The results are miles ahead of the dreary VHS releases this has received over the decades, once under the alternate title of *Beasts*. The mono audio is also clear and powerful for what it is. The disc also includes the (somewhat abbreviated) theatrical trailer and the usual reel of VCI previews.

TWITCH OF THE DEATH NERVE

Colour, 1971, 82m. / Directed by Mario Bava / Starring Claudine Auger, Luigi Pistilli / Image (US R0 NTSC) / WS (1.85:1) (16:9)

Thanks to his orgiastic feasts of gothic horror and comic book pop art, no one ever described Mario Bava as a restrained director. However, few could have anticipated the unbridled ferocity of his trendsetting 1971 shocker, *Reazione a catena (Chain Reaction)*, which turned up in Europe under such titles as *Antefatto, A Bay of Blood*, and *Ecologia del delitto* before terrorizing US drive-ins for years as *Last House - Part II* and, most unforgettably, *Twitch of the Death Nerve*. Here Bava essentially tears the horror genre apart from the ground up, dispensing with linear plotting or realistic characterization in favour of a mechanical, devious catalogue of murders, all served up with the tricky, sumptuous photography which gives his films their unforgettable artistic stamp. Even more than his earlier *Blood and Black Lace*, this is the body count movie par excellence.

In the haunting and darkly funny opening, an elderly countess (Isa Miranda) stares sadly through a rain-dappled window at her property surrounding a remote bay. Suddenly her wheelchair-bound body is seized up by a lariat, hoisting her back and choking the life from her throat. Her assailant nonchalantly steps outside and surveys his handiwork, then returns inside... only to receive a knife in the back for his trouble. Thus begins a mad, scurrying patchwork of fragmented storylines in which various residents and visitors become victim or predator, or sometimes both at once, in order to claim this valuable chunk of property. Watch and learn the fates of four partying youths, a Medusa-haired tarot freak (*A Hatchet for the Honeymoon*'s Laura Betti), the sinister squid-hunting local Simon (Claudio Camoso), and visiting married couple Renata (*Thunderball*'s Claudine Auger) and Albert (Luigi Pistilli). The solution to this bloody tangle of lives and motives will certainly surprise you and probably provoke a sick chuckle as well.

Though rarely acknowledged by the mainstream press, *Twitch* has gradually received credit as the progenitor of the slasher wave from the '80s (with Steve Miner's *Friday the 13th Part II* suffering the most direct and justified accusations of plagiarism). However, Bava's film is a more clever, subtle, and visually sumptuous affair than your standard stalk and kill yarn; even with limited means, he conjures up a swirling symphony of poetic images, from the rippling textures of the bay waters (even when strewn with corpses) to the macabre ochre glow behind a glass door during Renata's standout victim scene. The cheeky gore effects still shock today, including an unforgettable facial machete application, a unique shish-kebab variation, and a startling beheading, all laced with some '70s-styled helpings of nudity and sex. Stelvio Cipriani's deft score wavers between beautifully sustained and creepy beat rhythms (the main titles in particular) to the hilarious upbeat pop pastorale of the end credits, while the actors all seem to be having a ball before turning up as lambs to the slaughter. (Genre fans, look for an appearance by little Nicoletta Elmi, who also turned up in *Deep Red*, *Flesh for Frankenstein*, and Bava's *Baron Blood*, among many others.)

Image's DVD of this film (packaged as *Twitch of the Death Nerve* but containing the onscreen title of *A Bay of Blood*) obviously outclasses the notoriously bad earlier disc from Simitar. This widescreen version contains all of the gore scissored from the earlier letterboxed Redemption version, but most importantly, the colours and detail are strong enough to easily peg this as a Bava film. The compositions cleverly utilize every inch of the frame, and this presentation, stunningly enhanced for 16:9 displays, finally allows enough breathing room to allow Bava to work his spell. Just watch the opening sequence, in which the delicately colour-gelled lighting spills onto the ceiling and reflects off the furniture, becoming as vital a player in the murders as the actors

themselves. The mono soundtrack fares less successfully, with the sound and music displaying annoying distortion that often overwhelms or sometimes unintelligible dialogue.

The disc also includes the theatrical trailer under the alternate title of *Carnage* (in noticeably better shape than its earlier appearance on *Mad Ron's Prevues from Hell*), along with the standard Bava bio and photo gallery, a special tongue-in-cheek "Murder Menu" leading to each death scene, some outrageous radio spots, and the usual thorough, illuminating liner notes from Tim Lucas.

TWO DAYS IN THE VALLEY

Colour, 1996, 104m. / Directed by John Herzfeld / Starring Danny Aiello, Jeff Daniels / HBO (US R1 NTSC), EIV (UK R2 PAL) / WS (2.35:1) / DD5.1

Los Angeles. A washed-up hitman and an ice cool assassin are teamed up in an insurance scam. A snooty art dealer, contorted with kidney stone pains, is being cared for by his browbeaten but devoted assistant. A burnt out movie director has decided that suicide is the only option left open to him. An unbalanced vice cop, partnered with an over-eager novice, has made it his personal mission to clear the vicinity of undercover brothels. It's just another 48 hours of life and crime in The Valley.

A feisty little number with a *Pulp Fiction* flair for multiple interwoven plot threads and acid sharp wit; inevitably compared to Tarantino's film, *2 Days in the Valley* may be cut from the same cloth but it's never quite as ballsy and the dialogue is far less punchy. Spader does the ruthless killer bit to perfection whilst Aiello is superb as his disparate foil, the confused scapegoat in an ominous game. Daniels as the washed up and unhinged cop has rarely been better, in fact it's hard to believe that this is the same actor who played out moronically coarse flatulence scenes in *Dumb and Dumber*. Paul Mazursky's suicidal film director, seeking someone to home his dog, is a scene-stealer, whilst Greg Cruttwell's art dealer mines some genuine belly laughs, especially when he's in full flow and whinging like a demented marmoset. And we haven't yet mentioned Louise Fletcher, Glenne Headley, Eric Stoltz, Marsha Mason, Austin Pendleton, Keith Carradine... Violent, funny and erotic, with a divertingly eclectic cast, the seemingly unconnected vignettes of dishevelled and malcontent LA lives come together in an edifying wrap-up which sees the bad guys dead and the not-quite-so-bad guys surviving to fight another day. Director/writer Herzfeld manages to keep his narrative smooth and unpredictable enough that one's attention is held right up to the moment when a jubilant Aiello drives off into the sunset with new-found concubine Headley at his side. Oh, and any film that serves up a catfight between dishy Charlize Theron and drippy Teri Hatcher has to be worth a butcher's, wouldn't you say?

Great movie, shame about the Region 1 DVD. To be sure, the film itself is worth the admission price, delivered in an admirable 2.35:1 letterboxed transfer, albeit badly under-chaptered with just 12 breaks. But if it's extras you're seeking, forget it; beyond the standard trailer and some brief biographies, there's nothing here to tickle the palate. English and French language options are complemented by subtitles in English, French and Spanish. - TG

The UK disc features a trailer, featurette, B-roll, and soundbites. - ed.

TWO LANE BLACKTOP

Colour, 1971, 102m. / Directed by Monte Hellman / Starring James Taylor, Warren Oates / Anchor Bay (US R1 NTSC) / WS (2.35:1) (16:9) / DD5.1

Perhaps the strangest entry in the big studios' existential road race craze during the '70s, *Two-Lane Blacktop* immediately distinguishes itself from the likes of *Easy Rider* and *Vanishing Point* by offering bizarre, Godardian dialogue about car mechanics, delivered by rock musicians and established screen actors. Coupled with splendid widescreen photography and concise direction and editing by Monte Hellman (*The Shooting; China 9, Liberty 37*), the result is an underrated classic of '70s drive-in cinema.

Two buddies, the Driver (James Taylor) and the Mechanic (The Beach Boys' Dennis Wilson), tear back and forth across the country's highways in their '55 Chevy. After an encounter with the abrasive G.T.O. (Warren Oates), who drives - surprise! - a G.T.O., the boys decide to race each other to Washington, D.C. for their pink slips. Along the way the boys pick up a female hitchhiker (Laurie Bird), causing their already abstract relationship to deteriorate. The last word in automobile fetishism, *Two-Lane Blacktop* presents The Car (the Chevy) as a crucial character and the closest emotional link for the two younger men.

Though this bizarre scenario was hyped as a groundbreaking mainstream project, the film never really took off during its initial run, despite a legendary hype job from Esquire magazine. Thanks to a constantly growing cult following, coupled with the unavailability of the title to most venues due to music rights issues, the film's reputation began to soar, making it one of the most requested catalogue titles on home video. Of course, the presence of cult icons Taylor and Wilson didn't hurt; both of them give fine, understated performances, but Warren Oates easily steals the film in his best non-Peckinpah performance.

Over the past few years, a few sparse TV screenings on VH-1 and other channels, usually heavily censored, continued to whet fan's appetites, and *Two-Lane Blacktop* finally appeared on laserdisc from the Roan Group in a widescreen edition with all music intact. Anchor Bay's anamorphically enhanced DVD looks much better, with sharper resolution and very accurate colours. Since this film was early '70s and always looked like it was being projected on black leather, the visuals will always look a little gritty and heavily textured, but this is representative of its intended appearance. Not surprisingly, the 5.1 remix roars to life from the opening frames and never lets up; each channel constantly rumbles and putters throughout the film, though much of the intentionally obscured dialogue remains difficult to hear. Hellman provides a slow, studied commentary, which pauses often but does provide some nuggets of information, particularly concerning the music issue (which extends all the way to Bird muttering the Rolling Stones' "Satisfaction" in a greasy spoon). Strangely, all of the leads except for Taylor have already died, which contributes even further to the film's mystique and makes the bizarre, abrupt conclusion even more resonant.

The disc also includes the original trailer and a 15 minute short, "Monte Hellman: American Auteur," directed by George Hickenlooper. Featuring brief snippets from Hellman's films, this mini-documentary makes for fascinating if sketchy viewing and makes the commentary more enjoyable in context.

2001: A SPACE ODYSSEY

Colour, 1968, 139m. / Directed by Stanley Kubrick / Starring Keir Dullea, Gary Lockwood / Warner / WS (2.35:1) (16:9) / DD5.1

"I'm sorry, I can't do that, Dave..." Ape evolves into man. Man goes into space with computer. Man and computer do battle. Man experiences the next step in

evolution. While this summary may not do justice to the philosophical and visual wonder of Kubrick's science fiction masterpiece, it does basically convey the controversy that has surrounded the film since its release. What does it all mean? Like other films of its generation, particularly *Blow Up, 2001* ultimately forces viewers to form their own conclusions and offers some absolutely first rate eye candy along the way. While the human characters, represented primarily by Keir Dullea's Dave Bowman, may be withdrawn and chilly in true Kubrick style, the wrenching, three-dimensional villainy of the computer HAL hits all too close to home for a society which has become increasingly reliant on a screen and keyboard to express itself (um, wait a minute here...).

Kubrick's film remains primarily a matter of taste thanks to the extremely slow pace and difficult plotting, but from any point of view, it's an important film and demands to be seen.

Obviously the ideal way to see *2001* is in a theatre, preferably in Cinerama, but the home video versions have generally fared well. The first widescreen release from Criterion looked good but overly grainy, while MGM's meticulous 65mm restoration for laserdisc improved both the colour and clarity. The version was transferred verbatim to DVD without anamorphic enhancement for its first round through MGM and Warner, including a stint in the first (unsatisfying) Stanley Kubrick box set. A subsequent anamorphic transfer improves things somewhat, though nothing can really replicate the theatrical experience. The Dolby Digital 5.1 mix contains some effective directional effects but can't do much to spruce up the "space Muzak" score pieced together from pre-existing music (it's a shame Kubrick nixed Alex North's wonderful score, which could have taken this film to an even higher level). Incidentally, *2001* marked the first occasion Kubrick recut his work after its theatrical release; the film originally ran 12 minutes longer, but Kubrick made various trims for reasons which remain mysterious. Perhaps the excised footage will turn up someday, if it still exists. Bonuses here include a brief interview with author Arthur C. Clarke and the tedious US trailer.

TWO THOUSAND MANIACS!

Colour, 1964, 87m. / Directed by Herschell Gordon Lewis / Starring Connie Mason, Thomas Wood / Image (US R0 NTSC), Tartan (UK R0 PAL)

A quantum leap over *Blood Feast* in terms of filmmaking skill, *Two Thousand Maniacs!* trades in its predecessor's queasy laughs for a frightening, potent atmosphere of sunny dread. Instead of bombarding the viewer with splatter, *Maniacs* (whose title inspired the popular '80s alternative group, Ten Thousand Maniacs) allows the murders to grow out of the story, often delivering true shocks thanks to the agonizing build up and fiendish imagination of the executions.

While wandering the back roads of Florida, three Northern couples wind up in the little town of Pleasant Valley. Populated entirely by stereotypical grinning Southern yokels, the town welcomes its visitors with open arms and offers them free room and board. The main couple, Tom and his hitchhiking acquaintance, Terry (*Blood Feast*'s Thomas Wood and Connie Mason), begins to suspect something may be amiss, particularly when their fellow Yankees wind up disappearing- often before a convenient town barbecue turns up. Sure enough, this town is actually filled with malevolent ghosts bent on revenge for their slaughter at Yankee hands during the Civil War, a tradition they intend to hold up every one hundred years when the town reappears.

While the story takes a while to get going, with the first murder withheld until almost thirty minutes into the film, *Two Thousand Maniacs!* makes for engrossing and often chilling, sadistic viewing. The gore effects are uncomfortably accomplished, particularly a thumb slicing that still leaves audiences howling in shock. More outlandish feats include a man being drawn and quartered (though not as graphically as one might fear) and one poor soul tossed down a hill in a barrel spiked with nails. Mason's acting is still a liability, but her involvement and screen time have been wisely axed in favour of painting a broader, more effective canvas of countryfied terror that predates such efforts as *Deliverance*, *The Texas Chainsaw Massacre*, and *The Town that Dreaded Sundown*. Due to its mostly outdoor locales, *Two Thousand Maniacs!* lacks the same punchy colour schemes of *Blood Feast* but looks extremely impressive for a zero budget drive-in film.

Because of its conversion from a PAL source, the film runs slightly shorter here than its previous NTSC incarnations. Something Weird has lavished the same loving care on this title found on *Blood Feast*. Vraney, Lewis, and Friedman appear once again for a commentary track in which they recount the film's more ambitious production and numerous weird little anecdotes along the way. Also included is the original trailer (which once again focuses on the gore highlights), a surreal alternate French language track (which alas doesn't feature re-dubbing for the unforgettable theme song, "The South's Gonna Rise Again"), and sixteen minutes of outtakes, mostly consisting of alternate versions of scenes already in the film. The Tartan disc includes a different set of extras (mainly trailers) and an option to play the complete isolated musical soundtrack, jukebox-style.

TWO UNDERCOVER ANGELS

Colour, 1966, 75m. / Directed by Jess Franco / Starring Janine Reynaud, Rosanna Yanni / Anchor Bay (US R0 NTSC)

A cinematic companion piece to *Kiss Me Monster*, this film originally debuted in some areas of Europe under the extreme title, *Sadisterotica*, and was subsequently reissued as *Red Lips*. Under the former title this made an appearance on video first in the UK thanks to the fine folks at Redemption, and now after several years' delay, Americans can also savour its bizarre, scrappy charms.

A silly little piece that plays like a kinky remake of Roger Corman's *A Bucket of Blood*, the film kicks off with our two fetching detectives trading badly dubbed wisecracks as they attend a gallery of violent sculptures at a local art gallery. Upon noticing a striking resemblance between a local missing girl and one of the painting's victims, the Red Lips gals decide to investigate. Their mostly nonsensical journey takes them from swinging nightclubs to the lair of depraved artist Hoven who kidnaps girls with the aid of his hairy, wolfmanesque assistant, Morpho (a name that seems to pop up in an awful lot of Franco films).

Kitschy in the extreme, this film will delight Franco fans and is generally more inventive and fast-paced than *Kiss Me Monster* thanks to its darker air of twisted sexuality. A few camera setups even look a little bit like (gasp!) a Bava film.

While the *Sadisterotica* edition released in the UK was almost imperceptibly letterboxed at 1.58:1, the Anchor Bay transfer opens up the matte at the top of the frame and looks much better. The eye-popping colour designs look much better than one could ever expect from a film with such a low budget, and oddly enough, this contains the original European

title card instead of the inserted computer generated one from the Redemption version. Also includes an original trailer that probably didn't see the light of too many projector beams.

THE UGLY

Colour, 1996, 94m. / Directed by Scott Reynolds / Starring Paolo Rotondo, Rebecca Hobbs / Trimark (US R1 NTSC), Metrodome (UK R2 PAL) / WS (1.85:1) (16:9) / DD2.0

A remarkable fusion of psychological horror with artsy supernatural thrills, *The Ugly* is a New Zealand import hampered from notice thanks to an unworkable title and truly unappealing cover art (what were they thinking?). However, this is the kind of film whose reputation could easily build through word of mouth and the repeated viewings it richly deserves.

Dr. Karen Schumaker (Hobbs), a psychiatrist currently riding the wave of a media frenzy after freeing a noted serial killer, is called in to an institution at the request of its most notorious inmate, Simon Cartwright (Rotondo). The head of the institute (Ward, in a role tailor made for Jeffrey Combs) immediately reveals his disdain for Karen but begrudgingly allows her to question his patient. Through a startling mixture of flashbacks, shock cuts, and surreal fantasy images, Simon gradually unveils a nonsequential history of what made him the psycho he is today. After verbal and physical beatings at the hands of his unstable mother, grade school bullies, and his co-workers, Simon succumbed to the evil influence of "the ugly," his dark alter ego which forces him to kill at random to silence the voices within his head. Not surprisingly, Simon also turns out to be more clever and manipulative than he appears, and Karen finds herself pulled deeper and deeper into his seductive mania and ultimately must question the reality of what she sees around her.

While the premise may seem to tread on established serial killer favourites like *Seven, Silence of the Lambs*, and *Henry: Portrait of a Serial Killer, The Ugly* has quite a few nifty original surprises tucked up its sleeve. Most obviously, the film's startling use of colour gives it a texture and haunting resonance unlike any other in recent memory; the blood spilled during the violent killings is black as pitch, dreamlike red lighting appears from nowhere, and eerie pools of blue often appear in the background to preclude the ghostly appearances of

Simon's tormenters. The film also manipulates its audience through skilful use of sound, both through a subtly modulated Dolby soundtrack and, in one memorable sequence, alternating between deafening club music and complete silence to reflect two different characters' points of view. The two central performances are also extremely strong, and hopefully these actors will be seen again if this film ever reaches the eyes of anyone in Hollywood. Most amazingly, this is director Scott Reynolds' first feature film; one masterpiece out of the gate your first time around isn't too shabby, and he's definitely one to watch.

Trimark's DVD is generally satisfying; the extravagant gesture of an anamorphic transfer enhances the film's unsettling visual details, though it's still obviously not as crisp as more big studio releases. Though not mixed in 5.1, the soundtrack is effectively rendered and keeps the surround channels consistently active. This is definitely one film whose scare value increases exponentially with a good sound system. The unimpressive US video trailer is also included.

UN FLIC

Colour, 1971, 100m. / Directed by Jean-Pierre Melville / Starring Alain Delon, Richard Crenna / Anchor Bay (US R1 NTSC) / WS (1.85:1) (16:9)

 One of France's least heralded master directors, Jean-Pierre Melville was virtually unknown by most English speaking cineastes until hip and trendy talents like John Woo began singing his praises and noting his influence on such films as *The Killer*. Melville's only notable US release, 1967's masterful *Le Samouraï*, was thrown away under the title of *The Godson*, but in Europe it became a cult sensation and earned a new legion of followers for heartthrob Alain Delon. Best known to that point as the picture perfect, talented star of fare like Rene Clement's *Purple Noon*, Delon revealed a grittier side in front of Melville's camera and went on to star in two of the director's other masterpieces, 1970's frequently censored *The Red Circle* and Melville's last film, *Un Flic* (dubbed and barely shown by Allied Artists in 1975 as *Dirty Money*).

In the protracted and suspenseful opening sequence, a gang of robbers lay siege to a coastal town bank during a misty winter afternoon. Led by master criminal Simon (Richard Crenna), the looters escape and instigate plans for an audacious heist involving a moving train and a helicopter (the film's most famous and celebrated set piece). Meanwhile Simon's plans are being tracked by icy cool, jaded police commissioner Edouard Coleman (Delon), whose tumultuous relationship with fluffy-haired blonde Cathy (Catherine Deneuve) is waylaid by his regrettable friendship with Simon... who's also in love with Cathy. Eventually both men must put their friendship aside and face off in a battle of wits.

Fans of Michael Mann's *Heat* will undoubtedly be fascinated to see essentially the same storyline handled over twenty years earlier, right down to the same obsessive blue tint in every scene. Apart from the awkwardness of hearing Crenna dubbed in French, both he and Delon make for good Melvillian antagonists who share a common unspoken bond; it's also both fascinating and a bit unsettling to see Delon's chiselled looks fading into a more world weary, embittered visage that has obviously seen far too much. The supporting characters (including Deneuve) barely have a chance to register, with Melville devoting most of his attention to the two actors' line delivery, stances, and relationships with their natural and man made landscapes.

Given the sparse availability of Melville films on video around the world, apart from three non-subtitled anamorphic DVD releases in France and passable VHS editions of *Le Samouraï* and *Le Doulos*, Anchor Bay's release of *Un Flic* is a welcome turn against the tide. The presentation looks terrific, rendering this potentially tricky film's colour schemes with great skill and attention to detail. A few outside helicopter shots during the main robbery look a little muddy and shaky, but this is most likely a handicap carried over from the original materials. English language bootlegs of this title have made the rounds for a few years, but now they can thankfully be consigned to the trash bin. The disc also includes an insert reproducing the theatrical poster, as well as an oblique European trailer, which recuts the opening five minutes to very puzzling effect.

THE UNBEARABLE LIGHTNESS OF BEING

Colour, 1988, 172m. / Directed by Philip Kaufman / Starring Daniel Day-Lewis, Juliette Binoche, Lena Olin / Criterion (US R1 NTSC) / WS (1.85:1) (16:9) / DD 4.0

Philosophical novels usually make for very bad and pretentious cinema, with only the occasional fluke like *Slaughterhouse-Five* surviving the process from contemplative written word to concrete visual image. Milan Kundera's breathtaking novel, *The*

Unbearable Lightness of Being, is another of those rare survivors, thanks to Philip Kaufman's intelligent, understated direction and a marvellous ensemble cast. While those expecting a perfect replica of the book may be disappointed (the title, for instance, will be virtually meaningless for anyone who hasn't read it), this fascinating film easily deserves the Criterion treatment, which it has received in abundance.

Tomas (Daniel Day-Lewis, in his critical breakthrough role following *My Beautiful Laundrette*), a young doctor living in Prague in the late '60s, enjoys a promiscuous lifestyle thanks to a bevy of beautiful female patients passing through his door. His most constant lover, Sabina (Lena Olin), offers him physical and intellectual - but not emotional - satisfaction. During a vacation at a spa, Tomas meets Tereza (a very young Juliette Binoche), who strikes a resonant chord deep within him. They meet again in Prague, and while Tomas has misgivings about carrying on two relationships at the same time, the two women establish their own unique rapport. Tomas and Tereza grow closer as Sabina becomes entangled with the less charismatic Franz (Stealing Heaven's Derek De Lint). Their idyllic existence is shattered when the Soviet Union invades Prague, and all of them must adjust in their own way to the drastic new impositions being forced upon their lives.

While Kaufman experimented with the supernatural in his remake of *Invasion of the Body Snatchers,* his films more often possess a vague spiritual undercurrent that never quite manifests itself as something so obvious as a ghost or an elaborate special effect. *Henry & June* in particular seems to grow out of this film, which establishes sexual contact as one of the many means by which people communicate and build bonds that carry forth over vast distances and even time itself. The temporal manipulations of the final twenty minutes create a powerful effect in willing viewers which lingers long after the film has finished - indeed, after the last shot, one can easily get the feeling of passing into a strange, ethereal, and optimistic new plane. The performances are all pitch perfect, with Day-Lewis adopting a convincing Slavik accent. Some critics complained about the amount of sex and nudity throughout the film, though most of the sensuality is largely created in the viewer's mind. Nevertheless, Orion's original spicy video art landed this in the adult section of more than a few mainstream video stores.

Following a brief theatrical run, most of the film's loyal following discovered it on home video in an overly dark, Macrovision-smeared VHS version later reissued in somewhat better form on laserdisc by Orion. Criterion eventually released it on laserdisc in an improved transfer which still looks murky compared to this DVD. This anamorphic transfer finally resembles the big screen presentation - dense layers of white light, soft textured fabrics, and powdery landscapes. The Dolby surround soundtrack offers little in the way of separation effects, but the predominantly classical soundtrack seems fine, offering some basic stereo delineation like the original theatrical mix. Kaufman, who is tackling a film with Geoffrey Rush as the Marquis De Sade now that he's already conquered Henry Miller, provides an informative, extremely subdued commentary track in which he discusses his techniques for communicating with the actors and trying to convey the difficult concepts of Kundera's novel; the fact that he manages to remain lively and lucid for the entire three hour running time is something of a feat in itself.

UNBREAKABLE

Colour, 2000, 106m. / Directed by M. Night Shyamalan / Starring Bruce Willis, Samuel L. Jackson / Buena Vista (US R1 NTSC, UK R2 PAL) / WS (2.35:1) (16:9) / DD5.1

Having survived a catastrophic train crash in which everyone else aboard was killed, security guard David Dunn (Willis) is approached by enigmatic comic-art gallery owner Elijah Price (Jackson), who tries to convince him that he has superhuman powers. How else could he have walked away from such a disaster without so much as a scratch on him? Price himself is the precise antithesis, suffering from a debilitating disease that has rendered his bones fearfully brittle. Although Dunn dismisses Price's assertions as the ramblings of an eccentric, the man persists and eventually Dunn begins to discover things about himself that lead him to question his very existence.

Never mind your Superman and Spiderman; if a superhero really existed, what would he be like? That's the premise of M. N. Shyamalan's intriguing drama. Anyone out for a fright-punctuated journey to a shiver-down-the-spine conclusion a la the previous Willis-Shyamalan gig *The Sixth Sense* will find *Unbreakable* hard going. It's ponderous - at times almost sleep-inducingly so - and the "twist" ending isn't anywhere near as startling as the former film's. However, step into it with patience and an open mind and you'll not only find yourself rapidly falling under its spell, but will also be rewarded by Willis with what is possibly a career best performance. Even when shot from behind, the very manner in which he comports himself speaks volumes about Dunn's inner turmoil, loneliness (despite the fact he's married with a son) and overwhelming despair. The aforementioned ending is both abrupt and somewhat vexing, yet it could also theoretically suggest that the preceding two hours is but the opening chapter of an epic saga yet to unfold. Don't be surprised if an *Unbreakable 2* goes into production.

A lavish 2-disc set in super-slick packaging makes for a highly collectible DVD of Shyamalan's moody tale. The film itself is presented on the first disc, divided into 28 chapters and with options in English (DTS 5.1 Digital Surround or Dolby Digital 5.1 Surround), Spanish and French, plus subtitling in the former two only. Disc number 2 contains a small trove of additional goodies, doing away with the usual slew of TV spots and trailers in favour of two documentaries (one a behind the scenes featurette, the other a look at comic books and superheroes), a multi-angle replay of the pivotal train station sequence in the film, and a stunning half an hour of deleted scenes, every moment of which would have been pertinent had they been retained for the final cut. The less said about the vaguely conceited inclusion of a hideous video Shyamalan shot and appeared in as a youth the better. - TG

neighbourhood parking lot. They follow a lovely blonde woman to her home and force their way in where, as the film suddenly bursts into colour, they impale her on a huge knife. The victim, a Miss Lamb, is just the latest victim in a string of killings performed by two biker/restaurant owners, who take the choicest meats from their prey and provide plenty of business for their buddy, Mort the undertaker (Ray Dannis). Unfortunately, Miss Lamb also happened to be the secretary for a police detective who begins to smell a rat, particularly when the lunatics' restaurant serves suspiciously named plates like "Leg of Lamb." Carnage and hilarity ensue. Call it what you will, but *The Undertaker and His Pals* wastes no time during its one hour on the screen to pack in as many rib-nudging jokes and gory thrills as possible on its meagre budget. Apparently the Lewis-like atmosphere was potent enough to attract Z-movie director Ted V. Mikels, who picked it up as a co-feature for his *immortal The Corpse Grinders*. (Legend has it that some explicit, vivisection-like gore footage was trimmed out by Mikels before the release, but these trims appear to be either lost or a rumour.)

After years of cruddy VHS transfers, VCI's DVD looks much better (at least in the context of the film's history) and offers an approximation of the original eye-popping '60s-era colour schemes. Apart from some slight softness, the print is in very good shape and sports a clean, somewhat limited mono soundtrack. The disc also includes the highly memorable theatrical trailer, which makes repetitious use of the film's droning, a capella theme song.

THE UNDERTAKER AND HIS PALS

Colour, 1966, 61m. / Directed by David C. Graham / Starring Ray Dannis, Robert Lowery / VCI (US R1 NTSC)

A mostly forgotten early entry in the splatter sweepstakes, *The Undertaker and His Pals* explores much of the same territory as H.G. Lewis' legendary "Blood Trilogy." The difference here is that the filmmakers go for laughs when they're not splashing fake blood across the screen, though as a result it's somehow less amusing than the "serious," catastrophically acted *Blood Feast*. Still, *Undertaker* is a valuable and sometimes daring example of how graphic horror began to infiltrate the drive-ins during the beginning of the Vietnam era.

In the film's first and most striking sequence, we see sepia tone footage of bikers cruising around a

UP!

Colour, 1976, 80m. / Directed by Russ Meyer / Starring Raven De La Croix, Robert McLane / CTN (France R2 PAL)

Adolph Schwartz (Edward Schaaf) is mauled to death in his bathtub by a peckish piranha. His murder is still unsolved when into town comes full-bosomed Margo Winchester (De La Croix). Striking up a bargain with Sheriff Homer Johnson (Monte Bane) who keeps her out of jail for murdering the man who raped her, she gets a job as a waitress at Alice's Cafe, a local watering hole owned by bisexual husband and wife, the generously endowed Paul (McLane) and flirtatious Alice (Janet Wood). Business blossoms with Margo around, but no-one in town is quite who or what they seem, as she is soon to discover.

Raven De La Croix... rest assured you'll never forget her or her astounding anatomy once you've seen Russ Meyer's outrageous *Up!* High on nudity, low on plot, the story meanders along - with a helpful injection of narration (from Kitten Natividad as "The Greek Chorus") to keep the audience up to date with what's going on - to a violent and gruesome conclusion. Paddling the midwater between softcore and hardcore, this is without a doubt the most explicit of Meyer's films, which shouldn't necessarily be interpreted as a recommendation; only RM could treat brutal rape (twice) with such frivolity. The Nazi fuelled subtext of his earlier films reaches its apex here with a character, clearly meant to be Hitler, portrayed as a deviant masochistic homosexual. Suitably Meyeresque moments include comic alfresco intercourse between Wood and 2-ft-long strap-on-dildo-wearing Linda Sue Ragsdale ("Wait a minute, maybe we should talk about this..."), and the successful disarming of the gun-toting McLane with a large rubber marital aid. Associate produced by buxotic *Supervixens/Beneath the Valley of the Ultravixens* starlet Uschi Digard, this is time-wasting, tasteless smut as only lecherous old Russ could concoct.

Available under the title *Mega Vixens*, the French issued Region 2 presentation of *Up!* (with English or French sound and optional French subtitling) is fullscreen and divided by just 9 chapters. There's a generic trailer for all Meyer's movies thrown in for good measure, as well as an interactive "L'Univers de Russ Meyer" quiz and a textual interview/filmography/biography. - TG

VALENTINE

Colour, 2000, 95m. / Directed by Jamie Blanks / Starring David Boreanaz, Denise Richards / Warner (US R1 NTSC, UK R2 PAL) / WS (2.35:1) (16:9) / DD5.1

Critically lambasted and virtually ignored at the box office, *Valentine* proved to be a late and unwelcome addition to the rapidly dying neo-slasher revival. Taking a less grotesque angle on the romantic holiday than its less gimmicky '80s counterpart, *My Bloody Valentine*, this workmanlike yarn from director Jamie Blanks (who perpetrated the even more absurd *Urban Legends*) attempts to drag the straight-faced slasher/holiday formula into the modern age by injecting it with picture perfect young actors, glossy but uninspired photography, and a politically correct lack of gore or intense scares, coming up with a film that could have been interesting in another age but now comes out satisfying very few indeed.

Our story begins with a nerdy high school boy, Jeremy Melton, being brutally rejected by four girls at a dance before being humiliated under the bleachers with a trumped up claim of attempted rape. Faster than you can say Prom Night, all of the characters have now grown up, and each girl receives a sinister greeting for Valentine's Day (which somehow manages to actually stretch out for about three days, but never mind). Rich girl Dorothy (Jessica Capshaw) hates her new stepmom and allows her new boyfriend of one month to shack up in her house, while bitchy Paige (Denise Richards), Kate (Marley Shelton), and Lily (Jessica Cauffiel) spend most of their time blithely ignoring their nasty Valentine cards and attending pretentious art installations where one of them winds up harpooned by an arrow-wielding killer in a Cupid mask. The murderer also suffers from nosebleeds during moments of intense stress, a trait confined to poor Jeremy. As the body count climbs, the survivors must figure out which of the men in their lives could be the spurned boy, now grown up and desperate to avenge his broken heart.

Though *Valentine* is an abject failure as a horror film, it misfires for some very interesting reasons. The problem of adapting Tom Savage's complex novel was solved very simply by tossing out the story wholesale, focusing instead on a Cupid-faced killer and some inexplicable plotting that makes the work of Joe Eszterhas look almost competent in comparison. Some early sequences establishing the lead female characters are actually written and performed with a reasonable degree of snap; in fact, this might have been better as a dark comedy about the murderous perils of modern dating instead of a straight horror film. The top billed, underused David Boreanaz displays all of the vitality and emotional range he possesses on *Angel*, meaning his acting abilities are still anyone's guess, but Richards (a guilty pleasure actress to be sure) diverts one's attention with some tart one liners. The rest of the cast is bland and fails to make an impression, while Don Davis's score sounds like a more muted spin on his earlier work for *House on Haunted Hill*. The twist ending in the final shot is executed with some degree of panache and would actually be quite impressive if it weren't blatantly cribbed from Jack Sholder's superior *Alone in the Dark*.

As with most newer releases, *Valentine* contains the standard extras you would expect, including a commentary from Blanks that goes through the mechanics of each suspense sequence and elaborates

V

on the oft-reported story about how Warner ordered the digital removal of any gore that might have made the film interesting even on a visceral level. (However, the trite account of one victim's blood pooling out into the shape of a heart indicates these changes might not be such a bad thing after all.) The other supplements include the moody theatrical teaser, a video montage to a song from Orgy, and some disposable studio PR pieces passed off as a featurette. Not a bad deal for the extras and low price tag; too bad the main feature barely cuts it as a late night freebie on cable.

VALERIE
B&W, 1969, 95m. / Directed by Denis Héroux / Starring Danielle Ouimet, Pierre Paquette
L'INITIATION
Colour, 1970, 94m. / Directed by Denis Héroux / Starring Danielle Ouimet, Chantal Renaud
Lions Gate (Canada R1 NTSC)

Best known as the naive newlywed turned lesbian bloodsucker Valerie in *Daughters of Darkness*, French-Canadian actress Danielle Ouimet vanished from the international scene but left her own indelible mark in at least one true genre classic. However, her acting career actually stretched back a little earlier to 1969, when she caused a stir in the Quebec cinema community as another Valerie, this time a liberated woman born from the sexual revolution. The following year she reteamed with director/producer Denis Héroux for *L'initiation*, another mixture of softcore sex and social commentary also known as *Here and Now* (which happens to be the refrain of the catchy pop song over the opening credits). Fans of her vampire role will be surprised to see how relaxed and uninhibited she is in this pair of counterculture oddities, which play sort of like what Radley Metzger might have been like had he been French-Canadian and more in tune to the youth crowd of the time.

Undeniably a product of its time, *Valerie* follows the sexual misadventures of a young Catholic schoolgirl (Ouimet of course), first seen romping naked in front of a mirror, who decides to take off and experience real life in Quebec. After establishing a less than noble living as an exotic dancer and a woman for hire, she finally meets the man of her dreams but finds her chances for happiness thwarted by her seedy career choices. Though entertaining and crammed with stylish black and white photography, the film is hampered

somewhat by the reactionary underlying nature of its message that "loose" women are inferior or face difficult lives easily avoided by a good Catholic upbringing. Ouimet makes for a beguiling, erotically charged presence in the film, however, and she carried this persona over into her next film.

L'initiation concerns the sexual and intellectual awakening of Victoria (Chantal Renaud), a freckled good girl who enjoys an occasional skinny-dip but can't hold a candle to her best friend, Nadine (Ouimet), who enjoys rolling around naked on her inflatable swimming pool folding chair just to infuriate her mother. While Nadine goes through a string of men, the more cautious Victoria finally lands in the arms of Gervais (Jacques Riberolles), a middle aged French author visiting Canada who's teaching a literary course. Victoria's counterculture awakening broadens her horizons, allowing her to see how mind and body can be combined for a fuller daily existence. Incidentally, this scenario carried over into real life when Renaud and Riberolles began an affair during filming and took off to France together. Sort of like a hipper, faster, and more colourful version of *I Am Curious (Yellow)*, the film isn't really all that profound, but the performances are sincere, some moments generate authentic poignancy, and the vivid decors, pop music, and clothing make for a fetching time capsule.

Lions Gate has released both films as a two-sided, double feature DVD geared for the French-speaking Canadian market. Both films are presented in their original French language or dubbed in English; no subtitle options are available, but the dub is reasonably well done with suitably chosen voices. The English menu must be chosen to view the film in English; audio options cannot be switched on the fly while viewing the films. *Valerie* looks absolutely pristine in its open matte transfer and is one of the most beautiful black and white transfers to come down the road in quite a while. The subtly nuanced lighting comes through with razor sharp clarity, and there are no digital flaws to be spotted at all. *L'initiation* is mildly cropped from its original aspect ratio, approximately 1.78:1 judging from the slightly squeezed opening credit sequence (which look great in 16:9 playback). Colours are strong and the print is in excellent shape, though it doesn't look quite as dazzling as its companion feature.

The disc also includes extensive filmographies and bios for nearly every actor in each film; in fact, the bios are quite illuminating and loaded with facts relating directly to the production of the films. Also included is a nice new French language featurette in which Ouimet (now a TV hostess), Héroux, and other principals discuss the films and place them in their historical context. No subtitle options are offered, but those with a rudimentary knowledge of French should be able to get the idea. It's especially fascinating to see what Ouimet looks like now, and she comes off here as an elegant, charming, and high-spirited woman. Fans of hip '60s erotic cinema or Canadian films in general should find this one well worth picking up, and one can only wish Lions Gate's US releases were all this interesting.

VAMPIRES

Colour, 1998, 108m. / Directed by John Carpenter / Starring James Woods, Sheryl Lee / Columbia (US R1 NTSC, UK R2 PAL) / WS (2.35:1) (16:9) / DD5.1

 As far as vampire-western hybrids go, John Carpenter's *Vampires* must rank far below *Near Dark* and even *Sundown*. The concept of one of horror's few remaining living legends finally tackling a no holds barred vampire saga seemed promising, and while a few moments live up to the director's promise, the overall result is a crushing disappointment.

The film's first 20 minutes are gangbusters, with a squad of vampire hunters led by Jack Crow (James Woods) infiltrating a vampire hideout and laying waste to the bloodsuckers by cinching them to the back of a truck and hauling them out into daylight. When the fearless vampire killers (accompanied by their resident priest for hire) retire to a motel for some boozing and cheap sex, the "head vampire" (imposingly played by Thomas Ian Griffith) bursts in and causes more gory carnage than you've ever seen in an R-rated film. Unfortunately, things go off the rails - to the say the least - when Woods and his surviving sidekick, Daniel Baldwin, drag along the only surviving hooker, *Twin Peaks'* Sheryl Lee, who has been bitten and has thus established a telepathic link with Griffith. Also, the Catholic Church (represented by a sleepwalking Maximillian Schell) assigns a new priest (Tim Guinee) to accompany them, so Woods responds by repeatedly beating up the priest.

While Carpenter's anti-Catholic ruminations can be fun (*Prince of Darkness* is a prime example), here it's just a lame excuse for baiting controversy that just doesn't work. Furthermore, tying Lee naked to a bed for no good reason and having characters constantly call her a "no good half dead whore" leaves a pretty nasty aftertaste; while Carpenter may have been intending to simply convey the characters' misogyny, this attitude rubs off on the

entire film as a whole. Even at 108 minutes, this is very sluggish stuff; endless scenes unfold in dimly lit motel rooms and desert landscapes in some half-baked homage to Sam Peckinpah. However, even *Bring Me the Head of Alfredo Garcia* had more zip than *Vampires*, which tosses blood left and right in an attempt to wake up viewers but winds up flailing around in its own desperation. On the positive side, Gary Kibbe delivers some gorgeous widescreen anamorphic photography (no Super 35 bullstuff here, folks), even utilizing some *Ladyhawke*-style colour filters in some scenes to nice effect. Woods supplies a nicely twisted anti-hero performance, a welcome return to the genre after his memorable turn in *Videodrome*, and Guinee does a good job, relatively speaking, with a ridiculous part.

However flawed the film may be, Columbia has made a first rate DVD. The breathtaking transfer glows with pure, undistorted waves of crimson and orange, while the throbbing Dolby Digital 5.1 mix delivers each gunshot and Carpenter's moody electronic score with great panache. The audio commentary by Carpenter is miles ahead of his soporific comments for *In the Mouth of Madness*, though as usual he often resorts to simply play-by-play descriptions of the onscreen action. Though he missed the mark, at least he's still out there swinging in a genre being threatened to be consumed by inane teens-in-peril postmodern rip-offs; hopefully *Vampires'* successful turn at the box office will result in a Carpenter film more worthy of his name.

THE VAMPIRES' NIGHT ORGY

Colour, 1972, 79m. / Directed by León Klimovsky / Starring Jack Taylor, Dianik Zurakowska / Pagan (UK R2 PAL) / WS (2.35:1)

 Usually overlooked in the history of Spanish horror because it doesn't star Paul Naschy, this atmospheric and fairly rewarding vampire epic bears more in common with the gothic terrors being produced in Italy and other adjoining countries rather than the works of everyone's favourite "hombre lobo." Regular Naschy director León Klimovsky displays a sure hand in this, arguably his most artistically impressive horror achievement and a good introduction for Euro-sleaze newcomers.

In a setup common to many '70s supernatural tales, a busload of innocents takes an unexpected detour when the driver drops dead from a heart attack. The passengers, all future employees ranging from a chauffeur to a gardener at an aristocratic mansion, make their way to a seemingly deserted village. However, they do stumble upon the journeying Luis (Jess Franco regular Jack Taylor), whose car has broken down, at the town bar. That night one of the unlucky newcomers goes to investigate the village's empty streets and comes face to face with its inhabitants, who happen to sport fangs and a very nasty attitude. As their numbers dwindle, the humans attempt to piece together the mystery and find a way to escape with their lives.

Though relatively low on sleaze value considering its title, *The Vampires' Night Orgy* (*La orgia nocturna de los vampiros*) is rarely boring and sports a solid cast of vampires and victims. The always appealing Helga Liné turns up as the vampires' leader and could have used more screen time, while Taylor is a typically solid leading man. The scope photography makes the most of the spooky settings, which feel unnervingly genuine compared to the fog-bound sets of Hammer's vampire sagas. It may not have quite the delirious kick of the Spanish bloodsucking yarns that followed later, namely *Count Dracula's Great Love* and the criminally underrated *Saga of the Draculas*, but most will find their appetite for gothic chills well sated by this little gem.

Pagan's DVD of *The Vampires' Night Orgy* represents an alternate "clothed" edition of what was previously released on the public domain circuit in the US, primarily through Sinister Cinema. Bare breasts are replaced here with nighties, though some skin still slips through (including a brief bit not in the Sinister print). The restoration of the original anamorphic framing adds significantly to the its impact, while the print is in solid condition and, like the original elements, very subdued and greyish in terms of colour. It's grainier and duller looking compared to the sparkling results of, say, Anchor Bay, but a nice edition of this film at all on DVD is a cause for rejoicing. The disc also includes some interesting cast and crew bios, which contain some valuable bits of trivia for Eurofanatics.

VAMPYRES

Colour, 1974, 87m. / Directed by José Larraz / Starring Marianne Morris, Anulka / Anchor Bay (US NTSC R1) / WS (1.85:1) (16:9)

Fran and Miriam are murdered lovers who return from the grave to wreak havoc on promiscuous males. Posing as hitchhikers, the girls lure unsuspecting menfolk back to their remote mansion where they satiate their sexual and visceral desires upon them. But the nocturnal activities up at the

house have attracted the curiosity of a young couple camping nearby, and trouble looms as the woman's inquisitive traits compel her to investigate further.

From its taboo blood-on-breasts pre-credits carnage to the closing moments which cast a shadow of uncertainty over everything the audience has witnessed, *Vampyres* is an exhilarating, soul-penetrating tale, the shock value of which has endured, albeit now more than a quarter of a century old. There has never been denial on anybody's part that the two leads (both dubbed during post-production) were hired for their looks as opposed to any vestige of acting ability, yet it is rewarding that both Morris and Dziubinska should have turned in more worthy performances than one might expect, especially bearing in mind the criteria behind their employ.

Any small cracks where the lack of acting experience may have shown through were skilfully papered over with a strong supporting cast, notably Brian Deacon and an early turn by Michael Byrne. Stir Sally Faulkner, Murray Brown and Larraz stalwart Karl Lanchbury into the mix and you have one of those magical casts that could hardly have been improved upon.

Few productions of such limited funding can claim to be the subject of continued rejoice so long after their lensing, yet it is testament to the power of *Vampyres* that multiple viewings do nothing whatsoever to dilute its impact. Embroidered with lush visuals that boldly defy its meagre budget, to this day it remains one of the most haunting and atmospheric pieces ever committed to celluloid.

It is well documented that *Vampyres* was savagely emasculated upon its UK cinematic release in 1976, losing it almost 3 minutes of material to the censor's shears. This included a good deal of the sexual debauchery and a fair percentage of the blood-letting. Having been released in three incarnations on tape in Britain, all of them cut, Anchor Bay's 21-chapter region free DVD elicits mixed emotions. Struck from the original negative, the film itself bears little discernible wear and tear and with only the most minor traces of grain in the darker shots. Having seen the film in more formats and more often than I care to remember (or admit), I have never seen it looking this good before. But - and it's a ruefully galling but - contrary to what it says on the sleeve, this is not the "uncut and uncensored" manna from heaven that Anchor Bay would have liked us to believe. Regrettably it is missing a total of 29 seconds of precious footage from the murders of campers Harriet and John. Which sadly imbues this particular dish of ambrosia with a bitter tang.

The disc offers up several bonus extras, the highlight of which is commentary by director Jose Larraz and producer Brian Smedley-Aston. Spaniard Larraz is his usual gregarious, occasionally manic self, while Smedley-Aston's British reserve makes for a suitably more level-headed counterbalance. Also included is a brief textual resume of Larraz's work, a stills archive drawn from Smedley-Aston's own collection (nice, but disappointingly limited) and a pair of vastly different trailers. - TG

VAMPYROS LESBOS

Colour, 1970, 90m. / Directed by Jess Franco / Starring Soledad Miranda, Dennis Price / Synapse (US R1 NTSC) / WS (1.66:1), Second Sight (UK R2 PAL) / WS (1.66:1) (16:9)

Completely ignored in most English-speaking countries until the popularity of its soundtrack CD, Jess Franco's *Vampyros Lesbos* (or *Vampiros Lesbos*, as it's titled on the print) has long been a holy grail of European film collectors stuck with second rate, non-subtitled video bootlegs. The title alone causes the imagination to swim with images of slinky vampire vixens skulking through castles and biting their sapphic prey, but the film actually delivers something else entirely. Basically a transition piece between the stylish Franco classics *Succubus* and *The Female Vampire*, the film marks a fetishistic showpiece for the late Soledad Miranda, who graced such other Franco films as *Count Dracula* and the splendid *She Killed in Ecstasy*.

Like *Succubus*, this begins with an elaborate nightclub-style sequence relying on unabashed female nudity and surrealism. The lovely Countess Nadine Corody (Miranda) presides over her vampiric realm on an Iberian island, where unlucky travellers can often stumble into her web. Her latest prey, the lovely Linda Westinghouse (Ewa Stromberg), falls under the Countess' charms, unaware that she is a descendant of Count Dracula. Meanwhile the intrepid Doctor Seward (Paul Muller), a recurring Franco character lifted from Bram Stoker's novel, investigates the mysterious episodes of blood-drinking which plague the otherwise tranquil, sun-washed paradise.

The history of *Vampyros'* release on DVD has been somewhat tangled, as it originated on the videotape circuit usually culled from a German PAL master without subtitles. The first legitimate English subtitled version cropped up on UK VHS from Redemption, and a cleaned-up and very attractive variation on the same transfer (the original and most explicit German version, which contains far more exposed flesh than the mild Spanish cut titled *Las Vampiras*) was released on DVD in the US by Synapse.

The film isn't really as concerned with titillating thrills as the title might imply; the nudity is mostly matter of fact, with Franco devoting his attentions to the dreamlike pacing and weird, off-kilter atmosphere, similar to the luridly titled but elegant *A Virgin among the Living Dead*. While Miranda doesn't get the chance to function as much more than a sexual object, she does so quite magnificently and gives the film much of its visceral power. Of course, there's also the funky lounge soundtrack, something of an underground club legend already, which also popped up most strangely during a sequence in *Jackie Brown*.

The Synapse DVD itself is quite a beguiling treat, lovingly packaged and presented. Apart from the menu screen (which doesn't clearly show the option selected), Franco fans should find no room to quibble here, considering the film's bizarre pedigree (a Spanish film with French opening titles, dubbed in German and subtitled in English!). The optional subtitles don't offer much clarification for those who haven't seen the film in English, as this is definitely a visual-driven work from start to finish. The disc mercifully omits the silly fake "music video" from Redemption's VHS release, opting instead for the very long German theatrical trailer.

The Second Sight DVD in the UK was mastered from more pristine materials and sports a much more colourful appearance, enhanced for widescreen TVs and boasting razor sharp detail. The only drawback is slightly tighter framing, which knocks some of the compositions out of balance. The UK disc also features the trailer, an extensive photo gallery, and a particularly psychedelic cover.

THE VANISHING

Colour, 1988, 106m. / Directed by George Sluizer / Starring Bernard-Pierre Donnadieu, Gene Bervoets / Criterion (US R1 NTSC) / WS (1.78:1) (16:9), Image (US R1 NTSC)

A rare psychological thriller that actually lives up to that label, *The Vanishing (Spoorloos)* crept up in English language art theatres over two years after its completion and quietly scared the bejeezus out of

unsuspecting viewers. The film's structure and manner strongly recall the subdued, mannered suspense puzzles of Claude Chabrol, in which reality barely conceals the monstrous undercurrents of the human psyche, but here director George Sluizer goes one better by delivering a savage, emotional gut punch to the viewer including (but not limited to) the unforgettable final five minutes.

Vacationing Dutch couple Rex Hofman (Gene Bervoets) and Saskia Wagter (Johanna ter Steege) decide to take a holiday in France, and despite some minor squabbles about an empty gas tank, they seem perfectly happy. Rex even vows to never abandon Saskia, though this promise is put to the test when she mysteriously vanishes without a trace at a public rest stop. For three years Rex posts up signs and appears on television, doggedly searching for any clues leading to Saskia's disappearance. Rex turns down potential new girlfriends, instead obsessing over this tremendous unknown mystery in his life, and eventually his persistence pays off when Raymond (Bernard-Pierre Donnadieu) appears. A seemingly normal, happy family man, Raymond takes Rex on a road trip back through the past, during which flashbacks explain how Raymond's intellectually quizzical and perverse personality developed from childhood curiosity to full blown sociopathic tendencies. Only by hearing the whole story, Raymond explains, will Rex ever learn the truth about Saskia's disappearance, and ultimately the two men must test each other's wills to find true knowledge.

Totally devoid of any overt visual flashiness or stylistic tics, *The Vanishing* takes its time to develop its characters and establish how their interlocking psyches have led to such a dangerous, compelling situation. This is one of those haunting "car wreck" types of films, in which the occasional clutch of terror experienced while watching it is nothing compared to the delayed shock that kicks in an hour or so after viewing. (*Angel Heart* is another good example.) The three lead actors are all pitch perfect; though Donnadieu gets most of the standout moments with his quiet malignance, the two lovers are wholly convincing and establish enough of a bond to make the final resolution all the more powerful. Author Tim Krabbé does an expert job of translating his short but dense source novel, *The Golden Egg*, whose title relates to Saskia's dream and its symbolic implications in the final shot. However, this is a rare instance in which the film betters the novel, turning a good story into a lean,

precise, and ruthless screenplay. Unfortunately Sluizer agreed to remake this film under the same title for Fox, and the results (starring Jeff Bridges, Keifer Sutherland, Nancy Travis, and a young Sandra Bullock) pretty much trampled all over everything that made the original so potent and tacked on a gory, ineffective "happy" ending for good measure.

Though best experienced in a darkened, oppressive theatre, *The Vanishing* translates to the small screen with most of its subtle, macabre touches intact. Criterion's DVD is a marked improvement over the earlier Image/Wellspring laserdisc and DVD, which were slightly cropped to full frame and suffered from a soft video transfer with mediocre contrast. The new anamorphic edition looks excellent overall, and while it can't quite conceal the film's low budget origins, the blacks in particular look greatly improved. The optional subtitles also do a more efficient job of conveying the language difficulties as the language swerves back and forth between French and Dutch, and the extra visual information on the sides provides some minor but greatly needed breathing room. Evidently the 102 minute Wellspring version was taken from a time-compressed PAL transfer, as the Criterion version clocks in with an additional four minutes but appears to be identical in content. Some festival screenings reported an original running time of 111 minutes, and despite claims of a longer print from some bootleg video companies, verification of the content in this extended edition is still pending. The DVD also contains the original European theatrical trailer, which adequately conveys the nature of the film without blowing any of its major surprises.

VELVET GOLDMINE

Colour, 1998, 119m. / Directed by Todd Haynes / Starring Ewan McGregor, Jonathan Rhys Meyers / Buena Vista (US R1 NTSC), Cinema Club (UK R2 PAL) / WS (1.85:1) / DD5.1

The late '90s nostalgic burst of indie films geared around the '70s (*54*, *Last Days of Disco*, etc.) bore some strange fruit, but none can compare with *Velvet Goldmine*, a mind-spinning dose of dizzy Ken Russell camp splashed across a nonlinear storyline best described as a pansexual *Eddie and the Cruisers*. In 1984, ten years after the faked onstage assassination of Brit glam rock superstar Brian Slade (Rhys Meyers), reporter Christian Bale (a long way from Empire of the Sun) is assigned to do a retrospective on Slade's bizarre, short-lived career and subsequent disappearance. In classic *Citizen Kane* style, Bale tries to dig up the truth by interviewing people from Slade's past, particularly his ex-wife, Mandy (*Muriel's Wedding*'s Collette, effortlessly sliding her accents to convey an American party girl trying to mould into the London mod scene). Mandy relates tales of Slade's scandalous bisexual antics, his Bowie-styled onstage excesses, and his doomed relationship with Curt Wild (McGregor), a snarling, borderline insane Iggy Pop figure. Meanwhile Bale comes to terms with his own hidden glamorous impulses as Haynes spins out one colourful setpiece after another, beginning with the opening sequence which posits that pop superstars are all descended from Oscar Wilde, an alien glam god whose magical glitter brooch is passed from one successor to another over the ages.

Not one of Miramax's more sedate recent offerings, this will best be appreciated by anyone who can remember or identify with the glam rock era. If you've ever grinned through *Rocky Horror* or *Phantom of the Paradise*, you'll get it. Style rules over substance, gloriously so, and the cast is more than up to the task. McGregor's ferocious rock god will startle anyone introduced to him through *Star Wars* (though it's nothing compared to McGregor's excesses in *The Pillow Book*), and Sandy Powell's amazing costumes never fail to please and startle the eye. Most importantly, as the opening suggests, this is a film to be "played at maximum volume," with a continuously active rock soundtrack ranging from pitch-perfect Bryan Ferry covers to original pseudo-glam ditties crooned by Shudder to Think. Considering the influence of executive producer Michael Stipe, this attention to musical detail shouldn't be surprising, but this is clearly Haynes' show. Even featuring a brief Ken doll homage to his controversial *Superstar: The Karen Carpenter Story*, Haynes' opus fuses his flamboyant visual style (love the "Satellite of Love" sequence) with sly historical nods to famous '70s figures. Clocking in at two hours, the film overstays its welcome by about fifteen minutes but is a pleasurable ride nonetheless for anyone willing to surrender their senses to a complete battering.

The Miramax DVD is generally attractive if not outstanding; an anamorphic transfer would have been preferable, but this looks about as good as this low budget effort can for the moment. The room-pounding Dolby Digital soundtrack is serviced more effectively, with the music's glorious vinyl-tinged qualities preserved even in the home video medium. Also includes the US theatrical trailer; the UK disc adds a photo gallery and illustrated text supplements about the glam and glitter rock scene.

VENGEANCE

Colour, 1968, 99m. / Directed by Anthony Dawson (Antonio Margheriti) / Starring Richard Harrison / Image (US R0 NTSC) / WS (2.35:1) (16:9)

Though best known as the occasionally inspired hand behind such diverse Italian horror favourites as *Castle of Blood* and *Cannibal Apocalypse*, director Antonio Margheriti (or according to nearly every print in existence, Anthony M. Dawson - no relation to the *Dr. No* actor) often dabbled in a variety of B-movie subgenres. One of his stabs at the burgeoning spaghetti western niche, *Vengeance*, opened in its native country under the more florid title of *Joko invoca Dio... e muori (or Joko, Call to God and Die)*. Competent and rarely dull, the film obviously falls short of its direct inspiration, the Sergio Leone "Dollars" trilogy, but a dogged lead performance, solid atmosphere, some unexpected homoerotic undercurrents, and several surprising dashes of sadism make it worth checking out.

As usual, revenge and an elaborate back story form the crux of the anti-hero's motivations, this time beginning with a harrowing pre-credit sequence in which a young man is drawn and quartered by a sadistic posse. His friend, the half-breed Rocco (*Mad Dog Killer*'s Richard Harrison), had ridden with him during a plan to heist a large amount of gold, but treachery turned the whole deal sour. Now wandering aimlessly from town to town, Rocco becomes a vigilante, tearing through the traitors and possible sources of information (including the requisite belle, Jane, played by Mariangela Giordano). Along the way a number of colourful characters both villainous and friendly partake in bar brawls and showdowns, including a surprising appearance by the always memorable Werner Pochath, who later turned up in Dario Argento's *The Cat o' Nine Tails* and grossed out Euro-cultists with his leading role in *Mosquito*. The whole ordeal ends appropriately enough with an eerily filmed confrontation in a massive series of underground caverns, where destiny takes over to deal a new hand.

One of Margheriti's few films shot in scope, *Vengeance* sports some magnificent, amber-tinted cinematography but betrays the director's unease with wide framing, frequently boxing its characters to the centre of the screen and rarely taking full advantage of the expected wide open western scenery. In a sense this approach works for the film, however, giving it a queasy and off-kilter quality complemented by an unusually traditional orchestral score by renowned orchestrator Carlo Savina. Though not usually a terribly compelling leading man, Harrison handles his duties well enough as a dogged, angry protagonist, shooting some nasty glares into the camera but also maintaining enough charm and physical skill to keep the viewer rooting for him.

The Image DVD looks exceptionally good for a film of this vintage, and apart from the scratchy opening credits, which could easily have been spliced in from another print, the source material is in excellent condition. The decision to go with anamorphic enhancement results in a beautifully smooth, detailed presentation, and the colour schemes, which could have looked dull and muddy in a lesser transfer, are more impressive and nuanced here. The mono sound comes off well and bears no distracting signs of distortion. Apart from a nice poster reproduction on the poster the disc is devoid of extras, but fans of Euro-oaters will find this essential viewing all the same.

THE VENGEANCE OF SHE

Colour, 1968, 101m. / Directed by Cliff Owen / Starring John Richardson, Olinka Berova / WS (1.66:1) / Anchor Bay (US R1 NTSC)

Another cinematic spin-off from H. Rider Haggard's novel, Vengeance of She has been largely overshadowed by the popular original film, which featured Ursula Andress in one of her best roles. Ayesha, Andress' glamorous female ruler, was doomed to a fated romance with Killikrates (John Richardson), a tale which is continued in this sequel. Richardson returns again, this time convinced that Ayesha has been reincarnated as Carol (Olinka Berova), a young girl oblivious of her past who is summoned to the land of Kuma after a bizarre modern day opening in the Riviera. After many bad dreams and telepathic encounters, Carol begins to accept her destiny as a ruler, with the expected action-filled and violent consequences.

Less opulent than its predecessor but still compulsively entertaining, Vengeance of She boasts a more laid-back continental atmosphere accentuated by Mario Nascimbene's wonderful score, which effortlessly bounces from catchy lounge to full blooded orchestral adventure attacks. The performances are fairly wooden for the most part, understandable given the tone of the subject

matter, though Richardson still manages to mine some emotional texture out of his character. As Carol/Ayesha, Berova (who vanished for some reason) is little more than a clotheshorse here but manages to fill the challenging boots of Ms. Andress quite nicely.

Like the other Hammer DVDs, the quality is absolutely stellar in every respect. It's nice to see Hammer is preserving all of its titles so well, and the immaculate presentation of these prints really goes a long way to restoring the entertainment value to films once dismissed completely as ragged-looking late night TV fodder. As with the other titles, this includes both the trailer and TV spots, as well as a repro of the European poster design (with a very funny tagline that makes this look like some kind of fashion-conscious S&M epic).

VENUS IN FURS

B&W, 2000, 65m. / Directed by Maartje Seyferth & Victor Nieuwenhuijs / Starring Anne Van Der Ven / DVD Video International (US R1 NTSC) / DD2.0

One of the pioneering works of erotic fiction, Venus in Furs became a familiar title in popular culture after the Velvet Underground immortalized it with a tribute song on their classic Velvet Underground and Nico album, which in turn spawned a number of late '60s European films. The best among these was Jess Franco's 1969 adaptation, which retained the female protagonist's name and the S&M theme, but little else. Incidentally, the original memoir by Leopold von Sacher Masoch spawned the original term "masochism," and his real life wife eventually retaliated with an alternate erotic memoir of her own. It certainly took long enough, but a couple of Dutch filmmakers decided to actually make a film called Venus in Furs that faithfully follows the events of the book.

Shot in a slow, static, visually arresting style (in gorgeous black and white, no less), the film begins with the dejected Severin (Andre Arend Van Noord) resting in an empty town square reflecting on his relationship with Wanda (Anne Van Der Ven), who asked him to sign a contract vowing his status as her lover. Severin's day to day existence working on a train allows him to freely fantasize about his lover, who in some ways reminds him of his domineering fur coated aunt, who forced him to act as her servant when he was twelve. Naturally Severin got a sexual kick out of this relationship and willingly undergoes the same treatment from Wanda, with whom he descends into increasingly dangerous mind games.

Considering all it has going for it - a solid literary source, a nifty visual style, heaps of sex, and a lush soundtrack peppered with Mahler, Grieg, and Tchaikovsky - it's difficult to pinpoint exactly why *Venus in Furs* remains about as interesting to watch as paint drying. Part of the blame may lie with the two leads, who look more like wasted junkies than world weary European connoisseurs of sexual experimentation. The lousy English dubbing over the original dialogue (presumably Dutch) doesn't help, though thankfully verbal exchanges are kept to a minimum. (For those interested in the plot, however, the DVD offers subtitles in English, Dutch, German, Japanese, Italian, Spanish, and French!) Many scenes feel cribbed from better arty films, ranging from Peter Greenaway's *The Belly of an Architect* (note the opening scene and Severin's office wall papered with sketches) and Just Jaeckin's *Story of O,* which clearly inspired the finale. As an experiment, this is perhaps worth watching for some individual powerful images (such as a recurring low angle tracking shot of Wanda's high heeled shoes ascending a flight of stairs), but fans of Eurotica will find this one pretty tough going despite the heavy helpings of skin on display. The full frame image quality and the fairly well separated stereo sound are both fine, without any noticeable compression problems.

AMC) features several interviews and behind the scenes nuggets of information which are carried through to the other supplements, including stills, ad art, and the notorious alternate ending which was mercifully left on the floor over the years.

So does the film itself merit all this attention? Absolutely. A fetishistic masterpiece, *Vertigo* concerns "Scotty" Ferguson (James Stewart), a police detective whose involvement in the death of a fellow officer has left him cursed with an acute fear of heights. An old college chum, Gavin Elster (Tom Helmore), hires Scotty to follow Elster's wife, Madeleine (Kim Novak, never better), who may be possessed from beyond the grave by a distant relative. To reveal more, of course, would be heresy. Steeped in the obsessions that flicker through the rest of Hitchcock's work, this remains an achingly personal statement on the human instinct to reshape others into our own fabricated images and the consuming nature of passion even beyond death. Stewart, brilliantly cast against type, delivers a gutsy, terrifying performance unlike anything else he ever attempted. The film's relative failure at the box office at the time is understandable, as the film is about as anti-'50s as one can imagine, but its acceptance now in more jaded, self-analytical times seems highly appropriate. A magnificent film, definitely worthy of the multiple viewings and intense study it has finally received in recent years.

VERTIGO

Colour, 1958, 128m. / Directed by Alfred Hitchcock / Starring James Stewart, Kim Novak / Universal / WS (1.85:1) / DD5.1

The restoration of Hitchcock's *Vertigo* has already been covered exhaustively, even with an entire book devoted to the subject, but simply put, the film has never looked better than it does here. The eye-popping hues and exquisite cinematography easily shame the earlier MCA laserdisc, though a few quibbles can justifiably be made with the tampered "restored" soundtrack which adds and amplifies new sound effects like crumpling paper and footsteps to a distracting degree. On the other hand, Herrmann's score sounds terrific blasting from every available speaker instead of the old mono mix, and the plentiful extras cover everything you could want to know about the film. The entertaining and inform-ative restoration documentary (commissioned for

VERY BAD THINGS

Colour, 1998, 100m. / Directed by Peter Berg / Starring Christian Slater, Cameron Diaz / Polygram (US R1 NTSC) / WS (1.85:1) (16:9) / DD5.1

Black comedy is a very tricky balancing act, and as the violently opposed critical reaction of *Very Bad Things* demonstrates, even a successful one can't please everybody. First time director Peter Berg (*The Last Seduction*) displays a truly warped side of his personality here, and the absence of any likable characters may account for why many viewers expecting a jaunty gross-out fest like *There's Something About Mary* went flying for the exit doors.

Kyle (*Swingers'* Jon Favreau) decides to head out to Vegas with four of his buddies for a wild bachelor party, much to the disapproval of his wedding-obsessed fiancée, Laura (Cameron Diaz). Kyle's friends hire a hooker who offers to go way beyond topless dancing, and one of the guests (Piven) drags the girl off to the bathroom for a

V

cocaine-hazed sexual frenzy that winds up with the hooker dead on the floor. After another gruesome twist, the boys all wind up with a bloody mess on their hands and decide to dispose of it thanks to a few shovels and a barren stretch of desert land. Unfortunately, the truth can't stay buried for long as the five wind up backbiting each other and threatening to expose their deadly secret. In particular, married man Daniel Stern threatens to crack up, much to the distress of his tough-as-nails wife (Jeanne Tripplehorne). Worst of all, Slater, essentially doing a variation on his Jason Dean character from *Heathers* after too many self-starter courses, decides that murder is the fastest and easiest way to tie up the loose ends...

Bloody hip comedies in the post-Tarantino era can easily sink under the weight of their pretension without a strong script and cast to hold them up (*Things to Do in Denver When You're Dead*, for example), but at least *Very Bad Things* boasts a terrific ensemble of actors who wring each gory chuckle for all they're worth. Diaz in particular has a field day with what begins as a thankless part but manages to take an unexpected, deliciously nasty turn, and Tripplehorne threatens to steal the entire film with a raging freak-out scene that easily kicks her career back into overdrive after the debacle of *Waterworld*. Favreau is saddled with the most difficult part, a character that doesn't really do anything overtly horrible but becomes completely implicated by his willingness to go along with the increasing number of evil deeds piling up around him.. It doesn't work all the way through and the overabundance of screaming wears on one's nerves after a while, but at least they tried something different and pulled it off.

Polygram's anamorphic widescreen transfer looks fine, particularly during the neon-soaked Vegas scenes, and the spacious Dolby Digital mix makes inventive use of background music swirling around the exterior channels throughout the film. The letterboxed version is really the only way to go, since it looks much better than the pan-and-scan version also offered on the DVD (surprisingly, this was shot hardmatted at 1.85:1 and is not opened up to full frame). The DVD also includes filmographies for the major players, an alternate Dolby Surround track in English, Dolby Digital in French, and the original US trailer (which gives away far, far too much).

VIBRATION

B&W, 1968, 84m. / Directed by Torbjörn Axelman / Starring Essy Persson, Margareta Sjödin / First Run (US R1 NTSC) / WS (1.78:1)

As the 1960s drew to a close, European erotica really had its work cut out for it. In particular, Sweden, the country known for crashing American art houses with racy dramas, found itself competing with other countries like France and Italy to produce the latest *scandal du jour*. Budgets got bigger, acting got better, and plots became richer as directors tried to push the envelope, and no one benefited from this more than director and distributor Radley Metzger. *Vibration (Lejonsommar)* was released overseas hot on the heels of Metzger's *Therese and Isabelle,* also starring the fascinating and talented Essy Persson, and it shows the increasing influence of directors like Ingmar Bergman (who, lest we forget, was also promoted at first in the US more for his flashes of skin than his artistic merit). Arty editing, sundappled cinematography, and joyous sexuality are the order of the day here, and *Vibration* is a breezy reminder of what softcore was like just before Sweden's next big shocker export, *I Am Curious (Yellow)*.

During one tranquil summer, struggling writer Mauritz (Sven-Bertil Taube) takes a trip to a provincial Swedish island where he meets vivacious golden girl Barbro (Margareta Sjödin). The two begin a languorous affair mostly enjoyed in the great outdoors. Their idyllic love is torn apart, however, when his eye is caught by free spirit film actress Eliza (Persson), whose vacation plans include introducing Mauritz to the wonders of mod parties, motorcycle racing, and hot sex in greenhouses. Which lady will ultimately win his heart?

Vibration in many ways marks a strange collision between the dreamy eroticism for which Sweden had become known and the attempt to appeal to swinging teen audiences as well. The camera's tendency to drift in for painterly close ups of hands, feet, and other body parts makes for a dreamlike experience (and cuts down on dubbing problems as well), while the catchy lounge music keeps the story from drifting too far off into the ether. As usual Persson really dominates the screen when she appears, and as with Therese, the whole story is rendered as a flashback by the striking actress, who possesses an uncanny ability to change appearance from a world weary woman to a giggly schoolgirl with the flash of a smile.

Many of the Audubon transfers from First Run have been an erratic bag, but *Vibration* is easily among the cleanest and clearest of the bunch, most likely because completely new elements had to be used in absence of a prior video transfer. The letterboxing looks just right, and the print is almost entirely clean and free of distracting glitches. Contrast is excellent, with sharp detail reproduction. The dubbed English audio track is acceptable but wasn't anything to shout about in the beginning. The disc also includes a Persson gallery from the film, the striking Vibration US trailer, and a host of other Audubon trailers like *The Libertine* (when is that one going to get a decent letterboxed DVD release?), *Girls Who Like Girls, Therese and Isabelle, The Frightened Woman, Daniella by Night*, and Essy's big breakthrough film, *I, a Woman*. More on that one below.

VIDEODROME

Colour, 1982, 89m. / Directed by David Cronenberg / Starring James Woods, Deborah Harry / Universal (US R1 NTSC) / WS (1.85:1)

David Cronenberg's free-form masterpiece of philosophical kink still has teeth. For the uninitiated, James Woods stars as Max Renn, an underground porn TV pirate who stumbles upon a brutal new sex and torture program, "Videodrome." His girl of the moment, radio therapist Deborah Harry (yes, from Blondie, in her feature debut) becomes aroused by the show and reveals some nasty secrets of her own. Things just go downhill from there as Max finds his body and consciousness transformed by a techno-psychic battle between an extreme moral majority group and proponents of "the New Flesh."

Rarely linear and certain to put off newcomers, this relentless dissection of the human body as a moral and intellectual battlefield was a resounding flop on its initial release but has since gained a very strong following.

The DVD should continue to cement its critical respect; though hardly a pretty film, its gritty textures and ominous shadows grab the eye as never before, and the throbbing blues and reds are picture perfect. The Dolby Digital mono soundtrack is extremely clean and shows off Howard Shore's unnerving electronic score to its finest effect. The original trailer is also included, and it's a riot, consisting of cruddy first-grader animation that was probably responsible for the film's box office death.

For the record, yes, this is the same unrated version previously issued on video, containing a few nasty shots (notably Barry Convex's death scene) trimmed from theatrical prints. However, it does not contain the rejected scenes that appeared a few years ago on A&E's late night cable airings. While these snippets would have made an interesting supplement, their absence isn't much to cry about as Cronenberg himself was the one who excised them. Essential, if mind-threatening, viewing for the adventurous.

A VIEW TO A KILL

Colour, 1985, 130m. / Directed by John Glen / Starring Roger Moore, Christopher Walken / MGM / WS (2.35:1) (16:9) / DD5.1

Suspicious activity within the microchip manufacturing industry has James Bond (Moore) investigating millionaire businessman Max Zorin (Walken). 007 trails him to the outskirts of Paris, then on to San Francisco where Zorin plans to manipulate an earthquake which will result in the flooding of Silicon Valley, allowing him to monopolize the world production and supply of microchips.

By 1985 Roger Moore was only a couple of years shy of collecting his bus pass, and no amount of pancake could disguise the fact. Much as one might like jolly Roger, it stretches credibility to the zenith that fetching females such as Tanya Roberts, Fiona Fullerton and Mary Stavin would be queuing up to hop between the sheets with him, and consequently their flirtatious shenanigans verge on embarrassing. The previous Bond, *Octopussy*, was ballyhooed as "Bond's All Time High". *A View to a Kill*, with its ridiculously convoluted plotting, is Bond's all time low. The Parisian car capers are crummy, the foolish fire engine mischief in San Francisco is more suited to The Keystone Cops than a 007 thriller, and it takes more than blowing up another massive set (this time it's an abandoned silver mine) to disguise the shadow of mediocrity that hangs over the entire production. Perhaps most damaging of all, the pacing is sloth-like; if the middle third moved any slower it would be stationary. At least an infusion of palatable villainy - an admirably deranged Chris Walken, manic powerhouse Grace Jones and wily Patrick Bauchau (Argento's *Phenomena*) - distracts one from dwelling too much on the fact this is the worst Bond of them all. The glacial action during the pre-credits is quite good (until it degenerates into comic capers - didn't they learn anything from *Moonraker*?!) and the fisticuffs finale atop the Golden Gate Bridge is pretty reasonable too, even though Moore's stunt double is rather obvious.

If it's 007 you want and there's nothing else available, then this entry in the series will fill the bill adequately enough, after all, even at his weakest nobody does it better than Bond. But as an example of the formula at its well-oiled best, *A View to a Kill* fails miserably.

Poor movie, nice collection of extras. MGM's special edition DVD, which offers a 2.35:1 matted, 32-chapter print of the film additionally includes a behind the scenes overview, a second documentary studying the music of the Bond films, a single (slightly jokey) deleted scene, Duran Duran's cheap-looking music video, a commentary from director John Glen and members of the cast and crew, three trailers and four TV spots. Language options are English or Spanish and subtitles are provided in French and Spanish. - TG

THE VIKING QUEEN

Colour, 1967, 91m. / Directed by Don Chaffey / Starring Don Murray, Carita / Anchor Bay (US R1 NTSC) / WS (1.85:1)

Sporting one of the better Hammer girl film casts, *The Viking Queen* never transcends its basic pinup intentions but does continue to hold up as a fast-moving, literate, and eye-catching costume actioner. Perhaps because it features the same director *as Jason and the Argonauts* and *One Million Years B.C.,* the robust, straightforward treatment here keeps the silly chuckles in check for the most part, with an emphasis on story progression and brutal battle setpieces.

The shapely Carita (a make-up artist who gave up acting after this lone venture) portrays the titular queen, Salina, a peace-loving woman caught in the power struggles between England and Rome as an uprising stirs among the grumbling Druids. In the role of Justinian, American action star Don Murray lends some weight to the proceedings as Salina's forbidden love, while the well chosen supporting cast should please Hammer fans and horror buffs alike, including as it does Andrew Keir (Professor Quatermass himself), Adrienne Corri *(*from *Vampire Circus*), and Niall MacGinnis (also seen in *Curse of the Demon*), to name the most obvious. An entertaining and fairly stylish film, this is the kind of popcorn muncher completely forgotten after viewing.

As usual, the Anchor Bay DVD looks marvellous, perfectly letterboxed and boasting some truly dazzling candy-like colour schemes.

THE VIRGIN SUICIDES

Colour, 2000, 96m. / Directed by Sofia Coppola / Starring Kirsten Dunst, Kathleen Turner / Paramount (US R1 NTSC), Pathé (UK R2 PAL) / WS (1.85:1) (16:9) / DD5.1

This striking feature film debut for Sofia Coppola (her *Godfather III* days mercifully long behind her) deserves more than the lukewarm reception it received during a few small venue showings from Paramount's art film division. Sort of a fusion of *Picnic at Hanging Rock* by way of *The Ice Storm,* the deliberately slippery narrative relates the story of the five Lisbon girls, part of a suburban Michigan family "25 years ago," from the point of view of a group of bewildered neighbourhood boys attempting to untangle the clues and motivations leading to their premature suicides. The girls' ultimate deaths are given away by both the film's title and the opening monologue (by Giovanni Ribisi); given this unavoidable outcome, the viewer is instead guided through a surreal depiction of '70s suburbia as a battleground in which youthful innocence is ultimately suffocated.

The conservative and overly protective Mr. and Mrs. Lisbon (a frumpy looking James Woods and Kathleen Turner) attempt to maintain a portrait of normalcy even after the attempted wrist-slashing "cry for help" of their 13-year-old daughter, Cecilia (Hanna Hall). Upon Cecilia's return from the hospital, the Lisbons throw a party for the neighbourhood kids, which climaxes with Cecilia hurling herself out a window and landing on the spiked gate outside the family domicile. The most outgoing and sexually desired of the daughters, Lux (Kirsten Dunst), becomes the object of desire for high school stud Trip Fontaine (a less insufferable than usual Josh Hartnett). Trip convinces Mr. Lisbon to allow Lux to attend a post-game school dance, under the condition that the other girls have dates as well and remain under adult supervision for the entire evening. Unfortunately, teen hormones and emotional confusion thwart the evening, setting off a tragic chain of ultimately inexplicable events.

Aiming for the same sort of dreamy, detached responses generated by looking at faded '70s snapshots, Coppola deftly adapts Jeffrey Eugenides' novel and captures the wistful mixture of goofiness and tragedy that characterizes the coming-of-age experience. The treatment hardly aims for a realistic treatment of teen suicide, instead using it as a metaphor for the unfortunate and often stifling passage to adulthood (capped perfectly in a surreal, unexpected society party coda bathed entirely in hues of green). While the injection of celebrity cameos like Danny DeVito, Michael Pare, and Scott Glenn in minor roles proves to be a camera-waving distraction, the actors are all in top form, with Dunst adding yet another fetching performance to her already stunning roster. The often breathtaking cinematography utilizes a number of techniques including time lapse, split screen, and superimpositions to evoke the cinematic equivalent of a teen's stream of consciousness scribbling in a diary, while the borderline supernatural and horrific elements (such as the eerie appearances of Cecilia's ghost) are handled delicately without rupturing the story itself. A remarkable score by French electronica/pop group Air adds the perfect dreamlike sheen to the film, with a few startling nods to Goblin's *Dawn of the Dead* score thrown in for good measure.

Paramount's DVD of *The Virgin Suicides* does a terrific job of presenting a visually problematic film. The film grain apparent in many scenes is a deliberate stylistic choice, as are the often unnatural and oversaturated suffusions of colour, which could have been plucked from the cover of a record album. The expansive 5.1 soundtrack sounds superior to the film's theatrical presentation, with more thrust given to the score at several key moments without becoming overly showy, and dialogue is always clearly intelligible. Though Coppola does not provide a commentary track, an enlightening half hour documentary on Paramount's release adequately proves her skill behind the camera. Proud pa Francis Ford Coppola is shown on occasion during a visit to the set, often sitting back and chatting with Glenn, but there's no doubt who was really in charge. Eugenides and several cast members also appear for quick interviews, punctuated with behind the scenes footage from several key scenes.

The disc also includes the snappy theatrical trailer, a production and promotional photo gallery, and a marvellous video for Air's theme song, "Playground Love;" obviously filmed simultaneously during the production of the film, this is one of the cleverest uses of film and song promotion in recent memory. The Pathé UK features the same transfer but only contains the trailer as an extra.

VIY (THE VIJ)

Colour, 1967, 72m. / Directed by Aleksandr Ptushko and Georgi Kropachyov & Konstantin Yershov / Starring Leonid Kuralev / Ruscico (R0 NTSC) / DD5.1

This unique, underappreciated fusion of provincial fantasy and full-blooded horror has won over admirers in the West, even without acceptable English language versions available, thanks to its striking special effects sequences engineered by the great Aleksandr Ptushko (*The Day the Earth Froze*). However, his famous fairy tale aesthetics come into much darker play here, as he tackles the fantastic fiends of Nikolai Gogol's popular short story, "The Vij" (adapted much more loosely in Mario Bava's *Black Sunday*).

The simple storyline concerns a young, cocky lad named Khoma Brut (Leonid Kuralev), a seminary student in training for the priesthood, who loses his way into a dark forest and separates from his companions on the road. There he encounters a witch who carries him aloft for a dark moonlit adventure from which he barely escapes with his life. At a nearby village, the novice is asked by the locals to stay in their eerie wooden church for three nights to recite holy verses over the body of the wealthiest citizen's daughter (Natalya Varley); unfortunately, as he discovers while trapped for the first night in the church, the dead girl is also the witch... who rises from her coffin, stopped only by a holy circle of chalk drawn around the frightened seminarian. The villagers refuse to believe him the next day and force him to return for two more nights of unbridled horror, during which the sorceress unleashes all of the powers of the underworld to break the magic circle.

Running a tight 72 minutes, this film never overstays its welcome and wisely leaves the viewer wanting more. The second and third witch attacks are among Ptushko's finest work, as the witch rides her coffin in circles through the air, monsters pour from the walls, giant hands erupt from the floor, and "Viy" himself makes an appearance for the grand finale. The rest of the film is a skilful example of the balance between wonder and dread, with religion playing a prominent role from the opening moments to the final, ironic closing lines.

Thanks to Japanese laserdisc, *Viy* (or *The Vij*, depending on the print) became something of a grey market video staple, but the Ruscico DVD lifts it to a new level entirely. The stunning disc offers a virtually immaculate, restored video presentation, as well as multiple language options including soundtracks in Russian, English, and French (all skilfully remixed into 5.1) and subtitles in English, French, Dutch, Japanese, German, Russian, and so on. The atmospheric animated menus begin in

V

Russian but can be changed into English by clicking to the left. As if having this rare masterpiece of the supernatural in English on DVD weren't enough, the package is decked out with a mouth-watering array of extras. The theatrical trailer (in English, oddly enough) and a half hour documentary (in Russian with optional subtitles) about Gogol lead the pack, followed by three marvellous silent horror short films: "Satan Exultant," "The Queen of Spades," and the jarring "The Portrait," which is nearly worth the price tag by itself. Simply put, every self-respecting horror fan needs this DVD.

THE VOYEUR

Colour, 1993, 91m./ Directed by Tinto Brass / Starring Katarina Vasilassa, Francesco Casale / Nouveaux (UK R2 PAL), Dutch Filmworks (Holland R2 PAL) / WS (1.66:1)

One of Tinto's most popular titles, *The Voyeur (L'uomo che guarda)* is in many ways his definitive opus. Dodo (Francesco Casale), a university professor, languishes in his posh penthouse where he obsesses over the unusual habits of his luscious wife, Sylvia (Katarina Vasilissa), who comes and goes at odd hours day and night. Thanks to a handy peephole in the bathroom, Dodo also observes the carnal habits of his father, Alberto (Franco Branciaroli), who cavorts with his nubile nursemaid, Fausta (Cristina Garavaglia). Dodo flashes back to his own romantic dalliances both before and during his marriage, before the entire complex web of characters finally resolves itself in the tidy finale.

Beautifully scored by the reliable Riz Ortolani, *The Voyeur* is a good example of how structure and photography can make a softcore film gripping even during the long stretches when the characters aren't copulating, and Euro film buffs will probably savour what is most likely the closest Brass has come to the aesthetic heights of Radley Metzger and Walerian Borowczyk, for example.

The British DVD release is very slightly letter-boxed, features an attractive if slightly washed out transfer, and, like other Brass DVD releases, comes outfitted with a juicy still gallery. The BBFC reports an 8 second trim from the film, which is not immediately evident in the final cut but was most likely assigned to a lingering view of one of the fake prosthetic phalluses favoured over the real thing by Brass. The Dutch DVD release is intact, in Italian with Dutch subtitles.

WATER DROPS ON BURNING ROCKS

Colour, 1999, 80m. / Directed by François Ozon / Starring Bernard Giraudau, Malik Zidi / Zeitgeist (US R1 NTSC) / WS (1.66:1), Paramount (France R2 PAL) / WS (1.66:1) (16:9) / DD2.0

Apart from being gay and unbelievably prolific, directors François Ozon and the late Rainer Werner Fassbinder wouldn't seem to have much in common. Nevertheless the meeting of these two devious minds can be witnessed in the exquisitely cruel *Water Drops on Burning Rocks (Gouttes d'eau sur pierres brûlantes)*, based on an early, unproduced Fassbinder play. Impeccably cast and shot, *Water Drops* overcomes the stagy, prosaic nature of its source and displays the strength of both men who dramatically represent European art cinema at its most potent.

The four act story begins when Leopold (former heartthrob Bernard Giraudau), a fifty year old insurance salesman, brings home twenty year old Franz (Malik Zidi) to his swinging '70s Berlin apartment. Though Franz plans to marry Anna (Ludvine Sagnier), Leo quickly wins him over and turns him into his willing houseboy. Six months later the two have become a bickering couple, unable to separate sexual desire from the misery they thoughtlessly inflict on each other. When Leo goes out of town for business, Anna stops by to visit and tries to lure Franz back to her side. The situation becomes even more complicated when Leo returns early, just in time for the unexpected arrival of his ex-girlfriend, Vera (Anna Thomson), who has a few surprises of her own.

With its smooth editing and quirky sense of humour, *Water Drops* somehow never becomes depressing or overdone. The kitschy wallpaper, shag carpeting, and clothing somehow work perfectly in context with the film, though the undeniable centre-piece is the foursome's rousing dance routine to Tony Holiday's campy "Tanze Samba mit mir" (used in its entirety for the US trailer). The tone of the film is far more Ozon than Fassbinder; the dark, glossy Ballhaus visuals which made that German *enfant terrible*'s descents into misery so striking have been replaced by Ozon's austere, brightly lit, ironic compositions, more attuned to the wry but penetrating tactics of Ozon's earlier *Sitcom*. Critics have often made note of Ozon's penchant for shock value, though this "failing" actually seems less characteristic the more one sees of his work. Very little of the "edgy" material in *Water Drops*, from its

V

perverse plot twists to its oddly voluptuous female nudity, will seem especially novel to anyone familiar with '70s art cinema; instead Ozon appropriates the titillating elements to enhance his more serious study of human nature at its basest, where even the most sincere love can transform people into monsters.

Due to its recent vintage and wide palette of candy colours, *Water Drops* looks very good as expected on DVD, though the French version has an edge thanks to its anamorphic enhancement. The mild letterboxing looks about right, though the non-removable (but large and always legible) English subtitles on the US version may be obtrusive. Since it actually clocks in almost five minutes short of the original 85 minute running time (at least according to all of the film's international press info), the US disc may have originated from a PAL source, which would run slightly faster in NTSC (though the time drop still seems steep). Though the film sports a Dolby Digital/DTS credit, the disc is in standard surround and sounds just fine given the dialogue-driven nature of the film. Music receives some ambient support from the front speakers, and the showstopper dance routine has enough oomph to rattle the floors. Extras on the US disc include the aforementioned US trailer, the French trailer (which contains some spoilers but thankfully has no subs), bios and filmographies for Ozon and Fassbinder, a fun sing-along subtitle option for "Tanze Samba" in English or German, and an English translation for the German poem Franz recites twice in the film to poignant effect. The French disc (with optional English or French subs) includes an Ozon commentary, interviews with the four leads, and the 27 minute short film, "Une rose entre nous" (without subs, but still enjoyable).

WHAT EVER HAPPENED TO AUNT ALICE?

Colour, 1969, 101m. / Directed by Lee H. Katzin / Starring Geraldine Page, Ruth Gordon / Anchor Bay (US R1 NTSC) / WS (1.85:1) (16:9)

Now here's a fun little slice of Grand Guignol from the *Baby Jane* era. Geraldine Page has a field day as Claire Marrable, an Arizona society woman whose life is thrown into turmoil when her supposedly wealthy husband dies, leaving her only with a dagger, a stamp book, and a mountain of debt. Poor Claire has a hissyfit and kills off her housekeeper, then buries the body beneath a new pine tree beside her remote Tucson home. After performing a similar service for her next housekeeper, elderly Miss Tinsley (Mildred Dunnock), Claire's life begins to change. Alice Dimmock (Ruth Gordon) arrives to fill the now vacant housekeeper slot and seems to be a dream come true, complete with a hefty personal savings to invest in Claire's phoney stockbroker scheme. Since the number of pine trees seems to be growing exponentially, Alice's days are clearly numbered. Then single mom Harriet (Rosemary Forsyth) moves into the abandoned cottage next door, putting a serious strain on Claire's murderous financial plans. Harriet is also dating a racecar specialist, Mike (*The Brain from Planet Arous'* Robert Fuller), who figures into the plot much more than Claire suspects.

Following the success of his crazy old lady romps like *What Ever Happened to Baby Jane?* and *Hush... Hush, Sweet Charlotte* (with *The Dirty Dozen* thrown in there for some contrast), director Robert Aldrich went completely independent so he could produce pet projects like *The Killing of Sister George*. For this third instalment in his gothic series, he only stayed on as producer and turned over directing chores to Lee Katzin, a TV specialist who went on to do *The Phynx*. Katzin does a competent job here and mostly sits back to allow Page to run rampant, turning in a great villainous performance that ranks up there with her Southern belle gone bad in *The Beguiled*. You've just got to love any film in which Page denigrates a stray dog by declaring, "I will not have my lovingly cared for garden wrecked by that vagrant bitch!" Regular Aldrich composer Gerald Fried provides a loud, catchy score, complete with a theme song of course, and the arid desert setting produces some memorable, creepy visuals. The original "M" (or "Mature") rating was later changed to an "R" by the MPAA, though it would easily get a PG-13 today for a couple of bloodless head bonkings with a shovel. Morbid it may be, but this isn't a whole lot rougher than *Arsenic and Old Lace*. Unfortunately even Page's showstopping performance can't quite cover up the lame final scene; any viewer should be able to come up with at least a dozen variations more clever than what the screenwriter finally dreamed up.

Briefly released by Magnetic Video (now Fox) on VHS in the early '80s, *What Ever Happened to Aunt Alice?* (credited as *Whatever* on the posters) was notoriously hard to see for many years. Anchor Bay's DVD brings this film back to be savoured by its cult following and hopefully win over a few new fans in the process. The widescreen presentation looks close to immaculate, with only one or two blotches on the print keeping it from opening night quality. The colour is less vibrant than the Magnetic

W

tape, but this may be intentional considering how pumped up many of those early transfers were. The mono audio is fine but, as always, the music is often much louder than the dialogue and may cause lots of scrambling for the volume control. Thankfully the original trailer is included, and it's a doozy - lots of voices yelping "Aunt Alice! Aunt Alice!" during the story's more frenzied moments.

WHAT HAVE THEY DONE TO YOUR DAUGHTERS?

Colour, 1972, 85m. / Directed by Massimo Dallamano / Starring Giovanna Ralli, Claudio Cassinelli / Redemption (UK R0 PAL) / WS (2.35:1)

A textbook '70s Italian thriller, *What Have They Done to Your Daughters?* (originally *La polizia chiede aiuto*, or *The Police Cry for Help*) operates primarily as a cop procedural study crossed with a black-gloved giallo film. While this combination is hardly unique (e.g., the awful *Five Women for a Murderer*), Dallamano's film succeeds thanks to the sheer nastiness and forcefulness of its vision. Following the discovery of a nude fifteen-year-old girl hanged in an attic, the local police quickly uncover clues indicating she may have been murdered elsewhere and been framed as a suicide. The local Assistant D.A. (Giovanna Ralli, a great example of creative casting) teams up with the officer in charge (Claudio Cassinelli) for a grimy trip into the underbelly of the Italian urban scene, including a covert prostitute ring of underage girls. Meanwhile a cleaver-wielding killer stalks the investigating parties in his chic black leather motorcycle gear, forcing the police to unravel the corruption surrounding them before it's too late.

Displaying the same potentially unhealthy fixation with young schoolgirls in (and out of) their uniforms as his earlier *What Have They Done to Solange?*, cinematographer-turned-director Dallamano has lowered the sleaze content somewhat but delivers more standard gory thrills. In between some nonsensical rounds of suspect hunting and interrogations, the high speed killer himself provides all of the highlights. Whether tearing at frightening speed down a corridor or veering through the city streets on his bike, this is one of the more memorable '70s psychos (even if his identity isn't really all that important). One sequence involving his cleaver and a light switch will have Argento-jaded gorehounds squealing with glee, while other sordid goodies include multiple stabbings and a nasty morgue

inspection of a corpse ("cut up like a side of beef," as the ETC quote on the box exclaims). The occasionally slack pacing aside, Dallamano really knows how to arrange a set piece, such as Ralli's nocturnal pursuit through a parking deck and into an elevator. *Daughters* may not be the best place for Italo-sleaze neophytes to begin, but seasoned mystery vets will be grateful to have this obscure treat available in English at last. And be sure to look fast for Hitchcock vet Farley Granger (circa *The Slasher Is a Sex Maniac*) as a grieving father.

The British DVD from Salvation presents the film at an extremely wide aspect ratio, listed as 2.35:1 on the box but more like 2.50:1. The film was shot in a deliberately flat, *Kojak*-inspired style with over-lit rooms and drab colours; however, the transfer is as good as could be expected and displays only fleeting signs of wear and tear. The rousing score by Stelvio Cipriani, one of his very best, sounds just fine here in mono and should have anyone begging for a soundtrack release. Extras include the very long European, English language trailer and an assortment of still, video, and poster art.

WHEN A STRANGER CALLS

Colour, 1979, 97m. / Directed by Fred Walton / Starring Carol Kane, Charles Durning / Columbia (US, US R1 NTSC), WS (1.85:1: (16:9) / MIA (UK PAL R2)

One of the great scary word of mouth movies during the early '80s, *When a Stranger Calls* is a film people often mention discovering on TV or video without remembering the title. You know... it's the "Have you checked the children?" movie. Though never a huge financial hit, its influence has grown over the years, with *Urban Legend* even (erroneously) crediting the opening sequence as genuine modern folklore and *Scream* performing a twisty remake of its own during that legendary curtain raiser with Drew Barrymore.

Sweet teenage babysitter Jill (Carol Kane) arrives at the Mandrakis household in the suburbs to watch their children for the evening. Alone and content to busy herself with phone chatter and homework, she is unsettled to start receiving phone calls in which a male voice repeatedly asks, "Have you checked the children?" Jill's panic increases when she realizes the caller may be able to see her, and she calls the police for help. To say any more would be criminal. Flash forward several years later. The man responsible for the phone calls, Curt

Duncan (Tony Beckley), is a former British sailor being released from a mental institution. Unable to cope with modern society, he turns his attentions to a lovelorn middle aged woman named Tracy (Colleen Dewhurst) he met in a bar. Meanwhile Detective Clifford (Charles Durning), the man responsible for apprehending Curt years earlier, keeps an eye on him to ensure that Curt's psychotic urges don't kick in again. Nothing goes as planned, and soon even Jill is brought back into the terrifying loop for the film's twisty finale.

Skilfully directed by Fred Walton (who later returned to slasher territory with *April Fool's Day* and a remake of William Castle's *I Saw What You Did* - oh no, more phone horror!), this film noticeably sags after the powerhouse opening. All too obviously expanded from Walton's short film "The Babysitter" (which he probably came up with after watching Bob Clark's suspiciously similar *Black Christmas*), the plot avoids graphic bloodshed but can't sustain interest during Curt's long, long, long stalking of Dewhurst. Fortunately Walton reigns the story back in for the unexpected climax, which delivers one spectacular, unforgettable jolt and caps the film off on a high note. The dark urban setting during the midsection and a strange supporting cast (including *Superfly* himself, Ron O'Neal) keep things from getting too bogged down, making this an essential horror title but certainly not a classic.

One of the earliest films released on home video by Columbia, *When a Stranger Calls* has been the victim of shoddy, washed out transfers. Its vastly inferior sequel, *When a Stranger Calls Back*, is usually much easier to find and looks far better on tape. The British DVD release from MIA is a drab viewing option; the print is scratchy but watchable, suffering from splotchy, unstable blacks, which flutter during the darkest scenes (and there are a lot of them). The later US disc from Columbia offers full frame or widescreen options from a cleaner but still grainy print; either option offers visual information not present on the other, but the widescreen one appears more balanced.

THE WHIP AND THE BODY

Colour, 1963, 83m./ Directed by Mario Bava / Starring Daliah Lavi, Christopher Lee / VCI (US R0 NTSC) / WS (1.85:1)

The most overtly sexual of Mario Bava's gothic masterpieces, *The Whip and the Body* was rarely seen in its original form thanks to the threatening blend of S&M-themed romanticism and morbid horror. Thanks to home video, slightly differing

versions began to surface, ranging from the original European cut on Japanese laserdisc to an essentially complete US edition (under the title *What!*) with an alternate opening credits sequence. Even given this exposure, however, the film remains more widely discussed than actually seen, but admirers of early Bava gems like *Black Sunday* and *Black Sabbath* will find a similar treat for the senses here.

Cloistered in a seaside castle, the Menliff household is torn asunder by the return of black sheep son Kurt (Christopher Lee), a sadistic brute whose savage treatment of a local girl forced him to be banished years earlier. Meanwhile his fiancée, Nevenka (Daliah Lavi), has married his nice guy brother, Christian (Tony Kendall, aka Luciano Stella), and has a strange rapport with her father-in-law (Gustavo De Nardo). The housekeeper, Giorgia (Harriet White Medin), still resents Kurt's treatment of her daughter, who committed suicide with an ornate dagger now displayed in proper fetish fashion in a glass case. Angry over his father's continued denial to grant him status as an heir, Kurt encounters Nevenka on the beach and whips her furiously with a riding crop, an ordeal she accepts and apparently enjoys. Their love affair begins anew, but that evening Kurt is stabbed to death. Though Kurt's body is entombed, Nevenka experiences spectral encounters in which he enters her bedroom and whips her savagely. Strange deaths continue, and as the family deteriorates, the sadistic spirit of Kurt seems to hold sway over everyone involved.

Despite the potentially sordid subject matter, *The Whip and the Body* treats its subject with a finely restrained, poetic edge. The whipping scenes are mild by today's standards, especially in the wake of *Story of O*, but Lavi's feverish expressions still convey a palpable sense of delirium, hunger, and confusion. Likewise, Lee is an imposing and memorable presence in a rare appearance as a sexual predator and spirit, lurking in the shadows and rising occasionally into Bava's unmistakable pools of hellish green and blue lighting. Composer Carlo Rustichelli takes a break here from his standard lounge-oriented scores to provide an elegant, neo-classical score in keeping with the off-kilter romanticism of the film, rising to an appropriate crescendo during the memorable climax. Though not as overtly gruesome as other '60s horror titles, *The Whip and the Body* ultimately transcends its genre to stand as a challenging work of art. Newcomers to Bava would be advised to start elsewhere, but those already acquainted with the conventions of Italian gothic should find this most impressive.

After years of scratchy, faded videotapes, VCI's DVD of *The Whip and the Body* is nothing less than a revelation. The source material is in remarkable condition, particularly considering the rarity of the film itself, and thankfully it has been derived from a European source with the original opening titles (on red satin, natch, but newly generated). The US credits are also included as a supplement. The letter-boxing looks perfect, while the eerie chroma schemes come through even better than the Japanese version. Though all versions of the film were dubbed, the English dialogue track is just as acceptable as the Italian one, with optional English subtitles translated from the Italian also included for comparison. Tim Lucas returns for another multi-layered, finely arranged commentary track. Including more humorous asides than usual, he offers a breezy tour through Bava's gallery of morbid imagery with a sure hand, pointing out trivia about even the smallest background players and discussing a multitude of technical aspects. The DVD also contains a French trailer (under the title *Le corps et le fuet*, sans subtitles) along with trailers for *Blood and Black Lace* and, most surprisingly, Bava's magnificent *Planet of the Vampires*. A gallery of photos and posters rounds out this most unexpected and gratifying special edition.

WHITE ZOMBIE

B&W, 1932, 67m. / Directed by Victor Halperin / Starring Bela Lugosi, Madge Bellamy / Roan (US R1 NTSC)

While Universal and MGM were cranking out high profile horror titles in the wake of *Dracula* and *Frankenstein* back in the '30s, another strain of American horror films arose, commonly called "poverty row horrors." Formerly relegated to the darkest regions of fanzine appreciation, these films often used imagination to compensate for a lack of money, and *White Zombie* has justifiably been celebrated as the *Citizen Kane* of this peculiar and often fascinating subgenre.

Madeleine (Bellamy) and Neil (Harron), a young engaged couple visiting Haiti, are startled on a nocturnal carriage ride by the presence of shuffling workers who seem oblivious to their surroundings. Their local host (Cawthorn) greets them warmly but, it seems, is secretly infatuated with Madeleine and wants her for himself. He seeks the aid of sinister mill owner Murder Legendre (played by Lugosi of course - don't ya love that name?). It seems Murder is actually a voodoo master (yep, folks, this is the screen's first zombie movie) who uses the undead as slaves in his mill. Thanks to a few handy spells, he induces Madeleine into a state resembling death, then steals her "corpse" for his own private enjoyment (the viewer is left to fill in the blanks, but this seems to consist mostly of letting her roam around Murder's castle and play Liszt on the piano all day long). Of course, Neil is none too amused and decides to infiltrate Murder's imposing fortress, leading to a surprisingly rousing and poetic finale.

Rich with bizarre, beautiful imagery, *White Zombie* has been grabbing the attention of late night TV viewers for years despite its scrappy production and distribution history. Decent prints have been impossible to find, but the Roan Group with the aid of Sinister Cinema managed to piece together the finest extant materials to create a beautiful composite print originally released to great fan acclaim on laserdisc. The DVD looks even better, with further dirt removal and scratch repair; likewise, the transfer contains deeper blacks and more minute detail, particularly valuable when studying the film's striking sets and matte paintings.

Strangely, the Halperins never really hit paydirt like this again; even their sequel, *Revolt of the Zombies,* lacks the inventive spark that has made this a classic. While most of the performances are generally cardboard at best, Lugosi (famous for making only $800 from this one!) has a field day and delivers one of his most memorable characteriza-tions. His "hypnotic" eyes, used to famous effect in Tod Browning's *Dracula*, are once again utilized prominently here from the very first scene, but the other recurring images are far more compelling. The sequences involving the zombified Madeleine are particular visual highlights (she's not the world's greatest actress during the opening, so this is quite a relief), and the eerie shots of the zombie mill workers prove exactly why black and white photog-raphy was invented in the first place.

While the laserdisc was better packaged (it included original press kit material), the DVD boasts several new supplements. The most interesting, "Intimate Interviews," is a bizarre '30s promotional piece featuring a dim-witted journalist asking Lugosi inane questions about his career in "mystery films." Lugosi describes himself as a "lone wolf," explains his political asylum status to the blank-faced reporter, and eventually scares her off by staring off into space and intoning, "I'm coming." Thoroughly odd. Other bonuses include the 1952 sepia tone reissue trailer and running audio commentary.

WHITY

Colour, 1971, 95m. / Directed by Rainer Werner Fassbinder / Starring Günther Kaufmann, Hanna Schygulla / Fantoma (US R1 NTSC) / WS (2.35:1)

In his relatively brief lifespan, controversial and undeniably gifted director Rainer Werner Fassbinder churned out over forty films before overdosing in 1982, and his work managed to hit the mark more often than not. He started out in the '60s doing gritty "slice of life" films like *Gods of the Plague*, none of which were especially cheerful. However, beginning with the rarely seen musical western *Whity*, he turned towards a more stylized, formal approach which emphasized colour, set design, absurd plot twists, and of course, melodrama. Rarely screened outside Germany, *Whity* nevertheless caught on as a familiar title among the art house crowd, particularly after Fassbinder distilled its tumultuous production history into the story of another film, *Beware of a Holy Whore*.

Set in the late 1800s, this perverse epic takes place in the Southwestern household of Ben Nicholson (Ron Randell, the former Bulldog Drummond) and his highly disturbed family. Ben's trophy wife, the blonde Katherine (Katrin Schaake), sleeps with almost anything that moves, while his sons are either outrageously gay (Ulli Lommel) or mentally handicapped (Harry Bär). Each family member is fixated in a different way on Whity (Günther Kaufmann, Fassbinder's occasional lover and regular actor), the mulatto servant who tends to their pathetic needs. Whity's mother (Elaine Baker) is content to be a stereotypical "mammy" figure, but Whity has other plans, mostly involving his love for the sultry saloon singer, Hanna (the always magnificent Hanna Schygulla). After Ben reads his will aloud to the family (the film's most astounding scene), each member of the clan's demands on Whity escalate out of control to a murderous finale.

So bizarre that it can't even really be considered offensive, *Whity* twists the entire notion of American race relations and western clichés to create something entirely unearthly. The white cast members all sport bleached ivory make up, giving them the appearance of walking corpses, while Whity's mother sports a traditional and often alarming blackface. Whity himself and Hanna retain their natural skin tones, as do a few supporting characters (including R.W. himself in an amusing uncredited bit as a gunslinging barfly). Filmed on the same Spanish sets used for Sergio Leone's spaghetti westerns, this is truly an amazing looking film, saturated with vibrant colours even in the darkest scenes, and the cinematography by Michael Ballhaus (who later worked with Scorsese, Coppola, and many others) is never less than masterful. The actors do what they can under the circumstances, considering each character is insane and on edge in almost every scene.

The slow pacing of the film itself may not be to everyone's taste, but from a technical aspect, this disc is a stunner. The anamorphic image preserves the original Cinemascope framing, which lends an appropriate visually expansive flavour to this tawdry tale. The optional English subtitles are easily legible and synched well with the dialogue, though it appears that at least several portions of the film (Randell's scenes in particular) were shot in English and later dubbed into German. Several songs are also presented with British singers overdubbing the actors, resulting in a very odd and often incongruous soundtrack. However, the audio itself is very clear and does a fine job of showcasing the melancholy music score by the great Peer Raben. Ballhaus and Lommel (who later turned director with films like *The Boogeyman*) provide a fascinating audio commentary track, which covers not only this film but also the entire experience of working with Fassbinder. They remain appropriately sketchy about some of the more sordid, operatic aspects of the director's working patterns, but anyone interested should find plenty to chew on here. They also make some funny observations along the way, such as Lommel's comments during his character's seduction of Whity while dressed up in slinky Victoria's Secret undies.

THE WICKER MAN

Colour, 1973, 98/88m. / Directed by Robin Hardy / Starring Edward Woodward, Christopher Lee / Anchor Bay (US R1 NTSC), Warner (UK R2 PAL) / WS (1.85:1) (16:9) / DD5.1

Largely ignored in the final rush of Hammer horror films pouring out of England, *The Wicker Man* either confounded or impressed most first time viewers but became lost in a tangle of bad distribution, careless editing, and public indifference. Its reputation began to grow over the years until the film was finally regarded by many cultists as a classic, particularly after the full 102 minute cut surfaced in some theatres and on home video during the early 1980s. A horror film

W

more in intention and theme than in execution, *The Wicker Man* is a haunting, thoughtful exploration of faith and humanity vs. nature, cased deceptively in an entertaining narrative which also functions perfectly on its own terms as gruelling thriller.

Sergeant Howie (*The Equalizer*'s Edward Woodward), a sternly conservative Christian policeman in Scotland, decides to visit the nearby island of Summerisle after receiving a mysterious note indicating the disappearance of a young girl, Rowan Morrison. Upon his arrival Howie is confounded by the locals' claims that Rowan never existed, though various clues at the schoolhouse and among the community lead him to suspect otherwise. The pagan community shocks his staunch sensibilities with such rituals as maypole dancing, naked fire god worship, and celebrations of animal reincarnation, while the local leader, Lord Summerisle (Christopher Lee), proves to be an intelligent but uncooperative force to test his spirit indeed, while the innkeeper's comely daughter (Britt Ekland) offers a more sexual challenge. Howie comes to suspect that the missing girl may have suffered a not so pleasant fate, but his investigation takes him in a direction he could have never anticipated.

Best known for writing such tricky puzzles as *Frenzy, Sleuth*, and the underrated *Absolution*, Anthony Shaffer gets a rare possessory credit for this film, and indeed the dense narrative with a venomous sting fits in comfortably with his other work. Technical execution in other areas is excellent as well, however, from director Robin Hardy's confident pacing to the haunting score by Paul Giovanni, consisting of intentionally cloying folk music, which becomes more lewd and sinister as the film progresses. Though a few of the performers like Lee and Ingrid Pitt are familiar faces from Hammer, the tone here is quite different - indeed, it's unlike any other horror film, British or otherwise. The use of humour, eroticism, and animal imagery (most memorably frogs and snails) actually adds to the sense of unease, which is skilfully crafted in visual terms by using sunlight as a means to obstruct rather than illuminate.

Numerous accounts have already been written about the variant editions of *The Wicker Man* circulating over the years, so simply put, the Anchor Bay limited edition includes the theatrical 88 minute cut which most viewers first encountered and which was widely released as a budget title from Republic on VHS. Earlier videotape editions from Media and a more colourful, solid transfer from Magnum contained the restored 102 minute cut, which contains a more linear opening sequence establishing Howie's religious conviction

(represented in the shorter cut through brief, jagged flashbacks). The 88 minute cut also reshuffles numerous scenes and eliminates others; the most damning alternations include the elimination of the song "Gently Johnny" and the placement of Ekland's legendary nude dance far too early in the film. Similar to their extended edition of *Army of Darkness*, Anchor Bay has edited together the crystal clear, vibrant theatrical transfer where available with the restored sequences from a one inch video master, though inexplicably it looks more ragged, washed out, and pixellated here than on the Magnum tape. An explanatory card at the beginning of the extended cut explains the situation, and the effort that went into presenting both versions for comparison is worthwhile even if it will probably leave some first time viewers a little confused.

The theatrical cut (which is also available as a separate single disc release) boasts a reasonable 5.1 audio remix, though rear channel separation is negligible at best throughout most of the film. Music and sound effects are largely confined to the front speakers, while dialogue remains anchored in the centre. The extended cut (which runs 98 minutes instead of 102 for some reason but appears to be complete) is presented in mono.

Considering its video history, the shorter version will probably be more of a revelation for horror fans considering two out of three tape editions were already uncut; either way, the opportunity to compare them back to back is fascinating indeed. The theatrical disc contains several extras, most notably "The Wicker Man Enigma," a solid half hour documentary containing interviews with such principals as Lee, Woodward, Pitt, Hardy, Shaffer, and many more. The story behind the film's various versions and what materials are precisely still in existence still isn't quite answered clearly, though most notably one is left to ponder what extra scenes could have been contained in that unseen, even longer original negative that turned into highway fodder. Other extras include the rapidly edited theatrical trailer (which succeeds in blowing the ending for the film, so approach with caution!), a TV spot, and a smattering of radio spots, as well as a nifty Easter egg, all accessible from the fiery animated menus. The limited edition of 50,000 copies (which is actually far more than the entire disc runs of most titles) is housed in a wooden case containing two postcards with separate chapter listing and poster reproductions, while the discs are housed in a two-disc jewel case which can be tricky to pry out of the plastic housing inside the box.

The later UK Warner DVD contains the same versions and extras with the added bonus of an audio commentary featuring Woodward, Lee, and Hardy, along with bonus Easter Egg footage of them preparing for the discussion.

WILD THINGS

Colour, 1998, 116m. / Directed by John McNaughton / Starring Matt Dillon, Neve Campbell / Columbia (US R1 NTSC), EIV (UK R2 PAL) / WS (2.35:1) (16:9) / DD5.1

Sam Lombardo (Dillon), a respected counsellor at Blue Bay High School, is accused of rape by students Kelly Van Ryan (Denise Richards) and Suzie Toller (Neve Campbell). Although the case falls apart when it reaches court and Lombardo walks away with hefty financial recompense, unorthodox police detective Ray Duquette (Bacon) is intent on proving that the whole business was a money-making scam devised by the three of them.

Although the big ker-ching at the box office was undoubtedly down to the much hyped sapphic smooching between Richards and Campbell, there's a lot more to this spicy-as-salsa thriller than that. The intricate plot has more twists than you'll encounter in a heaped plate of fusilli pasta, so many in fact that the viewer is left dizzy attempting to rationalize each unpredictable turn of events. Every time you think you've got it all straight, director John McNaughton nonchalantly tosses another double-cross into the mix to throw you off kilter. Actually, the protagonists have so many hidden agendas between them that it takes a number of inserts during the closing credits to clarify some of the murkier details of the narrative. Where this could be interpreted as sloppy story telling, these explanatory segments act as the icing on a very rich and fruity celluloid cake. Dillon, Richards and Campbell are adequate - but no more than that - and Bacon shows off his dark side (and his wedding tackle) with suitable zeal. Theresa Russell and Robert Wagner offer good solid support, but the big revelation is Bill Murray in an (almost) straight role as the shyster lawyer who may or may not have a lot more involvement in the evil doings down in Blue Bay than is first apparent. High art it most certainly isn't, but *Wild Things* offers up enough brain-straining suspense, wry humour, steamy sexplay and wince-inducing violence to slake the thirst of the most demanding audience.

Columbia's Region 1 release of *Wild Things* is an above average affair; the premier quality 28-chapter feature aside, there are three deleted scenes (one of which plays without sound and is so brief as to render its inclusion pointless), a commentary from director McNaughton, and two trailers (one for *Wild Things*, the other for *Starship Troopers* for no other discernible reason than the fact Denise Richards stars in it). The double-sided disc offers a 2.35:1 theatrical presentation and a fullscreen pan and scan version. Language and subtitling options are available in English and French. - TG

THE WITCHES

Colour, 1966, 90m. / Directed by Cyril Frankel / Starring Joan Fontaine, Alec McCowen / Anchor Bay (US R1 NTSC) / WS (1.78:1) (16:9)

An occult vehicle tailored by Joan Fontaine (*Rebecca*) as her big screen comeback, *The Witches* was largely buried under the deluge of Hammer Films being released seemingly every other week during the mid-'60s. Shorn of such marketable elements as voluptuous maidens in distress or blood-dripping vampires, the film instead has to rely on such niceties as plot and atmosphere to hold the viewer's attention. While the final product isn't a complete success, *The Witches* is a nice try and a curious attempt by Hammer to do something out of the ordinary.

Our tale begins very shakily with fragile Gwen Mayfield (Fontaine) pushed over the edge to a complete nervous breakdown in Africa when she's assaulted by what appears to be some villagers toting around a big mask. A year later she lands a job as a schoolteacher in a quaint English village. The headmistress, Stephanie Bax (Kay Walsh), seems sensible enough, but the villagers are consumed by superstition and don't even have a local church. Bax's brother, Alan (Alec McCowen), failed to make the grade as a priest but still wears a clerical collar and fiddles with organ music anyway, while the slightly creepy Granny Rigg (cross-eyed Gwen Ffrangcon Davies from *The Devil Rides Out*) passes the time by shoving the hand of her granddaughter, Linda (Ingrid Brett), into a handy clothes mangler. Linda's boyfriend, Ronnie (*Village of the Damned*'s head tyke, Martin Stephens, almost unrecognizable here), tells Gwen about some of the sinister goings on and is promptly rewarded by falling into a coma. Soon Gwen comes to believe that witchcraft is at work in the tiny village, and Linda might be in line as a human sacrifice.

After its silly opening, *The Witches* settles nicely into a subdued, well-acted shocker relying mostly on implied menace and the skilful performances of its cast. Fontaine, Walsh, and McCowen are particular standouts, and the crisp photography makes the most of the sunny yet threatening locales. Unfortunately the plot takes a major detour at the one hour mark from which it never recovers, content instead to wrap things up with a silly interpretive dance of the witches looks for all the world like an outtake from *Showgirls*. The "surprise" villainess even dons an unforgettable piece of headgear made of candles and antlers. Well, at least it's different. Screenwriter Nigel Kneale (*Quatermass*) at least keeps the dialogue end afloat and in many ways foreshadowed the similarly plotted *The Wicker Man*.

Like its other Hammer titles, Anchor Bay has done a first rate job of bringing *The Witches* to DVD. Apart from approximately one irreparably damaged minute of washed out source material 45 minutes in, the print is in excellent shape with solid colours and detail. The strong mono track perfectly accentuates the dark, percussive score by Richard Rodney Bennett, while dialogue is clear and free of distortion. The disc also includes the trailer for the film's release in the US (where it bore the same title as its source novel, *The Devil's Own*), two TV spots, and the *World of Hammer* overview episode, "Wicked Women." Both this title and *Frankenstein Created Woman* have experienced some odd pressing problems, including the inability to load up on some players after a few viewings. Keep an eye on your discs!

THE WIZARD OF GORE

Colour, 1970, 96m. / Directed by Herschell Gordon Lewis / Starring Ray Sager, Judy Cler / Image (US R0 NTSC), Tartan (UK R0 PAL)

 The most conceptually outrageous film from gore pioneer H.G. Lewis, *The Wizard of Gore* extends the self-parody already creeping into his films into territory that can only be described as bizarre. The seemingly straightforward concept yields bizarre results from the opening scene, and many viewers may be left doubting their own sanity by the halfway point. Montag the Magnificent (Ray Sager), a hammy stage magician, draws in nightly crowds by performing "illusions" in which members of the audience are graphically dismembered. During one performance attended by daytime TV show hostess Sherry Carson (Judy Cler) and her cop boyfriend, Montag saws a woman in half with a chainsaw. The

woman appears to be unscathed after the magic act, but an hour later she turns up disembowelled in the middle of a restaurant. Some of the woman's blood winds up on Sherry's hand, and this "mark" endears her enough for Montag to agree to an appearance on her TV show. Meanwhile Montag continues his string of performances, which also involve a nail driven into a human head and a nasty sword swallowing. When Montag finally goes on the air, the film reaches an indescribable, existential climax that simply defies description.

While this film certainly delivers in the blood department, viewers shouldn't find the effects all that unsettling or tasteless. Lewis' distancing effect of reinforcing the audience's observer standpoint renders the violence strangely amusing, while Sager's over the top performance produces a huge number of laughs which may or may not be intentional. The film is noticeably less vibrant and colourful compared to Lewis' famous Blood Trilogy; the saturated interiors of *Blood Feast* have now been traded in for grimy city streets and drab set decoration, making this a far more typical 42nd Street offering.

Something Weird's DVD of *The Wizard of Gore* looks comparable to the old VHS editions; this film will never look all that impressive, but the disc gets the job done. Some print damage is evident during the first couple of minutes, while the majority of the source material is in good shape and looks suitably sleazy. The harshly recorded audio is faithfully reproduced here, for what that's worth, and the funky musical score must be heard to be believed. The disc also includes a very, very long theatrical trailer (in rough shape, but at least it exists!), and, on the US version, a feature length commentary by Lewis in which he expounds upon the various technical hurdles he faced when making this particular film. The UK disc includes a still gallery and liner notes by Billy Chainsaw. Not as well known or kitschy as his more famous *Blood* films, Lewis' little opus nevertheless should please the fans by offering up some whacked out food for thought along with the obvious helpings of animal guts and fake blood.

THE WOLF MAN

B&W, 1941, 70m. / Directed by George Waggner / Starring Claude Rains, Lon Chaney, Jr. / Universal (US R1 NTSC)

Universal had few pre-existing sources to use as inspiration for their enormously popular *The Wolf Man*, the best of their post-'30s monster films. The vague lycanthropic mythology of Eastern Europe,

not to mention the studio's earlier, much tamer *Werewolf of London*, made for a shaky springboard from which the crew had to create an entirely new set of rules for the title creature. Ironically, the public accepted everything in the film as legitimate monster folklore, and *The Wolf Man* has since inspired countless sequels and other films, almost always with the poor werewolf presented as a victimized hero.

Larry Talbot (Lon Chaney, Jr.) travels from America to his family's estate in Wales where he stays with his father, Sir John Talbot (Claude Rains), to cope with the death of his brother. Larry and a local girl go out at night and investigate a gypsy camp where they encounter the eccentric Bela (Bela Lugosi) and, of course, his memorable mother, Maleva (Maria Ouspenskaya). Out in the woods, Jenny is assaulted by a wolf; Larry saves her from the animal but winds up bitten in the process. Maleva informs Larry that he will become a werewolf during each full moon, and sure enough, he does. John and the lovely Gwen (Evelyn Ankers) don't believe Larry's anguished version of the facts, but out on the forest, the horrific truth comes to look them right in the face.

Though not as artistically dazzling as the first two Frankenstein films, *The Wolf Man* possesses its own peculiar charm and has deservedly remained a fan favourite over the decades. Rarely has a fog machine been put to better use, and the whole film is drenched in a creepy, melancholy atmosphere, capped off perfectly by the famous downbeat ending. Though filmed on sets, the film beautifully conveys a palpable sense of dread and inescapable fatalism that compensates for a few minor flaws in the dialogue and plotting. Chaney makes a terrific, pitiable leading man, and Rains is at his suave, compassionate best, with everyone else turning in memorable, finely etched supporting performances.

Another welcome entry in Universal's monster collection, *The Wolf Man* looks sharper and richer here than it ever has before, though restoration addicts will be dismayed to note that some rough print damage still exists, particularly during the opening credits and a couple of reel changes. Historian Tom Weaver contributes a scholarly commentary track, filled with some useful nuggets of information along the way, and Universal also produced a lively half hour documentary, "Monster by Moonlight." More expansive and cinema-oriented than their other documentaries in this series, this look at movie lycanthropy and this film's development from its early stages as a Boris Karloff project to its

final form boasts John Landis as an enthusiastic host (a nice choice, though it's a shame they couldn't get Joe Dante in there, too). The package is rounded off by the usual still and promotional art, as well as a tattered and virtually unwatchable trailer. (Incidentally, why has Universal only preserved its '50s reissue trailers for most horror films, and only one thrown in for each film title? Very odd.) Even horror fans who own *The Wolf Man* in its previous, uh, incarnations should be perfectly willing to upgrade to this version, which definitely delivers. Curl up and watch it under a bright, full moon.

THE WOLVES OF KROMER

Colour, 1999, 75m. / Directed by Will Gould / Starring James Layton, Lee Williams / First Run (US R1 NTSC) / WS (1.85:1) (16:9) / DD5.1

Since the 1970s we've had dozens of gay riffs on vampire lore, including such glossy big budget efforts as *Interview with the Vampire* and *The Lost Boys* which barely even attempted to conceal their sexual politics. Oddly, the werewolf legend has proven less fertile in this area, apart from the rib-nudging *Curse of the Queerwolf* and a few literary stabs in genre fiction. While it's hard to say exactly what the target audience was intended to be for *The Wolves of Kromer*, a low budget British production, the film certainly can't be compared to anything else, except for perhaps a gay, gender-twisted variation on *The Company of Wolves*.

Starting off with a fairy tale narration by none other than Boy George, we meet our two wolf heroes, cocky Gabriel (James Layton) and insecure Seth (Lee Williams) who is coming to terms with the realization that he's actually a wolf. Apart from playfully terrorizing passers-by in the woods and swiping the occasional bit of food and clothing to share with their pack, the boys lead a fairly benign existence despite the fearful rumours stirring within the village of Kromer. Meanwhile a scheming maid named Fanny (Rita Davies) schemes with her dim-witted friend, Doreen (Margaret Towner), to kill off her wealthy mistress and pin the blame on the innocent wolves. The influential priest (Kevin Moore) seizes the opportunity for a full scale witch hunt - err, wolf hunt - and incites the villagers into punishing the boys simply because they're different.

As a playful riff on familiar fairy tale conventions, *The Wolves of Kromer* is an interesting attempt to subvert expectations by using wolves to stand in for more familiar speeches involving persecution,

W

sexual identity confusion, and group hysteria. Seth's early "coming out" speech as a wolf is especially funny, though contrary to the plot summary on the box, this isn't really a comedy; instead it's a dark romantic fantasy with a very tragic undercurrent. However, director Will Gould seems afraid to push the gothic or subversive elements too far, as indicated by the odd happy ending closing credits, which seem to have stumbled in by accident from *Beautiful Thing*. Most of the actors do surprisingly well; in fact, it's hard to believe that the two leads were actually models with little prior acting experience. With their pointed ears, razor-sharp claws, and furry goth clothing, they make for an odd, compelling pair of protagonists, and it's certainly more subtle and wry than anything Joel Schumacher would have dreamed up.

With *The Wolves of Kromer*, First Run finally makes the leap into anamorphic transfers, and the results are quite pleasing. Some of the night scenes are overly dark (probably the way they were shot), but overall the transfer is very clear and colourful. The Dolby Digital 5.1 mix is also satisfying, particularly when it spreads out the music to emphasize its strange but effective mixture of orchestral instruments tinged with techno elements. Despite the 100 minute running time stated on the box, the film only clocks in at 75 minutes, missing the mark even with all of the supplements included. "On Location in Llanyblowel," a behind the scenes featurette, including interviews with the director, writer Charles Lambert (who also penned the source play), and the main actors, sprinkled with production footage. The running commentary track with Gould and Lambert is a generally affectionate and sometimes insightful account of the filming, and they point out enough anecdotes about the actors and production team to keep things moving along smoothly. Obviously this isn't a film for everyone, but it's a pleasant enough diversion and an interesting twist on the tried and true notion of monsters as outsiders.

THE WOMAN IN BLACK

Colour, 1989, 100m. / Directed by Herbert Wise / Starring Adrian Rawlins, Bernard Hepton / BFS (US R1 NTSC)

W

Anyone who claims old-fashioned ghost stories can't scare anymore would be well advised to take a look at *The Woman in Black*, unquestionably one of the most frightening films ever made for television - or any medium, for that matter. Steeped right to its core in a palpable sense of dread and inescapable doom, this is psychological terror at its finest and

makes more widely hailed attempts at "suggestive horror" look ridiculous by comparison.

In 1920s London, mild mannered solicitor and family man Arthur Kidd (Adrian Rawlins) is sent by his firm to handle the estate of a late client, one Alice Drablow. When he arrives at the small town near the isolated moor estate of Ms. Drablow, Arthur stops to save a young gypsy girl from certain death by a wooden cart and is confronted with the unnerving sight of a woman in black standing in the street, glaring malevolently at him with red-rimmed eyes. That night, miles away from any other human beings, Arthur settles into the Drablow house and goes through the personal effects. However, he has also incurred the wrath of the ghostly woman in black, who intends to pay Arthur back for the life he stole from her. And when he steps outside and looks at the empty moor, he repeatedly hears the horrifying sound of a horse carriage crashing, following by a child's hysterical screaming... What follows is not for those who intend to have a good night's sleep.

Exquisitely written (by *Quatermass* author Nigel Kneale, from Susan Hill's novel), scored (by Rachel Portman), and directed (by British miniseries vet Herbert Wise), *The Woman in Black* begins with a deceptively slow first act detailing Arthur's metropolitan lifestyle and the nature of his job. However, once the ghost story begins, the story relentlessly jangles the viewer's nerves with diabolical precision. The entire sequence with Kidd terrorized in the Drablow home is frightening enough, but the story then moves to a third act that turns the screws even tighter. In particular, one scene delivers such a blood-freezing jolt that only the stoniest viewer will be able to continue with the lights off. Really... it's that creepy. The novel was also adapted as a successful British stage play a few years later and reportedly is an equally traumatic experience.

Extremely difficult to track down on VHS, *The Woman in Black* has never managed to earn the reputation it deserves but will hopefully enjoy more word of mouth on DVD. The presentation from BFS looks as good as possible given the source material; the opening scenes were shot with a hazy, orange hue that looks intentionally soft. The rest of the film looks much sharper than the VHS edition, with some mild grain and scratchiness in the source material evident from time to time. The mono soundtrack can be played through both front channels, a smart move given the expansive and creepy nature of the music and sound effects. It may not be a demo piece, but every horror fan should check this one out. Grab some popcorn, turn down the lights... and try to make it through the night.

WOMEN IN REVOLT

Colour, 1971, 99m. / Directed by Paul Morrissey / Starring Viva, Candy Darling, Holly Woodlawn / Image (US R1 NTSC)

In retrospect, this is one of the funniest and most consistently surprising Paul Morrissey films, though the budgetary constraints may make this tough going for anyone unfamiliar with, for example, the zero-budget early efforts by John Waters. Warhol's most famous faux-women, Candy Darling, Jackie Curtis, and Holly Woodlawn (Trash) appear as gals from three different walks of life united in their participation in a homemade Women's Lib group. Candy decides she's had enough of her high class life (which entails having a long term affair with her brother), overly manly Jackie chucks her no-good boyfriend, and kept woman hussy Holly halts her endless string of sexual partners. All three take up lesbianism as the lifestyle of choice, leading to some bizarre and outrageous sequences culminating in a twisted on-the-air finale. Of course, this story is just a framework for Morrissey to spin his usual lengthy insult-loaded diatribes on current issues of the moment, and the performers don't let him down. Holly's opening freak-out screaming fit is a particular highlight, and Cagney and Lacey fans will be startled to see an early, very naked appearance by Martin Kove (who appeared the following year as a cop in Wes Craven's Last House on the Left). Unabashedly campy, trashy, and twisted, Women in Revolt is a perversely fascinating artefact of its era.

WONDERWALL

Colour, 1969, 74m. / Directed by Joe Massot / Starring Jack MacGowran, Jane Birkin / Rhino (US R1 NTSC) / DD5.1

Far better known as a soundtrack by The Beatles' George Harrison (and as an Oasis song) than an actual movie, Wonderwall is another attempt to depict the late '60s youth movement through the eyes of a stodgy, middle-aged character. Like many of its ilk, this look at free-

spirited, swinging London ultimately arrives at a conservative conclusion, but at least it allows its central character to freely indulge in psychedelic fantasies rather than simply observing them.

A sheltered professor named Oscar (The Exorcist's Jack MacGowran) spends his days looking at microscope samples and obeying the commands of those around him. However, his life changes when a beautiful young girl, Penny Lane (Jane Birkin), moves into the apartment next door along with her domineering, party-loving photographer boyfriend (Iain Quarrier). Through a hole in his wall, Oscar watches the young couple engage in several idylls with their models and visitors- some imagined, some real. Gradually reality and fantasy blur as the professor imagines himself as Penny's saviour, defeating her unworthy lover in a series of duels and confrontations laced with drug-like imagery. Oscar drills more holes and finds his own consciousness altering, which leads to a sudden and life-changing action for everyone involved.

Definitely a curio, this film isn't especially good and meanders around in a direction closer to aimless than impulsive. At least it features an excellent cast, reteaming Polanski vets MacGowran and Quarrier after Cul-de-sac and The Fearless Vampire Killers and featuring pop chanteuse and Euro film starlet Birkin in all her sexy '60s splendour. The production design also makes for delicious eye candy, with all of the fantasies and apartment observation scenes turning voyeurism and obsession into an innocent, delectable spectacle out of Willy Wonka's factory. Of course there's also the music, with Harrison mingling sitars, woodwinds, and rock beats into a pop fusion unlike any other. Simply put, Wonderwall works best when approached as a very long, free form music video rather than a traditional film, playing off the motifs of gallant nights, mid-life crises, and predatory relationships without anchoring them into a traditional cinematic structure.

Thanks no doubt to the resurgence of interest in mod pop culture in the wake of Austin Powers, Wonderwall was restored under the supervision of director Joe Massot (who went to co-write the even stranger Zachariah and helmed the landmark Led Zeppelin documentary, The Song Remains the Same). For his director's cut, Massot actually shortened the film from 93 minutes to 76, eliminating overlong establishing shots and various other little pieces of celluloid fat. The film definitely seems to move faster, a particular asset when compared to the overly sluggish first version. The original muddy soundtrack was also given a complete overhaul, using Harrison's original studio tapes to provide a far more spacious and crystal clear

W

soundscape. Not surprisingly the audio is in much better condition than the image on the DVD, which sports a vibrantly colourful but visibly battered print, marginally cropped from the 1.66:1 original (judging from the opening credits, anyway). The 5.1 mix on the other hand sounds terrific, and its clarity nearly dislocates it entirely from the moving images on the screen. The alternate 2.0 stereo track is quite lifeless in comparison.

The DVD also includes a short 11 minute film by Massot entitled "Reflections of Love," featuring an added soundtrack by Kula Shaker. Shot in Cinemascope and presented here letterboxed at 2.35:1, this short takes a swinging look at romance and marriage in London circa the late '60s, with footage of the Beatles and various urban locales interspersed with scenes of a young couple progressing towards the altar. The disc also includes a rough cut of a trailer with a time code visible in some shots, a gallery of the film's striking artwork by Marijke, a homemade "music video" for the recovered title song by Colin Manley and Tony Ashton of The Remo Four, the alternate opening credits with Harrison's original instrumental music, a scrap of outtake footage, a poem by John Lennon(?), and a short called "The Comic Art of Jack MacGowran," editing together some of his more memorable bits of physical comedy in the film. Another very quick little extra uses video images to accompany an isolation of the film's extended guitar riff performed by an uncredited Eric Clapton.

THE WORLD IS NOT ENOUGH

Colour, 1999, 123m. / Directed by Michael Apted / Starring Pierce Brosnan, Sophie Marceau / MGM / WS (2.35:1) (16:9) / DD5.1

 James Bond (Brosnan) is called in as bodyguard to wealthy oil heiress Elektra King (Marceau), who is under threat from fanatical terrorist Victor Zokas (Robert Carlyle), aka Renard the Fox. After a bungled attempt on their lives, Bond makes a discovery that indicates the mutual hatred between Elektra and Renard may not be quite as it seems...

The third time is definitely the charm. Kicking off with a double-whammy pre-credits sequence - including Bond gunning an armoured jetboat up the Thames in pursuit of slinky and treacherous Maria Grazia Cuccinotta, and culminating an explosive hot air balloon climax over the Millennium Dome - new man Michael Apted steers 007 through a meritorious thriller which rates as the best Bond since the 60s. There's a hastily improvised bungee jump from the top floor of a Bilbao office block, a dizzying race through an oil pipeline on a scouring rig booby-trapped with a plutonium bomb, a battle with paragliders on the ski slopes, an escape from an inferno inside a nuclear bunker, and an assault by helicopters equipped with rotary saw-blades.

The action aside, Neil Purvis and Robert Wade's script bestows the protagonists with plenty of depth and hidden agendas. Sophie Marceau, Robert Carlyle, Denise Richards (the latter far better than most critics would have one believe) and Robbie Coltrane are all worthy additions to the annals of Bond antagonists and allies. Special mention too for Desmond Llewelyn, playing out his 007 swansong as Q. He was in 17 of the official Bonds but by tragic default this one became his finest hour; a farewell shot as he descends into the floor of his workshop adopted a far greater poignancy than anyone could have foreseen when the actor was killed in a motoring accident shortly after the film's release.

Composer David Arnold consolidates the work he began with the previous film, proving himself the best 007 music-maker since John Barry departed in 1987. Make no mistake, *The World Is Not Enough* is more than enough, and contemporary Bond at his very best.

It's rare that a British DVD is superior to its American counterpart, but *The World Is Not Enough*'s Special Edition hit Region 2 with almost an hour's worth of material absent on the US version. The film itself - divided into 32 chapters - isn't quite fault-free; there are several instances when the audio levels dip suddenly during the louder passages. But the 2.35:1 picture quality is superb.

The extras comprise a "Making of *The World Is Not Enough*" documentary, plus two further 30-minute documentaries missing from the US disc, "The Bond Cocktail" and "Bond Down River" (the latter particularly interesting, focusing on the River Thames shoot). There are nine segments of varying length that delve into the effects, a promotional music video of the Garbage titles number (annoyingly altered from its original release version to include clips from the film), a montage of clips in tribute to Desmond Llewelyn, a trailer and a sampler of the Playstation game. Two commentaries are provided, the first from Director Michael Apted, the second from Production Designer Peter Lamont, Composer David Arnold and 2nd Unit Director Vic Armstrong. The sound and subtitling is in English only. - TG

WOYZECK

Colour, 1979, 80m. / Directed by Werner Herzog / Starring Klaus Kinski, Eva Mattes / Anchor Bay (US R1 NTSC) / WS 1.85:1 (16:9)

 Following the positive reception of his *Nosferatu* remake, director Werner Herzog turned again to the classics, albeit on a much smaller scale. His intimate rendition of Georg Büchner's harrowing play, *Woyzeck*, tackles its narrative in a style very similar to the stage adaptations of Robert Altman, such as *Streamers*. Static medium shots, oppressive interiors, a brief running time, and a limited number of characters make this a tasking experience, but not one without its own rewards for the patient.

Poor military officer Franz Woyzeck (Klaus Kinski) can't seem to have a moment's peace. His commanding officer forces him to perform an endless array of demeaning tasks (most notably shaving his superior's face with a straight razor), and Woyzeck's wife Marie (Eva Mattes) offers no support and seems to be cheating on him. The local doctors fail to alleviate his misery, and the onslaught of mental and physical anguish begins to take its toll on his rapidly deteriorating mind. How long can Woyzeck hold on before he finally snaps?

A compact chamber piece by Herzog standards, *Woyzeck* is often overlooked but still contains the director's favourite theme of mankind struggling against challenging obstacles, with fellow human beings replacing the daunting elements of nature in this case. Kinski's amazing, edgy performance adds much needed depth to the storyline, a straightforward account of one man's descent straight into hell. After over an hour of Herzog's detached camera calmly observing Woyzeck's disintegration, the violent final ten minutes pack a vicious punch. (Too bad the cover art completely spoils one of the key moments.) Though it may not be the best place to start for Herzog newcomers, *Woyzeck* represents both the filmmaker and his depraved muse, Kinski, at the height of their powers.

Previously released in the US on VHS by New Yorker, *Woyzeck* has been transferred as well as possible to DVD by Anchor Bay. The anamorphically enhanced image largely compensates for the cheap film stock and grainy '70s look the film has displayed over the years; Herzog's carefully modulated use of gold and brown shines through quite richly here. The optional English subtitles are likewise well paced and easy to read. Apart from the original German trailer (also with optional subs) and the usual cast/crew bios, this is a straightforward, no frills presentation. That's hardly surprising, though, given that even Herzog would be hard pressed to dissect the film for 80 minutes.

X - THE MAN WITH THE X-RAY EYES

Colour, 1963, 79m. / Directed by Roger Corman / Starring Ray Milland, Diana Van der Vlis / MGM (US R1 NTSC) / WS (1.85:1) (16:9)

 In 1959, Russ Meyer revolutionized the adult film industry with his softcore opus, *The Immoral Mr. Teas*, about a man with the ability to see through women's clothing. Four years later, Roger Corman took a serious, philosophical spin on the same subject *with X - The Man with X-Ray Eyes*, a haunting and unforgettable blend of science fiction and morality play.

Coming hot off his underrated turn in Corman's *The Premature Burial*, Ray Milland has one of his best latter day roles as Dr. James Xavier, a doctor who pioneers a new kind of eyedrops rendering the human eye capable of seeing through solid matter. Xavier's superiors at the hospital refuse to support his research, but he tests out his new discovery and uses it to save the life of a young girl. Unfortunately he immediately loses his job, a nasty turn of events immediately followed by the accidental death of a colleague which leaves Xavier on the run, fearing a murder rap. Now he's free to continue his addictive use of the eyedrops until he can see through much more than clothing, playing cards, and solid metal. While the talent comes in handy when he earns some cash as a mind reader at a carnival sideshow, he fearfully comes to realize that he can see well past the realm of normal perception, into something far more ghastly and dangerous than he could have imagined.

Though skimpy on traditional character development and elaborate plotting, *X* boasts a grand performance from Milland and stands as one of the best acid head movies before such a thing even existed. The see-through gimmick is exploited well by Corman, who uses a canny mixture of scientific jargon, comic relief, suspenseful chases, and ultimately Grand Guignol horror to demonstrate the numerous possibilities of such a hideous gift. The usual Corman collaborators are all here and working overtime, including composer Les Baxter (providing one of his oddest scores), cinematographer Floyd Crosby (working colourful wonders with an impoverished budget), and a supporting cast peppered with such familiar faces as Don Rickles and Dick Miller.

If any Roger Corman film demanded a commentary, this would be the one - and thankfully MGM didn't disappoint. The director turned B-movie mogul shares a number of recollections about the film, including his experience with Milland who was in the middle of a triple threat whammy at AIP (counting his self-directed apocalypse favourite, *Panic in Year Zero*). The film experienced something of a resurgence of fan interest in the wake of Stephen King's 1981 critical horror study, *Danse Macabre*, which also kicked off a rumour that Corman originally had Milland utter one chilling, final line that was ultimately cut from the film. Corman offers an explanation for this cinematic yarn, though you'll have to listen to find out the whole story. The transfer itself is a real eye popper (so to speak), with those swirling purples during the opening credits kicking off what turns into a riot of rainbow hues throughout the film. The source material is in excellent shape and looks much crisper than those awful cropped Warner videotapes and even the letterboxed but slightly soft Orion widescreen laserdisc. The disc also includes the psychedelic theatrical trailer; too bad AIP didn't bother giving this one a big reissue around the same time Fantasia was luring in the "alternative consciousness" crowd. It could have caused some real damage.

X THE UNKNOWN
B&W, 1956, 79m. / Directed by Leslie Norman / Starring Dean Jagger, Edward Chapman, Leo McKern / Anchor Bay (US R1 NTSC)

Before *The Blob*, Hammer Films took a stab at bringing shapeless, liquefied horror to the screen with *X the Unknown*, a less familiar follow up to the popular *The Quatermass Experiment (The Creeping Unknown)*. Though early in the studio's roster of classics, this small but interesting cautionary tale already contains many of the elements which distinguish Hammer at its best - namely Jimmy Sangster behind the screenplay, and James Bernard behind the music. Shot in moody back and white, this is an interesting early draft for their successes to come and of great historical interest to fans of British sci-fi and horror.

Several British soldiers are wounded by mysterious burns after their drilling causes a large crack in the earth... and a strange, gooey entity

crawls out. Scientist Adam Royston (Dean Jagger) investigates the menace crawling across the Scottish countryside, with many villagers continuing to be afflicted by its presence. An investigator (Leo McKern) for the local atomic energy commission joins the hunt, as the being grows and learns to adapt to its surroundings with terrifying results. Soon even women and children are under attack as Royston and his colleagues scramble against time to find a way of destroying this faceless monstrosity.

Fast-paced and entertaining, *X the Unknown* probably won't terrify any viewers now but still delivers some thrills if you're in the right frame of mind. The mud monster is a memorable creation, wiping men clean of their bones and emitting an unforgettable sound along the way. Despite his flagging career at the time, Jagger does a fine job as the lead and makes for a credible quasi-Quatermass protagonist, complete with the usual ambiguous finale. Had Nigel Kneale been behind this one as well, it could have qualified as a classic alongside the rest of its British sci-fi brethren.

Anchor Bay's DVD went through numerous delays over source material issues (much like *Quatermass II*, in fact), so the problems with this presentation should be taken with a grain of salt. Some sequences look absolutely pristine and dazzling, particularly the opening half hour, while others look more battered and dupey. Still, it's the best this film has ever looked on US shores. Some sources list an 81 minute running time for the British edition, so it may also be missing some footage. The disc also includes the original theatrical trailer and a reprise of the *World of Hammer* Sci-Fi episode.

X2000: THE FILMS OF FRANÇOIS OZON
Colour, 1994-98, 61m. / Directed by François Ozon / Starring Bruno Slagmulder, Sebastien Charles / Kim Stim (US R1 NTSC) / WS (1.66:1)
SEE THE SEA
Colour, 1997, 53m. / Directed by François Ozon / Paramount (France R2 PAL) / WS (1.66:1) (16:9)

One of the most consistently inventive and interesting directors of the "new" French cinema, François Ozon first made a name for himself with a series of shocking, unpredictable short films before embarking on a feature film career with 1998's *Sitcom*, a devilish mixture of grotesque horror, social satire, and John Waters style shock humour. Working at a furious pace, he has since churned out *Criminal Lovers*, *Water Drops on Burning Rocks*, *Under the Sand*, and *8 Women*. For those curious to see where it all started, this collection of four short films offers a good introduction to his work, though the easily offended should approach with caution.

The earliest film, 1994's "Action Vérité (Truth or Dare)," is a funny, jolting five minute piece in which four teenagers (two boys, two girls) sit on the floor and play the title game, culminating in an unforgettable punchline. "La Petite Morte (The Little Death)" (1995), the strongest narrative piece, concerns a young man named Paul (François Delaive) who resents his father and passes the time with his lover (Jaques Martial) by collecting pictures of people at the height of orgasm. His sister Camille (Camille Japy) arrives to tell Paul to tell him that their father has died; how he responds and his subsequent discoveries form the crux of the plot, with more than a few twists along the way. Exactly what its name implies, "Scènes de Lit (Bed Scenes)" (1997) presents seven couples of various configurations engaging in a variety of pillow talk, ranging from the erotic to the blatantly absurd, with each separated by a new title and cast list. Finally, the enigmatic "X2000" (1998) follows a hungover man (Bruno Slagmulder) awakening on New Year's Day, 2000, observing a pair of couples both during and following coitus, and pondering the existence of ants which swarm beneath his trash can and onto his foot. Though crammed with nudity, the eight minute short is fairly anti-erotic in nature, feeling more like a hazy late morning daydream than a real film.

Despite the short running times, these films offer a decent approximation of Ozon's skewed sense of humour and his ability to approach potentially repulsive subject matter with an odd impartiality. Though his visuals are rarely deliberately flashy, he exhibits a keen photographic eye and an ability to use editing and cinematic rhythm to create his own distinct voice as a director. Love him or hate him, there's thankfully no one else around quite like him.

Another good collection of his films, *See the Sea* (containing the title film and "My Summer Dress"), is available from New Yorker, who should really get around to releasing it on DVD along with *Sitcom* one of these days. The video quality on Kim Stim's DVD varies wildly depending on the source material. "X2000," the most recent of the bunch, looks quite fine and sharply transferred, but otherwise this is a mostly mixed bag in which the dullness of 16mm black definition results in some noticeable compression problems. Considering the brief running time of the entire program, the bit rate could have been much higher. Paramount France offers an alternate version under the title of *Regarde la mer (See the Sea),* including the excellent 52 minute title film (a Chabrol-like study of encroaching madness) as well as the aforementioned short films. All feature optional English subtitles.

YELLOW SUBMARINE

Colour, 1968, 90m. / Directed by George Dunning / MGM (US R1 NTSC, UK R2 PAL) / WS (1.66:1) / DD5.1

A cheerfully warped, insane animated feature, *Yellow Submarine* was a radical change of pace from the usual Disney fare of the time - not to mention the Beatles Saturday morning cartoon show which had become a pop culture staple. Many viewers, particularly children, find the film extremely difficult to grasp thirty years later; its phantasmagoric pop art landscapes and bizarre *non sequitur* humour are as far out of the mainstream as a G-rated cartoon can go. Of course, for those willing to fall into the groove and savour the numerous trippy delights on hand, this *Submarine* provides a very enjoyable ride.

The wicked Blue Meanies launch a diabolical attack upon the peaceful citizens of Pepperland. Old Captain Fred manages to escape in the title vehicle and obtains the assistance of the Fab Four themselves (well, sort of - they performed the songs but used stand-ins for the dialogue). John, Paul, George, and Ringo set off on a musical trip in which they pick up the Seussian Nowhere Man, encounter Lucy in the Sky with Diamonds, and wind up waging a flower-filled battle through song to reclaim Pepperland. To avoid any fan disappointment, the boys themselves make a live action appearance in the last scene to send the audience off on a high note. Though reminiscent in many ways of the popular Lewis Carroll-style nonsense children's poetry of the era, *Yellow Submarine* remains a unique creation and has inspired countless animators ever since, particularly Terry Gilliam.

The original British cut was altered significantly for US release, with one good musical number ("Hey Bulldog") deleted and some alternate footage added to soften the climax. Most of the songs were taken or adapted from *Sgt. Pepper's Lonely Hearts Club Band*, with three original numbers added and a fun, melodic score by George Martin filling in virtually every gap between the tunes.

The MGM DVD presents the much-ballyhooed restored edition, basically a sprucing up of the British version with eye-popping colour and a knockout new Dolby Digital 5.1 sound mix. The new soundtrack truly gives the film so much more depth that the original mono soundtrack is actually painful to listen to in comparison, and the source materials are in immaculate condition. Purists who owned the open matte version released several years ago may blanch at the imposition of a European aspect ratio (1.66:1) over the image, but since this is the maximum amount of picture information exhibited in theatres, the creators apparently intended for it to be seen this way.

The commentary by Dunning provides some valuable insight into the rushed, financially strapped conditions which somehow managed to produce a work of cinematic art, and the rest of the DVD lives up to the film's promise. For soundtrack fans, the entire score and songs are isolated without the disruptions of sound effects and dialogue - finally! Also, the documentary "Mod Odyssey" provides on-camera interviews to shed light on what can only be described as a labour of love for everyone involved; luckily, it appears everyone still feels the same way. The original trailer and numerous production drawings and preliminary artwork are also thrown in to keep fans busy for several hours. All in all, a great package, and Beatles fans in particular will be wishing all of their albums and movies sounded this good.

YOJIMBO

B&W, 1962,m. / Directed by Akira Kurosawa / Starring Toshiro Mifune, Eijiro Tono / Criterion (US R1 NTSC), BFI (UK R2 PAL), Mei Ah (HK R0 NTSC) / WS (2.35:1)

Many audiences have forgotten that, as the most "Western" of Japan's filmmakers, Kurosawa truly excelled at action films, and this remarkable feature shows him at his sword-slicing best. Extremely popular and widely acknowledged as one of Akira Kurosawa's finest films, *Yojimbo* has no difficulty living up to its reputation. Like many key Kurosawa titles (*Seven Samurai, The Hidden Fortress*), this was remade as a hit film for English speaking audiences in another genre, Sergio Leone's *A Fistful of Dollars* (and more recently by Walter Hill as *Last Man Standing*). Ironically, while Toho wound up getting a 15% cut of the profits from *Fistful* for lifting entire scenes

and shots from *Yojimbo*, no one bothered to point that Kurosawa himself had swiped the entire plot from Dashiell Hammett's first novel, *Red Harvest*, in which the Continental Op pits two small time crime families against each other in a Midwestern town. Controversy aside, *Yojimbo* is an extremely witty, fast-paced film and deservedly caught on outside its native country.

The Criterion DVD is a mostly satisfying presentation culled from the same master print used for the laserdisc. Though not quite as gorgeous as the terrible packaging claims, the print is mostly in good shape aside from the ratty looking American credits (complete with the alternate US title, *The Bodyguard*). Though the image conveys the essentials of the imaginative scope compositions, the original 2.35:1 framing has been pulled out to around 2.10:1, lopping off portions of some actors arranged at the edges of the frame. This doesn't affect the action sequences, however, and appears to be the only version Toho was willing to supply. Contrast and image quality are quite satisfying, however, given the condition of the print. The optional white English subtitles are placed below the frame; however, they're a little small for comfort and could cause serious eyestrain on an average size television.

A simultaneous overseas DVD release from Mei Ah features larger English subtitles and a somewhat different transfer. The Criterion DVD (and the subsequent UK DVD, which replicates the same master but adds on a commentary) also includes the original Japanese trailer with some amusing hyperbolic subtitles.

YOUNG FRANKENSTEIN

B&W, 1974, 105m. / Directed by Mel Brooks / Starring Gene Wilder, Marty Feldman / Fox (US R1 NTSC) / WS (1.85:1)

Baron Frankenstein (Wilder) is bequeathed the worldly goods of his late grandfather. Travelling to Transylvania he meets Igor (Feldman) and the sinister housekeeper of his grandfather's castle, Frau Blucher (Cloris Leachman). In spite of his good intentions, it isn't long before he finds himself irresistibly drawn to recreating his ancestor's experiments in the reanimation of dead tissue.

Although *Young Frankenstein* sends up Universal's classic films, it also treats them with a great deal of respect. Indeed, the efforts of Mel

Brooks (who co-wrote this with Gene Wilder) and his team certainly paid off, for *Young Frankenstein*, if not exactly a milestone on the comedic scale, is a minor classic in its own right, and would sit comfortably among Universal's own latter-day titles. Giving among their career finest performances are Wilder as Freddie Frankenstein ("That's Fronkonsteen!"), Teri Garr as his curvy lab assistant Inga, Cloris Leachman as sinister housekeeper Frau Blucher and Peter Boyle as the radically sympathetic "monster". Kenneth Mars and Gene Hackman deliver wonderful parodies of the characters from the original *Bride of Frankenstein*. However, this is primarily Marty Feldman's show. As Ygor ("It's pronounced Eye-gore"), he pilfers every sight gag and relishes in the cream of the script's snappy dialogue. Sitting watching the film alone, Brooks' passionate recollections of audience reaction upon its initial release might seem a little rose tinted; it's hard to believe that gags which at best raise a snigger ever had them rolling in the aisles. But having seen the film twice in jam-packed auditoriums back in the 1970s, I can validate these recollections; people were in stitches, myself along with them. Which is as good a piece of evidence as any that comedy is best savoured as a shared experience.

Fox's DVD contains a fine transfer of the black & white film (matted at a pleasing 1.85:1, with 28 chapter stops), plus a whole sackload of extra goodies. Audio commentary by Brooks combined with the extensive supplementary section tell you just about everything you could possibly want to know about the making of the film. One of the highlights among the extras is the inclusion of seven sequences deleted from the film's final cut. They're the highlight not because they're particularly entertaining, but because they allow you to appreciate how much the film benefited without them. Only a couple are funny and none of them would have improved the movie to any discernible degree. In fact, one extended sequence could have been the death of it. The piece in question consists of the reading of the late Baron's will, which would have been the first sequence up after the opening credits. It not only goes on for far too long, it's excruciatingly unfunny and could have ground the proceedings to a halt before the projection lamp had even got warm.

The section devoted to outtakes elicits a smile or two, though it consists primarily of the players collapsing in fits of giggles, more often than not instigated by Wilder's inability to keep a straight face. Patrick Cousans' excellent "making of" documentary (menu-listed at 36 minutes, but actually a more generous 42 minutes) is divided into 10 chapters. Dominated mainly by Wilder's recollections (not a bad thing), it also comprises material from cinematographer Gerald Hirschfeld, producer Michael Gruskoff and editors Bill Gordean and Stan Allen. Though Feldman is, of course, dead, Boyle, Khan, Mars, Garr and Leachman - even Brooks himself! - are all curiously conspicuous by their absence. The documentary also includes several amusing bloopers that aren't a part of the dedicated outtakes segment.

In addition there is a collection of trailers and TV spots which, although undoubtedly of interest to the completist, tend towards repetition and become a tad tedious when viewed en masse. Along with an expansive stills gallery, there are even some 1974 b/w television interviews (from Mexican TV no less!), conducted off-set with Wilder, Leachman and Feldman. Brooks' narration is adequate, though he's far too easily distracted; things get off to a strained start during the opening credits when he begins a story that he never really finishes, frequently being distracted to speak about the people whose names are appearing on screen. Fortunately he settles down and goes on to point out some interesting tidbits and impart several amusing anecdotes; often chuckling away to himself, he seems to enjoy his movie a great deal. Language options on the disc are English, Spanish and French, with subtitles available in English. - TG

YOU ONLY LIVE TWICE

Colour, 1967, 117m. / Directed by Lewis Gilbert / Starring Sean Connery, Donald Pleasence / MGM (US R1 NTSC) / WS (2.35:1) (16:9)

A U.S. space capsule is hijacked whilst orbiting the earth. America blames the Soviet Union but the British have a lead in Tokyo. Faking his own death so that he can investigate undercover, James Bond (Connery) teams up with Japanese Intelligence and exposes a mercenary SPECTRE plot that threatens to trigger World War III.

Celebrated children's author Roald Dahl gets out his typewriter, discards most of Ian Fleming's novel, whips Bond out of just-about-feasible terrain and deposits him in the land of the pretty-bloody-unlikely. Opening with our man getting riddled with bullets in a Hong Kong apartment, *You Only Live Twice* is bigger and brasher than any preceding Bond, but not necessarily the better for it. This is the one with the "Little Nellie" gyrocopter battling it out with a squadron of SPECTRE choppers, Bond marrying Japanese Agent Mie Hama as part of his cover (genuine matrimony being reserved for the next film in the series), the nippy Toyota sports car, the final revelation of master criminal Blofeld's face (a shaven-headed Donald Pleasence, upon whom Mike Myers later based *Austin Powers'* Dr. Evil), Karin Dor getting dunked into a pool full of piranhas, and, of course, the extinct volcano with a rocket launch site hidden beneath its fibreglass lake. The shot of the Ninja troops descending on ropes into Production Designer Ken Adam's remarkable set was awesome back in 1967 and still is today, even though its magnitude is diminished on the small screen. This was Lewis Gilbert's first Bond gig - he would return in the 70s for two Roger Moore episodes - and in spite of the many outlandish facets of the film he proves himself a worthy successor to the centre seat. Not one of the best, but damned good fun just the same.

In spite of the searingly beautiful quality of the 1967 movie (divided by 32 chapters, and accompanied by a commentary from director Lewis Gilbert and various folk who worked in front of and behind the cameras), MGM's special edition disc of *You Only Live Twice* feels slightly empty in the extras department. There is the requisite half-hour behind the scenes coverage, and an excellent 25-minute special entitled "Silhouettes: The James Bond Titles", which looks at the magnificent credits sequences over the years, with particular attention paid to the life and work of the late great Maurice Binder. This aside, however, all that remains is a storyboard sequence of Bond's plane flight with Helga Brandt, three trailers and a TV spot (all from its re-release with *Thunderball*) and seven radio spots. English and Spanish languages are provided, with subtitling in Spanish and French. - TG

ZACHARIAH

Colour, 1971, 93m. / Directed by George Englund / Starring Don Johnson, John Rubinstein / Anchor Bay (US R1 NTSC) / WS (1.85:1)

One of the more blissfully incoherent mainstream features of the 1970s, *Zachariah* comes off like the work of an acidhead trying to fuse together Ken Russell's *Tommy*, Conrad Rooks' *Siddhartha*, and Alejandro Jodorowsky's *El Topo*... only even stranger than it already sounds. Billed as "the first Electric Western," the film has now been tagged on video as "the first and only Electric Western." Whether that's a good thing will depend entirely on the viewer's individual taste.

Thanks to a mail order gun retrieved in the middle of the desert, young Zachariah (John Rubinstein) decides to go out into the frontier with his best buddy, Matthew (Don Johnson). An accidental shooting in a saloon convinces Zachariah that he could become a big time gunslinger, so the boys hook up with The Crackers, a band of outlaws better at guitar strumming than straight shootin'. The boys' loyalty is tested when their egos and outside forces threaten to tear them apart, and Zachariah is initiated into manhood by the sultry Belle Star (Pat Quinn, not the one from Rocky Horror). Sure enough, they're headed right for a showdown with each other. Will they regain their heads in time before someone bites the dust?

The major attraction of *Zachariah* is the fantastic soundtrack, which pounds and pulsates through virtually every scene. All of the various band members contribute impressively to the film, most memorably during the amusing Belle Star seduction. As a linear narrative, it isn't as clever or interesting as one might expect given the screenplay written by the Firesign Theatre (who subsequently disowned the film). On the other hand, camp movie fans will howl at the ridiculous gay subtext, which extends far beyond the young boys' pre-Village People outfits. In fact, *Zachariah* might make a good double feature with Nicholas Ray's outlandish lesbian western, *Johnny Guitar* or Paul Morrissey's *Lonesome Cowboys*. Don Johnson, a gay icon before his resurgence on *Miami Vice*, offers one of his better performances, though the emotional range of the finale is obviously beyond his reach. Along with *A Boy and His Dog* and *The Harrad Experiment,* this proves there used to be more to him than pastel suits and swaggering charm. Rubinstein, who had yet to break through with Pippin, gives an equally laid back performance and seems to be well within the spirit of the movie.

Unavailable since its brief VHS release from Magnetic Video in the very early '80s, *Zachariah* has been given an unlikely facelift from Anchor Bay on DVD. The letterboxing adds considerably the sides of the image and looks almost pristine (though non-anamorphic for some reason), apart from a couple of fleeting blemishes in the last two reels. The colour isn't as powerful as the Magnetic version ("electric blue" indeed), but the visuals are smoother and easier on the eyes, with an almost mind-boggling clarity of detail. While this film screams out for a stereo soundtrack, it has always existed in mono and is presented as such here.

A ZED AND TWO NOUGHTS

Colour, 1985, 115m. / Directed by Peter Greenaway / Starring Andréa Ferréol, Brian Deacon / Wellspring (US R0 NTSC) / WS (1.66:1)

Peter Greenaway's second feature film continued many of the obsessions already established in his experimental work: elaborate references to works of fine art, austere and painterly camerawork, confrontational subject matter, and a wholly unique view of sexuality and the human body. Here he tackles a dizzying number of topics including Darwinism vs. creationism, taxonomy, mortality, and the weird random patterns of fate. If that sounds too heady, well, he throws in some thrills for the groundlings, too, including bizarre time lapse decomposition films, rampant frontal nudity, bestiality, glass eating, and wicked black humour.

Twin zoologist brothers Oliver and Oswald Deuce (Brian and Eric Deacon, the latter also in *Vampyres*) find their lives shattered when their wives are killed in a car crash caused by a swan. The car's driver, Alba Bewick (Andréa Ferréol), loses a leg in a subsequent operation, and the brothers form a dependent relationship with her as they delve into the cosmic circumstances which cause such peculiar events. Their experiments include the aforementioned time lapse films on animals from the zoo and sex with the manipulative Venus de Milo (Frances Barber), all of which have unexpected consequences.

Thanks to another brilliant Michael Nyman score and breathtaking cinematography by Sacha Vierney (*Last Year at Marienbad*), *A Zed and Two Noughts* (that's "ZOO," of course) is one of Greenaway's most accomplished yet difficult films. Its rewards are generated by close attention and a willingness to submit to his intellectual gamesmanship, demands which may not be met by all viewers. Best appreciated after experiencing the most accessible *Drowning by Numbers* or *The Cook, the Thief, His Wife and Her Lover*, this is the equivalent of a final exam in a course of Greenaway cinema.

Zed has been most widely available in a very slightly letterboxed VHS edition from Pacific Arts and an optically censored Japanese laserdisc. The Wellspring DVD easily renders both of them obsolete and looks far better than anyone could have possibly expected, easily atoning for their lacklustre work on some of their Rohmer and Truffaut titles. The letterboxing reveals some additional symmetrical composition on the sides, and the intensely saturated colours look absolutely beautiful without any distracting smearing or bleeding. The biggest revelation, however, is the image clarity, which reveals whole new levels of detail in Vierney's stunning deep focus compositions. The source material looks derived from the internegative rather than the scratchy print used for the VHS edition, and the mono sound quality is also much more vivid and clearly defined. No extras apart from a handful of filmographies.

ZEDER

Colour, 1983, 98m. / Directed by Pupi Avati / Starring Gabriele Lavia, Anne Canovas / Image (US R1 NTSC)

When Pupi Avati's psychological horror film *Zeder* first hit US shores under the title *Revenge of the Dead*, more than a few Fulci and Romero fans were enraged after being suckered in by the misleading poster and video art. While the film does tangentially feature a few reanimated members of the undead, visceral thrills really aren't the name of the game here. Avati - who has since more or less abandoned the horror genre aside from a few vaguely supernatural films like *The Arcane Enchanter* and *The Bitter Chamber* - focuses on atmosphere and concepts, with the gradual accumulation of dread and helplessness driving the film rather than a succession of shocks.

A young journalist, Stefano (Gabriele Lavia), receives a used typewriter from his girlfriend, Alessandra (Anne Canovas). Out of curiosity (or boredom), he looks at the old ribbon inside and reconstructs the sentences last typed by its previous owner. After much headstrain, he deduces that Paolo Zeder, a scientist prominent in the 1950s, discovered that certain areas of the world are actually "K Zones" - supernatural landmarks where dead bodies may be brought back to life after being buried in the soil. Stefano digs further into the history of Zeder, and by tracing a number of strange unsolved deaths, he learns that a small group of followers holed out in an abandoned camp are determined to continue Zeder's studies by reviving a dead priest.

Methodically paced and extremely grim, *Zeder* was largely ignored by horror fans until Phil Hardy's *The Aurum Encyclopedia of Horror* began raving about Avati as an unsung genius. Suddenly everyone seemed to hail *Zeder* and its predecessor,

Z

Avati's *The House with Laughing Windows* (*La casa dalle finestre che ridono*), as the high points of Italian horror cinema. While *House* may indeed support this claim, *Zeder* suffers from such extreme appraisals, as it's neither quite a pioneering masterpiece nor a worthless rip-off.

Avati's impressive grip of cinematic vocabulary is quite evident here, and he manages to produce some genuinely unnerving sequences, particularly the finale in which a camera hidden inside a buried coffin produces some horrific results. On the other hand, Lavia, best known for his appearances in *Deep Red* and *Inferno*, makes for a flat, uninvolving leading man; he seems so sombre and skewed from his first moment onscreen that his subsequent descent doesn't quite build up the necessary unrelenting momentum. More noticeably, Riz Ortolani's loud, overbearing score has a tendency to squash subtle moments into sheer bombast. These quibbles aside, *Zeder* remains a highly rewarding film on its own terms, which some impatient viewers may not be willing to meet. As usual, Avati's sense of geography and local colour is impeccable, with oddball casting and a fascinating knack for turning mundane camera setups into magical landscapes of shadow and light.

Image's DVD improves somewhat in sharpness and visual composition upon the old Vestron VHS version, though the original print materials are noticeably in less than prime condition. Tears and dirt frequently rear their heads, particularly around reel changes, and Avati's washed out colour schemes will probably upset viewers expecting a Bava-like barrage of rainbow hues across the screen. The image is either open matte or very slightly cropped from 1.66:1 or less; in either case, no noticeable information seems to be missing; compositions appear balanced but the transfer seems to job slightly from left to right through most of the running time, creating a very odd, queasy sensation.

ZETA ONE

Colour, 1969, 82m. / Directed by Michael Cort / Starring Dawn Adams, James Robertson Justice / Image (US R0 NTSC), Salvation (UK R0 PAL)

Returning from his latest mission, special agent James Word (Hawdon) recounts a tale about a colony of female life forms from a parallel dimension known as Angvia, ruled by the exotic Zeta (Adams). When one of their number is captured and tortured by Earthbound adversary Major Bourdon (Justice), Zeta sends her warriors to annihilate all those who threaten to expose their secret world.

Based on "Island of the Planet", a photo-strip story that appeared in issues of the short-lived 1960s British skin mag "Zeta", this is strange stuff indeed. Alternatively known as *The Love Factor* and *Alien Women*, Tigon's *Zeta One* is an uneasy blend of science fiction, Bond-inspired spy thriller and grubby sex-comedy.

For all these elements, the prevailing impression one comes away with is that of a thinly disguised flesh show, and what delightful flesh director Michael Cort trotted out here: There's a roster of Hammer starlets - Yutte Stensgaard (who now detests the film, no doubt regretful that she acceded to frontal nudity), Valerie Leon, Kirsten Betts and Carol Hawkins - as well as Anna Gael (*Dracula pere et fils*), Nita Lorraine (from *Curse of the Crimson Altar*) and Brigitte Skay (also seen in Bava's *Twitch of the Death Nerve*). With this lot charging about the screen in little more than purple panties and blush-sparing nipple caps, one doesn't know where to look first!

The film is mostly distinctive for its placing of recognisable Thesps into uncharacteristic situations, case in point the scene in which Brit-comedy luminaries James Robertson Justice and Charles Hawtrey stand leering over a half-naked girl strapped to a torture rack. Taking all this into consideration, you'd think Cort had the perfect recipe for a "must-see" low-grade gem, right? Well, to a point yes, but *Zeta One* also suffers from that most heinous of all cinematic crimes; it's unforgivably slow. The first 15-minutes alone revolve around Hawdon coaxing Stensgaard into bed via a protracted game of strip poker and, believe me, 15-minutes worth of film was never such an endurance test. A painfully dated psychedelic curate's egg from a era whose like we'll not see again.

Although no-one's ever likely to invest money in a fully-fledged refurbishment job, and thus *Zeta One* will probably never look any better than it does here, the print used (which is presented fullscreen with noticeable cropping both to the left and the right) suffers from splice repairs, conspicuous patches of grain and murky, wildly unstable colours. On the extras front, there's a satisfyingly sizeable assortment of colour stills, lobby cards, video sleeve art and ad mats thrown in, but the real attraction for *Zeta* cultists will be the remarkably well-preserved copy of the scarcely seen original theatrical trailer.
- TG

ZOMBIE (ZOMBIE FLESH-EATERS)

Colour, 1979, 91m. / Directed by Lucio Fulci / Starring Tisa Farrow, Ian McCulloch / Anchor Bay (US R1 NTSC) / WS (2.35:1) / DD5.1, Stonevision (UK R2 PAL), Dragon (Germany R0 PAL) / WS (2.35:1)

Definitely a love it or hate it type of film, Lucio Fulci's *Zombie* is by far his most famous contribution to the horror genre and still ranks as one of the goriest features ever made. Fortunately, time has been very kind to this film; its guttersnipe nastiness now seems almost quaint and reassuring after two subsequent decades of jokey, watered-down horror hokum. Despite a draggy first third, Fulci really delivers the goods with this one, and the final two acts are an admirable escalation of pure nightmare on film.

The plot (what there is) follows Tisa Farrow (Mia's look-alike sister who appeared in *The Grim Reaper* and the excellent cult film *Fingers*) as she travels with Ian McCulloch from New York to the cursed tropical island of Matoul, where the dead have been coming back to life and attacking the locals. The mayhem all stems from the reckless mad scientist, Dr. Meynard (*The Haunting*'s Richard Johnson), who has been combining science with ancient voodoo rituals. Pretty soon, the entire cast (including Fulci regular Al Cliver and Auretta Gay) is fighting off hordes of the living dead, and the blood runs deep enough to require a raincoat.

Originally released under the title *Zombi 2* in Italy, Fulci's epic was intended as a pseudo-sequel to George Romero's profitable living dead classic, *Dawn of the Dead* (released in Europe as *Zombi*). However, Fulci opted to drop Romero's satiric approach and goes straight for the jugular, offering no social commentary or redeeming substance whatsoever. Of course, it's an easy film to attack; it lacks the flair of Fulci's *The Beyond* or *House by the Cemetery*, and on the whole, the acting is pretty awful. Farrow and McCulloch have little to do besides look neurotic, and Johnson skulks about in a haggard fashion and grumbles about the dead disturbing his work. The best acting award easily goes to the beautiful Olga Karlatos, who also enlivened Fulci's *Murderock* and is best known as Prince's mom in *Purple Rain*! She makes a very strong impression in the two scenes she has, particularly during the infamous close encounter between one of her eyes and a very large wooden splinter.

The VHS editions of *Zombie* from Wizard Video, Magnum Video (who also issued a long out-of-print pan and scan laserdisc), and a handful of public domain companies looked pretty wretched, suffering from greenish skin tones during the island scenes and muffled, scratchy audio. The Japanese laserdisc (under the *Zombi 2* title) looked substantially better, though the print was somewhat worn, with hissy sound. The Roan and Anchor Bay versions (on laserdisc and DVD respectively) feature a digitally remixed soundtrack in Dolby Digital, with some oddly recorded new sound effects. Of course, the dubbed voices still sound canned, and Fabio Frizzi's stirring music score doesn't sound as punchy as one might wish, but that can't be helped. Though the clarity of the picture is fine, the colours have been digitally enhanced and punched up a little too much for comfort on the laserdisc; for example, during a couple of faded scenes, the shadows glow an electric blue. Turn down the colour control on your monitor a bit, however, and the film looks as it should. On the other hand, the Anchor Bay DVD is too pale, washing out even the blues of the ocean scenes.

The fun bonus material includes the US theatrical trailer, a couple of TV spots, and some hilarious radio promos. Also, the commentary by Ian McCulloch provides quite a few chuckles, including his amazing comparison between Fulci and Preston Sturges! More often, though, the comments stray way off the subject and may not please Fulciphiles. In Britain there's a slightly cut version as *Zombie Flesh-Eaters*, marketed as the "Extreme Version;" it looks adequate enough. The German disc from Dragon, under the title *Woodoo*, is uncut, looks nicer than any of the other options, and also features an Antonella Fulci interview. Another edition from Media Blasters has also been projected at the time of this writing.

ZOMBIE LAKE

Colour, 1980, 83m. / Directed by J.A. Lazer (Jean Rollin and Julian de Laserna) / Starring Howard Vernon, Nadine Pascale
Image (US R1 NTSC) / WS (1.76:1) (16:9)

Often cited as the ultimate "so bad it's good" Euroschlock title, *Zombie Lake* is many things - most of them awful - but devotees of Grade Z European exploitation certainly won't find it dull. Packed with acres of bare skin, softcore groping, a maudlin storyline, and splashes of unconvincing but plentiful gore, this is about as low as they come on the Continental totem pole of zombie flicks, but doesn't that alone make it worth a look?

Z

While any semblance of a plot may be accidental, the film revolves around a lakeside town under siege by Nazi zombies left over from World War II. The first victim is a beautiful young skinny-dipper who gets groped to death by the helmeted underwater fiends, who sport military uniforms and bright green faces. The town mayor (Howard Vernon) is distraught by the crime, which repeats itself when a gang of uninhibited young schoolgirls decides to hop in the lake for a quick dip, too. Sweet little Helena (Annouchka, daughter of Eurociné head Daniel Lesoeur) deduces that the main blond zombie is actually the remnant of her dead soldier father, and the two form an unlikely bond as the entire town becomes zombie fodder around them.

Widely known as one of the fastest, cheapest, and most B-movie friendly European studios, Eurociné became a home for a wide variety of directors over the years. As with many of their titles, the authorship of *Zombie Lake* has been infernally difficult to pin down over the years. Originally Jess Franco was slated to direct (and thus Howard Vernon was signed to head up the cast), but he was unable to shoot the film (and instead wound up doing *Oasis of the Zombies* for the studio instead). The bulk of the film was handled by French erotic vampire specialist Jean Rollin, whose heart evidently wasn't in the project. However, the master's touch is still evident in some poetic gliding camera shots along the lake, some tender bits involving the Helena, and a funny extended Rollin cameo culminating in a bloody punchline. Franco fans will be especially amused by the blatant rehashing of Daniel White's haunting score for *The Female Vampire*, which once again becomes the catalyst for a rampage of erotic horror. Unfortunately *Zombie Lake* (or *Lake of the Living Dead* as it was sometimes shown in Europe) hardly ranks with either Franco or Rollin's best, but completists will find this oddly endearing little turkey worth a peek.

Zombie Lake haunted video stores for years in one of those great oversized VHS boxes from Wizard Video. The transfer was fuzzy and not very attractive, but it was decent for its time. This new transfer looks absolutely stunning in comparison; in fact, one has to wonder whether this film really deserves to look so pristine and clear in the first place. The framing measures out closer to 1.78:1 than the 1.66:1 aspect ratio listed on the box, but it looks just fine and appears more balanced than the cropped VHS version. Colours are extremely lifelike and strong (except for the cruddy green make up, of course), and the negative appears to have been stored with loving care in the Eurociné vaults for the past twenty years or so. The disc contains the same old cruddy English dub track as well as the far superior and almost lyrical French version. While there isn't an English subtitle option, returning viewers (and those who speak French) should try this option instead, as it imbues the film with at least a vague sense of poetry sabotaged by the clumsy English version. Along with the saucy European theatrical trailer, this includes the expected alternate clothed versions of the major nude scenes, which have turned up on some alternate tape versions over the years. Most of these are quite funny, as the formerly skinny-dipping girls now decide to get their long white dresses all soggy in the lake instead.

WEIRD ACTION AND BLACK CINEMA

ANGEL'S WILD WOMEN (Troma)
ASSAULT ON PRECINCT 13 (Image)
BIG BAD MAMA (New Concorde)
BIG BIRD CAGE, THE (New Concorde)
BILLY JACK (Ventura, Warner)
BILLY JACK GOES TO WASHINGTON (Ventura)
BLACK CAESAR (MGM)
BORN LOSERS (Ventura)
BROTHERHOOD OF THE WOLF (Universal)
CHAINED HEAT (New Concorde)
CLEOPATRA JONES (Warner)
CONFESSIONS OF A PSYCHO CAT (Image)
COOLEY HIGH (MGM)
COTTON COMES TO HARLEM (MGM)
CRIMSON RIVERS, THE (Columbia)
CRYING FREEMAN (Metropolitan)
DARKMAN (Universal)
DETROIT 9000 (Buena Vista)
DOLL SQUAD, THE (Image, MIA)
EBONY, IVORY AND JADE (Anchor Bay)
EL MARIACHI / DESPERADO (Columbia)
GRAND SLAM (Blue Underground)
HEAT (Warner)
HELL UP IN HARLEM (MGM)
I SPIT ON YOUR CORPSE (Troma)
I'M GONNA GIT YOU SUCKA! (MGM)
LEON / THE PROFESSIONAL (Columbia)
LOCK, STOCK AND TWO SMOKING BARRELS (Polygram)
MACON COUNTY LINE (Anchor Bay)
NIGHTHAWKS (Goodtimes)
ORIGINAL GANGSTAS (MGM)
PENITENTIARY (Xenon)
PENITENTIARY II (Xenon)
PLUNKETT & MACLEANE (Polygram
REVENGE OF THE STOLEN STARS (Image)
REVOLVER (Blue Underground)
RONIN (MGM)
SATAN'S SADISTS (Troma)
A SCREAM IN THE STREETS (Image)
SHAFT (Warner)
SHAFT IN AFRICA (Warner)
SHAFT'S BIG SCORE (Warner)
SHAOLIN DOLEMITE (Xenon)
SLAUGHTER (MGM)
SLAUGHTER'S BIG RIP-OFF (MGM)
SNATCH (Columbia)
10 VIOLENT WOMEN (Image)
TRIAL OF BILLY JACK, THE (Ventura)
TRUCK TURNER (MGM)
VIGILANTE (Anchor Bay)
VIOLENT CITY (Anchor Bay)
WARRIORS, THE (Paramount)
WILD ANGELS, THE (MGM)

WEIRD ANIMATION AND KIDS MOVIES

ALICE (First Run)
BEDKNOBS AND BROOMSTICKS (Buena Vista)
CARTOON NOIR (First Run)
FRITZ THE CAT (MGM)
NINE LIVES OF FRITZ THE CAT (MGM)
DIRTY DUCK, THE (New Concorde)
JAMES AND THE GIANT PEACH (Buena Vista)
THE NIGHTMARE BEFORE CHRISTMAS (Buena Vista)
WILLY WONKA AND THE CHOCOLATE FACTORY (Warner)
5,000 FINGERS OF DR. T (Columbia)
PERFECT BLUE (Manga)
VAMPIRE HUNTER D (Urban Vision)
VAMPIRE HUNTER D: BLOODLUST (AD Vision)
AKIRA (Pioneer)
SOUTH PARK (Warner)
SOUTH PARK: BIGGER, LONGER & UNCUT (Paramount, Warner)
WALLACE & GROMIT (Fox, Warner)
WITCHES, THE (Warner)

WEIRD MAINSTREAM, ARTHOUSE, AND UNDERGROUND

A MA SOEUR! (Tartan)
ABNORMAL: THE SINEMA OF NICK ZEDD (Music Video Distributors)
ALL THAT HEAVEN ALLOWS (Criterion)
ALMOST BLUE (Cecchi Gori)
AMARCORD (Criterion)
ANDREI RUBLEV (Criterion)
AMERICAN GIGOLO (Paramount)
AT HOME AMONG STRANGERS, A STRANGER AMONG HIS OWN (Ruscico)
AVALON (Panorama)
BAD LIEUTENANT (Artisan)
BADLANDS (Warner)
BALCONY, THE (Image)
BEAUTY AND THE BEAST (Criterion, BFI)
BEGOTTEN (World Artists)
BEING JOHN MALKOVICH (Universal)
BEYOND THE CLOUDS (Image)
BIG COMBO, THE (Image)
BIG HEAT, THE (Columbia)
BIG SLEEP, THE (Warner)
BIRDY (Columbia)
BLACKOUT, THE (Columbia)
BLUE GARDENIA, THE (Image)
BOOGIE NIGHTS (New Line)
BREAKING THE WAVES (Artisan)
BRINGING OUT THE DEAD (Paramount)
BUFFALO 66 (Universal)

FURTHER RECOMMENDATIONS

F U R T H E R   R E C O M M E N D A T I O N S

BURNT MONEY (PLATA QUIEMADA) (Filmax)
BUSINESS IS BUSINESS (Anchor Bay, Tartan)
CELOS (Sogepac)
CHOPPER (Image)
CITY OF WOMEN (New Yorker)
COCKFIGHTER (Anchor Bay)
COME DANCE WITH ME (Anchor Bay)
DAMAGE (New Line)
DAMNED, THE (CADUTA DEGLI DEI) (Medusa)
DANCER IN THE DARK (New Line)
DAY OF WRATH (Criterion)
DEATH ON THE NILE (Anchor Bay)
DECALOGUE, THE (Image)
DETOUR (Image)
DIABOLIQUE (Criterion)
DIVA (Anchor Bay)
D.O.A. (Image)
DON JUAN '73 (Home Vision)
DON'T LET ME DIE ON A SUNDAY (First Run)
DONNIE DARKO (Fox)
DOORS, THE (Artisan)
DYING OF LAUGHTER (Manga)
EASY RIDER (Columbia)
EDWARD SCISSORHANDS (Fox)
EMERALD FOREST, THE (MGM)
END OF THE AFFAIR, THE (Columbia)
ENDLESS NIGHT (Anchor Bay)
ENIGMA OF KASPAR HAUSER, THE (Anchor Bay)
ERASERHEAD (David Lynch, Universal)
EVA (Kino)
EVE'S BAYOU (Trimark)
EVIL UNDER THE SUN (Anchor Bay)
EXOTICA (Buena Vista)
FELLINI SATYRICON (MGM)
FELLINI'S ROMA (MGM)
FLOWERS IN THE ATTIC (Anchor Bay)
FRANCESCO (Simitar)
FUNERAL IN BERLIN (Paramount)
GANG OF FOUR (Image)
GOD'S LITTLE ACRE (Image)
GOING PLACES (Anchor Bay)
GRISSOM GANG, THE (Anchor Bay)
HEART OF GLASS (Anchor Bay)
HENRY AND JUNE (Universal)
I STAND ALONE (Strand)
INSOMNIA (Criterion)
IPCRESS FILE, THE (Anchor Bay)
JUBILEE (Second Sight)
JULIET OF THE SPIRITS (Criterion)
KIKA (Image)
KILLING OF SISTER GEORGE, THE (Anchor Bay)
KINGDOM, THE (Hong Kong, Feju)
KINGDOM II, THE (Hong Kong, Forel)
LADY FROM SHANGHAI (Columbia)
LAST TEMPTATION OF CHRIST (Criterion)

LE BOUCHER / LA FEMME INFIDELE (Artedis)
LE DERNIER COMBAT (Columbia)
LE MAGNIFIQUE (Image)
LE PROFESSIONEL (Image)
LE TROU (Criterion)
LEOPARD, THE (IL GATTOPARDO) (Medusa)
LES BONNES FEMMES (Kino)
LES FEMMES (Anchor Bay)
LIMEY, THE (Artisan)
LONE STAR (Warner)
LOST HIGHWAY (Cecchi Gori)
MACBETH (Columbia)
MAGNOLIA (New Line)
MAN OF FLOWERS (Image)
MARAT/SADE (MGM)
MEDIUM COOL (Paramount)
MISHIMA (Warner)
MOULIN ROUGE (Fox)
MURDER ON THE ORIENT EXPRESS (Studio Canal)
NAKED KISS, THE (Criterion)
NAUGHTY GIRL (Anchor Bay)
NIGHT HEAVEN FELL, THE (Home Vision)
NINTH CONFIGURATION, THE (Blue Dolphin)
NOT LOVE, JUST FRENZY (Image)
OF FREAKS AND MEN (Image)
OGRE, THE (Kino)
ORLANDO (Columbia)
OUT OF SIGHT (Universal)
OUT OF THE BLUE (Anchor Bay)
PI (Artisan)
PLEASE NOT NOW! (Anchor Bay)
PLUCKING THE DAISY (Home Vision)
QUADROPHENIA (Rhino)
RAINBOW, THE (Columbia)
RED DESERT, THE (Image)
RED SQUIRREL, THE (Tartan)
REQUIEM FOR A DREAM (Artisan)
RICHARD III (MGM)
RIFIFI (Criterion)
ROCCO AND HIS BROTHERS (Image)
ROMPER STOMPER (Fox)
RUSLAN AND LUDMILLA (Ruscico)
SALO' (Criterion, BFI)
SARAGOSSA MANUSCRIPT, THE (Image)
SCARLET EMPRESS, THE (Criterion)
SEBASTIANE (Second Sight)
SECRET OF ROAN INISH, THE (Columbia)
SERVANT, THE (Anchor Bay)
SHADOWS AND FOG (MGM)
SHOCK CORRIDOR (Criterion)
SID AND NANCY (MGM, Criterion)
SIDEWALKS OF BANGKOK (Image)
SISTER SISTER (Anchor Bay)
SITCOM (Paramount France)
SOLDIER OF ORANGE (Tartan)

SON DE MAR (Spain, Sogepaq)
STALKER (Ruscico)
STRAW DOGS (Anchor Bay)
SUDDEN FEAR (Image)
SUDDENLY, LAST SUMMER (Columbia)
TALE OF TIME LOST, THE (Ruscico)
TALES FROM THE GIMLI HOSPITAL (Kino)
TAXI DRIVER (Columbia)
TEN COMMANDMENTS, THE (Paramount)
THOSE WHO LOVE ME CAN TAKE THE TRAIN (Kino)
TITUS (Fox)
TRAINSPOTTING (Buena Vista)
TWIN PEAKS (Catalyst Logic)
UMBRELLAS OF CHERBOURG, THE (Wellspring)
UNBELIEVABLE TRUTH, THE (Anchor Bay)
UNBREAKABLE (Buena Vista)
VACAS (Tartan)
VOLAVERUNT (Spain, Columbia - PAL R2)
WAKING THE DEAD (USA)
WALKABOUT (Criterion)
WRITTEN ON THE WIND (Criterion)
YOUNG GIRLS OF ROCHEFORT, THE (Buena Vista)

WEIRD COMEDIES

ABBOTT & COSTELLO MEET FRANKENSTEIN (Universal)
ACID HOUSE, THE (VCI)
ARSENIC AND OLD LACE (Warner)
BELA LUGOSI MEETS A BROOKLYN GORILLA (Image)
BEETLEJUICE (Warner)
BEING JOHN MALKOVICH (USA)
BEST IN SHOW (Warner)
BIG LIEBOWSKI, THE (Polygram)
BILLY LIAR (Criterion)
BRITTANIA HOSPITAL (Anchor Bay)
BURBS, THE (Universal)
CANNIBAL WOMEN IN THE AVOCADO JUNGLE OF DEATH (Troma)
CANNIBAL! THE MUSICAL (Troma)
CARRY ON SCREAMING (Studio Canal)
DEAD MEN DON'T WEAR PLAID (Universal)
EARTH GIRLS ARE EASY (Artisan)
FOR YOUR HEIGHT ONLY (Simitar)
GROOVE TUBE, THE (Hen's Tooth)
HAIRSPRAY / PECKER (New Line)
HAPPINESS (Trimark)
HAROLD AND MAUDE (Paramount)
HARVEY (Universal)
HEATHERS (Anchor Bay)
HITCH HIKE TO HELL / KIDNAPPED CO-ED (Image)

HOLLYWOOD BOULEVARD (New Horizons)
HOW TO GET AHEAD IN ADVERTISING (Criterion)
HUDSUCKER PROXY, THE (Warner)
I WAS A TEENAGE ZOMBIE (Image)
JUDY BERLIN (Image)
KENTUCKY FRIED MOVIE (Anchor Bay)
LUST IN THE DUST (Anchor Bay)
MARRIED TO THE MOB (MGM)
MONTY PYTHON AND THE HOLY GRAIL (Columbia)
MONTY PYTHON'S THE MEANING OF LIFE (Image)
MONTY PYTHON: AND NOW FOR SOMETHING COMPLETELY DIFFERENT (Columbia)
MY SON THE VAMPIRE (Image)
NASHVILLE (Paramount)
NURSE BETTY (USA)
O BROTHER, WHERE ART THOU? (Buena Vista)
PEE WEE'S BIG ADVENTURE (Warner)
PINK FLAMINGOS / FEMALE TROUBLE (New Line)
PLAYER, THE (New Line)
POLYESTER / DESPERATE LIVING (New Line)
PUTNEY SWOPE (Rhino)
ROCK 'N' ROLL HIGH SCHOOL (New Concorde)
RUSHMORE (Criterion, Buena Vista)
SOMETHING WILD (MGM)
STRAIGHT TO HELL (International Licensing)
STRANGER THAN PARADISE (MGM)
THEY MIGHT BE GIANTS (Universal)
THIS IS SPINAL TAP (MGM)
THREE BUSINESSMEN (Anchor Bay)
TIME BANDITS (Criterion, Anchor Bay)
TOM THUMB (Warner)
TRAIN RIDE TO HOLLYWOOD (Anchor Bay)
TRUE STORIES (Warner)
UP IN SMOKE (Paramount)
WAITING FOR GUFFMAN (Warner)
WELCOME TO THE DOLLHOUSE (Columbia)
WET HOT AMERICAN SUMMER (USA)
WITHNAIL AND I (Criterion, Anchor Bay UK)
WORM EATERS, THE (Image)
YOUNG FRANKENSTEIN (Fox)

WEIRD EROTICA

AU PAIR GIRLS (Image)
BEHIND THE GREEN DOOR (Mitchell Bros.)
CAN YOU KEEP IT UP FOR A WEEK? (Image)
COUNTRY CUZZINS / MIDNIGHT PLOWBOY (Image)
DANIELLA BY NIGHT (First Run)
DEEP THROAT (VCA)
DEVIL IN MISS JONES, THE (VCX)

FURTHER RECOMMENDATIONS

DIARY OF A NUDIST / NAKED VENUS (Image)
DONNA LUPO, LA (Lantia)
EUGENIE (Wild East)
EUGENIE... THE STORY OF HER JOURNEY
INTO PERVERSION (Blue Underground)
EXHAUSTED (MG Media)
GUARDAMI (CVC)
KEY, THE (Cult Epics)
LATEX (VCA)
LET MY PUPPETS COME (VCA)
MIRANDA (Cult Epics)
NAKED CAME THE STRANGER (VCA)
91/2 WEEKS (MGM, Warner)
NOTORIOUS CLEOPATRA (Image)
PLEASE DON'T EAT MY MOTHER (Image)
PRETTY MODELS ALL IN A ROW (Rhino)
PRIVATE AFTERNOONS OF PAMELA MANN
(VCA)
SECRET SEX LIVES OF ROMEO & JULIET, THE
(Image)
SEX AND ZEN (Universe)
SEX AND ZEN III (Universe)
SHOCK (VCA)
TABOO (Standard Digital)
TOBACCO ROODY / SOUTHERN COMFORTS
(Image)
TOY BOX, THE / TOYS ARE NOT FOR
CHILDREN (Image)
TWO MOON JUNCTION (Columbia)
YELLOW TEDDY BEARS, THE (Image)

WEIRD CAMP

A*P*E (Image)
BEACH BLANKET BINGO (MGM)
BEACH PARTY (MGM)
BETSY, THE (Warner)
BIKINI BEACH (MGM)
BOXING HELENA (MGM)
CAN'T STOP THE MUSIC (Anchor Bay)
DR. GOLDFOOT AND THE BIKINI MACHINE
(MGM)
EEGAH! (Rhino)
GIRL IN GOLD BOOTS (Image)
HOW TO STUFF A WILD BIKINI (MGM)
MOMMIE DEAREST (Paramount)
PAJAMA PARTY (MGM)
SHANGHAI GESTURE, THE (Image)
SHOWGIRLS (MGM)
STUD, THE / BITCH, THE (Universal, R2 UK)
SUPERGIRL (Anchor Bay)
TEENAGE DOLL (Image)
XANADU (Universal)

WEIRD HORROR, MYSTERY AND SCIENCE FICTION

ADVENTURES OF BUCKAROO BANZAI
ACROSS THE 8TH DIMENSION (MGM)
AENIGMA (Image)
ALPHAVILLE (Criterion)
AMITYVILLE II: THE POSSESSION (CVC)
AND NOW THE SCREAMING STARTS (Image)
ASTOUNDING SHE-MONSTER, THE (Image)
ASYLUM OF SATAN (Image)
ATTACK OF THE PUPPET PEOPLE (MGM)
BAD TASTE (Anchor Bay)
BEACH GIRLS AND THE MONSTER (Image)
BEAST WITHIN, THE (MGM)
BEASTMASTER, THE (Anchor Bay)
BEGOTTEN (World Artists)
BLACK CAT, THE / THE FAT BLACK PUSSYCAT
(Image)
BLACK HOLE, THE (Anchor Bay)
BLADE RUNNER (Warner)
BLOB, THE ('88) (Columbia)
BLOOD BEAST TERROR, THE (Image)
BLOOD DOLLS (Full Moon)
BLOOD FOR DRACULA (Criterion)
BLOOD FREAK (Image)
BLOOD FROM THE MUMMY'S TOMB (Anchor
Bay)
BLOOD OF GHASTLY HORROR (Troma)
BLOOD ORGY OF THE SHE-DEVILS (Image)
BLOOD SIMPLE (Universal)
BLOODSTAINED SHADOW, THE (Anchor Bay)
BLOODSUCKING FREAKS (Troma)
BLOODY VAMPIRE (Beverly Wilshire)
BODY BAGS (Artisan)
BOOGEYMAN II (Image)
BOY AND HIS DOG, A (Slingshot)
BRAIN DEAD (New Concorde)
BRAINWAVES (Image)
BRAM STOKER'S DRACULA (Columbia)
BRIDES OF BLOOD (Image)
BRUISER (Trimark)
CANNIBAL APOCALYPSE (Image)
CASE OF THE BLOODY IRIS (Anchor Bay)
CASTLE FREAK (Full Moon)
CAT PEOPLE (Image, Universal)
CHRISTMAS EVIL (Troma)
CHURCH, THE (Anchor Bay)
CLASS OF NUKE 'EM HIGH (Troma)
COMA (Warner)
COMMUNION (Elite)
COMPANY OF WOLVES, THE (Germany)
CORPSE GRINDERS, THE (Image)
CORPSE GRINDERS 2, THE (Image)
CORRIDORS OF BLOOD (Image)
COUNT YORGA, VAMPIRE (MGM)

CRAFT, THE (Columbia)
CRAWLING EYE, THE (Image)
CRAWLING HAND, THE (Rhino)
CREATURE FROM THE BLACK LAGOON (Universal)
CRUCIBLE OF TERROR (Image)
CUJO (Artisan)
CUT AND RUN (Anchor Bay)
DAWN OF THE MUMMY (Laser Paradise)
DAY OF THE BEAST (EL DIA DE LA BESTIA) (Sogepaq)
DAY OF THE DEAD (Anchor Bay)
DEAD RINGERS (Criterion)
DEEP IN THE WOODS (Artisan)
DEF BY TEMPTATION (Troma)
DEVIL DOLL (Image)
DEVIL GIRL FROM MARS (Image)
DIE MONSTER, DIE! (MGM)
DINOSAURUS! (Image)
DOCTOR GORE (Image)
DONOVAN'S BRAIN (MGM)
DOOMWATCH (Image)
DR. DRACULA (Image)
DRACULA (BBC)
DRACULA, PRINCE OF DARKNESS (Anchor Bay)
DRACULA THE DIRTY OLD MAN / GUESS WHAT HAPPENED TO COUNT DRACULA (Image)
DRACULA VS. FRANKENSTEIN (Troma)
EATEN ALIVE (MANGIATI VIVI) (EC)
ESCAPE FROM L.A. (Paramount)
ESCAPE FROM NEW YORK (MGM)
ETERNAL, THE (Trimark)
EVIL DEAD 2 (Anchor Bay)
FACE OF FU MANCHU (Studio Canal) (as LE MASQUE DE FU MANCHU)
FANATIC (THE LAST HORROR FILM) (Troma)
FEVER (Studio)
FINAL PROGRAMME, THE (Anchor Bay)
FLASH GORDON (Image)
FLESH AND THE FIENDS, THE (Image)
FLIGHT TO MARS (Image)
FLY, THE / RETURN OF THE FLY (Fox)
FLY, THE / THE FLY II (Fox)
FORBIDDEN PLANET (MGM)
FRANKENSTEIN MEETS THE WOLFMAN / HOUSE OF FRANKENSTEIN (Universal)
FUNHOUSE, THE (Goodtimes)
GHASTLY ONES, THE / BLOODTHIRSTY BUTCHERS (Image)
GHOSTS OF MARS (Columbia)
GIANT FROM THE UNKNOWN (Image)
GINGER SNAPS (Artisan, Columbia)
GRAVEYARD OF HORROR (Image)
HABIT (Fox Lorber)
HANNIBAL (MGM)

HAUNTED (Artisan)
HAUNTED STRANGLER, THE (Image)
HEARSE, THE (Rhino)
HELTER SKELTER MURDERS (Image)
HENRY: PORTRAIT OF A SERIAL KILLER (Cult Epics)
HIDDEN, THE (New Line)
HIDEOUS SUN DEMON (Image)
HIGHLANDER (Anchor Bay, Artisan)
HIGHLANDER 2 (Artisan)
HILLS HAVE EYES 2, THE (Image)
HOMICIDAL (Columbia)
HORROR OF THE BLOOD MONSTERS (Image)
HOUSE OF THE SEVEN CORPSES (Image)
HOUSE WITH LAUGHING WINDOWS, THE (Image, Fox)
I BURY THE LIVING (MGM)
INVADERS FROM MARS (Image)
INVASION OF THE BODY SNATCHERS ('55) (Artisan)
INVASION OF THE BODY SNATCHERS ('78) (MGM)
ISLAND OF DEATH (Allstar)
ISLAND OF DR. MOREAU (New Line)
ISLAND OF DR. MOREAU (MGM)
JEEPERS CREEPERS (MGM)
KILLER CONDOM (Troma)
KISS OF THE VAMPIRE (Image)
LADY FRANKENSTEIN (DVD Drive-In)
LASERBLAST (Full Moon)
LAST HOUSE ON DEAD END STREET (Barrel)
LEGEND OF THE SEVEN GOLDEN VAMPIRES (Anchor Bay)
LIFEFORCE (MGM)
LIVING HEAD, THE (Rhino)
MAD DOCTOR OF BLOOD ISLAND (Image)
MAN FROM PLANET X, THE (MGM)
MANHUNTER (Anchor Bay)
MANIAC (Anchor Bay, Elite)
MANIAC COP (Elite)
MANSON (Beverly Wilshire)
MARS NEEDS WOMEN (MGM)
MARY SHELLEY'S FRANKENSTEIN (Columbia)
MAXIMUM OVERDRIVE (Anchor Bay)
MIND BENDERS, THE (Anchor Bay)
MONSTER FROM GREEN HELL (Image)
MONSTER THAT CHALLENGED THE WORLD, THE (MGM)
NIGHT FLIER, THE (HBO)
NIGHT STALKER, THE / NIGHT STRANGLER, THE (Anchor Bay)
NIGHT TRAIN TO TERROR (Simitar)
NIGHTMARE ON ELM STREET SERIES (New Line)
OLIVIA (Image)
PHANTASM II (Digital Entertainment)

F U R T H E R R E C O M M E N D A T I O N S

F U R T H E R   R E C O M M E N D A T I O N S

PHANTASM III (Digital Entertainment)
PHANTASM IV: OBLIVION (MGM)
PHANTOM OF THE RED HOUSE (Beverly Wilshire)
PLANET OF THE APES series (Fox)
PLAY MISTY FOR ME (Universal)
POPCORN (Elite)
PROGENY (Sterling)
PROWLER, THE (Blue Underground)
RAPE OF THE VAMPIRE (Image)
RATTLERS / SNAKE PEOPLE (Image)
REDNECK ZOMBIES (Troma)
REPTILICUS (MGM)
ROADKILL / MY SWEET SATAN (Exploited)
ROBOCOP (Criterion)
ROBOT MONSTER (Image)
ROBOT VS. THE AZTEC MUMMY (Beverly Wilshire)
SADIST, THE (AllDay)
SAMSON IN THE WAX MUSEUM (Beverly Wilshire)
SATAN'S CHEERLEADERS (VCI)
SATAN'S SCHOOL FOR GIRLS (Platinum Disc Corp.)
SCARS OF DRACULA (Anchor Bay)
SCHIZO (Image)
SECONDS (Paramount)
SESSION 9 (IVL)
SHADOW OF THE VAMPIRE (Universal)
SHE-CREATURE (Columbia)
SHE DEMONS (Image)
SHORT NIGHT OF THE GLASS DOLLS (Anchor Bay)
SILENCE OF THE LAMBS, THE (MGM, Criterion)
SLIME PEOPLE, THE (Rhino)
SORCERERS, THE (Metrodome)
STEPFORD WIVES, THE (Anchor Bay)
STIR OF ECHOES (Artisan)
STONE TAPE, THE (BFI)
STRAIT-JACKET (Columbia)
SWORD AND THE SORCERER, THE (Anchor Bay)
TEENAGE MONSTER (Image)
TEENAGERS FROM OUTER SPACE (Image)
TERROR FIRMER (Troma)
TERROR IN THE HAUNTED HOUSE (Rhino)
THERE'S NOTHING OUT THERE (Image)
TOOLBOX MURDERS, THE (Blue Underground, Vipco)
TOXIC AVENGER, THE (Troma)
TRACK OF THE VAMPIRE / NIGHTMARE CASTLE (Madacy)
TREMORS (Universal)
TROMEO AND JULIET (Troma)
TWICE TOLD TALES (MGM)
UNCLE SAM (Elite)

VAMP (Anchor Bay)
VAMPIRE HAPPENING, THE (Anchor Bay)
VAMPYR (Image)
VAULT OF HORROR (Vipco)
VILLAGE OF THE GIANTS (MGM)
WATCHER IN THE WOODS, THE (Anchor Bay)
WAX MASK (Image)
WHISTLE AND I'LL COME TO YOU (BFI)
WHO SAW HER DIE? (Anchor Bay)
WITCHFINDER GENERAL (Metrodome)
WORLD OF VAMPIRES, THE (Beverly Wilshire)
YOUNG HANNAH, QUEEN OF THE VAMPIRES (VCI)
ZARDOZ (Fox)

WEIRD ASIAN CINEMA

ANOTHER HEAVEN (Universe)
ARMOUR OF GOD (Universe, Buena Vista)
ARMOUR OF GOD II: OPERATION CONDOR (Universe, Buena Vista)
AS TEARS GO BY (Media Asia)
BATTLE ROYALE (Universe, Tartan)
BEASTCOPS (Media Asia)
BETTER TOMORROW, A (Media Asia, Anchor Bay)
BETTER TOMORROW 2, A (Media Asia, Anchor Bay)
BIG BOSS, THE (FISTS OF FURY) (Universe, Fox)
BLACK ANGEL, THE (Tokyo Bullet)
BLACK CAT (Media Asia)
BLACK CAT 2 (Media Asia)
BRIDE WITH WHITE HAIR, THE (Tai Seng)
BRIDE WITH WHITE HAIR 2, THE (Tai Seng)
BROTHER (Tartan, Universe)
BULLET IN THE HEAD, A (Media Asia)
CHINESE EROTIC GHOST STORY (Mei Ah)
CHINESE GHOST STORY, A (Media Asia)
CHINESE GHOST STORY 2, A (Media Asia)
CHINESE GHOST STORY 3, A (Media Asia)
DAYS OF BEING WILD (Media Asia)
DEAD OR ALIVE (Tartan)
DESTROY ALL MONSTERS (ADV Films)
DEVIL'S WOMAN (Universe)
DR. LAMB (Winson)
DREADNAUGHT (Media Asia)
DRUNKEN MASTER II (Warner)
EASTERN CONDORS (Universe)
EBOLA SYNDROME (Mo Asia)
ENTER THE DRAGON (Warner)
EROTIC NIGHTMARE (Winner's)
ETERNAL EVIL OF ASIA (Mei Ah)
EVIL DEAD TRAP 2 (Tokyo Shock, Japan Shock)
EXECUTIONERS, THE (Tai Seng)
FALLEN ANGELS (Image)

FIREWORKS (New Yorker)
FULL CONTACT (Media Asia, Mei Ah)
GAME OF DEATH (Universe, Fox)
GAMERA: THE PERFECT COLLECTION (Toshiba)
GINGKO BED, THE (Universe)
GODZILLA 2000 (Columbia)
GODZILLA VS MEGAGUIRUS (Universe)
GONIN (Ocean Shores)
GORGEOUS (Universe, Columbia)
GREEN SNAKE (Tai Seng)
GUINEA PIG (Japan Shock)
HARD BOILED (Media Asia, Criterion, Wellspring)
HEROIC TRIO, THE (Tai Seng, Universe)
IN THE REALM OF PASSION (Wellspring)
INUGAMI (Universe)
ISLE, THE (Universe)
JIGOKU (Eclipse)
JOINT SECURITY AREA (Modern)
KAIRO (Universe)
KAKASHI (Universe)
KILLER, THE (Universe, Criterion, Wellspring)
LONGEST NITE, THE (Universe)
MIRACLE FIGHTERS, THE (Media Asia)
MIRACLES (HK, Media Asia; US, Columbia)
NAKED BLOOD (Japan Shock)
NAKED KILLER (HK, Media Asia)
NAKED POISON (Universe)
NANG NAK (HK, Ocean Shores)
NEW DRAGON GATE INN (Hong Kong Legends)
NIGHTMARE (Universe)
NOBODY (Vanguard)
NOTORIOUS CONCUBINES, THE (Image)
NOWHERE TO HIDE (Korea, Spectrum)
ONCE A THIEF (HK, Media Asia)
ONCE UPON A TIME IN CHINA (Media Asia, Columbia)
PEEPING TOM, THE (Universe)
PEKING MAN, THE (Universe)
PEKING OPERA BLUES (Media Asia)
PHANTOM LOVER, THE (Tai Seng)
POSTMAN FIGHTS BACK, THE (Tai Seng)
PRISON ON FIRE (Tai Seng)
PRODIGAL SON, THE (Universe)
PULSE (Universe)
RAPED BY AN ANGEL (Universe)
RECORD, THE (Wide Sight)
RED TO KILL (Universe)
RING 2 (Tartan)
RUNNING OUT OF TIME (Media Asia)
RUSTED BODY (Japan Shock)
SAKUYA - THE SLAYER OF DEMONS (Universe)
SEVENTH CURSE, THE (Media Asia)
SNAKER (Universe, Winson)
SOUND FROM THE DARK (Universe)
ST. JOHN'S WORT (Universe)

STORY OF RICKY, THE (Media Asia, Media Blasters)
STREETFIGHTER, THE / RETURN OF THE STREETFIGHTER (Diamond)
STREETFIGHTER'S LAST REVENGE / SISTER STREETFIGHTER (Diamond)
SUBURB MURDER (Mei Ah)
SWORDSMAN II (Media Asia)
TELL ME SOMETHING (Edko)
TETSUO THE IRON MAN (Image)
TETSUO II (Tokyo Shock)
TO BE NUMBER ONE (Universe)
TOKYO EYES (Universe)
TOO MANY WAYS TO BE NO. 1 (City Laser)
UNGRATEFUL TINK (Universe)
UNTOLD STORY, THE (Tai Seng)
UNTOLD STORY 2, THE (Mei Ah)
UZUMAKI (Universe)
VIVA EROTICA (Universe)
WOMAN CALLED SADA ABE, A (Image)
WOMAN IN THE DUNES (Image)
ZERO WOMAN (Tokyo Shock)

WEIRD WESTERNS

BULLET FOR THE GENERAL, A (Anchor Bay)
COMPANEROS (Anchor Bay)
CUTTHROATS NINE (Eurovista)
HIGH PLAINS DRIFTER (Universal)
FISTFUL OF TRAILERS, A (Wild East)
KEOMA (Anchor Bay)
LONG RIDERS, THE (MGM)
MASSACRE TIME (Eurovista)
PALE RIDER (Warner)
TEXAS, ADIOS (Anchor Bay)

WEIRD SILENT

BELLS, THE (Image)
CABINET OF DR. CALIGARI (Image)
CAT AND THE CANARY, THE (Image)
DESTINY (Image)
DR. JEKYLL & MR. HYDE (Kino, Image)
HUNCHBACK OF NOTRE DAME, THE (Image)
LES VAMPIRES (Image)
NOSFERATU (Image)
PHANTOM OF THE OPERA (Image)

FURTHER RECOMMENDATIONS

SELECTED DIRECTORS INDEX

SELECTED DIRECTORS INDEX

SELECTED DIRECTORS INDEX

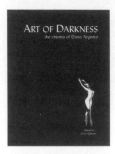